The Essential
PLATO

TRANSLATED BY
BENJAMIN JOWETT
WITH M. J. KNIGHT

INTRODUCTION BY
ALAIN DE BOTTON

THE ESSENTIAL
PLATO

CONTENTS

INTRODUCTION by Alain de Botton —————————— ix

PLATO'S LIFE —————————————————————— xvii
PLATO'S WRITING ——————————————————— xxxi
PLATO'S PHILOSOPHY ——————————————— li

THE REPUBLIC —————————————————————— 1

THE TRIAL AND DEATH OF SOCRATES   417

MENO
  The Immortality of the Soul ——————————— 419
EUTHYPHRO
  Piety and Impiety —————————————————— 473
APOLOGY
  The Defence of Socrates —————————————— 503
CRITO
  Socrates in Prison ————————————————— 547
PHAEDO
  The Last Day of Socrates' Life ————————— 569
THE SYMPOSIUM
  The Character of Socrates ——————————— 679
PHAEDRUS ——————————————————————— 763

SELECTIONS FROM CHARMIDES, LYSIS, OTHER DIALOGUES, AND THE LAWS   853

CHARMIDES
  Regarding Temperance ———————————— 855
LYSIS
  On Friendship ——————————————————— 895
LACHES
  Courage ———————————————————————— 931
PROTAGORAS
  The Unity of Virtue ————————————————— 969
EUTHYDEMUS
  Doctrinaire Politicians and True Philosophers ———— 1055

ION

    The Inspiration of the Poet _____ 1119

GORGIAS

    (1) The Good Man Desires, Not a Long, but a Virtuous Life_ 1141

ALCIBIADES I

    Socrates Humiliates Alcibiades by Showing Him His

    Inferiority to the Kings of Lacedaemon and of Persia _____ 1145

PARMENIDES

    The Meeting of Socrates and Parmenides at Athens.

    Criticism of the Ideas. _____ 1152

THEAETETUS

    (1) Socrates, a Midwife and the Son of a Midwife_____ 1168

    (2) The Lawyer and the Philosopher _____ 1171

SOPHIST

    The Pre-Socratic Philosophers and Their Puzzles_____ 1179

STATESMAN

    The Reign of Cronos_____ 1189

PHILEBUS

    The First Taste of Logic. The Art of Dialectic. _____ 1199

TIMAEUS

    (1) The Tale of Solon_____ 1203

    (2) The Balance of Mind and Body_____ 1212

CRITIAS, OR THE ISLAND OF ATLANTIS

    The Whole _____ 1217

THE LAWS   1238

BOOK I _____ 1240

    (1) The True Nature of Education _____ 1240

    (2) Man the Puppet of the Gods _____ 1242

BOOK II_____ 1244

    The Habit of Drinking Not to Be Encouraged in the State __ 1245

BOOK III _____ 1247

    The Origin of Government_____ 1247

BOOK IV_____ 1254

    (1) The Virtuous Tyrant_____ 1254

    (2) The Life of Virtue_____ 1259

BOOK V ———————————————————————— 1262
   (1) The Honor of the Soul. Precepts for a Virtuous Life. —— 1263
   (2) The Best and the Second-Best State ———————— 1272
   (3) Riches and Godliness ———————————————— 1276
BOOK VI ——————————————————————— 1279
BOOK VII ——————————————————————— 1279
   (1) The Good Citizen Must Not Lead an Inactive Life ——— 1280
   (2) The Education of the Young ———————————— 1283
BOOK VIII —————————————————————— 1288
BOOK IX ——————————————————————— 1289
BOOK X ———————————————————————— 1289
   The Three Classes of Unbelievers ——————————— 1291
BOOK XI ——————————————————————— 1308
   (1) The Evils of Retail Trade, and the Cure of Them ——— 1309
   (2) The Honor of Parents —————————————— 1312
BOOK XII ——————————————————————— 1315
   (1) The Good State in Its Intercourse with the World ——— 1316
   (2) The Burial of the Dead ————————————— 1319

AN INTRODUCTION TO PLATO

BY ALAIN DE BOTTON

1. Perhaps the most persuasive reason not to embark on an examined life comes from the feeling that it must already be too late. There seems little point in beginning to scrutinise one's ethical assumptions when others—more schooled and erudite than we, those privileged scholars who have none of our practical commitments—have studied for epochs and already contributed more than we will ever be able even to assimilate. This accumulation of knowledge, rather than being a cause for joy and an incentive to the development of our own mental life, functions simply as a depressant and a reason to abdicate independent thought. It seems neither necessary nor possible to add anything to the density of what has already been said.

2. This is a stance with which Plato, and the Socrates through whom he articulated his thoughts, was in the strongest disagreement.[1] Few philosophers have had more minimal views of what is required to pursue a thinking life than Plato did. For a start, it was not necessary to disengage from ordinary commitments. Philosophising could go on alongside shopping, working, bathing, loving; it was no alternative to an active life but its necessary complement. This point was emphasised by Plato's decision to develop Socrates' thoughts within dialogues set in quasi-novelistic contexts. The central tenets of Western philosophy are thus shown to unfold naturally during conversations between a man who didn't wash his cloak too frequently and some of his friends, as they strolled to the harbour and visited the gymnasium. The dialogues are strewn with banter

---

[1] Plato articulated almost all his thoughts through the historical figure of the philosopher Socrates, whom he had known as a young man in Athens. Here, when I refer to Socrates, I am talking exclusively of the Socrates found in Plato's dialogues.

and gossip unexpected in philosophical treatises, but because such static is part of existence, philosophy, its illuminator, has a duty not to shy from it.

As *Charmides* opens, we find Socrates, just returned from the siege of Potidaea, catching up with friends at the wrestling school opposite the temple of Basile, south of the Acropolis. They talk about the battle, and then the subject turns to a young man named Charmides, said to be extraordinarily pretty, who is on his way to the school. Socrates recounts his arrival:

> [Charmides] sat down between Critias and me. Great amusement was occasioned by every one pushing with might and main at his neighbour in order to make a place for him next to them, until at the two ends of the row one had to get up and the other was rolled away sideways. Now I, my friend, was beginning to feel awkward; my former bold belief in my powers of conversing with him had vanished . . . he looked at me in such an indescribable manner, and was about to ask a question. . . . I caught a sight of the inwards of his garment, and took the flame. Then I could no longer contain myself. (*Charmides*, p. 862)

Philosophy should not imply that it emerges from a vacuum; it is anchored in a world in which heads are lost after glimpses inside others' cloaks.

3. Plato offers further consolation to the underread. While the existence of libraries full of books that we have no time to open seems to debar us from ever making a contribution to knowledge, it is worth noting how little Socrates had read—Homer, perhaps some Thales, a little Anaxagoras, a scroll from Heraclitus: far less than his least-educated successor, far less than we. It is a humbling sign of how little we have done with the material, how unfairly we have blamed the flatness of our thoughts on the paucity of our reading. Ignorance of past explanations and the history of thought cannot be grounds for avoiding an examined life. There is no more inspiring aspect to Plato's Socratic dialogues than the inference that anyone seeking an answer to a tricky ethical point, anyone with a careful and flexible mind, may engage a friend in conversation on a city

street and stand an excellent chance of arriving at one or two great verities in under half an hour.

4. But Socrates was not popular with everyone. Anyone attending the theatrical festival of Dionysus on the sheltered southern slopes of the Acropolis in the spring of 423 would have caught the premiere of a comedy by a gifted playwright in his mid-twenties, already applauded and well-known for *The Acharnians* and *The Knights*. Aristophanes's new play, *The Clouds*, included a portrait of a middle-aged and bearded philosopher named Socrates, who would have been known—either personally or by sight—to most of the audience and who was subsequently acknowledged as one of the greatest figures in the history of Western philosophy.

Not that one would have guessed. The stage version of the august philosopher, however, spent his days in a basket suspended from a crane, because he claimed his mind worked better at high altitude. His thoughts were too urgent and profound to leave him a chance to wash or do any housework, which meant his cloaks were malodorous and his home riddled with vermin, but at least he was able to work out answers to some of the deepest philosophical questions, including: How many of its own lengths can a flea jump? And do gnats hum through their mouths or through their anuses? Though Aristophanes omitted elaborations on the results of Socrates' research, the audience must have had a good sense of the relevance of the enterprise.

5. Fleas or *Siphonaptera* (from the Greek *siphon*, tube or pipe, and *aptera*, wingless) range in size from 5.5 to 0.9 mm, depending on the branch of a family that includes the cat flea (*ctenocephalides felis*), the dog flea (*ctenocephalides canis*), the human flea (*Pulex irritans*), and the rabbit flea (*spilopsyllus cuniculi*). Propelling itself on two enlarged and bristled hind femurs, the dog flea, which measures an average of 1.52 mm, is capable of leaping 400 mm, or more than 263 times the length of its own body (400 ÷ 1.52 = 263.1578947), whereas the smaller rabbit flea (average size, 1.3 mm) can jump 380 mm, or 292 times its own body (380 mm ÷ 1.3 = 292.3076923).

As for the gnat, *culex pipiens pallens*, its sound emerges neither from its needlelike proboscis nor from its rear but rather from its wings, which vibrate between 550 and 650 times per second.

6. Beneath the caricature lies the familiar antagonism between philosophers and adherents of common sense. Whereas most humans rest soundly in the knowledge that fleas jump really rather far given how small they are and that gnats make a noise from somewhere, Socrates stood accused of a manic suspicion of simple explanation and a hunger for complicated but useless alternatives. The philosopher might have replied that in many cases, though perhaps not ones involving fleas, there can be a legitimate need for more complex, sustained inquiry than common sense allows. Dividing the playwright and the philosopher was a contrasting assessment of the worth and adequacy of ordinary explanations.

7. Socrates was not the first Greek to feel a need to probe beyond common sense. A century and a half before Aristophanes put Socrates in a basket, the philosopher Thales, in the town of Miletus on the shores of Asia Minor, had grown disenchanted with the loose explanations of certain phenomena offered by his contemporaries—for instance, for when eclipses of the sun occurred (every now and then), for how big the sun was (quite large), for how the earth was suspended in space (God knows), or for what the height of the Great Pyramid of Egypt was (huge).

By means of rational inquiry, Thales had succeeded in predicting the exact date of the next eclipse (May 28, 585 B.C.E.). He had also suggested that the sun was probably one 720th of the lunar orbit, that the earth was like a log sitting on a vast waterbed, and that the height of the Great Pyramid could be deduced by the theorem of similar triangles based on the relationship between a person's height and his or her shadow.

The philosopher Anaxagoras, who had died only a few years before the first performance of *The Clouds*, had in similar ways sought to attain a deeper understanding of the weather. Ignoring dominant religious accounts, he had argued that wind was not the work of the gods but the product of air rarefied by the sun, that thunder was created by a clash of clouds, and that lightning was the result of the friction of vapour. He became an expert at weather forecasting, traveled to Olympia wearing a thick mackintosh on an apparently perfect day, and astonished those around him when the dark clouds he'd predicted promptly massed and released a deluge, soaking those who—trusting common sense—had left home in linen tunics.

8. In embryonic form, these men displayed some key features of a philosophical approach that we find fully developed in Plato: a desire to go beyond everyday beliefs so as to find logical explanations why something should be thought true or false, and a corresponding refusal to be intimidated by long-established views backed only by the authority of religion or tradition, rather than by that of reason. Conclusions were valid because they were connected logically to premises, not because all the neighbours said so. This philosophical way of thinking could lead to thoughts that would sound implausible at first but might one day prove better than the commonsense views they challenged. Thinking philosophically could offer counterintuitive but superior advice, not least about what to wear on blue days in the Peloponnese.

9. Fortunately, Socrates did not devote himself to the study of how far fleas could jump. Nor did he think much about the weather or how high pyramids were. He examined the more pertinent issue of how to lead a good and happy life.

Socrates' contemporaries knew that leading a successful life was extraordinarily difficult, but they saw no challenge in working out what was required. Like the people around Thales and Anaxagoras, they seemed not to worry that their understanding might be a little casual or deficient. The subject was as unworthy of rational investigation as the jumping distances of fleas.

Socrates could not agree. There appeared to be a host of false or confusing aspects to the Athenian definition of an admirable person, and analysis of these lie at the heart of Plato's dialogues: Was money, as many said, really a prerequisite to virtue? Was justice only the interest of the stronger, as some younger politicians were arguing? Could only aristocrats be admirable? Was self-control possible without self-knowledge?

10. It was not normal to ask so many questions, but Socrates could not stop mulling, which prevented him from pursuing a regular career and even—as Aristophanes had hinted—from having more than an occasional bath. A friend of Socrates recounted that the

philosopher had once been struck dumb by a thought in the middle
of his military service:

> One morning he was thinking about something which he
> could not resolve; and he would not give up, but contin-
> ued thinking from early dawn until noon—there he stood
> fixed in thought; and at noon attention was drawn to him,
> and the rumor ran through the wondering crowd that
> Socrates had been standing and thinking about something
> ever since the break of day. At last, in the evening after
> supper, some Ionians out of curiosity (I should explain
> that this was not in winter but in summer), brought out
> their mats and slept in the open air that they might watch
> him and see whether he would stand all night. There he
> stood all night as well as all day and the following morn-
> ing; and with the return of light he offered up a prayer to
> the sun, and went his way. (*Symposium*, p. 758)

Socrates conceded that there were costs to thinking, referring to
himself as "[a] man who has never had the wit to be idle during his
whole life; but has been careless of what the many care about—
wealth, and family interests, and military offices, and speaking in the
assembly, and magistracies, and plots, and parties" (*Apology*, p. 538).

11. But Socrates did not depart from his conviction that the assumptions of others required scrutiny. His capacity to inspire and console
lay in his suggestion that popular views on how to lead one's life
(how much money to make, how to approach sex, what to think of
the gods)—views described as "normal" and so beyond question by
the majority—might upon examination reveal themselves to be
shakier than one thought, and that there could hence be a basis for
questioning common sense and leading an examined life.

PLATO'S LIFE

THERE is hardly another philosopher of antiquity
with whose life we are so intimately acquainted as
with Plato's; yet even in his case, tradition is often
uncertain and still more often incomplete. Born
some years after the commencement of the Pelopon-
nesian war, the son of an ancient aristocratic house,
favoured also by wealth, no less than birth, he must
have found in his education and surroundings abundant intellectual food; and even without the express
testimony of history, we might conclude that he
profited by these advantages to the fullest expansion
of his brilliant genius. Among the few further particulars that have descended to us respecting his
earlier years, our attention is principally drawn to
three points, important in their influence on his
mental development.

Of these we may notice first the general condition of his country, and the political position of his
family.

Plato's youth coincided with that unhappy period
succeeding the Sicilian defeat when all the faults of
the previous Athenian government were so terribly
avenged, all the disadvantages of unlimited democracy so nakedly exposed, all the pernicious results
of the self-seeking ethics and sophistical culture of
the time so unreservedly displayed. He himself
belonged to a social class and to a family which
regarded the existing constitution with undisguised,
and not always groundless discontent. Several of
his nearest relations were among the spokesmen of
the aristocratic party. But when that party had

itself been raised to power by the common enemy, on the ruins of Athenian greatness, it so misused its strength that the eyes of its blindest adherents were inevitably opened. It is easy to see how a noble, high-minded youth, in the midst of such experiences and influences, might be disgusted, not only with democracy, but with existing State systems in general, and take refuge in political Utopias, which would further tend to draw off his mind from the actual towards the ideal.

Again, there were other circumstances simultaneously working in the same direction. We know that Plato in his youth occupied himself with poetical attempts, and the artistic ability already evinced by some of his earliest writings, coupled with the poetical character of his whole system, would lead us to suppose that these studies went far beyond the superficiality of a fashionable pursuit. There is, therefore, little reason to doubt (however untrustworthy may be our more precise information on the subject) that he was intimate with the great poets of his country.

Lastly, he had, even before his acquaintance with Socrates, turned his attention to philosophy, and through Cratylus the Heraclitean had become acquainted with a doctrine which, in combination with other elements, essentially contributed to his later system.

All these influences, however, appear as of little importance by the side of Plato's acquaintance with Socrates. We can not, of course, say what direction his mind might have taken without this teacher, but the question may well remain unanswered. We know enough to prove from all historical traces that the deepest, most lasting, most decisive impression was produced by the philosophic reformer on his congenial disciple. Plato himself is said to have esteemed it as the highest of Fortune's favors, that he should have been born in the lifetime of Socrates, and later tradition has adorned with a significant myth the first meeting of the two men. But apart from this, the fact must always be regarded as one of those remarkable contingencies which are too important in their bearing on the course of history to be severed from it in our thought. During a long and confidential intercourse, Plato penetrated so deeply into the spirit of his distinguished friend that the portrait of that spirit which he was able to bequeath to us is at once the most faithful and the most ideal that we possess. Whether at that time he directed his attention to other teachers of philosophy, and if so, to what extent, we do not know; but it is scarcely credible that a youth so highly educated, and so eager for knowledge — whose first impulse, moreover, towards philosophy had not come from Socrates — should have made no attempt until his thirtieth year to inform himself as to the achievements of the earlier philosophers, should have learned nothing from his friend Euclid about the Eleatics, nor from Simmias and Cebes about Philolaus: that he should have inquired no further respecting the doctrines continually brought to the surface by the public lectures and disputations of the Sophists, and left unread the writings of Anaxagoras, so easily to be obtained in Athens. It is nevertheless probable that the overpowering influence of the Socratic teaching may have temporarily weakened his interest in the earlier natural philosophies, and that close and repeated study may afterwards have given him a deeper insight into their doctrines. Similarly, his own imaginative nature, under the restraining influence of his master's dialectic, was probably habituated to severer thought and more cautious investigation; perhaps, indeed, his

idealistic tendencies received at first an absolute
check; and conceptual science, together with the art
of forming concepts, was only to be attained by him
— a stranger like his contemporaries to all such
things — through the dry prosaic method of the Socratic inquiry. But Plato needed this schooling to
give him the repose and certainty of the scientific
method — to develope him from a poet into a philosopher; nor did he in the process permanently lose
anything for which his natural temperament designed
him. Socrates' conceptual philosophy had given him
a glance into a new world, and he forthwith set out
to explore it.

The tragic end of his aged master, a consummation which he seems at the outset to have thought
wholly impossible, must have been a fearful blow to
Plato; and one consequence of this shock, which still
seems long years afterwards to vibrate so sensibly in
the thrilling description of the Phædo, may have been
perhaps the illness which prevented the faithful disciple from attending his master at the last. We are,
however, more immediately concerned with the inquiry as to the effect of the fate of Socrates on Plato's
philosophic development and view of the world; and
if for this inquiry we are thrown upon conjectures,
these are not entirely devoid of probability. On the
one hand, for example, we shall find no difficulty in
understanding how his reverence for his departed
teacher was immeasurably increased by the destiny
which overtook him, and the magnanimity with which
he yielded to it; how the martyr of philosophy,
faithful unto death, became idealized in his heart and
memory as the very type of the true philosopher; how
principles tested by this fiery ordeal received in his
eyes the consecration of a higher truth; how at once
his judgment on the men and circumstances con-

cerned in the sacrifice of Socrates grew harder, and
his hope as to any political efficiency in those circumstances fainter; nay, how the general tendency
was fostered in him to contemplate reality in a
gloomy light, and to escape from the ills of the
present life into a higher, supersensuous world. On
the other hand, it may perhaps have been better for
his scientific growth that his connection with Socrates
lasted no longer than it did. During the years of
their intercourse he had made his teacher's spirit his
own, in completer fulness than was possible to any
of his fellow students; it was now for him to perfect the Socratic science by the addition of new elements, and to fit himself by the utmost expansion
in many directions for erecting it on an independent
basis: his apprenticeship (Lahrjahre) was over, his
travelling time (Wanderjahre) was come.

After the death of Socrates, Plato, with others of
his pupils, first betook himself to Megara, where a
circle of congenial minds had gathered round Euclid.
He afterwards undertook journeys which led him to
Egypt, Cyrene, Magna Græcia, and Sicily. Owing
to the meagreness, and sometimes the contradictori-
ness, of the traditions, it is impossible to ascertain
with certainty how long he continued in Megara,
when he commenced his travels, whether they immediately succeeded the Megaric sojourn, or a return
to Athens intervened; whether his stay in Athens was
long or short; and whether he had or had not become
a teacher of philosophy before his departure. But if
he really returned from Sicily only ten or twelve
years after the death of Socrates, there is great probability, and even some external evidence, that long
before his journey he had settled in Athens, and
there worked as teacher and author; even granting
that at this period his instructions were confined to

a select few, and that the opening of his school in
the Academy took place later on. What, in this
case, we are to think about the journey to Egypt
and Cyrene — whether the visit to Sicily was immediately connected with it, or whether Plato first
returned to Athens from Egypt, and only undertook the Italian journey after an interval of some
years, can not be certainly determined, but there is
a good deal in favor of the latter alternative.

If, indeed, Plato had already attained to manhood when he visited the countries of the south and
west; had already, that is, before his personal
acquaintance with the Italian Pythagoreans, found
the scientific bases of his system, and laid them
down in writings, these journeys can not have had
the striking effect on his philosophical development
which is often ascribed to them in ancient and
modern days. Besides the general enlargement of
his views and knowledge of human nature, his chief
gain from them seems to have consisted in a closer
acquaintance with the Pythagorean school (whose
principal written book he appears to have purchased), and in a deeper study of mathematics. To
this study, Theodorus is said to have introduced
him, and we have at any rate no proof against the
correctness of the statement. He may have received futher mathematical instruction from Archy-
tas and other Pythagoreans, so that we can
scarcely be wrong in connecting with this journey
his predilection for science, and his remarkable
knowledge of it: while, on the contrary, the stories
about the mathematical lore, priestly mysteries, and
political ideas which he is stated to have acquired
in Egypt, are in the highest degree improbable.
In Sicily, Plato visited the court of Dionysius the
elder. But in spite of his close intimacy with Dion,

he gave great offence there by his plain speaking,
and the tyrant in wrath delivered up the troublesome moralizer to the Spartan ambassador Pollis,
by whom he was exposed for sale in the slave-
market of Ægina. Ransomed by Anniceris, a
Cyrenian, he thence returned to his native city.

Plato seems now to have made his first formal
appearance as a teacher. Following the example
of Socrates, who had sought out intelligent youths
in the Gymnasia and other public places, — he, too,
first chose as the scene of his labours a gymnasium,
the Academy, whence, however, he subsequently
withdrew into his own garden, which was adjacent.
Concerning his manner of instruction tradition
tells us nothing; but if we consider how decidedly
he expresses himself against the rhetoricians who
made long speeches, but knew neither how to ask
questions nor how to answer them; and how low,
on the same ground, was his estimation of written
exposition, open to every misunderstanding and
abuse, — in comparison with the living personal
agency of conversation, — if we mark the fact, that
in his own works, the development of thought by
dialogue is a law, from which in his long literary
career he allowed himself not a single noteworthy
departure, — we can scarcely doubt that in his oral
teaching he remained true to these main principles.

On the other hand, however, we hear of a discourse on the Good, published by Aristotle and
some of his fellow pupils, and belonging to Plato's
later years. Aristotle himself mentions discourses
on Philosophy; and that these were not conversations, but in their general character at any rate
continuous discourses, is witnessed partly by express
testimony, partly by their internal evidence, which
can be taken in no other way. Also, there are many

portions of the Platonic system which from their nature could not well be imparted conversationally. It is most probable, therefore, that Plato, according to circumstances, made use of both forms; while the supposition must be admitted that as in his writings, so in his verbal instruction, question and answer gave place to unbroken exposition, in proportion, partly to the diminished vivacity of increasing years, partly to the necessary advance in his teaching, from preparatory inquiries to the dogmatic statement of his doctrine in detail.

That, side by side with the communications intended for the narrower circle of his friends, he should have given other discourses designed for the general public, is not likely. It is more credible that he may have brought his writings into connection with his spoken instruction, and imparted them to his scholars by way of stimulus to their memories. On this point, however, we are entirely without information. Plato doubtless combined with intellectual intercourse that friendly life-in-common to which he himself had been accustomed in the Socratic circle and the Pythagorean Society. With a philosopher so little able to separate philosophic from moral endeavour, it might be expected that community of knowledge would naturally grow into community of life. In this way he appears to have joined his scholars at stated intervals in social repasts. There can be no doubt, from what we know of his sentiments on the subject, that his instructions were altogether gratuitous; and if, on certain occasions, he accepted presents from some of his rich friends, there is no reason to conclude that such voluntary offerings were therefore customary among his disciples in the Academy.

Plato's sphere of work seemed to him to be

limited to this intellectual and educational activity,
more and more, as experience deepened his conviction that in the then state of Athens, no diplomatic
career was compatible with the principles he held.
The desire, however, that it might be otherwise was
none the less strong in him; and that he had not
abandoned the hope of somehow and somewhere
gratifying this desire is proved by his two great
political works, which are designed not merely to
set forth theoretical ideals, but at the same time to
exert a regulative influence on actual conditions.
Consequently though he, as little as his great master,
himself wished to be a statesman, both may certainly be credited with the aim of forming statesmen; and if he repudiated political activity in
circumstances which he considered hopeless, there
was, at the same time, nothing in his principles to
keep him back from it, should there arise a favorable opportunity for the realization of his ideas.
Such an opportunity seemed to offer after the death
of the elder Dionysius, when Dion, and, at his instigation, Dionysius the younger, invited him press-
ingly to Syracuse. Could this potentate indeed be
won over to Philosophy and to Plato's political
beliefs — (and of this Plato, or at any rate Dion,
appears certainly to have indulged a hope), the
most important results might be expected to follow,
not only in his own kingdom, but in all Sicily and
Magna Græcia, indeed throughout the Hellenic
states. Meanwhile the event proved, only too soon,
how insufficiently this hope was founded. When
Plato arrived in Syracuse, the young Prince received him most politely, and at first showed lively
interest in the philosopher and his endeavors; but
he very shortly became weary of these serious conversations, and when his jealousy of Dion, which

was not entirely groundless, had led to an open rupture with that statesman, and at length to the banishment of the latter, Plato must have been glad to escape from the painful position in which he found himself, by a second return home. Nevertheless, after some years, at the renewed solicitations of the tyrant and entreaties of his friends, he resolved upon yet another voyage to Sicily. His immediate aim was doubtless to attempt a reconciliation between Dion and Dionysius; to this may have linked themselves more distantly, new political hopes: the undertaking, however, turned out so unfortunately that Plato was even in considerable danger from the mistrust of the passionate prince, and only evaded it by the intervention of the Pythagoreans, who were then at the head of the Tarentine state. Whether, after his return, he approved of Dion's hostile aggression on Dionysius, we do not know; but for his own part, from this time, having now attained his seventieth year, he seems to have renounced all active interference with politics. The activity of his intellect, however, continued amidst the reverence of countrymen and foreigners, unabated till his death, which after a happy and peaceful old age, is said to have overtaken him at a wedding feast.

Even in antiquity, the character of Plato was the subject of many calumnies. The jests of the comic poets which have come down to us are indeed harmless enough, and concern the philosopher more than the man; but there are other reproaches, for the silencing of which Seneca's apology — that the life of a philosopher can never entirely correspond with his doctrine, — is scarcely sufficient. On the one hand, he is accused of connections, which, if proved, would forever throw a shadow on his mem·

ory; on the other of unfriendly, and even of hostile behavior towards several of his fellow disciples. He has also been charged with censoriousness and self-love; not to mention the seditious behavior after the death of Socrates which scandal has laid to his account. His relation with the Syracusan court was early made the handle for divers accusations, such as love of pleasure, avarice, flattery of tyrants; and his political character has especially suffered at the hands of those who were themselves unable to grasp his ideas. Lastly, if we are to believe his accusers, he not only, as an author, allowed himself numerous false assertions respecting his predecessors, but also such indiscriminate quotation from their works, that a considerable portion of his own writings can be nothing more than a robbery from them. All these complaints, however, so far as we are in a position to test them, appear so unfounded that scarcely a fraction of them will stand the process of investigation; and the rest are supported by such weak evidence, that they ought not to affect that reverence for the character of the philosopher which is certain to ensue from the perusal of his works. So far as a man may be judged by what he has written, only the very highest opinion can be formed of the personality of Plato. To appreciate him correctly, however, he must be measured by a standard that takes account of his natural disposition and historical place. Plato was a Greek, and he was proud of being one. He belonged to a rank and to a family, the prejudices as well as the advantages of which he was content to share. He lived at a time when Greece had touched the highest point of her national life, and was steadily declining from political greatness. His nature was ideal, adapted rather to artistic creation and scien-

tific research than to practical action; which tendency, nourished and confirmed by the whole course
of his life, and the strong influence of the Socratic
School, could not fail to be still further strength-
ened by his own political experiences. From such
a temperament and such influences might be evolved
all the virtues of a man and a philosopher, but
nought of the grandeur of a politician. Plato might
desire the very best for his country, and be ready to
sacrifice for her sake everything except his convictions: but that he should have thrown himself into
the turmoil of political life, for which he was quite
unfitted, — that he should have lavished his soul's
strength in propping up a constitution, the foundations of which he thought rotten, — that he should
have used means that he felt to be useless to stem
the torrent of opposing fate, — that he, like Demos-
thenes, should have led the forlorn hope among the
ruins of Grecian freedom, — would be too much to
expect. His province was to examine into State
problems and the conditions of their solution; their
practical realization he abandoned to others. Thus
inner disposition and outward circumstances alike
designed him for philosophy rather than state-
craft. But even his philosophy had to be pursued
differently from that of Socrates, nor could his habits
of life exactly resemble his master's. He desired to
be true in the main to the Socratic pattern, and by
no means to return to the mode of teaching adopted
by the Sophists. But aiming as he did at the formation and propagation of a comprehensive system,
— aphoristic conversation, conditioned by a hundred
accidental circumstances, was not enough for him;
he wanted more extensive machinery, skilled labor,
intellectual quiet; he wanted hearers who would
follow his inquiries in their entire connection, and

devote to them their whole time; his philosophy was forced to withdraw itself from street and market, within the precincts of a school.

Here already were many deviations from the Socratic way of life; many more sprang from Plato's own habits and inclinations, which were generally opposed to it. Simplicity and temperance were indeed required by his principles, and are expressly ascribed to him; but the entire freedom from wants and possessions to which Socrates attained, would not have suited a man of his education and circumstances. Himself full of artistic taste, he could not deny all worth to life's external adornments; extending his scientific research unreservedly to all reality, he could hardly, in ordinary life, be so indifferent to the outward, as they who, like Socrates, were satisfied with moral introspection. Socrates, in spite of his anti-democratic politics, was, by nature, a thorough man of the people: Plato's personality, like his philosophy, bears a more aristocratic stamp. He loves to shut himself up in his own circle, to ward off what is vulgar and disturbing; his interest and solicitude are not for all without distinction, but only or chiefly for the elect who are capable of sharing his culture, his knowledge, his view of life. The aristocracy of intelligence on which his State rests has deep roots in the character of Plato. But precisely to this circumstance are owing the grandeur and completeness that make his character in its particular sphere unique. As Plato in his capacity of philosopher unites the boldest idealism with rare acuteness of thought, a disposition for abstract critical inquiry with the freshness of artistic creativeness; — so does he, as a man, combine severity of moral principles with lively susceptibility for beauty, nobility and loftiness of mind with tenderness of feeling, passion with self-control, enthusiasm for his purpose with philosophic calm, gravity with mildness, magnanimity with human kindness, dignity with gentleness. He is great because he knew how to blend these apparently conflicting traits into unity, to complement opposites by means of each other, to develope on all sides the exuberance of his powers and capabilities into a perfect harmony, without losing himself in their multiplicity. That moral beauty and soundness of the whole life, which Plato, as a true Greek, requires before all things, he has, if his nature be truly represented in his works, brought to typical perfection in his own personality. Nor is the picture marred by incongruity of outward semblance with inward reality, for his bodily strength and beauty have been especially recorded. But throughout, the most striking peculiarity of the philosopher is that close connection of his character with his scientific aims, which he owes to the Socratic school. The moral perfection of his life is rooted in the clearness of his understanding; it is light of science which disperses the mists of his soul, and causes that Olympian serenity which breathes so refreshingly from his works. In a word, Plato's is an Apollo-like nature, and it is a fitting testimony to the impression produced by himself on his contemporaries, and by his writings on after generations, that many myths should have placed him, like Pythagoras, in the closest union with the god who, in the bright clearness of his spirit, was to the Greeks the very type of moral beauty, proportion, and harmony.

PLATO'S WRITINGS

THE most eloquent monument of the Platonic spirit, and the most important source for our knowledge of the Platonic doctrine, are in the writings of the philosopher himself. His literary activity extends over the greater part of his life, a period of more than fifty years, — and by a special favor of Fortune, it has so happened that not one of the works which he intended for publicity has been lost. This is at any rate a reasonable inference from the fact that no reliable trace of the existence of any Platonic writing no longer in our possession has come down to us; for the spuriousness of the lost dialogues of which we do hear is beyond question, and some other writings which might be supposed to be Platonic — the " Division " Discourses about Philosophy, and about the Good, " the unwritten doctrines " — originally never claimed to be the works of Plato at all. There is no ground even for thinking that any Platonic writing was ever more complete than it is now.

Fortune has indeed bestowed less care on the purity of the Platonic collection. Even the learned among the Greeks regarded as spurious several of the writings that bore Plato's name; the critics of our own century, sometimes unanimously, sometimes by an overwhelming majority, have rejected a still greater number; others are yet upon their trial, and among these, as formerly happened on the first appearance of Ast and Socher, is to be found more than one work the repudiation of which would con-siderably affect our apprehensions of the Platonic

philosophy. Though an exhaustive investigation of
this subject would exceed the limits of the present
treatise, we must to a certain extent examine it, and
notice the points of view on which our judgment of
it depends. With regard then first to the external
evidence, from the consideration of which every such
inquiry must start, — by far the most important is
that of Aristotle. For setting this aside, very few
remarks of ancient authors concerning the works of
Plato have been handed down to us, either from his
own or the succeeding century; and these relate
almost entirely to writings which Aristotle, too,
distinctly ascribes to Plato. Towards the end of the
third century, Aristophanes of Byzantium first arranged a portion of the works in those five Trilogies
which we know from Diog. iii. 61; and fully two centuries later, Thrasylus made a catalogue of them in
nine Tetralogies, which catalogue, with a few very
unimportant exceptions, contains all the writings
transmitted to us as Platonic. Grote thinks we may
place entire confidence, not only in the statements
of Aristophanes, but even in the catalogue of
Thrasylus. It can not be supposed, he argues, that
the school of Athens, which was continued in an unbroken line from its commencement, should not have
been completely and accurately informed of all that
its founder had written. On the contrary, there can
be no doubt that his very handwriting was carefully
preserved there: and the members of the Academy
were thus in a position to furnish the most trustworthy information to anyone who sought it, concerning the authenticity or the text of a Platonic
work. Such an opportunity would surely not have
been neglected by Demetrius Phalereus and his
successors at the founding of the Alexandrian Library. They would either have procured copies of

the original manuscripts of Plato, or have instituted inquiries in Athens as to the authenticity of the works which they received into their collection, causing a catalogue to be made of all the undoubted writings; and since Aristophanes certainly and Thrasylus probably, followed in their catalogues the Alexandrian tradition, the statements of these writers may be fairly supposed entitled to a high degree of credit. This theory, however, rests wholly upon a series of uncertain presuppositions. It may be that the original manuscripts of Plato, or copies of his works used by himself, were preserved in the Academy, though not a particle of historical evidence on the subject exists; but even supposing such to have been the case, who can guarantee that not only Plato's personal disciples, but their successors, were so convinced of the completeness of their collection, and so jealously watchful over its purity, as to deny admittance to every book not included in it, and represented to them as Platonic? Not to mention that there are many conceivable cases in which the manuscript collection in possession of the school might have to be completed by genuine Platonic works. And granted that the Academy had indeed never admitted any spurious writing into their library, how can we be sure that the Alexandrian librarians were equally scrupulous? They certainly might, on the above presupposition, have informed themselves in Athens as to the works which were there acknowledged to be authentic, but how can we know that they actually did this? There is not the slightest warrant for the assertion; but on the other hand we are told that the high prices paid for writings in Alexandria and Pergamus gave great encouragement to forgery, and that in particular many works were falsely attributed to Aristotle, in

order that they might be bought by Ptolemy Phila-
delphus. When we further consider the state of
literary criticism in the post Aristotelian period, it
seems unreasonable to credit the Alexandrians with
having tested the authenticity of works bearing illustrious names, so carefully and accurately as Grote
presupposes. The catalogues of Aristophanes and
Thrasylus therefore merely prove that the writings
they include were held to be Platonic at the time of
these grammarians; whether they really were so or
not, can only be determined by a particular inquiry
into each work, according to the general rules of
criticism.

The statements of Aristotle afford a much safer
criterion; but even with regard to these, the case is
by no means so simple as might be supposed. In
the first place, it is sometimes doubtful whether the
writing or the passage which refers to a saying of
Plato's in truth emanates from Aristotle; and this
doubt has already destroyed or weakened the argumentative force of some quotations. But even
though the Aristotelian authorship of a passage
apparently relating to Platonic writings be fully
established, the reference is not always of a kind that
implies an unequivocal recognition of the writings.
If not merely the name of the writing is given, but
also that of the author; if Aristotle says, " Plato remarks in the Timæus, Republic," &c., there can of
course be no hesitation as to his meaning. But not
unfrequently the writing in which some passage is
to be found is named without mention of its author;
or conversely, utterances and opinions are ascribed
to Plato, and nothing is stated concerning the writings in which they occur; or lastly, reference is made
to theories and expressions contained in our Platonic
collection. and yet there is no allusion either to Plato

as their author, or to a particular writing as their source. It also happens sometimes that a passage from some dialogue is quoted with an express mention of the dialogue, and yet is attributed to Socrates, and not to Plato. In all these cases, the question arises whether or not we can claim Aristotelian evidence for the Platonic origin of the writings concerned; but a portion of them only need occasion us any serious doubt. If Aristotle, in naming a dialogue, remarks, " Socrates here maintains this or that," he always means by it that Plato in this dialogue has put the remark into the mouth of Socrates. For not only does he employ the same mode of expression as to writings which he elsewhere most emphatically attributes to Plato, but he never quotes an opinion or a saying of Socrates from any writing that is not in our Platonic collection; though he must certainly have been acquainted with the Socratic dialogues of Xenophon, Æschines, and Antisthenes. Indeed the Socratic utterances are regarded by him as so completely identical with Plato's works, that he even designates the Laws as Socratic, although Socrates never appears in them, and is probably not intended by the Athenian stranger; and he quotes views which were entirely originated by Plato and put in the mouth of his master, simply as the views of Socrates, without any discrimination of the Platonic from the historic Socrates. If, therefore, a dialogue in our collection is thus treated by Aristotle, we may be certain that he considers it a work of Plato. The same holds good as to dialogues which are cited without the name either of Socrates or Plato. This kind of quotation only presupposes that the writing in question is known to the reader, and will not be mistaken for anything else; we therefore find it employed about other works that are universally famous; but among the philosophic writings which Aristotle mentions in this way, there is none which does not belong to our Platonic collection: the Platonic writings, as before remarked, are the only writings of the Socratic school to which he ever refers.   This circumstance makes it extremely probable that Aristotle really intends to ascribe all the writings quoted by him in this form to Plato, otherwise we should certainly have had a right to expect that those which he considered spurious, especially if in their style and treatment they might claim to be Platonic, would not have been introduced without some hint as to the true state of the case.   For he could not presuppose this to be necessarily known to his readers.

As to those passages which attribute to Plato or Socrates theories and sayings to be met with in the Platonic writings, but which do not mention the writings, Aristotle himself very often furnishes us with a proof that he is really referring to these by his use of the present tense: " Plato maintains," " Socrates says," and the like.   When he employs this form of expression, it is a sure indication that he has in his mind those Socratic or Platonic discourses which are laid down in writings; and when we find these very discourses in a work that tradition assures us to be Platonic, it is hardly possible to doubt that this is the work to which the quotation relates.   An appeal of this kind to Socratic or Platonic utterances, therefore, if these conditions fully obtain, has no less force than the literal mention of the particular writing, and the express acknowledgement of its Platonic origin. On the other hand, however, we must not conclude that Aristotle, whenever he makes use of the preterite in mentioning a doctrine of Socrates or Plato, refers only indirectly or not at all, to the writings that contain it.   Several cases are here to be distinguished.

In the first place, the perfect tense may properly be employed, and is very commonly employed by Aristotle, in quoting the sayings of Plato, or of the Platonic Socrates, from a writing. It is somewhat different with the narrative forms — the imperfect and aorist. These are only used in respect to Socrates when some theory is to be ascribed to the historic Socrates, supposing it to have become known to Aristotle through certain writings. For it might very well be said of the Platonic Socrates that he maintains something (in the present), or that something is in question as said by him (in the perfect), but not that he formerly has said something, because as this ideal person he exists for the reader of the Platonic writings, and for him only, in the present; he has no existence independently of the reader and belonging to the past. If, however, Plato himself is mentioned as having said or thought something, this consideration has no longer any force. His utterances are not merely sayings which are present to us in his works, but also acts which he completed in the compilation of those works; in that case, therefore, a historic tense, as well as a present, might be used in quoting them. Though this does not occur very frequently, it is sometimes to be met with, and we have consequently no right to conclude from the use of the preterite in the quotation of a Platonic saying, that it is not derived from any written work.

But there are also many passages in Aristotle where neither Plato nor any one of his dialogues is mentioned, but which have internal evidence to show that Aristotle in writing them had definitely in view particular works of Plato, and which very often allude to these unmistakably, though indirectly. The argumentative value of these passages can only be determined in each case by an appeal to the ordinary rules of criticism. The more perfect is the coincidence between the passage in Aristotle and the corresponding passage of a Platonic dialogue, and the less reason we have for supposing that the author of the dialogue made use of the Aristotelian writing, the clearer it becomes that the dialogue in question was known to Aristotle, and the greater the probability that this, like other portions of our Platonic collection, similarly quoted and employed, was recognised by him as genuine.

Among the writings that have been transmitted to us as Platonic, those which are most frequently criticised by Aristotle, with continual mention both of the author and the dialogue, are the three great expository works — the Republic, the Timæus, and the Laws. Besides these, the Phædo only is expressly designated by him as a work of Plato. The Phædrus is once named, and its definition of the soul is twice quoted as Platonic. The speech of Aristophanes from the Symposium is treated in a manner that presupposes the authenticity of that dialogue; and the same may be said of the allusions to the Gorgias, Meno, and Lesser Hippias. The Theætetus is not actually mentioned, but passages are adduced as from Platonic writings, which are only there to be found. Similarly the Philebus is not named by Aristotle; but in certain passages of his Ethics he evidently has it in mind, and in one of these passages he cites expressly from a Platonic exposition, propositions which the Philebus alone contains. We therefore can not doubt that he was acquainted with this dialogue and recognised its authenticity. There are also in the writings of Aristotle many indications, which sometimes taken independently, sometimes in their coincidence, unmistakably prove that both the Sophist and the Politicus were regarded by him as Platonic; and as the Politicus is plainly referred to in the Laws, it has the further support of all the evidence on the side of the latter. It is clear from the Rhetoric that the Apology was acknowledged by Aristotle; but some doubt exists with regard to the Menexenus. He nowhere mentions the Parmenides; there is only one minor particular, which may possibly be quoted from it. But if the Philebus really alludes to the Parmenides, the evidence for the one dialogue would indirectly apply to the other. The Protagoras, too, is never specified; but it was apparently known to Aristotle, and used by him as a historical authority. He seems also to have been acquainted with the Lysis, Charmides, and Laches; though this is not so certain as in the case of the Protagoras. It is still more doubtful whether or not two passages relate to the Cratylus and the Greater Hippias. The Euthydemus is indeed referred to by Eudemus; but the fallacies which Aristotle quotes from the sophist of that name are not to be found in the Platonic dialogue; and though certainly on the supposition of its genuineness, we should expect Aristotle to have used it in his examination of fallacies which often brought him in contact with it, this relation of the two expositions is not sufficiently established to serve as proof for the authenticity of the Euthydemus.

If, then, any dialogue in our collection is mentioned by Aristotle as Platonic, or used by him in a manner that presupposes it to be so, this circumstance is greatly in favor of its authenticity. For twenty years before the death of Plato, Aristotle was a member of the Platonic School at Athens; after that event he quitted the city, but returned twelve or thirteen years later for the rest of his life. That during the lifetime of the master any writing should have been falsely regarded as his work, by scholars who were already well instructed on the subject, or had the opportunity at any moment of becoming so, is quite impossible. Even in the generation succeeding his death, while Speusippus and Xenocrates were at the head of the Academy, and Aristotle and other personal disciples of Plato lived in Athens, this could only have occurred under quite peculiar conditions, and to a very limited extent. It is indeed conceivable that some one of the less important dialogues might after the death of Plato have been admitted even by his immediate disciples without previous acquaintance with it, as an earlier work that had escaped their attention, or under certain circumstances as a posthumous bequest. Cases of this kind have occurred in our own times, though we are so much richer than the ancients in resources, and more practised in literary criticism. It might still more easily happen that an imperfect sketch of Plato's, completed by another after his death — an unfinished writing, worked up by one of his disciples — might be received as wholly genuine, without accurate discrimination of the original from the later ingredients. But it is incredible that such things should frequently have repeated themselves in the first generation after the master's death; or that reputed works of his, which, had they existed, must on account of their importance have been owned during his lifetime by the School, should afterwards have emerged, and have been universally recognised. If the testimony of Aristotle to Platonic writings, so far as it is clear and undoubted, does not absolutely guarantee their authenticity, it is at all events so strong an argument in their favor, that only the weightiest internal evidence should be suffered to countervail it; and if any criticism of the Platonic collection starts from presuppositions requiring the rejection of numerous works recognised by

Aristotle, there is enough in this one circumstance to prove these presuppositions incorrect.

But if the evidence of Aristotle has this importance on the side of the writings from which he quotes, can we with certainty conclude that those about which he is silent are spurious? No one would maintain this without some qualification. Aristotle is not passing judgment on Plato's works as a literary historian who is bound to furnish a complete catalogue of them, and to tell all that he knows. Nor does he deal with them as a modern writer of the history of philosophy, whose object it is to combine their whole philosophic content into a representation of the Platonic theory; he only mentions them when occasion offers, in stating his own views, or criticising or opposing those of Plato and Socrates. We must not expect him, therefore, to name everything that is known to him as Platonic, but only such writings as it was necessary or desirable to mention for the purposes of any scientific discussion he might happen to be pursuing. Even this canon, however, must be cautiously applied. Plato's works are for us the sole, or at any rate the principal, source of our knowledge concerning his system: we cannot speak of the Platonic philosophy without continually recurring to them. In the case of Aristotle it was otherwise. He owes his knowledge of the Platonic doctrines in the first place to verbal communication and personal intercourse; in the second place only, to the writings of Plato. They were to him but subsidiary sources; in the exposition of the doctrines, he uses them sometimes for the confirmation of that which he already knows from Plato's oral discourses; but he has no occasion to enter more deeply into their contents except on subjects which were not examined in those discourses. Of such subjects, the most important seem to be the application

of philosophical principles to the explanation of
nature and to political institutions: hence the numerous quotations from the Republic, the Timæus, and
the Laws. The metaphysical bases of the system, on
the other hand, are indeed frequently and searchingly
criticised by Aristotle, but in by far the greater number of cases on the ground of Plato's discourses: the
propædeutic inquiries into the conception of knowledge, true virtue, and the art of governing, love, the
right scientific method, and its opposition to the
Sophistic teaching, are seldom touched upon. Only
one of the many passages from which we derive our
knowledge of the theory of ideas is quoted by him:
he makes no allusion to what is said on this subject
in the Republic, Timæus, Symposium, Phædrus, and
Theætetus; nor to the explanations of the Sophist,
Parmenides, and Philebus, though there was abundant opportunity for it. Even the well-known discussions of the Republic upon the Good are merely
glanced at with an uncertain hint, despite the frequent occasions when they might have been aptly
introduced. If we turn to those dialogues the authenticity of which has never been questioned, we find the
Protagoras, as before remarked, apparently made
use of in some passages, but it is never named, and
nothing is quoted from it as Platonic. The Theætetus is twice mentioned, the Gorgias and the Symposium once; and none of these quotations relate to the
main content of the dialogues — they are only incidental recollections of certain particulars in them, the
notice of which seems entirely fortuitous. All this
being considered, we may well hesitate to conclude
from Aristotle's silence with regard to any Platonic
writing, that he was unacquainted with it; and this
so much the more, as we do not even possess the whole
of Aristotle's works, and some lost writing or frag-

ment might very possibly contain citations from
dialogues for which we have now no Aristotelian
evidence. It is certainly surprising that Aristotle
should assert that Plato never inquired wherein the
participation of things in ideas consists; while in the
Parmenides the difficulties with which this theory has
to contend are clearly pointed out. But it is not
more surprising than that he should assail the doctrine of ideas with the question: "Who formed the
things of sense after the pattern of the ideas?" —
though it is distinctly stated in the Timæus that the
Creator of the world did this in looking on the eternal
archetypes. Nor, again, that he should maintain,
notwithstanding the well-known explanation in the
Phædo, often alluded to by himself — notwithstanding the doctrine in the Republic, of the Good being
the absolute end of the world — that the final cause
is not touched by the ideas. We should have expected
that in attacking Plato about the τρίτος ἄνθρωπος
Aristotle, had he been acquainted with the Parmenides, would have referred to the fact that in that
dialogue the same objection is raised. But might we
not also have expected after the further stricture:
"Plato ought then to assume ideas of art productions, mere relations, &c., which he does not," some
such remark as this: "In his writings he certainly
does speak of such ideas"? And in the discussions
concerning the Platonic theory of the world-soul,
should we not have anticipated some mention of the
passage in the Laws about the evil soul, which has
given so many handles to criticism? Many other
things besides these might reasonably have been
looked for on the supposition that the writings of
Plato had the same significance, as sources of his
doctrines, for Aristotle as for us, and were used by
him in a similar manner. But this we have no right

to presuppose; and therefore his not alluding to a writing is by no means sufficient to prove that it was unknown to him, or that he did not acknowledge it to be Platonic.

By means of Aristotle's testimony, supplemented sometimes from other quarters, we are thus enabled to ascribe a number of writings to Plato with all the certainty that can be attained in this way. These works acquaint us with the scientific and literary character of their author, and so furnish us with a criterion for the criticism of other works or portions of works which are either insufficiently supported by external evidence, or in their form or contents are open to suspicion. Great care, however, is necessary in fixing and applying this standard; and in some cases even the most cautious weighing of favorable and adverse considerations can not insure absolute certainty. In the first place we must decide, on which of the dialogues noticed by Aristotle our Platonic criterion is to be based. If we confine ourselves to those which he expressly attributes to Plato, we shall have only the Republic, the Timæus, the Phædo, and the Laws; and important as these works are, it is questionable whether they represent the scientific and literary individuality of the many-sided Plato exhaustively enough to make everything appear un-Platonic that at all departs from their type. If, on the other hand, we also take into account those writings of which Aristotle makes use without mentioning their author, or from which he quotes something that Plato has said, without naming the dialogue, — we find that the Philebus is as well attested as the Theætetus; the Sophist, Politicus, Meno, and the Lesser Hippias, as the Gorgias and Symposium; and all of them better than the Protagoras, the authenticity of which no one doubts. Our Platonic criterion must.

in this case, therefore be considerably wider than that of Ueberweg and Schaarschmidt. Moreover it must not be imagined that each divergence in a dialogue from those works considered normal is necessarily a proof of its spuriousness; these normal works them-selves present deviations one from the other, equal in importance to many that have formed the basis of adverse judgments. If it be objected against the Philebus that it wants dramatic liveliness, and the flow of conversational development, the Protagoras may be charged with meagreness of scientific content, with the entire failure of the theory of ideas, with the apparent barrenness of result in the whole inquiry, and the fatiguing prolixity of the discussion about the verse of Simonides. If the antinomic development of conceptions is peculiar to the Parmenides, and elaborate classifications to the Sophist and Politicus, — the Timæus stands alone not only in its theories of the Creator and antemundane matter, the mathematical construction of the elements, the arithmetical division, and distribution of the soul in space, but in its minute treatment of the whole subject of Physics, to which no other dialogue makes an approach. The Laws are separated by a far greater interval from the Republic and from the other normal works than from the Politicus, and in an artistic point of view are open to much graver criticism than the dialectical dialogues; the later form of the Platonic philosophy, known to us through Aristotle, has a much more abstruse and formal character than the logical and metaphysical statements of the Laws. We cannot, indeed, go quite so far as Grote, who sometimes speaks as if Plato in none of his works had the least regard to those already written, and thought nothing of contradicting himself in the most glaring manner, even in one and the same dialogue. But we ought not, on the other hand, to forget that so exuberant a spirit as Plato's was not limited for its expression to one particular form; that the purpose of a dialogue might make it necessary to emphasize some points in it, and to pass slightly over others: that the nature of a subject or the readers for whom it was intended might require the style of a work to be more or less ornate, and the treatment to be more or less popular; that much that now seems to us incomprehensible might be explained by special occasions and personal references; that as we might have anticipated, even without the evidence establishing it, during the sixty years of Plato's literary activity both his philosophy and his artistic method underwent a considerable change, and that on this account, if on no other, a standard derived from a portion of his works can not be applicable to them all without condition or modification. These considerations certainly render a decision concerning the genuineness of Platonic writings, so far as this depends on internal arguments, very difficult and complicated. It is not enough simply to compare one dialogue with others, we must inquire whether Plato, as we know him from his undoubted works, might be supposed to have produced the writing in question at a certain date and under certain circumstances. This of course can not always be answered with equal assurance, either affirmatively or negatively. It is sometimes hard to distinguish with perfect accuracy the work of a tolerably expert imitator from a less important work of the master; what is un-Platonic from what is unfinished, or the result of Plato's advanced age; and therefore it is almost unavoidable that among the dialogues which can be vouched for as Platonic, or the reverse, others should creep in, with respect to which a certain degree of probability is all we can attain. Those writings, however, on which our knowledge and estimate of the Platonic philosophy chiefly depend, can well maintain their ground in any impartial investigation; while, on the other hand, our general view of Platonism would be very little affected by the genuineness or spuriousness of several of the lesser dialogues.

It is impossible in this place to pursue this subject more particularly, or to discuss the reasons which may be urged for or against the Platonic origin of each work. But it seems necessary to point out those writings on which, as original sources of the Platonic philosophy, our exposition of that philosophy will be founded, if even the critical grounds which determine the position of these writings should not at once be explained, and receive only partial notice hereafter.

Our collection of Platonic works contains, besides those dialogues which even in ancient times were acknowledged to be spurious, thirty-five dialogues, thirteen letters, and a number of definitions, mostly relating to ethics. Among these there are a few — the Protagoras, Phædrus, Symposium, Gorgias, Theætetus, and Republic — the authenticity of which has never been questioned: the Phædo also has been as little affected by the suspicion of Panætius (if it really existed) — as the Timæus by Schelling's temporary doubt. The genuineness of all these works may be considered as fully established. There are, besides, several other important dialogues — the Philebus, Sophist, Politicus, Parmenides, and Cratylus, — which, in spite of the repeated assaults upon them in modern days, are certainly to be regarded as Platonic — not only on the strength of the Aristotelian testimony which can be cited for most of them, but

also on account of conclusive internal evidence. The
position of the Laws will be the subject of a future
discussion. There is all the less reason to mistrust
the Critias, since its contents, so far as they go, are
entirely in harmony with the opening of the Timæus.
The Meno is protected by a clear reference in the
Phædo, as well as by Aristotle's quotations; and
though not one of Plato's most perfect dialogues,
there is no good reason to suspect its authenticity.
The Euthydemus is at any rate made use of by Eudemus, and, though often attacked, may be easily defended, if we bear in mind the proper design of this
dialogue, and sufficiently discriminate between what
is seriously intended and what is satirical exaggeration or irony: it would be hard to deny to Plato on
trivial grounds so charming a sketch, abounding in
comic power and humor. The Apology, which was
known to Aristotle, is as little really doubtful as
the Crito: both are perfectly comprehensible if we
regard the one as in the main a true statement of
facts, and the other as apparently a freer representation of the motives which deterred Socrates from
flight. We may consider the Lysis, Charmides, and
Laches, with all of which Aristotle seems to have
been acquainted, to be youthful productions, written
when Plato had not as yet essentially advanced beyond the Socratic standpoint; the Lesser Hippias,
which is supported by very decisive Aristotelian evidence, as a first attempt; and the Euthyphro as an
occasional writing, of a slight and hasty character.
On the other hand, there are so many weighty internal arguments against the Menexenus, that notwithstanding the passages in Aristotle's Rhetoric, it is
difficult to believe this work Platonic: if Aristotle
really meant to attest it, we might suppose that in
this one instance he was deceived by a forgery ven-

tured upon soon after Plato's death. The Ion is
probably, and the Greater Hippias and First Alcibiades are still more probably, spurious. The remainder of the dialogues in our collection, the Second
Alcibiades, the Theages, the Anterasti, Hipparchus,
Minos, Clitophon, and Epinomis, have been rightly
abandoned almost unanimously by all modern critics
with the exception of Grote. It is impossible for a
moment to allow any genuineness to the Definitions;
and Karsten and Steinhart, following the example
of Meiners, Hermann, and others, have conclusively
shown that the Letters, as has so often happened,
were foisted upon their reputed author at various
dates.

It has indeed been questioned whether even the
undoubted works of Plato present a true picture of
his system. According to some, partly to increase
his own importance, partly as a precautionary measure, Plato designedly concealed in his writings the
real sense and connection of his doctrines, and only
disclosed this in secret to his more confidential pupils.
This notion has been, however, since Schleiermacher
justly and almost universally abandoned. It can be
supported neither on Platonic nor Aristotelian evidence: the assertions of later writers who transferred
their conceptions of the Pythagorean mystical doctrine to Plato, consequently prove nothing. It is
besides utterly incredible in itself that a philosopher
like Plato should have spent a long life in literary
labors, designed not to impart his views, but to hide
them; a purpose far more effectually and simply
carried out by silence. Further he himself assigns
the same content to the written as to the spoken
word, when he makes the aim of the one to be the
reminding us of the other. And Aristotle could not
have been aware of any essential difference between

Plato's oral and written teaching, otherwise he would
not have based his own exposition and criticism equally
on both, without ever drawing attention to the fact
that the true sense of the writings could only be determined by the spoken comments of their author. Still
less would he have taken the mythical or half mythical
portions in a literal manner, only possible to one who
had never conceived the idea of a secret doctrine pervading them. Nor can this theory be brought into
connection with Plato's habit of indirectly hinting at
his opinion and gradually arriving at it, instead of
distinctly stating it when formed; with his occasional pursuit, in pure caprice as it might seem, of
accidental digressions; with the confessions of ignorance or the doubting questions that, instead of a fixed
unequivocal decision, conclude many of the dialogues;
or with the method that in particular cases invests
philosophic thoughts with the many-colored veil of
the mythus. All this, it is true, is found in Plato;
and the reasons for such a method will hereafter
disclose themselves. Meanwhile the form of the dialogues will offer no insuperable hindrance to their
comprehension by anyone who has penetrated their
aim and plan, and learned to consider each in the
light of the whole, and as explicable only in its relation to others; nor again is there anything in this
form to weaken the belief that in the writings of
Plato we have trustworthy records of his philosophy.
If, lastly, we find in these writings, side by side with
philosophic inquiry, a considerable space allotted to
historical description and dramatic imagery, it is yet
easy in some cases to separate these elements, in
others to recognise the philosophic kernel which they
themselves contain.

PLATO'S PHILOSOPHY

THE Platonic philosophy is on the one side the completion of the Socratic; but on the other, an extension and an advance upon it. As Socrates in his philosophic inquiries concerned himself with the moral quite as much as with the intellectual life — as with him right action was inseparably united with right cognition, philosophy with morality and religion, being indeed one and the same thing — so is it in Plato; and as the aim of the one philosopher was to ground intelligence and conduct on conceptual knowledge, so to the other the standard of all action and of all convictions is the contemplation of universal ideas. Plato's views concerning the problem and principle of philosophy thus rest entirely on a Socratic basis. But that which had been with Socrates only a universal axiom became with Plato a system; that which the former had laid down as the principle of knowledge was announced by the latter as the principle of metaphysics. Socrates had sought that conceptual knowledge for which he claimed existence, but he had only reduced to their primary concept particular activities and phenomena in connection with the given case. He had never attempted to gain a whole from scientifically combined concepts, and thus to explain the totality of the Real. He confined himself on principle to ethical inquiries, and even these he pursued, not systematically, but in a merely inductory manner. It was Plato who first expanded the Socratic philosophy into a system, combined its ethics with the earlier natural philosophy, and founded both in dia-

lectics, or the pure science of ideas. But the necessity immediately became apparent of a principle not
only to guide thought in the scientific method, but
also to interpret material things in their essence and
existence. Plato, in transcending the Socratic ethics,
transcends also the Socratic acceptation of conceptual knowledge. The cognition of ideas, Socrates
had said, is the condition of all true knowledge and
right action. Therefore, concludes Plato, logical
thought is alone true knowledge. All other ways
of knowing — presentation, envisagement — afford
no scientific certainty of conviction. But if the
knowledge of the idea is alone real knowledge, this
can only be, according to Plato, because that alone
is a knowledge of the Real; because true Being
belongs exclusively to the essence of things presented
in the idea, and to all else, in proportion only as it
participates in the idea. Thus the idealizing of the
concept, which with Socrates had been a logical pos-
tulate involving a certain scientific dexterity, dialectical impulse, and dialectical art, was now raised
to the objective contemplation of the world, and
perfected into a system.

This, however, was impossible without introducing a sharper discrimination between intellectual
and moral activity. Their direct and unconditional
unity, which Socrates had demanded, can only be
maintained so long as no advance is made beyond
his general view of the two-sided problems. The
moment we proceed to particulars — either, on the
one hand, examining the conditions of scientific
thought, and directing that thought to subjects of
no immediate moral import; or, on the other, fixing
the attention more steadily on that which is peculiar
to moral activities and their various manifesta-
tions — we can no longer conceal from ourselves

that there is a difference, as well as a connection between knowledge and action. It will be shown hereafter that this difference forced itself upon Plato too: herein, however, as in his whole conception of philosophy, he is far less widely separated than Aristotle from his master. He distinguishes more sharply than the one between the moral direction of the will and scientific cognition, but does not therefore, like the other, make philosophy an exclusively theoretical activity. He completes the Socratic ethics not only with dialectical but with physical investigations: the latter, however, never prosper in his hands; and whatever may be the obligations of this branch of inquiry to Plato, it is certain that his genius and zeal for natural science were far inferior to those of Aristotle, and that his achievements in this department bear no comparison with those of his scholar, either in extent of knowledge, acuteness of observation, exactness of interpretation, or fruitfulness of result. He gives to concepts, as separate substances, the reality of Ideas; but in holding Ideas to be the only reality, and material things, as such, to be devoid of essence, and non-existent, he makes impossible to himself the explanation of the phenomenal world. He perfects the conceptual philosophy into a system, but is not impelled, like his successor, to enter deeply into particulars: to him the idea only is the true object of thought; the individual phenomenon possesses no interest. He can indeed make use of it to bring to light the idea in which it participates, but that thorough completeness with which Aristotle works his way through empirical data is not his concern. The study of particulars seems to him scarcely more than an intellectual pastime, and if he has for a while occupied himself with it, he always returns, as if wearied out, to the contempla·

tion of pure ideas. In this respect also, he stands
midway between Socrates and Aristotle; between
the philosopher who first taught the development of
the concept from presentation or envisagement, and
him who more completely than any other Greek
thinker has carried it into all the spheres of actual
existence. In the same proportion, however, that
Plato advanced beyond Socrates, it was inevitable
that he should go back to the pre-Socratic doctrines,
and regard as his co-disciples those who were then
seeking to apply those theories to the perfecting of
the Socratic doctrine. To what an extent he did both
is well known. Plato is the first of the Greek philosophers who not merely knew and made use of his
predecessors, but consciously completed their principles by means of each other, and bound them all
together in one higher principle. What Socrates had
taught with regard to the concept of knowledge;
Parmenides and Heraclitus, the Megarians and
Cynics, on the difference between knowledge and
opinion; Heraclitus, Zeno, and the Sophists, on the
subjectivity of sense perception — all this he built
up into a developed theory of knowledge. The
Eleatic principle of Being, and the Heraclitean of
Becoming, the doctrine of the unity and that of the
multiplicity of things, he has, in his doctrine of Ideas,
quite as much blended as opposed; while at the same
time he has perfected both by means of the Anaxa-
gorean conception of Spirit, the Megaro-Socratic
conception of the Good, and the idealised Pythagorean numbers. These latter, properly understood,
appear in the theory of the World-soul, and the
mathematical laws, as the mediating element between
the idea and the world of sense. Their one element,
the concept of the Unlimited, held absolutely and
combined with the Heraclitean view of the sensible

world, gives the Platonic definition of Matter. The cosmological part of the Pythagorean system is repeated in Plato's conception of the universe: while in his theory of the elements and of physics proper, Empedocles and Anaxagoras, and more distantly the Atomistic and older Ionic natural philosophies, find their echoes. His psychology is deeply coloured with the teaching of Anaxagoras on the immaterial nature of mind, and with that of Pythagoras on immortality. In his ethics, the Socratic basis can as little be mistaken as, in his politics, his sympathy with the Pythagorean aristocracy. Yet Plato is neither the envious imitator that calumny has called him, nor the irresolute eclectic, who only owed it to favoring circumstances that what was scattered about in earlier systems united in him to form a harmonious whole. We may say more truly that this blending of the rays of hitherto isolated genius into one focus is the work of his originality and the fruit of his philosophic principle. The Socratic conceptual philosophy is from the outset directed to the contemplation of things in all their aspects, the dialectic combination of those various definitions of which now one, and now another, is mistaken by a one-sided apprehension for the whole — to the reduction of the multiplicity of experience to its permanent base. Plato applies this method universally, seeking not merely the essential nature of moral activities, but the essential nature of the Real. He is thus inevitably directed towards the assumptions of his predecessors, which had all started from some true perception; but while these assumptions had related entirely and exclusively to one another, Plato's scientific principles required that he should fuse them all into a higher and more comprehensive theory of the world. As therefore Plato's knowledge of the earlier doctrines gave him the most decided impulse in the development of the Socratic teaching, it was conversely that development which alone enabled him to use the combined achievements of the other philosophers for his own system. The Socratic conceptual philosophy was transplanted by him into the fruitful and well-tilled soil of the previous natural philosophy, thence to appropriate to itself all kindred matter; and in thus permeating the older speculation with the spirit of Socrates, purifying and reforming it by dialectic, which was itself extended to metaphysical speculation, — in thus perfecting ethics by natural philosophy and natural philosophy by ethics — Plato has accomplished one of the greatest intellectual creations ever known. Philosophy could not indeed permanently remain in the form then given to it. Aristotle soon made very essential alterations in the theories of his master; the older Academy itself could not maintain them in their purity, and the later systems that thought to reproduce the system of Plato were self-deceived. But this is precisely Plato's greatness, — that he was able to give the progress of Philosophy an impulse so powerful, so far transcending the limits of his own system, and to proclaim the deepest principle of all right speculation — the Idealism of thought — with such energy, such freshness of youthful enthusiasm, that to him, despite all his scientific deficiencies, belongs the honor of forever conferring philosophic consecration on those in whom that principle lives.

In Plato's scientific method, also, we recognise the deepening, the purification and the progress of the Socratic philosophy. From the principle of conceptual knowledge arises, as its immediate consequence, that dialectic of which Socrates must be considered the author. But while Socrates contented himself with developing the concept out of mere envisagement, Plato further demanded that conceptual science should be drawn out by methodical classification into a system; while Socrates, in forming concepts, starts from the contingencies of the given case, and never goes beyond the particular, Plato requires that thought shall rise, by continued analysis, from conditioned to unconditioned, from the phenomenon to the idea, from particular ideas to the highest and most universal. The Socratic dialectic only set itself to gain the art of right thinking for the immediate use of individuals to purify their crude presentations into concepts: the practice of dialectic was therefore at the same time education; intellectual and moral activity coincided, as much for the work of the philosopher in itself as for its effect on others. The Platonic dialectic, on the other hand, was subservient to the formation of a system: it has, therefore, as compared with the Socratic, larger outlines and a more fixed form. What in the one was a matter of personal discipline, in the other becomes conscious method reduced to general rules; whereas the former aimed at educating individuals by true concepts, the latter seeks out the nature and connection of concepts, in themselves: it inquires not merely into moral problems and activities, but into the essential nature of the Real, proposing as its end a scientific representation of the universe. But Plato does not go so far in this direction as Aristotle; the technicalities of logic were not formed by him, as by his pupil, into an exact, minutely particularising theory; neither for the deviation nor for the systematic application of concepts does he summon to his aid such a mass of experimental material. He cares far less for that equal spread of scientific knowledge into all departments which Aristotle desired, than for the

contemplation of the idea as such. He regards the
Empirical partly as a mere help to the attainment
of the Idea — a ladder to be left behind if we would
gain the heights of thought; partly as a type of the
nature and inherent force of the ideas — a world of
shadows, to which the Philosopher only temporarily
descends, forthwith to return into the region of light
and of pure being. Whereas, therefore, Socrates in
the main confines himself to a search for concepts,
the cognition of which is for him moral education;
whereas Aristotle extends induction and demonstration, purely in the interests of science, over all the
Actual, — the special peculiarity of Plato is that
moral education, intellectual teaching, and, in science
itself, the formation of concepts and their development, in spite of partial separation, are yet, with
him, internally held together and united by their
common aim, both leading to that contemplation of
the idea, which is at the same time life in the idea.
This position is not indeed invariable. We see, in
the dialogues, Socratic induction at first decidedly
predominating over the constructive element, then
both intermingling, and, lastly, inductive preparation receding before systematic deduction; corresponding to which there is also a gradual change from
the form of conversation to that of continued exposition. But the fundamental character of the method
is never effaced; and however deeply Plato may
sometimes go into particulars, his ultimate design is
only to exhibit with all possible clearness and direct-
ness the Idea shining through the phenomenon; to
point out its reflection in the finite; to fill with its
light not only the intellect, but the whole man.
    This speciality in the philosophy of Plato explains
the form which he selected for its communication.
An artistic nature was indispensable for the produc-

tion of such a philosophy; conversely, this philosophy
would infallibly demand to be informed artistically.
The phenomenon, placed in such direct relation to
the idea, becomes a beautiful phenomenon; the perception of the idea in the phenomenon an æsthetic
perception.   Where science and life so completely
interpenetrate one another, as with Plato, science can
only impart itself in lively description; and as the
communicating medium is ideal, this description will
necessarily be poetical.   At the same time, however,
the exposition must be dialectical, if it is to correspond with the subject matter of conceptual philosophy.   Plato satisfies both these requirements in
the philosophic dialogue, by means of which he occupies a middle position between the personal converse
of Socrates and the purely scientific continuous exposition of Aristotle.   The Socratic conversation is
here idealised, the contingency of its motives and
conduct is corrected by a stricter method — the defects of personalities are covered by artistic treatment.   Yet the specialty of verbal intercourse, the
reciprocal kindling of thought, is still retained.   Philosophy is set forth, not merely as a doctrine, but as
a living power, in the person of the true philosopher,
and a moral and artistic effect is thus produced, of
a kind that would have been impossible to bare scientific inquiry.   Unbroken discourse is doubtless better
suited to the latter; and Plato himself shows this,
for in proportion as his scientific discussions gain in
depth and scope, they lose in freedom of conversational movement.   In the earlier works, this freedom
not unfrequently disturbs the clearness of the logic,
while in the dialectical dialogues of the middle order
it is more and more subordinated to the logical development of thought.   In the later writings, dialogue
is indeed employed with the accustomed skill for in-

troductory discussions or personal delineations; but
so far as the exposition of the system is concerned
it sinks into a mere form, and in the Timæus is discarded at the very commencement. We need not,
with Hermann, conclude from this that the form of
dialogue had for Plato a merely external value; that,
in fact, it was like some favorite and traditional
fashion of dress inherited from his predecessors,
adopted in his first attempts as a Socratic pupil, and
then adhered to out of piety and loyal attachment,
in opposition to general usage. He certainly had
an external motive for the choice of this form in
the conversations of his master, and a pattern for
its artistic treatment in dramatic poetry, especially
such as dealt with reflections, morals, and manners,
like that of Epicharmus, Sophron, and Euripides;
but it can not be proved that before his time dialogue
was already much in vogue for philosophic exposition; and even if it could, we might still be sure that
Plato, independent and creative as he was, and endowed with rare artistic feeling, would never on such
purely external grounds have held to a form all his
life long, even when it was most irksome to him,
that mere antiquity would not have determined him
in its choice, nor custom in its persistent employment, unless there had been the closest internal connection between that form and his whole conception
of philosophy. What this connection was Plato himself points out, when in the Phædrus he censures
writing, as compared with speech, with its inability
to defend itself, and its openness to all attacks and
misconceptions; for if this censure holds good of
written exposition in general, Plato must have been
conscious that even his dialogues could not entirely
escape it. Yet, on the other hand, his conviction of
the advantages of speech presupposes the design of

appropriating as far as possible those advantages to his writing, that " image of the living and animated word; " and if those advantages, in Plato's opinion, depend upon the art of scientific dialogue, we may reasonably derive from this his own application of that art. But the dialogues themselves manifest beyond possibility of mistake the design of compelling the reader, by their peculiar form, to the independent origination of thoughts. " Why should there so often be found in them, after the destruction of imaginary knowledge by the essentially Socratic method of proving ignorance, only isolated and apparently unconnected lines of inquiry? why should some of these be hidden by others? why should the argument at last resolve itself in apparent contradictions? unless Plato presupposes his reader to be capable of completing by his own active participation what is wanting in any given inquiry, of discovering the central point in that inquiry, and of subordinating all the rest to that one point — presupposes also that only such a reader will attain any conviction of having understood at all." The above-named peculiarities are unfavorable to the systematic objective development of science. Since, therefore, Plato has employed them with the most consummate art and the most deliberate intention, he must have had a special reason for it, and this can only be that he considered objective exposition as generally insufficient, and sought instead for some other manner which should stimulate the reader to possess knowledge as a self-generated thing, in which objective instruction should be conditioned by previous subjective culture. If this were the design of Plato, and he were at the same time convinced that the form of dialogue suited it better than continuous discourse, it naturally follows that he would select that form for his writings

Thought is to him a conversation of the soul with itself; philosophic communication, an engendering of truth in another; the logical element is therefore essentially dialogical. His writings, too, were probably in the first instance designed, not for the general public, but for his friends, to whom he himself would have imparted them: they were intended to remind those friends of the substance of the scientific conversations he was accustomed to carry on with them, or perhaps as a substitute for these. What therefore could be more natural than that he should adopt the form of their usual intercourse — that of the Socratic dialogue? Stricter science, in the sequel, wisely abandoned this form; but for Plato it was according to nature, and he stands alone and unapproached among all writers of philosophic dialogues, before and after him, because in the case of no other writer did the conditions under which his dialogues were produced exist in similar measure — in his person that rare combination of intellectual and artistic gifts, in his philosophy that equal perfection and inner fusion of the theoretical and practical, of the philosophic Eros, and of dialectic.

The central point of the dialogues is Socrates. Not only does he appear in most of them as the leader in conversation, in the rest as an acute and important listener and occasional speaker, but his personality is pre-eminently the bond which artistically unites the several pieces; and some of the most powerful and most delightful of the dialogues are devoted quite as much to the painting of this personality as to the philosophic development of doctrine. This trait is primarily a tribute of gratitude and veneration offered by the disciple to his master. Plato is conscious that he owes to Socrates what is best in his spiritual life, and, under this conviction, gives back to him in his writings the noblest fruits of the borrowed seed as his own. That Socrates should be brought forward was necessary, too, on artistic grounds; for the unity of the Platonic doctrine, and the intimate connection of all the writings devoted to it, could in no way be more artistically represented than by their association with one and the same personality; and that the personality of Socrates was far more suitable than any other; that a nobler, pleasanter picture — a picture more capable of idealisation — resulted from Plato's placing his opinions in the mouth of Socrates, instead of enunciating them himself, needs no proof.

His procedure has doubtless another and a deeper reason, rooted in the foundations of his manner of thought. Philosophy, according to his acceptation, being not merely a set of doctrines but the perfecting of the whole spiritual life; and science, not a finished, communicable system, apart from the person that knows, but personal activity and mental development, — true philosophy could only be represented in the perfect philosopher, in the personality, words, and demeanor of Socrates. This view of Philosophy is closely connected with another trait, by which Plato's literary individuality is marked with special clearness. This is his employment of myths, which he loves to combine with philosophic inquiry, and especially to bring forward for the opening or conclusion of a discussion. Here however, another motive comes into play. On the one side, the mythus is the expression of the religious and poetical character of the Platonic philosophy. Plato makes use of the traditions of the popular faith and of the mysteries (in which beneath the veil of fable he divines a deeper meaning) for the artistic representation of his ideas; he also extends and multiplies them by

original inventions, which rise from the transparent
personification of philosophic conceptions, into lively
epic description fully and exuberantly drawn out.
But, on the other side, the mythus is not a mere garment, thrown over a thought that had previously existed in a purely scientific shape; in many cases it is
for Plato a positive necessity, and his masterly use
of it is a consequence of the fact, that he does not turn
back upon the path of reflection to seek a picture for
his thought, but that from the very outset, like a creative artist, he thinks in pictures: that the mythus does
not reiterate that which the author has elsewhere
dialectically expressed, but seizes by anticipation, as
with a presentiment, that for which logical expression
is still wanting. The Platonic myths, in short, almost
always point to a gap in scientific knowledge: they
are introduced where something has to be set forth,
which the philosopher indeed acknowledges as true,
but which he has no means of establishing scientifically. This takes place chiefly in two cases: (1) when
it is required to explain the origin of material things,
the methodical derivation of which is impossible, according to the presuppositions of Plato's system;
and (2) when circumstances are to be described which
have no analogy with our present experience, and
which can not be more exactly delineated. The first
is found in the mythological cosmogony of the
Timæus; the second in the narrations concerning the
future life and the primeval history of man; for the
essential purport of these latter is also the determination of the state in which human society would find
itself under altered, ideal conditions. When Plato
in these cases adopts the mythical representation,
he indirectly confesses that his ordinary style would
be impossible to him. His myths are consequently
not only a proof of his artistic ability, and an effect

of the intimate relation still subsisting between his philosophy and his poetry, but they also betray the boundaries of his methodical thought. However admirable in themselves, therefore, they are, in a scientific point of view, rather a sign of weakness than of strength: they indicate the point at which it becomes evident that as yet he can not be wholly a philosopher, because he is still too much of a poet.

Plato's more comprehensive and methodical development of philosophy necessitates also a clearer distinction of its several branches with him than with earlier philosophers. Yet the dividing lines are not so sharply drawn in his writings as in those of Aristotle; nor is the precise determination of each branch quite certain. Modern writers have not unfrequently ascribed to Plato classifications which are manifestly alien to him; and the same is true of the previously mentioned attempts of the old grammarians to arrange his works according to their contents. Though the external evidence in its favor is insufficient, there is far more to be said for the theory that he divided the whole subject matter of philosophy into three parts: Dialectics (or Logic), Physics, and Ethics. For not only is this distribution presupposed by Aristotle and employed by Xenocrates, but the most important of the dialogues, in regard to their main subject, fall into three corresponding groups; though scarcely one dialogue is wholly contained in either. The Timæus, and, so far as Anthropology may be classed under Physics, the Phædo also, is physical as to contents; the Republic, Politicus, Philebus, Gorgias, ethical; the Theætetus, Sophist and Parmenides, dialectical. We may therefore venture to derive this division from Plato, though it is never brought forward in his writings, and at any rate can not be proved in the case of his oral discourses. But however

applicable it may be, it does not exhaust the philosophic content of the dialogues. It has already been
pointed out that in these the Socratic induction,—
discussion for scientific preparation and moral education, — is combined with systematic development of
doctrine, and at first even asserts itself to a far greater
extent. What place, then, is to be assigned to such
arguments? Where are we to arrange all those refu-
tations of popular opinion and of customary virtue,
of the Sophists and their Eudæmonistic theories —
all those passages which treat of the conception and
the method of knowledge, the oneness of virtue, and
the relation of knowledge to moral action, of philosophic love and the stages of its development? It is
usual to place one part of them under Dialectic,
another under Ethics. But by this procedure, either
the coherent exposition of these sciences is interrupted by elementary discussions which Plato, even
where he introduces them, has left far behind — or
the inquiries concerning true knowledge and right
action, always in him so closely intermingled, are
forced widely apart. To renounce an articulate
division of the exposition based on the contents, and
to adhere only to the conjectural arrangement of
the dialogues, seems unadvisable; for if we thus gain
a true representation of the order in which Plato pro-
pounded his thoughts, we get none of their internal
connection; and it is evident from the frequent discussion in widely distant dialogues of one and the
same thought, that the two orders do not necessarily
coincide. Unless we would follow Plato even in his
repetitions — in the want of perfect systematic clearness inseparable from his manner of explanation —
we must, in considering dialogues which are the
stronghold of any particular doctrine, adduce all
parallel instances from among the other dialogues

But if in this manner the order of the writings be once abandoned, we have no longer any reason for adhering to it at all; the problem will rather be to place ourselves at the inner source and centre of the Platonic system, and to rally round this nucleus the elements of that system, according to their internal relation in the mind of their author. On this subject Plato himself gives a pregnant hint. The highest division of the thinkable, he says, and the proper object of philosophy is this: "What the reason as such attains by means of the dialectic faculty, using the hypotheses not as first principles, but merely as hypotheses, like steps and points of departure, in order to reach out from them to the unconditioned, the first principle of all things; and laying hold of this, and then of that which follows from it, it again descends to the last step; so that it nowhere makes use of any sensible object but proceeds wholly from ideas, through ideas, to ideas." In this passage, and also in a noteworthy passage of Aristotle, a double way is clearly traced out for thought: the way from beneath, upward; and that from above, downward: the inductive ascent to the idea, effected by the cancelling of final hypotheses, and the systematic descent from the idea to the particular.

THE REPUBLIC

THE REPUBLIC

BOOK I

PERSONS OF THE DIALOGUE

SOCRATES, *who is the narrator.*   CEPHALUS.
GLAUCON.   THRASYMACHUS.
ADEIMANTUS.   CLEITOPHON.
POLEMARCHUS.

And others who are mute auditors.

The scene is laid in the house of Cephalus at the Piraeus; and the whole dialogue is narrated by Socrates the day after it actually took place to Timaeus, Hermocrates, Critias, and a nameless person, who are introduced in the Timaeus.

I WENT down yesterday to the Piraeus with Glaucon the son of Ariston, that I might offer up my prayers to the goddess;[1] and also because I wanted to see in what manner they would celebrate the festival, which was a new thing. I was delighted with the procession of the inhabitants; but that of the Thracians was equally, if not more, beautiful. When we had finished our prayers and viewed the spectacle, we turned in the direction of the city; and at that instant Polemarchus the son of Cephalus chanced to catch sight of us from a distance as we were starting on our way home, and told his servant to run and bid us wait for him. The servant took hold of me by the cloak behind, and said: Polemarchus desires you to wait.

[1] Bendis, the Thracian Artemis.

1

I turned round, and asked him where his master was.

There he is, said the youth, coming after you, if you will only wait.

Certainly we will, said Glaucon; and in a few minutes Polemarchus appeared, and with him Adeimantus, Glaucon's brother, Niceratus the son of Nicias, and several others who had been at the procession.

Polemarchus said to me: I perceive, Socrates, that you and your companion are already on your way to the city.

You are not far wrong, I said.

But do you see, he rejoined, how many we are?

Of course.

And are you stronger than all these? for if not, you will have to remain where you are.

May there not be the alternative, I said, that we may persuade you to let us go?

But can you persuade us, if we refuse to listen to you? he said.

Certainly not, replied Glaucon.

Then we are not going to listen; of that you may be assured.

Adeimantus added: Has no one told you of the torch-race on horseback in honor of the goddess which will take place in the evening?

With horses! I replied: That is a novelty. Will horsemen carry torches and pass them one to another during the race?

Yes, said Polemarchus, and not only so, but a festival will be celebrated at night, which you certainly ought to see. Let us rise soon after supper and see this festival; there will be a gathering of young men, and we will have a good talk. Stay then, and do not be perverse.

Glaucon said: I suppose, since you insist, that we must.

Very good, I replied.

Accordingly we went with Polemarchus to his house; and there we found his brothers Lysias and Euthydemus, and with them Thrasymachus the Chalcedonian, Charmantides the Paeanian, and Cleitophon the son of Aristonymus. There too was Cephalus the father of Polemarchus, whom I had not seen for a long time, and I thought him very much aged. He was seated on a cushioned chair, and had a garland on his head, for he had been sacrificing in the court; and there were some other chairs in the room arranged in a semicircle, upon which we sat down by him. He saluted me eagerly, and then he said: —

You don't come to see me, Socrates, as often as you ought: If I were still able to go and see you I would not ask you to come to me. But at my age I can hardly get to the city, and therefore you should come oftener to the Piraeus. For let me tell you, that the more the pleasures of the body fade away, the greater to me is the pleasure and charm of conversation. Do not then deny my request, but make our house your resort and keep company with these young men; we are old friends, and you will be quite at home with us.

I replied: There is nothing which for my part I like better, Cephalus, than conversing with aged men; for I regard them as travellers who have gone a journey which I too may have to go, and of whom I ought to inquire, whether the way is smooth and easy, or rugged and difficult. And this is a question which I should like to ask of you who have arrived at that time which the poets call the " threshold of old age " — Is life harder towards the end, or what report do you give of it?

I will tell you, Socrates, he said, what my own feeling is. Men of my age flock together; we are birds of a feather, as the old proverb says; and at our meetings the tale of my acquaintance commonly is — I can not eat, I can not drink; the pleasures of youth and love are fled away: there was a good time once, but now that is gone, and life is no longer life. Some complain of the slights which are put upon them by relations, and they will tell you sadly of how many evils their old age is the cause. But to me, Socrates, these complainers seem to blame that which is not really in fault. For if old age were the cause, I too being old, and every other old man, would have felt as they do. But this is not my own experience, nor that of others whom I have known. How well I remember the aged poet Sophocles, when in answer to the question, How does love suit with age, Sophocles, — are you still the man you were? Peace, he replied; most gladly have I escaped the thing of which you speak; I feel as if I had escaped from a mad and furious master. His words have often occurred to my mind since, and they seem as good to me now as at the time when he uttered them. For certainly old age has a great sense of calm and freedom; when the passions relax their hold, then, as Sophocles says, we are freed from the grasp not of one mad master only, but of many. The truth is, Socrates, that these regrets, and also the complaints about relations, are to be attributed to the same cause, which is not old age, but men's characters and tempers; for he who is of a calm and happy nature will hardly feel the pressure of age, but to him who is of an opposite disposition youth and age are equally a burden.

I listened in admiration, and wanting to draw him out, that he might go on — Yes, Cephalus, I said; but I rather suspect that people in general are not convinced by you when you speak thus; they think that old age sits lightly upon you, not because of your happy disposition, but because you are rich, and wealth is well known to be a great comforter.

You are right, he replied; they are not convinced: and there is something in what they say; not, however, so much as they imagine. I might answer them as Themistocles answered the Seriphian who was abusing him and saying that he was famous, not for his own merits but because he was an Athenian: " If you had been a native of my country or I of yours, neither of us would have been famous." And to those who are not rich and are impatient of old age, the same reply may be made; for to the good poor man old age can not be a light burden, nor can a bad rich man ever have peace with himself.

May I ask, Cephalus, whether your fortune was for the most part inherited or acquired by you?

Acquired! Socrates; do you want to know how much I acquired? In the art of making money I have been midway between my father and grandfather: for my grandfather, whose name I bear, doubled and trebled the value of his patrimony, that which he inherited being much what I possess now; but my father Lysanias reduced the property below what it is at present: and I shall be satisfied if I leave to these my sons not less but a little more than I received.

That was why I asked you the question, I replied, because I see that you are indifferent about money, which is a characteristic rather of those who have inherited their fortunes than of those who have acquired them; the makers of fortunes have a second love of money as a creation of their own, resembling the affection of authors for their own poems, or of parents for their children, besides that natural love of it for the sake of use and profit which is common to them and

all men. And hence they are very bad company, for
they can talk about nothing but the praises of wealth.

That is true, he said.

Yes, that is very true, but may I ask another question? — What do you consider to be the greatest
blessing which you have reaped from your wealth?

One, he said, of which I could not expect easily to
convince others. For let me tell you, Socrates, that
when a man thinks himself to be near death, fears and
cares enter into his mind which he never had before;
the tales of a world below and the punishment which
is exacted there of deeds done here were once a laughing matter to him, but now he is tormented with the
thought that they may be true: either from the weakness of age, or because he is now drawing nearer to
that other place, he has a clearer view of these things;
suspicions and alarms crowd thickly upon him, and
he begins to reflect and consider what wrongs he has
done to others. And when he finds that the sum of
his transgressions is great he will many a time like a
child start up in his sleep for fear, and he is filled
with dark forebodings. But to him who is conscious
of no sin, sweet hope, as Pindar charmingly says, is
the kind nurse of his age:

"Hope," he says, "cherishes the soul of him who lives in
justice and holiness, and is the nurse of his age and the companion of his journey; — hope which is mightiest to sway the
restless soul of man."

How admirable are his words! And the great
blessings of riches, I do not say to every man, but to a
good man, is, that he has had no occasion to deceive or
to defraud others, either intentionally or unintentionally; and when he departs to the world below he is not
in any apprehension about offerings due to the gods
or debts which he owes to men. Now to this peace of

mind the possession of wealth greatly contributes, and therefore I say, that, setting one thing against another, of the many advantages which wealth has to give, to a man of sense this is in my opinion the greatest.

Well said, Cephalus, I replied; but as concerning justice, what is it? — to speak the truth and to pay your debts — no more than this? And even to this are there not exceptions? Suppose that a friend when in his right mind has deposited arms with me and he asks for them when he is not in his right mind, ought I to give them back to him? No one would say that I ought or that I should be right in doing so, any more than they would say that I ought always to speak the truth to one who is in his condition.

You are quite right, he replied.

But then, I said, speaking the truth and paying your debts is not a correct definition of justice.

Quite correct, Socrates, if Simonides is to be believed, said Polemarchus interposing.

I fear, said Cephalus, that I must go now, for I have to look after the sacrifices, and I hand over the argument to Polemarchus and the company.

Is not Polemarchus your heir? I said.

To be sure, he answered, and went away laughing to the sacrifices.

Tell me then, O thou heir of the argument, what did Simonides say, and according to you truly say, about justice?

He said that the repayment of a debt is just, and in saying so he appears to me to be right.

I should be sorry to doubt the word of such a wise and inspired man, but his meaning, though probably clear to you, is the reverse of clear to me. For he certainly does not mean, as we were just now saying, that I ought to return a deposit of arms or of anything else to one who asks for it when he is not in his right senses; and yet a deposit can not be denied to be a debt.

True.

Then when the person who asks me is not in his right mind I am by no means to make the return?

Certainly not.

When Simonides said that the repayment of a debt was justice, he did not mean to include that case?

Certainly not; for he thinks that a friend ought always to do good to a friend and never evil.

You mean that the return of a deposit of gold which is to the injury of the receiver, if the two parties are friends, is not the repayment of a debt, — that is what you would imagine him to say?

Yes.

And are enemies also to receive what we owe to them?

To be sure, he said, they are to receive what we owe them, and an enemy, as I take it, owes to an enemy that which is due or proper to him — that is to say, evil.

Simonides, then, after the manner of poets, would seem to have spoken darkly of the nature of justice; for he really meant to say that justice is the giving to each man what is proper to him, and this he termed a debt.

That must have been his meaning, he said.

By heaven! I replied; and if we asked him what due or proper thing is given by medicine, and to whom, what answer do you think that he would make to us?

He would surely reply that medicine gives drugs and meat and drink to human bodies.

And what due or proper thing is given by cookery, and to what?

Seasoning to food.

And what is that which justice gives, and to whom?

If, Socrates, we are to be guided at all by the analogy of the preceding instances, then justice is the art which gives good to friends and evil to enemies.

That is his meaning then?

I think so.

And who is best able to do good to his friends and evil to his enemies in time of sickness?

The physician.

Or when they are on a voyage, amid the perils of the sea?

The pilot.

And in what sort of actions or with a view to what result is the just man most able to do harm to his enemy and good to his friend?

In going to war against the one and in making alliances with the other.

But when a man is well, my dear Polemarchus, there is no need of a physician?

No.

And he who is not on a voyage has no need of a pilot?

No.

Then in time of peace justice will be of no use?

I am very far from thinking so.

You think that justice may be of use in peace as well as in war?

Yes.

Like husbandry for the acquisition of corn?

Yes.

Or like shoemaking for the acquisition of shoes, — that is what you mean?

Yes.

And what similar use or power of acquisition has justice in time of peace?

In contracts, Socrates, justice is of use.

And by contracts you mean partnerships?

Exactly.

But is the just man or the skilful player a more useful and better partner at a game of draughts?

The skilful player.

And in the laying of bricks and stones is the just man a more useful or better partner than the builder?

Quite the reverse.

Then in what sort of partnership is the just man a better partner than the harp-player, as in playing the harp the harp-player is certainly a better partner than the just man?

In a money partnership.

Yes, Polemarchus, but surely not in the use of money; for you do not want a just man to be your counsellor in the purchase or sale of a horse; a man who is knowing about horses would be better for that, would he not?

Certainly.

And when you want to buy a ship, the shipwright or the pilot would be better?

True.

Then what is that joint use of silver or gold in which the just man is to be preferred?

When you want a deposit to be kept safely.

You mean when money is not wanted, but allowed to lie?

Precisely.

That is to say, justice is useful when money is useless?

That is the inference.

And when you want to keep a pruning-hook safe, then justice is useful to the individual and to the state; but when you want to use it, then the art of the vine-dresser?

Clearly.

And when you want to keep a shield or a lyre, and not to use them, you would say that justice is useful; but when you want to use them, then the art of the soldier or of the musician?

Certainly.

And so of all other things; — justice is useful when they are useless, and useless when they are useful?

That is the inference.

Then justice is not good for much. But let us consider this further point: Is not he who can best strike a blow in a boxing match or in any kind of fighting best able to ward off a blow?

Certainly.

And he who is most skilful in preventing or escaping [1] from a disease is best able to create one?

True.

And he is the best guard of a camp who is best able to steal a march upon the enemy?

Certainly.

Then he who is a good keeper of anything is also a good thief?

That, I suppose, is to be inferred.

Then if the just man is good at keeping money, he is good at stealing it?

That is implied in the argument.

Then after all the just man has turned out to be a thief. And this is a lesson which I suspect you must have learned out of Homer; for he, speaking of Autolycus, the maternal grandfather of Odysseus, who is a favorite of his, affirms that

He was excellent above all men in theft and perjury.

And so, you and Homer and Simonides are agreed that justice is an art of theft; to be practised however

---

[1] Reading φυλάξασθαι καὶ λαθεῖν, οὗτος, κ.τ.λ.

"for the good of friends and for the harm of enemies," — that was what you were saying?

No, certainly not that, although I do not now know
what I did say; but I still stand by the latter words.

Well, there is another question: By friends and
enemies do we mean those who are so really, or only
in seeming?

Surely, he said, a man may be expected to love
those whom he thinks good, and to hate those whom
he thinks evil.

Yes, but do not persons often err about good and
evil: many who are not good seem to be so, and conversely?

That is true.

Then to them the good will be enemies and the evil
will be their friends?

True.

And in that case they will be right in doing good to
the evil and evil to the good?

Clearly.

But the good are just and would not do an injustice?

True.

Then according to your argument it is just to injure those who do no wrong?

Nay, Socrates; the doctrine is immoral.

Then I suppose that we ought to do good to the just
and harm to the unjust?

I like that better.

But see the consequence: — Many a man who is
ignorant of human nature has friends who are bad
friends, and in that case he ought to do harm to them;
and he has good enemies whom he ought to benefit;
but, if so, we shall be saying the very opposite of that
which we affirmed to be the meaning of Simonides.

Very true, he said; and I think that we had better

correct an error into which we seem to have fallen in the use of the words " friend " and " enemy."

What was the error, Polemarchus? I asked.

We assumed that he is a friend who seems to be or who is thought good.

And how is the error to be corrected?

We should rather say that he is a friend who is, as well as seems, good; and that he who seems only, and is not good, only seems to be and is not a friend; and of an enemy the same may be said.

You would argue that the good are our friends and the bad our enemies?

Yes.

And instead of saying simply as we did at first, that it is just to do good to our friends and harm to our enemies, we should further say: It is just to do good to our friends when they are good and harm to our enemies when they are evil?

Yes, that appears to me to be the truth.

But ought the just to injure any one at all?

Undoubtedly he ought to injure those who are both wicked and his enemies.

When horses are injured, are they improved or deteriorated?

The latter.

Deteriorated, that is to say, in the good qualities of horses, not of dogs?

Yes, of horses.

And dogs are deteriorated in the good qualities of dogs, and not of horses?

Of course.

And will not men who are injured be deteriorated in that which is the proper virtue of man?

Certainly.

And that human virtue is justice?

To be sure.

Then men who are injured are of necessity made unjust?

That is the result.

But can the musician by his art make men unmusical?

Certainly not.

Or the horseman by his art make them bad horsemen?

Impossible.

And can the just by justice make men unjust, or speaking generally, can the good by virtue make them bad?

Assuredly not.

Any more than heat can produce cold?

It cannot.

Or drought moisture?

Clearly not.

Nor can the good harm any one!

Impossible.

And the just is the good?

Certainly.

Then to injure a friend or any one else is not the act of a just man, but of the opposite, who is the unjust?

I think that what you say is quite true, Socrates.

Then if a man says that justice consists in the repayment of debts, and that good is the debt which a just man owes to his friends, and evil the debt which he owes to his enemies, — to say this is not wise; for it is not true, if, as has been clearly shown, the injuring of another can be in no case just.

I agree with you, said Polemarchus.

Then you and I are prepared to take up arms against any one who attribute such a saying to Simonides or Bias or Pittacus, or any other wise man or seer?

I am quite ready to do battle at your side, he said. Shall I tell you whose I believe the saying to be? Whose?

I believe that Periander or Perdiccas or Xerxes or Ismenias the Theban, or some other rich and mighty man, who had a great opinion of his own power, was the first to say that justice is " doing good to your friends and harm to your enemies."

Most true, he said.

Yes, I said; but if this definition of justice also breaks down, what other can be offered?

Several times in the course of the discussion Thrasymachus had made an attempt to get the argument into his own hands, and had been put down by the rest of the company, who wanted to hear the end. But when Polemarchus and I had done speaking and there was a pause, he could no longer hold his peace; and, gathering himself up, he came at us like a wild beast, seeking to devour us. We were quite panic-stricken at the sight of him.

He roared out to the whole company: What folly, Socrates, has taken possession of you all? And why, sillybillies, do you knock under to one another? I say that if you want really to know what justice is, you should not only ask but answer, and you should not seek honor to yourself from the refutation of an opponent, but have your own answer; for there is many a one who can ask and can not answer. And now I will not have you say that justice is duty or advantage or profit or gain or interest, for this sort of nonsense will not do for me; I must have clearness and accuracy.

I was panic-stricken at his words, and could not look at him without trembling. Indeed I believe that if I had not fixed my eye upon him, I should have been struck dumb: but when I saw his fury rising, I looked at him first, and was therefore able to reply to him.

Thrasymachus, I said, with a quiver, don't be hard upon us. Polemarchus and I may have been guilty of a little mistake in the argument, but I can assure you that the error was not intentional. If we were seeking for a piece of gold, you would not imagine that we were " knocking under to one another," and so losing our chance of finding it. And why, when we are seeking for justice, a thing more precious than many pieces of gold, do you say that we are weakly yielding to one another and not doing our utmost to get at the truth? Nay, my good friend, we are most willing and anxious to do so, but the fact is that we can not. And if so, you people who know all things should pity us and not be angry with us.

How characteristic of Socrates! he replied, with a bitter laugh; — that's your ironical style! Did I not foresee — have I not already told you, that whatever he was asked he would refuse to answer, and try irony or any other shuffle, in order that he might avoid answering?

You are a philosopher, Thrasymachus, I replied, and well know that if you ask a person what numbers make up twelve, taking care to prohibit him whom you ask from answering twice six, or three times four, or six times two, or four times three, " for this sort of nonsense will not do for me," — then obviously, if that is your way of putting the question, no one can answer you. But suppose that he were to retort, " Thrasymachus, what do you mean? If one of these numbers which you interdict be the true answer to the question, am I falsely to say some other number which is not the right one? — is that your meaning? " — How would you answer him?

Just as if the two cases were at all alike! he said.

Why should they not be? I replied; and even if they are not, but only appear to be so to the person who is asked, ought he not to say what he thinks, whether you and I forbid him or not?

I presume then that you are going to make one of the interdicted answers?

I dare say that I may, notwithstanding the danger, if upon reflection I approve of any of them.

But what if I give you an answer about justice other and better, he said, than any of these? What do you deserve to have done to you?

Done to me! — as becomes the ignorant, I must learn from the wise — that is what I deserve to have done to me.

What, and no payment! a pleasant notion!

I will pay when I have the money, I replied.

But you have, Socrates, said Glaucon: and you, Thrasymachus, need be under no anxiety about money, for we will all make a contribution for Socrates.

Yes, he replied, and then Socrates will do as he always does — refuse to answer himself, but take and pull to pieces the answer of some one else.

Why, my good friend, I said, how can any one answer who knows and says that he knows, just nothing; and who, even if he has some faint notions of his own, is told by a man of authority not to utter them? The natural thing is, that the speaker should be some one like yourself who professes to know and can tell what he knows. Will you then kindly answer, for the edification of the company and of myself?

Glaucon and the rest of the company joined in my request, and Thrasymachus, as any one might see, was in reality eager to speak; for he thought that he had an excellent answer, and would distinguish himself. But

at first he affected to insist on my answering; at
length he consented to begin.   Behold, he said, the
wisdom of Socrates; he refuses to teach himself, and
goes about learning of others, to whom he never even
says Thank you.

That I learn of others, I replied, is quite true; but
that I am ungrateful I wholly deny.   Money I have
none, and therefore I pay in praise, which is all I
have; and how ready I am to praise any one who appears to me to speak well you will very soon find out
when you answer; for I expect that you will answer
well.

Listen, then, he said; I proclaim that justice is nothing else than the interest of the stronger.   And now
why do you not praise me?   But of course you won't.

Let me first understand you, I replied.   Justice,
as you say, is the interest of the stronger.   What,
Thrasymachus, is the meaning of this?   You can not
mean to say that because Polydamas, the pancratiast,
is stronger than we are, and finds the eating of beef
conducive to his bodily strength, that to eat beef is
therefore equally for our good who are weaker than
he is, and right and just for us?

That's abominable of you, Socrates; you take the
words in the sense which is most damaging to the
argument.

Not at all, my good sir, I said; I am trying to understand them; and I wish that you would be a little
clearer.

Well, he said, have you never heard that forms of
government differ; there are tyrannies, and there are
democracies, and there are aristocracies?

Yes, I know.

And the government is the ruling power in each
state?

Certainly.

And the different forms of government make laws democratical, aristocratical, tyrannical, with a view to their several interests; and these laws, which are made by them for their own interests, are the justice which they deliver to their subjects, and him who transgresses them they punish as a breaker of the law, and unjust. And that is what I mean when I say that in all states there is the same principle of justice, which is the interest of the government; and as the government must be supposed to have power, the only reasonable conclusion is, that everywhere there is one principle of justice, which is the interest of the stronger.

Now I understand you, I said; and whether you are right or not I will try to discover. But let me remark, that in defining justice you have yourself used the word "interest" which you forbade me to use. It is true, however, that in your definition the words "of the stronger" are added.

A small addition, you must allow, he said.

Great or small, never mind about that: we must first inquire whether what you are saying is the truth. Now we are both agreed that justice is interest of some sort, but you go on to say "of the stronger;" about this addition I am not so sure, and must therefore consider further.

Proceed.

I will; and first tell me, Do you admit that it is just for subjects to obey their rulers?

I do.

But are the rulers of states absolutely infallible, or are they sometimes liable to err?

To be sure, he replied, they are liable to err.

Then in making their laws they may sometimes make them rightly, and sometimes not?

True.

When they make them rightly, they make them agreeably to their interest; when they are mistaken, contrary to their interest; you admit that?

Yes.

And the laws which they make must be obeyed by their subjects, — and that is what you call justice?

Doubtless.

Then justice, according to your argument, is not only obedience to the interest of the stronger but the reverse?

What is that you are saying? he asked.

I am only repeating what you are saying, I believe. But let us consider: Have we not admitted that the rulers may be mistaken about their own interest in what they command, and also that to obey them is justice? Has not that been admitted?

Yes.

Then you must also have acknowledged justice not to be for the interest of the stronger, when the rulers unintentionally command things to be done which are to their own injury. For if, as you say, justice is the obedience which the subject renders to their commands, in that case, O wisest of men, is there any escape from the conclusion that the weaker are commanded to do, not what is for the interest, but what is for the injury of the stronger?

Nothing can be clearer, Socrates, said Polemarchus.

Yes, said Cleitophon, interposing, if you are allowed to be his witness.

But there is no need of any witness, said Polemarchus, for Thrasymachus himself acknowledges that rulers may sometimes command what is not for their own interest, and that for subjects to obey them is justice.

Yes, Polemarchus, — Thrasymachus said that for

subjects to do what was commanded by their rulers is just.

Yes, Cleitophon, but he also said that justice is the interest of the stronger, and, while admitting both these propositions, he further acknowledged that the stronger may command the weaker who are his subjects to do what is not for his own interest; whence follows that justice is the injury quite as much as the interest of the stronger.

But, said Cleitophon, he meant by the interest of the stronger what the stronger thought to be his interest, — this was what the weaker had to do; and this was affirmed by him to be justice.

Those were not his words, rejoined Polemarchus.

Never mind, I replied, if he now says that they are, let us accept his statement. Tell me, Thrasymachus, I said, did you mean by justice what the stronger thought to be his interest, whether really so or not?

Certainly not, he said. Do you suppose that I call him who is mistaken the stronger at the time when he is mistaken?

Yes, I said, my impression was that you did so, when you admitted that the ruler was not infallible but might be sometimes mistaken.

You argue like an informer, Socrates. Do you mean, for example, that he who is mistaken about the sick is a physician in that he is mistaken? or that he who errs in arithmetic or grammar is an arithmetician or grammarian at the time when he is making the mistake, in respect of the mistake? True, we say that the physician or arithmetician or grammarian has made a mistake, but this is only a way of speaking; for the fact is that neither the grammarian nor any other person of skill ever makes a mistake in so far as he is what his name implies; they none of them err unless their skill fails them, and then they cease to be skilled artists. No artist or sage or ruler errs at the time when he is what his name implies; though he is commonly said to err, and I adopted the common mode of speaking. But to be perfectly accurate, since you are such a lover of accuracy, we should say that the ruler, in so far as he is ruler, is unerring, and, being unerring, always commands that which is for his own interest; and the subject is required to execute his commands; and therefore, as I said at first and now repeat, justice is the interest of the stronger.

Indeed, Thrasymachus, and do I really appear to you to argue like an informer?

Certainly, he replied.

And do you suppose that I ask these questions with any design of injuring you in the argument?

Nay, he replied, " suppose " is not the word — I know it; but you will be found out, and by sheer force of argument you will never prevail.

I shall not make the attempt, my dear man; but to avoid any misunderstanding occurring between us in future, let me ask, in what sense do you speak of a ruler or stronger whose interest, as you were saying, he being the superior, it is just that the inferior should execute — is he a ruler in the popular or in the strict sense of the term?

In the strictest of all senses, he said. And now cheat and play the informer if you can; I ask no quarter at your hands. But you never will be able, never.

And do you imagine, I said, that I am such a madman as to try and cheat Thrasymachus? I might as well shave a lion.

Why, he said, you made the attempt a minute ago, and you failed.

Enough, I said, of these civilities. It will be better that I should ask you a question: Is the physician,

taken in that strict sense of which you are speaking,
a healer of the sick or a maker of money? And
remember that I am now speaking of the true physician.

A healer of the sick, he replied.

And the pilot — that is to say, the true pilot — is
he a captain of sailors or a mere sailor?

A captain of sailors.

The circumstance that he sails in the ship is not to
be taken into account; neither is he to be called a
sailor; the name pilot by which he is distinguished has
nothing to do with sailing, but is significant of his
skill and of his authority over the sailors.

Very true, he said.

Now, I said, every art has an interest?

Certainly.

For which the art has to consider and provide?

Yes, that is the aim of art.

And the interest of any art is the perfection of it —
this and nothing else?

What do you mean?

I mean what I may illustrate negatively by the
example of the body. Suppose you were to ask me
whether the body is self-sufficing or has wants, I
should reply: Certainly the body has wants; for the
body may be ill and require to be cured, and has therefore interests to which the art of medicine ministers;
and this is the origin and intention of medicine, as
you will acknowledge. Am I not right?

Quite right, he replied.

But is the art of medicine or any other art faulty
or deficient in any quality in the same way that the
eye may be deficient in sight or the ear fail of hearing, and therefore requires another art to provide for
the interests of seeing and hearing — has art in itself,
I say, any similar liability to fault or defect, and does

every art require another supplementary art to provide for its interests, and that another and another
without end? Or have the arts to look only after their
own interests? Or have they no need either of themselves or of another? — having no faults or defects,
they have no need to correct them, either by the exercise of their own art or of any other; they have only
to consider the interest of their subject-matter. For
every art remains pure and faultless while remaining
true — that is to say, while perfect and unimpaired.
Take the words in your precise sense, and tell me
whether I am not right.

Yes, clearly.

Then medicine does not consider the interest of
medicine, but the interest of the body?

True, he said.

Nor does the art of horsemanship consider the interests of the art of horsemanship, but the interests of
the horse; neither do any other arts care for themselves, for they have no needs; they care only for that
which is the subject of their art?

True, he said.

But surely, Thrasymachus, the arts are the superiors and rulers of their own subjects?

To this he assented with a good deal of reluctance.

Then, I said, no science or art considers or enjoins
the interest of the stronger or superior, but only the
interest of the subject and weaker?

He made an attempt to contest this proposition
also, but finally acquiesced.

Then, I continued, no physician, in so far as he is a
physician, considers his own good in what he prescribes, but the good of his patient; for the true physician is also a ruler having the human body as a subject, and is not a mere money-maker; that has been
admitted?

Yes.

And the pilot likewise, in the strict sense of the term, is a ruler of sailors and not a mere sailor.

That has been admitted.

And such a pilot and ruler will provide and prescribe for the interest of the sailor who is under him, and not for his own or the ruler's interest?

He gave a reluctant "Yes."

Then, I said, Thrasymachus, there is no one in any rule who, in so far as he is a ruler, considers or enjoins what is for his own interest, but always what is for the interest of his subject or suitable to his art; to that he looks, and that alone he considers in everything which he says and does.

When we had got to this point in the argument, and every one saw that the definition of justice had been completely upset, Thrasymachus, instead of replying to me, said: Tell me, Socrates, have you got a nurse?

Why do you ask such a question, I said, when you ought rather to be answering?

Because she leaves you to snivel, and never wipes your nose: she has not even taught you to know the shepherd from the sheep.

What makes you say that? I replied.

Because you fancy that the shepherd or neatherd fattens or tends the sheep or oxen with a view to their own good and not to the good of himself or his master; and you further imagine that the rulers of states, if they are true rulers, never think of their subjects as sheep, and that they are not studying their own advantage day and night. Oh, no; and so entirely astray are you in your ideas about the just and unjust as not even to know that justice and the just are in reality another's good; that is to say, the interest of the ruler and stronger, and the loss of the subject and servant; and injustice the opposite; for the unjust is lord over the truly simple and just: he is the stronger, and his subjects do what is for his interest, and minister to his happiness, which is very far from being their own. Consider further, most foolish Socrates, that the just is always a loser in comparison with the unjust. First of all, in private contracts: wherever the unjust is the partner of the just you will find that, when the partnership is dissolved, the unjust man has always more and the just less. Secondly, in their dealings with the State: when there is an income-tax, the just man will pay more and the unjust less on the same amount of income; and when there is anything to be received the one gains nothing and the other much. Observe also what happens when they take an office; there is the just man neglecting his affairs and perhaps suffering other losses, and getting nothing out of the public, because he is just; moreover he is hated by his friends and acquaintance for refusing to serve them in unlawful ways. But all this is reversed in the case of the unjust man. I am speaking, as before, of injustice on a large scale in which the advantage of the unjust is most apparent; and my meaning will be most clearly seen if we turn to that highest form of injustice in which the criminal is the happiest of men, and the sufferers or those who refuse to do injustice are the most miserable — that is to say tyranny, which by fraud and force takes away the property of others, not little by little but wholesale; comprehending in one, things sacred as well as profane, private and public; for which acts of wrong, if he were detected perpetrating any of them singly, he would be punished and incur great disgrace — they who do such wrong in particular cases are called robbers of temples, and man-stealers and burglars and swindlers and thieves. But when a man besides taking away the money of the citizens has made slaves of them, then, instead of these names of reproach, he is termed happy and blessed, not only by the citizens but by all who hear of his having achieved the consummation of injustice. For mankind censure injustice, fearing that they may be victims of it and not because they shrink from committing it. And thus, as I have shown, Socrates, injustice, when on a sufficient scale, has more strength and freedom and mastery than justice; and, as I said at first, justice is the interest of the stronger, whereas injustice is a man's own profit and interest.

Thrasymachus, when he had thus spoken, having, like a bath-man, deluged our ears with his words, had a mind to go away. But the company would not let him; they insisted that he should remain and defend his position; and I myself added my own humble request that he would not leave us. Thrasymachus, I said to him, excellent man, how suggestive are your remarks! And are you going to run away before you have fairly taught or learned whether they are true or not? Is the attempt to determine the way of man's life so small a matter in your eyes — to determine how life may be passed by each one of us to the greatest advantage?

And do I differ from you, he said, as to the importance of the inquiry?

You appear rather, I replied, to have no care or thought about us, Thrasymachus — whether we live better or worse from not knowing what you say you know, is to you a matter of indifference. Prithee, friend, do not keep your knowledge to yourself; we are a large party; and any benefit which you confer upon us will be amply rewarded. For my own part I openly declare that I am not convinced, and that I do not believe injustice to be more gainful than justice, even if uncontrolled and allowed to have free play. For, granting that there may be an unjust man who is able to commit injustice either by fraud or force, still this does not convince me of the superior advantage of injustice, and there may be others who are in the same predicament with myself. Perhaps we may be wrong; if so, you in your wisdom should convince us that we are mistaken in preferring justice to unjustice.

And how am I to convince you, he said, if you are not already convinced by what I have just said; what more can I do for you? Would you have me put the proof bodily into your souls?

Heaven forbid! I said; I would only ask you to be consistent; or, if you change, change openly and let there be no deception. For I must remark, Thrasymachus, if you will recall what was previously said, that although you began by defining the true physician in an exact sense, you did not observe a like exactness when speaking of the shepherd; you thought that the shepherd as a shepherd tends the sheep not with a view to their own good, but like a mere diner or banqueter with a view to the pleasures of the table; or, again, as a trader for sale in the market, and not as a shepherd. Yet surely the art of the shepherd is concerned only with the good of his subjects; he has only to provide the best for them, since the perfection of the art is already ensured whenever all the requirements of it are satisfied. And that was what I was saying just now about the ruler. I conceived that the art of the ruler, considered as ruler, whether in a state or in private life, could only regard the good of his flock or subjects; whereas you seem to think that the rulers in states, that is to say, the true rulers, like being in authority.

Think! Nay, I am sure of it.

Then why in the case of lesser offices do men never take them willingly without payment, unless under the idea that they govern for the advantage not of themselves but of others? Let me ask you a question: Are not the several arts different, by reason of their each having a separate function? And, my dear illustrious friend, do say what you think, that we may make a little progress.

Yes, that is the difference, he replied.

And each art gives us a particular good and not merely a general one — medicine, for example, gives us health; navigation, safety at sea, and so on?

Yes, he said.

And the art of payment has the special function of giving pay: but we do not confuse this with other arts, any more than the art of the pilot is to be confused with the art of medicine, because the health of the pilot may be improved by a sea voyage. You would not be inclined to say, would you, that navigation is the art of medicine, at least if we are to adopt your exact use of language?

Certainly not.

Or because a man is in good health when he receives pay you would not say that the art of payment is medicine?

I should not.

Nor would you say that medicine is the art of receiving pay because a man takes fees when he is engaged in healing?

Certainly not.

And we have admitted, I said, that the good of each art is specially confined to the art?

Yes.

Then, if there be any good which all artists have in common, that is to be attributed to something of which they all have the common use?

True, he replied.

And when the artist is benefited by receiving pay the advantage is gained by an additional use of the art of pay, which is not the art professed by him?

He gave a reluctant assent to this.

Then the pay is not derived by the several artists from their respective arts. But the truth is, that while the art of medicine gives health, and the art of the builder builds a house, another art attends them which is the art of pay. The various arts may be doing their own business and benefiting that over which they preside, but would the artist receive any benefit from his art unless he were paid as well?

I suppose not.

But does he therefore confer no benefit when he works for nothing?

Certainly, he confers a benefit.

Then now, Thrasymachus, there is no longer any doubt that neither arts nor governments provide for their own interests; but, as we were before saying, they rule and provide for the interests of their subjects who are the weaker and not the stronger — to their good they attend and not to the good of the superior. And this is the reason, my dear Thrasymachus, why, as I was just now saying, no one is willing to govern; because no one likes to take in hand the reformation of evils which are not his concern without remuneration. For, in the execution of his work, and in giving his orders to another, the true artist does not regard his own interest, but always that of his subjects; and therefore in order that rulers may be willing to rule, they must be paid in one of three modes of payment, money or honor, or a penalty for refusing.

What do you mean, Socrates? said Glaucon. The first two modes of payment are intelligible enough, but what the penalty is I do not understand, or how a penalty can be a payment.

You mean that you do not understand the nature of this payment which to the best men is the great inducement to rule? Of course you know that ambition and avarice are held to be, as indeed they are, a disgrace?

Very true.

And for this reason, I said, money and honor have no attraction for them; good men do not wish to be openly demanding payment for governing and so to get the name of hirelings, nor by secretly helping themselves out of the public revenues to get the name of thieves. And not being ambitious they do not care about honor. Wherefore necessity must be laid upon them, and they must be induced to serve from the fear of punishment. And this, as I imagine, is the reason why the forwardness to take office, instead of waiting to be compelled, has been deemed dishonorable. Now the worst part of the punishment is that he who refuses to rule is liable to be ruled by one who is worse than himself. And the fear of this, as I conceive, induces the good to take office, not because they would, but because they can not help — not under the idea that they are going to have any benefit or enjoyment themselves, but as a necessity, and because they are not able to commit the task of ruling to any one who is better than themselves, or indeed as good. For there is reason to think that if a city were composed entirely of good men, then to avoid office would be as much an object of contention as to obtain office is at present; then we should have plain proof that the true ruler is not meant by nature to regard his own interest, but that of his subjects; and every one who knew this would choose rather to receive a benefit from another than to have the trouble

of conferring one. So far am I from agreeing with
Thrasymachus that justice is the interest of the
stronger. This latter question need not be further
discussed at present; but when Thrasymachus says
that the life of the unjust is more advantageous than
that of the just, his new statement appears to me to
be of a far more serious character. Which of us has
spoken truly? And which sort of life, Glaucon, do
you prefer?

I for my part deem the life of the just to be the
more advantageous, he answered.

Did you hear all the advantages of the unjust
which Thrasymachus was rehearsing?

Yes, I heard him, he replied, but he has not convinced me.

Then shall we try to find some way of convincing
him, if we can, that he is saying what is not true?

Most certainly, he replied.

If, I said, he makes a set speech and we make another recounting all the advantages of being just,
and he answers and we rejoin, there must be a numbering and measuring of the goods which are claimed
on either side, and in the end we shall want judges to
decide; but if we proceed in our inquiry as we lately
did, by making admissions to one another, we shall
unite the offices of judge and advocate in our own
persons.

Very good, he said.

And which method do I understand you to prefer?
I said.

That which you propose.

Well, then, Thrasymachus, I said, suppose you
begin at the beginning and answer me. You say that
perfect injustice is more gainful than perfect justice?

Yes, that is what I say, and I have given you my
reasons.

And what is your view about them? Would you call one of them virtue and the other vice?

Certainly.

I suppose that you would call justice virtue and injustice vice?

What a charming notion! So likely too, seeing that I affirm injustice to be profitable and justice not.

What else then would you say?

The opposite, he replied.

And would you call justice vice?

No, I would rather say sublime simplicity.

Then would you call injustice malignity?

No; I would rather say discretion.

And do the unjust appear to you to be wise and good?

Yes, he said; at any rate those of them who are able to be perfectly unjust, and who have the power of subduing states and nations; but perhaps you imagine me to be talking of cutpurses. Even this profession if undetected has advantages, though they are not to be compared with those of which I was just now speaking.

I do not think that I misapprehend your meaning, Thrasymachus, I replied; but still I can not hear without amazement that you class injustice with wisdom and virtue, and justice with the opposite.

Certainly, I do so class them.

Now, I said, you are on more substantial and almost unanswerable ground; for if the injustice which you were maintaining to be profitable had been admitted by you as by others to be vice and deformity, an answer might have been given to you on received principles; but now I perceive that you will call injustice honorable and strong, and to the unjust you will attribute all the qualities which were attributed by us before to the just, seeing that you do not hesitate to rank injustice with wisdom and virtue.

You have guessed most infallibly, he replied.

Then I certainly ought not to shrink from going through with the argument so long as I have reason to think that you, Thrasymachus, are speaking your real mind; for I do believe that you are now in earnest and are not amusing yourself at our expense.

I may be in earnest or not, but what is that to you? — to refute the argument is your business.

Very true, I said; that is what I have to do: But will you be so good as answer yet one more question? Does the just man try to gain any advantage over the just?

Far otherwise; if he did he would not be the simple amusing creature which he is.

And would he try to go beyond just action?

He would not.

And how would he regard the attempt to gain an advantage over the unjust; would that be considered by him as just or unjust?

He would think it just, and would try to gain the advantage; but he would not be able.

Whether he would or would not be able, I said, is not to the point. My question is only whether the just man, while refusing to have more than another just man, would wish and claim to have more than the unjust?

Yes, he would.

And what of the unjust — does he claim to have more than the just man and to do more than is just?

Of course, he said, for he claims to have more than all men.

And the unjust man will strive and struggle to obtain more than the unjust man or action, in order that he may have more than all?

True.

We may put the matter thus, I said — the just does not desire more than his like but more than his unlike, whereas the unjust desires more than both his like and his unlike?

Nothing, he said, can be better than that statement.

And the unjust is good and wise, and the just is neither?

Good again, he said.

And is not the unjust like the wise and good and the just unlike them?

Of course, he said, he who is of a certain nature, is like those who are of a certain nature; he who is not, not.

Each of them, I said, is such as his like is?

Certainly, he replied.

Very good, Thrasymachus, I said; and now to take the case of the arts: you would admit that one man is a musician and another not a musician?

Yes.

And which is wise and which is foolish?

Clearly the musician is wise, and he who is not a musician is foolish.

And he is good in as far as he is wise, and bad in as far as he is foolish?

Yes.

And you would say the same sort of thing of the physician?

Yes.

And do you think, my excellent friend, that a musician when he adjusts the lyre would desire or claim to exceed or go beyond a musician in the tightening and loosening the strings?

I do not think that he would.

But he would claim to exceed the non-musician?

Of course.

And what would you say of the physician? In prescribing meats and drinks would he wish to go beyond another physician or beyond the practice of medicine?

He would not.

But he would wish to go beyond the non-physician?

Yes.

And about knowledge and ignorance in general; see whether you think that any man who has knowledge ever would wish to have the choice of saying or doing more than another man who has knowledge. Would he not rather say or do the same as his like in the same case?

That, I suppose, can hardly be denied.

And what of the ignorant? would he not desire to have more than either the knowing or the ignorant?

I dare say.

And the knowing is wise?

Yes.

And the wise is good?

True.

Then the wise and good will not desire to gain more than his like, but more than his unlike and opposite?

I suppose so.

Whereas the bad and ignorant will desire to gain more than both?

Yes.

But did we not say, Thrasymachus, that the unjust goes beyond both his like and unlike? Were not these your words?

They were.

And you also said that the just will not go beyond his like but his unlike?

Yes.

Then the just is like the wise and good, and the unjust like the evil and ignorant?

That is the inference.

And each of them is such as his like is?

That was admitted.

Then the just has turned out to be wise and good and the unjust evil and ignorant.

Thrasymachus made all these admissions, not fluently, as I repeat them, but with extreme reluctance; it was a hot summer's day, and the perspiration poured from him in torrents; and then I saw what I had never seen before, Thrasymachus blushing. As we were now agreed that justice was virtue and wisdom, and injustice vice and ignorance, I proceeded to another point:

Well, I said, Thrasymachus, that matter is now settled; but were we not also saying that injustice had strength; do you remember?

Yes, I remember, he said, but do not suppose that I approve of what you are saying or have no answer; if however I were to answer, you would be quite certain to accuse me of haranguing; therefore either permit me to have my say out, or if you would rather ask, do so, and I will answer " Very good," as they say to story-telling old women, and will nod " Yes " and " No."

Certainly not, I said, if contrary to your real opinion.

Yes, he said, I will, to please you, since you will not let me speak. What else would you have?

Nothing in the world, I said; and if you are so disposed I will ask and you shall answer.

Proceed.

Then I will repeat the question which I asked before, in order that our examination of the relative nature of justice and injustice may be carried on regularly. A statement was made that injustice is stronger and more powerful than justice, but now justice, having been identified with wisdom and virtue, is easily shown to be stronger than injustice, if injustice is ignorance; this can no longer be questioned by any one. But I want to view the matter, Thrasymachus, in a different way: You would not deny that a state may be unjust and may be unjustly attempting to enslave other states, or may have already enslaved them, and may be holding many of them in subjection?

True, he replied; and I will add that the best and most perfectly unjust state will be most likely to do so.

I know, I said, that such was your position; but what I would further consider is, whether this power which is possessed by the superior state can exist or be exercised without justice or only with justice.

If you are right in your view, and justice is wisdom, then only with justice; but if I am right, then without justice.

I am delighted, Thrasymachus, to see you not only nodding assent and dissent, but making answers which are quite excellent.

That is out of civility to you, he replied.

You are very kind, I said; and would you have the goodness also to inform me, whether you think that a state, or an army, or a band of robbers and thieves, or any other gang of evil-doers could act at all if they injured one another?

No indeed, he said, they could not.

But if they abstained from injuring one another, then they might act together better?

Yes.

And this is because injustice creates divisions and hatreds and fighting, and justice imparts har-

mony and friendship; is not that true, Thrasymachus?

I agree, he said, because I do not wish to quarrel
with you.

How good of you, I said; but I should like to know
also whether injustice, having this tendency to arouse
hatred, wherever existing, among slaves or among
freemen, will not make them hate one another and
set them at variance and render them incapable of
common action?

Certainly.

And even if injustice be found in two only, will
they not quarrel and fight, and become enemies to one
another and to the just?

They will.

And suppose injustice abiding in a single person,
would your wisdom say that she loses or that she
retains her natural power?

Let us assume that she retains her power.

Yet is not the power which injustice exercises of
such a nature that wherever she takes up her abode,
whether in a city, in an army, in a family, or in any
other body, that body is, to begin with, rendered incapable of united action by reason of sedition and
distraction; and does it not become its own enemy
and at variance with all that opposes it, and with the
just? Is not this the case?

Yes, certainly.

And is not injustice equally fatal when existing
in a single person; in the first place rendering him
incapable of action because he is not at unity with
himself, and in the second place making him an enemy
to himself and the just? Is not that true, Thrasymachus?

Yes.

And O my friend, I said, surely the gods are just?

Granted that they are.

But if so, the unjust will be the enemy of the gods, and the just will be their friends?

Feast away in triumph, and take your fill of the argument; I will not oppose you, lest I should displease the company.

Well then, proceed with your answers, and let me have the remainder of my repast. For we have already shown that the just are clearly wiser and better and abler than the unjust, and that the unjust are incapable of common action; nay more, that to speak as we did of men who are evil acting at any time vigorously together, is not strictly true, for if they had been perfectly evil, they would have laid hands upon one another; but it is evident that there must have been some remnant of justice in them, which enabled them to combine; if there had not been they would have injured one another as well as their victims; they were but half-villains in their enterprises; for had they been whole villains, and utterly unjust, they would have been utterly incapable of action. That, as I believe, is the truth of the matter, and not what you said at first. But whether the just have a better and happier life than the unjust is a further question which we also proposed to consider. I think that they have, and for the reasons which I have given; but still I should like to examine further, for no light matter is at stake, nothing less than the rule of human life.

Proceed.

I will proceed by asking a question: Would you not say that a horse has some end?

I should.

And the end or use of a horse or of anything would be that which could not be accomplished, or not so well accomplished, by any other thing?

I do not understand, he said.

Let me explain: Can you see, except with the eye?

Certainly not.

Or hear, except with the ear?

No.

These then may be truly said to be the ends of these organs?

They may.

But you can cut off a vine-branch with a dagger or with a chisel, and in many other ways?

Of course.

And yet not so well as with a pruning-hook made for the purpose?

True.

May we not say that this is the end of a pruning-hook?

We may.

Then now I think you will have no difficulty in understanding my meaning when I asked the question whether the end of anything would be that which could not be accomplished, or not so well accomplished, by any other thing?

I understand your meaning, he said, and assent.

And that to which an end is appointed has also an excellence? Need I ask again whether the eye has an end?

It has.

And has not the eye an excellence?

Yes.

And the ear has an end and an excellence also?

True.

And the same is true of all other things; they have each of them an end and a special excellence?

That is so.

Well, and can the eyes fulfil their end if they are

wanting in their own proper excellence and have a
defect instead?

How can they, he said, if they are blind and can
not see?

You mean to say, if they have lost their proper
excellence, which is sight, but I have not arrived at
that point yet. I would rather ask the question more
generally, and only inquire whether the things which
fulfil their ends fulfil them by their own proper excellence, and fail of fulfilling them by their own defect?

Certainly, he replied.

I might say the same of the ears; when deprived
of their own proper excellence they can not fulfil their
end?

True.

And the same observation will apply to all other
things?

I agree.

Well; and has not the soul an end which nothing
else can fulfil? for example, to superintend and command and deliberate and the like. Are not these functions proper to the soul, and can they rightly be assigned to any other?

To no other.

And is not life to be reckoned among the ends of
the soul?

Assuredly, he said.

And has not the soul an excellence also?

Yes.

And can she or can she not fulfil her own ends when
deprived of that excellence?

She can not.

Then an evil soul must necessarily be an evil
ruler and superintendent, and the good soul a good
ruler?

Yes, necessarily.

And we have admitted that justice is the excellence of the soul, and injustice the defect of the soul?

That has been admitted.

Then the just soul and the just man will live well, and the unjust man will live ill?

That is what your argument proves.

And he who lives well is blessed and happy, and he who lives ill the reverse of happy?

Certainly.

Then the just is happy, and the unjust miserable?

So be it.

But happiness and not misery is profitable.

Of course.

Then, my blessed Thrasymachus, injustice can never be more profitable than justice.

Let this, Socrates, he said, be your entertainment at the Bendidea.

For which I am indebted to you, I said, now that you have grown gentle towards me and have left off scolding. Nevertheless, I have not been well entertained; but that was my own fault and not yours. As an epicure snatches a taste of every dish which is successively brought to table, he not having allowed himself time to enjoy the one before, so have I gone from one subject to another without having discovered what I sought at first, the nature of justice. I left that inquiry and turned away to consider whether justice is virtue and wisdom or evil and folly; and when there arose a further question about the comparative advantages of justice and injustice, I could not refrain from passing on to that. And the result of the whole discussion has been that I know nothing at all. For I know not what justice is, and therefore I am not likely to know whether it is or is not a virtue, nor can I say whether the just man is happy or unhappy.

BOOK II

WITH these words I was thinking that I had made an end of the discussion; but the end, in truth, proved to be only a beginning. For Glaucon, who is always the most pugnacious of men, was dissatisfied at Thrasymachus' retirement; he wanted to have the battle out. So he said to me: Socrates, do you wish really to persuade us, or only to seem to have persuaded us, that to be just is always better than to be unjust?

I should wish really to persuade you, I replied, if I could.

Then you certainly have not succeeded. Let me ask you now: — How would you arrange goods — are there not some which we welcome for their own sakes, and independently of their consequences, as, for example, harmless pleasures and enjoyments, which delight us at the time, although nothing follows from them?

I agree in thinking that there is such a class, I replied.

Is there not also a second class of goods, such as knowledge, sight, health, which are desirable not only in themselves, but also for their results?

Certainly, I said.

And would you not recognize a third class, such as gymnastic, and the care of the sick, and the physician's art; also the various ways of money-making — these do us good but we regard them as disagreeable; and no one would choose them for their own sakes, but only for the sake of some reward or result which flows from them?

There is, I said, this third class also. But why do you ask?

Because I want to know in which of the three classes you would place justice?

In the highest class, I replied, — among those goods which he who would be happy desires both for their own sake and for the sake of their results.

Then the many are of another mind; they think that justice is to be reckoned in the troublesome class, among goods which are to be pursued for the sake of rewards and of reputation, but in themselves are disagreeable and rather to be avoided.

I know, I said, that this is their manner of thinking, and that this was the thesis which Thrasymachus was maintaining just now, when he censured justice and praised injustice. But I am too stupid to be convinced by him.

I wish, he said, that you would hear me as well as him, and then I shall see whether you and I agree. For Thrasymachus seems to me, like a snake, to have been charmed by your voice sooner than he ought to have been; but to my mind the nature of justice and injustice have not yet been made clear. Setting aside their rewards and results, I want to know what they are in themselves, and how they inwardly work in the soul. If you please, then, I will revive the argument of Thrasymachus. And first I will speak of the nature and origin of justice according to the common view of them. Secondly, I will show that all men who practise justice do so against their will, of necessity, but not as a good. And thirdly, I will argue that there is reason in this view, for the life of the unjust is after all better far than the life of the just — if what they say is true, Socrates, since I myself am not of their opinion. But still I acknowledge that I am perplexed when I hear the voices of Thrasymachus and myriads of others dinning in my ears; and, on the other hand, I have never yet heard the superiority of justice to injustice maintained by any one in a satisfactory way. I want to hear justice praised in respect of itself; then I shall be satisfied, and you are the person from whom I think that I am most likely to hear this; and therefore I will praise the unjust life to the utmost of my power, and my manner of speaking will indicate the manner in which I desire to hear you too praising justice and censuring injustice. Will you say whether you approve of my proposal?

Indeed I do; nor can I imagine any theme about which a man of sense would oftener wish to converse.

I am delighted, he replied, to hear you say so, and shall begin by speaking, as I proposed, of the nature and origin of justice.

They say that to do injustice is, by nature, good; to suffer injustice, evil; but that the evil is greater than the good. And so when men have both done and suffered injustice and have had experience of both, not being able to avoid the one and obtain the other, they think that they had better agree among themselves to have neither; hence there arise laws and mutual covenants; and that which is ordained by law is termed by them lawful and just. This they affirm to be the origin and nature of justice; — it is a mean or compromise, between the best of all, which is to do injustice and not be punished, and the worst of all, which is to suffer injustice without the power of retaliation; and justice, being at a middle point between the two, is tolerated not as a good, but as the lesser evil, and honored by reason of the inability of men to do injustice. For no man who is worthy to be called a man would ever submit to such an agreement if he were able to resist; he would be mad if he did. Such is the received account, Socrates, of the nature and origin of justice.

Now that those who practise justice do so involuntarily and because they have not the power to be unjust will best appear if we imagine something of this kind: having given both to the just and the unjust power to do what they will, let us watch and see whither desire will lead them; then we shall discover in the very act the just and unjust man to be proceeding along the same road, following their interest, which all natures deem to be their good, and are only diverted into the path of justice by the force of law. The liberty which we are supposing may be most completely given to them in the form of such a power as is said to have been possessed by Gyges, the ancestor of Croesus the Lydian.[1] According to the tradition, Gyges was a shepherd in the service of the king of Lydia; there was a great storm, and an earthquake made an opening in the earth at the place where he was feeding his flock. Amazed at the sight, he descended into the opening, where, among other marvels, he beheld a hollow brazen horse, having doors, at which he stooping and looking in saw a dead body of stature, as appeared to him, more than human, and having nothing on but a gold ring; this he took from the finger of the dead and reascended. Now the shepherds met together, according to custom, that they might send their monthly report about the flocks to the king; into their assembly he came having the ring on his finger, and as he was sitting among them he chanced to turn the collet of the ring inside his hand, when instantly he became invisible to the rest of the company and they began to speak of him as if he were no longer present. He was astonished at

Reading Γύγῃ τῷ Κροίσου τοῦ Λυδοῦ προγόνῳ.

this, and again touching the ring he turned the collet
outwards and reappeared; he made several trials of
the ring, and always with the same result — when he
turned the collet inwards he became invisible, when
outwards he reappeared. Whereupon he contrived
to be chosen one of the messengers who were sent to
the court; where as soon as he arrived he seduced the
queen, and with her help conspired against the king
and slew him, and took the kingdom. Suppose now
that there were two such magic rings, and the just
put on one of them and the unjust the other; no man
can be imagined to be of such an iron nature that he
would stand fast in justice. No man would keep his
hands off what was not his own when he could safely
take what he liked out of the market, or go into houses
and lie with any one at his pleasure, or kill or release
from prison whom he would, and in all respects be like
a God among men. Then the actions of the just
would be as the actions of the unjust; they would
both come at last to the same point. And this we
may truly affirm to be a great proof that a man is
just, not willingly or because he thinks that justice
is any good to him individually, but of necessity, for
wherever any one thinks that he can safely be unjust,
there he is unjust. For all men believe in their hearts
that injustice is far more profitable to the individual
than justice, and he who argues as I have been supposing, will say that they are right. If you could
imagine any one obtaining this power of becoming
invisible, and never doing any wrong or touching
what was another's, he would be thought by the
lookers-on to be a most wretched idiot, although they
would praise him to one another's faces, and keep up
appearances with one another from a fear that they
too might suffer injustice. Enough of this.
    Now. if we are to form a real judgment of the life

of the just and unjust, we must isolate them; there is no other way; and how is the isolation to be effected? I answer: Let the unjust man be entirely unjust, and the just man entirely just; nothing is to be taken away from either of them, and both are to be perfectly furnished for the work of their respective lives. First, let the unjust be like other distinguished masters of craft; like the skilful pilot or physician, who knows intuitively his own powers and keeps within their limits, and who, if he fails at any point, is able to recover himself. So let the unjust make his unjust attempts in the right way, and lie hidden if he means to be great in his injustice: (he who is found out is nobody:) for the highest reach of injustice is, to be deemed just when you are not. Therefore I say that in the perfectly unjust man we must assume the most perfect injustice; there is to be no deduction, but we must allow him, while doing the most unjust acts, to have acquired the greatest reputation for justice. If he have taken a false step he must be able to recover himself; he must be one who can speak with effect, if any of his deeds come to light, and who can force his way where force is required by his courage and strength, and command of money and friends. And at his side let us place the just man in his nobleness and simplicity, wishing, as Æschylus says, to be and not to seem good. There must be no seeming, for if he seem to be just he will be honored and rewarded, and then we shall not know whether he is just for the sake of justice or for the sake of honors and rewards; therefore, let him be clothed in justice only, and have no other covering; and he must be imagined in a state of life the opposite of the former. Let him be the best of men, and let him be thought the worst; then he will have been put to the proof; and we shall see whether he will be affected by the fear of infamy and its consequences. And let him continue thus to the hour of death; being just and seeming to be unjust. When both have reached the uttermost extreme, the one of justice and the other of injustice, let judgment be given which of them is the happier of the two.

Heavens! my dear Glaucon, I said, how energetically you polish them up for the decision, first one and then the other, as if they were two statues.

I do my best, he said. And now that we know what they are like there is no difficulty in tracing out the sort of life which awaits either of them. This I will proceed to describe; but as you may think the description a little too coarse, I ask you to suppose, Socrates, that the words which follow are not mine. — Let me put them into the mouths of the eulogists of injustice: They will tell you that the just man who is thought unjust will be scourged, racked, bound — will have his eyes burned out; and, at last, after suffering every kind of evil, he will be impaled: Then he will understand that he ought to seem only, and not to be, just; the words of Æschylus may be more truly spoken of the unjust than of the just. For the unjust is pursuing a reality; he does not live with a view to appearances — he wants to be really unjust and not to seem only: —

> " His mind has a soil deep and fertile,
> Out of which spring his prudent counsels." [1]

In the first place, he is thought just, and therefore bears rule in the city; he can marry whom he will, and give in marriage to whom he will; also he can trade and deal where he likes, and always to his own advantage, because he has no misgivings about injustice; and at every contest, whether in public or private, he

---

[1] Seven against Thebes, 574.

gets the better of his antagonists, and gains at their expense, and is rich, and out of his gains he can benefit his friends, and harm his enemies; moreover, he can offer sacrifices, and dedicate gifts to the gods abundantly and magnificently, and can honor the gods or any man whom he wants to honor in a far better style than the just, and therefore he is likely to be dearer than they are to the gods. And thus, Socrates, gods and men are said to unite in making the life of the unjust better than the life of the just.

I was going to say something in answer to Glaucon, when Adeimantus, his brother, interposed: Socrates, he said, you do not suppose that there is nothing more to be urged?

Why, what else is there? I answered.

The strongest point of all has not been even mentioned, he replied.

Well, then, according to the proverb, "Let brother help brother" — if he fails in any part do you assist him; although I must confess that Glaucon has already said quite enough to lay me in the dust, and take from me the power of helping justice.

Nonsense, he replied. But let me add something more: There is another side to Glaucon's argument about the praise and censure of justice and injustice, which is equally required in order to bring out what I believe to be his meaning. Parents and tutors are always telling their sons and their wards that they are to be just; but why? Not for the sake of justice, but for the sake of character and reputation; in the hope of obtaining for him who is reputed just some of those offices, marriages, and the like which Glaucon has enumerated among the advantages accruing to the unjust from the reputation of justice. More, however, is made of appearances by this class of persons than by the others; for they throw in the good opinion of the gods, and will tell you of a shower of benefits which the heavens, as they say, rain upon the pious; and this accords with the testimony of the noble Hesiod and Homer, the first of whom says, that the gods make the oaks of the just —

" To bear acorns at their summit, and bees in the middle;
And the sheep are bowed down with the weight of their fleeces," [1]

and many other blessings of a like kind are provided for them. And Homer has a very similar strain; for he speaks of one whose fame is —

" As the fame of some blameless king who, like a god,
    Maintains justice; to whom the black earth brings forth
    Wheat and barley, whose trees are bowed with fruit,
    And his sheep never fail to bear, and the sea gives him fish

Still grander are the gifts of heaven which Musaeus and his son [3] vouchsafe to the just; they take them down into the world below, where they have the saints lying on couches at a feast, everlastingly drunk, crowned with garlands; their ideas seem to be that an immortality of drunkenness is the highest meed of virtue. Some extend their rewards yet further; the posterity, as they say, of the faithful and just shall survive to the third and fourth generation. This is the style in which they praise justice. But about the wicked there is another strain; they bury them in a slough in Hades, and make them carry water in a sieve; also while they are yet living they bring them to infamy, and inflict upon them the punishments which Glaucon described as the portion of the just who are reputed to be unjust; nothing else does their invention supply. Such is their manner of praising the one and censuring the other.

Once more, Socrates, I will ask you to consider

---

[1] Hesiod, Works and Days, 230.   [2] Homer, Od. xix. 109.   [3] Eumolpus.

another way of speaking about justice and injustice, which is not confined to the poets, but is found in prose writers. The universal voice of mankind is always declaring that justice and virtue are honorable, but grievous and toilsome; and that the pleasures of vice and injustice are easy of attainment, and are only censured by law and opinion. They say also that honesty is for the most part less profitable than dishonesty; and they are quite ready to call wicked men happy, and to honor them both in public and private when they are rich or in any other way influential, while they despise and overlook those who may be weak and poor, even though acknowledging them to be better than the others. But most extraordinary of all is their mode of speaking about virtue and the gods: they say that the gods apportion calamity and misery to many good men, and good and happiness to the wicked. And mendicant prophets go to rich men's doors and persuade them that they have a power committed to them by the gods of making an atonement for a man's own or his ancestor's sins by sacrifices or charms, with rejoicings and feasts; and they promise to harm an enemy, whether just or unjust, at a small cost; with magic arts and incantations binding heaven, as they say, to execute their will. And the poets are the authorities to whom they appeal, now smoothing the path of vice with the words of Hesiod: —

" Vice may be had in abundance without trouble; the way is smooth and her dwelling-place is near. But before virtue the gods have set toil," [1]

and a tedious and uphill road: then citing Homer as a witness that the gods may be influenced by men; for he also says: —

[1] Hesiod, Works and Days, 287.

" The gods, too, may be turned from their purpose; and men pray to them and avert their wrath by sacrifices and soothing entreaties, and by libations and the odor of fat, when they have sinned and transgressed." [1]

And they produce a host of books written by Musaeus and Orpheus, who were children of the Moon and the Muses — that is what they say — according to which they perform their ritual, and persuade not only individuals, but whole cities, that expiations and atonements for sin may be made by sacrifices and amusements which fill a vacant hour, and are equally at the service of the living and the dead; the latter sort they call mysteries, and they redeem us from the pains of hell, but if we neglect them no one knows what awaits us.

He proceeded: And now when the young hear all this said about virtue and vice, and the way in which gods and men regard them, how are their minds likely to be affected, my dear Socrates, — those of them, I mean, who are quickwitted, and, like bees on the wing, light on every flower, and from all that they hear are prone to draw conclusions as to what manner of persons they should be and in what way they should walk if they would make the best of life? Probably the youth will say to himself in the words of Pindar —

" Can I by justice or by crooked ways of deceit ascend a loftier tower which may be a fortress to me all my days? "

For what men say is that, if I am really just and am not also thought just, profit there is none, but the pain and loss on the other hand are unmistakable. But if, though unjust, I acquire the reputation of justice, a heavenly life is promised to me. Since then, as philosophers prove, appearance tyrannizes over truth and is lord of happiness, to appearance I must

[1] Homer. Iliad, ix: 493.

devote myself. I will describe around me a picture and shadow of virtue to be the vestibule and exterior of my house; behind I will trail the subtle and crafty fox, as Archilochus, greatest of sages, recommends. But I hear some one exclaiming that the concealment of wickedness is often difficult; to which I answer, Nothing great is easy. Nevertheless, the argument indicates this, if we would be happy, to be the path along which we should proceed. With a view to concealment we will establish secret brotherhoods and political clubs. And there are professors of rhetoric who teach the art of persuading courts and assemblies; and so, partly by persuasion and partly by force, I shall make unlawful gains and not be punished. Still I hear a voice saying that the gods can not be deceived, neither can they be compelled. But what if there are no gods? or, suppose them to have no care of human things — why in either case should we mind about concealment? And even if there are gods, and they do care about us, yet we know of them only from tradition and the genealogies of the poets; and these are the very persons who say that they may be influenced and turned by " sacrifices and soothing entreaties and by offerings." Let us be consistent then, and believe both or neither. If the poets speak truly, why then we had better be unjust, and offer of the fruits of injustice; for if we are just, although we may escape the vengeance of heaven, we shall lose the gains of injustice; but, if we are unjust, we shall keep the gains, and by our sinning and praying, and praying and sinning, the gods will be propitiated, and we shall not be punished. " But there is a world below in which either we or our posterity will suffer for our unjust deeds." Yes, my friend, will be the reflection, but there are mysteries and atoning deities, and these have great power. That is what mighty cities declare; and the children of the gods, who were their poets and prophets, bear a like testimony.

On what principle, then, shall we any longer choose justice rather than the worst injustice? when, if we only unite the latter with a deceitful regard to appearances, we shall fare to our mind both with gods and men, in life and after death, as the most numerous and the highest authorities tell us. Knowing all this, Socrates, how can a man who has any superiority of mind or person or rank or wealth, be willing to honor justice; or indeed to refrain from laughing when he hears justice praised? And even if there should be some one who is able to disprove the truth of my words, and who is satisfied that justice is best, still he is not angry with the unjust, but is very ready to forgive them, because he also knows that men are not just of their own free will; unless, peradventure, there be some one whom the divinity within him may have inspired with a hatred of injustice, or who has attained knowledge of the truth — but no other man. He only blames injustice who, owing to cowardice or age or some weakness, has not the power of being unjust. And this is proved by the fact that when he obtains the power, he immediately becomes unjust as far as he can be.

The cause of all this, Socrates, was indicated by us at the beginning of the argument, when my brother and I told you how astonished we were to find that of all the professing panegyrists of justice — beginning with the ancient heroes of whom any memorial has been preserved to us, and ending with the men of our own time — no one has ever blamed injustice or praised justice except with a view to the glories, honors, and benefits which flow from them. No one has ever adequately described either in verse or prose the true essential nature of either of them abiding in the soul, and invisible to any human or divine eye; or shown that of all the things of a man's soul which he has within him, justice is the greatest good, and injustice the greatest evil. Had this been the universal strain, had you sought to persuade us of this from our youth upwards, we should not have been on the watch to keep one another from doing wrong, but every one would have been his own watchman, because afraid, if he did wrong, of harboring in himself the greatest of evils. I dare say that Thrasymachus and others would seriously hold the language which I have been merely repeating, and words even stronger than these about justice and injustice, grossly, as I conceive, perverting their true nature. But I speak in this vehement manner, as I must frankly confess to you, because I want to hear from you the opposite side; and I would ask you to show not only the superiority which justice has over injustice, but what effect they have on the possessor of them which makes the one to be a good and the other an evil to him. And please, as Glaucon requested of you, to exclude reputations; for unless you take away from each of them his true reputation and add on the false, we shall say that you do not praise justice, but the appearance of it; we shall think that you are only exhorting us to keep injustice dark, and that you really agree with Thrasymachus in thinking that justice is another's good and the interest of the stronger, and that injustice is a man's own profit and interest, though injurious to the weaker. Now as you have admitted that justice is one of that highest class of goods which are desired indeed for their results, but in a far greater degree for their own sakes — like sight or hearing or knowledge or health, or any other real and natural and not merely conven-

tional good — I would ask you in your praise of
justice to regard one point only: I mean the essential
good and evil which justice and injustice work in the
possessors of them.   Let others praise justice and
censure injustice, magnifying the rewards and
honors of the one and abusing the other; that is a
manner of arguing which, coming from them, I am
ready to tolerate, but from you who have spent your
whole life in the consideration of this question, unless
I hear the contrary from your own lips, I expect
something better.   And therefore, I say, not only
prove to us that justice is better than injustice, but
show what they either of them do to the possessor
of them, which makes the one to be a good and the
other an evil, whether seen or unseen by gods and
men.

I had always admired the genius of Glaucon and
Adeimantus, but on hearing these words I was quite
delighted, and said: Sons of an illustrious father, that
was not a bad beginning of the Elegiac verses which
the admirer of Glaucon made in honor of you after
you had distinguished yourselves at the battle of
Megara: —

" Sons of Ariston," he sang, " divine offspring of an illustrious
   hero."

The epithet is very appropriate, for there is something
truly divine in being able to argue as you have done
for the superiority of injustice, and remaining unconvinced by your own arguments.   And I do believe
that you are not convinced — this I infer from your
general character, for had I judged only from your
speeches I should have mistrusted you.   But now, the
greater my confidence in you, the greater is my difficulty in knowing what to say.   For I am in a strait
between two; on the one hand I feel that I am un-

equal to the task; and my inability is brought home to me by the fact that you were not satisfied with the answer which I made to Thrasymachus, proving, as I thought, the superiority which justice has over injustice. And yet I can not refuse to help, while breath and speech remain to me; I am afraid that there would be an impiety in being present when justice is evil spoken of and not lifting up a hand in her defence. And therefore I had best give such help as I can.

Glaucon and the rest entreated me by all means not to let the question drop, but to proceed in the investigation. They wanted to arrive at the truth, first, about the nature of justice and injustice, and secondly, about their relative advantages. I told them, what I really thought, that the inquiry would be of a serious nature, and would require very good eyes. Seeing then, I said, that we are no great wits, I think that we had better adopt a method which I may illustrate thus; suppose that a short-sighted person had been asked by some one to read small letters from a distance; and it occurred to some one else that they might be found in another place which was larger and in which the letters were larger — if they were the same and he could read the larger letters first, and then proceeds to the lesser — this would have been thought a rare piece of good fortune.

Very true, said Adeimantus; but how does the illustration apply to our inquiry?

I will tell you, I replied; justice, which is the subject of our inquiry, is, as you know, sometimes spoken of as the virtue of an individual, and sometimes as the virtue of a State.

True, he replied.

And is not a State larger than an individual?

It is.

Then in the larger the quantity of justice is likely to be larger and more easily discernible. I propose therefore that we inquire into the nature of justice and injustice, first as they appear in the State, and secondly in the individual, proceeding from the greater to the lesser and comparing them.

That, he said, is an excellent proposal.

And if we imagine the State in process of creation, we shall see the justice and injustice of the State in process of creation also.

I dare say.

When the State is completed there may be a hope that the object of our search will be more easily discovered.

Yes, far more easily.

But ought we to attempt to construct one? I said; for to do so, as I am inclined to think, will be a very serious task. Reflect therefore.

I have reflected, said Adeimantus, and am anxious that you should proceed.

A State, I said, arises, as I conceive, out of the needs of mankind; no one is self-sufficing, but all of us have many wants. Can any other origin of a State be imagined?

There can be no other.

Then, as we have many wants, and many persons are needed to supply them, one takes a helper for one purpose and another for another; and when these partners and helpers are gathered together in one habitation the body of inhabitants is termed a State.

True, he said.

And they exchange with one another, and one gives, and another receives, under the idea that the exchange will be for their good.

Very true.

Then, I said, let us begin and create in idea a State; and yet the true creator is necessity, who is the mother of our invention.

Of course, he replied.

Now the first and greatest of necessities is food, which is the condition of life and existence.

Certainly.

The second is a dwelling, and the third clothing and the like.

True.

And now let us see how our city will be able to supply this great demand: We may suppose that one man is a husbandman, another a builder, some one else a weaver — shall we add to them a shoemaker, or perhaps some other purveyor to our bodily wants?

Quite right.

The barest notion of a State must include four or five men.

Clearly.

And how will they proceed? Will each bring the result of his labors into a common stock? — the individual husbandman, for example, producing for four and laboring four times as long and as much as he need in the provision of food with which he supplies others as well as himself; or will he have nothing to do with others and not be at the trouble of producing for them, but provide for himself alone a fourth of the food in a fourth of the time, and in the remaining three fourths of his time be employed in making a house or a coat or a pair of shoes, having no partnership with others, but supplying himself all his own wants?

Adeimantus thought that he should aim at producing food only and not at producing everything.

Probably, I replied, that would be the better way; and when I hear you say this, I am myself reminded that we are not all alike; there are diversities of natures among us which are adapted to different occupations.

Very true.

And will you have a work better done when the workman has many occupations, or when he has only one?

When he has only one.

Further, there can be no doubt that a work is spoiled when not done at the right time?

No doubt.

For business is not disposed to wait until the doer of the business is at leisure; but the doer must follow up what he is doing, and make the business his first object.

He must.

And if so, we must infer that all things are produced more plentifully and easily and of a better quality when one man does one thing which is natural to him, and does it at the right time, and leaves other things.

Undoubtedly.

Then more than our citizens will be required; for the husbandman will not make his own plough or mattock, or other implements of agriculture, if they are to be good for anything. Neither will the builder make his tools — and he too needs many; and in like manner the weaver and shoemaker.

True.

Then carpenters, and smiths, and many other artisans, will be sharers in our little State, which is already beginning to grow?

True.

Yet even if we add neatherds, shepherds, and other

herdsmen, in order that our husbandmen may have oxen to plough with, and builders as well as husbandmen may have draught cattle, and curriers and weavers fleeces and hides, — still our State will not be very large.

That is true; yet neither will it be a very small State which contains all these.

Then, again, there is the situation of the city — to find a place where nothing need be imported is wellnigh impossible.

Impossible.

Then there must be another class of citizens who will bring the required supply from another city?

There must.

But if the trader goes empty-handed, having nothing which they require who would supply his need, he will come back empty-handed.

That is certain.

And therefore what they produce at home must be not only enough for themselves, but such both in quantity and quality as to accommodate those from whom their wants are supplied.

Very true.

Then more husbandmen and more artisans will be required?

They will.

Not to mention the importers and exporters, who are called merchants?

Yes.

Then we shall want merchants?

We shall.

And if merchandise is to be carried over the sea, skilful sailors will also be needed, and in considerable numbers?

Yes, in considerable numbers.

Then, again, within the city, how will they exchange their productions? To secure such an exchange was, as you will remember, one of our principal objects when we formed them into a society and constituted a State.

Clearly they will buy and sell.

Then they will need a market-place, and a money-token for purposes of exchange.

Certainly.

Suppose now that a husbandman, or an artisan, brings some production to market, and he comes at a time when there is no one to exchange with him, — is he to leave his calling and sit idle in the market-place?

Not at all; he will find people there who, seeing the want, undertake the office of salesmen. In well-ordered states they are commonly those who are the weakest in bodily strength, and therefore of little use for any other purpose; their duty is to be in the market, and to give money in exchange for goods to those who desire to sell and to take money from those who desire to buy.

This want, then, creates a class of retail-traders in our State. Is not " retailer " the term which is applied to those who sit in the market-place engaged in buying and selling, while those who wander from one city to another are called merchants?

Yes, he said.

And there is another class of servants, who are intellectually hardly on the level of companionship; still they have plenty of bodily strength for labor, which accordingly they sell, and are called, if I do not mistake, hirelings, hire being the name which is given to the price of their labor.

True.

Then hirelings will help to make up our population?

Yes.

And now, Adeimantus, is our State matured and perfected?

I think so.

Where, then, is justice, and where is injustice, and in what part of the State did they spring up?

Probably in the dealings of these citizens with one another. I can not imagine that they are more likely to be found anywhere else.

I dare say that you are right in your suggestion, I said; we had better think the matter out, and not shrink from the inquiry.

Let us then consider, first of all, what will be their way of life, now that we have thus established them. Will they not produce corn, and wine, and clothes, and shoes, and build houses for themselves? And when they are housed, they will work, in summer, commonly, stripped and barefoot, but in winter substantially clothed and shod. They will feed on barley-meal and flour of wheat, baking and kneading them, making noble cakes and loaves; these they will serve up on a mat of reeds or on clean leaves, themselves reclining the while upon beds strewn with yew or myrtle. And they and their children will feast, drinking of the wine which they have made, wearing garlands on their heads, and hymning the praises of the gods, in happy converse with one another. And they will take care that their families do not exceed their means; having an eye to poverty or war.

But, said Glaucon, interposing, you have not given them a relish to their meal.

True, I replied, I had forgotten; of course they must have a relish — salt, and olives, and cheese, and they will boil roots and herbs such as country people prepare; for a dessert we shall give them figs, and peas, and beans; and they will roast myrtle-berries and acorns at the fire, drinking in moderation. And with such a diet they may be expected to live in peace and health to a good old age, and bequeath a similar life to their children after them.

Yes, Socrates, he said, and if you were providing for a city of pigs, how else would you feed the beasts?

But what would you have, Glaucon? I replied.

Why, he said, you should give them the ordinary conveniences of life. People who are to be comfortable are accustomed to lie on sofas, and dine off tables, and they should have sauces and sweets in the modern style.

Yes, I said, now I understand: the question which you would have me consider is, not only how a State, but how a luxurious State is created; and possibly there is no harm in this, for in such a State we shall be more likely to see how justice and injustice originate. In my opinion the true and healthy constitution of the State is the one which I have described. But if you wish also to see a State at fever-heat, I have no objection. For I suspect that many will not be satisfied with the simpler way of life. They will be for adding sofas, and tables, and other furniture; also dainties, and perfumes, and incense, and courtesans, and cakes, all these not of one sort only, but in every variety; we must go beyond the necessaries of which I was at first speaking, such as houses, and clothes, and shoes: the arts of the painter and the embroiderer will have to be set in motion, and gold and ivory and all sorts of materials must be procured.

True, he said.

Then we must enlarge our borders; for the original healthy State is no longer sufficient. Now will the city have to fill and swell with a multitude of callings which are not required by any natural want; such as the whole tribe of hunters and actors, of whom one large class have to do with forms and colors; another will be the votaries of music — poets and their attendant train of rhapsodists, players, dancers, contractors; also makers of divers kinds of articles, including women's dresses. And we shall want more servants. Will not tutors be also in request, and nurses wet and dry, tirewomen and barbers, as well as confectioners and cooks; and swineherds, too, who were not needed and therefore had no place in the former edition of our State, but are needed now? They must not be forgotten: and there will be animals of many other kinds, if people eat them.

Certainly.

And living in this way we shall have much greater need of physicians than before?

Much greater.

And the country which was enough to support the original inhabitants will be too small now, and not enough?

Quite true.

Then a slice of our neighbors' land will be wanted by us for pasture and tillage, and they will want a slice of ours, if, like ourselves, they exceed the limit of necessity, and give themselves up to the unlimited accumulation of wealth?

That, Socrates, will be inevitable.

And so we shall go to war, Glaucon. Shall we not?

Most certainly, he replied.

Then, without determining as yet whether war does good or harm, thus much we may affirm, that now we have discovered war to be derived from causes which are also the causes of almost all the evils in States, private as well as public.

Undoubtedly.

And our State must once more enlarge; and this time the enlargement will be nothing short of a whole

army, which will have to go out and fight with the invaders for all that we have, as well as for the things
and persons whom we were describing above.

Why? he said; are they not capable of defending
themselves?

No, I said; not if we were right in the principle
which was acknowledged by all of us when we were
framing the State: the principle, as you will remember, was that one man can not practise many arts with
success.

Very true, he said.

But is not war an art?

Certainly.

And an art requiring as much attention as shoemaking?

Quite true.

And the shoemaker was not allowed by us to be a
husbandman, or a weaver, or a builder — in order that
we might have our shoes well made; but to him and
to every other worker was assigned one work for which
he was by nature fitted, and at that he was to continue
working all his life long and at no other; he was not
to let opportunities slip, and then he would become a
good workman. Now nothing can be more important
than that the work of a soldier should be well done.
But is war an art so easily acquired that a man may
be a warrior who is also a husbandman, or shoemaker,
or other artisan; although no one in the world would
be a good dice or draught player who merely took up
the game as a recreation, and had not from his earliest
years devoted himself to this and nothing else? No
tools will make a man a skilled workman, or master of
defence, nor be of any use to him who has not learned
how to handle them, and has never bestowed any attention upon them. How then will he who takes up a
shield or other implement of war become a good fighter

all in a day, whether with heavy-armed or any other kind of troops?

Yes, he said, the tools which would teach men their own use would be beyond price.

And the higher the duties of the guardian, I said, the more time, and skill, and art, and application will be needed by him?

No doubt, he replied.

Will he not also require natural aptitude for his calling?

Certainly.

Then it will be our duty to select, if we can, natures which are fitted for the task of guarding the city?

It will.

And the selection will be no easy matter, I said; but we must be brave and do our best.

We must.

Is not the noble youth very like a well-bred dog in respect of guarding and watching?

What do you mean?

I mean that both of them ought to be quick to see, and swift to overtake the enemy when they see him; and strong too if, when they have caught him, they have to fight with him.

All these qualities, he replied, will certainly be required by them.

Well, and your guardian must be brave if he is to fight well?

Certainly.

And is he likely to be brave who has no spirit, whether horse or dog or any other animal? Have you never observed how invincible and unconquerable is spirit and how the presence of it makes the soul of any creature to be absolutely fearless and indomitable?

I have.

Then now we have a clear notion of the bodily qualities which are required in the guardian.

True.

And also of the mental ones; his soul is to be full of spirit?

Yes.

But are not these spirited natures apt to be savage with one another, and with everybody else?

A difficulty by no means easy to overcome, he replied.

Whereas, I said, they ought to be dangerous to their enemies, and gentle to their friends; if not, they will destroy themselves without waiting for their enemies to destroy them.

True, he said.

What is to be done then? I said; how shall we find a gentle nature which has also a great spirit, for the one is the contradiction of the other?

True.

He will not be a good guardian who is wanting in either of these two qualities; and yet the combination of them appears to be impossible; and hence we must infer that to be a good guardian is impossible.

I am afraid that what you say is true, he replied.

Here feeling perplexed I began to think over what had preceded. — My friend, I said, no wonder that we are in a perplexity; for we have lost sight of the image which we had before us.

What do you mean? he said.

I mean to say that there do exist natures gifted with those opposite qualities.

And where do you find them?

Many animals, I replied, furnish examples of them; our friend the dog is a very good one: you know that well-bred dogs are perfectly gentle to their familiars and acquaintances, and the reverse to strangers.

Yes, I know.

Then there is nothing impossible or out of the order of nature in our finding a guardian who has a similar combination of qualities?

Certainly not.

Would not he who is fitted to be a guardian, besides the spirited nature, need to have the qualities of a philosopher?

I do not apprehend your meaning.

The trait of which I am speaking, I replied, may be also seen in the dog, and is remarkable in the animal.

What trait?

Why, a dog, whenever he sees a stranger, is angry; when an acquaintance, he welcomes him, although the one has never done any harm, nor the other any good. Did this never strike you as curious?

The matter never struck me before; but I quite recognize the truth of your remark.

And surely this instinct of the dog is very charming; — your dog is a true philosopher.

Why?

Why, because he distinguishes the face of a friend and of an enemy only by the criterion of knowing and not knowing. And must not an animal be a lover of learning who determines what he likes and dislikes by the test of knowledge and ignorance?

Most assuredly.

And is not the love of learning the love of wisdom, which is philosophy?

They are the same, he replied.

And may we not say confidently of man also, that he who is likely to be gentle to his friends and acquaintances, must by nature be a lover of wisdom and knowledge?

That we may safely affirm.

Then he who is to be a really good and noble guardian of the State will require to unite in himself philosophy and spirit and swiftness and strength?

Undoubtedly.

Then we have found the desired natures; and now that we have found them, how are they to be reared and educated? Is not this an inquiry which may be expected to throw light on the greater inquiry which is our final end — How do justice and injustice grow up in States? for we do not want either to omit what is to the point or to draw out the argument to an inconvenient length.

Adeimantus thought that the inquiry would be of great service to us.

Then, I said, my dear friend, the task must not be given up, even if somewhat long.

Certainly not.

Come then, and let us pass a leisure hour in story-telling, and our story shall be the education of our heroes.

By all means.

And what shall be their education? Can we find a better than the traditional sort? — and this has two divisions, gymnastic for the body, and music for the soul.

True.

Shall we begin education with music, and go on to gymnastic afterwards?

By all means.

And when you speak of music, do you include literature or not?

I do.

And literature may be either true or false?

Yes.

And the young should be trained in both kinds, and we begin with the false?

I do not understand your meaning, he said.

You know, I said, that we begin by telling children stories which, though not wholly destitute of truth, are in the main fictitious; and these stories are told them when they are not of an age to learn gymnastics.

Very true.

That was my meaning when I said that we must teach music before gymnastics.

Quite right, he said.

You know also that the beginning is the most important part of any work, especially in the case of a young and tender thing; for that is the time at which the character is being formed and the desired impression is more readily taken.

Quite true.

And shall we just carelessly allow children to hear any casual tales which may be devised by casual persons, and to receive into their minds ideas for the most part the very opposite of those which we should wish them to have when they are grown up?

We can not.

Then the first thing will be to establish a censorship of the writers of fiction, and let the censors receive any tale of fiction which is good, and reject the bad; and we will desire mothers and nurses to tell their children the authorized ones only. Let them fashion the mind with such tales, even more fondly than they mould the body with their hands; but most of those which are now in use must be discarded.

Of what tales are you speaking? he said.

You may find a model of the lesser in the greater, I said; for they are necessarily of the same type, and there is the same spirit in both of them.

Very likely, he replied; but I do not as yet know what you would term the greater.

Those, I said, which are narrated by Homer and

Hesiod, and the rest of the poets, who have ever been the great story-tellers of mankind.

But which stories do you mean, he said; and what fault do you find with them?

A fault which is most serious, I said; the fault of telling a lie, and, what is more, a bad lie.

But when is this fault committed?

Whenever an erroneous representation is made of the nature of gods and heroes, — as when a painter paints a portrait not having the shadow of a likeness to the original.

Yes, he said, that sort of thing is certainly very blamable; but what are the stories which you mean?

First of all, I said, there was that greatest of all lies in high places, which the poet told about Uranus, and which was a bad lie too, — I mean what Hesiod says that Uranus did, and how Cronus retaliated on him. The doings of Cronus, and the sufferings which in turn his son inflicted upon him, even if they were true, ought certainly not to be lightly told to young and thoughtless persons; if possible, they had better be buried in silence. But if there is an absolute necessity for their mention, a chosen few might hear them in a mystery, and they should sacrifice not a common [Eleusinian] pig, but some huge and unprocurable victim; and then the number of the hearers will be very few indeed.

Why, yes, said he, those stories are extremely ob- jectionable.

Yes, Adeimantus, they are stories not to be re- peated in our State; the young man should not be told that in committing the worst of crimes he is far from doing anything outrageous; and that even if he chas- tises his father when he does wrong, in whatever man- ner, he will only be following the example of the first and greatest among the gods.

I entirely agee with you, he said; in my opinion those stories are quite unfit to be repeated.

Neither, if we mean our future guardians to regard the habit of quarrelling among themselves as of all things the basest, should any word be said to them of the wars in heaven, and of the plots and fightings of the gods against one another, for they are not true. No, we shall never mention the battles of the giants, or let them be embroidered on garments; and we shall be silent about the innumerable other quarrels of gods and heroes with their friends and relatives. If they would only believe us we would tell them that quarrelling is unholy, and that never up to this time has there been any quarrel between citizens; this is what old men and old women should begin by telling children; and when they grow up, the poets also should be told to compose for them in a similar spirit.[1] But the narrative of Hephaestus binding Here his mother, or how on another occasion Zeus sent him flying for taking her part when she was being beaten, and all the battles of the gods in Homer — these tales must not be admitted into our State, whether they are supposed to have an allegorical meaning or not. For a young person can not judge what is allegorical and what is literal; anything that he receives into his mind at that age is likely to become indelible and unalterable; and therefore it is most important that the tales which the young first hear should be models of virtuous thoughts.

There you are right, he replied; but if any one asks where are such models to be found and of what tales are you speaking — how shall we answer him?

I said to him, You and I, Adeimantus, at this moment are not poets, but founders of a State: now the founders of a State ought to know the general forms

[1] Placing the comma after γραυσί, and not after γιγνομένοις.

in which poets should cast their tales, and the limits which must be observed by them, but to make the tales is not their business.

Very true, he said; but what are these forms of theology which you mean?

Something of this kind, I replied: — God is always to be represented as he truly is, whatever be the sort of poetry, epic, lyric or tragic, in which the representation is given.

Right.

And is he not truly good? and must he not be represented as such?

Certainly.

And no good thing is hurtful?

No, indeed.

And that which is not hurtful hurts not?

Certainly not.

And that which hurts not does no evil?

No.

And can that which does no evil be a cause of evil?

Impossible.

And the good is advantageous?

Yes.

And therefore the cause of well-being?

Yes.

It follows therefore that the good is not the cause of all things, but of the good only?

Assuredly.

Then God, if he be good, is not the author of all things, as the many assert, but he is the cause of a few things only, and not of most things that occur to men. For few are the goods of human life, and many are the evils, and the good is to be attributed to God alone; of the evils the causes are to be sought elsewhere, and not in him.

That appears to me to be most true, he said.

Then we must not listen to Homer or to any other poet who is guilty of the folly of saying that two casks

" Lie at the threshold of Zeus, full of lots, one of good, the other of evil lots," [1]

and that he to whom Zeus gives a mixture of the two

" Sometimes meets with evil fortune, at other times with good; "

but that he to whom is given the cup of unmingled ill,

" Him wild hunger drives o'er the beauteous earth."

And again —

" Zeus, who is the dispenser of good and evil to us."

And if any one asserts that the violation of oaths and treaties, which was really the work of Pandarus,[2] was brought about by Athene and Zeus, or that the strife and contention of the gods was instigated by Themis and Zeus,[3] he shall not have our approval; neither will we allow our young men to hear the words of Æschylus, that

" God plants guilt among men when he desires utterly to des- troy a house."

And if a poet writes of the sufferings of Niobe — the subject of the tragedy in which these iambic verses occur — or of the house of Pelops, or of the Trojan war or on any similar theme, either we must not per- mit him to say that these are the works of God, or if they are of God, he must devise some explanation of them such as we are seeking; he must say that God did what was just and right, and they were the better for being punished; but that those who are punished are miserable, and that God is the author of their misery — the poet is not to be permitted to say;

[1] Iliad xxiv. 527.　　[2] Iliad ii. 69:　　[3] Ib. xx.

though he may say that the wicked are miserable because they require to be punished, and are benefited by receiving punishment from God; but that God being good is the author of evil to any one is to be strenuously denied, and not to be said or sung or heard in verse or prose by any one whether old or young in any well-ordered commonwealth. Such a fiction is suicidal, ruinous, impious.

I agree with you, he replied, and am ready to give my assent to the law.

Let this then be one of our rules and principles concerning the gods, to which our poets and reciters will be expected to conform, — that God is not the author of all things, but of good only.

That will do, he said.

And what do you think of a second principle? Shall I ask you whether God is a magician, and of a nature to appear insidiously now in one shape, and now in another — sometimes himself changing and passing into many forms, sometimes deceiving us with the semblance of such transformations; or is he one and the same immutably fixed in his own proper image?

I can not answer you, he said, without more thought.

Well, I said; but if we suppose a change in anything, that change must be effected either by the thing itself, or by some other thing?

Most certainly.

And things which are at their best are also least liable to be altered or discomposed; for example, when healthiest and strongest, the human frame is least liable to be affected by meats and drinks, and the plant which is in the fullest vigor also suffers least from winds or the heat of the sun or any similar causes.

Of course.

And will not the bravest and wisest soul be least confused or deranged by any external influence?

True.

And the same principle, as I should suppose, applies to all composite things — furniture, houses, garments: when good and well made, they are least altered by time and circumstances.

Very true.

Then everything which is good, whether made by art or nature, or both, is least liable to suffer change from without?

True.

But surely God and the things of God are in every way perfect?

Of course they are.

Then he can hardly be compelled by external influence to take many shapes?

He can not.

But may he not change and transform himself?

Clearly, he said, that must be the case if he is changed at all.

And will he then change himself for the better and fairer, or for the worse and more unsightly?

If he change at all he can only change for the worse, for we can not suppose him to be deficient either in virtue or beauty.

Very true, Adeimantus; but then, would any one, whether God or man, desire to make himself worse?

Impossible.

Then it is impossible that God should ever be willing to change; being, as is supposed, the fairest and best that is conceivable, every God remains absolutely and forever in his own form.

That necessarily follows, he said, in my judgment.

Then, I said, my dear friend, let none of the poets tell us that

" The gods, taking the disguise of strangers from other lands, walk up and down cities in all sorts of forms; " [1]

and let no one slander Proteus and Thetis, neither let any one, either in tragedy or in any other kind of poetry, introduce Here disguised in the likeness of a priestess asking an alms

" For the life-giving daughters of Inachus the river of Argos; "

— let us have no more lies of that sort. Neither must we have mothers under the influence of the poets scaring their children with a bad version of these myths — telling how certain gods, as they say, " Go about by night in the likeness of so many strangers and in divers forms; " but let them take heed lest they make cowards of their children, and at the same time speak blasphemy against the gods.

Heaven forbid, he said.

But although the gods are themselves unchangeable, still by witchcraft and deception they may make us think that they appear in various forms?

Perhaps, he replied.

Well, but can you imagine that God will be willing to lie, whether in word or deed, or to put forth a phantom of himself?

I can not say, he replied.

Do you not know, I said, that the true lie, if such an expression may be allowed, is hated of gods and men?

What do you mean? he said.

I mean that no one is willingly deceived in that which is the truest and highest part of himself, or about the truest and highest matters; there, above all, he is most afraid of a lie having possession of him.

Still, he said, I do not comprehend you.

[1] Hom. Od. xvii 485.

The reason is, I replied, that you attribute some profound meaning to my words; but I am only saying that deception, or being deceived or uninformed about the highest realities in the highest part of themselves, which is the soul, and in that part of them to have and to hold the lie, is what mankind least like; — that, I say, is what they utterly detest.

There is nothing more hateful to them.

And, as I was just now remarking, this ignorance in the soul of him who is deceived may be called the true lie; for the lie in words is only a kind of imitation and shadowy image of a previous affection of the soul, not pure unadulterated falsehood. Am I not right?

Perfectly right.

The true lie is hated not only by the gods, but also by men?

Yes.

Whereas the lie in words is in certain cases useful and not hateful; in dealing with enemies — that would be an instance; or again, when those whom we call our friends in a fit of madness or illusion are going to do some harm, then it is useful and is a sort of medicine or preventive; also in the tales of mythology, of which we were just now speaking — because we do not know the truth about ancient times, we make falsehood as much like truth as we can, and so turn it to account.

Very true, he said.

But can any of these reasons apply to God? Can we suppose that he is ignorant of antiquity, and therefore has recourse to invention?

That would be ridiculous, he said.

Then the lying poet has no place in our idea of God?

I should say not.

Or perhaps he may tell a lie because he is afraid of enemies?

That is inconceivable.

But he may have friends who are senseless or mad?

But no mad or senseless person can be a friend of God.

Then no motive can be imagined why God should lie?

None whatever.

Then the superhuman and divine is absolutely incapable of falsehood?

Yes.

Then is God perfectly simple and true both in word and deed;[1] he changes not; he deceives not, either by sign or word, by dream or waking vision.

Your thoughts, he said, are the reflection of my own.

You agree with me then, I said, that this is the second type or form in which we should write and speak about divine things. The gods are not magicians who transform themselves, neither do they deceive mankind in any way.

I grant that.

Then, although we are admirers of Homer, we do not admire the lying dream which Zeus sends to Agamemnon; neither will we praise the verses of Æschylus in which Thetis says that Apollo at her nuptials

" Was celebrating in song her fair progeny whose days were to be long, and to know no sickness. And when he had spoken of my lot as in all things blessed of heaven he raised a note of triumph and cheered my soul. And I thought that the word of Phoebus, being divine and full of prophecy, would not fail. And now he himself who uttered the strain, he who was present at the banquet, and who said this — he it is who has slain my son." [2]

[1] Omitting κατὰ φαντασίας.   [2] From a lost play.

These are the kind of sentiments about the gods which will arouse our anger; and he who utters them shall be refused a chorus; neither shall we allow teachers to make use of them in the instruction of the young, meaning, as we do, that our guardians, as far as men can be, should be true worshippers of the gods and like them.

I entirely agree, he said, in these principles, and promise to make them my laws.

BOOK III

Such then, I said, are our principles of theology — some tales are to be told, and others are not to be told to our disciples from their youth upwards, if we mean them to honor the gods and their parents, and to value friendship with one another.

Yes; and I think that our principles are right, he said.

But if they are to be courageous, must they not learn other lessons besides these, and lessons of such a kind as will take away the fear of death? Can any man be courageous who has the fear of death in him?

Certainly not, he said.

And can he be fearless of death, or will he choose death in battle rather than defeat and slavery, who believes the world below to be real and terrible?

Impossible.

Then we must assume a control over the narrators of this class of tales as well as over the others, and beg them not simply to revile, but rather to commend the world below, intimating to them that their descriptions are untrue, and will do harm to our future warriors.

That will be our duty, he said.

Then, I said, we shall have to obliterate many obnoxious passages, beginning with the verses,

"I would rather be a serf on the land of a poor and portionless man than rule over all the dead who have come to nought." [1]

[1] Od. xi. 489.

We must also expunge the verse, which tells us how Pluto feared,

" Lest the mansions grim and squalid which the gods abhor should be seen both of mortals and immortals." [1]

And again: —

" O heavens! verily in the house of Hades there is soul and ghostly form but no mind at all! " [2]

Again of Tiresias: —

" [To him even after death did Persephone grant mind,] that he alone should be wise; but the other souls are flitting shades." [3]

Again: —

" The soul flying from the limbs had gone to Hades, lamenting her fate, leaving manhood and youth." [4]

Again:—

" And the soul, with shrilling cry, passed like smoke beneath the earth." [5]

And, —

" As bats in hollow of mystic cavern, whenever any of them has dropped out of the string and falls from the rock, fly shrilling and cling to one another, so did they with shrilling cry hold together as they moved." [6]

And we must beg Homer and the other poets not to be angry if we strike out these and similar passages, not because they are unpoetical, or unattractive to the popular ear, but because the greater the poetical charm of them, the less are they meet for the ears of boys and men who are meant to be free, and who should fear slavery more than death.

Undoubtedly.

Also we shall have to reject all the terrible and appalling names which describe the world below —

[1] Il. xx. 64.　　[2] Il. xxiii. 103.　　[3] Od. x. 495.　　[4] Il xvi. 856
[5] Ib. xxiii. 100.　　[6] Od. xxiv. 6.

Cocytus and Styx, ghosts under the earth, and sapless shades, and any similar words of which the very mention causes a shudder to pass through the inmost soul of him who hears them. I do not say that these horrible stories may not have a use of some kind; but there is a danger that the nerves of our guardians may be rendered too excitable and effeminate by them.

There is a real danger, he said.

Then we must have no more of them.

True.

Another and a nobler strain must be composed and sung by us.

Clearly.

And shall we proceed to get rid of the weepings and wailings of famous men?

They will go with the rest.

But shall we be right in getting rid of them? Reflect: our principle is that the good man will not consider death terrible to any other good man who is his comrade.

Yes; that is our principle.

And therefore he will not sorrow for his departed friend as though he had suffered anything terrible?

He will not.

Such an one, as we further maintain, is sufficient for himself and his own happiness, and therefore is least in need of other men.

True, he said.

And for this reason the loss of a son or brother, or the deprivation of fortune, is to him of all men least terrible.

Assuredly.

And therefore he will be least likely to lament, and will bear with the greatest equanimity any misfortune of this sort which may befall him.

Yes, he will feel such a misfortune far less than another.

Then we shall be right in getting rid of the lamentations of famous men, and making them over to women (and not even to women who are good for anything), or to men of a baser sort, that those who are being educated by us to be the defenders of their country may scorn to do the like.

That will be very right.

Then we will once more entreat Homer and the other poets not to depict Achilles,[1] who is the son of a goddess, first lying on his side, then on his back, and then on his face; then starting up and sailing in a frenzy along the shores of the barren sea; now taking the sooty ashes in both his hands [2] and pouring them over his head, or weeping and wailing in the various modes which Homer has delineated. Nor should he describe Priam the kinsman of the gods as praying and beseeching,

" Rolling in the dirt, calling each man loudly by his name." [3]

Still more earnestly will we beg of him at all events not to introduce the gods lamenting and saying,

" Alas! my misery! Alas! that I bore the bravest to my sorrow." [4]

But if he must introduce the gods, at any rate let him not dare so completely to misrepresent the greatest of the gods, as to make him say —

" O heavens! with my eyes verily I behold a dear friend of mine chased round and round the city, and my heart is sorrowful." [5]

Or again:—

" Woe is me that I am fated to have Sarpedon, dearest of men to me, subdued at the hands of Patroclus the son of Menoetius." [6]

[1] Il. xxiv. 10.   [2] Ib. xviii. 23.   [3] Ib. xxii. 414.   [4] Il. xviii. 54
[5] Ib. xxii. 168.   [6] Ib. xvi. 433.

For if, my sweet Adeimantus, our youth seriously listen to such unworthy representations of the gods, instead of laughing at them as they ought, hardly will any of them deem that he himself, being but a man, can be dishonored by similar actions; neither will he rebuke any inclination which may arise in his mind to say and do the like. And instead of having any shame or self-control, he will be always whining and lamenting on slight occasions.

Yes, he said, that is most true.

Yes, I replied; but that surely is what ought not to be, as the argument has just proved to us; and by that proof we must abide until it is disproved by a better.

It ought not to be.

Neither ought our guardians to be given to laughter. For a fit of laughter which has been indulged to excess almost always produces a violent reaction.

So I believe.

Then persons of worth, even if only mortal men, must not be represented as overcome by laughter, and still less must such a representation of the gods be allowed.

Still less of the gods, as you say, he replied.

Then we shall not suffer such an expression to be used about the gods as that of Homer when he describes how

"Inextinguishable laughter arose among the blessed gods, when they saw Hephaestus bustling about the mansion." [1]

On your views, we must not admit them.

On my views, if you like to father them on me; that we must not admit them is certain.

Again, truth should be highly valued; if, as we were saying, a lie is useless to the gods, and useful only as a medicine to men, then the use of such

[1] Ib. i. 599.

medicines should be restricted to physicians; private individuals have no business with them.

Clearly not, he said.

Then if any one at all is to have the privilege of lying, the rulers of the State should be the persons; and they, in their dealings either with enemies or with their own citizens, may be allowed to lie for the public good. But nobody else should meddle with anything of the kind; and although the rulers have this privilege, for a private man to lie to them in return is to be deemed a more heinous fault than for the patient or the pupil of a gymnasium not to speak the truth about his own bodily illnesses to the physician or to the trainer, or for a sailor not to tell the captain what is happening about the ship and the rest of the crew, and how things are going with himself or his fellow sailors.

Most true, he said.

If, then, the ruler catches anybody beside himself lying in the State,

" Any of the craftsmen, whether he be priest or physician or carpenter," [1]

he will punish him for introducing a practice which is equally subversive and destructive of ship or State.

Most certainly, he said, if our idea of the State is ever carried out.[2]

In the next place our youth must be temperate? Certainly.

Are not the chief elements of temperance, speaking generally, obedience to commanders and self-control in sensual pleasures?

True.

[1] Od. xvii. 383 sq.
[2] Or, "if his words are accompanied by actions."

Then we shall approve such language as that of Diomede in Homer,

> " Friend, sit still and obey my word," [1]

and the verses which follow,

> " The Greeks marched breathing prowess,[2]
> . . . . in silent awe of their leaders," [3]

and other sentiments of the same kind.

We shall.

What of this line,

> " O heavy with wine, who hast the eyes of a dog and the heart of a stag," [4]

and of the words which follow? Would you say that these, or any similar impertinences which private individuals are supposed to address to their rulers, whether in verse or prose, are well or ill spoken?

They are ill spoken.

They may very possibly afford some amusement, but they do not conduce to temperance. And therefore they are likely to do harm to our young men — you would agree with me there?

Yes.

And then, again, to make the wisest of men say that nothing in his opinion is more glorious than

> " When the tables are full of bread and meat, and the cupbearer carries round wine which he draws from the bowl and pours into the cups; " [5]

is it fit or conducive to temperance for a young man to hear such words? Or the verse

" The saddest of fates is to die and meet destiny from hunger "? [6]

What would you say again to the tale of Zeus, who,

[1] Il. iv. 412.　[2] Od. iii. 8.　[3] Ib. iv. 431.　[4] Ib. i. 225.　[5] Ib ix. 8
[6] Ib. xii. 342.

while other gods and men were asleep and he the only person awake, lay devising plans, but forgot them all in a moment through his lust, and was so completely overcome at the sight of Here that he would not even go into the hut, but wanted to lie with her on the ground, declaring that he had never been in such a state of rapture before, even when they first met one another

"Without the knowledge of their parents;"[1]

or that other tale of how Hephæstus, because of similar goings on, cast a chain around Ares and Aphrodite?[2]

Indeed, he said, I am strongly of opinion that they ought not to hear that sort of thing.

But any deeds of endurance which are done or told by famous men, these they ought to see and hear; as, for example, what is said in the verses,

"He smote his breast, and thus reproached his heart,
Endure, my heart; far worse has thou endured!"[3]

Certainly, he said.

In the next place, we must not let them be receivers of gifts or lovers of money.

Certainly not.

Neither must we sing to them of

"Gifts persuading gods, and persuading reverend kings."[4]

Neither is Phoenix, the tutor of Achilles, to be approved or deemed to have given his pupil good counsel when he told him that he should take the gifts of the Greeks and assist them;[5] but that without a gift he should not lay aside his anger. Neither will we believe or acknowledge Achilles himself to have been such a lover of money that he took Agamemnon's

[1] Il. xiv. 281.   [2] Od. viii. 266.   [3] Ib. xx. 17.
[4] Quoted by Suidas as attributed to Hesiod.   [5] Il. ix. 515.

gifts, or that when he had received payment he restored the dead body of Hector, but that without payment he was unwilling to do so.[1]

Undoubtedly, he said, these are not sentiments which can be approved.

Loving Homer as I do,[2] I hardly like to say that in attributing these feelings to Achilles, or in believing that they are truly attributed to him, he is guilty of downright impiety. As little can I believe the narrative of his insolence to Apollo, where he says,

"Thou hast wronged me, O far-darter, most abominable of deities. Verily I would be even with thee, if I had only the power;"[3]

or his insubordination to the river-god,[4] on whose divinity he is ready to lay hands; or his offering to the dead Patroclus of his own hair,[5] which had been previously dedicated to the other river-god Spercheius, and that he actually performed this vow; or that he dragged Hector round the tomb of Patroclus,[6] and slaughtered the captives at the pyre;[7] of all this I can not believe that he was guilty, any more than I can allow our citizens to believe that he, the wise Cheiron's pupil, the son of a goddess and of Peleus who was the gentlest of men and third in descent from Zeus, was so disordered in his wits as to be at one time the slave of two seemingly inconsistent passions, meanness, not untainted by avarice, combined with overweening contempt of gods and men.

You are quite right, he replied.

And let us equally refuse to believe, or allow to be repeated, the tale of Theseus son of Poseidon, or of Peirithous son of Zeus, going forth as they did to perpetrate a horrid rape; or of any other hero or son

[1] Ib. xxiv. 175. [2] Cf. *infra*, x. 595. [3] Il. xxii. 15 sq. [4] Lb. xxi. 130, 223 sq
[5] Il. xxiii. 151.   [6] Ib. xxii. 394.   [7] Ib. xxiii. 175.

of a god daring to do such impious and dreadful things as they falsely ascribe to them in our day: and let us further compel the poets to declare either that these acts were not done by them, or that they were not the sons of gods; — both in the same breath they shall not be permitted to affirm. We will not have them trying to persuade our youth that the gods are the authors of evil, and that heroes are no better than men — sentiments which, as we were saying, are neither pious nor true, for we have already proved that evil can not come from the gods.

Assuredly not.

And further they are likely to have a bad effect on those who hear them; for everybody will begin to excuse his own vices when he is convinced that similar wickednesses are always being perpetrated by —

" The kindred of the gods, the relatives of Zeus, whose ancestral altar, the altar of Zeus, is aloft in air on the peak of Ida,"

and who have

" the blood of deities yet flowing in their veins." [1]

And therefore let us put an end to such tales, lest they engender laxity of morals among the young.

By all means, he replied.

But now that we are determining what classes of subjects are or are not to be spoken of, let us see whether any have been omitted by us. The manner in which gods and demigods and heroes and the world below should be treated has been already laid down.

Very true.

And what shall we say about men? That is clearly the remaining portion of our subject.

Clearly so.

[1] From the Niobe of Æschylus.

But we are not in a condition to answer this question at present, my friend.

Why not?

Because, if I am not mistaken, we shall have to say
that about men poets and story-tellers are guilty of
making the gravest misstatements when they tell us
that wicked men are often happy, and the good miserable; and that injustice is profitable when undetected,
but that justice is a man's own loss and another's
gain — these things we shall forbid them to utter, and
command them to sing and say the opposite.

To be sure we shall, he replied.

But if you admit that I am right in this, then I
shall maintain that you have implied the principle
for which we have been all along contending.

I grant the truth of your inference.

That such things are or are not to be said about
men is a question which we can not determine until
we have discovered what justice is, and how naturally
advantageous to the possessor, whether he seem to be
just or not.

Most true, he said.

Enough of the subject of poetry: let us now speak
of the style; and when this has been considered, both
matter and manner will have been completely treated.

I do not understand what you mean, said Adeimantus.

Then I must make you understand; and perhaps I
may be more intelligible if I put the matter in this
way. You are aware, I suppose, that all mythology
and poetry is a narration of events, either past, present, or to come?

Certainly, he replied.

And narration may be either simple narration, or
imitation, or a union of the two?

That again, he said, I do not quite understand.

I fear that I must be a ridiculous teacher when I have so much difficulty in making myself apprehended. Like a bad speaker, therefore, I will not take the whole of the subject, but will break a piece off in illustration of my meaning. You know the first lines of the Iliad, in which the poet says that Chryses prayed Agamemnon to release his daughter, and that Agamemnon flew into a passion with him; whereupon Chryses, failing of his object, invoked the anger of the God against the Achæans. Now as far as these lines,

" And he prayed all the Greeks, but especially the two sons of Atreus, the chiefs of the people,"

the poet is speaking in his own person; he never leads us to suppose that he is any one else. But in what follows he takes the person of Chryses, and then he does all that he can to make us believe that the speaker is not Homer, but the aged priest himself. And in this double form he has cast the entire narrative of the events which occurred at Troy and in Ithaca and throughout the Odyssey.

Yes.

And a narrative it remains both in the speeches which the poet recites from time to time and in the intermediate passages?

Quite true.

But when the poet speaks in the person of another, may we not say that he assimilates his style to that of the person who, as he informs you, is going to speak?

Certainly.

And this assimilation of himself to another, either by the use of voice or gesture, is the imitation of the person whose character he assumes?

Of course.

Then in this case the narrative of the poet may be said to proceed by way of imitation?

Very true.

Or, if the poet everywhere appears and never conceals himself, then again the imitation is dropped, and his poetry becomes simple narration. However, in order that I may make my meaning quite clear, and that you may no more say, " I don't understand," I will show how the change might be effected. If Homer had said, " The priest came, having his daughter's ransom in his hands, supplicating the Achaeans, and above all the kings;" and then if, instead of speaking in the person of Chryses, he had continued in his own person, the words would have been, not imitation, but simple narration. The passage would have run as follows (I am no poet, and therefore I drop the metre), " The priest came and prayed the gods on behalf of the Greeks that they might capture Troy and return safely home, but begged that they would give him back his daughter, and take the ransom which he brought, and respect the God. Thus he spoke, and the other Greeks revered the priest and assented. But Agamemnon was wroth, and bade him depart and not come again, lest the staff and chaplets of the God should be of no avail to him — the daughter of Chryses should not be released, he said — she should grow old with him in Argos. And then he told him to go away and not to provoke him, if he intended to get home unscathed. And the old man went away in fear and silence, and, when he had left the camp, he called upon Apollo by his many names, reminding him of everything which he had done pleasing him, whether in building his temples, or in offering sacrifice, and praying that his good deeds might be returned to him, and that the Achaeans might expiate his tears by the arrows of the god," — and so on. In this way the whole becomes simple narrative.

I understand, he said.

Or you may suppose the opposite case — that the intermediate passages are omitted, and the dialogue only left.

That also, he said, I understand; you mean, for example, as in tragedy.

You have conceived my meaning perfectly; and if I mistake not, what you failed to apprehend before is now made clear to you, that poetry and mythology are, in some cases, wholly imitative — instances of this are supplied by tragedy and comedy; there is likewise the opposite style, in which the poet is the only speaker — of this the dithyramb affords the best example; and the combination of both is found in epic, and in several other styles of poetry. Do I take you with me?

Yes, he said; I see now what you meant.

I will ask you to remember also what I began by saying, that we had done with the subject and might proceed to the style.

Yes, I remember.

In saying this, I intended to imply that we must come to an understanding about the mimetic art, — whether the poets, in narrating their stories, are to be allowed by us to imitate, and if so, whether in whole or in part, and if the latter, in what parts; or should all imitation be prohibited?

You mean, I suspect, to ask whether tragedy and comedy shall be admitted into our State?

Yes, I said; but there may be more than this in question: I really do not know as yet, but whither the argument may blow, thither we go.

And go we will, he said.

Then, Adeimantus, let me ask you whether our

guardians ought to be imitators; or rather, has not this question been decided by the rule already laid down that one man can only do one thing well, and not many; and that if he attempt many, he will altogether fail of gaining much reputation in any?

Certainly.

And this is equally true of imitation; no one man can imitate many things as well as he would imitate a single one?

He can not.

Then the same person will hardly be able to play a serious part in life, and at the same time to be an imitator and imitate many other parts as well; for even when two species of imitation are nearly allied, the same persons cannot succeed in both, as, for example, the writers of tragedy and comedy — did you not just now call them imitations?

Yes, I did; and you are right in thinking that the same persons can not succeed in both.

Any more than they can be rhapsodists and actors at once?

True.

Neither are comic and tragic actors the same; yet all these things are but imitations.

They are so.

And human nature, Adeimantus, appears to have been coined into yet smaller pieces, and to be as incapable of imitating many things well, as of performing well the actions of which the imitations are copies.

Quite true, he replied.

If then we adhere to our original notion and bear in mind that our guardians, setting aside every other business, are to dedicate themselves wholly to the maintenance of freedom in the State, making this their craft, and engaging in no work which does not bear on this end, they ought not to practise or imitate anything else; if they imitate at all, they should imitate from youth upward only those characters which are suitable to their profession — the courageous, temperate, holy, free, and the like; but they should not depict or be skilful at imitating any kind of illiberality or baseness, lest from imitation they should come to be what they imitate. Did you never observe how imitations, beginning in early youth and continuing far into life, at length grow into habits and become a second nature, affecting body, voice, and mind?

Yes, certainly, he said.

Then, I said, we will not allow those for whom we profess a care and of whom we say that they ought to be good men, to imitate a woman, whether young or old, quarrelling with her husband, or striving and vaunting against the gods in conceit of her happiness, or when she is in affliction, or sorrow, or weeping; and certainly not one who is in sickness, love, or labor.

Very right, he said.

Neither must they represent slaves, male or female, performing the offices of slaves?

They must not.

And surely not bad men, whether cowards or any others, who do the reverse of what we have just been prescribing, who scold or mock or revile one another in drink or out of drink, or who in any other manner sin against themselves and their neighbors in word or deed, as the manner of such is. Neither should they be trained to imitate the action or speech of men or women who are mad or bad; for madness, like vice, is to be known but not to be practised or imitated.

Very true, he replied.

Neither may they imitate smiths or other artificers, or oarsmen, or boatswains, or the like?

How can they, he said, when they are not allowed

to apply their minds to the callings of any of these?

Nor may they imitate the neighing of horses, the bellowing of bulls, the murmur of rivers and roll of the ocean, thunder, and all that sort of thing?

Nay, he said, if madness be forbidden, neither may they copy the behavior of madmen.

You mean, I said, if I understand you aright, that there is one sort of narrative style which may be employed by a truly good man when he has anything to say, and that another sort will be used by a man of an opposite character and education.

And which are these two sorts? he asked.

Suppose, I answered, that a just and good man in the course of a narration comes on some saying or action of another good man, — I should imagine that he will like to personate him, and will not be ashamed of this sort of imitation: he will be most ready to play the part of the good man when he is acting firmly and wisely; in a less degree when he is overtaken by illness or love or drink, or has met with any other disaster. But when he comes to a character which is unworthy of him, he will not make a study of that; he will disdain such a person, and will assume his likeness, if at all, for a moment only when he is performing some good action; at other times he will be ashamed to play a part which he has never practised, nor will he like to fashion and frame himself after the baser models; he feels the employment of such an art, unless in jest, to be beneath him, and his mind revolts at it.

So I should expect, he replied.

Then he will adopt a mode of narration such as we have illustrated out of Homer, that is to say, his style will be both imitative and narrative; but there will be very little of the former, and a great deal of the latter. Do you agree?

Certainly, he said; that is the model which such a speaker must necessarily take.

But there is another sort of character who will narrate anything, and, the worse he is, the more unscrupulous he will be; nothing will be too bad for him: and he will be ready to imitate anything, not as a joke, but in right good earnest, and before a large company. As I was just now saying, he will attempt to represent the roll of thunder, the noise of wind and hail, or the creaking of wheels, and pulleys, and the various sounds of flutes, pipes, trumpets, and all sorts of instruments: he will bark like a dog, bleat like a sheep, or crow like a cock; his entire art will consist in imitation of voice and gesture, and there will be very little narration.

That, he said, will be his mode of speaking.

These, then, are the two kinds of style?

Yes.

And you would agree with me in saying that one of them is simple and has but slight changes; and if the harmony and rhythm are also chosen for their simplicity, the result is that the speaker, if he speaks correctly, is always pretty much the same in style, and he will keep within the limits of a single harmony (for the changes are not great), and in like manner he will make use of nearly the same rhythm?

That is quite true, he said.

Whereas the other requires all sorts of harmonies and all sorts of rhythms, if the music and the style are to correspond, because the style has all sorts of changes.

That is also perfectly true, he replied.

And do not the two styles, or the mixture of the two, comprehend all poetry, and every form of expression in words? No one can say anything except in one or other of them or in both together.

They include all, he said.

And shall we receive into our State all the three styles, or one only of the two unmixed styles? or would you include the mixed?

I should prefer only to admit the pure imitator of virtue.

Yes, I said, Adeimantus; but the mixed style is also very charming: and indeed the pantomimic, which is the opposite of the one chosen by you, is the popular style with children and their attendants, and with the world in general.

I do not deny it.

But I suppose you would argue that such a style is unsuitable to our State, in which human nature is not twofold or manifold, for one man plays one part only?

Yes; quite unsuitable.

And this is the reason why in our State, and in our State only, we shall find a shoemaker to be a shoemaker and not a pilot also, and a husbandman to be a husbandman and not a dicast also, and a soldier a soldier and not a trader also, and the same throughout?

True, he said.

And therefore when any one of these pantomimic gentlemen, who are so clever that they can imitate anything, comes to us, and makes a proposal to exhibit himself and his poetry, we will fall down and worship him as a sweet and holy and wonderful being; but we must also inform him that in our State such as he are not permitted to exist; the law will not allow them. And so when we have anointed him with myrrh, and set a garland of wool upon his head, we shall send him away to another city. For we mean to employ for our souls' health the rougher and severer poet or story-teller who will imitate the style of the virtuous

only, and will follow those models which we prescribed at first when we began the education of our
soldiers.

We certainly will, he said, if we have the power.

Then now, my friend, I said, that part of music or
literary education which relates to the story or myth
may be considered to be finished; for the matter and
manner have both been discussed.

I think so too, he said.

Next in order will follow melody and song.

That is obvious.

Every one can see already what we ought to say
about them, if we are to be consistent with ourselves.

I fear, said Glaucon, laughingly, that the word
" every one " hardly includes me, for I can not at the
moment say what they should be; though I may
guess.

At any rate you can tell that a song or ode has three
parts — the words, the melody, and the rhythm; that
degree of knowledge I may presuppose?

Yes, he said; so much as that you may.

And as for the words, there will surely be no difference between words which are and which are not
set to music; both will conform to the same laws, and
these have been already determined by us?

Yes.

And the melody and rhythm will depend upon the
words?

Certainly.

We were saying, when we spoke of the subject-
matter, that we had no need of lamentation and strains
of sorrow?

True.

And which are the harmonies expressive of sorrow?
You are musical, and can tell me.

The harmonies which you mean are the mixed or

tenor Lydian, and the full-toned or bass Lydian, and such like.

These then, I said, must be banished; even to women who have a character to maintain they are of no use, and much less to men.

Certainly.

In the next place, drunkenness and softness and indolence are utterly unbecoming the character of our guardians.

Utterly unbecoming.

And which are the soft or drinking harmonies?

The Ionian, he replied, and the Lydian; they are termed " relaxed."

Well, and are these of any military use?

Quite the reverse, he replied; and if so the Dorian and the Phrygian are the only ones which you have left.

I answered: Of the harmonies I know nothing, but I want to have one warlike, to sound the note or accent which a brave man utters in the hour of danger and stern resolve, or when his cause is failing, and he is going to wounds or death or is overtaken by some other evil, and at every such crisis meets the blows of fortune with firm step and a determination to endure; and another to be used by him in times of peace and freedom of action, when there is no pressure of necessity, and he is seeking to persuade God by prayer, or man by instruction and admonition, or on the other hand, when he is expressing his willingness to yield to persuasion or entreaty or admonition, and which represents him when by prudent conduct he has attained his end, not carried away by his success, but acting moderately and wisely under the circumstances, and acquiescing in the event. These two harmonies I ask you to leave; the strain of necessity and the strain of freedom, the strain of the unfortunate and the strain of the fortunate, the strain of courage, and the strain of temperance; these, I say, leave.

And these, he replied, are the Dorian and Phrygian harmonies of which I was just now speaking.

Then, I said, if these and these only are to be used in our songs and melodies, we shall not want multiplicity of notes or a panharmonic scale?

I suppose not.

Then we shall not maintain the artificers of lyres with three corners and complex scales, or the makers of any other many-stringed curiously-harmonized instruments?

Certainly not.

But what do you say to flute-makers and flute-players? Would you admit them into our State when you reflect that in this composite use of harmony the flute is worse than all the stringed instruments put together; even the panharmonic music is only an imitation of the flute?

Clearly not.

There remain then only the lyre and the harp for use in the city, and the shepherds may have a pipe in the country.

That is surely the conclusion to be drawn from the argument.

The preferring of Apollo and his instruments to Marsyas and his instruments is not at all strange, I said.

Not at all, he replied.

And so, by the dog of Egypt, we have been unconsciously purging the State, which not long ago we termed luxurious.

And we have done wisely, he replied.

Then let us now finish the purgation, I said. Next in order to harmonies, rhythms will naturally follow, and they should be subject to the same rules, for we ought not to seek out complex systems of metre, or metres of every kind, but rather to discover what rhythms are the expressions of a courageous and harmonious life; and when we have found them, we shall adapt the foot and the melody to words having a like spirit, not the words to the foot and melody. To say what these rhythms are will be your duty — you must teach me them, as you have already taught me the harmonies.

But, indeed, he replied, I can not tell you. I only know that there are some three principles of rhythm out of which metrical systems are framed, just as in sounds there are four notes [1] out of which all the harmonies are composed; that is an observation which I have made. But of what sort of lives they are severally the imitations I am unable to say.

Then, I said, we must take Damon into our counsels; and he will tell us what rhythms are expressive of meanness, or insolence, or fury, or other unworthiness, and what are to be reserved for the expression of opposite feelings. And I think that I have an indistinct recollection of his mentioning a complex Cretic rhythm; also a dactylic or heroic, and he arranged them in some manner which I do not quite understand, making the rhythms equal in the rise and fall of the foot, long and short alternating; and, unless I am mistaken, he spoke of an iambic as well as of a trochaic rhythm, and assigned to them short and long quantities.[2] Also in some cases he appeared to praise or censure the movement of the foot quite

---

[1] i.e. the four notes of the tetrachord.

[2] Socrates expresses himself carelessly in accordance with his assumed ignorance of the details of the subject. In the first part of the sentence he appears to be speaking of paeonic rhythms which are in the ratio of $\frac{3}{2}$; in the second part, of dactylic and anapaestic rhythms, which are in the ratio of 1; in the last clause, of iambic and trochaic rhythms, which are in the ratio of $\frac{1}{2}$ or $\frac{2}{1}$.

as much as the rhythm; or perhaps a combination of the two; for I am not certain what he meant. These matters, however, as I was saying, had better be referred to Damon himself, for the analysis of the subject would be difficult, you know?

Rather so, I should say.

But there is no difficulty in seeing that grace or the absence of grace is an effect of good or bad rhythm.

None at all.

And also that good and bad rhythm naturally assimilate to a good and bad style; and that harmony and discord in like manner follow style; for our principle is that rhythm and harmony are regulated by the words, and not the words by them.

Just so, he said, they should follow the words.

And will not the words and the character of the style depend on the temper of the soul?

Yes.

And everything else on the style?

Yes.

Then beauty of style and harmony and grace and good rhythm depend on simplicity, — I mean the true simplicity of a rightly and nobly ordered mind and character, not that other simplicity which is only an euphemism for folly?

Very true, he replied.

And if our youth are to do their work in life, must they not make these graces and harmonies their perpetual aim?

They must.

And surely the art of the painter and every other creative and constructive art are full of them, — weaving, embroidery, architecture, and every kind of manufacture; also nature, animal and vegetable, — in all of them there is grace or the absence of grace. And ugliness and discord and inharmonious motion are nearly allied to ill words and ill nature, as grace and harmony are the twin sisters of goodness and virtue and bear their likeness.

That is quite true, he said.

But shall our superintendence go no further, and are the poets only to be required by us to express the image of the good in their works, on pain, if they do anything else, of expulsion from our State? Or is the same control to be extended to other artists, and are they also to be prohibited from exhibiting the opposite forms of vice and intemperance and meanness and indecency in sculpture and building and the other creative arts; and is he who can not conform to this rule of ours to be prevented from practising his art in our State, lest the taste of our citizens be corrupted by him? We would not have our guardians grow up amid images of moral deformity, as in some noxious pasture, and there browse and feed upon many a baneful herb and flower day by day, little by little, until they silently gather a festering mass of corruption in their own soul. Let our artists rather be those who are gifted to discern the true nature of the beautiful and graceful; then will our youth dwell in a land of health, amid fair sights and sounds, and receive the good in everything; and beauty, the effluence of fair works, shall flow into the eye and ear, like a health-giving breeze from a purer region, and insensibly draw the soul from earliest years into likeness and sympathy with the beauty of reason.

There can be no nobler training than that, he replied.

And therefore, I said, Glaucon, musical training is a more potent instrument than any other, because rhythm and harmony find their way into the inward places of the soul, on which they mightily fasten, imparting grace, and making the soul of him who .is rightly educated graceful, or of him who is ill-educated ungraceful; and also because he who has received this true education of the inner being will most shrewdly perceive omissions or faults in art and nature, and with a true taste, while he praises and rejoices over and receives into his soul the good, and becomes noble and good, he will justly blame and hate the bad, now in the days of his youth, even before he is able to know the reason why; and when reason comes he will recognize and salute the friend with whom his education has made him long familiar.

Yes, he said, I quite agree with you in thinking that our youth should be trained in music and on the grounds which you mention.

Just as in learning to read, I said, we were satisfied when we knew the letters of the alphabet, which are very few, in all their recurring sizes and combinations; not slighting them as unimportant whether they occupy a space large or small, but everywhere eager to make them out; and not thinking ourselves perfect in the art of reading until we recognize them wherever they are found:

True —

Or, as we recognize the reflection of letters in the water, or in a mirror, only when we know the letters themselves; the same art and study giving us the knowledge of both:

Exactly —

Even so, as I maintain, neither we nor our guardians, whom we have to educate, can ever become musical until we and they know the essential forms of temperance, courage, liberality, magnificence, and their kindred, as well as the contrary forms, in all their combinations, and can recognize them and their images wherever they are found, not slighting them either in small things or great, but believing them all to be within the sphere of one art and study.

Most assuredly.

And when a beautiful soul harmonizes with a beautiful form, and the two are cast in one mould, that will be the fairest of sights to him who has an eye to see it?

The fairest indeed.

And the fairest is also the loveliest?

That may be assumed.

And the man who has the spirit of harmony will be most in love with the loveliest; but he will not love him who is of an inharmonious soul?

That is true, he replied, if the deficiency be in his soul; but if there be any merely bodily defect in another he will be patient of it, and will love all the same.

I perceive, I said, that you have or have had experiences of this sort, and I agree. But let me ask you another question: Has excess of pleasure any affinity to temperance?

How can that be? he replied; pleasure deprives a man of the use of his faculties quite as much as pain.

Or any affinity to virtue in general?

None whatever.

Any affinity to wantonness and intemperance?

Yes, the greatest.

And is there any greater or keener pleasure than that of sensual love?

No, nor a madder.

Whereas true love is a love of beauty and order — temperate and harmonious?

Quite true, he said.

Then no intemperance or madness should be allowed to approach true love?

Certainly not.

Then mad or intemperate pleasure must never be allowed to come near the lover and his beloved; neither of them can have any part in it if their love is of the right sort?

No, indeed, Socrates, it must never come near them.

Then I suppose that in the city which we are founding you would make a law to the effect that a friend should use no other familiarity to his love than a father would use to his son, and then only for a noble purpose, and he must first have the other's consent; and this rule is to limit him in all his intercourse, and he is never to be seen going further, or, if he exceeds, he is to be deemed guilty of coarseness and bad taste.

I quite agree, he said.

Thus much of music, which makes a fair ending; for what should be the end of music if not the love of beauty?

I agree, he said.

After music comes gymnastic, in which our youth are next to be trained.

Certainly.

Gymnastic as well as music should begin in early years; the training in it should be careful and should continue through life. Now my belief is, — and this is a matter upon which I should like to have your opinion in confirmation of my own, but my own belief is, — not that the good body by any bodily excellence improves the soul, but, on the contrary, that the good soul, by her own excellence, improves the body as far as this may be possible. What do you say?

Yes, I agree.

Then, to the mind when adequately trained, we shall be right in handing over the more particular care of the body; and in order to avoid prolixity we will now only give the general outlines of the subject.

Very good.

That they must abstain from intoxication has been already remarked by us; for of all persons a guardian should be the last to get drunk and not know where in the world he is.

Yes, he said; that a guardian should require an-other guardian to take care of him is ridiculous indeed.

But next, what shall we say of their food; for the men are in training for the great contest of all — are they not?

Yes, he said.

And will the habit of body of our ordinary athletes be suited to them?

Why not?

I am afraid, I said, that a habit of body such as they have is but a sleepy sort of thing, and rather perilous to health. Do you not observe that these athletes sleep away their lives, and are liable to most dangerous illnesses if they depart, in ever so slight a degree, from their customary regimen?

Yes, I do.

Then, I said, a finer sort of training will be required for our warrior athletes, who are to be like wakeful dogs, and to see and hear with the utmost keenness; amid the many changes of water and also of food, of summer heat and winter cold, which they will have to endure when on a campaign, they must not be liable to break down in health.

That is my view.

The really excellent gymnastic is twin sister of that simple music which we were just now describing.

How so?

Why, I conceive that there is a gymnastic which, like our music, is simple and good; and especially the military gymnastic.

What do you mean?

My meaning may be learned from Homer; he, you

know, feeds his heroes at their feasts, when they are campaigning, on soldiers' fare; they have no fish, although they are on the shores of the Hellespont, and they are not allowed boiled meats but only roast, which is the food most convenient for soldiers, requiring only that they should light a fire, and not involving the trouble of carrying about pots and pans.

True.

And I can hardly be mistaken in saying that sweet sauces are nowhere mentioned in Homer. In proscribing them, however, he is not singular; all professional athletes are well aware that a man who is to be in good condition should take nothing of the kind.

Yes, he said; and knowing this, they are quite right in not taking them.

Then you would not approve of Syracusan dinners, and the refinements of Sicilian cookery?

I think not.

Nor, if a man is to be in condition, would you allow him to have a Corinthian girl as his fair friend?

Certainly not.

Neither would you approve of the delicacies, as they are thought, of Athenian confectionery?

Certainly not.

All such feeding and living may be rightly compared by us to melody and song composed in the panharmonic style, and in all the rhythms.

Exactly.

There complexity engendered license, and here disease; whereas simplicity in music was the parent of temperance in the soul; and simplicity in gymnastic of health in the body.

Most true, he said.

But when intemperance and diseases multiply in a State, halls of justice and medicine are always being opened; and the arts of the doctor and the lawyer give themselves airs, finding how keen is the interest which not only the slaves but the freemen of a city take about them.

Of course.

And yet what greater proof can there be of a bad and disgraceful state of education than this, that not only artisans and the meaner sort of people need the skill of first-rate physicians and judges, but also those who would profess to have had a liberal education? Is it not disgraceful, and a great sign of the want of good-breeding, that a man should have to go abroad for his law and physic because he has none of his own at home, and must therefore surrender himself into the hands of other men whom he makes lords and judges over him?

Of all things, he said, the most disgraceful.

Would you say " most," I replied, when you consider that there is a further stage of the evil in which a man is not only a life-long litigant, passing all his days in the courts, either as plaintiff or defendant, but is actually led by his bad taste to pride himself on his litigiousness; he imagines that he is a master in dishonesty; able to take every crooked turn, and wriggle into and out of every hole, bending like a withy and getting out of the way of justice: and all for what? — in order to gain small points not worth mentioning, he not knowing that so to order his life as to be able to do without a napping judge is a far higher and nobler sort of thing. Is not that still more disgraceful?

Yes, he said, that is still more disgraceful.

Well, I said, and to require the help of medicine, not when a wound has to be cured, or on occasion of an epidemic, but just because, by indolence and a habit of life such as we have been describing, men fill themselves with waters and winds, as if their bodies were a marsh, compelling the ingenious sons of Asclepius to find more names for diseases, such as flatulence and catarrh; is not this, too, a disgrace?

Yes, he said, they do certainly give very strange and new-fangled names to diseases.

Yes, I said, and I do not believe that there were any such diseases in the days of Asclepius; and this I infer from the circumstance that the hero Eurypylus, after he has been wounded in Homer, drinks a posset of Pramnian wine well besprinkled with barley-meal and grated cheese, which are certainly inflammatory, and yet the sons of Asclepius who were at the Trojan war do not blame the damsel who gives him the drink, or rebuke Patroclus, who is treating his case.

Well, he said, that was surely an extraordinary drink to be given to a person in his condition.

Not so extraordinary, I replied, if you bear in mind that in former days, as is commonly said, before the time of Herodicus, the guild of Asclepius did not practise our present system of medicine, which may be said to educate diseases. But Herodicus, being a trainer, and himself of a sickly constitution, by a combination of training and doctoring found out a way of torturing first and chiefly himself, and secondly the rest of the world.

How was that? he said.

By the invention of lingering death; for he had a mortal disease which he perpetually tended, and as recovery was out of the question, he passed his entire life as a valetudinarian; he could do nothing but attend upon himself, and he was in constant torment whenever he departed in anything from his usual regimen, and so dying hard, by the help of science he struggled on to old age.

A rare reward of his skill!

Yes, I said; a reward which a man might fairly expect who never understood that, if Asclepius did not instruct his descendants in valetudinarian arts, the omission arose, not from ignorance or inexperience of such a branch of medicine, but because he knew that in all well-ordered states every individual has an occupation to which he must attend, and has therefore no leisure to spend in continually being ill. This we remark in the case of the artisan, but, ludicrously enough, do not apply the same rule to people of the richer sort.

How do you mean? he said.

I mean this: When a carpenter is ill he asks the physician for a rough and ready cure; an emetic or a purge or a cautery or the knife, — these are his remedies. And if some one prescribes for him a course of dietetics, and tells him that he must swathe and swaddle his head, and all that sort of thing, he replies at once that he has no time to be ill, and that he sees no good in a life which is spent in nursing his disease to the neglect of his customary employment; and therefore bidding good-bye to this sort of physician, he resumes his ordinary habits, and either gets well and lives and does his business, or, if his constitution fails, he dies and has no more trouble.

Yes, he said, and a man in his condition of life ought to use the art of medicine thus far only.

Has he not, I said, an occupation; and what profit would there be in his life if he were deprived of his occupation?

Quite true, he said.

But with the rich man this is otherwise; of him we do not say that he has any specially appointed work which he must perform, if he would live.

He is generally supposed to have nothing to do.

Then you never heard of the saying of Phocylides, that as soon as a man has a livelihood he should practise virtue?

Nay, he said, I think that he had better begin somewhat sooner.

Let us not have a dispute with him about this, I said; but rather ask ourselves: Is the practice of virtue obligatory on the rich man, or can he live without it? And if obligatory on him, then let us raise a further question, whether this dieting of disorders, which is an impediment to the application of the mind in carpentering and the mechanical arts, does not equally stand in the way of the sentiment of Phocylides?

Of that, he replied, there can be no doubt; such excessive care of the body, when carried beyond the rules of gymnastic, is most inimical to the practice of virtue.

[1] Yes, indeed, I replied, and equally incompatible with the management of a house, an army, or an office of state; and, what is most important of all, irreconcilable with any kind of study or thought or self-reflection — there is a constant suspicion that headache and giddiness are to be ascribed to philosophy, and hence all practising or making trial of virtue in the higher sense is absolutely stopped; for a man is always fancying that he is being made ill, and is in constant anxiety about the state of his body.

Yes, likely enough.

And therefore our politic Asclepius may be supposed to have exhibited the power of his art only to persons who, being generally of healthy constitution and habits of life, had a definite ailment; such as these he cured by purges and operations, and bade them live as usual, herein consulting the interests of the

[1] Making the answer of Socrates begin at καὶ γὰρ πρὸς κ. τ. λ.

State; but bodies which disease had penetrated
through and through he would not have attempted
to cure by gradual processes of evacuation and infu-
sion: he did not want to lengthen out good-for-nothing lives, or to have weak fathers begetting weaker
sons; — if a man was not able to live in the ordinary
way he had no business to cure him; for such a cure
would have been of no use either to himself, or to the
State.

Then, he said, you regard Asclepius as a statesman.

Clearly; and his character is further illustrated by
his sons. Note that they were heroes in the days of
old and practised the medicines of which I am speaking at the siege of Troy: You will remember how,
when Pandarus wounded Menelaus, they

" Sucked the blood out of the wound, and sprinkled soothing
remedies," [1]

but they never prescribed what the patient was afterwards to eat or drink in the case of Menelaus, any
more than in the case of Eurypylus; the remedies, as
they conceived, were enough to heal any man who
before he was wounded was healthy and regular in
his habits; and even though he did happen to drink
a posset of Pramnian wine, he might get well all the
same. But they would have nothing to do with unhealthy and intemperate subjects, whose lives were
of no use either to themselves or others; the art of
medicine was not designed for their good, and though
they were as rich as Midas, the sons of Asclepius
would have declined to attend them.

They were very acute persons, those sons of Asclepius.

Naturally so, I replied. Nevertheless, the tragedians and Pindar disobeying our behests, although

[1] Iliad iv. 218.

they acknowledge that Asclepius was the son of Apollo, say also that he was bribed into healing a rich man who was at the point of death, and for this reason he was struck by lightning. But we, in accordance with the principle already affirmed by us, will not believe them when they tell us both; — if he was the son of a god, we maintain that he was not avaricious; or, if he was avaricious, he was not the son of a god.

All that, Socrates, is excellent; but I should like to put a question to you: Ought there not to be good physicians in a State, and are not the best those who have treated the greatest number of constitutions good and bad? and are not the best judges in like manner those who are acquainted with all sorts of moral natures?

Yes, I said, I too would have good judges and good physicians. But do you know whom I think good?

Will you tell me?

I will, if I can. Let me however note that in the same question you join two things which are not the same.

How so? he asked.

Why, I said, you join physicians and judges. Now the most skilful physicians are those who, from their youth upwards, have combined with the knowledge of their art the greatest experience of disease; they had better not be robust in health, and should have had all manner of diseases in their own persons. For the body, as I conceive, is not the instrument with which they cure the body; in that case we could not allow them ever to be or to have been sickly; but they cure the body with the mind, and the mind which has become and is sick can cure nothing.

That is very true, he said.

But with the judge it is otherwise; since he governs mind by mind; he ought not therefore to have been trained among vicious minds, and to have associated with them from youth upwards, and to have gone through the whole calendar of crime, only in order that he may quickly infer the crimes of others as he might their bodily diseases from his own self-consciousness; the honorable mind which is to form a healthy judgment should have had no experience or contamination of evil habits when young. And this is the reason why in youth good men often appear to be simple, and are easily practised upon by the dishonest, because they have no examples of what evil is in their own souls.

Yes, he said, they are far too apt to be deceived.

Therefore, I said, the judge should not be young; he should have learned to know evil, not from his own soul, but from late and long observation of the nature of evil in others: knowledge should be his guide, not personal experience.

Yes, he said, that is the ideal of a judge.

Yes, I replied, and he will be a good man (which is my answer to your question) ; for he is good who has a good soul. But the cunning and suspicious nature of which we spoke, — he who has committed many crimes, and fancies himself to be a master in wickedness, when he is among his fellows, is wonderful in the precautions which he takes, because he judges of them by himself: but when he gets into the company of men of virtue, who have the experience of age, he appears to be a fool again, owing to his unseasonable suspicions; he can not recognize an honest man, because he has no pattern of honesty in himself; at the same time, as the bad are more numerous than the good, and he meets with them oftener, he thinks himself, and is by others thought to be, rather wise than foolish.

Most true, he said.

Then the good and wise judge whom we are seeking is not this man, but the other; for vice can not know virtue too, but a virtuous nature, educated by time, will acquire a knowledge both of virtue and vice: the virtuous, and not the vicious man has wisdom — in my opinion.

And in mine also.

This is the sort of medicine, and this is the sort of law, which you will sanction in your state. They will minister to better natures, giving health both of soul and of body; but those who are diseased in their bodies they will leave to die, and the corrupt and incurable souls they will put an end to themselves.

That is clearly the best thing both for the patients and for the State.

And thus our youth, having been educated only in that simple music which, as we said, inspires temperance, will be reluctant to go to law.

Clearly.

And the musician, who, keeping to the same track, is content to practise the simple gymnastic, will have nothing to do with medicine unless in some extreme case.

That I quite believe.

The very exercises and toils which he undergoes are intended to stimulate the spirited element of his nature, and not to increase his strength; he will not, like common athletes, use exercise and regimen to develop his muscles.

Very right, he said.

Neither are the two arts of music and gymnastic really designed, as is often supposed, the one for the training of the soul, the other for the training of the body.

What then is the real object of them?

I believe, I said, that the teachers of both have in view chiefly the improvement of the soul.

How can that be? he asked.

Did you never observe, I said, the effect on the mind itself of exclusive devotion to gymnastic, or the opposite effect of an exclusive devotion to music?

In what way shown? he said.

The one producing a temper of hardness and ferocity, the other of softness and effeminacy, I replied.

Yes, he said, I am quite aware that the mere athlete becomes too much of a savage, and that the mere musician is melted and softened beyond what is good for him.

Yet surely, I said, this ferocity only comes from spirit, which, if rightly educated, would give courage, but, if too much intensified, is liable to become hard and brutal.

That I quite think.

On the other hand the philosopher will have the quality of gentleness. And this also, when too much indulged, will turn to softness, but, if educated rightly, will be gentle and moderate.

True.

And in our opinion the guardians ought to have both these qualities?

Assuredly.

And both should be in harmony?

Beyond question.

And the harmonious soul is both temperate and courageous?

Yes.

And the inharmonious is cowardly and boorish?

Very true.

And, when a man allows music to play upon him

and to pour into his soul through the funnel of his ears those sweet and soft and melancholy airs of which we were just now speaking, and his whole life is past in warbling and the delights of song; in the first stage of the process the passion or spirit which is in him is tempered like iron, and made useful, instead of brittle and useless. But, if he carries on the softening and soothing process, in the next stage he begins to melt and waste, until he has wasted away his spirit and cut out the sinews of his soul; and he becomes a feeble warrior.

Very true.

If the element of spirit is naturally weak in him the change is speedily accomplished, but if he have a good deal, then the power of music weakening the spirit renders him excitable; — on the least provocation he flames up at once, and is speedily extinguished; instead of having spirit he grows irritable and passionate and is quite impracticable.

Exactly.

And so in gymnastics, if a man takes violent exercise and is a great feeder, and the reverse of a great student of music and philosophy, at first the high condition of his body fills him with pride and spirit, and he becomes twice the man that he was.

Certainly.

And what happens? if he do nothing else, and holds no converse with the Muses, does not even that intelligence which there may be in him, having no taste of any sort of learning or inquiry or thought or culture, grow feeble and dull and blind, his mind never waking up or receiving nourishment, and his senses not being purged of their mists?

True, he said.

And he ends by becoming a hater of philosophy, uncivilized, never using the weapon of persuasion, —

he is like a wild beast, all violence and fierceness, and knows no other way of dealing; and he lives in all ignorance and evil conditions, and has no sense of propriety and grace.

That is quite true, he said.

And as there are two principles of human nature, one the spirited and the other the philosophical, some God, as I should say, has given mankind two arts answering to them (and only indirectly to the soul and body), in order that these two principles (like the strings of an instrument) may be relaxed or drawn tighter until they are duly harmonized.

That appears to be the intention.

And he who mingles music with gymnastic in the fairest proportions, and best attempers them to the soul, may be rightly called the true musician and harmonist in a far higher sense than the tuner of the strings.

You are quite right, Socrates.

And such a presiding genius will be always required in our State if the government is to last.

Yes, he will be absolutely necessary.

Such, then, are our principles of nurture and education: Where would be the use of going into further details about the dances of our citizens, or about their hunting and coursing, their gymnastic and equestrian contests? For these all follow the general principle, and having found that, we shall have no difficulty in discovering them.

I dare say that there will be no difficulty.

Very good, I said; then what is the next question? Must we not ask who are to be rulers and who subjects?

Certainly.

There can be no doubt that the elder must rule the younger.

Clearly.

And that the best of these must rule.

That is also clear.

Now, are not the best husbandmen those who are most devoted to husbandry?

Yes.

And as we are to have the best of guardians for our city, must they not be those who have most the character of guardians?

Yes.

And to this end they ought to be wise and efficient, and to have a special care of the State?

True.

And a man will be most likely to care about that which he loves?

To be sure.

And he will be most likely to love that which he regards as having the same interests with himself, and that of which the good or evil fortune is supposed by him at any time most to affect his own?

Very true, he replied.

Then there must be a selection. Let us note among the guardians those who in their whole life show the greatest eagerness to do what is for the good of their country, and the greatest repugnance to do what is against her interests.

Those are the right men.

And they will have to be watched at every age, in order that we may see whether they preserve their resolution, and never, under the influence either of force or enchantment, forget or cast off their sense of duty to the State.

How cast off? he said.

I will explain to you, I replied. A resolution may go out of a man's mind either with his will or against his will; with his will when he gets rid of a falsehood and learns better, against his will whenever he is deprived of a truth.

I understand, he said, the willing loss of a resolution; the meaning of the unwilling I have yet to learn.

Why, I said, do you not see that men are unwillingly deprived of good, and willingly of evil? Is not to have lost the truth an evil, and to possess the truth a good? and you would agree that to conceive things as they are is to possess the truth?

Yes, he replied; I agree with you in thinking that mankind are deprived of truth against their will.

And is not this involuntary deprivation caused either by theft, or force, or enchantment?

Still, he replied, I do not understand you.

I fear that I must have been talking darkly, like the tragedians. I only mean that some men are changed by persuasion and that others forget; argument steals away the hearts of one class, and time of the other; and this I call theft. Now you understand me?

Yes.

Those again who are forced, are those whom the violence of some pain or grief compels to change their opinion.

I understand, he said, and you are quite right.

And you would also acknowledge that the enchanted are those who change their minds either under the softer influence of pleasure, or the sterner influence of fear?

Yes, he said; everything that deceives may be said to enchant.

Therefore, as I was just now saying, we must inquire who are the best guardians of their own conviction that what they think the interest of the State is to be the rule of their lives. We must watch them from their youth upwards, and make them perform actions in which they are most likely to forget or to be deceived, and he who remembers and is not deceived is to be selected, and he who fails in the trial is to be rejected. That will be the way?

Yes.

And there should also be toils and pains and conflicts prescribed for them, in which they will be made to give further proof of the same qualities.

Very right, he replied.

And then, I said, we must try them with enchantments — that is the sort of test — and see what will be their behavior: like those who take colts amid noise and tumult to see if they are of a timid nature, so must we take our youth amid terrors of some kind, and again pass them into pleasures, and prove them more thoroughly than gold is proved in the furnace, that we may discover whether they are armed against all enchantments, and of a noble bearing always, good guardians of themselves and of the music which they have learned, and retaining under all circumstances a rhythmical and harmonious nature, such as will be most serviceable to the individual and to the State. And he who at every age, as boy and youth and in mature life, has come out of the trial victorious and pure, shall be appointed a ruler and guardian of the State; he shall be honored in life and death, and shall receive sepulture and other memorials of honor, the greatest that we have to give. But him who fails, we must reject. I am inclined to think that this is the sort of way in which our rulers and guardians should be chosen and appointed. I speak generally, and not with any pretension to exactness.

And, speaking generally, I agree with you, he said.

And perhaps the word " guardian " in the fullest sense ought to be applied to this higher class only who preserve us against foreign enemies and maintain peace among our citizens at home, that the one may not have the will, or the others the power, to harm us. The young men whom we before called guardians may be more properly designated auxiliaries and supporters of the principles of the rulers.

I agree with you, he said.

How then may we devise one of those needful falsehoods of which we lately spoke — just one royal lie which may deceive the rulers, if that be possible, and at any rate the rest of the city?

What sort of lie? he said.

Nothing new, I replied; only an old Phoenician[1] tale of what has often occurred before now in other places, (as the poets say, and have made the world believe), though not in our time, and I do not know whether such an event could ever happen again, or could now even be made probable, if it did.

How your words seem to hesitate on your lips!

You will not wonder, I replied, at my hesitation when you have heard.

Speak, he said, and fear not.

Well then, I will speak, although I really know not how to look you in the face, or in what words to utter the audacious fiction, which I propose to communicate gradually, first to the rulers, then to the soldiers, and lastly to the people. They are to be told that their youth was a dream, and the education and training which they received from us, an appearance only; in reality during all that time they were being formed and fed in the womb of the earth, where they themselves and their arms and appurtenances were manufactured; when they were completed, the earth, their mother, sent them up; and so, their country being their mother and also their nurse, they

[1] Cp. Laws, 663 E.

are bound to advise for her good, and to defend her against attacks, and her citizens they are to regard as children of the earth and their own brothers.

You had good reason, he said, to be ashamed of the lie which you were going to tell.

True, I replied, but there is more coming; I have only told you half. Citizens, we shall say to them in our tale, you are brothers, yet God has framed you differently. Some of you have the power of command, and in the composition of these he has mingled gold, wherefore also they have the greatest honor; others he has made of silver, to be auxiliaries; others again who are to be husbandmen and craftsmen he has composed of brass and iron; and the species will generally be preserved in the children. But as all are of the same original stock, a golden parent will sometimes have a silver son, or a silver parent a golden son. And God proclaims as a first principle to the rulers, and above all else, that there is nothing which they should so anxiously guard, or of which they are to be such good guardians, as of the purity of the race. They should observe what elements mingle in their offspring; for if the son of a golden or silver parent has an admixture of brass and iron, then nature orders a transportation of ranks and the eye of the ruler must not be pitiful towards the child because he has to descend in the scale and become a husbandman or artisan, just as there may be sons of artisans who having an admixture of gold or silver in them are raised to honor, and become guardians or auxiliaries. For an oracle says that when a man of brass or iron guards the State, it will be destroyed. Such is the tale; is there any possibility of making our citizens believe in it?

Not in the present generation, he replied; there is

no way of accomplishing this; but their sons may be made to believe in the tale, and their sons' sons, and posterity after them.

I see the difficulty, I replied; yet the fostering of such a belief will make them care more for the city and for one another. Enough, however, of the fiction, which may now fly abroad upon the wings of rumor, while we arm our earth-born heroes, and lead them forth under the command of their rulers. Let them look round and select a spot whence they can best suppress insurrection, if any prove refractory within, and also defend themselves against enemies, who like wolves may come down on the fold from without; there let them encamp, and when they have encamped, let them sacrifice to the proper Gods and prepare their dwellings.

Just so, he said.

And their dwellings must be such as will shield them against the cold of winter and the heat of summer.

I suppose that you mean houses, he replied.

Yes, I said; but they must be the houses of soldiers, and not of shop-keepers.

What is the difference? he said.

That I will endeavor to explain, I replied. To keep watch-dogs, who, from want of discipline or hunger, or some evil habit or other, would turn upon the sheep and worry them, and behave not like dogs but wolves, would be a foul and monstrous thing in a shepherd?

Truly monstrous, he said.

And therefore every care must be taken that our auxiliaries, being stronger than our citizens, may not grow to be too much for them and become savage tyrants instead of friends and allies?

Yes, great care should be taken.

And would not a really good education furnish the best safeguard?

But they are well-educated already, he replied.

I can not be so confident, my dear Glaucon, I said; I am much more certain that they ought to be, and that true education, whatever that may be, will have the greatest tendency to civilize and humanize them in their relations to one another, and to those who are under their protection.

Very true, he replied.

And not only their education, but their habitations, and all that belongs to them, should be such as will neither impair their virtue as guardians, nor tempt them to prey upon the other citizens. Any man of sense must acknowledge that.

He must.

Then now let us consider what will be their way of life, if they are to realize our idea of them. In the first place, none of them should have any property of his own beyond what is absolutely necessary; neither should they have a private house or store closed against any one who has a mind to enter; their provisions should be only such as are required by trained warriors, who are men of temperance and courage; they should agree to receive from the citizens a fixed rate of pay, enough to meet the expenses of the year and no more; and they will go to mess and live together like soldiers in a camp. Gold and silver we will tell them that they have from God; the diviner metal is within them, and they have therefore no need of the dross which is current among them, and ought not to pollute the divine by any such earthly admixture; for that commoner metal has been the source of many unholy deeds, but their own is undefiled. And they alone of all the citizens may not touch or handle silver or gold, or be under the same roof with them, or wear them, or drink from them. And this will be their salvation, and they will be the saviors of the State. But should they ever acquire homes or lands or moneys of their own, they will become housekeepers and husbandmen instead of guardians, enemies and tyrants instead of allies of the other citizens; hating and being hated, plotting and being plotted against, they will pass their whole life in much greater terror of internal than of external enemies, and the hour of ruin, both to themselves and to the rest of the State, will be at hand. For all which reasons may we not say that thus shall our State be ordered, and that these shall be the regulations appointed by us for our guardians concerning their houses and all other matters?

Yes, said Glaucon.

BOOK IV

HERE Adeimantus interposed a question: How would you answer, Socrates, said he, if a person were to say that you are making[1] these people miserable, and that they are the cause of their own unhappiness; the city in fact belongs to them, but they are none the better for it; whereas other men acquire lands, and build large and handsome houses, and have everything handsome about them, offering sacrifices to the gods on their own account, and practising hospitality; moreover, as you were saying just now, they have gold and silver, and all that is usual among the favorites of fortune; but our poor citizens are no better than mercenaries who are quartered in the city and are always mounting guard?

Yes, I said; and you may add that they are only fed, and not paid in addition to their food, like other men; and therefore they can not, if they would, take a journey of pleasure; they have no money to spend on a mistress or any other luxurious fancy, which, as the world goes, is thought to be happiness; and many other accusations of the same nature might be added.

But, said he, let us suppose all this to be included in the charge.

You mean to ask, I said, what will be our answer?

Yes.

If we proceed along the old path, my belief, I said, is that we shall find the answer. And our answer will be that, even as they are, our guardians may very likely be the happiest of men; but that our aim in

[1] Or, "that for their own good you are making these people miserable."

133

founding the State was not the disproportionate happiness of any one class, but the greatest happiness of
the whole; we thought that in a State which is ordered
with a view to the good of the whole we should be
most likely to find justice, and in the ill-ordered State
injustice: and, having found them, we might then
decide which of the two is the happier. At present, I
take it, we are fashioning the happy State, not piece-
meal, or with a view of making a few happy citizens,
but as a whole; and by-and-by we will proceed to view
the opposite kind of State. Suppose that we were
painting a statue, and some one came up to us and
said, Why do you not put the most beautiful colors
on the most beautiful parts of the body — the eyes
ought to be purple, but you have made them black —
to him we might fairly answer, Sir, you would not
surely have us beautify the eyes to such a degree that
they are no longer eyes; consider rather whether, by
giving this and the other features their due proportion, we make the whole beautiful. And so I say
to you, do not compel us to assign to the guardians a
sort of happiness which will make them anything but
guardians; for we too can clothe our husbandmen in
royal apparel, and set crowns of gold on their heads,
and bid them till the ground as much as they like, and
no more. Our potters also might be allowed to repose
on couches, and feast by the fireside, passing round
the winecup, while their wheel is conveniently at hand,
and working at pottery only as much as they like;
in this way we might make every class happy — and
then, as you imagine, the whole State would be happy.
But do not put this idea into our heads; for, if we
listen to you, the husbandman will be no longer a
husbandman, the potter will cease to be a potter, and
no one will have the character of any distinct class in
the State. Now this is not of much consequence

where the corruption of society, and pretension to be what you are not, is confined to cobblers; but when the guardians of the laws and of the government are only seeming and not real guardians, then see how they turn the State upside down; and on the other hand they alone have the power of giving order and happiness to the State. We mean our guardians to be true saviors and not the destroyers of the State, whereas our opponent is thinking of peasants at a festival, who are enjoying a life of revelry, not of citizens who are doing their duty to the State. But, if so, we mean different things, and he is speaking of something which is not a State. And therefore we must consider whether in appointing our guardians we would look to their greatest happiness individually, or whether this principle of happiness does not rather reside in the State as a whole. But if the latter be the truth, then the guardians and auxiliaries, and all others equally with them, must be compelled or induced to do their own work in the best way. And thus the whole State will grow up in a noble order, and the several classes will receive the proportion of happiness which nature assigns to them.

I think that you are quite right.

I wonder whether you will agree with another remark which occurs to me.

What may that be?

There seem to be two causes of the deterioration of the arts.

What are they?

Wealth, I said, and poverty.

How do they act?

The process is as follows: When a potter becomes rich, will he, think you, any longer take the same pains with his art?

Certainly not.

He will grow more and more indolent and care-less?

Very true.

And the result will be that he becomes a worse potter?

Yes; he greatly deteriorates.

But, on the other hand, if he has no money, and can not provide himself with tools or instruments, he will not work equally well himself, nor will he teach his sons or apprentices to work equally well.

Certainly not.

Then, under the influence either of poverty or of wealth, workmen and their work are equally liable to degenerate?

That is evident.

Here, then, is a discovery of new evils, I said, against which the guardians will have to watch, or they will creep into the city unobserved.

What evils?

Wealth, I said, and poverty; the one is the parent of luxury and indolence, and the other of meanness and viciousness, and both of discontent.

That is very true, he replied; but still I should like to know, Socrates, how our city will be able to go to war, especially against an enemy who is rich and powerful, if deprived of the sinews of war.

There would certainly be a difficulty, I replied, in going to war with one such enemy; but there is no difficulty where there are two of them.

How so? he asked.

In the first place, I said, if we have to fight, our side will be trained warriors fighting against an army of rich men.

That is true, he said.

And do you not suppose, Adeimantus, that a single boxer who was perfect in his art would easily be a match for two stout and well-to-do gentlemen who were not boxers?

Hardly, if they came upon him at once.

What, not, I said, if he were able to run away and then turn and strike at the one who first came up? And supposing he were to do this several times under the heat of a scorching sun, might he not, being an expert, overturn more than one stout personage?

Certainly, he said, there would be nothing wonderful in that.

And yet rich men probably have a greater superiority in the science and practise of boxing than they have in military qualities.

Likely enough.

Then we may assume that our athletes will be able to fight with two or three times their own number?

I agree with you, for I think you right.

And suppose that, before engaging, our citizens send an embassy to one of the two cities, telling them what is the truth: Silver and gold we neither have nor are permitted to have, but you may; do you therefore come and help us in war, and take the spoils of the other city: Who, on hearing these words, would choose to fight against lean wiry dogs, rather than, with the dogs on their side, against fat and tender sheep?

That is not likely; and yet there might be a danger to the poor State if the wealth of many States were to be gathered into one.

But how simple of you to use the term State at all of any but our own!

Why so?

You ought to speak of other States in the plural number; not of them is a city, but many cities, as they say in the game. For indeed any city, however

small, is in fact divided into two, one the city of the
poor, the other of the rich; these are at war with one
another; and in either there are many smaller divisions,
and you would be altogether beside the mark if you
treated them all as a single State. But if you deal
with them as many, and give the wealth or power or
persons of the one to the others, you will always have
a great many friends and not many enemies. And
your State, while the wise order which has now been
prescribed continues to prevail in her, will be the
greatest of States, I do not mean to say in reputation
or appearance, but in deed and truth, though she
number not more than a thousand defenders. A
single State which is her equal you will hardly find,
either among Hellenes or barbarians, though many
that appear to be as great and many times greater.

That is most true, he said.

And what, I said, will be the best limit for our
rulers to fix when they are considering the size of the
State and the amount of territory which they are to
include, and beyond which they will not go?

What limit would you propose?

I would allow the State to increase so far as is
consistent with unity; that, I think, is the proper
limit.

Very good, he said.

Here then, I said, is another order which will have
to be conveyed to our guardians: Let our city be accounted neither large nor small, but one and self-
sufficing.

And surely, said he, this is not a very severe order
which we impose upon them.

And the other, said I, of which we were speaking
before is lighter still, — I mean the duty of degrading
the offspring of the guardians when inferior, and of
elevating into the rank of guardians the offspring of

the lower classes, when naturally superior. The intention was, that, in the case of the citizens generally, each individual should be put to the use for which nature intended him, one to one work, and then every man would do his own business, and be one and not many; and so the whole city would be one and not many.

Yes, he said; that is not so difficult.

The regulations which we are prescribing, my good Adeimantus, are not, as might be supposed, a number of great principles, but trifles all, if care be taken, as the saying is, of the one great thing, — a thing, however, which I would rather call, not, great, but sufficient for our purpose.

What may that be? he asked.

Education, I said, and nurture: If our citizens are well educated, and grow into sensible men, they will easily see their way through all these, as well as other matters which I omit; such, for example, as marriage, the possession of women and the procreation of children, which will all follow the general principle that friends have all things in common, as the proverb says.

That will be the best way of settling them.

Also, I said, the State, if once started well, moves with accumulating force like a wheel. For good nurture and education implant good constitutions, and these good constitutions taking root in a good education improve more **and** more, and this improvement affects the breed in man as in other animals.

Very possibly, he said.

Then to sum up: This is the point to which, above all, the attention of our rulers should be directed, — that music and gymnastic be preserved in their original form, and no innovation made. They must do their utmost to maintain them intact. And when any one says that mankind most regard

" The newest song which the singers have," [1]

they will be afraid that he may be praising, not new songs, but a new kind of song; and this ought not to be praised, or conceived to be the meaning of the poet; for any musical innovation is full of danger to the whole State, and ought to be prohibited. So Damon tells me, and I can quite believe him; — he says that when modes of music change, the fundamental laws of the State always change with them.

Yes, said Adeimantus; and you may add my suffrage to Damon's and your own.

Then, I said, our guardians must lay the foundations of their fortress in music?

Yes, he said; the lawlessness of which you speak too easily steals in.

Yes, I replied, in the form of amusement; and at first sight it appears harmless.

Why, yes, he said, and there is no harm; were it not that little by little this spirit of license, finding a home, imperceptibly penetrates into manners and customs; whence, issuing with greater force, it invades contracts between man and man, and from contracts goes on to laws and constitutions, in utter recklessness, ending at last, Socrates, by an overthrow of all rights, private as well as public.

Is that true? I said.

That is my belief, he replied.

Then, as I was saying, our youth should be trained from the first in a stricter system, for if amusements become lawless, and the youths themselves become lawless, they can never grow up into well-conducted and virtuous citizens.

[1] Od. i. 352.

Very true, he said.

And when they have made a good beginning in play, and by the help of music have gained the habit of good order, then this habit of order, in a manner how unlike the lawless play of the others! will accompany them in all their actions and be a principle of growth to them, and if there be any fallen places in the State will raise them up again.

Very true, he said.

Thus educated, they will invent for themselves any lesser rules which their predecessors have altogether neglected.

What do you mean?

I mean such things as these: — when the young are to be silent before their elders; how they are to show respect to them by standing and making them sit; what honor is due to parents; what garments or shoes are to be worn; the mode of dressing the hair; deportment and manners in general. You would agree with me?

Yes.

But there is, I think, small wisdom in legislating about such matters, — I doubt if it is ever done; nor are any precise written enactments about them likely to be lasting.

Impossible.

It would seem, Adeimantus, that the direction in which education starts a man, will determine his future life. Does not like always attract like?

To be sure.

Until some one rare and grand result is reached which may be good, and may be the reverse of good?

That is not to be denied.

And for this reason, I said, I shall not attempt to legislate further about them.

Naturally enough, he replied.

Well, and about the business of the agora, and the
ordinary dealings between man and man, or again
about agreements with artisans; about insult and
injury, or the commencement of actions, and the appointment of juries, what would you say? there may
also arise questions about any impositions and exac-
tions of market and harbor dues which may be required, and in general about the regulations of mar-
kets, police, harbors, and the like. But, oh heavens!
shall we condescend to legislate on any of these particulars?

I think, he said, that there is no need to impose laws
about them on good men; what regulations are necessary they will find out soon enough for themselves.

Yes, I said, my friend, if God will only preserve to
them the laws which we have given them.

And without divine help, said Adeimantus, they
will go on forever making and mending their laws
and their lives in the hope of attaining perfection.

You would compare them, I said, to those invalids
who, having no self-restraint, will not leave off their
habits of intemperance?

Exactly.

Yes, I said; and what a delightful life they lead!
they are always doctoring and increasing and com-
plicating their disorders, and always fancying that
they will be cured by any nostrum which anybody
advises them to try.

Such cases are very common, he said, with invalids
of this sort.

Yes, I replied; and the charming thing is that they
deem him their worst enemy who tells them the truth,
which is simply that, unless they give up eating and
drinking and wenching and idling, neither drug nor
cautery nor spell nor amulet nor any other remedy
will avail.

Charming! he replied. I see nothing charming in going into a passion with a man who tells you what is right.

These gentlemen, I said, do not seem to be in your good graces.

Assuredly not.

Nor would you praise the behavior of States which act like the men whom I was just now describing. For are there not ill-ordered States in which the citizens are forbidden under pain of death to alter the constitution; and yet he who most sweetly courts those who live under this régime and indulges them and fawns upon them and is skilful in anticipating and gratifying their humors is held to be a great and good statesman — do not these States resemble the persons whom I was describing?

Yes, he said; the States are as bad as the men; and I am very far from praising them.

But do you not admire, I said, the coolness and dexterity of these ready ministers of political corruption?

Yes, he said, I do; but not of all of them, for there are some whom the applause of the multitude has deluded into the belief that they are really statesmen, and these are not much to be admired.

What do you mean? I said; you should have more feeling for them. When a man can not measure, and a great many others who can not measure declare that he is four cubits high, can he help believing what they say?

Nay, he said, certainly not in that case.

Well, then, do not be angry with them; for are they not as good as a play, trying their hand at paltry reforms such as I was describing; they are always fancying that by legislation they will make an end of frauds in contracts, and the other rascalities which

I was mentioning, not knowing that they are in reality cutting off the heads of a hydra?

Yes, he said; that is just what they are doing.

I conceive, I said, that the true legislator will not trouble himself with this class of enactments whether concerning laws or the constitution either in an ill-ordered or in a well-ordered State; for in the former they are quite useless, and in the latter there will be no difficulty in devising them; and many of them will naturally flow out of our previous regulations.

What, then, he said, is still remaining to us of the work of legislation?

Nothing to us, I replied; but to Apollo, the god of Delphi, there remains the ordering of the greatest. and noblest and chiefest things of all.

Which are they? he said.

The institution of temples and sacrifices, and the entire service of gods, demigods, and heroes; also the ordering of the repositories of the dead, and the rites which have to be observed by him who would propitiate the inhabitants of the world below. These are matters of which we are ignorant ourselves, and as founders of a city we should be unwise in trusting them to any interpreter but our ancestral deity. He is the god who sits in the centre, on the navel of the earth, and he is the interpreter of religion to all mankind.

You are right, and we will do as you propose.

But where, amid all this, is justice? son of Ariston, tell me where. Now that our city has been made habitable, light a candle and search, and get your brother and Polemarchus and the rest of our friends to help, and let us see where in it we can discover justice and where injustice, and in what they differ from one another, and which of them the man who would be

happy should have for his portion, whether seen or
unseen by gods and men.

Nonsense, said Glaucon: did you not promise to
search yourself, saying that for you not to help justice in her need would be an impiety?

I do not deny that I said so; and as you remind
me, I will be as good as my word; but you must join.

We will, he replied.

Well, then, I hope to make the discovery in this
way: I mean to begin with the assumption that our
State, if rightly ordered, is perfect.

That is most certain.

And being perfect, is therefore wise and valiant
and temperate and just.

That is likewise clear.

And whichever of these qualities we find in the
State, the one which is not found will be the residue?

Very good.

If there were four things, and we were searching
for one of them, wherever it might be, the one sought
for might be known to us from the first, and there
would be no further trouble; or we might know the
other three first, and then the fourth would clearly
be the one left.

Very true, he said.

And is not a similar method to be pursued about
the virtues, which are also four in number?

Clearly.

First among the virtues found in the State, wisdom
comes into view, and in this I detect a certain peculiarity.

What is that?

The State which we have been describing is said to
be wise as being good in counsel?

Very true.

And good counsel is clearly a kind of knowledge.

for not by ignorance, but by knowledge, do men counsel well?

Clearly.

And the kinds of knowledge in a State are many and diverse?

Of course.

There is the knowledge of the carpenter; but is that the sort of knowledge which gives a city the title of wise and good in counsel?

Certainly not; that would only give a city the reputation of skill in carpentering.

Then a city is not to be called wise because possessing a knowledge which counsels for the best about wooden implements?

Certainly not.

Nor by reason of a knowledge which advises about brazen pots, he said, nor as possessing any other similar knowledge?

Not by reason of any of them, he said.

Nor yet by reason of a knowledge which cultivates the earth; that would give the city the name of agricultural?

Yes.

Well, I said, and is there any knowledge in our recently-founded State among any of the citizens which advises, not about any particular thing in the State, but about the whole, and considers how a State can best deal with itself and with other States?

There certainly is.

And what is this knowledge, and among whom is it found? I asked.

It is the knowledge of the guardians, he replied, and is found among those whom we were just now describing as perfect guardians.

And what is the name which the city derives from the possession of this sort of knowledge?

The name of good in counsel and truly wise.

And will there be in our city more of these true guardians or more smiths?

The smiths, he replied, will be far more numerous.

Will not the guardians be the smallest of all the classes who receive a name from the profession of some kind of knowledge?

Much the smallest.

And so by reason of the smallest part or class, and of the knowledge which resides in this presiding and ruling part of itself, the whole State, being thus con- stituted according to nature, will be wise; and this, which has the only knowledge worthy to be called wisdom, has been ordained by nature to be of all classes the least.

Most true.

Thus, then, I said, the nature and place in the State of one of the four virtues has somehow or other been discovered.

And, in my humble opinion, very satisfactorily dis- covered, he replied.

Again, I said, there is no difficulty in seeing the nature of courage, and in what part that quality re- sides which gives the name of courageous to the State.

How do you mean?

Why, I said, every one who calls any State cour- ageous or cowardly, will be thinking of the part which fights and goes out to war on the State's behalf.

No one, he replied, would ever think of any other.

The rest of the citizens may be courageous or may be cowardly, but their courage or cowardice will not, as I conceive, have the effect of making the city either the one or the other.

Certainly not.

The city will be courageous in virtue of a portion of herself which preserves under all circumstances that opinion about the nature of things to be feared and not to be feared in which our legislator educated them; and this is what you term courage.

I should like to hear what you are saying once more, for I do not think that I perfectly understand you.

I mean that courage is a kind of salvation.

Salvation of what?

Of the opinion respecting things to be feared, what they are and of what nature, which the law implants through education; and I mean by the words " under all circumstances " to intimate that in pleasure or in pain, or under the influence of desire or fear, a man preserves and does not lose this opinion. Shall I give you an illustration?

If you please.

You know, I said, that dyers, when they want to dye wool for making the true sea-purple, begin by selecting their white color first; this they prepare and dress with much care and pains, in order that the white ground may take the purple hue in full perfection. The dyeing then proceeds; and whatever is dyed in this manner becomes a fast color, and no washing either with lyes or without them can take away the bloom. But, when the ground has not been duly prepared, you will have noticed how poor is the look either of purple or of any other color.

Yes, he said; I know that they have a washed-out and ridiculous appearance.

Then now, I said, you will understand what our object was in selecting our soldiers, and educating them in music and gymnastic; we were contriving influences which would prepare them to take the dye of the laws in perfection, and the color of their opinion about dangers and of every other opinion was to be indelibly fixed by their nurture and training, not to be washed away by such potent lyes as pleasure —

mightier agent far in washing the soul than any soda or lye; or by sorrow, fear, and desire, the mightiest of all other solvents. And this sort of universal saving power of true opinion in conformity with law about real and false dangers I call and maintain to be courage, unless you disagree.

But I agree, he replied; for I suppose that you mean to exclude mere uninstructed courage, such as that of a wild beast or of a slave — this, in your opinion, is not the courage which the law ordains, and ought to have another name.

Most certainly.

Then I may infer courage to be such as you describe?

Why, yes, said I, you may, and if you add the words " of a citizen," you will not be far wrong; — hereafter, if you like, we will carry the examination further, but at present we are seeking not for courage but justice; and for the purpose of our inquiry we have said enough.

You are right, he replied.

Two virtues remain to be discovered in the State — first, temperance, and then justice which is the end of our search.

Very true.

Now, can we find justice without troubling ourselves about temperance?

I do not know how that can be accomplished, he said, nor do I desire that justice should be brought to light and temperance lost sight of; and therefore I wish that you would do me the favor of considering temperance first.

Certainly, I replied, I should not be justified in refusing your request.

Then consider, he said.

Yes, I replied; I will; and as far as I can at present see, the virtue of temperance has more of the nature of harmony and symphony than the preceding.

How so? he asked.

Temperance, I replied, is the ordering or controlling of certain pleasures and desires; this is curiously enough implied in the saying of " a man being his own master; " and other traces of the same notion may be found in language.

No doubt, he said.

There is something ridiculous in the expression " master of himself; " for the master is also the servant and the servant the master; and in all these modes of speaking the same person is denoted.

Certainly.

The meaning is, I believe, that in the human soul there is a better and also a worse principle; and when the better has the worse under control, then a man is said to be master of himself; and this is a term of praise: but when, owing to evil education or association, the better principle, which is also the smaller, is overwhelmed by the greater mass of the worse — in this case he is blamed and is called the slave of self and unprincipled.

Yes, there is reason in that.

And now, I said, look at our newly-created State, and there you will find one of these two conditions realized; for the State, as you will acknowledge, may be justly called master of itself, if the words " temperance " and " self-mastery " truly express the rule of the better part over the worse.

Yes, he said, I see that what you say is true.

Let me further note that the manifold and complex pleasures and desires and pains are generally found in children and women and servants, and in the freemen so called who are of the lowest and more numerous class.

Certainly, he said.

Whereas the simple and moderate desires which follow reason, and are under the guidance of mind and true opinion, are to be found only in a few, and those the best born and best educated.

Very true.

These two, as you may perceive, have a place in our State; and the meaner desires of the many are held down by the virtuous desires and wisdom of the few.

That I perceive, he said.

Then if there be any city which may be described as master of its own pleasures and desires, and master of itself, ours may claim such a designation?

Certainly, he replied.

It may also be called temperate, and for the same reasons?

Yes.

And if there be any State in which rulers and subjects will be agreed as to the question who are to rule, that again will be our State?

Undoubtedly.

And the citizens being thus agreed among themselves, in which class will temperance be found — in the rulers or in the subjects?

In both, as I should imagine, he replied.

Do you observe that we were not far wrong in our guess that temperance was a sort of harmony?

Why so?

Why, because temperance is unlike courage and wisdom, each of which resides in a part only, the one making the State wise and the other valiant; not so temperance, which extends to the whole, and runs through all the notes of the scale, and produces a harmony of the weaker and the stronger and the middle class, whether you suppose them to be stronger or weaker in wisdom or power or numbers or wealth, or anything else.   Most truly then may we deem temperance to be the agreement of the naturally superior and inferior, as to the right to rule of either, both in states and individuals.

I entirely agree with you.

And so, I said, we may consider three out of the four virtues to have been discovered in our State. The last of those qualities which make a state virtuous must be justice, if we only knew what that was.

The inference is obvious.

The time then has arrived, Glaucon, when, like huntsmen, we should surround the cover, and look sharp that justice does not steal away, and pass out of sight and escape us; for beyond a doubt she is somewhere in this country: watch therefore and strive to catch a sight of her, and if you see her first, let me know.

Would that I could! but you should regard me rather as a follower who has just eyes enough to see what you show him — that is about as much as I am good for.

Offer up a prayer with me and follow.

I will, but you must show me the way.

Here is no path, I said, and the wood is dark and perplexing; still we must push on.

Let us push on.

Here I saw something: Halloo! I said, I begin to perceive a track, and I believe that the quarry will not escape.

Good news, he said.

Truly, I said, we are stupid fellows.

Why so?

Why, my good sir, at the beginning of our inquiry, ages ago, there was justice tumbling out at our feet, and we never saw her; nothing could be more ridiculous.   Like people who go about looking for what they have in their hands — that was the way with us — we looked not at what we were seeking, but at what was far off in the distance; and therefore, I suppose, we missed her.

What do you mean?

I mean to say that in reality for a long time past we have been talking of justice, and have failed to recognize her.

I grow impatient at the length of your exordium.

Well then, tell me, I said, whether I am right or not: You remember the original principle which we were always laying down at the foundation of the State, that one man should practise one thing only, the thing to which his nature was best adapted; — now justice is this principle or a part of it.

Yes, we often said that one man should do one thing only.

Further, we affirmed that justice was doing one's own business, and not being a busybody; we said so again and again, and many others have said the same to us.

Yes, we said so.

Then to do one's own business in a certain way may be assumed to be justice. Can you tell me whence I derive this inference?

I can not, but I should like to be told.

Because I think that this is the only virtue which remains in the State when the other virtues of temperance and courage and wisdom are abstracted; and, that this is the ultimate cause and condition of the existence of all of them, and while remaining in them is also their preservative; and we were saying that if the three were discovered by us, justice would be the fourth or remaining one.

That follows of necessity.

If we are asked to determine which of these four

qualities by its presence contributes most to the excellence of the State, whether the agreement of rulers and subjects, or the preservation in the soldiers of the opinion which the law ordains about the true nature of dangers, or wisdom and watchfulness in the rulers, or whether this other which I am mentioning, and which is found in children and women, slave and freeman, artisan, ruler, subject, — the quality, I mean, of every one doing his own work, and not being a busybody, would claim the palm — the question is not so easily answered.

Certainly, he replied, there would be a difficulty in saying which.

Then the power of each individual in the State to do his own work appears to compete with the other political virtues, wisdom, temperance, courage.

Yes, he said.

And the virtue which enters into this competition is justice?

Exactly.

Let us look at the question from another point of view: Are not the rulers in a State those to whom you would entrust the office of determining suits at law?

Certainly.

And are suits decided on any other ground but that a man may neither take what is another's, nor be deprived of what is his own?

Yes; that is their principle.

Which is a just principle?

Yes.

Then on this view also justice will be admitted to be the having and doing what is a man's own, and belongs to him?

Very true.

Think, now, and say whether you agree with me or

not. Suppose a carpenter to be doing the business of
a cobbler, or a cobbler of a carpenter; and suppose
them to exchange their implements or their duties,
or the same person to be doing the work of both,
or whatever be the change; do you think that any
great harm would result to the State?

Not much.

But when the cobbler or any other man whom nature designed to be a trader, having his heart lifted
up by wealth or strength or the number of his followers, or any like advantage, attempts to force his
way into the class of warriors, or a warrior into that
of legislators and guardians, for which he is unfitted,
and either to take the implements or the duties of the
other; or when one man is trader, legislator, and warrior all in one, then I think you will agree with me in
saying that this interchange and this meddling of one
with another is the ruin of the State.

Most true.

Seeing then, I said, that there are three distinct
classes, any meddling of one with another, or the
change of one into another, is the greatest harm to the
State, and may be most justly termed evil-doing?

Precisely.

And the greatest degree of evil-doing to one's own
city would be termed by you injustice?

Certainly.

This then is injustice; and on the other hand when
the trader, the auxiliary, and the guardian each do
their own business, that is justice. and will make the
city just.

I agree with you.

We will not, I said, be over-positive as yet; but
if, on trial, this conception of justice be verified in the
individual as well as in the State, there will be no
longer any room for doubt: if it be not verified, we

must have a fresh inquiry. First let us complete the old investigation, which we began, as you remember, under the impression that, if we could previously examine justice on the larger scale, there would be less difficulty in discerning her in the individual. That larger example appeared to be the State, and accordingly we constructed as good a one as we could, knowing well that in the good State justice would be found. Let the discovery which we made be now applied to the individual — if they agree, we shall be satisfied; or, if there be a difference in the individual, we will come back to the State and have another trial of the theory. The friction of the two when rubbed together may possibly strike a light in which justice will shine forth, and the vision which is then revealed we will fix in our souls.

That will be in regular course; let us do as you say.

I proceeded to ask: When two things, a greater and less, are called by the same name, are they like or unlike in so far as they are called the same?

Like, he replied.

The just man then, if we regard the idea of justice only, will be like the just State?

He will.

And a State was thought by us to be just when the three classes in the State severally did their own business; and also thought to be temperate and valiant and wise by reason of certain other affections and qualities of these same classes?

True, he said.

And so of the individual; we may assume that he has the same three principles in his own soul which are found in the State; and he may be rightly described in the same terms, because he is affected in the same manner?

Certainly, he said.

Once more then, O my friend, we may have alighted upon an easy question — whether the soul has these three principles or not?

An easy question! Nay, rather, Socrates, the proverb holds that hard is the good.

Very true, I said; and I do not think that the method which we are employing is at all adequate to the accurate solution of this question; the true method is another and a longer one. Still we may arrive at a solution not below the level of the previous inquiry.

May we not be satisfied with that? he said; — under the circumstances, I am quite content.

I too, I replied, shall be extremely well satisfied.

Then faint not in pursuing the speculation, he said.

Must we not acknowledge, I said, that in each of us there are the same principles and habits which there are in the State; and that from the individual they pass into the State? — how else can they come there? Take the quality of passion or spirit; — it would be ridiculous to imagine that this quality, when found in States, is not derived from the individuals who are supposed to possess it, e. g. the Thracians, Scythians, and in general the northern nations; and the same may be said of the love of knowledge, which is the special characteristic of our part of the world, or of the love of money, which may, with equal truth, be attributed to the Phoenicians and Egyptians.

Exactly so, he said.

There is no difficulty in understanding this.

None whatever.

But the question is not quite so easy when we proceed to ask whether these principles are three or one; whether, that is to say, we learn with one part of our nature, are angry with another, and with a third part desire the satisfaction of our natural appetites: or whether the whole soul comes into play in each sort of action — to determine that is the difficulty.

Yes, he said; there lies the difficulty.

Then let us now try and determine whether they are the same or different.

How can we? he asked.

I replied as follows: The same thing clearly can not act or be acted upon in the same part or in relation to the same thing at the same time, in contrary ways; and therefore whenever this contradiction occurs in things apparently the same, we know that they are really not the same, but different.

Good.

For example, I said, can the same thing be at rest and in motion at the same time in the same part?

Impossible.

Still, I said, let us have a more precise statement of terms, lest we should hereafter fall out by the way. Imagine the case of a man who is standing and also moving his hands and his head, and suppose a person to say that one and the same person is in motion and at rest at the same moment — to such a mode of speech we should object, and should rather say that one part of him is in motion while another is at rest.

Very true.

And suppose the objector to refine still further, and to draw the nice distinction that not only parts of tops, but whole tops, when they spin round with their pegs fixed on the spot, are at rest and in motion at the same time (and he may say the same of anything which revolves in the same spot), his objection would not be admitted by us, because in such cases things are not at rest and in motion in the same parts of themselves; we should rather say that they have both an axis and a circumference; and that the axis stands still, for there is no deviation from the perpendicular; and that the circumference goes round. But if, while revolving, the axis inclines either to the right or left, forwards or backwards, then in no point of view can they be at rest.

That is the correct mode of describing them, he replied.

Then none of these objections will confuse us, or incline us to believe that the same thing at the same time, in the same part or in relation to the same thing, can act or be acted upon in contrary ways.

Certainly not, according to my way of thinking.

Yet, I said, that we may not be compelled to examine all such objections, and prove at length that they are untrue, let us assume their absurdity, and go forward on the understanding that hereafter, if this assumption turn out to be untrue, all the consequences which follow shall be withdrawn.

Yes, he said, that will be the best way.

Well, I said, would you not allow that assent and dissent, desire and aversion, attraction and repulsion, are all of them opposites, whether they are regarded as active or passive (for that makes no difference in the fact of their opposition)?

Yes, he said, they are opposites.

Well, I said, and hunger and thirst, and the desires in general, and again willing and wishing, — all these you would refer to the classes already mentioned. You would say — would you not? — that the soul of him who desires is seeking after the object of his desire; or that he is drawing to himself the thing which he wishes to possess: or again, when a person wants anything to be given him, his mind, longing for the realization of his desire, intimates his wish to have it by a nod of assent, as if he had been asked a question?

Very true.

And what would you say of unwillingness and dislike and the absence of desire; should not these be referred to the opposite class of repulsion and rejection?

Certainly.

Admitting this to be true of desire generally, let us suppose a particular class of desires, and out of these we will select hunger and thirst, as they are termed, which are the most obvious of them?

Let us take that class, he said.

The object of one is food, and of the other drink?

Yes.

And here comes the point: is not thirst the desire which the soul has of drink, and of drink only; not of drink qualified by anything else; for example, warm or cold, or much or little, or, in a word, drink of any particular sort: but if the thirst be accompanied by heat, then the desire is of cold drink; or, if accompanied by cold, then of warm drink; or, if the thirst be excessive, then the drink which is desired will be excessive; or, if not great, the quantity of drink will also be small: but thirst pure and simple will desire drink pure and simple, which is the natural satisfaction of thirst, as food is of hunger?

Yes, he said; the simple desire is, as you say, in every case of the simple object, and the qualified desire of the qualified object.

But here a confusion may arise; and I should wish to guard against an opponent starting up and saying that no man desires drink only, but good drink, or food only, but good food; for good is the universal object of desire, and thirst being a desire, will necessarily be thirst after good drink; and the same is true of every other desire.

Yes, he replied, the opponent might have something to say.

Nevertheless I should still maintain, that of relatives some have a quality attached to either term of the relation; others are simple and have their correlatives simple.

I do not know what you mean.

Well, you know of course that the greater is relative to the less?

Certainly.

And the much greater to the much less?

Yes.

And the sometime greater to the sometime less, and the greater that is to be to the less that is to be?

Certainly, he said.

And so of more and less, and of other correlative terms, such as the double and the half, or again, the heavier and the lighter, the swifter and the slower; and of hot and cold, and of any other relatives; — is not this true of all of them?

Yes.

And does not the same principle hold in the sciences? The object of science is knowledge (assuming that to be the true definition), but the object of a particular science is a particular kind of knowledge; I mean, for example, that the science of house-building is a kind of knowledge which is defined and distinguished from other kinds and is therefore termed architecture.

Certainly.

Because it has a particular quality which no other has?

Yes.

And it has this particular quality because it has an object of a particular kind; and this is true of the other arts and sciences?

Yes.

Now, then, if I have made myself clear, you will understand my original meaning in what I said about relatives. My meaning was, that if one term of a relation is taken alone, the other is taken alone; if one term is qualified, the other is also qualified. I do not mean to say that relatives may not be disparate, or that the science of health is healthy, or of disease necessarily diseased, or that the sciences of good and evil are therefore good and evil; but only that, when the term science is no longer used absolutely, but has a qualified object which in this case is the nature of health and disease, it becomes defined, and is hence called not merely science, but the science of medicine.

I quite understand, and I think as you do.

Would you not say that thirst is one of these essentially relative terms, having clearly a relation —

Yes, thirst is relative to drink.

And a certain kind of thirst is relative to a certain kind of drink; but thirst taken alone is neither of much nor little, nor of good nor bad, nor of any particular kind of drink, but of drink only?

Certainly.

Then the soul of the thirsty one, in so far as he is thirsty, desires only drink; for this he yearns and tries to obtain it?

That is plain.

And if you suppose something which pulls a thirsty soul away from drink, that must be different from the thirsty principle which draws him like a beast to drink: for, as we were saying, the same thing can not at the same time with the same part of itself act in contrary ways about the same.

Impossible.

No more than you can say that the hands of the archer push and pull the bow at the same time, but what you say is that one hand pushes and the other pulls.

Exactly so, he replied.

And might a man be thirsty, and yet unwilling to drink?

Yes, he said, it constantly happens.

And in such a case what is one to say? Would you not say that there was something in the soul bidding a man to drink, and something else forbidding him, which is other and stronger than the principle which bids him?

I should say so.

And the forbidding principle is derived from reason, and that which bids and attracts proceeds from passion and disease?

Clearly.

Then we may fairly assume that they are two, and that they differ from one another; the one with which a man reasons, we may call the rational principle of the soul, the other, with which he loves and hungers and thirsts and feels the flutterings of any other desire, may be termed the irrational or appetitive, the ally of sundry pleasures and satisfactions?

Yes, he said, we may fairly assume them to be different.

Then let us finally determine that there are two principles existing in the soul. And what of passion, or spirit? Is it a third, or akin to one of the preceding?

I should be inclined to say — akin to desire.

Well, I said, there is a story which I remember to have heard, and in which I put faith. The story is, that Leontius, the son of Aglaion, coming up one day from the Piraeus, under the north wall on the outside, observed some dead bodies lying on the ground at the place of execution. He felt a desire to see them, and also a dread and abhorrence of them; for a time he struggled and covered his eyes, but at length the desire got the better of him; and forcing them open, he ran up to the dead bodies, saying, Look, ye wretches, take your fill of the fair sight.

I have heard the story myself, he said.

The moral of the tale is, that anger at times goes to war with desire, as though they were two distinct things.

Yes; that is the meaning, he said.

And are there not many other cases in which we observe that when a man's desires violently prevail over his reason, he reviles himself, and is angry at the violence within him, and that in this struggle, which is like the struggle of factions in a State, his spirit is on the side of his reason; — but for the passionate or spirited element to take part with the desires when reason decides that she should not be opposed,[1] is a sort of thing which I believe that you never observed occurring in yourself, nor, as I should imagine, in any one else?

Certainly not.

Suppose that a man thinks he has done a wrong to another, the nobler he is the less able is he to feel indignant at any suffering, such as hunger, or cold, or any other pain which the injured person may inflict upon him — these he deems to be just, and, as I say, his anger refuses to be excited by them.

True, he said.

But when he thinks that he is the sufferer of the wrong, then he boils and chafes, and is on the side of what he believes to be justice; and because he suffers hunger or cold or other pain he is only the more determined to persevere and conquer. His noble spirit will not be quelled until he either slays or is slain; or until he hears the voice of the shepherd, that is, reason, bidding his dog bark no more.

[1] Reading μὴ δεῖν ἀντιπράττειν, without a comma after δεῖν.

The illustration is perfect, he replied; and in our State, as we were saying, the auxiliaries were to be dogs, and to hear the voice of the rulers, who are their shepherds.

I perceive, I said, that you quite understand me: there is, however, a further point which I wish you to consider.

What point?

You remember that passion or spirit appeared at first sight to be a kind of desire, but now we should say quite the contrary; for in the conflict of the soul spirit is arrayed on the side of the rational principle.

Most assuredly.

But a further question arises: Is passion different from reason also, or only a kind of reason; in which latter case, instead of three principles in the soul, there will be only two, the rational and the concupiscent; or rather, as the State was composed of three classes, traders, auxiliaries, counsellors, so may there not be in the individual soul a third element which is passion or spirit, and when not corrupted by bad education is the natural auxiliary of reason?

Yes, he said, there must be a third.

Yes, I replied, if passion, which has already been shown to be different from desire, turn out also to be different from reason.

But that is easily proved: — We may observe even in young children that they are full of spirit almost as soon as they are born, whereas some of them never seem to attain to the use of reason, and most of them late enough.

Excellent, I said, and you may see passion equally in brute animals, which is a further proof of the truth of what you are saying. And we may once more appeal to the words of Homer, which have been already quoted by us,

" He smote his breast, and thus rebuked his soul; " [1]

for in this verse Homer has clearly supposed the power which reasons about the better and worse to be different from the unreasoning anger which is rebuked by it.

Very true, he said.

And so, after much tossing, we have reached land, and are fairly agreed that the same principles which exist in the State exist also in the individual, and that they are three in number.

Exactly.

Must we not then infer that the individual is wise in the same way, and in virtue of the same quality which makes the State wise?

Certainly.

Also that the same quality which constitutes courage in the State constitutes courage in the individual, and that both the State and the individual bear the same relation to all the other virtues?

Assuredly.

And the individual will be acknowledged by us to be just in the same way in which the State is just?

That follows of course.

We can not but remember that the justice of the State consisted in each of the three classes doing the work of its own class?

We are not very likely to have forgotten, he said.

We must recollect that the individual in whom the several qualities of his nature do their own work will be just, and will do his own work?

Yes, he said, we must remember that too.

And ought not the rational principle, which is wise,

[1] Od. xx. 17. quoted supra.

and has the care of the whole soul, to rule, and the passionate or spirited principle to be the subject and ally?

Certainly.

And, as we were saying, the united influence of music and gymnastic will bring them into accord, nerving and sustaining the reason with noble words and lessons, and moderating and soothing and civilizing the wildness of passion by harmony and rhythm?

Quite true, he said.

And these two, thus nurtured and educated, and having learned truly to know their own functions, will rule [1] over the concupiscent, which in each of us is the largest part of the soul and by nature most insatiable of gain; over this they will keep guard, lest, waxing great and strong with the fulness of bodily pleasures, as they are termed, the concupiscent soul, no longer confined to her own sphere, should attempt to enslave and rule those who are not her natural-born subjects, and overturn the whole life of man?

Very true, he said.

Both together will they not be the best defenders of the whole soul and the whole body against attacks from without; the one counselling, and the other fighting under his leader, and courageously executing his commands and counsels?

True.

And he is to be deemed courageous whose spirit retains in pleasure and in pain the commands of reason about what he ought or ought not to fear?

---

[1] Reading προστατήσετον with Bekker; or, if the reading προστήσετον, which is found in the MSS., be adopted, then the nominative must be supplied from the previous sentence: "Music and gymnastic will place in authority over . . ." This is very awkward, and the awkwardness is increased by the necessity of changing the subject at τηρήσετον.

Right, he replied.

And him we call wise who has in him that little part which rules, and which proclaims these commands; that part too being supposed to have a knowledge of what is for the interest of each of the three parts and of the whole?

Assuredly.

And would you not say that he is temperate who has these same elements in friendly harmony, in whom the one ruling principle of reason, and the two subject ones of spirit and desire are equally agreed that reason ought to rule, and do not rebel?

Certainly, he said, that is the true account of temperance whether in the State or individual.

And surely, I said, we have explained again and again how and by virtue of what quality a man will be just.

That is very certain.

And is justice dimmer in the individual, and is her form different, or is she the same which we found her to be in the State?

There is no difference in my opinion, he said.

Because, if any doubt is still lingering in our minds, a few commonplace instances will satisfy us of the truth of what I am saying.

What sort of instances do you mean?

If the case is put to us, must we not admit that the just State, or the man who is trained in the principles of such a State, will be less likely than the unjust to make away with a deposit of gold or silver? Would any one deny this?

No one, he replied.

Will the just man or citizen ever be guilty of sacrilege or theft, or treachery either to his friends or to his country?

Never.

Neither will he ever break faith where there have been oaths or agreements?

Impossible.

No one will be less likely to commit adultery, or to dishonor his father and mother, or to fail in his religious duties?

No one.

And the reason is that each part of him is doing its own business, whether in ruling or being ruled?

Exactly so.

Are you satisfied then that the quality which makes such men and such states is justice, or do you hope to discover some other?

Not I, indeed.

Then our dream has been realized; and the suspicion which we entertained at the beginning of our work of construction, that some divine power must have conducted us to a primary form of justice, has now been verified?

Yes, certainly.

And the division of labor which required the carpenter and the shoemaker and the rest of the citizens to be doing each his own business, and not another's, was a shadow of justice, and for that reason it was of use?

Clearly.

But in reality justice was such as we were describing, being concerned however, not with the outward man, but with the inward, which is the true self and concernment of man: for the just man does not permit the several elements within him to interfere with one another, or any of them to do the work of others, — he sets in order his own inner life, and is his own master and his own law, and at peace with himself; and when he has bound together the three principles within him, which may be compared to the higher, lower, and middle notes of the scale, and the intermediate intervals — when he has bound all these together, and is no longer many, but has become one entirely temperate and perfectly adjusted nature, then he proceeds to act, if he has to act, whether in a matter of property, or in the treatment of the body, or in some affair of politics or private business; always thinking and calling that which preserves and co-operates with this harmonious condition, just and good action, and the knowledge which presides over it, wisdom, and that which at any time impairs this condition, he will call unjust action, and the opinion which presides over it ignorance.

You have said the exact truth, Socrates.

Very good; and if we were to affirm that we had discovered the just man and the just State, and the nature of justice in each of them, we should not be telling a falsehood?

Most certainly not.

May we say so, then?

Let us say so.

And now, I said, injustice has to be considered.

Clearly.

Must not injustice be a strife which arises among the three principles — a meddlesomeness, and inter-ference, and rising up of a part of the soul against the whole, an assertion of unlawful authority, which is made by a rebellious subject against a true prince, of whom he is the natural vassal, — what is all this confusion and delusion but injustice, and intem-perance and cowardice and ignorance, and every form of vice?

Exactly so.

And if the nature of justice and injustice be known, then the meaning of acting unjustly and being unjust, or, again, of acting justly, will also be perfectly clear?

What do you mean? he said.

Why, I said, they are like disease and health; being in the soul just what disease and health are in the body.

How so? he said.

Why, I said, that which is healthy causes health, and that which is unhealthy causes disease.

Yes.

And just actions cause justice, and unjust actions cause injustice?

That is certain.

And the creation of health is the institution of a natural order and government of one by another in the parts of the body; and the creation of disease is the production of a state of things at variance with this natural order?

True.

And is not the creation of justice the institution of a natural order and government of one by another in the parts of the soul, and the creation of injustice the production of a state of things at variance with the natural order?

Exactly so, he said.

Then virtue is the health and beauty and well-being of the soul, and vice the disease and weakness and deformity of the same?

True.

And do not good practices lead to virtue, and evil practices to vice?

Assuredly.

Still our old question of the comparative advantage of justice and injustice has not been answered: Which is the more profitable, to be just and act justly and practise virtue, whether seen or unseen of gods and men, or to be unjust and act unjustly, if only un-punished and unreformed?

In my judgment, Socrates, the question has now become ridiculous. We know that, when the bodily constitution is gone, life is no longer endurable, though pampered with all kinds of meats and drinks, and having all wealth and all power; and shall we be told that when the very essence of the vital principle is undermined and corrupted, life is still worth having to a man, if only he be allowed to do whatever he likes with the single exception that he is not to acquire justice and virtue, or to escape from injustice and vice; assuming them both to be such as we have described?

Yes, I said, the question is, as you say, ridiculous. Still, as we are near the spot at which we may see the truth in the clearest manner with our own eyes, let us not faint by the way.

Certainly not, he replied.

Come up hither, I said, and behold the various forms of vice, those of them, I mean, which are worth looking at.

I am following you, he replied: proceed.

I said, The argument seems to have reached a height from which, as from some tower of specula-tion, a man may look down and see that virtue is one, but that the forms of vice are innumerable; there being four special ones which are deserving of note.

What do you mean? he said.

I mean, I replied, that there appear to be as many forms of the soul as there are distinct forms of the State.

How many?

There are five of the State, and five of the soul, I said.

What are they?

The first, I said, is that which we have been describing, and which may be said to have two names, monarchy and aristocracy, accordingly as rule is exercised by one distinguished man or by many.

True, he replied.

But I regard the two names as describing one form only; for whether the government is in the hands of one or many, if the governors have been trained in the manner which we have supposed, the fundamental laws of the State will be maintained.

That is true, he replied.

BOOK V

Such is the good and true City or State, and the good and true man is of the same pattern; and if this is right every other is wrong; and the evil is one which affects not only the ordering of the State, but also the regulation of the individual soul, and is exhibited in four forms.

What are they? he said.

I was proceeding to tell the order in which the four evil forms appeared to me to succeed one another, when Polemarchus, who was sitting a little way off, just beyond Adeimantus, began to whisper to him: stretching forth his hand, he took hold of the upper part of his coat by the shoulder, and drew him towards him, leaning forward himself so as to be quite close and saying something in his ear, of which I only caught the words, " Shall we let him off, or what shall we do? "

Certainly not, said Adeimantus, raising his voice.

Who is it, I said, whom you are refusing to let off?

You, he said.

I repeated,[1] Why am I especially not to be let off?

Why, he said, we think that you are lazy, and mean to cheat us out of a whole chapter which is a very important part of the story; and you fancy that we shall not notice your airy way of proceeding; as if it were self-evident to everybody, that in the matter of women and children " friends have all things in common."

And was I not right, Adeimantus?

Yes, he said; but what is right in this particular

¹ Reading ἔτι ἐγὼ εἶπον.

case, like everything else, requires to be explained;
for community may be of many kinds. Please, therefore, to say what sort of community you mean. We
have been long expecting that you would tell us something about the family life of your citizens — how
they will bring children into the world, and rear them
when they have arrived, and, in general, what is the
nature of this community of women and children —
for we are of opinion that the right or wrong management of such matters will have a great and paramount
influence on the State for good or for evil. And now,
since the question is still undetermined, and you are
taking in hand another State, we have resolved, as
you heard, not to let you go until you give an account
of all this.

To that resolution, said Glaucon, you may regard
me as saying Agreed.

And without more ado, said Thrasymachus, you
may consider us all to be equally agreed.

I said, You know not what you are doing in thus
assailing me: What an argument are you raising
about the State! Just as I thought that I had finished, and was only too glad that I had laid this
question to sleep, and was reflecting how fortunate
I was in your acceptance of what I then said, you ask
me to begin again at the very foundation, ignorant of
what a hornet's nest of words you are stirring. Now
I foresaw this gathering trouble, and avoided it.

For what purpose do you conceive that we have
come here, said Thrasymachus, — to look for gold,
or to hear discourse?

Yes, but discourse should have a limit.

Yes, Socrates, said Glaucon, and the whole of life
is the only limit which wise men assign to the hearing
of such discourses. But never mind about us; take
heart yourself and answer the question in your own

way: What sort of community of women and children is this which is to prevail among our guardians? and how shall we manage the period between birth and education, which seems to require the greatest care? Tell us how these things will be.

Yes, my simple friend, but the answer is the reverse of easy; many more doubts arise about this than about our previous conclusions. For the practicability of what is said may be doubted; and looked at in another point of view, whether the scheme, if ever so practicable, would be for the best, is also doubtful. Hence I feel a reluctance to approach the subject, lest our aspiration, my dear friend, should turn out to be a dream only.

Fear not, he replied, for your audience will not be hard upon you; they are not sceptical or hostile.

I said: My good friend, I suppose that you mean to encourage me by these words.

Yes, he said.

Then let me tell you that you are doing just the reverse; the encouragement which you offer would have been all very well had I myself believed that I knew what I was talking about: to declare the truth about matters of high interest which a man honors and loves among wise men who love him need occasion no fear or faltering in his mind; but to carry on an argument when you are yourself only a hesitating inquirer, which is my condition, is a dangerous and slippery thing; and the danger is not that I shall be laughed at (of which the fear would be childish), but that I shall miss the truth where I have most need to be sure of my footing, and drag my friends after me in my fall. And I pray Nemesis not to visit upon me the words which I am going to utter. For I do indeed believe that to be an involuntary homicide is a less crime than to be a deceiver about beauty or good-

ness or justice in the matter of laws.[1] And that is a
risk which I would rather run among enemies than
among friends, and therefore you do well to encourage me.[2]

Glaucon laughed and said: Well then, Socrates,
in case you and your argument do us any serious
injury you shall be acquitted beforehand of the homicide, and shall not be held to be a deceiver; take
courage then and speak.

Well, I said, the law says that when a man is acquitted he is free from guilt, and what holds at law
may hold in argument.

Then why should you mind?

Well, I replied, I suppose that I must retrace my
steps and say what I perhaps ought to have said before in the proper place. The part of the men has
been played out, and now properly enough comes the
turn of the women. Of them I will proceed to speak,
and the more readily since I am invited by you.

For men born and educated like our citizens, the
only way, in my opinion, of arriving at a right conclusion about the possession and use of women and
children is to follow the path on which we originally
started, when we said that the men were to be the
guardians and watchdogs of the herd.

True.

Let us further suppose the birth and education of
our women to be subject to similar or nearly similar
regulations; then we shall see whether the result accords with our design.

What do you mean?

What I mean may be put into the form of a question, I said: Are dogs divided into hes and shes, or

---

[1] Or inserting καὶ before νομίμων : "a deceiver about beauty or goodness
or principles of justice or law."

[2] Reading ὥστε εὖ με παραμυθεῖ.

do they both share equally in hunting and in keeping watch and in the other duties of dogs? or do we entrust to the males the entire and exclusive care of the flocks, while we leave the females at home, under the idea that the bearing and suckling their puppies is labor enough for them?

No, he said, they share alike; the only difference between them is that the males are stronger and the females weaker.

But can you use different animals for the same purpose, unless they are bred and fed in the same way?

You can not.

Then, if women are to have the same duties as men, they must have the same nurture and education?

Yes.

The education which was assigned to the men was music and gymnastic.

Yes.

Then women must be taught music and gymnastic and also the art of war, which they must practise like the men?

That is the inference, I suppose.

I should rather expect, I said, that several of our proposals, if they are carried out, being unusual, may appear ridiculous.

No doubt of it.

Yes, and the most ridiculous thing of all will be the sight of women naked in the palaestra, exercising with the men, especially when they are no longer young; they certainly will not be a vision of beauty, any more than the enthusiastic old men who in spite of wrinkles and ugliness continue to frequent the gymnasia.

Yes, indeed, he said: according to present notions the proposal would be thought ridiculous.

But then, I said, as we have determined to speak

our minds, we must not fear the jests of the wits which will be directed against this sort of innovation; how they will talk of women's attainments both in music and gymnastic, and above all about their wearing armor and riding upon horseback!

Very true.

Yet having begun we must go forward to the rough places of the law; at the same time begging of these gentlemen for once in their life to be serious. Not long ago, as we shall remind them, the Hellenes were of the opinion, which is still generally received among the barbarians, that the sight of a naked man was ridiculous and improper; and when first the Cretans and then the Lacedaemonians introduced the custom, the wits of that day might equally have ridiculed the innovation.

No doubt.

But when experience showed that to let all things be uncovered was far better than to cover them up, and the ludicrous effect to the outward eye vanished before the better principle which reason asserted, then the man was perceived to be a fool who directs the shafts of his ridicule at any other sight but that of folly and vice, or seriously inclines to weigh the beautiful by any other standard but that of the good.[1]

Very true, he replied.

First, then, whether the question is to be put in jest or in earnest, let us come to an understanding about the nature of woman: Is she capable of sharing either wholly or partially in the actions of men, or not at all? And is the art of war one of those arts in which she can or can not share? That will be the best way of commencing the inquiry, and will probably lead to the fairest conclusion.

That will be much the best **way.**

[1] Reading with Paris A. καὶ καλοῦ . ͺ .

Shall we take the other side first and begin by arguing against ourselves; in this manner the adversary's position will not be undefended.

Why not? he said.

Then let us put a speech into the mouths of our opponents. They will say: " Socrates and Glaucon, no adversary need convict you, for you yourselves, at the first foundation of the State, admitted the principle that everybody was to do the one work suited to his own nature." And certainly, if I am not mistaken, such an admission was made by us. " And do not the natures of men and women differ very much indeed? " And we shall reply: Of course they do. Then we shall be asked, " Whether the tasks assigned to men and to women should not be different, and such as are agreeable to their different natures? " Certainly they should. " But if so, have you not fallen into a serious inconsistency in saying that men and women, whose natures are so entirely different, ought to perform the same actions? " — What defence will you make for us, my good Sir, against any one who offers these objections?

That is not an easy question to answer when asked suddenly; and I shall and I do beg of you to draw out the case on our side.

These are the objections, Glaucon, and there are many others of a like kind, which I foresaw long ago; they made me afraid and reluctant to take in hand any law about the possession and nurture of women and children.

By Zeus, he said, the problem to be solved is anything but easy

Why yes, I said, but the fact is that when a man is out of his depth, whether he has fallen into a little swimming bath or into mid ocean, he has to swim all the same.

Very true.

And must not we swim and try to reach the shore: we will hope that Arion's dolphin or some other miraculous help may save us?

I suppose so, he said.

Well then, let us see if any way of escape can be found. We acknowledged — did we not? that different natures ought to have different pursuits, and that men's and women's natures are different. And now what are we saying? — that different natures ought to have the same pursuits, — this is the inconsistency which is charged upon us.

Precisely.

Verily, Glaucon, I said, glorious is the power of the art of contradiction!

Why do you say so?

Because I think that many a man falls into the practice against his will. When he thinks that he is reasoning he is really disputing, just because he can not define and divide, and so know that of which he is speaking; and he will pursue a merely verbal opposition in the spirit of contention and not of fair discussion.

Yes, he replied, such is very often the case; but what has that to do with us and our argument?

A great deal; for there is certainly a danger of our getting unintentionally into a verbal opposition.

In what way?

Why we valiantly and pugnaciously insist upon the verbal truth, that different natures ought to have different pursuits, but we never considered at all what was the meaning of sameness or difference of nature, or why we distinguished them when we assigned different pursuits to different natures and the same to the same natures.

Why, no, he said, that was never considered by us.

I said: Suppose that by way of illustration we were to ask the question whether there is not an opposition in nature between bald men and hairy men; and if this is admitted by us, then, if bald men are cobblers, we should forbid the hairy men to be cobblers, and conversely?

That would be a jest, he said.

Yes, I said, a jest; and why? because we never meant when we constructed the State, that the opposition of natures should extend to every difference, but only to those differences which affected the pursuit in which the individual is engaged; we should have argued, for example, that a physician and one who is in mind a physician [1] may be said to have the same nature.

True.

Whereas the physician and the carpenter have different natures?

Certainly.

And if, I said, the male and female sex appear to differ in their fitness for any art or pursuit, we should say that such pursuit or art ought to be assigned to one or the other of them; but if the difference consists only in women bearing and men begetting children, this does not amount to a proof that a woman differs from a man in respect of the sort of education she should receive; and we shall therefore continue to maintain that our guardians and their wives ought to have the same pursuits.

Very true, he said.

Next, we shall ask our opponent how, in reference to any of the pursuits or arts of civic life, the nature of a woman differs from that of a man?

That will be quite fair.

And perhaps he, like yourself, will reply that to

• Reading ἰατρὸν μὲν καὶ ἰατρικὸν τὴν ψυχὴν ὄντα.

give a sufficient answer on the instant is not easy; but after a little reflection there is no difficulty.

Yes, perhaps.

Suppose then that we invite him to accompany us in the argument, and then we may hope to show him that there is nothing peculiar in the constitution of women which would affect them in the administration of the State.

By all means.

Let us say to him: Come now, and we will ask you a question: — when you spoke of a nature gifted or not gifted in any respect, did you mean to say that one man will acquire a thing easily, another with difficulty; a little learning will lead the one to discover a great deal; whereas the other, after much study and application, no sooner learns than he forgets; or again, did you mean, that the one has a body which is a good servant to his mind, while the body of the other is a hindrance to him? — would not these be the sort of differences which distinguish the man gifted by nature from the one who is ungifted?

No one will deny that.

And can you mention any pursuit of mankind in which the male sex has not all these gifts and qualities in a higher degree than the female? Need I waste time in speaking of the art of weaving, and the management of pancakes and preserves, in which womankind does really appear to be great, and in which for her to be beaten by a man is of all things the most absurd?

You are quite right, he replied, in maintaining the general inferiority of the female sex: although many women are in many things superior to many men, yet on the whole what you say is true.

And if so, my friend, I said, there is no special faculty of administration in a state which a woman

has because she is a woman, or which a man has by
virtue of his sex, but the gifts of nature are alike
diffused in both; all the pursuits of men are the pursuits of women also, but in all of them a woman is
inferior to a man.

Very true.

Then are we to impose all our enactments on men
and none of them on women?

That will never do.

One woman has a gift of healing, another not; one
is a musician, and another has no music in her nature?

Very true.

And one woman has a turn for gymnastic and
military exercises, and another is unwarlike and hates
gymnastics?

Certainly.

And one woman is a philosopher, and another is an
enemy of philosophy; one has spirit, and another is
without spirit?

That is also true.

Then one woman will have the temper of a
guardian, and another not. Was not the selection of
the male guardians determined by differences of this
sort?

Yes.

Men and women alike possess the qualities which
make a guardian; they differ only in their comparative strength or weakness.

Obviously.

And those women who have such qualities are to be
selected as the companions and colleagues of men
who have similar qualities and whom they resemble in
capacity and in character?

Very true.

And ought not the same natures to have the same
pursuits?

They ought.

Then, as we were saying before, there is nothing unnatural in assigning music and gymnastic to the wives of the guardians — to that point we come round again.

Certainly not.

The law which we then enacted was agreeable to nature, and therefore not an impossibility or mere aspiration; and the contrary practice, which prevails at present, is in reality a violation of nature.

That appears to be true.

We had to consider, first, whether our proposals were possible, and secondly whether they were the most beneficial?

Yes.

And the possibility has been acknowledged?

Yes.

The very great benefit has next to be established?

Quite so.

You will admit that the same education which makes a man a good guardian will make a woman a good guardian; for their original nature is the same?

Yes.

I should like to ask you a question.

What is it?

Would you say that all men are equal in excellence, or is one man better than another?

The latter.

And in the commonwealth which we were founding do you conceive the guardians who have been brought up on our model system to be more perfect men, or the cobblers whose education has been cobbling?

What a ridiculous question!

You have answered me, I replied: Well, and may we not further say that our guardians are the best of our citizens?

By far the best.

And will not their wives be the best women?

Yes, by far the best.

And can there be anything better for the interests of the State than that the men and women of a State should be as good as possible?

There can be nothing better.

And this is what the arts of music and gymnastic, when present in such manner as we have described, will accomplish?

Certainly.

Then we have made an enactment not only possible but in the highest degree beneficial to the State?

True.

Then let the wives of our guardians strip, for their virtue will be their robe, and let them share in the toils of war and the defence of their country; only in the distribution of labors the lighter are to be assigned to the women, who are the weaker natures, but in other respects their duties are to be the same. And as for the man who laughs at naked women exercising their bodies from the best of motives, in his laughter he is plucking

> " A fruit of unripe wisdom,"

and he himself is ignorant of what he is laughing at, or what he is about; — for that is, and ever will be, the best of sayings, *That the useful is the noble and the hurtful is the base.*

Very true.

Here, then, is one difficulty in our law about women, which we may say that we have now escaped; the wave has not swallowed us up alive for enacting that the guardians of either sex should have all their pursuits in common: to the utility and also to the possibility of this arrangement the consistency of the argument with itself bears witness.

Yes, that was a mighty wave which you have escaped.

Yes, I said, but a greater is coming; you will not think much of this when you see the next.

Go on; let me see.

The law, I said, which is the sequel of this and of all that has preceded, is to the following effect, — " that the wives of our guardians are to be common, and their children are to be common, and no parent is to know his own child, nor any child his parent."

Yes, he said, that is a much greater wave than the other; and the possibility as well as the utility of such a law are far more questionable.

I do not think, I said, that there can be any dispute about the very great utility of having wives and children in common; the possibility is quite another matter, and will be very much disputed.

I think that a good many doubts may be raised about both.

You imply that the two questions must be combined, I replied. Now I meant that you should admit the utility; and in this way, as I thought, I should escape from one of them, and then there would remain only the possibility.

But that little attempt is detected, and therefore you will please to give a defence of both.

Well, I said, I submit to my fate. Yet grant me a little favor: let me feast my mind with the dream as day dreamers are in the habit of feasting themselves when they are walking alone; for before they have discovered any means of effecting their wishes — that is a matter which never troubles them — they would rather not tire themselves by thinking about possibilities; but assuming that what they desire is already granted to them, they proceed with their plan, and delight in detailing what they mean to do when their wish has come true — that is a way which they have of not doing much good to a capacity which was never good for much. Now I myself am beginning to lose heart, and I should like, with your permission, to pass over the question of possibility at present. Assuming therefore the possibility of the proposal, I shall now proceed to inquire how the rulers will carry out these arrangements, and I shall demonstrate that our plan, if executed, will be of the greatest benefit to the State and to the guardians. First of all, then, if you have no objection, I will endeavor with your help to consider the advantages of the measure; and hereafter the question of possibility.

I have no objection; proceed.

First, I think that if our rulers and their auxiliaries are to be worthy of the name which they bear, there must be willingness to obey in the one and the power of command in the other; the guardians must themselves obey the laws, and they must also imitate the spirit of them in any details which are entrusted to their care.

That is right, he said.

You, I said, who are their legislator, having selected the men, will now select the women and give them to them; — they must be as far as possible of like natures with them; and they must live in common houses and meet at common meals. None of them will have anything specially his or her own; they will be together, and will be brought up together, and will associate at gymnastic exercises. And so they will be drawn by a necessity of their natures to have intercourse with each other — necessity is not too strong a word, I think?

Yes, he said; — necessity, not geometrical, but

another sort of necessity which lovers know, and which is far more convincing and constraining to the mass of mankind.

True, I said; and this, Glaucon, like all the rest, must proceed after an orderly fashion; in a city of the blessed, licentiousness is an unholy thing which the rulers will forbid.

Yes, he said, and it ought not to be permitted.

Then clearly the next thing will be to make matrimony sacred in the highest degree, and what is most beneficial will be deemed sacred?

Exactly.

And how can marriages be made most beneficial? — that is a question which I put to you, because I see in your house dogs for hunting, and of the nobler sort of birds not a few. Now, I beseech you, do tell me, have you ever attended to their pairing and breeding?

In what particulars?

Why, in the first place, although they are all of a good sort, are not some better than others?

True.

And do you breed from them all indifferently, or do you take care to breed from the best only?

From the best.

And do you take the oldest or the youngest, or only those of ripe age?

I choose only those of ripe age.

And if care was not taken in the breeding, your dogs and birds would greatly deteriorate?

Certainly.

And the same of horses and of animals in general?

Undoubtedly.

Good heavens! my dear friend, I said, what consummate skill will our rulers need if the same principle holds of the human species!

Certainly, the same principle holds; but why does this involve any particular skill?

Because, I said, our rulers will often have to practise upon the body corporate with medicines. Now you know that when patients do not require medicines, but have only to be put under a regimen, the inferior sort of practitioner is deemed to be good enough; but when medicine has to be given, then the doctor should be more of a man.

That is quite true, he said; but to what are you alluding?

I mean, I replied, that our rulers will find a considerable dose of falsehood and deceit necessary for the good of their subjects: we were saying that the use of all these things regarded as medicines might be of advantage.

And we were very right.

And this lawful use of them seems likely to be often needed in the regulations of marriages and births.

How so?

Why, I said, the principle has been already laid down that the best of either sex should be united with the best as often, and the inferior with the inferior, as seldom as possible; and that they should rear the offspring of the one sort of union, but not of the other, if the flock is to be maintained in first-rate condition. Now these goings on must be a secret which the rulers only know, or there will be a further danger of our herd, as the guardians may be termed, breaking out into rebellion.

Very true.

Had we not better appoint certain festivals at which we will bring together the brides and bridegrooms, and sacrifices will be offered and suitable hymeneal songs composed by our poets: the number of weddings is a matter which must be left to the discretion of the rulers, whose aim will be to preserve the average of population? There are many other things which they will have to consider, such as the effects of wars and diseases and any similar agencies, in order as far as this is possible to prevent the State from becoming either too large or too small.

Certainly, he replied.

We shall have to invent some ingenious kind of lots which the less worthy may draw on each occasion of our bringing them together, and then they will accuse their own ill-luck and not the rulers.

To be sure, he said.

And I think that our braver and better youth, besides their other honors and rewards, might have greater facilities of intercourse with women given them; their bravery will be a reason, and such fathers ought to have as many sons as possible.

True.

And the proper officers, whether male or female or both, for offices are to be held by women as well as by men —

Yes —

The proper officers will take the offspring of the good parents to the pen or fold, and there they will deposit them with certain nurses who dwell in a separate quarter; but the offspring of the inferior, or of the better when they chance to be deformed, will be put away in some mysterious, unknown place, as they should be.

Yes, he said, that must be done if the breed of the guardians is to be kept pure.

They will provide for their nurture, and will bring the mothers to the fold when they are full of milk, taking the greatest possible care that no mother recognizes her own child; and other wet-nurses may be engaged if more are required. Care will also be

taken that the process of suckling shall not be pro-
tracted too long; and the mothers will have no getting
up at night or other trouble, but will hand over all
this sort of thing to the nurses and attendants.

You suppose the wives of our guardians to have a
fine easy time of it when they are having children.

Why, said I, and so they ought. Let us, however,
proceed with our scheme. We were saying that the
parents should be in the prime of life?

Very true.

And what is the prime of life? May it not be
defined as a period of about twenty years in a woman's
life, and thirty in a man's?

Which years do you mean to include?

A woman, I said, at twenty years of age may begin
to bear children to the State, and continue to bear
them until forty; a man may begin at five-and-twenty,
when he has passed the point at which the pulse of life
beats quickest, and continue to beget children until
he be fifty-five.

Certainly, he said, both in men and women those
years are the prime of physical as well as of intellectual vigor.

Any one above or below the prescribed ages who
takes part in the public hymeneals shall be said to
have done an unholy and unrighteous thing;
the child of which he is the father, if it steals into life,
will have been conceived under auspices very unlike
the sacrifices and prayers, which at each hymeneal
priestesses and priests and the whole city will offer,
that the new generation may be better and more
useful than their good and useful parents, whereas
his child will be the offspring of darkness and strange
lust.

Very true, he replied.

And the same law will apply to any one of those

within the prescribed age who forms a connection with any woman in the prime of life without the sanction of the rulers; for we shall say that he is raising up a bastard to the State, uncertified and unconsecrated.

Very true, he replied.

This applies, however, only to those who are within the specified age: after that we allow them to range at will, except that a man may not marry his daughter or his daughter's daughter, or his mother or his mother's mother; and women, on the other hand, are prohibited from marrying their sons or fathers, or son's son or father's father, and so on in either direction. And we grant all this, accompanying the permission with strict orders to prevent any embryo which may come into being from seeing the light; and if any force a way to the birth, the parents must understand that the offspring of such an union can not be maintained, and arrange accordingly.

That also, he said, is a reasonable proposition. But how will they know who are fathers and daughters, and so on?

They will never know. The way will be this: — dating from the day of the hymeneal, the bridegroom who was then married will call all the male children who are born in the seventh and the tenth month afterwards his sons, and the female children his daughters, and they will call him father, and he will call their children his grandchildren, and they will call the elder generation grandfathers and grandmothers. All who were begotten at the time when their fathers and mothers came together will be called their brothers and sisters, and these, as I was saying, will be forbidden to intermarry. This, however, is not to be understood as an absolute prohibition of the marriage of brothers and sisters; if the lot favors them, and they receive the sanction of the Pythian oracle, the law will allow them.

Quite right, he replied.

Such is the scheme, Glaucon, according to which the guardians of our State are to have their wives and families in common. And now you would have the argument show that this community is consistent with the rest of our polity, and also that nothing can be better — would you not?

Yes, certainly.

Shall we try to find a common basis by asking of ourselves what ought to be the chief aim of the legislator in making laws and in the organization of a State, — what is the greatest good, and what is the greatest evil, and then consider whether our previous description has the stamp of the good or of the evil?

By all means.

Can there be any greater evil than discord and distraction and plurality where unity ought to reign? or any greater good than the bond of unity?

There can not.

And there is unity where there is community of pleasures and pains — where all the citizens are glad or grieved on the same occasions of joy and sorrow?

No doubt.

Yes; and where there is no common but only private feeling a State is disorganized — when you have one half of the world triumphing and the other plunged in grief at the same events happening to the city or the citizens?

Certainly.

Such differences commonly originate in a disagreement about the use of the terms " mine " and " not mine," " his " and " not his."

Exactly so.

And is not that the best-ordered State in which the

greatest number of persons apply the terms " mine "
and " not mine " in the same way to the same thing?

Quite true.

Or that again which most nearly approaches to the
condition of the individual — as in the body, when
but a finger of one of us is hurt, the whole frame,
drawn towards the soul as a centre and forming one
kingdom under the ruling power therein, feels the
hurt and sympathizes all together with the part
affected, and we say that the man has a pain in his
finger; and the same expression is used about any
other part of the body, which has a sensation of pain
at suffering or of pleasure at the alleviation of suffering.

Very true, he replied; and I agree with you that in
the best-ordered State there is the nearest approach
to this common feeling which you describe.

Then when any one of the citizens experiences any
good or evil, the whole State will make his case their
own, and will either rejoice or sorrow with him?

Yes, he said, that is what will happen in a well-
ordered State.

It will now be time, I said, for us to return to our
State and see whether this or some other form is most
in accordance with these fundamental principles.

Very good.

Our State like every other has rulers and subjects?

True.

All of whom will call one another citizens?

Of course.

But is there not another name which people give to
their rulers in other States?

Generally they call them masters, but in democratic
States they simply call them rulers.

And in our State what other name besides that of
citizens do the people give the rulers?

They are called saviours and helpers, he replied.

And what do the rulers call the people?

Their maintainers and foster-fathers.

And what do they call them in other States?

Slaves.

And what do the rulers call one another in other States?

Fellow-rulers.

And what in ours?

Fellow-guardians.

Did you ever know an example in any other State of a ruler who would speak of one of his colleagues as his friend and of another as not being his friend?

Yes, very often.

And the friend he regards and describes as one in whom he has an interest, and the other as a stranger in whom he has no interest?

Exactly.

But would any of your guardians think or speak of any other guardian as a stranger?

Certainly he would not; for every one whom they meet will be regarded by them either as a brother or sister, or father or mother, or son or daughter, or as the child or parent of those who are thus connected with him.

Capital, I said; but let me ask you once more: Shall they be a family in name only; or shall they in all their actions be true to the name? For example, in the use of the word "father," would the care of a father be implied and the filial reverence and duty and obedience to him which the law commands; and is the violator of these duties to be regarded as an impious and unrighteous person who is not likely to receive much good either at the hands of God or of man? Are these to be or not to be the strains which the children will hear repeated in their ears by all the citizens about those who are intimated to them to be their parents and the rest of their kinsfolk?

These, he said, and none other; for what can be more ridiculous than for them to utter the names of family ties with the lips only and not to act in the spirit of them?

Then in our city the language of harmony and concord will be more often heard than in any other. As I was describing before, when any one is well or ill, the universal word will be " with me it is well " or " it is ill."

Most true.

And agreeably to this mode of thinking and speaking, were we not saying that they will have their pleasures and pains in common?

Yes, and so they will.

And they will have a common interest in the same thing which they will alike call " my own," and having this common interest they will have a common feeling of pleasure and pain?

Yes, far more so than in other States.

And the reason of this, over and above the general constitution of the State, will be that the guardians will have a community of women and children?

That will be the chief reason.

And this unity of feeling we admitted to be the greatest good, as was implied in our own comparison of a well-ordered State to the relation of the body and the members, when affected by pleasure or pain?

That we acknowledge, and very rightly.

Then the community of wives and children among our citizens is clearly the source of the greatest good to the State?

Certainly.

And this agrees with the other principle which we

were affirming, — that the guardians were not to have houses or lands or any other property; their pay was to be their food, which they were to receive from the other citizens, and they were to have no private expenses; for we intended them to preserve their true character of guardians.

Right, he replied.

Both the community of property and the community of families, as I am saying, tend to make them more truly guardians; they will not tear the city in pieces by differing about " mine " and " not mine "; each man dragging any acquisition which he has made into a separate house of his own, where he has a separate wife and children and private pleasures and pains; but all will be affected as far as may be by the same pleasures and pains because they are all of one opinion about what is near and dear to them, and therefore they all tend towards a common end.

Certainly, he replied.

And as they have nothing but their persons which they can call their own, suits and complaints will have no existence among them; they will be delivered from all those quarrels of which money or children or relations are the occasion.

Of course they will.

Neither will trials for assault or insult ever be likely to occur among them. For that equals should defend themselves against equals we shall maintain to be honorable and right; we shall make the protection of the person a matter of necessity.

That is good, he said.

Yes; and there is a further good in the law; viz. that if a man has a quarrel with another he will satisfy his resentment then and there, and not proceed to more dangerous lengths.

Certainly.

To the elder shall be assigned the duty of ruling and chastising the younger.

Clearly.

Nor can there be a doubt that the younger will not strike or do any other violence to an elder, unless the magistrates command him; nor will he slight him in any way. For there are two guardians, shame and fear, mighty to prevent him: shame, which makes men refrain from laying hands on those who are to them in the relation of parents; fear, that the injured one will be succored by the others who are his brothers, sons, fathers.

That is true, he replied.

Then in every way the laws will help the citizens to keep the peace with one another?

Yes, there will be no want of peace.

And as the guardians will never quarrel among themselves there will be no danger of the rest of the city being divided either against them or against one another.

None whatever.

I hardly like even to mention the little meannesses of which they will be rid, for they are beneath notice: such, for example, as the flattery of the rich by the poor, and all the pains and pangs which men experience in bringing up a family, and in finding money to buy necessaries for their household, borrowing and then repudiating, getting how they can, and giving the money into the hands of women and slaves to keep — the many evils of so many kinds which people suffer in this way are mean enough and obvious enough, and not worth speaking of.

Yes, he said, a man has no need of eyes in order to perceive that.

And from all these evils they will be delivered, and

their life will be blessed as the life of Olympic victors and yet more blessed.

How so?

The Olympic victor, I said, is deemed happy in receiving a part only of the blessedness which is secured to our citizens, who have won a more glorious victory and have a more complete maintenance at the public cost. For the victory which they have won is the salvation of the whole State; and the crown with which they and their children are crowned is the fulness of all that life needs; they receive rewards from the hands of their country while living, and after death have an honorable burial.

Yes, he said, and glorious rewards they are.

Do you remember, I said, how in the course of the previous discussion some one who shall be nameless accused us of making our guardians unhappy — they had nothing and might have possessed all things — to whom we replied that, if an occasion offered, we might perhaps hereafter consider this question, but that, as at present advised, we would make our guardians truly guardians, and that we were fashioning the State with a view to the greatest happiness, not of any particular class, but of the whole?

Yes, I remember.

And what do you say, now that the life of our protectors is made out to be far better and nobler than that of Olympic victors — is the life of shoemakers, or any other artisans, or of husbandmen, to be compared with it?

Certainly not.

At the same time I ought here to repeat what I have said elsewhere, that if any of our guardians shall try to be happy in such a manner that he will cease to be a guardian, and is not content with this safe and harmonious life, which, in our judgment, is of all lives the best, but infatuated by some youthful conceit of happiness which gets up into his head shall seek to appropriate the whole state to himself, then he will have to learn how wisely Hesiod spoke, when he said, " half is more than the whole."

If he were to consult me, I should say to him: Stay where you are, when you have the offer of such a life.

You agree then, I said, that men and women are to have a common way of life such as we have described — common education, common children; and they are to watch over the citizens in common whether abiding in the city or going out to war; they are to keep watch together, and to hunt together like dogs; and always and in all things, as far as they are able, women are to share with the men? And in so doing they will do what is best, and will not violate, but preserve the natural relation of the sexes.

I agree with you, he replied.

The inquiry, I said, has yet to be made, whether such a community will be found possible — as among other animals, so also among men — and if possible, in what way possible?

You have anticipated the question which I was about to suggest.

There is no difficulty, I said, in seeing how war will be carried on by them.

How?

Why, of course they will go on expeditions together; and will take with them any of their children who are strong enough, that, after the manner of the artisan's child, they may look on at the work which they will have to do when they are grown up; and besides looking on they will have to help and be of use in war, and to wait upon their fathers and mothers. Did you never observe in the arts how the potters' boys look on and help, long before they touch the wheel?

Yes, I have.

And shall potters be more careful in educating their children and in giving them the opportunity of seeing and practising their duties than our guardians will be?

The idea is ridiculous, he said.

There is also the effect on the parents, with whom, as with other animals, the presence of their young ones will be the greatest incentive to valor.

That is quite true, Socrates; and yet if they are defeated, which may often happen in war, how great the danger is! the children will be lost as well as their parents, and the State will never recover.

True, I said; but would you never allow them to run any risk?

I am far from saying that.

Well, but if they are ever to run a risk should they not do so on some occasion when, if they escape disaster, they will be the better for it?

Clearly.

Whether the future soldiers do or do not see war in the days of their youth is a very important matter, for the sake of which some risk may fairly be incurred.

Yes, very important.

This then must be our first step, — to make our children spectators of war; but we must also contrive that they shall be secured against danger; then all will be well.

True.

Their parents may be supposed not to be blind to the risks of war, but to know, as far as human foresight can, what expeditions are safe and what dangerous?

That may be assumed.

And they will take them on the safe expeditions and be cautious about the dangerous ones?

True.

And they will place them under the command of experienced veterans who will be their leaders and teachers?

Very properly.

Still, the dangers of war can not be always foreseen; there is a good deal of chance about them?

True.

Then against such chances the children must be at once furnished with wings, in order that in the hour of need they may fly away and escape.

What do you mean? he said.

I mean that we must mount them on horses in their earliest youth, and when they have learned to ride, take them on horseback to see war: the horses must not be spirited and warlike, but the most tractable and yet the swiftest that can be had. In this way they will get an excellent view of what is hereafter to be their own business; and if there is danger they have only to follow their elder leaders and escape.

I believe that you are right, he said.

Next, as to war; what are to be the relations of your soldiers to one another and to their enemies? I should be inclined to propose that the soldier who leaves his rank or throws away his arms, or is guilty of any other act of cowardice, should be degraded into the rank of a husbandman or artisan. What do you think?

By all means, I should say.

And he who allows himself to be taken prisoner may as well be made a present of to his enemies; he is their lawful prey, and let them do what they like with him.

Certainly.

But the hero who has distinguished himself, what shall be done to him? In the first place, he shall receive honor in the army from his youthful comrades; every one of them in succession shall crown him. What do you say?

I approve.

And what do you say to his receiving the right hand of fellowship?

To that too, I agree.

But you will hardly agree to my next proposal.

What is your proposal?

That he should kiss and be kissed by them.

Most certainly, and I should be disposed to go further, and say: Let no one whom he has a mind to kiss refuse to be kissed by him while the expedition lasts. So that if there be a lover in the army, whether his love be youth or maiden, he may be more eager to win the prize of valor.

Capital, I said. That the brave man is to have more wives than others has been already determined: and he is to have first choices in such matters more than others, in order that he may have as many children as possible?

Agreed.

Again, there is another manner in which, according to Homer, brave youths should be honored; for he tells how Ajax,[1] after he had distinguished himself in battle, was rewarded with long chines, which seems to be a compliment appropriate to a hero in the flower of his age, being not only a tribute of honor but also a very strengthening thing.

Most true, he said.

Then in this, I said, Homer shall be our teacher; and we too, at sacrifices and on the like occasions, will honor the brave according to the measure of their

[1] Iliad. vii. 321.

valor, whether men or women, with hymns and those other distinctions which we were mentioning; also with

"seats of precedence, and meats and full cups;"[1]

and in honoring them, we shall be at the same time training them.

That, he replied, is excellent.

Yes, I said; and when a man dies gloriously in war shall we not say, in the first place, that he is of the golden race?

To be sure.

Nay, have we not the authority of Hesiod for affirming that when they are dead

"They are holy angels upon the earth, authors of good, averters of evil, the guardians of speech-gifted men"?[2]

Yes; and we accept his authority.

We must learn of the god how we are to order the sepulture of divine and heroic personages, and what is to be their special distinction; and we must do as he bids?

By all means.

And in ages to come we will reverence them and kneel before their sepulchres as at the graves of heroes. And not only they but any who are deemed preeminently good, whether they die from age, or in any other way, shall be admitted to the same honors.

That is very right, he said.

Next, how shall our soldiers treat their enemies? What about this?

In what respect do you mean?

First of all, in regard to slavery? Do you think it right that Hellenes should enslave Hellenic States, or allow others to enslave them, if they can help? Should not their custom be to spare them, considering

[1] Iliad, viii. 162.　　[2] Probably Works and Days, 121 foll.

the danger which there is that the whole race may one day fall under the yoke of the barbarians?

To spare them is infinitely better.

Then no Hellene should be owned by them as a slave; that is a rule which they will observe and advise the other Hellenes to observe.

Certainly, he said; they will in this way be united against the barbarians and will keep their hands off one another.

Next as to the slain; ought the conquerors, I said, to take anything but their armor? Does not the practice of despoiling an enemy afford an excuse for not facing the battle? Cowards skulk about the dead, pretending that they are fulfilling a duty, and many an army before now has been lost from this love of plunder.

Very true.

And is there not illiberality and avarice in robbing a corpse, and also a degree of meanness and womanishness in making an enemy of the dead body when the real enemy has flown away and left only his fighting gear behind him, — is not this rather like a dog who can not get at his assailant, quarrelling with the stones which strike him instead?

Very like a dog, he said.

Then we must abstain from spoiling the dead or hindering their burial?

Yes, he replied, we most certainly must.

Neither shall we offer up arms at the temples of the gods, least of all the arms of Hellenes, if we care to maintain good feeling with other Hellenes; and, indeed, we have reason to fear that the offering of spoils taken from kinsmen may be a pollution unless commanded by the god himself?

Very true.

Again, as to the devastation of Hellenic territory or the burning of houses, what is to be the practice?

May I have the pleasure, he said, of hearing your opinion?

Both should be forbidden, in my judgment; I would take the annual produce and no more. Shall I tell you why?

Pray do.

Why, you see, there is a difference in the names "discord" and "war," and I imagine that there is also a difference in their natures; the one is expressive of what is internal and domestic, the other of what is external and foreign; and the first of the two is termed discord, and only the second, war.

That is a very proper distinction, he replied.

And may I not observe with equal propriety that the Hellenic race is all united together by ties of blood and friendship, and alien and strange to the barbarians?

Very good, he said.

And therefore when Hellenes fight with barbarians and barbarians with Hellenes, they will be described by us as being at war when they fight, and by nature enemies, and this kind of antagonism should be called war; but when Hellenes fight with one another we shall say that Hellas is then in a state of disorder and discord, they being by nature friends; and such enmity is to be called discord.

I agree.

Consider then, I said, when that which we have acknowledged to be discord occurs, and a city is divided, if both parties destroy the lands and burn the houses of one another, how wicked does the strife appear! No true lover of his country would bring himself to tear in pieces his own nurse and mother: There might be reason in the conqueror depriving the conquered of their harvest, but still they would have the idea of peace in their hearts and would not mean to go on fighting forever.

Yes, he said, that is a better temper than the other.

And will not the city, which you are founding, be an Hellenic city?

It ought to be, he replied.

Then will not the citizens be good and civilized?

Yes, very civilized.

And will they not be lovers of Hellas, and think of Hellas as their own land, and share in the common temples?

Most certainly.

And any difference which arises among them will be regarded by them as discord only — a quarrel among friends, which is not to be called a war?

Certainly not.

Then they will quarrel as those who intend some day to be reconciled?

Certainly.

They will use friendly correction, but will not enslave or destroy their opponents; they will be correctors, not enemies?

Just so.

And as they are Hellenes themselves they will not devastate Hellas, nor will they burn houses, nor ever suppose that the whole population of a city — men, women, and children — are equally their enemies, for they know that the guilt of war is always confined to a few persons and that the many are their friends. And for all these reasons they will be unwilling to waste their lands and raze their houses; their enmity to them will only last until the many innocent sufferers have compelled the guilty few to give satisfaction?

I agree, he said, that our citizens should thus deal

with their Hellenic enemies; and with barbarians as
the Hellenes now deal with one another.

Then let us enact this law also for our guardians: —
that they are neither to devastate the lands of Hellenes
nor to burn their houses.

Agreed; and we may agree also in thinking that
these, like all our previous enactments, are very good.

But still I must say, Socrates, that if you are allowed to go on in this way you will entirely forget
the other question which at the commencement of this
discussion you thrust aside: — Is such an order of
things possible, and how, if at all? For I am quite
ready to acknowledge that the plan which you propose, if only feasible, would do all sorts of good to the
State. I will add, what you have omitted, that your
citizens will be the bravest of warriors, and will never
leave their ranks, for they will all know one another,
and each will call the other father, brother, son; and
if you suppose the women to join their armies,
whether in the same rank or in the rear, either as a
terror to the enemy, or as auxiliaries in case of need,
I know that they will then be absolutely invincible;
and there are many domestic advantages which might
also be mentioned and which I also fully acknowledge: but, as I admit all these advantages and as
many more as you please, if only this State of yours
were to come into existence, we need say no more
about them; assuming then the existence of the State,
let us now turn to the question of possibility and ways
and means — the rest may be left.

If I loiter [1] for a moment, you instantly make a
raid upon me, I said, and have no mercy; I have
hardly escaped the first and second waves, and you
seem not to be aware that you are now bringing upon
me the third, which is the greatest and heaviest.

[1] Reading στραγγευομένῳ.

When you have seen and heard the third wave, I think you will be more considerate and will acknowledge that some fear and hesitation was natural respecting a proposal so extraordinary as that which I have now to state and investigate.

The more appeals of this sort which you make, he said, the more determined are we that you shall tell us how such a State is possible: speak out and at once.

Let me begin by reminding you that we found our way hither in the search after justice and injustice.

True, he replied; but what of that?

I was only going to ask whether, if we have discovered them, we are to require that the just man should in nothing fail of absolute justice; or may we be satisfied with an approximation, and the attainment in him of a higher degree of justice than is to be found in other men?

The approximation will be enough.

We were inquiring into the nature of absolute justice and into the character of the perfectly just, and into injustice and the perfectly unjust, that we might have an ideal. We were to look at these in order that we might judge of our own happiness and unhappiness according to the standard which they exhibited and the degree in which we resembled them, but not with any view of showing that they could exist in fact.

True, he said.

Would a painter be any the worse because, after having delineated with consummate art an ideal of a perfectly beautiful man, he was unable to show that any such man could ever have existed?

He would be none the worse.

Well, and were we not creating an ideal of a perfect State?

To be sure.

And is our theory a worse theory because we are

unable to prove the possibility of a city being ordered in the manner described?

Surely not, he replied.

That is the truth, I said. But if, at your request, I am to try and show how and under what conditions the possibility is highest, I must ask you, having this in view, to repeat your former admissions.

What admissions?

I want to know whether ideals are ever fully realized in language? Does not the word express more than the fact, and must not the actual, whatever a man may think, always, in the nature of things, fall short of the truth? What do you say?

I agree.

Then you must not insist on my proving that the actual State will in every respect coincide with the ideal: if we are only able to discover how a city may be governed nearly as we proposed, you will admit that we have discovered the possibility which you demand; and will be contented. I am sure that I should be contented — will not you?

Yes, I will.

Let me next endeavor to show what is that fault in States which is the cause of their present maladministration, and what is the least change which will enable a State to pass into the truer form; and let the change, if possible, be of one thing only, or, if not, of two; at any rate, let the changes be as few and slight as possible.

Certainly, he replied.

I think, I said, that there might be a reform of the State if only one change were made, which is not a slight or easy though still a possible one.

What is it? he said.

Now then, I said, I go to meet that which I liken to the greatest of the waves; yet shall the word be spoken, even though the wave break and drown me in laughter and dishonor; and do you mark my words.

Proceed.

I said: *Until philosophers are kings, or the kings and princes of this world have the spirit and power of philosophy, and political greatness and wisdom meet in one, and those commoner natures who pursue either to the exclusion of the other are compelled to stand aside, cities will never have rest from their evils, — no, nor the human race, as I believe, — and then only will this our State have a possibility of life and behold the light of day.* Such was the thought, my dear Glaucon, which I would fain have uttered if it had not seemed too extravagant; for to be convinced that in no other State can there be happiness private or public is indeed a hard thing.

Socrates, what do you mean? I would have you consider that the word which you have uttered is one at which numerous persons, and very respectable persons too, in a figure pulling off their coats all in a moment, and seizing any weapon that comes to hand, will run at you might and main, before you know where you are, intending to do heaven knows what; and if you don't prepare an answer, and put yourself in motion, you will be " pared by their fine wits," and no mistake.

You got me into the scrape, I said.

And I was quite right; however, I will do all I can to get you out of it; but I can only give you good-will and good advice, and, perhaps, I may be able to fit answers to your questions better than another — that is all. And now, having such an auxiliary, you must do your best to show the unbelievers that you are right.

I ought to try, I said, since you offer me such invaluable assistance. And I think that, if there is to be a chance of our escaping, we must explain to them whom we mean when we say that philosophers are to rule in the State; then we shall be able to defend ourselves: There will be discovered to be some natures who ought to study philosophy and to be leaders in the State; and others who are not born to be philosophers, and are meant to be followers rather than leaders.

Then now for a definition, he said.

Follow me, I said, and I hope that I may in some way or other be able to give you a satisfactory explanation.

Proceed.

I dare say that you remember, and therefore I need not remind you, that a lover, if he is worthy of the name, ought to show his love, not to some one part of that which he loves, but to the whole.

I really do not understand, and therefore beg of you to assist my memory.

Another person, I said, might fairly reply as you do; but a man of pleasure like yourself ought to know that all who are in the flower of youth do somehow or other raise a pang or emotion in a lover's breast, and are thought by him to be worthy of his affectionate regards. Is not this a way which you have with the fair: one has a snub nose, and you praise his charming face; the hook-nose of another has, you say, a royal look; while he who is neither snub nor hooked has the grace of regularity: the dark visage is manly, the fair are children of the gods; and as to the sweet " honey pale," as they are called, what is the very name but the invention of a lover who talks in diminutives, and is not averse to paleness if appearing on the cheek of youth? In a word, there is no excuse which you will not make, and nothing which you will not say, in order not to lose a single flower that blooms in the spring-time of youth.

If you make me an authority in matters of love, for the sake of the argument, I assent.

And what do you say of lovers of wine? Do you not see them doing the same? They are glad of any pretext of drinking any wine.

Very good.

And the same is true of ambitious men; if they can not command an army, they are willing to command a file; and if they can not be honored by really great and important persons, they are glad to be honored by lesser and meaner people, — but honor of some kind they must have.

Exactly.

Once more let me ask: Does he who desires any class of goods, desire the whole class or a part only?

The whole.

And may we not say of the philosopher that he is a lover, not of a part of wisdom only, but of the whole?

Yes, of the whole.

And he who dislikes learning, especially in youth, when he has no power of judging what is good and what is not, such an one we maintain not to be a philosopher or a lover of knowledge, just as he who refuses his food is not hungry, and may be said to have a bad appetite and not a good one?

Very true, he said.

Whereas he who has a taste for every sort of knowledge and who is curious to learn and is never satisfied, may be justly termed a philosopher? Am I not right?

Glaucon said: If curiosity makes a philosopher, you will find many a strange being will have a title to the name. All the lovers of sights have a delight in learning, and must therefore be included. Musical amateurs, too, are a folk strangely out of place among philosophers, for they are the last persons in the world who would come to anything like a philosophical discussion, if they could help, while they run about at the Dionysiac festivals as if they had let out their ears to hear every chorus; whether the performance is in town or country — that makes no difference — they are there. Now are we to maintain that all these and any who have similar tastes, as well as the professors of quite minor arts, are philosophers?

Certainly not, I replied; they are only an imitation.

He said: Who then are the true philosophers?

Those, I said, who are lovers of the vision of truth.

That is also good, he said; but I should like to know what you mean?

To another, I replied, I might have a difficulty in explaining; but I am sure that you will admit a proposition which I am about to make.

What is the proposition?

That since beauty is the opposite of ugliness, they are two?

Certainly.

And inasmuch as they are two, each of them is one?

True again.

And of just and unjust, good and evil, and of every other class, the same remark holds; taken singly, each of them is one; but from the various combinations of them with actions and things and with one another, they are seen in all sorts of lights and appear many?

Very true.

And this is the distinction which I draw between the sight-loving, art-loving, practical class and those of whom I am speaking, and who are alone worthy of the name of philosophers.

How do you distinguish them? he said.

The lovers of sounds and sights, I replied, are, as I conceive, fond of fine tones and colors and forms and all the artificial products that are made out of them, but their mind is incapable of seeing or loving absolute beauty.

True, he replied.

Few are they who are able to attain to the sight of this.

Very true.

And he who, having a sense of beautiful things has no sense of absolute beauty, or who, if another lead him to a knowledge of that beauty is unable to follow — of such an one I ask, Is he awake or in a dream only? Reflect: is not the dreamer, sleeping or waking, one who likens dissimilar things, who puts the copy in the place of the real object?

I should certainly say that such an one was dreaming.

But take the case of the other, who recognizes the existence of absolute beauty and is able to distinguish the idea from the objects which participate in the idea, neither putting the objects in the place of the idea nor the idea in the place of the objects — is he a dreamer, or is he awake?

He is wide awake.

And may we not say that the mind of the one who knows has knowledge, and that the mind of the other, who opines only, has opinion?

Certainly.

But suppose that the latter should quarrel with us and dispute our statement, can we administer any soothing cordial or advice to him, without revealing to him that there is sad disorder in his wits?

We must certainly offer him some good advice, he replied.

Come, then, and let us think of something to say to him. Shall we begin by assuring him that he is welcome to any knowledge which he may have, and that we are rejoiced at his having it? But we should like to ask him a question: Does he who has knowledge know something or nothing? (You must answer for him.)

I answer that he knows something.

Something that is or is not?

Something that is; for how can that which is not ever be known?

And are we assured, after looking at the matter from many points of view, that absolute being is or may be absolutely known, but that the utterly nonexistent is utterly unknown?

Nothing can be more certain.

Good. But if there be anything which is of such a nature as to be and not to be, that will have a place intermediate between pure being and the absolute negation of being?

Yes, between them.

And, as knowledge corresponded to being and ignorance of necessity to not-being, for that intermediate between being and not-being there has to be discovered a corresponding intermediate between ignorance and knowledge, if there be such?

Certainly.

Do we admit the existence of opinion?

Undoubtedly.

As being the same with knowledge, or another faculty?

Another faculty.

Then opinion and knowledge have to do with different kinds of matter corresponding to this difference of faculties?

Yes.

And knowledge is relative to being and knows being. But before I proceed further I will make a division.

What division?

I will begin by placing faculties in a class by themselves: they are powers in us, and in all other things, by which we do as we do. Sight and hearing, for example, I should call faculties. Have I clearly explained the class which I mean?

Yes, I quite understand.

Then let me tell you my view about them. I do not see them, and therefore the distinctions of figure, color, and the like, which enable me to discern the differences of some things, do not apply to them. In speaking of a faculty I think only of its sphere and its result; and that which has the same sphere and the same result I call the same faculty, but that which has another sphere and another result I call different. Would that be your way of speaking?

Yes.

And will you be so very good as to answer one more question? Would you say that knowledge is a faculty, or in what class would you place it?

Certainly knowledge is a faculty, and the mightiest of all faculties.

And is opinion also a faculty?

Certainly, he said; for opinion is that with which we are able to form an opinion.

And yet you were acknowledging a little while ago that knowledge is not the same as opinion?

Why, yes, he said: how can any reasonable being ever identify that which is infallible with that which errs?

An excellent answer, proving, I said, that we are quite conscious of a distinction between them.

Yes.

Then knowledge and opinion having distinct powers have also distinct spheres or subject-matters?

That is certain.

Being is the sphere or subject-matter of knowledge, and knowledge is to know the nature of being?

Yes.

And opinion is to have an opinion?

Yes.

And do we know what we opine? or is the subject-matter of opinion the same as the subject-matter of knowledge?

Nay, he replied, that has been already disproven; if difference in faculty implies difference in the sphere or subject-matter, and if, as we were saying, opinion and knowledge are distinct faculties, then the sphere of knowledge and of opinion can not be the same.

Then if being is the subject-matter of knowledge, something else must be the subject-matter of opinion?

Yes, something else.

Well then, is not-being the subject-matter of opinion? or, rather, how can there be an opinion at all about not-being? Reflect: when a man has an opinion, has he not an opinion about something? Can he have an opinion which is an opinion about nothing?

Impossible.

He who has an opinion has an opinion about some one thing?

Yes.

And not-being is not one thing but, properly speaking, nothing?

True.

Of not-being, ignorance was assumed to be the necessary correlative; of being, knowledge?

True, he said.

Then opinion is not concerned either with being or with not-being?

Not with either.

And can therefore neither be ignorance nor knowledge?

That seems to be true.

But is opinion to be sought without and beyond either of them, in a greater clearness than knowledge, or in a greater darkness than ignorance?

In neither.

Then I suppose that opinion appears to you to be darker than knowledge, but lighter than ignorance?

Both; and in no small degree.

And also to be within and between them?

Yes.

Then you would infer that opinion is intermediate?

No question.

But were we not saying before, that if anything appeared to be of a sort which is and is not at the same time, that sort of thing would appear also to lie in the interval between pure being and absolute not-being; and that the corresponding faculty is neither knowledge nor ignorance, but will be found in the interval between them?

True.

And in that interval there has now been discovered something which we call opinion?

There has.

Then what remains to be discovered is the object which partakes equally of the nature of being and not-being, and can not rightly be termed either, pure and simple; this unknown term, when discovered, we may truly call the subject of opinion, and assign each to their proper faculty, — the extremes to the faculties of the extremes and the mean to the faculty of the mean.

True.

This being premised, I would ask the gentleman who is of opinion that there is no absolute or unchangeable idea of beauty — in whose opinion the beautiful is the manifold — he, I say, your lover of beautiful sights, who can not bear to be told that the beautiful is one, and the just is one, or that anything is one — to him I would appeal, saying, Will you be so very kind, sir, as to tell us whether, of all these beautiful things, there is one which will not be found ugly; or of the just, which will not be found unjust; or of the holy, which will not also be unholy?

No, he replied; the beautiful will in some point of view be found ugly; and the same is true of the rest.

And may not the many which are doubles be also halves? — doubles, that is, of one thing, and halves of another?

Quite true.

And things great and small, heavy and light, as they are termed, will not be denoted by these any more than by the opposite names?

True; both these and the opposite names will always attach to all of them.

And can any one of those many things which are called by particular names be said to be this rather than not to be this?

He replied: They are like the punning riddles which are asked at feasts or the children's puzzle about the eunuch aiming at the bat, with what he hit him, as they say in the puzzle, and upon what the bat was sitting. The individual objects of which I am speaking are also a riddle, and have a double sense: nor can you fix them in your mind, either as being or not-being, or both, or neither.

Then what will you do with them? I said. Can

they have a better place than between being and not-being? For they are clearly not in greater darkness or negation than not-being, or more full of light and existence than being.

That is quite true, he said.

Thus then we seem to have discovered that the many ideas which the multitude entertain about the beautiful and about all other things are tossing about in some region which is half-way between pure being and pure not-being?

We have.

Yes; and we had before agreed that anything of this kind which we might find was to be described as matter of opinion, and not as matter of knowledge; being the intermediate flux which is caught and detained by the intermediate faculty.

Quite true.

Then those who see the many beautiful, and who yet neither see absolute beauty, nor can follow any guide who points the way thither; who see the many just, and not absolute justice, and the like, — such persons may be said to have opinion but not knowledge?

That is certain.

But those who see the absolute and eternal and immutable may be said to know, and not to have opinion only?

Neither can that be denied.

The one love and embrace the subjects of knowledge, the other those of opinion? The latter are the same, as I dare say you will remember, who listened to sweet sounds and gazed upon fair colors, but would not tolerate the existence of absolute beauty.

Yes, I remember.

Shall we then be guilty of any impropriety in calling them lovers of opinion rather than lovers of wisdom, and will they be very angry with us for thus describing them?

I shall tell them not to be angry; no man should be angry at what is true.

But those who love the truth in each thing are to be called lovers of wisdom and not lovers of opinion.

Assuredly.

BOOK VI

AND thus, Glaucon, after the argument has gone a weary way, the true and the false philosophers have at length appeared in view.

I do not think, he said, that the way could have been shortened.

I suppose not, I said; and yet I believe that we might have had a better view of both of them if the discussion could have been confined to this one subject and if there were not many other questions awaiting us, which he who desires to see in what respect the life of the just differs from that of the unjust must consider.

And what is the next question? he asked.

Surely, I said, the one which follows next in order. Inasmuch as philosophers only are able to grasp the eternal and unchangeable, and those who wander in the region of the many and variable are not philosophers, I must ask you which of the two classes should be the rulers of our State?

And how can we rightly answer that question?

Whichever of the two are best able to guard the laws and institutions of our State — let them be our guardians.

Very good.

Neither, I said, can there be any question that the guardian who is to keep anything should have eyes rather than no eyes?

There can be no question of that.

And are not those who are verily and indeed wanting in the knowledge of the true being of each thing, and who have in their souls no clear pattern, and are unable as with a painter's eye to look at the absolute truth and to that original to repair, and having perfect vision of the other world to order the laws about beauty, goodness, justice in this, if not already ordered, and to guard and preserve the order of them — are not such persons, I ask, simply blind?

Truly, he replied, they are much in that condition.

And shall they be our guardians when there are others who, besides being their equals in experience and falling short of them in no particular of virtue, also know the very truth of each thing?

There can be no reason, he said, for rejecting those who have this greatest of all great qualities; they must always have the first place unless they fail in some other respect.

Suppose then, I said, that we determine how far they can unite this and the other excellences.

By all means.

In the first place, as we began by observing, the nature of the philosopher has to be ascertained. We must come to an understanding about him, and, when we have done so, then, if I am not mistaken, we shall also acknowledge that such an union of qualities is possible, and that those in whom they are united, and those only, should be rulers in the State.

What do you mean?

Let us suppose that philosophical minds always love knowledge of a sort which shows them the eternal nature not varying from generation and corruption.

Agreed.

And further, I said, let us agree that they are lovers of all true being; there is no part whether greater or less, or more or less honorable, which they are willing to renounce; as we said before of the lover and the man of ambition.

True.

And if they are to be what we were describing, is there not another quality which they should also possess?

What quality?

Truthfulness: they will never intentionally receive into their mind falsehood, which is their detestation, and they will love the truth.

Yes, that may be safely affirmed of them.

" May be," my friend, I replied, is not the word; say rather, " must be affrmed: " for he whose nature is amorous of anything can not help loving all that belongs or is akin to the object of his affections.

Right, he said.

And is there anything more akin to wisdom than truth?

How can there be?

Can the same nature be a lover of wisdom and a lover of falsehood?

Never.

The true lover of learning then must from his earliest youth, as far as in him lies, desire all truth?

Assuredly.

But then again, as we know by experience, he whose desires are strong in one direction will have them weaker in others; they will be like a stream which has been drawn off into another channel.

True.

He whose desires are drawn towards knowledge in every form will be absorbed in the pleasures of the soul, and will hardly feel bodily pleasure — I mean, if he be a true philosopher and not a sham one.

That is most certain.

Such an one is sure to be temperate and the reverse of covetous; for the motives which make another man desirous of having and spending, have no place in his character.

Very true.

Another criterion of the philosophical nature has also to be considered.

What is that?

There should be no secret corner of illiberality; nothing can be more antagonistic than meanness to a soul which is ever longing after the whole of things both divine and human.

Most true, he replied.

Then how can he who has magnificence of mind and is the spectator of all time and all existence, think much of human life?

He can not.

Or can such an one account death fearful?

No indeed.

Then the cowardly and mean nature has no part in true philosophy?

Certainly not.

Or again: can he who is harmoniously constituted, who is not covetous or mean, or a boaster, or a coward — can he, I say, ever be unjust or hard in his dealings?

Impossible.

Then you will soon observe whether a man is just and gentle, or rude and unsociable; these are the signs which distinguish even in youth the philosophical nature from the unphilosophical.

True.

There is another point which should be remarked.

What point?

Whether he has or has not a pleasure in learning; for no one will love that which gives him pain, and in which after much toil he makes little progress.

Certainly not.

And again, if he is forgetful and retains nothing of what he learns, will he not be an empty vessel?

That is certain.

Laboring in vain, he must end in hating himself and his fruitless occupation?

Yes.

Then a soul which forgets can not be ranked among genuine philosophic natures; we must insist that the philosopher should have a good memory?

Certainly.

And once more, the inharmonious and unseemly nature can only tend to disproportion?

Undoubtedly.

And do you consider truth to be akin to proportion or to disproportion?

To proportion.

Then, besides other qualities, we must try to find a naturally well-proportioned and gracious mind, which will move spontaneously towards the true being of everything.

Certainly.

Well, and do not all these qualities, which we have been enumerating, go together, and are they not, in a manner, necessary to a soul, which is to have a full and perfect participation of being?

They are absolutely necessary, he replied.

And must not that be a blameless study which he only can pursue who has the gift of a good memory, and is quick to learn, — noble, gracious, the friend of truth, justice, courage, temperance, who are his kindred?

The god of jealousy himself, he said, could find no fault with such a study.

And to men like him. I said, when perfected by years and education, and to these only you will entrust the State.

Here Adeimantus interposed and said: To these statements, Socrates, no one can offer a reply; but when you talk in this way, a strange feeling passes over the minds of your hearers: They fancy that they are led astray a little at each step in the argument, owing to their own want of skill in asking and answering questions; these littles accumulate, and at the end of the discussion they are found to have sustained a mighty overthrow and all their former notions appear to be turned upside down. And as unskilful players of draughts are at last shut up by their more skilful adversaries and have no piece to move, so they too find themselves shut up at last; for they have nothing to say in this new game of which words are the counters; and yet all the time they are in the right. The observation is suggested to me by what is now occurring. For any one of us might say, that although in words he is not able to meet you at each step of the argument, he sees as a fact that the votaries of philosophy, when they carry on the study, not only in youth as a part of education, but as the pursuit of their maturer years, most of them become strange monsters, not to say utter rogues, and that those who may be considered the best of them are made useless to the world by the very study which you extol.

Well, and do you think that those who say so are wrong?

I can not tell, he replied; but I should like to know what is your opinion.

Hear my answer; I am of opinion that they are quite right.

Then how can you be justified in saying that cities will not cease from evil until philosophers rule in them, when philosophers are acknowledged by us to be of no use to them?

You ask a question, I said, to which a reply can only be given in a parable.

Yes, Socrates; and that is a way of speaking to which you are not at all accustomed, I suppose.

I perceive, I said, that you are vastly amused at having plunged me into such a hopeless discussion; but now hear the parable, and then you will be still more amused at the meagreness of my imagination: for the manner in which the best men are treated in their own States is so grievous that no single thing on earth is comparable to it; and therefore, if I am to plead their cause, I must have recourse to fiction, and put together a figure made up of many things, like the fabulous unions of goats and stags which are found in pictures. Imagine then a fleet or a ship in which there is a captain who is taller and stronger than any of the crew, but he is a little deaf and has a similar infirmity in sight, and his knowledge of navigation is not much better. The sailors are quarrelling with one another about the steering — every one is of opinion that he has a right to steer, though he has never learned the art of navigation and can not tell who taught him or when he learned, and will further assert that it can not be taught, and they are ready to cut in pieces any one who says the contrary. They throng about the captain, begging and praying him to commit the helm to them; and if at any time they do not prevail, but others are preferred to them, they kill the others or throw them overboard, and having first chained up the noble captain's senses with drink or some narcotic drug, they mutiny and take possession of the ship and make free with the stores; thus, eating and drinking, they proceed on their voyage in such manner as might be expected of them. Him who is their partisan and cleverly aids them in their plot for getting the ship out of the captain's hands into their own whether by force or persuasion, they compliment with the name of sailor, pilot, able seaman, and abuse the other sort of man, whom they call a good-for-nothing; but that the true pilot must pay attention to the year and seasons and sky and stars and winds, and whatever else belongs to his art, if he intends to be really qualified for the command of a ship, and that he must and will be the steerer, whether other people like or not — the possibility of this union of authority with the steerer's art has never seriously entered into their thoughts or been made part of their calling.[1] Now in vessels which are in a state of mutiny and by sailors who are mutineers, how will the true pilot be regarded? Will he not be called by them a prater, a star-gazer, a good-for-nothing?

Of course, said Adeimantus.

Then you will hardly need, I said, to hear the interpretation of the figure, which describes the true philosopher in his relation to the State; for you understand already.

Certainly.

Then suppose you now take this parable to the gentleman who is surprised at finding that philosophers have no honor in their cities; explain it to him and try to convince him that their having honor would be far more extraordinary.

I will.

Say to him, that, in deeming the best votaries of philosophy to be useless to the rest of the world, he is right; but also tell him to attribute their uselessness to the fault of those who will not use them, and not to themselves. The pilot should not humbly beg the sailors to be commanded by him — that is not the

---

[1] Or, applying ὅπως δὲ κυβερνήσει to the mutineers, "But only understand-ing (ἐπαίοντας) that he (the mutinous pilot) must rule in spite of other people, never considering that there is an art of command which may be practised in combination with the pilot's art."

order of nature; neither are " the wise to go to the doors of the rich " — the ingenious author of this saying told a lie — but the truth is, that, when a man is ill, whether he be rich or poor, to the physician he must go, and he who wants to be governed, to him who is able to govern. The ruler who is good for anything ought not to beg his subjects to be ruled by him; although the present governors of mankind are of a different stamp; they may be justly compared to the mutinous sailors, and the true helmsmen to those who are called by them good-for-nothings and star-gazers.

Precisely so, he said.

For these reasons, and among men like these, philosophy, the noblest pursuit of all, is not likely to be much esteemed by those of the opposite faction; not that the greatest and most lasting injury is done to her by her opponents, but by her own professing followers, the same of whom you suppose the accuser to say, that the greater number of them are arrant rogues, and the best are useless; in which opinion I agreed.

Yes.

And the reason why the good are useless has now been explained?

True.

Then shall we proceed to show that the corruption of the majority is also unavoidable, and that this is not to be laid to the charge of philosophy any more than the other?

By all means.

And let us ask and answer in turn, first going back to the description of the gentle and noble nature. Truth, as you will remember, was his leader, whom he followed always and in all things; failing in this, he was an impostor, and had no part or lot in true philosophy.

Yes, that was said.

Well, and is not this one quality, to mention no others, greatly at variance with present notions of him?

Certainly, he said.

And have we not a right to say in his defence, that the true lover of knowledge is always striving after being — that is his nature; he will not rest in the multiplicity of individuals which is an appearance only, but will go on — the keen edge will not be blunted, nor the force of his desire abate until he have attained the knowledge of the true nature of every essence by a sympathetic and kindred power in the soul, and by that power drawing near and mingling and becoming incorporate with very being, having begotten mind and truth, he will have knowledge and will live and grow truly, and then, and not till then, will he cease from his travail.

Nothing, he said, can be more just than such a description of him.

And will the love of a lie be any part of a philosopher's nature? Will he not utterly hate a lie?

He will.

And when truth is the captain, we can not suspect any evil of the band which he leads?

Impossible.

Justice and health of mind will be of the company, and temperance will follow after?

True, he replied.

Neither is there any reason why I should again set in array the philosopher's virtues, as you will doubtless remember that courage, magnificence, apprehension, memory, were his natural gifts. And you objected that, although no one could deny what I then said, still, if you leave words and look at facts, the persons who are thus described are some of them manifestly useless, and the greater number utterly depraved; we were then led to inquire into the grounds of these accusations, and have now arrived at the point of asking why are the majority bad, which question of necessity brought us back to the examination and definition of the true philosopher.

Exactly.

And we have next to consider the corruptions of the philosophic nature, why so many are spoiled and so few escape spoiling — I am speaking of those who were said to be useless but not wicked — and, when we have done with them, we will speak of the imitators of philosophy, what manner of men are they who aspire after a profession which is above them and of which they are unworthy, and then, by their manifold inconsistencies, bring upon philosophy, and upon all philosophers, that universal reprobation of which we speak.

What are these corruptions? he said.

I will see if I can explain them to you. Every one will admit that a nature having in perfection all the qualities which we required in a philosopher, is a rare plant which is seldom seen among men.

Rare indeed.

And what numberless and powerful causes tend to destroy these rare natures!

What causes?

In the first place there are their own virtues, their courage, temperance, and the rest of them, every one of which praiseworthy qualities (and this is a most singular circumstance) destroys and distracts from philosophy the soul which is the possessor of them.

That is very singular, he replied.

Then there are all the ordinary goods of life — beauty, wealth, strength, rank, and great connections in the State — you understand the sort of things

— these also have a corrupting and distracting effect.

I understand; but I should like to know more precisely what you mean about them.

Grasp the truth as a whole, I said, and in the right way; you will then have no difficulty in apprehending the preceding remarks, and they will no longer appear strange to you.

And how am I to do so? he asked.

Why, I said, we know that all germs or seeds, whether vegetable or animal, when they fail to meet with proper nutriment or climate or soil, in proportion to their vigor, are all the more sensitive to the want of a suitable environment, for evil is a greater enemy to what is good than to what is not.

Very true.

There is reason in supposing that the finest natures, when under alien conditions, receive more injury than the inferior, because the contrast is greater.

Certainly.

And may we not say, Adeimantus, that the most gifted minds, when they are ill-educated, become pre-eminently bad? Do not great crimes and the spirit of pure evil spring out of a fulness of nature ruined by education rather than from any inferiority, whereas weak natures are scarcely capable of any very great good or very great evil?

There I think that you are right.

And our philosopher follows the same analogy — he is like a plant which, having proper nurture, must necessarily grow and mature into all virtue, but, if sown and planted in an alien soil, becomes the most noxious of all weeds, unless he be preserved by some divine power. Do you really think, as people so often say, that our youth are corrupted by Sophists, or that private teachers of the art corrupt them in any degree worth speaking of? Are not the public who say these things the greatest of all Sophists? And do they not educate to perfection young and old, men and women alike, and fashion them after their own hearts?

When is this accomplished? he said.

When they meet together, and the world sits down at an assembly, or in a court of law, or a theatre, or a camp, or in any other popular resort, and there is a great uproar, and they praise some things which are being said or done, and blame other things, equally exaggerating both, shouting and clapping their hands, and the echo of the rocks and the place in which they are assembled redoubles the sound of the praise or blame — at such a time will not a young man's heart, as they say, leap within him? Will any private training enable him to stand firm against the overwhelming flood of popular opinion? or will he be carried away by the stream? Will he not have the notions of good and evil which the public in general have — he will do as they do, and as they are, such will he be?

Yes, Socrates; necessity will compel him.

And yet, I said, there is a still greater necessity, which has not been mentioned.

What is that?

The gentle force of attainder or confiscation or death, which, as you are aware, these new Sophists and educators, who are the public, apply when their words are powerless.

Indeed they do; and in right good earnest.

Now what opinion of any other Sophist, or of any private person, can be expected to overcome in such an unequal contest?

None, he replied.

No, indeed, I said, even to make the attempt is a great piece of folly; there neither is, nor has been,

nor is ever likely to be, any different type of character [1] which has had no other training in virtue but
that which is supplied by public opinion [1] — I speak,
my friend, of human virtue only; what is more than
human, as the proverb says, is not included: for I
would not have you ignorant that, in the present evil
state of governments, whatever is saved and comes
to good is saved by the power of God, as we may
truly say.

I quite assent, he replied.

Then let me crave your assent also to a further
observation.

What are you going to say?

Why, that all those mercenary individuals, whom
the many call Sophists and whom they deem to be
their adversaries, do, in fact, teach nothing but the
opinion of the many, that is to say, the opinions of
their assemblies; and this is their wisdom. I might
compare them to a man who should study the tempers
and desires of a mighty strong beast who is fed by
him — he would learn how to approach and handle
him, also at what times and from what causes he is
dangerous or the reverse, and what is the meaning
of his several cries, and by what sounds, when another
utters them, he is soothed or infuriated; and you may
suppose further, that when, by continually attending
upon him, he has become perfect in all this, he calls
his knowledge wisdom, and makes of it a system or
art, which he proceeds to teach, although he has no
real notion of what he means by the principles or
passions of which he is speaking, but calls this honorable and that dishonorable, or good or evil, or
just or unjust, all in accordance with the tastes and
tempers of the great brute. Good he pronounces to
be that in which the beast delights and evil to be that

[1] Or, taking παρά in another sense, "trained to virtue on their principles."

which he dislikes; and he can give no other account of them except that the just and noble are the necessary, having never himself seen, and having no power of explaining to others the nature of either, or the difference between them, which is immense. By heaven, would not such an one be a rare educator?

Indeed he would.

And in what way does he who thinks that wisdom is the discernment of the tempers and tastes of the motley multitude, whether in painting or music, or, finally, in politics, differ from him whom I have been describing? For when a man consorts with the many, and exhibits to them his poem or other work of art or the service which he has done the State, making them his judges [1] when he is not obliged, the so-called necessity of Diomede will oblige him to produce whatever they praise. And yet the reasons are utterly ludicrous which they give in confirmation of their own notions about the honorable and good. Did you ever hear any of them which were not?

No, nor am I likely to hear.

You recognize the truth of what I have been saying? Then let me ask you to consider further whether the world will ever be induced to believe in the existence of absolute beauty rather than of the many beautiful, or of the absolute in each kind rather than of the many in each kind?

Certainly not.

Then the world can not possibly be a philosopher?

Impossible.

And therefore philosophers must inevitably fall under the censure of the world?

They must.

And of individuals who consort with the mob and seek to please them?

[1] Putting a comma after τῶν ἀναγκαίων.

That is evident.

Then, do you see any way in which the philosopher can be preserved in his calling to the end? and remember what we were saying of him, that he was to have quickness and memory and courage and magnificence — these were admitted by us to be the true philosopher's gifts.

Yes.

Will not such an one from his early childhood be in all things first among all, especially if his bodily endowments are like his mental ones?

Certainly, he said.

And his friends and fellow-citizens will want to use him as he gets older for their own purposes?

No question.

Falling at his feet, they will make requests to him and do him honor and flatter him, because they want to get into their hands now, the power which he will one day possess.

That often happens, he said.

And what will a man such as he is be likely to do under such circumstances, especially if he be a citizen of a great city, rich and noble, and a tall proper youth? Will he not be full of boundless aspirations, and fancy himself able to manage the affairs of Hellenes and of barbarians, and having got such notions into his head will he not dilate and elevate himself in the fulness of vain pomp and senseless pride?

To be sure he will.

Now, when he is in this state of mind, if some one gently comes to him and tells him that he is a fool and must get understanding, which can only be got by slaving for it, do you think that, under such adverse circumstances, he will be easily induced to listen?

Far otherwise.

And even if there be some one who through inherent goodness or natural reasonableness has had his eyes opened a little and is humbled and taken captive by philosophy, how will his friends behave when they think that they are likely to lose the advantage which they were hoping to reap from his companionship? Will they not do and say anything to prevent him from yielding to his better nature and to render his teacher powerless, using to this end private intrigues as well as public prosecutions?

There can be no doubt of it.

And how can one who is thus circumstanced ever become a philosopher?

Impossible.

Then were we not right in saying that even the very qualities which make a man a philosopher may, if he be ill-educated, divert him from philosophy, no less than riches and their accompaniments and the other so-called goods of life?

We were quite right.

Thus, my excellent friend, is brought about all that ruin and failure which I have been describing of the natures best adapted to the best of all pursuits; they are natures which we maintain to be rare at any time; this being the class out of which come the men who are the authors of the greatest evil to States and individuals; and also of the greatest good when the tide carries them in that direction; but a small man never was the doer of any great thing either to individuals or to States.

That is most true, he said.

And so philosophy is left desolate, with her marriage rite incomplete: for her own have fallen away and forsaken her, and while they are leading a false and unbecoming life, other unworthy persons, seeing that she has no kinsmen to be her protectors, enter in and dishonor her; and fasten upon her the reproaches which, as you say, her reprovers utter, who affirm of her votaries that some are good for nothing, and that the greater number deserve the severest punishment.

That is certainly what people say.

Yes; and what else would you expect, I said, when you think of the puny creatures who, seeing this land open to them — a land well stocked with fair names and showy titles — like prisoners running out of prison into a sanctuary, take a leap out of their trades into philosophy; those who do so being probably the cleverest hands at their own miserable crafts? For, although philosophy be in this evil case, still there remains a dignity about her which is not to be found in the arts. And many are thus attracted by her whose natures are imperfect and whose souls are maimed and disfigured by their meannesses, as their bodies are by their trades and crafts. Is not this unavoidable?

Yes.

Are they not exactly like a bald little tinker who has just got out of durance and come into a fortune; he takes a bath and puts on a new coat, and is decked out as a bridegroom going to marry his master's daughter, who is left poor and desolate?

A most exact parallel.

What will be the issue of such marriages? Will they not be vile and bastard?

There can be no question of it.

And when persons who are unworthy of education approach philosophy and make an alliance with her who is in a rank above them, what sort of ideas and opinions are likely to be generated? [1] Will they not be sophisms captivating to the ear,[1] having nothing in them genuine, or worthy of or akin to true wisdom?

[1] Or, "will they not deserve to be called sophisms," . . .

No doubt, he said.

Then, Adeimantus, I said, the worthy disciples of philosophy will be but a small remnant: perchance some noble and well-educated person, detained by exile in her service, who in the absence of corrupting influences remains devoted to her; or some lofty soul born in a mean city, the politics of which he contemns and neglects; and there may be a gifted few who leave the arts, which they justly despise, and come to her; — or peradventure there are some who are restrained by our friend Theages' bridle; for everything in the life of Theages conspired to divert him from philosophy; but ill-health kept him away from politics. My own case of the internal sign is hardly worth mentioning, for rarely, if ever, has such a monitor been given to any other man. Those who belong to this small class have tasted how sweet and blessed a possession philosophy is, and have also seen enough of the madness of the multitude; and they know that no politician is honest, nor is there any champion of justice at whose side they may fight and be saved. Such an one may be compared to a man who has fallen among wild beasts — he will not join in the wickedness of his fellows, but neither is he able singly to resist all their fierce natures, and therefore seeing that he would be of no use to the State or to his friends, and reflecting that he would have to throw away his life without doing any good either to himself or others, he holds his peace, and goes his own way. He is like one who, in the storm of dust and sleet which the driving wind hurries along, retires under the shelter of a wall; and seeing the rest of mankind full of wickedness, he is content, if only he can live his own life and be pure from evil or unrighteousness, and depart in peace and good-will, with bright hopes.

Yes, he said, and he will have done a great work before he departs.

A great work — yes; but not the greatest, unless he find a State suitable to him; for in a State which is suitable to him, he will have a larger growth and be the savior of his country, as well as of himself.

The causes why philosophy is in such an evil name have now been sufficiently explained: the injustice of the charges against her has been shown — is there anything more which you wish to say?

Nothing more on that subject, he replied; but I should like to know which of the governments now existing is in your opinion the one adapted to her.

Not any of them, I said; and that is precisely the accusation which I bring against them — not one of them is worthy of the philosophic nature, and hence that nature is warped and estranged; — as the exotic seed which is sown in a foreign land becomes denaturalized, and is wont to be overpowered and to lose itself in the new soil, even so this growth of philosophy, instead of persisting, degenerates and receives another character. But if philosophy ever finds in the State that perfection which she herself is, then will be seen that she is in truth divine, and that all other things, whether natures of men or institutions, are but human; — and now, I know, that you are going to ask, What that State is:

No, he said; there you are wrong, for I was going to ask another question — whether it is the State of which we are the founders and inventors, or some other?

Yes, I replied, ours in most respects; but you may remember my saying before, that some living authority would always be required in the State having the same idea of the constitution which guided you when as legislator you were laying down the laws.

That was said, he replied.

Yes, but not in a satisfactory manner; you frightened us by interposing objections, which certainly showed that the discussion would be long and difficult; and what still remains is the reverse of easy.

What is there remaining?

The question how the study of philosophy may be so ordered as not to be the ruin of the State: All great attempts are attended with risk; "hard is the good," as men say.

Still, he said, let the point be cleared up, and the inquiry will then be complete.

I shall not be hindered, I said, by any want of will, but, if at all, by a want of power: my zeal you may see for yourselves; and please to remark in what I am about to say how boldly and unhesitatingly I declare that States should pursue philosophy, not as they do now, but in a different spirit.

In what manner?

At present, I said, the students of philosophy are quite young; beginning when they are hardly past childhood, they devote only the time saved from moneymaking and housekeeping to such pursuits; and even those of them who are reputed to have most of the philosophic spirit, when they come within sight of the great difficulty of the subject, I mean dialectic, take themselves off. In after life when invited by some one else, they may, perhaps, go and hear a lecture, and about this they make much ado, for philosophy is not considered by them to be their proper business: at last, when they grow old, in most cases they are extinguished more truly than Heracleitus' sun, inasmuch as they never light up again.[1]

But what ought to be their course?

[1] Heracleitus said that the sun was extinguished every evening and relighted every morning.

Just the opposite. In childhood and youth their study, and what philosophy they learn, should be suited to their tender years: during this period while they are growing up towards manhood, the chief and special care should be given to their bodies that they may have them to use in the service of philosophy; as life advances and the intellect begins to mature, let them increase the gymnastics of the soul; but when the strength of our citizens fails and is past civil and military duties, then let them range at will and engage in no serious labor, as we intend them to live happily here, and to crown this life with a similar happiness in another.

How truly in earnest you are, Socrates! he said; I am sure of that; and yet most of your hearers, if I am not mistaken, are likely to be still more earnest in their opposition to you, and will never be convinced; Thrasymachus least of all.

Do not make a quarrel, I said, between Thrasymachus and me, who have recently become friends, although, indeed, we were never enemies; for I shall go on striving to the utmost until I either convert him and other men, or do something which may profit them against the day when they live again, and hold the like discourse in another state of existence.

You are speaking of a time which is not very near.

Rather, I replied, of a time which is as nothing in comparison with eternity. Nevertheless, I do not wonder that the many refuse to believe; for they have never seen that of which we are now speaking realized; they have seen only a conventional imitation of philosophy, consisting of words artificially brought together, not like these of ours having a natural unity. But a human being who in word and work is perfectly moulded, as far as can be, into the proportion and likeness of virtue — such a man ruling in a city

which bears the same image, they have never yet seen,
neither one nor many of them — do you think that
they ever did?

No indeed.

No, my friend, and they have seldom, if ever, heard
free and noble sentiments; such as men utter when
they are earnestly and by every means in their power
seeking after truth for the sake of knowledge, while
they look coldly on the subtleties of controversy, of
which the end is opinion and strife, whether they meet
with them in the courts of law or in society.

They are strangers, he said, to the words of which
you speak.

And this was what we foresaw, and this was the
reason why truth forced us to admit, not without fear
and hesitation, that neither cities nor States nor individuals will ever attain perfection until the small
class of philosophers whom we termed useless but
not corrupt are providentially compelled, whether
they will or not, to take care of the State, and until a
like necessity be laid on the State to obey them;[1] or
until kings, or if not kings, the sons of kings or princes,
are divinely inspired with a true love of true philosophy.   That either or both of these alternatives are
impossible, I see no reason to affirm: if they were so,
we might indeed be justly ridiculed as dreamers and
visionaries.   Am I not right?

Quite right.

If then, in the countless ages of the past, or at the
present hour in some foreign clime which is far away
and beyond our ken, the perfected philosopher is or
has been or hereafter shall be compelled by a superior
power to have the charge of the State, we are ready to
assert to the death, that this our constitution has been,
and is — yea, and will be whenever the Muse of Phi-

[1] Reading κατηκόῳ or κατηκόοις.

losophy is queen. There is no impossibility in all this; that there is a difficulty, we acknowledge ourselves.

My opinion agrees with yours, he said.

But do you mean to say that this is not the opinion of the multitude?

I should imagine not, he replied.

O my friend, I said, do not attack the multitude: they will change their minds, if, not in an aggressive spirit, but gently and with the view of soothing them and removing their dislike of over-education, you show them your philosophers as they really are and describe as you were just now doing their character and profession, and then mankind will see that he of whom you are speaking is not such as they supposed — if they view him in this new light, they will surely change their notion of him, and answer in another strain.[1] Who can be at enmity with one who loves them, who that is himself gentle and free from envy will be jealous of one in whom there is no jealousy? Nay, let me answer for you, that in a few this harsh temper may be found but not in the majority of mankind.

I quite agree with you, he said.

And do you not also think, as I do, that the harsh feeling which the many entertain towards philosophy originates in the pretenders, who rush in uninvited, and are always abusing them, and finding fault with them, who make persons instead of things the theme of their conversation? and nothing can be more unbecoming in philosophers than this.

It is most unbecoming.

For he, Adeimantus, whose mind is fixed upon true being, has surely no time to look down upon the

---

[1] Reading ἢ καὶ ἐὰν οὕτω θεῶνται without a question, and ἀλλοίαν τοι : or, retaining the question and taking ἀλλοίαν δόξαν in a new sense: " Do you mean to say really that, viewing him in this light, they will be of another mind from yours, and answer in another strain? "

affairs of earth, or to be filled with malice and envy, contending against men; his eye is ever directed towards things fixed and immutable, which he sees neither injuring nor injured by one another, but all in order moving according to reason; these he imitates, and to these he will, as far as he can, conform himself. Can a man help imitating that with which he holds reverential converse?

Impossible.

And the philosopher holding converse with the divine order, becomes orderly and divine, as far as the nature of man allows; but like every one else, he will suffer from detraction.

Of course.

And if a necessity be laid upon him of fashioning, not only himself, but human nature generally, whether in States or individuals, into that which he beholds elsewhere, will he, think you, be an unskilful artificer of justice, temperance, and every civil virtue?

Anything but unskilful.

And if the world perceives that what we are saying about him is the truth, will they be angry with philosophy? Will they disbelieve us, when we tell them that no State can be happy which is not designed by artists who imitate the heavenly pattern?

They will not be angry if they understand, he said. But how will they draw out the plan of which you are speaking?

They will begin by taking the State and the manners of men, from which, as from a tablet, they will rub out the picture, and leave a clean surface. This is no easy task. But whether easy or not, herein will lie the difference between them and every other legislator, — they will have nothing to do either with individual or State, and will inscribe no laws, until they have either found, or themselves made, a clean surface.

They will be very right, he said.

Having effected this, they will proceed to trace an outline of the constitution?

No doubt.

And when they are filling in the work, as I conceive, they will often turn their eyes upwards and downwards: I mean that they will first look at absolute justice and beauty and temperance, and again at the human copy; and will mingle and temper the various elements of life into the image of a man; and this they will conceive according to that other image, which, when existing among men, Homer calls the form and likeness of God.

Very true, he said.

And one feature they will erase, and another they will put in, until they have made the ways of men, as far as possible, agreeable to the ways of God?

Indeed, he said, in no way could they make a fairer picture.

And now, I said, are we beginning to persuade those whom you described as rushing at us with might and main, that the painter of constitutions is such an one as we were praising; at whom they were so very indignant because to his hands we committed the State; and are they growing a little calmer at what they have just heard?

Much calmer, if there is any sense in them.

Why, where can they still find any ground for objection? Will they doubt that the philosopher is a lover of truth and being?

They would not be so unreasonable.

Or that his nature, being such as we have delineated, is akin to the highest good?

Neither can they doubt this.

But again, will they tell us that such a nature,

placed under favorable circumstances, will not be perfectly good and wise if any ever was? Or will they prefer those whom we have rejected?

Surely not.

Then will they still be angry at our saying, that, until philosophers bear rule, States and individuals will have no rest from evil, nor will this our imaginary State ever be realized?

I think that they will be less angry.

Shall we assume that they are not only less angry but quite gentle, and that they have been converted and for very shame, if for no other reason, can not refuse to come to terms?

By all means, he said.

Then let us suppose that the reconciliation has been effected. Will any one deny the other point, that there may be sons of kings or princes who are by nature philosophers?

Surely no man, he said.

And when they have come into being will any one say that they must of necessity be destroyed; that they can hardly be saved is not denied even by us; but that in the whole course of ages no single one of them can escape — who will venture to affirm this?

Who indeed!

But, said I, one is enough; let there be one man who has a city obedient to his will, and he might bring into existence the ideal polity about which the world is so incredulous.

Yes, one is enough.

The ruler may impose the laws and institutions which we have been describing, and the citizens may possibly be willing to obey them?

Certainly.

And that others should approve, of what we ap= prove, is no miracle or impossibility?

I think not.

But we have sufficiently shown, in what has preceded, that all this, if only possible, is assuredly for the best.

We have.

And now we say not only that our laws, if they could be enacted, would be for the best, but also that the enactment of them, though difficult, is not impossible.

Very good.

And so with pain and toil we have reached the end of one subject, but more remains to be discussed; — how and by what studies and pursuits will the saviors of the constitution be created, and at what ages are they to apply themselves to their several studies?

Certainly.

I omitted the troublesome business of the possession of women, and the procreation of children, and the appointment of the rulers, because I knew that the perfect State would be eyed with jealousy and was difficult of attainment; but that piece of cleverness was not of much service to me, for I had to discuss them all the same. The women and children are now disposed of, but the other question of the rulers must be investigated from the very beginning. We were saying, as you will remember, that they were to be lovers of their country, tried by the test of pleasures and pains, and neither in hardships, nor in dangers, nor at any other critical moment were to lose their patriotism — he was to be rejected who failed, but he who always came forth pure, like gold tried in the refiner's fire, was to be made a ruler, and to receive honors and rewards in life and after death. This was the sort of thing which was being said, and then the argument turned aside and veiled her face; not liking to stir the question which has now arisen.

I perfectly remember, he said.

Yes, my friend, I said, and I then shrank from hazarding the bold word; but now let me dare to say — that the perfect guardian must be a philosopher.

Yes, he said, let that be affirmed.

And do not suppose that there will be many of them; for the gifts which were deemed by us to be essential rarely grow together; they are mostly found in shreds and patches.

What do you mean? he said.

You are aware, I replied, that quick intelligence, memory, sagacity, cleverness, and similar qualities, do not often grow together, and that persons who possess them and are at the same time high-spirited and magnanimous are not so constituted by nature as to live orderly and in a peaceful and settled manner; they are driven any way by their impulses, and all solid principle goes out of them.

Very true, he said.

On the other hand, those steadfast natures which can better be depended upon, which in a battle are impregnable to fear and immovable, are equally immovable when there is anything to be learned; they are always in a torpid state, and are apt to yawn and go to sleep over any intellectual toil.

Quite true.

And yet we were saying that both qualities were necessary in those to whom the higher education is to be imparted, and who are to share in any office or command.

Certainly, he said.

And will they be a class which is rarely found?

Yes, indeed.

Then the aspirant must not only be tested in those labors and dangers and pleasures which we mentioned before, but there is another kind of probation which we did not mention — he must be exercised also in many kinds of knowledge, to see whether the soul will be able to endure the highest of all, or will faint under them, as in any other studies and exercises.

Yes, he said, you are quite right in testing him. But what do you mean by the highest of all knowledge?

You may remember, I said, that we divided the soul into three parts; and distinguished the several natures of justice, temperance, courage, and wisdom?

Indeed, he said, if I had forgotten, I should not deserve to hear more.

And do you remember the word of caution which preceded the discussion of them? [1]

To what do you refer?

We were saying, if I am not mistaken, that he who wanted to see them in their perfect beauty must take a longer and more circuitous way, at the end of which they would appear; but that we could add on a popular exposition of them on a level with the discussion which had preceded. And you replied that such an exposition would be enough for you, and so the inquiry was continued in what to me seemed to be a very inaccurate manner; whether you were satisfied or not, it is for you to say.

Yes, he said, I thought and the others thought that you gave us a fair measure of truth.

But, my friend, I said, a measure of such things which in any degree falls short of the whole truth is not fair measure; for nothing imperfect is the measure of anything, although persons are too apt to be contented and think that they need search no further.

Not an uncommon case when people are indolent.

Yes, I said; and there can not be any worse fault in a guardian of the State and of the laws.

[1] Cp. IV 435 D.

True.

The guardian then, I said, must be required to take the longer circuit, and toil at learning as well as at gymnastics, or he will never reach the highest knowledge of all which, as we were just now saying, is his proper calling.

What, he said, is there a knowledge still higher than this — higher than justice and the other virtues?

Yes, I said, there is. And of the virtues too we must behold not the outline merely, as at present — nothing short of the most finished picture should satisfy us. When little things are elaborated with an infinity of pains, in order that they may appear in their full beauty and utmost clearness, how ridiculous that we should not think the highest truths worthy of attaining the highest accuracy!

A right noble thought; [1] but do you suppose that we shall refrain from asking you what is this highest knowledge?

Nay, I said, ask if you will; but I am certain that you have heard the answer many times, and now you either do not understand me or, as I rather think, you are disposed to be troublesome; for you have often been told that the idea of good is the highest knowledge, and that all other things become useful and advantageous only by their use of this. You can hardly be ignorant that of this I was about to speak, concerning which, as you have often heard me say, we know so little; and, without which, any other knowledge or possession of any kind will profit us nothing. Do you think that the possession of all other things is of any value if we do not possess the good? or the knowledge of all other things if we have no knowledge of beauty and goodness?

---

[1] Or, separating καὶ μάλα from ἄξιον, "True, he said, and a noble thought." or ἄξιον τὸ διανόημα may be a gloss.

Assuredly not.

You are further aware that most people affirm pleasure to be the good, but the finer sort of wits say it is knowledge?

Yes.

And you are aware too that the latter can not explain what they mean by knowledge, but are obliged after all to say knowledge of the good?

How ridiculous!

Yes, I said, that they should begin by reproaching us with our ignorance of the good, and then presume our knowledge of it — for the good they define to be knowledge of the good, just as if we understood them when they use the term " good " — this is of course ridiculous.

Most true, he said.

And those who make pleasure their good are in equal perplexity; for they are compelled to admit that there are bad pleasures as well as good.

Certainly.

And therefore to acknowledge that bad and good are the same?

True.

There can be no doubt about the numerous difficulties in which this question is involved.

There can be none.

Further, do we not see that many are willing to do or to have or to seem to be what is just and honorable without the reality; but no one is satisfied with the appearance of good — the reality is what they seek; in the case of the good, appearance is despised by every one.

Very true, he said.

Of this then, which every soul of man pursues and makes the end of all his actions, having a presentiment that there is such an end, and yet hesitating because neither knowing the nature nor having the same assurance of this as of other things, and therefore losing whatever good there is in other things, — of a principle such and so great as this ought the best men in our State, to whom everything is entrusted, to be in the darkness of ignorance?

Certainly not, he said.

I am sure, I said, that he who does not know how the beautiful and the just are likewise good will be but a sorry guardian of them; and I suspect that no one who is ignorant of the good will have a true knowledge of them.

That, he said, is a shrewd suspicion of yours.

And if we only have a guardian who has this knowledge our State will be perfectly ordered?

Of course, he replied; but I wish that you would tell me whether you conceive this supreme principle of the good to be knowledge or pleasure, or different from either?

Aye, I said, I knew all along that a fastidious gentleman [1] like you would not be contented with the thoughts of other people about these matters.

True, Socrates; but I must say that one who like you has passed a lifetime in the study of philosophy should not be always repeating the opinions of others, and never telling his own.

Well, but has any one a right to say positively what he does not know?

Not, he said, with the assurance of positive certainty; he has no right to do that: but he may say what he thinks, as a matter of opinion.

And do you not know, I said, that all mere opinions are bad, and the best of them blind? You would not deny that those who have any true notion without

[1] Reading ἀνὴρ καλός: or reading ἀνὴρ καλῶς, " I quite well knew from the very first, that you, etc."

intelligence are only like blind men who feel their way along the road?

Very true.

And do you wish to behold what is blind and crooked and base, when others will tell you of brightness and beauty?

Still, I must implore you, Socrates, said Glaucon, not to turn away just as you are reaching the goal; if you will only give such an explanation of the good as you have already given of justice and temperance and the other virtues, we shall be satisfied.

Yes, my friend, and I shall be at least equally satisfied, but I can not help fearing that I shall fail, and that my indiscreet zeal will bring ridicule upon me. No, sweet sirs, let us not at present ask what is the actual nature of the good, for to reach what is now in my thoughts would be an effort too great for me. But of the child of the good who is likest him, I would fain speak, if I could be sure that you wished to hear — otherwise, not.

By all means, he said, tell us about the child, and you shall remain in our debt for the account of the parent.

I do indeed wish, I replied, that I could pay, and you receive, the account of the parent, and not, as now, of the offspring only; take, however, this latter by way of interest,[1] and at the same time have a care that I do not render a false account, although I have no intention of deceiving you.

Yes, we will take all the care that we can: proceed.

Yes, I said, but I must first come to an understanding with you, and remind you of what I have mentioned in the course of this discussion, and at many other times.

What?

The old story, that there is a many beautiful and a

[1] A play upon τόκος, which means both " offspring " and " interest "

many good, and so of other things which we describe
and define; to all of them the term " many " is applied.

True, he said.

And there is an absolute beauty and an absolute
good, and of other things to which the term " many "
is applied there is an absolute; for they may be
brought under a single idea, which is called the essence of each.

Very true.

The many, as we say, are seen but not known, and
the ideas are known but not seen.

Exactly.

And what is the organ with which we see the visible
things?

The sight, he said.

And with the hearing, I said, we hear, and with the
other senses perceive the other objects of sense?

True.

But have you remarked that sight is by far the
most costly and complex piece of workmanship which
the artificer of the senses ever contrived?

No, I never have, he said.

Then reflect: has the ear or voice need of any third
or additional nature in order that the one may be able
to hear and the other to be heard?

Nothing of the sort.

No, indeed, I replied; and the same is true of most,
if not all, the other senses — you would not say that
any of them requires such an addition?

Certainly not.

But you see that without the addition of some other
nature there is no seeing or being seen?

How do you mean?

Sight being, as I conceive, in the eyes, and he who
has eyes wanting to see; color being also present in

them, still unless there be a third nature specially adapted to the purpose, the owner of the eyes will see nothing and the colors will be invisible.

Of what nature are you speaking?

Of that which you term light, I replied.

True, he said.

Noble, then, is the bond which links together sight and visibility, and great beyond other bonds by no small difference of nature; for light is their bond, and light is no ignoble thing?

Nay, he said, the reverse of ignoble.

And which, I said, of the gods in heaven would you say was the lord of this element? Whose is that light which makes the eye to see perfectly and the visible to appear?

You mean the sun, as you and all mankind say.

May not the relation of sight to this deity be described as follows?

How?

Neither sight nor the eye in which sight resides is the sun?

No.

Yet of all the organs of sense the eye is the most like the sun?

By far the most like.

And the power which the eye possesses is a sort of effluence which is dispensed from the sun?

Exactly.

Then the sun is not sight, but the author of sight who is recognized by sight?

True, he said.

And this is he whom I call the child of the good, whom the good begat in his own likeness, to be in the visible world, in relation to sight and the things of sight, what the good is in the intellectual world in relation to mind and the things of mind:

Will you be a little more explicit? he said.

Why, you know, I said, that the eyes, when a person directs them towards objects on which the light of day is no longer shining, but the moon and stars only, see dimly, and are nearly blind; they seem to have no clearness of vision in them?

Very true.

But when they are directed towards objects on which the sun shines, they see clearly and there is sight in them?

Certainly.

And the soul is like the eye: when resting upon that on which truth and being shine, the soul perceives and understands, and is radiant with intelligence; but when turned towards the twilight of becoming and perishing, then she has opinion only, and goes blinking about, and is first of one opinion and then of another, and seems to have no intelligence?

Just so.

Now, that which imparts truth to the known and the power of knowing to the knower is what I would have you term the idea of good, and this you will deem to be the cause of science,[1] and of truth in so far as the latter becomes the subject of knowledge; beautiful too, as are both truth and knowledge, you will be right in esteeming this other nature as more beautiful than either; and, as in the previous instance, light and sight may be truly said to be like the sun, and yet not to be the sun, so in this other sphere, science and truth may be deemed to be like the good, but not the good; the good has a place of honor yet higher.

What a wonder of beauty that must be, he said, which is the author of science and truth, and yet surpasses them in beauty; for you surely can not mean to say that pleasure is the good?

[1] Reading διανοοῦ.

God forbid, I replied; but may I ask you to consider the image in another point of view?

In what point of view?

You would say, would you not, that the sun is not only the author of visibility in all visible things, but of generation and nourishment and growth, though he himself is not generation?

Certainly.

In like manner the good may be said to be not only the author of knowledge to all things known, but of their being and essence, and yet the good is not essence, but far exceeds essence in dignity and power.

Glaucon said, with a ludicrous earnestness: By the light of heaven, how amazing!

Yes, I said, and the exaggeration may be set down to you; for you made me utter my fancies.

And pray continue to utter them; at any rate let us hear if there is anything more to be said about the similitude of the sun.

Yes, I said, there is a great deal more.

Then omit nothing, however slight.

I will do my best, I said; but I should think that a great deal will have to be omitted.

I hope not, he said.

You have to imagine, then, that there are two ruling powers, and that one of them is set over the intellectual world, the other over the visible. I do not say heaven, lest you should fancy that I am playing upon the name (οὐρανός, ὁρατός). May I suppose that you have this distinction of the visible and intelligible fixed in your mind?

I have.

Now take a line which has been cut into two unequal [1] parts, and divide each of them again in the same proportion, and suppose the two main divisions

[1] Reading ἄνισα.

to answer, one to the visible and the other to the intelligible, and then compare the subdivisions in respect of their clearness and want of clearness, and you will find that the first section in the sphere of the visible consists of images. And by images I mean, in the first place, shadows, and in the second place, reflections in water and in solid, smooth and polished bodies and the like: Do you understand?

Yes, I understand.

Imagine, now, the other section, of which this is only the resemblance, to include the animals which we see, and everything that grows or is made.

Very good.

Would you not admit that both the sections of this division have different degrees of truth, and that the copy is to the original as the sphere of opinion is to the sphere of knowledge?

Most undoubtedly.

Next proceed to consider the manner in which the sphere of the intellectual is to be divided.

In what manner?

Thus: — There are two subdivisions, in the lower of which the soul uses the figures given by the former division as images; the inquiry can only be hypothetical, and instead of going upwards to a principle descends to the other end; in the higher of the two, the soul passes out of hypotheses, and goes up to a principle which is above hypotheses, making no use of images [1] as in the former case, but proceeding only in and through the ideas themselves.

I do not quite understand your meaning, he said.

Then I will try again; you will understand me better when I have made some preliminary remarks. You are aware that students of geometry, arithmetic, and the kindred sciences assume the odd and the even

---

[1] Reading ὥσπερ ἐκεῖνο εἰκόνων.

and the figures and three kinds of angles and the like in their several branches of science; these are their hypotheses, which they and everybody are supposed to know, and therefore they do not deign to give any account of them either to themselves or others; but they begin with them, and go on until they arrive at last, and in a consistent manner, at their conclusion?

Yes, he said, I know.

And do you not know also that although they make use of the visible forms and reason about them, they are thinking not of these, but of the ideals which they resemble; not of the figures which they draw, but of the absolute square and the absolute diameter, and so on — the forms which they draw or make, and which have shadows and reflections in water of their own, are converted by them into images, but they are really seeking to behold the things themselves, which can only be seen with the eye of the mind?

That is true.

And of this I spoke as the intelligible, although in the search after it the soul is compelled to use hypotheses; not ascending to a first principle, because she is unable to rise above the region of hypothesis, but employing the objects of which the shadows below are resemblances in their turn as images, they having in relation to the shadows and reflections of them a greater distinctness, and therefore a higher value.

I understand, he said, that you are speaking of the province of geometry and the sister arts.

And when I speak of the other division of the intelligible, you will understand me to speak of that other sort of knowledge which reason herself attains by the power of dialectic, using the hypotheses not as first principles, but only as hypotheses — that is to say, as steps and points of departure into a world which is above hypotheses, in order that she may soar beyond them to the first principle of the whole; and clinging to this and then to that which depends on this, by successive steps she descends again without the aid of any sensible object, from ideas, through ideas, and in ideas she ends.

I understand you, he replied; not perfectly, for you seem to me to be describing a task which is really tremendous; but, at any rate, I understand you to say that knowledge and being, which the science of dialectic contemplates, are clearer than the notions of the arts, as they are termed, which proceed from hypotheses only: these are also contemplated by the understanding, and not by the senses: yet, because they start from hypotheses and do not ascend to a principle, those who contemplate them appear to you not to exercise the higher reason upon them, although when a first principle is added to them they are cognizable by the higher reason. And the habit which is concerned with geometry and the cognate sciences I suppose that you would term understanding and not reason, as being intermediate between opinion and reason.

You have quite conceived my meaning, I said; and now, corresponding to these four divisions, let there be four faculties in the soul — reason answering to the highest, understanding to the second, faith (or conviction) to the third, and perception of shadows to the last — and let there be a scale of them, and let us suppose that the several faculties have clearness in the same degree that their objects have truth.

I understand, he replied, and give my assent, and accept your arrangement.

BOOK VII

AND now, I said, let me show in a figure how far
our nature is enlightened or unenlightened: — Behold! human beings living in an underground den,
which has a mouth open towards the light and reaching all along the den; here they have been from their
childhood, and have their legs and necks chained so
that they can not move, and can only see before them,
being prevented by the chains from turning round
their heads. Above and behind them a fire is blazing
at a distance, and between the fire and the prisoners
there is a raised way; and you will see, if you look, a
low wall built along the way, like the screen which
marionette players have in front of them, over which
they show the puppets.

I see.

And do you see, I said, men passing along the wall
carrying all sorts of vessels, and statues and figures
of animals made of wood and stone and various
materials, which appear over the wall? Some of them
are talking, others silent.

You have shown me a strange image, and they are
strange prisoners.

Like ourselves, I replied; and they see only their
own shadows, or the shadows of one another, which
the fire throws on the opposite wall of the cave?

True, he said; how could they see anything but the
shadows if they were never allowed to move their
heads?

And of the objects which are being carried in like
manner they would only see the shadows?

Yes, he said.

And if they were able to converse with one another, would they not suppose that they were naming what was actually before them? [1]

Very true.

And suppose further that the prison had an echo which came from the other side, would they not be sure to fancy when one of the passers-by spoke that the voice which they heard came from the passing shadow?

No question, he replied.

To them, I said, the truth would be literally nothing but the shadows of the images.

That is certain.

And now look again, and see what will naturally follow if the prisoners are released and disabused of their error. At first, when any of them is liberated and compelled suddenly to stand up and turn his neck round and walk and look towards the light, he will suffer sharp pains; the glare will distress him, and he will be unable to see the realities of which in his former state he had seen the shadows; and then conceive some one saying to him, that what he saw before was an illusion, but that now, when he is approaching nearer to being and his eye is turned towards more real existence, he has a clearer vision, — what will be his reply? And you may further imagine that his instructor is pointing to the objects as they pass and requiring him to name them, — will he not be perplexed? Will he not fancy that the shadows which he formerly saw are truer than the objects which are now shown to him?

Far truer.

And if he is compelled to look straight at the light, will he not have a pain in his eyes which will make him

[1] Reading παρόντα.

turn away to take refuge in the objects of vision which he can see, and which he will conceive to be in reality clearer than the things which are now being shown to him?

True, he said.

And suppose once more, that he is reluctantly dragged up a steep and rugged ascent, and held fast until he is forced into the presence of the sun himself, is he not likely to be pained and irritated? When he approaches the light his eyes will be dazzled, and he will not be able to see anything at all of what are now called realities.

Not all in a moment, he said.

He will require to grow accustomed to the sight of the upper world. And first he will see the shadows best, next the reflections of men and other objects in the water, and then the objects themselves; then he will gaze upon the light of the moon and the stars and the spangled heaven; and he will see the sky and the stars by night better than the sun or the light of the sun by day?

Certainly.

Last of all he will be able to see the sun, and not mere reflections of him in the water, but he will see him in his own proper place, and not in another; and he will contemplate him as he is.

Certainly.

He will then proceed to argue that this is he who gives the season and the years, and is the guardian of all that is in the visible world, and in a certain way the cause of all things which he and his fellows have been accustomed to behold?

Clearly, he said, he would first see the sun and then reason about him.

And when he remembered his old habitation, and the wisdom of the den and his fellow-prisoners, do

you not suppose that he would felicitate himself on
the change, and pity them?

Certainly, he would.

And if they were in the habit of conferring honors
among themselves on those who were quickest to observe the passing shadows and to remark which of
them went before, and which followed after, and
which were together; and who were therefore best
able to draw conclusions as to the future, do you think
that he would care for such honors and glories, or
envy the possessors of them? Would he not say with
Homer,

" Better to be the poor servant of a poor master,"

and to endure anything, rather than think as they do
and live after their manner?

Yes, he said, I think that he would rather suffer
anything than entertain these false notions and live
in this miserable manner.

Imagine once more, I said, such an one coming
suddenly out of the sun to be replaced in his old situation; would he not be certain to have his eyes full of
darkness?

To be sure, he said.

And if there were a contest, and he had to compete
in measuring the shadows with the prisoners who had
never moved out of the den, while his sight was still
weak, and before his eyes had become steady (and the
time which would be needed to acquire this new habit
of sight might be very considerable), would he not be
ridiculous? Men would say of him that up he went
and down he came without his eyes ; and that it was
better not even to think of ascending; and if any one
tried to loose another and lead him up to the light,
let them only catch the offender, and they would put
him to death.

No question, he said.

This entire allegory, I said, you may now append, dear Glaucon, to the previous argument; the prison-house is the world of sight, the light of the fire is the sun, and you will not misapprehend me if you interpret the journey upwards to be the ascent of the soul into the intellectual world according to my poor belief, which, at your desire, I have expressed — whether rightly or wrongly God knows. But, whether true or false, my opinion is that in the world of knowledge the idea of good appears last of all, and is seen only with an effort; and, when seen, is also inferred to be the universal author of all things beautiful and right, parent of light and of the lord of light in this visible world, and the immediate source of reason and truth in the intellectual; and that this is the power upon which he who would act rationally either in public or private life must have his eye fixed.

I agree, he said, as far as I am able to understand you.

Moreover, I said, you must not wonder that those who attain to this beatific vision are unwilling to descend to human affairs; for their souls are ever hastening into the upper world where they desire to dwell; which desire of theirs is very natural, if our allegory may be trusted.

Yes, very natural.

And is there anything surprising in one who passes from divine contemplations to the evil state of man, misbehaving himself in a ridiculous manner; if, while his eyes are blinking and before he has become accustomed to the surrounding darkness, he is compelled to fight in courts of law, or in other places, about the images or the shadows of images of justice, and is endeavoring to meet the conceptions of those who have never yet seen absolute justice?

Anything but surprising, he replied.

Any one who has common sense will remember that the bewilderments of the eyes are of two kinds, and arise from two causes, either from coming out of the light or from going into the light, which is true of the mind's eye, quite as much as of the bodily eye; and he who remembers this when he sees any one whose vision is perplexed and weak, will not be too ready to laugh; he will first ask whether that soul of man has come out of the brighter life, and is unable to see because unaccustomed to the dark, or having turned from darkness to the day is dazzled by excess of light. And he will count the one happy in his condition and state of being, and he will pity the other; or, if he have a mind to laugh at the soul which comes from below into the light, there will be more reason in this than in the laugh which greets him who returns from above out of the light into the den.

That, he said, is a very just distinction.

But then, if I am right, certain professors of education must be wrong when they say that they can put a knowledge into the soul which was not there before, like sight into blind eyes.

They undoubtedly say this, he replied.

Whereas, our argument shows that the power and capacity of learning exists in the soul already; and that just as the eye was unable to turn from darkness to light without the whole body, so too the instrument of knowledge can only by the movement of the whole soul be turned from the world of becoming into that of being, and learn by degrees to endure the sight of being, and of the brightest and best of being, or in other words, of the good.

Very true.

And must there not be some art which will effect conversion in the easiest and quickest manner; not implanting the faculty of sight, for that exists already, but has been turned in the wrong direction, and is looking away from the truth?

Yes, he said, such an art may be presumed.

And whereas the other so-called virtues of the soul seem to be akin to bodily qualities, for even when they are not originally innate they can be implanted later by habit and exercise, the virtue of wisdom more than anything else contains a divine element which always remains, and by this conversion is rendered useful and profitable; or, on the other hand, hurtful and useless. Did you never observe the narrow intelligence flashing from the keen eye of a clever rogue — how eager he is, how clearly his paltry soul sees the way to his end; he is the reverse of blind, but his keen eye-sight is forced into the service of evil, and he is mischievous in proportion to his cleverness?

Very true, he said.

But what if there had been a circumcision of such natures in the days of their youth; and they had been severed from those sensual pleasures, such as eating and drinking, which, like leaden weights, were attached to them at their birth, and which drag them down and turn the vision of their souls upon the things that are below — if, I say, they had been released from these impediments and turned in the opposite direction, the very same faculty in them would have seen the truth as keenly as they see what their eyes are turned to now.

Very likely.

Yes, I said; and there is another thing which is likely, or rather a necessary inference from what has preceded, that neither the uneducated and uninformed of the truth, nor yet those who never make an end of their education, will be able ministers of State; not the former, because they have no single aim of duty which is the rule of all their actions, private as well as public; nor the latter, because they will not act at all except upon compulsion, fancying that they are already dwelling apart in the islands of the blest.

Very true, he replied.

Then, I said, the business of us who are the founders of the State will be to compel the best minds to attain that knowledge which we have already shown to be the greatest of all — they must continue to ascend until they arrive at the good; but when they have ascended and seen enough we must not allow them to do as they do now.

What do you mean?

I mean that they remain in the upper world: but this must not be allowed; they must be made to descend again among the prisoners in the den, and partake of their labors and honors, whether they are worth having or not.

But is not this unjust? he said; ought we to give them a worse life, when they might have a better?

You have again forgotten, my friend, I said, the intention of the legislator, who did not aim at making any one class in the State happy above the rest; the happiness was to be in the whole State, and he held the citizens together by persuasion and necessity, making them benefactors of the State, and therefore benefactors of one another; to this end he created them, not to please themselves, but to be his instruments in binding up the State.

True, he said, I had forgotten.

Observe, Glaucon, that there will be no injustice in compelling our philosophers to have a care and providence of others; we shall explain to them that in other States, men of their class are not obliged to share in the toils of politics: and this is reasonable, for they grow up at their own sweet will, and the government would rather not have them. Being self-taught, they can not be expected to show any gratitude for a culture which they have never received. But we have brought you into the world to be rulers of the hive, kings of yourselves and of the other citizens, and have educated you far better and more perfectly than they have been educated, and you are better able to share in the double duty. Wherefore each of you, when his turn comes, must go down to the general underground abode, and get the habit of seeing in the dark. When you have acquired the habit, you will see ten thousand times better than the inhabitants of the den, and you will know what the several images are, and what they represent, because you have seen the beautiful and just and good in their truth. And thus our State, which is also yours, will be a reality, and not a dream only, and will be administered in a spirit unlike that of other States, in which men fight with one another about shadows only and are distracted in the struggle for power, which in their eyes is a great good. Whereas the truth is that the State in which the rulers are most reluctant to govern is always the best and most quietly governed, and the State in which they are most eager, the worst.

Quite true, he replied.

And will our pupils, when they hear this, refuse to take their turn at the toils of State, when they are allowed to spend the greater part of their time with one another in the heavenly light?

Impossible, he answered; for they are just men, and the commands which we impose upon them are just; there can be no doubt that every one of them will take office as a stern necessity, and not after the fashion of our present rulers of State.

Yes, my friend, I said; and there lies the point. You must contrive for your future rulers another and a better life than that of a ruler, and then you may have a well-ordered State; for only in the State which offers this, will they rule who are truly rich, not in silver and gold, but in virtue and wisdom, which are the true blessings of life. Whereas if they go to the administration of public affairs, poor and hungering after their own private advantage, thinking that hence they are to snatch the chief good, order there can never be; for they will be fighting about office, and the civil and domestic broils which thus arise will be the ruin of the rulers themselves and of the whole State.

Most true, he replied.

And the only life which looks down upon the life of political ambition is that of true philosophy. Do you know of any other?

Indeed, I do not, he said.

And those who govern ought not to be lovers of the task? For, if they are, there will be rival lovers, and they will fight.

No question.

Who then are those whom we shall compel to be guardians? Surely they will be the men who are wisest about affairs of State, and by whom the State is best administered, and who at the same time have other honors and another and a better life than that of politics?

They are the men, and I will choose them, he replied.

And now shall we consider in what way such guardians will be produced, and how they are to be brought from darkness to light, — as some are said to have ascended from the world below to the gods?

By all means, he replied.

The process, I said, is not the turning over of an oyster-shell,[1] but the turning round of a soul passing from a day which is little better than night to the true day of being, that is, the ascent from below,[2] which we affirm to be true philosophy?

Quite so.

And should we not inquire what sort of knowledge has the power of effecting such a change?

Certainly.

What sort of knowledge is there which would draw the soul from becoming to being? And another consideration has just occurred to me: You will remember that our young men are to be warrior athletes?

Yes, that was said.

Then this new kind of knowledge must have an additional quality?

What quality?

Usefulness in war.

Yes, if possible.

There were two parts in our former scheme of education, were there not?

Just so.

There was gymnastic which presided over the growth and decay of the body, and may therefore be regarded as having to do with generation and corruption?

True.

Then that is not the knowledge which we are seeking to discover?

No.

But what do you say of music, what also entered to a certain extent into our former scheme?

Music, he said, as you will remember, was the

---

[1] In allusion to a game in which two parties fled or pursued according as an oyster-shell which was thrown into the air fell with the dark or light side uppermost. [2] Reading οὖσαν ἐπάνοδον.

counterpart of gymnastic, and trained the guardians by the influences of habit, by harmony making them harmonious, by rhythm rhythmical, but not giving them science; and the words, whether fabulous or possibly true, had kindred elements of rhythm and harmony in them. But in music there was nothing which tended to that good which you are now seeking.

You are most accurate, I said, in your recollection; in music there certainly was nothing of the kind. But what branch of knowledge is there, my dear Glaucon, which is of the desired nature; since all the useful arts were reckoned mean by us?

Undoubtedly; and yet if music and gymnastic are excluded, and the arts are also excluded, what remains?

Well, I said, there may be nothing left of our special subjects; and then we shall have to take something which is not special, but of universal application.

What may that be?

A something which all arts and sciences and intelligences use in common, and which every one first has to learn among the elements of education.

What is that?

The little matter of distinguishing one, two, and three — in a word, number and calculation: — do not all arts and sciences necessarily partake of them?

Yes.

Then the art of war partakes of them?

To be sure.

Then Palamedes, whenever he appears in tragedy, proves Agamemnon ridiculously unfit to be a general. Did you never remark how he declares that he had invented number, and had numbered the ships and set in array the ranks of the army at Troy; which implies that they had never been numbered before, and

Agamemnon must be supposed literally to have been incapable of counting his own feet — how could he if he was ignorant of number? And if that is true, what sort of general must he have been?

I should say a very strange one, if this was as you say.

Can we deny that a warrior should have a knowledge of arithmetic?

Certainly he should, if he is to have the smallest understanding of military tactics, or indeed, I should rather say, if he is to be a man at all.

I should like to know whether you have the same notion which I have of this study?

What is your notion?

It appears to me to be a study of the kind which we are seeking, and which leads naturally to reflection, but never to have been rightly used; for the true use of it is simply to draw the soul towards being.

Will you explain your meaning? he said.

I will try, I said; and I wish you would share the inquiry with me, and say " yes " or " no " when I attempt to distinguish in my own mind what branches of knowledge have this attracting power, in order that we may have clearer proof that arithmetic is, as I suspect, one of them.

Explain, he said.

I mean to say that objects of sense are of two kinds; some of them do not invite thought because the sense is an adequate judge of them; while in the case of other objects sense is so untrustworthy that further inquiry is imperatively demanded.

You are clearly referring, he said, to the manner in which the senses are imposed upon by distance, and by painting in light and shade.

No, I said, that is not at all my meaning.

Then what is your meaning?

When speaking of uninviting objects, I mean those which do not pass from one sensation to the opposite; inviting objects are those which do; in this latter case the sense coming upon the object, whether at a distance or near, gives no more vivid idea of anything in particular than of its opposite. An illustration will make my meaning clearer: — here are three fingers — a little finger, a second finger, and a middle finger.

Very good.

You may suppose that they are seen quite close: And here comes the point.

What is it?

Each of them equally appears a finger, whether seen in the middle or at the extremity, whether white or black, or thick or thin — it makes no difference; a finger is a finger all the same. In these cases a man is not compelled to ask of thought the question what is a finger? for the sight never intimates to the mind that a finger is other than a finger.

True.

And therefore, I said, as we might expect, there is nothing here which invites or excites intelligence.

There is not, he said.

But is this equally true of the greatness and smallness of the fingers? Can sight adequately perceive them? and is no difference made by the circumstance that one of the fingers is in the middle and another at the extremity? And in like manner does the touch adequately perceive the qualities of thickness or thinness, of softness or hardness? And so of the other senses; do they give perfect intimations of such matters? Is not their mode of operation on this wise — the sense which is concerned with the quality of hardness is necessarily concerned also with the quality of softness, and only intimates to the soul that the same thing is felt to be both hard and soft?

You are quite right, he said.

And must not the soul be perplexed at this intimation which the sense gives of a hard which is also soft? What, again, is the meaning of light and heavy, if that which is light is also heavy, and that which is heavy, light?

Yes, he said, these intimations which the soul receives are very curious and require to be explained.

Yes, I said, and in these perplexities the soul naturally summons to her aid calculation and intelligence, that she may see whether the several objects announced to her are one or two.

True.

And if they turn out to be two, is not each of them one and different?

Certainly.

And if each is one, and both are two, she will conceive the two as in a state of division, for if they were undivided they could only be conceived of as one?

True.

The eye certainly did see both small and great, but only in a confused manner; they were not distinguished.

Yes.

Whereas the thinking mind, intending to light up the chaos, was compelled to reverse the process, and look at small and great as separate and not confused.

Very true.

Was not this the beginning of the inquiry "What is great?" and "What is small?"

Exactly so.

And thus arose the distinction of the visible and the intelligible.

Most true.

This was what I meant when I spoke of impressions which invited the intellect, or the reverse — those which are simultaneous with opposite impressions, invite thought; those which are simultaneous do not.

I understand, he said, and agree with you.

And to which class do unity and number belong?

I do not know, he replied.

Think a little and you will see that what has preceded will supply the answer; for if simple unity could be adequately perceived by the sight or by any other sense, then, as we were saying in the case of the finger, there would be nothing to attract towards being; but when there is some contradiction always present, and one is the reverse of one and involves the conception of plurality, then thought begins to be aroused within us, and the soul perplexed and wanting to arrive at a decision asks " What is absolute unity? " This is the way in which the study of the one has a power of drawing and converting the mind to the contemplation of true being.

And surely, he said, this occurs notably in the case of one; for we see the same thing to be both one and infinite in multitude?

Yes, I said; and this being true of one must be equally true of all number?

Certainly.

And all arithmetic and calculation have to do with number?

Yes.

And they appear to lead the mind towards truth?

Yes, in a very remarkable manner.

Then this is knowledge of the kind for which we are seeking, having a double use, military and philosophical; for the man of war must learn the art of number or he will not know how to array his troops, and the philosopher also, because he has to rise out of the sea of change and lay hold of true being, and therefore he must be an arithmetician.

That is true.

And our guardian is both warrior and philosopher?

Certainly.

Then this is a kind of knowledge which legislation may fitly prescribe; and we must endeavor to persuade those who are to be the principal men of our State to go and learn arithmetic, not as amateurs, but they must carry on the study until they see the nature of numbers with the mind only; nor again, like merchants or retail-traders, with a view to buying or selling, but for the sake of their military use, and of the soul herself; and because this will be the easiest way for her to pass from becoming to truth and being.

That is excellent, he said.

Yes, I said, and now having spoken of it, I must add how charming the science is! and in how many ways it conduces to our desired end, if pursued in the spirit of a philosopher, and not of a shopkeeper!

How do you mean?

I mean, as I was saying, that arithmetic has a very great and elevating effect, compelling the soul to reason about abstract number, and rebelling against the introduction of visible or tangible objects into the argument. You know how steadily the masters of the art repel and ridicule any one who attempts to divide absolute unity when he is calculating, and if you divide, they multiply,[1] taking care that one shall continue one and not become lost in fractions.

That is very true.

Now, suppose a person were to say to them: O my

[1] Meaning either (1) that they integrate the number because they deny the possibility of fractions; or (2) that division is regarded by them as a process of multiplication, for the fractions of one continue to be units.

friends, what are these wonderful numbers about which you are reasoning, in which, as you say, there is a unity such as you demand, and each unit is equal, invariable, indivisible, — what would they answer?

They would answer, as I should conceive, that they were speaking of those numbers which can only be realized in thought.

Then you see that this knowledge may be truly called necessary, necessitating as it clearly does the use of the pure intelligence in the attainment of pure truth?

Yes; that is a marked characteristic of it.

And have you further observed, that those who have a natural talent for calculation are generally quick at every other kind of knowledge; and even the dull, if they have had an arithmetical training, although they may derive no other advantage from it, always become much quicker than they would otherwise have been.

Very true, he said.

And indeed, you will not easily find a more difficult study, and not many as difficult.

You will not.

And, for all these reasons, arithmetic is a kind of knowledge in which the best natures should be trained, and which must not be given up.

I agree.

Let this then be made one of our subjects of education. And next, shall we inquire whether the kindred science also concerns us?

You mean geometry?

Exactly so.

Clearly, he said, we are concerned with that part of geometry which relates to war; for in pitching a camp, or taking up a position, or closing or extending the lines of an army, or any other military manœuvre,

whether in actual battle or on a march, it will make
all the difference whether a general is or is not a
geometrician.

Yes, I said, but for that purpose a very little of
either geometry or calculation will be enough; the
question relates rather to the greater and more advanced part of geometry — whether that tends in any
degree to make more easy the vision of the idea of
good; and thither, as I was saying, all things tend
which compel the soul to turn her gaze towards that
place, where is the full perfection of being, which she
ought, by all means, to behold.

True, he said.

Then if geometry compels us to view being, it concerns us; if becoming only, it does not concern us?

Yes, that is what we assert.

Yet anybody who has the least acquaintance with
geometry will not deny that such a conception of the
science is in flat contradiction to the ordinary language of geometricians.

How so?

They have in view practice only, and are always
speaking, in a narrow and ridiculous manner, of
squaring and extending and applying and the like —
they confuse the necessities of geometry with those
of daily life; whereas knowledge is the real object
of the whole science.

Certainly, he said.

Then must not a further admission be made?

What admission?

That the knowledge at which geometry aims is
knowledge of the eternal, and not of aught perishing
and transient.

That, he replied, may be readily allowed, and is
true.

Then, my noble friend, geometry will draw the soul

towards truth, and create the spirit of philosophy, and raise up that which is now unhappily allowed to fall down.

Nothing will be more likely to have such an effect.

Then nothing should be more sternly laid down than that the inhabitants of your fair city should by all means learn geometry. Moreover the science has indirect effects, which are not small.

Of what kind? he said.

There are the military advantages of which you spoke, I said; and in all departments of knowledge, as experience proves, any one who has studied geometry is infinitely quicker of apprehension than one who has not.

Yes indeed, he said, there is an infinite difference between them.

Then shall we propose this as a second branch of knowledge which our youth will study?

Let us do so, he replied.

And suppose we make astronomy the third — what do you say?

I am strongly inclined to it, he said; the observation of the seasons and of months and years is as essential to the general as it is to the farmer or sailor.

I am amused, I said, at your fear of the world, which makes you guard against the appearance of insisting upon useless studies; and I quite admit the difficulty of believing that in every man there is an eye of the soul which, when by other pursuits lost and dimmed, is by these purified and re-illumined; and is more precious far than ten thousand bodily eyes, for by it alone is truth seen. Now there are two classes of persons: one class of those who will agree with you and will take your words as a revelation; another class to whom they will be utterly unmeaning, and who will naturally deem them to be idle tales, for they see no sort of profit which is to be obtained from them. And therefore you had better decide at once with which of the two you are proposing to argue. You will very likely say with neither, and that your chief aim in carrying on the argument is your own improvement; at the same time you do not grudge to others any benefit which they may receive.

I think that I should prefer to carry on the argument mainly on my own behalf.

Then take a step backward, for we have gone wrong in the order of the sciences.

What was the mistake? he said.

After plane geometry, I said, we proceeded at once to solids in revolution, instead of taking solids in themselves; whereas after the second dimension the third, which is concerned with cubes and dimensions of depth, ought to have followed.

That is true, Socrates; but so little seems to be known as yet about these subjects.

Why, yes, I said, and for two reasons: — in the first place, no government patronizes them; this leads to a want of energy in the pursuit of them, and they are difficult; in the second place, students can not learn them unless they have a director. But then a director can hardly be found, and even if he could, as matters now stand, the students, who are very conceited, would not attend to him. That, however, would be otherwise if the whole State became the director of these studies and gave honor to them; then disciples would want to come, and there would be continuous and earnest search, and discoveries would be made; since even now, disregarded as they are by the world, and maimed of their fair proportions, and although none of their votaries can tell the use of them, still these studies force their way by their natural charm, and very likely, if they had the help of the State, they would some day emerge into light.

Yes, he said, there is a remarkable charm in them. But I do not clearly understand the change in the order. First you began with a geometry of plane surfaces?

Yes, I said.

And you placed astronomy next, and then you made a step backward?

Yes, and I have delayed you by my hurry; the ludicrous state of solid geometry, which in natural order, should have followed, made me pass over this branch and go on to astronomy, or motion of solids.

True, he said.

Then assuming that the science now omitted would come into existence if encouraged by the State, let us go on to astronomy, which will be fourth.

The right order, he replied. And now, Socrates, as you rebuked the vulgar manner in which I praised astronomy before, my praise shall be given in your own spirit. For every one, as I think, must see that astronomy compels the soul to look upwards and leads us from this world to another.

Every one but myself, I said; to every one else this may be clear, but not to me.

And what then would you say?

I should rather say that those who elevate astronomy into philosophy appear to me to make us look downwards and not upwards.

What do you mean? he asked.

You, I replied, have in your mind a truly sublime conception of our knowledge of the things above. And I dare say that if a person were to throw his head back and study the fretted ceiling, you would still think that his mind was the percipient, and not his eyes. And you are very likely right, and I may be a simpleton: but, in my opinion, that knowledge only which is of being and of the unseen can make the soul look upwards, and whether a man gapes at the heavens or blinks on the ground, seeking to learn some particular of sense, I would deny that he can learn, for nothing of that sort is matter of science; his soul is looking downwards, not upwards, whether his way to knowledge is by water or by land, whether he floats, or only lies on his back.

I acknowledge, he said, the justice of your rebuke. Still, I should like to ascertain how astronomy can be learned in any manner more conducive to that knowledge of which we are speaking?

I will tell you, I said: The starry heaven which we behold is wrought upon a visible ground, and therefore, although the fairest and most perfect of visible things, must necessarily be deemed inferior far to the true motions of absolute swiftness and absolute slowness, which are relative to each other, and carry with them that which is contained in them, in the true number and in every true figure. Now, these are to be apprehended by reason and intelligence, but not by sight.

True, he replied.

The spangled heavens should be used as a pattern and with a view to that higher knowledge; their beauty is like the beauty of figures or pictures excellently wrought by the hand of Daedalus, or some other great artist, which we may chance to behold; any geometrician who saw them would appreciate the exquisiteness of their workmanship, but he would never dream of thinking that in them he could find the true equal or the true double, or the truth of any other proportion.

No, he replied, such an idea would be ridiculous.

And will not a true astronomer have the same feeling when he looks at the movements of the stars?

Will he not think that heaven and the things in heaven are framed by the Creator of them in the most perfect manner? But he will never imagine that the proportions of night and day, or of both to the month, or of the month to the year, or of the stars to these and to one another, and any other things that are material and visible can also be eternal and subject to no deviation — that would be absurd; and it is equally absurd to take so much pains in investigating their exact truth.

I quite agree, though I never thought of this before.

Then, I said, in astronomy, as in geometry, we should employ problems, and let the heavens alone if we would approach the subject in the right way and so make the natural gift of reason to be any of real use.

That, he said, is a work infinitely beyond our present astronomers.

Yes, I said; and there are many other things which must also have a similar extension given to them, if our legislation is to be of any value. But can you tell me of any other suitable study?

No, he said, not without thinking.

Motion, I said, has many forms, and not one only; two of them are obvious enough even to wits no better than ours; and there are others, as I imagine, which may be left to wiser persons.

But where are the two?

There is a second, I said, which is the counterpart of the one already named.

And what may that be?

The second, I said, would seem relatively to the ears to be what the first is to the eyes; for I conceive that as the eyes are designed to look up at the stars, so are the ears to hear harmonious motions; and these are sister sciences — as the Pythagoreans say, and we, Glaucon, agree with them?

Yes, he replied.

But this, I said, is a laborious study, and therefore we had better go and learn of them; and they will tell us whether there are any other applications of these sciences. At the same time, we must not lose sight of our own higher object.

What is that?

There is a perfection which all knowledge ought to reach, and which our pupils ought also to attain, and not to fall short of, as I was saying that they did in astronomy. For in the science of harmony, as you probably know, the same thing happens. The teachers of harmony compare the sounds and consonances which are heard only, and their labor, like that of the astronomers, is in vain.

Yes, by heaven! he said; and 'tis as good as a play to hear them talking about their condensed notes, as they call them; they put their ears close alongside of the strings like persons catching a sound from their neighbor's wall [1] — one set of them declaring that they distinguish an intermediate note and have found the least interval which should be the unit of measurement; the others insisting that the two sounds have passed into the same — either party setting their ears before their understanding.

You mean, I said, those gentlemen who tease and torture the strings and rack them on the pegs of the instrument: I might carry on the metaphor and speak after their manner of the blows which the plectrum gives, and make accusations against the strings, both of backwardness and forwardness to sound; but this would be tedious, and therefore I will only say that

[1] Or, "close alongside of their neighbor's instruments, as if to catch a sound from them."

these are not the men, and that I am referring to the Pythagoreans, of whom I was just now proposing to inquire about harmony. For they too are in error, like the astronomers; they investigate the numbers of the harmonies which are heard, but they never attain to problems — that is to say, they never reach the natural harmonies of number, or reflect why some numbers are harmonious and others not.

That, he said, is a thing of more than mortal knowledge.

A thing, I replied, which I would rather call useful; that is, if sought after with a view to the beautiful and good; but if pursued in any other spirit, useless.

Very true, he said.

Now, when all these studies reach the point of inter-communion and connection with one another, and come to be considered in their mutual affinities, then, I think, but not till then, will the pursuit of them have a value for our objects; otherwise there is no profit in them.

I suspect so; but you are speaking, Socrates, of a vast work.

What do you mean? I said; the prelude or what? Do you not know that all this is but the prelude to the actual strain which we have to learn? For you surely would not regard the skilled mathematician as a dialectician?

Assuredly not, he said; I have hardly ever known a mathematician who was capable of reasoning.

But do you imagine that men who are unable to give and take a reason will have the knowledge which we require of them?

Neither can this be supposed.

And so, Glaucon, I said, we have at last arrived at the hymn of dialectic. This is that strain which is of the intellect only, but which the faculty of sight will nevertheless be found to imitate; for sight, as you may remember, was imagined by us after a while to behold the real animals and stars, and last of all the sun himself. And so with dialectic; when a person starts on the discovery of the absolute by the light of reason only, and without any assistance of sense, and perseveres until by pure intelligence he arrives at the perception of the absolute good, he at last finds himself at the end of the intellectual world, as in the case of sight at the end of the visible.

Exactly, he said.

Then this is the progress which you call dialectic?

True.

But the release of the prisoners from chains, and their translation from the shadows to the images and to the light, and the ascent from the underground den to the sun, while in his presence they are vainly trying to look on animals and plants and the light of the sun, but are able to perceive even with their weak eyes the images [1] in the water [which are divine], and are the shadows of true existence (not shadows of images cast by a light of fire, which compared with the sun is only an image) — this power of elevating the highest principle in the soul to the contemplation of that which is best in existence, with which we may compare the raising of that faculty which is the very light of the body to the sight of that which is brightest in the material and visible world — this power is given, as I was saying, by all that study and pursuit of the arts which has been described.

I agree in what you are saying, he replied, which may be hard to believe, yet, from another point of view, is harder still to deny. This however is not a theme to be treated of in passing only, but will have

[1] Omitting ἐνταῦθα δὲ πρὸς φαντάσματα. The word θεῖα is bracketed by Stallbaum.

to be discussed again and again. And so, whether our conclusion be true or false, let us assume all this, and proceed at once from the prelude or preamble to the chief strain,[1] and describe that in like manner. Say, then, what is the nature and what are the divisions of dialectic, and what are the paths which lead thither; for these paths will also lead to our final rest.

Dear Glaucon, I said, you will not be able to follow me here, though I would do my best, and you should behold not an image only but the absolute truth, according to my notion. Whether what I told you would or would not have been a reality I can not venture to say; but you would have seen something like reality; of that I am confident.

Doubtless, he replied.

But I must also remind you, that the power of dialectic alone can reveal this, and only to one who is a disciple of the previous sciences.

Of that assertion you may be as confident as of the last.

And assuredly no one will argue that there is any other method of comprehending by any regular process all true existence or of ascertaining what each thing is in its own nature; for the arts in general are concerned with the desires or opinions of men, or are cultivated with a view to production and construction, or for the preservation of such productions and constructions; and as to the mathematical sciences which, as we were saying, have some apprehension of true being — geometry and the like — they only dream about being, but never can they behold the waking reality so long as they leave the hypotheses which they use unexamined, and are unable to give an account of them. For when a man knows not his own first prin-

[1] A play upon the word νόμος, which means both " law " and " strain "

ciple, and when the conclusion and intermediate steps are also constructed out of he knows not what, how can he imagine that such a fabric of convention can ever become science?

Impossible, he said.

Then dialectic, and dialectic alone, goes directly to the first principle and is the only science which does away with hypotheses in order to make her ground secure; the eye of the soul, which is literally buried in an outlandish slough, is by her gentle aid lifted upwards; and she uses as handmaids and helpers in the work of conversion, the sciences which we have been discussing. Custom terms them sciences, but they ought to have some other name, implying greater clearness than opinion and less clearness than science: and this, in our previous sketch, was called understanding. But why should we dispute about names when we have realities of such importance to consider?

Why indeed, he said, when any name will do which expresses the thought of the mind with clearness?

At any rate, we are satisfied, as before, to have four divisions; two for intellect and two for opinion, and to call the first division science, the second understanding, the third belief, and the fourth perception of shadows, opinion being concerned with becoming, and intellect with being; and so to make a proportion:

As being is to becoming, so is pure intellect to opinion.
And as intellect is to opinion, so is science to belief, and understanding to the perception of shadows.

But let us defer the further correlation and sub-division of the subjects of opinion and of intellect, for it will be a long inquiry, many times longer than this has been.

As far as I understand, he said, I agree.

And do you also agree, I said, in describing the

dialectician as one who attains a conception of the essence of each thing? And he who does not possess and is therefore unable to impart this conception, in whatever degree he fails, may in that degree also be said to fail in intelligence? Will you admit so much?

Yes, he said; how can I deny it?

And you would say the same of the conception of the good? Until the person is able to abstract and define rationally the idea of good, and unless he can run the gauntlet of all objections, and is ready to disprove them, not by appeals to opinion, but to absolute truth, never faltering at any step of the argument — unless he can do all this, you would say that he knows neither the idea of good nor any other good; he apprehends only a shadow, if anything at all, which is given by opinion and not by science; — dreaming and slumbering in this life, before he is well awake here, he arrives at the world below, and has his final quietus.

In all that I should most certainly agree with you.

And surely you would not have the children of your ideal State, whom you are nurturing and educating — if the ideal ever becomes a reality — you would not allow the future rulers to be like posts,[1] having no reason in them, and yet to be set in authority over the highest matters?

Certainly not.

Then you will make a law that they shall have such an education as will enable them to attain the greatest skill in asking and answering questions?

Yes, he said, you and I together will make it.

Dialectic, then, as you will agree, is the coping-stone of the sciences, and is set over them; no other science can be placed higher — the nature of knowledge can no further go?

[1] γραμμάς, literally "lines," probably the starting-point of a race-course.

I agree, he said.

But to whom we are to assign these studies, and in what way they are to be assigned, are questions which remain to be considered.

Yes, clearly.

You remember, I said, how the rulers were chosen before?

Certainly, he said.

The same natures must still be chosen, and the preference again given to the surest and the bravest, and, if possible, to the fairest; and, having noble and generous tempers, they should also have the natural gifts which will facilitate their education.

And what are these?

Such gifts as keenness and ready powers of acquisition; for the mind more often faints from the severity of study than from the severity of gymnastics: the toil is more entirely the mind's own, and is not shared with the body.

Very true, he replied.

Further, he of whom we are in search should have a good memory, and be an unwearied solid man who is a lover of labor in any line; or he will never be able to endure the great amount of bodily exercise and to go through all the intellectual discipline and study which we require of him.

Certainly, he said; he must have natural gifts.

The mistake at present is, that those who study philosophy have no vocation, and this, as I was before saying, is the reason why she has fallen into disrepute: her true sons should take her by the hand and not bastards.

What do you mean?

In the first place, her votary should not have a lame or halting industry — I mean, that he should not be half industrious and half idle: as, for example, when a man is a lover of gymnastic and hunting, and all other bodily exercises, but a hater rather than a lover of the labor of learning or listening or inquiring. Or the occupation to which he devotes himself may be of an opposite kind, and he may have the other sort of lameness.

Certainly, he said.

And as to truth, I said, is not a soul equally to be deemed halt and lame which hates voluntary falsehood and is extremely indignant at herself and others when they tell lies, but is patient of involuntary falsehood, and does not mind wallowing like a swinish beast in the mire of ignorance, and has no shame at being detected?

To be sure.

And, again, in respect of temperance, courage, magnificence, and every other virtue, should we not carefully distinguish between the true son and the bastard? for where there is no discernment of such qualities states and individuals unconsciously err; and the state makes a ruler, and the individual a friend, of one who, being defective in some part of virtue, is in a figure lame or a bastard.

That is very true, he said.

All these things, then, will have to be carefully considered by us; and if only those whom we introduce to this vast system of education and training are sound in body and mind, justice herself will have nothing to say against us, and we shall be the saviors of the constitution and of the State; but, if our pupils are men of another stamp, the reverse will happen, and we shall pour a still greater flood of ridicule on philosophy than she has to endure at present.

That would not be creditable.

Certainly not, I said; and yet perhaps, in thus turning jest into earnest I am equally ridiculous.

In what respect?

I had forgotten, I said, that we were not serious and spoke with too much excitement. For when I saw philosophy so undeservedly trampled under foot of men I could not help feeling a sort of indignation at the authors of her disgrace: and my anger made me too vehement.

Indeed! I was listening, and did not think so.

But I, who am the speaker, felt that I was. And now let me remind you that, although in our former selection we chose old men, we must not do so in this. Solon was under a delusion when he said that a man when he grows old may learn many things — for he can no more learn much than he can run much; youth is the time for any extraordinary toil.

Of course.

And, therefore, calculation and geometry and all the other elements of instruction, which are a preparation for dialectic, should be presented to the mind in childhood; not, however, under any notion of forcing our system of education.

Why not?

Because a freeman ought not to be a slave in the acquisition of knowledge of any kind. Bodily exercise, when compulsory, does no harm to the body; but knowledge which is acquired under compulsion obtains no hold on the mind.

Very true.

Then, my good friend, I said, do not use compulsion, but let early education be a sort of amusement; you will then be better able to find out the natural bent.

That is a very rational notion, he said.

Do you remember that the children, too, were to be taken to see the battle on horseback; and that if there were no danger they were to be brought close up and, like young hounds, have a taste of blood given them?

Yes, I remember.

The same practice may be followed, I said, in all these things — labors, lessons, dangers — and he who is most at home in all of them ought to be enrolled in a select number.

At what age?

At the age when the necessary gymnastics are over: the period whether of two or three years which passes in this sort of training is useless for any other purpose; for sleep and exercise are unpropitious to learning; and the trial of who is first in gymnastic exercises is one of the most important tests to which our youth are subjected.

Certainly, he replied.

After that time those who are selected from the class of twenty years old will be promoted to higher honor, and the sciences which they learned without any order in their early education will now be brought together, and they will be able to see the natural relationship of them to one another and to true being.

Yes, he said, that is the only kind of knowledge which takes lasting root.

Yes, I said; and the capacity for such knowledge is the great criterion of dialectical talent; the comprehensive mind is always the dialectical.

I agree with you, he said.

These, I said, are the points which you must consider; and those who have most of this comprehension, and who are most steadfast in their learning, and in their military and other appointed duties, when they have arrived at the age of thirty will have to be chosen by you out of the select class, and elevated to higher honor; and you will have to prove them by the help of dialectic, in order to learn which of them is able to give up the use of sight and the other senses, and in company with truth to attain absolute being: And here, my friend, great caution is required.

Why great caution?

Do you not remark, I said, how great is the evil which dialectic has introduced?

What evil? he said.

The students of the art are filled with lawlessness.

Quite true, he said.

Do you think that there is anything so very unnatural or inexcusable in their case? or will you make allowance for them?

In what way make allowance?

I want you, I said, by way of parallel, to imagine a supposititious son who is brought up in great wealth; he is one of a great and numerous family, and has many flatterers. When he grows up to manhood, he learns that his alleged are not his real parents; but who the real are he is unable to discover. Can you guess how he will be likely to behave towards his flatterers and his supposed parents, first of all during the period when he is ignorant of the false relation, and then again when he knows? Or shall I guess for you?

If you please.

Then I should say, that while he is ignorant of the truth he will be likely to honor his father and his mother and his supposed relations more than the flatterers; he will be less inclined to neglect them when in need, or to do or say anything against them; and he will be less willing to disobey them in any impor tant matter.

He will.

But when he has made the discovery, I should imagine that he would diminish his honor and regard for them, and would become more devoted to the flat‑ terers; their influence over him would greatly in‑ crease; he would now live after their ways, and openly associate with them, and, unless he were of an un‑ usually good disposition, he would trouble himself no more about his supposed parents or other relations.

Well, all that is very probable. But how is the image applicable to the disciples of philosophy?

In this way: you know that there are certain prin‑ ciples about justice and honor, which were taught us in childhood, and under their parental authority we have been brought up, obeying and honoring them.

That is true.

There are also opposite maxims and habits of pleasure which flatter and attract the soul, but do not influence those of us who have any sense of right, and they continue to obey and honor the maxims of their fathers.

True.

Now, when a man is in this state, and the question‑ ing spirit asks what is fair or honorable, and he answers as the legislator has taught him, and then arguments many and diverse refute his words, until he is driven into believing that nothing is honorable any more than dishonorable, or just and good any more than the reverse, and so of all the notions which he most valued, do you think that he will still honor and obey them as before?

Impossible.

And when he ceases to think them honorable and natural as heretofore, and he fails to discover the true, can he be expected to pursue any life other than that which flatters his desires?

He can not.

And from being a keeper of the law he is converted into a breaker of it?

Unquestionably.

Now all this is very natural in students of philosophy such as I have described, and also, as I was just now saying, most excusable.

Yes, he said; and, I may add, pitiable.

Therefore, that your feelings may not be moved to pity about our citizens who are now thirty years of age, every care must be taken in introducing them to dialectic.

Certainly.

There is a danger lest they should taste the dear delight too early; for youngsters, as you may have observed, when they first get the taste in their mouths, argue for amusement, and are always contradicting and refuting others in imitation of those who refute them; like puppy-dogs, they rejoice in pulling and tearing at all who come near them.

Yes, he said, there is nothing which they like better.

And when they have made many conquests and received defeats at the hands of many, they violently and speedily get into a way of not believing anything which they believed before, and hence, not only they, but philosophy and all that relates to it is apt to have a bad name with the rest of the world.

Too true, he said.

But when a man begins to get older, he will no longer be guilty of such insanity; he will imitate the dialectician who is seeking for truth, and not the eristic, who is contradicting for the sake of amusement; and the greater moderation of his character will increase instead of diminishing the honor of the pursuit.

Very true, he said.

And did we not make special provision for this, when we said that the disciples of philosophy were to be orderly and steadfast, not, as now, any chance aspirant or intruder?

Very true.

Suppose, I said, the study of philosophy to take the place of gymnastics and to be continued diligently and earnestly and exclusively for twice the number of years which were passed in bodily exercise — will that be enough?

Would you say six or four years? he asked.

Say five years, I replied; at the end of the time they must be sent down again into the den and compelled to hold any military or other office which young men are qualified to hold: in this way they will get their experience of life, and there will be an opportunity of trying whether, when they are drawn all manner of ways by temptation, they will stand firm or flinch.

And how long is this stage of their lives to last?

Fifteen years, I answered; and when they have reached fifty years of age, then let those who still survive and have distinguished themselves in every action of their lives and in every branch of knowledge come at last to their consummation: the time has now arrived at which they must raise the eye of the soul to the universal light which lightens all things, and behold the absolute good; for that is the pattern according to which they are to order the State and the lives of individuals, and the remainder of their own lives also; making philosophy their chief pursuit, but, when their turn comes, toiling also at politics and ruling for the public good, not as though they were performing some heroic action, but simply as a matter of duty; and when they have brought up in each generation others like themselves and left them in their place to be governors of the State, then they will depart to the Islands of the Blest and dwell there; and the city will give them public memorials and sacrifices and honor them, if the Pythian oracle consent, as demigods, but if not, as in any case blessed and divine.

You are a sculptor, Socrates, and have made statues of our governors faultless in beauty.

Yes, I said, Glaucon, and of our governesses too; for you must not suppose that what I have been saying applies to men only and not to women as far as their natures can go.

There you are right, he said, since we have made them to share in all things like the men.

Well, I said, and you would agree (would you not?) that what has been said about the State and the government is not a mere dream, and although difficult not impossible, but only possible in the way which has been supposed; that is to say, when the true philosopher kings are born in a State, one or more of them, despising the honors of this present world which they deem mean and worthless, esteeming above all things right and the honor that springs from right, and regarding justice as the greatest and most necessary of all things, whose ministers they are, and whose principles will be exalted by them when they set in order their own city?

How will they proceed?

They will begin by sending out into the country all the inhabitants of the city who are more than ten years old, and will take possession of their children, who will be unaffected by the habits of their parents; these they will train in their own habits and laws, I mean in the laws which we have given them: and in this way the State and constitution of which we were speaking will soonest and most easily attain happiness, and the nation which has such a constitution will gain most.

Yes, that will be the best way. And I think

Socrates, that you have very well described how, if ever, such a constitution might come into being.

Enough then of the perfect State, and of the man who bears its image — there is no difficulty in seeing how we shall describe him.

There is no difficulty, he replied; and I agree with you in thinking that nothing more need be said.

BOOK VIII

AND so, Glaucon, we have arrived at the conclusion that in the perfect State wives and children are to be in common; and that all education and the pursuits of war and peace are also to be common, and the best philosophers and the bravest warriors are to be their kings?

That, replied Glaucon, has been acknowledged.

Yes, I said; and we have further acknowledged that the governors, when appointed themselves, will take their soldiers and place them in houses such as we were describing, which are common to all, and contain nothing private, or individual; and about their property, you remember what we agreed?

Yes, I remember that no one was to have any of the ordinary possessions of mankind; they were to be warrior athletes and guardians, receiving from the other citizens, in lieu of annual payment, only their maintenance, and they were to take care of themselves and of the whole State.

True, I said; and now that this division of our task is concluded, let us find the point at which we digressed, that we may return into the old path.

There is no difficulty in returning; you implied, then as now, that you have finished the description of the State: you said that such a State was good, and that the man was good who answered to it, although, as now appears, you had more excellent things to relate both of State and man. And you said further, that if this was the true form, then the others were false; and of the false forms, you said, as I remember, that there were four principal ones, and that their defects, and the defects of the individuals corresponding to them, were worth examining. When we had seen all the individuals, and finally agreed as to who was the best and who was the worst of them, we were to consider whether the best was not also the happiest, and the worst the most miserable. I asked you what were the four forms of government of which you spoke, and then Polemarchus and Adeimantus put in their word; and you began again, and have found your way to the point at which we have now arrived.

Your recollection, I said, is most exact.

Then, like a wrestler, he replied, you must put yourself again in the same position; and let me ask the same questions, and do you give me the same answer which you were about to give me then.

Yes, if I can, I will, I said.

I shall particularly wish to hear what were the four constitutions of which you were speaking.

That question, I said, is easily answered: the four governments of which I spoke, so far as they have distinct names, are, first, those of Crete and Sparta, which are generally applauded; what is termed oligarchy comes next; this is not equally approved, and is a form of government which teems with evils: thirdly, democracy, which naturally follows oligarchy, although very different: and lastly comes tyranny, great and famous, which differs from them all, and is the fourth and worst disorder of a State. I do not know, do you? of any other constitution which can be said to have a distinct character. There are lordships and principalities which are bought and sold, and some other intermediate forms of government. But these are nondescripts and may be found equally among Hellenes and among barbarians.

Yes, he replied, we certainly hear of many curious forms of government which exist among them.

Do you know, I said, that governments vary as the dispositions of men vary, and that there must be as many of the one as there are of the other? For we can not suppose that States are made of "oak and rock," and not out of the human natures which are in them, and which in a figure turn the scale and draw other things after them?

Yes, he said, the States are as men are; they grow out of human characters.

Then if the constitutions of States are five, the dispositions of individual minds will also be five?

Certainly.

He who answers to aristocracy, and whom we rightly call just and good, we have already described.

We have.

Then let us now proceed to describe the inferior sort of natures, being the contentious and ambitious, who answer to the Spartan polity; also the oligarchical, democratical, and tyrannical. Let us place the most just by the side of the most unjust, and when we see them we shall be able to compare the relative happiness or unhappiness of him who leads a life of pure justice or pure injustice. The inquiry will then be completed. And we shall know whether we ought to pursue injustice, as Thrasymachus advises, or in accordance with the conclusions of the argument to prefer justice.

Certainly, he replied, we must do as you say.

Shall we follow our old plan, which we adopted with a view to clearness, of taking the State first and then proceeding to the individual, and begin with the government of honor? — I know of no name for such a government other than timocracy, or perhaps timarchy. We will compare with this the like char-

acter in the individual; and, after that, consider
oligarchy and the oligarchical man; and then again
we will turn our attention to democracy and the
democratical man; and lastly, we will go and view
the city of tyranny, and once more take a look into
the tyrant's soul, and try to arrive at a satisfactory
decision.

That way of viewing and judging of the matter
will be very suitable.

First, then, I said, let us inquire how timocracy
(the government of honor) arises out of aristocracy
(the government of the best). Clearly, all political
changes originate in divisions of the actual governing power; a government which is united, however
small, can not be moved.

Very true, he said.

In what way, then, will our city be moved, and in
what manner will the two classes of auxiliaries and
rulers disagree among themselves or with one another? Shall we, after the manner of Homer, pray
the Muses to tell us " how discord first arose?" Shall
we imagine them in solemn mockery, to play and
jest with us as if we were children, and to address
us in a lofty tragic vein, making believe to be in
earnest?

How would they address us?

After this manner: — A city which is thus constituted can hardly be shaken; but, seeing that everything which has a beginning has also an end, even
a constitution such as yours will not last forever, but
will in time be dissolved. And this is the dissolution: — In plants that grow in the earth, as well as
in animals that move on the earth's surface, fertility
and sterility of soul and body occur when the circum-
ferences of the circles of each are completed, which in
short-lived existences pass over a short space, and in

long-lived ones over a long space. But to the knowledge of human fecundity and sterility all the wisdom and education of your rulers will not attain; the laws which regulate them will not be discovered by an intelligence which is alloyed with sense, but will escape them, and they will bring children into the world when they ought not. Now that which is of divine birth has a period which is contained in a perfect number,[1] but the period of human birth is comprehended in a number in which first increments by involution and evolution [or squared and cubed] obtaining three intervals and four terms of like and unlike, waxing and waning numbers, make all the terms commensurable and agreeable to one another.[2] The base of these (3) with a third added (4) when combined with five (20) and raised to the third power furnishes two harmonies; the first a square which is a hundred times as great (400 = 4 × 100),[3] and the other a figure having one side equal to the former, but oblong,[4] consisting of a hundred numbers squared upon rational diameters of a square (i. e. omitting fractions), the side of which is five (7 × 7 = 49 × 100 = 4900), each of them being less by one (than the perfect square which includes the fractions, sc. 50) or less by [5] two perfect squares of irrational diameters (of a square the side of which is five = 50 + 50 = 100); and a hundred cubes of three (27 × 100 = 2700 + 4900 + 400 = 8000). Now this number

[1] i. e. a cyclical number, such as 6, which is equal to the sum of its divisors 1, 2, 3, so that when the circle or time represented by 6 is completed, the lesser times or rotations represented by 1, 2, 3 are also completed.

[2] Probably the numbers 3, 4, 5, 6 of which the three first = the sides of the Pythagorean triangle. The terms will then be 3^3, 4^3, 5^3, which together $= 6^3 = 216$.

[3] Or the first a square which is 100 × 100 = 10,000. The whole number will then be 17,500 = a square of 100, and an oblong of 100 by 75.

[4] Reading προμήκη δέ.

[5] Or, "consisting of two numbers squared upon irrational diameters," etc. = 100. For other explanations of the passage see Introduction.

represents a geometrical figure which has control over the good and evil of births. For when your guardians are ignorant of the law of births, and unite bride and bridegroom out of season, the children will not be goodly or fortunate. And though only the best of them will be appointed by their predecessors, still they will be unworthy to hold their fathers' places, and when they come into power as guardians, they will soon be found to fail in taking care of us, the Muses, first by undervaluing music; which neglect will soon extend to gymnastic; and hence the young men of your State will be less cultivated. In the succeeding generation rulers will be appointed who have lost the guardian power of testing the metal of your different races, which, like Hesiod's, are of gold and silver and brass and iron. And so iron will be mingled with silver, and brass with gold, and hence there will arise dissimilarity and inequality and irregularity, which always and in all places are causes of hatred and war. This the Muses affirm to be the stock from which discord has sprung, wherever arising; and this is their answer to us.

Yes, and we may assume that they answer truly.

Why, yes, I said, of course they answer truly; how can the Muses speak falsely?

And what do the Muses say next?

When discord arose, then the two races were drawn different ways: the iron and brass fell to acquiring money and land and houses and gold and silver; but the gold and silver races, not wanting money but having the true riches in their own nature, inclined towards virtue and the ancient order of things. There was a battle between them, and at last they agreed to distribute their land and houses among individual owners; and they enslaved their friends and maintainers, whom they had formerly protected in the condition of freemen, and made of them subjects and servants; and they themselves were engaged in war and in keeping a watch against them.

I believe that you have rightly conceived the origin of the change.

And the new government which thus arises will be of a form intermediate between oligarchy and aristocracy?

Very true.

Such will be the change, and after the change has been made, how will they proceed? Clearly, the new State, being in a mean between oligarchy and the perfect State, will partly follow one and partly the other, and will also have some peculiarities.

True, he said.

In the honor given to rulers, in the abstinence of the warrior class from agriculture, handicrafts, and trade in general, in the institution of common meals, and in the attention paid to gymnastics and military training — in all these respects this State will resemble the former.

True.

But in the fear of admitting philosophers to power, because they are no longer to be had simple and earnest, but are made up of mixed elements; and in turning from them to passionate and less complex characters, who are by nature fitted for war rather than peace; and in the value set by them upon military stratagems and contrivances, and in the waging of everlasting wars — this State will be for the most part peculiar.

Yes.

Yes, I said; and men of this stamp will be covetous of money, like those who live in oligarchies; they will have a fierce secret longing after gold and silver, which they will hoard in dark places, having magazines and treasuries of their own for the deposit and concealment of them; also castles which are just nests for their eggs, and in which they will spend large sums on their wives, or on any others whom they please.

That is most true, he said.

And they are miserly because they have no means of openly acquiring the money which they prize; they will spend that which is another man's on the gratification of their desires, stealing their pleasures and running away like children from the law, their father: they have been schooled not by gentle influences but by force, for they have neglected her who is the true Muse, the companion of reason and philosophy, and have honored gymnastic more than music.

Undoubtedly, he said, the form of government which you describe is a mixture of good and evil.

Why, there is a mixture, I said; but one thing, and one thing only, is predominantly seen, — the spirit of contention and ambition; and these are due to the prevalence of the passionate or spirited element.

Assuredly, he said.

Such is the origin and such the character of this State, which has been described in outline only; the more perfect execution was not required, for a sketch is enough to show the type of the most perfectly just and most perfectly unjust; and to go through all the States and all the characters of men, omitting none of them, would be an interminable labor.

Very true, he replied.

Now what man answers to this form of government — how did he come into being, and what is he like?

I think, said Adeimantus, that in the spirit of contention which characterizes him, he is not unlike our friend Glaucon.

Perhaps, I said, he may be like him in that one point; but there are other respects in which he is very different.

In what respects?

He should have more of self-assertion and be less cultivated, and yet a friend of culture; and he should be a good listener, but no speaker. Such a person is apt to be rough with slaves, unlike the educated man, who is too proud for that; and he will also be courteous to freemen, and remarkably obedient to authority; he is a lover of power and a lover of honor; claiming to be a ruler, not because he is eloquent, or on any ground of that sort, but because he is a soldier and has performed feats of arms; he is also a lover of gymnastic exercises and of the chase.

Yes, that is the type of character which answers to timocracy.

Such an one will despise riches only when he is young; but as he gets older he will be more and more attracted to them, because he has a piece of the avaricious nature in him, and is not single-minded towards virtue, having lost his best guardian.

Who was that? said Adeimantus.

Philosophy, I said, tempered with music, who comes and takes up her abode in a man, and is the only savior of his virtue throughout life.

Good, he said.

Such, I said, is the timocratical youth, and he is like the timocratical State.

Exactly.

His origin is as follows: — He is often the young son of a brave father, who dwells in an ill-governed city, of which he declines the honors and offices, and will not go to law, or exert himself in any way, but is ready to waive his rights in order that he may escape trouble.

And how does the son come into being?

The character of the son begins to develop when he hears his mother complaining that her husband has no place in the government, of which the consequence is that she has no precedence among other women. Further, when she sees her husband not very eager about money, and instead of battling and railing in the law courts or assembly, taking whatever happens to him quietly; and when she observes that his thoughts always centre in himself, while he treats her with very considerable indifference, she is annoyed, and says to her son that his father is only half a man and far too easy-going: adding all the other complaints about her own ill-treatment which women are so fond of rehearsing.

Yes, said Adeimantus, they give us plenty of them, and their complaints are so like themselves.

And you know, I said, that the old servants also, who are supposed to be attached to the family, from time to time talk privately in the same strain to the son; and if they see any one who owes money to his father, or is wronging him in any way, and he fails to prosecute them, they tell the youth that when he grows up he must retaliate upon people of this sort, and be more of a man than his father. He has only to walk abroad and he hears and sees the same sort of thing: those who do their own business in the city are called simpletons, and held in no esteem, while the busy-bodies are honored and applauded. The result is that the young man, hearing and seeing all these things — hearing, too, the words of his father, and having a nearer view of his way of life, and making comparisons of him and others — is drawn opposite ways: while his father is watering and nourishing the rational principle in his soul, the others are encouraging the passionate and appetitive; and he being not originally of a bad nature, but having kept bad company, is at last brought by their joint influence to a middle point, and gives up the kingdom which is within him to the middle principle of contentiousness and passion, and becomes arrogant and ambitious.

You seem to me to have described his origin perfectly.

Then we have now, I said, the second form of government and the second type of character?

We have.

Next, let us look at another man who, as Æschylus says,

"Is set over against another State;"

or rather, as our plan requires, begin with the State.

By all means.

I believe that oligarchy follows next in order.

And what manner of government do you term oligarchy?

A government resting on a valuation of property, in which the rich have power and the poor man is deprived of it.

I understand, he replied.

Ought I not to begin by describing how the change from timocracy to oligarchy arises?

Yes.

Well, I said, no eyes are required in order to see how the one passes into the other.

How?

The accumulation of gold in the treasury of private individuals is the ruin of timocracy; they invent illegal modes of expenditure; for what do they or their wives care about the law?

Yes, indeed.

And then one, seeing another grow rich, seeks to rival him, and thus the great mass of the citizens become lovers of money.

Likely enough.

And so they grow richer and richer, and the more they think of making a fortune the less they think of virtue; for when riches and virtue are placed together in the scales of the balance, the one always rises as the other falls.

True.

And in proportion as riches and rich men are honored in the State, virtue and the virtuous are dishonored.

Clearly.

And what is honored is cultivated, and that which has no honor is neglected.

That is obvious.

And so at last, instead of loving contention and glory, men become lovers of trade and money; they honor and look up to the rich man, and make a ruler of him, and dishonor the poor man.

They do so.

They next proceed to make a law which fixes a sum of money as the qualification of citizenship; the sum is higher in one place and lower in another, as the oligarchy is more or less exclusive; and they allow no one whose property falls below the amount fixed to have any share in the government. These changes in the constitution they effect by force of arms, if intimidation has not already done their work.

Very true.

And this, speaking generally, is the way in which oligarchy is established.

Yes. he said; but what are the characteristics of

this form of government, and what are the defects of which we were speaking?[1]

First of all, I said, consider the nature of the qualification. Just think what would happen if pilots were to be chosen according to their property, and a poor man were refused permission to steer, even though he were a better pilot?

You mean that they would shipwreck?

Yes; and is not this true of the government of anything?[2]

I should imagine so.

Except a city? — or would you include a city?

Nay, he said, the case of a city is the strongest of all, inasmuch as the rule of a city is the greatest and most difficult of all.

This, then, will be the first great defect of oligarchy?

Clearly.

And here is another defect which is quite as bad.

What defect?

The inevitable division: such a State is not one, but two States, the one of poor, the other of rich men; and they are living on the same spot and always conspiring against one another.

That, surely, is at least as bad.

Another discreditable feature is, that, for a like reason, they are incapable of carrying on any war. Either they arm the multitude, and then they are more afraid of them than of the enemy; or, if they do not call them out in the hour of battle, they are oligarchs indeed, few to fight as they are few to rule. And at the same time their fondness for money makes them unwilling to pay taxes.

How discreditable!

And, as we said before, under such a constitution

[1] Cp. supra, 544 C.   [2] Omitting ἢ τινος.

the same persons have too many callings — they are husbandmen, tradesmen, warriors, all in one. Does that look well?

Anything but well.

There is another evil which is, perhaps, the greatest of all, and to which this State first begins to be liable.

What evil?

A man may sell all that he has, and another may acquire his property; yet after the sale he may dwell in the city of which he is no longer a part, being neither trader, nor artisan, nor horseman, nor hoplite, but only a poor, helpless creature.

Yes, that is an evil which also first begins in this State.

The evil is certainly not prevented there; for oligarchies have both the extremes of great wealth and utter poverty.

True.

But think again: In his wealthy days, while he was spending his money, was a man of this sort a whit more good to the State for the purposes of citizenship? Or did he only seem to be a member of the ruling body, although in truth he was neither ruler nor subject, but just a spendthrift?

As you say, he seemed to be a ruler, but was only a spendthrift.

May we not say that this is the drone in the house who is like the drone in the honeycomb, and that the one is the plague of the city as the other is of the hive?

Just so, Socrates.

And God has made the flying drones, Adeimantus, all without stings, whereas of the walking drones he has made some without stings but others have dreadful stings; of the stingless class are those who in their old age end as paupers; of the stingers come all the criminal class, as they are termed.

Most true, he said.

Clearly then, whenever you see paupers in a State, somewhere in that neighborhood there are hidden away thieves and cut-purses and robbers of temples, and all sorts of malefactors.

Clearly.

Well, I said, and in oligarchical States do you not find paupers?

Yes, he said; nearly everybody is a pauper who is not a ruler.

And may we be so bold as to affirm that there are also many criminals to be found in them, rogues who have stings, and whom the authorities are careful to restrain by force?

Certainly, we may be so bold.

The existence of such persons is to be attributed to want of education, ill-training, and an evil constitution of the State?

True.

Such, then, is the form and such are the evils of oligarchy; and there may be many other evils.

Very likely.

Then oligarchy, or the form of government in which the rulers are elected for their wealth, may now be dismissed. Let us next proceed to consider the nature and origin of the individual who answers to this State.

By all means.

Does not the timocratical man change into the oligarchical on this wise?

How?

A time arrives when the representative of timocracy has a son: at first he begins by emulating his father and walking in his footsteps, but presently he sees him of a sudden foundering against the State as upon a sunken reef, and he and all that he has is lost; he may have been a general or some other high officer who is brought to trial under a prejudice raised by informers, and either put to death, or exiled, or deprived of the privileges of a citizen, and all his property taken from him.

Nothing more likely.

And the son has seen and known all this — he is a ruined man, and his fear has taught him to knock ambition and passion headforemost from his bosom's throne; humbled by poverty he takes to money-making and by mean and miserly savings and hard work gets a fortune together. Is not such an one likely to seat the concupiscent and covetous element on the vacant throne and to suffer it to play the great king within him, girt with tiara and chain and scimitar?

Most true, he replied.

And when he has made reason and spirit sit down on the ground obediently on either side of their sovereign, and taught them to know their place, he compels the one to think only of how lesser sums may be turned into larger ones, and will not allow the other to worship and admire anything but riches and rich men, or to be ambitious of anything so much as the acquisition of wealth and the means of acquiring it.

Of all changes, he said, there is none so speedy or so sure as the conversion of the ambitious youth into the avaricious one.

And the avaricious, I said, is the oligarchical youth?

Yes, he said; at any rate the individual out of whom he came is like the State out of which oligarchy came.

Let us then consider whether there is any likeness between them.

Very good.

First, then, they resemble one another in the value which they set upon wealth?

Certainly.

Also in their penurious, laborious character; the individual only satisfies his necessary appetites, and confines his expenditure to them; his other desires he subdues, under the idea that they are unprofitable.

True.

He is a shabby fellow, who saves something out of everything and makes a purse for himself; and this is the sort of man whom the vulgar applaud. Is he not a true image of the State which he represents?

He appears to me to be so; at any rate money is highly valued by him as well as by the State.

You see that he is not a man of cultivation, I said.

I imagine not, he said; had he been educated he would never have made a blind god director of his chorus, or given him chief honor.[1]

Excellent! I said. Yet consider: Must we not further admit that owing to this want of cultivation there will be found in him dronelike desires as of pauper and rogue, which are forcibly kept down by his general habit of life?

True.

Do you know where you will have to look if you want to discover his rogueries?

Where must I look?

You should see him where he has some great opportunity of acting dishonestly, as in the guardianship of an orphan.

Aye.

It will be clear enough then that in his ordinary

[1] Reading καὶ ἐτίμα μάλιστα. Εὖ, ἦν δ' ἐγώ, according to Schneider's excellent emendation.

dealings which give him a reputation for honesty he coerces his bad passions by an enforced virtue; not making them see that they are wrong, or taming them by reason, but by necessity and fear constraining them, and because he trembles for his possessions.

To be sure.

Yes, indeed, my dear friend, but you will find that the natural desires of the drone commonly exist in him all the same whenever he has to spend what is not his own.

Yes, and they will be strong in him too.

The man, then, will be at war with himself; he will be two men, and not one; but, in general, his better desires will be found to prevail over his inferior ones.

True.

For these reasons such an one will be more respectable than most people; yet the true virtue of a unanimous and harmonious soul will flee far away and never come near him.

I should expect so.

And surely, the miser individually will be an ignoble competitor in a State for any prize of victory, or other object of honorable ambition; he will not spend his money in the contest for glory; so afraid is he of awakening his expensive appetites and inviting them to help and join in the struggle; in true oligarchical fashion he fights with a small party only of his resources, and the result commonly is that he loses the prize and saves his money.

Very true.

Can we any longer doubt, then, that the miser and moneymaker answers to the oligarchical State?

There can be no doubt.

Next comes democracy; of this the origin and nature have still to be considered by us; and then we will inquire into the ways of the democratic man, and bring him up for judgment.

That, he said, is our method.

Well, I said, and how does the change from oligarchy into democracy arise? Is it not on this wise? — The good at which such a State aims is to become as rich as possible, a desire which is insatiable?

What then?

The rulers, being aware that their power rests upon their wealth, refuse to curtail by law the extravagance of the spendthrift youth because they gain by their ruin; they take interest from them and buy up their estates and thus increase their own wealth and importance?

To be sure.

There can be no doubt that the love of wealth and the spirit of moderation can not exist together in citizens of the same state to any considerable extent; one or the other will be disregarded.

That is tolerably clear.

And in oligarchical States, from the general spread of carelessness and extravagance, men of good family have often been reduced to beggary?

Yes, often.

And still they remain in the city; there they are, ready to sting and fully armed, and some of them owe money, some have forfeited their citizenship; a third class are in both predicaments; and they hate and conspire against those who have got their property, and against everybody else, and are eager for revolution.

That is true.

On the other hand, the men of business, stooping as they walk, and pretending not even to see those whom they have already ruined, insert their sting — that is, their money — into some one else who is not on his guard against them, and recover the parent sum many times over multiplied into a family of children: and so they make drone and pauper to abound in the State.

Yes, he said, there are plenty of them — that is certain.

The evil blazes up like a fire; and they will not extinguish it, either by restricting a man's use of his own property, or by another remedy:

What other?

One which is the next best, and has the advantage of compelling the citizens to look to their characters:— Let there be a general rule that every one shall enter into voluntary contracts at his own risk, and there will be less of this scandalous money-making, and the evils of which we were speaking will be greatly lessened in the State.

Yes, they will be greatly lessened.

At present the governors, induced by the motives which I have named, treat their subjects badly; while they and their adherents, especially the young men of the governing class, are habituated to lead a life of luxury and idleness both of body and mind; they do nothing, and are incapable of resisting either pleasure or pain.

Very true.

They themselves care only for making money, and are as indifferent as the pauper to the cultivation of virtue.

Yes, quite as indifferent.

Such is the state of affairs which prevails among them. And often rulers and their subjects may come in one another's way, whether on a journey or on some other occasion of meeting, on a pilgrimage or a march, as fellow-soldiers or fellow-sailors; aye and they may observe the behavior of each other in the very moment of danger — for where danger is, there is no fear that the poor will be despised by the rich -— and very likely the wiry sunburnt poor man may be placed in battle at the side of a wealthy one who has never spoiled his complexion and has plenty of superfluous flesh — when he sees such an one puffing and at his wits'-end, how can he avoid drawing the conclusion that men like him are only rich because no one has the courage to despoil them? And when they meet in private will not people be saying to one another "Our warriors are not good for much"?

Yes, he said, I am quite aware that this is their way of talking.

And, as in a body which is diseased the addition of a touch from without may bring on illness, and sometimes even when there is no external provocation a commotion may arise within — in the same way wherever there is weakness in the State there is also likely to be illness, of which the occasion may be very slight, the one party introducing from without their oligarchical, the other their democratical allies, and then the State falls sick, and is at war with herself; and may be at times distracted, even when there is no external cause.

Yes, surely.

And then democracy comes into being after the poor have conquered their opponents, slaughtering some and banishing some, while to the remainder they give an equal share of freedom and power; and this is the form of government in which the magistrates are commonly elected by lot.

Yes, he said, that is the nature of democracy, whether the revolution has been effected by arms, or whether fear has caused the opposite party to withdraw.

And now what is their manner of life, and what sort of a government have they? for as the government is, such will be the man.

Clearly, he said.

In the first place, are they not free; and is not the city full of freedom and frankness — a man may say and do what he likes?

'Tis said so, he replied.

And where freedom is, the individual is clearly able to order for himself his own life as he pleases?

Clearly.

Then in this kind of State there will be the greatest variety of human natures?

There will.

This, then, seems likely to be the fairest of States, being like an embroidered robe which is spangled with every sort of flower.[1] And just as women and children think a variety of colors to be of all things most charming, so there are many men to whom this State, which is spangled with the manners and characters of mankind, will appear to be the fairest of States.

Yes.

Yes, my good Sir, and there will be no better in which to look for a government.

Why?

Because of the liberty which reigns there — they have a complete assortment of constitutions; and he who has a mind to establish a State, as we have been doing, must go to a democracy as he would go to a bazaar at which they sell them, and pick out the one that suits him; then, when he has made his choice, he may found his State.

He will be sure to have patterns enough.

And there being no necessity, I said, for you to govern in this State, even if you have the capacity, or to be governed, unless you like, or to go to war when the rest go to war, or to be at peace when others are at peace, unless you are so disposed —

---

[1] Omitting τί μήν ; ἔφη.

there being no necessity also, because some law forbids you to hold office or be a dicast, that you should not hold office or be a dicast, if you have a fancy — is not this a way of life which for the moment is supremely delightful?

For the moment, yes.

And is not their humanity to the condemned [1] in some cases quite charming? Have you not observed how, in a democracy, many persons, although they have been sentenced to death or exile, just stay where they are and walk about the world — the gentleman parades like a hero, and nobody sees or cares?

Yes, he replied, many and many a one.

See too, I said, the forgiving spirit of democracy, and the " don't care " about trifles, and the disregard which she shows of all the fine principles which we solemnly laid down at the foundation of the city — as when we said that, except in the case of some rarely gifted nature, there never will be a good man who has not from his childhood been used to play amid things of beauty and make of them a joy and a study — how grandly does she trample all these fine notions of ours under her feet, never giving a thought to the pursuits which make a statesman, and promoting to honor any one who professes to be the people's friend.

Yes, she is of a noble spirit.

These and other kindred characteristics are proper to democracy, which is a charming form of government, full of variety and disorder, and dispensing a sort of equality to equals and unequals alike.

We know her well.

Consider now, I said, what manner of man the individual is, or rather consider, as is the case of the State, how he comes into being.

[1] Or, "the philosophical temper of the condemned."

Very good, he said.

Is not this the way — he is the son of the miserly and oligarchical father who has trained him in his own habits?

Exactly.

And, like his father, he keeps under by force the pleasures which are of the spending and not of the getting sort, being those which are called unnecessary?

Obviously.

Would you like, for the sake of clearness, to distinguish which are the necessary and which are the unnecessary pleasures?

I should.

Are not necessary pleasures those of which we can not get rid, and of which the satisfaction is a benefit to us? And they are rightly called so, because we are framed by nature to desire both what is beneficial and what is necessary, and can not help it.

True.

We are not wrong therefore in calling them necessary?

We are not.

And the desires of which a man may get rid, if he takes pains from his youth upwards — of which the presence, moreover, does no good, and in some cases the reverse of good -- shall we not be right in saying that all these are unnecessary?

Yes, certainly.

Suppose we select an example of either kind, in order that we may have a general notion of them?

Very good.

Will not the desire of eating, that is, of simple food and condiments, in so far as they are required for health and strength, be of the necessary class?

That is what I should suppose.

The pleasure of eating is necessary in two ways; it

does us good and it is essential to the continuance of
life?

Yes.

But the condiments are only necessary in so far as
they are good for health?

Certainly.

And the desire which goes beyond this, of more
delicate food, or other luxuries, which might generally
be got rid of, if controlled and trained in youth, and is
hurtful to the body, and hurtful to the soul in the
pursuit of wisdom and virtue, may be rightly called
unnecessary?

Very true.

May we not say that these desires spend, and that
the others make money because they conduce to production?

Certainly.

And of the pleasures of love, and all other pleasures,
the same holds good?

True.

And the drone of whom we spoke was he who was
surfeited in pleasures and desires of this sort, and was
the slave of the unnecessary desires, whereas he who
was subject to the necessary only was miserly and
oligarchical?

Very true.

Again, let us see how the democratical man grows
out of the oligarchical: the following, as I suspect, is
commonly the process.

What is the process?

When a young man who has been brought up as we
were just now describing, in a vulgar and miserly
way, has tasted drones' honey and has come to associate with fierce and crafty natures who are able to
provide for him all sorts of refinements and varieties
of pleasure — then, as you may imagine, the change

will begin of the oligarchical principle within him into the democratical?

Inevitably.

And as in the city like was helping like, and the change was effected by an alliance from without assisting one division of the citizens, so too the young man is changed by a class of desires coming from without to assist the desires within him, that which is akin and alike again helping that which is akin and alike?

Certainly.

And if there be any ally which aids the oligarchical principle within him, whether the influence of a father or of kindred, advising or rebuking him, then there arises in his soul a faction and an opposite faction, and he goes to war with himself.

It must be so.

And there are times when the democratical principle gives way to the oligarchical, and some of his desires die, and others are banished; a spirit of reverence enters into the young man's soul and order is restored.

Yes, he said, that sometimes happens.

And then, again, after the old desires have been driven out, fresh ones spring up, which are akin to them, and because he their father does not know how to educate them, wax fierce and numerous.

Yes, he said, that is apt to be the way.

They draw him to his old associates, and holding secret intercourse with them, breed and multiply in him.

Very true.

At length they seize upon the citadel of the young man's soul, which they perceive to be void of all accomplishments and fair pursuits and true words, which make their abode in the minds of men who are

dear to the gods, and are their best guardians and sentinels.

None better.

False and boastful conceits and phrases mount upwards and take their place.

They are certain to do so.

And so the young man returns into the country of the lotus-eaters, and takes up his dwelling there in the face of all men; and if any help be sent by his friends to the oligarchical part of him, the aforesaid vain conceits shut the gate of the king's fastness; and they will neither allow the embassy itself to enter, nor if private advisers offer the fatherly counsel of the aged will they listen to them or receive them. There is a battle and they gain the day, and then modesty, which they call silliness, is ignominiously thrust into exile by them, and temperance, which they nickname unmanliness, is trampled in the mire and cast forth; they persuade men that moderation and orderly expenditure are vulgarity and meanness, and so, by the help of a rabble of evil appetites, they drive them beyond the border.

Yes, with a will.

And when they have emptied and swept clean the soul of him who is now in their power and who is being initiated by them in great mysteries, the next thing is to bring back to their house insolence and anarchy and waste and impudence in bright array having garlands on their heads, and a great company with them, hymning their praises and calling them by sweet names; insolence they term breeding, and anarchy liberty, and waste magnificence, and impudence courage. And so the young man passes out of his original nature, which was trained in the school of necessity, into the freedom and libertinism of useless and unnecessary pleasures.

Yes, he said, the change in him is visible enough.

After this he lives on, spending his money and labor and time on unnecessary pleasures quite as much as on necessary ones; but if he be fortunate, and is not too much disordered in his wits, when years have elapsed, and the heyday of passion is over — supposing that he then re-admits into the city some part of the exiled virtues, and does not wholly give himself up to .their successors — in that case he balances his pleasures and lives in a sort of equilibrium, putting the government of himself into the hands of the one which comes first and wins the turn; and when he has had enough of that, then into the hands of another; he despises none of them but encourages them all equally.

Very true, he said.

Neither does he receive or let pass into the fortress any true word of advice; if any one says to him that some pleasures are the satisfactions of good and noble desires, and others of evil desires, and that he ought to use and honor some and chastise and master the others — whenever this is repeated to him he shakes his head and says that they are all alike, and that one is as good as another.

Yes, he said; that is the way with him.

Yes, I said, he lives from day to day indulging the appetite of the hour; and sometimes he is lapped in drink and strains of the flute; then he becomes a water-drinker, and tries to get thin; then he takes a turn at gymnastics; sometimes idling and neglecting everything, then once more living the life of a philosopher; often he is busy with politics, and starts to his feet and says and does whatever comes into his head; and, if he is emulous of any one who is a warrior, off he is in that direction, or of men of business, once more in that. His life has neither law nor order;

and this distracted existence he terms joy and bliss and freedom; and so he goes on.

Yes, he replied, he is all liberty and equality.

Yes, I said; his life is motley and manifold and an epitome of the lives of many; — he answers to the State which we described as fair and spangled. And many a man and many a woman will take him for their pattern, and many a constitution and many an example of manners is contained in him.

Just so.

Let him then be set over against democracy; he may truly be called the democratic man.

Let that be his place, he said.

Last of all comes the most beautiful of all, man and State alike, tyranny and the tyrant; these we have now to consider.

Quite true, he said.

Say then, my friend, In what manner does tyranny arise? — that it has a democratic origin is evident.

Clearly.

And does not tyranny spring from democracy in the same manner as democracy from oligarchy — I mean, after a sort?

How?

The good which oligarchy proposed to itself and the means by which it was maintained was excess of wealth — am I not right?

Yes.

And the insatiable desire of wealth and the neglect of all other things for the sake of money-getting was also the ruin of oligarchy?

True.

And democracy has her own good, of which the insatiable desire brings her to dissolution?

What good?

Freedom, I replied; which, as they tell you in a democracy, is the glory of the State — and that therefore in a democracy alone will the freeman of nature deign to dwell.

Yes; the saying is in everybody's mouth.

I was going to observe, that the insatiable desire of this and the neglect of other things introduces the change in democracy, which occasions a demand for tyranny.

How so?

When a democracy which is thirsting for freedom has evil cup-bearers presiding over the feast, and has drunk too deeply of the strong wine of freedom, then, unless her rulers are very amenable and give a plentiful draught, she calls them to account and punishes them, and says that they are cursed oligarchs.

Yes, he replied, a very common occurrence.

Yes, I said; and loyal citizens are insultingly termed by her slaves who hug their chains and men of naught; she would have subjects who are like rulers, and rulers who are like subjects: these are men after her own heart, whom she praises and honors both in private and public. Now, in such a State, can liberty have any limit?

Certainly not.

By degrees the anarchy finds a way into private houses, and ends by getting among the animals and infecting them.

How do you mean?

I mean that the father grows accustomed to descend to the level of his sons and to fear them, and the son is on a level with his father, he having no respect or reverence for either of his parents; and this is his freedom, and the metic is equal with the citizen and the citizen with the metic, and the stranger is quite as good as either.

Yes, he said, that is the way.

And these are not the only evils, I said — there are several lesser ones: In such a state of society the master fears and flatters his scholars, and the scholars despise their masters and tutors; young and old are all alike; and the young man is on a level with the old, and is ready to compete with him in word or deed; and old men condescend to the young and are full of pleasantry and gaiety; they are loth to be thought morose and authoritative, and therefore they adopt the manners of the young.

Quite true, he said.

The last extreme of popular liberty is when the slave bought with money, whether male or female. is just as free as his or her purchaser; nor must 1 forget to tell of the liberty and equality of the two sexes in relation to each other.

Why not, as Æschylus says, utter the word which rises to our lips?

That is what I am doing, I replied; and I must add that no one who does not know would believe, how much greater is the liberty which the animals who are under the dominion of man have in a democracy than in any other State: for truly, the she-dogs, as the proverb says, are as good as their she-mistresses, and the horses and asses have a way of marching along with all the rights and dignities of freemen; and they will run at anybody who comes in their way if he does not leave the road clear for them: and all things are just ready to burst with liberty.

When I take a country walk, he said, I often experience what you describe. You and I have dreamed the same thing.

And above all, I said, and as the result of all, see how sensitive the citizens become; they chafe impatiently at the least touch of authority, and at length, as you know, they cease to care even for the laws, written or unwritten; they will have no one over them.

Yes, he said, I know it too well.

Such, my friend, I said, is the fair and glorious beginning out of which springs tyranny.

Glorious indeed, he said. But what is the next step?

The ruin of oligarchy is the ruin of democracy; the same disease magnified and intensified by liberty overmasters democracy — the truth being that the excessive increase of anything often causes a reaction in the opposite direction; and this is the case not only in the seasons and in vegetable and animal life, but above all in forms of government.

True.

The excess of liberty, whether in States or individuals, seems only to pass into excess of slavery.

Yes, the natural order.

And so tyranny naturally arises out of democracy, and the most aggravated form of tyranny and slavery out of the most extreme form of liberty?

As we might expect.

That, however, was not, as I believe, your question — you rather desired to know what is that disorder which is generated alike in oligarchy and democracy, and is the ruin of both?

Just so, he replied.

Well, I said, I meant to refer to the class of idle spendthrifts, of whom the more courageous are the leaders and the more timid the followers, the same whom we were comparing to drones, some stingless, and others having stings.

A very just comparison.

These two classes are the plagues of every city in

which they are generated, being what phlegm and bile are to the body. And the good physician and law-giver of the State ought, like the wise bee-master, to keep them at a distance and prevent, if possible, their ever coming in; and if they have anyhow found a way in, then he should have them and their cells cut out as speedily as possible.

Yes, by all means, he said.

Then, in order that we may see clearly what we are doing, let us imagine democracy to be divided, as indeed it is, into three classes; for in the first place freedom creates rather more drones in the democratic than there were in the oligarchical State.

That is true.

And in the democracy they are certainly more intensified.

How so?

Because in the oligarchical State they are disqualified and driven from office, and therefore they can not train or gather strength; whereas in a democracy they are almost the entire ruling power, and while the keener sort speak and act, the rest keep buzzing about the bema and do not suffer a word to be said on the other side; hence in democracies almost everything is managed by the drones.

Very true, he said.

Then there is another class which is always being severed from the mass.

What is that?

They are the orderly class, which in a nation of traders is sure to be the richest.

Naturally so.

They are the most squeezable persons and yield the largest amount of honey to the drones.

Why, he said, there is little to be squeezed out of people who have little.

And this is called the wealthy class, and the drones feed upon them.

That is pretty much the case, he said.

The people are a third class, consisting of those who work with their own hands; they are not politicians, and have not much to live upon. This, when assembled, is the largest and most powerful class in a democracy.

True, he said; but then the multitude is seldom willing to congregate unless they get a little honey.

And do they not share? I said. Do not their leaders deprive the rich of their estates and distribute them among the people; at the same time taking care to reserve the larger part for themselves?

Why, yes, he said, to that extent the people do share.

And the persons whose property is taken from them are compelled to defend themselves before the people as they best can?

What else can they do?

And then, although they may have no desire of change, the others charge them with plotting against the people and being friends of oligarchy?

True.

And the end is that when they see the people, not of their own accord, but through ignorance, and because they are deceived by informers, seeking to do them wrong, then at last they are forced to become oligarchs in reality; they do not wish to be, but the sting of the drones torments them and breeds revolution in them.

That is exactly the truth.

Then come impeachments and judgments and trials of one another.

True.

The people have always some champion whom they set over them and nurse into greatness.

Yes, that is their way.

This and no other is the root from which a tyrant springs; when he first appears above ground he is a protector.

Yes, that is quite clear.

How then does a protector begin to change into a tyrant? Clearly when he does what the man is said to do in the tale of the Arcadian temple of Lycæan Zeus.

What tale?

The tale is that he who has tasted the entrails of a single human victim minced up with the entrails of other victims is destined to become a wolf. Did you never hear it?

O yes.

And the protector of the people is like him; having a mob entirely at his disposal, he is not restrained from shedding the blood of kinsmen; by the favorite method of false accusation he brings them into court and murders them, making the life of man to disappear, and with unholy tongue and lips tasting the blood of his fellow citizens; some he kills and others he banishes, at the same time hinting at the abolition of debts and partition of lands: and after this, what will be his destiny? Must he not either perish at the hands of his enemies, or from being a man become a wolf — that is, a tyrant?

Inevitably.

This, I said, is he who begins to make a party against the rich?

The same.

After a while he is driven out, but comes back, in spite of his enemies, a tyrant full grown.

That is clear.

And if they are unable to expel him, or to get him condemned to death by a public accusation, they conspire to assassinate him.

Yes, he said, that is their usual way.

Then comes the famous request for a body-guard, which is the device of all those who have got thus far in their tyrannical career — " Let not the people's friend," as they say, " be lost to them."

Exactly.

The people readily assent; all their fears are for him — they have none for themselves.

Very true.

And when a man who is wealthy and is also accused of being an enemy of the people sees this, then, my friend, as the oracle said to Crœsus,

" By pebbly Hermus' shore he flees and rests not, and is not ashamed to be a coward." [1]

And quite right too, said he, for if he were, he would never be ashamed again.

But if he is caught he dies.

Of course.

And he, the protector of whom we spoke, is to be seen, not " larding the plain " with his bulk, but himself the overthrower of many, standing up in the chariot of State with the reins in his hand, no longer protector, but tyrant absolute.

No doubt, he said.

And now let us consider the happiness of the man, and also of the State in which a creature like him is generated.

Yes, he said, let us consider that.

At first, in the early days of his power, he is full of smiles, and he salutes every one whom he meets; — he to be called a tyrant, who is making promises in

[1] Herod. i. 55.

public and also in private! liberating debtors, and distributing land to the people and his followers, and wanting to be so kind and good to every one!

Of course, he said.

But when he has disposed of foreign enemies by conquest or treaty, and there is nothing to fear from them, then he is always stirring up some war or other, in order that the people may require a leader.

To be sure.

Has he not also another object, which is that they may be impoverished by payment of taxes, and thus compelled to devote themselves to their daily wants and therefore less likely to conspire against him?

Clearly.

And if any of them are suspected by him of having notions of freedom, and of resistance to his authority, he will have a good pretext for destroying them by placing them at the mercy of the enemy; and for all these reasons the tyrant must be always getting up a war.

He must.

Now he begins to grow unpopular.

A necessary result.

Then some of those who joined in setting him up, and who are in power, speak their minds to him and to one another, and the more courageous of them cast in his teeth what is being done.

Yes, that may be expected.

And the tyrant, if he means to rule, must get rid of them; he can not stop while he has a friend or an enemy who is good for anything.

He can not.

And therefore he must look about him and see who is valiant, who is high-minded, who is wise, who is wealthy; happy man, he is the enemy of them all, and

must seek occasion against them whether he will or
no, until he has made a purgation of the State.

Yes, he said, and a rare purgation.

Yes, I said, not the sort of purgation which the
physicians make of the body; for they take away the
worse and leave the better part, but he does the reverse.

If he is to rule, I suppose that he can not help
himself.

What a blessed alternative, I said: — to be compelled to dwell only with the many bad, and to be by
them hated, or not to live at all!

Yes, that is the alternative.

And the more detestable his actions are to the citizens the more satellites and the greater devotion in
them will he require?

Certainly.

And who are the devoted band, and where will he
procure them?

They will flock to him, he said, of their own accord,
if he pays them.

By the dog! I said, here are more drones, of every
sort and from every land.

Yes, he said, there are.

But will he not desire to get them on the spot?

How do you mean?

He will rob the citizens of their slaves; he will
then set them free and enroll them in his body-
guard.

To be sure, he said; and he will be able to trust
them best of all.

What a blessed creature, I said, must this tyrant
be; he has put to death the others and has these for his
trusted friends.

Yes, he said; they are quite of his sort.

Yes, I said, and these are the new citizens whom

he has called into existence, who admire him and are his companions, while the good hate and avoid him.

Of course.

Verily, then, tragedy is a wise thing and Euripides a great tragedian.

Why so?

Why, because he is the author of the pregnant saying,

"Tyrants are wise by living with the wise;"

and he clearly meant to say that they are the wise whom the tyrant makes his companions.

Yes, he said, and he also praises tyranny as godlike; and many other things of the same kind are said by him and by the other poets.

And therefore, I said, the tragic poets being wise men will forgive us and any others who live after our manner if we do not receive them into our State, because they are the eulogists of tyranny.

Yes, he said, those who have the wit will doubtless forgive us.

But they will continue to go to other cities and attract mobs, and hire voices fair and loud and persuasive, and draw the cities over to tyrannies and democracies.

Very true.

Moreover, they are paid for this and receive honor — the greatest honor, as might be expected, from tyrants, and the next greatest from democracies; but the higher they ascend our constitution hill, the more their reputation fails, and seems unable from shortness of breath to proceed further.

True.

But we are wandering from the subject: Let us therefore return and inquire how the tyrant will main--

tain that fair and numerous and various and ever-changing army of his.

If, he said, there are sacred treasures in the city, he will confiscate and spend them; and in so far as the fortunes of attainted persons may suffice, he will be able to diminish the taxes which he would otherwise have to impose upon the people.

And when these fail?

Why, clearly, he said, then he and his boon companions, whether male or female, will be maintained out of his father's estate.

You mean to say that the people, from whom he has derived his being, will maintain him and his companions?

Yes, he said; they can not help themselves.

But what if the people fly into a passion, and aver that a grown-up son ought not to be supported by his father, but that the father should be supported by the son? The father did not bring him into being, or settle him in life, in order that when his son became a man he should himself be the servant of his own servants and should support him and his rabble of slaves and companions; but that his son should protect him, and that by his help he might be emancipated from the government of the rich and aristocratic, as they are termed. And so he bids him and his companions depart, just as any other father might drive out of the house a riotous son and his undesirable associates.

By heaven, he said, then the parent will discover what a monster he has been fostering in his bosom; and, when he wants to drive him out, he will find that he is weak and his son strong.

Why, you do not mean to say that the tyrant will use violence? What! beat his father if he opposes him?

Yes, he will, having first disarmed him.

Then he is a parricide, and a cruel guardian of an aged parent; and this is real tyranny, about which there can be no longer a mistake: as the saying is, the people who would escape the smoke which is the slavery of freemen, has fallen into the fire which is the tyranny of slaves. Thus liberty, getting out of all order and reason, passes into the harshest and bitterest form of slavery.

True, he said.

Very well; and may we not rightly say that we have sufficiently discussed the nature of tyranny, and the manner of the transition from democracy to tyranny?

Yes, quite enough, he said.

BOOK IX

LAST of all comes the tyrannical man; about whom we have once more to ask, how is he formed out of the democratical? and how does he live, in happiness or in misery?

Yes, he said, he is the only one remaining.

There is, however, I said, a previous question which remains unanswered.

What question?

I do not think that we have adequately determined the nature and number of the appetites, and until this is accomplished the inquiry will always be confused.

Well, he said, it is not too late to supply the omission.

Very true, I said; and observe the point which I want to understand: Certain of the unnecessary pleasures and appetites I conceive to be unlawful; every one appears to have them, but in some persons they are controlled by the laws and by reason, and the better desires prevail over them — either they are wholly banished or they become few and weak; while in the case of others they are stronger, and there are more of them.

Which appetites do you mean?

I mean those which are awake when the reasoning and human and ruling power is asleep; then the wild beast within us, gorged with meat or drink, starts up and having shaken off sleep, goes forth to satisfy his desires; and there is no conceivable folly or crime — not excepting incest or any other unnatural

346

union, or parricide, or the eating of forbidden food —
which at such a time, when he has parted company
with all shame and sense, a man may not be ready to
commit.

Most true, he said.

But when a man's pulse is healthy and temperate,
and when before going to sleep he has awakened his
rational powers, and fed them on noble thoughts and
inquiries, collecting himself in meditation; after having first indulged his appetites neither too much nor
too little, but just enough to lay them to sleep, and
prevent them and their judgments and pains from
interfering with the higher principle — which he
leaves in the solitude of pure abstraction, free to contemplate and aspire to the knowledge of the unknown,
whether in past, present, or future: when again he has
allayed the passionate element, if he has a quarrel
against any one — I say, when, after pacifying the
two irrational principles, he rouses up the third, which
is reason, before he takes his rest, then, as you know,
he attains truth most nearly, and is least likely to be
the sport of fantastic and lawless visions.

I quite agree.

In saying this I have been running into a digression; but the point which I desire to note is that in
all of us, even in good men, there is a lawless wild-
beast nature, which peers out in sleep. Pray, consider whether I am right, and you agree with me.

Yes, I agree.

And now remember the character which we attributed to the democratic man. He was supposed from
his youth upwards to have been trained under a
miserly parent, who encouraged the saving appetites
in him, but discountenanced the unnecessary, which
aim only at amusement and ornament?

True.

And then he got into the company of a more refined, licentious sort of people, and taking to all their wanton ways rushed into the opposite extreme from an abhorrence of his father's meanness. At last, being a better man than his corruptors, he was drawn in both directions until he halted midway and led a life, not of vulgar and slavish passion, but of what he deemed moderate indulgence in various pleasures. After this manner the democrat was generated out of the oligarch?

Yes, he said; that was our view of him, and is so still.

And now, I said, years will have passed away, and you must conceive this man, such as he is, to have a son, who is brought up in his father's principles.

I can imagine him.

Then you must further imagine the same thing to happen to the son which has already happened to the father: — he is drawn into a perfectly lawless life, which by his seducers is termed perfect liberty; and his father and friends take part with his moderate desires, and the opposite party assist the opposite ones. As soon as these dire magicians and tyrant-makers find that they are losing their hold on him, they contrive to implant in him a master passion, to be lord over his idle and spendthrift lusts — a sort of monstrous winged drone — that is the only image which will adequately describe him.

Yes, he said, that is the only adequate image of him.

And when his other lusts, amid clouds of incense and perfumes and garlands and wines, and all the pleasures of a dissolute life, now let loose, come buzzing around him, nourishing to the utmost the sting of desire which they implant in his drone-like nature, then at last this lord of the soul, having Madness for the captain of his guard, breaks out into a frenzy; and if he finds in himself any good opinions or appetites in process of formation,[1] and there is in him any sense of shame remaining, to these better principles he puts an end, and casts them forth until he has purged away temperance and brought in madness to the full.

Yes, he said, that is the way in which the tyrannical man is generated.

And is not this the reason why of old love has been called a tyrant?

I should not wonder.

Further, I said, has not a drunken man also the spirit of a tyrant?

He has.

And you know that a man who is deranged and not right in his mind, will fancy that he is able to rule, not only over men, but also over the gods?

That he will.

And the tyrannical man in the true sense of the word comes into being when, either under the influ-ence of nature, or habit, or both, he becomes drunken, lustful, passionate? O my friend, is not that so?

Assuredly.

Such is the man and such is his origin. And next, how does he live?

Suppose, as people facetiously say, you were to tell me.

I imagine, I said, at the next step in his progress, that there will be feasts and carousals and revellings and courtezans, and all that sort of thing; Love is the lord of the house within him, and orders all the con-cerns of his soul.

That is certain.

Yes; and every day and every night desires grow up many and formidable, and their demands are many.

[1] Or "opinions or appetites such as are deemed to be good."

They are indeed, he said.

His revenues, if he has any, are soon spent.

True.

Then comes debt and the cutting down of his prop‧ erty.

Of course.

When he has nothing left, must not his desires, crowding in the nest like young ravens, be crying aloud for food; and he, goaded on by them, and especially by love himself, who is in a manner the captain of them, is in a frenzy, and would fain discover whom he can defraud or despoil of his property, in order that he may gratify them?

Yes, that is sure to be the case.

He must have money, no matter how, if he is to escape horrid pains and pangs.

He must.

And as in himself there was a succession of pleasures, and the new got the better of the old and took away their rights, so he being younger will claim to have more than his father and his mother, and if he has spent his own share of the property, he will take a slice of theirs.

No doubt he will.

And if his parents will not give way, then he will try first of all to cheat and deceive them.

Very true.

And if he fails, then he will use force and plunder them.

Yes, probably.

And if the old man and woman fight for their own, what then, my friend? Will the creature feel any compunction at tyrannizing over them?

Nay, he said, I should not feel at all comfortable about his parents.

But, O heavens! Adeimantus, on account of some

new-fangled love of a harlot, who is anything but a
necessary connection, can you believe that he would
strike the mother who is his ancient friend and necessary to his very existence, and would place her under
the authority of the other, when she is brought under
the same roof with her; or that, under like circumstances, he would do the same to his withered old
father, first and most indispensable of friends, for the
sake of some newly-found blooming youth who is the
reverse of indispensable?

Yes, indeed, he said; I believe that he would.

Truly, then, I said, a tyrannical son is a blessing
to his father and mother.

He is indeed, he replied.

He first takes their property, and when that fails,
and pleasures are beginning to swarm in the hive of
his soul, then he breaks into a house, or steals the garments of some nightly wayfarer; next he proceeds to
clear a temple. Meanwhile the old opinions which he
had when a child, and which gave judgment about
good and evil, are overthrown by those others which
have just been emancipated, and are now the body-
guard of love and share his empire. These in his democratic days, when he was still subject to the laws and
to his father, were only let loose in the dreams of sleep.
But now that he is under the dominion of Love, he
becomes always and in waking reality what he was
then very rarely and in a dream only; he will commit
the foulest murder, or eat forbidden food, or be guilty
of any other horrid act. Love is his tyrant, and lives
lordly in him and lawlessly, and being himself a king,
leads him on, as a tyrant leads a State, to the performance of any reckless deed by which he can maintain himself and the rabble of his associates, whether
those whom evil communications have brought in from
without, or those whom he himself has allowed to

break loose within him by reason of a similar evil nature in himself. Have we not here a picture of his way of life?

Yes, indeed, he said.

And if there are only a few of them in the State, and the rest of the people are well disposed, they go away and become the body-guard or mercenary soldiers of some other tyrant who may probably want them for a war; and if there is no war, they stay at home and do many little pieces of mischief in the city.

What sort of mischief?

For example, they are the thieves, burglars, cut-purses, foot-pads, robbers of temples, man-stealers of the community; or if they are able to speak they turn informers, and bear false witness, and take bribes.

A small catalogue of evils, even if the perpetrators of them are few in number.

Yes, I said; but small and great are comparative terms, and all these things, in the misery and evil which they inflict upon a State, do not come within a thousand miles of the tyrant; when this noxious class and their followers grow numerous and become conscious of their strength, assisted by the infatuation of the people, they choose from among themselves the one who has most of the tyrant in his own soul, and him they create their tyrant.

Yes, he said, and he will be the most fit to be a tyrant.

If the people yield, well and good; but if they resist him, as he began by beating his own father and mother, so now, if he has the power, he beats them, and will keep his dear old fatherland or motherland, as the Cretans say, in subjection to his young retainers whom he has introduced to be their rulers and masters. This is the end of his passions and desires.

Exactly.

When such men are only private individuals and before they get power, this is their character; they associate entirely with their own flatterers or ready tools; or if they want anything from anybody, they in their turn are equally ready to bow down before them: they profess every sort of affection for them; but when they have gained their point they know them no more.

Yes, truly.

They are always either the masters or servants and never the friends of anybody; the tyrant never tastes of true freedom or friendship.

Certainly not.

And may we not rightly call such men treacherous?

No question.

Also they are utterly unjust, if we were right in our notion of justice?

Yes, he said, and we were perfectly right.

Let us then sum up in a word, I said, the character of the worst man: he is the waking reality of what we dreamed.

Most true.

And this is he who being by nature most of a tyrant bears rule, and the longer he lives the more of a tyrant he becomes.

That is certain, said Glaucon, taking his turn to answer.

And will not he who has been shown to be the wickedest, be also the most miserable? and he who has tyrannized longest and most, most continually and truly miserable; although this may not be the opinion of men in general?

Yes, he said, inevitably.

And must not the tyrannical man be like the tyrannical State, and the democratical man like the democratical State; and the same of the others?

Certainly.

And as State is to State in virtue and happiness, so is man in relation to man?

To be sure.

Then comparing our original city, which was under a king, and the city which is under a tyrant, how do they stand as to virtue?

They are the opposite extremes, he said, for one is the very best and the other is the very worst.

There can be no mistake, I said, as to which is which, and therefore I will at once inquire whether you would arrive at a similar decision about their relative happiness and misery. And here we must not allow ourselves to be panic-stricken at the apparition of the tyrant, who is only a unit and may perhaps have a few retainers about him; but let us go as we ought into every corner of the city and look all about, and then we will give our opinion.

A fair invitation, he replied; and I see, as every one must, that a tyranny is the wretchedest form of government, and the rule of a king the happiest.

And in estimating the men too, may I not fairly make a like request, that I should have a judge whose mind can enter into and see through human nature? he must not be like a child who looks at the outside and is dazzled at the pompous aspect which the tyrannical nature assumes to the beholder, but let him be one who has a clear insight. May I suppose that the judgment is given in the hearing of us all by one who is able to judge, and has dwelt in the same place with him, and been present at his daily life and known him in his family relations, where he may be seen stripped of his tragedy attire, and again in the hour of public danger — he shall tell us about the happiness and misery of the tyrant when compared with other men?

That again, he said, is a very fair proposal.

Shall I assume that we ourselves are able and experienced judges and have before now met with such a person? We shall then have some one who will answer our inquiries.

By all means.

Let me ask you not to forget the parallel of the individual and the State; bearing this in mind, and glancing in turn from one to the other of them, will you tell me their respective conditions?

What do you mean? he asked.

Beginning with the State, I replied, would you say that a city which is governed by a tyrant is free or enslaved?

No city, he said, can be more completely enslaved.

And yet, as you see, there are freemen as well as masters in such a State?

Yes, he said, I see that there are — a few; but the people, speaking generally, and the best of them are miserably degraded and enslaved.

Then if the man is like the State, I said, must not the same rule prevail? his soul is full of meanness and vulgarity — the best elements in him are enslaved; and there is a small ruling part, which is also the worst and maddest.

Inevitably.

And would you say that the soul of such an one is the soul of a freeman, or of a slave?

He has the soul of a slave, in my opinion.

And the State which is enslaved under a tyrant is utterly incapable of acting voluntarily?

Utterly incapable.

And also the soul which is under a tyrant (I am speaking of the soul taken as a whole) is least capable of doing what she desires; there is a gadfly which goads her, and she is full of trouble and remorse?

Certainly.

And is the city which is under a tyrant rich or poor?

Poor.

And the tyrannical soul must be always poor and insatiable?

True.

And must not such a State and such a man be always full of fear?

Yes, indeed.

Is there any State in which you will find more of lamentation and sorrow and groaning and pain?

Certainly not.

And is there any man in whom you will find more of this sort of misery than in the tyrannical man, who is in a fury of passions and desires?

Impossible.

Reflecting upon these and similar evils, you held the tyrannical State to be the most miserable of States?

And I was right, he said.

Certainly, I said. And when you see the same evils in the tyrannical man, what do you say of him?

I say that he is by far the most miserable of all men.

There, I said, I think that you are beginning to go wrong.

What do you mean?

I do not think that he has as yet reached the utmost extreme of misery.

Then who is more miserable?

One of whom I am about to speak.

Who is that?

He who is of a tyrannical nature, and instead of leading a private life has been cursed with the further misfortune of being a public tyrant.

From what has been said, I gather that you are right.

Yes, I replied, but in this high argument you should

be a little more certain, and should not conjecture only; for of all questions, this respecting good and evil is the greatest.

Very true, he said.

Let me then offer you an illustration, which may, I think, throw a light upon this subject.

What is your illustration?

The case of rich individuals in cities who possess many slaves: from them you may form an idea of the tyrant's condition, for they both have slaves; the only difference is that he has more slaves.

Yes, that is the difference.

You know that they live securely and have nothing to apprehend from their servants?

What should they fear?

Nothing. But do you observe the reason of this?

Yes; the reason is, that the whole city is leagued together for the protection of each individual.

Very true, I said. But imagine one of these owners, the master say of some fifty slaves, together with his family and property and slaves, carried off by a god into the wilderness, where there are no free-men to help him — will he not be in an agony of fear lest he and his wife and children should be put to death by his slaves?

Yes, he said, he will be in the utmost fear.

The time has arrived when he will be compelled to flatter divers of his slaves, and make many promises to them of freedom and other things, much against his will — he will have to cajole his own servants.

Yes, he said, that will be the only way of saving himself.

And suppose the same god, who carried him away, to surround him with neighbors who will not suffer one man to be the master of another, and who, if they could catch the offender, would take his life?

His case will be still worse, if you suppose him to be everywhere surrounded and watched by enemies.

And is not this the sort of prison in which the tyrant will be bound — he who being by nature such as we have described, is full of all sorts of fears and lusts? His soul is dainty and greedy, and yet alone, of all men in the city, he is never allowed to go on a journey, or to see the things which other freemen desire to see, but he lives in his hole like a woman hidden in the house, and is jealous of any other citizen who goes into foreign parts and sees anything of interest.

Very true, he said.

And amid evils such as these will not he who is ill-governed in his own person — the tyrannical man, I mean — whom you just now decided to be the most miserable of all — will not he be yet more miserable when, instead of leading a private life, he is constrained by fortune to be a public tyrant? He has to be master of others when he is not master of himself: he is like a diseased or paralytic man who is compelled to pass his life, not in retirement, but fighting and combating with other men.

Yes, he said, the similitude is most exact.

Is not his case utterly miserable? and does not the actual tyrant lead a worse life than he whose life you determined to be the worst?

Certainly.

He who is the real tyrant, whatever men may think, is the real slave, and is obliged to practise the greatest adulation and servility, and to be the flatterer of the vilest of mankind. He has desires which he is utterly unable to satisfy, and has more wants than any one, and is truly poor, if you know how to inspect the whole soul of him: all his life long he is beset with fear and is full of convulsions and distractions, even as the State which he resembles: and surely the resemblance holds?

Very true, he said.

Moreover, as we were saying before, he grows worse from having power: he becomes and is of necessity more jealous, more faithless, more unjust, more friendless, more impious, than he was at first; he is the purveyor and cherisher of every sort of vice, and the consequence is that he is supremely miserable, and that he makes everybody else as miserable as himself.

No man of any sense will dispute your words.

Come then, I said, and as the general umpire in theatrical contests proclaims the result, do you also decide who in your opinion is first in the scale of happiness, and who second, and in what order the others follow: there are five of them in all — they are the royal, timocratical, oligarchical, democratical, tyrannical.

The decision will be easily given, he replied; they shall be choruses coming on the stage, and I must judge them in the order in which they enter, by the criterion of virtue and vice, happiness and misery.

Need we hire a herald, or shall I announce, that the son of Ariston [the best] has decided that the best and justest is also the happiest, and that this is he who is the most royal man and king over himself; and that the worst and most unjust man is also the most miserable, and that this is he who being the greatest tyrant of himself is also the greatest tyrant of his State?

Make the proclamation yourself, he said.

And shall I add, " whether seen or unseen by gods and men "?

Let the words be added.

Then this, I said, will be our first proof; and there is another, which may also have some weight.

What is that?

The second proof is derived from the nature of the soul: seeing that the individual soul, like the State, has been divided by us into three principles, the division may, I think, furnish a new demonstration.

Of what nature?

It seems to me that to these three principles three pleasures correspond; also three desires and governing powers.

How do you mean? he said.

There is one principle with which, as we were saying, a man learns, another with which he is angry; the third, having many forms, has no special name, but is denoted by the general term appetitive, from the extraordinary strength and vehemence of the desires of eating and drinking and the other sensual appetites which are the main elements of it; also money-loving, because such desires are generally satisfied by the help of money.

That is true, he said.

If we were to say that the loves and pleasures of this third part were concerned with gain, we should then be able to fall back on a single notion; and might truly and intelligibly describe this part of the soul as loving gain or money.

I agree with you.

Again, is not the passionate element wholly set on ruling and conquering and getting fame?

True.

Suppose we call it the contentious or ambitious — would the term be suitable?

Extremely suitable.

On the other hand, every one sees that the principle of knowledge is wholly directed to the truth, and cares less than either of the others for gain or fame.

Far less.

"Lover of wisdom," "lover of knowledge," are

tides which we may fitly apply to that part of the soul?

Certainly.

One principle prevails in the souls of one class of men, another in others, as may happen?

Yes.

Then we may begin by assuming that there are three classes of men — lovers of wisdom, lovers of honor, lovers of gain?

Exactly.

And there are three kinds of pleasure, which are their several objects?

Very true.

Now, if you examine the three classes of men, and ask of them in turn which of their lives is pleasantest, each will be found praising his own and depreciating that of others: the money-maker will contrast the vanity of honor or of learning if they bring no money with the solid advantages of gold and silver?

True, he said.

And the lover of honor — what will be his opinion? Will he not think that the pleasure of riches is vulgar, while the pleasure of learning, if it brings no distinction, is all smoke and nonsense to him?

Very true.

And are we to suppose,[1] I said, that the philosopher sets any value on other pleasures in comparison with the pleasure of knowing the truth, and in that pursuit abiding, ever learning, not so far indeed from the heaven of pleasure? Does he not call the other pleasures necessary, under the idea that if there were no necessity for them, he would rather not have them?

There can be no doubt of that, he replied.

Since, then, the pleasures of each class and the life

[1] Reading with Grasere and Hermann τί οἰώμεθα, and omitting οὐδὲη which is not found in the best MSS.

of each are in dispute, and the question is not which
life is more or less honorable, or better or worse, but
which is the more pleasant or painless — how shall we
know who speaks truly?

I can not myself tell, he said.

Well, but what ought to be the criterion? Is any
better than experience and wisdom and reason?

There can not be a better, he said.

Then, I said, reflect. Of the three individuals,
which has the greatest experience of all the pleasures
which we enumerated? Has the lover of gain, in
learning the nature of essential truth, greater experience of the pleasure of knowledge than the philosopher has of the pleasure of gain?

The philosopher, he replied, has greatly the advantage; for he has of necessity always known the
taste of the other pleasures from his childhood upwards: but the lover of gain in all his experience has
not of necessity tasted — or, I should rather say, even
had he desired, could hardly have tasted — the sweetness of learning and knowing truth.

Then the lover of wisdom has a great advantage
over the lover of gain, for he has a double experience?

Yes, very great.

Again, has he greater experience of the pleasures of
honor, or the lover of honor of the pleasures of wisdom?

Nay, he said, all three are honored in proportion as
they attain their object; for the rich man and the
brave man and the wise man alike have their crowd
of admirers, and as they all receive honor they all have
experience of the pleasures of honor; but the delight
which is to be found in the knowledge of true being
is known to the philosopher only.

His experience, then, will enable him to judge better than any one?

Far better.

And he is the only one who has wisdom as well as experience?

Certainly.

Further, the very faculty which is the instrument of judgment is not possessed by the covetous or ambitious man, but only by the philosopher?

What faculty?

Reason, with whom, as we were saying, the decision ought to rest.

Yes.

And reasoning is peculiarly his instrument?

Certainly.

If wealth and gain were the criterion, then the praise or blame of the lover of gain would surely be the most trustworthy?

Assuredly.

Or if honor or victory or courage, in that case the judgment of the ambitious or pugnacious would be the truest?

Clearly.

But since experience and wisdom and reason are the judges —

The only inference possible, he replied, is that pleasures which are approved by the lover of wisdom and reason are the truest.

And so we arrive at the result, that the pleasure of the intelligent part of the soul is the pleasantest of the three, and that he of us in whom this is the ruling principle has the pleasantest life.

Unquestionably, he said, the wise man speaks with authority when he approves of his own life.

And what does the judge affirm to be the life which is next, and the pleasure which is next?

Clearly that of the soldier and lover of honor; who is nearer to himself than the money-maker.

Last comes the lover of gain?

Very true, he said.

Twice in succession, then, has the just man over-thrown the unjust in this conflict; and now comes the third trial, which is dedicated to Olympian Zeus the savior: a sage whispers in my ear that no pleasure except that of the wise is quite true and pure — all others are a shadow only; and surely this will prove the greatest and most decisive of falls?

Yes, the greatest; but will you explain yourself?

I will work out the subject and you shall answer my questions.

Proceed.

Say, then, is not pleasure opposed to pain?

True.

And there is a neutral state which is neither pleasure nor pain?

There is.

A state which is intermediate, and a sort of repose of the soul about either — that is what you mean?

Yes.

You remember what people say when they are sick?

What do they say?

That after all nothing is pleasanter than health. But then they never knew this to be the greatest of pleasures until they were ill.

Yes, I know, he said.

And when persons are suffering from acute pain, you must have heard them say that there is nothing pleasanter than to get rid of their pain?

I have.

And there are many other cases of suffering in which the mere rest and cessation of pain, and not any positive enjoyment, is extolled by them as the greatest pleasure?

Yes, he said; at the time they are pleased and well content to be at rest.

Again, when pleasure ceases, that sort of rest or cessation will be painful?

Doubtless, he said.

Then the intermediate state of rest will be pleasure and will also be pain?

So it would seem.

But can that which is neither become both?

I should say not.

And both pleasure and pain are motions of the soul, are they not?

Yes.

But that which is neither was just now shown to be rest and not motion, and in a mean between them?

Yes.

How, then, can we be right in supposing that the absence of pain is pleasure, or that the absence of pleasure is pain?

Impossible.

This then is an appearance only and not a reality; that is to say, the rest is pleasure at the moment and in comparison of what is painful, and painful in comparison of what is pleasant; but all these representations, when tried by the test of true pleasure, are not real but a sort of imposition?

That is the inference.

Look at the other class of pleasures which have no antecedent pains and you will no longer suppose, as you perhaps may at present, that pleasure is only the cessation of pain, or pain of pleasure.

What are they, he said, and where shall I find them?

There are many of them: take as an example the pleasures of smell, which are very great and have no antecedent pains; they come in a moment, and when they depart leave no pain behind them.

Most true, he said.

Let us not, then, be induced to believe that pure pleasure is the cessation of pain, or pain of pleasure.

No.

Still, the more numerous and violent pleasures which reach the soul through the body are generally of this sort — they are reliefs of pain.

That is true.

And the anticipations of future pleasures and pains are of a like nature?

Yes.

Shall I give you an illustration of them?

Let me hear.

You would allow, I said, that there is in nature an upper and lower and middle region?

I should.

And if a person were to go from the lower to the middle region, would he not imagine that he is going up; and he who is standing in the middle and sees whence he has come, would imagine that he is already in the upper region, if he has never seen the true upper world?

To be sure, he said; how can he think otherwise?

But if he were taken back again he would imagine, and truly imagine, that he was descending?

No doubt.

All that would arise out of his ignorance of the true upper and middle and lower regions?

Yes.

Then can you wonder that persons who are inexperienced in the truth, as they have wrong ideas about many other things, should also have wrong ideas about pleasure and pain and the intermediate state; so that when they are only being drawn towards the painful they feel pain and think the pain which they experience to be real, and in like manner, when drawn away from pain to the neutral or intermediate state, they firmly believe that they have reached the goal of satiety and pleasure; they, not knowing pleasure, err in contrasting pain with the absence of pain, which is like contrasting black with gray instead of white — can you wonder, I say, at this?

No, indeed; I should be much more disposed to wonder at the opposite.

Look at the matter thus: — Hunger, thirst, and the like, are inanitions of the bodily state?

Yes.

And ignorance and folly are inanitions of the soul?

True.

And food and wisdom are the corresponding satisfactions of either?

Certainly.

And is the satisfaction derived from that which has less or from that which has more existence the truer?

Clearly, from that which has more.

What classes of things have a greater share of pure existence in your judgment — those of which food and drink and condiments and all kinds of sustenance are examples, or the class which contains true opinion and knowledge and mind and all the different kinds of virtue? Put the question in this way: — Which has a more pure being — that which is concerned with the invariable, the immortal, and the true, and is of such a nature, and is found in such natures; or that which is concerned with and found in the variable and mortal, and is itself variable and mortal?

Far purer, he replied, is the being of that which is concerned with the invariable.

And does the essence of the invariable partake of knowledge in the same degree as of essence?

Yes, of knowledge in the same degree.

And of truth in the same degree?

Yes.

And, conversely, that which has less of truth will also have less of essence?

Necessarily.

Then, in general, those kinds of things which are in the service of the body have less of truth and essence than those which are in the service of the soul?

Far less.

And has not the body itself less of truth and essence than the soul?

Yes.

What is filled with more real existence, and actually has a more real existence, is more really filled than that which is filled with less real existence and is less real?

Of course.

And if there be a pleasure in being filled with that which is according to nature, that which is more really filled with more real being will more really and truly enjoy true pleasure; whereas that which participates in less real being will be less truly and surely satisfied, and will participate in an illusory and less real pleasure?

Unquestionably.

Those then who know not wisdom and virtue, and are always busy with gluttony and sensuality, go down and up again as far as the mean; and in this region they move at random throughout life, but they never pass into the true upper world; thither they neither look, nor do they ever find their way, neither are they truly filled with true being, nor do they taste of pure and abiding pleasure. Like cattle, with their eyes always looking down and their heads stooping to the earth, that is, to the dining table, they fatten and feed and breed, and, in their excessive love of these delights, they kick and butt at one another with horns and hoofs which are made of iron; and they kill one another by reason of their insatiable lust. For they fill themselves with that which is not substantial, and the part of themselves which they fill is also unsubstantial and incontinent.

Verily, Socrates, said Glaucon, you describe the life of the many like an oracle.

Their pleasures are mixed with pains — how can they be otherwise? For they are mere shadows and pictures of the true, and are colored by contrast, which exaggerates both light and shade, and so they implant in the minds of fools insane desires of themselves; and they are fought about as Stesichorus says that the Greeks fought about the shadow of Helen at Troy in ignorance of the truth.

Something of that sort must inevitably happen.

And must not the like happen with the spirited or passionate element of the soul? Will not the passionate man who carries his passion into action, be in the like case, whether he is envious and ambitious, or violent and contentious, or angry and discontented, if he be seeking to attain honor and victory and the satisfaction of his anger without reason or sense?

Yes, he said, the same will happen with the spirited element also.

Then may we not confidently assert that the lovers of money and honor, when they seek their pleasures under the guidance and in the company of reason and knowledge, and pursue after and win the pleasures which wisdom shows them, will also have the truest pleasures in the highest degree which is attainable to them, inasmuch as they follow truth; and they will have the pleasures which are natural to them, if that which is best for each one is also most natural to him?

Yes, certainly; the best is the most natural.

And when the whole soul follows the philosophical

principle, and there is no division, the several parts are just, and do each of them their own business, and enjoy severally the best and truest pleasures of which they are capable?

Exactly.

But when either of the two other principles prevails, it fails in attaining its own pleasure, and compels the rest to pursue after a pleasure which is a shadow only and which is not their own?

True.

And the greater the interval which separates them from philosophy and reason, the more strange and illusive will be the pleasure?

Yes.

And is not that farthest from reason which is at the greatest distance from law and order?

Clearly.

And the lustful and tyrannical desires are, as we saw, at the greatest distance?

Yes.

And the royal and orderly desires are nearest?

Yes.

Then the tyrant will live at the greatest distance from true or natural pleasure, and the king at the least?

Certainly.

But if so, the tyrant will live most unpleasantly, and the king most pleasantly?

Inevitably.

Would you know the measure of the interval which separates them?

Will you tell me?

There appear to be three pleasures, one genuine and two spurious: now the transgression of the tyrant reaches a point beyond the spurious; he has run away from the region of law and reason, and taken up his

abode with certain slave pleasures which are his satellites, and the measure of his inferiority can only be
expressed in a figure.

How do you mean?

I assume, I said, that the tyrant is in the third place
from the oligarch; the democrat was in the middle?

Yes.

And if there is truth in what has preceded, he will
be wedded to an image of pleasure which is thrice
removed as to truth from the pleasure of the oligarch?

He will.

And the oligarch is third from the royal; since we
count as one royal and aristocratical?

Yes, he is third.

Then the tyrant is removed from true pleasure by
the space of a number which is three times three?

Manifestly.

The shadow then of tyrannical pleasure determined
by the number of length will be a plane figure.

Certainly.

And if you raise the power and make the plane a
solid, there is no difficulty in seeing how vast is the
interval by which the tyrant is parted from the
king.

Yes; the arithmetician will easily do the sum.

Or if some person begins at the other end and
measures the interval by which the king is parted from
the tyrant in truth of pleasure, he will find him, when
the multiplication is completed, living 729 times more
pleasantly, and the tyrant more painfully by this
same interval.

What a wonderful calculation! And how enormous is the distance which separates the just from the
unjust in regard to pleasure and pain!

Yet a true calculation, I said, and a number which
nearly concerns human life, if human beings are

concerned with days and nights and months and years.[1]

Yes, he said, human life is certainly concerned with them.

Then if the good and just man be thus superior in pleasure to the evil and unjust, his superiority will be infinitely greater in propriety of life and in beauty and virtue?

Immeasurably greater.

Well, I said, and now having arrived at this stage of the argument, we may revert to the words which brought us hither: Was not some one saying that injustice was a gain to the perfectly unjust who was reputed to be just?

Yes, that was said.

Now then, having determined the power and quality of justice and injustice, let us have a little conversation with him.

What shall we say to him?

Let us make an image of the soul, that he may have his own words presented before his eyes.

Of what sort?

An ideal image of the soul, like the composite creations of ancient mythology, such as the Chimera or Scylla or Cerberus, and there are many others in which two or more different natures are said to grow into one.

There are said to have been such unions.

Then do you now model the form of a multitudinous, many-headed monster, having a ring of heads of all manner of beasts, tame and wild, which he is able to generate and metamorphose at will.

You suppose marvellous powers in the artist; but, as language is more pliable than wax or any similar substance, let there be such a model as you propose.

[1] 729 *nearly* equals the number of days and nights in the year.

Suppose now that you make a second form as of a lion, and a third of a man, the second smaller than the first, and the third smaller than the second.

That, he said, is an easier task; and I have made them as you say.

And now join them, and let the three go into one.

That has been accomplished.

Next fashion the outside of them into a single image, as of a man, so that he who is not able to look within, and sees only the outer hull, may believe the beast to be a single human creature.

I have done so, he said.

And now, to him who maintains that it is profitable for the human creature to be unjust, and unprofitable to be just, let us reply that, if he be right, it is profitable for this creature to feast the multitudinous monster and strengthen the lion and the lion-like qualities, but to starve and weaken the man, who is consequently liable to be dragged about at the mercy of either of the other two; and he is not to attempt to familiarize or harmonize them with one another — he ought rather to suffer them to fight and bite and devour one another.

Certainly, he said; that is what the approver of injustice says.

To him the supporter of justice makes answer that he should ever so speak and act as to give the man within him in some way or other the most complete mastery over the entire human creature. He should watch over the many-headed monster like a good husbandman, fostering and cultivating the gentle qualities, and preventing the wild ones from growing; he should be making the lion-heart his ally, and in common care of them all should be uniting the several parts with one another and with himself.

Yes, he said, that is quite what the maintainer of justice will say.

And so from every point of view, whether of pleasure, honor, or advantage, the approver of justice is right and speaks the truth, and the disapprover is wrong and false and ignorant?

Yes, from every point of view.

Come, now, and let us gently reason with the unjust, who is not intentionally in error. " Sweet Sir," we will say to him, " what think you of things esteemed noble and ignoble? Is not the noble that which subjects the beast to the man, or rather to the god in man; and the ignoble that which subjects the man to the beast? " He can hardly avoid saying Yes — can he now?

Not if he has any regard for my opinion.

But, if he agrees so far, we may ask him to answer another question: " Then how would a man profit if he received gold and silver on the condition that he was to enslave the noblest part of him to the worst? Who can imagine that a man who sold his son or daughter into slavery for money, especially if he sold them into the hands of fierce and evil men, would be the gainer, however large might be the sum which he received? And will any one say that he is not a miserable caitiff who remorselessly sells his own divine being to that which is most godless and detestable? Eriphyle took the necklace as the price of her husband's life, but he is taking a bribe in order to compass a worse ruin."

Yes, said Glaucon, far worse — I will answer for him.

Has not the intemperate been censured of old, because in him the huge multiform monster is allowed to be too much at large?

Clearly.

And men are blamed for pride and bad temper when the lion and serpent element in them disproportionately grows and gains strength?

Yes.

And luxury and softness are blamed, because they relax and weaken this same creature, and make a coward of him?

Very true.

And is not a man reproached for flattery and meanness who subordinates the spirited animal to the unruly monster, and, for the sake of money, of which he can never have enough, habituates him in the days of his youth to be trampled in the mire, and from being a lion to become a monkey?

True, he said.

And why are mean employments and manual arts a reproach? Only because they imply a natural weakness of the higher principle; the individual is unable to control the creatures within him, but has to court them, and his great study is how to flatter them.

Such appears to be the reason.

And therefore, being desirous of placing him under a rule like that of the best, we say that he ought to be the servant of the best, in whom the Divine rules; not as Thrasymachus supposed, to the injury of the servant, but because every one had better be ruled by divine wisdom dwelling within him; or, if this be impossible, then by an external authority, in order that we may be all, as far as possible, under the same government, friends and equals.

True, he said.

And this is clearly seen to be the intention of the law, which is the ally of the whole city; and is seen also in the authority which we exercise over children, and the refusal to let them be free until we have established in them a principle analogous to the constitution of a state, and by cultivation of this higher element have set up in their hearts a guardian and ruler like our own, and when this is done they may go their ways.

Yes, he said, the purpose of the law is manifest.

From what point of view, then, and on what ground can we say that a man is profited by injustice or intemperance or other baseness, which will make him a worse man, even though he acquire money or power by his wickedness?

From no point of view at all.

What shall he profit, if his injustice be undetected and unpunished? He who is undetected only gets worse, whereas he who is detected and punished has the brutal part of his nature silenced and humanized; the gentler element in him is liberated, and his whole soul is perfected and ennobled by the acquirement of justice and temperance and wisdom, more than the body ever is by receiving gifts of beauty, strength and health, in proportion as the soul is more honorable than the body.

Certainly, he said.

To this nobler purpose the man of understanding will devote the energies of his life. And in the first place, he will honor studies which impress these qualities on his soul, and will disregard others?

Clearly, he said.

In the next place, he will regulate his bodily habit and training, and so far will he be from yielding to brutal and irrational pleasures, that he will regard even health as quite a secondary matter; his first object will be not that he may be fair or strong or well, unless he is likely thereby to gain temperance, but he will always desire so to attemper the body as to preserve the harmony of the soul?

Certainly he will, if he has true music in him.

And in the acquisition of wealth there is a principle of order and harmony which he will also observe; he will not allow himself to be dazzled by the foolish applause of the world, and heap up riches to his own infinite harm?

Certainly not, he said.

He will look at the city which is within him, and take heed that no disorder occur in it, such as might arise either from superfluity or from want; and upon this principle he will regulate his property and gain or spend according to his means.

Very true.

And, for the same reason, he will gladly accept and enjoy such honors as he deems likely to make him a better man; but those, whether private or public, which are likely to disorder his life, he will avoid?

Then, if that is his motive, he will not be a statesman.

By the dog of Egypt, he will! in the city which is his own he certainly will, though in the land of his birth perhaps not, unless he have a divine call.

I understand; you mean that he will be a ruler in the city of which we are the founders, and which exists in idea only; for I do not believe that there is such an one anywhere on earth?

In heaven, I replied, there is laid up a pattern of it, methinks, which he who desires may behold, and beholding, may set his own house in order.[1] But whether such an one exists, or ever will exist in fact is no matter; for he will live after the manner of that city, having nothing to do with any other.

I think so, he said.

[1] Or "take up his abode there."

BOOK X

OF the many excellences which I perceive in the order of our State, there is none which upon reflection pleases me better than the rule about poetry.

To what do you refer?

To the rejection of imitative poetry, which certainly ought not to be received; as I see far more clearly now that the parts of the soul have been distinguished.

What do you mean?

Speaking in confidence, for I should not like to have my words repeated to the tragedians and the rest of the imitative tribe — but I do not mind saying to you, that all poetical imitations are ruinous to the understanding of the hearers, and that the knowledge of their true nature is the only antidote to them.

Explain the purport of your remark.

Well, I will tell you, although I have always from my earliest youth had an awe and love of Homer, which even now makes the words falter on my lips, for he is the great captain and teacher of the whole of that charming tragic company; but a man is not to be reverenced more than the truth, and therefore I will speak out.

Very good, he said.

Listen to me then, or rather, answer me.

Put your question.

Can you tell me what imitation is? for I really do not know.

A likely thing, then, that I should know.

Why not? for the duller eye may often see a thing sooner than the keener.

Very true, he said; but in your presence, even if I had any faint notion, I could not muster courage to utter it. Will you inquire yourself?

Well then, shall we begin the inquiry in our usual manner: Whenever a number of individuals have a common name, we assume them to have also a corresponding idea or form: — do you understand me?

I do.

Let us take any common instance; there are beds and tables in the world — plenty of them, are there not?

Yes.

But there are only two ideas or forms of them — one the idea of a bed, the other of a table.

True.

And the maker of either of them makes a bed or he makes a table for our use, in accordance with the idea — that is our way of speaking in this and similar instances — but no artificer makes the ideas themselves: how could he?

Impossible.

And there is another artist, — I should like to know what you would say of him.

Who is he?

One who is the maker of all the works of all other workmen.

What an extraordinary man!

Wait a little, and there will be more reason for your saying so. For this is he who is able to make not only vessels of every kind, but plants and animals, himself and all other things — the earth and heaven, and the things which are in heaven or under the earth; he makes the gods also.

He must be a wizard and no mistake.

Oh! you are incredulous, are you? Do you mean that there is no such maker or creator, or that in one sense there might be a maker of all these things but in another not? Do you see that there is a way in which you could make them all yourself?

What way?

An easy way enough; or rather, there are many ways in which the feat might be quickly and easily accomplished, none quicker than that of turning a mirror round and round — you would soon enough make the sun and the heavens, and the earth and yourself, and other animals and plants, and all the other things of which we were just now speaking, in the mirror.

Yes, he said; but they would be appearances only.

Very good, I said, you are coming to the point now. And the painter too is, as I conceive, just such another — a creator of appearances, is he not?

Of course.

But then I suppose you will say that what he creates is untrue. And yet there is a sense in which the painter also creates a bed?

Yes, he said, but not a real bed.

And what of the maker of the bed? were you not saying that he too makes, not the idea which, according to our view, is the essence of the bed, but only a particular bed?

Yes, I did.

Then if he does not make that which exists he can not make true existence, but only some semblance of existence; and if any one were to say that the work of the maker of the bed, or of any other workman, has real existence, he could hardly be supposed to be speaking the truth.

At any rate, he replied, philosophers would say that he was not speaking the truth.

No wonder, then, that his work too is an indistinct expression of truth.

No wonder.

Suppose now that by the light of the examples just offered we inquire who this imitator is?

If you please.

Well then, here are three beds: one existing in nature, which is made by God, as I think that we may say — for no one else can be the maker?

No.

There is another which is the work of the carpenter?

Yes.

And the work of the painter is a third?

Yes.

Beds, then, are of three kinds, and there are three artists who superintend them: God, the maker of the bed, and the painter?

Yes, there are three of them.

God, whether from choice or from necessity, made one bed in nature and one only; two or more such ideal beds neither ever have been nor ever will be made by God.

Why is that?

Because even if He had made but two, a third would still appear behind them which both of them would have for their idea, and that would be the ideal bed and not the two others.

Very true, he said.

God knew this, and He desired to be the real maker of a real bed, not a particular maker of a particular bed, and therefore He created a bed which is essentially and by nature one only.

So we believe.

Shall we, then, speak of Him as the natural author or maker of the bed?

Yes, he replied; inasmuch as by the natural process of creation He is the author of this and of all other things.

And what shall we say of the carpenter — is not he also the maker of the bed?

Yes.

But would you call the painter a creator and maker?

Certainly not.

Yet if he is not the maker, what is he in relation to the bed?

I think, he said, that we may fairly designate him as the imitator of that which the others make.

Good, I said; then you call him who is third in the descent from nature an imitator?

Certainly, he said.

And the tragic poet is an imitator, and therefore, like all other imitators, he is thrice removed from the king and from the truth?

That appears to be so.

Then about the imitator we are agreed. And what about the painter? — I would like to know whether he may be thought to imitate that which originally exists in nature, or only the creations of artists?

The latter.

As they are or as they appear? you have still to determine this.

What do you mean?

I mean, that you may look at a bed from different points of view, obliquely or directly or from any other point of view, and the bed will appear different, but there is no difference in reality. And the same of all things.

Yes, he said, the difference is only apparent.

Now let me ask you another question: Which is the art of painting designed to be — an imitation of things as they are, or as they appear — of appearance or of reality?

Of appearance.

Then the imitator, I said, is a long way off the truth,

and can do all things because he lightly touches on a small part of them, and that part an image. For example: A painter will paint a cobbler, carpenter, or any other artist, though he knows nothing of their arts; and, if he is a good artist, he may deceive children or simple persons, when he shows them his picture of a carpenter from a distance, and they will fancy that they are looking at a real carpenter.

Certainly.

And whenever any one informs us that he has found a man who knows all the arts, and all things else that anybody knows, and every single thing with a higher degree of accuracy than any other man — whoever tells us this, I think that we can only imagine him to be a simple creature who is likely to have been deceived by some wizard or actor whom he met, and whom he thought all-knowing, because he himself was unable to analyze the nature of knowledge and ignorance and imitation.

Most true.

And so, when we hear persons saying that the tragedians, and Homer, who is at their head, know all the arts and all things human, virtue as well as vice, and divine things too, for that the good poet can not compose well unless he knows his subject, and that he who has not this knowledge can never be a poet, we ought to consider whether here also there may not be a similar illusion. Perhaps they may have come across imitators and been deceived by them; they may not have remembered when they saw their works that these were but imitations thrice removed from the truth, and could easily be made without any knowledge of the truth, because they are appearances only and not realities? Or, after all, they may be in the right, and poets do really know the things about which they seem to the many to speak so well?

The question, he said, should by all means be considered.

Now do you suppose that if a person were able to make the original as well as the image, he would seriously devote himself to the image-making branch? Would he allow imitation to be the ruling principle of his life, as if he had nothing higher in him?

I should say not.

The real artist, who knew what he was imitating, would be interested in realities and not in imitations; and would desire to leave as memorials of himself works many and fair; and, instead of being the author of encomiums, he would prefer to be the theme of them.

Yes, he said, that would be to him a source of much greater honor and profit.

Then, I said, we must put a question to Homer; not about medicine, or any of the arts to which his poems only incidentally refer: we are not going to ask him, or any other poet, whether he has cured patients like Asclepius, or left behind him a school of medicine such as the Asclepiads were, or whether he only talks about medicine and other arts at second-hand; but we have a right to know respecting military tactics, politics, education, which are the chiefest and noblest subjects of his poems, and we may fairly ask him about them. " Friend Homer," then we say to him, " if you are only in the second remove from truth in what you say of virtue, and not in the third — not an image maker or imitator — and if you are able to discern what pursuits make men better or worse in private or public life, tell us what State was ever better governed by your help? The good order of Lacedaemon is due to Lycurgus, and many other cities great and small have been similarly benefited by others; but who says that you have been a good legislator to them and have done them any good? Italy and Sicily boast of Charondas, and there is Solon who is renowned among us; but what city has anything to say about you?" Is there any city which he might name?

I think not, said Glaucon; not even the Homerids themselves pretend that he was a legislator.

Well, but is there any war on record which was carried on successfully by him, or aided by his counsels, when he was alive?

There is not.

Or is there any invention [1] of his, applicable to the arts or to human life, such as Thales the Milesian or Anacharsis the Scythian, and other ingenious men have conceived, which is attributed to him?

There is absolutely nothing of the kind.

But, if Homer never did any public service, was he privately a guide or teacher of any? Had he in his lifetime friends who loved to associate with him, and who handed down to posterity an Homeric way of life, such as was established by Pythagoras who was so greatly beloved for his wisdom, and whose followers are to this day quite celebrated for the order which was named after him?

Nothing of the kind is recorded of him. For surely, Socrates, Creophylus, the companion of Homer, that child of flesh, whose name always makes us laugh, might be more justly ridiculed for his stupidity, if, as is said, Homer was greatly neglected by him and others in his own day when he was alive?

Yes, I replied, that is the tradition. But can you imagine, Glaucon, that if Homer had really been able to educate and improve mankind — if he had possessed knowledge and not been a mere imitator — can you imagine, I say, that he would not have had many followers, and been honored and loved by them?

[1] Omitting εἰς.

Protagoras of Abdera, and Prodicus of Ceos, and a host of others, have only to whisper to their contemporaries: " You will never be able to manage either your own house or your own State until you appoint us to be your ministers of education " — and this ingenious device of theirs has such an effect in making men love them that their companions all but carry them about on their shoulders. And is it conceivable that the contemporaries of Homer, or again of Hesiod, would have allowed either of them to go about as rhapsodists, if they had really been able to make mankind virtuous? Would they not have been as unwilling to part with them as with gold, and have compelled them to stay at home with them? Or, if the master would not stay, then the disciples would have followed him about everywhere, until they had got education enough?

Yes, Socrates, that, I think, is quite true.

Then must we not infer that all these poetical individuals, beginning with Homer, are only imitators; they copy images of virtue and the like, but the truth they never reach? The poet is like a painter who, as we have already observed, will make a likeness of a cobbler though he understands nothing of cobbling; and his picture is good enough for those who know no more than he does, and judge only by colors and figures.

Quite so.

In like manner the poet with his words and phrases [1] may be said to lay on the colors of the several arts, himself understanding their nature only enough to imitate them; and other people, who are as ignorant as he is, and judge only from his words, imagine that if he speaks of cobbling, or of military tactics, or of anything else, in metre and harmony and rhythm, he

[1] Or, " with his nouns and verbs "

speaks very well — such is the sweet influence which melody and rhythm by nature have. And I think that you must have observed again and again what a poor appearance the tales of poets make when stripped of the colors which music puts upon them, and recited in simple prose.

Yes, he said.

They are like faces which were never really beautiful, but only blooming; and now the bloom of youth has passed away from them?

Exactly.

Here is another point: The imitator or maker of the image knows nothing of true existence; he knows appearances only. Am I not right?

Yes.

Then let us have a clear understanding, and not be satisfied with half an explanation.

Proceed.

Of the painter we say that he will paint reins, and he will paint a bit?

Yes.

And the worker in leather and brass will make them?

Certainly.

But does the painter know the right form of the bit and reins? Nay, hardly even the workers in brass and leather who make them; only the horseman who knows how to use them — he knows their right form.

Most true.

And may we not say the same of all things?

What?

That there are three arts which are concerned with all things: one which uses, another which makes, a third which imitates them?

Yes.

And the excellence or beauty or truth of every

structure, animate or inanimate, and of every action of man, is relative to the use for which nature or the artist has intended them.

True.

Then the user of them must have the greatest experience of them, and he must indicate to the maker the good or bad qualities which develop themselves in use; for example, the flute-player will tell the flute-maker which of his flutes is satisfactory to the performer; he will tell him how he ought to make them, and the other will attend to his instructions?

Of course.

The one knows and therefore speaks with authority about the goodness and badness of flutes, while the other, confiding in him, will do what he is told by him?

True.

The instrument is the same, but about the excellence or badness of it the maker will only attain to a correct belief; and this he will gain from him who knows, by talking to him and being compelled to hear what he has to say, whereas the user will have knowledge?

True.

But will the imitator have either? Will he know from use whether or no his drawing is correct or beautiful? or will he have right opinion from being compelled to associate with another who knows and gives him instructions about what he should draw?

Neither.

Then he will no more have true opinion than he will have knowledge about the goodness or badness of his imitations?

I suppose not.

The imitative artist will be in a brilliant state of intelligence about his own creations?

Nay, very much the reverse.

And still he will go on imitating without knowing what makes a thing good or bad, and may be expected therefore to imitate only that which appears to be good to the ignorant multitude?

Just so.

Thus far then we are pretty well agreed that the imitator has no knowledge worth mentioning of what he imitates. Imitation is only a kind of play or sport, and the tragic poets, whether they write in Iambic or in Heroic verse, are imitators in the highest degree?

Very true.

And now tell me, I conjure you, has not imitation been shown by us to be concerned with that which is thrice removed from the truth?

Certainly.

And what is the faculty in man to which imitation is addressed?

What do you mean?

I will explain: The body which is large when seen near, appears small when seen at a distance?

True.

And the same objects appear straight when looked at out of the water, and crooked when in the water; and the concave becomes convex, owing to the illusion about colors to which the sight is liable. Thus every sort of confusion is revealed within us; and this is that weakness of the human mind on which the art of conjuring and of deceiving by light and shadow and other ingenious devices imposes, having an effect upon us like magic.

True.

And the arts of measuring and numbering and weighing come to the rescue of the human understanding — there is the beauty of them — and the apparent greater or less, or more or heavier, no longer have the mastery over us, but give way before calculation and measure and weight?

Most true.

And this, surely, must be the work of the calculating and rational principle in the soul?

To be sure.

And when this principle measures and certifies that some things are equal, or that some are greater or less than others, there occurs an apparent contradiction?

True.

But were we not saying that such a contradiction is impossible — the same faculty can not have contrary opinions at the same time about the same thing?

Very true.

Then that part of the soul which has an opinion contrary to measure is not the same with that which has an opinion in accordance with measure?

True.

And the better part of the soul is likely to be that which trusts to measure and calculation?

Certainly.

And that which is opposed to them is one of the inferior principles of the soul?

No doubt.

This was the conclusion at which I was seeking to arrive when I said that painting or drawing, and imitation in general, when doing their own proper work, are far removed from truth, and the companions and friends and associates of a principle within us which is equally removed from reason, and that they have no true or healthy aim.

Exactly.

The imitative art is an inferior who marries an inferior, and has inferior offspring.

Very true.

And is this confined to the sight only, or does it extend to the hearing also, relating in fact to what we term poetry?

Probably the same would be true of poetry.

Do not rely, I said, on a probability derived from the analogy of painting; but let us examine further and see whether the faculty with which poetical imitation is concerned is good or bad.

By all means.

We may state the question thus: — Imitation imitates the actions of men, whether voluntary or involuntary, on which, as they imagine, a good or bad result has ensued, and they rejoice or sorrow accordingly. Is there anything more?

No, there is nothing else.

But in all this variety of circumstances is the man at unity with himself — or rather, as in the instance of sight there was confusion and opposition in his opinions about the same things, so here also is there not strife and inconsistency in his life? Though I need hardly raise the question again, for I remember that all this has been already admitted; and the soul has been acknowledged by us to be full of these and ten thousand similar oppositions occurring at the same moment?

And we were right, he said.

Yes, I said, thus far we were right; but there was an omission which must now be supplied.

What was the omission?

Were we not saying that a good man, who has the misfortune to lose his son or anything else which is most dear to him, will bear the loss with more equanimity than another?

Yes.

But will he have no sorrow, or shall we say that

although he can not help sorrowing, he will moderate his sorrow?

The latter, he said, is the truer statement.

Tell me: will he be more likely to struggle and hold out against his sorrow when he is seen by his equals, or when he is alone?

It will make a great difference whether he is seen or not.

When he is by himself he will not mind saying or doing many things which he would be ashamed of any one hearing or seeing him do?

True.

There is a principle of law and reason in him which bids him resist, as well as a feeling of his misfortune which is forcing him to indulge his sorrow?

True.

But when a man is drawn in two opposite directions, to and from the same object, this, as we affirm, necessarily implies two distinct principles in him?

Certainly.

One of them is ready to follow the guidance of the law?

How do you mean?

The law would say that to be patient under suffering is best, and that we should not give way to impatience, as there is no knowing whether such things are good or evil; and nothing is gained by impatience; also, because no human thing is of serious importance, and grief stands in the way of that which at the moment is most required.

What is most required? he asked.

That we should take counsel about what has happened, and when the dice have been thrown order our affairs in the way which reason deems best; not, like children who have had a fall, keeping hold of the part struck and wasting time in setting up a howl, but always accustoming the soul forthwith to apply a remedy, raising up that which is sickly and fallen, banishing the cry of sorrow by the healing art.

Yes, he said, that is the true way of meeting the attacks of fortune.

Yes, I said; and the higher principle is ready to follow this suggestion of reason?

Clearly.

And the other principle, which inclines us to recollection of our troubles and to lamentation, and can never have enough of them, we may call irrational, useless, and cowardly?

Indeed, we may.

And does not the latter — I mean the rebellious principle — furnish a great variety of materials for imitation? Whereas the wise and calm temperament, being always nearly equable, is not easy to imitate or to appreciate when imitated, especially at a public festival when a promiscuous crowd is assembled in a theatre. For the feeling represented is one to which they are strangers.

Certainly.

Then the imitative poet who aims at being popular is not by nature made, nor is his art intended, to please or to affect the rational principle in the soul; but he will prefer the passionate and fitful temper, which is easily imitated?

Clearly.

And now we may fairly take him and place him by the side of the painter, for he is like him in two ways: first, inasmuch as his creations have an inferior degree of truth — in this, I say, he is like him; and he is also like him in being concerned with an inferior part of the soul; and therefore we shall be right in refusing to admit him into a well-ordered State, because he awakens and nourishes and strengthens the feelings and impairs the reason. As in a city when the evil are permitted to have authority and the good are put out of the way, so in the soul of man, as we maintain, the imitative poet implants an evil constitution, for he indulges the irrational nature which has no discernment of greater and less, but thinks the same thing at one time great and at another small — he is a manufacturer of images and is very far removed from the truth.[1]

Exactly.

But we have not yet brought forward the heaviest count in our accusation: — the power which poetry has of harming even the good (and there are very few who are not harmed), is surely an awful thing?

Yes, certainly, if the effect is what you say.

Hear and judge: The best of us, as I conceive, when we listen to a passage of Homer, or one of the tragedians, in which he represents some pitiful hero who is drawling out his sorrows in a long oration, or weeping, and smiting his breast — the best of us, you know, delight in giving way to sympathy, and are in raptures at the excellence of the poet who stirs our feelings most.

Yes, of course I know.

But when any sorrow of our own happens to us, then you may observe that we pride ourselves on the opposite quality — we would fain be quiet and patient; this is the manly part, and the other which delighted us in the recitation is now deemed to be the part of a woman.

Very true, he said.

Now can we be right in praising and admiring another who is doing that which any one of us would abominate and be ashamed of in his own person?

No, he said, that is certainly not reasonable.

[1] Reading εἰδωλοποιοῦντα . . . ἀφεστῶτα.

Nay, I said, quite reasonable from one point of view.

What point of view?

If you consider, I said, that when in misfortune we feel a natural hunger and desire to relieve our sorrow by weeping and lamentation, and that this feeling which is kept under control in our own calamities is satisfied and delighted by the poets; — the better nature in each of us, not having been sufficiently trained by reason or habit, allows the sympathetic element to break loose because the sorrow is another's; and the spectator fancies that there can be no disgrace to himself in praising and pitying any one who comes telling him what a good man he is, and making a fuss about his troubles; he thinks that the pleasure is a gain, and why should he be supercilious and lose this and the poem too? Few persons ever reflect, as I should imagine, that from the evil of other men something of evil is communicated to themselves. And so the feeling of sorrow which has gathered strength at the sight of the misfortunes of others is with difficulty repressed in our own.

How very true!

And does not the same hold also of the ridiculous? There are jests which you would be ashamed to make yourself, and yet on the comic stage, or indeed in private, when you hear them, you are greatly amused by them, and are not at all disgusted at their unseemliness; — the case of pity is repeated; — there is a principle in human nature which is disposed to raise a laugh, and this which you once restrained by reason, because you were afraid of being thought a buffoon, is now let out again; and having stimulated the risible faculty at the theatre, you are betrayed unconsciously to yourself into playing the comic poet at home.

Quite true, he said.

And the same may be said of lust and anger and all the other affections, of desire and pain and pleasure, which are held to be inseparable from every action — in all of them poetry feeds and waters the passions instead of drying them up; she lets them rule, although they ought to be controlled, if mankind are ever to increase in happiness and virtue.

I can not deny it.

Therefore, Glaucon, I said, whenever you meet with any of the eulogists of Homer declaring that he has been the educator of Hellas, and that he is profitable for education and for the ordering of human things, and that you should take him up again and again and get to know him and regulate your whole life according to him, we may love and honor those who say these things — they are excellent people, as far as their lights extend; and we are ready to acknowledge that Homer is the greatest of poets and first of tragedy writers; but we must remain firm in our conviction that hymns to the gods and praises of famous men are the only poetry which ought to be admitted into our State. For if you go beyond this and allow the honeyed muse to enter, either in epic or lyric verse, not law and the reason of mankind, which by common consent have ever been deemed best, but pleasure and pain will be the rulers in our State.

That is most true, he said.

And now since we have reverted to the subject of poetry, let this our defence serve to show the reasonableness of our former judgment in sending away out of our State an art having the tendencies which we have described; for reason constrained us. But that she may not impute to us any harshness or want of politeness, let us tell her that there is an ancient quarrel between philosophy and poetry; of which there are many proofs, such as the saying of " the yelping hound howling at her lord," or of one " mighty in the vain talk of fools," and " the mob of sages circumventing Zeus," and the " subtle thinkers who are beggars after all; " and there are innumerable other signs of ancient enmity between them. Notwithstanding this, let us assure our sweet friend and the sister arts of imitation, that if she will only prove her title to exist in a well-ordered State we shall be delighted to receive her — we are very conscious of her charms; but we may not on that account betray the truth. I dare say, Glaucon, that you are as much charmed by her as I am, especially when she appears in Homer?

Yes, indeed, I am greatly charmed.

Shall I propose, then, that she be allowed to return from exile, but upon this condition only — that she make a defence of herself in lyrical or some other metre?

Certainly.

And we may further grant to those of her defenders who are lovers of poetry and yet not poets the permission to speak in prose on her behalf: let them show not only that she is pleasant but also useful to States and to human life, and we will listen in a kindly spirit; for if this can be proved we shall surely be the gainers — I mean, if there is a use in poetry as well as a delight?

Certainly, he said, we shall be the gainers.

If her defence fails, then, my dear friend, like other persons who are enamored of something, but put a restraint upon themselves when they think their desires are opposed to their interests, so too must we after the manner of lovers give her up, though not without a struggle. We too are inspired by that love of poetry which the education of noble States has implanted in us, and therefore we would have her appear at her best and truest; but so long as she is unable to make good her defence, this argument of ours shall be a charm to us, which we will repeat to ourselves while we listen to her strains; that we may not fall away into the childish love of her which captivates the many. At all events we are well aware [1] that poetry being such as we have described is not to be regarded seriously as attaining to the truth; and he who listens to her, fearing for the safety of the city which is within him, should be on his guard against her seductions and make our words his law.

Yes, he said, I quite agree with you.

Yes, I said, my dear Glaucon, for great is the issue at stake, greater than appears, whether a man is to be good or bad. And what will any one be profited if under the influence of honor or money or power, aye, or under the excitement of poetry, he neglect justice and virtue?

Yes, he said; I have been convinced by the argument, as I believe that any one else would have been.

And yet no mention has been made of the greatest prizes and rewards which await virtue.

What, are there any greater still? If there are, they must be of an inconceivable greatness.

Why, I said, what was ever great in a short time? The whole period of three score years and ten is surely but a little thing in comparison with eternity?

Say rather " nothing," he replied.

And should an immortal being seriously think of this little space rather than of the whole?

Of the whole, certainly. But why do you ask?

Are you not aware, I said, that the soul of man is immortal and imperishable?

He looked at me in astonishment, and said: No, by

---

[1] Or, if we accept Madvig's ingenious but unnecessary emendation ἀσόμεθα, " At all events we will sing, that " etc.

heaven: And are you really prepared to maintain this?

Yes, I said, I ought to be, and you too — there is no difficulty in proving it.

I see a great difficulty; but I should like to hear you state this argument of which you make so light.

Listen then.

I am attending.

There is a thing which you call good and another which you call evil?

Yes, he replied.

Would you agree with me in thinking that the corrupting and destroying element is the evil, and the saving and improving element the good?

Yes.

And you admit that everything has a good and also an evil; as ophthalmia is the evil of the eyes and disease of the whole body; as mildew is of corn, and rot of timber, or rust of copper and iron: in everything, or in almost everything, there is an inherent evil and disease?

Yes, he said.

And anything which is infected by any of these evils is made evil, and at last wholly dissolves and dies?

True.

The vice and evil which is inherent in each is the destruction of each; and if this does not destroy them there is nothing else that will; for good certainly will not destroy them, nor again, that which is neither good nor evil.

Certainly not.

If, then, we find any nature which having this inherent corruption can not be dissolved or destroyed, we may be certain that of such a nature there is no destruction?

That may be assumed.

Well, I said, and is there no evil which corrupts the soul?

Yes, he said, there are all the evils which we were just now passing in review: unrighteousness, intemperance, cowardice, ignorance.

But does any of these dissolve or destroy her? — and here do not let us fall into the error of supposing that the unjust and foolish man, when he is detected, perishes through his own injustice, which is an evil of the soul. Take the analogy of the body: The evil of the body is a disease which wastes and reduces and annihilates the body; and all the things of which we were just now speaking come to annihilation through their own corruption attaching to them and inhering in them and so destroying them. Is not this true?

Yes.

Consider the soul in like manner. Does the injustice or other evil which exists in the soul waste and consume her? do they by attaching to the soul and inhering in her at last bring her to death, and so separate her from the body?

Certainly not.

And yet, I said, it is unreasonable to suppose that anything can perish from without through affection of external evil which could not be destroyed from within by a corruption of its own?

It is, he replied.

Consider, I said, Glaucon, that even the badness of food, whether staleness, decomposition, or any other bad quality, when confined to the actual food, is not supposed to destroy the body; although, if the badness of food communicates corruption to the body, then we should say that the body has been destroyed by a corruption of itself, which is disease, brought on by this; but that the body, being one thing, can be destroyed by the badness of food, which is another, and which does not engender any natural infection — this we shall absolutely deny?

Very true.

And, on the same principle, unless some bodily evil can produce an evil of the soul, we must not suppose that the soul, which is one thing, can be dissolved by any merely external evil which belongs to another?

Yes, he said, there is reason in that.

Either, then, let us refute this conclusion, or, while it remains unrefuted, let us never say that fever, or any other disease, or the knife put to the throat, or even the cutting up of the whole body into the minutest pieces, can destroy the soul, until she herself is proved to become more unholy or unrighteous in consequence of these things being done to the body; but that the soul, or anything else if not destroyed by an internal evil, can be destroyed by an external one, is not to be affirmed by any man.

And surely, he replied, no one will ever prove that the souls of men become more unjust in consequence of death.

But if some one who would rather not admit the immortality of the soul boldly denies this, and says that the dying do really become more evil and unrighteous, then, if the speaker is right, I suppose that injustice, like disease, must be assumed to be fatal to the unjust, and that those who take this disorder die by the natural inherent power of destruction which evil has, and which kills them sooner or later, but in quite another way from that in which, at present, the wicked receive death at the hands of others as the penalty of their deeds?

Nay, he said, in that case injustice, if fatal to the unjust, will not be so very terrible to him, for he will be delivered from evil. But I rather suspect the opposite to be the truth, and that injustice which, if it have the power, will murder others, keeps the murderer alive — aye, and well awake too; so far removed is her dwelling-place from being a house of death.

True, I said; if the inherent natural vice or evil of the soul is unable to kill or destroy her, hardly will that which is appointed to be the destruction of some other body, destroy a soul or anything else except that of which it was appointed to be the destruction.

Yes, that can hardly be.

But the soul which can not be destroyed by an evil, whether inherent or external, must exist forever, and if existing forever, must be immortal?

Certainly.

That is the conclusion, I said; and, if a true conclusion, then the souls must always be the same, for if none be destroyed they will not diminish in number. Neither will they increase, for the increase of the immortal natures must come from something mortal, and all things would thus end in immortality.

Very true.

But this we can not believe — reason will not allow us — any more than we can believe the soul, in her truest nature, to be full of variety and difference and dissimilarity.

What do you mean? he said.

The soul, I said, being, as is now proven, immortal, must be the fairest of compositions and can not be compounded of many elements?

Certainly not.

Her immortality is demonstrated by the previous argument, and there are many other proofs; but to see her as she really is, not as we now behold her, marred by communion with the body and other miseries, you must contemplate her with the eye of reason, in her original purity; and then her beauty will be revealed, and justice and injustice and all the things which we have described will be manifested more clearly. Thus far, we have spoken the truth concerning her as she appears at present, but we must remember also that we have seen her only in a condition which may be compared to that of the sea-god Glaucus, whose original image can hardly be discerned because his natural members are broken off and crushed and damaged by the waves in all sorts of ways, and incrustations have grown over them of seaweed and shells and stones, so that he is more like some monster than he is to his own natural form. And the soul which we behold is in a similar condition, disfigured by ten thousand ills. But not there, Glaucon, not there must we look.

Where then?

At her love of wisdom. Let us see whom she affects, and what society and converse she seeks in virtue of her near kindred with the immortal and eternal and divine; also how different she would become if wholly following this superior principle, and borne by a divine impulse out of the ocean in which she now is, and disengaged from the stones and shells and things of earth and rock which in wild variety spring up around her because she feeds upon earth, and is overgrown by the good things of this life as they are termed: then you would see her as she is, and know whether she have one shape only or many, or what her nature is. Of her affections and of the forms which she takes in this present life I think that we have now said enough.

True, he replied.

And thus, I said, we have fulfilled the conditions of the argument; [1] we have not introduced the rewards

[1] Reading ἀπελυσάμεθα.

and glories of justice, which, as you were saying, are to be found in Homer and Hesiod; but justice in her own nature has been shown to be best for the soul in her own nature. Let a man do what is just, whether he have the ring of Gyges or not, and even if in addition to the ring of Gyges he put on the helmet of Hades.

Very true.

And now, Glaucon, there will be no harm in further enumerating how many and how great are the rewards which justice and the other virtues procure to the soul from gods and men, both in life and after death.

Certainly not, he said.

Will you repay me, then, what you borrowed in the argument?

What did I borrow?

The assumption that the just man should appear unjust and the unjust just: for you were of opinion that even if the true state of the case could not possibly escape the eyes of gods and men, still this admission ought to be made for the sake of the argument, in order that pure justice might be weighed against pure injustice. Do you remember?

I should be much to blame if I had forgotten.

Then, as the cause is decided, I demand on behalf of justice that the estimation in which she is held by gods and men and which we acknowledge to be her due should now be restored to her by us;[1] since she has been shown to confer reality, and not to deceive those who truly possess her, let what has been taken from her be given back, that so she may win that palm of appearance which is hers also, and which she gives to her own.

The demand, he said, is just.

[1] Reading ἡμῶν.

In the first place, I said — and this is the first thing which you will have to give back — the nature both of the just and unjust is truly known to the gods.

Granted.

And if they are both known to them, one must be the friend and the other the enemy of the gods, as we admitted from the beginning?

True.

And the friend of the gods may be supposed to receive from them all things at their best, excepting only such evil as is the necessary consequence of former sins?

Certainly.

Then this must be our notion of the just man, that even when he is in poverty or sickness, or any other seeming misfortune, all things will in the end work together for good to him in life and death: for the gods have a care of any one whose desire is to become just and to be like God, as far as man can attain the divine likeness, by the pursuit of virtue?

Yes, he said; if he is like God he will surely not be neglected by him.

And of the unjust may not the opposite be supposed?

Certainly.

Such, then, are the palms of victory which the gods give the just?

That is my conviction.

And what do they receive of men? Look at things as they really are, and you will see that the clever unjust are in the case of runners, who run well from the starting-place to the goal but not back again from the goal: they go off at a great pace, but in the end only look foolish, slinking away with their ears draggling on their shoulders, and without a crown; but the true runner comes to the finish and receives the prize and is crowned. And this is the way with the just; he who endures to the end of every action and occasion of his entire life has a good report and carries off the prize which men have to bestow.

True.

And now you must allow me to repeat of the just the blessings which you were attributing to the fortunate unjust. I shall say of them, what you were saying of the others, that as they grow older, they become rulers in their own city if they care to be; they marry whom they like and give in marriage to whom they will; all that you said of the others I now say of these. And, on the other hand, of the unjust I say that the greater number, even though they escape in their youth, are found out at last and look foolish at the end of their course, and when they come to be old and miserable are flouted alike by stranger and citizen; they are beaten and then come those things unfit for ears polite, as you truly term them; they will be racked and have their eyes burned out, as you were saying. And you may suppose that I have repeated the remainder of your tale of horrors. But will you let me assume, without reciting them, that these things are true?

Certainly, he said, what you say is true.

These, then, are the prizes and rewards and gifts which are bestowed upon the just by gods and men in this present life, in addition to the other good things which justice of herself provides.

Yes, he said; and they are fair and lasting.

And yet, I said, all these are as nothing either in number or greatness in comparison with those other recompenses which await both just and unjust after death. And you ought to hear them, and then both just and unjust will have received from us a full payment of the debt which the argument owes to them.

Speak, he said; there are few things which I would more gladly hear.

Well, I said, I will tell you a tale; not one of the tales which Odysseus tells to the hero Alcinous, yet this too is a tale of a hero, Er the son of Armenius, a Pamphylian by birth. He was slain in battle, and ten days afterwards, when the bodies of the dead were taken up already in a state of corruption, his body was found unaffected by decay, and carried away home to be buried. And on the twelfth day, as he was lying on the funeral pile, he returned to life and told them what he had seen in the other world. He said that when his soul left the body he went on a journey with a great company, and that they came to a mysterious place at which there were two openings in the earth; they were near together, and over against them were two other openings in the heaven above. In the intermediate space there were judges seated, who commanded the just, after they had given judgment on them and had bound their sentences in front of them, to ascend by the heavenly way on the right hand; and in like manner the unjust were bidden by them to descend by the lower way on the left hand; these also bore the symbols of their deeds, but fastened on their backs. He drew near, and they told him that he was to be the messenger who would carry the report of the other world to men, and they bade him hear and see all that was to be heard and seen in that place. Then he beheld and saw on one side the souls departing at either opening of heaven and earth when sentence had been given on them; and at the two other openings other souls, some ascending out of the earth dusty and worn with travel, some descending out of heaven clean and bright. And arriving ever and anon they seemed to have come from a long journey, and they went forth with gladness into the meadow, where

they encamped as at a festival; and those who knew
one another embraced and conversed, the souls which
came from earth curiously inquiring about the things
above, and the souls which came from heaven about
the things beneath. And they told one another of
what had happened by the way, those from below
weeping and sorrowing at the remembrance of the
things which they had endured and seen in their journey beneath the earth (now the journey lasted a thousand years), while those from above were describing
heavenly delights and visions of inconceivable beauty.
The story, Glaucon, would take too long to tell; but
the sum was this: — He said that for every wrong
which they had done to any one they suffered tenfold;
or once in a hundred years — such being reckoned to
be the length of man's life, and the penalty being thus
paid ten times in a thousand years. If, for example,
there were any who had been the cause of many deaths,
or had betrayed or enslaved cities or armies, or been
guilty of any other evil behavior, for each and all of
their offences they received punishment ten times
over, and the rewards of beneficence and justice and
holiness were in the same proportion. I need hardly
repeat what he said concerning young children dying
almost as soon as they were born. Of piety and impiety to gods and parents, and of murderers,[1] there
were retributions other and greater far which he described. He mentioned that he was present when one
of the spirits asked another, " Where is Ardiaeus the
Great? " (Now this Ardiaeus lived a thousand years
before the time of Er: he had been the tyrant of some
city of Pamphylia, and had murdered his aged father
and his elder brother, and was said to have committed
many other abominable crimes.) The answer of the
other spirit was: " He comes not hither and will never

---

[1] Reading αὐτόχειρας.

come. And this," said he, "was one of the dreadful sights which we ourselves witnessed. We were at the mouth of the cavern, and, having completed all our experiences, were about to reascend, when of a sudden Ardiaeus appeared and several others, most of whom were tyrants; and there were also besides the tyrants private individuals who had been great criminals: they were just, as they fancied, about to return into the upper world, but the mouth, instead of admitting them, gave a roar, whenever any of these incurable sinners or some one who had not been sufficiently punished tried to ascend; and then wild men of fiery aspect, who were standing by and heard the sound, seized and carried them off; and Ardiaeus and others they bound head and foot and hand, and threw them down and flayed them with scourges, and dragged them along the road at the side, carding them on thorns like wool, and declaring to the passers-by what were their crimes, and that [1] they were being taken away to be cast into hell." And of all the many terrors which they had endured, he said that there was none like the terror which each of them felt at that moment, lest they should hear the voice; and when there was silence, one by one they ascended with exceeding joy. These, said Er, were the penalties and retributions, and there were blessings as great.

Now when the spirits which were in the meadow had tarried seven days, on the eighth they were obliged to proceed on their journey, and, on the fourth day after, he said that they came to a place where they could see from above a line of light, straight as a column, extending right through the whole heaven and through the earth, in color resembling the rainbow, only brighter and purer; another day's journey brought them to the place, and there, in the midst of the light,

[1] Reading καὶ ὅτι.

they saw the ends of the chains of heaven let down
from above: for this light is the belt of heaven, and
holds together the circle of the universe, like the under-
girders of a trireme. From these ends is extended the
spindle of Necessity, on which all the revolutions turn.
The shaft and hook of this spindle are made of steel,
and the whorl is made partly of steel and also partly
of other materials. Now the whorl is in form like the
whorl used on earth; and the description of it implied
that there is one large hollow whorl which is quite
scooped out, and into this is fitted another lesser one,
and another, and another, and four others, making
eight in all, like vessels which fit into one another; the
whorls show their edges on the upper side, and on
their lower side all together form one continuous
whorl. This is pierced by the spindle, which is driven
home through the centre of the eighth. The first and
outermost whorl has the rim broadest, and the seven
inner whorls are narrower, in the following proportions — the sixth is next to the first in size, the fourth
next to the sixth; then comes the eighth; the seventh
is fifth, the fifth is sixth, the third is seventh, last and
eighth comes the second. The largest [or fixed stars]
is spangled, and the seventh [or sun] is brightest; the
eighth [or moon] colored by the reflected light of the
seventh; the second and fifth [Saturn and Mercury]
are in color like one another, and yellower than the
preceding; the third [Venus] has the whitest light;
the fourth [Mars] is reddish; the sixth [Jupiter] is
in whiteness second. Now the whole spindle has the
same motion; but, as the whole revolves in one direction, the seven inner circles move slowly in the other,
and of these the swiftest is the eighth; next in swiftness are the seventh, sixth, and fifth, which move together; third in swiftness appeared to move according to the law of this reversed motion the fourth; the

third appeared fourth and the second fifth. The spindle turns on the knees of Necessity; and on the upper surface of each circle is a siren, who goes round with them, hymning a single tone or note. The eight together form one harmony; and round about, at equal intervals, there is another band, three in number, each sitting upon her throne: these are the Fates, daughters of Necessity, who are clothed in white robes and have chaplets upon their heads, Lachesis and Clotho and Atropos, who accompany with their voices the harmony of the sirens — Lachesis singing of the past, Clotho of the present, Atropos of the future; Clotho from time to time assisting with a touch of her right hand the revolution of the outer circle of the whorl or spindle, and Atropos with her left hand touching and guiding the inner ones, and Lachesis laying hold of either in turn, first with one hand and then with the other.

When Er and the spirits arrived, their duty was to go at once to Lachesis; but first of all there came a prophet who arranged them in order; then he took from the knees of Lachesis lots and samples of lives, and having mounted a high pulpit, spoke as follows: " Hear the word of Lachesis, the daughter of Necessity. Mortal souls, behold a new cycle of life and mortality. Your genius will not be allotted to you, but you will choose your genius; and let him who draws the first lot have the first choice, and the life which he chooses shall be his destiny. Virtue is free, and as a man honors or dishonors her he will have more or less of her; the responsibility is with the chooser — God is justified." When the Interpreter had thus spoken he scattered lots indifferently among them all, and each of them took up the lot which fell near him, all but Er himself (he was not allowed), and each as he took his lot perceived the number which he had obtained. Then the Interpreter placed on the ground before them the samples of lives; and there were many more lives than the souls present, and they were of all sorts. There were lives of every animal and of man in every condition. And there were tyrannies among them, some lasting out the tyrant's life, others which broke off in the middle and came to an end in poverty and exile and beggary; and there were lives of famous men, some who were famous for their form and beauty as well as for their strength and success in games, or, again, for their birth and the qualities of their ancestors; and some who were the reverse of famous for the opposite qualities. And of women likewise; there was not, however, any definite character in them, because the soul, when choosing a new life, must of necessity become different. But there was every other quality, and they all mingled with one another, and also with elements of wealth and poverty, and disease and health; and there were mean states also. And here, my dear Glaucon, is the supreme peril of our human state; and therefore the utmost care should be taken. Let each one of us leave every other kind of knowledge and seek and follow one thing only, if peradventure he may be able to learn and may find some one who will make him able to learn and discern between good and evil, and so to choose always and everywhere the better life as he has opportunity. He should consider the bearing of all these things which have been mentioned severally and collectively upon virtue; he should know what the effect of beauty is when combined with poverty or wealth in a particular soul, and what are the good and evil consequences of noble and humble birth, of private and public station, of strength and weakness, of cleverness and dullness, and of all the natural and acquired gifts of the soul, and the operation of them

when conjoined; he will then look at the nature of
the soul, and from the consideration of all these qualities he will be able to determine which is the better
and which is the worse; and so he will choose, giving
the name of evil to the life which will make his soul
more unjust, and good to the life which will make his
soul more just; all else he will disregard. For we
have seen and know that this is the best choice both in
life and after death. A man must take with him into
the world below an adamantine faith in truth and
right, that there too he may be undazzled by the desire
of wealth or the other allurements of evil, lest, coming
upon tyrannies and similar villainies, he do irremedi-
able wrongs to others and suffer yet worse himself;
but let him know how to choose the mean and avoid
the extremes on either side, as far as possible, not only
in this life but in all that which is to come. For this
is the way of happiness.

And according to the report of the messenger from
the other world this was what the prophet said at the
time: " Even for the last comer, if he chooses wisely
and will live diligently, there is appointed a happy
and not undesirable existence. Let not him who
chooses first be careless, and let not the last despair."
And when he had spoken, he who had the first choice
came forward and in a moment chose the greatest
tyranny; his mind having been darkened by folly and
sensuality, he had not thought out the whole matter
before he chose, and did not at first sight perceive that
he was fated, among other evils, to devour his own
children. But when he had time to reflect, and saw
what was in the lot, he began to beat his breast and
lament over his choice, forgetting the proclamation
of the prophet; for, instead of throwing the blame of
his misfortune on himself, he accused chance and the
gods, and everything rather than himself. Now he

was one of those who came from heaven, and in a former life had dwelt in a well-ordered State, but his virtue was a matter of habit only, and he had no philosophy. And it was true of others who were similarly overtaken, that the greater number of them came from heaven and therefore they had never been schooled by trial, whereas the pilgrims who came from earth having themselves suffered and seen others suffer were not in a hurry to choose. And owing to this inexperience of theirs, and also because the lot was a chance, many of the souls exchanged a good destiny for an evil or an evil for a good. For if a man had always on his arrival in this world dedicated himself from the first to sound philosophy, and had been moderately fortunate in the number of the lot, he might, as the messenger reported, be happy here, and also his journey to another life and return to this, instead of being rough and underground, would be smooth and heavenly. Most curious, he said, was the spectacle — sad and laughable and strange; for the choice of the souls was in most cases based on their experience of a previous life. There he saw the soul which had once been Orpheus choosing the life of a swan out of enmity to the race of women, hating to be born of a woman because they had been his murderers; he beheld also the soul of Thamyras choosing the life of a nightingale; birds, on the other hand, like the swan and other musicians, wanting to be men. The soul which obtained the twentieth [1] lot chose the life of a lion, and this was the soul of Ajax the son of Telamon, who would not be a man, remembering the injustice which was done him in the judgment about the arms. The next was Agamemnon, who took the life of an eagle, because, like Ajax, he hated human nature by reason of his sufferings. About the middle

[1] Reading εἰκοστήν.

came the lot of Atalanta; she, seeing the great fame
of an athlete, was unable to resist the temptation: and
after her there followed the soul of Epeus the son of
Panopeus passing into the nature of a woman cunning
in the arts; and far away among the last who chose,
the soul of the jester Thersites was putting on the
form of a monkey. There came also the soul of
Odysseus having yet to make a choice, and his lot happened to be the last of them all. Now the recollection
of former toils had disenchanted him of ambition, and
he went about for a considerable time in search of the
life of a private man who had no cares; he had some
difficulty in finding this, which was lying about and
had been neglected by everybody else; and when he
saw it, he said that he would have done the same had
his lot been first instead of last, and that he was delighted to have it. And not only did men pass into
animals, but I must also mention that there were
animals tame and wild who changed into one another
and into corresponding human natures — the good
into the gentle and the evil into the savage, in all sorts
of combinations.

All the souls had now chosen their lives, and they
went in the order of their choice to Lachesis, who sent
with them the genius whom they had severally chosen,
to be the guardian of their lives and the fulfiller of the
choice: this genius led the souls first to Clotho, and
drew them within the revolution of the spindle impelled by her hand, thus ratifying the destiny of each;
and then, when they were fastened to this, carried
them to Atropos, who spun the threads and made
them irreversible, whence without turning round they
passed beneath the throne of Necessity; and when
they had all passed, they marched on in a scorching
heat to the plain of Forgetfulness, which was a barren
waste destitute of trees and verdure; and then towards

evening they encamped by the river of Unmindfulness, whose water no vessel can hold; of this they were all obliged to drink a certain quantity, and those who were not saved by wisdom drank more than was necessary; and each one as he drank forgot all things. Now after they had gone to rest, about the middle of the night there was a thunderstorm and earthquake, and then in an instant they were driven upwards in all manner of ways to their birth, like stars shooting. He himself was hindered from drinking the water. But in what manner or by what means he returned to the body he could not say; only, in the morning, awakening suddenly, he found himself lying on the pyre.

And thus, Glaucon, the tale has been saved and has not perished, and will save us if we are obedient to the word spoken; and we shall pass safely over the river of Forgetfulness and our soul will not be defiled. Wherefore my counsel is, that we hold fast ever to the heavenly way and follow after justice and virtue always, considering that the soul is immortal and able to endure every sort of good and every sort of evil. Thus shall we live dear to one another and to the gods, both while remaining here and when, like conquerors in the games who go round to gather gifts, we receive our reward. And it shall be well with us both in this life and in the pilgrimage of a thousand years which we have been describing.

THE TRIAL
AND DEATH
OF
SOCRATES

MENO

INTRODUCTION

THIS Dialogue begins abruptly with a question of Meno, who asks "whether virtue can be taught." Socrates replies that he does not as yet know what virtue is, and has never known any one who did. "Then he can not have met Gorgias when he was at Athens." Yes, Socrates had met him, but he has a bad memory, and has forgotten what Gorgias said. Will Meno tell him his own notion, which is probably not very different from that of Gorgias? "O yes — nothing easier; there is the virtue of a man, of a woman, of an old man, and of a child; there is a virtue of every age and state of life, all of which may be easily described."

Socrates reminds Meno that this is only an enumeration of the virtues and not a definition of the notion which is common to them all. Meno tries again; this time he defines virtue to be "the power of command." But to this, again, exceptions are taken. For there must be a virtue of those who obey, as well as of those who command; and the power of command must be justly or not unjustly exercised. Meno is ever ready to admit that justice is virtue: "Would you say virtue or a virtue, for there are other virtues, such as courage, temperance, and the like; just as round is a figure, and black and white are colors, and yet there are other figures and other colors. Let Meno take the examples of figure and color, and try to define them." Meno confesses his inability, and after a process of interrogation, in which Socrates explains to him the nature of a "simile in multis," Socrates himself defines figure as "the accompaniment of color." But some one may object that he does not know the meaning of the word "color;" and if he is a candid friend, and not a mere disputant, Socrates is willing to furnish him with a simpler and more philosophical definition, in which no disputed word is allowed to intrude: "Figure is the limit of form." Meno imperiously insists that he must still have a definition of color. To which, after some playful raillery, Socrates is induced to reply, "that color is the effluence of form in due proportion to the sight." This definition is exactly suited to the taste of Meno, who welcomes the familiar language of Gorgias

419

and Empedocles. Socrates is of opinion that the more abstract or dialectical definition of figure is far better.

Now that Meno has been made to understand the nature of a general definition, he answers in the spirit of a Greek gentleman, and in the words of a poet, " that virtue is to delight in things honorable, and to have the power of getting them." This is a nearer approximation than he has yet made to a complete definition, and, regarded as a piece of proverbial or popular morality is not far from the truth. But the objection is urged " that the honorable is the good," and as every one desires the good, the point of the definition is contained in the last words, " the power of getting them." " And they must be got justly or with justice." The definition will then stand thus: " Virtue is the power of getting good with justice." But justice is a part of virtue, and therefore virtue is the getting of good with a part of virtue. The definition repeats the word defined.

Meno complains that the conversation of Socrates has the effect of a torpedo's shock upon him. When he talks with other persons he has plenty to say about virtue; in the presence of Socrates, his thoughts seem to desert him. Socrates replies that he is only the cause of perplexity in others, because he is himself perplexed. He proposes to continue the inquiry. But how, asks Meno, can he inquire either into what he knows or into what he does not know? This is a sophistical puzzle, which, as Socrates remarks, saves a great deal of trouble to him who accepts it. But the puzzle has a real difficulty latent under it, to which Socrates replies in a figure. The difficulty is the origin of knowledge.

He professes to have heard from priests and priestesses, and from the poet Pindar, of an immortal soul which is always learning and forgetting in successive periods of existence, wandering over all places of the upper and under world, having seen and known all things at one time or other, and by association out of one thing capable of recovering all. For nature is of one kindred; and every soul has a seed or germ which may be developed into all knowledge. The existence of this latent knowledge is further proved by the interrogation of one of Meno's slaves, who, in the skilful hands of Socrates, is made to acknowledge some elementary relations of geometrical figures. The theorem that the square of the diagonal is double the square of the side — that famous discovery of primitive mathematics, in honor of which the legendary Pythagoras is said to have sacrificed a hecatomb — is elicited from him. The first step in the process of teaching has made him conscious of his own ignorance. He has had the " torpedo's shock " given him, and is the better for the operation. But whence had the uneducated man this knowledge? He had never learned geometry in this world; nor was it born with him; he must therefore have had it in a previous existence.

After Socrates has given this specimen of the true nature of teaching, the original question of the teachableness of virtue is renewed. Again he professes a desire to know " what virtue is " first. But he is willing to argue the question, as mathematicians say, under an hypothesis. He will assume that if virtue is knowledge, then virtue can be taught.

Socrates has no difficulty in showing that virtue is a good, and that goods, whether of body or mind, must be under the direction of knowledge. Upon the assumption just made, then, virtue is teachable. But where are the teachers? There are none found. This is extremely discouraging. Virtue is no sooner discovered to be teachable, than the discovery follows that it is not taught. Virtue, therefore, is and is not teachable.

In this dilemma an appeal is made to Anytus, who is a respectable and well-to-do citizen of the old school, and happens to be present. He is asked " whether Meno shall go to the Sophists and be taught." The very suggestion of this throws him into a rage. " To whom, then, shall Meno go? " asks Socrates. To any Athenian gentleman — to the great Athenian statesmen of past times. Socrates replies here, that Themistocles, Pericles, and other great men, never taught their sons anything worth learning; and they would surely, if they could, have imparted to them their own political wisdom. Anytus is angry at the imputation which is supposed to be cast on his favorite statesmen, and breaks off with a significant threat.

Socrates returns to the consideration of the question " whether virtue is teachable," which was denied on the ground that there are no teachers of it: (for the Sophists are bad teachers, and the rest of the world do not profess to teach.) But there is another point which we failed to observe, and in which Gorgias has never instructed Meno, nor Prodicus Socrates. This is the nature of right opinion. For virtue may be under the guidance of right opinion as well as knowledge; and right opinion is for practical purposes as good as knowledge, but is incapable of being taught, and is also liable to " walk off," because not bound by the tie of the cause. This is the sort of instinct which is possessed by statesmen who are not wise or knowing persons, but only inspired or divine. The higher virtue, which is identical with knowledge, is an ideal only. If the statesman had this knowledge, and could teach what he knew, he would be like Tiresias in the world below, — "he alone would have wisdom, while the rest flit as shadows."

This Dialogue is an attempt to answer the question, Can virtue be taught? No one would either ask or answer such a question in modern times. But in the age of Socrates it was only by an effort that the mind could rise to a general notion of virtue as distinct from the particular virtues of courage, liberality, and the like. And when a hazy conception of this was attained, it was only by a further effort that the question of the teachableness of virtue could be resolved.

The answer which is given by Plato is paradoxical enough, and seems rather intended to stimulate than to satisfy inquiry. Virtue is knowledge, and therefore virtue can be taught. But virtue is not taught, and therefore in this higher and ideal sense there is no virtue and no knowledge. The teaching of the Sophists is confessedly inadequate, and Meno, who is their pupil, is ignorant of the very nature of general terms. He can only produce out of their armory the sophism, "that you can neither inquire into what you know nor into what you do not know;" to which Socrates replies by his theory of reminiscence.

To the doctrine that virtue is knowledge, Plato has been constantly tending in the previous Dialogues. But here the new truth is no sooner found than it seems to vanish away. "If there is knowledge, there must be teachers; and where are the teachers?" There is no knowledge in the higher sense of systematic, connected, reasoned knowledge, such as may one day be attained, and such as Plato himself seems to see in some far off vision of a single science. And there are no teachers in the higher sense of the word; that is to say, no real teachers who will arouse the spirit of inquiry in their pupils, and not merely instruct them in rhetoric or impart to them ready-made information for a fee of "one" or of "fifty drachms." Plato is desirous of deepening the notion of education, and therefore he asserts the seeming paradox that there are no educators.

But there is still a possibility which must not be overlooked. Even if there is no knowledge, as has been proved by "the wretched state of education," there may be right opinion. This is a sort of guessing or divination which rests on no knowledge of causes, and is incommunicable to others. This is what our statesmen have, as is proved by the circumstance that they are unable to impart their knowledge to others. Those who are possessed of this gift can not be said to be men of science or philosophers, but they are inspired and divine.

There is no trace of irony in this curious passage, which forms the concluding portion of the dialogue. Nor again does Plato mean to intimate that the supernatural or divine is the true basis of human life. To him knowledge, if only attainable in this world, is of all things the most divine. But, like other philosophers, he is willing to admit that " probability is the guide of life;" and at the same time is desirous to contrast " the wisdom which governs the world" with true wisdom. There are many instincts, judgments, and anticipations of the human mind which can not be reduced to rule, and of which the grounds can not always be given in words. A person may have some skill or latent experience which he is able to use himself and is yet unable to teach others, because he has no principles, and is not able to collect or arrange his ideas. He has practice, but not theory; art, but not science. This is a true fact of psychology, which is recognized by Plato in this passage.

Also here, as in the Phaedrus, Plato appears to acknowledge an unreasoning element in the higher nature of man. The philosopher only has knowledge, and yet the statesman and the poet are inspired. There may be a sort of irony in regarding in this way the gifts of genius. But there is no reason to suppose that he is deriding them any more than he is deriding the phenomena of love or of enthusiasm in the Symposium, or of oracles in the Apology, or of divine intimations when he is speaking of the daemonium of Socrates. He recognizes the lower form of right opinion, as well as the higher one of science, in the spirit of one who desires to include in his philosophy every aspect of human life; just as he recognizes the existence of popular opinion as a fact, and the Sophists as the expression of it.

This Dialogue contains the first intimation of the doctrine of reminiscence and of the immortality of the soul. It may be observed that the fanciful notion of preëxistence is combined with a true view of the unity of knowledge, and of the association of ideas. The germs of two valuable principles of education may also be gathered from the " doctrine of priests and priestesses:" (1) that true knowledge is a knowledge of causes; and (2) that the process of learning consists not in what is brought to the learner, but in what is drawn out of him. The philosophy of ideas is here presented in a less developed form than in the Phaedo and Phaedrus. Nothing is said of the preexistence of ideas of justice, temperance, and the like. Nor is Socrates positive of anything but the duty of inquiry. The doctrine of reminiscence too is explained in a manner more in accordance with fact and experience out of the affinities of nature. Modern philosophy says that all things in nature are dependent on one another; the ancient philosopher has the same truth latent in his mind when he says that out of one thing all the rest may be recovered.

Some lesser traits of the dialogue may be noted also, such as the acute observation that Meno prefers the familiar definition, which is embellished with poetical language, to the better and truer one; or (2) the shrewd reflection, which may admit of an application to modern as well as to ancient teachers, that the Sophists having made large fortunes, this must surely be a criterion of their powers of teaching, for that no man could get a living by shoemaking who was not a good shoemaker; or (3) the remark conveyed, almost in a word, that the verbal sceptic is saved the labor of thought and inquiry. Characteristic also of the temper of the Socratic inquiry is, (4) the proposal to discuss the teachableness of virtue under an hypothesis, after the manner of the mathematicians, and (5) the repetition of the favorite doctrine which occurs so frequently in the earlier and more Socratic Dialogues, and gives a color to all of them — that mankind only desire evil through ignorance.

The character of Meno, like that of Critias, has no relation to the actual circumstances of his life. Plato is silent about his treachery to the ten thousand Greeks, which Xenophon has recorded, as he is also silent about the crimes of Critias. He is a Thessalian Alcibiades, rich and luxurious — a spoiled child of fortune, and is described as the hereditary friend of the great king. Like Alcibiades, he is inspired with an ardent desire of knowledge, and is equally willing to learn of Socrates and the Sophists. He may be regarded as standing in the same relation to Gorgias as Hippocrates in the Protagoras to the other great Sophist. He is the sophisticated youth on whom Socrates tries his cross-examining powers, with a view of exhibiting him and his teachers in their true light, just as in the Charmides, the Lysis, and the Euthydemus, he makes ingenuous boyhood the subject of a similar experiment. Socrates treats Meno in a half playful manner, and tries to exhibit him to himself and to the reader as ignorant of the very elements of dialectics, in which the Sophists have failed to instruct their disciple.

Anytus is the type of the narrow-minded man of the world, who is indignant at innovation, and equally detests the popular teacher and the true philosopher. He seems, like Aristophanes, to regard the new opinions, whether of Socrates or the Sophists, as fatal to Athenian greatness. He is of the same class as Callicles in the Gorgias, but of a different variety; the immoral and sophistical doctrines of Callicles are not attributed to him. The moderation with which he is described is remarkable, if he be the accuser of Socrates; and this seems to be indicated by his parting words. Perhaps Plato may have been desirous of showing that the accusation of Socrates was not to be attributed to badness or malevolence, but rather to a tendency in men's minds. Or he may have been regardless of the historical truth of the characters of his dialogue, as in the case of Meno and Critias. Like Chaerephon the real Anytus was a democrat, and had joined Thrasybulus in the conflict with the thirty.

MENO

PERSONS OF THE DIALOGUE

MENO.   A SLAVE OF MENO.
SOCRATES.   ANYTUS.

Meno. CAN you tell me, Socrates, whether virtue is acquired by teaching or by practice; or if neither by teaching nor by practice, then whether it comes to man by nature, or in what other way?

Socrates. O Meno, there was a time when the Thessalians were famous among the other Hellenes only for their riches and their riding; but now, if I am not mistaken, they are equally famous for their wisdom, especially at Larisa, which is the native city of your friend Aristippus. And this is Gorgias' doing; for when he came there, the flower of the Aleuadae, of whom your lover Aristippus is one, and the other chiefs of the Thessalians, fell in love with his wisdom. And he has taught you the habit of answering questions in a grand and bold style, which becomes those who know, and is the style in which he himself answers all comers; and any Hellene who likes may ask him anything. How different is our lot! my dear Meno. Here at Athens there is a dearth of the commodity, and all wisdom seems to have emigrated from us to you. I am certain that if you were to ask any Athenian whether virtue was natural or acquired, he would laugh in your face, and say: Stranger, you have far too good an opinion of me; if I were inspired I might answer your question. But now I literally do not know what virtue is, and much less whether it is acquired by teaching or not. And I myself, Meno, living as I do in this region of poverty, am as poor as the rest of the citizens; and I confess with shame that I know literally nothing about virtue; and when I do not know the " quid " of anything how can I know the " quale? " How, if I knew nothing at all of Meno, could I tell if he was fair, or the opposite of fair; rich and noble, or the reverse of rich and noble? Do you think that I could?

Men. No, indeed. But are you in earnest, Socrates, in saying that you do not know what virtue is? And am I to carry back this report of you to Thessaly?

Soc. Not only that, my dear boy, but you may say further that I have never known of any one else who did, in my judgment.

Men. Then you have never met Gorgias when he was at Athens?

Soc. Yes, I have.

Men. And did you not think that he knew?

Soc. I have not a good memory, Meno, and therefore I can not now tell what I thought of him at the time. And I dare say that he did know, and that you know what he said: please, therefore, to remind me of what he said; or, if you would rather, tell me your own view, for I dare say that you and he think much alike.

Men. True.

Soc. Then as he is not here, never mind him, and do you tell me. By the gods, Meno, be generous, and tell me what you say that virtue is; for I shall be truly delighted to find that I have been mistaken, and that you and Gorgias do really know what I have been saying that I have never found anybody who knew.

Men. There will be no difficulty, Socrates, in answering that. Take first the virtue of a man: his virtue is to know how to administer the state, in the administration of which he will benefit his friends and damage his enemies, and will take care not to suffer damage himself. A woman's virtue may also be easily described: her virtue is to order her house, and keep what is indoors, and obey her husband. Every age, every condition of life, young or old, male or female, bond or free, has a different virtue: there are virtues numberless, and no lack of definitions of them; for virtue is relative to the actions and ages of each of us in all that we do. And the same may be said of vice, Socrates.

Soc. How fortunate I am, Meno! When I ask you for one virtue, you present me with a swarm of them, which are in your keeping. Suppose that I carry on the figure of the swarm, and ask of you, What is the nature of the bee? and you answer that there are many kinds of bees, and I reply: But do bees differ as bees, because there are many and different kinds of them; or are they not rather to be distinguished by some other quality, as for example beauty, size, or shape? How would you answer that?

Men. I should answer that bees do not differ from one another, as bees.

Soc. And suppose that I went on to say: That is what I want to know, Meno; tell me what is that quality in which they do not differ, but are all alike; — you would be able to answer that?

Men. I should.

Soc. And so of the virtues, however many and different they may be, they have all a common nature which makes them virtues; and on this he who would answer the question, "What is virtue?" would do well to have his eye fixed. Do you understand?

Men. I am beginning to understand; but I do not as yet take hold of the question as I could wish.

Soc. When you say, Meno, that there is one virtue

of a man, another of a woman, another, of a child, and so on; does this apply only to virtue, or would you say the same of health, and size, and strength? Or is the nature of health always the same, whether in man or woman?

Men. I should say that health, regarded as health, is the same, whether of man or woman.

Soc. And is not this true of size and strength? If a woman is strong, she will be strong by reason of the same form and of the same strength subsisting in her which there is in the man. I mean to say that strength, as strength, whether of man or woman, is the same. Is there any difference?

Men. I think not.

Soc. And will not virtue, as virtue, be the same, whether in a child or in a grown-up person, in a woman or in a man?

Men. I can not help feeling, Socrates, that this case is not like the others.

Soc. Why? Were you not saying that the virtue of a man was to order a state, and the virtue of a woman was to order a house?

Men. I did say that.

Soc. And can either house or state or anything be well ordered without temperance and without justice?

Men. Certainly not.

Soc. Then they who order a state or a house temperately or justly order them with temperance and justice?

Men. Certainly.

Soc. Then both men and women, if they are to be good men and women, must have the same virtues of temperance and justice?

Men. True.

Soc. And can either a young man or an old one be good, if they are intemperate and unjust?

Men. They can not.

Soc. They must be temperate and just?

Men. Yes.

Soc. Then all men are good in the same way, and by participation in the same virtues?

Men. That is the inference.

Soc. And they surely would not have been good in the same way, unless their virtue had been the same?

Men. They would not.

Soc. Then now that the sameness of all virtue has been proven, try and remember what you and Gorgias say that virtue is.

Men. Will you have one definition of them all?

Soc. That is what I am seeking.

Men. What can I say but that virtue is the power of governing mankind?

Soc. And does this definition of virtue include all virtue? Is virtue the same in a child and in a slave, Meno? Ought the child to govern his father, or the slave his master; and would he who governed be any longer a slave?

Men. I think not, Socrates.

Soc. No, indeed; there would be small reason in that. Yet once more, fair friend; according to you, virtue is " the power of governing; " but do you not add " justly " and not unjustly?

Men. Yes, Socrates; I agree to that, for justice is virtue.

Soc. Would you say " virtue," Meno, or " a virtue? "

Men. What do you mean?

Soc. I mean as I might say about anything; that a round, for example, is " a figure " and not simply " figure," and I should say this because there are other figures.

Men. Quite right; and that is just what I am saying about virtue — that there are other virtues as well as justice.

Soc. What are they? tell me the names of them, as I would tell you the names of the other figures if you asked me.

Men. Courage and temperance and wisdom and magnificence are virtues; and there are many others.

Soc. Yes, Meno; and again we are in the same case: in searching after one virtue we have found many, though not in the same way as before; but we have been unable to find the common element which runs through them all.

Men. Why, Socrates, even now I am not able to follow you in the attempt to get at one common notion of virtue as of other things.

Soc. No wonder; but I will try to arrive a little nearer if I can, for you know that all things have a common notion. Suppose now that some one asked you the question which I asked before: Meno, he would say, what is figure? And if you answered "roundness," he would reply to you, in my way of speaking, by asking whether you would say that roundness is "figure" or "a figure;" and you would answer "a figure."

Men. Certainly.

Soc. And for this reason — that there are other figures?

Men. Yes.

Soc. And if he proceeded to ask, what other figures are there? you would have told him.

Men. I should.

Soc. And if he similarly asked what color is, and you answered whiteness, and the questioner rejoined, Would you say that whiteness is color or a color? you would reply, A color, because there are other colors as well.

Men. I should.

Soc. And if he had said, Tell me what they are, you would have told him of other colors which are colors just as much as whiteness.

Men. Yes.

Soc. And suppose that he were to pursue the matter in my way, he would say: Ever and anon we are landed in particulars, but this is not what I want; tell me then, since you call them by a common name, and say that they are all figures, even when opposed to one another, what is that common nature which you designate as figure — which comprehends straight as well as round, and is no more one than the other — would you not say that?

Men. Yes.

Soc. And in saying that, you do not mean to say that the round is round any more than straight, or the straight any more straight than round?

Men. Certainly not.

Soc. You only assert that the round figure is not more a figure than the straight, or the straight than the round?

Men. That is true.

Soc. What then is this which is called figure? Try and answer. Suppose that when a person asked you this question either about figure or color, you were to reply, Man, I do not understand what you want, or know what you are saying; he would look rather astonished and say: Do you not understand that I am looking for the "simile in multis?" And then he might put the question in another form: Meno, he might say, what is that "simile in multis" which you call figure, and which includes not only round and straight figures, but all? Could you not answer that question, Meno? I wish that you would try; the attempt will be good practice with a view to the answer about virtue.

Men. I would rather that you should answer, Socrates.

Soc. Shall I indulge you?

Men. By all means.

Soc. And then you will tell me about virtue?

Men. I will.

Soc. Then I must do my best, for there is a prize to be won.

Men. Certainly.

Soc. Well, I will try and explain to you what figure is. What do you say to this answer? — Figure is the only thing that always follows color. I hope that you are satisfied with that, as I am sure I should be content if you would let me have a similar definition of virtue.

Men. But that, Socrates, is a simple answer.

Soc. Why simple?

Men. Because you say that figure is that which always follows color; but if a person says that he does not know what color is, any more than what figure is — what sort of answer would you have given him?

Soc. I should have told him the truth. And if he were a philosopher of the eristic and antagonistic sort, I should say to him: You have my answer, and if I am wrong, your business is to take up the argument and refute me. But if I were talking as you and I now are, as between friends, I should reply in a milder strain and more in the dialectician's way; that is to say, I should not only speak the truth, but I should make use of premisses which the person interrogated would be willing to admit. And this is the way in which I shall approach you. You will acknowledge, will you not, that there is such a thing as an end, or termination, or extremity? — all of which words I use in the same sense, although I am aware that Prodicus might quarrel with us about this: but still you, I am sure, would speak of a thing as ended or terminated — that is all which I am saying — not anything very difficult.

Men. Yes, I should; and I believe that I understand your meaning.

Soc. And you will speak of a surface and also of a solid, as for example in geometry.

Men. Yes.

Soc. Well then, you are now in a condition to understand my definition of figure. I define figure to be that in which the solid ends; or, more concisely, as the limit of solid.

Men. And now, Socrates, what is color?

Soc. You are outrageous, Meno, in thus plaguing a poor old man to give you an answer, when you won't take the trouble of remembering what is Gorgias' definition of virtue.

Men. When you have told me what I ask, I will tell you, Socrates.

Soc. A man who was blindfolded has only to hear you talking, and he would know that you are a fair creature and have still many lovers.

Men. Why do you say that?

Soc. Why, because you always speak in imperatives: like all beauties when they are in their prime, you are tyrannical; and also, as I suspect, you have found out that I have a weakness for the fair, and therefore I must humor you and answer.

Men. Please do.

Soc. Would you like me to answer you after the manner of Gorgias, which is familiar to you?

Men. I should very much like that.

Soc. Do not he and Empedocles say that there are certain effluences of existence?

Men. Certainly.

Soc. And passages into which and through which the effluences pass?

Men. Exactly.

Soc. And some of the effluences fit into the passages, and some of them are too small or too large?

Men. True.

Soc. And there is such a thing as sight?

Men. Yes.

Soc. And now, as Pindar says, " read my meaning: " — color is an effluence of form, commensurate with sight, and sensible.

Men. That, Socrates, appears to me to be an admirable answer.

Soc. Why, yes, because it is just such an one as you have been in the habit of hearing: and your wit will have discovered that you may explain in the same way the nature of sound and smell, and of many other similar phenomena.

Men. Quite true.

Soc. The answer, Meno, was in the orthodox solemn vein, and therefore was more acceptable to you than the other answer about figure.

Men. Yes.

Soc. And yet, O son of Alexidemus, I can not help thinking that the other was the better; and I am sure that you would be of the same opinion, if you would only stay and be initiated, and were not compelled, as you said yesterday, to go away before the mysteries.

Men. But I will gladly stay, Socrates, if you will give me many such answers.

Soc. Well then, for my own sake as well as for yours, I will do my very best; but I am afraid that I shall not be able to give you very many as good: and now, in your turn, you are to fulfil your promise, and tell me what virtue is in the universal; and do not make a singular into a plural, as the facetious say of those who break a thing, but deliver virtue to me whole and sound and not broken into a number of pieces. I have given you the pattern.

Men. Well then, Socrates, virtue, as I take it, is the love and attainment of the honorable; that is what the poet says, and I say too —

" Virtue is the desire and power of attaining the honorable."

Soc. And does he who desires the honorable also desire the good?

Men. Certainly.

Soc. Then are there some who desire the evil and others who desire the good! Do not all men, my dear sir, desire good?

Men. No, I do not think that.

Soc. There are some who desire evil?

Men. Yes.

Soc. Do you mean that they think the evils which they desire to be good; or do they know that they are evil and yet desire them?

Men. Both, as I think.

Soc. And do you really imagine, Meno, that a man knows evils to be evils and desires them notwithstanding?

Men. Certainly I do.

Soc. And desire is of possession?

Men. Yes, of possession.

Soc. And does he think that the evils will do good to him who possesses them, or does he know that they will do him harm?

Men. There are some who think that the evils will do them good, and others who know that they will do them harm.

Soc. And, in your opinion, do those who think

that they will do them good know that they are evils?

Men. No, I certainly do not think that.

Soc. Can anything be clearer than that those who are ignorant of the evils do not desire them, but they desire what they suppose to be good when they are really evils, and they who do not know them to be evils, and suppose them to be good, desire good?

Men. Yes, in that case.

Soc. Well, and do those who, as you say, desire evils, and think that evils are hurtful to the possessor of them, know that they will be hurt by them?

Men. They must know that.

Soc. And do they not suppose that they are miserable in the degree that they are hurt?

Men. That again they must believe.

Soc. And are not the miserable ill-fated?

Men. Yes, indeed.

Soc. And does any one desire to be miserable and ill-fated?

Men. I should say not, Socrates.

Soc. But if there is no one who desires to be miserable, there is no one, Meno, who desires evil; for what is misery but the desire and possession of evil?

Men. That appears to be the truth, Socrates, and I admit that nobody desires evil.

Soc. And yet, were you not saying just now that virtue is the desire and power of attaining good?

Men. Yes, I did say that.

Soc. But granting that, then the desire of good is common to all, and one man is no better than another in that?

Men. True.

Soc. And if one man is not better than another in desiring good, he must be better in the power of attaining good?

Men. Exactly.

Soc. Then, according to your definition, virtue would appear to be the power of attaining good?

Men. I entirely approve, Socrates, of the manner in which you view this matter.

Soc. Then now let us see whether this is true from another point of view; for I dare say that you are right. What you say is, that virtue is the power of attaining good?

Men. Yes.

Soc. And you would say that goods are such as health and wealth and the possession of gold and silver, and having office and honor in the state — these are what you would call goods?

Men. Yes, all these.

Soc. Then, according to Meno, who is the hereditary friend of the great king, virtue is the power of getting silver and gold; and would you add piously, justly, or do you deem this of no consequence? And is any mode of acquisition, even if unjust or dishonest, equally to be regarded as virtue?

Men. Not virtue, Socrates, but vice.

Soc. Then justice or temperance or holiness, or some other part of virtue, as would appear, must accompany the acquisition, and without them the mere acquisition of good will not be virtue.

Men. Why, how can there be virtue without these?

Soc. And the non-acquisition of gold and silver in a dishonest manner may be equally virtue?

Men. True.

Soc. Then the acquisition of such goods is no more virtue than the non-acquisition of them, but whatever is accompanied by justice or honesty is virtue, and whatever is devoid of justice is vice?

Men. There can be no doubt about that, in my judgment.

Soc. And were we not saying just now that justice, temperance, and the like, were each of them a part of virtue?

Men. Yes.

Soc. And so, Meno, this is the way in which you mock me.

Men. Why do you say that, Socrates?

Soc. Why, because I asked you to deliver virtue into my hands whole and unbroken, and I gave you a pattern according to which you were to frame your answer; and you have already forgotten this, and tell me that virtue is the power of attaining good justly, or with justice — thus acknowledging justice to be a part of virtue.

Men. Yes.

Soc. Then it follows from your own admissions, that virtue is doing what you do with a part of virtue; for justice and the like are each of them parts of virtue.

Men. What of that?

Soc. What of that! Why, did not I ask you to tell me the nature of virtue as a whole? And you are very far from telling me this; but declare every action to be virtue which is done with a part of virtue; as though you had already told me the whole of virtue, and as if I should know what the whole was when frittered away into little pieces. And, therefore, my dear Meno, I fear that I must begin again and repeat the same question: What is virtue? for otherwise, I can only say, that every action done with a part of virtue is virtue; what else is the meaning of saying that every action done with justice is virtue? Don't you think that the question requires to be repeated; for can any one who does not know virtue know a part of virtue?

Men. No; I do not say that he can.

Soc. Do you remember how, in the example of figure, we rejected any answer given in terms which were as yet unexplained or unadmitted?

Men. Yes, Socrates; and we were right in that.

Soc. Well, my friend, do as we did then: and do not suppose that we can explain to any one the nature of virtue as a whole through some unexplained portion of virtue, or anything at all in that fashion; for that only leads to a repetition of the old question, What is virtue? Now, am I not right?

Men. I believe that you are.

Soc. Then begin again, and answer me, What, according to you and your friend, is the definition of virtue?

Men. O Socrates; I used to be told, before I knew you, that you are always puzzling yourself and others; and now you are casting your spells over me, and I am simply getting bewitched and enchanted, and am at my wits' end. And if I may venture to make a jest upon you, you seem to me both in your appearance and in your power over others to be very like the flat torpedo fish, who torpifies those who come near him with the touch, as you have now torpified me, I think. For my soul and my tongue are really torpid, and I do not know how to answer you; and though I have been delivered of an infinite variety of speeches about virtue before now, and to many persons — and very good ones they were, as I thought — now I can not even say what virtue is. And I think that you are very wise in not voyaging and going away from home, for if you did in other places as you do in Athens, you would be cast into prison as a magician.

Soc. You are a rogue, Meno, and had all but caught me.

Men. What do you mean, Socrates?

Soc. I can tell why you made a simile about me.

Men. Why, do you think?

Soc. In order that I might make another simile about you. For I know that all pretty young gentlemen like to have pretty similes made about them; and well they may: but I shall not return the compliment. As to my being a torpedo, if the torpedo is torpid as well as the cause of torpidity in others, then indeed I am a torpedo, but not otherwise; for I perplex others, not because I am clear, but because I am utterly perplexed myself. And now I know not what virtue is, and you seem to be in the same case, although you did once know before you touched me. However, I have no objection to join with you in the inquiry.

Men. And how will you inquire, Socrates, into that which you know not? What will you put forth as the subject of inquiry? And if you find what you want, how will you ever know that this is what you did not know?

Soc. I know, Meno, what you mean; but just see what a tiresome dispute you are introducing. You argue that a man can not inquire either about that which he knows, or about that which he does not know; for he knows, and therefore has no need to inquire about that — nor about that which he does not know; for he does not know that about which he is to inquire.

Men. Well, Socrates, and is not the argument sound?

Soc. I think not.

Men. Why not?

Soc. I will tell you why. I have heard from certain wise men and women who spoke of things divine that —

Men. What did they say?

Soc. They spoke of a glorious truth, as I conceive.

Men. What was that? and who were they?

Soc. Some of them were priests and priestesses,

who have studied how they might be able to give a reason of their profession: there have been poets also, such as the poet Pindar and other inspired men. And what they say is — mark, now, and see whether their words are true — they say that the soul of man is immortal, and at one time has an end, which is termed dying, and at another time is born again, but is never destroyed. And the moral is, that a man ought to live always in perfect holiness. For in the ninth year Persephone sends the souls of those from whom she has received the penalty of ancient crime back again into the light of this world, and these are they who become noble kings and mighty men and great in wisdom and are called saintly heroes in after ages. The soul, then, as being immortal, and having been born again many times, and having seen all things that there are, whether in this world or in the world below, has knowledge of them all; and it is no wonder that she should be able to call to remembrance all that she ever knew about virtue, and about everything; for as all nature is akin, and the soul has learned all things, there is no difficulty in her eliciting, or as men say learning, all out of a single recollection, if a man is strenuous and does not faint; for all inquiry and all learning is but recollection. And therefore we ought not to listen to this sophistical argument about the impossibility of inquiry: that is a saying which will make us idle, and is sweet only to the sluggard; but the other saying will make us active and enterprising. In that confiding, I will gladly inquire with you into the nature of virtue.

Men. Yes, Socrates; but what do you mean by saying that we do not learn, and that what we call learning is only a process of recollection? Can you teach me that?

Soc. I told you, Meno, that you were a rogue, and

now you ask whether I can teach you, when I am saying that there is no teaching, but only recollection; and thus you imagine that you will involve me in a contradiction.

Men. Indeed, Socrates, I protest that I had no such intention. I only asked the question from habit; but if you can prove to me that what you say is true, I wish that you would.

Soc. That is no easy matter, but I will try to please you to the utmost of my power. Suppose that you call one of your numerous attendants, that I may demonstrate on him.

Men. Certainly. Come hither, boy.

Soc. He is Greek, and speaks Greek, does he not?

Men. Yes; he was born in the house.

Soc. Attend now to the questions which I ask him, and observe whether he learns of me or only remembers.

Men. I will.

Soc. Tell me, boy, do you know that a figure like this is a square?

Boy. I do.

Soc. And you know that a square figure has these four lines equal?

Boy. Certainly.

Soc. And these lines which I have drawn through the middle of the square are also equal?

Boy. Yes.

Soc. A square may be of any size?

Boy. Certainly.

Soc. And if one side of the figure be of two feet, and the other side be of two feet, how much will the whole be? Let me explain: if in one direction the space was of two feet, and in the other direction of one foot, the whole would be of two feet taken once?

Boy. Yes.

Soc. But since this side is also of two feet, there are twice two feet?

Boy. There are.

Soc. Then the square is of twice two feet?

Boy. Yes.

Soc. And how many are twice two feet? count and tell me.

Boy. Four, Socrates.

Soc. And might there not be another square twice as large as this, and having like this the lines equal?

Boy. Yes.

Soc. And of how many feet will that be?

Boy. Of eight feet.

Soc. And now try and tell me the length of the line which forms the side of that double square: this is two feet — what will that be?

Boy. Clearly, Socrates, that will be double.

Soc. Do you observe, Meno, that I am not teaching the boy anything, but only asking him questions; and now he fancies that he knows how long a line is necessary in order to produce a figure of eight square feet; does he not?

Men. Yes.

Soc. And does he really know?

Men. Certainly not.

Soc. He only guesses that [because the square is double], the line is double.

Men. True.

Soc. Observe him while he recalls the steps in regular order. (*To the Boy.*) Tell me, boy, do you assert that a double space comes from a double line? Remember that I am not speaking of an oblong, but of a square, and of a square twice the size of this one — that is to say of eight feet; and I want to know whether you still say that a double square comes from a double line?

Boy. Yes.

Soc. But does not this line become doubled if we add another such line here?

Boy. Certainly.

Soc. And four such lines will make a space containing eight feet?

Boy. Yes.

Soc. Let us describe such a figure: is not that what you would say is the figure of eight feet?

Boy. Yes.

Soc. And are there not these four divisions in the figure, each of which is equal to the figure of four feet?

Boy. True.

Soc. And is not that four times four?

Boy. Certainly.

Soc. And four times is not double.

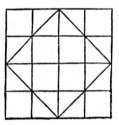

Boy. No, indeed.

Soc. But how much?

Boy. Four times as much.

Soc. Therefore the double line, boy, has formed a space, not twice, but four times as much.

Boy. True.

Soc. And four times four are sixteen — are they not?

Boy. Yes.

Soc. What line would give you a space of eight feet, as this gives one of sixteen feet; — do you see?

Boy. Yes.

Soc. And the space of four feet is made from this half line?

Boy. Yes.

Soc. Good; and is not a space of eight feet twice the size of this, and half the size of the other?

Boy. Certainly.

Soc. Such a space, then, will be made out of a line greater than this one, and less than that one?

Boy. Yes; that is what I think.

Soc. Very good; I like to hear you say what you think. And now tell me, is not this a line of two feet and that of four?

Boy. Yes.

Soc. Then the line which forms the side of eight feet ought to be more than this line of two feet, and less than the other of four feet?

Boy. It ought.

Soc. Try and see if you can tell me how much it will be.

Boy. Three feet.

Soc. Then if we add a half to this line of two, that will be the line of three. Here are two and there is one; and on the other side, here are two also and there is one: and that makes the figure of which you speak?

Boy. Yes.

Soc. But if there are three feet this way and three feet that way, the whole space will be three times three feet?

Boy. That is evident.

Soc. And how much are three times three feet?

Boy. Nine.

Soc. And how much is the double of four?

Boy. Eight.

Soc. Then the figure of eight is not made out of a line of three?

Boy. No.

Soc. But from what line? — tell me exactly; and if you would rather not reckon, try and show me the line.

Boy. Indeed, Socrates, I do not know.

Soc. Do you see, Meno, what advances he has made in his power of recollection? He did not know at first, and he does not know now, what is the side of a figure of eight feet: but then he thought that he knew, and answered confidently as if he knew, and had no difficulty; but now he has a difficulty, and neither knows nor fancies that he knows.

Men. True.

Soc. Is he not better off in knowing his ignorance?

Men. I think that he is.

Soc. If we have made him doubt, and given him the " torpedo's shock," have we done him any harm?

Men. I think not.

Soc. We have certainly done something that may assist him in finding out the truth of the matter; and now he will wish to remedy his ignorance, but then he would have been ready to tell all the world that the double space should have a double side.

Men. True.

Soc. But do you suppose that he would ever have inquired or learned what he fancied that he knew and did not know, until he had fallen into perplexity under the idea that he did not know, and had desired to know?

Men. I think not, Socrates.

Soc. Then he was the better for the torpedo's touch?

Men. I think that he was.

Soc. Mark now the farther development. I shall only ask him, and not teach him, and he shall share the inquiry with me: and do you watch and see if you find me telling or explaining anything to him, instead of eliciting his opinion. Tell me, boy, is not this a square of four feet which I have drawn?

Boy. Yes.

Soc. And now I add another square equal to the former one?

Boy. Yes.

Soc. And a third, which is equal to either of them?

Boy. Yes.

Soc. Suppose that we fill up the vacant corner.

Boy. Very good.

Soc. Here, then, there are four equal spaces?

Boy. Yes.

Soc. And how many times is this space larger than this?

Boy. Four times.

Soc. But it ought to have been twice only, as you will remember.

Boy. True.

Soc. And does not this line, reaching from corner to corner, bisect each of these spaces?

Boy. Yes.

Soc. And are there not here four equal lines which contain this space?

Boy. There are.

Soc. Look and see how much this space is.

Boy. I do not understand.

Soc. Has not each interior line cut off half of the four spaces?

Boy. Yes.

Soc. And how many such spaces are there in this division?

Boy. Four.

Soc. And how many in this?

Boy. Two.

Soc. And four is how many times two?

Boy. Twice.

Soc. And this space is of how many feet?

Boy. Of eight feet.

Soc. And from what line do you get this figure?

Boy. From this.

Soc. That is, from the line which extends from corner to corner?

Boy. Yes.

Soc. And that is the line which the learned call the diagonal. And if this is the proper name, then you, Meno's slave, are prepared to affirm that the double space is the square of the diagonal?

Boy. Certainly, Socrates.

Soc. What do you say of him, Meno? Were not all these answers given out of his own head?

Men. Yes, they were all his own.

Soc. And yet, as we were just now saying, he did not know?

Men. True.

Soc. And yet he had those notions in him?

Men. Yes.

Soc. Then he who does not know still has true notions of that which he does not know?

Men. He has.

Soc. And at present these notions are just wakening up in him, as in a dream; but if he were frequently asked the same questions, in different forms, he would know as well as any one at last?

Men. I dare say.

Soc. Without any one teaching him he will recover his knowledge for himself, if he is only asked questions?

Men. Yes.

Soc. And this spontaneous recovery in him is recollection?

Men. True.

Soc. And this knowledge which he now has must he not either have acquired or always possessed?

Men. Yes.

Soc. But if he always possessed this knowledge he would always have known; or if he has acquired the knowledge, he could not have acquired it in this life, unless he has been taught geometry; for he may be made to do the same with all geometry and every other branch of knowledge. Now, has any one ever taught him? You must know that, if, as you say, he was born and bred in your house.

Men. And I am certain that no one ever did teach him.

Soc. And yet has he not the knowledge?

Men. That, Socrates, is most certain.

Soc. But if he did not acquire this knowledge in this life, then clearly he must have had and learned it at some other time?

Men. That is evident.

Soc. And that must have been the time when he was not a man?

Men. Yes.

Soc. And if there have been always true thoughts in him, both at the time when he was and was not a man, which only need to be awakened into knowledge by putting questions to him, his soul must have always possessed this knowledge, for he always either was or was not a man?

Men. That is clear.

Soc. And if the truth of all things always existed in the soul, then the soul is immortal. Wherefore be of good cheer, and try to recollect what you do not know, or rather do not remember.

Men. I feel, somehow, that I like what you are saying.

Soc. And I, Meno, like what I am saying. Some things I have said of which I am not altogether confident. But that we shall be better and braver and less helpless if we think that we ought to inquire, than we should have been if we indulged in the idle fancy that there was no knowing and no use in searching

after what we know not; — that is a theme upon which
I am ready to fight, in word and deed, to the utmost
of my power.

Men. That again, Socrates, appears to me to be
well said.

Soc. Then, as we are agreed that a man should
inquire about that which he does not know, shall you
and I make an effort to inquire together into the nature of virtue?

Men. By all means, Socrates. And yet I would
rather return to my original question, Whether virtue comes by instruction, or by nature, or is gained in
some other way?

Soc. Had I the command of you as well as of myself, Meno, I would not have inquired whether virtue
is given by instruction or not, until we had first ascertained " what virtue is." But as you never think of
controlling yourself, but only of controlling him who
is your slave, and this is your notion of freedom, I
must yield to you, for I can not help. And therefore
I have now to inquire into the qualities of that of
which I do not at present know the nature. At any
rate, will you condescend a little, and allow the question " Whether virtue is given by instruction, or in
any other way," to be argued upon hypothesis? As
the geometrician, when he is asked whether a certain
triangle is capable of being described in a certain
circle, will reply: " I can not tell you as yet; but I will
offer a hypothesis which may assist us in forming a
conclusion: If the space be such that when you have
drawn along the line given by it another figure, the
original figure is reduced by a space equal to that
which is added,[1] then one consequence follows, and if
this is impossible then some other; and therefore I
wish to assume a hypothesis before I tell you whether

[1] Or, in simpler phrase, " If so much be taken from the triangle."

this triangle is capable of being included in the circle: " — that is a geometrical hypothesis. And we too, as we know not the nature and qualities of virtue, must ask, whether virtue is or is not taught, under a hypothesis: as thus, if virtue is of such a class of mental goods, will it be taught or not? Let the first hypothesis be that virtue is or is not knowledge, — in that case will it be taught or not? or, as we were just now saying, " remembered? " For there is no use in disputing about the name. But is virtue taught or not? or rather, does not every one see that knowledge alone is taught?

Men. I agree.

Soc. Then if virtue is knowledge, virtue will be taught?

Men. Certainly.

Soc. Then now we have made a quick end of this question: if virtue is of such a nature, it will be taught; and if not, not?

Men. Certainly.

Soc. And the next question is, whether virtue is knowledge or of another species?

Men. Yes, that appears to be the question which comes next in order.

Soc. Do we not say that virtue is a good? This is a hypothesis which is not set aside.

Men. Certainly.

Soc. Now, if there be any sort of good which is parted from knowledge, virtue may be that good; but if knowledge embraces all good, then we shall be right in thinking that knowledge is some sort of good?

Men. True.

Soc. And virtue makes us good?

Men. Yes.

Soc. And if we are good, then we are profitable; for all good things are profitable?

Men. Yes.

Soc. Then virtue is profitable?

Men. That is the only inference.

Soc. Then now let us see what are the things that severally profit us. Health and strength, and beauty and wealth — these, as we say, are the sort of things which profit us?

Men. True.

Soc. And yet these things may also sometimes do us harm: would you not admit that?

Men. Yes.

Soc. And what is the guiding principle which makes them profitable or the reverse? Are they not profitable when they are rightly used, and hurtful when they are not rightly used?

Men. Certainly.

Soc. Next, let us consider the goods of the soul: these are temperance, justice, courage, quickness of apprehension, memory, magnificence, and the like?

Men. Surely.

Soc. And such of these as are not knowledge, but of another sort, are sometimes profitable and sometimes hurtful; as, for example, courage, which has no prudence, but is only a sort of confidence? When a man has no sense he is harmed by courage, but when he has sense he is profited?

Men. True.

Soc. And the same may be said of temperance and quickness of apprehension; whatever things are learned or done with sense are profitable, but when done without sense they are hurtful?

Men. Very true.

Soc. And in general, all that the soul attempts or endures, when under the guidance of wisdom, ends in happiness; but when she is under the guidance of folly, in the opposite?

Men. That appears to be true.

Soc. If then virtue is a good of the soul, and is to be profitable, it must be wisdom or prudence, since some of the goods of the soul are either profitable or hurtful by the addition of wisdom or of folly; and therefore if virtue is profitable, virtue must be a sort of wisdom or prudence?

Men. That is my view.

Soc. And the other goods, such as wealth and the like, of which we were just now saying that they are sometimes good and sometimes evil, are they not also made profitable or hurtful, accordingly as the soul guides and uses them rightly or wrongly — as in the soul generally, wisdom is the useful and folly the hurtful guide?

Men. True.

Soc. And the wise soul guides them rightly, and the foolish soul wrongly?

Men. Yes.

Soc. And is not this universally true of human nature? All other things hang upon the soul, and the things of the soul hang upon wisdom, if they are to be good; and according to this view of the question that which profits is wisdom — and virtue, as we say, is profitable?

Men. Certainly.

Soc. And thus we arrive at the conclusion that virtue is either wholly or partly wisdom?

Men. I think that what you are saying, Socrates, is very true.

Soc. But if this is true, then the good are not by nature good?

Men. I think not.

Soc. If they had been, there would assuredly have been discerners of characters among us who would have known our future great men; and we should

have taken them on their showing, and when we had
got them, we should have kept them in the citadel out
of the way of harm, and set a stamp upon them more
than upon gold, in order that no one might tamper
with them; and then when they grew up they would
have been useful to the state?

Men. Yes, Socrates, that would have been the way.

Soc. But if the good are not by nature good, are
they made good by instruction?

Men. There is no other alternative, Socrates. On
the supposition that virtue is knowledge, there can
be no doubt that virtue is taught.

Soc. Yes, indeed; but what if the supposition is
erroneous?

Men. I certainly thought just now that we were
right.

Soc. Yes, Meno; but a principle which has any
soundness should stand firm not only now and then,
but always and forever.

Men. Well; and why are you so slow of heart to
believe that knowledge is virtue?

Soc. I will try and tell you why, Meno. I do not
retract the assertion that if virtue is knowledge it may
be taught; but I fear that I have some reason in doubting whether virtue is knowledge: for consider now
and say whether virtue, or anything that is taught,
must not have teachers and disciples?

Men. Surely.

Soc. And again, may not that art of which there
are neither teachers nor disciples be assumed to be
incapable of being taught?

Men. True; but do you think that there are no
teachers of virtue?

Soc. I have certainly often inquired whether there
were any, and taken great pains to find them, and
have never succeeded; and many have assisted me in

the search, and they were the persons whom I thought the most likely to know. Here is Anytus, who is sitting by us at the very moment when he is wanted; he is the person whom we should ask. In the first place, he is the son of a wealthy and wise father, Anthemion, who acquired his wealth, not by accident or gift, like Ismenias the Theban (who has recently made himself as rich as a Polycrates), but by his own skill and industry, and he is a well-conditioned, modest man, not insolent, or overbearing, or annoying; moreover, he has given his son a good education, as the Athenian people certainly appear to think, for they choose him to fill the highest offices. And these are the sort of men from whom you are likely to learn whether there are any teachers of virtue, and who they are. Please, Anytus, to help me and your friend Meno in answering our question, Who are the teachers? Consider the matter thus: If we wanted Meno to be a good physician, to whom should we send him? Should we not send him to the physicians?

Any. Certainly.

Soc. Or if we wanted him to be a good cobbler, should we not send him to the cobblers?

Any. Yes.

Soc. And so forth?

Any. Yes.

Soc. Let me trouble you with one more question. When we say that we should be right in sending him to the physicians if we wanted him to be a physician, do we mean that we should be right in sending him to those who profess the art, rather than to those who don't, and to those who demand payment for teaching the art, and profess to teach it to any one who will come and learn? If we were right in sending him, would that be the reason?

Any. Yes.

Soc. And might not the same be said of flute-playing, and of the other arts? No man who wanted to
make a man a flute-player would refuse to send him
to those who profess to teach the art for money, and
trouble other persons to give him instruction who do
not profess to teach, and never had a disciple in that
branch of knowledge which we want him to acquire —
that would be the height of folly.

Any. Yes, by Zeus, and of ignorance too.

Soc. Very good. And now you are in a position to
advise with me about my friend Meno. He has been
saying to me, Anytus, that he desires to attain that
wisdom and virtue, by which men order the state or
the house, and honor their parents, and know when
to receive and when to send away citizens and
strangers, as a good man should. Now, to whom
ought we to send him in order that he may learn this
virtue? Does not the previous argument imply
clearly that he ought to go to those who profess and
avouch that they are the common teachers of Hellas,
and are ready to impart instruction to any one who
likes, at a fixed price?

Any. Whom do you mean, Socrates?

Soc. You surely know, do you not, Anytus, that
these are the people whom mankind describe as
Sophists?

Any. By Heracles, Socrates, forbear! I only hope
that no friend or kinsman or acquaintance of mine,
whether citizen or stranger, will ever be so mad as to
allow himself to be corrupted by them; for they are a
manifest pest and corrupting influence of those who
have to do with them.

Soc. What do you mean, Anytus? Of all the
people who profess that they know how to do men
good, are these the only ones who not only do them
no good, but positively corrupt those who are en-

trusted to them? That is very singular. And moreover, in return they publicly demand money. Indeed,
I can not believe this; for I know of a single man,
Protagoras, who made more out of his craft than the
illustrious Pheidias, or any ten other statuaries. How
could that be? A mender of old shoes, or patcher up
of clothes, who made the shoes or clothes worse than
he received them, could not have remained thirty days
undetected, and would very soon have starved;
whereas, during more than forty years, Protagoras
was corrupting his disciples, and sending them from
him worse than he received them, and yet all Hellas
failed in detecting him. For, if I am not mistaken,
he was about seventy years old at his death, forty of
which were spent in the practice of his profession;
and during all that time he had a good reputation,
which to this day he retains: and not only Protagoras,
but many others have a good reputation; some who
lived before him, and others who are still living. Now,
when you say that they deceived and corrupted the
youth, are they to be supposed to have corrupted them
intentionally or unintentionally? Can those who were
deemed by many to be the wisest men of Hellas have
been out of their minds?

Any. Out of their minds! No, Socrates; the young
men who gave their money to them were out of their
minds, and their relations and guardians who entrusted them to their care were still more out of their
minds, and most of all the cities who allowed them to
come in and did not drive them out, citizen or stranger
alike.

Soc. Has any of the Sophists wronged you, Anytus? What makes you so angry with them?

Any. No, indeed, neither I nor any of my belong-
ings has ever had, nor would I suffer them to have,
anything to do with them.

Soc. Then you are entirely unacquainted with them?

Any. And I have no wish to be acquainted.

Soc. Then, my dear friend, how can you know whether a thing is good or bad of which you are wholly ignorant?

Any. Quite well; I am quite sure that I know what manner of men these are, whether I know them or not.

Soc. You must be a diviner, Anytus, for I really can not make out, judging from your own words, how, if you are not acquainted with them, you know about them. But I am not inquiring of you who are the teachers who will corrupt Meno (let them be, if you please, the Sophists) ; I only ask you to tell him who there is in this great city who will teach him how to become eminent in the virtues which I was just now describing. He is the friend of your family, and you will oblige him.

Any. Why don't you tell him?

Soc. I have told him whom I supposed to be the teachers of these things; but I learn from you that I am utterly at fault, and I dare say that you are right. And now I wish that you, on your part, would tell me to whom among the Athenians he should go. Whom would you name?

Any. Why single out individuals? Any Athenian gentleman, taken at random, if he will mind him, will do him far more good than the Sophists.

Soc. And did those gentlemen grow of themselves; and without having been taught by any one, were they nevertheless able to teach others that which they never learned themselves?

Any. I imagine that they learned of the previous generation of gentlemen. Have there not been many good men in this city?

Soc. Yes, certainly, Anytus; and many good statesmen also there always have been, and there are still, in the city of Athens. But the question is whether they were also good teachers of their own virtue; — not whether there are, or have been, good men, but whether virtue can be taught, is the question which we have been discussing. Now, do we mean to say that the good men of our own and of other times knew how to impart to others that virtue which they had themselves; or is this virtue incapable of being communicated or imparted by one man to another? That is the question which I and Meno have been arguing. Look at the matter in your own way. Would you not admit that Themistocles was a good man?

Any. Certainly; no man better.

Soc. And must not he then have been a good teacher, if any man ever was a good teacher, of his own virtue?

Any. Yes, certainly, — if he wanted to be that.

Soc. But would he not have wanted? He would, at any rate, have desired to make his own son a good man and a gentleman; he could not have been jealous of him, or have intentionally abstained from imparting to him his own virtue. Did you never hear that he made Cleophantus, who was his son, a famous horseman? — he would stand upright on horseback and hurl a javelin; and many other marvellous things he could do which his father had him taught; and in anything which the skill of a master could teach him he was well trained. Have you not heard from our elders of this?

Any. I have.

Soc. Then no one could say that his son showed any want of capacity?

Any. Possibly not.

Soc. But did any one, old or young, ever say in your hearing that Cleophantus, the son of Themistocles, was a wise or good man, as his father was?

Any. I have certainly never heard that.

Soc. And if virtue could have been taught, would he have sought to train him in these sort of accomplishments, and allowed him who, as you must remember, was his own son, to be no better than his neighbors in those qualities in which he himself excelled?

Any. Indeed, indeed, I think not.

Soc. Here then is a teacher of virtue whom you admit to be among the best men of the past. Let us take another, — Aristides, the son of Lysimachus: would you not acknowledge that he was a good man?

Any. To be sure, I should.

Soc. And did not he train his son Lysimachus better than any other Athenian in all that could be done for him by the help of masters? But what has been the result? Is he a bit better than any other mortal? He is an acquaintance of yours, and you see what he is like. There is Pericles, again, magnificent in his wisdom; and he, as you know, had two sons, Paralus and Xanthippus.

Any. I know.

Soc. And you know, also, that he taught them to be unrivalled horsemen, and had them trained in music and gymnastics and all sorts of arts — in these respects they were on a level with the best — and had he no wish to make good men of them? Nay, he must have wished that. But I suspect that virtue could not be taught. And that you may not suppose that the incompetent teachers are the meaner sort of Athenians and few in number, remember again that Thucydides had two sons, Melesias and Stephanus, whom he trained chiefly in wrestling; and they too had an excellent education, and were the best wrestlers in Athens: one of them he committed to the care of Xanthias, and the other of Eudorus, who had the reputation of being the most celebrated wrestlers of that day. Do you remember them?

Any. I have heard of them.

Soc. Now, can there be a doubt that Thucydides, who had his children taught wrestling, at a considerable expense, would have taught them to be good men, which would have cost him nothing, if virtue could have been taught? Will you reply that he was a mean man, and had not many friends among the Athenians and allies? Nay, but he was of a great family, and a man of influence at Athens and in all Hellas, and, if virtue could have been taught, he would have found out some one either in or out of Hellas who would have made good men of his sons, if he could not himself spare the time from cares of state. Again I suspect, friend Anytus, that virtue is not a thing which can be taught?

Any. Socrates, I think that you are too ready to speak evil of men: and, if you will take my advice, I would recommend you to be careful. Perhaps there is no city in which it is not easier to do men harm than to do them good, and this is certainly the case at Athens, as I believe that you know.

Soc. O Meno, I think that Anytus is in a rage. And he may well be in a rage, for he thinks, in the first place, that I am defaming these gentlemen; and then, in the second place, he thinks that he is one of them. But when he understands, which he does not at present, what is the meaning of defamation, he will forgive me. Meanwhile I will return to you, Meno; for I suppose that there are gentlemen in your region too?

Men. Certainly there are.

Soc. And are they willing to teach the young? and do they profess to be teachers? and do they agree that virtue is taught?

Men. No indeed, Socrates, they are anything but agreed; and you may hear them saying at one time that virtue can be taught, and then again the reverse.

Soc. Can we call them teachers who do not acknowledge the possibility of their own vocation?

Men. I think not, Socrates.

Soc. And what do you think of these Sophists, who are the only professors? Do they seem to you to be teachers of virtue?

Men. I often wonder, Socrates, that you never hear Gorgias promising to teach virtue: and when he hears others promising this he only laughs at them; but he thinks that you ought to teach men to speak.

Soc. Then do you not think that the Sophists are teachers?

Men. I can not tell you, Socrates; like the rest of the world, I am in doubt, and sometimes I think that they are teachers and sometimes not.

Soc. And are you aware that not you only and other political men have doubts whether virtue can be taught or not, but that Theognis the poet says the very same thing — are you aware of that?

Men. Where does he imply that?

Soc. In the elegiac verses, in which he says: —

" Eat and drink and sit with the mighty, and make yourself agreeable to them; for from the good you will learn what is good, but if you mix with the bad you will lose the intelligence which you already have."

Do you observe that here he seems to imply that virtue can be taught?

Men. Clearly.

Soc. But in some other verses he shifts about and says: —

"If understanding could be created and put into a man, then they (who were able to accomplish this) would have obtained great rewards."

And again: —

"Never did a bad son spring from a good sire because he heard the voice of instruction; not by teaching will you ever make a bad man into a good one."

And this, as you may remark, is a contradiction of the other.

Men. That is palpable.

Soc. And is there anything else of which the teachers and professors are not only asserted not to be teachers of others, but to be ignorant themselves of that which they profess to teach and bad at the knowledge of that which they preach; and about which the acknowledged "gentlemen" are themselves saying sometimes that "this thing can be taught," and sometimes not. Can you say that they are teachers of authority whose ideas are in this state of confusion?

Men. I should say, certainly not.

Soc. But if neither the Sophists nor the gentlemen are teachers, clearly there can be no other teachers?

Men. No.

Soc. And if there are no teachers, neither are there disciples?

Men. Agreed.

Soc. And we have admitted that a thing can not be taught of which there are neither teachers nor disciples?

Men. We have.

Soc. And there are no teachers of virtue to be found anywhere?

Men. There are not.

Soc. And if there are no teachers neither are there scholars?

Men. I think that is true.

Soc. Then virtue can not be taught?

Men. Not if we are right in our view. But I can not believe, Socrates, that there are no good men in the state. And if there are, how did they come into existence?

Soc. I am afraid, Meno, that you and I are not good for much, and that Gorgias has been as poor an educator of you as Prodicus has been of me. Certainly we shall have to look to ourselves, and try to find some one who will help to improve us. This I say, because I observe that in the previous discussion none of us remarked that right and good action is possible to man under other guidance than that of knowledge; — and indeed if this be denied, there is no seeing how there can be any good men at all.

Men. How do you mean, Socrates?

Soc. I mean this — that good men must necessarily be useful or profitable. Were we not right in admitting that?

Men. Yes.

Soc. And in supposing that they will be useful only if they are true guides of action — in that we were also right?

Men. Yes.

Soc. But we do not seem to have been right in saying that knowledge only was the right and good guide of action.

Men. What do you mean by the word " right? "

Soc. I will explain. If a man knew the way to Larisa, or anywhere else, and went to the place and led others thither, would he not be a right and good guide?

Men. Certainly.

Soc. And a person who had a right opinion about the way, but had never been and did not know, might be a good guide also, might he not?

Men. Certainly.

Soc. And while he has true opinion about that which the other knows, he will be just as good a guide if he thinks the truth, as if he knows the truth?

Men. Exactly.

Soc. Then true opinion is as good a guide to correct action as wisdom; and that was the point which we omitted in our speculation about the nature of virtue, when we said that wisdom only is the guide of right action; whereas there is also right opinion.

Men. True.

Soc. Then right opinion is not less useful than knowledge?

Men. The difference, Socrates, is only that he who has knowledge will always be right; but he who has right opinion will sometimes be right, and sometimes not right.

Soc. What do you mean? Can he be wrong who has right opinion, as long as he has right opinion?

Men. I admit the cogency of that, and therefore, Socrates, allowing this, I wonder that knowledge should be preferred to right opinion — or why they should ever differ.

Soc. And shall I explain this wonder to you?

Men. Do tell me.

Soc. You would not wonder if you had ever observed the images of Daedalus; but perhaps you have not got them in your country?

Men. Why do you refer to them?

Soc. Because they require to be fastened in order

to keep them, and if they are not fastened they will run away.

Men. Well, what of that?

Soc. I mean to say that it is not much use possess‹ ing one of them if they are at liberty, for they will walk off like runaway slaves; but when fastened, they are of great value, for they are really beautiful works of art. Now this is an illustration of the nature of true opinions: while they abid‹ with us they are beautiful and fruitful, but they run away out of the human soul, and do not remain long, and therefore they are not of much value until they are fastened by the tie of the cause; and this fastening of them, friend Meno, is recollection, as has been already agreed by us. But when they are bound, in the first place, they have the nature of knowledge; and, in the second place, they are abiding. And this is why knowledge is more honorable and excellent than true opinion, because fastened by a chain.

Men. Yes indeed, Socrates, that I should conjecture to be the truth.

Soc. I too speak not as one who knows; and yet that knowledge differs from true opinion is not a matter of conjecture with me. There are not many things which I should affirm that I knew, but that is most certainly one of them.

Men. You are right, Socrates.

Soc. And am I not right also in saying that true opinion is as good a guide in the performance of an action as knowledge?

Men. That also appears to me to be true.

Soc. Then right opinion is not a whit inferior to knowledge, or less useful in action; nor is the man who has right opinion inferior to him who has knowledge?

Men. That is true.

Soc. And surely the good man has been acknowledged by us to be useful?

Men. Yes.

Soc. Seeing then that men become good and useful to states, not only because they have knowledge, but because they have right opinion, and neither knowledge nor right opinion is given to man by nature or acquired by him — (do you think that either of them is given by nature?

Men. Not I.)

Soc. Then if they are not given by nature, neither are the good by nature good?

Men. Certainly not.

Soc. And nature being excluded, the next question was whether virtue is acquired by teaching?

Men. Yes.

Soc. If virtue was wisdom, then, as we thought, it was taught?

Men. Yes.

Soc. And if it was taught it was wisdom?

Men. Certainly.

Soc. And if there were teachers, it might be taught; and if there were no teachers, not?

Men. True.

Soc. But surely we acknowledged that there were no teachers of virtue?

Men. Yes.

Soc. Then we acknowledged that it was not taught, and was not wisdom?

Men. Certainly.

Soc. And yet we admitted that it was a good?

Men. Yes.

Soc. And the right guide is useful and good?

Men. Certainly.

Soc. And the only right guides are knowledge and true opinion — these are the guides of man; for things which happen by chance are not under the guidance of man: but the guidance of man are true opinion and knowledge.

Men. I think so too.

Soc. But if virtue is not taught, neither is virtue knowledge.

Men. Clearly not.

Soc. Then of two good and useful things, one, which is knowledge, has been set aside, and can not be supposed to be our guide in political life.

Men. I think not.

Soc. And therefore not by any wisdom, and not because they were wise, did Themistocles and those others of whom Anytus spoke govern states. And this was the reason why they were unable to make others like themselves — because their virtue was not grounded on knowledge.

Men. That is probably true, Socrates.

Soc. But if not by knowledge, the only alternative which remains is that statesmen must have guided states by right opinion, which is in politics what divination is in religion; for diviners and also prophets say many things truly, but they know not what they say.

Men. Very true.

Soc. And may we not, Meno, truly call those men divine who, having no understanding, yet succeed in many a grand deed and word?

Men. Certainly.

Soc. Then we shall also be right in calling those divine whom we were just now speaking of as diviners and prophets, as well as all poets. Yes, and statesmen above all may be said to be divine and illumined, being inspired and possessed of God, in which condition they say many grand things, not knowing what they say.

Men. Yes.

Soc. And the women too, Meno, call good men divine; and the Spartans, when they praise a good man, say " that he is a divine man."

Men. And I think, Socrates, that they are right; although very likely our friend Anytus may take offence at the name.

Soc. I do not care; as for Anytus, there will be another opportunity of talking with him. To sum up our inquiry — the result seems to be, if we are at all right in our view, that virtue is neither natural nor acquired, but an instinct given by God to the virtuous. Nor is the instinct accompanied by reason, unless there may be supposed to be among statesmen any one who is also the educator of statesmen. And if there be such an one, he may be said to be among the living what Tiresias was among the dead, who " alone," according to Homer, " of those in the world below, has understanding; but the rest flit as shadows."

Men. That is excellent, Socrates.

Soc. Then, Meno, the conclusion is that virtue comes to the virtuous by the gift of God. But we shall never know the certain truth until, before asking how virtue is given, we inquire into the actual nature of virtue. I fear that I must go away, but do you, now that you are persuaded yourself, persuade our friend Anytus. And don't let him be so exasperated; for if you can persuade him you will have done some service to the Athenian people.

EUTHYPHRO

INTRODUCTION

In the Meno Anytus had parted from Socrates with the threatening words: "That in any city, and particularly in the city of Athens, it is easier to do men harm than to do them good;" and Socrates was anticipating another opportunity of talking with him. In the Euthyphro Socrates is already awaiting his trial for impiety in the porch of the King Archon. But before the trial proceeds, Plato would like to put the world on their trial, and convince them of ignorance in that very matter touching which Socrates is accused. An incident which may perhaps really have occurred in the family of Euthyphro, a learned Athenian diviner and soothsayer, furnishes the occasion of the discussion.

This Euthyphro and Socrates are represented as meeting in the porch of the Archon. Both have legal business in hand. Socrates is defendant in a suit for impiety which Meletus has brought against him (it is remarked by the way that he is not a likely man himself to have brought a suit against another); and Euthyphro too is plaintiff in an action for murder, which he has brought against his own father. The latter has originated in the following manner: — A poor dependant of the family of Euthyphro had slain one of their domestic slaves in Naxos. The guilty person was bound and thrown into a ditch by the command of Euthyphro's father, who sent to the interpreters of religion at Athens to ask what should be done with him. Before the messenger came back the criminal had died from hunger and exposure.

This is the origin of the charge of murder which Euthyphro brings against his father. Socrates is confident that before he could have taken upon himself the responsibility of such a prosecution, he must have been perfectly informed of the nature of piety and impiety; and as he is going to be tried for impiety, he thinks that he can not do better than learn of Euthyphro (who will be admitted by all men, including the judges, to be an unimpeachable authority) what piety is, and what is impiety. What then is piety?

Euthyphro, who, in the abundance of his knowledge, is very

473

willing to undertake all the responsibility, replies: That piety is doing as I do, prosecuting your father (if he is guilty) on a charge of murder; doing as the gods do — as Zeus did to Cronos, and Cronos to Uranus.

Socrates has a dislike to these tales of mythology, and he fancies that this dislike of his may be the reason why he is charged with impiety. "Are they really true?" "Yes, they are;" and Euthyphro will gladly tell Socrates some more of them. But Socrates would like first of all to have a more satisfactory answer to the question, "What is piety?" "Doing as I do, charging a father with murder" may be a single instance of piety, but can hardly be regarded as a general definition.

Euthyphro replies, that "Piety is what is dear to the gods, and impiety is what is not dear to them." But may there not be differences of opinion, as among men, so also among the gods? Especially about good and evil, which have no fixed rule, and are precisely the sort of differences which give rise to quarrels. And therefore what may be dear to one god may not be dear to another, and the same action may be both pious and impious; e. g. your chastisement of your father, Euthyphro, may be dear or pleasing to Zeus, but not pleasing to Cronos or Uranus.

Euthyphro answers that there is no difference of opinion, either among gods or men, as to the propriety of punishing a murderer. Yes, rejoins Socrates, when they know him to be a murderer; but that assumes the point at issue. If all the circumstances of the case are considered, are you able to show that your father was guilty of murder, or that all the gods are agreed in approving of your prosecution of him? And must you not allow that what is hated by one god may be liked by another? Waiving this last, however, Socrates proposes to amend the definition, and say that "what all the gods love is pious, and what they all hate is impious." To this Euthyphro agrees.

Socrates proceeds to analyze the new form of the definition. He shows that in other cases the act precedes the state; e. g. the act of being carried, loved, etc., precedes the state of being carried, loved, etc., and therefore that which is dear to the gods is dear to the gods because it is first loved of them, not loved of them because it is dear to them. But the pious or holy is loved by the gods because it is pious or holy, which is equivalent to saying, that it is loved by them because it is dear to them. Here then appears to be a contradiction, — Euthyphro has been giving an attribute or accident of piety only, and not the essence. Euthyphro acknowledges himself that his explanations seem to walk away or go round in a circle, like the moving figures of Daedalus, the ancestor of Socrates, who has communicated his art to his descendants.

Socrates, who is desirous of stimulating the indolent intelligence of Euthyphro, raises the question in another manner: " Is all the pious just? " " Yes." " Is all the just pious? " " No." " Then what part of justice is piety? " Euthyphro replies that piety is that part of justice which " attends " to the gods, as there is another part of justice which " attends " to men. But what is the meaning of " attending " to the gods? The word " attending," when applied to dogs, horses, and men, implies that in some way they are made better. But how do pious or holy acts make the gods any better? Euthyphro explains that he means by pious acts, acts of ministration. Yes; but the ministrations of the husbandman, the physician, and the builder have an end. To what end do we minister to the gods, and what do we help them to accomplish? Euthyphro replies, that there is not time for all these difficult questions to be resolved; and he would rather say simply that piety is knowing how to please the gods in word and deed, by prayers and sacrifices. In other words, says Socrates, piety is " a science of asking and giving " — asking what we want and giving what they want; in short, a mode of doing business between gods and men. But although they are the givers of all good, how can we give them any good in return? " Nay, but we give them honor." Then we give them not what is beneficial, but what is pleasing or dear to them; and this is what has been already disproved.

Socrates, although weary of the subterfuges and evasions of Euthyphro, remains unshaken in his conviction that he must know the nature of piety, or he would never have prosecuted his old father. He is still hoping that he will condescend to instruct him. But Euthyphro is in a hurry and can not stay. And Socrates' last hope of knowing the nature of piety before he is prosecuted for impiety has disappeared.

The Euthyphro is manifestly designed to contrast the real nature of piety and impiety with the popular conceptions of them. But although the popular conceptions are overthrown, Plato does not offer any definition of his own: as in the Laches and Lysis, he exhibits the subject of the Dialogue in several different lights, but fails to answer explicitly his main question.

Euthyphro is a religionist, and is elsewhere spoken of as the author of a philosophy of names, by whose " prancing steeds "

Socrates in the Cratylus is carried away. He has the conceit and self-confidence of a Sophist; no doubt that he is right in prosecuting his father has ever entered into his mind. Like a Sophist too, and perhaps like most educated men of his age, he is incapable either of framing a general definition or of following the course of an argument. But he is not a bad man, and he is friendly to Socrates, whose familiar sign he recognizes with interest. Moreover he is the enemy of Meletus, who, as he thinks, is availing himself of the popular dislike to innovations in religion in order to injure Socrates; at the same time he is amusingly confident that he has weapons in his own armory which would be more than a match for him. He is quite sincere in his prosecution of his father, who has accidentally been guilty of homicide, and is not wholly free from blame. To purge away the crime appears to him in the light of a duty, whoever may be the criminal.

Thus begins the contrast between the religion of the letter, or of the narrow and unenlightened conscience, and the higher notion of religion which Socrates vainly endeavors to elicit from him. " Piety is doing as I do " is the first idea of religion which is suggested to his mind, and may be regarded as the definition of popular religion in all ages. Greek mythology hardly admitted of the distinction between accidental homicide and murder: that the pollution of blood was the same in both cases is also the feeling of the Athenian diviner. He is ready to defend his conduct by the examples of the gods. These are the very tales which Socrates can not abide; and his dislike of which, as he suspects, has branded him with the reputation of impiety. Here is one answer to the question, " Why Socrates was put to death," suggested by the way. Another is conveyed in the words, " The Athenians do not care about any man being thought wise until he begins to make other men wise; and then for some reason or other they are angry: " which may be said to be the rule of popular toleration in most other countries, and not at Athens only.

The next definition, " Piety is that which is loved of the gods," is shipwrecked on a refined distinction between the state and the act, corresponding respectively to the adjective ($\phi\iota\lambda o\nu$) and the participle ($\phi\iota\lambda o\acute{\upsilon}\mu\epsilon\nu o\nu$), or rather perhaps to the participle and the verb ($\phi\iota\lambda o\acute{\upsilon}\mu\epsilon\nu o\nu$ and $\phi\iota\lambda\epsilon\hat{\iota}\tau\alpha\iota$). The words " loved of the gods " express an attribute only, and not the essence of piety. Then follows the third and last definition " Piety is a part of justice." Thus far Socrates has proceeded in placing religion on a moral foundation. To which the soothsayer adds, " attending upon the gods." When further interrogated by Socrates as to the nature of this " attention to the gods," he replies, that piety is an affair of business, a science of giving and asking, and the like. Socrates points out the latent anthropomorphism of these notions. But when we expect him to go on and show that the true service of the gods is the service of the spirit, and the coöperation with them in all things true and good, he stops short; this was a lesson which the soothsayer could not have been made to understand, and which every one must learn for himself.

There seem to be altogether three aims or interests in this little Dialogue: (1) the dialectical development of the idea of piety; (2) the antithesis of true and false religion, which is carried to a certain extent only; (3) the defence of Socrates.

The subtle connection of this Dialogue with the Apology and the Crito, the holding back of the conclusion; the insight into the religious world; the dramatic power and play of the two characters; the inimitable irony, are reasons for believing that it is a genuine Platonic writing. The spirit in which the popular representations of mythology are denounced recalls the Republic. The virtue of piety has been already mentioned as one of five in the Protagoras, but is not reckoned among the four cardinal virtues of the Republic.

EUTHYPHRO

PERSONS OF THE DIALOGUE

SOCRATES.   EUTHYPHRO.

SCENE: — The Porch of the King Archon

Euthyphro. WHY have you left the Lyceum, Socrates? and what are you doing in the porch of the King Archon? Surely you can not be engaged in an action before the king, as I am.

Socrates. Not in an action, Euthyphro; impeachment is the word which the Athenians use.

Euth. What! I suppose that some one has been prosecuting you, for I can not believe that you are the prosecutor of another.

Soc. Certainly not.

Euth. Then some one else has been prosecuting you?

Soc. Yes.

Euth. And who is he?

Soc. A young man who is little known, Euthyphro; and I hardly know him: his name is Meletus, and he is of the deme of Pitthis. Perhaps you may remember his appearance; he has a beak, and long straight hair, and a beard which is ill grown.

Euth. No, I do not remember him, Socrates. And what is the charge which he brings against you?

Soc. What is the charge? Well, a very serious charge, which shows a good deal of character in the young man, and for which he is certainly not to be despised. He says he knows how the youth are corrupted and who are their corruptors. I fancy that

he must be a wise man, and seeing that I am anything but a wise man, he has found me out, and is
going to accuse me of corrupting his young friends.
And of this our mother the state is to be the judge.
Of all our political men he is the only one who seems
to me to begin in the right way, with the cultivation
of virtue in youth; he is a good husbandman, and takes
care of the shoots first, and clears away us who are
the destroyers of them. That is the first step; he will
afterwards attend to the elder branches; and if he goes
on as he has begun, he will be a very great public
benefactor.

Euth. I hope that he may; but I rather fear,
Socrates, that the reverse will turn out to be the truth.
My opinion is that in attacking you he is simply aiming a blow at the state in a sacred place. But in what
way does he say that you corrupt the young?

Soc. He brings a wonderful accusation against me,
which at first hearing excites surprise: he says that I
am a poet or maker of gods, and that I make new gods
and deny the existence of old ones; this is the ground
of his indictment.

Euth. I understand, Socrates; he means to attack
you about the familiar sign which occasionally, as you
say, comes to you. He thinks that you are a neologian,
and he is going to have you up before the court for
this. He knows that such a charge is readily received,
for the world is always jealous of novelties in religion.
And I know that when I myself speak in the assembly
about divine things, and foretell the future to them,
they laugh at me as a madman; and yet every word
that I say is true. But they are jealous of all of us.
I suppose that we must be brave and not mind them.

Soc. Their laughter, friend Euthyphro, is not a
matter of much consequence. For a man may be
thought wise; but the Athenians, I suspect, do not

care much about this, until he begins to make other men wise; and then for some reason or other, perhaps, as you say, from jealousy, they are angry.

Euth. I have no desire to try conclusions with them about this.

Soc. I dare say that you don't make yourself common, and are not apt to impart your wisdom. But I have a benevolent habit of pouring out myself to everybody, and would even pay for a listener, and I am afraid that the Athenians know this; and therefore, as I was saying, if the Athenians would only laugh at me as you say that they laugh at you, the time might pass gaily enough in the court; but perhaps they may be in earnest, and then what the end will be you soothsayers only can predict.

Euth. I dare say that the affair will end in nothing, Socrates, and that you will win your cause; and I think that I shall win mine.

Soc. And what is your suit? and are you the pursuer or defendant, Euthyphro?

Euth. I am pursuer.

Soc. Of whom?

Euth. You will think me mad when I tell you whom I am pursuing.

Soc. Why, has the fugitive wings?

Euth. Nay, he is not very volatile at his time of life.

Soc. Who is he?

Euth. My father.

Soc. Your father! good heavens, you don't mean that?

Euth. Yes.

Soc. And of what is he accused?

Euth. Murder, Socrates.

Soc. By the powers, Euthyphro! how little does the common herd know of the nature of right and truth. A man must be an extraordinary man and have made great strides in wisdom, before he could have seen his way to this.

Euth. Indeed, Socrates, he must have made great strides.

Soc. I suppose that the man whom your father murdered was one of your relatives; if he had been a stranger you would never have thought of prosecuting him.

Euth. I am amused, Socrates, at your making a distinction between one who is a relation and one who is not a relation; for surely the pollution is the same in either case, if you knowingly associate with the murderer when you ought to clear yourself by proceeding against him. The real question is whether the murdered man has been justly slain. If justly, then your duty is to let the matter alone; but if unjustly, then even if the murderer is under the same roof with you and eats at the same table, proceed against him. Now the man who is dead was a poor dependant of mine who worked for us as a field laborer at Naxos, and one day in a fit of drunken passion he got into a quarrel with one of our domestic servants and slew him. My father bound him hand and foot and threw him into a ditch, and then sent to Athens to ask of a diviner what he should do with him. Meantime he had no care or thought of him, being under the impression that he was a murderer; and that even if he did die there would be no great harm. And this was just what happened. For such was the effect of cold and hunger and chains upon him, that before the messenger returned from the diviner, he was dead. And my father and family are angry with me for taking the part of the murderer and prosecuting my father. They say that he did not kill him, and if he did, the dead man was but a murderer, and I ought not to take any notice, for that a son is impious who prosecutes a father. That shows, Socrates, how little they know of the opinions of the gods about piety and impiety.

Soc. Good heavens, Euthyphro! and have you such a precise knowledge of piety and impiety, and of divine things in general, that, supposing the circumstances to be as you state, you are not afraid that you too may be doing an impious thing in bringing an action against your father?

Euth. The best of Euthyphro, and that which distinguishes him, Socrates, from other men, is his exact knowledge of all these matters. What should I be good for without that?

Soc. Rare friend! I think that I can not do better than be your disciple, before the trial with Meletus comes on. Then I shall challenge him, and say that I have always had a great interest in religious questions, and now, as he charges me with rash imaginations and innovations in religion, I have become your disciple. Now you, Meletus, as I shall say to him, acknowledge Euthyphro to be a great theologian, and sound in his opinions; and if you think that of him you ought to think the same of me, and not have me into court; you should begin by indicting him who is my teacher, and who is the real corruptor, not of the young, but of the old; that is to say, of myself whom he instructs, and of his old father whom he admonishes and chastises. And if Meletus refuses to listen to me, but will go on, and will not shift the indictment from me to you, I can not do better than say in the court that I challenged him in this way.

Euth. Yes, Socrates; and if he attempts to indict me I am mistaken if I don't find a flaw in him; the court shall have a great deal more to say to him than to me.

Soc. I know that, dear friend; and that is the reason why I desire to be your disciple. For I observe that no one, not even Meletus, appears to notice you; but his sharp eyes have found me out at once, and he has indicted me for impiety. And therefore, I adjure you to tell me the nature of piety and impiety, which you said that you knew so well, and of murder, and the rest of them. What are they? Is not piety in every action always the same? and impiety, again, is not that always the opposite of piety, and also the same with itself, having, as impiety, one notion which includes whatever is impious?

Euth. To be sure, Socrates.

Soc. And what is piety, and what is impiety?

Euth. Piety is doing as I am doing; that is to say, prosecuting any one who is guilty of murder, sacrilege, or of any other similar crime — whether he be your father or mother, or some other person, that makes no difference — and not prosecuting them is impiety. And please to consider, Socrates, what a notable proof I will give you of the truth of what I am saying, which I have already given to others: — of the truth, I mean, of the principle that the impious, whoever he may be, ought not to go unpunished. For do not men regard Zeus as the best and most righteous of the gods? — and even they admit that he bound his father (Cronos) because he wickedly devoured his sons, and that he too had punished his own father (Uranus) for a similar reason, in a nameless manner. And yet when I proceed against my father, they are angry with me. This is their inconsistent way of talking when the gods are concerned, and when I am concerned.

Soc. May not this be the reason, Euthyphro, why I am charged with impiety — that I can not away with these stories about the gods? and therefore I suppose that people think me wrong. But, as you who are well informed about them approve of them, I can not do better than assent to your superior wisdom. For what else can I say, confessing as I do, that I know nothing of them. I wish you would tell me whether you really believe that they are true?

Euth. Yes, Socrates; and things more wonderful still, of which the world is in ignorance.

Soc. And do you really believe that the gods fought with one another, and had dire quarrels, battles, and the like, as the poets say, and as you may see represented in the works of great artists? The temples are full of them; and notably the robe of Athene, which is carried up to the Acropolis at the great Panathenaea, is embroidered with them. Are all these tales of the gods true, Euthyphro?

Euth. Yes, Socrates; and, as I was saying, I can tell you, if you would like to hear them, many other things about the gods which would quite amaze you.

Soc. I dare say; and you shall tell me them at some other time when I have leisure. But just at present I would rather hear from you a more precise answer, which you have not as yet given, my friend, to the question, What is " piety? " In reply, you only say that piety is, Doing as you do, charging your father with murder?

Euth. And that is true, Socrates.

Soc. I dare say, Euthyphro, but there are many other pious acts.

Euth. There are.

Soc. Remember that I did not ask you to give me two or three examples of piety, but to explain the general idea which makes all pious things to be pious Do you not recollect that there was one idea which made the impious impious, and the pious pious?

Euth. I remember.

Soc. Tell me what this is, and then I shall have a standard to which I may look, and by which I may measure the nature of actions, whether yours or any one's else, and say that this action is pious, and that impious?

Euth. I will tell you, if you like.

Soc. I should very much like.

Euth. Piety, then, is that which is dear to the gods, and impiety is that which is not dear to them.

Soc. Very good, Euthyphro; you have now given me just the sort of answer which I wanted. But whether it is true or not I can not as yet tell, although I make no doubt that you will prove the truth of your words.

Euth. Of course.

Soc. Come, then, and let us examine what we are saying. That thing or person which is dear to the gods is pious, and that thing or person which is hateful to the gods is impious. Was not that said?

Euth. Yes, that was said.

Soc. And that seems to have been very well said too?

Euth. Yes, Socrates, I think that; it was certainly said.

Soc. And further, Euthyphro, the gods were admitted to have enmities and hatreds and differences — that was also said?

Euth. Yes, that was said.

Soc. And what sort of difference creates enmity and anger? Suppose for example that you and I, my good friend, differ about a number; do differences of this sort make us enemies and set us at variance with one another? Do we not go at once to calculation, and end them by a sum?

Euth. True.

Soc. Or suppose that we differ about magnitudes,

do we not quickly put an end to that difference by measuring?

Euth. That is true.

Soc. And we end a controversy about heavy and light by resorting to a weighing-machine?

Euth. To be sure.

Soc. But what differences are those which, because they can not be thus decided, make us angry and set us at enmity with one another? I dare say the answer does not occur to you at the moment, and therefore I will suggest that this happens when the matters of difference are the just and unjust, good and evil, honorable and dishonorable. Are not these the points about which, when differing, and unable satisfactorily to decide our differences, we quarrel, when we do quarrel, as you and I and all men experience?

Euth. Yes, Socrates, that is the nature of the differences about which we quarrel.

Soc. And the quarrels of the gods, noble Euthyphro, when they occur, are of a like nature?

Euth. They are.

Soc. They have differences of opinion, as you say, about good and evil, just and unjust, honorable and dishonorable: there would have been no quarrels among them, if there had been no such differences — would there now?

Euth. You are quite right.

Soc. Does not every man love that which he deems noble and just and good, and hate the opposite of them?

Euth. Very true.

Soc. But then, as you say, people regard the same things, some as just and others as unjust; and they dispute about this, and there arise wars and fightings among them.

Euth. Yes, that is true.

Soc. Then the same things, as appears, are hated by the gods and loved by the gods, and are both hateful and dear to them?

Euth. True.

Soc. Then upon this view the same things, Euthyphro, will be pious and also impious?

Euth. That, I suppose, is true.

Soc. Then, my friend, I remark with surprise that you have not answered what I asked. For I certainly did not ask what was that which is at once pious and impious: and that which is loved by the gods appears also to be hated by them. And therefore, Euthyphro, in thus chastising your father you may very likely be doing what is agreeable to Zeus but disagreeable to Cronos or Uranus, and what is acceptable to Hephaestus but unacceptable to Here, and there may be other gods who have similar differences of opinion.

Euth. But I believe, Socrates, that all the gods would be agreed as to the propriety of punishing a murderer: there would be no difference of opinion about that.

Soc. Well, but speaking of men, Euthyphro, did you ever hear any one arguing that a murderer or any sort of evil-doer ought to be let off?

Euth. I should rather say that they are always arguing this, especially in courts of law: they commit all sorts of crimes, and there is nothing that they will not do or say in order to escape punishment.

Soc. But do they admit their guilt, Euthyphro, and yet say that they ought not to be punished?

Euth. No; they do not.

Soc. Then there are some things which they do not venture to say and do: for they do not venture to argue that the guilty are to be unpunished, but they deny their guilt, do they not?

Euth. Yes.

Soc. Then they do not argue that the evil-doer should not be punished, but they argue about the fact of who the evil-doer is, and what he did and when?

Euth. True.

Soc. And the gods are in the same case, if as you imply they quarrel about just and unjust, and some of them say that they wrong one another, and others of them deny this. For surely neither God nor man will ever venture to say that the doer of evil is not to be punished: — you don't mean to tell me that?

Euth. That is true, Socrates, in the main.

Soc. But they join issue about particulars; and this applies not only to men but to the gods; if they dispute at all they dispute about some act which is called in question, and which some affirm to be just, others to be unjust. Is not that true?

Euth. Quite true.

Soc. Well then, my dear friend Euthyphro, do tell me, for my better instruction and information, what proof have you that in the opinion of all the gods a servant who is guilty of murder, and is put in chains by the master of the dead man, and dies because he is put in chains before his corrector can learn from the interpreters what he ought to do with him, dies unjustly; and that on behalf of such an one a son ought to proceed against his father and accuse him of murder. How would you show that all the gods absolutely agree in approving of his act? Prove to me that, and I will applaud your wisdom as long as you live.

Euth. That would not be an easy task, although I could make the matter very clear indeed to you.

Soc. I understand; you mean to say that I am not so quick of apprehension as the judges: for to them you will be sure to prove that the act is unjust, and hateful to the gods.

Euth. Yes indeed, Socrates; at least if they will listen to me.

Soc. But they will be sure to listen if they find that you are a good speaker. There was a notion that came into my mind while you were speaking; I said to myself: " Well, and what if Euthyphro does prove to me that all the gods regarded the death of the serf as unjust, how do I know anything more of the nature of piety and impiety? for granting that this action may be hateful to the gods, still these distinctions have no bearing on the definition of piety and impiety, for that which is hateful to the gods has been shown to be also pleasing and dear to them." And therefore, Euthyphro, I don't ask you to prove this; I will suppose, if you like, that all the gods condemn and abominate such an action. But I will amend the definition so far as to say that what all the gods hate is impious, and what they love pious or holy; and what some of them love and others hate is both or neither. Shall this be our definition of piety and impiety?

Euth. Why not, Socrates?

Soc. Why not! certainly, as far as I am concerned, Euthyphro. But whether this admission will greatly assist you in the task of instructing me as you promised, is a matter for you to consider.

Euth. Yes, I should say that what all the gods love is pious and holy, and the opposite which they all hate, impious.

Soc. Ought we to inquire into the truth of this, Euthyphro, or simply to accept the mere statement on our own authority and that of others?

Euth. We should inquire; and I believe that the statement will stand the test of inquiry.

Soc. That, my good friend, we shall know better in a little while. The point which I should first wish

to understand is whether the pious or holy is beloved
by the gods because it is holy, or holy because it is
beloved of the gods.

Euth. I don't understand your meaning, Socrates.

Soc. I will endeavor to explain: we speak of carrying and we speak of being carried, of leading and
being led, seeing and being seen. And here is a difference, the nature of which you understand.

Euth. I think that I understand.

Soc. And is not that which is beloved distinct from
that which loves?

Euth. Certainly.

Soc. Well; and now tell me, is that which is carried in this state of carrying because it is carried, or
for some other reason?

Euth. No; that is the reason.

Soc. And the same is true of that which is led and
of that which is seen?

Euth. True.

Soc. And a thing is not seen because it is visible,
but conversely, visible because it is seen; nor is a thing
in the state of being led because it is led, or in the
state of being carried because it is carried, but the
converse of this. And now I think, Euthyphro, that
my meaning will be intelligible; and my meaning is,
that any state of action or passion implies previous
action or passion. It does not become because it is
becoming, but it is becoming because it comes; neither
does it suffer because it is in a state of suffering, but
it is in a state of suffering because it suffers. Do you
admit that?

Euth. Yes.

Soc. Is not that which is loved in some state either
of becoming or suffering?

Euth. Yes.

Soc. And the same holds as in the previous instances; the state of being loved follows the act of being loved, and not the act the state.

Euth. That is certain.

Soc. And what do you say of piety, Euthyphro: is not piety, according to your definition, loved by all the gods?

Euth. Yes.

Soc. Because it is pious or holy, or for some other reason?

Euth. No, that is the reason.

Soc. It is loved because it is holy, not holy because it is loved?

Euth. Yes.

Soc. And that which is in a state to be loved of the gods, and is dear to them, is in a state to be loved of them because it is loved of them?

Euth. Certainly.

Soc. Then that which is loved of God, Euthyphro, is not holy, nor is that which is holy loved of God, as you affirm; but they are two different things.

Euth. How do you mean, Socrates?

Soc. I mean to say that the holy has been acknowledged by us to be loved of God because it is holy, not to be holy because it is loved.

Euth. Yes.

Soc. But that which is dear to the gods is dear to them because it is loved by them, not loved by them because it is dear to them.

Euth. True.

Soc. But, friend Euthyphro, if that which is holy is the same as that which is dear to God, and that which is holy is loved as being holy, then that which is dear to God would have been loved as being dear to God; but if that which is dear to God is dear to him because loved by him, then that which is holy would have been holy because loved by him. But now you see that the reverse is the case, and that they are quite different from one another. For one ($\theta\epsilon o\phi\iota\lambda\grave{\epsilon}s$) is of a kind to be loved because it is loved, and the other ($\H{o}\sigma\iota o\nu$) is loved because it is of a kind to be loved. Thus you appear to me, Euthyphro, when I ask you what is the essence of holiness, to offer an attribute only, and not the essence — the attribute of being loved by all the gods. But you still refuse to explain to me the nature of piety. And therefore, if you please, I will ask you not to hide your treasure, but to tell me once more what piety or holiness really is, whether dear to the gods or not (for that is a matter about which we will not quarrel). And what is impiety?

Euth. I really do not know, Socrates, how to say what I mean. For somehow or other our arguments, on whatever ground we rest them, seem to turn round and walk away.

Soc. Your words, Euthyphro, are like the handiwork of my ancestor Daedalus; and if I were the sayer or propounder of them, you might say that this comes of my being his relation; and that this is the reason why my arguments walk away and won't remain fixed where they are placed. But now, as the notions are your own, you must find some other gibe, for they certainly, as you yourself allow, show an inclination to be on the move.

Euth. Nay, Socrates, I shall still say that you are the Daedalus who sets arguments in motion; not I, certainly, make them move or go round, for they would never have stirred, as far as I am concerned.

Soc. Then I must be a greater than Daedalus; for whereas he only made his own inventions to move, I move those of other people as well. And the beauty of it is, that I would rather not. For I would give the wisdom of Daedalus, and the wealth of Tantalus, to be able to detain them and keep them fixed. But enough of this. As I perceive that you are indolent, I will myself endeavor to show you how you might instruct me in the nature of piety; and I hope that you will not grudge your labor. Tell me, then, — Is not that which is pious necessarily just?

Euth. Yes.

Soc. And is, then, all which is just pious? or, is that which is pious all just, but that which is just only in part and not all pious?

Euth. I don't understand you, Socrates.

Soc. And yet I know that you are as much wiser than I am, as you are younger. But, as I was saying, revered friend, the abundance of your wisdom makes you indolent. Please to exert yourself, for there is no real difficulty in understanding me. What I mean I may explain by an illustration of what I do not mean. The poet (Stasinus) sings —

" Of Zeus, the author and creator of all these things,
You will not tell: for where there is fear there is also reverence."

And I disagree with this poet. Shall I tell you in what I disagree?

Euth. By all means.

Soc. I should not say that where there is fear there is also reverence; for I am sure that many persons fear poverty and disease, and the like evils, but I do not perceive that they reverence the objects of their fear.

Euth. Very true.

Soc. But where reverence is, there is fear; for he who has a feeling of reverence and shame about the commission of any action, fears and is afraid of an ill reputation.

Euth. No doubt.

Soc. Then we are wrong in saying that where there

is fear there is also reverence; and we should say, where there is reverence there is also fear. But there is not always reverence where there is fear; for fear is a more extended notion, and reverence is a part of fear, just as the odd is a part of number, and number is a more extended notion than the odd. I suppose that you follow me now?

Euth. Quite well.

Soc. That was the sort of question which I meant to raise when asking whether the just is the pious, or the pious the just; and whether there may not be justice where there is not always piety; for justice is the more extended notion of which piety is only a part. Do you agree in that?

Euth. Yes; that, I think, is correct.

Soc. Then, now, if piety is a part of justice, I suppose that we inquire what part? If you had pursued the injury in the previous cases; for instance, if you had asked me what is an even number, and what part of number the even is, I should have had no difficulty in replying, a number which represents a figure having two equal sides. Do you agree?

Euth. Yes.

Soc. In like manner, I want you to tell me what part of justice is piety or holiness; that I may be able to tell Meletus not to do me injustice, or indict me for impiety; as I am now adequately instructed by you in the nature of piety or holiness, and their opposites.

Euth. Piety or holiness, Socrates, appears to me to be that part of justice which attends to the gods, as there is the other part of justice which attends to men.

Soc. That is good, Euthyphro; yet still there is a little point about which I should like to have further information, What is the meaning of " attention? "

For attention can hardly be used in the same sense when applied to the gods as when applied to other things. For instance, horses are said to require attention, and not every person is able to attend to them, but only a person skilled in horsemanship. Is not that true?

Euth. Quite true.

Soc. I should suppose that the art of horsemanship is the art of attending to horses?

Euth. Yes.

Soc. Nor is every one qualified to attend to dogs, but only the huntsman.

Euth. True.

Soc. And I should also conceive that the art of the huntsman is the art of attending to dogs?

Euth. Yes.

Soc. As the art of the oxherd is the art of attending to oxen?

Euth. Very true.

Soc. And as holiness or piety is the art of attending to the gods? — that would be your meaning, Euthyphro?

Euth. Yes.

Soc. And is not attention always designed for the good or benefit of that to which the attention is given? As in the case of horses, you may observe that when attended to by the horseman's art they are benefited and improved, are they not?

Euth. True.

Soc. As the dogs are benefited by the huntsman's art, and the oxen by the art of the oxherd, and all other things are tended or attended for their good and not for their hurt?

Euth. Certainly, not for their hurt.

Soc. But for their good?

Euth. Of course.

Soc. And does piety or holiness, which has been defined as the art of attending to the gods, benefit or improve them? Would you say that when you do a holy act you make any of the gods better?

Euth. No, no; that is certainly not my meaning.

Soc. Indeed, Euthyphro, I did not suppose that this was your meaning; far otherwise. And that was the reason why I asked you the nature of this attention, because I thought that this was not your meaning.

Euth. You do me justice, Socrates; for that is not my meaning.

Soc. Good: but I must still ask what is this attention to the gods which is called piety?

Euth. It is such, Socrates, as servants show to their masters.

Soc. I understand — a sort of ministration to the gods.

Euth. Exactly.

Soc. Medicine is also a sort of ministration or service, tending to the attainment of some object — would you not say health?

Euth. Yes.

Soc. Again, there is an art which ministers to the ship-builder with a view to the attainment of some result?

Euth. Yes, Socrates, with a view to the building of a ship.

Soc. As there is an art which ministers to the house-builder with a view to the building of a house?

Euth. Yes.

Soc. And now tell me, my good friend, about this art which ministers to the gods: what work does that help to accomplish? For you must surely know if, as you say, you are of all men living the one who is best instructed in religion.

Euth. And that is true, Socrates.

Soc. Tell me then, oh tell me — what is that fair work which the gods do by the help of us as their ministers?

Euth. Many and fair, Socrates, are the works which they do.

Soc. Why, my friend, and so are those of a general. But the chief of them is easily told. Would you not say that victory in war is the chief of them?

Euth. Certainly.

Soc. Many and fair, too, are the works of the husbandman, if I am not mistaken; but his chief work is the production of food from the earth?

Euth. Exactly.

Soc. And of the many and fair things which the gods do, which is the chief and principal one?

Euth. I have told you already, Socrates, that to learn all these things accurately will be very tiresome. Let me simply say that piety is learning how to please the gods in word and deed, by prayers and sacrifices. That is piety, which is the salvation of families and states, just as the impious, which is unpleasing to the gods, is their ruin and destruction.

Soc. I think that you could have answered in much fewer words the chief question which I asked, Euthyphro, if you had chosen. But I see plainly that you are not disposed to instruct me: else why, when we had reached the point, did you turn aside? Had you only answered me I should have learned of you by this time the nature of piety. Now, as the asker of a question is necessarily dependent on the answerer, whither he leads I must follow; and can only ask again, what is the pious, and what is piety? Do you mean that they are a sort of science of praying and sacrificing?

Euth. Yes, I do.

Soc. And sacrificing is giving to the gods, and prayer is asking of the gods?

Euth. Yes, Socrates.

Soc. Upon this view, then, piety is a science of asking and giving?

Euth. You understand me capitally, Socrates.

Soc. Yes, my friend; the reason is that I am a votary of your science, and give my mind to it, and therefore nothing which you say will be thrown away upon me. Please then to tell me, what is the nature of this service to the gods? Do you mean that we prefer requests and give gifts to them?

Euth. Yes, I do.

Soc. Is not the right way of asking to ask of them what we want?

Euth. Certainly.

Soc. And the right way of giving is to give to them in return what they want of us. There would be no meaning in an art which gives to any one that which he does not want.

Euth. Very true, Socrates.

Soc. Then piety, Euthyphro, is an art which gods and men have of doing business with one another?

Euth. That is an expression which you may use, if you like.

Soc. But I have no particular liking for anything but the truth. I wish, however, that you would tell me what benefit accrues to the gods from our gifts. That they are the givers of every good to us is clear; but how we can give any good thing to them in return is far from being equally clear. If they give everything and we give nothing, that must be an affair of business in which we have very greatly the advantage of them.

Euth. And do you imagine, Socrates, that any

benefit accrues to the gods from what they receive of us?

Soc. But if not, Euthyphro, what sort of gifts do we confer upon the gods?

Euth. What should we confer upon them, but tributes of honor; and, as I was just now saying, what is pleasing to them?

Soc. Piety, then, is pleasing to the gods, but not beneficial or dear to them?

Euth. I should say that nothing could be dearer.

Soc. Then once more the assertion is repeated that piety is dear to the gods?

Euth. No doubt.

Soc. And when you say this, can you wonder at your words not standing firm, but walking away? Will you accuse me of being the Daedalus who makes them walk away, not perceiving that there is another and far greater artist than Daedalus who makes them go round in a circle; and that is yourself: for the argument, as you will perceive, comes round to the same point. I think that you must remember our saying that the holy or pious was not the same as that which is loved of the gods. Do you remember that?

Euth. I do.

Soc. And do you not see that what is loved of the gods is holy, and that this is the same as what is dear to them?

Euth. True.

Soc. Then either we were wrong in that admission; or, if we were right then, we are wrong now.

Euth. I suppose that is the case.

Soc. Then we must begin again and ask, What is piety? That is an inquiry which I shall never be weary of pursuing as far as in me lies; and I entreat you not to scorn me, but to apply your mind to the utmost, and tell me the truth. For, if any man knows, you are he; and therefore I shall detain you, like Proteus, until you tell. For if you had not certainly known the nature of piety and impiety, I am confident that you would never, on behalf of a serf, have charged your aged father with murder. You would not have run such a risk of doing wrong in the sight of the gods, and you would have had too much respect for the opinions of men. I am sure, therefore, that you know the nature of piety and impiety. Speak out then, my dear Euthyphro, and do not hide your knowledge.

Euth. Another time, Socrates; for I am in a hurry, and must go now.

Soc. Alas! my companion, and will you leave me in despair? I was hoping that you would instruct me in the nature of piety and impiety, so that I might have cleared myself of Meletus and his indictment. Then I might have proved to him that I had been converted by Euthyphro, and had done with rash innovations and speculations, in which I had indulged through ignorance, and was about to lead a better life.

APOLOGY

INTRODUCTION

In what relation the Apology of Plato stands to the **real de-**
fence of Socrates, there are no means of determining. It certainly agrees in tone and character with the description of Xenophon, who says in the Memorabilia that Socrates might have
been acquitted " if in any moderate degree he would have con-
ciliated the favor of the dicasts; " and who informs us in another
passage, on the testimony of Hermogenes, the friend of Socrates, that he had no wish to live; and that the divine sign refused to allow him to prepare a defence, and also that Socrates
himself declared this to be unnecessary, on the ground that all
his life long he had been preparing against that hour. For the
speech breathes throughout a spirit of defiance, " ut non supplex
aut reus sed magister aut dominus videretur esse judicum " (Cic.
de Orat. i. 54); and the loose and desultory style is an imitation
of the " accustomed manner " in which Socrates spoke in " the
agora and among the tables of the money-changers." The allusion in the Crito may, perhaps, be adduced as a further evidence of the literal accuracy of some parts. But in the main
it must be regarded as the ideal of Socrates, according to Plato's
conception of him, appearing in the greatest and most public
scene of his life, and in the height of his triumph, when he is
weakest, and yet his mastery over mankind is greatest, and the
habitual irony of his life acquires a new meaning and a sort of
tragic pathos in the face of death. The facts of his life are
summed up, and the features of his character are brought out
as if by accident in the course of the defence. The looseness of
the style, the seeming want of arrangement of the topics, is
found to result in a perfect work of art, which is the portrait
of Socrates.

Yet some of the topics may have been actually used by Socrates; and the recollection of his very words may have rung
in the ears of his disciple. The Apology of Plato may be compared generally with those speeches of Thucydides in which he
has embodied his conception of the lofty character and policy
of the great Pericles, and which at the same time furnish a com-

503

mentary on the situation of affairs from the point of view of the historian. So in the Apology there is an ideal rather than a literal truth; much is said that ought to have been said but was not said, and is only Plato's view of the situation. And we may perhaps even indulge in the fancy that the actual defence of Socrates was as much greater than the Platonic defence as the master was greater than the disciple. But in any case, some of the words actually used have probably been preserved. It is significant that Plato is said to have been present at the defence, as he is also said to have been absent at the last scene in the Phaedo. Is it fanciful to suppose that he meant to give the stamp of authenticity to the one and not to the other? — especially when we remember that these two passages are the only ones in which Plato makes mention of himself. Moreover, the Apology appears to combine the common characteristics both of the Xenophontean and Platonic Socrates, while the Phaedo passes into a region of thought which is very characteristic of Plato, but not of his master.

There is not much in the other Dialogues which can be compared with the Apology. The same recollection of his master may have been present to the mind of Plato when depicting the sufferings of the Just in the Republic. The Crito may also be regarded as a sort of appendage to the Apology, in which Socrates, who has defied the judges, is nevertheless represented as scrupulously obedient to the laws. The idealization of the sufferer is carried still further in the Gorgias, in which the thesis is maintained, that " to suffer is better than to do evil; " and the art of rhetoric is described as only useful for the purpose of self-accusation. The parallelisms which occur in the so-called Apology of Xenophon are not worth noticing, because the writing in which they are contained is manifestly spurious. The statements of the Memorabilia respecting the trial and death of Socrates agree generally with Plato; but they have lost the flavor of Socratic irony in the narrative of Xenophon.

The Apology or Platonic defence of Socrates is divided into three parts: 1st. The defence properly so called; 2nd. The shorter address in mitigation of the penalty; 3rd. The last words of prophetic rebuke and exhortation.

The first part commences with an apology for his colloquial style; he is, as he has always been, the enemy of rhetoric, and knows of no rhetoric but truth; he will not falsify his character by making a speech. Then he proceeds to divide his accusers into two classes; first, there is the nameless accuser — public opinion. All the world from their earliest years had heard that he was a corruptor of youth, and had seen him caricatured in the Clouds of Aristophanes. Secondly, there are the professed accusers, who are but the mouth-piece of the others. The accusations of both might be summed up in a formula. The first say, " Socrates is an evil-doer and a curious person, searching into things under the earth and above the heaven; and making the worse appear the better cause, and teaching all this to others." The second, " Socrates is an evil-doer and corruptor of the youth, who does not receive the gods whom the state receives, but introduces other new divinities." These last appear to have been the words of the actual indictment, of which the previous formula is a parody.

The answer begins by clearing up a confusion. In the representations of the comic poets, and in the opinion of the multitude, he had been confounded with the teachers of physical science and with the Sophists. But this was an error. For both of them he professes a respect in the open court, which contrasts with his manner of speaking about them in other places. But at the same time he shows that he is not one of them. Of natural philosophy he knows nothing; not that he despises such pursuits, but the fact is that he is ignorant of them, and never says a word about them. Nor does he receive money for teaching; that is another mistaken notion, for he has nothing to teach. But he commends Evenus for teaching virtue at such a moderate rate. Something of the " accustomed irony," which may perhaps be expected to sleep in the ear of the multitude, is lurking here.

He then goes on to explain the reason why he is in such an evil name. That had arisen out of a peculiar mission which he had taken upon himself. The enthusiastic Chaerephon (probably in anticipation of the answer which he received) had gone to Delphi and asked the oracle if there was any man wiser than Socrates; and the answer was, that there was no man wiser. What could be the meaning of this — that he who knew nothing, and knew that he knew nothing, should be declared by the oracle to be the wisest of men? Reflecting upon this, he determined to refute the oracle by finding " a wiser; " and first he went to the politicians, and then to the poets, and then to the craftsmen, but always with the same result — he found that they knew nothing, or hardly anything more than himself; and that the little advantage which in some cases they possessed was more than counterbalanced by their conceit of knowledge. He knew nothing, and knew that he knew nothing: they knew little or nothing, and imagined that they knew all things. Thus he had passed his life as a sort of missionary in detecting the pretended wisdom of mankind; and this occupation had quite absorbed him and taken him away both from public and private affairs. Young men of the richer sort had made a pastime of the same pursuit, "which was not unamusing." And hence bitter enmities had arisen; the professors of knowledge had revenged themselves by calling him a villainous corruptor of the youth, and by repeating the commonplaces about atheism and materialism and sophistry, which are the stock-accusations against all philosophers when there is nothing else to be said of them.

The second accusation he meets by interrogating Meletus, who is present and can be interrogated. "If he is the corruptor, who is the improver of the citizens?" "All mankind." But how absurd, how contrary to analogy is this! How inconceivable too, that he should make the citizens worse when he has to live with them. This surely can not be intentional; and if unintentional, he ought to have been instructed by Meletus, and not accused in the court.

But there is another part of the indictment which says that he teaches men not to receive the gods whom the city receives, and has other new gods. "Is that the way in which he is supposed to corrupt the youth?" "Yes, that is the way." "Has he only new gods, or none at all?" "None at all." "What, not even the sun and moon?" "No; why, he says that the sun is a stone, and the moon earth." That, replies Socrates, is the old confusion about Anaxagoras; the Athenian people are not so ignorant as to attribute to the influence of Socrates notions which have found their way into the drama, and may be learned at the theatre. Socrates undertakes to show that Meletus (rather unjustifiably) has been compounding a riddle in this part of the indictment: "There are no gods, but Socrates believes in the existence of the sons of gods, which is absurd."

Leaving Meletus, who has had enough words spent upon him, he returns to his original accusers. The question may be asked, Why will he persist in following a profession which leads him to death? Why — because he must remain at his post where the god has placed him, as he remained at Potidaea, and Amphipolis, and Delium, where the generals placed him. Besides, he is not so overwise as to imagine that he knows whether death is a good or an evil; and he is certain that desertion of his duty is an evil. Anytus is quite right in saying that they should never have indicted him if they meant to let him go. For he will certainly obey God rather than man; and will continue to preach to all men of all ages the necessity of virtue and improvement; and if they refuse to listen to him he will persevere and reprove them. This is his way of corrupting the youth, which he will not cease to follow in obedience to the god, even if a thousand deaths await him.

He is desirous that they should not put him to death — not for his own sake, but for theirs; because he is their heaven-sent friend (and they will never have such another), or, as he may be ludicrously described, the gadfly who stirs the generous steed into motion. Why then has he never taken part in public affairs? Because the familiar divine voice has hindered him; if he had been a public man, and fought for the right, as he would certainly have fought against the many, he would not have lived, and could therefore have done no good. Twice in public matters he has risked his life for the sake of justice — once at the trial of the generals; and again in resistance to the tyrannical commands of the Thirty.

But, though not a public man, he has passed his days in instructing the citizens without fee or reward; this was his mission. Whether his disciples have turned out well or ill, he can not justly be charged with the result, for he never promised to teach them anything. They might come if they liked, and they might stay away if they liked: and they did come, because they found an amusement in hearing the pretenders to wisdom detected. If they had been corrupted, their elder relatives (if not themselves) might surely appear in court and witness against him, and there is an opportunity still for them to do this. But their fathers and brothers all appear in court (including " this " Plato), to witness on his behalf; and if their relatives are corrupted, at least they are uncorrupted; " and they are my witnesses. For they know that I am speaking the truth, and that Meletus is lying."

This is about all that he has to say. He will not entreat the judges to spare his life; neither will he present a spectacle of weeping children, although he, too, is not made of " rock or oak." Some of the judges themselves may have complied with this practice on similar occasions, and he trusts that they will not be angry with him for not following their example. But he feels that such conduct brings discredit on the name of Athens: he feels, too, that the judge has sworn not to give away justice; and he can not be guilty of the impiety of asking the judge to forswear himself, when he is himself being tried for impiety.

As he expected, and probably intended, he is convicted. And now the tone of the speech, instead of being more conciliatory, becomes more lofty and commanding. Anytus proposes death as the penalty: and what counter-proposition shall he make? He, the benefactor of the Athenian people, whose whole life has been spent in doing them good, should at least have the Olympic victor's reward of maintenance in the prytaneum. Or why should he propose any counter-penalty when he does not know whether death, which Anytus proposes, is a good or an evil? and he is certain that imprisonment is an evil, exile is an evil. Loss of money might be no evil, but then he has none to give; perhaps he can make up a mina. Let that then be the penalty, or, if his friends wish, thirty minae; for this they will be excellent securities.

(*He is condemned to death.*)

He is an old man already, and the Athenians will gain nothing but disgrace by depriving him of a few years of life. Perhaps he could have escaped, if he had chosen to throw down his arms and entreat for his life. But he does not at all repent of the manner of his defence; he would rather die in his own fashion than live in theirs. For the penalty of unrighteousness is swifter than death, and that has already overtaken his accusers as death will soon overtake him.

And now, as one who is about to die, he will prophesy to them. They have put him to death in order to escape the necessity of giving an account of their lives. But his death " will be the seed " of many disciples who will convict them of their evil ways, and will come forth to reprove them in harsher terms, because they are younger and more inconsiderate.

He would like to say a few words, while there is time, to those who would have acquitted him. He wishes them to know that the divine sign never interrupted him in the course of his defence; the reason of which, as he conjectures, is that the death to which he is going is a good and not an evil. For either death is a long sleep, the best of sleeps, or a journey to another world in which the souls of the dead are gathered together, and in which there may be a hope of seeing the heroes of old — in which, too, there are just judges; and as all are immortal, there can be no fear of any one being put to death for his opinions.

Nothing evil can happen to the good man either in life or death, and his own death has been permitted by the gods, because it was better for him to depart; and therefore he forgives his judges because they have done him no harm, although they never meant to do him any good.

He has a last request to make to them — that they will trouble his sons as he has troubled them, if they appear to prefer riches to virtue, or to think themselves something when they are nothing.

" Few persons will be found to wish that Socrates should have defended himself otherwise," — if, as we must add, his defence was that with which Plato has provided him. But leaving this question, which does not admit of a precise solution, we may go on to ask what was the impression which Plato in the Apology intended to leave of the character and conduct of his master in the last great scene? Did he intend to represent him (1) as employing sophistries; (2) as designedly irritating the judges? Or are these sophistries to be regarded as belonging to the age in which he lived and to his personal character, and this apparent haughtiness as flowing from the natural elevation of his position?

For example, when he says that it is absurd to suppose that one man is the corruptor and all the rest of the world the improvers of the youth; or, when he argues that he never could have corrupted the men with whom he had to live; or, when he proves his belief in the gods because he believes in the sons of gods, is he serious or jesting? It may be observed that these sophisms all occur in his cross-examination of Meletus, who is easily foiled and mastered in the hands of the great dialectician. Perhaps he regarded these answers as all of them good enough for his accuser (he makes very light of him throughout). Also it may be noted that there is a touch of irony in all of them, which takes them out of the category of sophistry.

That the manner in which he defends himself about the lives of his disciples is not satisfactory, can hardly be denied. Fresh in the memory of the Athenians, and detestable as they deserved to be to the newly restored democracy, were the names of Alcibiades, Critias, Charmides. It is obviously not a sufficient answer that Socrates had never professed to teach them any-- thing, and is therefore not justly chargeable with their crimes. Yet the defence, when taken out of this ironical form, is doubtless sound: that his teaching had nothing to do with their evil lives. Here. then, the sophistry is rather in form than in substance, though we might desire that to such a serious charge Socrates had given a more serious answer.

Truly characteristic of Socrates is another point in his answer, which may also be regarded as sophistical. He says that " if he has corrupted the youth, he must have corrupted them involuntarily." In these words the Socratic doctrine of the involuntariness of evil is clearly intended to be conveyed. But if, as Socrates argues, all evil is involuntary, then all criminals ought to be admonished and not punished. Here again, as in the former instance, the defence of Socrates, which is untrue practically, may yet be true in some ideal or transcendental sense. The commonplace reply, that if he had been guilty of corrupting the youth their relations would surely have witnessed against him, with which he concludes this part of his defence, is more satisfactory.

Again, when Socrates argues that he must believe in the gods because he believes in the sons of gods, we must remember that this is a refutation not of the original indictment, which is consistent enough — " Socrates does not receive the gods whom the city receives, and has other new divinities " — but of the interpretation put upon the words by Meletus, who has affirmed that he is a downright atheist. To this Socrates fairly answers, in accordance with the ideas of the time, that a downright atheist can not believe in the sons of gods or in divine things. The notion that demons or lesser divinities are the sons of gods is not to be regarded as ironical or sceptical. But the love of argument may certainly have led Plato to relapse into the mythological point of view, and prevented him from observing that the reasoning is only formally corect.

The second question, whether Plato meant to represent Socrates as needlessly braving or irritating his judges, must also be answered in the negative. His irony, his superiority, his audacity, " regarding not the person of man," necessarily flow out of the loftiness of his situation. He is not acting a part upon a great occasion, but he is what he has been all his life long, " a king of men." He would rather not appear insolent, if he could avoid this (οὐχ ὡς αὐθαδιζόμενος τοῦτο λέγω). He is not desirous of hastening his own end, for life and death are simply indifferent to him. But neither will he say or do anything which might avert the penalty; he can not have his tongue bound, even in the " throat of death: " his natural character must appear. He is quite willing to make his defence to posterity and to the world, for that is a true defence. But such a defence as would be acceptable to his judges and might procure an acquittal, it is not in his nature to make. With his actual accusers he will only fence and play. The singularity of the mission which he ascribes to himself is a great reason for believing that he is serious in his account of the motives which actuated him. The dedication of his life to the improvement of his fellow-citizens is not so remarkable as the ironical spirit in which he goes about doing good to all men only in vindication of the credit of the oracle, and in the vain hope of finding a wiser man than himself. Yet this singular and almost accidental character of his mission agrees with the divine sign which, according to our notions, is equally accidental and irrational, and is nevertheless accepted by him as the guiding principle in his life. Nor must we forget that Socrates is nowhere represented to us as a freethinker or sceptic. There is no reason whatever to doubt his sincerity when he implies his belief in the divinity of the sun and moon, or when he speculates on the possibility of seeing and knowing the heroes of the Trojan war in another world. On the other hand, his hope of immortality is uncertain; — he also conceives of death as a long sleep (in this respect differing from the Phaedo), and at last falls back on resignation to the divine will, and the certainty that no evil can happen to the good man either in life or death. His absolute truthfulness seems to hinder him from asserting positively more than this. The irony of Socrates is not a mask which he puts on at will, but flows necessarily out of his character and out of his relation to mankind. This, which is true of him generally, is especially true of the last memorable act in which his life is summed up. Such irony is not impaired but greatly heightened by a sort of natural simplicity.

It has been remarked that the prophecy at the end of a new generation of teachers who would rebuke and exhort the Athenian people in harsher and more violent terms, as far as we know, was never fulfilled. No inference can be drawn from this circumstance as to the probability of their having been actually uttered. They express the aspiration of the first martyr of philosophy, that he would leave behind him many followers, accompanied by the not unnatural feeling that they would be fiercer and more inconsiderate in their words when emancipated from his control.

The above remarks must be understood as applying with any degree of certainty to the Platonic Socrates only. For, however probable it may be that these or similar words may have been spoken by Socrates himself, we can not exclude the possibility, that like so much else, e. g. the wisdom of Critias, the poem of Solon, the virtues of Charmides, they may have been due only to the imagination of Plato.

APOLOGY

How you have felt, O men of Athens, at hearing the speeches of my accusers, I cannot tell; but I know that their persuasive words almost made me forget who I was: — such was the effect of them; and yet they have hardly spoken a word of truth. But many as their falsehoods were, there was one of them which quite amazed me; — I mean when they told you to be upon your guard, and not to let yourselves be deceived by the force of my eloquence. They ought to have been ashamed of saying this, because they were sure to be detected as soon as I opened my lips and displayed my deficiency: they certainly did appear to be most shameless in saying this, unless by the force of eloquence they mean the force of truth; for then I do indeed admit that I am eloquent. But in how different a way from theirs! Well, as I was saying, they have hardly uttered a word, or not more than a word, of truth; but you shall hear from me the whole truth: not, however, delivered after their manner, in a set oration duly ornamented with words and phrases. No, indeed! but I shall use the words and arguments which occur to me at the moment; for I am certain that this is right, and that at my time of life I ought not to be appearing before you, O men of Athens, in the character of a juvenile orator — let no one expect this of me. And I must beg of you to grant me one favor, which is this — If you hear me using the same words in my

513

defence which I have been in the habit of using, and which most of you may have heard in the agora, and at the tables of the money-changers, or anywhere else, I would ask you not to be surprised at this, and not to interrupt me. For I am more than seventy years of age, and this is the first time that I have ever appeared in a court of law, and I am quite a stranger to the ways of the place; and therefore I would have you regard me as if I were really a stranger, whom you would excuse if he spoke in his native tongue, and after the fashion of his country; — that I think is not an unfair request. Never mind the manner, which may or may not be good; but think only of the justice of my cause, and give heed to that: let the judge decide justly and the speaker speak truly.

And first, I have to reply to the older charges and to my first accusers, and then I will go on to the later ones. For I have had many accusers, who accused me of old, and their false charges have continued during many years; and I am more afraid of them than of Anytus and his associates, who are dangerous, too, in their own way. But far more dangerous are these, who began when you were children, and took possession of your minds with their falsehoods, telling of one Socrates, a wise man, who speculated about the heaven above, and searched into the earth beneath, and made the worse appear the better cause. These are the accusers whom I dread; for they are the circulators of this rumor, and their hearers are too apt to fancy that speculators of this sort do not believe in the gods. And they are many, and their charges against me are of ancient date, and they made them in days when you were impressible — in childhood, or perhaps in youth — and the cause when heard went by default, for there was none to answer. And hardest of all, their names I do not know and can not tell; unless in the chance case of a comic poet. But the main body of these slanderers who from envy and malice have wrought upon you — and there are some of them who are convinced themselves, and impart their convictions to others — all these, I say, are most difficult to deal with; for I can not have them up here, and examine them, and therefore I must simply fight with shadows in my own defence, and examine when there is no one who answers. I will ask you then to assume with me, as I was saying, that my opponents are of two kinds; one recent, the other ancient: and I hope that you will see the propriety of my answering the latter first, for these accusations you heard long before the others, and much oftener.

Well, then, I will make my defence, and I will endeavor in the short time which is allowed to do away with this evil opinion of me which you have held for such a long time; and I hope that I may succeed, if this be well for you and me, and that my words may find favor with you. But I know that to accomplish this is not easy — I quite see the nature of the task. Let the event be as God wills: in obedience to the law I make my defence.

I will begin at the beginning, and ask what the accusation is which has given rise to this slander of me, and which has encouraged Meletus to proceed against me. What do the slanderers say? They shall be my prosecutors, and I will sum up their words in an affidavit. " Socrates is an evil-doer, and a curious person, who searches into things under the earth and in heaven, and he makes the worse appear the better cause; and he teaches the aforesaid doctrines to others." That is the nature of the accusation, and that is what you have seen yourselves in the comedy of Aristophanes, who has introduced a man whom he calls Socrates, going about and saying that he can walk in the air, and talking a deal of nonsense concerning matters of which I do not pretend to know either much or little -- not that I mean to say anything disparaging of any one who is a student of natural philosophy. I should be very sorry if Meletus could lay that to my charge. But the simple truth is, O Athenians, that I have nothing to do with these studies. Very many of those here present are witnesses to the truth of this, and to them I appeal. Speak then, you who have heard me, and tell your neighbors whether any of you have ever known me hold forth in few words or in many upon matters of this sort. . . . You hear their answer. And from what they say of this you will be able to judge of the truth of the rest.

As little foundation is there for the report that I am a teacher, and take money; that is no more true than the other. Although, if a man is able to teach, I honor him for being paid. There is Gorgias of Leontium, and Prodicus of Ceos, and Hippias of Elis, who go the round of the cities, and are able to persuade the young men to leave their own citizens, by whom they might be taught for nothing, and come to them, whom they not only pay, but are thankful if they may be allowed to pay them. There is actually a Parian philosopher residing in Athens, of whom I have heard; and I came to hear of him in this way: — I met a man who has spent a world of money on the sophists, Callias, the son of Hipponicus, and knowing that he had sons, I asked him: "Callias," I said, "if your two sons were foals or calves, there would be no difficulty in finding some one to put over them; we should hire a trainer of horses, or a farmer probably, who would improve and perfect them in their own proper virtue and excellence; but as they are

human beings, whom are you thinking of placing
over them? Is there any one who understands human
and political virtue? You must have thought about
this as you have sons; is there any one?" "There
is," he said. "Who is he?" said I; "and of what
country? and what does he charge?" "Evenus the
Parian," he replied; "he is the man, and his charge
is five minae." Happy is Evenus, I said to myself, if
he really has this wisdom, and teaches at such a modest charge. Had I the same, I should have been very
proud and conceited; but the truth is that I have no
knowledge of the kind, O Athenians.

I dare say that some one will ask the question,
"Why is this, Socrates, and what is the origin of these
accusations of you: for there must have been something strange which you have been doing? All this
great fame and talk about you would never have
arisen if you had been like other men: tell us, then,
why this is, as we should be sorry to judge hastily
of you." Now I regard this as a fair challenge, and
I will endeavor to explain to you the origin of this
name of "wise," and of this evil fame. Please to
attend then. And although some of you may think
that I am joking, I declare that I will tell you the
entire truth. Men of Athens, this reputation of mine
has come of a certain sort of wisdom which I possess.
If you ask me what kind of wisdom, I reply, such
wisdom as is attainable by man, for to that extent I
am inclined to believe that I am wise; whereas the
persons of whom I was speaking have a superhuman
wisdom, which I may fail to describe, because I have
it not myself; and he who says that I have, speaks
falsely, and is taking away my character. And here,
O men of Athens, I must beg you not to interrupt
me, even if I seem to say something extravagant.
For the word which I will speak is not mine. I will

refer you to a wisdom who is worthy of credit, and will tell you about my wisdom — whether I have any, and of what sort — and that witness shall be the God of Delphi. You must have known Chaerephon; he was early a friend of mine, and also a friend of yours, for he shared in the exile of the people, and returned with you. Well, Chaerephon, as you know, was very impetuous in all his doings, and he went to Delphi and boldly asked the oracle to tell him whether — as I was saying, I must beg you not to interrupt — he asked the oracle to tell him whether there was any one wiser than I was, and the Pythian prophetess answered, that there was no man wiser. Chaerephon is dead himself; but his brother, who is in court, will confirm the truth of this story.

Why do I mention this? Because I am going to explain to you why I have such an evil name. When I heard the answer, I said to myself, What can the god mean? and what is the interpretation of this riddle? for I know that I have no wisdom, small or great. What then can he mean when he says that I am the wisest of men? And yet he is a god, and can not lie; that would be against his nature. After long consideration, I at last thought of a method of trying the question. I reflected that if I could only find a man wiser than myself, then I might go to the god with a refutation in my hand. I should say to him, " Here is a man who is wiser than I am; but you said that I was the wisest." Accordingly I went to one who had the reputation of wisdom, and observed him — his name I need not mention; he was a politician whom I selected for examination — and the result was as follows: When I began to talk with him, I could not help thinking that he was not really wise, although he was thought wise by many, and wiser still by himself; and I went and tried to explain to

him that he thought himself wise, but was not really
wise; and the consequence was that he hated me, and
his enmity was shared by several who were present
and heard me. So I left him, saying to myself, as
I went away: Well, although I do not suppose that
either of us knows anything really beautiful and good,
I am better off than he is, — for he knows nothing,
and thinks that he knows. I neither know nor think
that I know. In this latter particular, then, I seem
to have slightly the advantage of him. Then I went
to another who had still higher philosophical pretensions, and my conclusion was exactly the same. I
made another enemy of him, and of many others
besides him.

After this I went to one man after another, being
not unconscious of the enmity which I provoked, and
I lamented and feared this: but necessity was laid
upon me, — the word of God, I thought, ought to be
considered first. And I said to myself, Go I must
to all who appear to know, and find out the meaning
of the oracle. And I swear to you, Athenians, by
the dog I swear! — for I must tell you the truth —
the result of my mission was just this: I found that
the men most in repute were all but the most foolish;
and that some inferior men were really wiser and
better. I will tell you the tale of my wanderings and
of the " Herculean " labors, as I may call them, which
I endured only to find at last the oracle irrefutable.
When I left the politicians, I went to the poets;
tragic, dithyrambic, and all sorts. And there, I said
to myself, you will be detected; now you will find
out that you are more ignorant than they are. Accordingly, I took them some of the most elaborate
passages in their own writings, and asked what was
the meaning of them — thinking that they would
teach me something. Will you believe me? I am

almost ashamed to speak of this, but still I must say that there is hardly a person present who would not have talked better about their poetry than they did themselves. That showed me in an instant that not by wisdom do poets write poetry, but by a sort of genius and inspiration; they are like diviners or soothsayers who also say many fine things, but do not understand the meaning of them. And the poets appeared to me to be much in the same case; and I further observed that upon the strength of their poetry they believed themselves to be the wisest of men in other things in which they were not wise. So I departed, conceiving myself to be superior to them for the same reason that I was superior to the politicians.

At last I went to the artisans, for I was conscious that I knew nothing at all, as I may say, and I was sure that they knew many fine things; and in this I was not mistaken, for they did know many things of which I was ignorant, and in this they certainly were wiser than I was. But I observed that even the good artisans fell into the same error as the poets; — because they were good workmen they thought that they also knew all sorts of high matters, and this defect in them overshadowed their wisdom — therefore I asked myself on behalf of the oracle, whether I would like to be as I was, neither having their knowledge nor their ignorance, or like them in both; and I made answer to myself and the oracle that I was better off as I was.

This investigation has led to my having many enemies of the worst and most dangerous kind, and has given occasion also to many calumnies. And I am called wise, for my hearers always imagine that I myself possess the wisdom which I find wanting in others: but the truth is, O men of Athens, that God

only is wise; and in this oracle he means to say that
the wisdom of men is little or nothing; he is not
speaking of Socrates, he is only using my name as
an illustration, as if he said, He, O men, is the wisest
who, like Socrates, knows that his wisdom is in truth
worth nothing. And so I go my way, obedient to
the god, and make inquisition into the wisdom of any
one, whether citizen or stranger, who appears to be
wise; and if he is not wise, then in vindication of the
oracle I show him that he is not wise; and this occupation quite absorbs me, and I have no time to give
either to any public matter of interest or to any concern of my own, but I am in utter poverty by reason
of my devotion to the god.

There is another thing: — young men of the richer
classes, who have not much to do, come about me of
their own accord; they like to hear the pretenders
examined, and they often imitate me, and examine
others themselves; there are plenty of persons, as
they soon enough discover, who think that they know
something, but really know little or nothing; and
then those who are examined by them instead of being
angry with themselves are angry with me: This confounded Socrates, they say; this villainous misleader
of youth! — and then if somebody asks them, Why,
what evil does he practise or teach? they do not know,
and can not tell; but in order that they may not
appear to be at a loss, they repeat the ready-made
charges which are used against all philosophers about
teaching things up in the clouds and under the earth,
and having no gods, and making the worse appear
the better cause; for they do not like to confess that
their pretence of knowledge has been detected —
which is the truth; and as they are numerous and
ambitious and energetic, and are all in battle array
and have persuasive tongues, they have filled your

ears with their loud and inveterate calumnies. And this is the reason why my three accusers, Meletus and Anytus and Lycon, have set upon me; Meletus, who has a quarrel with me on behalf of the poets; Anytus, on behalf of the craftsmen; Lycon, on behalf of the rhetoricians: and as I said at the beginning, I can not expect to get rid of this mass of calumny all in a moment. And this, O men of Athens, is the truth and the whole truth; I have concealed nothing, I have dissembled nothing. And yet, I know that this plainness of speech makes them hate me, and what is their hatred but a proof that I am speaking the truth? — this is the occasion and reason of their slander of me, as you will find out either in this or in any future inquiry.

I have said enough in my defence against the first class of my accusers; I turn to the second class who are headed by Meletus, that good and patriotic man, as he calls himself. And now I will try to defend myself against them: these new accusers must also have their affidavit read. What do they say? Something of this sort: — That Socrates is a doer of evil, and corruptor of the youth, and he does not believe in the gods of the state, and has other new divinities of his own. That is the sort of charge; and now let us examine the particular counts. He says that I am a doer of evil, who corrupt the youth; but I say, O men of Athens, that Meletus is a doer of evil, and the evil is that he makes a joke of a serious matter, and is too ready at bringing other men to trial from a pretended zeal and interest about matters in which he really never had the smallest interest. And the truth of this I will endeavor to prove.

Come hither, Meletus, and let me ask a question of you. You think a great deal about the improvement of youth?

Yes I do.

Tell the judges, then, who is their improver; for you must know, as you have taken the pains to discover their corruptor, and are citing and accusing me before them. Speak, then, and tell the judges who their improver is. Observe, Meletus, that you are silent, and have nothing to say. But is not this rather disgraceful, and a very considerable proof of what I was saying, that you have no interest in the matter? Speak up, friend, and tell us who their improver is.

The laws.

But that, my good sir, is not my meaning. I want to know who the person is, who, in the first place, knows the laws.

The judges, Socrates, who are present in court.

What, do you mean to say, Meletus, that they are able to instruct and improve youth?

Certainly they are.

What, all of them, or some only and not others?

All of them.

By the goddess Here, that is good news! There are plenty of improvers, then. And what do you say of the audience, — do they improve them?

Yes, they do.

And the senators?

Yes, the senators improve them.

But perhaps the ecclesiasts corrupt them? — or do they too improve them?

They improve them.

Then every Athenian improves and elevates them; all with the exception of myself; and I alone am their corruptor? Is that what you affirm?

That is what I stoutly affirm.

I am very unfortunate if that is true. But suppose I ask you a question: Would you say that this also holds true in the case of horses? Does one man do

them harm and all the world good? Is not the exact
opposite of this true? One man is able to do them
good, or at least not many; — the trainer of horses,
that is to say, does them good, and others who have
to do with them rather injure them? Is not that true,
Meletus, of horses, or any other animals? Yes, certainly. Whether you and Anytus say yes or no, that
is no matter. Happy indeed would be the condition
of youth if they had one corruptor only, and all the
rest of the world were their improvers. And you,
Meletus, have sufficiently shown that you never had
a thought about the young: your carelessness is seen
in your not caring about the matters spoken of in
this very indictment.

And now, Meletus, I must ask you another question: Which is better, to live among bad citizens, or
among good ones? Answer, friend, I say; for that
is a question which may be easily answered. Do not
the good do their neighbors good, and the bad do them
evil?

Certainly.

And is there any one who would rather be injured
than benefited by those who live with him? Answer,
my good friend, the law requires you to answer —
does any one like to be injured?

Certainly not.

And when you accuse me of corrupting and deteri-
orating the youth, do you allege that I corrupt them
intentionally or unintentionally?

Intentionally, I say.

But you have just admitted that the good do their
neighbors good, and the evil do them evil. Now, is
that a truth which your superior wisdom has recognized thus early in life, and am I, at my age, in such
darkness and ignorance as not to know that if a man
with whom I have to live is corrupted by me. I am

very likely to be harmed by him, and yet I corrupt him, and intentionally, too; — that is what you are saying and of that you will never persuade me or any other human being. But either I do not corrupt them, or I corrupt them unintentionally, so that on either view of the case you lie. If my offence is unintentional, the law has no cognizance of unintentional offences: you ought to have taken me privately, and warned and admonished me; for if I had been better advised, I should have left off doing what I only did unintentionally — no doubt I should; whereas you hated to converse with me or teach me, but you indicted me in this court, which is a place not of instruction, but of punishment.

I have shown, Athenians, as I was saying, that Meletus has no care at all, great or small, about the matter. But still I should like to know, Meletus, in what I am affirmed to corrupt the young. I suppose you mean, as I infer from your indictment, that I teach them not to acknowledge the gods which the state acknowledges, but some other new divinities or spiritual agencies in their stead. These are the lessons which corrupt the youth, as you say.

Yes, that I say emphatically.

Then, by the gods, Meletus, of whom we are speaking, tell me and the court, in somewhat plainer terms, what you mean! for I do not as yet understand whether you affirm that I teach others to acknowledge some gods, and therefore do believe in gods, and am not an entire atheist — this you do not lay to my charge; — but only that they are not the same gods which the city recognizes — the charge is that they are different gods. Or, do you mean to say that I am an atheist simply, and a teacher of atheism?

I mean the latter — that you are a complete atheist.

That is an extraordinary statement, Meletus. Why

do you say that? Do you mean that I do not believe in the godhead of the sun or moon, which is the common creed of all men?

I assure you, judges, that he does not believe in them; for he says that the sun is stone, and the moon earth.

Friend Meletus, you think that you are accusing Anaxagoras: and you have but a bad opinion of the judges, if you fancy them ignorant to such a degree as not to know that these doctrines are found in the books of Anaxagoras the Clazomenian, who is full of them. And these are the doctrines which the youth are said to learn of Socrates, when there are not unfrequently exhibitions of them at the theatre [1] (price of admission one drachma at the most); and they might cheaply purchase them, and laugh at Socrates if he pretends to father such eccentricities. And so, Meletus, you really think that I do not believe in any god?

I swear by Zeus that you believe absolutely in none at all.

You are a liar, Meletus, not believed even by yourself. For I can not help thinking, O men of Athens, that Meletus is reckless and impudent, and that he has written this indictment in a spirit of mere wantonness and youthful bravado. Has he not compounded a riddle, thinking to try me? He said to himself: — I shall see whether this wise Socrates will discover my ingenious contradiction, or whether I shall be able to deceive him and the rest of them. For he certainly does appear to me to contradict himself in the indictment as much as if he said that Socrates is guilty of not believing in the gods, and yet of believing in them — but this surely is a piece of fun.

[1] Probably in allusion to Aristophanes who caricatured, and to Euripides who borrowed the notions of Anaxagoras, as well as to other dramatic poets.

I should like you, O men of Athens, to join me in
examining in what I conceive to be his inconsistency;
and do you, Meletus, answer. And I must remind
you that you are not to interrupt me if I speak in my
accustomed manner.

Did ever man, Meletus, believe in the existence of
human things, and not human beings? . . . I wish,
men of Athens, that he would answer, and not be
always trying to get up an interruption. Did ever
any man believe in horsemanship, and not in horses?
or in flute-playing, and not in flute-players? No, my
friend; I will answer to you and to the court, as you
refuse to answer for yourself. There is no man who
ever did. But now please to answer the next question: Can a man believe in spiritual and divine agencies, and not in spirits or demigods?

He can not.

I am glad that I have extracted that answer, by the
assistance of the court; nevertheless you swear in the
indictment that I teach and believe in divine or spiritual agencies (new or old, no matter for that); at
any rate, I believe in spiritual agencies, as you say
and swear in the affidavit; but if I believe in divine
beings, I must believe in spirits or demigods; — is not
that true? Yes, that is true, for I may assume that
your silence gives assent to that. Now what are
spirits or demigods? are they not either gods or the
sons of gods? Is that true?

Yes, that is true.

But this is just the ingenious riddle of which I was
speaking: the demigods or spirits are gods, and you
say first that I don't believe in gods, and then again
that I do believe in gods; that is, if I believe in demigods. For if the demigods are the illegitimate sons
of gods, whether by the nymphs or by any other mothers, as is thought, that, as all men will allow, neces-

sarily implies the existence of their parents. You might as well affirm the existence of mules, and deny that of horses and asses. Such nonsense, Meletus, could only have been intended by you as a trial of me. You have put this into the indictment because you had nothing real of which to accuse me. But no one who has a particle of understanding will ever be convinced by you that the same men can believe in divine and superhuman things, and yet not believe that there are gods and demigods and heroes.

I have said enough in answer to the charge of Meletus: any elaborate defence is unnecessary; but as I was saying before, I certainly have many enemies, and this is what will be my destruction if I am destroyed; of that I am certain; — not Meletus, nor yet Anytus, but the envy and detraction of the world, which has been the death of many good men, and will probably be the death of many more; there is no danger of my being the last of them.

Some one will say: And are you not ashamed, Socrates, of a course of life which is likely to bring you to an untimely end? To him I may fairly answer: There you are mistaken: a man who is good for anything ought not to calculate the chance of living or dying; he ought only to consider whether in doing anything he is doing right or wrong — acting the part of a good man or of a bad. Whereas, according to your view, the heroes who fell at Troy were not good for much, and the son of Thetis above all, who altogether despised danger in comparison with disgrace; and when his goddess mother said to him, in his eagerness to slay Hector, that if he avenged his companion Patroclus, and slew Hector, he would die himself — " Fate," as she said, " waits upon you next after Hector; " he, hearing this, utterly despised danger and death, and instead of fearing them, feared rather to live in dishonor, and not to avenge his friend. " Let me die next," he replies, " and be avenged of my enemy, rather than abide here by the beaked ships, a scorn and a burden of the earth." Had Achilles any thought of death and danger? For wherever a man's place is, whether the place which he has chosen or that in which he has been placed by a commander, there he ought to remain in the hour of danger; he should not think of death or of anything, but of disgrace. And this, O men of Athens, is a true saying.

Strange, indeed, would be my conduct, O men of Athens, if I who, when I was ordered by the generals whom you chose to command me at Potidaea and Amphipolis and Delium, remained where they placed me, like any other man, facing death; if, I say, now, when, as I conceive and imagine, God orders me to fulfil the philosopher's mission of searching into myself and other men, I were to desert my post through fear of death, or any other fear; that would indeed be strange, and I might justly be arraigned in court for denying the existence of the gods, if I disobeyed the oracle because I was afraid of death: then I should be fancying that I was wise when I was not wise. For this fear of death is indeed the pretence of wisdom, and not real wisdom, being the appearance of knowing the unknown; since no one knows whether death, which they in their fear apprehend to be the greatest evil, may not be the greatest good. Is there not here conceit of knowledge, which is a disgraceful sort of ignorance? And this is the point in which, as I think, I am superior to men in general, and in which I might perhaps fancy myself wiser than other men, — that whereas I know but little of the world below, I do not suppose that I know: but I do know that injustice and disobedience to a better,

whether God or man, is evil and dishonorable, and
I will never fear or avoid a possible good rather than
a certain evil. And therefore if you let me go now,
and reject the counsels of Anytus, who said that if
I were not put to death I ought not to have been prosecuted, and that if I escape now, your sons will all
be utterly ruined by listening to my words — if you
say to me, Socrates, this time we will not mind Anytus, and will let you off, but upon one condition, that
you are not to inquire and speculate in this way any
more, and that if you are caught doing this again
you shall die; — if this was the condition on which you
let me go, I should reply: Men of Athens, I honor
and love you; but I shall obey God rather than you,
and while I have life and strength I shall never cease
from the practice and teaching of philosophy, exhorting any one whom I meet after my manner, and convincing him, saying: O my friend, why do you, who
are a citizen of the great and mighty and wise city of
Athens, care so much about laying up the greatest
amount of money and honor and reputation, and so
little about wisdom and truth and the greatest improvement of the soul, which you never regard or
heed at all? Are you not ashamed of this? And if
the person with whom I am arguing, says: Yes, but
I do care; I do not depart or let him go at once; I
interrogate and examine and cross-examine him, and
if I think that he has no virtue, but only says that
he has, I reproach him with undervaluing the greater,
and overvaluing the less. And this I should say to
every one whom I meet, young and old, citizen and
alien, but especially to the citizens, inasmuch as they
are my brethren. For this is the command to God,
as I would have you know; and I believe that to this
day no greater good has ever happened in the state
than my service to the God. For I do nothing but

go about persuading you all, old and young alike, not to take thought for your persons or your properties, but first and chiefly to care about the greatest improvement of the soul. I tell you that virtue is not given by money, but that from virtue come money and every other good of man, public as well as private. This is my teaching, and if this is the doctrine which corrupts the youth, my influence is ruinous indeed. But if any one says that this is not my teaching, he is speaking an untruth. Wherefore, O men of Athens, I say to you, do as Anytus bids or not as Anytus bids, and either acquit me or not; but whatever you do, know that I shall never alter my ways, not even if I have to die many times.

Men of Athens, do not interrupt, but hear me; there was an agreement between us that you should hear me out. And I think that what I am going to say will do you good: for I have something more to say, at which you may be inclined to cry out; but I beg that you will not do this. I would have you know, that if you kill such an one as I am, you will injure yourselves more than you will injure me. Meletus and Anytus will not injure me: they can not; for it is not in the nature of things that a bad man should injure a better than himself. I do not deny that he may, perhaps, kill him, or drive him into exile, or deprive him of civil rights; and he may imagine, and others may imagine, that he is doing him a great injury: but in that I do not agree with him; for the evil of doing as Anytus is doing — of unjustly taking away another man's life — is greater far. And now, Athenians, I am not going to argue for my own sake, as you may think, but for yours, that you may not sin against the God, or lightly reject his boon by condemning me. For if you kill me you will not easily find another like me, who, if I may use such a ludicrous figure of speech, am a sort of gadfly, given to the state by the God; and the state is like a great and noble steed who is tardy in his motions owing to his very size, and requires to be stirred into life. I am that gadfly which God has given the state, and all day long and in all places am always fastening upon you, arousing and persuading and reproaching you. And as you will not easily find another like me, I would advise you to spare me. I dare say that you may feel irritated at being suddenly awakened when you are caught napping; and you may think that if you were to strike me dead as Anytus advises, which you easily might, then you would sleep on for the remainder of your lives, unless God in his care of you gives you another gadfly. And that I am given to you by God is proved by this: — that if I had been like other men, I should not have neglected all my own concerns or patiently seen the neglect of them during all these years, and have been doing yours, coming to you individually like a father or elder brother, exhorting you to regard virtue; this, I say, would not be like human nature. And had I gained anything, or if my exhortations had been paid, there would have been some sense in that; but now, as you will perceive, not even the impudence of my accusers dares to say that I have ever exacted or sought pay of any one; they have no witness of that. And I have a witness of the truth of what I say; my poverty is a sufficient witness.

Some one may wonder why I go about in private giving advice and busying myself with the concerns of others, but do not venture to come forward in public and advise the state. I will tell you the reason of this. You have often heard me speak of an oracle or sign which comes to me, and is the divinity which Meletus ridicules in the indictment. This sign I have had ever since I was a child. The sign is a voice which comes to me and always forbids me to do something which I am going to do, but never commands me to do anything, and this is what stands in the way of my being a politician. And rightly, as I think. For I am certain, O men of Athens, that if I had engaged in politics, I should have perished long ago, and done no good either to you or to myself. And don't be offended at my telling you the truth: for the truth is, that no man who goes to war with you or any other multitude, honestly struggling against the commission of unrighteousness and wrong in the state, will save his life; he who will really fight for the right, if he would live even for a little while, must have a private station and not a public one.

I can give you as proofs of this, not words only, but deeds, which you value more than words. Let me tell you a passage of my own life which will prove to you that I should never have yielded to injustice from any fear of death, and that if I had not yielded I should have died at once. I will tell you a story — tasteless perhaps and commonplace, but nevertheless true. The only office of state which I ever held, O men of Athens, was that of senator: the tribe Antiochis, which is my tribe, had the presidency at the trial of the generals who had not taken up the bodies of the slain after the battle of Arginusae; and you proposed to try them all together, which was illegal, as you all thought afterwards; but at the time I was the only one of the Prytanes who was opposed to the illegality, and I gave my vote against you; and when the orators threatened to impeach and arrest me, and have me taken away, and you called and shouted, I made up my mind that I would run the risk, having law and justice with me, rather than take part in your injustice because I feared imprisonment and death.

This happened in the days of the democracy. But when the oligarchy of the Thirty was in power, they sent for me and four others into the rotunda, and bade us bring Leon the Salaminian from Salamis, as they wanted to execute him. This was a specimen of the sort of commands which they were always giving with the view of implicating as many as possible in their crimes; and then I showed, not in word only but in deed, that, if I may be allowed to use such an expression, I cared not a straw for death, and that my only fear was the fear of doing an unrighteous or unholy thing. For the strong arm of that oppressive power did not frighten me into doing wrong; and when we came out of the rotunda the other four went to Salamis and fetched Leon, but I went quietly home. For which I might have lost my life, had not the power of the Thirty shortly afterwards come to an end. And to this many will witness.

Now do you really imagine that I could have survived all these years, if I had led a public life, supposing that like a good man I had always supported the right and had made justice, as I ought, the first thing? No indeed, men of Athens, neither I nor any other. But I have been always the same in all my actions, public as well as private, and never have I yielded any base compliance to those who are slanderously termed my disciples, or to any other. For the truth is that I have no regular disciples: but if any one likes to come and hear me while I am pursuing my mission, whether he be young or old, he may freely come. Nor do I converse with those who pay only, and not with those who do not pay; but any one, whether he be rich or poor, may ask and answer me and listen to my words; and whether he turns out to be a bad man or a good one, that can not be justly laid to my charge, as I never taught him anything.

And if any one says that he has ever learned or heard anything from me in private which all the world has not heard, I should like you to know that he is speaking an untruth.

But I shall be asked, Why do people delight in continually conversing with you? I have told you already, Athenians, the whole truth about this: they like to hear the cross-examination of the pretenders to wisdom; there is amusement in this. And this is a duty which the God has imposed upon me, as I am assured by oracles, visions, and in every sort of way in which the will of divine power was ever signified to any one. This is true, O Athenians; or, if not true, would be soon refuted. For if I am really corrupting the youth, and have corrupted some of them already, those of them who have grown up and have become sensible that I gave them bad advice in the days of their youth should come forward as accusers and take their revenge; and if they do not like to come themselves, some of their relatives, fathers, brothers, or other kinsmen, should say what evil their families suffered at my hands. Now is their time. Many of them I see in the court. There is Crito, who is of the same age and of the same deme with myself, and there is Critobulus his son, whom I also see. Then again there is Lysanias of Sphettus, who is the father of Aeschines — he is present; and also there is Antiphon of Cephisus, who is the father of Epigenes; and there are the brothers of several who have associated with me. There is Nicostratus the son of Theosdotides, and the brother of Theodotus (now Theodotus himself is dead, and therefore he, at any rate, will not seek to stop him); and there is Paralus the son of Demodocus, who had a brother Theages; and Adeimantus the son of Ariston, whose brother Plato is present; and Aeantodorus, who is the brother of

Apollodorus, whom I also see. I might mention a great many others, any of whom Meletus should have produced as witnesses in the course of his speech; and let him still produce them, if he has forgotten — I will make way for him. And let him say, if he has any testimony of the sort which he can produce. Nay, Athenians, the very opposite is the truth. For all these are ready to witness on behalf of the corruptor, of the destroyer of their kindred, as Meletus and Anytus call me; not the corrupted youth only — there might have been a motive for that — but their uncorrupted elder relatives. Why should they too support me with their testimony? Why, indeed, except for the sake of truth and justice, and because they know that I am speaking the truth, and that Meletus is lying.

Well, Athenians, this and the like of this is nearly all the defence which I have to offer. Yet a word more. Perhaps there may be some one who is offended at me, when he calls to mind how he himself on a similar, or even a less serious occasion, had recourse to prayers and supplications with many tears, and how he produced his children in court, which was a moving spectacle, together with a posse of his relations and friends; whereas I, who am probably in danger of my life, will do none of these things. Perhaps this may come into his mind, and he may be set against me, and vote in anger because he is displeased at this. Now if there be such a person among you, which 1 am far from affirming, I may fairly reply to him: My friend, I am a man, and like other men, a creature of flesh and blood, and not of wood or stone, as Homer says; and I have a family, yes, and sons, O Athenians, three in number, one of whom is growing up, and the two others are still young; and yet I will not bring any of them hither in order to petition you for an acquittal. And why not? Not from any self-will or disregard of you. Whether I am or am not afraid of death is another question, of which I will not now speak. But my reason simply is, that I feel such conduct to be discreditable to myself, and you, and the whole state. One who has reached my years, and who has a name for wisdom, whether deserved or not, ought not to demean himself. At any rate, the world has decided that Socrates is in some way superior to other men. And if those among you who are said to be superior in wisdom and courage, and any other virtue, demean themselves in this way, how shameful is their conduct! I have seen men of reputation, when they have been condemned, behaving in the strangest manner: they seemed to fancy that they were going to suffer something dreadful if they died, and that they could be immortal if you only allowed them to live; and I think that they were a dishonor to the state, and that any stranger coming in would say of them that the most eminent men of Athens, to whom the Athenians themselves give honor and command, are no better than women. And I say that these things ought not to be done by those of us who are of reputation; and if they are done, you ought not to permit them; you ought rather to show that you are more inclined to condemn, not the man who is quiet, but the man who gets up a doleful scene, and makes the city ridiculous.

But, setting aside the question of dishonor, there seems to be something wrong in petitioning a judge, and thus procuring an acquittal instead of informing and convincing him. For his duty is, not to make a present of justice, but to give judgment; and he has sworn that he will judge according to the laws and not according to his own good pleasure; and neither he nor we should get into the habit of perjuring ourselves — there can be no piety in that. Do not then require me to do what I consider dishonorable and impious and wrong, especially now, when I am being tried for impiety on the indictment of Meletus. For if, O men of Athens, by force of persuasion and entreaty, I could overpower your oaths, then I should be teaching you to believe that there are no gods, and convict myself, in my own defence, of not believing in them. But that is not the case; for I do believe that there are gods, and in a far higher sense than that in which any of my accusers believe in them. And to you and to God I commit my cause, to be determined by you as is best for you and me.

There are many reasons why I am not grieved, O men of Athens, at the vote of condemnation. I expected this, and am only surprised that the votes are so nearly equal; for I had thought that the majority against me would have been far larger; but now, had thirty votes gone over to the other side, I should have been acquitted. And I may say that I have escaped Meletus. And I may say more; for without the assistance of Anytus and Lycon, he would not have had a fifth part of the votes, as the law requires, in which case he would have incurred a fine of a thousand drachmae, as is evident.

And so he proposes death as the penalty. And what shall I propose on my part, O men of Athens? Clearly that which is my due. And what is that which I ought to pay or to receive? What shall be done to the man who has never had the wit to be idle during his whole life; but has been careless of what the many care about — wealth, and family interests, and military offices, and speaking in the assembly, and magistracies, and plots, and parties. Reflecting that I

was really too honest a man to follow in this way
and live, I did not go where I could do no good to you
or to myself; but where I could do the greatest good
privately to every one of you, thither I went, and
sought to persuade every man among you, that he
must look to himself, and seek virtue and wisdom
before he looks to his private interests, and look to
the state before he looks to the interests of the state;
and that this should be the order which he observes in
all his actions. What shall be done to such an one?
Doubtless some good thing, O men of Athens, if he
has his reward; and the good should be of a kind
suitable to him. What would be a reward suitable
to a poor man who is your benefactor, who desires
leisure that he may instruct you? There can be no
more fitting reward than maintenance in the Prytaneum, O men of Athens, a reward which he deserves
far more than the citizen who has won the prize at
Olympia in the horse or chariot race, whether the
chariots were drawn by two horses or by many. For
I am in want, and he has enough; and he only gives
you the appearance of happiness, and I give you the
reality. And if I am to estimate the penalty justly,
I say that maintenance in the Prytaneum is the just
return.

Perhaps you may think that I am braving you in
saying this, as in what I said before about the tears
and prayers. But that is not the case. I speak rather
because I am convinced that I never intentionally
wronged any one, although I can not convince you of
that — for we have had a short conversation only;
but if there were a law at Athens, such as there is in
other cities, that a capital cause should not be decided
in one day, then I believe that I should have convinced you; but now the time is too short. I can not
in a moment refute great slanders; and, as I am con-

vinced that I never wronged another, I will assuredly not wrong myself. I will not say of myself that I deserve any evil, or propose any penalty. Why should I? Because I am afraid of the penalty of death which Meletus proposes? When I do not know whether death is a good or an evil, why should I propose a penalty which would certainly be an evil? Shall I say imprisonment? And why should I live in prison, and be the slave of the magistrates of the year — of the eleven? Or shall the penalty be a fine, and imprisonment until the fine is paid? There is the same objection. I should have to lie in prison, for money I have none, and can not pay. And if I say exile (and this may possibly be the penalty which you will affix), I must indeed be blinded by the love of life, if I do not consider that when you, who are my own citizens, can not endure my discourses and words, and have found them so grievous and odious that you would fain have done with them, others are likely to endure me. No indeed, men of Athens, that is not very likely. And what a life should I lead, at my age, wandering from city to city, living in ever-changing exile, and always being driven out! For I am quite sure that into whatever place I go, as here so also there, the young men will come to me; and if I drive them away, their elders will drive me out at their desire; and if I let them come, their fathers and friends will drive me out for their sakes.

Some one will say: Yes, Socrates, but can not you hold your tongue, and then you may go into a foreign city, and no one will interfere with you? Now I have great difficulty in making you understand my answer to this. For if I tell you that this would be a disobedience to a divine command, and therefore that I can not hold my tongue, you will not believe that I am serious; and if I say again that the greatest good

of man is daily to converse about virtue, and all that
concerning which you hear me examining myself and
others, and that the life which is unexamined is not
worth living — that you are still less likely to believe.
And yet what I say is true, although a thing of which
it is hard for me to persuade you. Moreover, I am
not accustomed to think that I deserve any punishment. Had I money I might have proposed to give
you what I had, and have been none the worse. But
you see that I have none, and can only ask you to
proportion the fine to my means. However, I think
that I could afford a mina, and therefore I propose
that penalty: Plato, Crito, Critobulus, and Apollodorus, my friends here, bid me say thirty minae, and
they will be the sureties. Well, then, say thirty
minae, let that be the penalty; for that they will be
ample security to you.

Not much time will be gained, O Athenians, in
return for the evil name which you will get from the
detractors of the city, who will say that you killed
Socrates, a wise man; for they will call me wise even
although I am not wise when they want to reproach
you. If you had waited a little while, your desire
would have been fulfilled in the course of nature.
For I am far advanced in years, as you may perceive,
and not far from death. I am speaking now only
to those of you who have condemned me to death.
And I have another thing to say to them: You think
that I was convicted through deficiency of words —
I mean, that if I had thought fit to leave nothing
undone, nothing unsaid, I might have gained an
acquittal. Not so; the deficiency which led to my
conviction was not of words — certainly not. But I
had not the boldness or impudence or inclination to

address you as you would have liked me to address you, weeping and wailing and lamenting, and saying and doing many things which you have been accustomed to hear from others, and which, as I say, are unworthy of me. But I thought that I ought not to do anything common or mean in the hour of danger: nor do I now repent of the manner of my defence, and I would rather die having spoken after my manner, than speak in your manner and live. For neither in war nor yet at law ought any man to use every way of escaping death. For often in battle there is no doubt that if a man will throw away his arms, and fall on his knees before his pursuers, he may escape death; and in other dangers there are other ways of escaping death, if a man is willing to say and do anything. The difficulty, my friends, is not in avoiding death, but in avoiding unrighteousness; for that runs faster than death. I am old and move slowly, and the slower runner has overtaken me, and my accusers are keen and quick, and the faster runner, who is unrighteousness, has overtaken them. And now I depart hence condemned by you to suffer the penalty of death, and they too go their ways condemned by the truth to suffer the penalty of villainy and wrong; and I must abide by my award — let them abide by theirs. I suppose that these things may be regarded as fated, — and I think that they are well.

And now, O men who have condemned me, I would fain prophesy to you; for I am about to die, and that is the hour in which men are gifted with prophetic power. And I prophesy to you who are my murderers, that immediately after my death punishment far heavier than you have inflicted on me will surely await you. Me you have killed because you wanted to escape the accuser, and not to give an account of your lives. But that will not be as you suppose: far otherwise. For I say that there will be more accusers of you than there are now; accusers whom hitherto I have restrained: and as they are younger they will be more severe with you, and you will be more offended at them. For if you think that by killing men you can avoid the accuser censuring your lives, you are mistaken; that is not a way of escape which is either possible or honorable; the easiest and the noblest way is not to be crushing others, but to be improving yourselves. This is the prophecy which I utter before my departure to the judges who have condemned me.

Friends, who would have acquitted me, I would like also to talk with you about this thing which has happened, while the magistrates are busy, and before I go to the place at which I must die. Stay then awhile, for we may as well talk with one another while there is time. You are my friends, and I should like to show you the meaning of this event which has happened to me. O my judges — for you I may truly call judges — I should like to tell you of a wonderful circumstance. Hitherto the familiar oracle within me has constantly been in the habit of opposing me even about trifles, if I was going to make a slip or error about anything; and now as you see there has come upon me that which may be thought, and is generally believed to be, the last and worst evil. But the oracle made no sign of opposition, either as I was leaving my house and going out in the morning, or when I was going up into this court, or while I was speaking, at anything which I was going to say; and yet I have often been stopped in the middle of a speech, but now in nothing I either said or did touching this matter has the oracle opposed me. What do I take to be the explanation of this? I will tell you. I regard this as a proof that what has happened to me is a good, and that those of us who think that death is an evil are in error. This is a great proof to me of what I am saying, for the customary sign would surely have opposed me had I been going to evil and not to good.

Let us reflect in another way, and we shall see that there is great reason to hope that death is a good, for one of two things: — either death is a state of nothingness and utter unconsciousness, or, as men say, there is a change and migration of the soul from this world to another. Now if you suppose that there is no consciousness, but a sleep like the sleep of him who is undisturbed even by the sight of dreams, death will be an unspeakable gain. For if a person were to select the night in which his sleep was undisturbed even by dreams, and were to compare with this the other days and nights of his life, and then were to tell us how many days and nights he had passed in the course of his life better and more pleasantly than this one, I think that any man, I will not say a private man, but even the great king will not find many such days or nights, when compared with the others. Now if death is like this, I say that to die is gain; for eternity is then only a single night. But if death is the journey to another place, and there, as men say, all the dead are, what good, O my friends and judges, can be greater than this? If indeed when the pilgrim arrives in the world below, he is delivered from the professors of justice in this world, and finds the true judges who are said to give judgment there, Minos and Rhadamanthus and Aeacus and Triptolemus, and other sons of God who were righteous in their own life, that pilgrimage will be worth making. What would not a man give if he might converse with Orpheus and Musaeus and Hesiod and Homer?

Nay, if this be true, let me die again and again. I, too, shall have a wonderful interest in a place where I can converse with Palamedes, and Ajax the son of Telamon, and other heroes of old, who have suffered death through an unjust judgment; and there will be no small pleasure, as I think, in comparing my own sufferings with theirs. Above all, I shall be able to continue my search into true and false knowledge; as in this world, so also in that; I shall find out who is wise, and who pretends to be wise, and is not. What would not a man give, O judges, to be able to examine the leader of the great Trojan expedition; or Odysseus or Sisyphus, or numberless others, men and women too! What infinite delight would there be in conversing with them and asking them questions! For in that world they do not put a man to death for this; certainly not. For besides being happier in that world than in this, they will be immortal, if what is said is true.

Wherefore, O judges, be of good cheer about death, and know this of a truth — that no evil can happen to a good man, either in life or after death. He and his are not neglected by the gods; nor has my own approaching end happened by mere chance. But I see clearly that to die and be released was better for me; and therefore the oracle gave no sign. For which reason, also, I am not angry with my accusers or my condemners; they have done me no harm, although neither of them meant to do me any good; and for this I may gently blame them.

Still I have a favor to ask of them. When my sons are grown up, I would ask you, O my friends, to punish them; and I would have you trouble them, as I have troubled you, if they seem to care about riches, or anything, more than about virtue; or if they pretend to be something when they are really nothing, — then reprove them, as I have reproved you, for not caring about that for which they ought to care, and thinking that they are something when they are really nothing. And if you do this, I and my sons will have received justice at your hands.

The hour of departure has arrived, and we go our ways — I to die, and you to live. Which is better God only knows.

CRITO

INTRODUCTION

THE Crito seems intended to exhibit the character of Socrates in one light only, not as the philosopher, fulfilling a divine mission and trusting in the will of heaven, but simply as the good citizen, who having been unjustly condemned is willing to give up his life in obedience to the laws of the state.

The days of Socrates are drawing to a close; the fatal ship has been seen off Sunium, as he is informed by his aged friend and contemporary Crito, who visits him before the dawn has broken; he himself has been warned in a dream that on the third day he must depart. Time is precious, and Crito has come early in order to gain his consent to a plan of escape. This can be easily accomplished by his friends, who will incur no danger in making the attempt to save him, but will be disgraced forever if they allow him to perish. He should think of his duty to his children, and not play into the hands of his enemies. Money is already provided by Crito as well as by Simmias and others, and he will have no difficulty in finding friends in Thessaly and other places.

Socrates is afraid that Crito is but pressing upon him the opinions of the many: whereas, all his life long he has followed the dictates of reason only and the opinion of the one wise or skilled man. There was a time when Crito himself had allowed the propriety of this. And although some one will say "the many can kill us," that makes no difference; but a good life, that is to say a just and honorable life, is alone to be valued. All considerations of loss of reputation or injury to his children should be dismissed: the only question is whether he would be right in attempting to escape. Crito, who is a disinterested person not having the fear of death before his eyes, shall answer this for him. Before he was condemned they had often held discussions, in which they agreed that no man should either do evil, or return evil for evil, or betray the right. Are these principles to be altered because the circumstances of Socrates are altered? Crito admits that they remain the same. Then is his

547

escape consistent with the maintenance of them? To this Crito is unable or unwilling to reply.

Socrates proceeds: — Suppose the laws of Athens to come and remonstrate with him: they will ask "Why does he seek to overturn them?" and if he replies, "they have injured him," will not the laws answer, "Yes, but was that the agreement? Has he any objection to make to them which would justify him in overturning them? Was he not brought into the world and educated by their help, and are they not his parents? He might have left Athens and gone where he pleased, but he has lived there for seventy years more constantly than any other citizen." Thus he has clearly shown that he acknowledged the agreement which he can not now break without dishonor to himself and danger to his friends. Even in the course of the trial he might have proposed exile as the penalty, but then he declared that he preferred death to exile. And whither will he direct his footsteps? In any well-ordered state the laws will consider him as an enemy. Possibly in a land of misrule like Thessaly he may be welcomed at first, and the unseemly narrative of his escape regarded by the inhabitants as an amusing tale. But if he offends them he will have to learn another sort of lesson. Will he continue to give lectures in virtue? That would hardly be decent. And how will his children be the gainers if he takes them into Thessaly, and deprives them of Athenian citizenship? Or if he leaves them behind, does he expect that they will be better taken care of by his friends because he is in Thessaly? Will not true friends care for them equally whether he is alive or dead?

Finally, they exhort him to think of justice first, and of life and children afterwards. He may now depart in peace and innocence, a sufferer and not a doer of evil. But if he breaks agreements, and returns evil for evil, they will be angry with him while he lives; and their brethren the laws of the world below will receive him as an enemy. Such is the mystic voice which is always murmuring in his ears.

That Socrates was not a good citizen was a charge made against him during his lifetime, which has been often repeated in later ages. The crimes of Alcibiades, Critias, and Charmides, who had been his pupils, were still recent in the memory of the now restored democracy. The fact that he had been neutral in the death-struggle of Athens was not likely to conciliate popular good-will. Plato, writing probably in the next generation, undertakes the defence of his friend and master in this particular, not to the Athenians of his day, but to posterity and the world at large.

Whether such an incident ever really occurred as the visit of Crito and the proposal of escape is uncertain: Plato could easily have invented far more than that; and in the selection of Crito, the aged friend, as the fittest person to make the proposal to Socrates, we seem to recognize the hand of the artist. Whether any one who has been subjected by the laws of his country to an unjust judgment is right in attempting to escape, is a thesis about which casuists might disagree. Shelley is of opinion that Socrates " did well to die," but not for the " sophistical " reasons which Plato has put into his mouth. And there would be no difficulty in arguing that Socrates should have lived and preferred to a glorious death the good which he might still be able to perform. " A skilful rhetorician would have had much to say about that." It may be remarked however that Plato never intended to answer the question of casuistry, but only to exhibit the ideal of patient virtue which refuses to do the least evil in order to avoid the greatest, and to show Socrates, his master, maintaining in death the opinions which he had professed in his life. Not " the world," but the " one wise man," is still the philosopher's paradox in his last hours.

CRITO

PERSONS OF THE DIALOGUE

SOCRATES.   CRITO.

SCENE: — The Prison of Socrates.

Socrates. WHY have you come at this hour, Crito? it must be quite early?

Crito. Yes, certainly.

Soc. What is the exact time?

Cr. The dawn is breaking.

Soc. I wonder that the keeper of the prison would let you in.

Cr. He knows me, because I often come, Socrates; moreover, I have done him a kindness.

Soc. And are you only just come?

Cr. No, I came some time ago.

Soc. Then why did you sit and say nothing, instead of awakening me at once?

Cr. Why, indeed, Socrates, I myself would rather not have all this sleeplessness and sorrow. But I have been wondering at your peaceful slumbers, and that was the reason why I did not awaken you, because I wanted you to be out of pain. I have always thought you happy in the calmness of your temperament; but never did I see the like of the easy, cheerful way in which you bear this calamity.

Soc. Why, Crito, when a man has reached my age he ought not to be repining at the prospect of death.

Cr. And yet other old men find themselves in similar misfortunes, and age does not prevent them from repining.

Soc. That may be. But you have not told me why you come at this early hour.

Cr. I come to bring you a message which is sad and painful; not, as I believe, to yourself, but to all of us who are your friends, and saddest of all to me.

Soc. What! I suppose that the ship has come from Delos, on the arrival of which I am to die?

Cr. No, the ship has not actually arrived, but she will probably be here to-day, as persons who have come from Sunium tell me that they left her there; and therefore to-morrow, Socrates, will be the last day of your life.

Soc. Very well, Crito; if such is the will of God, I am willing; but my belief is that there will be a delay of a day.

Cr. Why do you say this?

Soc. I will tell you. I am to die on the day after the arrival of the ship?

Cr. Yes; that is what the authorities say.

Soc. But I do not think that the ship will be here until to-morrow; this I gather from a vision which I had last night, or rather only just now, when you fortunately allowed me to sleep.

Cr. And what was the nature of the vision?

Soc. There came to me the likeness of a woman, fair and comely, clothed in white raiment, who called to me and said: O Socrates,

" The third day hence to Phthia shalt thou go."

Cr. What a singular dream, Socrates!

Soc. There can be no doubt about the meaning, Crito, I think.

Cr. Yes; the meaning is only too clear. But, Oh! my beloved Socrates, let me entreat you once more to take my advice and escape. For if you die I shall not only lose a friend who can never be replaced, but there is another evil: people who do not know you and me will believe that I might have saved you if I had been willing to give money, but that I did not care. Now, can there be a worse disgrace than this — that I should be thought to value money more than the life of a friend? For the many will not be persuaded that I wanted you to escape, and that you refused.

Soc. But why, my dear Crito, should we care about the opinion of the many? Good men, and they are the only persons who are worth considering, will think of these things truly as they happened.

Cr. But do you see, Socrates, that the opinion of the many must be regarded, as is evident in your own case, because they can do the very greatest evil to any one who has lost their good opinion.

Soc. I only wish, Crito, that they could; for then they could also do the greatest good, and that would be well. But the truth is, that they can do neither good nor evil: they can not make a man wise or make him foolish; and whatever they do is the result of chance.

Cr. Well, I will not dispute about that; but please to tell me, Socrates, whether you are not acting out of regard to me and your other friends: are you not afraid that if you escape hence we may get into trouble with the informers for having stolen you away, and lose either the whole or a great part of our property; or that even a worse evil may happen to us? Now, if this is your fear, be at ease; for in order to save you we ought surely to run this, or even a greater risk; be persuaded, then, and do as I say.

Soc. Yes, Crito, that is one fear which you mention, but by no means the only one.

Cr. Fear not. There are persons who at no great cost are willing to save you and bring you out of prison; and as for the informers, you may observe that they are far from being exorbitant in their demands; a little money will satisfy them. My means, which, as I am sure, are ample, are at your service, and if you have a scruple about spending all mine, here are strangers who will give you the use of theirs; and one of them, Simmias the Theban, has brought a sum of money for this very purpose; and Cebes and many others are willing to spend their money too. I say therefore, do not on that account hesitate about making your escape, and do not say, as you did in the court, that you will have a difficulty in knowing what to do with yourself if you escape. For men will love you in other places to which you may go, and not in Athens only; there are friends of mine in Thessaly, if you like to go to them, who will value and protect you, and no Thessalian will give you any trouble. Nor can I think that you are justified, Socrates, in betraying your own life when you might be saved; this is playing into the hands of your enemies and destroyers; and moreover I should say that you were betraying your children; for you might bring them up and educate them; instead of which you go away and leave them, and they will have to take their chance; and if they do not meet with the usual fate of orphans, there will be small thanks to you. No man should bring children into the world who is unwilling to persevere to the end in their nurture and education. But you are choosing the easier part, as I think, not the better and manlier, which would rather have become one who professes virtue in all his actions, like yourself. And indeed, I am ashamed not only of you, but of us who are your friends, when I reflect that this entire business of yours will be attributed to our want of courage. The trial need never have come on, or might have been brought to another issue; and the end of all, which is the crowning absurdity, will seem to have been permitted by us, through cowardice and baseness, who might have saved you, as you might have saved yourself, if we had been good for anything (for there was no difficulty in escaping) ; and we did not see how disgraceful, Socrates, and also miserable all this will be to us as well as to you. Make your mind up then, or rather have your mind already made up, for the time of deliberation is over, and there is only one thing to be done, which must be done, if at all, this very night, and which any delay will render all but impossible; I beseech you therefore, Socrates, to be persuaded by me, and to do as I say.

Soc. Dear Crito, your zeal is invaluable, if a right one; but if wrong, the greater the zeal the greater the evil; and therefore we ought to consider whether these things shall be done or not. For I am and always have been one of those natures who must be guided by reason, whatever the reason may be which upon reflection appears to me to be the best; and now that this fortune has come upon me, I can not put away the reasons which I have before given: the principles which I have hitherto honored and revered I still honor, and unless we can find other and better principles on the instant, I am certain not to agree with you; no, not even if the power of the multitude could inflict many more imprisonments, confiscations, deaths, frightening us like children with hobgoblin terrors. But what will be the fairest way of considering the question? Shall I return to your old argument about the opinions of men? some of which are to be regarded, and others, as we were saying, are not to be regarded. Now were we right in maintaining this before I was condemned? And has the argu‑ment which was once good now proved to be talk for the sake of talking; — in fact an amusement only, and altogether vanity? That is what I want to con‑sider with your help, Crito: — whether, under my present circumstances, the argument appears to be in any way different or not; and is to be allowed by me or disallowed. That argument, which, as I be‑lieve, is maintained by many who assume to be author‑ities, was to the effect, as I was saying, that the opin‑ions of some men are to be regarded, and of other men not to be regarded. Now you, Crito, are a disinter‑ested person who are not going to die to-morrow — at least, there is no human probability of this, and you are therefore not liable to be deceived by the circum‑stances in which you are placed. Tell me then, whether I am right in saying that some opinions, and the opinions of some men only, are to be valued, and other opinions, and the opinions of other men, are not to be valued. I ask you whether I was right in maintaining this?

Cr. Certainly.

Soc. The good are to be regarded, and not the bad?

Cr. Yes.

Soc. And the opinions of the wise are good, and the opinions of the unwise are evil?

Cr. Certainly.

Soc. And what was said about another matter? Was the disciple in gymnastics supposed to attend to the praise and blame and opinion of every man, or of one man only — his physician or trainer, who‑ever that was?

Cr. Of one man only.

Soc. And he ought to fear the censure and wel‑come the praise of that one only, and not of the many?

Cr. That is clear.

Soc. And he ought to live and train, and eat and drink in the way which seems good to his single master who has understanding, rather than according to the opinion of all other men put together?

Cr. True.

Soc. And if he disobeys and disregards the opinion and approval of the one, and regards the opinion of the many who have no understanding, will he not suffer evil?

Cr. Certainly he will.

Soc. And what will the evil be, whither tending and what affecting, in the disobedient person?

Cr. Clearly, affecting the body; that is what is destroyed by the evil.

Soc. Very good; and is not this true, Crito, of other things which we need not separately enumerate? In the matter of just and unjust, fair and foul, good and evil, which are the subjects of our present consultation, ought we to follow the opinion of the many and to fear them; or the opinion of the one man who has understanding, and whom we ought to fear and reverence more than all the rest of the world: and whom deserting we shall destroy and injure that principle in us which may be assumed to be improved by justice and deteriorated by injustice; — is there not such a principle?

Cr. Certainly there is, Socrates.

Soc. Take a parallel instance: — if, acting under the advice of men who have no understanding, we destroy that which is improvable by health and deteriorated by disease — when that has been destroyed, I say, would life be worth having? And that is — the body?

Cr. Yes.

Soc. Could we live, having an evil and corrupted body?

Cr. Certainly not.

Soc. And will life be worth having, if that higher part of man be depraved, which is improved by justice and deteriorated by injustice? Do we suppose that principle, whatever it may be in man, which has to do with justice and injustice, to be inferior to the body?

Cr. Certainly not.

Soc. More honored, then?

Cr. Far more honored.

Soc. Then, my friend, we must not regard what the many say of us: but what he, the one man who has understanding of just and unjust, will say, and what the truth will say. And therefore you begin in error when you suggest that we should regard the opinion of the many about just and unjust, good and evil, honorable and dishonorable. — Well, some one will say, " but the many can kill us."

Cr. Yes, Socrates; that will clearly be the answer.

Soc. That is true: but still I find with surprise that the old argument is, as I conceive, unshaken as ever. And I should like to know whether I may say the same of another proposition — that not life, but a good life, is to be chiefly valued?

Cr. Yes, that also remains.

Soc. And a good life is equivalent to a just and honorable one — that holds also?

Cr. Yes, that holds.

Soc. From these premisses I proceed to argue the question whether I ought or ought not to try and escape without the consent of the Athenians: and if I am clearly right in escaping, then I will make the attempt; but if not, I will abstain. The other considerations which you mention, of money and loss of character and the duty of educating children, are, as I fear, only the doctrines of the multitude, who would be as ready to call people to life, if they were able, as they are to put them to death — and with as little reason. But now, since the argument has thus far prevailed, the only question which remains to be considered is, whether we shall do rightly either in escaping or in suffering others to aid in our escape and paying them in money and thanks, or whether we shall not do rightly; and if the latter, then death or any other calamity which may ensue on my remaining here must not be allowed to enter into the calculation.

Cr. I think that you are right, Socrates; how then shall we proceed?

Soc. Let us consider the matter together, and do you either refute me if you can, and I will be convinced; or else cease, my dear friend, from repeating to me that I ought to escape against the wishes of the Athenians: for I am extremely desirous to be persuaded by you, but not against my own better judgment. And now please to consider my first position, and do your best to answer me.

Cr. I will do my best.

Soc. Are we to say that we are never intentionally to do wrong, or that in one way we ought and in another way we ought not to do wrong, or is doing wrong always evil and dishonorable, as I was just now saying, and as has been already acknowledged by us? Are all our former admissions which were made within a few days to be thrown away? And have we, at our age, been earnestly discoursing with one another all our life long only to discover that we are no better than children? Or are we to rest assured, in spite of the opinion of the many, and in spite of consequences whether better or worse, of the truth of what was then said, that injustice is always an evil and dishonor to him who acts unjustly? Shall we affirm that?

Cr. Yes.

Soc. Then we must do no wrong?

Cr. Certainly not.

Soc. Nor when injured injure in return, as the many imagine; for we must injure no one at all?

Cr. Clearly not.

Soc. Again, Crito, may we do evil?

Cr. Surely not, Socrates.

Soc. And what of doing evil in return for evil, which is the morality of the many — is that just or not?

Cr. Not just.

Soc. For doing evil to another is the same as injuring him?

Cr. Very true.

Soc. Then we ought not to retaliate or render evil for evil to any one, whatever evil we may have suf‧fered from him. But I would have you consider, Crito, whether you really mean what you are saying. For this opinion has never been held, and never will be held, by any considerable number of persons; and those who are agreed and those who are not agreed upon this point have no common ground, and can only despise one another when they see how widely they differ. Tell me, then, whether you agree with and assent to my first principle, that neither injury nor retaliation nor warding off evil by evil is ever right. And shall that be the premiss of our argument? Or do you decline and dissent from this? For this has been of old and is still my opinion; but, if you are of another opinion, let me hear what you have to say. If, however, you remain of the same mind as formerly, I will proceed to the next step.

Cr. You may proceed, for I have not changed my mind.

Soc. Then I will proceed to the next step, which

may be put in the form of a question: — Ought a man to do what he admits to be right, or ought he to betray the right?

Cr. He ought to do what he thinks right.

Soc. But if this is true, what is the application? In leaving the prison against the will of the Athenians, do I wrong any? or rather do I not wrong those whom I ought least to wrong? Do I not desert the principles which were acknowledged by us to be just? What do you say?

Cr. I can not tell, Socrates; for I do not know.

Soc. Then consider the matter in this way: — Imagine that I am about to play truant (you may call the proceeding by any name which you like), and the laws and the government come and interrogate me: " Tell us, Socrates," they say; " what are you about? are you going by an act of yours to overturn us — the laws and the whole state, as far as in you lies? Do you imagine that a state can subsist and not be overthrown, in which the decisions of law have no power, but are set aside and overthrown by individuals?" What will be our answer, Crito, to these and the like words? Any one, and especially a clever rhetorician, will have a good deal to urge about the evil of setting aside the law which requires a sentence to be carried out; and we might reply, " Yes; but the state has injured us and given an unjust sentence." Suppose I say that?

Cr. Very good, Socrates.

Soc. " And was that our agreement with you?" the law would say; " or were you to abide by the sentence of the state?" And if I were to express astonishment at their saying this, the law would probably add: " Answer, Socrates, instead of opening your eyes: you are in the habit of asking and answering questions. Tell us what complaint you have to make against us which justifies you in attempting to destroy us and the state? In the first place did we not bring you into existence? Your father married your mother by our aid and begat you. Say whether you have any objection to urge against those of us who regulate marriage?" None, I should reply. "Or against those of us who regulate the system of nurture and education of children in which you were trained? Were not the laws, who have the charge of this, right in commanding your father to train you in music and gymnastic?" Right, I should reply. "Well then, since you were brought into the world and nurtured and educated by us, can you deny in the first place that you are our child and slave, as your fathers were before you? And if this is true you are not on equal terms with us; nor can you think that you have a right to do to us what we are doing to you. Would you have any right to strike or revile or do any other evil to a father or to your master, if you had one, when you have been struck or reviled by him, or received some other evil at his hands? — you would not say this? And because we think right to destroy you, do you think that you have any right to destroy us in return, and your country as far as in you lies? And will you, O professor of true virtue, say that you are justified in this? Has a philosopher like you failed to discover that our country is more to be valued and higher and holier far than mother or father or any ancestor, and more to be regarded in the eyes of the gods and of men of understanding? also to be soothed, and gently and reverently entreated when angry, even more than a father, and if not persuaded, obeyed? And when we are punished by her, whether with imprisonment or stripes, the punishment is to be endured in silence; and if she lead us to wounds or death in battle, thither we follow as is right; neither may any one yield or retreat or leave his rank, but whether in battle or in a court of law, or in any other place, he must do what his city and his country order him; or he must change their view of what is just: and if he may do no violence to his father or mother, much less may he do violence to his country." What answer shall we make to this, Crito? Do the laws speak truly, or do they not?

Cr. I think that they do.

Soc. Then the laws will say: " Consider, Socrates, if this is true, that in your present attempt you are going to do us wrong. For, after having brought you into the world, and nurtured and educated you, and given you and every other citizen a share in every good that we had to give, we further proclaim and give the right to every Athenian, that if he does not like us when he has come of age and has seen the ways of the city, and made our acquaintance, he may go where he pleases and take his goods with him; and none of us laws will forbid him or interfere with him. Any of you who does not like us and the city, and who wants to go to a colony or to any other city, may go where he likes, and take his goods with him. But he who has experience of the manner in which we order justice and administer the state, and still remains, has entered into an implied contract that he will do as we command him. And he who disobeys us is, as we maintain, thrice wrong; first, because in disobeying us he is disobeying his parents; secondly, because we are the authors of his education; thirdly, because he has made an agreement with us that he will duly obey our commands; and he neither obeys them nor convinces us that our commands are wrong; and we do not rudely impose them, but give them the alternative of obeying or convincing us;—that is what we offer, and he does neither. These are the sort of accusations to which, as we were saying, you, Socrates, will be exposed if you accomplish your intentions; you, above all other Athenians." Suppose I ask, why is this? they will justly retort upon me that I above all other men have acknowledged the agreement. " There is clear proof," they will say, " Socrates, that we and the city were not displeasing to you. Of all Athenians you have been the most constant resident in the city, which, as you never leave, you may be supposed to love. For you never went out of the city either to see the games, except once when you went to the Isthmus, or to any other place unless when you were on military service; nor did you travel as other men do. Nor had you any curiosity to know other states or their laws: your affections did not go beyond us and our state; we were your special favorites, and you acquiesced in our government of you; and this is the state in which you begat your children, which is a proof of your satisfaction. Moreover, you might, if you had liked, have fixed the penalty at banishment in the course of the trial — the state which refuses to let you go now would have let you go then. But you pretended that you preferred death to exile, and that you were not grieved at death. And now you have forgotten these fine sentiments, and pay no respect to us the laws, of whom you are the destroyer; and are doing what only a miserable slave would do, running away and turning your back upon the compacts and agreements which you made as a citizen. And first of all answer this very question: Are we right in saying that you agreed to be governed according to us in deed, and not in word only? Is that true or not?" How shall we answer that, Crito? Must we not agree?

Cr. There is no help, Socrates.

Soc. Then will they not say: " You, Socrates, are

breaking the covenants and agreements which you made with us at your leisure, not in any haste or under any compulsion or deception, but having had seventy years to think of them, during which time you were at liberty to leave the city, if we were not to your mind, or if our covenants appeared to you to be unfair. You had your choice, and might have gone either to Lacedaemon or Crete, which you often praise for their good government, or to some other Hellenic or foreign state. Whereas you, above all other Athenians, seemed to be so fond of the state, or, in other words, of us her laws (for who would like a state that has no laws), that you never stirred out of her; the halt, the blind, the maimed were not more stationary in her than you were. And now you run away and forsake your agreements. Not so, Socrates, if you will take our advice; do not make yourself ridiculous by escaping out of the city.

" For just consider, if you transgress and err in this sort of way, what good will you do either to yourself or to your friends? That your friends will be driven into exile and deprived of citizenship, or will lose their property, is tolerably certain; and you yourself, if you fly to one of the neighboring cities, as, for example, Thebes or Megara, both of which are well-governed cities, will come to them as an enemy, Socrates, and their government will be against you, and all patriotic citizens will cast an evil eye upon you as a subverter of the laws, and you will confirm in the minds of the judges the justice of their own condemnation of you. For he who is a corruptor of the laws is more than likely to be corruptor of the young and foolish portion of mankind. Will you then flee from well-ordered cities and virtuous men? and is existence worth having on these terms? Or will you go to them without shame, and talk to them, Socrates?

And what will you say to them? What you say here about virtue and justice and institutions and laws being the best things among men. Would that be decent of you? Surely not. But if you go away from well-governed states to Crito's friends in Thessaly, where there is a great disorder and license, they will be charmed to have the tale of your escape from prison, set off with ludicrous particulars of the manner in which you were wrapped in a goatskin or some other disguise, and metamorphosed as the fashion of runaways is — that is very likely; but will there be no one to remind you that in your old age you violated the most sacred laws from a miserable desire of a little more life. Perhaps not, if you keep them in a good temper; but if they are out of temper you will hear many degrading things; you will live, but how? — as the flatterer of all men, and the servant of all men; and doing what? — eating and drinking in Thessaly, having gone abroad in order that you may get a dinner. And where will be your fine sentiments about justice and virtue then? Say that you wish to live for the sake of your children, that you may bring them up and educate them — will you take them into Thessaly and deprive them of Athenian citizenship? Is that the benefit which you would confer upon them? Or are you under the impression that they will be better cared for and educated here if you are still alive, although absent from them; for that your friends will take care of them? Do you fancy that if you are an inhabitant of Thessaly they will take care of them, and if you are an inhabitant of the other world they will not take care of them? Nay; but if they who call themselves friends are truly friends, they surely will.

"Listen, then, Socrates, to us who have brought you up. Think not of life and children first, and of justice afterwards, but of justice first, that you may be justified before the princes of the world below. For neither will you nor any that belong to you be happier or holier or juster in this life, or happier in another, if you do as Crito bids. Now you depart in innocence, a sufferer and not a doer of evil; a victim, not of the laws, but of men. But if you go forth, returning evil for evil, and injury for injury, breaking the covenants and agreements which you have made with us, and wronging those whom you ought least to wrong, that is to say, yourself, your friends, your country, and us, we shall be angry with you while you live, and our brethren, the laws in the world below, will receive you as an enemy; for they will know that you have done your best to destroy us. Listen, then, to us and not to Crito."

This is the voice which I seem to hear murmuring in my ears, like the sound of the flute in the ears of the mystic; that voice, I say, is humming in my ears, and prevents me from hearing any other. And I know that anything more which you may say will be vain. Yet speak, if you have anything to say.

Cr. I have nothing to say, Socrates.

Soc. Then let me follow the intimations of the will of God.

PHAEDO

INTRODUCTION

AFTER an interval of some months or years, and at Phlius a
town of Sicyon, the tale of the last hours of Socrates is narrated
to Echecrates and other Phliasians by Phaedo the " beloved disciple." The Dialogue necessarily takes the form of a narrative,
because Socrates has to be described acting as well as speaking.
The minutest particulars of the event are interesting to distant
friends, and the narrator has an equal interest in them.

During the voyage of the sacred ship to and from Delos,
which has occupied thirty days, the execution of Socrates has
been deferred. (Cp. Xen. Mem. iv. 8. 2.) The time has been
passed by him in conversation with a select company of disciples.
But now the holy season is over, and the disciples meet earlier
than usual in order that they may converse with Socrates for the
last time. Those who were present, and those who might have
been expected to be present, are specially mentioned. There are
Simmias and Cebes, two disciples of Philolaus whom Socrates
" by his enchantments has attracted from Thebes " (Mem. iii. 11.
17), Crito the aged friend, the attendant of the prison, who is
as good as a friend — these take part in the conversation. There
are present also, Hermogenes, from whom Xenophon derived his
information about the trial of Socrates (Mem. iv. 8. 4), the
" madman " Apollodorus, Euclid and Terpsion from Megara,
Ctesippus, Antisthenes, Menexenus, and some other less-known
members of the Socratic circle, all of whom are silent auditors.
Aristippus and Plato are noted as absent. Soon the wife and
children of Socrates are sent away, under the direction of Crito;
he himself has just been released from chains, and is led by this
circumstance to make the natural remark that " pleasure follows
pain." (Observe that Plato is preparing the way for his doctrine
of the alternation of opposites.) " Aesop would have represented
them in a fable as a two-headed creature of the gods." The
mention of Aesop reminds Cebes of a question which had been
asked by Evenus the poet: " Why Socrates, who was not a poet,
while in prison had been putting Aesop into verse? " — " Because
several times in his life he had been warned in dreams that he
should make music; and as he was about to die and was not

569

certain what was the meaning of this, he wished to fulfil the admonition in the letter as well as in the spirit, by writing verses as well as by cultivating philosophy. Tell Evenus this and bid him follow me in death." "He is not the sort of man to do that, Socrates." "Why, is he not a philosopher?" "Yes." "Then he will be willing to die, although he will not take his own life, for that is held not to be right."

Cebes asks why men say that suicide is not right, if death is to be accounted a good? Well, (1) according to one explanation, because man is a prisoner, and is not allowed to open the door of his prison and run away — this is the truth in a "mystery." Or rather, perhaps, (2) because man is not his own property, but a possession of the gods, and he has no right to make away with that which does not belong to him. But why, asks Cebes, if he is a possession of the gods, will he wish to die and leave them? for he is under their protection; and surely he can not take better care of himself than they take of him. Simmias explains that Cebes is really referring to Socrates, whom they think too unmoved at the prospect of leaving the gods and his friends. Socrates answers that he is going to other gods who are wise and good, and perhaps to better friends; and he professes that he is ready to defend himself against the charge of Cebes. They shall be his judges, and he hopes that he will be more successful in convincing them than he had been in convincing the court.

The philosopher desires death — which the wicked world will insinuate that he also deserves: and perhaps he does, but not in any sense which they are capable of understanding. Enough of them: the real question is, What is the nature of that death which he desires? Death is the separation of soul and body — and the philosopher desires such a separation. He would like to be freed from the dominion of bodily pleasures and of the senses, which are always perturbing his mental vision. He wants to get rid of eyes and ears, and with the light of the mind only to behold the light of truth. All the evils and impurities and necessities of men come from the body. And death separates him from these evils, which in this life he can not wholly cast aside. Why then should he repine when the hour of separation arrives? Why, if he is dead while he lives, should he fear that other death, through which alone he can behold wisdom in her purity?

Besides, the philosopher has notions of good and evil unlike those of other men. For they are courageous because they are afraid of greater dangers, and temperate because they desire greater pleasures. But he disdains this balancing of pleasures and pains; he knows no virtue but that which is the companion of wisdom. All the virtues, including wisdom, are regarded by him only as purifications of the soul. And this was the meaning of the founders of the mysteries when they said, " Many are the wand-bearers but few are the mystics." (Cp. Matt. xxii. 14: " Many are called, but few are chosen.") And in the hope that he is one of these mystics, Socrates is now departing. This is his answer to those who charge him with indifference at the prospect of leaving the gods and his friends.

Still, a fear is expressed that the soul upon leaving the body, may vanish away like smoke or air. Socrates in answer appeals first of all to the old Orphic tradition that the souls of the dead are in the world below, and that the living come from them. This he attempts to found on a philosophical assumption that all opposites — e. g. less, greater; weaker, stronger; sleeping, waking; life, death — are generated out of each other. Nor can this process of generation be only a passage from living to dying, for then all would end in death. The perpetual sleeper (Endymion) would be no longer distinguished, for all the world would sink in rest. The circle of nature is not complete unless the living come from the dead as well as pass to them.

The favorite Platonic doctrine of reminiscence is then adduced as a confirmation of the preëxistence of the soul. Some proofs of this doctrine are demanded. One proof given is the same as that of the Meno, and is derived from the latent knowledge of mathematics, which may be elicited from an unlearned person when a diagram is presented to him. Again, there is a power of association, which from seeing Simmias may remember Cebes, or from seeing a picture of Simmias may remember Simmias. The lyre may recall the player of the lyre, and equal pieces of wood or stone may be associated with the higher notion of absolute equality. But here observe that material equalities fall short of the conception of absolute equality with which they are compared, and which is the measure of them. And the measure or standard must be prior to that which is measured, the idea of equality prior to the visible equals. And if prior to them, then prior also to the perceptions of the senses which recall them, and therefore either given before birth or at birth. But all men have not this knowledge, nor have any without a process of reminiscence; and this is a proof that it is not innate or given at birth (unless indeed it was given **and taken away at the same** instant, which is absurd). But if not given to men in birth, it must have been given before birth — this is the only alternative which remains. And if we had ideas in a former state, then our souls must have existed and must have had intelligence in a former state. The preëxistence of the soul stands or falls with the doctrine of ideas.

It is objected by Simmias and Cebes that these arguments only prove a former and not a future existence. Socrates answers this objection by recalling the previous argument, in which he had shown that the living had come from the dead. But the fear that the soul at departing may vanish into air (especially if there is a wind blowing at the time) has not yet been charmed away. He proceeds: When we fear that the soul will vanish away, let us ask ourselves what is that which we suppose to be liable to dissolution? Is it the simple or the compound, the unchanging or the changing, the invisible idea or the visible object of sense? Clearly the latter and not the former; and therefore not the soul, which in her own pure thought is unchangeable, and only when using the senses descends into the region of change. Again, the soul commands, the body serves: in this respect too the soul is akin to the divine, and the body to the mortal. And in every point of view the soul is the image of divinity and immortality, and the body of the human and mortal. And whereas the body is liable to speedy dissolution, the soul is almost if not quite indissoluble. Yet even the body may be preserved for ages by the embalmer's art; how much more the soul returning into herself on her way to the good and wise God! She has been practising death all her life long, and is now finally released from the errors and follies and passions of men, and forever dwells in the company of the gods.

But the soul which is polluted and engrossed by the corporeal, and has no eye except that of the senses, and is weighed down by the bodily appetites, can not attain to this abstraction. In her fear of the world below she lingers about her sepulchre, a ghostly apparition, saturated with sense, and therefore visible. At length she enters into the body of some animal of a nature congenial to her former life of sensuality or violence, and becomes an ass or a wolf or a kite. And of these earthly souls the happiest are those who have practised virtue without philosophy; they are allowed to pass into gentle and civil natures, such as bees and ants. But only the philosopher who departs pure is permitted to enter the company of the gods. This is the reason why he abstains from fleshly lusts, and not from the fear of loss or disgrace, which are the motives of other men. He too has been a captive, and the willing agent of his own captivity. But philosophy has spoken to him, and he has heard her voice; she has gently entreated him, and brought his soul out of the " miry clay," and purged away the mists of passion and the illusions of sense which envelope her, and taught her to resist the influence of pleasures and pains, which are like nails fastening her to the body. To that prison-house she will not return; and therefore she abstains from bodily pleasures — not from a desire of having more or greater ones, which is the exchange of commerce and not of virtue, but because she knows that only in the calm of pleasures and passions she will behold the light of truth.

Simmias and Cebes remain in doubt; but they are unwilling to raise objections at such a time. Socrates wonders at this. Let them regard him rather as the swan, who, having sung the praises of Apollo all his life long, sings at his death more lustily than ever. Simmias acknowledges that there is cow-ardice in not probing truth to the bottom. " And if truth divine and inspired is not to be had, then let a man take the best of human notions, and upon this frail bark let him sail through life." He proceeds to state his difficulty: It has been argued that the soul is invisible and incorporeal, and therefore immortal, and prior to the body. But is not the soul acknowledged to be a harmony, and has she not the same relation to the body, as the harmony — which like her is invisible — has to the lyre? And yet the harmony does not survive the lyre. Cebes has also an objection, which like Simmias he expresses in a figure. He is willing to admit that the soul is more lasting than the body. But the more lasting nature of the soul does not prove her im-mortality; for after having worn out many bodies in a single life, and many more in successive births and deaths, she may at last perish, or, as Socrates afterwards restates the objection, the very act of birth may be the beginning of her death, and the last body may survive the last soul, just as the coat of an old weaver is left behind him after he is dead, although a man is more last-ing than his coat. And he who would prove the immortality of the soul, must prove not only that the soul outlives one or many bodies, but that she outlives them all.

The audience, like the chorus in a play, for a moment inter-pret the feelings of the actors; there is a temporary depression. and then the inquiry is resumed. It is a melancholy reflection that arguments, like men, are apt to be deceivers; and those who have been often deceived become distrustful both of arguments and of friends. But this unfortunate experience should not make us either haters of men or haters of arguments. The hatred of arguments is equally mistaken, whether we are going to live or die. At the approach of death Socrates desires to be impartial, and yet he can not help feeling that he has too great an interest in the truth of his own argument. And therefore he wishes his friends to examine and refute him, if they think that he is not speaking the truth.

Socrates requests Simmias and Cebes to state their objections again. They do not go to the length of denying the preëxistence of ideas. Simmias is of opinion that the soul is a harmony of the body. But the admission of the preëxistence of ideas, and therefore of the soul, is at variance with this. For a harmony is an effect, whereas the soul is not an effect, but a cause; a harmony follows, but the soul leads; a harmony admits of degrees, and the soul has no degrees. Again, upon the supposition that the soul is a harmony, why is one soul better than another? Are they more or less harmonized, or is there one harmony within another? But the soul does not admit of degrees, and can not therefore be more or less harmonized. Further, the soul is often engaged in resisting the affections of the body, as Homer describes Odysseus "rebuking his heart." Could he have written this under the idea that the soul is a harmony of the body? Nay rather, are we not contradicting Homer and ourselves in affirming anything of the sort?

The goddess Harmonia, as Socrates playfully terms the argument of Simmias, has been happily disposed of; and now an answer has to be given to the Theban Cadmus. Socrates recapitulates the argument of Cebes, which, as he remarks, involves the whole question of natural growth or causation; about this he proposes to narrate his own mental experience. When he was young he had puzzled himself with physics: he had inquired into the growth and decay of animals, and the origin of thought, until at last he began to doubt the self-evident fact that growth is the result of eating and drinking, and thus he arrived at the conclusion that he was not meant for such inquiries. Nor was he less perplexed with notions of comparison and number. At first he had imagined himself to understand differences of greater and less, and to know that ten is two more than eight, and the like. But now those very notions appeared to him to contain a contradiction. For how can one be divided into two? or two be compounded into one? These are difficulties which Socrates can not answer. Of generation and destruction he knows nothing. But he has a confused notion of another method in which matters of this sort are to be investigated.

Then he heard some one reading out of a book of Anaxagoras, that mind is the cause of all things. And he said to himself: If mind is the cause of all things, mind must dispose them all for the best. The new teacher will show me this "order of the best" in man and nature. How great had been his hopes and how great his disappointment! For he found that his new friend was anything but consistent in his use of mind as a cause, and that he soon introduced winds, waters, and other eccentric notions. It was as if a person had said that Socrates is sitting here because he is made up of bones and muscles, instead of telling the true reason — that he is here because the Athenians have thought good to sentence him to death, and he has thought good to await his sentence. Had his bones and muscles been left by him to their own ideas of right, they would long ago have taken themselves off. But surely there is a great confusion of the cause and condition in all this. And this confusion also leads people into all sorts of erroneous theories about the position and motions of the earth. None of them know how much stronger than any Atlas is the power of the best. But this "best" is still undiscovered; and in inquiring after the cause, we can only hope to attain the second best.

Now there is a danger in the contemplation of the nature of things, as there is a danger in looking at the sun during an eclipse, unless the precaution is taken of looking only at the image reflected in the water, or in a glass. And I was afraid, says Socrates, that I might injure the eye of the soul. I thought that I had better return to the old and safe method of ideas. Though I do not mean to say that he who contemplates existence through the medium of ideas sees only through a glass darkly, any more than he who contemplates actual effects.

If the existence of ideas is granted to him, Socrates is of opinion that he will then have no difficulty in proving the immortality of the soul. He will only ask for a further admission: — that beauty is the cause of the beautiful, greatness the cause of the great, smallness of the small, and so on of other things. Thus he avoids the contradictions of greater and less (greater by reason of that which is smaller!), of addition and subtraction, and the other difficulties of relation. These subtleties he is for leaving to wiser heads than his own; he prefers to test ideas by their consequences, and, if asked to give an account of them, goes back to some higher idea or hypothesis which appears to him to be the best, until at last he arrives at a resting-place.

The doctrine of ideas, which has long ago received the assent of the Socratic circle, is now affirmed by the Phliasian auditor to command the assent of any men of sense. The narrative is continued; Socrates is desirous of explaining how opposite ideas may appear to coëxist but do not really coëxist in the same thing or person. For example, Simmias may be said to have greatness and also smallness, because he is greater than Socrates and less than Phaedo. And yet Simmias is not really great and also small, but only when compared to Phaedo and Socrates. I use the illustration, says Socrates, because I want to show you not only that ideal opposites exclude one another, but also the opposites in us. I, for example, having the attribute of smallness remain small, and can not become great: the smallness in me drives out greatness.

One of the company here remarked that this was inconsistent with the old assertion that opposites generated opposites. But that, replies Socrates, was affirmed, not of opposite ideas either in us or in nature, but of opposite things — not of life and death, but of individuals living and dying. When this objection has been removed, Socrates proceeds: This doctrine of the mutual exclusion of opposites is not only true of the opposites themselves, but of things which are inseparable from them. For example, cold and heat are opposed; and fire, which is inseparable from heat, can not coëxist with cold, or snow, which is inseparable from cold, with heat. Again, the number three excludes the number four, because three is an odd number and four is an even number, and the odd is opposed to the even. Thus we are able to proceed a step beyond "the safe and simple answer." We may say, not only that the odd excludes the even, but that the number three, which participates in oddness, excludes the even. And in like manner, not only does life exclude death, but the soul, of which life is the inseparable attribute, also excludes death. And that of which life is the inseparable attribute is by the force of the terms imperishable. If the odd principle were imperishable, then the number three would not perish, but remove on the approach of the even principle. But the immortal is imperishable; and therefore the soul on the approach of death does not perish but removes.

Thus all objections appear to be finally silenced. And now the application has to be made: If the soul is immortal, "what manner of persons ought we to be?" having regard not only to time but to eternity. For death is not the end of all, and the wicked is not released from his evil by death; but every one carries with him into the world below that which he is and that which he becomes, and that only.

For after death the soul is carried away to judgment, and when she has received her punishment returns to earth in the course of ages. The wise soul is conscious of her situation, and follows the attendant angel who guides her through the windings of the world below; but the impure soul wanders hither and thither without a guide, and is carried at last to her own place, as the pure soul is also carried away to hers. " In order that you may understand this, I must first describe to you the nature and conformation of the earth."

Now the whole earth is a globe placed in the centre of the heavens, and is maintained there by the perfection of balance. That which we call the earth is only a small hollow, of which there are many; but the true earth is above, and is a finer and subtler element, and is full of precious stones and bright colors, of which the stones and colors in our earth are but fragments and reflections, and the earth itself is corroded and crusted over just as the shore is by the sea. And if, like birds, we could fly to the surface of the air, in the same manner that fishes come to the top of the sea, then we should behold the true earth and the true heaven and the true stars. This heavenly earth is of divers colors, sparkling with jewels brighter than gold and whiter than any snow, having flowers and fruits innumerable. And the inhabitants dwell some on the shore of the sea of air, others in " islets of the blest," and they hold converse with the gods, and behold the sun, moon and stars as they truly are, and their other blessedness is of a piece with this.

But the interior of the earth has other and deeper hollows, and one huge chasm or opening called Tartarus, into which vast streams of water and fire are ever flowing to and fro, of which small portions find their way to the surface and form seas and rivers and volcanoes. There is perpetual inhalation and exhalation of the air rising and falling as the waters pass into the depths of the earth and return again, in their course forming lakes and rivers, but never descending below the centre of the earth, the opposite side of which is a precipice to the rivers on both sides. The rivers are many and mighty, and there are four principal ones, Oceanus, Acheron, Pyriphlegethon, and Cocytus. Oceanus is the river which encircles the earth; Acheron takes an opposite direction, and after flowing under the earth and in desert places at last reaches the Acherusian lake, and this is the river at which the dead await their return to earth. Pyriphlegethon is a stream of fire, which coils around the earth and flows into the depths of Tartarus. The fourth river (Cocytus) is that which is called by the poets the Stygian river, and falls into, and forms the lake Styx, receiving strange powers in the waters. This river, too, falls into Tartarus.

The dead are first of all judged according to their deeds, and those who are incurable are thrust into Tartarus, from which they never come out. Those who have only committed venial sins are first purified of them, and then rewarded for the good which they have done. Those who have committed crimes, great indeed, but not unpardonable, are thrust into Tartarus, but are cast forth at the end of the year on the shores of the rivers, where they stand crying to their victims to let them come out, and if they prevail, then they are let out and their sufferings cease; if not, they are borne in a ceaseless whirl along the rivers of Tartarus. The pure souls also receive their reward, and have their abode in the upper earth, and a select few in still fairer " mansions."

Socrates is not prepared to insist on the literal accuracy of this description, but he is confident that something of the kind is true. He who has sought after the pleasures of knowledge and rejected the pleasures of the body, has reason to be of good hope at the approach of death, whose voice is already heard calling to him, and will be heard calling by all men.

The hour has come at which he must drink the poison, and not much remains to be done. How shall they bury him? That is a question which he refuses to entertain, for they are not burying him, but his dead body. His friends had once been sureties that he would remain, and they shall now be sureties that he has run away. Yet he would not die without the customary ceremonies of washing and burial. Shall he make a libation of the poison? In the spirit he will, but not in the letter. One request he utters in the very act of death, which has been a puzzle to after ages. The puzzle has been occasioned by the simplicity of his words, for there is no reason to suppose that they have any hidden meaning. With a sort of irony he remembers that a trifling religious duty is still unfulfilled, just as above he is represented as desirous before he departs to make a few verses in order to satisfy a scruple about the meaning of a dream.

1. The doctrine of the immortality of the soul has such a great interest for all mankind that they are apt to rebel against any

examination of the nature of their belief. They do not like to acknowledge that this, as well as the other " eternal ideas " of man, has a history in time, which may be traced in Greek poetry or philosophy, and also in the Hebrew Scriptures. They convert feeling into reasoning, and throw a network of dialectics over that which is really a deeply-rooted instinct. In the same temper which Socrates reproves in himself they are disposed to think that even bad arguments will do no harm, for they will die with them, and while they live they will gain by the delusion. But there is a better and higher spirit to be gathered from the Phaedo, as well as from the other writings of Plato, which says that first principles should be most constantly reviewed, and that the highest subjects demand of us the greatest accuracy.

2. Modern philosophy is perplexed at this whole question, which is sometimes fairly given up and handed over to the realm of faith. The perplexity should not be forgotten by us when we attempt to submit the Phaedo of Plato to the requirements of logic. For what idea can we form of the soul when separated from the body? Or how can the soul be united with the body and still be independent? Is the soul related to the body as the ideal to the real, or as the whole to the parts, or as the subject to the object, or as the cause to the effect, or as the end to the means? Shall we say with Aristotle, that the soul is the entelechy or form of an organized living body? or with Plato, that she has a life of her own? Is the Pythagorean image of the harmony, or of the monad, the truer expression? Is the soul related to the body as sight to the eye, or as the boatman to his boat? And in another state of being is the soul to be conceived of as vanishing into infinity, hardly possessing an existence which she can call her own, as in the pantheistic system of Spinoza and others? or as an individual spirit informed with another body and retaining the impress of her former character? Or is the opposition of soul and body a mere illusion, and the true self neither soul nor body, but the union of the two in the " I " which is above them? And is death the assertion of this individuality in the higher nature, and the falling away into nothingness of the lower? Or are we vainly attempting to pass the boundaries of human thought? The body and the soul seem to be inseparable, not only in fact, but in our conceptions of them; and any philosophy which too closely unites them, or too widely separates them, either in this life or in another, disturbs the balance of human nature. Neither Plato nor any other philosopher has

perfectly adjusted them, or been perfectly consistent with him-self in describing their relation to one another.

3. Again, believing in the immortality of the soul, we must still ask the question of Socrates, " what is that which we sup-pose to be immortal? " Is it the personal and individual element in us, or the spiritual and universal? Is it the principle of knowledge or of goodness, or the union of the two? Is it the mere force of life which is determined to be, or the consciousness of self which can not be got rid of, or the fire of genius which refuses to be extinguished? Or is there a hidden being which is allied to the Author of all existence, who is because he is per-fect, and to whom our ideas of perfection give us a title to be-long? Whatever answer is given by us to these questions, there still remains the necessity of allowing the permanence of evil, if not forever, at any rate for a time, in order that the wicked " may not have too good a bargain." For the annihilation of evil at death, or the eternal duration of it, seem to involve equal difficulties in the moral order of the universe. Sometimes we are led by our feelings, rather than by our reason, to think of the good and wise only as existing in another life. Why should the mean, the weak, the idiot, the infant, the herd of men who have never in any proper sense the use of reason, reappear with blink-ing eyes in the light of another world? But our second thought is that the hope of humanity is a common one, and that all or none have a right to immortality. Reason does not allow us to suppose that we have any greater claims than others, and ex-perience sometimes reveals to us unexpected flashes of the higher nature in those whom we had despised. Such are some of the distracting thoughts which press upon us when we attempt to assign any form to our conceptions of a future state.

4. Again, ideas must be given through something; and we are always prone to argue about the soul from analogies of outward things which may serve to embody our thoughts, but are also partly delusive. For we can not reason from the natural to the spiritual, or from the outward to the inward. The progress of physiological science, without bringing us nearer to the great secret, has perhaps tended to remove some erroneous notions respecting the relations of body and mind, and in this we have the advantage of the ancients. But no one imagines that any seed of immortality is to be discerned in our mortal frames. The result seems to be that those who have thought most deeply on the immortality of the soul, have been content to rest their belief on the agreement of the more enlightened part of mankind.

and on the inseparable connection of such a doctrine with the existence of a God, and our ideas of divine justice — also in a less degree on the impossibility of thinking otherwise of those whom we reverence in this world. And after all has been said, the figure, the analogy, the argument, are felt to be only approx-imations in different forms to the expression of the common sentiment of the human heart.

5. The Phaedo of Plato may also be regarded as a dialectical approximation to the truth of immortality. Beginning in mystery, Socrates, in the intermediate part of the Dialogue, attempts to bring the doctrine of a future life into connection with his theory of knowledge. In proportion as he succeeds in this, the individual seems to disappear in a more general notion of the soul; the contemplation of ideas " under the form of eternity " takes the place of past and future states of existence. His language may be compared to that of some modern philosophers, who speak of eternity, not in the sense of perpetual duration of time, but as an ever-present quality of the soul. Yet at the conclusion of the Dialogue, having " arrived at the end of the intellectual world," he replaces the veil of mythology, and describes the soul and her attendant genius in the language of the mysteries or of a disciple of Zoroaster. Nor can we fairly demand of Plato a consistency which is wanting among ourselves, who acknowledge that another world is beyond the range of human thought, and yet are always seeking to represent the mansions of heaven or hell in the colors of the painter, or in the descriptions of the poet or rhetorician.

6. The doctrine of the immortality of the soul was not new to the Greeks in the age of Socrates, but, like the unity of God, had a foundation in the popular belief. The old Homeric notion of a gibbering ghost flitting away to Hades; or of a few illustrious heroes enjoying the isles of the blest; or of an existence divided between the two; or the Hesiodic, of righteous spirits, who become guardian angels, — had given place in the mysteries and the Orphic poets to representations, partly fanciful, of a future state of rewards and punishments. The reticence of the Greeks on public occasions and in some part of their literature respecting this " underground " religion, is not to be taken as a measure of the diffusion of such beliefs. If Pericles in the funeral oration is silent on the consolations of immortality, the poet Pindar and the tragedians on the other hand constantly assume the continued existence of the dead in an upper or under world. Darius and Laius are still alive; Antigone will be dear

to her brethren after death; the way to the palace of Cronos
is found by those who "have thrice departed from evil." The
tragedy of the Greeks is not "rounded" by this life, but is
deeply set in decrees of fate and mysterious workings of powers
beneath the earth. In the caricature of Aristophanes there is
also a witness to the common sentiment. The Ionian and Pythagorean philosophies arose, and some new elements were added
to the popular belief. The individual must find an expression
as well as the world. Either the soul was supposed to exist in
the form of a magnet or of a particle of fire, or light, or air, or
water; or of a number or of a harmony of number; or to be or
have, like the stars, a principle of motion. At length Anaxagoras, hardly distinguishing between life and mind, or between
mind human and divine, attained the pure abstraction; and this,
like the other abstractions of Greek philosophy, sank deep into
the human intelligence. The opposition of the intelligible and
the sensible, and of God to the world, supplied an analogy which
assisted in the separation of soul and body. If ideas were separable from phenomena, mind was also separable from matter;
if the ideas were eternal, the mind that conceived them was eternal too. As the unity of God was more distinctly acknowledged
the conception of the human soul became more developed. The
succession, or alternation of life and death, had occurred to
Heracleitus. The Eleatic Parmenides had stumbled upon the
modern thesis, that "thought and being are the same." The
eastern belief in transmigration defined the sense of individuality; and some, like Empedocles, fancied that the blood which
they had shed in another state of being was crying against them,
and that for thirty thousand years they were to be "fugitives
and vagabonds upon the earth." The desire of recognizing a
lost love or friend in the world below is a natural feeling which,
in that age as well as in every other, has given distinctness to
the hope of immortality. Nor were ethical considerations wanting, partly derived from the necessity of punishing the greater
sort of criminals, whom no avenging power of this world could
reach. The voice of conscience, too, was heard reminding the
good man that he was not altogether innocent. To these indistinct longings and fears an expression was given in the mysteries and Orphic poets: a "heap of books," passing under the
names of Musaeus and Orpheus in Plato's time were filled with
notions of an under world.

7. Yet probably the belief in the individuality of the soul after
death had but a feeble hold on the Greek mind. Like the per-

sonality of God, the personality of man in a future state was not inseparably bound up with the reality of his existence. For the distinction between the personal and impersonal, and also between the divine and human, was far less marked to the Greek than to ourselves. And as Plato readily passes from the notion of the good to that of God, he also passes almost imperceptibly to himself and his reader from the future life of the individual soul to the eternal being of the absolute soul. There has been a clearer statement and a clearer denial of the belief in modern times than is found in early Greek philosophy, and hence the comparative silence on the whole subject which is often remarked in ancient writers, and particularly in Aristotle. For Plato and Aristotle are not further removed in their teaching about the immortality of the soul than they are in their theory of knowledge.

8. That in an age when logic was beginning to mould human thought, Plato should have cast his belief in immortality into a logical form, is not surprising. And when we consider how much the doctrine of ideas was also one of words, we can not wonder that he should have fallen into verbal fallacies: early logic is always mistaking the truth of the form for the truth of the matter. It is easy to see that the alternation of opposites is not the same as the generation of them out of each other; and that the generation of them out of each other, which is the first argument in the Phaedo, is at variance with their mutual exclusion of each other, whether in themselves or in us, which is the last. For even if we admit the distinction which he draws between the opposites and the things which have the opposites, still individuals fall under the latter class; and we have to pass out of the region of human hopes and fears to a conception of an abstract soul which is the impersonation of the ideas. Such a conception, which in Plato himself is but half expressed, is unmeaning to us, and relative only to a particular stage in the history of thought. The doctrine of reminiscence is also a fragment of a former world, which has no place in the philosophy of modern times. But Plato had the wonders of psychology just opening to him, and he had not the explanation of them which is supplied by the analysis of language and the history of the human mind. The question, "Whence come our abstract ideas?" he could only answer by an imaginary hypothesis. Nor is it difficult to see that his crowning argument is purely verbal, and is but the expression of an instinctive confidence put into a logical form: — "The soul is immortal because it con-

tains a principle of imperishableness." Nor does he himself
seem at all to be aware that nothing is added to human knowledge by his " safe and simple answer," that beauty is the cause
of the beautiful; and that he is merely reasserting the Eleatic
being " divided by the Pythagorean numbers," against the Heracleitean doctrine of perpetual generation. The answer to the
" very serious question " of generation and destruction is really
the denial of them. For this he would substitute, as in the Republic, a system of ideas, tested not by experience, but by their
consequences, and not explained by actual causes, but by a
higher, that is, more general notion: consistency with themselves is all that is required of them.

9. To deal fairly with such arguments they should not only
not be separated from the age to which they belong, but they
should be translated as far as possible into their modern equiv-
alents. " If the ideas of men are eternal, their souls are eternal,
and if not the ideas, then not the souls." Such an argument
stands nearly in the same relation to Plato and his age, as the
argument from the existence of God to immortality among ourselves. " If God exists, then the soul exists after death; and
if there is no God, there is no existence of the soul after death."
For the ideas are to his mind the reality, the truth, the principle
of permanence, as well as of mind and order in the world. When
Simmias and Cebes say that they are more strongly persuaded
of the existence of ideas than they are of the immortality of
the soul, they represent fairly enough the order of thought in
Greek philosophy. And we might say in the same way that
we are more certain of the existence of God than we are of the
immortality of the soul, and are led by the belief in the one to
a belief in the other. The parallel, as Socrates would say, is
not perfect, but agrees in as far as the mind in either case is
regarded, as dependent on something above and beyond herself.
Nor need we shrink from pressing the analogy one step further:
" We are more certain of our ideas of truth and right than we
are of the existence of God, and are led on in the order of thought
from one to the other."

10. The main argument of the Phaedo is derived from the
existence of eternal ideas of which the soul is a partaker; the
other argument of the alternation of opposites is replaced by this.
And there have not been wanting philosophers of the idealist
school who have imagined that the doctrine of the immortality
of the soul is a theory of knowledge only, and that in all that
precedes Plato is preparing for this. Such a view is far from

lying on the surface of the Phaedo, and seems to be inconsistent with the Gorgias and the Republic. Those who maintain it are immediately compelled to renounce the shadow which they have grasped, as a play of words only. But the truth is, that Plato in his argument for the immortality of the soul has collected many elements of proof or persuasion, ethical and mythological as well as dialectical, which are not easily to be reconciled with one another; and he is as much in earnest about his doctrine of retribution, which is repeated in all his more ethical writings, as about his theory of knowledge. And while we may fairly translate the dialectical into the language of Hegel, and the religious and mythological into the language of Dante or Bunyan, the ethical speaks to us still in the same voice, reaching across the ages.

11. Two arguments of this sort occur in the Phaedo. The first may be described as the aspiration of the soul after another sort of being. Like the Oriental or Christian ascetic, the philosopher is seeking to withdraw from impurities of sense, to leave the world and the things of the world, and to find his higher self. Plato recognizes in these aspirations the foretaste of immortality; as Butler and Addison in modern times have argued, the one from the moral tendencies of mankind, the other from the progress of the soul towards perfection. In using this argument Plato has certainly confused the soul which has left the body, with the soul of the good and wise. Such a confusion was natural, and arose partly out of the antithesis of soul and body. The soul in her own essence, and the soul " clothed upon " with virtues and graces, were easily interchanged with one another, because on a subject which passes expression the distinctions of language can hardly be maintained.

12. The other ethical proof of the immortality of the soul is derived from the necessity of retribution. The wicked would be too well off if their evil deeds came to an end. It is not to be supposed that an Ardiaeus, an Archelaus, an Ismenias could ever have suffered the penalty of their crimes in this world. The manner in which this retribution is accomplished Plato represents under the figure of mythology. Doubtless he felt that it was easier to improve than to invent, and that in religion especially the traditional form was required in order to give verisimilitude to the myth. The myth too is far more probable to that age than to ours, and may fairly be regarded as " one guess among many " about the nature of the earth, which he cleverly supports by the indications of geology. Not that he

insists on the absolute truth of his own particular notions: " no man of sense will be confident of that; but he will be confident that something of the kind is true." As in other passages, he wins belief for his fictions by the moderation of his statements; he does not, like Dante or Swedenborg, allow himself to be deceived by his own creations.

The Dialogue must be read in the light of the situation. And first of all we are struck by the calmness of the scene. Like the spectators at the time, we can not pity Socrates; his mien and his language are so noble and fearless. He is the same as he ever was, but milder and gentler, and he has in no degree lost his interest in dialectics; the argument is the greatest gain to him, and he will not forego the delight of it in compliance with the jailer's intimation that he should not heat himself with talking. Some other traits of his character may be noted; for example, the courteous manner in which he inclines his head to the last objector, or the ironical touch, " Me already, as the tragic poet would say, the voice of fate calls; " or the depreciation of the arguments with which ''he comforted himself and them; " or the allusion to the possibility of finding another teacher among barbarous races; or the mysterious reference to another science (mathematics?) of generation and destruction for which he is vainly feeling. There is no change in him; only now he is invested with a sort of sacred character, as the prophet or priest of Apollo the God of the festival, in whose honor he first of all composes a hymn, and then like the swan pours forth his dying lay. Perhaps the extreme elevation of Socrates above his own situation, and the ordinary interests of life (compare his *jeu d'esprit* about his burial) create in the mind of the reader an impression stronger than could be derived from arguments that such an one, in his own language, has in him " a principle which does not admit of death."

The other persons of the Dialogue may be considered under two heads: (1) private friends; (2) the respondents in the argument.

First there is Crito, who has been already introduced to us; he is the equal in years of Socrates, and stands in quite a different relation to him from his younger disciples. He is a man of the world who is rich and prosperous, the best friend of Socrates, who wants to know his last commands, in whose presence he talks to his family, and who performs the last duty of closing his eyes. It is observable too that Crito shows no aptitude for philosophical discussions. Nor among the friends of Socrates must the jailer be forgotten, who seems to have been introduced by Plato in order to show the impression made by the extraordinary man on the common. The gentle nature of the man is indicated by his weeping at the announcement of his errand and then turning away, and also by the words of Socrates to his disciples: "How charming the man is! since I have been in prison he was always coming to me, and has been as good as could be to me." We are reminded too that he has retained this gentle nature amid scenes of death and violence by the contrasts which he draws between the behavior of Socrates and of others when about to die.

Another person who takes no part in the philosophical discussion is the excitable Apollodorus, the same who, in the Symposium, of which he is the narrator, is called "the madman," and who testifies his grief by the most violent emotions. Phaedo is also present, the "beloved disciple" as he may be termed, who is described, if not "leaning on his bosom," as seated next to Socrates, who is playing with his hair. At a particular point the argument is described as falling before the attack of Simmias. A sort of despair is introduced in the minds of the company. The effect of this is heightened by the description of Phaedo, who has been the eye-witness of the scene, and by the sympathy of his Phliasian auditors who are beginning to think "that they too can never trust an argument again." Like Apollodorus, Phaedo himself takes no part in the argument. But the calmness of his behavior, "veiling his face" when he can no longer contain his tears, contrasts with the passionate cries of the other.

The two principal interlocutors are Simmias and Cebes, the disciples of Philolaus the Pythagorean philosopher of Thebes. Simmias is described in the Phaedrus as fonder of an argument than any man living; and Cebes, although finally persuaded by Socrates, is said to be the most incredulous of human beings. It is Cebes who at the commencement of the Dialogue raises the question why "suicide is unlawful," and who first supplies the doctrine of recollection as a confirmation of the argument of the preëxistence of the soul. It is Cebes who urges that the preexistence does not necessarily involve the future existence of the soul, and who brings forward the argument of the weaver and his coat. To Simmias, on the other hand, is attributed the notion that the soul is a harmony, which is naturally put into the mouth of a Pythagorean disciple. It is Simmias, too, who first remarks on the uncertainty of human knowledge, and only at last concedes to the argument such a qualified approval as is consistent with the feebleness of the human faculties.

There is no proof that the conversation was ever actually held, and the place of the Dialogue in the series is doubtful. The doctrine of ideas is certainly carried beyond the Socratic point of view; in no other of the writings of Plato is the theory of them so completely developed. Whether the belief in immortality can be attributed to Socrates or not is uncertain; the silence of the Memorabilia, and of the earlier Dialogues of Plato, is an argument to the contrary. Yet in the Cyropaedia Xenophon has put language into the mouth of the dying Cyrus which recalls the Phaedo, and may perhaps have been derived from the teaching of Socrates.

The Phaedo, as has been already intimated, is not one of the Socratic Dialogues of Plato; nor, on the other hand, can it be assigned to that later period of the Platonic writings at which the ideas appear to be forgotten. Without pretending to determine the real time of composition, the Meno, Euthyphro, Apology, Phaedo, Symposium may be conveniently read by us in this order as illustrative of the life of Socrates. Another chain may be formed of the Meno, Phaedo, Phaedrus in which the immortality of the soul is connected with the doctrine of ideas. In the Meno the theory of ideas is based on the ancient belief in transmigration, which reappears again in the Phaedrus as well as in the Republic and Timaeus, and in all of them is connected with a doctrine of retribution. In the Phaedrus the immortality of the soul is supposed to rest on the conception of the soul as a principle of motion, whereas in the Republic the argument turns on the natural continuance of the soul, which, if not destroyed by her own proper evil, can hardly be destroyed by any other. The soul of man in the Timaeus is derived from the Supreme Creator, and either returns after death to her kindred star, or descends into the lower life of an animal. The Apology expresses the same view as the Phaedo, but with less confidence; the probability of death being a long sleep is not excluded. The Theaetetus also describes, in a digression, the desire of the soul to fly away and be with God — " and to fly to him is to be like him." Lastly, the Symposium may be observed to resemble as well as to differ from the Phaedo. While the first notion of immortality is only in the way of natural procreation or of posthumous fame and glory, the higher vision of beauty, like the good in the Republic, is the vision of the eternal idea. So deeply rooted in Plato's mind is the belief in immortality; so various are the forms of expression which he employs.

Some elements of the drama may be noted in all the Dialogues of Plato. The Phaedo is the tragedy of which Socrates is the protagonist and Simmias and Cebes the secondary performers. No Dialogue has a greater unity of subject and feeling. Plato has certainly fulfilled the condition of Greek, or rather of all art, which requires that scenes of death and suffering should be clothed in beauty. The gathering of the friends at the commencement of the Dialogue, the dejection of the audience at the temporary overthrow of the argument, the picture of Socrates playing with the hair of Phaedo, the final scene in which Socrates alone retains his composure — are masterpieces of art. The chorus at the end might have interpreted the feeling of the play: " There can no evil happen to a good man in life or death."

PHAEDO

PERSONS OF THE DIALOGUE

Phaedo, *who is the narrator of*
the Dialogue to
Echecrates *of Phlius*
Socrates.
Attendant of the Prison.

Apollodorus.
Simmias.
Cebes.
Crito.

Scene :— The Prison of Socrates.
Place of the Narration :— Phlius.

Echecrates. Were you yourself, Phaedo, in the prison with Socrates on the day when he drank the poison?

Phaedo. Yes, Echecrates, I was.

Ech. I wish that you would tell me about his death. What did he say in his last hours? We were informed that he died by taking poison, but no one knew anything more; for no Phliasian ever goes to Athens now, and a long time has elapsed since any Athenian found his way to Phlius, and therefore we had no clear account.

Phaed. Did you not hear of the proceedings at the trial?

Ech. Yes; some one told us about the trial, and we could not understand why, having been condemned, he was put to death, as appeared, not at the time, but long afterwards. What was the reason of this?

Phaed. An accident, Echecrates. The reason was that the stern of the ship which the Athenians send to Delos happened to have been crowned on the day before he was tried.

Ech. What is this ship?

591

Phaed. This is the ship in which, as the Athenians say, Theseus went to Crete when he took with him the fourteen youths, and was the savior of them and of himself. And they were said to have vowed to Apollo at the time, that if they were saved they would make an annual pilgrimage to Delos. Now this custom still continues, and the whole period of the voyage to and from Delos, beginning when the priest of Apollo crowns the stern of the ship, is a holy season, during which the city is not allowed to be polluted by public executions; and often, when the vessel is detained by adverse winds, there may be a very considerable delay. As I was saying, the ship was crowned on the day before the trial, and this was the reason why Socrates lay in prison and was not put to death until long after he was condemned.

Ech. What was the manner of his death, Phaedo? What was said or done? And which of his friends had he with him? Or were they not allowed by the authorities to be present? And did he die alone?

Phaed. No; there were several of his friends with him.

Ech. If you have nothing to do, I wish that you would tell me what passed, as exactly as you can.

Phaed. I have nothing to do, and will try to gratify your wish. For to me too there is no greater pleasure than to have Socrates brought to my recollection; whether I speak myself or hear another speak of him.

Ech. You will have listeners who are of the same mind with you, and I hope that you will be as exact as you can.

Phaed. I remember the strange feeling which came over me at being with him. For I could hardly believe that I was present at the death of a friend, and therefore I did not pity him, Echecrates; his mien and his language were so noble and fearless in the hour of death that to me he appeared blessed. I thought that in going to the other world he could not be without a divine call, and that he would be happy, if any man ever was, when he arrived there; and therefore I did not pity him as might seem natural at such a time. But neither could I feel the pleasure which I usually felt in philosophical discourse (for philosophy was the theme of which we spoke). I was pleased and I was also pained, because I knew that he was soon to die, and this strange mixture of feeling was shared by us all; we were laughing and weeping by turns, especially the excitable Apollodorus — you know the sort of man?

Ech. Yes.

Phaed. He was quite overcome; and I myself, and all of us were greatly moved.

Ech. Who were present?

Phaed. Of native Athenians there were, besides Apollodorus, Critobulus and his father Crito, Hermogenes, Epigenes, Aeschines, and Antisthenes; likewise Ctesippus of the deme of Paeania, Menexenus, and some others; but Plato, if I am not mistaken, was ill.

Ech. Were there any strangers?

Phaed. Yes, there were; Simmias the Theban, and Cebes, and Phaedondes; Euclid and Terpsion, who came from Megara.

Ech. And was Aristippus there, and Cleombrotus?

Phaed. No, they were said to be in Aegina.

Ech. Any one else?

Phaed. I think that these were about all.

Ech. And what was the discourse of which you spoke?

Phaed. I will begin at the beginning, and endeavor to repeat the entire conversation. You must understand that we had been previously in the habit of assembling early in the morning at the court in which the trial was held, and which is not far from the prison. There we remained talking with one another until the opening of the prison doors (for they were not opened very early), and then went in and generally passed the day with Socrates. On the last morning the meeting was earlier than usual; this was owing to our having heard on the previous evening that the sacred ship had arrived from Delos, and therefore we agreed to meet very early at the accustomed place. On our going to the prison, the jailer who answered the door, instead of admitting us, came out and bade us wait and he would call us. " For the eleven," he said, " are now with Socrates; they are taking off his chains, and giving orders that he is to die to-day." He soon returned and said that we might come in. On entering we found Socrates just released from chains, and Xanthippe, whom you know, sitting by him, and holding his child in her arms. When she saw us she uttered a cry and said, as women will: " O Socrates, this is the last time that either you will converse with your friends, or they with you." Socrates turned to Crito and said: " Crito, let some one take her home." Some of Crito's people accordingly led her away, crying out and beating herself. And when she was gone, Socrates, sitting up on the couch, began to bend and rub his leg, saying, as he rubbed: How singular is the thing called pleasure, and how curiously related to pain, which might be thought to be the opposite of it; for they never come to a man together, and yet he who pursues either of them is generally compelled to take the other. They are two, and yet they grow together out of one head or stem; and I can not help thinking that if Aesop had noticed them, he would have made a fable about God trying to reconcile their strife, and when he could not, he fastened their heads together;

and this is the reason why when one comes the other follows, as I find in my own case pleasure comes following after the pain in my leg which was caused by the chain.

Upon this Cebes said: I am very glad indeed, Socrates, that you mentioned the name of Aesop. For that reminds me of a question which has been asked by others, and was asked of me only the day before yesterday by Evenus the poet, and as he will be sure to ask again, you may as well tell me what I should say to him, if you would like him to have an answer. He wanted to know why you who never before wrote a line of poetry, now that you are in prison are putting Aesop into verse, and also composing that hymn in honor of Apollo.

Tell him, Cebes, he replied, that I had no idea of rivalling him or his poems; which is the truth, for I knew that I could not do that. But I wanted to see whether I could purge away a scruple which I felt about certain dreams. In the course of my life I have often had intimations in dreams " that I should make music." The same dream came to me sometimes in one form, and sometimes in another, but always saying the same or nearly the same words: Make and cultivate music, said the dream. And hitherto I had imagined that this was only intended to exhort and encourage me in the study of philosophy, which has always been the pursuit of my life, and is the noblest and best of music. The dream was bidding me do what I was already doing, in the same way that the competitor in a race is bidden by the spectators to run when he is already running. But I was not certain of this, as the dream might have meant music in the popular sense of the word, and being under sentence of death, and the festival giving me a respite, I thought that I should be safer if I satisfied the scruple, and, in obedience to the dream, composed a few verses before I departed. And first I made a hymn in honor of the god of the festival, and then considering that a poet, if he is really to be a poet or maker, should not only put words together but make stories, and as I have no invention, I took some fables of Aesop, which I had ready at hand and knew, and turned them into verse. Tell Evenus this, and bid him be of good cheer; say that I would have him come after me if he be a wise man, and not tarry; and that to-day I am likely to be going, for the Athenians say that I must.

Simmias said: What a message for such a man! having been a frequent companion of his I should say that, as far as I know him, he will never take your advice unless he is obliged.

Why, said Socrates. Is not Evenus a philosopher?

I think that he is, said Simmias.

Then he, or any man who has the spirit of philosophy, will be willing to die, though he will not take his own life, for that is held not to be right.

Here he changed his position, and put his legs off the couch on to the ground, and during the rest of the conversation he remained sitting.

Why do you say, inquired Cebes, that a man ought not to take his own life, but that the philosopher will be ready to follow the dying?

Socrates replied: And have you, Cebes and Simmias, who are acquainted with Philolaus, never heard him speak of this?

I never understood him, Socrates.

My words, too, are only an echo; but I am very willing to say what I have heard: and indeed, as I am going to another place, I ought to be thinking and talking of the nature of the pilgrimage which I am about to make. What can I do better in the interval between this and the setting of the sun?

Then tell me, Socrates, why is suicide held not to be right? as I have certainly heard Philolaus affirm when he was staying with us at Thebes; and there are others who say the same, although none of them has ever made me understand him.

But do your best, replied Socrates, and the day may come when you will understand. I suppose that you wonder why, as most things which are evil may be accidentally good, this is to be the only exception (for may not death, too, be better than life in some cases?), and why, when a man is better dead, he is not permitted to be his own benefactor, but must wait for the hand of another.

By Jupiter! yes, indeed, said Cebes laughing, and speaking in his native Doric.

I admit the appearance of inconsistency, replied Socrates; but there may not be any real inconsistency after all in this. There is a doctrine uttered in secret that man is a prisoner who has no right to open the door of his prison and run away; this is a great mystery which I do not quite understand. Yet I too believe that the gods are our guardians, and that we are a possession of theirs. Do you not agree?

Yes, I agree to that, said Cebes.

And if one of your own possessions, an ox or an ass, for example, took the liberty of putting himself out of the way when you had given no intimation of your wish that he should die, would you not be angry with him, and would you not punish him if you could?

Certainly, replied Cebes.

Then there may be reason in saying that a man should wait, and not take his own life until God summons him, as he is now summoning me.

Yes, Socrates, said Cebes, there is surely reason in that. And yet how can you reconcile this seemingly true belief that God is our guardian and we his possessions, with that willingness to die which we were attributing to the philosopher? That the wisest of men should be willing to leave this service in which they are ruled by the gods who are the best of rulers, is not reasonable, for surely no wise man thinks that when set at liberty he can take better care of himself than the gods take of him. A fool may perhaps think this — he may argue that he had better run away from his master, not considering that his duty is to remain to the end, and not to run away from the good, and that there is no sense in his running away. But the wise man will want to be ever with him who is better than himself. Now this, Socrates, is the reverse of what was just now said; for upon this view the wise man should sorrow and the fool rejoice at passing out of life.

The earnestness of Cebes seemed to please Socrates. Here, said he, turning to us, is a man who is always inquiring, and is not to be convinced all in a moment, nor by every argument.

And in this case, added Simmias, his objection does appear to me to have some force. For what can be the meaning of a truly wise man wanting to fly away and lightly leave a master who is better than himself. And I rather imagine that Cebes is referring to you; he thinks that you are too ready to leave us, and too ready to leave the gods who, as you acknowledge, are our good rulers.

Yes, replied Socrates; there is reason in that. And this indictment you think that I ought to answer as if I were in court?

That is what we should like, said Simmias.

Then I must try to make a better impression upon you than I did when defending myself before the judges. For I am quite ready to acknowledge, Simmias and Cebes, that I ought to be grieved at death, if I were not persuaded that I am going to other gods who are wise and good (of this I am as certain as I can be of anything of the sort), and to men departed (though I am not so certain of this) who are better than those whom I leave behind; and therefore I do not grieve as I might have done, for I have good hope that there is yet something remaining for the dead, and as has been said of old, some far better thing for the good than for the evil.

But do you mean to take away your thoughts with you, Socrates, said Simmias? Will you not communicate them to us?—the benefit is one in which we too may hope to share. Moreover, if you succeed in convincing us, that will be an answer to the charge against yourself.

I will do my best, replied Socrates. But you must first let me hear what Crito wants; he was going to say something to me.

Only this, Socrates, replied Crito: — the attendant who is to give you the poison has been telling me that you are not to talk much, and he wants me to let you know this; for that by talking, heat is increased, and this interferes with the action of the poison; those who excite themselves are sometimes obliged to drink the poison two or three times.

Then, said Socrates, let him mind his business and be prepared to give the poison two or three times, if necessary; that is all.

I was almost certain that you would say that, replied Crito; but I was obliged to satisfy him.

Never mind him, he said.

And now I will make answer to you, O my judges, and show that he who has lived as a true philosopher has reason to be of good cheer when he is about to die, and that after death he may hope to receive the greatest good in the other world. And how this may be, Simmias and Cebes, I will endeavor to explain. For I deem that the true disciple of philosophy is likely to be misunderstood by other men; they do not perceive that he is ever pursuing death and dying; and if this is true, why, having had the desire of death all his life long, should he repine at the arrival of that which he has been always pursuing and desiring?

Simmias laughed and said: Though not in a laughing humor, I swear that I can not help laughing, when I think what the wicked world will say when they hear this. They will say that this is very true, and our people at home will agree with them in saying that the life which philosophers desire is truly death, and that they have found them out to be deserving of the death which they desire.

And they are right, Simmias, in saying this, with the exception of the words " they have found them out;" for they have not found out what is the nature of this death which the true philosopher desires, or how he deserves or desires death. But let us leave them and have a word with ourselves: Do we believe that there is such a thing as death?

To be sure, replied Simmias.

And is this anything but the separation of soul and body? And being dead is the attainment of this separation when the soul exists in herself, and is parted from the body and the body is parted from the soul — that is death?

Exactly: that and nothing else, he replied.

And what do you say of another question, my friend, about which I should like to have your opinion, and the answer to which will probably throw light on our present inquiry: Do you think that the philosopher ought to care about the pleasures — if they are to be called pleasures — of eating and drinking?

Certainly not, answered Simmias.

And what do you say of the pleasures of love — should he care about them?

By no means.

And will he think much of the other ways of indulging the body, for example, the acquisition of costly raiment, or sandals or other adornments of the body? Instead of caring about them, does he not rather despise anything more than nature needs? What do you say?

I should say that the true philosopher would despise them.

Would you not say that he is entirely concerned with the soul and not with the body? He would like, as far as he can, to be quit of the body and turn to the soul.

That is true.

In matters of this sort philosophers, above all other men, may be observed in every sort of way to dissever the soul from the body.

That is true.

Whereas, Simmias, the rest of the world are of opinion that a life which has no bodily pleasures and no part in them is not worth having; but that he who thinks nothing of bodily pleasures is almost as though he were dead.

That is quite true.

What again shall we say of the actual acquirement of knowledge? — is the body, if invited to share in the inquiry, a hinderer or a helper? I mean to say, have sight and hearing any truth in them? Are they not, as the poets are always telling us, inaccurate witnesses? and yet, if even they are inaccurate and indistinct, what is to be said of the other senses? — for you will allow that they are the best of them?

Certainly, he replied.

Then when does the soul attain truth? — for in attempting to consider anything in company with the body she is obviously deceived.

Yes, that is true.

Then must not existence be revealed to her in thought, if at all?

Yes.

And thought is best when the mind is gathered into herself and none of these things trouble her — neither sounds nor sights nor pain nor any pleasure, — when she has as little as possible to do with the body, and has no bodily sense or feeling, but is aspiring after being?

That is true.

And in this the philosopher dishonors the body; his soul runs away from the body and desires to be alone and by herself?

That is true.

Well, but there is another thing, Simmias: Is there or is there not an absolute justice?

Assuredly there is.

And an absolute beauty and absolute good?

Of course.

But did you ever behold any of them with your eyes?

Certainly not.

Or did you ever reach them with any other bodily sense? (and I speak not of these alone, but of absolute greatness, and health, and strength, and of the essence or true nature of everything). Has the reality of them ever been perceived by you through the bodily organs? or rather, is not the nearest approach to the knowledge of their several natures made by him who so orders his intellectual vision as to have the most exact conception of the essence of that which he considers?

Certainly.

And he attains to the knowledge of them in their highest purity who goes to each of them with the mind alone, not allowing when in the act of thought the intrusion or introduction of sight or any other sense in the company of reason, but with the very light of the mind in her clearness penetrates into the very light of truth in each; he has got rid, as far as he can, of eyes and ears and of the whole body, which he conceives of only as a disturbing element, hindering the soul from the acquisition of knowledge when in company with her — is not this the sort of man who, if ever man did, is likely to attain the knowledge of existence?

There is admirable truth in that, Socrates, replied Simmias.

And when they consider all this, must not true philosophers make a reflection, of which they will speak to one another in such words as these: We have found, they will say, a path of speculation which seems to bring us and the argument to the conclusion, that while we are in the body, and while the soul is mingled with this mass of evil, our desire will not be satisfied, and our desire is of the truth. For the body is a source of endless trouble to us by reason of the mere requirement of food; and also is liable to diseases which overtake and impede us in the search after truth: and by filling us as full of loves, and lusts, and fears, and fancies, and idols, and every sort of folly, prevents our ever having, as people say, so much as a thought. For whence come wars, and fightings, and factions? whence but from the body and the lusts of the body? For wars are occasioned by the love of money, and money has to be acquired for the sake and in the service of the body; and in consequence of all these things the time which ought to be given to philosophy is lost. Moreover, if there is time and an inclination towards philosophy, yet the body introduces a turmoil and confusion and fear into the course of speculation, and hinders us from seeing the truth; and all experience shows that if we would have pure knowledge of anything we must be quit of the body, and the soul in herself must behold all things in themselves: then, I suppose, that we shall attain that which we desire, and of which we say that we are lovers, and that is wisdom; not while we live, but after death, as the argument shows; for if while in company with the body, the soul can not have pure knowledge, one of two things seems to follow — either knowledge is not to be attained at all, or, if at all, after death. For then, and not till then, the soul will be in herself alone and without the body. In this present life, I reckon that we make the nearest approach to knowledge when we have the least possible concern or interest in the body, and are not saturated with the bodily nature, but remain pure until the hour when God himself is pleased to release us. And then the foolishness of the body will be cleared away and we shall be pure and hold converse with other pure souls, and know of ourselves the clear light everywhere; and this is surely the light of truth. For no impure thing is allowed to approach the pure. These are the sort of words, Simmias, which the true lovers of wisdom can not help saying to one another, and thinking. You will agree with me in that?

Certainly, Socrates.

But if this is true, O my friend, then there is great hope that, going whither I go, I shall there be satisfied with that which has been the chief concern of you and me in our past lives. And now that the hour of departure is appointed to me, this is the hope with which I depart, and not I only, but every man who believes that he has his mind purified.

Certainly, replied Simmias.

And what is purification but the separation of the soul from the body, as I was saying before; the habit of the soul gathering and collecting herself into herself, out of all the courses of the body; the dwelling in her own place alone, as in another life, so also in this, as far as she can; — the release of the soul from the chains of the body?

Very true, he said.

And what is that which is termed death, but this very separation and release of the soul from the body?

To be sure, he said.

And the true philosophers, and they only, study and are eager to release the soul. Is not the separation and release of the soul from the body their especial study?

That is true.

And, as I was saying at first, there would be a ridiculous contradiction in men studying to live as nearly as they can in a state of death, and yet repining when death comes.

Certainly.

Then Simmias, as the true philosophers are ever studying death, to them, of all men, death is the least terrible. Look at the matter in this way: — how inconsistent of them to have been always enemies of the body, and wanting to have the soul alone, and when this is granted to them, to be trembling and repining; instead of rejoicing at their departing to that place where, when they arrive, they hope to gain that which in life they loved (and this was wisdom), and at the same time to be rid of the company of their enemy. Many a man has been willing to go to the world below in the hope of seeing there an earthly love, or wife, or son, and conversing with them. And will he who is a true lover of wisdom, and is persuaded in like manner that only in the world below he can worthily enjoy her, still repine at death? Will he not depart with joy? Surely, he will, my friend, if he be a true philosopher. For he will have a firm conviction that there only, and nowhere else, he can find wisdom in her purity. And if this be true, he would be very absurd, as I was saying, if he were to fear death.

He would indeed, replied Simmias.

And when you see a man who is repining at the approach of death, is not his reluctance a sufficient proof that he is not a lover of wisdom, but a lover of the body, and probably at the same time a lover of either money or power, or both?

That is very true, he replied.

There is a virtue, Simmias, which is named courage. Is not that a special attribute of the philosopher?

Certainly.

Again, there is temperance. Is not the calm, and control, and disdain of the passions which even the many call temperance, a quality belonging only to those who despise the body, and live in philosophy?

That is not to be denied.

For the courage and temperance of other men, if you will consider them, are really a contradiction.

How is that, Socrates?

Well, he said, you are aware that death is regarded by men in general as a great evil.

That is true, he said.

And do not courageous men endure death because they are afraid of yet greater evils?

That is true.

Then all but the philosophers are courageous only from fear, and because they are afraid; and yet that a man should be courageous from fear, and because he is a coward, is surely a strange thing.

Very true.

And are not the temperate exactly in the same case?
They are temperate because they are intemperate —
which may seem to be a contradiction, but is nevertheless the sort of thing which happens with this foolish
temperance. For there are pleasures which they must
have, and are afraid of losing; and therefore they
abstain from one class of pleasures because they are
overcome by another: and whereas intemperance is
defined as " being under the dominion of pleasure,"
they overcome only because they are overcome by
pleasure. And that is what I mean by saying that
they are temperate through intemperance.

That appears to be true.

Yet the exchange of one fear or pleasure or pain
for another fear or pleasure or pain, which are
measured like coins, the greater with the less, is not
the exchange of virtue. O my dear Simmias, is there
not one true coin for which all things ought to exchange? — and that is wisdom; and only in exchange
for this, and in company with this, is anything truly
bought or sold, whether courage or temperance or
justice. And is not all true virtue the companion of
wisdom, no matter what fears or pleasures or other
similar goods or evils may or may not attend her?
But the virtue which is made up of these goods, when
they are severed from wisdom and exchanged with one
another, is a shadow of virtue only, nor is there any
freedom or health or truth in her; but in the true exchange there is a purging away of all these things,
and temperance, and justice, and courage, and wisdom
herself, are a purgation of them. And I conceive that
the founders of the mysteries had a real meaning and
were not mere triflers when they intimated in a figure
long ago that he who passed unsanctified and un-
initiated into the world below will live in a slough, but
that he who arrives there after initiation and purifica-

tion will dwell with the gods. For "many," as they say in the mysteries, "are the thyrsus-bearers, but few are the mystics," — meaning, as I interpret the words, the true philosophers. In the number of whom I have been seeking, according to my ability, to find a place during my whole life; — whether I have sought in a right way or not, and whether I have succeeded or not, I shall truly know in a little while, if God will, when I myself arrive in the other world: that is my belief. And now Simmias and Cebes, I have answered those who charge me with not grieving or repining at parting from you and my masters in this world; and I am right in not repining, for I believe that I shall find other masters and friends who are as good in the world below. But all men can not receive this, and I shall be glad if my words have any more success with you than with the judges of Athenians.

Cebes answered: I agree, Socrates, in the greater part of what you say. But in what relates to the soul, men are apt to be incredulous; they fear that when she leaves the body her place may be nowhere, and that on the very day of death she may be destroyed and perish — immediately on her release from the body, issuing forth like smoke or air and vanishing away into nothingness. For if she could only hold together and be herself after she was released from the evils of the body, there would be good reason to hope, Socrates, that what you say is true. But much persuasion and many arguments are required in order to prove that when the man is dead the soul yet exists, and has any force or intelligence.

True, Cebes, said Socrates; and shall I suggest that we talk a little of the probabilities of these things?

I am sure, said Cebes, that I should greatly like to know your opinion about them.

I reckon, said Socrates, that no one who heard me now, not even if he were one of my old enemies, the comic poets, could accuse me of idle talking about matters in which I have no concern. Let us then, if you please, proceed with the inquiry.

Whether the souls of men after death are or are not in the world below, is a question which may be argued in this manner: — The ancient doctrine of which I have been speaking affirms that they go from hence into the other world, and return hither, and are born from the dead. Now if this be true, and the living come from the dead, then our souls must be in the other world, for if not, how could they be born again? And this would be conclusive, if there were any real evidence that the living are only born from the dead; but if there is no evidence of this, then other arguments will have to be adduced.

That is very true, replied Cebes.

Then let us consider this question, not in relation to man only, but in relation to animals generally, and to plants, and to everything of which there is generation, and the proof will be easier. Are not all things which have opposites generated out of their opposites? I mean such things as good and evil, just and unjust — and there are innumerable other opposites which are generated out of opposites. And I want to show that this holds universally of all opposites; I mean to say, for example, that anything which becomes greater must become greater after being less.

True.

And that which becomes less must have been once greater and then become less.

Yes.

And the weaker is generated from the stronger, and the swifter from the slower.

Very true.

And the worst is from the better, and the more just is from the more unjust?

Of course.

And is this true of all opposites? and are we convinced that all of them are generated out of opposites?

Yes.

And in this universal opposition of all things, are there not also two intermediate processes which are ever going on, from one to the other, and back again; where there is a greater and a less there is also an intermediate process of increase and diminution, and that which grows is said to wax, and that which decays to wane?

Yes, he said.

And there are many other processes, such as division and composition, cooling and heating, which equally involve a passage into and out of one another. And this holds of all opposites, even though not always expressed in words — they are generated out of one another, and there is a passing or process from one to the other of them?

Very true, he replied.

Well, and is there not an opposite of life, as sleep is the opposite of waking?

True, he said.

And what is that?

Death, he answered.

And these then are generated, if they are opposites, the one from the other, and have there their two inter mediate processes also?

Of course.

Now, said Socrates, I will analyze one of the two pairs of opposites which I have mentioned to you, and also its intermediate processes, and you shall analyze the other to me. The state of sleep is opposed to the state of waking, and out of sleeping waking is generated, and out of waking, sleeping; and the process of generation is in the one case falling asleep, and in the other waking up. Are you agreed about that?

Quite agreed.

Then, suppose that you analyze life and death to me in the same manner. Is not death opposed to life?

Yes.

And they are generated one from the other?

Yes.

What is generated from life?

Death.

And what from death?

I can only say in answer — life.

Then the living, whether things or persons, Cebes, are generated from the dead?

That is clear, he replied.

Then the inference is that our souls are in the world below?

That is true.

And one of the true processes or generations is visible — for surely the act of dying is visible?

Surely, he said.

And may not the other be inferred as the complement of nature, who is not to be supposed to go on one leg only? And if not, a corresponding process of generation in death must also be assigned to her?

Certainly, he replied.

And what is that process?

Revival.

And revival, if there be such a thing, is the birth of the dead into the world of the living?

Quite true.

Then here is a new way in which we arrive at the inference that the living come from the dead, just as the dead come from the living; and if this is true, then the souls of the dead must be in some place out of which they come again. And this, as I think, has been satisfactorily proved.

Yes, Socrates, he said; all this seems to flow necessarily out of our previous admissions.

And that these admissions were not unfair, Cebes, he said, may be shown, as I think, in this way: If generation were in a straight line only, and there were no compensation or circle in nature, no turn or return into one another, then you know that all things would at last have the same form and pass into the same state, and there would be no more generation of them.

What do you mean? he said.

A simple thing enough, which I will illustrate by the case of sleep, he replied. You know that if there were no compensation of sleeping and waking, the story of the sleeping Endymion would in the end have no meaning, because all other things would be asleep too, and he would not be thought of. Or if there were composition only, and no division of substances, then the chaos of Anaxagoras would come again. And in like manner, my dear Cebes, if all things which partook of life were to die, and after they were dead remained in the form of death, and did not come to life again, all would at last die, and nothing would be alive — how could this be otherwise? For if the living spring from any others who are not the dead, and they die, must not all things at last be swallowed up in death?

There is no escape from that, Socrates, said Cebes; and I think that what you say is entirely true.

Yes, he said, Cebes, I entirely think so too; and we are not walking in a vain imagination: but I am confident in the belief that there truly is such a thing as living again, and that the living spring from the dead, and that the souls of the dead are in existence.

and that the good souls have a better portion than the evil.

Cebes added: Your favorite doctrine, Socrates, that knowledge is simply recollection, if true, also necessarily implies a previous time in which we learned that which we now recollect. But this would be impossible unless our soul was in some place before existing in the human form; here then is another argument of the soul's immortality.

But tell me, Cebes, said Simmias, interposing, what proofs are given of this doctrine of recollection? I am not very sure at this moment that I remember them.

One excellent proof, said Cebes, is afforded by questions. If you put a question to a person in a right way, he will give a true answer of himself, but how could he do this unless there were knowledge and right reason already in him? And this is most clearly shown when he is taken to a diagram or to anything of that sort.

But if, said Socrates, you are still incredulous, Simmias, I would ask you whether you may not agree with me when you look at the matter in another way; — I mean, if you are still incredulous as to whether knowledge is recollection?

Incredulous, I am not, said Simmias; but I want to have this doctrine of recollection brought to my own recollection, and, from what Cebes has said, I am beginning to recollect and be convinced: but I should still like to hear what more you have to say.

This is what I should say, he replied: — We should agree, if I am not mistaken, that what a man recollects he must have known at some previous time.

Very true.

And what is the nature of this recollection? And, in asking this, I mean to ask, whether when a person has already seen or heard or in any way perceived anything, and he knows not only that, but something else of which he has not the same but another knowledge, we may not fairly say that he recollects that which comes into his mind. Are we agreed about that?

What do you mean?

I mean what I may illustrate by the following instance: — The knowledge of a lyre is not the same as the knowledge of a man?

True.

And yet what is the feeling of lovers when they recognize a lyre, or a garment, or anything else which the beloved has been in the habit of using? Do not they, from knowing the lyre, form in the mind's eye an image of the youth to whom the lyre belongs? And this is recollection: and in the same way any one who sees Simmias may remember Cebes; and there are endless other things of the same nature.

Yes, indeed, there are, — endless, replied Simmias.

And this sort of thing, he said, is recollection, and is most commonly a process of recovering that which has been forgotten through time and inattention.

Very true, he said.

Well; and may you not also from seeing the picture of a horse or a lyre remember a man? and from the picture of Simmias, you may be led to remember Cebes?

True.

Or you may also be led to the recollection of Simmias himself?

True, he said.

And in all these cases, the recollection may be derived from things either like or unlike?

That is true.

And when the recollection is derived from like

things, then there is sure to be another question, which
is — whether the likeness of that which is recollected
is in any way defective or not?

Very true, he said.

And shall we proceed a step further, and affirm that
there is such a thing as equality, not of wood with
wood, or of stone with stone, but that, over and above
this, there is equality in the abstract? Shall we affirm
this?

Affirm, yes, and swear to it, replied Simmias, with
all the confidence in life.

And do we know the nature of this abstract essence?

To be sure, he said.

And whence did we obtain this knowledge? Did
we not see equalities of material things, such as pieces
of wood and stones, and gather from them the idea
of an equality which is different from them? — you
will admit that? Or look at the matter again in this
way: — Do not the same pieces of wood or stone appear at one time equal, and at another time unequal?

That is certain.

But are real equals ever unequal? or is the idea of
equality ever inequality?

That surely was never yet known, Socrates.

Then these (so-called) equals are not the same with
the idea of equality?

I should say, clearly not, Socrates.

And yet from these equals, although differing from
the idea of equality, you conceived and attained that
idea?

Very true, he said.

Which might be like, or might be unlike them?

Yes.

But that makes no difference: whenever from seeing one thing you conceived another, whether like or

unlike, there must surely have been an act of recollection?

Very true.

But what would you say of equal portions of wood and stone, or other material equals? and what is the impression produced by them? Are they equals in the same sense as absolute equality? or do they fall short of this in a measure?

Yes, he said, in a very great measure too.

And must we not allow, that when I or any one look at any object, and perceive that the object aims at being some other thing, but falls short of, and can not attain to it, — he who makes this observation must have had a previous knowledge of that to which, as he says, the other, although similar, was inferior?

Certainly.

And has not this been our own case in the matter of equals and of absolute equality?

Precisely.

Then we must have known absolute equality previously to the time when we first saw the material equals, and reflected that all these apparent equals aim at this absolute equality, but fall short of it?

That is true.

And we recognize also that this absolute equality has only been known, and can only be known, through the medium of sight or touch, or of some other sense. And this I would affirm of all such conceptions.

Yes, Socrates, as far as the argument is concerned, one of them is the same as the other.

And from the sense then is derived the knowledge that all sensible things aim at an idea of equality of which they fall short — is not that true?

Yes.

Then before we began to see or hear or perceive in any way, we must have had a knowledge of absolute equality, or we could not have referred to that the equals which are derived from the senses? — for to that they all aspire, and of that they fall short?

That, Socrates, is certainly to be inferred from the previous statements.

And did we not see and hear and acquire our other senses as soon as we were born?

Certainly.

Then we must have acquired the knowledge of the ideal equal at some time previous to this?

Yes.

That is to say, before we were born, I suppose?

True.

And if we acquired this knowledge before we were born, and were born having it, then we also knew before we were born and at the instant of birth not only the equal or the greater or the less, but all other ideas; for we are not speaking only of equality absolute, but of beauty, good, justice, holiness, and all which we stamp with the name of essence in the dialectical process, when we ask and answer questions. Of all this we may certainly affirm that we acquired the knowledge before birth?

That is true.

But if, after having acquired, we have not forgotten that which we acquired, then we must always have been born with knowledge, and shall always continue to know as long as life lasts — for knowing is the acquiring and retaining knowledge and not forgetting. Is not forgetting, Simmias, just the losing of knowledge?

Quite true, Socrates.

But if the knowledge which we acquired before birth was lost by us at birth, and if afterwards by the use of the senses we recovered that which we previously knew, will not that which we call learning be a process of recovering our knowledge, and may not this be rightly termed recollection by us?

Very true.

For this is clear — that when we perceived something, either by the help of sight, or hearing, or some other sense, there was no difficulty in receiving from this a conception of some other thing like or unlike which had been forgotten and which was associated with this; and therefore, as I was saying, one of two alternatives follows: — either we had this knowledge at birth, and continued to know through life; or, after birth, those who are said to learn only remember, and learning is recollection only.

Yes, that is quite true, Socrates.

And which alternative, Simmias, do you prefer? Had we the knowledge at our birth, or did we remember afterwards the things which we knew previously to our birth?

I can not decide at the moment.

At any rate you can decide whether he who has knowledge ought or ought not to be able to give a reason for what he knows.

Certainly, he ought.

But do you think that every man is able to give a reason about these very matters of which we are speaking?

I wish that they could, Socrates, but I greatly fear that to-morrow at this time there will be no one able to give a reason worth having.

Then you are not of opinion, Simmias, that all men know these things?

Certainly not.

Then they are in process of recollecting that which they learned before?

Certainly.

But when did our souls acquire this knowledge? — not since we were born as men?

Certainly not.

And therefore, previously?

Yes.

Then, Simmias, our souls must have existed before they were in the form of man — without bodies, and must have had intelligence.

Unless indeed you suppose, Socrates, that these notions were given us at the moment of birth; for this is the only time that remains.

Yes, my friend, but when did we lose them? for they are not in us when we are born — that is admitted. Did we lose them at the moment of receiving them, or at some other time?

No, Socrates, I perceive that I was unconsciously talking nonsense.

Then may we not say, Simmias, that if, as we are always repeating, there is an absolute beauty, and goodness, and essence in general, and to this, which is now discovered to be a previous condition of our being, we refer all our sensations, and with this compare them — assuming this to have a prior existence, then our souls must have had a prior existence, but if not, there would be no force in the argument. There can be no doubt that if these absolute ideas existed before we were born, then our souls must have existed before we were born, and if not the ideas, then not the souls.

Yes, Socrates; I am convinced that there is precisely the same necessity for the existence of the soul before birth, and of the essence of which you are speaking: and the argument arrives at a result which happily agrees with my own notion. For there is nothing which to my mind is so evident as that beauty, good, and other notions of which you were just now speaking, have a most real and absolute existence; and I am satisfied with the proof.

Well, but is Cebes equally satisfied? for I must convince him too.

I think, said Simmias, that Cebes is satisfied: although he is the most incredulous of mortals, yet I believe that he is convinced of the existence of the soul before birth. But that after death the soul will continue to exist is not yet proven even to my own satisfaction. I can not get rid of the feelings of the many to which Cebes was referring — the feeling that when the man dies the soul may be scattered, and that this may be the end of her. For admitting that she may be generated and created in some other place, and may have existed before entering the human body, why after having entered in and gone out again may she not herself be destroyed and come to an end?

Very true, Simmias, said Cebes; that our soul existed before we were born was the first half of the argument, and this appears to have been proven; that the soul will exist after death as well as before birth is the other half of which the proof is still wanting, and has to be supplied.

But that proof, Simmias and Cebes, has been already given, said Socrates, if you put the two arguments together — I mean this and the former one, in which we admitted that everything living is born of the dead. For if the soul existed before birth, and in coming to life and being born can be born only from death and dying, must she not after death continue to exist, since she has to be born again? surely the proof which you desire has been already furnished. Still I suspect that you and Simmias would be glad to probe the argument further: like children, you are haunted with a fear that when the soul leaves the body, the wind may really blow her away and scatter her; especially if a man should happen to die in stormy weather and not when the sky is calm.

Cebes answered with a smile: Then, Socrates, you must argue us out of our fears — and yet, strictly speaking, they are not our fears, but there is a child within us to whom death is a sort of hobgoblin; him too we must persuade not to be afraid when he is alone with him in the dark.

Socrates said: Let the voice of the charmer be applied daily until you have charmed him away.

And where shall we find a good charmer of our fears, Socrates, when you are gone?

Hellas, he replied, is a large place, Cebes, and has many good men, and there are barbarous races not a few: seek for him among them all, far and wide, sparing neither pains nor money; for there is no better way of using your money. And you must not forget to seek for him among yourselves too; for he is nowhere more likely to be found.

The search, replied Cebes, shall certainly be made. And now, if you please, let us return to the point of the argument at which we digressed.

By all means, replied Socrates; what else should I please?

Very good, he said.

Must we not, said Socrates, ask ourselves some question of this sort? — What is that which, as we imagine, is liable to be scattered away, and about which we fear? and what again is that about which we have no fear? And then we may proceed to inquire whether that which suffers dispersion is or is not of the nature of soul — our hopes and fears as to our own souls will turn upon that.

That is true, he said.

Now the compound or composite may be supposed to be naturally capable of being dissolved in like man-

ner as of being compounded; but that which is uncompounded, and that only, must be, if anything is,
indissoluble.

Yes; that is what I should imagine, said Cebes.

And the uncompounded may be assumed to be the
same and unchanging, whereas the compound is always changing and never the same?

That I also think, he said.

Then now let us return to the previous discussion.
Is that idea or essence, which in the dialectical process
we define as essence or true existence — whether essence of equality, beauty, or anything else — are these
essences, I say, liable at times to some degree of
change? or are they each of them always what they
are, having the same simple self-existent and unchanging forms, and not admitting of variation at all,
or in any way, or at any time?

They must be always the same, Socrates, replied
Cebes.

And what would you say of the many beautiful —
whether men or horses or garments or any other things
which may be called equal or beautiful, — are they all
unchanging and the same always, or quite the reverse?
May they not rather be described as almost always
changing and hardly ever the same, either with themselves or with one another?

The latter, replied Cebes; they are always in a
state of change.

And these you can touch and see and perceive with
the senses, but the unchanging things you can only
perceive with the mind — they are invisible· and are
not seen?

That is very true, he said.

Well then, he added, let us suppose that there are
two sorts of existences — one seen, the other unseen.

Let us suppose them.

The seen is the changing, and the unseen is the unchanging?

That may be also supposed.

And, further, is not one part of us body, and the rest of us soul?

To be sure.

And to which class may we say that the body is more alike and akin?

Clearly to the seen: no one can doubt that.

And is the soul seen or not seen?

Not by man, Socrates.

And by " seen " and " not seen " is meant by us that which is or is not visible to the eye of man?

Yes, to the eye of man.

And what do we say of the soul? — is that seen or not seen?

Not seen.

Unseen then?

Yes.

Then the soul is more like to the unseen, and the body to the seen?

That is most certain, Socrates.

And were we not saying long ago that the soul when using the body as an instrument of perception, that is to say, when using the sense of sight or hearing or some other sense (for the meaning of perceiving through the body is perceiving through the senses) — were we not saying that the soul too is then dragged by the body into the region of the changeable, and wanders and is confused; the world spins round her, and she is like a drunkard when under their influence?

Very true.

But when returning into herself she reflects; then she passes into the realm of purity, and eternity, and immortality, and unchangeableness, which are her kin-

dred, and with them she ever lives, when she is by
herself and is not let or hindered; then she ceases
from her erring ways, and being in communion with
the unchanging is unchanging. And this state of the
soul is called wisdom?

That is well and truly said, Socrates, he replied.

And to which class is the soul more nearly alike and
akin, as far as may be inferred from this argument,
as well as from the preceding one?

I think, Socrates, that, in the opinion of every one
who follows the argument, the soul will be infinitely
more like the unchangeable — even the most stupid
person will not deny that.

And the body is more like the changing?

Yes.

Yet once more consider the matter in this light:
When the soul and the body are united, then nature
orders the soul to rule and govern, and the body to
obey and serve. Now which of these two functions
is akin to the divine? and which to the mortal? Does
not the divine appear to you to be that which naturally
orders and rules, and the mortal that which is subject
and servant?

True.

And which does the soul resemble?

The soul resembles the divine, and the body the
mortal — there can be no doubt of that, Socrates.

Then reflect, Cebes: is not the conclusion of the
whole matter this — that the soul is in the very likeness of the divine, and immortal, and intelligible, and
uniform, and indissoluble, and unchangeable; and the
body is in the very likeness of the human, and mortal,
and unintelligible, and multiform, and dissoluble, and
changeable. Can this, my dear Cebes, be denied?

No indeed.

But if this is true, then is not the body liable to

speedy dissolution? and is not the soul almost or altogether indissoluble?

Certainly.

And do you further observe, that after a man is dead, the body, which is the visible part of man, and has a visible framework, which is called a corpse, and which would naturally be dissolved and decomposed and dissipated, is not dissolved or decomposed at once, but may remain for a good while, if the constitution be sound at the time of death, and the season of the year favorable? For the body when shrunk and embalmed, as is the custom in Egypt, may remain almost entire through infinite ages; and even in decay, still there are some portions, such as the bones and ligaments, which are practically indestructible. You allow that?

Yes.

And are we to suppose that the soul, which is invisible, in passing to the true Hades, which like her is invisible, and pure, and noble, and on her way to the good and wise God, whither, if God will, my soul is also soon to go, — that the soul, I repeat, if this be her nature and origin, is blown away and perishes immediately on quitting the body, as the many say? That can never be, my dear Simmias and Cebes. The truth rather is, that the soul which is pure at departing draws after her no bodily taint, having never voluntarily had connection with the body, which she is ever avoiding, herself gathered into herself; for such abstraction has been the study of her life. And what does this mean but that she has been a true disciple of philosophy, and has practised how to die easily? And is not philosophy the practice of death?

Certainly.

That soul, I say, herself invisible, departs to the invisible world — to the divine and immortal and rational: thither arriving, she lives in bliss and is released from the error and folly of men, their fears and wild passions and all other human ills, and forever dwells, as they say of the initiated, in company with the gods? Is not this true, Cebes?

Yes, said Cebes, beyond a doubt.

But the soul which has been polluted, and is impure at the time of her departure, and is the companion and servant of the body always, and is in love with and fascinated by the body and by the desires and pleasures of the body, until she is led to believe that the truth only exists in a bodily form, which a man may touch and see and taste and use for the purposes of his lusts, — the soul, I mean, accustomed to hate and fear and avoid the intellectual principle, which to the bodily eye is dark and invisible, and can be attained only by philosophy; — do you suppose that such a soul as this will depart pure and unalloyed?

That is impossible, he replied.

She is engrossed by the corporeal, which the continual association and constant care of the body have made natural to her.

Very true.

And this, my friend, may be conceived to be that heavy, weighty, earthy element of sight by which such a soul is depressed and dragged down again into the visible world, because she is afraid of the invisible and of the world below — prowling about tombs and sepulchres, in the neighborhood of which, as they tell us, are seen certain ghostly apparitions of souls which have not departed pure, but are cloyed with sight and therefore visible.[1]

[1] Compare Milton, Comus, 463 foll.: —

> " But when lust,
> By unchaste looks, loose gestures, and foul talk,
> But most by lewd and lavish act of sin,
> Lets in defilement to the inward parts,

That is very likely, Socrates.

Yes, that is very likely, Cebes; and these must be the souls, not of the good, but of the evil, who are compelled to wander about such places in payment of the penalty of their former evil way of life; and they continue to wander until the desire which haunts them is satisfied and they are imprisoned in another body. And they may be supposed to be fixed in the same natures which they had in their former life.

What natures do you mean, Socrates?

I mean to say that men who have followed after gluttony, and wantonness, and drunkenness, and have had no thought of avoiding them, would pass into asses and animals of that sort. What do you think?

I think that exceedingly probable.

And those who have chosen the portion of injustice, and tyranny, and violence, will pass into wolves, or hawks and kites; — whither else can we suppose them to go?

Yes, said Cebes; that is doubtless the place of natures such as theirs.

And there is no difficulty, he said, in assigning to all of them places answering to their several natures and propensities?

There is not, he said.

Even among them some are happier than others; and the happiest both in themselves and their place of abode are those who have practised the civil and social virtues which are called temperance and justice, and

> The soul grows clotted by contagion,
> Imbodies, and imbrutes, till she quite lose
> The divine property of her first being.
> Such are those thick and gloomy shadows damp
> Oft seen in charnel vaults and sepulchres,
> Lingering, and sitting by a new made grave,
> As loath to leave the body that it lov'd,
> And linked itself by carnal sensuality
> To a degenerate and degraded state."

are acquired by habit and attention without philosophy and mind.

Why are they the happiest?

Because they may be expected to pass into some
gentle social nature which is like their own, such as
that of bees or ants, or even back again into the form
of man, and just and moderate men spring from them.

That is not impossible.

But he who is a philosopher or lover of learning,
and is entirely pure at departing, is alone permitted
to reach the gods. And this is the reason, Simmias
and Cebes, why the true votaries of philosophy abstain
from all fleshly lusts, and endure and refuse to give
themselves up to them, — not because they fear poverty or the ruin of their families, like the lovers of
money, and the world in general; nor like the lovers
of power and honor, because they dread the dishonor
or disgrace of evil deeds.

No, Socrates, that would not become them, said
Cebes.

No indeed, he replied; and therefore they who have
a care of their souls, and do not merely live in the
fashions of the body, say farewell to all this; they will
not walk in the ways of the blind: and when philosophy offers them purification and release from evil,
they feel that they ought not to resist her influence,
and to her they incline, and whither she leads they
follow her.

What do you mean, Socrates?

I will tell you, he said. The lovers of knowledge
are conscious that their souls when philosophy receives
them, are simply fastened and glued to their bodies:
the soul is only able to view existence through the bars
of a prison, and not in her own nature; she is wallowing in the mire of all ignorance; and philosophy, seeing the terrible nature of her confinement, and that

the captive through desire is led to conspire in her own captivity (for the lovers of knowledge are aware that this was the original state of the soul, and that when she was in this state philosophy received and gently counselled her, and wanted to release her, pointing out to her that the eye is full of deceit, and also the ear and the other senses, and persuading her to retire from them in all but the necessary use of them, and to be gathered up and collected into herself, and to trust only to herself and her own intuitions of absolute existence, and mistrust that which comes to her through others and is subject to vicissitude) — philosophy shows her that this is visible and tangible, but that what she sees in her own nature is intellectual and invisible. And the soul of the true philosopher thinks that she ought not to resist this deliverance, and therefore abstains from pleasures and desires and pains and fears, as far as she is able; reflecting that when a man has great joys or sorrows or fears or desires, he suffers from them, not the sort of evil which might be anticipated — as for example, the loss of his health or property which he has sacrificed to his lusts — but he has suffered an evil greater far, which is the greatest and worst of all evils, and one of which he never thinks.

And what is that, Socrates? said Cebes.

Why this: When the feeling of pleasure or pain in the soul is most intense, all of us naturally suppose that the object of this intense feeling is then plainest and truest: but this is not the case.

Very true.

And this is the state in which the soul is most enthralled by the body.

How is that?

Why, because each pleasure and pain is a sort of nail which nails and rivets the soul to the body, and engrosses her and makes her believe that to be true which the body affirms to be true; and from agreeing with the body and having the same delights she is obliged to have the same habits and ways, and is not likely ever to be pure at her departure to the world below, but is always saturated with the body; so that she soon sinks into another body and there germinates and grows, and has therefore no part in the communion of the divine and pure and simple.

That is most true, Socrates, answered Cebes.

And this, Cebes, is the reason why the true lovers of knowledge are temperate and brave; and not for the reason which the world gives.

Certainly not.

Certainly not! For not in that way does the soul of a philosopher reason; she will not ask philosophy to release her in order that when released she may deliver herself up again to the thraldom of pleasures and pains, doing a work only to be undone again, weaving instead of unweaving her Penelope's web. But she will make herself a calm of passion, and follow reason, and dwell in her, beholding the true and divine (which is not matter of opinion), and thence derive nourishment. Thus she seeks to live while she lives, and after death she hopes to go to her own kindred and to be freed from human ills. Never fear, Simmias and Cebes, that a soul which has been thus nurtured and has had these pursuits, will at her departure from the body be scattered and blown away by the winds and be nowhere and nothing.

When Socrates had done speaking, for a considerable time there was silence; he himself and most of us appeared to be meditating on what had been said; only Cebes and Simmias spoke a few words to one another. And Socrates observing this asked them what they thought of the argument, and whether there was anything wanting? For, said he, much is still open to suspicion and attack, if any one were disposed to sift the matter thoroughly. If you are talking of something else I would rather not interrupt you, but if you are still doubtful about the argument do not hesitate to say exactly what you think, and let us have anything better which you can suggest; and if I am likely to be of any use, allow me to help you.

Simmias said: I must confess, Socrates, that doubts did arise in our minds, and each of us was urging and inciting the other to put the question which we wanted to have answered and which neither of us liked to ask, fearing that our importunity might be troublesome under present circumstances.

Socrates smiled, and said: O Simmias, how strange that is; I am not very likely to persuade other men that I do not regard my present situation as a misfortune, if I am unable to persuade you, and you will keep fancying that I am at all more troubled now than at any other time. Will you not allow that I have as much of the spirit of prophecy in me as the swans? For they, when they perceive that they must die, having sung all their life long, do then sing more than ever, rejoicing in the thought that they are about to go away to the god whose ministers they are. But men, because they are themselves afraid of death, slanderously affirm of the swans that they sing a lament at the last, not considering that no bird sings when cold, or hungry, or in pain, not even the nightingale, nor the swallow, nor yet the hoopoe; which are said indeed to tune a lay of sorrow, although I do not believe this to be true of them any more than of the swans. But because they are sacred to Apollo, and have the gift of prophecy, and anticipate the good things of another world, therefore they sing and rejoice in that day more than ever they did before. And

I too, believing myself to be the consecrated servant of the same God, and the fellow-servant of the swans, and thinking that I have received from my master gifts of prophecy which are not inferior to theirs, would not go out of life less merrily than the swans. Cease to mind then about this, but speak and ask anything which you like, while the eleven magistrates of Athens allow.

Well, Socrates, said Simmias, then I will tell you my difficulty, and Cebes will tell you his. For I dare say that you, Socrates, feel as I do, how very hard or almost impossible is the attainment of any certainty about questions such as these in the present life. And yet I should deem him a coward who did not prove what is said about them to the uttermost, or whose heart failed him before he had examined them on every side. For he should persevere until he has attained one of two things: either he should discover or learn the truth about them; or, if this is impossible, I would have him take the best and most irrefragable of human notions, and let this be the raft upon which he sails through life — not without risk, as I admit, if he can not find some word of God which will more surely and safely carry him. And now, as you bid me, I will venture to question you, as I should not like to reproach myself hereafter with not having said at the time what I think. For when I consider the matter, either alone or with Cebes, the argument does certainly appear to me, Socrates, to be not sufficient.

Socrates answered: I dare say, my friend, that you may be right, but I should like to know in what respect the argument is not sufficient.

In this respect, replied Simmias: — might not a person use the same argument about harmony and the lyre — might he not say that harmony is a thing invisible, incorporeal, fair, divine, abiding in the lyre

which is harmonized, but that the lyre and the strings
are matter and material, composite, earthy, and akin
to mortality? And when some one breaks the lyre, or
cuts and rends the strings, then he who takes this view
would argue as you do, and on the same analogy, that
the harmony survives and has not perished; for you
can not imagine, as he would say, that the lyre without
the strings, and the broken strings themselves remain,
and yet that the harmony, which is of heavenly and
immortal nature and kindred, has perished — and
perished too before the mortal. That harmony, he
would say, certainly exists somewhere, and the wood
and strings will decay before that decays. For I suspect, Socrates, that the notion of the soul which we
are all of us inclined to entertain, would also be yours,
and that you too would conceive the body to be strung
up, and held together, by the elements of hot and cold,
wet and dry, and the like, and that the soul is the harmony or due proportionate admixture of them. And,
if this is true, the inference clearly is, that when the
strings of the body are unduly loosened or overstrained
through disorder or other injury, then the soul, though
most divine, like other harmonies of music or of works
of art, of course perishes at once; although the material
remains of the body may last for a considerable time,
until they are either decayed or burned. Now if any
one maintained that the soul, being the harmony of the
elements of the body, first perishes in that which is
called death, how shall we answer him?

Socrates looked round at us as his manner was, and
said with a smile: Simmias has reason on his side; and
why does not some one of you who is abler than myself
answer him? for there is force in his attack upon me.
But perhaps, before we answer him, we had better
also hear what Cebes has to say against the argument
— this will give us time for reflection, and when both

of them have spoken, we may either assent to them,
if their words appear to be in consonance with the
truth, or if not, we may take up the other side, and
argue with them. Please to tell me then, Cebes, he
said, what was the difficulty which troubled you?

Cebes said: I will tell you. My feeling is that the
argument is still in the same position, and open to the
same objections which were urged before; for I am
ready to admit that the existence of the soul before
entering into the bodily form has been very ingeniously, and, as I may be allowed to say, quite sufficiently proven; but the existence of the soul after
death is still, in my judgment, unproven. Now my
objection is not the same as that of Simmias; for I am
not disposed to deny that the soul is stronger and more
lasting than the body, being of opinion that in all such
respects the soul very far excels the body. Well then,
says the argument to me, why do you remain unconvinced? — When you see that the weaker is still in
existence after the man is dead, will you not admit that
the more lasting must also survive during the same
period of time? Now I, like Simmias, must employ a
figure; and I shall ask you to consider whether the
figure is to the point. The parallel which I will suppose is that of an old weaver, who dies, and after his
death somebody says: — He is not dead, he must be
alive; and he appeals to the coat which he himself wove
and wore, and which is still whole and undecayed. And
then he proceeds to ask of some one who is incredulous,
whether a man lasts longer, or the coat which is in use
and wear; and when he is answered that a man lasts
far longer, thinks that he has thus certainly demonstrated the survival of the man, who is the more lasting, because the less lasting remains. But that,
Simmias, as I would beg you to observe, is not the
truth; every one sees that he who talks thus is talking

nonsense. For the truth is, that this weaver, having worn and woven many such coats, though he outlived several of them, was himself outlived by the last; but this is surely very far from proving that a man is slighter and weaker than a coat. Now the relation of the body to the soul may be expressed in a similar figure; for you may say with reason that the soul is lasting, and the body weak and shortlived in comparison. And every soul may be said to wear out many bodies, especially in the course of a long life. For if while the man is alive the body deliquesces and decays, and yet the soul always weaves her garment anew and repairs the waste, then of course, when the soul perishes, she must have on her last garment, and this only will survive her; but then again, when the soul is dead, the body will at last show its native weakness, and soon pass into decay. And therefore this is an argument on which I would rather not rely as proving that the soul exists after death. For suppose that we grant even more than you affirm as within the range of possibility, and besides acknowledging that the soul existed before birth, admit also that after death the souls of some are existing still, and will exist, and will be born and die again and again, and that there is a natural strength in the soul which will hold out and be born many times — for all this, we may be still inclined to think that she will weary in the labors of successive births, and may at last succumb in one of her deaths and utterly perish; and this death and dissolution of the body which brings destruction to the soul may be unknown to any of us, for no one of us can have had any experience of it: and if this be true, then I say that he who is confident in death has but a foolish confidence, unless he is able to prove that the soul is altogether immortal and imperishable. But if he is not able to prove this, he who is about to die will always have reason to fear that when the body is dis-united, the soul also may utterly perish.

All of us, as we afterwards remarked to one another, had an unpleasant feeling at hearing them say this. When we had been so firmly convinced before, now to have our faith shaken seemed to introduce a confusion and uncertainty, not only into the previous argument, but into any future one; either we were not good judges, or there were no real grounds of belief.

Ech. There I feel with you — indeed I do, Phaedo, and when you were speaking, I was beginning to ask myself the same question: What argument can I ever trust again? For what could be more convincing than the argument of Socrates, which has now fallen into discredit? That the soul is a harmony is a doctrine which has always had a wonderful attraction for me, and, when mentioned, came back to me at once, as my own original conviction. And now I must begin again and find another argument which will assure me that when the man is dead the soul dies not with him. Tell me, I beg, how did Socrates proceed? Did he appear to share the unpleasant feeling which you mention? or did he receive the interruption calmly and give a sufficient answer? Tell us, as exactly as you can, what passed.

Phaed. Often, Echecrates, as I have admired Socrates, I never admired him more than at that moment. That he should be able to answer was nothing, but what astonished me was, first, the gentle and pleasant and approving manner in which he regarded the words of the young men, and then his quick sense of the wound which had been inflicted by the argument, and his ready application of the healing art. He might be compared to a general rallying his defeated and broken army, urging them to follow him and return to the field of argument.

Ech. How was that?

Phaed. You shall hear, for I was close to him on his right hand, seated on a sort of stool, and he on a couch which was a good deal higher. Now he had a way of playing with my hair, and then he smoothed my head, and pressed the hair upon my neck, and said: — To-morrow, Phaedo, I suppose that these fair locks of yours will be severed.

Yes, Socrates, I suppose that they will, I replied.

Not so, if you will take my advice.

What shall I do with them? I said.

To-day, he replied, and not to-morrow, if this argument dies and can not be brought to life again by us, you and I will both shave our locks: and if I were you, and could not maintain my ground against Simmias and Cebes, I would myself take an oath, like the Argives, not to wear hair any more until I had renewed the conflict and defeated them.

Yes, I said; but Heracles himself is said not to be match for two.

Summon me then, he said, and I will be your Iolaus until the sun goes down.

I summon you rather, I said, not as Heracles summoning Iolaus, but as Iolaus might summon Heracles.

That will be all the same, he said. But first let us take care that we avoid a danger.

And what is that? I said.

The danger of becoming misologists, he replied, which is one of the very worst things that can happen to us. For as there are misanthropists or haters of men, there are also misologists or haters of ideas, and both spring from the same cause, which is ignorance of the world. Misanthropy arises from the too great confidence of inexperience; — you trust a man and think him altogether true and good and faithful, and then in a little while he turns out to be false and knavish;

and then another and another, and when this has happened several times to a man, especially within the
circle of his own most trusted friends, as he deems
them, and he has often quarrelled with them, he at last
hates all men, and believes that no one has any good
in him at all. I dare say that you must have observed
this.

Yes, I said.

And is not this discreditable? The reason is, that a
man, having to deal with other men, has no knowledge
of them; for if he had knowledge, he would have
known the true state of the case, that few are the good
and few the evil, and that the great majority are in
the interval between them.

How do you mean? I said.

I mean, he replied, as you might say of the very
large and very small — that nothing is more uncommon than a very large or very small man; and this
applies generally to all extremes, whether of great and
small, or swift and slow, or fair and foul, or black and
white: and whether the instances you select be men or
dogs or anything else, few are the extremes, but many
are in the mean between them. Did you never observe
this?

Yes, I said, I have.

And do you not imagine, he said, that if there were
a competition of evil, the first in evil would be found
to be very few?

Yes, that is very likely, I said.

Yes, that is very likely, he replied; not that in this
respect arguments are like men — there I was led on
by you to say more than I had intended; but the point
of comparison was, that when a simple man who has
no skill in dialectics believes an argument to be true
which he afterwards imagines to be false, whether
really false or not, and then another and another, he

has no longer any faith left, and great disputers, as
you know, come to think at last that they have grown
to be the wisest of mankind; for they alone perceive
the utter unsoundness and instability of all arguments,
or indeed, of all things, which, like the currents in
the Euripus, are going up and down in never-ceasing
ebb and flow.

That is quite true, I said.

Yes, Phaedo, he replied, and very melancholy too,
if there be such a thing as truth or certainty or power
of knowing at all, that a man should have lighted upon
some argument or other which at first seemed true and
then turned out to be false, and instead of blaming
himself and his own want of wit, because he is annoyed, should at last be too glad to transfer the blame
from himself to arguments in general; and for ever
afterwards should hate and revile them, and lose the
truth and knowledge of existence.

Yes, indeed, I said; that is very melancholy.

Let us then, in the first place, he said, be careful of
admitting into our souls the notion that there is no
truth or health or soundness in any arguments at all;
but let us rather say that there is as yet no health in us,
and that we must quit ourselves like men and do our
best to gain health — you and all other men with a
view to the whole of your future life, and I myself
with a view to death. For at this moment I am sensible that I have not the temper of a philosopher; like
the vulgar, I am only a partisan. For the partisan,
when he is engaged in a dispute, cares nothing about
the rights of the question, but is anxious only to convince his hearers of his own assertions. And the difference between him and me at the present moment is
only this — that whereas he seeks to convince his
hearers that what he say is true, I am rather seeking
to convince myself; to convince my hearers is a second-

ary matter with me. And do but see how much I gain by this. For if what I say is true, then I do well to be persuaded of the truth; but if there be nothing after death, still, during the short time that remains, I shall save my friends from lamentations, and my ignorance will not last, and therefore no harm will be done. This is the state of mind, Simmias and Cebes, in which I approach the argument. And I would ask you to be thinking of the truth and not of Socrates: agree with me, if I seem to you to be speaking the truth; or if not, withstand me might and main, that I may not deceive you as well as myself in my enthusiasm, and like the bee, leave my sting in you before I die.

And now let us proceed, he said. And first of all let me be sure that I have in my mind what you were saying. Simmias, if I remember rightly, has fears and misgivings whether the soul, being in the form of harmony, although a fairer and diviner thing than the body, may not perish first. On the other hand, Cebes appeared to grant that the soul was more lasting than the body, but he said that no one could know whether the soul, after having worn out many bodies, might not perish herself and leave her last body behind her; and that this is death, which is the destruction not of the body but of the soul, for in the body the work of destruction is ever going on. Are not these, Simmias and Cebes, the points which we have to consider?

They both agreed to this statement of them.

He proceeded: And did you deny the force of the whole preceding argument, or of a part only?

Of a part only, they replied.

And what did you think, he said, of that part of the argument in which we said that knowledge was recollection only, and inferred from this that the soul must have previously existed somewhere else before she was enclosed in the body? Cebes said that he had been

wonderfully impressed by that part of the argument,
and that his conviction remained unshaken. Simmias
agreed, and added that he himself could hardly imagine the possibility of his ever thinking differently
about that.

But, rejoined Socrates, you will have to think differently, my Theban friend, if you still maintain that
harmony is a compound, and that the soul is a harmony
which is made out of strings set in the frame of the
body; for you will surely never allow yourself to say
that a harmony is prior to the elements which compose
the harmony.

No, Socrates, that is impossible.

But do you not see that you *are* saying this when
you say that the soul existed before she took the form
and body of man, and was made up of elements which
as yet had no existence? For harmony is not a sort of
thing like the soul, as you suppose; but first the lyre,
and the strings, and the sounds exist in a state of discord, and then harmony is made last of all, and
perishes first. And how can such a notion of the soul
as this agree with the other?

Not at all, replied Simmias.

And yet, he said, there surely ought to be harmony
when harmony is the theme of discourse.

There ought, replied Simmias.

But there is no harmony, he said, in the two propositions that knowledge is recollection, and that the
soul is a harmony. Which of them then will you
retain?

I think, he replied, that I have a much stronger
faith, Socrates, in the first of the two, which has been
fully demonstrated to me, than in the latter, which
has not been demonstrated at all, but rests only on
probable and plausible grounds; and I know too well
that these arguments from probabilities are impostors.

and unless great caution is observed in the use of them, they are apt to be deceptive — in geometry, and in other things too. But the doctrine of knowledge and recollection has been proven to me on trustworthy grounds; and the proof was that the soul must have existed before she came into the body, because to her belongs the essence of which the very name implies existence. Having, as I am convinced, rightly accepted this conclusion, and on sufficient grounds, I must, as I suppose, cease to argue or allow others to argue that the soul is a harmony.

Let me put the matter, Simmias, he said, in another point of view: Do you imagine that a harmony or any other composition can be in a state other than that of the elements, out of which it is compounded?

Certainly not.

Or do or suffer anything other than they do or suffer?

He agreed.

Then a harmony does not lead the parts or elements which make up the harmony, but only follows them.

He assented.

For harmony can not possibly have any motion, or sound, or other quality which is opposed to the parts.

That would be impossible, he replied.

And does not every harmony depend upon the manner in which the elements are harmonized?

I do not understand you, he said.

I mean to say that a harmony admits of degrees, and is more of a harmony, and more completely a harmony, when more completely harmonized, if that be possible; and less of a harmony, and less completely a harmony, when less harmonized.

True.

But does the soul admit of degrees? or is one soul

in the very least degree more or less, or more or less completely, a soul than another?

Not in the least.

Yet surely one soul is said to have intelligence and virtue, and to be good, and another soul is said to have folly and vice, and to be an evil soul: and this is said truly?

Yes, truly.

But what will those who maintain the soul to be a harmony say of this presence of virtue and vice in the soul? — will they say that here is another harmony, and another discord, and that the virtuous soul is harmonized, and herself being harmony has another harmony within her, and that the vicious soul is inharmonical and has no harmony within her?

I can not say, replied Simmias; but I suppose that something of that kind would be asserted by those who take this view.

And the admission is already made that no soul is more a soul than another; and this is equivalent to admitting that harmony is not more or less harmony, or more or less completely a harmony?

Quite true.

And that which is not more or less a harmony is not more or less harmonized?

True.

And that which is not more or less harmonized can not have more or less of harmony, but only an equal harmony?

Yes, an equal harmony.

Then one soul not being more or less absolutely a soul than another, is not more or less harmonized?

Exactly.

And therefore has neither more nor less of harmony or of discord?

She has not.

And having neither more nor less of harmony or of discord, one soul has no more vice or virtue than another, if vice be discord and virtue harmony?

Not at all more.

Or speaking more correctly, Simmias, the soul, if she is a harmony, will never have any vice; because a harmony, being absolutely a harmony, has no part in the inharmonical.

No.

And therefore a soul which is absolutely a soul has no vice?

How can she have, consistently with the preceding argument?

Then, according to this, if the souls of all animals are equally and absolutely souls, they will be equally good?

I agree with you, Socrates, he said.

And can all this be true, think you? he said; and are all these consequences admissible — which nevertheless seem to follow from the assumption that the soul is a harmony?

Certainly not, he said.

Once more, he said, what ruling principle is there of human things other than the soul, and especially the wise soul? Do you know of any?

Indeed, I do not.

And is the soul in agreement with the affections of the body? or is she at variance with them? For example, when the body is hot and thirsty, does not the soul incline us against drinking? and when the body is hungry, against eating? And this is only one instance out of ten thousand of the opposition of the soul to the things of the body.

Very true.

But we have already acknowledged that the soul, being a harmony, can never utter a note at variance with the tensions and relaxations and vibrations and other affections of the strings out of which she is composed; she can only follow, she can not lead them?

Yes, he said, we acknowledged that, certainly.

And yet do we not now discover the soul to be doing the exact opposite — leading the elements of which she is believed to be composed; almost always opposing and coercing them in all sorts of ways throughout life, sometimes more violently with the pains of medicine and gymnastic; then again more gently; — threatening and also reprimanding the desires, passions, fears, as if talking to a thing which is not herself, as Homer in the Odyssee represents Odysseus doing in the words: —

> " He beat his breast, and thus reproached his heart:
> Endure, my heart; far worse hast thou endured! "

Do you think that Homer could have written this under the idea that the soul is a harmony capable of being led by the affections of the body, and not rather of a nature which leads and masters them; and herself a far diviner thing than any harmony?

Yes, Socrates, I quite agree to that.

Then, my friend, we can never be right in saying that the soul is a harmony, for that would clearly contradict the divine Homer as well as ourselves.

True, he said.

Thus much, said Socrates, of Harmonia, your Theban goddess, Cebes, who has not been ungracious to us, I think; but what shall I say to the Theban Cadmus, and how shall I propitiate him?

I think that you will discover a way of propitiating him, said Cebes; I am sure that you have answered the argument about harmony in a manner that I could never have expected. For when Simmias mentioned his objection, I quite imagined that no answer could be given to him, and therefore I was surprised at finding that this argument could not sustain the first onset of yours, and not impossibly the other, whom you call Cadmus, may share a similar fate.

Nay, my good friend, said Socrates, let us not boast, lest some evil eye should put to flight the word which I am about to speak. That, however, may be left in the hands of those above; while I draw near in Homeric fashion, and try the mettle of your words. Briefly, the sum of your objection is as follows: — You want to have proven to you that the soul is imperishable and immortal, and you think that the philosopher who is confident in death has but a vain and foolish confidence, if he thinks that he will fare better than one who has led another sort of life, in the world below, unless he can prove this: and you say that the demonstration of the strength and divinity of the soul, and of her existence prior to our becoming men, does not necessarily imply her immortality. Granting that the soul is longlived, and has known and done much in a former state, still she is not on that account immortal; and her entrance into the human form may be a sort of disease which is the beginning of dissolution, and may at last, after the toils of life are over, end in that which is called death. And whether the soul enters into the body once only or many times, that, as you would say, makes no difference in the fears of individuals. For any man, who is not devoid of natural feeling, has reason to fear, if he has no knowledge or proof of the soul's immortality. That is what I suppose you to say, Cebes, which I designedly repeat, in order that nothing may escape us, and that you may, if you wish, add or subtract anything.

But, said Cebes, as far as I see at present, I have nothing to add or subtract; you have expressed my meaning.

Socrates paused awhile, and seemed to be absorbed in reflection. At length he said: This is a very serious inquiry which you are raising, Cebes, involving the whole question of generation and corruption, about which I will, if you like, give you my own experience; and you can apply this, if you think that anything which I say will avail towards the solution of your difficulty.

I should very much like, said Cebes, to hear what you have to say.

Then I will tell you, said Socrates. When I was young, Cebes, I had a prodigious desire to know that department of philosophy which is called Natural Science; this appeared to me to have lofty aims, as being the science which has to do with the causes of things, and which teaches why a thing is, and is created and destroyed; and I was always agitating myself with the consideration of such questions as these: — Is the growth of animals the result of some decay which the hot and cold principle contract, as some have said? Is the blood the element with which we think, or the air, or the fire? or perhaps nothing of this sort — but the brain may be the originating power of the perceptions of hearing and sight and smell, and memory and opinion may come from them, and science may be based on memory and opinion when no longer in motion, but at rest. And then I went on to examine the decay of them, and then to the things of heaven and earth, and at last I concluded that I was wholly incapable of these inquiries, as I will satisfactorily prove to you. For I was fascinated by them to such a degree that my eyes grew blind to things that I had seemed to myself, and also to others, to know quite well; and I forgot what I had before thought to be self-evident, that the growth of man is the result of eating and drinking; for when by the digestion of

food flesh is added to flesh and bone to bone, and whenever there is an aggregation of congenial elements,
the lesser bulk becomes larger and the small man
greater. Was not that a reasonable notion?

Yes, said Cebes, I think so.

Well; but let me tell you something more. There
was a time when I thought that I understood the
meaning of greater and less pretty well; and when I
saw a great man standing by a little one, I fancied
that one was taller than the other by a head; or one
horse would appear to be greater than another horse:
and still more clearly did I seem to perceive that ten
is two more than eight, and that two cubits are more
than one, because two is twice one.

And what is now your notion of such matters? said
Cebes.

I should be far enough from imagining, he replied,
that I knew the cause of any of them, indeed I should,
for I can not satisfy myself that when one is added to
one, the one to which the addition is made becomes two,
or that the two units added together make two by
reason of the addition. For I cannot understand how,
when separated from the other, each of them was one
and not two, and now, when they are brought together, the mere juxtaposition of them can be the
cause of their becoming two: nor can I understand
how the division of one is the way to make two;
for then a different cause would produce the same
effect, — as in the former instance the addition and
juxtaposition of one to one was the cause of two, in
this the separation and subtraction of one from the
other would be the cause. Nor am I any longer
satisfied that I understand the reason why one or anything else either is generated or destroyed or is at all,
but I have in my mind some confused notion of another method, and can never admit this.

Then I heard some one who had a book of Anaxagoras, as he said, out of which he read that mind was the disposer and cause of all, and I was quite delighted at the notion of this, which appeared admirable, and I said to myself: If mind is the disposer, mind will dispose all for the best, and put each particular in the best place; and I argued that if any one desired to find out the cause of the generation or destruction or existence of anything, he must find out what state of being or suffering or doing was best for that thing, and therefore a man had only to consider the best for himself and others, and then he would also know the worse, for that the same science comprised both. And I rejoiced to think that I had found in Anaxagoras a teacher of the causes of existence such as I desired, and I imagined that he would tell me first whether the earth is flat or round; and then he would further explain the cause and the necessity of this, and would teach me the nature of the best and show that this was best; and if he said that the earth was in the centre, he would explain that this position was the best, and I should be satisfied if this were shown to me, and not want any other sort of cause. And I thought that I would then go on and ask him about the sun and moon and stars, and that he would explain to me their comparative swiftness, and their returnings and various states, and how their several affections, active and passive, were all for the best. For I could not imagine that when he spoke of mind as the disposer of them, he would give any other account of their being as they are, except that this was best; and I thought that when he had explained to me in detail the cause of each and the cause of all, he would go on to explain to me what was best for each and what was best for all. I had hopes which I would not have sold for much, and I seized the books and read them as fast as

I could in my eagerness to know the better and the worse.

What hopes I had formed, and how grievously was I disappointed! As I proceeded, I found my philosopher altogether forsaking mind or any other principle of order, but having recourse to air, and ether, and water, and other eccentricities. I might compare him to a person who began by maintaining generally that mind is the cause of the actions of Socrates, but who, when he endeavored to explain the causes of my several actions in detail, went on to show that I sit here because my body is made up of bones and muscles; and the bones, as he would say, are hard and have ligaments which divide them, and the muscles are elastic, and they cover the bones, which have also a covering or environment of flesh and skin which contains them; and as the bones are lifted at their joints by the contraction or relaxation of the muscles, I am able to bend my limbs, and this is why I am sitting here in a curved posture; — that is what he would say, and he would have a similar explanation of my talking to you, which he would attribute to sound, and air, and hearing, and he would assign ten thousand other causes of the same sort, forgetting to mention the true cause, which is, that the Athenians have thought fit to condemn me, and accordingly I have thought it better and more right to remain here and undergo my sentence; for I am inclined to think that these muscles and bones of mine would have gone off to Megara or Boeotia — by the dog of Egypt they would, if they had been guided only by their own idea of what was best, and if I had not chosen as the better and nobler part, instead of playing truant and running away, to undergo any punishment which the state inflicts. There is surely a strange confusion of causes and conditions in all this. It may be said, indeed, that without bones and muscles and the other parts of the body I can not execute my purposes. But to say that I do as I do because of them, and that this is the way in which mind acts, and not from the choice of the best, is a very careless and idle mode of speaking. I wonder that they can not distinguish the cause from the condition, which the many, feeling about in the dark, are always mistaking and misnaming. And thus one man makes a vortex all round and steadies the earth by the heaven; another gives the air as a support to the earth, which is a sort of broad trough. Any power which in disposing them as they are disposes them for the best never enters into their minds, nor do they imagine that there is any superhuman strength in that; they rather expect to find another Atlas of the world who is stronger and more everlasting and more containing than the good is, and are clearly of opinion that the obligatory and containing power of the good is as nothing; and yet this is the principle which I would fain learn if any one would teach me. But as I have failed either to discover myself, or to learn of any one else, the nature of the best, I will exhibit to you, if you like, what I have found to be the second best mode of inquiring into the cause.

I should very much like to hear that, he replied.

Socrates proceeded: — I thought that as I had failed in the contemplation of true existence, I ought to be careful that I did not lose the eye of my soul; as people may injure their bodily eye by observing and gazing on the sun during an eclipse, unless they take the precaution of only looking at the image reflected in the water, or in some similar medium. That occurred to me, and I was afraid that my soul might be blinded altogether if I looked at things with my eyes or tried by the help of the senses to apprehend them. And I thought that I had better have recourse to

ideas, and seek in them the truth of existence. I dare
say that the simile is not perfect — for I am very far
from admitting that he who contemplates existences
through the medium of ideas, sees them only " through
a glass darkly," any more than he who sees them in
their working and effects. However, this was the
method which I adopted: I first assumed some principle which I judged to be the strongest, and then I
affirmed as true whatever seemed to agree with this,
whether relating to the cause or to anything else; and
that which disagreed I regarded as untrue. But I
should like to explain my meaning clearly, as I do not
think that you understand me.

No indeed, replied Cebes, not very well.

There is nothing new, he said, in what I am about
to tell you; but only what I have been always and
everywhere repeating in the previous discussion and
on other occasions: I want to show you the nature of
that cause which has occupied my thoughts, and I
shall have to go back to those familiar words which
are in the mouth of every one, and first of all assume
that there is an absolute beauty and goodness, and
greatness, and the like; grant me this, and I hope to be
able to show you the nature of the cause, and to prove
the immortality of the soul.

Cebes said: You may proceed at once with the proof,
as I readily grant you this.

Well, he said, then I should like to know whether
you agree with me in the next step; for I can not help
thinking that if there be anything beautiful other than
absolute beauty, that can only be beautiful in as far as
it partakes of absolute beauty — and this I should say
of everything. Do you agree in this notion of the
cause?

Yes, he said, I agree.

He proceeded: I know nothing and can understand

nothing of any other of those wise causes which are alleged; and if a person says to me that the bloom of color, or form, or anything else of that sort is a source of beauty, I leave all that, which is only confusing to me, and simply and singly, and perhaps foolishly, hold and am assured in my own mind that nothing makes a thing beautiful but the presence and participation of beauty in whatever way or manner obtained; for as to the manner I am uncertain, but I stoutly contend that by beauty all beautiful things become beautiful. That appears to me to be the only safe answer that I can give, either to myself or to any other, and to that I cling, in the persuasion that I shall never be overthrown, and that I may safely answer to myself or any other, that by beauty beautiful things become beautiful. Do you not agree to that?

Yes, I agree.

And that by greatness only great things become great and greater greater, and by smallness the less become less.

True.

Then if a person remarks that A is taller by a head than B, and B less by a head than A, you would refuse to admit this, and would stoutly contend that what you mean is only that the greater is greater by, and by reason of, greatness, and the less is less only by, or by reason of, smallness; and thus you would avoid the danger of saying that the greater is greater and the less less by the measure of the head, which is the same in both, and would also avoid the monstrous absurdity of supposing that the greater man is greater by reason of the head, which is small. Would you not be afraid of that?

Indeed, I should, said Cebes, laughing.

In like manner you would be afraid to say that ten exceeded eight by, and by reason of, two; but would say by, and by reason of, number; or that two cubits exceed one cubit by a half, but by magnitude? — that is what you would say, for there is the same danger in both cases.

Very true, he said.

Again, would you not be cautious of affirming that the addition of one to one, or the division of one, is the cause of two? And you would loudly asseverate that you know of no way in which anything comes into existence except by participation in its own proper essence, and consequently, as far as you know, the only cause of two is the participation in duality; that is, the way to make two, and the participation in one is the way to make one. You would say: I will let alone puzzles of division and addition — wiser heads than mine may answer them; inexperienced as I am, and ready to start, as the proverb says, at my own shadow, I can not afford to give up the sure ground of a principle. And if any one assails you there, you would not mind him, or answer him, until you had seen whether the consequences which follow agree with one another or not, and when you are further required to give an explanation of this principle, you would go on to assume a higher principle, and the best of the higher ones until you found a resting-place; but you would not confuse the principle and the consequences in your reasoning, like the Eristics — at least if you wanted to discover real existence. Not that this confusion signifies to them who never care or think about the matter at all, for they have the wit to be well pleased with themselves however great may be the turmoil of their ideas. But you, if you are a philosopher, will, I believe, do as I say.

What you say is most true, said Simmias and Cebes, both speaking at once.

Ech. Yes, Phaedo; and I don't wonder at their

assenting. Any one who has the least sense will acknowledge the wonderful clearness of Socrates' reasoning.

Phaed. Certainly, Echecrates; and that was the feeling of the whole company at the time.

Ech. Yes, and equally of ourselves, who were not of the company, and are now listening to your recital. But what followed?

Phaed. After all this was admitted, and they had agreed about the existence of ideas and the participation in them of the other things which derive their names from them, Socrates, if I remember rightly, said: —

This is your way of speaking; and yet when you say that Simmias is greater than Socrates and less than Phaedo, do you not predicate of Simmias both greatness and smallness?

Yes, I do.

But still you allow that Simmias does not really exceed Socrates, as the words may seem to imply, because he is Simmias, but by reason of the size which he has; just as Simmias does not exceed Socrates because he is Simmias, any more than because Socrates is Socrates, but because he has smallness when compared with the greatness of Simmias?

True.

And if Phaedo exceeds him in size, this is not because Phaedo is Phaedo, but because Phaedo has greatness relatively to Simmias, who is comparatively smaller?

That is true.

And therefore Simmias is said to be great, and is also said to be small, because he is in a mean between them, exceeding the smallness of the one by his greatness, and allowing the greatness of the other to exceed his smallness. He added, laughing, I am speaking like a book, but I believe that what I am saying is true.

Simmias assented to this.

The reason why I say this, is that I want you to agree with me in thinking, not only that absolute greatness will never be great and also small, but that greatness in us or in the concrete will never admit the small or admit of being exceeded: instead of this one of two things will happen, either the greater will fly or retire before the opposite, which is the less, or at the advance of the less will cease to exist; but will not, if allowing or admitting smallness, be changed by that; even as I, having received and admitted smallness when compared with Simmias, remain just as I was, and am the same small person. And as the idea of greatness can not condescend ever to be or become small, in like manner the smallness in us can not be or become great; nor can any other opposite which remains the same ever be or become its own opposite, but either passes away or perishes in the change.

That, replied Cebes, is quite my notion.

One of the company, though I do not exactly remember which of them, on hearing this, said: By heaven, is not this the direct contrary of what was admitted before — that out of the greater came the less and out of the less the greater, and that opposites were simply generated from opposites; whereas now this seems to be utterly denied.

Socrates inclined his head to the speaker and listened. I like your courage, he said, in reminding us of this. But you do not observe that there is a difference in the two cases. For then we were speaking of opposites in the concrete, and now of the essential opposite which, as is affirmed, neither in us nor in nature can ever be at variance with itself: then, my

friend, we were speaking of things in which opposites are inherent and which are called after them,
but now about the opposites which are inherent in
them and which give their name to them; these essential opposites will never, as we maintain, admit of
generation into or out of one another. At the same
time, turning to Cebes, he said: Were you at all disconcerted, Cebes, at our friend's objection?

That was not my feeling, said Cebes; and yet I can
not deny that I am apt to be disconcerted.

Then we are agreed after all, said Socrates, that
the opposite will never in any case be opposed to
itself?

To that we are quite agreed, he replied.

Yet once more let me ask you to consider the question from another point of view, and see whether you
agree with me: — There is a thing which you term
heat, and another thing which you term cold?

Certainly.

But are they the same as fire and snow?

Most assuredly not.

Heat is not the same as fire, nor is cold the same
as snow?

No.

And yet you will surely admit, that when snow,
as was before said, is under the influence of heat, they
will not remain snow and heat; but at the advance
of the heat, the snow will either retire or perish?

Very true, he replied.

And the fire too at the advance of the cold will
either retire or perish; and when the fire is under the
influence of the cold, they will not remain as before,
fire and cold.

That is true, he said.

And in some cases the name of the idea is not confined to the idea; but anything else which, not being

the idea, exists only in the form of the idea, may also lay claim to it. I will try to make this clearer by an example. — The odd number is always called by the name of odd?

Very true.

But is this the only thing which is called odd? Are there not other things which have their own name, and yet are called odd, because, although not the same as oddness, they are never without oddness? — that is what I mean to ask — whether numbers such as the number three are not of the class of odd. And there are many other examples: would you not say, for example, that three may be called by its proper name, and also be called odd, which is not the same with three? and this may be said not only of three but also of five, and every alternate number — each of them without being oddness is odd, and in the same way two and four, and the whole series of alternate numbers, has every number even, without being evenness. Do you admit that?

Yes, he said, how can I deny that?

Then now mark the point at which I am aiming: — not only do essential opposites exclude one another, but also concrete things, which, although not in themselves opposed, contain opposites; these, I say, also reject the idea which is opposed to that which is contained in them, and at the advance of that they either perish or withdraw. There is the number three for example; — will not that endure annihilation or anything sooner than be converted into an even number, remaining three?

Very true, said Cebes.

And yet, he said, the number two is certainly not opposed to the number three?

It is not.

Then not only do opposite ideas repel the advance

of one another, but also there are other things which repel the approach of opposites.

That is quite true, he said.

Suppose, he said, that we endeavor, if possible, to determine what these are.

By all means.

Are they not, Cebes, such as compel the things of which they have possession, not only to take their own form, but also the form of some opposite?

What do you mean?

I mean, as I was just now saying, and have no need to repeat to you, that those things which are possessed by the number three must not only be three in number, but must also be odd.

Quite true.

And on this oddness, of which the number three has the impress, the opposite idea will never intrude?

No.

And this impress was given by the odd principle?

Yes.

And to the odd is opposed the even?

True.

Then the idea of the even number will never arrive at three?

No.

Then three has no part in the even?

None.

Then the triad or number three is uneven?

Very true.

To return then to my distinction of natures which are not opposites, and yet do not admit opposites: as in this instance, three, although not opposed to the even, does not any the more admit of the even, but always brings the opposite into play on the other side; or as two does not receive the odd, or fire the cold — from these examples (and there are many more of them) perhaps you may be able to arrive at the general conclusion, that not only opposites will not re-ceive opposites, but also that nothing which brings the opposite will admit the opposite of that which it brings in that to which it is brought. And here let me recapitulate — for there is no harm in repetition. The number five will not admit the nature of the even, any more than ten, which is the double of five, will admit the nature of the odd — the double, though not strictly opposed to the odd, rejects the odd altogether. Nor again will parts in the ratio of 3:2, nor any fraction in which there is a half, nor again in which there is a third, admit the notion of the whole, al-though they are not opposed to the whole. You will agree to that?

Yes, he said, I entirely agree and go along with you in that.

And now, he said, I think that I may begin again; and to the question which I am about to ask I will beg you to give not the old safe answer, but another, of which I will offer you an example; and I hope that you will find in what has been just said another foundation which is as safe. I mean that if any one asks you " what that is, the inherence of which makes the body hot," you will reply not heat (this is what I call the safe and stupid answer), but fire, a far bet-ter answer, which we are now in a condition to give. Or if any one asks you " why a body is diseased," you will not say from disease, but from fever; and instead of saying that oddness is the cause of odd numbers, you will say that monad is the cause of them: and so of things in general, as I dare say that you will understand sufficiently without my adducing any fur-ther examples.

Yes, he said, I quite understand you.

Tell me, then, what is that the inherence of which will render the body alive?

The soul, he replied.

And is this always the case?

Yes, he said, of course.

Then whatever the soul possesses, to that she comes bearing life?

Yes, certainly.

And is there any opposite to life?

There is, he said.

And what is that?

Death.

Then the soul, as has been acknowledged, will never receive the opposite of what she brings. And now, he said, what did we call that principle which repels the even?

The odd.

And that principle which repels the musical, or the just?

The unmusical, he said, and the unjust.

And what do we call that principle which does not admit of death?

The immortal, he said.

And does the soul admit of death?

No.

Then the soul is immortal?

Yes, he said.

And may we say that this is proven?

Yes, abundantly proven, Socrates, he replied.

And supposing that the odd were imperishable, must not three be imperishable?

Of course.

And if that which is cold were imperishable, when the warm principle came attacking the snow, must not the snow have retired whole and unmelted — for

it could never have perished, nor could it have remained and admitted the heat?

True, he said.

Again, if the uncooling or warm principle were
imperishable, the fire when assailed by cold would not
have perished or have been extinguished, but would
have gone away unaffected?

Certainly, he said.

And the same may be said of the immortal: if the
immortal is also imperishable, the soul when attacked
by death can not perish; for the preceding argument
shows that the soul will not admit of death, or ever be
dead, any more than three or the odd number will
admit of the even, or fire, or the heat in the fire, of
the cold. Yet a person may say: " But although the
odd will not become even at the approach of the even,
why may not the odd perish and the even take the
place of the odd? " Now to him who makes this objection, we can not answer that the odd principle is
imperishable; for this has not been acknowledged, but
if this had been acknowledged, there would have been
no difficulty in contending that at the approach of
the even the odd principle and the number three took
up their departure; and the same argument would
have held good of fire and heat and any other thing

Very true.

And the same may be said of the immortal: if the
immortal is also imperishable, then the soul will be imperishable as well as immortal; but if not, some other
proof of her imperishableness will have to be given.

No other proof is needed, he said; for if the immortal, being eternal, is liable to perish, then nothing
is imperishable.

Yes, replied Socrates, all men will agree that God,
and the essential form of life, and the immortal in
general, will never perish.

Yes, all men, he said — that is true; and what is more, gods, if I am not mistaken, as well as men.

Seeing then that the immortal is indestructible, must not the soul, if she is immortal, be also imperishable?

Most certainly.

Then when death attacks a man, the mortal portion of him may be supposed to die, but the immortal goes out of the way of death and is preserved safe and sound?

True.

Then, Cebes, beyond question, the soul is immortal and imperishable, and our souls will truly exist in another world!

I am convinced, Socrates, said Cebes, and have nothing more to object; but if my friend Simmias, or any one else, has any further objection, he had better speak out, and not keep silence, since I do not know how there can ever be a more fitting time to which he can defer the discussion, if there is anything which he wants to say or have said.

But I have nothing more to say, replied Simmias; nor did I see any room for uncertainty, except that which arises necessarily out of the greatness of the subject and the feebleness of man, and which I can not help feeling.

Yes, Simmias, replied Socrates, that is well said: and more than that, first principles, even if they appear certain, should be carefully considered; and when they are satisfactorily ascertained, then, with a sort of hesitating confidence in human reason, you may, I think, follow the course of the argument; and if this is clear, there will be no need for any further inquiry.

That, he said, is true.

But then, O my friends, he said, if the soul is really immortal, what care should be taken of her, not only in respect of the portion of time which is called life, but of eternity! And the danger of neglecting her from this point of view does indeed appear to be awful. If death had only been the end of all, the wicked would have had a good bargain in dying, for they would have been happily quit not only of their body, but of their own evil together with their souls. But now, as the soul plainly appears to be immortal, there is no release or salvation from evil except the attainment of the highest virtue and wisdom. For the soul when on her progress to the world below takes nothing with her but nurture and education; which are indeed said greatly to benefit or greatly to injure the departed, at the very beginning of his pilgrimage in the other world.

For after death, as they say, the genius of each individual, to whom he belonged in life, leads him to a certain place in which the dead are gathered together for judgment, whence they go into the world below, following the guide, who is appointed to conduct them from this world to the other: and when they have there received their due and remained their time, another guide brings them back again after many revolutions of ages. Now this journey to the other world is not, as Aeschylus says in the Telephus, a single and straight path — no guide would be wanted for that, and no one could miss a single path; but there are many partings of the road, and windings, as I must infer from the rites and sacrifices which are offered to the gods below in places where three ways meet on earth. The wise and orderly soul is conscious of her situation, and follows in the path; but the soul which desires the body, and which, as I was relating before, has long been fluttering about the lifeless frame and the world of sight, is after many struggles and many sufferings hardly and with violence carried away by

her attendant genius, and when she arrives at the place
where the other souls are gathered, if she be impure
and have done impure deeds, or been concerned in
foul murders or other crimes which are the brothers of
these, and the works of brothers in crime — from that
soul every one flees and turns away; no one will be her
companion, no one her guide, but alone she wanders
in extremity of evil until certain times are fulfilled,
and when they are fulfilled, she is borne irresistibly
to her own fitting habitation; as every pure and just
soul which has passed through life in the company and
under the guidance of the gods has also her own
proper home.

Now the earth has divers wonderful regions, and is
indeed in nature and extent very unlike the notions of
geographers, as I believe on the authority of one who
shall be nameless.

What do you mean, Socrates? said Simmias. I
have myself heard many descriptions of the earth, but
I do not know in what you are putting your faith, and
I should like to know.

Well, Simmias, replied Socrates, the recital of a
tale does not, I think, require the art of Glaucus; and
I know not that the art of Glaucus could prove the
truth of my tale, which I myself should never be able
to prove, and even if I could, I fear, Simmias, that
my life would come to an end before the argument
was completed. I may describe to you, however, the
form and regions of the earth according to my conception of them.

That, said Simmias, will be enough.

Well then, he said, my conviction is, that the earth
is a round body in the centre of the heavens, and therefore has no need of air or any similar force as a support, but is kept there and hindered from falling or
inclining any way by equability of the surrounding

heaven and by her own equipoise. For that which, being in equipoise, is in the centre of that which is equably diffused, will not incline any way in any degree, but will always remain in the same state and not deviate. And this is my first notion.

Which is surely a correct one, said Simmias.

Also I believe that the earth is very vast, and that we who dwell in the region extending from the river Phasis to the Pillars of Heracles along the borders of the sea, are just like ants or frogs about a marsh, and inhabit a small portion only, and that many others dwell in many like places. For I should say that in all parts of the earth there are hollows of various forms and sizes, into which the water and the mist and the air collect; and that the true earth is pure and in the pure heaven, in which also are the stars — that is the heaven which is commonly spoken of as the ether, of which this is but the sediment collecting in the hollows of the earth. But we who live in these hollows are deceived into the notion that we are dwelling above on the surface of the earth; which is just as if a creature who was at the bottom of the sea were to fancy that he was on the surface of the water, and that the sea was the heaven through which he saw the sun and the other stars, — he having never come to the surface by reason of his feebleness and sluggishness, and having never lifted up his head and seen, nor ever heard from one who had seen, this other region which is so much purer and fairer than his own. Now this is exactly our case: for we are dwelling in a hollow of the earth, and fancy that we are on the surface; and the air we call the heaven, and in this we imagine that the stars move. But this is also owing to our feebleness and sluggishness, which prevent our reaching the surface of the air: for if any man could arrive at the exterior limit, or take the wings of a bird and fly upward, like a fish who puts his head out and sees this world, he would see a world beyond; and, if the nature of man could sustain the sight, he would acknowledge that this was the place of the true heaven and the true light and the true stars. For this earth, and the stones, and the entire region which surrounds us, are spoiled and corroded, like the things in the sea which are corroded by the brine; for in the sea too there is hardly any noble or perfect growth, but clefts only, and sand, and an endless slough of mud; and even the shore is not to be compared to the fairer sights of this world. And greater far is the superiority of the other. Now of that upper earth which is under the heaven, I can tell you a charming tale, Simmias, which is well worth hearing.

And we, Socrates, replied Simmias, shall be charmed to listen.

The tale, my friend, he said, is as follows: — In the first place, the earth, when looked at from above, is like one of those balls which have leather coverings in twelve pieces, and is of divers colors, of which the colors which painters use on earth are only a sample. But there the whole earth is made up of them, and they are brighter far and clearer than ours; there is a purple of wonderful lustre, also the radiance of gold, and the white which is in the earth is whiter than any chalk or snow. Of these and other colors the earth is made up, and they are more in number and fairer than the eye of man has ever seen; and the very hollows (of which I was speaking) filled with air and water are seen like light flashing amid the other colors, and have a color of their own, which gives a sort of unity to the variety of earth. And in this fair region everything that grows — trees, and flowers, and fruits — are in a like degree fairer than any here; and there are hills, and stones in them in a like degree

smoother, and more transparent, and fairer in color
than our highly-valued emeralds and sardonyxes and
jaspers, and other gems, which are but minute fragments of them: for there all the stones are like our
precious stones, and fairer still. The reason of this is,
that they are pure, and not, like our precious stones,
infected or corroded by the corrupt briny elements
which coagulate among us, and which breed foulness
and disease both in earth and stones, as well as in
animals and plants. They are the jewels of the upper
earth, which also shines with gold and silver and the
like, and they are visible to sight and large and abundant and found in every region of the earth, and
blessed is he who sees them. And upon the earth are
animals and men, some in a middle region, others
dwelling about the air as we dwell about the sea;
others in islands which the air flows round, near the
continent: and in a word, the air is used by them as
the water and the sea are by us, and the ether is to
them what the air is to us. Moreover, the temperament of their season is such that they have no disease,
and live much longer than we do, and have sight and
hearing and smell, and all the other senses, in far
greater perfection, in the same degree that air is purer
than water or the ether than air. Also they have
temples and sacred places in which the gods really
dwell, and they hear their voices and receive their
answers, and are conscious of them and hold converse
with them, and they see the sun, moon, and stars as
they really are, and their other blessedness is of a piece
with this.

Such is the nature of the whole earth, and of the
things which are around the earth; and there are
divers regions in the hollows on the face of the globe
everywhere, some of them deeper and also wider than
that which we inhabit, others deeper and with a nar-

rower opening than ours, and some are shallower and
wider; all have numerous perforations, and passages
broad and narrow in the interior of the earth, connecting them with one another; and there flows into and
out of them, as into basins, a vast tide of water, and
huge subterranean streams of perennial rivers, and
springs hot and cold, and a great fire, and great rivers
of fire, and streams of liquid mud, thin or thick (like
the rivers of mud in Sicily, and the lava streams which
follow them), and the regions about which they happen to flow are filled up with them. And there is a
sort of swing in the interior of the earth which moves
all this up and down. Now the swing is on this wise:
— There is a chasm which is the vastest of them all,
and pierces right through the whole earth; this is that
which Homer describes in the words: —

" Far off, where is the inmost depth beneath the earth; "

and which he in other places, and many other poets,
have called Tartarus. And the swing is caused by the
streams flowing into and out of this chasm, and they
each have the nature of the soil through which they
flow. And the reason why the streams are always
flowing in and out, is that the watery element has no
bed or bottom, and is surging and swinging up and
down, and the surrounding wind and air do the same;
they follow the water up and down, hither and thither,
over the earth — just as in respiring the air is always
in process of inhalation and exhalation; — and the
wind swinging with the water in and out produces
fearful and irresistible blasts: when the waters retire
with a rush into the lower parts of the earth, as they
are called, they flow through the earth into those
regions, and fill them up as with the alternate motion
of a pump, and then when they leave those regions
and rush back hither, they again fill the hollows here,

and when these are filled, flow through subterranean channels and find their way to their several places, forming seas, and lakes, and rivers, and springs. Thence they again enter the earth, some of them making a long circuit into many lands, others going to few places and those not distant; and again fall into Tartarus, some at a point a good deal lower than that at which they rose, and others not much lower, but all in some degree lower than the point of issue. And some burst forth again on the opposite side, and some on the same side, and some wind round the earth with one or many folds like the coils of a serpent, and descend as far as they can, but always return and fall into the lake. The rivers on either side can descend only to the centre and no further, for to the rivers on both sides the opposite side is a precipice.

Now these rivers are many, and mighty, and diverse, and there are four principle ones, of which the greatest and outermost is that called Oceanus, which flows round the earth in a circle; and in the opposite direction flows Acheron, which passes under the earth through desert places, into the Acherusian lake: this is the lake to the shores of which the souls of the many go when they are dead, and after waiting an appointed time, which is to some a longer and to some a shorter time, they are sent back again to be born as animals. The third river rises between the two, and near the place of rising pours into a vast region of fire, and forms a lake larger than the Mediterranean Sea, boiling with water and mud; and proceeding muddy and turbid, and winding about the earth, comes, among other places, to the extremities of the Acherusian lake, but mingles not with the waters of the lake, and after making many coils about the earth plunges into Tartarus at a deeper level. This is that Pyriphle-gethon, as the stream is called, which throws up jets of fire in all sorts of places. The fourth river goes out on the opposite side, and falls first of all into a wild and savage region, which is all of a dark blue color, like lapis lazuli; and this is that river whch is called the Stygian river, and falls into and forms the Lake Styx, and after falling into the lake and receiving strange powers in the waters, passes under the earth, winding round in the opposite direction to Pyriphlegethon and meeting in the Acherusian lake from the opposite side. And the water of this river too mingles with no other, but flows round in a circle and falls into Tartarus over against Pyriphlegethon; and the name of this river, as the poets say, is Cocytus.

Such is the nature of the other world; and when the dead arrive at the place to which the genius of each severally conveys them, first of all, they have sentence passed upon them, as they have lived well and piously or not. And those who appear to have lived neither well nor ill, go to the river Acheron, and mount such conveyances as they can get, and are carried in them to the lake, and there they dwell and are purified of their evil deeds, and suffer the penalty of the wrongs which they have done to others, and are absolved, and receive the rewards of their good deeds according to their deserts. But those who appear to be incurable by reason of the greatness of their crimes — who have committed many and terrible deeds of sacrilege, murders foul and violent, or the like — such are hurled into Tartarus which is their suitable destiny, and they never come out. Those again who have committed crimes, which, although great, are not unpardonable — who in a moment of anger, for example, have done violence to a father or a mother, and have repented for the remainder of their lives, or, who have taken the life of another under the like extenuating circumstances — these are plunged into Tartarus, the pains of which they are compelled to undergo for a year, but at the end of the year the wave casts them forth — mere homicides by way of Cocytus, parricides and matricides by Pyriphlegethon — and they are borne to the Acherusian lake, and there they lift up their voices and call upon the victims whom they have slain or wronged, to have pity on them, and to receive them, and to let them come out of the river into the lake. And if they prevail, then they come forth and cease from their troubles; but if not, they are carried back again into Tartarus and from thence into the rivers unceasingly, until they obtain mercy from those whom they have wronged: for that is the sentence inflicted upon them by their judges. Those also who are remarkable for having led holy lives are released from this earthly prison, and go to their pure home which is above, and dwell in the purer earth; and those who have duly purified themselves with philosophy, live henceforth altogether without the body, in mansions fairer far than these, which may not be described, and of which the time would fail me to tell.

Wherefore, Simmias, seeing all these things, what ought not we to do in order to obtain virtue and wisdom in this life? Fair is the prize, and the hope great!

I do not mean to affirm that the description which I have given of the soul and her mansions is exactly true — a man of sense ought hardly to say that. But I do say that, inasmuch as the soul is shown to be immortal, he may venture to think, not improperly or unworthily, that something of the kind is true. The venture is a glorious one, and he ought to comfort himself with words like these, which is the reason why I lengthen out the tale. Wherefore, I say, let a man be of good cheer about his soul, who has cast away the pleasures and ornaments of the body as alien to him, and rather hurtful in their effects, and has followed after the pleasures of knowledge in this life; who has adorned the soul in her own proper jewels, which are temperance, and justice, and courage, and nobility, and truth — in these arrayed she is ready to go on her journey to the world below, when her time comes. You, Simmias and Cebes, and all other men, will depart at some time or other. Me already, as the tragic poet would say, the voice of fate calls. Soon I must drink the poison; and I think that I had better repair to the bath first, in order that the women may not have the trouble of washing my body after I am dead.

When he had done speaking, Crito said: And have you any commands for us, Socrates — anything to say about your children, or any other matter in which we can serve you?

Nothing particular, he said: only, as I have always told you, I would have you look to yourselves; that is a service which you may always be doing to me and mine as well as to yourselves. And you need not make professions; for if you take no thought for yourselves, and walk not according to the precepts which I have given you, not now for the first time, the warmth of your professions will be of no avail.

We will do our best, said Crito. But in what way would you have us bury you?

In any way that you like; only you must get hold of me, and take care that I do not walk away from you. Then he turned to us, and added with a smile: — I can not make Crito believe that I am the same Socrates who has been talking and conducting the argument; he fancies that I am the other Socrates whom he will soon see, a dead body — and he asks, How shall he bury me? And though I have spoken many words in the endeavor to show that when I have drunk the poison I shall leave you and go to the joys of the blessed, — these words of mine, with which I comforted you and myself, have had, as I perceive, no effect upon Crito. And therefore I want you to be surety for me now, as he was surety for me at the trial: but let the promise be of another sort; for he was my surety to the judges that I would remain, but you must be my surety to him that I shall not remain, but go away and depart; and then he will suffer less at my death, and not be grieved when he sees my body being burned or buried. I would not have him sorrow at my hard lot, or say at the burial, Thus we lay out Socrates, or, Thus we follow him to the grave or bury him; for false words are not only evil in themselves, but they infect the soul with evil. Be of good cheer, then, my dear Crito, and say that you are burying my body only, and do with that as is usual, and as you think best.

When he had spoken these words, he arose and went into the bath-chamber with Crito, who bid us wait; and we waited, talking and thinking of the subject of discourse, and also of the greatness of our sorrow; he was like a father of whom we were being bereaved, and we were about to pass the rest of our lives as orphans. When he had taken the bath his children were brought to him — (he had two young sons and an elder one) ; and the women of his family also came, and he talked to them and gave them a few directions in the presence of Crito; and he then dismissed them and returned to us.

Now the hour of sunset was near, for a good deal of time had passed while he was within. When he came out, he sat down with us again after his bath, but not much was said. Soon the jailer, who was the servant of the eleven, entered and stood by him, saying: — To you, Socrates, whom I know to be the noblest and gentlest and best of all who ever came to this place, I will not impute the angry feelings of other men, who rage and swear at me, when, in obedience to the authorities, I bid them drink the poison — indeed, I am sure that you will not be angry with me; for others, as you are aware, and not I, are the guilty cause. And so fare you well, and try to bear lightly what must needs be; you know my errand. Then bursting into tears he turned away and went out.

Socrates looked at him and said: I return your good wishes, and will do as you bid. Then turning to us, he said, How charming the man is: since I have been in prison he has always been coming to see me, and at times he would talk to me, and was as good as could be to me, and now see how generously he sorrows for me. But we must do as he says, Crito; let the cup be brought, if the poison is prepared: if not, let the attendant prepare some.

Yet, said Crito, the sun is still upon the hill-tops, and many a one has taken the draught late, and after the announcement has been made to him, he has eaten and drunk, and indulged in sensual delights; do not hasten then, there is still time.

Socrates said: Yes, Crito, and they of whom you speak are right in doing thus, for they think that they will gain by the delay; but I am right in not doing thus, for I do not think that I should gain anything by drinking the poison a little later; I should be sparing and saving a life which is already gone; I could only laugh at myself for this. Please then to do as I say, and not to refuse me.

Crito, when he heard this, made a sign to the servant; and the servant went in, and remained for some time, and then returned with the jailer carrying the cup of poison. Socrates said: You, my good friend,

who are experienced in these matters, shall give me
directions how I am to proceed. The man answered:
You have only to walk about until your legs are heavy,
and then to lie down, and the poison will act. At the
same time he handed the cup to Socrates, who in the
easiest and gentlest manner, without the least fear or
change of color or feature, looking at the man with all
his eyes, Echecrates, as his manner was, took the cup
and said: What do you say about making a libation
out of this cup to any god? May I, or not? The
man answered: We only prepare, Socrates, just so
much as we deem enough. I understand, he said: yet
I may and must pray to the gods to prosper my
journey from this to that other world — may this
then, which is my prayer, be granted to me. Then
holding the cup to his lips, quite readily and cheer-
fully he drank off the poison. And hitherto most of
us had been able to control our sorrow; but now when
we saw him drinking, and saw too that he had finished
the draught, we could no longer forbear, and in spite
of myself my own tears were flowing fast; so that I
covered my face and wept over myself, for certainly I
was not weeping over him, but at the thought of my
own calamity in having lost such a companion. Nor
was I the first, for Crito, when he found himself unable to restrain his tears, had got up and moved away,
and I followed; and at that moment, Apollodorus,
who had been weeping all the time, broke out into a
loud cry which made cowards of us all. Socrates
alone retained his calmness: What is this strange
outcry? he said. I sent away the women mainly in
order that they might not offend in this way, for I
have heard that a man should die in peace. Be quiet
then, and have patience. When we heard that, we
were ashamed, and refrained our tears; and he walked
about until, as he said, his legs began to fail, and then

he lay on his back, according to the directions, and
the man who gave him the poison now and then looked
at his feet and legs; and after a while he pressed his
foot hard, and asked him if he could feel; and he said,
No; and then his leg, and so upwards and upwards,
and showed us that he was cold and stiff. And he felt
then himself and said: When the poison reaches the
heart, that will be the end. He was beginning to grow
cold about the groin, when he uncovered his face, for
he had covered himself up, and said (they were his
last words) — he said: Crito, I owe a cock to
Asclepius; will you remember to pay the debt? The
debt shall be paid, said Crito; is there anything else?
There was no answer to this question; but in a minute
or two a movement was heard, and the attendants uncovered him; his eyes were set, and Crito closed his
eyes and mouth.

Such was the end, Echecrates, of our friend, whom
I may truly call the wisest, and justest, and best of
all men whom I have ever known.

THE SYMPOSIUM

INTRODUCTION

OF all the works of Plato the Symposium is the most perfect in form, and may be truly thought to contain more than any commentator has ever dreamed of; or, as Goethe said of one of his own writings, more than the author himself knew. For in philosophy as in prophecy glimpses of the future may often be conveyed in words which could hardly have been understood or interpreted at the time when they were uttered. More than any other Platonic work the Symposium is Greek both in style and subject, having a beauty " as of a statue," while the companion Dialogue of the Phaedrus is marked by a sort of Gothic irregularity. More too than in any other part of his writings, Plato is emancipated from former philosophies. The genius of Greek art seems to triumph over the traditions of Pythagorean, Eleatic, or Megarian systems, and " the old quarrel of poetry and philosophy " has at least a superficial reconcilement.

An unknown person who had heard of the discourses in praise of love spoken by Socrates and others at the banquet of Agathon is desirous of having an authentic account of them, which he thinks that he can obtain from Apollodorus, the same excitable, or rather " mad " friend of Socrates, who has already appeared in the Phaedo. He had imagined that the discourses were recent. There he is mistaken: but they are still fresh in the memory of his informant, who had just been repeating them to Glaucon, and is quite prepared to have another rehearsal of them in a walk from the Piraeus to Athens. He had not indeed been present himself, but he had heard them from the best authority. Aristodemus, who is described as having been in past times a sort of humble but inseparable attendant of Socrates, had reported them to him.

The narrative which he had heard was as follows: —

Aristodemus meeting Socrates in holiday attire, is invited by him to a banquet at the house of Agathon, who had been sacrificing in thanksgiving for his tragic victory on the day previous. But no sooner has he entered the house than he finds that Socrates is missing — he has stayed behind in a fit of abstraction, and does not appear until the banquet is half over.

Some raillery passes between him and the host, and then the question is asked, " What shall they do about drinking? as they had been all well drunk on the day before, and drinking on two successive days is a bad thing." This is confirmed by the authority of Eryximachus the physician, who further proposes that instead of listening to the flute-girl and her " noise " they shall hold discourses in honor of love, one after another, going from left to right as they are sitting at the table. All of them agree to this, and Phaedrus, who is the " father " of the idea which he has previously communicated to Eryximachus, begins as follows : —

He descants first of all upon the antiquity of love, which is proved by the authority of the poets, and then upon the benefits which he gives to man. The greatest of these is the sense of honor and dishonor. The lover is ashamed to be seen by the beloved doing or suffering any cowardly or mean act. And a state or army which was made up only of lovers and their loves would be invincible. For love will convert the veriest coward into an inspired hero.

And there have been true loves not only of men but of women also. Such was the love of Alcestis, who dared to die for her husband, and as a reward was allowed to come again from the dead. But Orpheus, the cowardly harper, who went down to Hades alive, that he might bring back his wife, was mocked with an apparition only, and the gods afterwards contrived his death as a punishment of his impudence. The hero Achilles affords an instance of similar devotion; for he was willing to avenge his lover Patroclus, although he knew that his own death would immediately follow: and the gods, who honor the love of the beloved above that of the lover, rewarded him, and sent him to the islands of the blest.

Pausanias, who was sitting next, then takes up the tale. He says that Phaedrus should have distinguished the heavenly love from the earthly, before he praised either. For there are two loves, as there are two Aphrodites — one the heavenly, who has no mother and is the elder and wiser goddess, and the other, the daughter of Zeus and Dione, who is popular and common. The first of the two loves has a noble purpose, and delights only in the intelligent nature of man, and is faithful to the end, and has no shadow of wantonness or lust. The second is the coarser kind of love, which is a love of the body rather than of the soul, and is apt to be a love of women and boys as well as of men. Now actions vary according to the manner of their performance; and this applies to love as well as to every other sort of action. Moreover there is a difference of opinion about the propriety of male loves. Some, like the Boeotians, approve of them; others, like the Ionians, and most of the barbarians, disapprove of them; partly because they are aware of the political dangers which ensue from them, as may be seen in the instance of Harmodius and Aristogeiton. At Athens and Sparta there is an apparent contradiction about them. For at times they are encouraged, and then the lover is allowed to play all sorts of fantastic tricks; he may swear and forswear himself (and " at lovers' perjuries they say Jove laughs "); he may be a servant, and lie on a mat at the door of his love, without any loss of character; but there are also times when elders look grave and guard their young relations, and personal remarks are made. The truth is that some of these loves are disgraceful and others honorable. The vulgar love of the body which takes wings and flies away when the bloom of youth is over, is disgraceful, as is also the interested love of power or wealth; but the love of the noble mind is lasting. The lover should be tested, and the beloved should not be too ready to yield. The rule in our country is that the beloved may do the same service to the lover in the way of virtue which the lover may do to him.

This voluntary service rendered for the sake of virtue and wisdom is permitted among us; and when these two customs — one the love of youth, the other the practice of virtue and philosophy — meet in one, then the lovers may lawfully unite. Nor is there any disgrace to a disinterested lover in being deceived: but the interested lover is doubly disgraced, for if he loses his love he loses his character; whereas the noble love of the other remains the same, although the object of his love is unworthy: for nothing can be nobler than love for the sake of virtue. This is that love of the heavenly goddess which is of great price to individuals and cities, making them work together for their improvement.

The turn of Aristophanes comes next; but he has the hiccough, and therefore proposes that Eryximachus the physician shall cure him or speak in his turn. Eryximachus is ready to do both, and speaks as follows: —

He agrees with Pausanias in maintaining that there are two kinds of love; but his art has led him to the conclusion that the empire of this double love extends over all things, and is to be found in animals and plants as well as in man. In the human body also there are two loves; and the art of medicine shows which is the good and which is the bad love, and persuades the body to accept the good and reject the bad, and reconciles conflicting elements and makes them friends. Every art, gymnastic and husbandry as well as medicine, is the reconciliation of opposites; and this is what Heracleitus meant, when he spoke of a harmony of opposites: but in strictness he should rather have spoken of a harmony which succeeds opposites, for an agreement of disagreements there can not be. Music too is concerned with the principles of love in their application to harmony and rhythm. In the abstract, all is simple, and we are not troubled with the twofold love; but when they are applied in education with their accompaniments of song and metre, then the discord begins. Then the old tale has to be repeated of fair Urania and the coarse Polyhymnia, who must be indulged sparingly, just as in my own art of medicine care must be taken that the taste of the epicure be gratified without inflicting upon him the attendant penalty of disease.

There is a similar harmony or disagreement in the course of the seasons and in the relations of moist and dry, hot and cold, hoar frost and blight; and diseases of all sorts spring from the excesses or disorders of the element of love. The knowledge of this in relation to the heavenly bodies is termed astronomy, and in relation to the gods is called divination. For divination is the peacemaker of gods and men, and works by a knowledge of the tendencies of merely human loves to piety and impiety. Such is the power of love; and that love which is just and temperate has the greatest power, and is the source of all our happiness and friendship with the gods and with one another. I dare say that I have omitted to mention many things which you, Aristophanes, may supply, as I perceive that you are cured of the hiccough.

Aristophanes, who has been cured of the hiccough, now speaks: —

He professes to open a new vein of discourse, in which he begins by treating of the origin of human nature. The sexes were originally three, men, women, and the union of the two; and they were made round, having four hands, four feet, two faces on a round neck, and the rest to correspond. Terrible was their strength and swiftness; and they were essaying to scale heaven and attack the gods. Doubt reigned in the celestial councils; the gods were divided between the desire of quelling the pride of man and the fear of losing the sacrifices. At last Zeus hit upon an expedient. Let us cut them in two, he said; then they will only have half their strength, and we shall have twice as many sacrifices. He spake, and split them as you might split an egg with an hair; and when this was done, he told Apollo to give their faces a twist and rearrange their persons, taking out the wrinkles and tying the skin in a knot about the navel. The two halves went about looking for one another, and were ready to die of hunger in one another's arms. Then Zeus invented an adjustment of the sexes, which enabled them to marry and go their way to the business of life. Now the characters of men differ accordingly as they are derived from the original man or the original woman, or the original man-woman. Those who come from the man-woman are lascivious and adulterous; those who come from the woman form female attachments; those who are a section of the male follow the male and embrace him, and in him all their desires centre. They can not tell what they want of one another, but they live in pure and manly affection and can not be separated. If Hephaestus were to come to them and propose that they should be melted into one and remain one in this world and in the world below, they would acknowledge that this was the very expression of their want. For love is the desire of the whole, and the pursuit of the whole is called love. There was a time when the two sexes were only one, but now God has halved them, — much as the Lacedaemonians have cut up the Arcadians, — and if they don't behave themselves he will quarter them, and they will hop about with half a nose and face in basso relievo. Wherefore let us exhort all men to piety, that we may obtain the goods of which love is the author, and be reconciled to God, and find our own true loves, which rarely happens in this world. And now I must beg you not to suppose that I am alluding to Pausanias and Agathon, for my words refer to all mankind everywhere.

Some raillery ensues first between Aristophanes and Eryximachus and then between Agathon and Socrates, which threatens to grow into an argument. This is speedily repressed by Phaedrus, who reminds the disputants of their tribute to the god. Agathon's speech follows.

He will speak of the god first and then of his gifts. He is the fairest and blessedest and best of the gods, and also the youngest, having had no existence in the old days of Iapetus and Cronos when the gods were at war. The things that were done then were done of necessity and not of love. For love is young and dwells in soft places, — not like Ate in Homer, walking on the skulls of men, but in their hearts and souls, which are soft enough. He is all flexibility and grace, and his habitation is among the flowers, and he can not do or suffer wrong; for all men serve and obey him of their own free will, and where there is love there is obedience, and where obedience is, there is justice; for none can be wronged of his own free will. And he is temperate as well as just, for he is the ruler of the desires, and if he rules them he must be temperate. Also he is courageous, for he is the conqueror of the lord of war. And he is wise too; for he is a poet, and the author of poesy in others. He created the animals; he is the inventor of the arts; all the gods are his subjects; he is the fairest and best in himself, and the cause of what is fairest and best in others; he makes men to be of one mind at a banquet, filling them with affection and emptying them of disaffection; the pilot, helper, defender, savior of men, in whose footsteps let every man follow, chanting a strain of love. Such is the discourse, half playful, half serious, which I dedicate to the god.

The turn of Socrates comes next. He begins by remarking satirically that he has not understood the terms of the original agreement, for he fancied that they meant to speak the true praises of love, but now he finds that they only say what is good of him, whether true or false. He begs to be absolved from speaking falsely, but he is willing to speak the truth, and proposes to begin by questioning Agathon. The result of his questions may be summed up as follows: —

Love is of something, and that which love desires is not that which love is or has; for no man desires that which he is or has. And love is of the beautiful, and therefore love has not the beautiful. And the beautiful is the good, and therefore, in wanting and desiring the beautiful, love also wants and desires the good. Socrates professes to have put the same questions and have obtained the same answers from Diotima, a wise woman of Mantinea, who, like Agathon, had spoken first of love and then of his works. Socrates, like Agathon, had told her that love is a mighty god and also fair, and she had shown him in return that love was neither, but in a mean between fair and foul, good and evil, and not a god at all, but only a great demon or intermediate being, who conveys to the gods the prayers of men, and to men the commands of the gods.

Socrates asks: Who are his father and mother? To this Diotima replies that he is the son of Plenty and Poverty, and partakes of the nature of both, and is full and starved by turns. Like his mother he is poor and squalid, lying on mats at doors like his father he is full of arts and resources, and is in a mean between ignorance and knowledge. And in this he resembles the philosopher who is also in a mean between the wise and the ignorant. Such is the nature of love, who is not to be confused with the beloved.

But love desires the beautiful; and then arises the question, What does he desire of the beautiful? He desires, of course, the possession of the beautiful; — but what is given by that? For the beautiful let us substitute the good, and we have no difficulty in seeing that the possession of the good is happiness, and that love is the desire of this. But the meaning of the term has been too often confined to one sort of love, whereas love is really coëxtensive with the good. And love desires not only the good, but the everlasting possession of the good. Why then is there all this flutter and excitement about love? Because all men and women at a certain age are desirous of bringing to the birth. And love is not of beauty only, but of birth in beauty; this is the principle of immortality in a mortal creature. And when beauty approaches, then the conceiving power is benign and diffuse, but when foulness, she is averted and morose.

But why again does this extend not only to men but also to animals? Because they too have an instinct of immortality. Even in the same individual there is a perpetual succession as well of the parts of the material body as of the thoughts and desires of the mind; nay, even knowledge comes and goes. There is no sameness of existence, but the new mortality is always taking the place of the old. This is why parents love their children — for the sake of immortality; and this is why men love the immortality of fame. For the creative soul creates not children, but conceptions of wisdom and virtue, such as poets and other creators have invented. And the noblest creations of all are those of legislators, in honor of whom temples have been raised. Who would not sooner have these children of the mind than the ordinary human ones?

I will now initiate you, she said, into the greater mysteries; for he who would proceed in due course should love first one fair form, and then many, and learn the connection of them; and from beautiful bodies he should proceed to beautiful minds, and the beauty of laws and institutions, until he perceives that all beauty is of one kindred; and from institutions he should go on to the sciences, until at last the vision is revealed to him of a single science of universal beauty, and then he will behold the everlasting nature which is the cause of all, and will be near the end. In the contemplation of that supreme being of love he will be purified of earthly leaven, and will behold beauty, not with the bodily eye, but with the eye of the mind, and will bring forth true creations of virtue and wisdom, and be the friend of God and heir of immortality.

Such, Phaedrus, is the tale which I heard from the stranger of Mantinea, and which you may call the encomium of love, or what you please.

The company applaud the speech of Socrates, and Aristophanes is about to say something, when suddenly a band of revellers breaks into the court, and the voice of Alcibiades is heard asking for Agathon. He is led in drunk, and welcomed by Agathon, whom he has come to crown with a garland. He is placed on a couch at his side, but suddenly, on recognizing Socrates, he starts up, and a sort of conflict is carried on between them, which Agathon is requested to appease. Alcibiades insists that they shall drink, and has a large wine-cooler filled, which he first empties himself, and then fills again and passes on to Socrates. He is informed of the nature of the entertainment; he is willing to join, if only in the character of a drunken and disappointed lover he may be allowed to sing the praises of Socrates.

He begins by comparing Socrates first to the masks of Silenus, which have images of the gods inside them; and, secondly, to Marsyas the flute-player. For Socrates produces the same effect with the voice which Marsyas did with the flute. He is the great speaker and enchanter who ravishes the souls of men, the convincer of hearts too, as he has convinced Alcibiades, and made him ashamed of his mean and miserable life. He has suffered agonies from him, and is at his wit's end. He was in hopes that Socrates would fall in love with him; this as he thought would give him a wonderful opportunity of receiving lessons of wisdom. He narrates the failure of his design. He then proceeds to mention some other particulars of the life of Socrates; how they were at Potidaea together, where Socrates showed his superior powers of enduring cold and fatigue; how on one occasion he had stood for an entire day and night absorbed in reflection amid the wonder of the spectators; how on another occasion he had saved Alcibiades' life; how at the battle of Delium, after the defeat, he might be seen stalking about like a pelican, rolling his eyes. The sum of all is, that he is the most wonderful of human beings, and absolutely unlike any one but a satyr. Like the satyr in his language too; for he uses the commonest words as the outward mask of the divinest truths.

When Alcibiades has done speaking, a dispute begins between him and Agathon and Socrates. Socrates piques Alcibiades by a pretended affection for Agathon. Presently another band of revellers appears, who introduce disorder into the feast; the sober part of the company, Eryximachus, Phaedrus, and others, withdraw; and Aristodemus, the follower of Socrates, sleeps during the whole of a long winter's night. When he wakes at cockcrow the revellers are nearly all asleep. Only Socrates, Aristophanes, and Agathon hold out; they are drinking out of a large goblet, which they pass round, and Socrates is explaining to the two others, who are half asleep, that the genius of tragedy is the same as that of comedy, and that the writer of tragedy ought to be a writer of comedy also. And first Aristophanes drops, and then, as the day is dawning, Agathon. Socrates, having laid them to rest, goes to his daily avocations until the evening.

If it be true that there are more things in the Symposium of Plato than any commentator has dreamed of, it is also true that many things have been imagined which are not really to be found there. Some writings hardly admit of a more distinct interpretation than a musical composition; and every reader may form his own accompaniment of thought or feeling to the strain which he hears. The Symposium of Plato is a work of this character, and hardly admits of being rendered in any other words but the writer's own. There are so many half-lights and cross-lights, so much of the color of mythology, and of the manner of sophistry, adhering — rhetoric and poetry, the playful and the serious, are so subtly intermingled in it, and vestiges of old philosophy so curiously blend with germs of future knowledge, that agreement among interpreters is not to be expected. The expression " poema magis putandum quam comicorum poetarum," which has been applied to all the writings of Plato, is especially applicable to the Symposium.

The power of love is represented in the Symposium as running through all nature and all being: at one end descending to animals and plants, and attaining to the highest vision of truth at the other. In an age when man was seeking for an expression of the world around him, the conception of love greatly affected him. One of the first distinctions of language and of mythology was that of gender; and at a later period the ancient physicist, anticipating modern science, saw, or thought that he saw, a sex in plants; there were elective affinities among the elements, marriages of earth and heaven. Love became a mythic personage, whom philosophy, borrowing from poetry, converted into an efficient cause of creation. As of number and figure, the traces of the existence of love were everywhere discerned; and in the Pythagorean list of opposites male and female were ranged side by side with odd and even, finite and infinite.

But Plato seems also to be aware that there is a mystery of love not only in nature, but in man, extending far beyond the mere immediate relation of the sexes. He is conscious that the highest and noblest things in the world are not easily severed from the sensual desires, or may even be regarded as a spiritualized form of them. We may observe that Socrates himself is not represented as originally unimpassioned, but as one who has overcome his passions; the secret of his power over others partly lies in his passionate but self-controlled nature. Love is with Plato not merely the feeling usually so called, but the mystical contemplation of the beautiful and the good. The same passion which may wallow in the mire is capable of rising to the highest summit — of penetrating to the inmost secret of philosophy. The unity of knowledge, the consistency of the warring elements of the world, the enthusiasm of knowledge when first beaming upon mankind, the relativity of ideas to the human mind, and of the human mind to ideas, are all included, consciously or unconsciously, in Plato's doctrine of love.

The successive speeches in praise of love are all of them characteristic of the speakers, and contribute in various degrees to the final result; they are all designed to prepare the way for Socrates, who gathers up the threads anew, and skims the highest points of each of them. But they are not to be regarded as the stages of an idea, rising above one another to a climax. They are fanciful, partly facetious performances, "yet also having a certain degree of seriousness," which the successive speakers dedicate to the god. All of them are rhetorical and poetical rather than dialectical; they do not aim at truth, but only at appearance. When the turn of Socrates comes round, he can not be allowed to disturb the arrangement, and therefore he throws his argument into the form of a speech. And on the occasion of a banquet, good manners would not allow him to win a victory either over his host or any of the guests. The advantage which he gains over Agathon is ingeniously represented as having been already gained over himself by Diotima. At the same time he maintains his own profession of ignorance.

The speeches are attested to us by the very best authority. The madman Apollodorus, who for three years past has made a daily study of the actions of Socrates — to whom the world is summed up in the words "Great is Socrates" — he has heard them from another "madman" who was the shadow of Socrates in days of old, like him going about barefooted, and who had been present at the time. Would you desire better witness? We may observe, by the way, (1) how the very appearance of Aristodemus by himself is a sufficient indication to Agathon that Socrates has been left behind; also, (2) how the courtesy of Agathon anticipates the excuse which Socrates was to have made on Aristodemus' behalf for coming uninvited; (3) how the story of the fit or trance of Socrates is confirmed by the mention which Alcibiades makes of a similar fit of abstraction occurring when he was serving with the army at Potidaea; like (4) the drinking powers of Socrates and his love of the fair, which receive a similar attestation in the concluding scene; or the attachment of Aristodemus, who is not forgotten when Socrates takes his departure. (5) We may notice the manner in which Socrates himself regards the first five speeches, not as true, but as fanciful and exaggerated encomiums of the god Love; (6) the ruling passion of Socrates for dialectics, who will argue with Agathon instead of making a speech, and will only speak at all upon the condition that he is allowed to speak the truth. We may note also (7) the characteristic Platonic remark which occurs in the speech of Eryximachus, that "confusion first begins in the concrete;" and the touch of Socratic irony, (8) which admits of a wide application and reveals a deep insight into the world; that in speaking of holy things and persons there is a general understanding that you should praise them, not that you should speak the truth of them — this is the sort of praise which Socrates is unable to give. Lastly we may remark that the banquet is a real banquet after all, at which love is the theme of discourse, and huge quantities of wine are drunk.

The discourse of Phaedrus is half-mythical, half-ethical; and he himself, true to the character which is given him in the Dialogue which bears his name, is half-sophist, half-enthusiast. He is the critic of poetry also, who compares Homer and Aeschylus in the insipid and irrational manner of the schools of the day, characteristically reasoning about the probability of matters which do not admit of reasoning. The age of love, the great blessing of having a lover, the incentive which love is to daring deeds, the examples of Alcestis and Achilles, are the chief themes of his discourse. The love of women is regarded by him as almost on an equality with that of men; and he takes occasion to remark that the lover has a diviner being, and that therefore the gods favor the return of love which is made to him more than the original sentiment of the lover.

There is something of a sophistical ring in the speech of Phaedrus, which recalls the first speech in imitation of Lysias, occurring in the Dialogue called the Phaedrus. This is still more marked in the speech of Pausanias which follows; and which is at once hyperlogical in form and also extremely confused and pedantic. Plato is attacking the logical feebleness of the sophists and rhetoricians, through their pupils; of course, " playing both sides of the game," as in the Phaedrus; but it is not necessary in order to understand him that we should discuss the fairness of his mode of proceeding. The love of Pausanias for Agathon has already been touched upon in the Protagoras, and is alluded to by Aristophanes. Hence he is naturally the upholder of male loves, which, like all the other affections or actions of men, he regards as varying according to the manner of their performance; thus the question of morals is converted into one of manners. Like the sophists and like Plato himself, though in a different sense, he begins his discussion by an appeal to mythology, and distinguishes between the elder and younger love. The value which he attributes to such loves as motives to virtue and philosophy is greatly at variance with modern and Christian notions, but is in accordance with Hellenic sentiment. For it is impossible to deny that some of the best and greatest of the Greeks indulged in attachments, which Plato in the Laws, no less than the universal opinion of Christendom, has stigmatized as unnatural. Pausanias is very earnest in insisting on the innocence of such loves, when pursued in a right spirit; and he speaks of them as generally approved of among the Hellenes and disapproved by the barbarians, the latter for the sophistical reason that they are inimical to tyrants. The speech as a whole is " more words than matter," such as might certainly have been composed by a pupil of Lysias and Prodicus, although there is no hint given that Plato is designing to parody them.

Plato transposes the two next speeches, as in the Republic he would transpose the virtues and the mathematical sciences. This is done partly to avoid monotony, partly for the sake of making Aristophanes " the cause of wit in others," and also in order to bring the comic and tragic poet into juxtaposition, as if by accident. A suitable " expectation " of Aristophanes is raised by the ludicrous circumstance of his having the hiccough, which is appropriately cured by his substitute, the physician Eryximachus. To Eryximachus Love is the good physician; he sees everything as an intelligent physicist, and, like many professors of his art in modern times, attempts to reduce the moral to the physical; or recognizes one law of love which pervades them both. There are loves and strifes of the body as well as of the mind. Like Hippocrates the Asclepiad, he is a disciple of Heracleitus, whose conception of the harmony of opposites he explains in a new way as the harmony after discord; to his common sense, as to that of many moderns as well as ancients, the identity of contradictories is an absurdity. His notion of love may be summed up as the harmony of man with himself in soul as well as body, and of all things in heaven and earth with one another.

Aristophanes is ready to laugh and make laugh before he opens his mouth, just as Socrates, true to his character, is ready to argue before he begins to speak. He expresses the very genius of the old comedy, its coarse and forcible imagery, and the license of its language in speaking about the gods. He has no sophistical notions about love, which is brought back by him to its common-sense meaning of love between intelligent beings. His account of the origin of the sexes has the greatest (comic) probability and verisimilitude. Nothing in Aristophanes is more truly Aristophanic than the description of the human monster whirling round on four arms and four legs, eight in all, with incredible rapidity. Yet there is a mixture of earnestness in this jest; three serious principles seem to be insinuated: — first, that man can not exist in isolation; he must be reunited if he is to be perfected; secondly, that love is the mediator and reconciler of poor, divided human nature: thirdly, that the loves of this world are an indistinct anticipation of an ideal union which is not yet realized.

The speech of Agathon is conceived in a higher strain, and receives the real, if half-ironical, approval of Socrates. It is the speech of the tragic poet and a sort of poem, like tragedy, moving among the gods of Olympus, and not among the elder or Orphic deities. In the idea of the antiquity of love he can not agree; love is not of the old time, but present and youthful ever. The speech may be compared with that speech of Socrates in the Phaedrus, in which he describes himself as talking dithyrambs. It is at once a preparation for Socrates and a foil to him. The rhetoric of Agathon elevates the soul to "sunlit heights," but at the same time contrasts with the natural and necessary eloquence of Socrates. Agathon contributes the distinction between love and the works of love, and also hints incidentally that love is always of beauty, which Socrates afterwards elevates into a principle. While the consciousness of discord is stronger in the comic poet Aristophanes, Agathon, the tragic poet, has a deeper sense of harmony and reconciliation, and speaks of Love as the creator and artist.

All the earlier speeches embody common opinions colored with a tinge of philosophy. They furnish the material out of which Socrates proceeds to form his discourse, starting, as in other places, from mythology and the opinions of men. From Phaedrus he takes the thought that love is stronger than death; from Pausanias, that the true love is akin to intellect and political activity; from Eryximachus, that love is a universal phenomenon and the great power of nature; from Aristophanes, that love is the child of want, and is not merely the love of the congenial or of the whole, but (as he adds) of the good; from Agathon, that love is of beauty — not however of beauty only, but of birth of beauty.

The speech of the day begins with a short argument which overthrows not only Agathon but all of them, by the help of a distinction which has escaped them. Extravagant praises have been ascribed to Love as the author of every good; no sort of encomium was too high for him, whether deserved and true or not. But Socrates has no talent for speaking anything but the truth, and if he is to speak the truth of Love he must honestly confess that he is not a good at all: for love is of the good, and no man can desire that which he has. This piece of dialectics is ascribed to Diotima, the wise woman of Mantineia, who has already urged upon Socrates the argument which he urges against Agathon.

But Diotima, the prophetess of Mantineia, whose sacred and superhuman character raises her above the ordinary proprieties of women, has taught Socrates far more than this about the art and mystery of love. She has taught him that love is another aspect of philosophy. The same want in the human soul which is satisfied in the vulgar by the procreation of children, may become the highest aspiration of intellectual desire. As the Christian might speak of hungering and thirsting after righteousness; or of divine loves under the figure of human ("This is a great mystery, but I speak concerning Christ and the church "); as the mediæval saint might speak of the " fruitio Dei," so the absorption and annihilation of all other loves and desires in the love of knowledge is a feeling that was at least intelligible to the Greek of the fifth century before Christ. To most men reason and passion appear to be antagonistic both in idea and fact. The union of the greatest comprehension of knowledge and the burning intensity of love is a contradiction in nature, which may have existed in a far-off primeval age in the mind of some Hebrew prophet or other Eastern sage, but has now become an imagination only. Yet this " passion of the reason " is the theme of the Symposium of Plato. And as there is no impossibility in supposing that " one king, or son of a king, may be a philosopher," so also there is a probability that there may be some few — perhaps one or two in a whole generation — in whom the light of truth may not lack the warmth of desire. And if there be such natures, no one will be disposed to deny that " from them flow most of the benefits of individuals and states."

Yet there is a higher region in which love is not only felt, but satisfied, in the perfect beauty of eternal knowledge, beginning with the beauty of earthly things, and at last by regular steps reaching a beauty in which all existence is seen harmonious and one. The limited affection is enlarged, and enabled to behold the ideal beauty of all things. This ideal beauty of the Symposium is the ideal good of the Republic; regarded not with the eye of knowledge, but of faith and desire. The one seems to say to us " the idea is love," the other " the idea is truth." In both the lover of wisdom is the " spectator of all time and all existence." This is a sort of " mystery " in which Plato also obscurely intimates the interpenetration of the moral and intellectual faculties.

The divine image of beauty that resides within Socrates has been revealed; the Silenus mask, or outward man, has now to be exhibited. The description of Socrates is placed side by side with the speech of Socrates; one is the complement of the other. At the height of divine inspiration, when the force of nature can no further go, as if by way of contrast to this extreme idealism or mysticism, Alcibiades, accompanied by a troop of revellers, staggers in, and in his drunken state is able to tell of things which he would have been ashamed to mention, if he had been sober. The state of his affections towards Socrates, unintelligible to us and perverted as they appear, is a perfect illustration of the power ascribed to the loves of men in the speech of Pausanias. Indeed, he is confident that the whole company will sympathize with him; several of them have been in love with Socrates, and, like himself, have been deceived by him. The singular part of this confession is the combination of the most degrading passion with the desire of virtue and improvement. The pangs of philosophy and of love work together on this abandoned soul. Such an union is not wholly untrue to human nature, in which there is a mixture of good and evil, far surpassing in subtlety any powers of human imagination to conceive. The Platonic Socrates (for of the real Socrates this may be doubted: cp. Xenophon's Mem. I. 2, 29, 30) does not appear to regard the greatest evil of Greek life as matter of abhorrence, but as a subject for irony, and is far from resenting the imputation of such attachments. Nor does Plato feel any repugnance, such as would be felt in modern times, in bringing his great master and hero into connection with nameless crimes. He is contented with representing him as a sort of saint, who has won " the Olympian victory " over the temptations of human nature. The fault of taste, which to us appears glaring, and which was recognized by the Greeks of a later age, was not perceived by Plato himself. Still more surprising is the fact itself, that the elevation of sentiment, which is regarded by Plato as the first step in the upward progress of the philosopher, is aroused not by female beauty, but by the beauty of youth, which alone seems to have been capable of inspiring the modern feeling of romance in the Greek mind. The passion which was unsatisfied by the love of women, took the spurious form of an enthusiasm for the ideal of beauty — a worship as of some godlike image of an Apollo or Antinous. Thus wide is the gulf which separates a portion of Hellenic sentiment in the age of Plato (for about the opinion of Plato himself, as of Socrates, respecting these male loves we are in the same perplexity which he attributes to his countrymen,) not only from Christian, but from Homeric feeling.

The character here attributed to Alcibiades is hardly less remarkable than that of Socrates. He is the impersonation of lawlessness — " the lion's whelp, who ought not to be reared in the city," yet not without a certain generosity which gained the hearts of men, — strangely fascinated by Socrates, and possessed of a genius which might have been either the destruction or salvation of Athens. The dramatic interest of the character is heightened by the recollection of his after history. He seems to have been present to the mind of Plato in the description of the democratic man of the Republic.

There is no criterion of the date of the Symposium, except that which is furnished by the allusion to the division of Arcadia after the destruction of Mantineia. This took place in the year B. C. 384, which is the forty-fourth year of Plato's life. The Symposium can not therefore be regarded as a youthful work. As Mantineia was restored in the year 369, the composition of the Dialogue will probably fall between 384 and 369. Whether the recollection of the event is more likely to have been renewed at the destruction or restoration of the city, rather than at some intermediate period, is a consideration not worth raising.

The Symposium is closely connected with the Phaedrus both in style and matter. They are the only Dialogues of Plato in which the subject of love is considered at length. In both philosophy is regarded as a sort of enthusiasm or madness. Philosophy in the Phaedo might also be described as " dying for love." But while the Phaedo and Phaedrus look backwards and forwards to past and future states of existence, the Symposium is bounded by this world. The intellectual and ethical are held in solution with the physical. Philosophy is not death, or abstraction from life: in and through the sensible world we rise to the ideal. Nor is the eternity of knowledge asserted; but only the eternal succession of knowledge. The immortality is not personal, but an immortality of the race. The Lysis may be compared as containing the first suggestion of the questions finally answered in the speech of Socrates.

The Symposium of Xenophon, in which Socrates describes himself as a pander, and also discourses of the difference between sensual and sentimental love, likewise offers several interesting points of comparison. But the suspicion which hangs over other writings of Xenophon, and the numerous minute references to the Phaedrus and Symposium, throw a doubt on the genuineness of the work. The Symposium of Xenophon, if written by him at all, would certainly show that he wrote against Plato, and was acquainted with his works. Of this there is no trace in the Memorabilia. Such a rivalry is more characteristic of an imitator than of an original writer. This (so-called) Symposium of Xenophon may therefore have no more title to be regarded as genuine than the confessedly spurious Apology.

There are no means of determining the relative order in time of the Phaedo, Symposium, Phaedrus. The order which has been adopted in this translation rests on no other principle than the desire to bring together in a series the memorials of the life of Socrates.

THE SYMPOSIUM

PERSONS OF THE DIALOGUE

APOLLODORUS, *who repeats to his companion the dialogue which he had heard from Aristodemus, and had already once narrated to Glaucon.*

PHAEDRUS.

PAUSANIAS.

ERYXIMACHUS.

ARISTOPHANES

AGATHON.

SOCRATES.

ALCIBIADES.

A TROOP OF REVELLERS.

SCENE: — The House of Agathon.

I BELIEVE that I am prepared with an answer. For the day before yesterday I was coming from my own home at Phalerum to the city, and one of my acquaintance, who had caught a sight of the back of me at a distance, in merry mood commanded me to halt: Apollodorus, he cried, O thou man of Phalerum, halt! So I did as I was bid; and then he said, I was looking for you, Apollodorus, only just now, that I might hear about the discourses in praise of love, which were delivered by Socrates, Alcibiades, and others, at Agathon's supper. Phoenix, the son of Philip, told another person who told me of them, and he said that you knew; but he was himself very indistinct, and I wish that you would give me an account of them. Who but you should be the reporter of the words of your friend? And first tell me, he said, were you present at this meeting?

Your informant, Glaucon, I said, must have been very indistinct indeed, if you imagine that the occasion was recent, or that I could have been present.

Why, yes, he replied, that was my impression.

But how is that possible? I said. For Agathon has not been in Athens for many years, (are you aware of that?) and my acquaintance with Socrates, of whose every action and word I now make a daily study, is not as yet of three years' standing. I used to be running about the world, thinking that I was doing something, and would have done anything rather than be a philosopher; I was almost as miserable as you are now.

Well, he said, cease from jesting, and tell me when the meeting occurred.

In our boyhood, I replied, when Agathon won the prize with his first tragedy, on the day after that on which he and his chorus offered the sacrifice of victory.

That is a long while ago, he said; and who told you — did Socrates?

No indeed, I replied, but the same person who told Phoenix; — he was a little fellow, who never wore any shoes, Aristodemus, of the deme of Cydathenaeum. He had been at this feast; and I think that there was no one in those days who was a more devoted admirer of Socrates. Moreover, I asked Socrates about the truth of some parts of his narrative, and he confirmed them. Then, said Glaucon, let us have the tale over again; is not the road to Athens made for conversation? And so we walked, and talked of the discourses on love; and therefore, as I said at first, I am prepared with an answer, and will have another rehearsal, if you like. For I love to speak or to hear others speak of philosophy; there is the greatest pleasure in that, to say nothing of the profit. But when I hear any other discourses, especially those of you rich men and traders, they are irksome to me; and I pity you who are my companions, because you always think that you are hard at work when really you are idling. And I dare say that you pity me in return, whom you regard as an unfortunate wight, which I perhaps am. But I certainly know of you what you only think of me — there is the difference.

Companion. I see, Apollodorus, that you are just the same — always speaking evil of yourself, and of others; and I do believe that you pity all mankind, beginning with yourself and including everybody else with the exception of Socrates, true in this to your old name, which, however deserved, I know not how you acquired, of Apollodorus the madman; for your humor is always to be out of humor with yourself and with everybody except Socrates.

Apollodorus. Yes, friend, and I am proved to be mad, and out of my wits, because I have these notions of myself and you; no other evidence is required.

Com. I have no wish to dispute about that, Apollodorus; but let me renew my request that you would repeat the tale of love.

Apoll. Well, the tale of love was on this wise: — But perhaps I had better begin at the beginning, and endeavor to repeat to you the words as Aristodemus gave them.

He said that he met Socrates fresh from the bath and sandalled; and as the sight of the sandals was unusual, he asked him whither he was going that he was so fine.

To a banquet at Agathon's, he replied, whom I refused yesterday, fearing the crowd that there would be at his sacrifice, but promising that I would come to-day instead; and I have put on my finery because he is a fine creature. What say you to going with me unbidden?

Yes, I replied, I will go with you, if you like.

Follow then, he said, and let us demolish the proverb that

" To the feasts of lesser men the good unbidden go; "

instead of which our proverb will run that

" To the feasts of the good unbidden go the good; "

and this alteration may be supported by the authority of Homer, who not only demolishes but literally outrages this proverb. For, after picturing Agamemnon as the most valiant of men, he makes Menelaus, who is but a soft-hearted warrior, come of his own accord [1] to the sacrificial feast of Agamemnon, the worse to the better.

I am afraid, Socrates, said Aristodemus, that I shall rather be the inferior person, who, like Menelaus in Homer,

" To the feasts of the wise unbidden goes."

But I shall say that I was bidden of you, and then you will have to make the excuse.

" Two going together,"

he replied, in Homeric fashion, may invent an excuse by the way.[2]

This was the style of their conversation as they went along; and a comical thing happened — Socrates stayed behind in a fit of abstraction, and desired Aristodemus, who was waiting, to go on before him. When he reached the house of Agathon he found the doors wide open, and a servant coming out met him, and led him at once into the banqueting-hall in which the guests were reclining, for the banquet was about to begin. Welcome, Aristodemus, said Agathon, you are just in time to sup with us; if you come on any other errand put that off, and make one of us, as I

---

[1] Iliad, xvii. 588. [2] Iliad, x. 224.

was looking for you yesterday and meant to have asked you, if I could have found you. But what have you done with Socrates?

I turned round and saw that Socrates was missing, and I had to explain that he had been with me a moment before, and that I came by his invitation.

You were quite right in coming, said Agathon; but where is he himself?

He was behind me just now, as I entered, he said, and I can not think what has become of him.

Go and look for him, boy, said Agathon, and bring him in; do you, Aristodemus, meanwhile take the place by Eryximachus.

Then he said that the attendant assisted him to wash, and that he lay down, and presently another servant came in and said that our friend Socrates had retired into the portico of the neighboring house. " There he is fixed, and when I call to him," said the servant, " he will not stir."

How strange, said Agathon; then you must call him again, and keep calling him.

Let him alone, said my informant; he has just a habit of stopping anywhere and losing himself without any reason; don't disturb him, as I believe he will soon appear.

Well, if you say that, I will not interfere with him, said Agathon. My domestics, who on these occasions become my masters, shall entertain us as their guests. " Put on the table whatever you like," he said to the servants, " as usual when there is no one to give you orders, which I never do. Imagine that you are our hosts, and that I and the company are your guests; and treat us well, and then we shall commend you." After this they supped; and during the meal Agathon several times expressed a wish to send for Socrates, but Aristodemus would not allow him; and when the feast was half over — for the fit, as usual, was not of long duration — Socrates entered. Agathon, who was reclining alone at the end of the table, begged that he would take the place next to him; that I may touch the sage, he said, and get some of that wisdom which came into your mind in the portico. For I am certain that you would not have left until you had found what you were seeking.

How I wish, said Socrates, taking his place as he was desired, that wisdom could be infused through the medium of touch, out of the full into the empty man, like the water which the wool sucks out of the full vessel into an empty one; in that case how much I should prize sitting by you! For you would have filled me full of gifts of wisdom, plenteous and fair, in comparison of which my own is of a very mean and questionable sort, no better than a dream; but yours is bright and only beginning, and was manifested forth in all the splendor of youth the day before yesterday in the presence of more than thirty thousand Hellenes.

You are insolent, said Agathon; and you and I will have to settle hereafter who bears off the palm of wisdom, and of this Dionysus shall be the judge; but at present you are better occupied with the banquet.

Socrates took his place on the couch; and when the meal was ended, and the libations offered, and after a hymn had been sung to the god, and there had been the usual ceremonies, — as they were about to commence drinking, Pausanias reminded them that they had had a bout yesterday, from which he and most of them were still suffering, and they ought to be allowed to recover, and not go on drinking to-day. He would therefore ask, How the drinking could be made easiest?

I entirely agree, said Aristophanes, that we should, by all means, get off the drinking, having been myself one of those who were yesterday drowned in drink.

I think that you are right, said Eryximachus, the son of Acumenus; but I should like to hear one other person speak. What are the inclinations of our host?

I am not able to drink, said Agathon.

Then, said Eryximachus, the weak heads like myself, Aristodemus, Phaedrus, and others who never can drink, are fortunate in finding that the stronger ones are not in a drinking mood. (I do not include Socrates, who is an exceptional being, and able either to drink or to abstain.) Well, then, as the company seem indisposed to drink much, I may be forgiven for saying, as a physician, that drinking is a bad practice, which I never, if I can help, follow, and certainly do not recommend to another, least of all to any one who still feels the effects of yesterday's carouse.

I always follow what you advise, and especially what you prescribe as a physician, rejoined Phaedrus the Myrrhinusian, and the rest of the company, if they are wise, will do the same.

All agreed that drinking was not to be the order of the day. Then, said Eryximachus, as you are all agreed that drinking is to be voluntary, and that there is to be no compulsion, I move, in the next place, that the flute-girl, who has just made her appearance, be told to go away; she may play to herself, or, if she has a mind, to the women who are within. But on this day let us have conversation instead; and, if you will allow me, I will tell you what sort of conversation. This proposal having been accepted, Eryximachus proceeded as follows: —

I will begin, he said, after the manner of Melanippe in Euripides,

" Not mine the word "

which I am about to speak, but that of Phaedrus. For he is in the habit of complaining that, whereas other gods have poems and hymns made in their honor by the poets, who are so many, the great and glorious god, Love, has not a single panegyrist or encomiast. Many sophists also, as for example the excellent Prodicus, have descanted in prose on the virtues of Heracles and other heroes; and, what is still more extraordinary, I have met with a philosophical work in which the utility of salt has been made the theme of an eloquent discourse; and many other like things have had a like honor bestowed upon them. And only to think that there should have been an eager interest created about them, and yet that to this day, as Phaedrus well and truly says, no one has ever dared worth· ily to hymn Love's praises. This mighty deity has been neglected wholly! Now I want to offer Phaedrus a contribution to his feast; nor do I see how the present company can, at this moment, do anything better than honor the god Love. And if you agree to this, there will be no lack of conversation; for I mean to propose that each of us in turn shall make a discourse in honor of Love. Let us have the best which he can make; and Phaedrus, who is sitting first on the left hand, and is the father of the thought, shall begin.

No one will oppose that, Eryximachus, said Socrates; I certainly can not refuse to speak on the only subject of which I profess to have any knowledge, and Agathon and Pausanias will surely assent; and there can be no doubt of Aristophanes, who is always in the company of Dionysus and Aphrodite; nor will any one disagree of those whom I see around me. The proposal, as I am aware, may seem hard upon us whose place is last; but that does not matter if we hear some good speeches first. Let Phaedrus begin the praise of Love, and good luck to him. All the company expressed their assent, and desired him to do as Socrates bade him.

Aristodemus did not recollect all that was said, nor do I recollect all that he related to me; but I will tell you what I thought most worthy of remembrance, and what the chief speakers said.

Phaedrus began by affirming that Love is a mighty god, and wonderful among gods and men, but especially wonderful in his birth. For that he is the eldest of the gods is an honor to him; and a proof of this is, that of his parents there is no memorial; neither poet nor prose-writer has ever affirmed that he had any. As Hesiod says: —

> " First Chaos came, and then broad-bosomed Earth,
> The everlasting seat of all that is,
> And Love."

In other words, after Chaos, the Earth and Love, these two came into being. Also Parmenides sings of the generation of the gods: —

> " First in the train of gods, he moulded Love."

And Acusilaus agrees with Hesiod. Thus numerous are the witnesses which acknowledge Love to be the eldest of the gods. And not only is he the eldest, he is also the source of the greatest benefits to us. For I know not any greater blessing to a young man beginning life than a virtuous lover, or to the lover than a beloved youth. For the principle which ought to be the guide of men who would nobly live — that principle, I say, neither kindred, nor honor, nor wealth nor any other motive is able to implant as surely as love. Of what am I speaking? Of the sense of honor and dishonor, without which neither states nor individuals ever do any good or great work. And I say that a lover who is detected in doing any dishonorable act, or submitting through cowardice when any dishonor is done to him by another, will be more pained at being detected by his beloved than at being seen by his father, or his companions, or any one else. And the beloved has the same feeling about his love, when he again is seen on any disgraceful occasion. And if there were only some way of contriving that a state or an army should be made up of lovers and their loves, they would be the very best governors of their own city, abstaining from all dishonor, and emulating one another in honor; and when fighting at one another's side, although a mere handful, they would overcome all men. For what lover would not choose rather to be seen by all mankind than by his beloved, either when abandoning his post or throwing away his arms? He would be ready to die a thousand deaths rather than endure this. Or who would desert his beloved or fail him in the hour of danger? The veriest coward would become an inspired hero, equal to the bravest, at such a time; Love would inspire him. That courage which, as Homer says, the god breathes into the soul of heroes, Love of himself infuses into the lover.

Love will make men dare to die for their beloved; and women as well as men. Of this, Alcestis, the daughter of Pelias, is a monument to all Hellas; for she was willing to lay down her life on behalf of her husband, when no one else would, although he had a father and mother; but the tenderness of her love so far exceeded theirs, that they seemed to be as strangers to their own son, having no concern with him; and so noble did this action of hers appear, not only to men but also to the gods, that among the many who have done virtuously she was one of the very few to whom the gods have granted the privilege of returning to earth, in admiration of her virtue; such exceeding honor is paid by them to the devotion and virtue of love. But Orpheus, the son of Oeagrus, because he appeared to them to be a cowardly harper, who did not dare to die for love, like Alcestis, but contrived to go down alive to Hades, was sent back by them without effecting his purpose; to him they showed an apparition only of her whom he sought, but herself they would not give up; moreover, they afterwards caused him to suffer death at the hands of women, as the punishment of his intrusiveness. Far other was the reward of the true love of Achilles towards his lover Patroclus — his lover and not his love (the notion that Patroclus was the beloved one is a foolish error into which Aeschylus has fallen, for Achilles was surely the fairer of the two, fairer also than all the other heroes; and he was much younger, as Homer informs us, and he had no beard). And greatly as the gods honor the virtue of love, still the return of love on the part of the beloved to the lover is more admired and valued and rewarded by them, for the lover has a nature more divine and more worthy of worship. Now Achilles was quite aware, for he had been told by his mother, that he might avoid death and return home, and live to a good old age, if he abstained from slaying Hector. Nevertheless he gave his life to revenge his friend, and dared to die, not only on his behalf, but after his death. Wherefore the gods honored him even above Alcestis, and sent him to the Islands of the Blest. These are my reasons for affirming that Love is the eldest and noblest and mightiest of the gods, and the chiefest author and giver of happiness and virtue, in life and after death.

This, or something like this, was the speech of Phaedrus: and some other speeches followed which

Aristodemus did not remember; the next which he repeated was that of Pausanias, who observed that the proposal of Phaedrus was too indiscriminate, and that Love ought not to be praised in this unqualified manner. If there were only one Love, then what he said would be well enough; but since there are more Loves than one, he should have begun by determining which of them was to be the theme of our praises. I will amend this defect, he said; and first of all I will tell you which Love is worthy of praise, and then try to hymn the praiseworthy one in a manner worthy of the god. For we all know that Love is inseparable from Aphrodite, and if there were only one Aphrodite there would be only one Love; but as there are two goddesses there must be two Loves. For am I not right in asserting that there are two goddesses? The elder one, having no mother, who is called the heavenly Aphrodite — she is the daughter of Uranus; the younger, who is the daughter of Zeus and Dione, whom we call common; and the other Love who is her fellow-worker may and must also have the name of common, as the other is called heavenly. All the gods ought to have praise given to them, but still I must discriminate the attributes of the two Loves. For actions vary according to the manner of their performance. Take for example, that which we are now doing, drinking, singing and talking — these actions are not in themselves either good or evil, but turn out in this or that way according to the mode of performing them; and when well done they are good, and when wrongly done they are evil; and in like manner not every love, but only that which has a noble purpose, is noble and worthy of praise. But the Love who is the son of the common Aphrodite is essentially common, and has no discrimination, being such as the meaner sort of men feel, and is apt to be of women

as well as of youths, and is of the body rather than of
the soul — the most foolish beings are the objects of
this love which desires only to gain an end, but never
thinks of accomplishing the end nobly, and therefore
does good and evil quite indiscriminately. The goddess who is his mother is far younger, and she was
born of the union of the male and female, and partakes of both sexes. But the son of the heavenly
Aphrodite is sprung from a mother in whose birth
the female has no part, but she is from the male only;
this is that love which is of youths only, and the goddess being older has nothing of wantonness. Those
who are inspired by this love turn to the male, and
delight in him who is the more valiant and intelligent
nature; any one may recognize the pure enthusiasts
in the very character of their attachments. For they
love not boys, but intelligent beings whose reason is
beginning to be developed, much about the time at
which their beards begin to grow. And in choosing
them as their companions, they mean to be faithful to
them, and to pass their whole life with them, and be
with them, and not to take them in their inexperience,
and deceive them, and play the fool with them, or
run away from one to another of them. But the love
of young boys should be forbidden by law, because
their future is uncertain; they may turn out good or
bad, either in body or soul, and the affection which is
devoted to them may be thrown away; in this the good
are a law to themselves, and the coarser sort of lovers
ought to be restrained by force, as we restrain or attempt to restrain them from fixing their affections on
women of free birth. For the abuse of a thing brings
discredit on the lawful use, and this has led some to
deny the lawfulness of love when they see the impropriety and evil of attachments of this sort; for surely
nothing that is decorously and lawfully done can

justly be censured. Now in most cities the practice about love is determined by a simple rule, and is easily intelligible. But here and in Lacedaemon there is a perplexity, — in Elis and Boeotia, having no gifts of eloquence, they are very straightforward; the universal sentiment is simply in favor of these connections, and no one, whether young or old, has anything to say to their discredit. The reason is, as I suppose, that they are men of few words in those parts, and therefore the lovers do not like the trouble of pleading their suit. But in Ionia and other places, and generally in countries which are subject to the barbarians, loves of youths share the evil repute of philosophy and gymnastics, because they are inimical to tyranny; for the interests of rulers require that their subjects should be poor in spirit, and that there should be no strong bond of friendship or society among them, and love, above all other motives, is likely to inspire this, as our Athenian tyrants learned by experience; for the love of Aristogeiton and the constancy of Harmodius had a strength which undid their power. And, therefore, the ill-repute into which these attachments have fallen is to be ascribed to the evil condition of those who make them to be ill-reputed; that is to say, to the rapacity of the governors and the cowardice of the governed; on the other hand, the indiscriminate honor which is given to them in some countries is attributable to the laziness of those who hold this opinion of them. There is yet a more excellent way of legislating about them, which is our own way; but this, as I was saying, is rather perplexing. For, observe that open loves are held to be more honorable than secret ones, and that the love of the noblest and highest, even if their persons are less beautiful than others, is especially honorable. Consider, too, how great is the encouragement which all the world gives to the lover; neither is he supposed to be doing anything dishonorable; but if he succeeds he is praised, and if he fail he is blamed. And in the pursuit of his love the custom of mankind allows him to do many strange things, which philosophy would bitterly censure if they were done from any motive of interest, or wish for office or power. He may pray, and entreat, and supplicate, and swear, and be a servant of servants, and lie on a mat at the door; in any other case friends and enemies would be equally ready to prevent him, but now there is no friend who will be ashamed of him and admonish him, and no enemy will charge him with meanness or flattery; the actions of a lover have a grace which ennobles them; and custom has decided that they are highly commendable and that there is no loss of character in them; and, what is yet more strange, he only may swear and forswear himself (this is what the world says), and the gods will forgive his transgression, for there is no such thing as a lover's oath. Such is the entire liberty which gods and men allow the lover, and which in our part of the world the custom confirms. And this is one side of the question, which may make a man fairly think that in this city to love and to be loved is held to be a very honorable thing. But when there is a new regime, and parents forbid their sons to talk with their lovers, and place them under a tutor's care, and their companions and equals are personal in their remarks when they see anything of this sort going on, and their elders refuse to silence them and do not reprove their words; any one who reflects on this will, on the contrary, think that we hold these practices to be disgraceful. But the truth, as I imagine, and as I said at first, is, that whether such practices are honorable or whether they are dishonorable is not a simple question; they are honorable to him who follows them honorably, dishonorable to him who follows them dishonorably. There is dishonor in yielding to the evil, or in an evil manner; but there is honor in yielding to the good, or in an honorable manner. Evil is the vulgar lover who loves the body rather than the soul, and who is inconstant because he is a lover of the inconstant, and therefore when the bloom of youth which he was desiring is over, he takes wings and flies away, in spite of all his words and promises; whereas the love of the noble mind, which is in union with the unchangeable, is everlasting. The custom of our country would have them both proven well and truly, and would have us yield to the one sort of love and avoid the other; testing them in contests and trials, which will show to which of the two classes the lover and the beloved respectively belong. And this is the reason why, in the first place, a hasty attachment is held to be dishonorable, because time is the true test of this as of most other things; and then again there is a dishonor in being overcome by the love of money, wealth, or of political power, whether a man suffers and is frightened into surrender at the loss of them, or is unable to rise above the advantages of them. For none of these things are of a permanent or lasting nature; not to mention that no generous friendship ever sprung from them. There remains, then, only one way of honorable attachment which custom allows in the beloved, and this is the way of virtue; any service which the lover did was not to be accounted flattery or dishonor, and the beloved has also one way of voluntary service which is not dishonorable, and this is virtuous service.

For we have a custom, and according to our custom any one who does service to another under the idea that he will be improved by him either in wisdom, or in some other particular of virtue — such a voluntary service as this, I say, is not regarded as a dishonor, and is not open to the charge of flattery. And these two customs, one the love of youth, and the other the practice of philosophy and virtue in general, ought to meet in one, and then the beloved may honorably indulge the lover. For when the lover and beloved come together, having each of them a law, and the lover on his part is ready to confer any favor that he rightly can on his gracious loving one, and the other is ready to yield any compliance that he rightly can to him who is to make him wise and good; the one capable of communicating wisdom and virtue, the other seeking after knowledge, and making his object education and wisdom; when the two laws of love are fulfilled and meet in one — then, and then only, may the beloved yield with honor to the lover. Nor when love is of this disinterested sort is there any disgrace in being deceived, but in every other case there is equal disgrace in being or not being deceived. For he who is gracious to his lover under the impression that he is rich, and is disappointed of his gains because he turns out to be poor, is disgraced all the same: for he has done his best to show that he would turn himself to any one's uses base for the sake of money, and this is not honorable. But on the same principle he who lives for the sake of virtue, and in the hope that he will be improved by his lover's company, shows himself to be virtuous, even though the object of his affection be proved to be a villain, and to have no virtue; and if he is deceived he has committed a noble error. For he has proved that for his part he will do anything for anybody for the sake of virtue and improvement, and nothing can be nobler than this. Thus noble in every case is the acceptance of another for the sake of virtue. This is that love which is the love of the heavenly goddess, and is heavenly, and of great price to individuals and cities, making the lover and the beloved alike eager in the work of their own improvement. But all other loves are the offspring of the common or vulgar goddess. To you, Phaedrus, I offer this my encomium of love, which is as good as I could make on the sudden.

When Pāusănĭās cāme tŏ ă pāuse (this is the balanced way in which I have been taught by the wise to speak), Aristodemus said that the turn of Aristophanes was next, but that either he had eaten too much, or from some other cause he had the hiccough, and was obliged to change with Eryximachus the physician, who was reclining on the couch below him. Eryximachus, he said, you ought either to stop my hiccough, or to speak in my turn until I am better.

I will do both, said Eryximachus: I will speak in your turn, and do you speak in mine; and while I am speaking let me recommend you to hold your breath, and if this fails, then to gargle with a little water; and if the hiccough still continues, tickle your nose with something and sneeze; and if you sneeze once or twice, even the most violent hiccough is sure to go. In the meantime I will take your turn, and you shall take mine. I will do as you prescribe, said Aristophanes, and now get on.

Eryximachus spoke as follows: Seeing that Pausanias made a fair beginning, and but a lame ending, I will endeavor to supply his deficiency. I think that he has rightly distinguished two kinds of love. But my art instructs me that this double love is to be found in all animals and plants, and I may say in all that is; and is not merely an affection of the soul of man towards the fair, or towards anything; that, I say, is a view of the subject which I seem to have gathered from my own art of medicine, which shows me how great and wonderful and universal is this deity, whose empire is over all that is, divine as well as human. And from medicine I will begin that I may do honor to my art. For there are in the human body two loves, which are confessedly different and unlike, and being unlike, have loves and desires which are unlike; and the desire of the healthy is one, and the desire of the diseased is another; and, as Pausanias says, the good are to be accepted, and the bad are not to be accepted; and so too in the body the good and healthy elements are to be indulged, and the bad elements and the elements of desire are not to be indulged, but discouraged. And this is what the physician has to do, and in this the art of medicine consists: for medicine may be regarded generally as the knowledge of the loves and desires of the body, and how to fill or empty them; and the good physician is he who is able to separate fair love from foul, or to convert one into the other; and if he is a skilful practitioner, he knows how to eradicate and how to implant love, whichever is required, and he can reconcile the most hostile elements in the constitution, and make them friends. Now the most hostile are the most opposite, such as hot and cold, moist and dry, bitter and sweet, and the like. And my ancestor, Asclepius, knowing how to implant friendship and accord in these elements, was the creator of our art, as our friends the poets here tell us, and I believe them; and not only medicine in every branch, but the arts of gymnastic and husbandry are under his dominion. Any one who pays the least attention will also perceive that in music there is the same reconciliation of opposites; and I suppose that this must have been the meaning of Heracleitus, although his words are not accurate; for he says that one is united by disunion, like the harmony of the bow and the lyre. Now there is an ab-

surdity in saying that harmony is disagreement or is
composed of elements which are still in a state of disagreement. But perhaps what he really meant to say
was that harmony is composed of differing notes of
higher or lower pitch which disagreed once, but are
now reconciled by the art of music; for if the higher
and lower notes still disagree, there could be no
harmony, as is indeed evident. For harmony is a
symphony, and symphony is an agreement; but an
agreement of disagreements while they disagree can
not exist; there is no harmony of discord and disagreement. This may be illustrated by rhythm, which is
composed of elements short and long, once differing
and now in accord; which accordance, as in the former
instance, medicine, so in this, music implants, making
love and unison to grow up among them: and thus
music, too, is concerned with the principles of love in
their application to harmony and rhythm. Again,
in the abstract principles of harmony and rhythm
there is no difficulty in discerning them, for as yet
love has no double nature. But when you want to
use them in actual life, either in the composition of
music or in the correct performance of airs or metres
composed already, which latter is called education,
then the difficulty begins, and the good artist is
needed. Then the old tale has to be repeated of fair
and heavenly love — the love of Urania the fair and
heavenly muse, and of the duty of accepting the temperate, and the intemperate only that they may become temperate, and of preserving their love; and
again, of the vulgar Polyhymnia, who must be used
with circumspection that the pleasure may not generate licentiousness; just as in my own art great skill
is shown in gratifying the taste of the epicure without
inflicting upon him the attendant evil of disease.
The conclusion is that in music, in medicine, in all

other things human as well as divine, both loves
ought to be noted as far as may be, for they are both
present.

The course of the season is also full of both principles; and when, as I was saying, the elements of hot
and cold, moist and dry, attain the harmonious love
of one another and blend in temperance and harmony,
they bring to men, animals and vegetables health and
wealth, and do them no harm; whereas the wantonness
and overbearingness of the other love affecting the
seasons is a great injurer and destroyer, and is the
source of pestilence, and brings many different sorts
of diseases on animals and plants; for hoar-frost and
hail and blight spring from the excesses and disorders
of these elements of love, the knowledge of which in
relation to the revolutions of the heavenly bodies and
the seasons of the year is termed astronomy. Further-
more all sacrifices and the whole art of divination,
which is the art of communion between gods and
men — these, I say, are concerned only with the
salvation and healing power of love. For all impiety
is likely to ensue if, instead of accepting and honoring
and reverencing the harmonious love in all his actions,
a man honors the other love, whether in his feelings
towards gods or parents, towards the living or the
dead. Wherefore the business of divination is to see
to these loves and to heal them, and divination is the
peacemaker of gods and men, working by a knowledge of the religious or irreligious tendencies which
exist in merely human loves. Such is the great and
mighty, or rather universal, force of all love. And
that love, especially, which is concerned with the good,
and which is perfected in company with temperance
and justice, whether among gods or men, has the
greatest power, and is the source of all our happiness
and harmony and friendship with the gods which are

above us, and with one another. I dare say that I
have omitted several things which might be said in
praise of Love, but this was not intentional, and you,
Aristophanes, may now supply the omission or take
some other line of commendation; as I perceive that
you are cured of the hiccough.

Yes, said Aristophanes, who followed, the hiccough
is gone; not, however, until I applied the sneezing;
and I wonder whether the principle of order in the
human frame requires these sort of noises and ticklings, for I no sooner applied the sneezing than I was
cured.

Eryximachus said: Take care, friend Aristophanes,
you are beginning with a joke, and I shall have to
watch if you talk nonsense; and the interruption will
be occasioned by your own fault.

You are very right, said Aristophanes, laughing,
and I will retract what I said; and do you please not
to watch me, as I fear that in what I am going to say,
instead of making others laugh, which is to the manner born of our muse and would be all the better, I
shall only be laughed at by them.

Do you expect to shoot your bolt and escape,
Aristophanes? Well, if you are very careful and
have a due sense of responsibility, I may be induced
to let you off.

Aristophanes professed to open another vein of discourse; he had a mind to praise Love in another way,
not like that either of Pausanias or Eryximachus.
Mankind, he said, judging by their neglect of him,
have never, as I think, at all understood the power
of Love. For if they had understood him they would
surely have built noble temples and altars, and offered
solemn sacrifices in his honor; but this is not done, and
certainly ought to be done: for of all the gods he is the
best friend of men, the helper and the healer of the

ills which are the great obstruction to the happiness of the race. I shall rehearse to you his power, and you may repeat what I say to the rest of the world. And first let me treat of the nature and state of man; for the original human nature was not like the present, but different. In the first place, the sexes were originally three in number, not two as they are now; there was man, woman, and the union of the two, having a name corresponding to this double nature; this once had a real existence, but is now lost, and the name only is preserved as a term of reproach. In the second place, the primeval man was round and had four hands and four feet, back and sides forming a circle, one head with two faces, looking opposite ways, set on a round neck and precisely alike; also four ears, two privy members, and the remainder to correspond. When he had a mind he could walk as men now do, and he could also roll over and over at a great rate, leaning on his four hands and four feet, eight in all, like tumblers going over and over with their legs in the air; this was when he wanted to run fast. Now there were these three sexes, because the sun, moon, and earth are three; and the man was originally the child of the sun, the woman of the earth, and the man-woman of the moon, which is made up of sun and earth, and they were all round and moved round and round like their parents. Terrible was their might and strength, and the thoughts of their hearts were great, and they made an attack upon the gods; and of them is told the tale of Otus and Ephialtes who, as Homer says, dared to scale heaven, and would have laid hands upon the gods. Doubt reigned in the councils of Zeus and of the gods. Should they kill them and annihilate the race with thunderbolts, as they had done the giants, then there would be an end of the sacrifice and worship which men offered to them; but, on the other hand, the gods could not suffer their insolence to be unrestrained. At last, after a good deal of reflection, Zeus discovered a way. He said: " I have a notion which will humble their pride and mend their manners; they shall continue to exist, but I will cut them in two and then they will be diminished in strength and increased in numbers; this will have the advantage of making them more profitable to us. They shall walk upright on two legs, and if they continue insolent and won't be quiet, I will split them again and they shall hop about on a single leg." He spoke and cut them in two, like a sorb-apple which is halved for pickling, or as you might divide an egg with a hair; and as he cut them one after another, he bade Apollo give the face and the half of the neck a turn in order that the man might contemplate the section of himself: this would teach him a lesson of humility. He was also to heal their wounds and compose their forms. Apollo twisted the face and pulled the skin all round over that which in our language is called the belly, like the purses which draw in, and he made one mouth at the centre, which he fastened in a knot (this is called the navel) ; he also moulded the breast and took out most of the wrinkles, much as a shoemaker might smooth out leather upon a last; he left a few, however, in the region of the belly and navel, as a memorial of the primeval change. After the division the two parts of man, each desiring his other half, came together, and threw their arms about one another eager to grow into one, and would have perished from hunger without ever making an effort, because they did not like to do anything apart; and when one of the halves died and the other survived, the survivor sought another mate, whether the section of an entire man or of an entire woman, which had usurped the name of man and woman, and clung to that. And this was being the destruction of them, when Zeus in pity invented a new plan: he turned the parts of generation round in front, for this was not always their position, and they sowed the seed no longer as hitherto like grasshoppers in the ground, but in one another; and after the transposition the male generated in the female in order that by the mutual embraces of man and woman they might breed, and the race might continue; or if man came to man they might be satisfied, and rest and go their ways to the business of life: so ancient is the desire of one another which is implanted in us, reuniting our original nature, making one of two, and healing the state of man. Each of us when separated is but the indenture of a man, having one side only like a flat fish, and he is always looking for his other half. Men who are a section of that double nature which was once called Androgynous are lascivious; adulterers are generally of this breed, and also adulterous and lascivious women: the women who are a section of the woman don't care for men, but have female attachments; the female companions are of this sort. But the men who are a section of the male follow the male, and while they are young, being a piece of the man, they hang about him and embrace him, and they are themselves the best of boys and youths, because they have the most manly nature. Some indeed assert that they are shameless, but this is not true; for they do not act thus from any want of shame, but because they are valiant and manly, and have a manly countenance, and they embrace that which is like them. And these when they grow up are our statesmen, and these only, which is a great proof of the truth of what I am saying. And when they reach manhood they are lovers of youth, and are not naturally inclined to marry or beget children, which they do, if at all, only in obedience to the law, but they are satisfied if they may be allowed to live unwedded; and such a nature is prone to love and ready to return love, always embracing that which is akin to him. And when one of them finds his other half, whether he be a lover of youth or a lover of another sort, the pair are lost in an amazement of love and friendship and intimacy, and one will not be out of the other's sight, as I may say, even for a moment: these are they who pass their lives with one another; yet they could not explain what they desire of one another. For the intense yearning which each of them has towards the other does not appear to be the desire of intercourse, but of something else which the soul desires and can not tell, and of which she has only a dark and doubtful presentiment. Suppose Hephaestus, with his instruments, to come to the pair who are lying side by side and say to them, "What do you people want of one another?" they would be unable to explain. And suppose further, that when he saw their perplexity he said: "Do you desire to be wholly one; always day and night to be in one another's company? for if this is what you desire, I am ready to melt you into one and let you grow together, so that being two you shall become one, and while you live live a common life as if you were a single man, and after your death in the world below still be one departed soul instead of two — I ask whether this is what you lovingly desire, and whether you are satisfied to attain this?" — there is not a man among them when he heard this who would deny or who would not acknowledge that this meeting and melting in one another's arms, this becoming one instead of two, was the very expression of his ancient need. And the reason is that human nature was originally one and we were a whole, and the desire and pursuit of the whole is called love.

There was a time, I say, when the two were one, but now because of this wickedness of men God has dispersed us, as the Arcadians were dispersed into villages by the Lacedaemonians. And if we are not obedient to the gods there is a danger that we shall be split up again and go about in basso-relievo, like the figures having only half a nose which are sculptured on columns, and that we shall be like tallies. Wherefore let us exhort all men to piety, that we may avoid the evil and obtain the good, of which Love is the lord and leader; and let no one oppose him — he is the enemy of the gods who opposes him. For if we are friends of God and reconciled to him we shall find our own true loves, which rarely happens in this world. I am serious, and therefore I must beg Eryximachus not to make fun or to find any allusion to Pausanias and Agathon, who, as I believe, are of the manly sort such as I have been describing. But my words have a wider application — they include men and women everywhere; and I believe that if all of us obtained our love, and each one had his particular beloved, thus returning to his original nature, then our race would be happy. And if this would be best of all, that which would be best under present circumstances would be the nearest approach to such an union; and that will be the attainment of a congenial love. Therefore we shall do well to praise the god Love, who is the author of this gift, and who is also our greatest benefactor, leading us in this life back to our own nature, and giving us high hopes for the future, that if we are pious, he will restore us to our original state, and heal us and make us happy and blessed. This, Eryximachus, is my discourse of love, which, although different from yours, I must beg you to leave unassailed by the shafts of your ridicule, in order that each may have his turn; each, or rather either, for Agathon and Socrates are the only ones left.

Indeed, I am not going to attack you, said Eryximachus, for I thought your speech charming, and did I not know that Agathon and Socrates are masters in the art of love, I should be really afraid that they would have nothing to say, after all the world of things which have been said already. But, for all that, I am not without hopes.

Socrates said: You did your part well, Eryximachus; but if you were as I am now, or rather as I shall be when Agathon has spoken, you would, indeed, be in a great strait.

You want to cast a spell over me, Socrates, said Agathon, in the hope that I may be disconcerted, thinking of the anticipation which the theatre has of my fine speech.

I should be strangely forgetful, Agathon, replied Socrates, of the courage and magnanimity which you showed when your own compositions were about to be exhibited, coming upon the stage with the actors and facing the whole theatre altogether undismayed, if I thought that your nerves could be fluttered at a small party of friends.

Do you think, Socrates, said Agathon, that my head is so full of the theatre as not to know how much more formidable to a man of sense a few good judges are than many fools?

Nay, replied Socrates, I should be very wrong in attributing to you, Agathon, that or any other want of refinement. And I am quite aware that if you happened to meet with any one whom you thought wise, you would care for his opinion much more than for that of the many. But then we, having been a part of the foolish many in the theatre, can not be regarded as the select wise; though I know that if you chanced to light upon a really wise man, you would be ashamed of disgracing yourself before him — would you not?

Yes, said Agathon.

But you would not be ashamed of disgracing yourself before the many?

Here Phaedrus interrupted them, saying: Don't answer him, my dear Agathon; for if he can only get a partner with whom he can talk, especially a good-looking one, he will no longer care about the completion of our plan. Now I love to hear him talk; but just at present I must not forget the encomium on Love which I ought to receive from him and every one. When you and he have paid the tribute to the god, then you may talk.

Very good, Phaedrus, said Agathon; I see no reason why I should not proceed with my speech, as I shall have other opportunities of conversing with Socrates. Let me say first how I ought to speak, and then speak.

The previous speakers, instead of praising the god Love, or unfolding his nature, appear to have congratulated mankind on the benefits which he confers upon them. But I would rather praise the god first, and then speak of his gifts; this is always the right way of praising everything. May I express unblamed then, that of all the blessed gods he is the blessedest and the best? And also the fairest, which I prove in this way: for, in the first place, Phaedrus, he is the youngest, and of his youth he is himself the witness, fleeing out of the way of age, which is swift enough surely, swifter than most of us like: yet he can not be overtaken by him; he is not a bird of that feather; youth and love live and move together — like to like, as the proverb says. There are many things which Phaedrus said about Love in which I agree with him; but I can not agree that he is older

than Iapetus and Kronos — that is not the truth; as
I maintain, he is the youngest of the gods, and youthful ever. The ancient things of which Hesiod and
Parmenides speak, if they were done at all, were done
of necessity and not of love; had love been in those
days, there would have been no chaining or mutilation
of the gods, or other violence, but peace and sweetness, as there is now in heaven, since the rule of Love
began. Love is young and also tender; he ought to
have a poet like Homer to describe his tenderness, as
Homer says of Ate, that she is a goddess and tender: —

> " Her feet are tender, for she sets her steps,
> Not on the ground but on the heads of men: "

which is an excellent proof of her tenderness, because
she walks not upon the hard but upon the soft. Let
us adduce a similar proof of the tenderness of Love;
for he walks not upon the earth, nor yet upon the
skulls of men, which are hard enough, but in the hearts
and souls of men: in them he walks and dwells and
has his home. Not in every soul without exception,
for where there is hardness he departs, where there
is softness there he dwells; and clinging always with
his feet and in all manner of ways in the softest of
soft places, how can he be other than the softest of all
things? And he is the youngest as well as the ten-
derest, and also he is of flexile form; for without flex-
ure he could not enfold all things, or wind his way
into and out of every soul of man without being discovered, if he were hard. And a proof of his flexibility and symmetry of form is his grace, which is
universally admitted to be in an especial manner the
attribute of Love; ungrace and love are always at
war with one another. The fairness of his complexion
is revealed by his habitation among the flowers; for

he dwells not amid unflowering or fading beauties, whether of body or soul or aught else, but in the place of flowers and scents, there he dwells and abides. Enough of his beauty — of which, however, there is more to tell. But I must now speak of his virtue: his greatest glory is that he can neither do nor suffer wrong from any god or any man; for he suffers not by force if he suffers, for force comes not near him, neither does he act by force. For all serve him of their own free will, and where there is love as well as obedience, there, as the laws which are the lords of the city say, is justice. And not only is he just but exceedingly temperate, for Temperance is the acknowledged ruler of the pleasures and desires, and no pleasure ever masters Love; he is their master and they are his servants; and if he conquers them he must be temperate indeed. As to courage, even the God of War is no match for him; he is the captive and Love is the lord, for love, the love of Aphrodite, masters him, as the tale runs; and the master is stronger than the servant. And if he conquers the bravest of all he must be himself the bravest. Of his courage and justice and temperance I have spoken; but I have yet to speak of his wisdom, and I must try to do my best, according to the measure of my ability. For in the first place he is a poet (and here, like Eryximachus, I magnify my art), and he is also the source of poesy in others, which he could not be if he were not himself a poet. And at the touch of him every one becomes a poet, even though he had no music in him before; this also is a proof that Love is a good poet and accomplished in all the musical arts; for no one can give to another that which he has not himself, or teach that of which he has no knowledge. Who will deny that the creation of the animals is his doing? Are they not all the works of his wisdom, born and begotten of him? And as to the artists, do we not know that he only of them whom love inspires has the light of fame? — he whom love touches not walks in darkness. The arts of medicine and archery and divination were discovered by Apollo, under the guidance of love and desire, so that he too is a disciple of love. Also the melody of the Muses, the metallurgy of Hephaestus, the weaving of Athene, the empire of Zeus over gods and men, are all due to love, who was the inventor of them. Love set in order the empire of the gods — the love of beauty, as is evident, for of deformity there is no love. And formerly, as I was saying, dreadful deeds were done among the gods, because of the rule of necessity; but now since the birth of love, and from the love of the beautiful, has sprung every good in heaven and earth. Therefore, Phaedrus, I say of love that he is the fairest and best in himself, and the cause of what is fairest and best in all other things. And I have a mind to say of him in verse that he is the god who

> " Gives peace on earth and calms the stormy deep,
> Who stills the waves and bids the sufferer sleep."

He makes men to be of one mind at a banquet such as this, fulfilling them with affection and emptying them of disaffection. In sacrifices, banquets, dances, he is our lord — supplying kindness and banishing unkindness, giving friendship and forgiving enmity, the joy of the good, the wonder of the wise, the amazement of the gods; desired by those who have no part in him, and precious to those who have the better part in him; parent of delicacy, luxury, desire, fondness, softness, grace; careful of the good, uncareful of the evil. In every word, work, wish, fear — pilot, helper, defender, savior; glory of gods and men, leader best and brightest: in whose footsteps let every man follow, chanting a hymn and joining in that fair strain with which love charms the souls of gods and men. Such is the discourse, Phaedrus, half playful, yet having a certain measure of seriousness, which, according to my ability, I dedicate to the god.

When Agathon had done speaking, Aristodemus said that there was a general cheer; the fair youth was thought to have spoken in a manner worthy of himself, and of the god. And Socrates, looking at Eryximachus, said: Tell me, son of Acumenus, was I not a prophet? Did I not anticipate that Agathon would make a wonderful oration and, that I should be in a strait?

I think, said Eryximachus, that you were right in the first anticipation, but not in the second.

Why, my dear friend, said Socrates, must not I or any one be in a strait who has to speak after such a rich and varied discourse as that? I am especially struck with the beauty of the concluding words — who could listen to them without amazement? When I reflected on the immeasurable inferiority of my own powers, I was ready to run away for shame, if there had been any escape. For I was reminded of Gorgias, and at the end of his speech I fancied that Agathon was shaking at me the Gorginian or Gorgonian head of the great master of rhetoric, which was simply to turn me and my speech into stone, as Homer says, and strike me dumb. And then I perceived how foolish I had been in consenting to take my turn with you in praising love, and saying that I too was a master of the art, when I really had no idea of the meaning of the word " praise," which appears to be another name for glorification, whether true or false; in which sense of the term I am unable to praise anything. For I in my simplicity imagined that the topics of praise should be true; this was to be the foundation, and that out of them the speaker was to choose the best and arrange them in the best order. And I felt quite proud, and thought that I could speak as well as another, as I knew the nature of true praise. Whereas I see now that the intention was to attribute to love every species of greatness and glory, whether really belonging to him or not, without regard to truth or falsehood — that was no matter; for the original proposal seems to have been not that you should praise, but only that you should appear to praise him. And you attribute to love every imaginable form of praise, and say that "he is all this," "the cause of all this," in order that you may exhibit him as the fairest and best of all; and this of course imposes on the unwary, but not on those who know him: and a noble and solemn hymn of praise have you rehearsed. But as I misunderstood the nature of the praise when I said that I would take my turn, I must beg to be absolved from the promise which (as Euripides would say) was a promise of the lips and not of the mind. Farewell then to such a strain: for that is not my way of praising; no, indeed, I can not attain to that. But if you like to hear the truth about love, I am ready to speak in my own manner, though I will not make myself ridiculous by entering into any rivalry with you. Say then, Phædrus, whether you would like to have the truth about love, spoken in any words and in any order which may happen to come into my mind at the time. Will that be agreeable to you?

Aristodemus said that Phædrus and the company bid him take his own course. Then, he said, let me have your permission first to ask Agathon a few more questions, in order that I may take his admissions as the premisses of my discourse.

I grant the permission, said Phaedrus: put your questions. Socrates then proceeded as follows: —

In the magnificent discourse which you have uttered, I think that you were right, my dear Agathon, in saying that you would begin with the nature of love and then afterwards speak of his works — that is a way of beginning which I very much approve. And as you have spoken thus eloquently of the nature of love, will you answer me a further question? — Is love the love of something or of nothing? And here I must explain myself: I do not want you to say that love is the love of a father or the love of a mother — that would be ridiculous; but to answer as you would, if I asked is a father a father of something? to which you would find no difficulty in replying, of a son or daughter: and that would be right.

Very true, said Agathon.

And you would say the same of a mother?

He assented.

Yet let me ask you one more question in order further to illustrate my meaning. Is not a brother to be regarded essentially as a brother of something?

Certainly, he replied.

That is, of a brother or sister?

Yes, he said.

And now, said Socrates, I will ask about love: — Is love of something or of nothing?

Of something, surely, he replied.

Keep in mind what this is, and tell me what I want to know — whether love desires that of which love is.

Yes, surely.

And does he possess, or does he not possess, that which he loves and desires?

Probably not, I should say.

Nay, replied Socrates, I would have you consider

whether necessarily is not rather the word. The inference that he who desires something is in want of something, and that he who desires nothing is in want of nothing, is in my judgment, Agathon, absolutely and necessarily true. What do you think?

I think with you, said Agathon, in that.

Very good. And would he who is great desire to be great, or he who is strong desire to be strong?

That would be inconsistent with our previous admissions.

True. For he who is anything can not want to be that which he is?

Very true.

But if, added Socrates, a man being strong desired to be strong, or being swift desired to be swift, or being healthy desired to be healthy (for any one may be imagined to desire any quality which he already has), in these cases there might be an objection raised — they might be said to desire that which they have already. I give the example in order that we may avoid misconception. For as you may see, Agathon, these persons must be supposed to have their respective advantages at the time, whether they choose or not; and surely no man can desire that which he has. And therefore, when a person says, I am well and wish to be well, or I am rich and wish to be rich, and I desire simply what I have; we shall reply to him: "You, my friend, having wealth and health and strength, want to have the continuance of them; for at this moment, whether you choose or no, you have them. And when you say, I desire that which I have and nothing else, is not your meaning that you want to have what you now have in the future?" He must allow this?

He must, said Agathon.

Then, said Socrates, this is equivalent to desiring

not what he has or possesses already, but that what he has may be preserved to him in the future?

Very true, he said.

Then he and every one who desires, desires that which he has not already, and which is future and not present, and which he has not, and is not, and of which he is in want; — these are the sort of things which love and desire seek?

Very true, he said.

Then now, said Socrates, let us recapitulate the argument. First, is not love of something, and of something too which is wanting to a man?

Yes, he replied.

Remember further what you said in your speech, or if you do not remember I will remind you: you said that the love of the beautiful disposes the empire of the gods, for that of deformed things there is no love — did you not say something like that?

Yes, said Agathon.

Yes, my friend, and the remark is a just one. And if this is true, love is the love of beauty and not of deformity?

He assented.

And the admission has been already made that love is of that which a man wants and has not?

True, he said.

Then love wants and has not beauty?

Certainly, he replied.

And would you call that beautiful which wants and does not possess beauty?

Certainly not.

Then would you still say that love is beautiful?

Agathon replied: I fear that I did not understand what I was saying.

Nay, Agathon, replied Socrates; but I should like

to ask you one more question: — Is not the good also the beautiful?

Yes.

Then in wanting the beautiful, love wants also the good?

I can not refute you, Socrates, said Agathon. And let us suppose that what you say is true.

Say rather, dear Agathon, that you can not refute the truth; for Socrates is easily refuted.

And now I will take my leave of you, and rehearse the tale of love which I heard once upon a time from Diotima of Mantineia, who was a wise woman in this and many other branches of knowledge. She was the same who deferred the plague of Athens ten years by a sacrifice, and was my instructress in the art of love. In the attempt which I am about to make I shall pursue Agathon's method, and begin with his admissions, which are nearly if not quite the same which I made to the wise woman when she questioned me: this will be the easiest way, and I shall take both parts myself as well as I can. For, like Agathon, she spoke first of the being and nature of love, and then of his works. And I said to her in nearly the same words which he used to me, that love was a mighty god, and likewise fair; and she proved to me as I proved to him that, in my way of speaking about him, love was neither fair nor good. " What do you mean, Diotima," I said, " is love then evil and foul? " " Hush," she cried; " is that to be deemed foul which is not fair? " " Certainly," I said. " And is that which is not wise, ignorant? do you not see that there is a mean between wisdom and ignorance? " " And what is this? " I said. " **Right** opinion," she replied; " which, as you know, being incapable of giving a reason, is not knowledge (for how could knowledge be devoid of reason? nor again, ignorance, for neither can ignorance attain the truth), but is clearly something which is a mean between ignorance and wisdom." "Quite true," I replied. "Do not then insist," she said, "that what is not fair is of necessity foul, or what is not good evil; or infer that because love is not fair and good he is therefore foul and evil; for he is in a mean between them." "Well," I said, "love is surely admitted by all to be a great god." "By those who know or by those who don't know?" "By all." "And how, Socrates," she said with a smile, "can love be acknowledged to be a great god by those who say that he is not a god at all?" "And who are they?" I said. "You and I are two of them," she replied. "How can that be?" I said. "That is very intelligible," she replied; "as you yourself would acknowledge that the gods are happy and fair — of course you would — would you dare to say that any god was not?" "Certainly not," I replied. "And you mean by the happy, those who are the possessors of things good or fair?" "Yes." "And you admitted that love, because he was in want, desires those good and fair things of which he is in want?" "Yes, I admitted that." "But how can he be a god who has no share in the good or the fair?" "That is not to be supposed." "Then you see that you also deny the deity of love."

"What then is love?" I asked; "Is he mortal?" "No." "What then?" "As in the former instance, he is neither mortal nor immortal, but in a mean between them." "What is he then, Diotima?" "He is a great spirit (δαίμων), and like all that is spiritual he is intermediate between the divine and the mortal." "And what is the nature of this spiritual power?" I said. "This is the power," she said, "which interprets and conveys to the gods the prayers and sacrifices of men, and to men the commands and rewards of the gods; and this power spans the chasm which divides them, and in this all is bound together, and through this the arts of the prophet and the priest, their sacrifices and mysteries and charms, and all prophecy and incantation, find their way. For God mingles not with man; and through this power all the intercourse and speech of God with man, whether awake or asleep, is carried on. The wisdom which understands this is spiritual; all other wisdom, such as that of arts or handicrafts, is mean and vulgar. Now these spirits or intermediate powers are many and divine, and one of them is love." "And who," I said, "was his father, and who his mother?" "The tale," she said, "will take time; nevertheless I will tell you. On the birthday of Aphrodite there was a feast of the gods, at which the god Poros or Plenty, who is the son of Metis or Discretion, was one of the guests. When the feast was over, Penia or Poverty, as the manner was, came about the doors to beg. Now Plenty, who was the worse for nectar (there was no wine in those days), came into the garden of Zeus and fell into a heavy sleep; and Poverty considering her own straitened circumstances, plotted to have him for a husband, and accordingly she lay down at his side and conceived Love, who partly because he is naturally a lover of the beautiful, and because Aphrodite is herself beautiful, and also because he was born on Aphrodite's birthday is her follower and attendant. And as his parentage is, so also are his fortunes. In the first place he is always poor, and anything but tender and fair, as the many imagine him; and he is hard-featured and squalid, and has no shoes, nor a house to dwell in; on the bare earth exposed he lies under the open heaven, in the streets, or at the doors of houses, taking his rest; and like his mother he is always in distress. Like his father too, whom he also partly resembles, he is always plotting against the fair and good; he is bold, enterprising, strong, a hunter of men, always at some intrigue or other, keen in the pursuit of wisdom, and never wanting resources; a philosopher at all times, terrible as an enchanter, sorcerer, sophist; for as he is neither mortal nor immortal, he is alive and flourishing at one moment when he is in plenty, and dead at another moment, and again alive by reason of his father's nature. But that which is always flowing in is always flowing out, and so he is never in want and never in wealth, and he is also in a mean between ignorance and knowledge. The truth of the matter is just this: No god is a philosopher or seeker after wisdom, for he is wise already; or does any one else who is wise seek after wisdom. Neither do the ignorant seek after wisdom. For herein is the evil of ignorance, that he who is neither good nor wise is nevertheless satisfied: he feels no want, and has therefore no desire." " But who then, Diotima," I said, " are the lovers of wisdom, if they are neither the wise nor the foolish? " " A child may answer that question," she replied; " they are those who, like love, are in a mean between the two. For wisdom is a most beautiful thing, and love is of the beautiful; and therefore love is also a philosopher or lover of wisdom, and being a lover of wisdom is in a mean between the wise and the ignorant. And this again is a quality which Love inherits from his parents; for his father is wealthy and wise, and his mother poor and foolish. Such, my dear Socrates, is the nature of the spirit Love. The error in your conception of him was very natural, and as I imagine from what you say, has arisen out of a confusion of love and the beloved — this made you think that love was all beautiful. For the beloved is the truly beautiful, delicate, and perfect and blessed; but the principle of love is of another nature, and is such as I have described."

I said: "O thou stranger woman, thou sayest well, and now, assuming love to be such as you say, what is the use of him?" "That, Socrates," she replied, "I will proceed to unfold: of his nature and birth I have already spoken; and you acknowledge that love is of the beautiful. But some one will say: Of the beautiful in what, Socrates and Diotima — or rather let me put the question more clearly, and ask: When a man loves the beautiful, what does he love?" I answered her "That the beautiful may be his." "Still," she said, "The answer suggests a further question, which is this: What is given by the possession of beauty?" "That," I replied, "is a question to which I have no answer ready." "Then," she said, "let me put the word 'good' in the place of the beautiful, and repeat the question: What does he who loves the good desire?" "The possession of the good," I said. "And what does he gain who possesses the good?" "Happiness," I replied; "there is no difficulty in answering that." "Yes," she said, "the happy are made happy by the acquisition of good things. Nor is there any need to ask why a man desires happiness; the answer is already final." "That is true," I said. "And is this wish and this desire common to all? and do all men always desire their own good, or only some men? — what think you?" "All men," I replied; "the desire is common to all." "But all men, Socrates," she rejoined, "are not said to love, but only some of them; and you say that all men are always loving the same things." "I myself wonder," I said, "why that is." "There is nothing to wonder at," she replied; "the reason is that one part of love is separated off and receives the name of the whole, but the other parts have other names." "Give an example."

I said. She answered me as follows: " There is poetry, which, as you know, is complex and manifold. And all creation or passage of non-being into being is poetry or making, and the processes of all art are creative; and the masters of arts are all poets." " Very true." " Still," she said, " you know that they are not called poets, but have other names; the generic term ' poetry ' is confined to that specific art which is separated off from the rest of poetry, and is concerned with music and metre; and this is what is called poetry, and they who possess this kind of poetry are called poets." " Very true," I said. " And the same holds of love. For you may say generally that all desire of good and happiness is due to the great and subtle power of love; but those who, having their affections set upon him, are yet diverted into the paths of money-making or gymnastic philosophy, are not called lovers — the name of the genus is reserved for those whose devotion takes one form only — they alone are said to love, or to be lovers." " In that," I said, " I am of opinion that you are right." " Yes," she said, " and you hear people say that lovers are seeking for the half of themselves; but I say that they are seeking neither for the half, nor for the whole, unless the half or the whole be also a good. And they will cut off their own hands and feet and cast them away, if they are evil; for they love them not because they are their own, but because they are good, and dislike them not because they are another's, but because they are evil. There is nothing which men love but the good. Do you think that there is?" " Indeed," I answered, " I should say not." " Then," she said, " the conclusion of the whole matter is, that men love the good." " Yes," I said. " To which may be added that they love the possession of the good?" " Yes, that may be added." " And not only the pos-

session, but the everlasting possession of the good?"
"That may be added too." "Then, love," she said,
"may be described generally as the love of the everlasting possession of the good?" "That is most
true," I said.

"Then if this be the nature of love, can you tell me
further," she said, "what is the manner of the pursuit? what are they doing who show all this eagerness
and heat which is called love? Answer me that."
"Nay, Diotima," I said, "if I had known I should
not have wondered at your wisdom, or have come to
you to learn." "Well," she said, "I will teach you;
— love is only birth in beauty, whether of body or
soul." "The oracle requires an explanation," I said;
"I don't understand you." "I will make my meaning clearer," she replied. "I mean to say, that all
men are bringing to the birth in their bodies and in
their souls. There is a certain age at which human
nature is desirous of procreation; and this procreation
must be in beauty and not in deformity: and this is
the mystery of man and woman, which is a divine
thing, for conception and generation are a principle
of immortality in the mortal creature. And in the
inharmonical they can never be. But the deformed is
always inharmonical with the divine, and the beautiful
harmonious. Beauty, then, is the destiny or goddess
of parturition who presides at birth, and therefore
when approaching beauty the conceiving power is
propitious, and diffuse, and benign, and begets and
bears fruit: on the appearance of foulness she frowns
and contracts in pain, and is averted and morose, and
shrinks up, and not without a pang refrains from conception. And this is the reason why, when the hour
of conception arrives, and the teeming nature is full,
there is such a flutter and ecstasy about beauty whose
approach is the alleviation of pain. For love,

Socrates, is not, as you imagine, the love of the beautiful only." " What then?" " The love of generation and birth in beauty." " Yes," I said. " Yes, indeed," she replied. " But why of birth?" I said. " Because to the mortal, birth is a sort of eternity and immortality," she replied; " and as has been already admitted, all men will necessarily desire immortality together with good, if love is of the everlasting possession of the good."

And this she taught me at various times when she spoke of love. And on another occasion she said to me, " What is the reason, Socrates, of this love, and the attendant desire? See you not how all animals, birds as well as beasts, in their desire of procreation, are in agony when they take the infection of love; — this begins with the desire of union, to which is added the care of offspring, on behalf of whom the weakest are ready to battle against the strongest even to the uttermost, and to die for them, and will let themselves be tormented with hunger or suffer anything in order to maintain their offspring. Man may be supposed to do this from reason; but why should animals have these passionate feelings? Can you tell me why?" Again I replied, that I did not know. She said to me: " And do you expect ever to become a master in the art of love, if you do not know this?" " But that," I said, " Diotima, is the reason why I come to you, because, as I have told you already, I am aware that I want a teacher; and I wish that you would explain to me this and the other mysteries of love." " Marvel not at this," she said, " if you believe that love is of the immortal, as we have already admitted; for here again, and on the same principle too, the mortal nature is seeking as far as is possible to be everlasting and immortal: and this is only to be attained by generation, because the new is always left in the place of the old. For even in the same individual there is succession and not absolute unity: a man is called the same; but yet in the short interval which elapses between youth and age, and in which every animal is said to have life and identity, he is undergoing a perpetual process of loss and reparation — hair, flesh, bones, blood, and the whole body are always changing. And this is true not only of the body, but also of the soul, whose habits, tempers, opinions, desires, pleasures, pains, fears, never remain the same in any one of us, but are always coming and going. And what is yet more surprising is, that this is also true of knowledge; and not only does knowledge in general come and go, so that in this respect we are never the same; but particular knowledge also experiences a like change. For what is implied in the word " recollection," but the departure of knowledge, which is ever being forgotten and is renewed and preserved by recollection, appearing to be the same although in reality new, according to that law of succession by which all mortal things are preserved, not by absolute sameness of existence, but by substitution, the old worn-out mortality leaving another new and similar one behind — unlike the immortal in this, which is always the same and not another? And in this way, Socrates, the mortal body, or mortal anything, partakes of immortality; but the immortal in another way. Marvel not then at the love which all men have of their offspring; for that universal love and interest is for the sake of immortality."

When I heard this, I was astonished, and said: " Is this really true, O thou wise Diotima? " And she answered with all the authority of a sophist: " Of that, Socrates, you may be assured; — think only of the ambition of men, and you will marvel at their senselessness, unless you consider how they are stirred

by the love of an immortality of fame. They are
ready to run risks greater far than they would have
run for their children, and to spend money and undergo any amount of toil, and even to die for the sake
of leaving behind them a name which shall be eternal.
Do you imagine that Alcestis would have died on
behalf of Admetus, or Achilles after Patroclus, or
your own Codrus in order to preserve the kingdom
for his sons, if they had not imagined that the memory
of their virtues, which is still retained among us,
would be immortal? Nay," she said, " for I am persuaded that all men do all things for the sake of the
glorious fame of immortal virtue, and the better they
are the more they desire this; for they are ravished
with the desire of the immortal.

" Men whose bodies only are creative, betake themselves to women and beget children — this is the character of their love; their offspring, as they hope, will
preserve their memory and give them the blessedness
and immortality which they desire in the future. But
creative souls — for there are men who are more
creative in their souls than in their bodies — conceive
that which is proper for the soul to conceive or retain.
And what are these conceptions? — wisdom and virtue in general. And such creators are all poets and
other artists who may be said to have invention. But
the greatest and fairest sort of wisdom by far is that
which is concerned with the ordering of states and
families, and which is called temperance and justice.
And he who in youth has the seed of these implanted
in him and is himself inspired, when he comes to
maturity desires to beget and generate. And he
wanders about seeking beauty that he may beget
offspring — for in deformity he will beget nothing —
and embraces the beautiful rather than the deformed;
and when he finds a fair and noble and well-nurtured

soul, and there is union of the two in one person, he gladly embraces him, and to such an one he is full of fair speech about virtue and the nature and pursuits of a good man; and he tries to educate him; and at the touch and presence of the beautiful he brings forth the beautiful which he conceived long before, and the beautiful is ever present with him and in his memory even when absent, and in company they tend that which he brings forth, and they are bound together by a far nearer tie and have a closer friendship than those who beget mortal children, for the children who are their common offspring are fairer and more immortal. Who, when he thinks of Homer and Hesiod and other great poets, would not rather have their children than any ordinary human ones? Who would not emulate them in the creation of children such as theirs, which have preserved their memory and given them everlasting glory? Or who would not have such children as Lycurgus left behind to be the saviors, not only of Lacedaemon, but of Hellas, as one may say? There is Solon, too, who is the revered father of Athenian laws; and many others there are in many other places, both among Hellenes and barbarians. All of them have done many noble works, and have been the parents of virtue of every kind, and many temples have been raised in honor of their children, which were never raised in honor of the mortal children of any one.

" These are the lesser mysteries of love, into which even you, Socrates, may enter; to the greater and more hidden ones which are the crown of these, and to which, if you pursue them in a right spirit, they will lead, I know not whether you will be able to attain. But I will do my utmost to inform you, and do you follow if you can. For he who would proceed rightly in this matter should begin in youth to turn to beautiful forms; and first, if his instructor guide him rightly, he should learn to love one such form only — out of that he should create fair thoughts; and soon he would himself perceive that the beauty of one form is truly related to the beauty of another; and then if beauty in general is his pursuit, how foolish would he be not to recognize that the beauty in every form is one and the same! And when he perceives this he will abate his violent love of the one, which he will despise and deem a small thing, and will become a lover of all beautiful forms; this will lead him on to consider that the beauty of the mind is more honorable than the beauty of the outward form. So that if a virtuous soul have but a little comeliness, he will be content to love and tend him, and will search out and bring to the birth thoughts which may improve the young, until his beloved is compelled to contemplate and see the beauty of institutions and laws, and understand that all is of one kindred, and that personal beauty is only a trifle; and after laws and institutions he will lead him on to the sciences, that he may see their beauty, being not like a servant in love with the beauty of one youth or man or institution, himself a slave mean and calculating, but looking at the abundance of beauty and drawing towards the sea of beauty, and creating and beholding many fair and noble thoughts and notions in boundless love of wisdom; until at length he grows and waxes strong, and at last the vision is revealed to him of a single science, which is the science of beauty everywhere. To this I will proceed; please to give me your very best attention.

"For he who has been instructed thus far in the things of love, and who has learned to see the beautiful in due order and succession, when he comes toward the end will suddenly perceive a nature of wondrous beauty — and this, Socrates, is that final cause of all our former toils, which in the first place is everlasting — not growing and decaying, or waxing and waning; in the next place not fair in one point of view and foul in another, or at one time or in one relation or at one place fair, at another time or in another relation or at another place foul, as if fair to some and foul to others, or in the likeness of a face or hands or any other part of the bodily frame, or in any form of speech or knowledge, nor existing in any other being; as for example, an animal, whether in earth or heaven, but beauty only, absolute, separate, simple, and everlasting, which without diminution and without increase, or any change, is imparted to the ever-growing and perishing beauties of all other things. He who under the influence of true love rising upward from these begins to see that beauty, is not far from the end. And the true order of going or being led by another to the things of love, is to use the beauties of earth as steps along which he mounts upwards for the sake of that other beauty, going from one to two, and from two to all fair forms, and from fair forms to fair actions, and from fair actions to fair notions, until from fair notions he arrives at the notion of absolute beauty, and at last knows what the essence of beauty is. This, my dear Socrates," said the stranger of Mantineia, " is that life above all others which man should live, in the contemplation of beauty absolute; a beauty which if you once beheld, you would see not to be after the measure of gold, and garments, and fair boys and youths, which when you now behold you are in fond amazement, and you and many a one are content to live seeing only and conversing with them without meat or drink, if that were possible — you only want to be with them and to look at them. But what if man had eyes to see the true beauty — the divine beauty, I mean, pure and clear and unalloyed, not clogged with the pollutions of mortality, and all the colors and vanities of human life — thither looking, and holding converse with the true beauty divine and simple, and bringing into being and educating true creations of virtue and not idols only? Do you not see that in that communion only, beholding beauty with the eye of the mind, he will be enabled to bring forth, not images of beauty, but realities; for he has hold not of an image but of a reality, and bringing forth and educating true virtue to become the friend of God and be immortal, if mortal man may. Would that be an ignoble life?"

Such, Phaedrus — and I speak not only to you, but to all men — were the words of Diotima; and I am persuaded of their truth. And being persuaded of them, I try to persuade others, that in the attainment of this end human nature will not easily find a better helper than love. And therefore, also, I say that every man ought to honor him as I myself honor him, and walk in his ways, and exhort others to do the same, even as I praise the power and spirit of love according to the measure of my ability now and ever.

The words which I have spoken, you, Phaedrus, may call an encomium of love, or anything else which you please.

When Socrates had done speaking, the company applauded, and Aristophanes was beginning to say something in answer to the allusion which Socrates had made to his own speech, when suddenly there was a great knocking at the door of the house, as of revellers, and the sound of a flute-girl was heard. Agathon told the attendants to go and see who were the intruders. "If they are friends of ours," he said, "invite them in, but if not say that the drinking is over." A little while afterwards they heard the voice of Alcibiades resounding in the court; he was in a great state of intoxication, and kept roaring and shouting "Where is Agathon? Lead me to Agathon," and at length, supported by the flute-girl and some of his companions, he found his way to them. "Hail friends," he said, appearing at the door crowned with a massive garland of ivy and wall-flowers, and having his head flowing with ribands. "Will you have a very drunken man as a companion of your revels? Or shall I crown Agathon, as was my intention in coming, and go my way? For I was unable to come yesterday, and therefore I come today, carrying on my head these ribands, that taking them from my own head, I may crown the head of this fairest and wisest of men, as I may be allowed to call him. Will you laugh at me because I am drunk? Yet I know very well that I am speaking the truth, although you may laugh. But first tell me whether I shall come in on the understanding that I am drunk. Will you drink with me or not?"

The company were vociferous in begging that he would take his place among them, and Agathon specially invited him. Thereupon he was led in by the people who were with him; and as he was being led he took the crown and ribands from his head, intending to crown Agathon, and had them before his eyes; this prevented him from seeing Socrates, who made way for him, and Alcibiades took the vacant place between Agathon and Socrates, and in taking the place he embraced Agathon and crowned him. Take off his sandals, said Agathon, and let him make a third on the same couch.

By all means; but who makes the third partner in our revels? said Alcibiades, turning round and starting up as he caught sight of Socrates. By Heracles, he said, what is this? here is Socrates always lying in wait for me, and always, as his way is, coming out at all sorts of unsuspected places: and now, what have you to say for yourself, and why are you lying here, where I perceive that you have contrived to find a place, not by a professor or lover of jokes, like Aristophanes, but by the fairest of the company?

Socrates turned to Agathon and said: I must ask you to protect me, Agathon; for this passion of his has grown quite a serious matter. Since I became his admirer I have never been allowed to speak to any other fair one, or so much as to look at them. If I do he goes wild with envy and jealousy, and not only abuses me but can hardly keep his hands off me, and at this moment he may do me some harm. Please to see to this, and either reconcile me to him, or, if he attempts violence, protect me, as I am in bodily fear of his mad and passionate attempts.

There can never be reconciliation between you and me, said Alcibiades; but for the present I will defer your chastisement. And I must beg you, Agathon, to give me back some of the ribands that I may crown the marvellous head of this universal despot — I would not have him complain of me for crowning you, and neglecting him, who in conversation is the conqueror of all mankind; and this not once only, as you were the day before yesterday, but always. Then taking some of the ribands, he crowned Socrates, and again reclined. When he had lain down again, he said: You seem, my friends, to be sober, which is a thing not to be endured; you must drink — for that was the agreement which I made with you — and I elect myself master of the feast until you are well drunk. Let us have a large goblet, Agathon, or rather, he said, addressing the attendant, bring me that wine-cooler. The wine-cooler was a vessel holding more than two quarts which caught his eye —

this he filled and emptied, and bid the attendant fill it again for Socrates. Observe, my friends, said Alcibiades, that my ingenious device will have no effect on Socrates, for he can drink any quantity of wine and not be at all nearer being drunk. Socrates drank the cup which the attendant filled for him.

Eryximachus said: What is this, Alcibiades? Are we to have neither conversation nor singing over our cups; but simply to drink as if we were thirsty?

Alcibiades replied: Hail, worthy son of a most wise and worthy sire.

The same to you, said Eryximachus; but what shall we do?

That I leave to you, said Alcibiades.

" The wise physician skilled our wounds to heal "

shall prescribe and we will obey. What do you want?

Well, Eryximachus said: Before you appeared a resolution was agreed to by us that each one in turn should speak a discourse in praise of love, and as good a one as he could: this was passed round from left to right; and as all of us have spoken, and you have not spoken but have well drunken, you ought to speak, and then impose upon Socrates any task which you please, and he on his right hand neighbor, and so on.

That is good, Eryximachus, said Alcibiades; and yet the comparison of a drunken man's speech with those of sober men is hardly fair; and I should like to know, sweet friend, whether you really believe what Socrates was just now saying; for I can assure you that the very reverse is the fact, and that if I praise any one but himself in his presence, whether God or man, he will hardly keep his hands off me.

For shame, said Socrates.

By Poseidon, said Alcibiades, there is no use in

your denying this, for no creature will I praise in your presence.

Well then take your own course, said Eryximachus, and if you like praise Socrates.

What do you think, Eryximachus? said Alcibiades; shall I attack him and inflict the punishment in your presence?

What are you about? said Socrates; are you going to raise a laugh at me? Is that the meaning of your praise?

I am going to speak the truth, if you will permit me.

I not only permit you but exhort you to speak the truth.

Then I will begin at once, said Alcibiades, and if I say anything that is not true, you may interrupt me if you will, and say that I speak falsely, though my intention is to speak the truth. But you must not wonder if I speak any how as things come into my mind; for the fluent and orderly enumeration of all your wonderful qualities is not a task the accomplishment of which is easy to a man in my condition.

I shall praise Socrates in a figure which shall appear to him to be a caricature, and yet I do not mean to laugh at him, but only to speak the truth. I say then, that he is exactly like the masks of Silenus, which may be seen sitting in the statuaries' shops, having pipes and flutes in their mouths; and they are made to open in the middle, and there are images of gods inside them. I say also that he is like Marsyas the satyr. You will not deny, Socrates, that your face is like that of a satyr. Aye, and there is a resemblance in other points too. For example, you are a bully, — that I am in a position to prove by the evidences of witnesses, if you will not confess. And are you not a flute-player? That you are, and a far more wonderful performer than Marsyas. For he indeed with instruments charmed the souls of men by the power of his breath, as the performers of his music do still: for the melodies of Olympus are derived from the teaching of Marsyas, and these, whether they are played by a great master or by a miserable flute-girl, have a power which no others have; they alone possess the soul and reveal the wants of those who have needs of gods and mysteries, because they are inspired. But you produce the same effect with the voice only, and do not require the flute: that is the difference between you and him. When we hear any other speaker, even a very good one, his words produce absolutely no effect upon us in comparison, whereas the very fragments of you and your words, even at second-hand, and however imperfectly repeated, amaze and possess the souls of every man, woman, and child who comes within hearing of them. And if I were not afraid that you would think me drunk, I would have sworn as well as spoken to the influence which they have always had and still have over me. For my heart leaps within me more than that of any Corybantian reveller, and my eyes rain tears when I hear them. And I observe that many others are affected in the same way. I have heard Pericles and other great orators, but though I thought that they spoke well, I never had any similar feeling; my soul was not stirred by them, nor was I angry at the thought of my own slavish state. But this Marsyas has often brought me to such a pass, that I have felt as if I could hardly endure the life which I am leading (this, Socrates, you admit); and I am conscious that if I did not shut my ears against him, and fly from the voice of the siren, he would detain me until I grew old sitting at his feet. For he makes me confess that I ought not to live as I do, neglecting the wants of my own soul, and busying myself with the concerns of the Athenians; therefore I hold my ears and tear myself away from him. And he is the only person who ever made me ashamed, which you might think not to be in my nature, and there is no one else who does the same. For I know that I can not answer him or say that I ought not to do as he bids, but when I leave his presence the love of popularity gets the better of me. And therefore I run away and fly from him, and when I see him I am ashamed of what I have confessed to him. And many a time I wish that he were dead, and yet I know that I should be much more sorry than glad, if he were to die: so that I am at my wit's end.

And this is what I and many others have suffered from the flute-playing of this satyr. Yet hear me once more while I show you how exact the image is, and how marvellous his power. For I am sure that none of you know him; but I know him and will describe him, as I have begun. See you how fond he is of the fair? He is always with them and is always being smitten by them, and then again he knows nothing and is ignorant of all things — that is the appearance which he puts on. Is he not like a Silenus in this? Yes, surely: that is, his outer mask, which is the carved head of the Silenus; but when he is opened, what temperance there is, as I may say to you, O my companions in drink, residing within. Know you that beauty and wealth and honor, at which the many wonder, are of no account with him, and are utterly despised by him: he regards not at all the persons who are gifted with them; mankind are nothing to him; all his life is spent in mocking and flouting at them. But when I opened him, and looked within at his serious purpose, I saw in him divine and golden images of such fascinating beauty that I was ready to do in a moment whatever Socrates commanded: (they may have escaped the observation of others, but I saw them). Now I thought that he was seriously enamored of my beauty, and this appeared to be a grand opportunity of hearing him tell what he knew, for I had a wonderful opinion of the attractions of my youth. In the prosecution of this design, when I next went to him, I sent away the attendant who usually accompanied me (I will confess the whole truth, and beg you to listen; and if I speak falsely, do you, Socrates, expose the falsehood). Well, he and I were alone together, and I thought that when there was nobody with us, I should hear him speak the language of love as lovers do, and I was delighted. Not a word; he conversed as usual, and spent the day with me and then went away. Afterwards I challenged him to the palaestra; and he wrestled and closed with me several times alone; I fancied that I might succeed in this way. Not a bit; there was no use in that. Lastly, as I had failed hitherto, I thought that I must use stronger measures and attack him boldly, as I had begun, and not give him up until I saw how the matter stood. So I invited him to supper, just as if he were a fair youth, and I a designing lover. He was not easily persuaded to come; he did, however, after a while accept the invitation, and when he came the first time, he wanted to go away at once as soon as supper was over, and I had not the face to detain him. The second time, still in pursuance of my design, after we had supped, I went on conversing far into the night, and when he wanted to go away, I pretended that the hour was late and that he had better remain. So he lay down on the next couch to me, the same on which he had supped, and there was no one else in the apartment. All this may be told without shame to any one. But what follows I could hardly tell you if I were sober. Yet as the proverb says, " In vino veritas," whether there is in boys or not; and therefore I must speak. Nor, again, should I be justified in concealing the lofty actions of Socrates as I come to praise him. Moreover I have felt the pang; and he who has suffered, as they say, is willing to tell his fellow-sufferers only, as they alone will be likely to understand him, and will not be extreme in judging of the sayings or doings which have been wrung from his agony. For I have been bitten by the viper too; I have known in my soul, or in my heart, or in some other part, that worst of pangs, more violent in ingenuous youth than any serpent's tooth, the pang of philosophy, which will make a man say or do anything. And you whom I see around me, your Phaedrus, your Agathon, your Eryximachus, your Pausanias, your Aristodemus, your Aristophanes, all of you, and I need not say Socrates himself, have all had experience of the same madness and passion of philosophy. Therefore listen and excuse my doings then and my sayings now. But let the attendants and other profane and unmannered persons close the doors of their ears.

When the lamp was put out and the servants had gone away, I thought that I must be plain with him and have no more ambiguity. So I gave him a shake, and I said: " Socrates, are you asleep?" " No," he said. " Do you know what I am meditating?" " What is that? " he said. " I think," I replied, " that of all the lovers whom I have ever had you are the only one who is worthy of me, and you appear to be too modest to speak. Now I feel that I should be a fool to refuse you this or any other favor, and therefore I come to lay at your feet all that I have and all that my friends have, in the hope that you will assist me in the way of virtue, which I desire above all things, and in which I believe that you can help me better than any one else. And I am certainly of opinion that I should have more reason to be ashamed of what wise men would say if I were to refuse a favor to such as you, than of what fools would say if I granted it." When he heard this, he said in his ironical manner: " Friend Alcibiades, you have indeed an elevated aim if what you say is true, and if there really is in me any power by which you may become better; truly you must see in me some rare beauty of a kind infinitely higher than that which I see in you. And if, seeing this, you mean to share with me and to exchange beauty for beauty, you will have greatly the advantage of me; you will gain real beauty in return for appearance — gold in exchange for brass. But look again, sweet friend, and see whether you are not deceived in me. The mind begins to grow critical when the bodily eye fails, and you have not come to that yet." Hearing this, I said: " I have told you my purpose, which is quite serious, and do you consider what you think best for you and me." " That is good," he said; " at some other time then we will consider and act as seems best about this and about other matters." When I heard this answer, I fancied that he was smitten, and that my arrows had wounded him, and so without waiting to hear more I got up, and throwing my coat about him crept under his threadbare cloak, as the time of year was winter, and there I lay during the whole night having this wonderful monster in my arms. You won't deny this, Socrates. And yet, notwithstanding all this, he was so superior to my solicitations, so contemptuous and derisive and disdainful of my beauty — which really, as I believe, had some attractions — hear, O judges; for judges you shall be of the haughty virtue of Socrates — that in the morning when I awoke (let all the gods and goddesses be my witnesses) I arose as from the couch of a father or an elder brother.

What do you suppose must have been my feelings after this rejection at the thought of my own dishonor? And yet I could not help wondering at his natural temperance and self-restraint and courage. I never could have thought that I should have met with a man like him in wisdom and endurance. Neither could I be angry with him or renounce his company, any more than I could hope to win him. For I well knew that if Ajax could not be wounded by steel, much less he by money; and I had failed in my only chance of captivating him. So I wandered about and was at my wit's end; no one was ever more hopelessly enslaved by another. All this, as I should explain, happened before he and I went on the expedition to Potidaea; there we messed together, and I had the opportunity of observing his extraordinary power of sustaining fatigue and going without food when our supplies were intercepted at any place, as will happen with an army. In the faculty of endurance he was superior not only to me but to everybody; there was no one to be compared to him. Yet at a festival he was the only person who had any real powers of enjoyment, and though not willing to drink, he could if compelled beat us all at that, and the most wonderful thing of all was that no human being had ever seen Socrates drunk; and that, if I am not mistaken, will soon be tested. His endurance of cold was also surprising. There was a severe frost, for the winter in that region is really tremendous, and everybody else either remained indoors, or if they went out had on no end of clothing, and were well shod, and had their feet swathed in felt and fleeces: in the midst of this, Socrates, with his bare feet on the ice, and in his ordinary dress, marched better than any of the other soldiers who had their shoes on, and they looked daggers at him because he seemed to despise them.

I have told you one tale, and now I must tell you another, which is worth hearing, of the doings and sufferings of this enduring man while he was on the expedition. One morning he was thinking about something which he could not resolve; and he would not give up, but continued thinking from early dawn until noon — there he stood fixed in thought; and at noon attention was drawn to him, and the rumor ran through the wondering crowd that Socrates had been standing and thinking about something ever since the break of day. At last, in the evening after supper, some Ionians out of curiosity (I should explain that this was not in winter but in summer), brought out their mats and slept in the open air that they might watch him and see whether he would stand all night. There he stood all night as well as all day and the following morning; and with the return of light he offered up a prayer to the sun, and went his way. I will also tell, if you please — and indeed I am bound to tell — of his courage in battle; for who but he saved my life? Now this was the engagement in which I received the prize of valor: for I was wounded and he would not leave me, but he rescued me and my arms; and he ought to have received the prize of valor which the generals wanted to confer on me partly on account of my rank, and I told them so (this Socrates will not impeach or deny), but he was more eager than the generals that I and not he should have the prize. There was another occasion on which he was very noticeable; this was in the flight of the army after the battle of Delium, and I had a better opportunity of seeing him than at Potidaea as I was myself on horseback, and therefore comparatively out of danger. He and Laches were retreating as the troops were in flight, and I met them and told them not to be discouraged, and promised to remain with them; and there you might see him, Aristophanes, as you describe, just as he is in the streets of Athens, stalking like a pelican, and rolling his eyes, calmly contemplating enemies as well as friends, and making very intelligible to anybody, even from a distance, that whoever attacks him will be likely to meet with a stout resistance; and in this way he and his companion escaped — for these are the sort of persons who are never touched in war; they only pursue those who are running away headlong. I particularly observed how superior he was to Laches in presence of mind. Many are the wonders of Socrates which I might narrate in his praise; most of his ways might perhaps be paralleled in others, but the most astonishing thing of all is his absolute unlikeness to any human being that is or ever has been. You may imagine Brasidas and others to have been like Achilles; or you may imagine Nestor and Antenor to have been like Pericles; and the same may be said of other famous men, but of this strange being you will never be able to find any likeness however remote, either among men who now are or who ever have been, except that which I have already suggested of Silenus and the satyrs; and this is an allegory not only of himself, but also of his words. For, although I forgot to mention this before, his words are ridiculous when you first hear them; he clothes himself in language that is as the skin of the wanton satyr — for his talk is of pack-asses and smiths and cobblers and curriers, and he is always repeating the same things in the same words, so that an ignorant man who did not know him might feel disposed to laugh at him; but he who pierces the mask and sees what is within will find that they are the only words which have a meaning in them, and also the most divine, abounding in fair examples of virtue, and of the largest discourse, or rather extending to the whole duty of a good and honorable man.

This, friends, is my praise of Socrates. I have added my blame of him for his ill-treatment of me; and he has ill-treated not only me, but Charmides the son of Glaucon, and Euthydemus the son of Diocles, and many others in the same way — beginning as their lover he has ended by making them pay their addresses to him. Wherefore I say to you, Agathon, " Be not deceived by him; learn from me and take warning, and don't be a fool and learn by experience," as the proverb says.

When Alcibiades had done speaking, there was a laugh at his plainness of speech, as he seemed to be still in love with Socrates. You are sober, Alcibiades, said Socrates, or you would never have gone about to hide the purpose of your satyr's praises, for all this long story is only an ingenious circumlocution, the point of which comes in by the way at the end; you want to get up a quarrel between me and Agathon, and your notion is that I ought to love you and nobody else, and that you and you only ought to love Agathon. But the plot of this Satyric or Silenic drama has been detected, and you must not allow him, Agathon, to set us at variance.

I believe you are right, said Agathon, and I am disposed to think that his intention in placing himself between you and me was only to divide us; but he shall gain nothing by that move, as I will go and lie in the couch next to you.

Yes, yes, replied Socrates, by all means come here and lie on the couch below me.

Alas, said Alcibiades, how am I fooled by this man;

he is determined to get the better of me at every turn.
I do beseech you, allow Agathon to lie between us.

Impossible, said Socrates, as you praised me, and I
ought to praise my neighbor on the right, he will be
out of order in praising me again when he ought
rather to be praised by me, and I must entreat you to
consent to this, and not be jealous, for I have a great
desire to praise the youth.

Ha! ha! cried Agathon, I will rise instantly, that
I may be praised by Socrates.

The usual way, said Alcibiades, where Socrates is,
no one else has any chance with the fair, and now how
readily has he invented a specious reason for attracting Agathon to himself.

Agathon arose in order that he might take his place
on the couch by Socrates, when suddenly a band of
revellers entered, and spoiled the order of the banquet.
Some one who was going out having left the door
open, they had found their way in, and made themselves at home; great confusion ensued, and every one
was compelled to drink large quantities of wine. Aristodemus said that Eryximachus, Phaedrus, and others
went away — he himself fell asleep, and as the nights
were long took a good rest: he was awakened towards
daybreak by a crowing of cocks, and when he awoke,
the others were either asleep, or had gone away; there
remained awake only Socrates, Aristophanes, and
Agathon, who were drinking out of a large goblet
which they passed round, and Socrates was discoursing to them. Aristodemus did not hear the beginning
of the discourse, and he was only half awake, but the
chief thing which he remembered, was Socrates insisting to the other two that the genius of comedy was the
same as that of tragedy, and that the writer of tragedy
ought to be a writer of comedy also. To this they were
compelled to assent, being sleepy, and not quite under-

standing his meaning. And first of all Aristophanes dropped, and then, when the day was already dawning, Agathon. Socrates, when he had put them to sleep, rose to depart, Aristodemus, as his manner was, following him. At the Lyceum he took a bath and passed the day as usual; and when evening came he retired to rest at his own home.

PHAEDRUS

INTRODUCTION

THE Phaedrus is closely connected with the Symposium, and may be regarded either as introducing or following it. The two Dialogues together contain the whole philosophy of Plato on the nature of love, which in the Republic and in the later writings of Plato is only introduced playfully or as a figure of speech. But in the Phaedrus and Symposium love and philosophy join hands, and one is an aspect of the other. The spiritual and emotional part is elevated into the ideal, to which in the Symposium mankind are described as looking forward, and which in the Phaedrus, as well as in the Phaedo, they are seeking to recover from a former state of existence. Whether the subject of the Dialogue is love or rhetoric, or the union of the two, or the relation of philosophy to love and to art in general, will be hereafter considered.

Phaedrus has been passing the day with Lysias, the celebrated rhetorician, and is going to refresh himself by taking a walk outside the wall, when he is met by Socrates, who professes that he will not leave him until he has delivered up the speech with which Lysias has regaled him, and which he is carrying about in his mind, or more probably in a book hidden under his cloak, and is intending to study as he walks. The imputation is not denied, and the two agree to direct their steps out of the public way along the stream of the Ilissus towards a plane-tree which is seen in the distance. There, lying down amidst pleasant sounds and scents, they will read the speech of Lysias. The country is a novelty to Socrates, who never goes out of the town; and hence he is full of admiration for the beauties of nature, of which he seems for the first time to be conscious.

In the course of their walk Phaedrus asks the opinion of Socrates respecting the local tradition of Boreas and Oreithyia. Socrates, after a satirical allusion to the " rationalizers " of his day, replies that he has no time for these " nice " interpretations of mythology; " the proper study of mankind is man," who is a far more complex and wonderful being than the serpent Typhon. When they have reached the plane-tree, Phaedrus pulls out the speech and reads.

The speech consists of a foolish paradox which is to the effect that the non-lover ought to be accepted rather than the lover — because he is more rational, more agreeable, more enduring, less suspicious, less hurtful, less boastful, less engrossing, and because there are more of them, and for a great many other reasons which are equally unmeaning. Phaedrus is captivated with the beauty of the periods, and wants to make Socrates say that nothing was or ever could be better written. Socrates does not think much of the matter, but then he has only attended to the form, and in the form he thinks that he has detected repetitions and other marks of haste. He can not agree with Phaedrus in the extreme value which he sets upon this performance, because he is afraid of doing injustice to Anacreon and Sappho and other great writers, and is almost inclined to think that he himself, or rather some power residing within him, could make a speech better than that of Lysias on the same theme, and also different from his, if he may be allowed to have a few commonplaces which all speakers must equally employ.

Phaedrus is delighted at the prospect of having another speech, and promises that he will set up a golden statue of Socrates at Delphi, if he keeps his word. Some raillery ensues, and at length Socrates, conquered by the threat that he shall never hear a speech of Lysias again unless he fulfils his promise, veils his face and begins.

The first part of his speech is a somewhat prosaic discussion of the opposition between desire and opinion guided by reason. But he has not proceeded far when he fancies that he detects in himself an unusual flow of eloquence — this he can only attribute to the inspiration of the place, which appears to be dedicated to the nymphs. Starting from the philosophical basis which has been already laid down, he proceeds to show how many advantages the non-lover has over the lover. The one leads to softness and poverty and exclusiveness, and is full of all sorts of unpleasantness; "crabbed age and youth" have to "live together," and the sight and the ways of the old are mighty disagreeable to the young. Or if they part company, then the spectacle may be seen of the lover running away from the beloved, who pursues him with vain reproaches, and demands his reward which the other refuses to pay. The lover turns virtuous when the hour of payment arrives, and the beloved learns too late, after all his pains and disagreeables, that as wolves love lambs so lovers love their loves. Here is the end; the "other" or "non-lover" part of the speech had better be understood, for if in the censure of the lover Socrates has broken out in verse, what will he do in his praise of the non-lover? He has said his say and is preparing to go away.

Phaedrus begs him to remain, at any rate until the heat of noon has passed; he thinks that they may as well have a little more conversation before they go. Socrates, who has risen to go, recognizes the oracular sign which forbids him to depart until he has done penance. His conscience has been awakened, and like Stesichorus over Helen he will sing a palinode for having blasphemed the majesty of love. His palinode takes the form of a myth.

Socrates begins his tale with a glorification of madness, which he divides into four kinds: first, there is the art of divination or prophecy — this, in a vein similar to that of the Cratylus, he connects with madness by an etymological explanation (" 'tis all one reckoning, save the phrase is a little variations "); secondly, there is the art of purification by mysteries; thirdly, poetry or the inspiration of the Muses, without which no man can enter their temple. All this shows that madness is one of heaven's blessings, and may sometimes be a great deal better than sense. There is also a fourth kind of madness which cannot be explained without inquiring into the nature of the soul.

The soul is immortal, for she is the source of all motion both in herself and in others. Of her true and divine form it would be long to tell, but she may be described in a figure as a composite being made up of a charioteer and a pair of winged steeds. The steeds of the gods are immortal, but ours are one mortal and the other immortal. The immortal soul soars upwards into the heavens, but the mortal drops her plumes and is draggled upon the earth.

Now the nature of the wings is to rise and carry the downward element into the upper world — there to behold beauty, wisdom, goodness, and the other things of God by which the soul is nourished. On a certain day Zeus the lord of heaven goes forth in a winged chariot; and an array of gods and demi-gods and of human souls in their train, follows him. There are glorious and blessed sights in the interior of heaven, and he who will may freely behold them. The great vision of all is seen at the feast of the gods, when they ascend the heights of heaven — all but Hestia, who is left at home to keep house. The horses of the gods glide readily upwards and stand upon the outside, and are carried round in the revolutions of the spheres, and gaze upon the world beyond. But of this world beyond the heavens, who can tell? There is an essence formless, colorless, intangible, perceived by the mind only, circling above in the place of true knowledge. The divine mind in her revolution enjoys this fair prospect, and beholds justice, temperance, and knowledge in their everlasting essence. When fulfilled with the sight of them she returns home, and the charioteer puts up the horses in their stable, and gives them ambrosia to eat and nectar to drink. This is the life of the gods; and the human soul tries to reach the same heights, but hardly succeeds; and sometimes the head of the charioteer rises above, and sometimes sinks below the fair vision, and is at last obliged, after much contention, to turn away and leave the plain of truth. Yet if she has followed in the train of any god and once beheld truth she is preserved harmless, and is carried round in the next revolution of the spheres; and if always following, and always seeing the truth, then forever harmless. But if she drops her wings and falls to the earth, then she takes the form of man, and the soul which has seen most of the truth passes into a philosopher or lover; that which has seen truth in the second degree, into a king or warrior; the third, into a householder or money-maker; the fourth, into a gymnast; the fifth, into a prophet, or mystic; the sixth, into a poet, or imitator; the seventh, into a husbandman or craftsman; the eighth, into a sophist, or demagogue; the ninth, into a tyrant. In all these conditions he who lives righteously improves, and he who lives unrighteously deteriorates his lot. Ten thousand years elapse before the souls of men in general can regain their first estate, and have their wings restored to them. And the soul of a man may descend into a beast, and return again into the form of man. But the form of man can only be acquired at all by those who have once beheld truth, for the soul of man alone apprehends the universal; and this is the recollection of that knowledge which she attained when in the company of the gods. At the end of every thousand years the soul has another choice, and may go upwards or downwards. Only the soul of a philosopher or lover who has three times in succession chosen the better life may receive wings and go her way in three thousand years.

For the soul in her own nature having the vision of true being remembers in her condition here those glorious sights of justice and temperance and wisdom and truth which she once gazed upon when in company with the heavenly choir. Then she celebrated holy mysteries and beheld blessed apparitions shining in pure light, herself pure and not as yet entombed in the oyster-shell of the body. And still she is eager to depart, and like a bird is fluttering and looking upwards, and is therefore esteemed mad. Such a light of other days is spread over her when she remembers that beauty which alone of the ideas has any visible representation on earth. For wisdom has no outward form, and is "too dazzling bright for mortal eye." Now the corrupted nature, when blindly excited by the vision of beauty, only rushes on to enjoy, and wallows like a quadruped in sensual pleasures. But the true mystic, who has seen the many sights of bliss, when he beholds a godlike form or face is ravished with delight, and if he were not afraid of being thought mad he would fall down and worship. Then the stiffened wing begins to relax and grow again. At the sight of earthly beauty the memory of the heavenly is recalled; desire which has been imprisoned, pours over the soul of the lover; the germ of the wing unfolds, and stings and pangs at birth, like the cutting of teeth, are everywhere felt. Father and mother, and goods and laws, and proprieties are nothing to him; his beloved is his physician, who can alone cure his pain. An apocryphal sacred writer says that mortals call him love, but the immortals call him dove, or the winged one, in order to represent the force of his wings — at any rate this is his nature. Now the characters of lovers depend upon the god whom they followed in the other world, and they choose their loves in this world accordingly. The followers of Ares are fierce and violent; those of Zeus seek out some philosophical and imperial nature; the attendants of Here find a royal love; and in like manner the followers of every god seek a love who is in his likeness, and they communicate to him the nature which they have received from their god. The manner in which they take their love is as follows: —

I told you about the charioteer and two steeds, the one a noble animal who is guided by word and admonition only, the other an ill-looking villain who will hardly yield to blow or spur. Together all three, who are a figure of the soul, approach the vision of love. And now a conflict begins. The ill-conditioned steed rushes on to enjoy, but the charioteer, who beholds the beloved with awe, falls back in adoration, and forces both the steeds on their haunches; again the evil steed rushes forwards and pulls shamelessly. Then a still more fearful conflict ensues; the charioteer dropping at the very start jerks violently the bit from the clenched teeth of the brute, and pulling harder than ever at the reins, covers his tongue and jaws with blood, and forces him to rest his hocks and haunches with pain upon the ground. When this has happened several times, the villain is tamed and humbled, and from that time forward the soul of the lover follows the beloved in modesty and holy fear. And now their bliss is consummated; the same image of love dwells in the breast of either; and if they have self-control, they pass their lives in the greatest happiness which is attainable by man — they live masters of themselves and conquer in one of the three heavenly victories. But if they choose the lower life of ambition they may still have a happy destiny, though inferior, because they have not the approval of the whole soul. At last they leave the body and proceed on their pilgrim's progress, and those who have once begun can never go back. When the time comes they receive their wings and fly away, and the lovers have the same wings.

Socrates concludes: —

These are the blessings of love, and thus I have made my recantation in finer language than before, but this was only in order to please Phaedrus. If I said what was wrong at first, please to attribute my error to Lysias, who ought to study philosophy instead of rhetoric, and then he will not mislead his disciple Phaedrus.

Phaedrus is afraid that he will lose conceit of Lysias, and that Lysias will be out of conceit with himself, and leave off making speeches, as the politicians have been deriding him. Socrates is of opinion that there is small danger of this, and that the politicians are themselves the great rhetoricians of the age, who desire to obtain immortality by the authorship of laws, and therefore there can be no disgrace, nothing with which anybody could reproach Lysias in being a writer, but there may be disgrace in being a bad one.

And what is good or bad writing or speaking? There is time to consider that question. For by the discussion of such questions man lives, and not by the indulgence of bodily pleasures. And the grasshoppers who are chirruping around may carry our words to the Muses, who are their patronesses; for the grasshoppers were human beings themselves in a world before the Muses, and when the Muses came they died of hunger for the love of song. And they carry to them in heaven the report of those who honor them on earth.

The first rule of good speaking is to know and speak truth; true art is truth, says a Spartan proverb, whereas rhetoric is a mode of enchanting the soul, which makes things appear good and evil, like and unlike, according to the fancy of the speaker.

Still, mankind are deceived, not all at once, but by degrees, and therefore he who would either impose on others or escape imposition must know the truth.

Socrates then proposes that they shall use the two speeches as illustrations of the art of rhetoric; first distinguishing between the debatable and undisputed class of subjects. In the debatable class there ought to be a definition of all disputed matters. But there was no such definition in the speech of Lysias; nor is there any order or connection in his words any more than in a nursery rhyme. With this he compares the regular divisions of the other speech, which was his own (and yet not his own, for the local deities must have inspired him). This "fancy" of his will be found to embody two principles; first, that of synthesis or the comprehension of parts in a whole; secondly, analysis, or the resolution of the whole into parts. These are the processes of division and generalization which are so dear to the dialectician, that king of men. But this is dialectic and not rhetoric; of which the remains are but scanty after order and arrangement have been subtracted. There is nothing left but a heap of "ologies" and other technical terms invented by Theodorus, Evenus, Tisias, Gorgias, and others who have rules for everything, and who teach how to be short or long at pleasure. Prodicus showed his good sense in saying that there was a better thing than either being short or long, which was to be of a convenient length.

Still, notwithstanding the absurdities of Polus and others, rhetoric has great power in public assemblies. This, however, is not given by these technical rules, but is the gift of genius. The real art is always being confused by rhetoricians with the preliminaries of the art. The perfection of oratory is the perfection of all things; but for this the art of rhetoric can do little, and the art which does this little is of another kind from that which is taught by the rhetoricians.

Pericles, the most accomplished of all speakers, derived his art not from rhetoric but from the philosophy of nature which he learned from Anaxagoras. The true rhetoric is like medicine, and the rhetorician has to consider the natures of men's souls as the physician considers the natures of their bodies. Such and such persons are to be affected in this way, such and such others in that; he must know the times and the seasons for saying this or that. This is not an easy task, and this, if there be such an art, is the art of rhetoric.

I know that there are some professors of the art who maintain that probability is stronger than truth. But we maintain that probability is engendered by likeness of the truth which is best attained by the knowledge of the truth, and that the aim of the good man should not be to please or persuade his fellow-servants, but to please his good masters who are the gods. Rhetoric has a fair beginning in this.

Enough of the art of speaking; let us now proceed to consider the true use of writing. There is an old Egyptian tale of Theuth, the inventor of writing, showing his invention to the god Thamuz, who told him that he would only spoil men's memories and take away their understandings. From this tale, which young Athens will probably scorn, may be gathered the lesson that writing is inferior to speech. For writing is like a picture which can give no answer to a question, and has only a deceitful likeness of a living creature. It has no power of adaptation, but uses the same words for all. It is a sort of bastard and not a legitimate son of knowledge, and when an attack is made upon this illegitimate progeny neither the parent nor any one else is there to defend it. The husbandman will not seriously incline to sow his seed in such a hot-bed or garden of Adonis; he will rather sow in the natural soil of the human soul which has depth of earth; and he will anticipate this natural process by writing, if at all, only as a remedy against old age. The natural growth will be far nobler, and bring forth fruit not only in his own but in other minds.

The conclusion of the whole matter is just this, — that until a man knows the truth, and the manner of adapting the truth to the natures of other men, he can not be a good orator; also, that the living is better than the written word, and that the principles of justice and truth when delivered by word of mouth are the legitimate offspring of a man's own bosom, and their lawful descendants take up their abode in others. Such an orator as he is who has them, you and I would fain become. And to all composers in the world who are poets, orators, legislators, we hereby announce that if their compositions are based upon these principles then they are not only poets, orators, statesmen, but philosophers. All the rest are mere flatterers and putters together of words. This is the message which Phaedrus undertakes to carry to Lysias from the local deities, and Socrates will himself carry a similar message to his favorite Isocrates, whose future distinction as a great rhetorician he prophesies. The heat of the day has passed and, after offering up a prayer to Pan and the nymphs, Socrates and Phaedrus depart.

There are two principal controversies which have been raised about the Phaedrus; the first relates to the subject, the second to the date of the Dialogue.

There seems to be a notion that the work of a great artist like Plato could not fail in unity, and that the unity of a dialogue requires a single subject. But the conception of unity really applies in very different degrees and ways to different kinds of art; to a statue, for example, far more than to any kind of literary composition, and to some species of literature far more than to others. Nor does the dialogue appear to be a style of composition in which the requirement of unity is most stringent; nor should the idea of unity derived from one sort of art be hastily transferred to another. The double titles of several of the Platonic Dialogues seem to indicate that this severer unity was not attempted by Plato. The Republic is divided between the search after justice and the construction of the ideal state; the Parmenides between the criticism of the Platonic ideas and of the Eleatic one or being; the Gorgias between the art of speaking and the nature of the good; the Sophist between the detection of the Sophist and the correlation of ideas. The Theaetetus, the Politicus, and the Philebus, have also digressions which are but remotely connected with the main subject.

Thus the comparison of Plato's other writings, as well as the reason of the thing, lead us to the conclusion that we are not to expect to find one idea pervading a whole work, but one, two, or more, as the invention of the writer may suggest or his fancy wander. If each dialogue were confined to the development of a single idea, this would appear on the face of the dialogue, nor could any controversy be raised as to whether the Phaedrus treated of love or rhetoric. But the truth is that Plato subjects himself to no rule of this sort. Like every great artist he gives unity of form to the different and apparently distracting topics which he brings together. He works freely and is not to be supposed to have arranged every part of the dialogue before he begins to write. He fastens or weaves together the frame of his discourse loosely and imperfectly, and which is the warp and which is the woof is not always easy to determine.

The subjects of the Phaedrus (exclusive of the short introductory passage about mythology which is suggested by the local tradition) are first the false or conventional art of rhetoric; secondly, love or the inspiration of beauty and knowledge which is described as madness; thirdly, dialectic or the art of composition and division; fourthly, the true rhetoric, which is based upon dialectic; fifthly, the superiority of the spoken over the written word. The continuous thread which appears and reappears throughout is rhetoric; this is the ground into which the rest of the Dialogue is inlaid, in parts embroidered with fine words " in order to please Phaedrus." The speech of Lysias, and the first speech of Socrates are examples of the false rhetoric, as the second speech of Socrates is adduced as an instance of the true. But the true rhetoric is based upon dialectic, and dialectic is a sort of inspiration akin to love; they are two aspects of philosophy in which the technicalities of rhetoric are absorbed. Thus the example becomes also the deeper theme of discourse. The true knowledge of things in heaven and earth is based upon enthusiasm or love of the ideas; and the true order of speech or writing proceeds according to them. Love, again, has three degrees: first, of interested love corresponding to the conventionalities of rhetoric; secondly, of disinterested or mad love, fixed on objects of sense and answering, perhaps, to poetry; thirdly, of disinterested love directed towards the unseen, answering to dialectic or the science of the ideas. Lastly, the art of rhetoric in the lower sense is found to rest on a knowledge of the natures and characters of men, which Socrates at the commencement of the Dialogue has described as his own peculiar study.

Thus amid the appearance of discord a very tolerable degree of uniformity begins to arise; there are many threads of connection which are not visible at first sight. At the same time the Phaedrus, although one of the most beautiful of the Platonic dialogues, may be admitted to have more of the character of a " tour de force," and has certainly more of the " quidlibet audendi potestas " than any other.

The first speech is composed " in that balanced style in which the wise love to talk." The characteristics of rhetoric are insipidity, mannerism, and monotonous parallelism of clauses. There is more rhythm than reason; the creative power of imagination is wanting.

" 'Tis Greece, but living Greece no more."

Plato has seized by anticipation the spirit which hung over Greek literature for a thousand years afterwards. Yet doubtless there were some who, like Phaedrus, felt a delight in the harmonious cadence and the pedantic reasoning of the rhetoricians newly imported from Sicily, which had ceased to be awakened in them by really great works, such as the poems of Anacreon or Sappho or the orations of Pericles. That the first speech was really written by Lysias is improbable. Like the poem of Solon, or the story of Thamuz and Theuth, or the funeral oration of Aspasia (if genuine), or the pretence of Socrates in the Cratylus that his knowledge of philology is derived from Euthyphro, the invention is really due to the imagination of Plato, and may be compared to the parodies of the Sophists in the Protagoras. Numerous fictions of this sort occur in the dialogues, and the gravity of Plato has sometimes imposed upon his commentators. The introduction of a considerable writing of another would seem not to be in keeping with a great work of art, and has no parallel elsewhere.

In the second speech Socrates is exhibited as beating the rhetoricians at their own weapons; he " an unpractised man and they masters of the art." True to his character he must, however, profess that the speech which he makes is not his own, for he knows nothing of himself. The superiority of this speech over the first seems to consist chiefly in a better arrangement of the topics; a lesser merit is the greater liveliness of Socrates, which hurries him into verse and relieves the monotony of the style; and he gives an apparent weight to his words by going back to general maxims.

Both speeches are strongly condemned by Socrates as sinful and blasphemous towards the god Love, and as worthy only of some haunt of sailors to which good manners were unknown. The meaning of this and other wild language to the same effect, which is introduced by way of contrast to the formality of the two speeches (Socrates has a sense of relief when he has escaped from the trammels of rhetoric) seems to be that the two speeches proceed upon the supposition that love is and ought to be interested, and that no such thing as a real or disinterested passion, which would be at the same time lasting, could be conceived.

This is what Socrates proposes to recant in the famous myth, which is a sort of parable, and like other parables ought not to receive too minute an interpretation. In all such allegories there is a great deal which is merely ornamental, and the interpreter has to separate the important from the unimportant. Socrates himself has given the right clue when, in using his own discourse afterwards as the text for his examination of rhetoric, he characterizes it as a " partly true and tolerably credible mythus," in which amid poetical figures, order and arrangement were not forgotten.

The soul is described in magnificent language as the self-moved and the source of motion in all other things. This is the philosophical theme or proem of the whole. But ideas must be given through something, and under the pretext that to realize the true nature of the soul would be not only tedious but impossible, we at once pass on to describe the souls of gods as well as men under the figure of two winged steeds and a charioteer. No connection is traced between the soul as the great motive power and the triple soul which is thus imaged. There is no difficulty in seeing that the charioteer represents the reason, or that the black horse is the symbol of the sensual or concupiscent element of human nature. The white horse also represents rational impulse, but the description, " a lover of honor and modesty and temperance, and a follower of true glory," though kindred, does not at once recall the " spirit " of the Republic. The two steeds really correspond in a figure more nearly to the appetitive and moral or semi-rational soul of Aristotle. And thus for the first time, perhaps, in the history of philosophy, we have represented to us the threefold division of psychology. The image of the charioteer and the steeds has been compared with a similar image which occurs in the verses of Parmenides; but it is important to remark that the horses of Parmenides have no allegorical meaning, and that the poet is only describing his own approach in a chariot to the regions of light and the house of the goddess of truth.

The triple soul has had a previous existence, in which following in the train of some god, from whom she derived her character, she beheld partially and imperfectly the vision of absolute truth. All her after existence, passed in many forms of men and animals, is spent in regaining this. In the various stages of this long struggle she is sorely let and hindered by the animal desires of the inferior or concupiscent steed. Again and again she beholds the flashing beauty of the beloved. But before that vision can be finally enjoyed the animal desires must be subjected.

The moral or spiritual element in man is represented by the immortal steed which, like $\theta\nu\mu\grave{o}s$ in the Republic, always sides with the reason. Both are dragged out of their course by the furious impulses of desire. In the end something is conceded to the desires, after they have been finally humbled and overpowered. And yet the way of philosophy, or perfect love of the unseen is total abstinence from bodily delights. " But all men can not receive this saying: " in the lower life of ambition they may be taken off their guard and stoop to folly unawares, and then, although they do not attain to the highest bliss, yet if they have once conquered they may be happy enough.

The language of the Meno and the Phaedo as well as of the Phaedrus, seems to show that at one time of his life Plato was quite serious in maintaining a former state of existence. His mission was to realize the abstract; in that all good and truth, all the hopes of this and another life seemed to centre. It was another kind of knowledge to him — a second world distinct from that of sense, which seemed to exist within him far more truly than the fleeting objects of sense which are without him. When we are once able to imagine the intense power which abstract ideas exercised over the mind of Plato, we see that there was no more difficulty to him in realizing the eternal existence of them and of the human minds which were associated with them — in the past and future than in the present. The difficulty was not how they could exist, but how they could fail to exist. In the attempt to regain this " saving " knowledge of the ideas, the sense was found to be as great an enemy as the desires; and hence two things which to us seem quite distinct are inextricably blended in the representation of Plato.

Thus far we may believe that Plato was serious in his conception of the soul as a motive power, in his reminiscence of a former state of being, in his elevation of the reason over sense and passion, and perhaps in his doctrine of transmigration. Was he equally serious in the rest? For example, are we to attribute his tripartite division of the soul to the gods? Or is this merely assigned to them by way of parallelism with men? The latter is the more probable; for the horses of the gods are both white, i. e. their every impulse is in harmony with reason; their dualism, on the other hand, only carries out the figure of the chariot. Is he serious, again, in regarding love as " a madness? " That seems to arise out of the antithesis to the former conception of love. At the same time he appears to intimate here, as in the Ion, Apology, Meno, and elsewhere, that there is a faculty in man, whether to be termed in modern language genius, or inspiration, or idealism, which can not be reduced to rule and measure. Perhaps, too, he is ironically repeating the common language of mankind about philosophy, and is turning their jest into a sort of earnest. Or is he serious in holding that each soul bears the character of a god? Perhaps he had no other account to give of the differences of human characters to which he afterwards refers. It seems to be characteristic of the irony of Socrates to mix up sense and nonsense in such a way that no exact line can be drawn between them. And allegory helps to increase this sort of confusion.

As is often the case in the parables and prophecies of Scripture, the meaning is allowed to break through the figure, and the details are not always consistent. When the charioteers and their steeds stand upon the dome of heaven they behold the intangible, invisible essences which are not objects of sight. This is because the force of language can no further go. Nor can we dwell much on the circumstance, that at the completion of ten thousand years all are to return to the place from whence they came; because he also represents this as dependent on their own good conduct in the successive stages of existence. Nor again can we attribute anything to the accidental inference which would also follow, that even a tyrant may live righteously in the condition of life to which fate has called him (" he aiblins might, I dinna ken "). But this would be much at variance with Plato himself and with Greek notions generally. He is much more serious in distinguishing men from animals by their recognition of the universal which they have known in a former state, and in denying that this gift of reason can ever be obliterated or lost. In the language of some modern theologians he might be said to maintain the " final perseverance " of those who have entered on their pilgrim's progress. Other intimations of a " metaphysic " or " theology " of the future may also be discerned in him: (1) The moderate predestinarianism which here, as in the Republic, acknowledges the element of chance in human life, and yet asserts the freedom and responsibility of man; (2) The recognition of a moral as well as an intellectual principle in man under the image of an immortal steed; (3) The notion that the divine nature exists by the contemplation of ideas of virtue and justice — or, in other words, the assertion of the essentially moral nature of God; (4) Again, there is the hint that human life is a life of aspiration only, and that the true ideal is not to be found in art; (5) There occurs the first trace of the distinction between certain and contingent matter; (6) The conception of the soul itself as the motive power and reason of the universe.

The conception of the philosopher, or the philosopher and lover in one, as a sort of madman, may be compared with the Republic and Theaetetus, in both of which the philosopher is regarded as a stranger and monster upon the earth. The whole myth, like the other myths of Plato, describes in a figure things which are beyond the range of human faculties, or inaccessible to the knowledge of the age. That philosophy should be represented as the inspiration of love is a conception that has already become familiar to us in the Symposium, and is the expression partly of Plato's enthusiasm for the idea, and is also an indication of the real power exercised by the passion of friendship over the mind of the Greek. The master in the art of love knew that there was a mystery in these feelings and their associations, and especially in the contrast of the sensible and permanent which is afforded by them; and he sought to explain this, as he explained universal ideas, by a reference to a former state of existence. The capriciousness of love is also derived by him from an attachment to some god in a former world. The singular remark that the beloved is more affected than the lover at the final consummation of their love, seems likewise to have a psychological truth.

We may now pass on to the second part of the Dialogue, which is a criticism on the first. Rhetoric is assailed on various grounds: first, as expecting to deceive, without a knowledge of the truth; and secondly, as ignoring the distinction between certain and probable matter. The three speeches are then passed in review: the first of them has no definition of the nature of love, and no order in the topics (being in these respects far inferior to the second); while the third of them is found (though a fancy of the hour) to be framed upon real dialectical principles. But dialectic is not rhetoric; nothing on that subject is to be found in the endless treatises of rhetoric, however prolific in hard names. When Plato has sufficiently put them to the test of ridicule he touches, as with the point of a needle, the real error of this as well as of much modern literature and writing upon the arts, which is the confusion of preliminary knowledge with creative power. No attainments will provide the speaker with genius; and the sort of attainments which can alone be of any value are the higher philosophy and the power of psychological analysis, which is given by dialectic, not by the rules of the rhetoricians.

Dialectic may be variously defined, either as the power of dividing a whole into parts, and of uniting the parts in a whole, or as the process of the mind talking with herself. The latter view seems to have led Plato to the par. dox that speech is superior to writing, in which he may seem also to be doing an injustice to himself. For the truth is, that speech and writing can not be fairly compared in the manner which Plato suggests. The contrast of the living and dead word, as well as the exam ple of Socrates, which he has represented in the form of the dialogue, seem to have misled him. For speech and writing have really different functions; the one is more transitory, more diffuse, more elastic and capable of adaptation to moods and times; the other is more permanent, more concentrated, and is uttered not to this or that person or audience, but to all the world. In the Politicus the paradox is carried further; the mind or will of the king is preferred to the written law.

The chief criteria for determining the date of the Dialogue are (1) the ages of Lysias and Isocrates; (2) the character of the work.

Lysias was born in the year 458; Isocrates in the year 436, about seven years before the birth of Plato. The first of the two great rhetoricians is described as in the zenith of his fame; the second as still young and full of promise. Now it is argued that this must have been written in the youth of Isocrates, when the promise was still unfulfilled. And thus we should have to assign the Dialogue to a year not later than 406, when Isocrates was thirty and Plato twenty-three years of age, and while Socrates himself was still alive.

Those who argue in this way seem not to reflect how easily Plato can " invent Egyptians or anything else," and how careless he is of historical truth or probability. Who would suspect that the wise Critias, the virtuous Charmides, had ended their lives among the thirty tyrants? Who would imagine that Lysias, who is here assailed by Socrates, is the son of his old friend Cephalus? Or that Isocrates himself is the enemy of Plato and his school? No arguments can be drawn from the appropriateness or inappropriateness of the characters of Plato. (Else, perhaps, it might be further argued, that judging from their extant remains, insipid rhetoric is far more characteristic of Isocrates than of Lysias.) But Plato makes use of names which have often hardly any connection with the historical characters to whom they belong. In this instance the comparative favor shown to Isocrates may possibly be accounted for by the circumstance of his belonging to the aristocratical, as Lysias to the democratical party.

Few persons will be inclined to suppose, in the superficial manner of some ancient critics, that a dialogue which treats of love must necessarily have been written in youth. As little weight can be attached to the argument that he had probably visited Egypt before he wrote the story of Theuth and Thamuz. For there is no real proof that he ever was in Egypt; and even if he was, he might have known or invented Egyptian traditions before he went there. The late ,date of the Phaedrus is really to be proved by other arguments than these: the maturity of the thought, the perfection of the style, the insight, the relation to the other Platonic Dialogues, seem to contradict the notion that it could have been the work of a youth of twenty or twenty-three years of age. The cosmological notion of the mind as the *primum mobile,* and the admission of impulse into the immortal nature, afford grounds for assigning a much later date. Add to this that the picture of Socrates, though in some lesser particulars, e. g. his going without sandals, his habit of remaining within the walls, his emphatic declaration that his study is human nature, an exact resemblance, is in the main the Platonic and not the real Socrates. Can we suppose " the young man to have told such lies " about his master while he was still alive? Moreover, when two Dialogues are so closely connected as the Phaedrus and Symposium, there is great improbability in supposing that one of them was written at least twenty years after the other. The conclusion seems to be, that the Dialogue was written at some comparatively late but unknown period of Plato's life, after he had deserted the purely Socratic point of view, but before he had entered on the more abstract speculations of the Sophist or the Philebus. Comparing the divisions of the soul, the doctrine of transmigration, the isolation of the philosophic life, and the general character of the style, we shall not be far wrong in placing the Phaedrus in the neighborhood of the Republic; remarking only that allowance must be made for the poetical element in the Phaedrus, which, while falling short of the Republic in definite philosophic results, seems to have glimpses of a truth beyond.

Two short passages, which are unconnected with the main subject of the Dialogue, may seem to merit a more particular notice: (1) the *locus classicus* about mythology; (2) the tale of the grasshoppers.

The first passage is remarkable as showing that Plato was entirely free from what may be termed the Euhemerism of his age. (For there were Euhemerists in Greece before Euhemerus.) Other philosophers, like Anaxagoras, had found in Homer and mythology hidden meanings. Plato, with a truer instinct, rejects these attractive interpretations; he regards the invention of them as an " unfortunate " way of employing a man's mind and time. They are endless, and they draw a man off from the knowledge of himself. There is a latent criticism, and also a poetical sense in Plato, which at once enable him to discard them, and yet in another way to make the fullest use of poetry and mythology as a vehicle of thought and feeling. The " sophistical " interest of Phaedrus, the little touch about the two versions of the story, the ironical manner in which these explanations are set aside, " the common opinion about them is enough for me," may be noted in passing; also the general agreement between the tone of this speech and the remark of Socrates which follows afterwards, " I am a diviner, but a poor one."

The tale of the grasshoppers is naturally suggested by the surrounding scene. Yet we must not forget also, that they are the representatives of the Athenians as children of the soil. Under the image of the lively chirruping grasshoppers who inform the Muses in heaven who honors them on earth, Plato intends to represent an Athenian audience. The story is introduced, apparently, to mark a change of subject, and also, like several other allusions which occur in the course of the Dialogue, in order to preserve the scene in the recollection of the reader.

PHAEDRUS

PERSONS OF THE DIALOGUE

SOCRATES.   PHAEDRUS.

SCENE :— Under a plane-tree, by the banks of the Ilissus.

Socrates. My dear Phaedrus, whence come you, and whither are you going?

Phaedrus. I am come from Lysias the son of Cephalus, and I am going to take a walk outside the wall, for I have been with him ever since the early dawn, which is a long while, and our common friend Acumenus advises me to walk in the country; he says that this is far more refreshing than walking in the courts.

Soc. There he is right. Lysias then, I suppose, was in the city?

Phaedr. Yes, he was with Epicrates, at the house of Morychus; that house which is near the temple of Olympian Zeus.

Soc. And how did he entertain you? Can I be wrong in supposing that Lysias gave you a feast of discourse?

Phaedr. You shall hear, if you have leisure to stay and listen.

Soc. And would I not regard the conversation of you and Lysias as " a thing of higher import," as I may say in the words of Pindar, " than any business? "

Phaedr. Will you go on?

Soc. And will you go on with the narration?

Phaedr. My tale, Socrates, is one of your sort, for the theme which occupied us was love — after a fashion: Lysias imagined a fair youth who was being tempted, but not by a lover; and this was the point: he ingeniously proved that the non-lover should be accepted rather than the lover.

Soc. O that is noble of him. And I wish that he would say a poor man rather than a rich, and an old man rather than a young one; he should meet the case of me, and all of us, and then his words would indeed be charming, and of public utility; and I am so eager to hear them that if you walk all the way to Megara, and when you have reached the wall come back, as Herodicus recommends, without going in, I will not leave you.

Phaedr. What do you mean, Socrates? How can you imagine that I, who am quite unpractised, can remember or do justice to an elaborate work, which the greatest rhetorician of the day spent a long time in composing. Indeed, I can not; I would give a great deal if I could.

Soc. I believe that I know Phaedrus about as well as I know myself, and I am very sure that he heard the words of Lysias, not once only, but again and again he made him say them, and Lysias was very willing to gratify him; at last, when nothing else would satisfy him, he got hold of the book, and saw what he wanted — this was his morning's occupation — and then when he was tired with sitting, he went out to take a walk, not until, as I believe, he had simply learned by heart the entire discourse, which may not have been very long; and as he was going to take a walk outside the wall in order that he might practise, he saw a certain lover of discourse who had the same complaint as himself; — he saw and rejoiced; now thought he, " I shall have a partner in my revels." And he invited him to come with him. But when the lover of discourse asked to hear the tale, he gave himself airs and said, " No I can't," as if he didn't like; although, if the hearer had refused, the end would have been that he would have made him listen whether he would or no. Therefore, Phaedrus, as he will soon speak in any case, begs him to speak at once.

Phaedr. As you don't seem very likely to let me off until I speak in some way, the best thing that I can do is to speak as I best may.

Soc. That is a very true observation of yours.

Phaedr. I will do my best, for believe me, Socrates, I did not learn the very words; O no, but I have a general notion of what he said, and will repeat concisely, and in order, the several arguments by which the case of the non-lover was proved to be superior to that of the lover; let me begin at the beginning.

Soc. Yes, my friend; but you must first of all show what you have got in your left hand under your cloak, for that roll, as I suspect, is the actual discourse. Now, much as I love you, I would not have you suppose that I am going to have your memory exercised upon me, if you have Lysias himself here.

Phaedr. Enough; I see that I have no hope of practising upon you. But if I am to read, where would you please to sit?

Soc. Turn this way; let us go to the Ilissus, and sit down at some quiet spot.

Phaedr. I am fortunate in not having my sandals, and as you never have any, I think that we may go along the brook and cool our feet in the water; this is the easiest way, and at mid-day and in the summer is far from being unpleasant.

Soc. Lead on, and look out for a place in which we can sit down.

Phaedr. Do you see that tallest plane-tree in the distance?

Soc. Yes.

Phaedr. There are shade and gentle breezes, and grass on which we may either sit or lie down.

Soc. Move on.

Phaedr. I should like to know, Socrates, whether the place is not somewhere here at which Boreas is said to have carried off Orithyia from the banks of the Ilissus.

Soc. That is the tradition.

Phaedr. And is this the exact spot? The little stream is delightfully clear and bright; I can fancy that there might be maidens playing near.

Soc. I believe that the spot is not exactly here, but about a quarter of a mile lower down, where you cross to the temple of Agra, and I think that there is some sort of altar of Boreas at the place.

Phaedr. I don't recollect; but I wish that you would tell me whether you believe this tale.

Soc. The wise are doubtful, and if, like them, I also doubted, there would be nothing very strange in that. I might have a rational explanation that Orithyia was playing with Pharmacia, when a northern gust carried her over the neighboring rocks; and this being the manner of her death, she was said to have been carried away by Boreas. There is a discrepancy, however, about the locality, as according to another version of the story she was taken from the Areopagus, and not from this place. Now I quite acknowledge that these explanations are very nice, but he is not to be envied who has to give them; much labor and ingenuity will be required of him; and when he has once begun, he must go on and rehabilitate centaurs and chimeras dire. Gorgons and winged steeds flow in apace, and numberless other inconceivable and impossible monstrosities and marvels of nature. And if he is sceptical about them, and would fain reduce them all to the rules of probability,

this sort of crude philosophy will take up all his time.
Now I have certainly not time for this; shall I tell
you why? I must first know myself, as the Delphian
inscription says; and I should be absurd indeed, if
while I am still in ignorance of myself I were to be
curious about that which is not my business. And
therefore I say farewell to all this; the common opinion is enough for me. For, as I was saying, I want
to know not about this, but about myself. Am I
indeed a wonder more complicated and swollen with
passion than the serpent Typho, or a creature of a
gentler and simpler sort, to whom Nature has given
a diviner and lowlier destiny? But here let me ask
you, friend: Is not this the plane-tree to which you
were conducting us?

Phaedr. Yes, this is the tree.

Soc. Yes, indeed, and a fair and shady resting-
place, full of summer sounds and scents. There is the
lofty and spreading plane-tree, and the agnus castus
high and clustering, in the fullest blossom and the
greatest fragrance; and the stream which flows beneath the plane-tree is deliciously cold to the feet.
Judging from the ornaments and images, this must
be a spot sacred to Achelous and the Nymphs; moreover, there is a sweet breeze, and the grasshoppers
chirrup; and the greatest charm of all is the grass
like a pillow gently sloping to the head. My dear
Phaedrus, you have been an admirable guide.

Phaedr. I always wonder at you, Socrates; for
when you are in the country, you really are like a
stranger who is being led about by a guide. Do you
ever cross the border? I rather think that you never
venture even outside the gates.

Soc. Very true, my good friend; and I hope that
you will excuse me when you hear the reason, which
is, that I am a lover of knowledge, and the men who

dwell in the city are my teachers, and not the trees, or the country. Though I do, indeed, believe that you have found a spell with which to draw me out of the city into the country, as hungry cows are led by shaking before them a bait of leaves or fruit. For only hold up the bait of discourse, and you may lead me all round Attica, and over the wide world. And now having arrived, I intend to lie down, and do you choose any posture in which you can read best. Begin.

Phaedr. Listen. " You know my views of our common interest, and I do not think that I ought to fail in the object of my suit, because I am not your lover: for the kindnesses of lovers are afterwards regretted by them when their passion ceases, but non-lovers have no time of repentance, because they are free and not subject to necessity, and they confer their benefits as far as they are able, in the way which is most conducive to their own interest. Then again, lovers remember how they have neglected their interests, for the sake of their loves; they consider the benefits which they have conferred on them; and when to these they add the troubles which they have endured, they think that they have long ago paid all that is due to them. But the non-lover has no such tormenting recollections; he has never neglected his affairs or quarrelled with his relations; he has no troubles to reckon up, or excuses to allege; for all has gone smoothly with him. What remains, then, but that he should freely do what will gratify the beloved? But you will say that the lover is more to be esteemed, because his love is thought to be greater; for he is willing to say and do what is hateful to other men, in order to please his beloved: well, that, if true, is only a proof that he will prefer any future love to his present, and will injure his old love at the pleasure of the new. And how can a man reasonably sacrifice himself to one who is possessed with a malady which no experienced person would attempt to cure, for the patient himself admits that he is not in his right mind, and acknowledges that he is wrong in his mind, but is unable, as he says, to control himself. How, if he came to his right mind, could he imagine that the desires were good which he conceived when in his wrong mind? Then again, there are many more non-lovers than lovers; and, therefore, you will have a larger choice, and are far more likely to find among them a compatible friend. And if you fear common opinion, and would avoid publicity and reproach, the lover, who is always thinking that other men are as emulous of him as he is of them, will be sure to boast of his successes, and make a show of them openly in the pride of his heart; — he wants others to know that his labor has not been lost; but the non-lover is more his own master, and is desirous of solid good, and not of the vainglory of men. Again, the lover may be generally seen and known following the beloved (this is his regular occupation), and when they are observed to exchange two words they are supposed to meet about some affair of love, either past or future; but when non-lovers meet, no one asks the reason why, because people know that talking is natural, whether friendship or mere pleasure is the motive. And, again, if you fear the fickleness of friendship, consider that in any other case a quarrel might be a mutual calamity; but now, when you have given up what is most precious to you, you will be the great loser, and therefore, you will have reason in being more afraid of the lover, for his vexations are many, and he is always fancying that everything is against him. And for this reason he debars his beloved from society; he will not have you intimate with the wealthy, lest they should exceed him in wealth, or with men of education, lest they should be his superiors in knowledge; and he is equally afraid of the power of any other good. He would persuade you to have nothing to do with them, in order that he may have you all to himself, and if, out of regard to your own interest, you have more sense than to comply with this desire, a quarrel will ensue. But those who are non-lovers, and whose success in love is the reward of their superiority, will not be jealous of the companions of their beloved, but will rather hate those who refuse to be his companions, thinking that their refusal is a mark of contempt, and that he would be benefited by having companions; more love than hatred may be expected to come of that. Many lovers also have loved the person of a youth before they knew his character, or were acquainted with his domestic relations; so that when their passion has passed away, there is no knowing whether they will continue to be his friends; whereas, in the case of non-lovers who were always friends, the friendship is not lessened by sensual delights; but the recollection of these remains with them, and is an earnest of good things to come. Further, I say that you are likely to be improved by me, whereas the lover will spoil you. For they praise your words and actions in a bad way; partly, they are afraid of offending you, and partly, their judgment is weakened by their passion: for lovers are singular beings when disappointed in love — they deem that painful which is not painful to others, and when successful they can not help praising that which ought not to give them pleasure; so that the beloved is a far more appropriate object of pity than of envy. But if you listen to me, in the first place, I, in my intercourse with you, shall not regard present enjoyment, but future advantage, being not conquered by love, but conquering myself; nor for small causes taking violent offences, but even

when the cause is great, slowly laying up little wrath
—unintentional offences I shall forgive, and intentional ones I shall try to prevent; and these are the
marks of a friendship which will last. But if you
think that only a lover can be a firm friend, you ought
to consider that, if this were true, we should set small
value on sons, or fathers, or mothers; nor should we
ever have loyal friends, for our love of them arises not
from passion, but from other associations. Further, if
we ought to confer favors on those who are the most
eager suitors, we ought to confer them not on the most
virtuous, but on the most needy; for they are the persons who will be most relieved, and will therefore be
the most grateful; and, in general, when you make a
feast, invite not your friend, but the beggar and the
empty soul, for they will love you, and attend you,
and come about your doors, and will be the
best pleased, and the most grateful, and will invoke
blessings on your head. But, perhaps, you will say
that you ought not to give to the most importunate,
but to those who are best able to reward you; nor to the
lover only, but to those who are worthy of love; nor to
those who will enjoy the charm of your youth, but to
those who will share their goods with you in age; nor
to those who, having succeeded, will glory in their
success to others, but to those who will be modest and
hold their peace; nor to those who care about you for
a moment only, but to those who will continue your
friends for life; nor to those who, when their passion
is over, will pick a quarrel with you, but rather to those
who, when the bloom of youth is over, will show their
own virtue. Remember what I have said; and consider this also, that friends admonish the lover under
the idea that his way of life is bad, but no one of his
kindred ever yet censured the non-lover, or thought
that he was ill-advised about his own interests.

" Perhaps you will ask me whether I propose that you should indulge every non-lover. To which I reply that not even the lover would advise you to indulge all lovers, for the favor is less in the just estimation of the receiver and more difficult to hide from the world. Now love ought to be for the advantage of both parties and for the injury of neither.

" I believe that I have said enough; but if there is anything more which you desire or which needs to be supplied, ask and I will answer."

Now, Socrates, what do you think? Is not the discourse excellent, especially the language?

Soc. Yes indeed, admirable; the effect on me was ravishing. And this I owe to you, Phaedrus, for I observed you while reading to be in an ecstasy, and thinking that you are more experienced in these matters than I am, I followed your example, and, like you, became inspired with a divine frenzy.

Phaedr. Indeed, you are pleased to be merry.

Soc. Do you mean that I am not in earnest?

Phaedr. Now, don't talk in that way, Socrates, but let me have your real opinion; I adjure you, by the god of friendship, to tell me whether you think that any Hellene could have said more or spoken better on the same subject.

Soc. Well, but are you and I expected to praise the sentiments of the author, or only the clearness, and roundness, and accuracy, and tournure of the language? As to the first I willingly submit to your better judgment, for I am unworthy to form an opinion, having only attended to the rhetorical manner; and I was doubting whether Lysias himself would be able to defend that; for I thought, though I speak under correction, that he repeated himself two or three times, either from want of words or from want of pains; and also, he appeared to me wantonly ambitious of showing how well he could say the same thing in two or three ways.

Phaedr. Nonsense, Socrates; that was his exhaustive treatment of the subject; for he omitted nothing; — this is the special merit of the speech, and I do not think that any one could have made a fuller or better.

Soc. I can not go so far as that with you. Ancient sages, men and women, who have spoken and written of these things, would rise up in judgment against me, if I lightly assented to you.

Phaedr. Who are they, and where did you hear anything better than this?

Soc. I am sure that I must have heard; I don't remember at this moment from whom; perhaps from Sappho the fair, Anacreon the wise; or, possibly, from a prose writer. What makes me say this? Why, because I perceive that my bosom is full, and that I could make another speech as good as that of Lysias, and different. Now I am certain that this is not an invention of my own, for I am conscious that I know nothing, and therefore I can only infer that I have been filled through the ears, like a pitcher from the waters of another, though I have actually forgotten in my stupidity who was my informant.

Phaedr. That is grand. But never mind where you heard the discourse or of whom; let that, if you will, be a mystery not to be divulged even at my earnest desire. But do as you say; promise to make another and better oration of equal length on the same subject, with other arguments; and I, like the nine Archons, will promise to set up a golden image at Delphi, not only of myself, but of you, and as large as life.

Soc. You are a dear golden simpleton if you suppose me to mean that Lysias has altogether missed the mark, and that I can make a speech from which all his arguments are to be excluded. The worst of authors will say something that is to the point. Who, for example, could speak on this thesis of yours without praising the discretion of the non-lover and blaming the folly of the lover? These are the common-places which must come in (for what else is there to be said?) and must be allowed and excused; the only merit is in the arrangement of them, for there can be none in the invention; but when you leave the common-places, then there may be some originality.

Phaedr. I admit that there is reason in that, and I will be reasonable too, and will allow you to start with the premiss that the lover is more disordered in his wits than the non-lover; and if you go on after that and make a longer and better speech than Lysias, and use other arguments, then I say again that a statue you shall have of beaten gold, and take your place by the colossal offering of the Cypselids at Olympia.

Soc. Is not the lover serious, because only in fun I lay a finger upon his love? And so, Phaedrus, you really imagine that I am going to improve upon his ingenuity?

Phaedr. There I have you as you had me, and you must speak " as you best can," and no mistake. And don't let us have the vulgar exchange of " tu quoque " as in a comedy, or compel me to say to you as you said to me, " I know Socrates as well as I know myself, and he was wanting to speak, but he gave himself airs." Rather I would have you consider that from this place we stir not until you have unbosomed yourself of the speech; for here are we all alone, and I am stronger, remember, and younger than you; therefore perpend, and do not compel me to use violence.

Soc. But, my sweet Phaedrus, how can I ever compete with Lysias in an extempore speech? He is a master in his art and I am an untaught man.

Phaedr. You see how matters stand; and therefore let there be no more pretences; for, indeed, I know the word that is irresistible.

Soc. Then don't say it.

Phaedr. Yes, but I will; and my word shall be an oath. "I say, or rather swear" — but what god will be the witness of my oath? — "I swear by this plane-tree, that unless you repeat the discourse here, in the face of the plane-tree, I will never tell you another; never let you have word of another!"

Soc. Villain! I am conquered; the poor lover of discourse has no more to say.

Phaedr. Then why are you still at your tricks?

Soc. I am not going to play tricks now that you have taken the oath, for I can not allow myself to be starved.

Phaedr. Proceed.

Soc. Shall I tell you what I will do?

Phaedr. What?

Soc. I will veil my face and gallop through the discourse as fast as I can, for if I see you, I shall feel ashamed and not know what to say.

Phaedr. Only go on and you may do as you please.

Soc. Come, O ye Muses, melodious (λιγεῖαι), as ye are called, whether you have received this name from the character of your strains, or because the Melians are a musical race, help, O help me in the tale which my good friend desires me to rehearse, for the good of his friend whom he always deemed wise and will now deem wiser than ever.

Once upon a time there was a fair boy, or, more properly speaking, a youth; he was very fair and had a great many lovers; and there was one special cunning one, who had persuaded the youth that he did not love him, but he really loved him all the same; and one day as he was paying his addresses to him, he used this very argument — that he ought to accept the non-lover rather than the lover; and his words were as follow: —

" All good counsel begins in the same way; a man should know what he is advising about, or his counsel will come to nought. But people imagine that they know about the nature of things, when they don't know about them, and, not agreeing at the beginning, they end, as might be expected, in contradicting one another and themselves. Now you and I must not be guilty of the error which we condemn in others; but as our question is whether the lover or non-lover is to be preferred, let us first of all agree in defining the nature and power of love, and then, keeping our eyes upon this and to this appealing let us further inquire whether love brings advantage or disadvantage.

" Every one sees that love is a desire, and we know also that non-lovers desire the beautiful and good. Now in what way is the lover to be distinguished from the non-lover? Let us note that in every one of us there are two guiding and ruling principles which lead us whither they will; one is the natural desire of pleasure, the other is an acquired opinion which is in search of the best; and these two are sometimes in harmony and then again at war, and sometimes the one, sometimes the other conquers. When opinion conquers, and by the help of reason leads us to the best, the conquering principle is called temperance; but when desire, which is devoid of reason, rules in us and drags us to pleasure, that power of misrule is called excess. Now excess has many names, and many members, and many forms, and any of these forms when marked gives a name to the bearer of the name, neither honorable nor desirable. The desire of eating, which gets the better of the higher reason and the other desires, is called gluttony, and he who is possessed by this is called a glutton; the tyrannical desire of drink, which inclines the possessor of the desire to drink, has a name which is only too obvious; and the same may be said of the whole family of desires and their names, whichever of them happens to be dominant. And now I think that you will perceive the drift of my discourse; but as every spoken word is in a manner plainer than the unspoken, I had better say further that the irrational desire which overcomes the tendency of opinion towards right, and is led away to the enjoyment of beauty, and especially of personal beauty, by the desires which are her kindred — that desire, I say, the conqueror and leader of the rest, and waxing strong from having this very power, is called the power of love."

And now, dear Phaedrus, I shall pause for an instant to ask whether you do not think me, as I appear to myself, inspired?

Phaedr. Yes, Socrates, you seem to have a very unusual flow of words.

Soc. Listen to me, then, in silence; for surely the place is holy; so that you must not wonder, if, as I proceed, I appear to be in a divine fury, for already I am getting into dithyrambics.

Phaedr. That is quite true.

Soc. And that I attribute to you. But hear what follows, and perhaps the fit may be averted; all is in their hands above. And now I will go on talking to my youth. Listen: —

Thus, my friend, we have declared and determined the nature of love. Keeping this in view, let us now inquire what advantage or disadvantage is likely to ensue from the lover or the non-lover to him who accepts their advances.

He who is the victim of his passions and the slave of pleasure will of course desire to make his beloved as agreeable to himself as possible. Now to him who is not in his right senses that is agreeable which is not opposed to him, but that which is equal or superior is hateful to him, and therefore the lover will not brook any superiority or equality on the part of his beloved; he is always employed in reducing him to inferiority. And the ignorant is the inferior of the wise, the coward of the brave, the slow of speech of the speaker, the dull of the clever. These are the sort of natural and inherent defects in the mind of the beloved which enhance the delight of the lover, and there are acquired defects which he must produce in him, or he will be deprived of his fleeting joy. And therefore he can not help being jealous, and will debar him from the advantages of society which would make a man of him, and especially from that society which would have given him wisdom. That is to say, he will be compelled to banish from him divine philosophy, in his excessive fear lest he should come to be despised in his eyes; and there is no greater injury which he can inflict on him than this. Moreover, he will contrive that he shall be wholly ignorant, and in everything dependent on himself; he is to be the delight of his lover's heart, and a curse to himself. Verily, a lover is a profitable guardian and associate for him in all that relates to his mind.

Let us next see how his master, whose law of life is pleasure and not good, will keep and train the body of his servant. Will he not choose a beloved who is delicate rather than sturdy and strong? One brought up in shady bowers and not in the bright sun, not practised in manly exercises or dried by perspiration, but knowing only a soft and luxurious diet, instead of the hues of health having only the colors of paint and ornament, and the rest of a piece? — such a life as any one can imagine and which I need not detail at length. But I may sum up all that I have to say in a word, and pass on. Such a person in war, or in any of the great exigencies in life, will be the anxiety of his friends and also of his lover, and certainly not the terror of his enemies; which nobody can deny.

And now let us tell what advantage or disadvantage the beloved will receive from the guardianship and society of his lover in the matter of his possessions; that is the next point to consider. All men will see, and the lover above all men, that his own first wish is to deprive his beloved of his dearest and best and most sacred possessions, father, mother, kindred, friends, all whom he thinks may be hinderers or reprovers of their sweet converse; he will even cast a jealous eye upon his gold and silver or other property, because these make him a less easy and manageable prey, and hence he is of necessity displeased at the possession of them and rejoices at their loss; and he would like him to be wifeless, childless, homeless, as well; and the longer the better, for the longer he is all this, the longer he will enjoy him.

There are some sort of animals, such as flatterers, which are dangerous and mischievous enough, and yet nature has mingled a temporary pleasure and grace in their composition. You may say that a courtesan is hurtful, and disapprove of such creatures and their practices, and yet for the time they are very pleasant. But the lover is not only mischievous to his love, he is also extremely unpleasant to live with. Equals, as the proverb says, delight in equals; equality of years inclines them to the same pleasures, and similarity begets friendship, and yet you may have more than enough even of this, and compulsion is always said to be grievous. Now the lover is not only unlike his beloved, but he forces himself upon him. For he is old and his love is young, and neither day nor night

will he leave him if he can help; and necessity and
the sting of desire drive him on, and allure him with
the pleasure which he receives from seeing, hearing,
touching, perceiving him. And therefore he is delighted to fasten upon him and to minister to him.
But what pleasure or consolation can the beloved be
receiving all this time? Must he not feel the extremity of disgust when he looks at an old withered face
and the remainder to match, which even in a description is not agreeable, and quite detestable when you
are forced into daily contact with them; moreover he
is jealously watched and guarded against everything
and everybody, and has to hear misplaced and exaggerated praises of himself, and censures as inappro-
priate, which are quite intolerable when the man is
sober, and, besides being intolerable, are published all
over the world in all their shamelessness and weari-
someness when he is drunk.

And not only while his love continues is he mischievous and unpleasant, but when his love ceases he
becomes a perfidious enemy of him on whom he show-
ered his oaths and prayers and promises, and yet could
hardly prevail upon him to tolerate the tedium of his
company even from motives of interest. The time
of payment arrives, and now he is the servant of another master; instead of love and infatuation, wisdom
and temperance are his bosom's lords; the man has
changed, but the beloved is not aware of this; he asks
for a return and recalls to his recollection former acts
and words, for he fancies that he is talking to the same
person, and the other, being ashamed and not having
the courage to tell him that he has changed, and not
knowing how to make good his promises, has now
grown virtuous and temperate; he does not want to
do as he did or to be as he was before. Therefore he
runs away and can but end a defaulter; quick as the

spinning of a teetotum [1] he changes pursuit into flight,
and the other is compelled to follow him with passion
and imprecation, not knowing that he ought never
from the first to have accepted a demented lover instead of a sensible non-lover; and that in making
such a choice he was yielding to a faithless, morose,
envious, disagreeable being, hurtful to his estate, hurtful to his bodily constitution, and still more hurtful
to the cultivation of his mind, which is and ever will
be the most honorable possession both of gods and
men. Consider this, fair youth, and know that in the
friendship of the lover there is no real kindness; he
has an appetite and wants to feed upon you.

" As wolves love lambs so lovers love their loves."

But, as I said before, I am speaking in verse, and
therefore I had better make an end; that is enough.

Phaedr. I thought that you were only half-way and
were going to make a similar speech about all the
advantages of accepting the non-lover. Why don't
you go on?

Soc. Does not your simplicity observe that I have
got out of dithyrambics into epics; and if my censure
was in verse, what will my praise be? Don't you see
that I am already overtaken by the Nymphs to whom
you have mischievously exposed me? And therefore
I will only add that the non-lover has all the advantages in which the lover is charged with being deficient. And now I will say no more; there has been
enough said of both of them. Leaving the tale to its
fate, I will cross the river and make the best of my
way home, lest a worse thing be inflicted upon me by
you.

Phaedr. Not yet, Socrates; not until the heat of
the day has passed; don't you see that the hour is

[1] Lit. an oyster-shell.

noon, and the sun is standing over our heads? Let us rather stay and talk over what has been said, and then return in the cool.

Soc. Your love of discourse, Phaedrus, is superhuman, simply marvellous, and I do not believe that there is any one of your contemporaries who in one way or another has either made or been the cause of others making an equal number of speeches. I would except Simmias the Theban, but all the rest are far behind you. And now I do verily believe that you have been the cause of another.

Phaedr. That is good news. But what do you mean?

Soc. I mean to say that as I was about to cross the stream the usual sign was given to me; that is the sign which never bids but always forbids me to do what I am going to do; and I thought that I heard a voice saying in my ear that I had been guilty of impiety, and that I must not go away until I had made an atonement. Now I am a diviner, though not a very good one, but I have enough religion for my own needs, as you might say of a bad writer — his writing is good enough for him. And, O my friend, how singularly prophetic is the soul! For at the time I had a sort of misgiving, and, like Ibycus, " I was troubled," and I suspected that I might be receiving honor from men at the expense of sinning against the gods. Now I am aware of the error.

Phaedr. What error?

Soc. That was a dreadful speech which you brought with you, and you made me utter one as bad.

Phaedr. How was that?

Soc. Foolish, I say, and in a degree impious; and what can be more dreadful than this?

Phaedr. Nothing, if the speech was really such as you describe.

Soc. Well, and is not Eros, the son of Aphrodite, a mighty god?

Phaedr. That is the language of mankind about him.

Soc. But that was not the language of Lysias' speech any more than of that other speech uttered through my lips when under the influence of your enchantments, and which I may call yours and not mine. For love, if he be a god or divine, can not be evil. Yet this was the error of both our speeches. There was also a solemnity about them which was truly charming: they had no truth or honesty in them, and yet they pretended to be something, hoping to succeed in deceiving the manikins of earth and be famous among them. And therefore I must have a purgation. And now I bethink me of an ancient purgation of mythological error which was devised, not by Homer, for he never had the wit to discover why he was blind, but by Stesichorus, who was a philosopher and knew the reason why; and, therefore, when he lost his eyes, for that was the penalty which was inflicted upon him for reviling the lovely Helen, he purged himself. And the purgation was a recantation, which began with the words: —

" That was a lie of mine when I said that thou never embarkedst on the swift ships, or wentest to the walls of Troy."

And when he had completed his poem, which is called " the recantation," immediately his sight returned to him. Now I will be wiser than either Stesichorus or Homer, in that I am going to make a recantation before I lose mine; and this I will attempt, not as before, veiled and ashamed, but with forehead bold and bare.

Phaedr. There is nothing which I should like better to hear.

Soc. Only think, my good Phaedrus, what an utter want of delicacy was shown in the two discourses; I mean, in my own and in the one which you recited out of the book. Would not any one who was himself of a noble and gentle nature, and who loved or ever had loved a nature like his own, when he heard us speaking of the petty causes of lovers' jealousies, and of their exceeding animosities, and the injuries which they do to their beloved, have imagined that our ideas of love were taken from some haunt of sailors to which good manners were unknown — he would certainly never have admitted the justice of our censure?

Phaedr. Certainly not.

Soc. Therefore, because I blush at the thought of this person, and also because I am afraid of the god Love, I desire to wash down that gall and vinegar with a wholesome draught; and I would counsel Lysias not to delay, but to write another discourse, which shall prove "ceteris paribus" that the lover ought to be accepted rather than the non-lover.

Phaedr. Be assured that he shall. You shall speak the praises of the lover, and Lysias shall be made to write them in another discourse. I will compel him to do this.

Soc. You will be true to your nature in that, and therefore I believe you.

Phaedr. Speak, and fear not.

Soc. But where is the fair youth whom I was addressing, and who ought to listen, in order that he may not be misled by one side before he has heard the other?

Phaedr. He is close at hand, and always at your service.

Soc. Know then, fair youth, that the former discourse was that of a finely-scented gentleman, who is all myrrh and fragrance, named Phaedrus, the son of Vain Man. And this is the recantation of Stesichorus the pious, who comes from the town of Desire, and is to the following effect: That was a lie in which I said that the beloved ought to accept the non-lover and reject the lover, because the one is sane, and the other mad. For that might have been truly said if madness were simply an evil; but there is also a madness which is the special gift of heaven, and the source of the chiefest blessings among men. For prophecy is a madness, and the prophetess at Delphi and the priestesses of Dodona, when out of their senses have conferred great benefits on Hellas, both in public and private life, but when in their senses few or none. And I might also tell you how the Sibyl and other persons, who have had the gift of prophecy, have told the future of many an one and guided them aright; but that is obvious, and would be tedious.

There will be more reason in appealing to the ancient inventors of names, who, if they had thought madness a disgrace or dishonor, would never have called prophecy, which is the noblest of arts, by the very same name (μαντική, μανική) as madness, thus inseparably connecting them; but they must have thought that there was an inspired madness which was no disgrace; for the two words, μαντική and μανική, are really the same, and the letter τ is only a modern and tasteless insertion. And this is confirmed by the name which they gave to the rational investigation of futurity, whether made by the help of birds or other signs; this as supplying from the reasoning faculty insight and information to human thought (νοῦς and ἱστορία), they originally termed οἰονοιστική, but the word has been lately altered and made sonorous by the modern introduction of the letter Omega (οἰονοιστική and οἰωνιστική), and in proportion as (μαντική or) prophecy is higher and more perfect than divination both in name and reality, in the same proportion as the ancients testify, is madness superior to a sane mind ($\sigma\omega\phi\rho o\sigma\acute{v}\nu\eta$), for the one is only of human, but the other of divine origin. Again, where plagues and mightiest woes have bred in a race, owing to some ancient wrath, there madness, lifting up her voice and flying to prayers and rites, has come to the rescue of those who are in need; and he who has part in this gift, and is truly possessed and duly out of his mind, is by the use of purifications and mysteries made whole and delivered from evil, future as well as present, and has a release from the calamity which afflicts him. There is also a third kind of madness, which is a possession of the Muses; this enters into a delicate and virgin soul, and there inspiring frenzy, awakens lyric and all other numbers; with these adorning the myriad actions of ancient heroes for the instruction of posterity. But he who, not being inspired and having no touch of madness in his soul, comes to the door and thinks that he will get into the temple by the help of art — he, I say, and his poetry are not admitted; the sane man is nowhere at all when he enters into rivalry with the madman.

I might tell of many other noble deeds which have sprung from inspired madness. And therefore, let no one frighten or flutter us by saying that temperate love is preferable to mad love, but let him further show, if he would carry off the palm, that love is not sent by the gods for any good to lover or beloved. And we, on our part, will prove in answer to him that the madness of love is the greatest of heaven's blessings, and the proof shall be one which the wise will receive, and the witling disbelieve. And, first of all, let us inquire what is the truth about the affections and actions of the soul, divine as well as human. And thus we begin our proof:

The soul is immortal, for that is immortal which is ever in motion; but that which moves and is moved by another, in ceasing to move ceases also to live. Therefore, only that which is self-moving, never failing of self, never ceases to move, and is the fountain and beginning of motion to all that moves besides. Now, the beginning is unbegotten, for that which is begotten has a beginning; but the beginning has no beginning, for if a beginning were begotten of something, that would have no beginning. But that, which is unbegotten must also be indestructible; for if beginning were destroyed, there could be no beginning out of anything, nor anything out of a beginning; and all things must have a beginning. And therefore the self-moving is the beginning of motion; and this can neither be destroyed nor begotten, for in that case the whole heavens and all generation would collapse and stand still, and never again have motion or birth. But if the self-moving is immortal, he who affirms that self-motion is the very idea and essence of the soul will not be put to confusion. For the body which is moved from without is soulless; but that which is moved from within has a soul, and this is involved in the nature of the soul. But if the soul be truly affirmed to be the self-moving, then must she also be without beginning, and immortal. Enough of the soul's immortality.

Her form is a theme of divine and large discourse; human language may, however, speak of this briefly, and in a figure. Let our figure be of a composite nature — a pair of winged horses and a charioteer. Now the winged horses and the charioteer of the gods are all of them noble, and of noble breed, while ours are mixed; and we have a charioteer who drives them in a pair, and one of them is noble and of noble origin, and the other is ignoble and of ignoble origin; and, as might be expected, there is a great deal of trouble in managing them. I will endeavor to explain to you in what way the mortal differs from the immortal creature. The soul or animate being has the care of the inanimate, and traverses the whole heaven in divers forms appearing; — when perfect and fully winged she soars upward, and is the ruler of the universe; while the imperfect soul loses her feathers, and drooping in her flight at last settles on the solid ground — there, finding a home, she receives an earthly frame which appears to be self-moved, but is really moved by her power; and this composition of soul and body is called a living and mortal creature. For no such union can be reasonably believed, or at all proved to be other than mortal; although fancy may imagine a god whom, not having seen nor surely known, we invent — such an one, an immortal creature having a body, and having also a soul which have been united in all time. Let that, however, be as God wills, and be spoken of acceptably to him. But the reason why the soul loses her feathers should be explained, and is as follows:

The wing is intended to soar aloft and carry that which gravitates downwards into the upper region, which is the dwelling of the gods; and this is that element of the body which is most akin to the divine. Now the divine is beauty, wisdom, goodness, and the like; and by these the wing of the soul is nourished, and grows apace; but when fed upon evil and foulness, and the like, wastes and falls away. Zeus, the mighty lord holding the reins of a winged chariot, leads the way in heaven, ordering all and caring for all; and there follows him the heavenly array of gods and demi-gods, divided into eleven bands; for only Hestia is left at home in the house of heaven; but the rest of the twelve greater deities march in their appointed order. And they see in the interior of heaven many blessed sights; and there are ways to and fro, along which the happy gods are passing, each one fulfilling his own work; and any one may follow who pleases, for jealousy has no place in the heavenly choir. This is within the heaven. But when they go to feast and festival, then they move right up the steep ascent, and mount the top of the dome of heaven. Now the chariots of the gods, self-balanced, upward glide in obedience to the rein; but the others have a difficulty, for the steed who has evil in him, if he has not been properly trained by the charioteer, gravitates and inclines and sinks towards the earth: — and this is the hour of agony and extremest conflict of the soul. For the immortal souls, when they are at the end of their course, go out and stand upon the back of heaven, and the revolution of the spheres carries them round, and they behold the world beyond. Now of the heaven which is above the heavens, no earthly poet has sung or ever will sing in a worthy manner. But I must tell, for I am bound to speak truly when speaking of the truth. The colorless and formless and intangible essence is visible to the mind, which is the only lord of the soul. Circling around this in the region above the heavens is the place of true knowledge. And as the divine intelligence, and that of every other soul which is rightly nourished, is fed upon mind and pure knowledge, such an intelligent soul is glad at once more beholding being; and feeding on the sight of truth is replenished, until the revolution of the worlds brings her round again to the same place. During the revolution she beholds justice, temperance, and knowledge absolute, not in the form of generation or of relation, which men call existence, but knowledge absolute in existence absolute; and beholding other existences in like manner, and feeding upon them, she passes down into the interior of the heavens and returns home, and there the charioteer putting up his horses at the stall, gives them ambrosia to eat and nectar to drink.

This is the life of the gods; but of other souls, that which follows God best and is likest to him lifts the head of the charioteer into the outer world, and is carried round in the revolution, troubled indeed by the steeds, and beholding true being, but hardly; another rises and falls, and sees, and again fails to see by reason of the unruliness of the steeds. The rest of the souls are also longing after the upper world and they all follow, but not being strong enough they sink into the gulf, as they are carried round, plunging, treading on one another, striving to be first; and there is confusion and the extremity of effort, and many of them are lamed or have their wings broken through the ill-driving of the charioteers; and all of them after a fruitless toil go away without being initiated into the mysteries of being, and are nursed with the food of opinion. The reason of their great desire to behold the plain of truth is that the food which is suited to the highest part of the soul comes out of that meadow; and the wing on which the soul soars is nourished with this. And there is a law of the goddess Retribution, that the soul which attains any vision of truth in company with the god is preserved from harm until the next period, and he who always attains is always unharmed. But when she is unable to follow, and fails to behold the vision of truth, and through some ill-hap sinks beneath the double load of forgetfulness and vice, and her feathers fall from her and she drops to earth, then the law ordains that this soul shall in the first generation pass, not into that of any other animal, but only of man; and the soul which has seen most of truth shall come to the birth as a philosopher, or artist, or musician, or lover; that which has seen truth in the second degree shall be a righteous king or warrior or lord; the soul which is of the third class shall be a politician, or economist, or trader; the fourth shall be a lover of gymnastic toils, or a physician; the fifth a prophet or hierophant; to the sixth a poet or imitator will be appropriate; to the seventh the life of an artisan or husbandman; to the eighth that of a sophist or demagogue; to the ninth that of a tyrant; — all these are states of probation, in which he who lives righteously improves, and he who lives unrighteously deteriorates his lot.

Ten thousand years must elapse before the soul can return to the place from whence she came, for she can not grow her wings in less; only the soul of a philosopher, guileless and true, or the soul of a lover, who is not without philosophy, may acquire wings in the third recurring period of a thousand years: and if they choose this life three times in succession, then they have their wings given them, and go away at the end of three thousand years. But the others receive judgment when they have completed their first life, and after the judgment they go, some of them to the houses of correction which are under the earth, and are punished; others to some place in heaven whither they are lightly borne by justice, and there they live in a manner worthy of the life which they led here when in the form of men. And at the end of the first thousand years the good souls and also the evil souls both come to cast lots and choose their second life, and they may take any that they like. And then the soul of the man may pass into the life of a beast, or from the beast again into the man. But the soul of him who has never seen the truth will not pass into the human form, for man ought to have intelligence, as they say, " secundum speciem," proceeding from many particulars of sense to one conception of reason; and this is the recollection of those things which our soul once saw when in company with God — when looking down from above on that which we now call being and upwards towards the true being. And therefore the mind of the philosopher alone has wings; and this is just, for he is always, according to the measure of his abilities, clinging in recollection to those things in which God abides, and in beholding which He is what he is. And he who employs aright these memories is ever being initiated into perfect mysteries and alone becomes truly perfect. But, as he forgets earthly interests and is rapt in the divine, the vulgar deem him mad, and rebuke him; they do not see that he is inspired.

Thus far I have been speaking of the fourth and last kind of madness, which is imputed to him who, when he sees the beauty of earth, is transported with the recollection of the true beauty; he would like to fly away, but he can not; he is like a bird fluttering and looking upward and careless of the world below; and he is therefore esteemed mad. And I have shown that this is of all inspirations the noblest and best, and comes of the best, and that he who has part or lot in this madness is called a lover of the beautiful. For as has been already said, every soul of man has in the way of nature beheld true being; this was the condition of her passing into the form of man. But all men do not easily recall the things of the other world; they may have seen them for a short time only, or they may have been unfortunate when they fell to earth, and may have lost the memory of the holy things which they saw there through some evil and corrupting association. Few there are who retain the remembrance of them sufficiently; and they, when they behold any image of that other world, are rapt in amazement; but they are ignorant of what this means, because they have no clear perceptions. For there is no light in the earthly copies of justice or temperance or any of the higher qualities which are precious to souls: they are seen but through a glass dimly; and there are few who, going to the images, behold in them the realities, and they only with difficulty. They might have seen beauty shining in brightness, when, with the happy band following in the train of Zeus, as we philosophers did, or with other gods as others did, they saw a vision and were initiated into most blessed mysteries, which we celebrated in our state of innocence; and having no feeling of evils as yet to come; beholding apparitions innocent and simple and calm and happy as in a mystery; shining in pure light, pure ourselves and not yet enshrined in that living tomb which we carry about, now that we are imprisoned in the body, as in an oyster-shell. Let me linger thus long over the memory of scenes which have passed away.

But of beauty, I repeat again that we saw her there shining in company with the celestial forms; and coming to earth we find her here too, shining in clearness through the clearest aperture of sense. For sight is the keenest of our bodily senses; though not by that is wisdom seen, for her loveliness would have been transporting if there had been a visible image of her, and this is true of the loveliness of the other ideas as well. But beauty only has this portion, that she is at once the loveliest and also the most apparent. Now he who has not been lately initiated or who has become corrupted, is not easily carried out of this world to the sight of absolute beauty in the other; he looks only at that which has the name of beauty in this world, and instead of being awed at the sight of her, like a brutish beast he rushes on to enjoy and beget; he takes wantonness to his bosom, and is not afraid or ashamed of pursuing pleasure in violation of nature. But he whose initiation is recent, and who has been the spectator of many glories in the other world, is amazed when he sees any one having a god-like face or form, which is the expression or imitation of divine beauty; and at first a shudder runs through him, and some "misgiving" of a former world steals over him; then looking upon the face of his beloved as of a god he reverences him, and if he were not afraid of being thought a downright madman, he would sacrifice to his beloved as to the image of a god; then as he gazes on him there is a sort of reaction, and the shudder naturally passes into an unusual heat and perspiration; for, as he receives the effluence of beauty through the eyes, the wing moistens and he warms. And as he warms, the parts out of which the wing grew, and which had been hitherto closed and rigid, and had prevented the wing from shooting forth are melted, and as nourishment streams upon him, the lower end of the wing begins to swell and grow from the root upwards, extending under the whole soul — for once the whole was winged. Now during this process the whole soul is in a state of effervescence and irritation, like the state of irritation and pain in the gums at the time of cutting teeth; in like manner the soul when beginning to grow wings has inflammation and pains and ticklings, and when looking at the beauty of youth she receives the sensible warm traction of particles which flow towards her, therefore called attraction ($ἵμερος$), and is refreshed and warmed by them, and then she ceases from her pain with joy. But when she is separated and her moisture fails, then the orifices of the passages out of which the wing shoots dry up and close, and intercept the germ of the wing; which, being shut up within in company with desire, throbbing as with the pulsations of an artery, pricks the aperture which is nearest, until at length the entire soul is pierced and maddened and pained, and at the recollection of beauty is again delighted. And from both of them together the soul is oppressed at the strangeness of her condition, and is in a great strait and excitement, and in her madness can neither sleep by night nor abide in her place by day. And wherever she thinks that she will behold the beautiful one, thither in her desire she runs. And when she has seen him, and drunk rivers of desire, her constraint is loosened, and she is refreshed, and has no more pangs and pains; and this is the sweetest of all pleasures at the time, and is the reason why the soul of the lover never forsakes his beautiful one, whom he esteems above all; he has forgotten his mother and brethren and companions, and he thinks nothing of the neglect and loss of his property; and as to the rules and proprieties of life, on which he formerly prided himself, he now despises them, and is ready to sleep and serve, wherever he is allowed, as near as he can to his beautiful one who is not only the object of his worship, but the only physician who can heal him in his extreme agony. And this state, my dear imaginary youth, is by men called love, and among the gods has a name which you, in your simplicity, may be inclined to mock; there are two lines in honor of love in the Homeric Apocrypha in which the name occurs. One of them is rather outrageous, and is not quite metrical; they are as follow: —

" Mortals call him Eros (love),
 But the immortals call him Pteros (fluttering dove),
 Because fluttering of wings is a necessity to him."

You may believe this or not as you like. At any rate the loves of lovers and their causes are such as I have described.

Now the lover who is the attendant of Zeus is better able to bear the winged god, and can endure a heavier burden; but the attendants and companions of Ares, when under the influence of love, if they fancy that they have been at all wronged, are ready to kill and put an end to themselves and their beloved. And in like manner he who follows in the train of any other god honors him, and imitates him as far as he is able while the impression lasts; and this is his way of life and the manner of his behavior to his beloved and to every other in the first period of his earthly existence. Every one chooses the object of his affections according to his character, and this he makes his god, and fashions and adorns as a sort of image which he is to fall down and worship. The followers of Zeus desire that their beloved should have a soul like him; and, therefore, they seek some philosophical and imperial nature, and when they have found him and loved him, they do all they can to create such a nature in him, and if they have no experience hitherto, they learn of any one who can teach them, and themselves follow in the same way. And they have the less difficulty in finding the nature of their own god in themselves, because they have been compelled to gaze intensely on him; their recollection clings to him, and they become possessed by him, and receive his character and ways, as far as man can participate in God. These they attribute to the beloved, and they love him all the more, and if they draw inspiration from Zeus, like the Bacchic Nymphs, they pour this out upon him in order to make him as like their god as possible. But those who are the followers of Hera seek a royal love, and when they have found him they do the same with him; and in like manner the followers of Apollo, and of every other god walking in the ways of their god, seek a love who is to be like their god, and when they have found him, they themselves imitate their god, and persuade their love to do the same, and bring him into harmony with the form and ways of the god as far as they can; for they have no feelings of envy or mean enmity towards their beloved, but they do their utmost to create in him the greatest likeness of themselves and the god whom they honor. And the desire of the lover, if effected, and the initiation of which I speak into the mysteries of true love, is thus fair and blissful to the beloved when he is chosen by the lover who is driven mad by love. Now the beloved or chosen one is taken captive in the following manner: —

As I said at the beginning of this tale, I divided each soul into three parts, two of them having the forms of horses and the third that of a charioteer; and one of the horses was good and the other bad, but I have not yet explained the virtue and vice of either, and to that I will now proceed. The well-conditioned horse is erect and well-formed; he has a lofty neck and an aquiline nose, and his color is white, and he has dark eyes and is a lover of honor and modesty and temperance, and the follower of true glory; he needs not the touch of the whip, but is guided by word and admonition only. Whereas the other is a large mis-shapen animal, put together anyhow; he has a strong short neck; he is flat-faced and of a dark color, grey-eyed and bloodshot, the mate of insolence and pride, shag-eared, deaf, hardly yielding to blow or spur. Now when the charioteer beholds the vision of love, and has his whole soul warmed with sense, and is full of tickling and desire, the obedient steed then as always under the government of shame, refrains himself from leaping on the beloved; but the other, instead of heeding the blows of the whip, prances away and gives all manner of trouble to his companion and to the char-

ioteer, and urges them on toward the beloved and
reminds them of the joys of love. They at first indig-
nantly oppose him and will not be urged on to do
terrible and unlawful deeds; but at last, when there is
no end of evil, they yield and suffer themselves to be
led on to do as he bids them. And now they are at
the spot and behold the flashing beauty of the beloved.
But when the charioteer sees that, his memory is carried to the true beauty, and he beholds her in company
with Modesty set in her holy place. And when he
sees her he is afraid and falls back in adoration, and
in falling is compelled to pull back the reins, which he
does with such force as to bring both the steeds on
their haunches, the one willing and unresisting, the
unruly one very unwilling; and when they have gone
back a little, the one is overflowing with shame and
wonder, and pours forth rivers of perspiration over
the entire soul; the other, when the pain is over which
the bridle and the fall had given him, having with difficulty taken breath, is full of wrath and reproaches,
which he heaps upon the charioteer and his fellow-
steed, as though from want of courage and manhood
they had been false to their agreement and guilty of
desertion. And, when they again decline, he forces
them on, and will scarce yield to their request that
he would wait until another time. Returning at the
appointed hour, they make as if they had forgotten,
and he reminds them, fighting and neighing and dragging them, until at length he on the same thoughts
intent, forces them to draw near. And when they are
near he stoops his head and puts up his tail, and takes
the bit in his mouth and pulls shamelessly. Then the
charioteer is worse off than ever; he drops at the very
start, and with still greater violence draws the bit out
of the teeth of the wild steed and covers his abusive
tongue and jaws with blood, and forces his legs and

haunches to the ground and punishes him sorely. And when this has happened several times and the villain has ceased from his wanton way, he is tamed and humbled, and follows the will of the charioteer, and when he sees the beautiful one he is ready to die of fear. And from that time forward the soul of the lover follows the beloved in modesty and holy fear.

And so the beloved who, like a god, has received every true and loyal service from his lover, not in pretence but in reality, being also himself of a nature friendly to his admirer, if in former days he has blushed to own his passion and turned away his lover, because his youthful companions or others slanderously told him that he would be disgraced, now as years advance, at the appointed age and time is led to receive him into communion. For fate which has ordained that there shall be no friendship among the evil has also ordained that there shall ever be friendship among the good. And when he has received him into communion and intimacy, then the beloved is amazed at the good will of the lover; he recognizes that the inspired friend is worth all other friendship or kinships, which have nothing of friendship in them in comparison. And as he continues to feel this and approaches and embraces him, in gymnastic exercises and at other times of meeting, then does the fountain of that stream, which Zeus when he was in love with Ganymede called desire, overflow upon the lover, and some enters into his soul, and some when he is filled flows out again, and as a breeze or an echo leaps from the smooth rocks and rebounds to them again, so does the stream of beauty, passing the eyes which are the natural doors and windows of the soul, return again to the beautiful one; there arriving and fluttering the passages of the wings, and watering them and inclining them to grow, and filling the soul of the beloved also with love. And thus he loves, but he knows not what; he does not understand and can not explain his own state; he appears to have caught the infection of another's eye; the lover is his mirror in whom he is beholding himself, but he is not aware of this. When he is with the lover, both cease from their pain, but when he is away then he longs as he is longed for, and has love's image, love for love (Anteros) lodging in his breast, which he calls and deems not love but friendship only, and his desire is as the desire of the other, but weaker; he wants to see him, touch him, kiss, embrace him, and not long afterwards his desire is accomplished. Now, when they meet, the wanton steed of the lover has a word to say to the charioteer; he would like to have a little pleasure as a return for many pains, but the wanton steed of the beloved says not a word, for he is bursting with passion which he understands not, but he throws his arms round the lover and embraces him as his dearest friend; and, when they are side by side, he is not in a state in which he can refuse the lover anything, if he ask him, while his fellow-steed and the charioteer oppose him with shame and reason. After this their happiness depends upon their self-control; if the better elements of the mind which lead to order and philosophy prevail, then they pass their life in this world in happiness and harmony — masters of themselves and orderly — enslaving the vicious and emancipating the virtuous elements; and when the end comes, being light and ready to fly away, they conquer in one of the three heavenly or truly Olympian victories; nor can human discipline or divine inspiration confer any greater blessing on man than this. If, on the other hand, they leave philosophy and lead the lower life of ambition, then, probably in the dark or in some other careless hour, the two wanton animals take the two souls

when off their guard and bring them together, and
they accomplish that desire of their hearts which to
the many is bliss; and this having once enjoyed they
continue to enjoy, yet rarely because they have not
the approval of the whole soul. They too are dear,
but not so dear to one another as the others, either at
the time of their love or afterwards. They consider
that they have given and taken from each other the
most sacred pledges, and they may not break them
and fall into enmity. At last they pass out of the
body, unwinged, but eager to soar, and thus obtain no
mean reward of love and madness. For those who
have once begun the heavenward pilgrimage may not
go down again to darkness and the journey beneath
the earth, but they live in light always; happy companions in their pilgrimage, and when the time comes
at which they receive their wings they have the same
plumage because of their love.

Thus great are the heavenly blessings which the
friendship of a lover will confer on you, my youth.
Whereas the attachment of the non-lover which is
just a vulgar compound of temperance and niggardly
earthly ways and motives, will breed meanness —
praised by the vulgar as virtue in your inmost soul;
will send you bowling round the earth during a period
of nine thousand years, and leave you a fool in the
world below.

And thus, dear Eros, I have made and paid my
recantation, as well as I could and as fairly as I could;
the poetical figures I was compelled to use, because
Phaedrus would have them. And now forgive the
past and accept the present, and be gracious and mer-
ciful to me, and do not deprive me of sight or take
from me the art of love, but grant that I may be yet
more esteemed in the eyes of the fair. And if Phaedrus or I myself said anything objectionable in our

first speeches, blame Lysias, who is the father of the brat, and let us have no more of his progeny; bid him study philosophy, like his brother Polemarchus; and then his lover Phaedrus will no longer halt between two, but dedicate himself wholly to love and philosophical discourses.

Phaedr. I say with you, Socrates, may this come true if this be for my good. But why did you make this discourse of yours so much finer than the other? I wonder at that. And I begin to be afraid that I shall lose conceit of Lysias, even if he be willing to make another as long as yours, which I doubt. For one of our politicians lately took to abusing him on this very account; he would insist on calling him a speech-writer. So that a feeling of pride may probably induce him to give up writing.

Soc. That is an amusing notion; but I think that you are a little mistaken in your friend if you imagine that he is frightened at every noise; and, possibly, you think that his assailant was in earnest?

Phaedr. I thought, Socrates, that he was. And you are aware that the most powerful and considerable men among our statesmen are ashamed of writing speeches and leaving them in a written form because they are afraid of posterity, and do not like to be called sophists.

Soc. I don't know whether you are aware, Phaedrus, that the " sweet elbow " [1] of which the proverb speaks is really derived from the long and difficult arm of the Nile. And you appear to be equally unaware of the fact that this sweet elbow of theirs is also a long arm. For there is nothing of which great politicians are so fond as of writing speeches, which they bequeath to posterity. And when they write

---

[1] A proverb, like " the grapes are sour," applied to pleasures which can not be had, meaning sweet things which are out of the reach of the mouth.

them, out of gratitude to their admirers, they append their names at the top.

Phaedr. What do you mean? I don't understand.

Soc. Why, don't you know that when a politician writes, he begins with the names of his approvers?

Phaedr. How is that?

Soc. Why, he begins thus: " Be it enacted by the senate, the people, or both, as a certain person who was the author proposed; " and then he rehearses all his titles, and proceeds to display his own wisdom to his admirers with a great flourish in what is often a long and tedious composition. Now what is that sort of thing but a regular piece of authorship?

Phaedr. True.

Soc. And if the law is passed, then, like the poet, he leaves the theatre in high delight; but if the law is rejected and he is done out of his speech-making, and not thought good enough to write, then he and his party are in mourning.

Phaedr. Very true.

Soc. This shows how far they are from despising, or rather how highly they value the practice of writing.

Phaedr. No doubt.

Soc. And when the king or orator has the power, as Lycurgus or Solon or Darius had, of attaining an immortality of authorship in a state, is he not thought by posterity, when they see his writings, and does he not think himself, while he is yet alive, to be like a god?

Phaedr. That is true.

Soc. Then do you think that any one of this class who may be ill-disposed to Lysias would ever make it a reproach against him that he is an author?

Phaedr. Not upon your view; for according to you he would be reproaching him with his own favorite pursuit.

Soc. Any one may see that there is no disgrace in the fact of writing?

Phaedr. Certainly not.

Soc. There may however be a disgrace in writing, not well, but badly.

Phaedr. That is true.

Soc. And what is well and what is badly — need we ask Lysias, or any other poet or orator, who ever wrote or will write either a political or any other work, in metre or out of metre, poet or prose writer, to teach us this?

Phaedr. Need we? What motive has a man to live if not for the pleasure of discourse? Surely he would not live for the sake of bodily pleasures, which almost always have previous pain as a condition of them, and therefore are rightly called slavish.

Soc. There is time yet. And I can fancy that the grasshoppers who are still chirruping in the sun over our heads are talking to one another and looking at us. What would they say if they saw that we also, like the many, are not talking but slumbering at midday, lulled by their voices, too indolent to think? They would have a right to laugh at us, and might imagine that we are slaves coming to our place of resort, who like sheep lie asleep at noon about the fountain. But if they see us discoursing, and like Odysseus sailing by their siren voices, they may perhaps, out of respect, give us of the gifts which they receive of the gods and give to men.

Phaedr. What gifts do you mean? I never heard of any.

Soc. A lover of music like yourself ought surely to have heard the story of the grasshoppers, who are said to have been human beings in an age before the Muses. And when the Muses came and song appeared they were ravished with delight; and singing always, never thought of eating and drinking, until at last they forgot and died. And now they live again in the grasshoppers; and this is the return which the Muses make to them — they hunger no more, neither thirst any more, but are always singing from the moment that they are born, and never eating or drinking; and when they die they go and inform the Muses in heaven who honors them on earth. They win the love of Terpsichore for the dancers by their report of them; of Erato for the lovers, and of the other Muses for those who do them honor, according to the several ways of honoring them; — of Calliope the eldest Muse, and of her who is next to her for the votaries of philosophy; for these are the Muses who are chiefly concerned with heaven and the ideas, divine as well as human, and they have the sweetest utterance. For many reasons, then, we ought always to talk and not to sleep at mid-day.

Phaedr. Let us talk.

Soc. Shall we discuss the rules of writing and speech as we were proposing?

Phaedr. Very good.

Soc. Is not the first rule of good speaking that the mind of the speaker should know the truth of what he is going to say?

Phaedr. And yet, Socrates, I have heard that he who would be an orator has nothing to do with true justice, but only with that which is likely to be approved by the many who sit in judgment; nor with the truly good or honorable, but only with public opinion about them, and that from this source and not from the truth come the elements of persuasion.

Soc. Any words of the wise ought to be regarded and not trampled under foot, for there is probably something in them, and perhaps there may be something in this which is worthy of attention.

Phaedr. Very true.

Soc. Let us put the matter thus: — Suppose that I persuaded you to buy a horse and go to the wars. Neither of us knew what a horse was like, but I knew that you believed a horse to be the longest-eared of domestic animals.

Phaedr. That would be ridiculous.

Soc. There is something more ridiculous coming. Suppose, now, that I was in earnest and went and composed a speech in honor of an ass, whom I entitled a horse, beginning: " A noble animal and a most use-ful possession, especially in war, and you may get on his back and fight, and he will carry baggage or any-thing."

Phaedr. That would be most ridiculous.

Soc. Ridiculous! Yes; but is not even a ridiculous friend better than a dangerous enemy?

Phaedr. Certainly.

Soc. And when the orator instead of putting an ass in the place of a horse, puts good for evil, being him-self as ignorant of their true nature as the city on which he imposes is ignorant; and having studied the notions of the multitude, persuades them to do evil instead of good, — what will be the harvest which rhetoric will be likely to gather after the sowing of that fruit?

Phaedr. Anything but good.

Soc. Perhaps, however, rhetoric has been getting too roughly handled by us, and she might answer: What amazing nonsense is this! As if I forced any man to learn to speak in ignorance of the truth! Whatever my advice may be worth, I should have told him to arrive at the truth first, and then come to me. At the same time I boldly assert that mere knowl-edge of the truth will not give you the art of per-suasion.

Phaedr. There is reason in the lady's defence of herself.

Soc. Yes, I admit that, if the argument which she has yet in store bear witness that she is an art at all. But I seem to hear them arraying themselves on the opposite side, declaring that she speaks not true, and that rhetoric is not an art but only a dilettante amusement. Lo! a Spartan appears, and says that there never is nor ever will be a real art of speaking which is unconnected with the truth.

Phaedr. And what are these arguments, Socrates? Bring them out that we may examine them.

Soc. Come out, children of my soul, and convince Phaedrus, who is the father of similar beauties, that he will never be able to speak about anything unless he be trained in philosophy. And let Phaedrus answer you.

Phaedr. Put the question.

Soc. Is not rhetoric, taken generally, a universal art of enchanting the mind by arguments; which is practised not only in courts and public assemblies, but in private houses also, having to do with all matters, great as well as small, good and bad alike, and is in all equally right, and equally to be esteemed — that is what you have heard?

Phaedr. Nay, not exactly that; but I should rather say that I have heard the art confined to speaking and writing in law-suits, and to speaking in public assemblies — not extended farther.

Soc. Then I suppose that you have only heard of the rhetoric of Nestor and Odysseus, which they composed in their leisure hours when at Troy, and never of Palamedes?

Phaedr. No more than of Nestor and Odysseus, unless Gorgias is your Nestor, and Thrasymachus and Theodorus your Odysseus.

Soc. Perhaps that is my meaning. But let us leave them. And do you tell me, instead, what are plaintiff and defendant doing in a law-court — are they not contending?

Phaedr. Exactly.

Soc. About the just and unjust — that is the matter in dispute?

Phaedr. Yes.

Soc. And he who is practised in the art will make the same thing appear to the same persons to be at one time just and at another time unjust, if he has a mind?

Phaedr. Exactly.

Soc. And when he speaks in the assembly, he will make the same things seem good to the city at one time, and at another time the reverse of good?

Phaedr. That is true.

Soc. Have we not heard of the Eleatic Palamedes (Zeno), who has an art of speaking which makes the same things appear to his hearers like and unlike, one and many, at rest and in motion too?

Phaedr. Very true.

Soc. The art of disputation, then, is not confined to the courts and the assembly, but is one and the same in every use of language; this is that art, if such an art there be, which finds a likeness of everything to which a likeness can be found, and draws into the light of day the likenesses and disguises which are used by others?

Phaedr. How do you mean?

Soc. Let me put the matter thus: When will there be more chance of deception — when the difference is large or small?

Phaedr. When the difference is small.

Soc. And you will be less likely to be discovered in passing by degrees into the other extreme than when you go all at once?

Phaedr. Of course.

Soc. He, then, who would deceive others, and not be deceived, must exactly know the real likenesses and differences of things?

Phaedr. Yes, he must.

Soc. And if he is ignorant of the true nature of anything, how can he ever distinguish the greater or less degree of likeness to other things of that which he does not know?

Phaedr. He can not.

Soc. And when men are deceived, and their notions are at variance with realities, it is clear that the error slips in through some resemblances?

Phaedr. Yes, that is the way.

Soc. Then he who would be a master of the art must know the real nature of everything; or he will never know either how to contrive or how to escape the gradual departure from truth into the opposite of truth which is effected by the help of resemblances?

Phaedr. He will not.

Soc. He then, who being ignorant of the truth catches at appearances, will only attain an art of rhetoric which is ridiculous and is not an art at all?

Phaedr. That may be expected.

Soc. Shall I propose that we look for examples ot good and bad art, according to our notion of them, in the speech of Lysias which you have in your hand, and in my own speech?

Phaedr. Nothing could be better; and indeed I think that our previous argument has been too barren of illustrations.

Soc. Yes; and the two speeches afford a good illustration of the way in which the speaker who knows the truth may playfully draw away the hearts of his hearers. This piece of good fortune I attribute to the local deities; and, perhaps, the prophets of the Muses who are singing over our heads may have imparted their inspiration to me. For I do not imagine that I have any rhetorical art myself.

Phaedr. I will not dispute that; only please to go forward.

Soc. Suppose that you read me the first words of Lysias' speech?

Phaedr. " You know my views of our common interest, and I do not think that I ought to fail in the object of my suit because I am not your lover. For lovers repent when —— "

Soc. Enough. Now, shall I point out the rhetorical error of those words?

Phaedr. Yes.

Soc. Every one is aware that about some things we are agreed, whereas about other things we differ.

Phaedr. I think that I understand you; but will you explain yourself?

Soc. When any one speaks of iron and silver, is not the same thing present in the minds of all?

Phaedr. Certainly.

Soc. But when any one speaks of justice and goodness, there is every sort of disagreement, and we are at odds with one another and with ourselves?

Phaedr. Precisely.

Soc. Then in some things we agree, but not in others?

Phaedr. That is true.

Soc. In which are we more likely to be deceived, and in which has rhetoric the greater power?

Phaedr. Clearly, in the class which admits of error.

Soc. Then the rhetorician ought to make a regular division, and acquire a distinct notion of both classes, as well of that in which the many err, as of that in which they do not err?

Phaedr. He who made such a distinction would have an excellent principle.

Soc. Yes; and in the next place he must have a keen eye for the observation of particulars in speaking, and not make a mistake about the class to which they are to be referred.

Phaedr. Certainly.

Soc. Now to which class does love belong — to the debatable or to the undisputed class?

Phaedr. To the debatable class surely; for if not, do you think that any one would have allowed you to say as you did, that love is an evil both to the lover and the beloved, and also the greatest possible good?

Soc. Capital. But will you tell me whether I defined love at the beginning of my speech? for, having been in an ecstasy, I can not well remember.

Phaedr. Yes, indeed; that you did, and no mistake.

Soc. Then I perceive that the Nymphs of Achelous and Pan the son of Hermes, who inspired me, were far better rhetoricians than Lysias the son of Cephalus. Alas! how inferior to them he is! But perhaps I am mistaken; and Lysias at the commencement of his lover's speech did insist on our supposing love to be something or other which he fancied him to be, and that in relation to this something he fashioned and framed the remainder of his discourse. Suppose we read him over again.

Phaedr. If you please; but you will not find what you want.

Soc. Read, that I may have his exact words.

Phaedr. "You know my views of our common interest; and I do not think that I ought to fail in the object of my suit because I am not your lover, for lovers repent of the kindnesses which they have shown, when their love is over."

Soc. Here he appears to have done just the reverse

of what he ought; for he has begun at the end, and is
swimming on his back through the flood of words to
the place of starting.   His address to the fair youth
commences with reference to the conclusion of his love.
Am I not right, sweet Phaedrus?

Phaedr. Yes, indeed, Socrates; he does begin at the
end.

Soc. Then as to the other topics — are they not a
mass of confusion?   Is there any principle in them?
Why should the next topic or any other topic follow
in that order?   I can not help fancying in my ignorance that he wrote freely off just what came into his
head, but I dare say that you would recognize a rhetorical necessity in the succession of the several parts
of the composition?

Phaedr. You have too good an opinion of me if you
think that I have any such insight into his principles
of composition.

Soc. At any rate, you will allow that every discourse ought to be a living creature, having its own
body and head and feet; there ought to be a middle,
beginning, and end, which are in a manner agreeable
to one another and to the whole?

Phaedr. Certainly.

Soc. Can this be said of the discourse of Lysias?
See whether you can find any more connections in his
words than in the epitaph, which is said by some to
have been inscribed on the grave of Midas the
Phrygian.

Phaedr. What is there remarkable in the epitaph?

Soc. The epitaph is as follows:

> " I am a maiden of brass;
> I lie on the tomb of Midas,
> While waters flow and tall trees grow,
> Here am I.

On Midas' tearful tomb I lie;
I am to tell the passers by
That Midas sleeps in earth below."

Now in this rhyme whether a line comes first or comes last, that, as you will perceive, makes no difference.

Phaedr. You are making fun of that oration of ours.

Soc. Well, I will say no more about your friend lest I should give offence to you; although I think that he might furnish many other examples of what a man ought to avoid. But I will proceed to the other speech, which, as I think, is also suggestive to students of rhetoric.

Phaedr. In what way?

Soc. The two speeches, as you may remember, were of an opposite character, the one argued that the lover and the other that the non-lover ought to be accepted.

Phaedr. And right manfully.

Soc. You should rather say " madly; " and that was the argument of them, for, as I said, " love is a madness."

Phaedr. Yes.

Soc. And there were two kinds of madness; one produced by human infirmity, the other by a divine release from the ordinary ways of men.

Phaedr. True.

Soc. The divine madness was subdivided into four kinds, prophetic, initiatory, poetic, erotic, having four gods presiding over them; the first was the inspiration of Apollo, the second that of Dionysus, the third that of the Muses, the fourth that of Aphrodite and Eros. In the description of the last kind of madness, which was also the best, being a sort of figure of love, we mingled a tolerably credible and possibly true, though partly erring myth, which was also a hymn in honor of Eros, who is your lord and also mine, Phaedrus, and the guardian of fair children, and to him we sung the hymn in measured and solemn form.

Phaedr. I know that I had great pleasure in listening to the tale.

Soc. Let us take this instance and examine how the transition was made from blame to praise.

Phaedr. What do you mean.

Soc. I mean to say that the composition was mostly playful. Yet in these chance fancies of the hour were involved two principles which would be charming if they could· be fixed by art.

Phaedr. What are they?

Soc. First, the comprehension of scattered particulars in one idea; — the speaker defines his several notions in order that he may make his meaning clear, as in our definition of love, which whether true or false certainly gave clearness and consistency to the discourse.

Phaedr. What is the other principle, Socrates?

Soc. Secondly, there is the faculty of division according to the natural ideas or members, not breaking any part as a bad carver might. But, as the body may be divided into a left side and into a right side, having parts right and left, so in the two discourses there was assumed, first of all, the general idea of unreason, and then one of the two proceeded to divide the parts of the left side and did not desist until he found in them an evil or left-handed love which the speaker justly reviled; and the other leading us to the right portion in which madness lay, found another love, having the same name, but yet divine, which he held up before us and applauded as the author of the greatest benefits.

Phaedr. That is most true.

Soc. I am a great lover of these processes of division

and generalization; they help me to speak and think.
And if I find any man who is able to see unity and
plurality in nature, him I follow, and walk in his step
as if he were a god. And those who have this art, I
have hitherto been in the habit of calling dialecticians;
but God knows whether the name is right or not.
And I should like to know what name you would give
to your or Lysias' disciples, and whether this may not
be that famous art of rhetoric which Thrasymachus
and others practise? Skilful speakers they are, and
impart their skill to any one who will consent to worship them as kings and to bring them gifts.

Phaedr. Yes, they are royal men; but their art is
not the same with the art of those whom you call, and
rightly, in my opinion, dialecticians. Still we are in
the dark about rhetoric.

Soc. What do you mean? The remains of the art,
when all this has been taken away, must be of rare
value; and are not at all to be despised by you and me.
But what are the remains? — tell me that.

Phaedr. There is a great deal surely to be found in
books of rhetoric?

Soc. Yes; thank you for reminding me of that,
there is the prooemium, if I remember rightly — that
is what you mean — the niceties of the art?

Phaedr. Yes.

Soc. There follows the statement of facts, and upon
that witnesses; thirdly, proofs; fourthly, probabilities
are to come; the great Byzantian artist also speaks, if
I am not mistaken, of confirmation and superconfir-
mation.

Phaedr. You mean the excellent Theodorus.

Soc. Yes; and he tells how refutation or further
refutation is to be managed, whether in accusation or
defence. I need hardly mention the Parian Evenus,
who first invented indirect allusions and incidental

praises, and also censures, of which this wise man made a *memoria technica* in verse. But shall

" I to dumb forgetfulness consign "

Tisias and Gorgias, who are not ignorant that probability is superior to truth, and who by force of argument make the little appear great and the great little, and the new old and the old new, and have discovered universal forms, either short or going on to infinity. I remember Prodicus laughing when I told him of this; he said that he had himself discovered the true rule of art, which was to be neither long nor short, but of a convenient length.

Phaedr. Well done, Prodicus.

Soc. Then there is Hippias of Elis, who probably agrees with him.

Phaedr. Yes.

Soc. And there is also Polus, who has schools of diplasiology, and gnomology, and eikonology, and who teaches in them the words of which Licymnius made him a present; they were to give a polish.

Phaedr. Had not Protagoras something of the same sort?

Soc. Yes, rules of correctness and many other fine precepts; for the " sorrows of a poor old man," or any other pathetic case, no one is better than the Chalcedonian giant; he can put a whole company of people into a passion and out of one again by his mighty magic, and is first-rate at inventing or disposing of any sort of calumny on any grounds or none. All of them agree in asserting that a speech should end in a recapitulation, though they do not all agree in the use of this word.

Phaedr. You mean that there should be a summing up of the arguments in order to remind the hearers of them.

Soc. I have now said all that I have to say of the art of rhetoric: have you anything to add?

Phaedr. Not much, nor very important.

Soc. Leave the unimportant and let us bring the really important question into the light of day, which is: What power this art of rhetoric has, and when?

Phaedr. A very great power in public meetings.

Soc. Yes, that is true. But I should like to know whether you have the same feeling as I have about the rhetoricians? To me there seems to be a great many holes in their web.

Phaedr. Give an example.

Soc. I will. Suppose a person to come to your friend Eryximachus, or to his father Acumenus, and say to him: " I know how to apply drugs which shall have either a heating or a cooling effect, and I can give a vomit and also a purge, and all that sort of thing; and knowing all this, as I do, I claim to be a physician and a teacher of physic " — what do you suppose that they would say?

Phaedr. They would be sure to ask him whether he knew " to whom " he would give them, and " when," and " how much."

Soc. And suppose that he were to reply: " No; I know nothing of that; I expect those whom I have taught all this to do that of themselves."

Phaedr. They would reply that he is a madman or a pedant who fancies that he is a physician, because he has read something in a book, or has stumbled on a few drugs, although he has no real understanding of the art of medicine.

Soc. And suppose a person were to come to Sophocles or Euripides and say that he knows how to make a long speech about a small matter, and a short speech about a great matter, and also a sorrowful speech, or a terrible, or threatening speech, or any other kind of speech, and in teaching this fancies that he is teaching the art of tragedy?

Phaedr. They too would surely laugh at him if he fancies that tragedy is anything but the arranging of these elements in a manner suitable to one another and to the whole.

Soc. But I do not suppose that they would be rude to him or revile him. Would they not treat him as a musician would treat a man who thinks that he is a harmonist because he knows how to pitch the highest and lowest note; happening to meet such an one he would not say to him savagely, " Fool, you are mad! " Oh, no; he would rather say to him in a gentle and musical tone of voice: " My good friend, he who would be a harmonist must certainly know this, and yet he may understand nothing of harmony if he has not got beyond your stage of knowledge, for you only know the preliminaries of harmony and not harmonies."

Phaedr. Very true.

Soc. And would not Sophocles say to the display of the would-be tragedian, that this was not tragedy but the preliminaries of tragedy, and would not Acumenus say to the would-be doctor that this was not medicine but the preliminaries of medicine?

Phaedr. Very true.

Soc. And if Adrastus the mellifluous or Pericles heard of these wonderful arts, brachylogies and eikonologies and all the hard names which we have been endeavoring to draw into the light of day, what would they say? Instead of losing temper and applying uncomplimentary epithets, as you and I have been doing to the authors of such an imaginary art, their superior wisdom would rather censure us, as well as them. Have a little patience, Phaedrus and Socrates, they would say, and don't be angry with those who from some want of dialectical skill are unable to define the nature of rhetoric, and consequently suppose that they have found the art in the preliminary conditions of the art, and when they have taught these to others, fancy that they have been teaching the whole art of rhetoric; but as to persuasion in detail and unity of composition, that they regard as an easy thing with which their disciples may supply themselves.

Phaedr. I quite admit, Socrates, that the art of rhetoric which these men teach and of which they write is such as you describe — in that I agree with you. But I still want to know where and how the true art of rhetoric and persuasion is to be acquired.

Soc. The perfection of oratory is, or rather must be, like the perfection of all things, partly given by nature; but this is assisted by art, and if you have the natural power you will be famous as a rhetorician, if you only add knowledge and practice, and in either you may fall short. But the art, as far as there is an art, of rhetoric does not lie in the direction of Tisias or Thrasymachus.

Phaedr. But in what direction then?

Soc. I should conceive that Pericles was the most accomplished of rhetoricians.

Phaedr. What of that?

Soc. All the higher arts require much discussion and lofty contemplation of nature; this is the source of sublimity and perfect comprehensive power. And this, as I conceive, was the quality which, in addition to his natural gifts, Pericles acquired from his happening to know Anaxagoras. He was imbued with the higher philosophy, and attained the knowledge of mind and matter, which was the favorite theme of Anaxagoras, and hence he drew what was applicable to his art.

Phaedr. Explain.

Soc. Rhetoric is like medicine.

Phaedr. How is that?

Soc. Why, because medicine has to define the nature of the body and rhetoric of the soul — if you would proceed, not empirically but scientifically, in the one case to impart health and strength by giving medicine and food, in the other to implant the conviction which you require by the right use of words and principles.

Phaedr. You are probably right in that.

Soc. And do you think that you can know the nature of the soul intelligently without knowing the nature of the whole?

Phaedr. Hippocrates the Asclepiad says that this is the only method of procedure by which the nature even of the body can be understood.

Soc. Yes, friend, and he says truly. Still, we ought not to be content with the name of Hippocrates, but to examine and see whether he has reason on his side.

Phaedr. True.

Soc. Then consider what this is which Hippocrates says, and which right reason says about this or any other nature. Ought we not to consider first whether that which we wish either to learn or to teach is simple or multiform, and if simple, then to inquire what power this has of acting or being acted upon by other, and if multiform, then to number the forms; and see first in the case of one of them, and then in the case of all of them, the several powers which they by nature have of doing or suffering.

Phaedr. That will be the way.

Soc. The method which has not this analysis is like the groping of a blind man. Yet, surely, he who is an artist ought not to admit of a comparison with the blind, or deaf; but he who imparts rules of speech in an artist-like or scientific manner will particularly set forth the nature of that to which he gives his rules, which I suppose is the soul.

Phaedr. Certainly.

Soc. His whole effort is directed towards this, for in this he seeks to produce conviction.

Phaedr. Yes.

Soc. Then clearly, Thrasymachus or any one else who elaborates a system of rhetoric will give an exact description of the nature of the soul; which he will make to appear either as single and same, or, like the body, multiform. That is what we should call showing the nature of the soul.

Phaedr. Exactly.

Soc. He will next proceed to speak of the instruments by which the soul acts or is affected in any way.

Phaedr. True.

Soc. Thirdly, having arranged men and speeches, and their modes and affections in different classes, and fitted them into one another, he will point out the connection between them — he will show why one is naturally persuaded by a particular form of argument, and another not.

Phaedr. That will certainly be a very good way.

Soc. Yes, that is the true and only way in which any subject can be set forth or treated by rules of art, whether in speaking or writing. But the writers of the present day, at whose feet you have sat, improperly conceal all this about the soul which they know quite well. Nor, until they adopt our method of reading and writing, can we admit that they write by rules of art.

Phaedr. What is our method?

Soc. I can not give you the exact details; but I should like to tell you generally, as far as I can, how a man ought to proceed according to rules of art.

Phaedr. Let me hear.

Soc. Oratory is the art of enchanting the soul, and therefore he who would be an orator has to learn the differences of human souls — they are so many and of such a nature, and from them come the differences between man and man — he will then proceed to divide speeches into their different classes. Such and such persons, he will say, are affected by this or that kind of speech in this or that way, and he will tell you why; he must have a theoretical notion of them first, and then he must see them in action, and be able to follow them with all his senses about him, or he will never get beyond the precepts of his masters. But when he is able to say what persons are persuaded by what arguments, and recognize the individual about whom he used to theorize as actually present to him, and say to himself, " This is he and this is the sort of man who ought to have that argument applied to him in order to convince him of this; " — when he has attained the knowledge of all this, and knows also when he should speak and when he should abstain from speaking, and when he should make use of pithy sayings, pathetic appeals, aggravated effects, and all the other figures of speech; — when, I say, he knows the times and seasons of all these things, then, and not till then, he is perfect and a consummate master of his art; but if he fail in any of these points, whether in speaking or teaching or writing them, and says that he speaks by rules of art, he who denies this has the better of him. Well, the teacher will say, is this Phaedrus and Socrates, your account of the art of rhetoric, or am I to look for another?

Phaedr. He must take this, Socrates, for there is no possibility of another, and yet the creation of such an art is not easy.

Soc. That is true; and therefore let us turn the

matter up and down, and see whether there may not be a shorter and easier road; there is no use in taking the longer and more difficult way when there is a shorter and easier one. And I wish that you would try and remember whether there is anything which you have heard from Lysias or any one else which might be of service to us.

Phaedr. If trying would avail, then I might; but I fear that I can not remember anything at the moment.

Soc. Suppose I tell you something which somebody who knows told me.

Phaedr. Certainly.

Soc. May not the wolf, as the proverb says, claim a hearing?

Phaedr. Do you say what can be said for him.

Soc. Well, they say that there is no use in putting a solemn face on a matter, or in going round and round, until you arrive at the beginning of all things; for that when the question is of justice and good, as I said at first, or a question in which men are concerned who are just and good, either by nature or habit, he who would be a skilful rhetorician has no need of truth — for that in courts of law men literally care nothing about truth, but only about conviction: and this is based on probability, to which he who would be a skilful orator should therefore give his whole attention. And they say also that there are cases in which the actual facts ought to be withheld, and only the probabilities should be told either in accusation or defence, and that always in speaking the orator should run after probability, and say good-bye to the truth. And the observance of this principle throughout a speech furnishes the whole art.

Phaedr. That is what the professors of rhetoric do actually say, Socrates, for I remember that although we have touched upon this matter but slightly, the point is all-important with them.

Soc. I dare say that you are familiar with Tisias. Does he not define probability to be that which the many think?

Phaedr. Certainly, he does.

Soc. I believe that he has a clever and ingenious case of this sort: — He supposes a feeble and valiant man to have assaulted a strong and cowardly one, and to have robbed him of his coat or of something or other; he is brought into court, and then Tisias says that both parties should tell lies: the coward should say that he was assaulted by more men than one; the other should prove that they were alone, and should use this argument: " How could a man like me have assaulted a man like him? " The other will not like to confess his own cowardice, and will therefore invent some other lie which his adversary will thus gain an opportunity of refuting. These and others like them are the precepts of the doctors of the art. Am I not right, Phaedrus?

Phaedr. Certainly.

Soc. I can not help feeling that this is a wonderfully mysterious art which Tisias has discovered, or whoever the gentleman was, or whatever his name or country may have been who was the discoverer. Shall we say a word to him or not?

Phaedr. What shall we say to him?

Soc. Let us tell him that, before he appeared, you and I were saying that probability was engendered in the minds of the many by the likeness of the truth, and were setting forth that he who knew the truth would always know how best to discover the resemblances of the truth. If he has anything further to say about the art of speaking we should like to hear him; but if not, we are satisfied with our own view, that unless a man estimates the various characters of his hearers and is able to divide existences into classes and to sum them up in single ideas, he will never be a skilful rhetorician even within the limits of human power. And this art he will not attain without a great deal of trouble, which a good man ought to undergo, not for the sake of speaking and acting before men, but in order that he may be able to say what is acceptable to God and in all things to act acceptably to Him as far as in him lies; for there is a saying of wiser men than ourselves, that a man of sense should not try to please his fellow-servants (at least this should not be his principal object) but his good and noble masters, so that, if the way is long and circuitous, marvel not at this; for, where the end is great, there the way may be permitted to be long, but not for lesser ends such as yours. Truly, the argument may say, Tisias, that if you do not mind going so far, rhetoric has a fair beginning in this.

Phaedr. I think, Socrates, that this is admirable, if only practicable.

Soc. But even to fail in an honorable object is honorable.

Phaedr. True.

Soc. I think that enough has been said of a true and false art of speaking.

Phaedr. Certainly.

Soc. But there is something yet to be said of propriety and impropriety of writing.

Phaedr. Yes.

Soc. Do you know how you can speak or act about rhetoric in a manner which will be acceptable to God?

Phaedr. No, indeed. Do you?

Soc. I have heard a tradition of antiquity, whether true or not antiquity only knows. If we had the truth ourselves, do you think that we should care much about the opinions of men?

Phaedr. That is a question which needs no answer; but I wish that you would tell me what you say that you have heard.

Soc. At the Egyptian city of Naucratis, there was a famous old god, whose name was Theuth; the bird which is called the Ibis was sacred to him, and he was the inventor of many arts, such as arithmetic and calculation and geometry and astronomy and draughts and dice, but his great discovery was the use of letters. Now in those days Thamus was the king of the whole of Upper Egypt, which is the district surrounding that great city which is called by the Hellenes Egyptian Thebes, and they call the god himself Ammon. To him came Theuth and showed his inventions, desiring that the other Egyptians might be allowed to have the benefit of them; he went through them, and Thamus inquired about their several uses, and praised some of them and censured others, as he approved or disapproved of them. There would be no use in repeating all that Thamus said to Theuth in praise or blame of the various arts. But when they came to letters, This, said Theuth, will make the Egyptians wiser and give them better memories; for this is the cure of forgetfulness and of folly. Thamus replied: O most ingenious Theuth, he who has the gift of invention is not always the best judge of the utility or inutility of his own inventions to the users of them. And in this instance a paternal love of your own child has led you to say what is not the fact; for this invention of yours will create forgetfulness in the learners' souls, because they will not use their memories; they will trust to the external written characters and not remember of themselves. You have found a specific, not for memory but for reminiscence, and you give your disciples only the pretence of wisdom; they will be hearers of many things and will have learned nothing; they will appear to be omniscient and will generally know nothing; they will be tiresome, having the reputation of knowledge without the reality.

Phaedr. Yes, Socrates, you can easily invent tales of Egypt, or of any other country that you like.

Soc. There was a tradition in the temple of Dodona that oaks first gave prophetic utterances. The men of that day, unlike in their simplicity to young philosophy, deemed that if they heard the truth even from " oak or rock," that was enough for them; whereas, you seem to think not of the truth but of the speaker, and of the country from which the truth comes.

Phaedr. I acknowledge the justice of your rebuke; and I think that the Theban is right in his view about letters.

Soc. He would be a simple person, and quite without understanding of the oracles Thamus and Ammon, who should leave in writing or receive in writing any art under the idea that the written word would be intelligible or certain; or who deemed that writing was at all better than knowledge and recollection of the same matters.

Phaedr. That is most true.

Soc. I can not help feeling, Phaedrus, that writing is unfortunately like painting; for the creations of the painter have the attitude of life, and yet if you ask them a question they preserve a solemn silence. And the same may be said of speeches. You would imagine that they had intelligence, but if you want to know anything and put a question to one of them, the speaker always gives one unvarying answer. And when they have been once written down they are tossed about anywhere among those who do and among those who do not understand them. And they have no reticences or proprieties towards different classes of persons; and, if they are unjustly assailed or abused, their parent is needed to protect his offspring, for they can not protect or defend themselves.

Phaedr. That again is most true.

Soc. May we not imagine another kind of writing or speaking far better than this is, and having far greater power — which is one of the same family, but lawfully begotten? Let us see what his origin is.

Phaedr. Who is he, and what do you mean about his origin?

Soc. I am speaking of an intelligent writing which is graven in the soul of him who has learned, and can defend itself, and knows when to speak and when to be silent.

Phaedr. You mean the word of knowledge which has a living soul, and of which the written word is properly no more than an image?

Soc. Yes, of course that is what I mean. And I wish that you would let me ask you a question: Would a husbandman, who is a man of sense, take the seeds, which he values and which he wishes to be fruitful, and in sober earnest plant them during the heat of summer, in some garden of Adonis, that he may rejoice when he sees them in eight days appearing in beauty (at least he does that, if at all, only as the show of a festival); but those about which he is in earnest he sows in fitting soil, and practises husbandry, and is satisfied if in eight months they arrive at perfection?

Phaedr. Yes, ·Socrates, that will be his way when he is in earnest; he will do the other, as you say, only as an amusement.

Soc. And can we suppose that he who knows the just and good and honorable has less understanding in reference to his own seeds than the husbandman?

Phaedr. Certainly not.

Soc. Then he will not seriously incline to write them in water with pen and ink or in dumb characters which have not a word to say for themselves and can not adequately express the truth?

Phaedr. No, that is not likely.

Soc. No, that is not likely — in the garden of letters he will plant them only as an amusement, or he will write them down as memorials against the forgetfulness of old age, to be treasured by him and his equals when they, like him, have one foot in the grave; and he will rejoice in beholding their tender growth; and they will be his pastime while others are watering the garden of their souls with banqueting and the like.

Phaedr. A pastime, Socrates, as noble as the other is ignoble, when a man is able to pass time merrily in the representation of justice and the like.

Soc. True, Phaedrus. But nobler far is the serious pursuit of the dialectician, who finds a congenial soul, and then with knowledge engrafts and sows words which are able to help themselves and him who planted them, and are not unfruitful, but have in them seeds which may bear fruit in other natures, nurtured in other ways — making the seed everlasting and the possessors happy to the utmost extent of human happiness.

Phaedr. Yes, indeed, that is far nobler.

Soc. And now, Phaedrus, having agreed upon the premisses we may decide about the conclusion.

Phaedr. About what conclusion?

Soc. About Lysias, whom we censured, and his art of writing, and his discourses, and the rhetorical skill or want of skill which was shown in them; for he brought us to this point. And I think that we are now pretty well informed about the nature of art and its opposite.

Phaedr. Yes, I think with you; but I wish that you would repeat what was said.

Soc. Until a man knows the truth of the several particulars of which he is writing or speaking, and is able to define them as they are, and having defined them again to divide them until they can be no longer divided, and until in like manner he is able to discern the nature of the soul and discover the different modes of discourse which are adapted to different natures, and to arrange and dispose them in such a way that the simple form of speech may be addressed to the simpler nature, and the complex and composite to the complex nature — until he has accomplished all this, he will be unable to handle arguments according to rules of art, as far as their nature allows them to be subjected to art, either for the purpose of teaching or persuading; — that is the view which is implied in the whole preceding argument.

Phaedr. Yes, that was our view, certainly.

Soc. Secondly, as to the justice of the censure which was passed on speaking or writing discourses — did not our previous argument show — ?

Phaedr. Show what?

Soc. That whether Lysias or any other writer that ever was or will be, whether private man or statesman, writes a political treatise in his capacity of legislator, and fancies that there is a great certainty and clearness in his performance, the fact of his writing as he does is only a disgrace to him, whatever men may say. For entire ignorance about the nature of justice and injustice, and good and evil, and the inability to distinguish the dream from the reality, can not in truth be otherwise than disgraceful to him, even though he have the applause of the whole world.

Phaedr. Certainly.

Soc. But he who thinks that in the written word

there is necessarily much which is not serious, and that neither poetry nor prose, spoken or written, are of any great value — if, like the compositions of the rhapsodes, they are only recited in order to be believed, and not with any view to criticism or instruction; and who thinks that even the best of them are but a reminiscence of what we know, and that only in principles of justice and goodness and nobility taught and communicated orally and written in the soul, which is the true way of writing, is there clearness and perfection and seriousness; and that such principles are like legitimate offspring; — being, in the first place, that which the man finds in his own bosom; secondly, the brethren and descendants and relations of this which has been duly implanted in the souls of others; and who cares for them and no others — this is the right sort of man; and you and I, Phaedrus, would pray that we may become like him.

Phaedr. That is most assuredly my desire and prayer.

Soc. And now the play is played out; and of rhetoric enough. Go and tell Lysias that to the fountain and school of the Nymphs we went down, and were bidden by them to convey a message to him and to other composers of speeches — to Homer and other writers of poems, whether set to music or not. And to Solon and the writers of political documents, which they term laws, we are to say that if their compositions are based on knowledge of the truth, and they can defend or prove them, when they are put to the test, by spoken arguments, which leave their writings poor in comparison of them, then they are not only poets, orators, legislators, but worthy of a higher name.

Phaedr. What name is that?

Soc. Wise, I may not call them; for that is a great

name which belongs to God only, — lovers of wisdom or philosophers is their modest and befitting title.

Phaedr. Very good.

Soc. And he who can not rise above his own compilations and compositions, which he has been long patching and piecing, adding some and taking away some, may be justly called poet or speech-maker or law-maker.

Phaedr. Certainly.

Soc. Now go and tell this to your companion.

Phaedr. But there is also a friend of yours who ought not to be forgotten.

Soc. Who is that?

Phaedr. Isocrates the fair.

Soc. What of him?

Phaedr. What message shall we send to him?

Soc. Isocrates is still young, Phaedrus; but I am willing to risk a prophecy concerning him.

Phaedr. What would you prophesy?

Soc. I think that he has a genius which soars above the orations of Lysias, and he has a character of a finer mould. My impression of him is that he will marvellously improve as he grows older, and that all former rhetoricians will be as children in comparison of him. And I believe that he will not be satisfied with this, but that some divine impulse will lead him to things higher still. For there is an element of philosophy in his nature. This is the message which comes from the gods dwelling in this place, and which I will myself deliver to Isocrates, who is my delight; and do you give the other to Lysias who is yours.

Phaedr. I will; and now as the heat is abated let us depart.

Soc. Should we not offer up a prayer first of all to the local deities?

Phaedr. By all means.

Soc. Beloved Pan, and all ye other gods who haunt this place, give me beauty in the inward soul; and may the outward and inward man be at one. May I reckon the wise to be the wealthy, and may I have such a quantity of gold as none but the temperate can carry. Anything more? That prayer, I think, is enough for me.

Phaedr. Ask the same for me, for friends should have all things in common.

Soc. Let us go.

SELECTIONS FROM CHARMIDES, LYSIS, OTHER DIALOGUES AND THE LAWS

CHARMIDES

INTRODUCTION

THE subject of the Charmides is Temperance, which may also
be rendered Moderation, Modesty, Discretion, Wisdom, without
completely exhausting by all these terms the various associations
of the word. It may be described as " mens sana in corpore
sano," the harmony or due proportion of the higher and lower
elements of human nature which " makes a man his own master,"
according to the definition of the Republic. In the accompanying translation the word has been rendered in different places
either Temperance or Wisdom, as the connection seemed to
require.

The beautiful youth, Charmides, who is also the most temperate of human beings, is asked by Socrates, " What is Temperance? " He answers characteristically, (1) " Quietness."
" But temperance is a fine and noble thing; and quietness in
many or most cases is not so fine a thing as quickness." He
tries again and says (2) that temperance is modesty. But this
again is set aside by a sophistical application of Homer: for
temperance is good as well as noble, and Homer has declared
that " modesty is not good for a needy man." (3) Once more
Charmides makes the attempt. This time he gives a definition
which he has heard, and of which he insinuates that Critias is
the author: " Temperance is doing one's own business." But
the artisan who makes another man's shoes may be temperate,
and yet he is not doing his own business. How is this riddle
to be explained?

Critias, who takes the place of Charmides, distinguishes in
his answer between " making " and " doing," and with the help
of a misapplied quotation from Hesiod assigns to the words
" doing " and " work " an exclusively good sense: temperance
is doing one's own business; — (4) is doing good.

Still an element of knowledge is wanting which Critias is

readily induced to admit at the suggestion of Socrates; and, in the spirit of Socrates and of Greek life generally, proposes as a fifth definition, (5) Temperance is self-knowledge. But all sciences have a subject: number is the subject of arithmetic, health of medicine — what is the subject of temperance or wisdom? The answer is that (6) Temperance is the knowledge of what a man knows and of what he does not know. But this is contrary to analogy; there is no vision of vision, but only of visible things; no love of loves, but only of beautiful things; how then can there be a knowledge of knowledge? That which is older, heavier, lighter, is older, heavier, and lighter than something else, not than itself, and this seems to be true of all relative notions — the object of relation is outside of them; at any rate they can only have relation to themselves in the form of that object. Whether there are any such cases of reflex relation or not, and whether that sort of knowledge which we term Temperance is of this reflex nature, has yet to be determined by the great metaphysician. But even if knowledge can know itself, how does the knowledge of what we know imply the knowledge of what we do not know? Besides this, knowledge is an abstraction only, and will not inform us of any particular subject, such as medicine, building, and the like. It may tell us that we or other men know something, but can never tell what we know.

But admitting further that there is such a knowledge of what we know and do not know, which would supply a rule and measure of all things, still there would be no good in this. For temperance is a good, and the knowledge which temperance gives must be of a kind which will do us good. But this universal knowledge does not tend to our happiness or good: the only kind of knowledge which brings happiness is the knowledge of good and evil. To this Critias replies that the science or knowledge of good and evil, and all the other sciences, are regulated by the higher science or knowledge of knowledge. Socrates replies by again dividing the abstract from the concrete, and asks how this knowledge conduces to happiness in the same definite way that medicine conduces to health.

And now, after making all these concessions, which are really inadmissible, we are still as far as ever from ascertaining the nature of temperance, which Charmides has already discovered, and had therefore better rest in the knowledge that the more temperate he is the happier he will be, and not trouble himself with the speculations of Socrates.

In this Dialogue may be noted (1) the Greek ideal of beauty and goodness, the vision of the fair soul in the fair body, realized in the beautiful Charmides; (2) The true conception of medicine as a science of the whole as well as the parts, and of the mind as well as the body, which is playfully intimated in the story of the Thracian; (3) The tendency of the age to verbal distinctions, which here, as in the Protagoras and Cratylus, are ascribed to the ingenuity of Prodicus; also the interpretations or rather parodies of Homer and Hesiod, which are eminently characteristic of Plato and of his age; (4) The germ of an ethical principle contained in the notion that temperance is " doing one's own business," which in the Republic (such is the shifting character of the Platonic philosophy) is given as the definition, not of temperance, but of justice; (5) The beginnings of logic and metaphysics implied in the two questions, whether there can be a science of science? and whether the knowledge of what you know is the same as the knowledge of what you do not know? also in the distinction between " what you know," and " that you know;" here arises the first conception of an absolute self-determined science (the claims of which, however, are set aside by Socrates); as well as the first suggestion of the difficulty of the abstract and concrete, and one of the earliest anticipations of the relation of subject and object, and of the subjective element in knowledge; (6) The conception of a science of good and evil also first occurs here, and may be regarded as an anticipation of the Philebus and Republic, as well as of moral philosophy in later ages.

The dramatic interest of the Dialogue chiefly centres in the youth Charmides, with whom Socrates talks in the kindly spirit of an elder. Some contrast appears to be intended between his youthful simplicity and ingenuousness and the dialectical and rhetorical arts of Critias, who is the grown-up man of the world, not without a tincture of philosophy. But neither in this nor in any other of the dialogues of Plato is that most hated of Athenians displayed in his true character. He is simply a cultivated person who, like his kinsman Plato, is ennobled by the connection of his family with Solon, and had been the follower, if not the disciple, both of Socrates and of the Sophists. In the argument he is not unfair, if allowance is made for a slight rhetorical tendency, and for some desire to save his reputation with the company; in some respects he is nearer the truth than Socrates. Nothing in his language or behavior is unbecoming the guardian of the beautiful Charmides. His love of reputation, which is characteristically Greek, contrasts with the utter absence of this quality and profession of ignorance on the part of Socrates.

The definitions of temperance proceed in regular order from the popular to the philosophical. The first two are simple enough and partially true, like the first thoughts of an intelligent youth; the third, which is a real contribution to ethical philosophy, is perverted by the ingenuity of Socrates, and hardly rescued by an equal perversion on the part of Critias. The remaining definitions have a higher aim, which is to introduce the element of knowledge, and at last to unite good and truth in a single science. But the time has not yet arrived for the realization of this vision of metaphysical philosophy. Hence we see with surprise that Plato, who in his other writings identifies good and knowledge, here opposes them, and asks, almost in the spirit of Aristotle, how can there be a knowledge of knowledge, and even if attainable, how can such a knowledge be of any use?

The relations of knowledge and virtue are again brought forward in the companion Dialogues of the Lysis and Laches; and also in the Protagoras and Euthydemus.

CHARMIDES, OR TEMPERANCE

PERSONS OF THE DIALOGUE

SOCRATES, *who is the narrator.*   CHARMIDES.
CHAEREPHON.   CRITIAS.

SCENE: —The Palaestra of Taureas, which is near the Porch of the King Archon.

YESTERDAY evening I returned from the army at Potidaea, and having been a good while away, I thought that I would go and look at my old haunts. So I went into the palaestra of Taureas, which is over against the temple adjoining the porch of the King Archon, and there I found a number of persons, most of whom I knew, but not all. My visit was unexpected, and no sooner did they see me entering than they saluted me from afar on all sides; and Chaerephon, who is a kind of madman, started up and ran to me, seizing my hand, and saying, How did you escape, Socrates? — (I should explain that an engagement had taken place at Potidaea not long before we came away, the news of which had only just reached Athens.)

You see, I replied, that here I am.

There was a report, he said, that the engagement was very severe, and that many of our acquaintance had fallen.

That, I replied, was not far from the truth.

I suppose, he said, that you were present.

I was.

859

Then sit down, and tell us the whole story, which as yet we have only heard imperfectly.

I took the place which he assigned to me, by the side of Critias the son of Callaeschrus, and when I had saluted him and the rest of the company, I told them the news from the army, and answered their several inquiries.

Then, when there had been enough of this, I, in my turn, began to make inquiries about matters at home — about the present state of philosophy, and about the youth. I asked whether any of them were remarkable for beauty or sense, or both. Critias, glancing at the door, invited my attention to some youths who were coming in, and talking noisily to one another, followed by a crowd. Of the beauties, Socrates, he said, I fancy that you will soon be able to form a judgment. For those who are just entering are the advanced guard of the great beauty of the day, and he is likely to be not far off himself.

Who is he, I said; and who is his father?

Charmides, he replied, is his name; he is my cousin, and the son of my uncle Glaucon: I rather think that you know him, although he was not grown up at the time of your departure.

Certainly, I know him, I said, for he was remarkable even then when he was still a child, and now I should imagine that he must be almost a young man.

You will see, he said, in a moment what progress he has made and what he is like. He had scarcely said the word, when Charmides entered.

Now you know, my friend, that I can not measure anything, and of the beautiful, I am simply such a measure as a white line is of chalk; for almost all young persons are alike beautiful in my eyes. But at that moment, when I saw him coming in, I must admit that I was quite astonished at his beauty and stature; all the world seemed to be enamored of him; amazement and confusion reigned when he entered; and a troop of lovers followed him. That grown-up men like ourselves should have been affected in this way was not surprising, but I observed that there was the same feeling among the boys; all of them, down to the very least child, turned and looked at him as if he had been a statue.

Chaerephon called me and said: What do you think of him, Socrates? Has he not a beautiful face?

That he has, indeed, I said.

But you would think nothing of his face, he replied, if you could see his naked form: he is absolutely perfect.

And to this they all agreed.

By Heracles, I said, there never was such a paragon, if he has only one other slight addition.

What is that? said Critias.

If he has a noble soul; and being of your house, Critias, he may be expected to have this.

He is as fair and good within, as he is without, replied Critias.

Shall we ask him then, I said, to show us, not his body, but his soul, naked and undisguised? he is just of an age at which he will like to talk.

That he will, said Critias, and I can tell you that he is a philosopher already, and also a considerable poet, not in his own opinion only, but in that of others.

That, my dear Critias, I replied, is a distinction which has long been in your family, and is inherited by you from Solon. But why don't you call him, and show him to us? for even if he were younger than he is, there could be no impropriety in his talking to us in the presence of you, who are his guardian and cousin.

Very well, he said; then I will call him; and turning to the attendant, he said, Call Charmides, and tell him that I want him to come and see a physician about the illness of which he spoke to me the day before yesterday. Then again addressing me, he added: He has been complaining lately of having a headache when he rises in the morning: now why should you not make believe to him that you know a cure for the headache?

There will be no difficulty about that, I said, if he comes.

He will be sure to come, he replied.

He came as he was bidden, and sat down between Critias and me. Great amusement was occasioned by every one pushing with might and main at his neighbor in order to make a place for him next to them, until at the two ends of the row one had to get up and the other was rolled over sideways. Now I, my friend, was beginning to feel awkward; my former bold belief in my powers of conversing with him had vanished. And when Critias told him that I was the person who had the cure, he looked at me in such an indescribable manner, and was about to ask a question; and then all the people in the palaestra crowded about us, and, O rare! I caught a sight of the inwards of his garment, and took the flame. Then I could no longer contain myself. I though how well Cydias understood the nature of love, when, in speaking of a fair youth, he warns some one " not to bring the fawn in the sight of the lion lest he devour him," for I felt that I had been overcome by a sort of wild-beast appetite. But I controlled myself, and when he asked me if I knew the cure of the headache, I answered, but with an effort, that I did know.

And what is it? he said.

I replied that it was a kind of leaf, which required to be accompanied by a charm, and if a person would repeat the charm at the same time that he used the cure, he would be made whole; but that without the charm the leaf would be of no avail.

Then I will write out the charm from your dictation, he said.

With my good will? I said, or without my good will?

With your good will, Socrates, he said, laughing.

Very good, I said; and are you quite sure that you know my name?

I ought to know you, he replied, for there is a great deal said about you among my companions; and I remember when I was a child seeing you in company with my cousin Critias.

That is very good of you, I said; and will make me more at home with you in explaining the nature of the charm; I was thinking that I might have a difficulty about this. For the charm will do more, Charmides, than only cure the headache. I dare say that you may have heard eminent physicians say to a patient who comes to them with bad eyes, that they can not cure his eyes by themselves, but that if his eyes are to be cured, his head must be treated; and then again they say that to think of curing the head alone, and not the rest of the body also, is the height of folly. And arguing in this way they apply their methods to the whole body, and try to treat and heal the whole and the part together. Did you ever observe that this is what they say?

Yes, he said.

And they are right, and you would agree with them?

Yes, he said, certainly I should.

His approving answers reassured me, and I began by degrees to regain confidence, and the vital heat returned. Such, Charmides, I said, is the nature of the charm. Now I learned it when serving with the army, of one of the physicians of the Thracian king, Zamolxis. He was one of those who are said to give immortality. This Thracian told me that the Greek physicians are quite right in these notions of theirs, which I was mentioning, as far as they go; but Zamolxis, he added, our king, who is also a god, says further, "that as you ought not to attempt to cure the eyes without the head, or the head without the eyes, so neither ought you to attempt to cure the body without the soul; and this," he said, "is the reason why the cure of many diseases is unknown to the physicians of Hellas, because they are ignorant of the whole, which ought to be studied also; for the part can never be well unless the whole is well." For all good and evil, whether in the body or in human nature, originates, as he declared, in the soul, and overflows from thence, as from the head into the eyes. And therefore if the head and the body are to be well, you must begin by curing the soul; that is the first thing. And the cure, my dear youth, has to be effected by the use of certain charms, and these charms are fair words; and by them temperance is implanted in the soul, and where temperance is, there health is speedily imparted, not only to the head, but to the whole body. And he who taught me the cure and the charm added a special direction; " Let no one," he said, " persuade you to cure the head, until he has first given you his soul to be cured by the charm. For this," he said, " is the great error of our day in the treatment of the human body, that physicians separate the soul from the body." And he added with emphasis, at the same time making me swear to his words, " let no one, however rich, or noble, or fair, persuade you to give him the cure, without the charm." Now I have sworn, and I must keep my oath, and therefore if you will allow me to apply the Thracian charm first to your soul, as the stranger directed, I will afterwards proceed to apply the cure to your head. But if not, I do not know what I am to do with you, my dear Charmides.

Critias, when he heard this, said: The headache will be an unexpected benefit to my young relation, if the pain in his head compels him to improve his mind: and I can tell you, Socrates, that Charmides is not only preëminent in beauty among his equals, but also in that quality which is given by the charm; and this, as you say, is temperance, is it not?

Yes, I said.

Then let me tell you that he is the most temperate of human beings, and for his age inferior to none in any quality.

Yes, I said, Charmides; and indeed I think that you ought to excel others in all good qualities; for if I am not mistaken there is no one present who could easily point out two Athenian houses, the alliance of which was likely to produce a better or nobler son than the two from which you are sprung. There is your father's house, which is descended from Critias the son of Dropidas, whose family has been commemorated in the panegyrical verses of Anacreon, Solon, and many other poets, as famous for beauty and virtue and all other high fortune: and your mother's house is equally distinguished; for your maternal uncle, Pyrilampes, never met with his equal in Persia at the court of the great king, or on the whole continent in all the places to which he went as ambassador, for stature and beauty; that whole family is not a whit inferior to the other. Having such ancestors you ought to be first in all things, and as far as I can see, sweet son of Glaucon, your outward form is no dishonor to them. And if you have temperance as well as beauty, as Critias declares, then blessed art thou, dear Charmides, in being the son of thy mother. And this is the question: if this gift of temperance is already yours, as Critias declares, and you are temperate enough, in that case you have no need of any charms, whether of Zamolxis, or of Abaris the Hyperborean, and I may as well give you the cure of the head at once; but if you are wanting in these qualities, I must use the charm before I give you the medicine. Please, therefore, to inform me whether you admit the truth of what Critias has been saying about your gift of temperance, or are you wanting in this particular?

Charmides blushed, and the blush heightened his beauty, for modesty is becoming in youth; he then said very ingenuously, that he really could not say at once, either yes, or no, in answer to the question which I had asked: For, said he, if I affirm that I am not temperate, that would be a strange thing to say of myself, and also I should have to give the lie to Critias, and many others, who think that I am temperate, as he tells you: but, on the other hand, if I say that I am, I shall have to praise myself, which would be ill manners; and therefore I have no answer to make to you.

I said to him: That is a natural reply, Charmides, and I think that you and I may as well inquire together whether you have this quality about which I am asking or not; and then you will not be compelled to say what you do not like; neither shall I be a rash practitioner of medicine: therefore, if you please, I will join with you in the inquiry, but I will not press you if you would rather not.

There is nothing which I should like better, he said; and as far as I am concerned you may proceed in the way which you think best.

I think, I said, that I had better begin by asking you, What is Temperance? for you must have an opinion about this: if temperance abides in you, she must give some intimation of her nature and qualities, which may enable you to form some notion of her. Is not that true?

Yes, he said, that I think is true.

And as you speak Greek, I said, you can surely describe what this appears to be, which you have within you.

Certainly, he said.

In order, then, that I may form a conjecture whether you have temperance abiding in you or not, tell me, I said, what, in your opinion, is Temperance?

At first he hesitated, and was very unwilling to answer: then he said that he thought temperance was doing things orderly and quietly, such things for example as walking in the streets, and talking, or anything else of that nature. In a word, he said, I should answer that, in my opinion, temperance is quietness.

Are you right, Charmides? I said. No doubt the opinion is held that the quiet are the temperate; but let us see whether they are right who say this; and first tell me whether you would not acknowledge temperance to be of the class of the honorable and good?

Yes.

But which is best when you are at the writing-master's, to write the same letters quickly or quietly?

Quickly.

And to read quickly or slowly?

Quickly again.

And in playing the lyre, or wrestling, quickness or cleverness are far better than quietness and slowness?

Yes.

And the same holds in boxing and the pancratium?

Certainly.

And in leaping and running, and bodily exercises generally, quickness and agility are good; slowness, and inactivity, and quietness, are bad?

That is evident.

Then, I said, in all bodily actions, not quietness, but the greatest agility and quickness, is noblest and best?

Yes, certainly.

And is temperance a good?

Yes.

Then, in reference to the body, not quietness, but quickness will be the higher degree of temperance, if temperance is a good?

True, he said.

And which, I said, is better — facility in learning, or difficulty in learning?

Facility.

Yes, I said; and facility in learning is learning quickly, and difficulty in learning is learning quietly and slowly?

True.

And is it not better to teach one another quickly and energetically, rather than quietly and slowly?

Yes.

And to call to mind, and to remember, quickly and readily — that is also better than to remember quietly and slowly?

Yes.

And is not shrewdness a quickness or cleverness of the soul, and not a quietness?

True.

And is it not best to understand what is said, whether at the writing-master's or the music-master's, or anywhere else, not as quietly as possible, but as quickly as possible?

Yes.

And when the soul inquires, and in deliberations, not the quietest, as I imagine, and he who with difficulty deliberates and discovers, is thought worthy of praise, but he who does this most easily and quickly?

That is true, he said.

And in all that concerns either body or soul, swiftness and activity are clearly better than slowness and quietness?

That, he said, is the inference.

Then temperance is not quietness, nor is the temperate life quiet, upon this view; for the life which is temperate is supposed to be the good. And of two things, one is true, — either never, or very seldom, do the quiet actions in life appear to be better than the quick and energetic ones; or, granting ever so much that of the nobler sort of actions, there are as many quiet, as quick and vehement ones: still, even if we admit this, temperance will not be acting quietly any more than acting quickly and vehemently, either in walking, talking, or anything else; nor will the quiet life be more temperate than the unquiet, seeing that temperance is reckoned by us in the class of good and honorable, and the quick have been shown to be as good as the quiet.

I think, he said, Socrates, that you are right in saying that.

Then once more, Charmides, I said, fix your attention, and look within; consider the effect which temperance has upon yourself, and the nature of that which has the effect. Think over that, and, like a brave youth, tell me — What is temperance?

After a moment's pause, in which he made a real manly effort to think, he said: My opinion is, Socrates, that temperance makes a man ashamed or modest, and that temperance is the same as modesty.

Very good, I said; and did you not admit, just now, that temperance is honorable?

Yes, certainly, he said.

And the temperate are also good?

Yes.

And can that be good which does not make men good?

Certainly not.

And you would infer that temperance is not only honorable, but also good?

That is my opinion.

Well, I said; and surely you would agree with Homer when he says,

" Modesty is not good for a needy man "?

Yes, he said; I agree to that.

Then I suppose that modesty is and is not good?

That is plain.

But temperance, whose presence makes men only good, and not bad, is always good?

That appears to me to be as you say.

Then the inference is, that temperance can not be modesty — if temperance is a good, and if modesty is as much an evil as a good?

All that, Socrates, appears to me to be true; but I should like to know what you think about another definition of temperance, which I just now remember to have heard from some one, who said, " That temperance is doing our own business." Was he right who affirmed that?

You young monster! I said; this is what Critias, or some philosopher has told you.

Some one else, then, said Critias; for certainly I have not.

But what matter, said Charmides, from whom I heard this?

No matter at all, I replied; for the point is not who said the words, but whether they are true or not.

There you are in the right, Socrates, he replied.

To be sure, I said; yet I doubt whether we shall ever be able to discover their truth or falsehood; for they are a riddle.

What makes you think that? he said.

Because, I said, he who uttered them seems to me to have meant one thing, and said another. Is the scribe, for example, to be regarded as doing nothing when he reads or writes?

I should rather think that he was doing something.

And does the scribe write or read, or teach you boys to write or read, your own names only, or did you write your enemies' names as well as your own and your friends'?

As much one as the other.

And was there anything meddling or intemperate in this?

Certainly not.

And yet, if reading and writing are the same as doing, you were doing what was not your own business?

But they are the same as doing.

And the healing art, my friend, and building, and weaving, and doing anything whatever which is done by art, all come under the head of doing?

Certainly.

And do you think that a state would be well ordered by a law which compelled every man to weave and wash his own coat, and make his own shoes, and his own flask and strigil, and other implements, on this principle of every one doing and performing his own, and abstaining from what is not his own?

I think not, he said.

But, I said, a temperate state will be a well-ordered state.

Of course, he replied.

Then temperance, I said, will not be doing one's own business; at least not in this way, or not doing these sort of things?

Clearly not.

Then, as I was just now saying, he who declared that temperance is a man doing his own business had another and a hidden meaning; for I don't think that he could have been such a fool as to mean this. Was he a fool who told you, Charmides?

Nay, he replied, I certainly thought him a very wise man.

Then I am quite certain that he put forth this as a riddle: he meant to say that there was a difficulty in a man knowing what is his own business.

I dare say, he replied.

And what, then, is the meaning of a man doing his own business? Can you tell me?

Indeed, I can not, he said; and I shouldn't wonder if he who said this had no notion of his own meaning. And in saying this he laughed slyly, and looked at Critias.

Critias had long been showing uneasiness, for he felt that he had a reputation to maintain with Charmides and the rest of the company. He had, however, hitherto managed to restrain himself; but now he could no longer forbear, and his eagerness satisfied me of the truth of my suspicion, that Charmides had heard this answer about temperance from Critias. And Charmides, who did not want to answer himself, but to make Critias answer, tried to stir him up. He went on pointing out that he had been refuted, and at this Critias got angry, and, as I thought, was rather inclined to quarrel with him; just as a poet might quarrel with an actor who spoiled his poems in repeating them; so he looked hard at him and said —

Do you imagine, Charmides, that the author of the definition of temperance did not understand the meaning of his own words, because you don't understand them?

Why, at his age, I said, most excellent Critias, he can hardly be expected to understand; but you, who are older, and have studied, may well be assumed to know the meaning of them; and therefore, if you agree with him, and accept his definition of temperance, I would much rather argue with you than with him about the truth or falsehood of the definition.

I entirely agree, said Critias, and accept the definition.

Very good, I said; and now let me repeat my question — Do you admit, as I was just now saying, that all craftsmen make or do something.

I do.

And do they make or do their own business only, or that of others also?

They make that of others also.

And are they temperate, seeing that they make not for themselves or their own business only?

Why not? he said.

No objection on my part, I said, but there may be a difficulty on his who proposes as a definition of temperance, " doing one's own business," and then says that there is no reason why those who do the business of others should not be temperate.

Nay, said he; did I ever acknowledge that those who do the business of others are temperate? I said, those who make, not those who do.

What! I asked; do you mean to say that doing and making are not the same?

No more, he replied, than making or working are the same: that I have learned from Hesiod, who says that "work is no disgrace." Now do you imagine that if he had meant by working such things as you were describing, he would have said that there was no disgrace in them? in making shoes, for example, or in selling pickles, or sitting for hire in a house of ill fame. That, Socrates, is not to be supposed: but, as I imagine, he distinguished making from action and work; and, while admitting that the making anything might sometimes become a disgrace, when the employment was not honorable, thought that work was never any disgrace at all. For things nobly and usefully made he called works; and such makings he called workings, and doings; and he must be supposed to have called such things only man's proper business, and what is hurtful, not his business: and in that sense Hesiod, and any other wise man, may be reasonably supposed to call him wise who does his own work.

O Critias, I said, no sooner had you opened your mouth, than I pretty well knew that you would call that which is proper to a man, and that which is his own, good; and that the making of the good you would call doings, for I have heard Prodicus drawing endless distinctions about names. Now I have no objection to your giving names any sense that you please, if you will only tell me what you mean by them. Please then to begin again, and be a little plainer. Do you not mean that this doing or making, or whatever is the word which you would use, of good actions, is temperance?

I do, he said.

Then not he who does evil, but he who does good, is temperate?

Yes, he said; and you would agree to that.

Never mind whether I agree or not; as yet we are only concerned with your meaning.

Well, he answered; I mean to say, that he who does evil, and not good, is not temperate; and that he is temperate who does good, and not evil: for temperance I define in plain words to be the doing of good actions.

And you may be very likely right in that, I said; but I am curious to know whether you imagine that temperate men are ignorant of their own temperance?

I do not imagine that, he said.

And yet were you not saying, not so very long ago, that craftsmen might be temperate in doing another's work, as well as their own?

Yes, I was, he replied; but why do you refer to that?

I have no particular reason, but I wish you would tell me whether a physician who cures a patient may do good to himself and good to another also?

I think that he may.

And he who does this does his duty. And does not he who does his duty act temperately or wisely?

Yes, he acts wisely.

But must the physician necessarily know when his treatment is likely to prove beneficial, and when not? or must the craftsman necessarily know when he is likely to be benefited, and when not to be benefited, by the work which he is doing?

I suppose not.

Then, I said, he may sometimes do good or harm, and not know what he is himself doing, and yet, in doing good, as you say, he has done temperately or wisely. Was not that your statement?

Yes.

Then, as would seem, in doing good, he may act

wisely or temperately, and be wise or temperate, but not know his own wisdom or temperance?

But that, Socrates, he said, is impossible; and therefore if that is, as you imply, the necessary consequence of any of my previous admissions, I would rather withdraw them, and not be ashamed to confess that I was mistaken, than admit that a man can be temperate or wise, who does not know himself. For self-knowledge would certainly be maintained by me to be the very essence of knowledge, and in this I agree with him who dedicated the inscription, " Know thyself! " at Delphi. That word, if I am not mistaken, is put there as a sort of salutation which the god addresses to those who enter the temple; as much as to say that the ordinary salutation of " Hail! " is not right, and that the exhortation "'Be temperate! '" would be a far better way of saluting one another. The notion of him who dedicated the inscription was, as I believe, that the god speaks to those who enter his temple not as men speak; but, when a worshipper enters, the first word which he hears is " Be temperate! " This, however, like a prophet he expresses in a sort of riddle, for " Know thyself! " and " Be temperate! " are the same, as I maintain, and as the writing implies, and yet they may be easily misunderstood; and succeeding sages who added " Never too much," or " Give a pledge, and evil is nigh at hand," would appear to have misunderstood them; for they imagined that " Know thyself! " was a piece of advice which the god gave, and not his salutation of the worshippers at their first coming in; and they wrote their inscription under the idea that they would give equally useful pieces of advice. Shall I tell you, Socrates, why I say all this? My object is to leave the previous discussion (in which I know not whether you or I are more right, but, at any rate, no clear result was attained), and to raise a new one in which I will attempt to prove, if you deny, that temperance is self-knowledge.

Yes, I said, Critias; but you come to me as though I professed to know about the questions which I ask, and as though I could, if only I would, agree with you. Whereas the fact is that I am, as you are, an inquirer into the truth of your proposition; and when I have inquired, I will say whether I agree with you or not. Please then to allow me time to reflect.

Reflect, he said.

I am reflecting, I replied, and discover that temperance, or wisdom, if implying a knowledge of anything, must be a science, and a science of something.

Yes, he said; the science of itself.

And is not medicine, I said, the science of health?

True.

And suppose, I said, that I were asked by you what is the use or effect of medicine, which is this science of health, I should answer that medicine is of very great use in producing health, which, as you will admit, is an excellent effect.

Granted.

And if you were to ask me, what is the result or effect of architecture, which is the science of building, I should say, houses, and so of other arts, which all have their different results. Now I want you, Critias, to answer a similar question about temperance, or wisdom, to which you ought to know the answer, if, as you say, wisdom or temperance is the science of itself. Admitting this, I ask, what good work, worthy of the name, does wisdom effect? Answer me that.

That is not the true way of pursuing the inquiry, Socrates, he said; for wisdom is not like the other sciences, any more than they are like one another: but you proceed as if they were alike. For tell me, he said, what result is there of computation or geometry, in the same sense as a house is the result of building, or a garment of weaving, or any other work of any other art? Can you show me any such result of them? You can not.

That is true, I said; but still each of these sciences has a subject which is different from the science. I can show you that the art of computation has to do with odd and even numbers in their numerical relations to themselves and to each other. Is not that true?

Yes, he said.

And the odd and even numbers are not the same with the art of computation?

They are not.

The art of weighing, again, has to do with lighter and heavier; but the art of weighing is one thing, and the heavy and the light another. Do you admit that?

Yes.

Now, I want to know, what is that which is not wisdom, and of which wisdom is the science?

That is precisely the old error, Socrates, he said. You come asking in what wisdom differs from the other sciences; and then you carry on the inquiry, as if they were alike: but that is not the case, for all the other sciences are of something else, and not of themselves; but that alone is a science of other sciences, and of itself. And of this, as I believe, you are very well aware; and that you are only doing what you denied that you were doing just now, leaving the argument and trying to refute me.

And what if I am refuting you? How can you think that I have any other motive in this but what I should have in examining into myself? which motive would be just a fear of my unconsciously fancying that I knew something of which I was ignorant.

And at this moment I pursue the inquiry chiefly for my own sake, and perhaps in some degree also for the sake of my other friends. For is not the discovery of things as they truly are a common good to all mankind?

Yes, certainly, Socrates, he said.

Then, I said, be of good cheer, sweet sir, and give your opinion in answer to the question which I asked, without minding whether Critias or Socrates is the person refuted; attend only to the argument, and see what will come of the refutation.

I think that you are right, he replied; and I will do as you say.

Tell me, then, I said, what you mean to affirm about wisdom.

I mean, he said, that wisdom is the only science which is the science of itself and of the other sciences as well.

But the science of science, I said, will also be the science of the absence of science.

Very true, he said.

Then the wise or temperate man, and he only, will know himself, and be able to examine what he knows or does not know, and see what others know, and think that they know and do really know; and what they do not know, and fancy that they know, when they do not. No other person will be able to do this. And this is the state and virtue of wisdom, or temperance, and self-knowledge, which is just knowing what a man knows, and what he does not know. That is your view?

Yes, he said.

Now then, I said, making an offering of the third or last argument to Zeus the Savior, let us once more begin, and ask, in the first place, whether this knowledge that you know and do not know what you know and do not know is possible; and in the second place, whether, even if quite possible, such knowledge is of any use.

That is what we must consider, he said.

And here, Critias, I said, I hope that you will find a way out of a difficulty into which I have got myself. Shall I tell you the difficulty?

By all means, he replied.

Does not what you have been saying, if true, amount to this: that there must be a science which is wholly a science of itself, and also of other sciences, and that the same is also the science of the absence of science?

True.

But consider how monstrous this is, my friend: in any parallel case, the impossibility will be transparent to you.

How is that? and in what cases do you mean?

In such cases as this: Suppose that there is a kind of vision which is not like ordinary vision, but a vision of itself and of other sorts of vision, and of the defect of them, which in seeing sees no color, but only itself and other sorts of vision. Do you think that there is such a kind of vision?

Certainly not.

Or is there a kind of hearing which hears no sound at all, but only itself and other sorts of hearing, or the defects of them?

There is not.

Or take all the senses: can you imagine that there is any sense of itself and of other senses, but which is incapable of perceiving the objects of the senses?

I think not.

Could there be any desire which is not the desire of any pleasure, but of itself, and of all other desires?

Certainly not.

Or can you imagine a wish which wishes for no good, but only for itself and all other wishes?

I should answer, No.

Or would you say that there is a love which is not the love of beauty, but of itself and of other loves?

I should not.

Or did you ever know of a fear which fears itself or other fears, but has no object of fear?

I never did, he said.

Or of an opinion which is an opinion of itself and of other opinions, and which has no opinion on the subjects of opinion in general?

Certainly not.

But surely we are assuming a science of this kind, which, having no subject-matter, is a science of itself and of the other sciences; for that is what is affirmed. Now this is strange, if true: however, we must not as yet absolutely deny the possibility of such a science; let us rather consider the matter.

You are quite right.

Well then, this science of which we are speaking is a science of something, and is of a nature to be a science of something?

Yes.

Just as that which is greater is of a nature to be greater than something?[1]

Yes.

Which is less, if the other is to be conceived as greater?

To be sure.

And if we could find something which is at once greater than self, and greater than other great things,

---

[1] Socrates is intending to show that science differs from the object of science, as any other relative differs from the object of relation. A relation to self as well as to other things involves in the case of comparison of magnitudes an absolute contradiction; and in other cases, as in the case of the senses, is hardly conceivable.

but not greater than those things in comparison of which the others are greater, then that thing would have the property of being greater and also less than itself?

That, Socrates, he said, is the inevitable inference.

Or if there be a double which is double of other doubles and of itself, they will be halves; for the half is relative to the double?

That is true.

And that which is greater than itself will also be less, and that which is heavier will also be lighter, and that which is older will also be younger: and the same of other things; that which has a nature relative to self will retain also the nature of its object. I mean to say, for example, that hearing is, as we say, of sound or voice. Is that true?

Yes.

Then if hearing hears itself, it must hear a voice; for there is no other way of hearing.

Certainly.

And sight also, my excellent friend, if it sees itself must see a color, for sight can not see that which has no color.

No.

Then do you see, Critias, that in several of the examples which have been recited the notion of a relation to self is altogether inadmissible, and in other cases hardly credible — inadmissible, for example, in the case of magnitudes, numbers, and the like.

Very true.

But in the case of hearing, and the power of self-motion, and the power of heat to burn, this relation to self will be regarded as incredible by some, but perhaps not by others. And some great man, my friend, is wanted, who will satisfactorily determine for us, whether there is nothing which has an inherent property of relation to self, or some things only and not others; and whether in this latter class, if there be such a class, that science which is called wisdom or temperance is included. I altogether distrust my own power of determining this: I am not certain whether there is such a science of science at all; and even if there be, I should not acknowledge this to be wisdom or temperance, until I can also see whether such a knowledge would or would not do us any good; for I have an impression that temperance is a benefit and a good. And therefore, O son of Callaeschrus, as you maintain that temperance or wisdom is a science of science, and also of the absence of science, I will request you to show in the first place, as I was saying before, the possibility, and in the second place, the advantage, of such a science; and then perhaps you may satisfy me that you are right in your view of temperance.

Critias heard me say this, and saw that I was in a difficulty; and as one person when another yawns in his presence catches the infection of yawning from him, so did he seem to be driven into a difficulty by my difficulty. But as he had a reputation to maintain, he was ashamed to admit before the company that he could not answer my challenge or decide the question at issue; and he made an unintelligible attempt to hide his perplexity. In order that the argument might proceed, I said to him, Well then, Critias, if you like, let us assume that there may be this science of science; whether the assumption is right or wrong may be hereafter investigated. But fully admitting this, will you tell me how such a science enables us to distinguish what we know or do not know, which, as we were saying, is self-knowledge or wisdom. That is what we were saying?

Yes, Socrates, he said; and that I think is certainly

true: for he who has that science or knowledge which knows itself will become like that knowledge which he has, in the same way that he who has swiftness will be swift, and he who has beauty will be beautiful, and he who has knowledge will know. In the same way he who has that knowledge which is the knowledge of itself, will know himself.

I do not doubt, I said, that a man will know himself, when he possesses that which has self-knowledge: but what necessity is there that, having this, he should know what he knows and what he does not know?

Because, Socrates, they are the same.

Very likely, I said; but I remain as stupid as ever; for still I fail to comprehend how this knowing what you know and do not know is the same as the knowledge of self.

What do you mean? he said.

This is what I mean, I replied: I will admit that there is a science of science, but can this do more than determine that of two things one is and the other is not science or knowledge?

No, just that.

Then is knowledge or want of knowledge of health the same as knowledge or want of knowledge of justice?

Certainly not.

The one is medicine, and the other is politics; but that of which we are speaking is knowledge pure and simple.

Very true.

And if a man knows only, and has only knowledge of knowledge, and has no further knowledge of health and justice, the probability is that he will only know that he knows something, and has a certain knowledge, whether concerning himself or other men.

True.

But how will this knowledge or science teach him to know what he knows? Say that he knows health; — not wisdom or temperance, but the art of medicine has taught him that; — and he has learned harmony from the art of music, and building from the art of building, — neither, from wisdom or temperance: and the same of other things.

That is evident.

But how will wisdom, regarded only as a knowledge of knowledge or science of science, ever teach him that he knows health, or that he knows building?

That is impossible.

Then he who is ignorant of this will only know that he knows, but not what he knows?

True.

Then wisdom or being wise appears to be not the knowledge of the things which we do or do not know, but only the knowledge that we know and do not know?

That is the inference.

Then he who has this knowledge will not be able to examine whether a pretender knows or does not know that which he says that he knows: he will only know that he has a knowledge of some kind; but wisdom will not show him of what the knowledge is?

Plainly not.

Neither will he be able to distinguish the pretender in medicine from the true physician, nor between any other true and false possessor of knowledge. Let us consider the matter in this way: If the wise man or any other man wants to distinguish the true physician from the false, what is he to do? He will not talk to him about medicine; and that, as we are saying, is the only thing which the physician understands.

True.

And he certainly knows nothing of science, for this has been assumed to be the province of wisdom.

True.

But then again, if medicine is a science, neither will the physician know anything of medicine.

Exactly.

The wise man will indeed know that the physician has some kind of science or knowledge; but when he wants to discover the nature of this he will ask, What is the subject-matter? For each science is distinguished, not as science, but by the nature of the subject. Is not that true?

Yes; that is quite true.

And medicine is distinguished from other sciences as having the subject-matter of health and disease?

Yes.

And he who would inquire into the nature of medicine must pursue the inquiry into health and disease, and not into what is extraneous?

True.

And he who judges rightly will judge of the physician as a physician in what relates to these?

He will.

He will consider whether what he says is true, and whether what he does is right in relation to these?

He will.

But can any one appreciate either without having a knowledge of medicine?

He can not.

Nor any one but the physician, not even the wise man, as appears; for that would require him to be a physician as well as a wise man?

Very true.

Then, assuredly, wisdom or temperance, if only a science of science, and of the absence of science or knowledge, will not be able to distinguish the physician who knows from one who does not know but pretends or thinks that he knows, or any other professor of anything at all; like any other artist, he will only know his fellow in art or wisdom, and no one else.

That is evident, he said.

But then what profit, Critias, I said, is there any longer in wisdom or temperance which yet remains, if this is wisdom? If, indeed, as we were supposing at first, the wise man had been able to distinguish what he knew and did not know, and that he knew the one and did not know the other, and to recognize a similar faculty of discernment in others, there would certainly have been a great advantage in being wise; for then we should never have made a mistake, but have passed through life the unerring guides of ourselves and of those who were under us; and we should not have attempted to do what we did not know, but we should have found out those who knew, and confided in them; nor should we have allowed those who were under us to do anything which they were not likely to do well; and they would be likely to do well just that of which they had knowledge; and the house or state which was ordered or administered under the guidance of wisdom would have been well ordered, and everything else of which wisdom was the lord; for truth guiding, and error having been expelled, in all their doings, men would have done well, and would have been happy. Was not this, Critias, what we spoke of as the great advantage of wisdom — to know what is known and what is unknown to us?

Very true, he said.

And now you perceive, I said, that no such science is to be found anywhere.

I perceive, he said.

May we assume then, I said, that wisdom, viewed in this new light merely as a knowledge of knowledge and ignorance, has this advantage: — that he who possesses such knowledge will more easily learn anything that he learns; and that everything will be clearer to him, because, in addition to the knowledge of individuals, he sees the science, and this also will better enable him to test the knowledge which others have of what he knows himself; whereas the inquirer who is without this knowledge may be supposed to have a feebler and weaker insight? Are not these, my friend, the real advantages which are to be gained from wisdom? And are not we looking and seeking after something more than is to be found in her?

That is very likely, he said.

That is very likely, I said; and very likely, too, we have been inquiring to no purpose. I am led to infer this, because I observe that if this is wisdom, some strange consequences would follow. Let us, if you please, assume the possibility of this science of sciences, and further admit and allow, as was originally suggested, that wisdom is the knowledge of what we know and do not know. Assuming all this, still, upon further consideration, I am doubtful, Critias, whether wisdom, if such as this, would do us any good. For I think we were wrong in supposing, as we were saying just now, that such wisdom ordering the government of house or state would be a great benefit.

How is that? he said.

Why, I said, we were far too ready to admit the great benefits which mankind would obtain from their severally doing the things which they knew, and committing to others who knew the things of which they are ignorant.

Were we not right, he said, in making that admission?

I think not, I said.

That is certainly strange, Socrates.

By the dog of Egypt, I said, I am of your opinion about that: and that was in my mind when I said that strange consequences would follow, and that I was afraid we were on the wrong track; for however ready we may be to admit that this is wisdom, I certainly can not make out what good this sort of thing does to us.

What do you mean? he said; I wish that you could make me understand what you mean.

I dare say that what I am saying is nonsense, I replied; and yet if a man has any feeling of what is due to himself, he can not let the thought which comes into his mind pass away unheeded and unexamined.

I like that, he said.

Hear, then, I said, my own dream; whether coming through the horn or the ivory gate, I can not tell. The dream is this: Let us suppose that wisdom is such as we are now defining, and that she has absolute sway over us; then each action will be done according to the arts or sciences, and no one professing to be a pilot when he is not, or any physician or general, or any one else pretending to know matters of which he is ignorant, will deceive or elude us; our health will be improved; our safety at sea, and also in battle, will be assured; our coats and shoes, and all other instruments and implements will be well made, because the workmen will be good and true. Aye, and if you please, you may suppose that prophecy, which is the knowledge of the future, will be under the control of wisdom, and that she will deter deceivers and set up the true prophet in their place as the revealer of the future. Now I quite agree that mankind, thus provided, would live and act according to knowledge, for wisdom would watch and prevent ignorance from intruding on us. But we have not as yet discovered why, because we act according to knowledge, we act well and are happy, my dear Critias.

Yet I think, he replied, that you will hardly find any other end of right action, if you reject knowledge.

And of what is this knowledge? I said. Just answer me that small question. Do you mean a knowledge of shoemaking?

God forbid.

Or of working in brass?

Certainly not.

Or in wool, or wood, or anything of that sort?

No, I do not.

Then, I said, we are giving up the doctrine that he who lives according to knowledge is happy, for these live according to knowledge, and yet they are not allowed by you to be happy; but I think that you mean to confine happiness to particular individuals who live according to knowledge, such for example as the prophet, who, as I was saying, knows the future.

Yes, I mean him, but there are others as well.

Yes, I said, some one who knows the past and present as well as the future, and is ignorant of nothing. Let us suppose that there is such a person, and if there is, you will allow that he is the most knowing of all living men.

Certainly he is.

Yet I should like to know one thing more: which of the different kinds of knowledge makes him happy? or do all equally make him happy?

Not all equally, he replied.

But which most tends to make him happy? the knowledge of what past, present, or future thing? May I infer this to be the knowledge of the game of draughts?

Nonsense about the game of draughts.

Or of computation?

No.

Or of health?

That is nearer the truth, he said.

And that knowledge which is nearest of all, I said, is the knowledge of what?

The knowledge with which he discerns good and evil.

Monster! I said; you have been carrying me round in a circle, and all this time hiding from me the fact that the life according to knowledge is not that which makes men act rightly and be happy, not even if all the sciences be included, but that this has to do with one science only, that of good and evil. For, let me ask you, Critias, whether, if you take away this science from all the rest, medicine will not equally give health, and shoemaking equally produce shoes, and the art of the weaver clothes? — whether the art of the pilot will not equally save our lives at sea, and the art of the general in war?

Quite so.

And yet, my dear Critias, none of these things will be well or beneficially done, if the science of the good be wanting.

That is true.

But that science is not wisdom or temperance, but a science of human advantage; not a science of other sciences, or of ignorance, but of good and evil: and if this be of use, then wisdom or temperance will not be of use.

And why, he replied, will not wisdom be of use? For if we really assume that wisdom is a science of sciences, and has a sway over other sciences, surely she will have this particular science of the good under her control, and in this way will benefit us.

And will wisdom give health? I said; is not this rather the effect of medicine? Or does wisdom do the work of any of the other arts, and do not they do, each of them, their own work? Have we not long ago asseverated that knowledge is only the knowledge of knowledge and of ignorance, and of nothing else?

That is clear.

Another art is concerned with health.

Another.

The art of health is different.

Yes, different.

Nor does wisdom give advantage, my good friend; for that again we have just now been attributing to another art.

Very true.

How then can wisdom be advantageous, giving no advantage?

That, Socrates, is certainly inconceivable.

You see then, Critias, that I was not far wrong in fearing that I could have no sound notion about wisdom; I was quite right in depreciating myself; for that which is admitted to be the best of all things would never have seemed to us useless, if I had been good for anything at an inquiry. But now I have been utterly defeated, and have failed to discover what that is to which the imposer of names gave this name of temperance or wisdom. And yet many more admissions were made by us than could be really granted; for we admitted that there was a science of science, although the argument said No, and protested against this; and we admitted further, that this science knew the works of the other sciences (although this too was denied by the argument), because we wanted to show that the wise man had knowledge of what he knew and did not know; also we nobly disregarded, and never even considered, the impossibility of a man knowing in a sort of way that which he does not know at all; for our assumption was, that he knows that which he does not know; than which nothing, as I think, can be more irrational. And yet, after finding

us so easy and good-natured, the inquiry is still unable
to discover the truth; but mocks us to a degree, and
has gone out of its way to prove the inutility of that
which we admitted only by a sort of supposition and
fiction to be the true definition of temperance or wisdom: which result, as far as I am concerned, is not so
much to be lamented, I said. But for your sake,
Charmides, I am very sorry — that you, having such
beauty and such wisdom and temperance of soul,
should have no profit or good in life from your wisdom and temperance. And still more am I grieved
about the charm which I learned with so much pain,
and to so little profit, from the Thracian, for the sake
of a thing which is nothing worth. I think indeed that
there is a mistake, and that I must be a bad inquirer,
for I am persuaded that wisdom or temperance is
really a great good; and happy are you if you possess
that good. And therefore examine yourself, and see
whether you have this gift and can do without the
charm; for if you can, I would rather advise you to
regard me simply as a fool who is never able to reason
out anything; and to rest assured that the more wise
and temperate you are, the happier you will be.

Charmides said: I am sure that I do not know,
Socrates, whether I have or have not this gift of wisdom and temperance: for how can I know whether I
have that, the very nature of which even you and
Critias, as you say, are unable to discover? — (not
that I believe you.) And further, I am sure,
Socrates, that I do need the charm, and as far as I am
concerned, I shall be willing to be charmed by you
daily, until you say that I have had enough.

Very good, Charmides, said Critias; if you do this
I shall have a proof of your temperance, that is, if you
allow yourself to be charmed by Socrates. and never
desert him at all.

You may depend on my following and not deserting him, said Charmides: if you who are my guardian command me, I should be very wrong not to obey you.

And I do command you, he said.

Then I will do as you say, and begin this very day.

You sirs, I said, what are you conspiring about?

We are not conspiring, said Charmides, we have conspired already.

And are you about to use violence, without even going through the forms of justice?

Yes, I shall use violence, he replied, since he orders me; and therefore you had better consider well.

But the time for consideration has passed, I said, when violence is employed; and you, when you are determined on anything, and in the mood of violence, are irresistible.

Do not you resist me then, he said.

I will not resist you, I replied.

LYSIS, OR FRIENDSHIP

INTRODUCTION

No answer is given in the Lysis to the question, "What is Friendship?" any more than in the Charmides to the question, "What is Temperance?" There are several resemblances in the two Dialogues: the same youthfulness and sense of beauty pervades both of them; they are alike rich in the description of Greek life. The question is again raised of the relation of knowledge to virtue and good, which also recurs in the Laches; and Socrates appears again as the elder friend of the two boys Lysis and Menexenus. In the Charmides, as also in the Laches, he is described as middle-aged; in the Lysis he is advanced in years.

The Dialogue consists of two scenes or conversations which seem to have no relation to each other. The first is a conversation between Socrates and Lysis, who, like Charmides, is an Athenian youth of noble descent and of great beauty, goodness, and intelligence: this is carried on in the absence of Menexenus, who is called away to take part in a sacrifice. Socrates asks Lysis whether his father and mother do not love him very much? "Yes, that they do." "Then of course they allow him to do exactly as he likes." "Of course not: the very slaves have more liberty than he has." "But how is this?" "The reason is that he is not old enough." "No; the real reason is that he is not wise enough." "For are there not some things which he is allowed to do, although he is not allowed to do others?" "Yes, because he knows them, and does not know the others." This leads to the conclusion that all men everywhere will trust him in what he knows, but not in what he does not know; for in such matters he will be unprofitable to them, and do them no good. And no one will love him, if he does them no good; and he can only do them good by knowledge; and as he is still without knowledge, he has no conceit of knowledge. In this manner Socrates reads a lesson to Hippothales, the foolish lover of Lysis, respecting the style of conversation which he should address to his beloved.

After the return of Menexenus, Socrates, at the request of Lysis, asks him a new question: "What is friendship? You,

895

Menexenus, who have a friend already, can tell me, who am always longing to find one, what is the secret of this great blessing."

When one man loves another, which is the friend — he who loves, or he who is loved? or are both friends? From the first of these suppositions they are driven to the second; and from the second to the third; and neither the two boys nor Socrates are satisfied with any of them. Socrates turns to the poets, who affirm that God brings like to like (Homer), and to philosophers (Empedocles), who assert also that like is the friend of like. But the bad are not friends, for they are not even like themselves, and still less are they like one another. And the good have no need of one another, and therefore do not care about one another. Moreover there are others who say that likeness is a cause of aversion, and unlikeness of love and friendship; and they too adduce the authority of poets and philosophers in support of their doctrines; for Hesiod says that "potter is jealous of potter, bard of bard;" and subtle doctors tell us that "moist is the friend of dry, hot of cold," and the like. But neither can their doctrine be maintained; for then the just would be the friend of the unjust, good of evil.

Thus we arrive at the conclusion that like is not the friend of like, nor unlike of unlike; and therefore good is not the friend of good, nor evil of evil, nor good of evil, nor evil of good. What remains but that the indifferent, which is neither good nor evil, should be the friend (not of the indifferent, for that would be "like the friend of like," but) of the good?

But why should the indifferent have this attachment to the good? There are circumstances under which such an attachment would be natural. Suppose the indifferent, say the human body, to be desirous of getting rid of some evil, such as disease, which is not essential but only accidental to it (for if the evil were essential the body would cease to be indifferent, and would become evil) — in such a case the indifferent becomes a friend of the good for the sake of getting rid of the evil. In this intermediate "indifferent" position the philosopher or lover of wisdom stands: he is not wise, and yet not unwise, but he has ignorance accidentally clinging to him, and he yearns for wisdom as the cure of the evil.

After this explanation has been received with triumphant accord, a fresh dissatisfaction begins to steal over the mind of Socrates: Must not friendship be for the sake of some ulterior end? and what can that final cause or end of friendship be, other than the good? But the good is desired by us only as the cure of evil; and therefore if there were no evil there would be no friendship. Some other explanation then has to be devised. May not desire be the source of friendship? And desire is of what a man wants and of what is congenial to him. But then again, the congenial can not be the same as the like; for like can not be the friend of like. Nor can the congenial be explained as the good; for good is not the friend of good, as has been also shown. The problem is unsolved, and the three friends, Socrates, Lysis, and Menexenus, are still unable to find out what a friend is.

Thus, as in the Charmides and Laches, and several of the other Dialogues of Plato, no conclusion is arrived at. The dialogue is what would be called in the language of Thrasyllus tentative or inquisitive. The subject is continued in the Phaedrus and Symposium, and treated, with a manifest reference to the Lysis, in the eighth and ninth books of the Nicomachean Ethics of Aristotle. As in other writings of Plato (for example, the Republic), there is a progress from unconscious morality, illustrated by the unconscious friendship of the two youths, and also by the sayings of the poets ("who are our fathers in wisdom," and yet only tell us half the truth, and in this particular instance are not much improved upon by the philosophers), to a more comprehensive notion of friendship. This, however, is far from being cleared of its perplexity. Two notions appear to be struggling or balancing in the mind of Socrates: — First, the sense that friendship arises out of human needs and wants; Secondly, that the higher form or ideal of friendship exists only for the sake of the good. That friends are not necessarily either like or unlike, is also a truth confirmed by experience. But the use of the terms " like " or " good " is too strictly limited; Socrates has allowed himself to be carried away by a sort of eristic or illogical logic against which the truest definition of friendship would be unable to stand. The sense of the interdependence of good and evil, and the allusion to the possibility of the nonexistence of evil, are very curious.

The dialectical interest is fully sustained by the dramatic accompaniments. Observe, first, the scene, which is a Greek Palaestra, at a time when a sacrifice is going on, and the Hermaea are in course of celebration; secondly, the " accustomed irony " of Socrates, who declares, as in the Symposium, that he is ignorant of all other things, but claims to have a knowledge of the mysteries of love. There are also several contrasts of character;

first of the dry, caustic Ctesippus, of whom Socrates professes a humorous sort of fear, and Hippothales the flighty lover, who murders sleep by bawling out the name of his beloved; also there is a contrast between the false, exaggerated, sentimental love of Hippothales towards Lysis, and the simple and innocent friendship of the boys with one another. Some difference appears to be intended between the characters of the more talkative Menexenus and the reserved and simple Lysis. Socrates draws out the latter by a new sort of irony, which is sometimes adopted in talking to children, and consists in asking a leading question which can only be answered in a sense contrary to the intention of the question: " Your father and mother of course allow you to drive the chariot? " " No they don't." When Menexenus returns, the serious dialectic begins.

LYSIS, OR FRIENDSHIP

PERSONS OF THE DIALOGUE

SOCRATES, *who is the narrator.*   MENEXENUS.
HIPPOTHALES.   LYSIS.

CTESIPPUS.

SCENE: —A newly-erected Palaestra outside the walls of Athens.

I WAS going from the Academy straight to the Lyceum, intending to take the outer road, which is close under the wall. When I came to the postern gate of the city, which is by the fountain of Panops, I fell in with Hippothales, the son of Hieronymus, and Ctesippus the Paeanian, and a company of young men who were standing with them. Hippothales, seeing me approach, asked whence I came and whither I was going.

I am going, I replied, from the Academy straight to the Lyceum.

Then come straight to us, he said, and put in here; you may as well.

Who are you, I said; and where am I to come?

He showed me an enclosed space and an open door over against the wall. And there, he said, is the building at which we all meet: and a goodly company we are.

And what is this building, I asked; and what sort of entertainment have you?

The building, he replied, is a newly-erected Palaestra; and the entertainment is generally conversation to which you are welcome.

Thank you, I said; and is there any teacher there?

Yes, he said, your old friend and admirer, Miccus.

Indeed, I replied; he is a very eminent professor.

Are you disposed, he said, to go with me and see them?

Yes, I said; but I should like to know first, what is expected of me, and who is the favorite among you.

Some persons have one favorite, Socrates, and some another, he said.

And who is yours? I asked: tell me that, Hippothales.

At this he blushed; and I said to him, O Hippothales, thou son of Hieronymus! do not say that you are, or that you are not, in love; the confession is too late; for I see not only that you are in love, but that you are already far gone in your love. Simple and foolish as I am, the Gods have given me the power of understanding these sort of affections.

At this he blushed more and more.

Ctesippus said: I like to see you blushing, Hippothales, and hesitating to tell Socrates the name; when, if he were with you but for a very short time, he would be plagued to death by hearing of nothing else. Indeed, Socrates, he has literally deafened us, and stopped our ears with the praises of Lysis; and if he is a little intoxicated, there is every likelihood that we may have our sleep murdered with a cry of Lysis. His performances in prose are bad enough, but nothing at all in comparison with his verse; and when he drenches us with his poems and other compositions, that is really too bad; and what is even worse, is his manner of singing them to his love; this he does in a voice which is truly appalling, and we can not help hearing him: and now he has a question put to him by you, and lo! he is blushing.

Who is Lysis? I said: I suppose that he must be young; for the name does not recall any one to me.

Why, he said, his father being a very well-known man, he retains his patronymic, and is not as yet commonly called by his own name; but, although you do not know his name, I am sure that you must know his face, for that is quite enough to distinguish him.

But tell me whose son he is, I said.

He is the eldest son of Democrates, of the deme of Aexonè.

Ah, Hippothales, I said; what a noble and really perfect love you have found! I wish that you would favor me with the exhibition which you have been making to the rest of the company, and then I shall be able to judge whether you know what a lover ought to say about his love, either to the youth himself, or to others.

Nay, Socrates, he said; you surely do not attach any weight to what he is saying.

Do you mean, I said, that you disown the love of the person whom he says that you love?

No; but I deny that I make verses or address compositions to him.

He is not in his right mind, said Ctesippus; he is talking nonsense, and is stark mad.

O Hippothales, I said, if you have ever made any verses or songs in honor of your favorite, I do not want to hear them; but I want to know the purport of them, that I may be able to judge of your mode of approaching your fair one.

Ctesippus will be able to tell you, he said; for if, as he avers, I talk to him of nothing else, he must have a very accurate knowledge and recollection of that.

Yes, indeed, said Ctesippus; I know only too well; and very ridiculous the tale is: for although he is a lover, and very devotedly in love, he has nothing particular to talk about to his beloved which a child might not say.　Now is not that ridiculous?　He can only speak of the wealth of Democrates, which the whole city celebrates, and grandfather Lysis, and the other ancestors of the youth, and their stud of horses, and their victory at the Pythian games, and at the Isthmus, and at Nemea with four horses and single horses; and these he sings and says, and greater twaddle still. For the day before yesterday he made a poem in which he described how Heracles, who was a connection of the family, was entertained by an ancestor of Lysis as his relation; this ancestor was himself the son of Zeus and the daughter of the founder of the deme. And these are the sort of old wives' tales which he sings and recites to us, and we are obliged to listen to him.

When I heard this, I said: O ridiculous Hippothales! how can you be making and singing hymns in honor of yourself before you have won?

But my songs and verses, he said, are not in honor of myself, Socrates.

You think not, I said.

But what are they, then? he replied.

Most assuredly, I said, those songs are all in your own honor; for if you win your beautiful love, your discourses and songs will be a glory to you, and may be truly regarded as hymns of praise composed in honor of you who have conquered and won such a love; but if he slips away from you, the more you have praised him, the more ridiculous you will look at having lost this fairest and best of blessings; and this is the reason why the wise lover does not praise his beloved until he has won him, because he is afraid of accidents.　There is also another danger; the fair, when any one praises or magnifies them, are filled with the spirit of pride and vain-glory. Is not that true?

Yes, he said.

And the more vain-glorious they are, the more difficult is the capture of them?

I believe that.

What should you say of a hunter who frightened away his prey, and made the capture of the animals which he is hunting more difficult?

He would be a bad hunter, that is clear.

Yes; and if, instead of soothing them, he were to infuriate them with words and songs, that would show a great want of wit: don't you agree with me?

Yes.

And now reflect, Hippothales, and see whether you are not guilty of all these errors in writing poetry. For I can hardly suppose that you will affirm a man to be a good poet who injures himself by his poetry.

Assuredly not, he said: I should be a fool if I said that; and this makes me desirous, Socrates, of taking you into my counsels, and I shall be glad of any further advice which you may have to offer. Will you tell me by what words or actions I may become endeared to my love?

That is not easy to determine, I said; but if you will bring your love to me, and will let me talk with him, I may perhaps be able to show you how to converse with him, instead of singing and reciting in the fashion of which you are accused.

There will be no difficulty in bringing him, he replied; if you will only go into the house with Ctesippus, and sit down and talk, he will come of himself; for he is fond of listening, Socrates. And as this is the festival of the Hermaea, there is no separation of young men and boys, but they are all mixed up together. He will be sure to come: but if he does not come, Ctesippus, with whom he is familiar, and whose relation Menexenus is his great friend, shall call him.

That will be the way, I said. Thereupon I and Ctesippus went towards the Palaestra, and the rest followed.

Upon entering we found that the boys had just been sacrificing; and this part of the festival was nearly come to an end. They were all in white array, and games at dice were going on among them. Most of them were in the outer court amusing themselves; but some were in a corner of the Apodyterium playing at odd and even with a number of dice, which they took out of little wicker baskets. There was also a circle of lookers on, one of whom was Lysis. He was standing among the other boys and youths, having a crown upon his head, like a fair vision, and not less worthy of praise for his goodness than for his beauty. We left them, and went over to the opposite side of the room, where we found a quiet place, and sat down; and then we began to talk. This attracted Lysis, who was constantly turning round to look at us — he was evidently wanting to come to us. For a time he hesitated and had not the courage to come alone; but first of all, his friend Menexenus came in out of the court in the interval of his play, and when he saw Ctesippus and myself, came and sat by us; and then Lysis, seeing him, followed, and sat down with him; and the other boys joined. I should observe that Hippothales, when he saw the crowd, got behind them, where he thought that he would be out of sight of Lysis, lest he should anger him; and there he stood and listened.

I turned to Menexenus, and said: Son of Demophon, which of you two youths is the elder?

That is a matter of dispute between us, he said.

And which is the nobler? Is that a matter of dispute too?

Yes, certainly.

And another disputed point is, which is the fairer? The two boys laughed.

I sha'n't ask which is the richer, I said; for you two are friends, are you not?

Certainly, they replied.

And friends have all things in common, so that one of you can be no richer than the other, if you say truly that you are friends.

They assented. I was about to ask which was the juster of the two, and which was the wiser of the two; but at this moment Menexenus was called away by some one who came and said that the gymnastic-master wanted him. As I imagine, he had to offer sacrifice. So he went away, and I asked Lysis some more questions. I dare say, Lysis, I said, that your father and mother love you very much.

That they do, he said.

And they would wish you to be perfectly happy.

Yes.

But do you think that any one is happy who is in the condition of a slave, and who can not do what he likes?

I should think not indeed, he said.

And if your father and mother love you, and desire that you should be happy, no one can doubt that they are very ready to promote your happiness.

Certainly, he replied.

And do they then permit you to do what you like, and never rebuke you or hinder you from doing what you desire?

Yes, indeed, Socrates; there are a great many things which they hinder me from doing.

What do you mean? I said. Do they want you to be happy, and yet hinder you from doing what you like? — for example, if you want to mount one of your father's chariots, and take the reins at a race, they will not allow you to do that; they will prevent you?

Certainly, he said, they will not allow me to do that.

Whom then will they allow?

There is a charioteer, whom my father pays for driving.

And do they trust a hireling more than you? and may he do what he likes with the horses? and do they pay him for this?

They do.

But I dare say that you may take the whip and guide the mule-cart if you like; — they will permit that?

Permit me! no they won't.

Then, I said, may no one use the whip to the mules?

Yes, he said, the muleteer.

And is he a slave or a free man?

A slave, he said.

And do they esteem a slave of more value than you who are their son? And do they entrust their property to him rather than to you? and allow him to do what he likes, when you may not? Answer me now: Are you your own master, or do they not even allow that?

Nay, he said; of course they do not allow that.

Then you have a master?

Yes, my tutor; there he is.

And is he a slave?

To be sure; he is our slave, he replied.

Surely, I said, this is a strange thing, that a free man should be governed by a slave. And what does he do with you?

He takes me to my teachers.

You don't mean to say that your teachers also rule over you?

Of course they do.

Then I must say that your father is pleased to inflict many lords and masters on you. But at any rate when you go home to your mother, she will let you have your own way, and will not interfere with your happiness; her wool, or the piece of cloth she is weaving, are at your disposal: I am sure that there is nothing to hinder you from touching her wooden spathe, or her comb, or any other of her spinning implements.

Nay, Socrates, he replied, laughing; not only does she hinder me, but I should be beaten, if I were to touch one of them.

Well, I said, that is amazing. And did you ever behave ill to your father or your mother?

No, indeed, he replied.

But why then are they so terribly anxious to prevent you from being happy, and doing as you like? — keeping you all day long in subjection to another, and, in a word, doing nothing which you desire; so that you have no good, as would appear, out of their great possessions, which are under the control of anybody rather than of you, and have no use of your own fair person, which is committed to the care of a shepherd; while you, Lysis, are master of nobody, and can do nothing?

Why, he said, Socrates, the reason is that I am not of age.

I doubt whether that is the real reason, I said; for as far as that goes, I should imagine that your father Democrates, and your mother, do permit you to do many things already, and do not wait until you are of age: for example, if they want anything read or written, you, I presume, would be the first person in the house who is summoned by them.

Very true.

And you would be allowed to write or read the letters in any order which you please, or take up the lyre and tune the notes, and play with the fingers, or strike with the plectrum, exactly as you please, and neither father nor mother would interfere with you.

That is true, he said.

Then what can be the reason, Lysis, I said, why they allow you to do the one and not the other?

I suppose, he said, that the reason is that I understand the one, and not the other.

Yes, my dear youth, I said, the reason is not any deficiency of years, but a deficiency of knowledge; and whenever your father thinks that you are wiser than he is, he will instantly commit himself and his possessions to you.

That I believe.

Aye, I said; and about your neighbor, too, does not the same rule hold as about your father? If he is satisfied that you know more of housekeeping than he does, will he continue to administer his affairs himself, or will he commit them to you?

I think that he will commit them to me.

And will not the Athenian people, too, entrust their affairs to you when they see that you have wisdom enough for his?

Yes.

Now, I said, let me put a case. Suppose the great king to have an eldest son, who is the Prince of Asia; and you and I go to him and establish to his satisfaction that we are better cooks than his son, will he not entrust to us the prerogative of making soup, and putting in anything that we like while the boiling is going on, rather than to the Prince of Asia, who is his son?

To us, clearly.

And we shall be allowed to throw in salt by handfuls, whereas the son will not be allowed to put in as much as he can take up between his fingers?

Of course.

Or suppose again that the son has bad eyes, will he allow him, or will he not allow him, to touch his own eyes if he thinks that he has no knowledge of medicine?

He will not allow him.

Whereas, if we are supposed to have a knowledge of medicine, he will allow us to open the eyes wide and sprinkle ashes upon them, because he supposes that we know what is best?

That is true.

And everything in which we appear to him to be wiser than himself or his son he will commit to us?

That is very true, Socrates, he replied.

Then now, my dear youth, I said, you perceive that in things which we know every one will trust us, — Hellenes and barbarians, men and women, — and we may do as we please, and no one will like to interfere with us; and we are free, and masters of others; and these things will be really ours, for we shall turn them to our good. But in things of which we have no understanding, no one will trust us to do as seems good to us — they will hinder us as far as they can; and not only strangers, but father and mother, and the friend, if there be one, who is dearer still, will also hinder us; and we shall be subject to others; and these things will not be ours, for we shall turn them to no good. Do you admit that?

He assented.

And shall we ever be friends to others? and will any others love us, in as far as we are useless to them?

Certainly not.

Neither can your father or mother love you, nor

can anybody love anybody else, in as far as they are useless to them?

No.

And therefore, my boy, if you are wise, all men will be your friends and kindred, for you will be useful and good; but if you are not wise, neither father, nor mother, nor kindred, nor any one else, will be your friends. And not having yet attained to wisdom, can you have high thoughts about that of which you have no thoughts?

How can I? he said.

And you have no wisdom, for you require a teacher? True.

And you are not conceited, having nothing of which to be conceited?

Indeed, Socrates, I think not.

When I heard him say this, I turned to Hippothales, and was very nearly making a blunder, for I had a mind to say to him: That is the way, Hippothales, in which you should talk to your beloved, humbling and lowering him, and not as you do, puffing him up and spoiling him. But I saw that he was in great excitement and confusion at what had been said; and I remembered that, although he was in the neighborhood, he did not want to be seen by Lysis, so I thought better and refrained.

In the meantime Menexenus came back and sat down in his place by Lysis; and Lysis, in a childish and affectionate manner, whispered privately in my ear, so that Menexenus should not hear: Do, Socrates, tell Menexenus what you have been telling me.

Suppose that you tell him yourself, Lysis, I replied; for I am sure that you were attending.

That I was, he replied.

Try, then, to remember the words, and be as exact

as you can in repeating them to him, and if you have forgotten anything, ask me again the next time that you see me.

I will be sure to do that, Socrates; but go on telling him something new, and let me hear, as long as I am allowed to stay.

I certainly can not refuse, I said, as you ask me; but then, as you know, Menexenus is very pugnacious, and therefore you must come to the rescue if he attempts to upset me.

Yes, indeed, he said; he is very pugnacious, and that is the reason why I want you to argue with him.

That I may make a fool of myself?

No, indeed, he said; but that you may put him down.

That is no easy matter, I replied; for he is a terrible fellow — a pupil of Ctesippus. And there is Ctesippus: do you see him?

Never mind, Socrates, you shall argue with him.

Well, I suppose I must, I replied.

Hereupon Ctesippus complained that we were talking in secret, and keeping the feast to ourselves.

I shall be happy, I said, to let you have a share. Here is Lysis, who does not understand something that I was saying, and wants me to ask Menexenus, who, as he thinks, will be able to answer.

And why don't you ask him? he said.

Very well, I said, I will ask him; and do you, Menexenus, answer. But first I must tell you that I am one who from my childhood upward have set my heart upon a certain thing. All people have their fancies; some desire horses, and others dogs; and some are fond of gold, and others of honor. Now, I have no violent desire of any of these things; but I have a passion for friends; and I would rather have a good friend than the best cock or quail in the world: I would even go further, and say than a horse or dog. Yea, by the dog of Egypt, I should greatly prefer a real friend to all the gold of Darius, or even to Darius himself: I am such a lover of friends as that. And when I see you and Lysis, at your early age, so easily possessed of his treasure, and so soon, he of you, and you of him, I am amazed and delighted, seeing that I myself, although I am now advanced in years, am so far from having made a similar acquisition, that I do not even know in what way a friend is acquired. But this is the question which I want to ask you, as you have experience: tell me then, when one loves another, is the lover or the beloved the friend; or may either be the friend?

Either, he said, may be the friend.

Do you mean, I said, that if only one of them loves the other, they are mutual friends?

Yes, he said; that is my meaning.

But what if the lover is not loved in return? That is a possible case.

Yes.

Or is, perhaps, even hated? for that is a fancy which lovers sometimes have. Nothing can exceed their love; and yet they imagine either that they are not loved in return, or that they are hated. Is not that true?

Yes, he said, quite true.

In that case, the one loves, and the other is loved?

Yes.

Then which is the friend of which? Is the lover the friend of the beloved, whether he be loved in return, or hated; or is the beloved the friend; or is there no friendship at all on either side, unless they both love one another?

There would seem to be none at all.

Then that is at variance with our former notion.

That appears to be true.

Then no one is a friend to his friend who does not love in return?

I think not.

Then they are not lovers of horses, whom the horses do not love in return; nor lovers of quails, nor of dogs, nor of wine, nor of gymnastic exercises, who have no return of love; no, nor of wisdom, unless wisdom loves them in return. Or perhaps they do love them, but they are not beloved by them; and the poet was wrong who sings: —

" Happy the man to whom his children are dear, and steeds having single hoofs, and dogs of chase, and the stranger of another land."

I do not think that he was wrong.

Then you think that he is right?

Yes.

Then, Menexenus, the conclusion is, that what is beloved may be dear, whether loving or hating: for example, very young children, too young to love, or even hating their father or mother when they are punished by them, are never dearer to them than at the time when they are hating them.

I think that is true, he said.

Then on this view, not the lover, but the beloved, is the friend or dear one; and the hated one, and not the hater, is the enemy?

That is plain.

Then many men are loved by their enemies, and hated by their friends, and are the friends of their enemies, and the enemies of their friends — that follows if the beloved is dear, and not the lover: but this, my dear friend, is an absurdity, or, I should rather say, an impossibility.

That, Socrates, I believe to be true.

But then, if not the enemy, the lover will be the friend, of that which is loved?

True.

And the hater will be the enemy of that which is hated?

Certainly.

Yet there is no avoiding the admission in this, as in the preceding instance, that a man may love one who is not his friend, or who may be his enemy. There are cases in which a lover loves, and is not loved, or is perhaps hated; and a man may be the enemy of one who is not his enemy, and is even his friend: for example, when he loves that which does not hate him, or even hates that which loves him.

That appears to be true.

But if the lover is not a friend, nor the beloved a friend, nor both together, what are we to say? Whom are we to call friends to one another? Do any remain?

Indeed, Socrates, I can not find any.

But, O Menexenus! 1 said, may we not have been altogether wrong in our conclusions?

I am sure that we have been wrong, Socrates, said Lysis. And he blushed at his own words, as if he had not intended to speak, but the words escaped him involuntarily in his eagerness; there was no mistaking his attentive look while he was listening.

I was pleased at the interest which was shown by Lysis, and I wanted to give Menexenus a rest, so I turned to him, and said, I think, Lysis, that what you say is true, and that we, if we had been right, should never have gone so far wrong; let us proceed no further in this direction (for the road seems to be getting troublesome), but take the other in which the poets will be our guide; for they are to us in a manner the fathers and authors of wisdom, and they speak of friends in no light or trivial manner, but God himself, as they say, makes them and draws them to one another; and this they express, if I am not mistaken, in the following words: —

" God is ever drawing like towards like, and making them acquainted."

I dare say that you have heard those words.

Yes, he said; I have.

And have you not also met with the treatises of philosophers who say that like must love like? they are the people who go talking and writing about nature and the universe.

That is true, he said.

And are they right in saying that?

They may be.

Perhaps, I said, about half right, or probably altogether right, if their meaning were rightly apprehended by us. For the more a bad man has to do with a bad man, and the more nearly he is brought into contact with him, the more he will be likely to hate him, for he injures him, and injurer and injured can not be friends. Is not that true?

Yes, he said.

Then one half of the saying is untrue, if the wicked are like one another?

That is true.

But people really mean, as I suppose, that the good are like one another, and friends to one another; and that the bad, as is often said of them, are never at unity with one another or with themselves, but are passionate and restless: and that which is at variance and enmity with itself is not likely to be in union or harmony with any other thing. Don't you agree to that?

Yes, I do.

Then, my friend, those who say that the like is

friendly to the like mean to intimate, if I do not misapprehend, that the good only is the friend of the
good, and of him only; but that the evil never attains
to any real friendship, either with good or evil. Do
you agree?

He nodded assent.

Then now we know how to answer the question
" Who are friends? " for the argument supplies the
answer, " That the good are friends."

Yes, he said, that is true.

Yes, I replied; and yet I am not quite satisfied
with this. Shall I tell you what I suspect? I will.
Assuming that like, inasmuch as he is like, is the
friend of like, and useful to him — or rather let me
try another way of putting the matter: Can like do
any good or harm to like which he could not do to
himself, or suffer anything from his like which he
would not suffer from himself? And if neither can
be of any use to the other, how can they be loved by
one another? Can they now?

They can not.

And can he who is not loved be a friend?

Certainly not.

But say that the like is not the friend of the like
in as far as he is like; still the good may be the friend
of the good in as far as he is good.

True.

But then again, will not the good, in as far as he
is good, be sufficient for himself? And he who is
sufficient wants nothing — that is implied in the word
sufficient?

Of course not.

And he who wants nothing will desire nothing?

He will not.

Neither can he love that which he does not desire?

He can not.

And he who loves not is not a lover or friend?

Clearly not.

What place then is there for friendship, if, when absent, good men have no desire of one another (for when alone they are sufficient for themselves), and when present have no use of one another? How can such persons ever be induced to value one another?

They can not.

And friends they can not be, unless they value one another?

Very true.

But see now, Lysis, how we are being deceived in all this; are we not entirely wrong?

How is that? he said.

Have I not heard some one say, as I just now recollect, that the like is the greatest enemy of the like, the good of the good? — and in fact he quoted the authority of Hesiod, who says, " That potter quarrels with potter, bard with bard, beggar with beggar; " and of all other things he also says " That of necessity the most like are most full of envy, strife, and hatred of one another, and the most unlike of friendship. For the poor man is compelled to be the friend of the rich, and the weak requires the aid of the strong, and the sick man of the physician; every one who knows not has to love and court him who knows." And indeed he went on to say in grandiloquent language, that the idea of friendship existing between similars is not the truth, but the very reverse of the truth, and that the most opposed are the most friendly; for that everything desires not like but unlike: for example, the dry desires the moist, the cold the hot, the bitter the sweet, the sharp the blunt, the void the full, the full the void, and so of all other things; for the opposite is the food of the opposite, whereas like receives nothing from like. And I thought that he was a charming man who said this, and that he spoke well. What do the rest of you say?

I should say, at first hearing, that he is right, said Menexenus.

Then are we to say that the greatest friendship is of opposites?

Exactly.

Yes, Menexenus; but will not that be a monstrous answer? and will not the all-wise eristics be down upon us in triumph, and ask, fairly enough, whether love is not the very opposite of hate? and what answer shall we make to them? must we not admit that they speak truly?

That we must.

They will ask whether the enemy is the friend of the friend, or the friend the friend of the enemy?

Neither, he replied.

Well, but is a just man the friend of the unjust, or the temperate of the intemperate, or the good of the bad?

I do not see how that is possible.

And yet, I said, if friendship goes by contraries, the contraries must be friends.

They must.

Then neither like and like nor unlike and unlike are friends.

I suppose not.

And yet there is a further consideration: may not all these notions of friendship be erroneous? but still may there not be cases in which that which is neither good nor bad is the friend of the good?

How do you mean? he said.

Why really, I said, the truth is that I don't know; but my head is dizzy with thinking of the argument, and therefore I hazard the conjecture, that the beautiful is the friend, as the old proverb says. Beauty is certainly a soft, smooth, slippery thing, and therefore of a nature which easily slips in and permeates our souls. And I further add that the good is the beautiful. You will agree to that?

Yes.

This I say from a sort of notion that what is neither good nor evil is the friend of the beautiful and the good, and I will tell you why I am inclined to think this: I assume that there are three principles — the good, the bad, and that which is neither good nor bad. What do you say to that?

I agree.

And neither is the good the friend of the good, nor the evil of the evil, nor the good of the evil; — that the preceding argument will not allow; and therefore the only alternative is — if there be such a thing as friendship or love at all — that what is neither good nor evil must be the friend, either of the good, or of that which is neither good nor evil, for nothing can be the friend of the bad.

True.

Nor can like be the friend of like, as we were just now saying.

True.

Then that which is neither good nor evil can have no friend which is neither good nor evil.

That is evident.

Then the good alone is the friend of that only which is neither good nor evil.

That may be assumed to be certain.

And does not this seem to put us in the right way? Just remark, that the body which is in health requires neither medical nor any other aid, but is well enough; and the healthy man has no love of the physician, because he is in health.

He has none.

But the sick loves him, because he is sick?

Certainly.

And sickness is an evil, and the art of medicine a good and useful thing?

Yes.

But the human body, viewed as a body, is neither good nor evil?

True.

And the body is compelled by reason of disease to court and make friends of the art of medicine?

Yes.

Then that which is neither good nor evil becomes the friend of good, by reason of the presence of evil?

That is the inference.

And clearly this must have happened before that which was neither good nor evil had become altogether corrupted with the element of evil, for then it would not still desire and love the good; for, as we were saying, the evil can not be the friend of the good.

That is impossible.

Further, I must observe that some substances are assimilated when others are present with them; and there are some which are not assimilated: take, for example, the case of an ointment or color which is put on another substance.

Very good.

In such a case, is the substance which is anointed the same as the color or ointment?

What do you mean? he said.

This is what I mean, I said: Suppose that I were to cover your auburn locks with white lead, would they be really white, or would they only appear to be white?

They would only appear to be white, he replied.

And yet whiteness would be present in them. But that would not make them at all the more white, notwithstanding the presence of white in them — they would be neither white nor black.

True.

But when old age superinduces in them the same color, then they become assimilated, and are white by the presence of white.

Certainly.

Now I want to know whether in all cases a substance is assimilated by the presence of another substance; or must the presence be after a peculiar sort?

The latter, he said.

Then that which is neither good nor evil may be in the presence of evil, and not be wholly evil, and that has happened before now?

True.

Then when anything is in the presence of evil, but is not as yet evil, the presence of good arouses the desire of good in that thing; but the presence of evil, which makes a thing evil, takes away the desire and friendship of the good; for that which was once both good and evil has now become evil only, and the good had no friendship with the evil?

None.

And therefore we say that those who are already wise, whether Gods or men, are no longer lovers of wisdom; nor can they be lovers of wisdom, who are ignorant to the extent of being evil, for no evil or ignorant person is a lover of wisdom. There remain those who have the misfortune to be ignorant, but are not yet hardened in their ignorance, or void of understanding, and do not as yet fancy that they know what they do not know: and therefore those who are the lovers of wisdom are as yet neither good nor bad. But the bad do not love wisdom any more than the good; for, as we have already seen, neither unlike is the friend of unlike, nor like of like. You remember that?

Yes, they both said.

And so, Lysis and Menexenus, we have discovered the nature of friendship: there can be no doubt of that. Friendship is the love which the neither good nor evil has of the good, when the evil is present, either in the soul, or in the body, or anywhere.

They both agreed and entirely assented, and for a moment I rejoiced and was satisfied like a huntsman whose prey is within his grasp. But then a suspicion came across me, and I fancied unaccountably that the conclusion was untrue, and I felt pained, and said, Alas! Lysis and Menexenus, I am afraid that we have been grasping at a shadow.

Why do you say that? said Menexenus.

I am afraid, I said, that the argument about friendship is false: arguments, like men, are often pretenders.

How is that? he asked.

Well, I said; look at the matter in this way: a friend is the friend of some one.

Certainly he is.

And has he a motive and object in being a friend, or has he no motive and object?

He has a motive and object.

And is the object which makes him a friend dear to him, or neither dear nor hateful to him?

I don't quite follow you, he said.

I do not wonder at that, I said. But perhaps, if I put the matter in another way, you will be able to follow me, and my own meaning will be clearer to myself. The sick man, as I was just now saying, is the friend of the physician — is he not?

Yes.

And he is the friend of the physician because of disease, and for the sake of health?

Yes.

And disease is an evil?

Certainly.

And what of health? I said. Is that good or evil, or neither?

Good, he replied.

And we were saying, I believe, that the body being neither good nor evil, because of disease, that is to say because of evil, is the friend of medicine, and medicine is a good: and medicine has entered into this friendship for the sake of health, and health is a good.

True.

And is health a friend, or not a friend?

A friend.

And disease is an enemy?

Yes.

Then that which is neither good nor evil is the friend of the good because of the evil and hateful, and for the sake of the good and the friend?

That is clear.

Then the friend is a friend for the sake of the friend, and because of the enemy?

That is to be inferred.

Then at this point, my boys, let us take heed, and be on our guard against deceptions. I will no more say that the friend is the friend of the friend, and the like of the like, which has been declared by us to be an impossibility; but, in order that this new statement may not delude us, let us attentively examine another point, which is this: medicine, as we were saying, is a friend, or dear to us for the sake of health?

Yes.

And health is also dear?

Certainly.

And if dear, then dear for the sake of something?
Yes.

And surely this object must also be dear, as is implied in our previous admissions?
Yes.

And that something dear involves something else dear?
Yes.

But then, proceeding in this way, we shall at last come to an end, and arrive at some first principle of friendship or dearness which is not capable of being referred to any other, for the sake of which, as we maintain, all other things are dear.
Certainly.

My fear is that all those other things, which, as we say, are dear for the sake of that other, are illusions and deceptions only, of which that other is the reality or true principle of friendship. Let me put the matter thus: Suppose the case of a great treasure (this may be a son, who is more precious to his father than all his other treasures); would not the father, who values his son above all things, value other things also for the sake of his son? I mean, for instance, if he knew that his son had drunk hemlock, and the father thought that wine would save him, he would value the wine?
Certainly.

And also the vessel which contains the wine?
Certainly.

But he does not therefore value the three measures of wine, or the earthen vessel which contains them, equally with his son? Is not this rather the true state of the case? All this anxiety of his has regard not to the means which are provided for the sake of an object, but to the object for the sake of which they are provided. And although we may often say that gold and silver are highly valued by us, that is not the truth; for the truth is that there is a further object, whatever that may be, which we value most of all, and for the sake of which gold and all our other possessions are acquired by us. Am I not right?

Yes, certainly.

And may not the same be said of the friend? That which is only dear to us for the sake of something else is improperly said to be dear, but the truly dear is that in which all these so-called dear friendships terminate.

That, he said, appears to be true.

And the truly dear or ultimate principle of friendship is not for the sake of any other or further dear.

True.

Then the notion is at an end that friendship has not any further object. But are we therefore to infer that the good is the friend?

That is my view.

Then is the good loved for the sake of the evil? Let me put the case in this way: Suppose that of the three principles, good, evil, and that which is neither good nor evil, there remained only the good and the neutral, and that evil went far away, and in no way affected soul or body, nor ever at all that class of things which, as we say, are neither good nor evil in themselves; — would the good be of any use, or other than useless to us? For if there were nothing to hurt us any longer, we should have no need of anything that would do us good. Then would be clearly seen that we did but love and desire the good because of the evil, and as the remedy of the evil, which was the disease; but if there had been no disease, there would have been no need of a remedy. Is not this the nature of the good — to be loved because of the evil, by us who are between the two? but there is no use in the good for its own sake.

I suppose that is true.

Then the final principle of friendship, in which all other friendships which are relative only were supposed by us to terminate, is of another and a different nature from them. For they are called dear because of another dear or friend. But with the true friend or dear, the case is quite the reverse; for that is proved to be dear because of the hated, and if the hated were away, the loved would no longer stay.

That is true, he replied: at least, that is implied in the argument.

But, oh! will you tell me, I said, whether if evil were to perish, we should hunger any more, or thirst any more, or have any similar affection? Or may we suppose that hunger will remain while men and animals remain, but not so as to be hurtful? And the same of thirst and the other affections, — that they will remain, but will not be evil because evil has perished? Or shall I say rather, that to ask what either would be or would not be has no meaning, for who can tell? This only we know, that in our present condition hunger may injure us, and may also benefit us. Is not that true?

Yes.

And in like manner thirst or any similar desire may sometimes be a good and sometimes an evil to us, and sometimes neither one nor the other?

To be sure.

But is there any reason why, because evil perishes, that which is not evil should also perish?

None.

Then, even if evil perishes, the desires which are neither good nor evil will remain?

That is evident.

And must not a man love that which he desires and affects?

He must.

Then, even if evil perishes, there may still remain some elements of love or friendship?

Yes.

But not, if evil is the cause of friendship: for in that case nothing will be the friend of any other thing after the destruction of evil; for the effect can not remain when the cause is destroyed.

True.

And have we not been saying that the friend loves something for a reason? and the reason was because of the evil which leads the neither good nor evil to love the good?

Very true.

But now our view is changed, and there must be some other cause of friendship?

I suppose that there must.

May not the truth be that, as we were saying, desire is the cause of friendship; for that which desires is dear to that which is desired at the time of desire? and may not the other theory have been just a long story about nothing?

That is possibly true.

But surely, I said, he who desires, desires that of which he is in want?

Yes.

And that of which he is in want is dear to him?

True.

And he is in want of that of which he is deprived?

Certainly.

Then love, and desire, and friendship would appear to be of the natural or congenial. That, Lysis and Menexenus, is the inference.

They assented.

Then if you are friends, you must have natures which are congenial to one another?

Certainly, they both said.

And I say, my boys, that no one who loves or desires another would ever have loved or desired or affected him, if he had not been in some way congenial to him, either in his soul, or in his character, or in his manners, or in his form.

Yes, yes, said Menexenus. But Lysis was silent.

Then, I said, the conclusion is, that what is of a congenial nature must be loved.

That follows, he said.

Then the true lover, and not the counterfeit, must be loved by his love.

Lysis and Menexenus gave a faint assent to this; and Hippothales changed into all manner of colors with delight.

Here, intending to revise the argument, I said: Can we point out any difference between the congenial and the like? For if that is possible, then I think, Lysis and Menexenus, there may be some sense in our argument about friendship. But if the congenial is only the like, how will you get rid of the other argument, of the uselessness of like to like in as far as they are like; for to say that what is useless is dear, would be absurd? Suppose, then, that we agree to distinguish between the congenial and the like — in the intoxication of argument, that may perhaps be allowed.

Very true.

And shall we further say that the good is congenial, and the evil uncongenial to every one? Or again that the evil is congenial to the evil, and the good to the good; or that which is neither good nor evil to that which is neither good nor evil.

They agreed to the latter alternative.

Then, my boys, we have again fallen into the old discarded error; for the unjust will be the friend of the unjust, and the bad of the bad, as well as the good of the good.

That appears to be true.

But again if we say that the congenial is the same as the good, in that case the good will only be the friend of the good.

True.

But that too was a position of ours which, as you will remember, has been already refuted by ourselves.

We remember.

Then what is to be done? Or rather is there anything to be done? I can only, like the wise men who argue in courts, sum up the arguments. If neither the beloved, nor the lover, nor the like, nor the unlike, nor the good, nor the congenial, nor any other of whom we spoke — for there were such a number of them that I can't remember them — if, I say, none of these are friends, I know not what remains to be said.

Here I was going to invite the opinion of some older person, when suddenly we were interrupted by the tutors of Lysis and Menexenus, who came upon us like an evil apparition with their brothers, and bade them go home, as it was getting late. At first, we and the bystanders drove them off; but afterwards, as they would not mind, and only went on shouting in their barbarous dialect, and got angry, and kept calling the boys — they appeared to us to have been drinking rather too much at the Hermaea, which made them difficult to manage — we fairly gave way and broke up the company.

I said, however, a few words to the boys at parting: O Menexenus and Lysis, will not the bystanders go away, and say, " Here is a jest; you two boys, and I, an old boy, who would fain be one of you, imagine ourselves to be friends, and we have not as yet been able to discover what is a friend! "

LACHES, OR COURAGE

INTRODUCTION

Lysimachus, the son of Aristides the Just, and Melesias, the son of the elder Thucydides, two aged men, who live together, are desirous of educating their sons in the best manner. Their own education, as often happens with the sons of great men, has been neglected; and they are resolved that their children shall have more care taken of them, than they received themselves at the hands of their fathers.

At their request, Nicias and Laches have accompanied them to see a man named Stesilaus fighting in heavy armor. The two fathers ask the two generals what they think of this exhibition, and whether they would advise that their sons shou'l acquire the accomplishment. Nicias and Laches are quite willing to give their opinion; but they suggest that Socrates should be invited to take part in the consultation. He is a stranger to Lysimachus, but is afterwards recognized as the son of his old friend Sophroniscus, with whom " he never had a difference to the hour of his death." Socrates is also known to Nicias, to whom he had introduced the excellent Damon, musician and sophist, as a tutor for his son, and to Laches, who had witnessed his heroic behavior at the battle of Delium.

Socrates, as he is younger than either Nicias or Laches, prefers to wait until they have delivered their opinions, which they give in a characteristic manner. Nicias, the tactician, is very much in favor of the new art, which he describes as the gymnastics of war — useful when the ranks are formed, and still more useful when they are broken; creating a general interest in military studies, and greatly adding to the appearance of the soldier in the field. Laches, the blunt warrior, is of opinion that such an art is not knowledge, and can not be of any value, because the Lacedaemonians, those great masters of arms, neglect it. His own experience in actual service has taught him that these pretenders are useless and ridiculous. This man Stesilaus has been seen by him on board ship making a very sorry exhibition of himself. The possession of the art will make the coward rash, and subject the courageous, if he chance to make a slip, to invidious remarks. And now let Socrates be taken into counsel. As they differ he must decide.

931

Socrates would rather not decide the question by a plurality of votes: in such a serious matter as the education of a friend's children, he would rather consult the one skilled person who has had masters, and has works to show as evidences of his skill. This is not himself; for he has never been able to pay the sophists for instructing him, and has never had the wit to do or discover anything. But Nicias and Laches are older and richer than he is: they have had teachers, and perhaps have made discoveries; and he would have trusted them entirely, if they had not been diametrically opposed.

Lysimachus here proposes to resign the argument into the hands of the younger part of the company, as he is old, and has a bad memory. He earnestly requests Socrates to remain; — in this showing, as Nicias says, how little he knows the man, who will certainly not go away until he has cross-examined the company about their past lives. Nicias has often submitted to this process; and Laches is quite willing to learn from Socrates, because his actions, in the true Dorian mode, correspond to his words.

Socrates proceeds: We might ask who are our teachers? But a better and more thorough way of examining the question will be to ask, " What is Virtue? " — or rather, to restrict the inquiry to that part of virtue which is concerned with the use of weapons — " What is Courage? " Laches thinks that he knows this: (1) " He is courageous who remains at his post." But some nations fight flying, after the manner of Aeneas in Homer; or as the heavy-armed Spartans also did at the battle of Plataea. (2) Socrates wants a more general definition, not only of military courage, but of courage of all sorts, both amid pleasures and pains. Laches replies that this universal courage is endurance. But courage is a good thing, and mere endurance may be hurtful and injurious. Therefore (3) the element of intelligence must be added. But then again unintelligent endurance may often be more courageous than the intelligent — the bad than the good. How is this contradiction to be solved? Socrates and Laches are not set " to the Dorian mode " of words and actions; for their words are all confusion, although their actions are courageous. Still they must " endure " in an argument about endurance. Laches is very willing, and is quite sure that he knows what courage is, if he could only tell.

Nicias is now appealed to; and in reply he offers a definition which he has heard from Socrates himself, to the effect that (1) " Courage is intelligence." Laches derides this; and Socrates inquires, " What sort of intelligence? " to which Nicias replies, " Intelligence of things terrible." " But every man knows the things to be dreaded in his own art." " No they do not. They may predict results, but can not tell whether they are really terrible; only the courageous man can do that." Laches draws the inference that the courageous man is either a soothsayer or a god.

Again, in Nicias' way of speaking, the term " courageous " must be denied to animals or children, because they do not know the danger. Against this inversion of the ordinary use of language Laches reclaims, but is in some degree mollified by a compliment to his own courage. Still, he does not like to see an Athenian statesman and general descending to sophistries of this sort. Socrates resumes the argument. Courage has been defined to be intelligence or knowledge of the terrible; and courage is not all virtue, but only one of the virtues. The terrible is in the future, and therefore the knowledge of the terrible is a knowledge of the future. But there can be no knowledge of future good or evil separated from a knowledge of the good and evil of the past or present; that is to say, of all good and evil. Courage, therefore, is the knowledge of good and evil generally. But he who has the knowledge of good and evil generally, must not only have courage, but also temperance, justice, and every other virtue. Thus, a single virtue would be the same as all virtues. And after all the two generals, and Socrates, the hero of Delium, are still in ignorance of the nature of courage. They must go to school again, boys, old men and all.

Some points of resemblance, and some points of difference, appear in the Laches when compared with the Charmides and Lysis. There is less of poetical and simple beauty, and more of dramatic interest and power. They are richer in the externals of the scene; the Laches has more play and development of character. In the Lysis and Charmides the youths are the central figures, and frequent allusions are made to the place of meeting, which is a palaestra. Here the place of meeting, which is also a palaestra, is quite forgotten, and the boys play a subordinate part. The *séance* is of old and elder men, of whom Socrates is the youngest.

First is the aged Lysimachus, who may be compared with Cephalus in the Republic, and, like him, withdraws from the argument. Melesias, who is only his shadow, also subsides into silence. Both of them have been ill-educated, as is shown in a striking manner by the circumstance that Lysimachus, the friend of Sophroniscus, has never heard of the fame of Socrates, his son; they belong to different circles. The characters of the two generals, Nicias and Laches, are first indicated by their opinions on the exhibitions of the man fighting in heavy armor. The more thoughtful Nicias is quite ready to accept the new art, which Laches treats in the spirit of ridicule, and seems to think that this, or any other military question, may be settled by asking, "What do the Lacedaemonians say to this?" The one clearly inclines to tactics and arts of fence; the other is an enemy to innovation, and relies on native courage. It is to be noted that one of them is supposed to be a hearer of Socrates; the other is only acquainted with his actions. Laches is the admirer of the Dorian mode; and into his mouth the remark is put that there are some persons who, never having been taught, are better than those who have.

In the discussion of the main thesis of the Dialogue — "What is Courage?" the antagonism of the two characters is still more clearly brought out; and in this, as in the preliminary question, the truth is parted between them. Gradually, and not without difficulty, Laches is made to pass on from the more popular to the more philosophical; it has never occurred to him that there was any other courage than that of the soldier; and only by an effort of the mind can he frame a general notion at all. No sooner has this general notion been formed than it evanesces before the dialectic of Socrates; and Nicias appears from the other side with the Socratic doctrine, that courage is knowledge. But to this Socrates himself replies, that knowledge is of past, present, and future, and such a definition of virtue would make courage equivalent to all virtue. In this part of the Dialogue the contrast between the mode of cross-examination which is practised by Laches and by Socrates, and the manner in which the definition of Laches is made to approximate to that of Nicias, are well worthy of attention.

Thus, with some intimation of the connection and unity of virtue and knowledge, we arrive at no distinct result. The two aspects of courage are never harmonized. The knowledge which in the Protagoras is explained as the faculty of estimating pleasures and pains is here lost in an unmeaning and transcendental conception. Yet several true intimations of the nature of courage are allowed to appear: (1) That courage is moral as well as physical; (2) That true courage is inseparable from knowledge, and yet (3) is based on a sort of natural instinct. Laches exhibits one aspect of courage; Nicias the other. The perfect image and harmony of both is only realized in Socrates himself.

LACHES, OR COURAGE

PERSONS OF THE DIALOGUE.

LYSIMACHUS, *son of Aristides.*   NICIAS.
MELESIAS, *son of Thucydides.*   LACHES.
THEIR SONS.   SOCRATES.

Lys. YOU have seen the exhibition of the man fighting in armor, Nicias and Laches, but we did not tell you at the time the reason why my friend Melesias and I asked you to go with us and see him. I think that we may as well confess this, for we certainly ought not to have any reserve with you. The reason was, that we were intending to ask your advice. Some laugh at the very notion of advising others, and when they are asked will not say what they think. They guess at the wishes of the person who asks them, and answer according to his, and not according to their own, opinion. But as we know that you are good judges, and will say exactly what you think, we have taken you into our counsels. And the matter about which I am making all this preface is just this: Melesias and I have two sons; that is his son, and he is named Thucydides, after his grandfather; and this is mine, who is also called, after his grandfather, Aristides. Now, we are resolved to take the greatest care of the youths, and not to let them run about as they like, which is too often the way with the young, when they are no longer children, but to begin at once and do the utmost that we can for them. And knowing that you have sons of your own, we thought that you were most likely to have attended to their training

and improvement, and, if you have not, we may remind you that you ought to have attended to them,
and would invite you to assist us in the fulfilment of
a common duty. I will tell you, Nicias and Laches,
even at the risk of being tedious, how we came to
think of this. Melesias and I live together, and our
two sons live with us; and now, as I was saying at
first, we are going to confess to you. Both of us often
talk to the lads about the many noble deeds which our
fathers did in war and peace — in the management
of the allies, and also of the affairs of the city; but
neither of us has any deeds of his own which he can
show. Now we are somewhat ashamed of this contrast being seen by them, and we blame our fathers
for letting us be spoiled in the days of our youth,
while they were occupied with the concerns of others;
and this we point out to the lads, and tell them that
they will not grow up to honor if they are rebellious
and take no pains about themselves; but that if they
take pains they may, perhaps, become worthy of the
names which they bear. They, on their part, promise
to comply with our wishes; and our care is to discover
what studies or pursuits are likely to be most improving to them. Some one told us of this art of using
weapons, which, he said, was an excellent accomplishment for a young man to learn; and he praised the
man whose exhibition you have seen, and told us to
go and see him. And we determined to go, and to
get you to accompany us, and if you did not object,
we thought that we would take counsel with you about
the education of our sons. That is the matter about
which we wanted to talk with you; and we hope that
you will give us your opinion about this, and about
any other studies or pursuits which may or may not
be desirable for a young man to learn. Please to say
whether you object to our proposal.

Nic. As far as I am concerned, Lysimachus and Melesias, I applaud your purpose, and will gladly assist you; and I believe that you, Laches, will be equally glad.

La. Certainly, Nicias; and I quite approve of the remark which Lysimachus made about his own father, and the father of Melesias, and which is applicable, not only to them, but to us, and to every one who is occupied with public affairs. As he says, they are too apt to be negligent and careless of their own children and their private concerns. There is much truth in that remark of yours, Lysimachus. But why do you not consult our friend Socrates, instead of consulting us, about the education of the youths? he is of the same deme with you, and is always passing his time in places in which the youth have any noble study or pursuit, such as you are inquiring after.

Lys. Why, Laches, has Socrates ever attended to matters of this sort?

La. Certainly, Lysimachus.

Nic. That I have the means of knowing as well as Laches; for quite lately he supplied me with a teacher of music for my sons, — Damon, the disciple of Agathocles, who is a most accomplished man in every way, as well as a musician, and a companion of inestimable value for young men at their age.

Lys. Those who have reached my age, Socrates and Nicias and Laches, fall out of acquaintance with the young, because they are generally detained at home by old age; but I hope that you, O son of Sophroniscus, will let your fellow demesmen have the benefit of any advice which you are able to give them. And I have a claim upon you as an old friend of your father; for I and he were always companions and friends, and to the hour of his death there never was a difference between us; and now it comes back to me, at the mention of your name, that I have heard these lads talking to one another at home, and often speaking of Socrates in terms of the highest praise; but I have never thought to ask them whether the son of Sophroniscus was the person whom they meant. Tell me, my boy, whether this is the Socrates of whom you have often spoken?

Son. Certainly, father, this is he.

Lys. I am delighted to hear, Socrates, that you maintain the name of your father, who was a most excellent man; and I further rejoice at the prospect of our family ties being renewed.

La. Indeed, Lysimachus, you ought not to give him up; for I can assure you that I have seen him maintaining, not only his father's, but also his country's name. He was my companion in the retreat from Delium, and I can tell you that if others had only been like him, the honor of our country would have been maintained, and the great defeat would never have occurred.

Lys. That is very high praise, which is given you, Socrates, by faithful witnesses and for deserts like these. And let me tell you the pleasure which I feel in hearing of your fame; and I hope that you will regard me as one of your best friends; indeed you ought to have visited us long ago, and reckoned us among your friends; but now, from this day forward, as we have at last found one another out, do as I say — come and make acquaintance with me, and with these young men, that I may continue your friend, as I was your father's. I shall expect you to do this, and shall venture to remind you. But what say you of the matter of which I was speaking — the art of fighting in armor? Is that a practice in which the lads may be advantageously instructed?

Soc. I will endeavor to advise you, Lysimachus, as

far as I can in this matter, and also in every way will comply with your wishes; but as I am younger and not so experienced, I think that I ought to hear what my elders have to say first, and to learn of them, and if I have anything to add, then I may venture to give my opinion to them as well as to you. Suppose, Nicias, that one of you speaks first.

Nic. I have no objection, Socrates; and my opinion is that the acquirement of this art is in many ways useful to young men. There is an advantage in their being employed during their leisure hours in a way which tends to improve their bodily constitution, and not in the way in which young men are too apt to be employed. No sort of gymnastics could be harder exercise; and this, and the art of riding, are of all arts most befitting to a freeman; for they only who are thus trained in the use of implements of war are trained in the conflict which is set before us, or in that on which the conflict turns. Moreover in actual battle this sort of acquirement will be of some use, when you have to fight in a line with a number of others; and will be of the greatest use when the ranks are broken and you have to fight singly; either in pursuit, when you are attacking some one who is defending himself, or in flight, when you have to defend yourself against an assailant. Certainly he who possessed the art could not meet with any harm at the hands of a single person, or perhaps of several; and in any case he would have a great advantage. Further, this sort of skill inclines a man to other noble lessons; for every man who has learned how to fight in arms will desire to learn the proper arrangement of an army, which is the sequel of the lesson: and when he has learned this, and his ambition is once fired, he will go on to learn the complete art of the general. There is no difficulty in seeing that the knowledge and practice of other military arts will be useful and valuable to a man; and this lesson may be the beginning of them. Let me add a further advantage, which is by no means a slight one, — that this science will make any man a great deal more valiant and self-possessed in the field. And I will not disdain to mention, what to some may appear to be a small matter, that he will make a better appearance at the right time; that is to say, at the time when his appearance will strike terror into his enemies. My opinion then, Lysimachus, is, as I say, that the youths should be instructed in this art, and for the reasons which I have given. But I shall be very glad to hear Laches, if he has another view.

La. I should not like to say, Nicias, that any kind of knowledge is not to be learned; for all knowledge appears to be a good: and if, as Nicias and as the teachers of it affirm, this art of fence is really a species of knowledge, then it ought to be learned; but if not, and if those who profess it are deceivers only; or if it be knowledge, but not of a valuable sort; then what is the use of learning it? I say this, because I think that if it had been really valuable, the Lacedaemonians, whose whole life is passed in finding out and practising the arts which give them an advantage over other nations in war, would have discovered this one. And even if they had not, still these professors of the art would certainly not have failed to discover that of all the Hellenes the Lacedaemonians have the greatest interest in such matters, and that a master of the art who was honored among them would have been sure to have made his fortune among other nations, just as a tragic poet would who is honored among ourselves; which is the reason why he who fancies that he can write a tragedy does not go on a peregrination into the neighboring states, but rushes hither straight, and exhibits at Athens; and this is natural. Whereas

I perceive that these fighters in armor regard Lacedaemon as a sacred inviolable territory, which they do not touch with the point of their foot; but they make a circuit of the neighboring states, and would rather exhibit to any others than to the Spartans; and particularly to those who would themselves acknowledge that they are by no means first-rate in the arts of war. Further, Lysinachus, I have encountered a good many of these gentlemen in actual service, and have taken their measure, which I can give you at once; for none of these masters of fence has ever been distinguished in war, — there has been a sort of fatality about this: whereas, in all other arts, the men of note have been always those who have practised the art; but these appear to be a most unfortunate exception. For example, this very Stesilaus, whom you and I have just witnessed exhibiting in all that crowd and making such great professions of his powers, I have seen at another time making, in sober truth, an involuntary exhibition of himself, which was a far better spectacle. He was a marine on board a ship, which struck a transport vessel, and was armed with a weapon, half spear, half scythe, the singularity of which was worthy of the singularity of the man. To make a long story short, I will only tell you what happened to this notable invention of the scythe-spear. He was fighting, and the scythe end caught in the rigging of the other ship, and stuck fast; and he tugged, but was unable to get his weapon free. The two ships were passing one another. He first ran along his own ship holding on to the spear; but as the other ship passed by and drew him after as he was holding on, he let the spear slip through his hand until he retained only the end of the handle. The people in the transport clapped their hands, and laughed at his ridiculous figure; and when some one threw a stone, which fell on the deck at his feet, and he quitted his hold of the scythe-spear, the crew of his own trireme also burst out laughing; they could not refrain when they beheld the weapon waving in the air, suspended from the transport. Now I do not deny that there may be something in such an art, as Nicias asserts: but I tell you my experience, and, as I said at first, my opinion is, that whether this be an art which is of some slight advantage, or not an art at all, but only an imposition; in either case there is no use in such an acquirement. For my opinion is, that if the professor of this art be a coward, he will be likely to become rash, and his character will be only more notorious; or if he be brave, and fail ever so little, other men will be on the watch, and he will be greatly traduced: for there is a jealousy of such pretenders; and unless a man be preëminent in valor, he can not help being ridiculous, if he says that he has this skill in weapons. Such is my judgment, Lysimachus, of the desirableness of this art; but, as I said at first, ask Socrates, and do not let him go until he has given you his opinion of the matter.

Lys. I am going to ask this favor of you, Socrates; as is the more necessary because the two doctors disagree, and some one is needed to decide between them. Had they agreed, this might not have been required. But as Laches has voted one way and Nicias another, I should like to hear with which of our two friends you agree.

Soc. What, Lysimachus, are you for going by the opinion of the majority?

Lys. Why, yes, Socrates; what other way is there?

Soc. And would you agree in that, Melesias? If you were deliberating about the gymnastic training of your son, would you follow the advice of the majority of us, or the opinion of the one who had been trained and exercised under a skilful master?

Mel. I should take the advice of the latter, Socrates; as would be reasonable.

Soc. His one vote would be worth more than the vote of all us four?

Mel. Certainly.

Soc. And for this reason, as I imagine, — because a good decision is based on knowledge and not on numbers?

Mel. To be sure.

Soc. Must we not then first of all ask, whether there is any one of us who has knowledge in that about which we are deliberating? If there is, let us take his advice, though he be one only, and not mind the others; if there is not, let us seek further counsel. Is this a slight matter about which you and Lysimachus are deliberating? Are you not risking the greatest of your possessions? For children are your riches; and upon their turning out well or ill will depend the whole order of their father's house.

Mel. That is true.

Soc. Great care, then, is required in the matter?

Mel. Certainly.

Soc. Suppose, as I was just now saying, that we were considering, or wanting to consider, who was the best trainer. Should we not decide in his favor who knew and had practised the art, and had the best teachers?

Mel. I think that we should.

Soc. But would there not arise a prior question about the nature of the art of which we want to find the masters?

Mel. I do not understand.

Soc. Let me try to make my meaning plainer then. I do not think that we have as yet decided what that is about which we are consulting, when we ask which of us is skilled in that, and which of us has or has not had a teacher of the art.

Nic. Why, Socrates, is not the question whether young men ought or ought not to learn the art of fighting in armor?

Soc. Yes, Nicias; but there is also a prior question, which I may illustrate in this way: When a person considers about applying a medicine to the eyes, would you say that he is consulting about the medicine or about the eyes?

Nic. About the eyes.

Soc. And when he considers if he shall set a bridle on a horse, he thinks of the horse and not of the bridle?

Nic. True.

Soc. And in a word, when he considers anything for the sake of another thing, he thinks of the end and not of the means?

Nic. Certainly.

Soc. And when you call in an adviser, you should see whether he is skilful in the accomplishment of the end which you have in view, as well as of the means?

Nic. Most true.

Soc. And at present we have in view some kind of knowledge, the end of which is the soul of youth?

Nic. Yes.

Soc. The question is, Which of us is skilful or successful in the treatment of the soul, and which of us has had good teachers?

La. Well but Socrates; did you never observe that some persons, who have had no teachers, are more skilful than those who have, in some things?

Soc. Yes, Laches, I have observed that; but you would not be very willing to trust them if they only professed to be masters of their art, unless they could show some proof of their skill or excellence in one or more works.

La. That is true.

Soc. And therefore, Laches and Nicias, as Lysimachus and Melesias, in their anxiety to improve the minds of their sons, have asked our advice about them, we too should inform them who our teachers were, if we say that we have any, and prove them to be men of merit and experienced trainers of the minds of youth and really our teachers. Or if any of us says that he has no teacher, but that he has works to show of his own; then he should point out to them, what Athenians or strangers, bond or free, he is generally acknowledged to have improved. But if he can show neither teachers nor works, then they should ask him to look out for others; and not to run the risk of spoiling the children of friends, which is the most formidable accusation that can be brought against any one by his near and dear relations. As for myself, Lysimachus and Melesias, I am the first to confess that I have never had a teacher; although I have always from my earliest youth desired to have one. But I am too poor to give money to the Sophists, who are the only professors of moral improvement; and to this day I have never been able to discover the art myself, though I should not be surprised if Nicias or Laches may have learned or discovered it; for they are far wealthier than I am, and may therefore have learned of others. And they are older too; so that they have had more time to make the discovery. And I really believe that they are able to educate a man; for unless they had been confident in their own knowledge, they would never have spoken thus decidedly of the pursuits which are advantageous or hurtful to a young man. I repose confidence in both of them; but I do not understand why they differ from one another.

And therefore, Lysimachus, as Laches suggests that you should detain me, and not let me go until I have answered, I in turn earnestly beseech and advise you to detain Laches and Nicias, and question them. I would have you say to them: Socrates says that he has no knowledge of the matter, and that he is unable to decide which of you speaks truly; neither discoverer nor student is he of anything of the kind. But you, Laches and Nicias, should either of you tell us who is the most skilful educator whom you have ever known; and whether you invented the art yourselves, or learned of another; and if you learned, who were your respective teachers, and who were their brothers in the art; and then, if you are too much occupied in politics to teach us yourselves, let us go to them, and present them with gifts, or make interest with them, or both, in the hope that they may be induced to take charge of all our families, in order that they may not grow up inferior, and disgrace their ancestors. But if you are yourselves original discoverers in that field, give us some proof of your skill. Who are they who, having been inferior persons, have become under your care good and noble? For if this is your first attempt at education, there is a danger that you may be trying the experiment, not on the "vile corpus" of a Carian slave, but on your own sons, or the sons of your friend; and as the proverb says, "break the large vessel in learning to make pots." Tell us then, what qualities you claim or do not claim. Make them tell you this, Lysimachus, and do not let them off.

Lys. I very much approve of the words of Socrates, my friends; but you, Nicias and Laches, must determine whether you will be questioned, and give an explanation about matters of this sort. Assuredly, I and Melesias would be greatly pleased to hear you answer the questions which Socrates asks, if you will: for I began by saying that we took you into our counsels because we thought you would be likely to have attended to the subject, especially as you have children who, like our own, are nearly of an age to be educated. Suppose, then, if you have no objection, that you take Socrates into partnership; and do you and he ask and answer one another's questions: for, as he has well said, we are deliberating about the most important of our concerns. I hope that you will see fit to comply with our request.

Nic. I see very clearly, Lysimachus, that you have only known Socrates' father, and have no acquaintance with Socrates himself: at least, you can only have known him when he was a child, and may have met him among his fellow-tribesmen, in company with his father, at a sacrifice, or at some other gathering. You clearly show that you have never known him since he arrived at manhood.

Lys. Why do you say that, Nicias?

Nic. You don't seem to be aware that any one to whom Socrates has an intellectual affinity is liable to be drawn into an argument with him; and whatever subject may be started by him, he will be continually carried round and round by him, until at last he finds that he has to give an account both of his present and past life; and when he is once entangled, Socrates will not let him go until he has completely and thoroughly sifted him. Now I am used to his ways; and I know that he will certainly do this: and also I know that I myself will be the sufferer; for I am fond of his company, Lysimachus. Neither do I think that there is any harm in being reminded of the evil which we are, or have been, doing: he who does not fly from reproof will be sure to take more heed of his after life; he will wish and desire to learn as long as he lives, as Solon says, and will not think that old age of itself brings wisdom. To me, to be cross-examined by Socrates is neither unusual nor unpleasant; indeed, I knew all along that where Socrates was, the argument would soon pass from our sons to ourselves; and therefore, as I say, as far as I am concerned, I am quite willing to discourse with Socrates in his own manner; but you had better ask our friend Laches what his feeling may be.

La. I have but one feeling, Nicias, or (shall I say?) two feelings, about discussions. And to some I may seem to be a lover, and to others a hater of discourse; for when I hear a man discoursing of virtue, or of any sort of wisdom, who is a true man and worthy of his theme, I am delighted beyond measure: and I compare the man and his words, and note the harmony and correspondence of them. And such an one I deem to be the true musician, having in himself a fairer harmony than that of the lyre, or any pleasant instrument of music; for truly he has in his own life a harmony of words and deeds arranged, not in the Ionian, or in the Phrygian mode, nor yet in the Lydian, but in the true Hellenic mode, which is the Dorian, and no other. Such a one makes me merry with the sound of his voice; and when I hear him I am thought to be a lover of discourse; so eager am I in drinking in his words. But when I hear a man of opposite character, I am annoyed; and the better he speaks the more I hate him, and then I seem to be a hater of discourse. As to Socrates, I have no knowledge of his words: but of old, as would seem, I have had experience of his deeds; and his deeds show that free and noble sentiments may be expected from him. And if his words accord, then I am of one mind with him, and shall be delighted to be interrogated by a man such as he is, and shall not be annoyed at having to learn of him: for I agree with Solon, "that I would fain grow old, learning many things." But I must be allowed to add of the good only. Socrates must be willing to allow that he is a good teacher, or I shall be a dull and uncongenial pupil: but that the teacher is younger, or not as yet in repute — anything of that sort is of no account with me. And therefore, Socrates, I give you notice that you may teach and confute me as much as ever you like, and also learn of me anything which I know. Such is the opinion which I have had of you ever since that day on which you were my companion in danger, and gave an unmistakable proof of your valor. Therefore, say whatever you like, and do not mind about the difference of our ages.

Soc. I can not say that either of you show any reluctance to take counsel and advise with me.

Lys. But that is our business, in which I regard you as having a common interest; for I reckon you as one of us. Please then to take my place, and find out from Nicias and Laches what we want to know, for the sake of the youths, and talk and advise with them: for I am old, and my memory is bad; and I do not remember the questions which I am going to ask, or the answers to them; and if there is any interruption I am quite lost. I will therefore beg of you to carry on the proposed discussion by yourselves; and I will listen, and Melesias and I will act upon your conclusions.

Soc. Let us, Nicias and Laches, comply with the request of Lysimachus and Melesias. There would be no harm in asking ourselves the question which was first proposed to us: Who have been our own instructors in this sort of training, and whom we have made better? But the other mode of carrying on the inquiry will bring us to the same point, and will be more like proceeding from first principles. For if we knew that the addition of something would improve some other thing, and were able to make the addition, then, clearly, we must know how that about which we are advising may be best and most easily attained. Perhaps you do not understand what I mean. Then let me make my meaning plainer in this way. Suppose we know that the addition of sight makes better the eyes which possess this gift, and also were able to impart sight to the eyes, then, clearly, we should know the nature of sight, when asked how this gift of sight may be best and most easily attained; for if we knew neither what sight is, nor what hearing is, we should not be very good medical advisers about the eyes, or the ears, or about the best mode of giving sight and hearing to them.

La. That is true, Socrates.

Soc. And are not our two friends, Laches, at this very moment inviting us to consider in what way the gift of virtue may be imparted to their sons for the improvement of their minds?

La. Very true.

Soc. Then must we not first know the nature of virtue? For how, if we are wholly ignorant of this, can we advise any one about the best mode of attaining it?

La. I do not think that we can, Socrates.

Soc. Then, Laches, we may presume that we know the nature of virtue?

La. Yes.

Soc. And that which we know we must surely be able to tell?

La. Certainly.

Soc. I would not have us begin, my friend, with inquiring about the whole of virtue; for that may be too much for us: let us first consider whether we have a sufficient knowledge of a part; that will probably be an easier mode of proceeding.

La. Let us do as you say, Socrates.

Soc. Then which of the parts of virtue shall we select? Must we not select that to which the use of arms is supposed to conduce? And is not that generally supposed to be courage?

La. Yes, certainly.

Soc. Then, Laches, suppose that we first set about determining the nature of courage, and in the second place proceed to inquire how the young men may attain this quality of courage, as far as this is to be effected by the help of studies and pursuits. Try, and see whether you can tell me what is courage.

La. Indeed, Socrates, that is soon answered: he is a man of courage who remains at his post, and does not run away, but fights against the enemy; of that you may be very certain.

Soc. That is good, Laches; and yet I fear that I did not express myself clearly; and therefore you have answered not the question which I intended to ask, but another.

La. What do you mean, Socrates?

Soc. I will endeavor to explain; you would call a man courageous, who remains at his post, and fights with the enemy?

La. Certainly I should.

Soc. And so should I; but what would you say of another man, who fights flying, instead of remaining?

La. How flying?

Soc. Why, as the Scythians are said to fight, flying as well as pursuing; and as Homer says in praise of the horses of Aeneas, that they knew how to pursue, and fly quickly hither and thither; and he passes an encomium on Aeneas himself, as having a knowledge of fear or flight, and calls him an author of fear or flight.

La. Yes, Socrates, and there Homer is right; for he was speaking of chariots, as you were speaking of the Scythian cavalry, who have that way of fighting; but the heavy-armed Greek fights, as I say, remaining in his rank.

Soc. And yet, Laches, you must except the Lacedaemonians at Plataea, who, when they came upon the light shields of the Persians, are said not to have been willing to stand and fight, and to have fled; but when the ranks of the Persians were broken, they turned upon them like cavalry, and won the battle.

La. That is true.

Soc. That was my meaning when I said that I was to blame in having put my question badly, and that this was the reason of your answering badly. For I meant to ask you not only about the courage of heavy-armed soldiers, but about the courage of cavalry, and every other style of soldier; and not only who are courageous in war, but who are courageous in perils by sea, and who in disease, or poverty, or again in politics, are courageous; and not only who are courageous against pain or fear, but mighty to contend against desires and pleasures, either fixed in their rank or turning upon their enemy. There is this sort of courage, is there not?

La. Certainly, Socrates.

Soc. And all these are courageous, but some have courage in pleasures, and some in pains; some in desires, and some in fears; and some are cowards under the same conditions, as I should imagine.

La. Very true.

Soc. Now I was asking about courage and cowardice in general. And I will begin with courage, and once more ask, What is that common quality, which is the same in all these cases, and which is called courage? Do you understand now what I mean?

La. Not over well.

Soc. I mean this: As I might ask what is that quality which is called quickness, and which is found in running, playing the lyre, speaking, learning, and in many other similar actions, or rather which we possess in nearly every action that can be mentioned of arms or legs, mouth, voice, mind; — would you not apply the term quickness to all of them?

La. Quite true.

Soc. And suppose I were to be asked by some one: What is that common quality, Socrates, which, in all these uses of the word, you call quickness? I should say that which accomplishes much in a little time — that I call quickness in running, speaking, and every other sort of action.

La. You would be quite correct.

Soc. And now, Laches, do you try and tell me, What is that common quality which is called courage, and which includes all the various uses of the term when applied both to pleasure and pain, and in all the cases which I was just now mentioning?

La. I should say that courage is a sort of endurance of the soul, if I am to speak of the universal nature which pervades them all.

Soc. But that is what we must do if we are to answer the question. And yet I can not say that every kind of endurance is, in my opinion, to be deemed courage. Hear my reason: I am sure, Laches, that you would consider courage to be a very noble quality.

La. Most noble, certainly.

Soc. And you would say that a wise endurance is also good and noble?

La. Very noble.

Soc. But what would you say of a foolish endurance? Is not that, on the other hand, to be regarded as evil and hurtful?

La. True.

Soc. And is anything noble which is evil and hurtful?

La. I ought not to say that, Socrates.

Soc. Then you would not admit that sort of endurance to be courage — for that is not noble, but courage is noble?

La. You are right.

Soc. Then, according to you, only the wise endurance is courage?

La. True.

Soc. But as to the epithet " wise," — wise in what? In all things small as well as great? For example, if a man endures in spending his money wisely, knowing that by spending he will acquire more in the end, do you call him courageous?

La. Assuredly not.

Soc. Or, for example, if a man is a physician, and his son, or some patient of his, has inflammation of the lungs, and begs that he may be allowed to eat or drink something, and the other refuses; is that courage?

La. No; that is not courage at all, any more than the last.

Soc. Again, take the case of one who endures in war, and is willing to fight, and wisely calculates and knows that others will help him, and that there will be fewer and inferior men against him than there are with him; and suppose that he has also advantages of position; — would you say of such a one who endures with all this wisdom and preparation, that he, or some man in the opposing army who is in the opposite circumstances to these and yet endures and remains at his post, is the braver?

La. I should say that the latter, Socrates, was the braver.

Soc. But, surely, this is a foolish endurance in comparison with the other?

La. That is true.

Soc. And you would say that he who in an engagement of cavalry endures, having the knowledge of horsemanship, is not so courageous as he who endures, having no knowledge of horsemanship?

La. That is my view.

Soc. And he who endures, having a knowledge of the use of the sling, or the bow, or any other art, is not so courageous as he who endures, not having such a knowledge?

La. True.

Soc. And he who descends into a well, and dives, and holds out in this or any similar action, having no knowledge of diving, or the like, is, as you would say, more courageous than those who have this knowledge?

La. Why, Socrates, what else can a man say?

Soc. Nothing, if that is what he thinks.

La. But that is what I do think.

Soc. And yet men who thus run risks and endure are but foolish, Laches, in comparison of those who do the same things, having the skill to do them.

La. That is true.

Soc. But foolish boldness and endurance appeared before to be base and hurtful to us.

La. Quite true.

Soc. Whereas courage was acknowledged to be a noble quality.

La. True.

Soc. And now on the contrary we are saying that the foolish endurance, which was before held in dishonor, is courage.

La. Very true.

Soc. And are we right in saying that?

La. Indeed, Socrates, I am sure that we are not right.

Soc. Then according to your statement, you and I, Laches, are not attuned to the Dorian mode, which is a harmony of words and deeds; for our deeds are not in accordance with our words. Any one would say that we had courage who saw us in action, but not, I imagine, he who heard us talking about courage just now.

La. That is most true.

Soc. And is this condition of ours satisfactory?

La. Quite the reverse.

Soc. Suppose, however, that we admit our principle to a certain extent.

La. What principle? And what are we to admit?

Soc. The principle of endurance. Let us too endure and persevere in the inquiry, and then courage will not laugh at our faint-heartedness in searching for courage; which after all may, very likely, be endurance.

La. I am ready to go on, Socrates; and yet I am unused to investigations of this sort. But the spirit of controversy has been aroused in me by what has been said; and I am really grieved at being thus unable to express my meaning. For I fancy that I do know the nature of courage; but, somehow or other, she has slipped away from me, and I can not get hold of her and tell her nature.

Soc. But, my dear friend, should not the good sportsman follow the track, and not be lazy?

La. Certainly, he should.

Soc. And shall we invite Nicias to join us? he may be better at the sport than we are. What do you say?

La. I should like that.

Soc. Come then, Nicias, and do what you can to

help your friends, who are tossing on the waves of argument, and at the last gasp: you see our extremity, and may save us, and also settle your own opinion, if you will tell us what you think about courage.

Nic. I have been thinking, Socrates, that you and Laches are not defining courage in the right way; for you have forgotten an excellent saying which I have heard from your own lips.

Soc. What is that, Nicias?

Nic. I have often heard you say that " Every man is good in that in which he is wise, and bad in that in which he is unwise."

Soc. That is certainly true, Nicias.

Nic. And therefore if the brave man is good, he is also wise.

Soc. Do you hear him, Laches?

La. Yes, I hear him, but I don't quite understand him.

Soc. I think that I understand him; and he appears to me to mean that courage is a sort of wisdom.

La. What sort of wisdom, Socrates?

Soc. That is a question which you must ask of Nicias.

La. Yes.

Soc. Tell him then, Nicias, what you mean by this wisdom; for you surely do not mean the wisdom which plays on the flute?

Nic. Certainly not.

Soc. Nor the wisdom which plays the lyre?

Nic. No.

Soc. But what is this knowledge then, and of what?

La. I think that you put the question to him very well, Socrates; and I would like him to say what is the nature of this knowledge or wisdom.

Nic. I mean to say, Laches, that courage is the

knowledge of that which inspires fear or confidence in war, or in anything.

La. How strangely he is talking, Socrates.

Soc. What makes you say that, Laches?

La. What makes me say that? Why, surely courage is one thing, and wisdom another.

Soc. That is just what Nicias denies.

La. Yes, that is what he denies in his foolishness.

Soc. Shall we enlighten him instead of abusing him?

Nic. Laches does not want to enlighten me, Socrates; but having been proved to be talking nonsense himself, he wants to prove that I have been doing the same.

La. Very true, Nicias; and you are talking nonsense, as I shall endeavor to show. Let me ask you a question: Do not physicians know the dangers of disease? or do the courageous know them? or are the physicians the same as the courageous?

Nic. Not at all.

La. No more than the husbandmen who know the dangers of husbandry, or other masters of crafts, who have a knowledge of that which inspires them with fear or confidence in their own crafts, and yet they are not courageous a whit the more for that.

Soc. What is Laches saying, Nicias; he appears to be saying something.

Nic. Yes, he is saying something, but something which is not true.

Soc. How is that?

Nic. Why, because he does not see that the physician's knowledge only extends to the nature of health and disease: he can tell the sick man that, and nothing more. Do you imagine, Laches, that the physician knows whether health or disease is the more terrible to a man? Had not many a man better never

get up from a sick bed? I should like to know
whether you think that life is always better than death.
May not death often be the better of the two?

La. Yes, I certainly think that.

Nic. And do you think that the same things are
terrible to those to whom to die is better, and to those
to whom to live is better?

La. Certainly not.

Nic. And do you suppose that the physician or any
other artist knows this, or any one indeed, except he
who is skilled in the grounds of fear and hope? And
him I call the courageous.

Soc. Do you understand his meaning, Laches?

La. Yes; I suppose that, in his way of speaking,
the soothsayers are courageous. For who but one of
them can know to whom to die or to live is better?
And yet, Nicias, would you allow that you are yourself a soothsayer, or are you neither soothsayer nor
courageous?

Nic. What! do you mean to say that the soothsayer ought to know the grounds of hope or fear?

La. Indeed I do: who but he?

Nic. Much rather I should say he of whom I speak;
for the soothsayer ought to know only the signs of
things that are about to come to pass, whether death
or disease, or loss of property, or victory, or defeat
in war, or in any sort of contest; but to whom the
suffering or not suffering of these things will be for
the best, can no more be decided by the soothsayer
than by one who is no soothsayer.

La. I can not understand what Nicias would be
at, Socrates; for he represents the courageous man
as neither a soothsayer, nor a physician, nor in any
other character, unless he means to say that he is a
god. My opinion is that he does not like honestly
to confess that he is talking nonsense, but that he

shuffles up and down in order to conceal the difficulty into which he has got himself. You and I, Socrates, might have practised a similar shuffle just now, if we had only wanted to avoid the appearance of contradiction. And if we had been arguing in a court of law there might have been reason in this; but why should a man deck himself out with vain words at a meeting of friends such as this?

Soc. I quite agree with you, Laches, that he should not. But perhaps Nicias is serious, and not merely talking for the sake of talking. Let us ask him to explain what he means, and if he has reason on his side we will agree with him; if not, we will instruct him.

La. Do you, Socrates, if you like, ask him: I think that I have asked enough.

Soc. I don't see why I should not; and my question will do for both of us.

La. Very good.

Soc. Then tell me, Nicias, or rather tell us, for Laches and I are partners in the argument: Do you mean to affirm that courage is the knowledge of the grounds of hope and fear?

Nic. I do.

Soc. And that is a very special knowledge which is not possessed by the physician or prophet, who will not be courageous unless they superadd this particular knowledge. That is what you were saying?

Nic. I was.

Soc. Then courage is not a thing which every pig would have, any more than he would have knowledge, as the proverb says?

Nic. I think not.

Soc. Clearly not, Nicias; not even such a big pig as the Crommyonian sow would be called by you courageous. And this I say not as a joke, but because I think that he who assents to your doctrine, that courage is the knowledge of the grounds of fear and hope, can not allow that any wild beast is courageous, unless he admits that a lion, or a leopard, or perhaps a boar, or any other animal, has a degree of wisdom which but a few human beings, and these only with difficulty, attain. He who takes your view of courage must affirm that a lion, and a stag, and a bull, and a monkey, have equally little pretensions to courage.

La. Capital, Socrates; by the gods, that is truly good. And I hope, Nicias, that you will tell us whether these animals, which we all admit to be courageous, are really wiser than mankind; or whether you will have the boldness, in the face of universal opinion, to deny their courage.

Nic. Why, Laches, I don't call animals or any other things courageous, which have no fear of dangers, because they are ignorant of them, but fearless and senseless only. Do you think that I should call little children courageous, which fear no dangers because they know none? There is a difference, as I should imagine, between fearlessness and courage. Now I am of opinion that thoughtful courage is a quality possessed by very few, but that rashness, and boldness, and fearlessness, which has no forethought, are very common qualities possessed by many men, many women, many children, many animals. And you, and men in general, call by the term " courageous " actions which I call rash, and my courageous actions are wise actions.

La. Behold, Socrates, how admirably, as he thinks, he dresses himself out in words, while seeking to deprive of the honor of courage those whom all the world acknowledges to be courageous.

Nic. Be of good cheer, Laches; for I am quite

willing to say of you and also of Lamachus, and of many other Athenians, that you are courageous and therefore wise.

La. I could answer that; but I would not have you cast in my teeth that I am a haughty Aexonian.

Soc. I would not have you answer him, for I fancy, Laches, that you have not discovered whence his wisdom comes; he has got all this from my friend Damon, and Damon is always with Prodicus, who, of all the Sophists, is considered to be the best taker to pieces of words of this sort.

La. Yes, Socrates; and the examination of such niceties is a much more suitable employment for a Sophist than for a great statesman whom the city chooses to preside over her.

Soc. But still, my sweet friend, a great statesman is just the man to have a great mind. And I think that the view which is implied in Nicias' definition of courage is worthy of examination.

La. Then examine for yourself, Socrates.

Soc. That is what I am going to do, my dear friend. Don't, however, suppose that I shall let you out of the partnership; for I shall expect you to apply your mind, and join with me in the consideration of the question.

La. I do not object if you think that I ought.

Soc. Yes, I do; and I must beg of you, Nicias, to begin again. You remember that we originally considered courage to be a part of virtue.

Nic. Very true.

Soc. And you yourself said that this was a part, and that there were many other parts, all of which together are called virtue.

Nic. Certainly.

Soc. Do you agree with me about the parts? For 1 say that justice, temperance, and the like, are all of them parts of virtue as well as courage. Would you not say the same?

Nic. Certainly.

Soc. Well then, about that we are agreed. And now let us proceed a step, and see whether we are equally agreed about the fearful and the hopeful. Let me tell you my own opinion, and if I am wrong you shall set me right: my opinion is that the terrible and the hopeful are the things which do or do not create fear, and that fear is not of the present, nor of the past, but is of future and expected evil. Do you not agree to that, Laches?

La. Yes, Socrates, entirely.

Soc. That is my view, Nicias; the terrible things, as I should say, are the evils which are future; and the hopeful are the good or not evil things which are future. Do you or do you not agree in this?

Nic. I agree.

Soc. And the knowledge of these things you call courage?

Nic. Precisely.

Soc. And now let me see whether you agree with Laches and myself in a third point.

Nic. What is that?

Soc. I will tell you. He and I have a notion that there is not one knowledge or science of the past, another of the present, a third of what will be and will be best in the future; but that of all three there is one science only: for example, there is one science of medicine which is concerned with the inspection of health equally in all times, present, past, and future; and of husbandry in like manner, which is concerned with the productions of the earth. And as to the general's art, you yourself will be my witnesses, that the general has to think of the future as well as the present; and he considers that he is not to be the servant of the soothsayer, but his master, because he knows better what is happening or is likely to happen in war: and accordingly the law places the soothsayer under the general, and not the general under the soothsayer. Am I not correct, Laches?

La. Quite correct.

Soc. And do you, Nicias, also acknowledge that the same science has understanding of the same things, whether future, present, or past?

Nic. Yes, indeed, Socrates; that is my opinion.

Soc. And courage, my friend, is, as you say, a knowledge of the fearful and of the hopeful?

Nic. Yes.

Soc. And the fearful, and the hopeful, are admitted to be future goods and future evils?

Nic. True.

Soc. And the same science has to do with the same things in the future or at any time?

Nic. That is true.

Soc. Then courage is not the science which is concerned with the fearful and hopeful, for they are future only; and courage, like the other sciences, is concerned not only with good and evil of the future, but of the present, and past, and of any time?

Nic. That, as I suppose, is true.

Soc. Then the answer which you have given, Nicias, includes only a third part of courage; but our question extended to the whole nature of courage: and according to your view, that is, according to your present view, courage is not only the knowledge of the hopeful and the fearful, but seems to include nearly every good and evil without reference to time. What do you say to that alteration in your statement?

Nic. I agree to that, Socrates.

Soc. But then, my dear friend, if a man knew all

good and evil, and how they are, and have been, and
will be produced, would he not be perfect, and wanting in no virtue, whether justice, or temperance, or
holiness? He would possess them all, and he would
know which were dangers and which were not, and
guard against them whether they were supernatural
or natural; and he would provide the good, as he
would know how to deal with gods or men.

Nic. I think, Socrates, that there is a great deal of
truth in what you say.

Soc. But then, Nicias, courage, according to this
new definition of yours, instead of being a part of
virtue only, will be all virtue?

Nic. I suppose that is true.

Soc. But we were saying that courage is one of the
parts of virtue?

Nic. Yes, that was what we were saying.

Soc. And that is in contradiction with our present
view?

Nic. That appears to be the case.

Soc. Then, Nicias, we have not discovered what
courage is.

Nic. We have not.

La. And yet, friend Nicias, I imagined that you
would have made the discovery, as you were so contemptuous of the answers which I made to Socrates.
I had very great hopes that you would have been
enlightened by the wisdom of Damon.

Nic. I perceive, Laches, that you think nothing of
having displayed your ignorance of the nature of
courage, but you look only to see whether I have not
made a similar display; and if we are both equally
ignorant of the things which a man who is good for
anything should know, that, I suppose, will be of no
consequence. You certainly appear to me very like
the rest of the world, looking at your neighbor and

not at yourself. I am of opinion that enough has been said on the subject of discussion; and if anything has been imperfectly said, that may be hereafter corrected by the help of Damon, whom you think to deride, although you have never seen him, and with the help of others. And when I am satisfied myself, I will freely impart my satisfaction to you, for I think that you are very much in want of knowledge.

La. You are a philosopher, Nicias; of that I am aware: nevertheless I would recommend Lysimachus and Melesias not to take you and me as advisers about the education of their children; but, as I said at first, they should ask Socrates; and if my sons were old enough, I would have asked him myself.

Nic. To that I quite agree, if Socrates is willing to take them under his charge. I should not wish for any one else to be the tutor of Niceratus. But I observe that when I mention the matter to him he recommends to me some other tutor and refuses himself. Perhaps he may be more ready to listen to you, Lysimachus.

Lys. He ought, Nicias: for certainly I would do things for him which I would not do for many others. What do you say, Socrates — will you comply? And are you ready to give assistance in the improvement of the youths?

Soc. Indeed, Lysimachus, I should be very wrong in refusing to aid in the improvement of anybody. And if I had shown in this conversation that I had a knowledge which Nicias and Laches have not, then I admit that you would be right in inviting me to perform this duty; but as we are all in the same perplexity, why should one of us be preferred to another? I certainly think that no one should; and under these circumstances, let me offer you a piece of advice (and this need not go further than ourselves).

I maintain, my friends, that every one of us should seek out the best teacher whom he can find, first for ourselves, and then for the youth, regardless of expense or anything. But I can not advise that we remain as we are. And if any one laughs at us for going to school at our age, I would quote to them the authority of Homer, who says, that

" Modesty is not good for a needy man."

Let us then, regardless of the remarks which are made upon us, make the education of the youths our own education.

Lys. I like your proposal, Socrates; and as I am the oldest, I am also the most eager to go to school with the boys. Let me beg a favor of you: come to my house to-morrow at dawn, and we will advise about these matters. For the present, let us make an end of the conversation.

Soc. I will come to you to-morrow, Lysimachus, as you propose, God willing.

PROTAGORAS

INTRODUCTION

THE Protagoras, like several of the Dialogues of Plato, is put into the mouth of Socrates, who describes a conversation which had taken place between himself and the great Sophist at the house of Callias—"the man who had spent more upon the Sophists than all the rest of the world, and in which the learned Hippias and the grammarian Prodicus had also shared, as well as Alcibiades and Critias, both of whom said a few words — in the presence of a distinguished company consisting of disciples of Protagoras and of leading Athenians belonging to the Socratic circle. The Dialogue commences with a request on the part of Hippocrates that Socrates would introduce him to the celebrated teacher. He has come before the dawn had risen to testify his zeal. Socrates moderates his excitement and advises him to find out "what Protagoras will make of him," before he becomes his pupil.

They go together to the house of Callias; and Socrates, after explaining the purpose of their visit to Protagoras, asks the question "What he will make of Hippocrates?" Protagoras answers that he will make a better and a wiser man." "But in what will he be better?"—Socrates desires to have a more precise answer. Protagoras replies, "That he will teach him prudence in affairs private and public; in short, the science or knowledge of human life."

This, as Socrates admits, is a noble profession: but he is doubtful — or rather would have been, if Protagoras had not assured him of it — whether such knowledge can be taught. And this for two reasons: (1) Because the Athenian people, who recognize in their assemblies the distinction between the skilled and the unskilled, do not recognize any distinction between the trained politician and the untrained; (2) Because the wisest and best Athenian citizens do not teach their sons political virtue. Will Protagoras explain this anomaly to him?

Protagoras explains his views in the form of an apologue, in which, after Prometheus had given men the arts, Zeus is represented as sending Hermes to them, bearing with him Justice and

Reverence. These are not, like the arts, to be imparted to a few only, but all men are to be partakers of them. Therefore the Athenian people are right in distinguishing between the skilled and unskilled in the arts, and not between skilled and unskilled politicians. (1) For all men have the political virtues to a certain degree, and whether they have them or not are obliged to say that they have them. A man would be thought a madman who professed an art which he did not know; and he would be equally thought a madman if he did not profess a virtue which he had not. (2) And that the political virtues can be taught and acquired, in the opinion of the Athenians, is proved by the fact that they punish evil-doers, with a view to prevention, of course — mere retribution is for beasts, and not for men. (3) Another proof of this is the education of youth, which begins almost as soon as they can speak, and is continued by the state, when they pass out of the control of their parents. (4) Nor is there any inconsistency in wise and good fathers having foolish and worthless sons; for (a) in the first place the young do not learn of their fathers only, but of all the citizens; and (b) this is partly a matter of chance and of natural gifts: the sons of a great statesman are not necessarily great statesmen any more than the sons of a good artist are necessarily good artists. (5) The error of Socrates lies in supposing that there are no teachers, when all men are teachers. Only a few, like Protagoras himself, are somewhat better than others.

Socrates is highly delighted, and quite satisfied with this explanation of Protagoras. But he has still a doubt lingering in his mind. Protagoras has spoken of the virtues: are they many, or one? are they parts of a whole, or different names of the same thing? Protagoras replies that they are parts, like the parts of a face, which have their several functions, and no one part is like any other part. This admission, which has been somewhat hastily made, is now taken up and cross-examined by Socrates:

" Is justice just, and is holiness holy? And are justice and holiness opposed to one another? " — " Then justice is unholy." Protagoras would rather say that justice is different from holiness, and yet in a certain point of view nearly the same. He does not, however, escape in this way from the cunning of Socrates, who entangles him into an admission that everything has but one opposite. Folly, for example, is opposed to wisdom; and folly is also opposed to temperance; and therefore temperance and wisdom are the same. And holiness has been already admitted to be nearly the same as justice. Temperance, therefore, has now to be compared with justice.

Protagoras, whose temper begins to get a little ruffled at the process to which he has been subjected, is aware that he will soon be compelled by the dialectics of Socrates to admit that the temperate is the just. He therefore defends himself with his favorite weapon; that is to say, he makes a long speech not much to the point, which elicits the applause of the audience.

Here occurs a sort of interlude, which commences with a declaration on the part of Socrates that he can not follow a long speech, and therefore he must beg Protagoras to speak shorter. As Protagoras declines to accommodate him, he rises to depart, but is detained by Callias, who thinks him unreasonable in not allowing Protagoras the liberty which he takes himself of speaking as he likes. But Alcibiades answers that the two cases are not parallel. For Socrates admits his inability to speak long; will Protagoras in like manner acknowledge his inability to speak short?

Counsels of moderation are urged first in a few words by Critias, and then by Prodicus in balanced and sententious language: and Hippias proposes an umpire. But who is to be the umpire? rejoins Socrates; he would rather suggest as a compromise that Protagoras shall ask, and he will answer. To this Protagoras yields a reluctant assent.

Protagoras selects as the thesis of his questions a poem of Simonides of Ceos, in which he professes to find a contradiction. First the poet says,

"Hard is it to become good,"

and then reproaches Pittacus for having said, "Hard is it to be good." How is this to be reconciled? Socrates, who is familiar with the poem, is embarrassed at first, and invokes the aid of Prodicus the Cean, who must come to the help of his countryman, but apparently only with the intention of flattering him into absurdities. First a distinction is drawn between to be, and to become: to become good is difficult; to be good is easy. Then the word difficult or hard is explained to mean "evil" in the Cean dialect. To this Prodicus assents; but when Protagoras reclaims, Socrates slily withdraws Prodicus from the fray, under the pretence that his assent was only intended to test the wits of his adversary. He then proceeds to give another and more elaborate explanation of the whole passage. The explanation is as follows: —

The Lacedaemonians are great philosophers (although this is a fact which is not generally known); and the soul of their philosophy is brevity, which was also the style of primitive antiquity and of the seven sages. Now Pittacus had a saying, "Hard is it to be good:" Simonides was jealous of the fame of this saying, and wrote a poem which was designed to controvert it. No, says he, Pittacus; not "hard to be good," but "hard to become good." Socrates proceeds to argue in a highly impressive manner that the whole composition is intended as an attack upon Pittacus. This, though manifestly absurd, is accepted by the company, and meets with the special approval of Hippias, who has however a favorite interpretation of his own, which he is requested by Alcibiades to defer.

The argument is now resumed, not without some disdainful remarks of Socrates on the practice of introducing the poets, who ought not to be allowed, any more than flute-girls, to come into good society. Men's own thoughts should supply them with the materials for 'discussion. A few soothing flatteries are addressed to Protagoras by Callias and Socrates, and then the old question is repeated, "Whether the virtues are one or many?" To which Protagoras is now disposed to reply, that four out of the five virtues are in some degree similar; but he still contends that the fifth, courage, is wholly dissimilar. Socrates proceeds to undermine the last stronghold of the adversary, first obtaining from him the admission that all virtue is in the highest degree good:

The courageous are the confident; and the confident are those who know their business or profession: those who have no such knowledge and are still confident are madmen. This is admitted. Then, says Socrates, courage is knowledge — an inference which Protagoras evades by drawing a futile distinction between the courageous and the confident in a fluent speech.

Socrates renews the attack from another side: he would like to know whether pleasure is not the only good, and pain the only evil? Protagoras seems to doubt the morality or propriety of assenting to this; he would rather say that "some pleasures are good, some pains are evil," which is also the opinion of the generality of mankind. What does he think of knowledge? does he agree with the common opinion about this also, that knowledge is overpowered by passion? or does he hold that knowledge is power? Protagoras agrees that knowledge is certainly a governing power.

This, however, is not the doctrine of men in general, who maintain that many who know what is best, act contrary to their knowledge under the influence of pleasure. But this opposition of good and evil is really the opposition of a greater or lesser amount of pleasure. Pleasures are evils because they end in pain, and pains are good because they end in pleasures. Thus pleasure is seen to be the only good; and the only evil is the preference of the lesser pleasure to the greater. But then comes in the illusion of distance. Some art of mensuration is required in order to show us pleasures and pains in their true proportion. This art of mensuration is a kind of knowledge, and knowledge is thus proved once more to be the governing principle of human life, and ignorance the origin of all evil: for no one prefers the less pleasure to the greater, or the greater pain to the less, except from ignorance. The argument is drawn out in an imaginary " dialogue within a dialogue," conducted by Socrates and Protagoras on the one part, and the rest of the world on the other. Hippias and Prodicus, as well as Protagoras, admit the soundness of the conclusion.

Socrates then applies this new conclusion to the case of courage — the only virtue which still holds out against the assaults of the Socratic dialectic. No one chooses the evil or refuses the good except through ignorance. This explains why cowards refuse to go to war: — because they form a wrong estimate of good, and honor, and pleasure. And why are the courageous willing to go to war? — because they form a right estimate of pleasures and pains, of things terrible and not terrible. Courage then is knowledge, and cowardice is ignorance. And the five virtues, which were originally maintained to have five different natures, after having been easily reduced to two only, are at last resolved in one. The assent of Protagoras to this last position is extracted with great difficulty.

Socrates concludes by professing his disinterested love of the truth, and remarks on the singular manner in which he and his adversary had changed sides. Protagoras began by asserting, and Socrates by denying, the teachableness of virtue, and now the latter ends by affirming that virtue is knowledge, which is the most teachable of all things, while Protagoras has been striving to show that virtue is not knowledge, and this is almost equivalent to saying that virtue can not be taught. He is not satisfied with the result, and would like to renew the inquiry with the help of Protagoras in a different order, asking (1) What virtue is, and (2) Whether virtue can be taught. Protagoras declines this offer, but commends Socrates' earnestness and mode of discussion.

The Protagoras is often supposed to be full of difficulties. These are partly imaginary and partly real. The imaginary ones are: (1) Chronological, — which were pointed out in ancient times by Athenaeus, and are noticed by Schleiermacher and others, and relate to the impossibility of all the persons in the Dialogue meeting at any one time, whether in the year 425 B. C., or in any other. But Plato, like other writers of fiction, aims only at the probable, and has shown in other Dialogues (e. g. the Symposium and Republic) an extreme disregard of the historical accuracy which is sometimes demanded of him. (2) The exact place of the Protagoras among the Dialogues, and the date of composition, have also been much disputed. But there are no criteria which afford any real grounds for determining the date of composition; and the affinities of the Dialogues, when they are not indicated by Plato himself, must always to some extent remain uncertain. (3) There is another class of difficulties, which may be ascribed to preconceived notions of commentators, who imagine that Protagoras the Sophist ought always to be in the wrong, and his adversary Socrates in the right; or that in this or that passage — e. g. in the explanation of good as pleasure — Plato is inconsistent with himself; or that the Dialogue fails in unity, and has not a proper " beginning, middle, and ending." They seem to forget that Plato is a dramatic writer who throws his thoughts into both sides of the argument, and certainly does not aim at any unity which is inconsistent with freedom, and with a natural or even wild manner of treating his subject; also that his mode of revealing the truth is by lights and shadows, and far off and opposing points of view, and not by dogmatic statements or definite results.

The real difficulties arise out of the extreme subtlety of the work, which, as Socrates says of the poem of Simonides, is a most perfect piece of art. There are dramatic contrasts and interests, threads of philosophy broken and resumed, satirical reflections on mankind, veils thrown over truths which are lightly suggested, and all woven together in a single design, and moving towards one end.

In the introductory scene Plato raises the expectation that a " great personage " is about to appear on the stage (perhaps with a further view of showing that he is destined to be overthrown by a greater still, who makes no pretensions). Before introducing Hippocrates to him, Socrates thinks proper to warn the youth of the dangers of "influence," of the invidious nature of which Protagoras is also sensible. Hippocrates readily adopts the suggestion of Socrates that he shall learn the accomplishments which befit an Athenian gentleman of Protagoras, and let alone his "sophistry." There is nothing however in the introduction which leads to the inference that Plato intended to blacken the character of the Sophists; he only makes a little merry at their expense.

The " great personage " is somewhat ostentatious, but frank and honest. He is introduced on a stage which is worthy of him — at the house of the rich Callias, in which are congregated the noblest and wisest of the Athenians. He considers openness to be the best policy, and particularly mentions his own liberal mode of dealing with his pupils, as if in answer to the favorite accusation of the Sophists that they received pay. He is remarkable for the good temper which he exhibits throughout the discussion under the trying and often sophistical cross-examination of Socrates. Although once or twice ruffled, and reluctant to continue the discussion, he parts company on perfectly good terms, and appears to be, as he says of himself, the " least jealous of mankind."

Nor is there anything in the sentiments of Protagoras which impairs this pleasing impression of the grave and weighty old man. His real defect is that he is inferior to Socrates in dialectics. The opposition between him and Socrates is not the opposition of good and bad, true and false, but of the old art of rhetoric and the new science of interrogation and argument; also of the irony of Socrates and the self-assertion of the Sophists. There is quite as much truth on the side of Protagoras as of Socrates; but the truth of Protagoras is based on common sense and common maxims of morality, while that of Socrates is paradoxical or transcendental, and though full of meaning and insight, hardly intelligible to the rest of mankind.

For example: (1) one of the noblest statements to be found in antiquity about the preventive nature of punishment is put into the mouth of Protagoras; (2) he is clearly right also in maintaining that virtue can be taught (which Socrates himself, at the end of the Dialogue, is disposed to concede); and also (3) in his explanation of the phenomenon that good fathers have bad sons; (4) he is right also in observing that the virtues are not like the arts, gifts, or attainments of special individuals, but the common property of all: this, which in all ages has been the strength and weakness of ethics and politics, is deeply seated in human nature; (5) there is a sort of half truth in the notion that all civilized men are teachers of virtue; and (6) the religious allegory should be noticed, in which the arts are said to be given by Prometheus (who stole them), whereas justice and reverence and the political virtues could only be imparted by Zeus. It is observable also (7) in the latter part of the Dialogue, when Socrates is arguing that " pleasure is the only good," Protagoras deems it more in accordance with his character to maintain that " some pleasures only are good."

There is no reason to suppose that in all this Plato is depicting an imaginary Protagoras; at any rate, he is showing us the teaching of the Sophists under the milder aspect under which he once regarded them. Nor is there any reason to doubt that Socrates is equally an historical character, paradoxical, ironical, tiresome, but seeking for the unity of virtue and knowledge as for a precious treasure; willing to rest this even on a calculation of pleasure, and irresistible here, as everywhere in Plato, in his intellectual superiority.

The aim of Socrates, and of the Dialogue, is to show the unity of virtue. In the determination of this question the identity of virtue and knowledge is found to be involved. But if virtue and knowledge are one, then virtue can be taught; the end of the Dialogue returns to the beginning. Had Protagoras been allowed by Plato to make the Aristotelian distinction, and say that virtue is not knowledge, but is accompanied with knowledge; or to point out with Aristotle that the same quality may have more than one opposite; or with Plato himself in the Phaedo to deny that good is a mere exchange of a greater pleasure for a less — the unity of virtue and the identity of virtue and knowledge would have required to be proved by other arguments.

The victory of Socrates over Protagoras is in every way complete when their minds are fairly brought together. Protagoras falls before him after two or three blows. Socrates partially gains his object in the first part, and completely in the second. Nor does he appear at any disadvantage when subjected to " the question " by Protagoras. He succeeds in making his two " friends," Prodicus and Hippias, ludicrous by the way; he also makes a long speech in defence of the poem of Simonides, after the manner of the Sophists, showing, as Alcibiades says, that he is only pretending to have a bad memory.

Not having the whole of this poem before us, it is impossible for us to answer certainly the question of Protagoras, how the two passages of Simonides are to be reconciled. We can only follow the indications given by Plato himself. But it seems likely that the reconcilement offered by Socrates is only a caricature of the methods of interpretation which were practised by the Sophists — for the following reasons: (1) The transparent irony of the previous interpretations given by Socrates. (2) The ludicrous opening of the speech in which the Lacedaemonians are described as the true philosophers, and Laconic brevity as the true form of philosophy, evidently with an allusion to Protagoras' long speeches. (3) The manifest futility and absurdity of the explanation of ἐμῶν ἐπαίνημι ἀλαθέως, which is hardly consistent with the rational interpretation of the rest of the poem. The opposition of εἶναι and γενέσθαι seems also intended to express the rival doctrines of Socrates and Protagoras, and is a sort of facetious commentary on their differences. (4) The general treatment in Plato both of the Poets and the Sophists, who are their interpreters, and whom he delights to identify with them. (5) The depreciating spirit in which Socrates speaks of the introduction of the poets as a substitute for original conversation, which is intended to contrast with Protagoras' exaltation of the study of them — this again is hardly consistent with the serious defence of Simonides. (6) The marked approval of Hippias, who is supposed at once to catch the familiar sound, just as in the previous conversation Prodicus is represented as ready to accept any distinctions of language however absurd. At the same time Hippias is desirous of substituting a new interpretation of his own; as if the words might really be made to mean anything, and were only to be regarded as affording a field for the ingenuity of the interpreter.

This curious passage is, therefore, to be regarded as Plato's satire on the tedious and hypercritical arts of interpretation which prevailed in his own day, and may be compared with his condemnation of the same arts when applied to mythology in the Phaedrus, and with his other parodies, e. g. with the second speech in the Phaedrus and with the Menexenus. Several lesser touches of satire appear in it, e. g. the claim of philosophy advanced for the Lacedaemonians, which is a parody of the claims advanced for the Poets by Protagoras; the mistake of the Laconizing set in supposing that the Lacedaemonians are a great nation because they bruise their ears; the far-fetched notion, which is " really too bad," that Simonides uses the Lesbian (?) word, ἐπαίνημι, because he is addressing a Lesbian. The whole may also be considered as a satire on those who spin pompous theories out of nothing.

All the interests and contrasts of character in a great dramatic work like the Protagoras are not easily exhausted. The impressiveness of the scene should not be lost upon us, or the gradual substitution of Socrates in the second part for Protagoras in the first. There is Alcibiades, who is compelled by the necessity of his nature to be a partisan, lending effectual aid to Socrates; there is Critias assuming the tone of impartiality; Callias there as always inclining to the Sophist, but eager for any intellectual repast; Prodicus, who finds an opportunity for displaying his distinctions of language; Hippias, for exhibiting his vanity and superficial knowledge of natural philosophy. Both of these have been previously a good deal damaged by the mock sublime description of them in the introduction. It may be remarked that Protagoras is consistently presented to us throughout as the teacher of moral and political virtue; there is no allusion to the theories of sensation which are attributed to him elsewhere, or to his denial of the existence of the gods; he is the religious rather than the irreligious teacher in this Dialogue. Also it may be observed that Socrates shows him as much respect as is consistent with his own ironical character.

It remains to be considered in what relation the Protagoras stands to the other Dialogues of Plato. That it is one of the earlier or purely Socratic works — perhaps the last, as it is certainly the greatest of them — is indicated by the absence of all allusion to the doctrine of reminiscence; and also probably by the different attitude assumed towards the teaching and persons of the Sophists in some of the later Dialogues. The Charmides, Laches, Lysis, all touch on the question of the relation of knowledge to virtue, and may be regarded, if not as preliminary studies or sketches of the more important work, at any rate as closely connected with it. The Io and Hippias contain discussions of the Poets, which offer a parallel to the ironical criticism of the verses of Simonides, and are conceived in a similar spirit. The affinity of the Protagoras to the Meno is more doubtful. For there, although the same question is discussed, " whether virtue can be taught," and the relation of Meno to the Sophists is much the same as that of Hippocrates, the answer to the question is supplied out of the doctrine of ideas; the real Socrates is already passing into the Platonic one. At a later stage of the Platonic philosophy we shall find that both the paradox and the solution of it appear to have been retracted. The Phaedo, the Gorgias, and the Philebus offer further corrections of the teaching of the Protagoras; in all of them the doctrine that virtue is pleasure,

or that pleasure is the chief or only good, is distinctly renounced.

Thus after many preparations and oppositions, both of the
characters of men and aspects of the truth, especially of the
popular and philosophical aspect; and after many interruptions
and detentions by the way, which, as Theodorus says in the
Theaetetus, are quite as agreeable as the argument, we arrive
at the great Socratic thesis that virtue is knowledge. This is
an aspect of the truth which was lost almost as soon as it was
found; and yet has to be recovered by every one for himself
who would pass the limits of proverbial and popular philosophy.
It is not to be regarded only as a passing stage in the history of
the human mind, but as an anticipation of the reconcilement of
the moral and intellectual elements of human nature.

PROTAGORAS

PERSONS OF THE DIALOGUE

SOCRATES, *who is the narrator of the Dialogue to his Companion.*
HIPPOCRATES.
ALCIBIADES.
CRITIAS.

PROTAGORAS,
HIPPIAS,
PRODICUS,
} *Sophists.*

CALLIAS, *a wealthy Athenian.*

SCENE — The House of Callias.

Com. WHERE do you come from, Socrates? And yet I need hardly ask the question, as I know that you have been in chase of the fair Alcibiades. I saw him the day before yesterday; and he had got a beard like a man, — and he is a man, as I may tell you in your ear. But I thought that he was still very charming.

Soc. What of his beard? Are you not of Homer's opinion, who says that

" Youth is most charming when the beard first appears " ?

And that is now the charm of Alcibiades.

Com. Well, and how do matters proceed? Have you been visiting him, and was he gracious to you?

Soc. Yes, I thought that he was very gracious; and especially to-day, for I have just come from him, and he has been helping me in an argument. But shall I tell you a strange thing? Although he was present, I never attended to him, and several times he quite passed out of my mind.

Com. What is the meaning of this? Has anything happened between you and him? For surely you can not have discovered a fairer love than he is; certainly not in this city of Athens.

Soc. Yes, much fairer.

Com. What do you mean — a citizen or a foreigner?

Soc. A foreigner.

Com. Of what country?

Soc. Of Abdera.

Com. And is this stranger really in your opinion fairer than the son of Cleinias?

Soc. And is not the wiser always the fairer, sweet friend?

Com. But have you really met, Socrates, with some wise one?

Soc. Yes; I would say rather, with the wisest of all living men, if you are willing to accord that title to Protagoras.

Com. What! Do you mean to say that Protagoras is in Athens?

Soc. Yes; he has been here two days.

Com. And do you just come from an interview with him?

Soc. Yes; and I have heard and said many things.

Com. Then, if you have no engagement, suppose that you sit down and tell me what passed, and my attendant shall give up his place to you.

Soc. To be sure; and I shall be grateful to you for listening.

Com. Thank you, too, for telling us.

Soc. That is thank you twice over. Listen then: —

Last night, or rather very early this morning, Hippocrates, the son of Apollodorus and the brother of Phason, gave a tremendous thump with his staff at my door; some one opened to him, and he came rushing in and bawled out: Socrates, are you awake or asleep?

I knew his voice, and said: Hippocrates, is that you? and do you bring any news?

Good news, he said; nothing but good.

Very good, I said; but what news? and why have you come here at this unearthly hour?

He drew nearer to me and said: Protagoras is come.

Yes, I said; he came two days ago: have you only just heard of his arrival?

Yes, indeed, he said; I heard yesterday evening.

At the same time he felt for the truckle-bed, and sat down at my feet, and then he said: I heard yesterday, quite late in the evening, on my return from Oenoe whither I had gone in pursuit of my runaway slave Satyrus — as I was going to have told you if some other matter had not come in the way; — on my return, when we had done supper and were about to retire to rest, my brother said to me: Protagoras is come. And I was going to you at once, if I had not considered that the night was far spent. But when sleep relaxed her hold on me after my toil, I got up and came hither direct.

I, who knew the very courageous madness of the man, said: What is the matter? has Protagoras robbed you of anything?

He replied, laughing: Yes, indeed he has, Socrates, of the wisdom which he keeps to himself.

But, surely, I said, if you give him money, and make friends with him, he will make you as wise as he is himself.

Would to heaven, he replied, that he would! He might take all that I have, and all that my friends have, if he would. And that is why I have come to you now, in order that you may speak to him on my behalf; for I am young, and also I have never seen nor heard him; (when he visited Athens before I was but a child;) and all men praise him, Socrates, as being the most accomplished of speakers. There is no reason why we should not go to him at once, and then we shall find him at home. He lodges, as I hear, with Callias the son of Hipponicus. Let us start.

I replied: Not yet, my good friend; the hour is too early. But let us rise and take a turn in the court and wait there until daybreak, and when the day breaks, then we will go; for Protagoras is generally at home, and we shall be sure to find him; never fear.

Upon this we got up and walked about in the court, and I thought that I would make trial of the strength of his resolution. So I examined him and put questions to him. Tell me, Hippocrates, I said, as you are going to Protagoras, and will be paying your money to him, what is he to whom you are going? and what will he make of you? If you were going to Hippocrates, the Coan, the Asclepiad, and were about to give him your money, and some one said to you: As being what, do you give money to your namesake Hippocrates, O Hippocrates? what would you answer?

I should say, he replied, that I give money to him as a physician.

And what will he make of you?

A physician, he said.

And if you went to Polycleitus the Argive, or Pheidias the Athenian, and intended to give them money, and some one were to ask you: As being what, do you give this money to Polycleitus and Pheidias? what would you answer?

I should answer, as being statuaries.

And what will they make of you?

A statuary, of course.

Well now, I said, you and I are going to Protagoras, and we are ready to pay him money for you. If our own means are sufficient, and we can gain him with these, we shall be too glad; but if not, then we are to spend your friends' money as well. Now suppose, that while we are in this intense state of excitement, some one were to say to us: Tell me, Socrates, and you Hippocrates, as being what, are you going to pay money to Protagoras? how should we answer him? I know that Pheidias is a sculptor, and Homer is a poet; but what appellation is given to Protagoras? how is he designated?

They call him a Sophist, Socrates, he replied.

Then we are going to pay our money to him in the character of a Sophist?

Certainly.

But suppose a person were to ask this further question: And how about yourself? what will Protagoras make you, if you go to see him?

He answered, with a blush upon his face (for the day was just beginning to dawn, so that I could see him): Unless this differs in some way from the former instances, I suppose that he will make a Sophist of me.

And are you not, in sober earnest ashamed, I said, at having to appear before the Hellenes in the character of a Sophist?

Indeed, Socrates, if I am to confess the truth, I am.

But why do you assume, Hippocrates, that the instruction of Protagoras is of this nature? and why may you not learn of him in the same way that you learned the arts of the grammarian, or musician, or trainer, not with the view of making any of them a profession, but only as a part of education, and because a private gentleman and freeman ought to know them?

Just so, he said; and that, in my opinion, is a far truer account of the teaching of Protagoras.

I said: I wonder whether you know what you are doing?

And what am I doing?

You are going to commit your soul to the care of a man whom you call a Sophist. And yet I hardly think that you know what a Sophist is; and if not, then you do not even know whether you are committing your soul to good or evil.

I certainly think that I do know, he replied.

Then tell me, what do you imagine that he is?

I take him to be one who is wise and knowing, he replied, as his name implies.

And might you not, I said, affirm this of the painter and the carpenter also; are not they, too, wise and knowing? But suppose a person were to ask us: In what are the painters wise? We should answer: In what relates to the making of likenesses, and similarly of other things. And if he were further to ask: What is the wisdom of the Sophist, and what is the manufacture over which he presides? how should we answer him?

How should we answer him, Socrates? What other answer could there be but that he presides over the art which makes men eloquent?

Yes, I replied, that is very likely a true, but not a sufficient answer; for a further question is involved: About what does the Sophist make a man eloquent? The player on the lyre may be supposed to make a man eloquent about that which he makes him understand, that is about playing the lyre. Is not that true?

Yes.

Then about what does the Sophist make him eloquent? must not he make him eloquent in that which he understands?

Yes, that may be assumed.

And what is that which the Sophist knows and makes his disciple know?

Indeed, he said, that I can not tell.

Then I proceeded to say: Well, but are you aware of the danger which you are incurring? If you were going to commit the body to some one, and there was a risk of your getting good or harm from him, would you not carefully consider and ask the opinion of your friends and kindred, and deliberate many days as to whether you should give him the care of your body? But when the soul is in question, which you hold to be of far more value than the body, and upon the well or ill-being of which depends your all, — about this you never consulted either with your father or with your brother or with any one of us who are your companions. But no sooner does this foreigner appear, than you instantly commit your soul to his keeping. In the evening, as you say, you hear of him, and in the morning you go to him, never deliberating, or taking the opinion of any one as to whether you ought to intrust yourself to him or not; — you have quite made up your mind that you will be a pupil of Protagoras, and are prepared to expend all the property of yourself and of your friends in carrying out at any price this determination, although, as you admit, you do not know him, and have never spoken with him: and you call him a Sophist, but are manifestly ignorant of what a Sophist is; and yet you are going to commit yourself to his keeping.

When he heard me say this he replied: That I suppose, Socrates, is the conclusion which I must draw from your words.

I proceeded: Is not a Sophist, Hippocrates, one who deals wholesale or retail in the food of the soul? To me that appears to be the sort of man.

And what, Socrates, is the food of the soul?

Surely, I said, knowledge is the food of the soul; and we must take care, my friend, that the Sophist does not deceive us when he praises what he sells, like the dealers wholesale or retail who sell the food of the body; for they praise indiscriminately all their goods, without knowing what are really beneficial or hurtful: neither do their customers know, with the exception of any trainer or physician who may happen to buy of them. In like manner those who carry about the wares of knowledge, and make the round of the cities, and sell or retail them to any customer who is in want of them, praise them all alike; and I should not wonder, O my friend, if many of them were really ignorant of their effect upon the soul; and their customers equally ignorant, unless he who buys of them happens to be a physician of the soul. If, therefore, you have understanding of what is good and evil, you may safely buy knowledge of Protagoras or of any one; but if not then, O my friend, pause, and do not hazard your dearest interests at a game of chance. For there is far greater peril in buying knowledge than in buying meat and drink: the one you purchase of the wholesale or retail dealer, and carry them away in other vessels, and before you receive them into the body as food, you may deposit them at home and call in any experienced friend who knows what is good to be eaten or drunken, and what not, and how much, and when; and hence the danger of purchasing them is not so great. But when you buy the wares of knowledge you can not carry them away in another vessel; they have been sold to you, and you must take them into the soul and go your way, either greatly harmed or greatly benefited by the lesson: and therefore we should think about this and take counsel with our elders; for we are still young — too young to determine such a matter. And now let us go, as we were intending, and hear Protagoras; and when we have heard what he has to say, we may take counsel

of others; for not only is Protagoras at the house of
Callias, but there is Hippias of Elis, and, if I am not
mistaken, Prodicus of Ceos, and several other wise
men.

To this we agreed, and proceeded on our way until
we reached the vestibule of the house; and there we
stopped in order to finish a dispute which had arisen
as we were going along; and we stood talking in the
vestibule until we had finished and come to an understanding. And I think that the door-keeper, who
was a eunuch, and who was probably annoyed at the
great inroad of the Sophists, must have heard us talking. At any rate, when we knocked at the door,
and he opened and saw us, he grumbled: They are
Sophists — he is not at home; and instantly gave the
door a hearty bang with both his hands. Again we
knocked, and he answered without opening: Did you
not hear me say that he is not at home, fellows? But,
my friend, I said, we are not Sophists, and we are not
come to see Callias; fear not, for we want to see
Protagoras; and I must request you to announce us.
At last, after a good deal of difficulty, the man was
persuaded to open the door.

When we entered, we found Protagoras taking a
walk in the portico; and next to him, on one side,
were walking Callias, the son of Hipponicus, and
Paralus, the son of Pericles, who, by the mother's
side, is his half-brother, and Charmides, the son of
Glaucon. On the other side of him were Xanthippus,
the other son of Pericles, Philippides, the son of
Philomelus; also Antimoerus of Mende, who of all
the disciples of Protagoras is the most famous, and
intends to make sophistry his profession. A train of
listeners followed him, of whom the greater part appeared to be foreigners, who accompanied Protagoras
out of the various cities through which he journeyed,

Now he, like Orpheus, attracted them by his voice, and they followed the attraction. I should mention also that there were some Athenians in the company. Nothing delighted me more than the precision of their movements: they never got into his way at all; but when he and those who were with him turned back, then the band of listeners divided into two parts on either side; he was always in front, and they wheeled round and took their places behind him in perfect order.

After him, as Homer says [1], " I lifted up my eyes and saw " Hippias the Elean sitting in the opposite portico on a chair of state, and around him were seated on benches Eryximachus, the son of Acumenus, and Phaedrus the Myrrhinusian, and Andron the son of Androtion, and there were strangers whom he had brought with him from his native city of Elis, and some others: they appeared to be asking Hippias certain physical and astronomical questions, and he, *ex cathedrà,* was determining their several questions to them, and discoursing of them.

Also, " my eyes beheld Tantalus; " [2] for Prodicus the Cean was at Athens: he had been put into a room which, in the days of Hipponicus, was a storehouse; but, as the house was full, Callias had cleared this out and made the room into a guest-chamber. Now Prodicus was still in bed, wrapped up in sheepskins and bedclothes, of which there seemed to be a great heap; and there were sitting by him on the couches near, Pausanias of the deme of Cerameis, and with Pausanias was a youth quite young, who is certainly remarkable for his good looks, and if I am not mistaken, is also of a fair and gentle nature. I think that I heard him called Agathon, and my suspicion is

---

[1] Od. xi. 601 foll. [2] Od. xi. 582.

that he is the beloved of Pausanias. There was this youth, and also there were the two Adeimantuses, one the son of Cepis, and the other of Leucolophides, and some others. I was very anxious to hear what Prodicus was saying, for he seemed to me to be an extraordinarily wise and divine man; but I was not able to get into the inner circle, and his fine deep voice made an echo in the room which rendered his words inaudible.

No sooner had we entered than there followed us Alcibiades the beautiful, as you say, and I believe you; and also Critias the son of Callaeschrus.

On entering we stopped a little, in order to look about us, and then walked up to Protagoras, and I said: Protagoras, my friend Hippocrates and I have come to see you.

Do you wish, he said, to speak with me alone, or in the presence of others?

That is as you please, I said: you shall determine when you have heard the object of our visit.

And what is that? he said.

I must explain, I said, that my friend Hippocrates is a native Athenian; he is the son of Apollodorus, and of a great and prosperous house, and he is himself in natural ability quite a match for those of his own age. I believe that he aspires to political eminence; and this he thinks that conversation with you is most likely to procure for him: now it is for you to decide whether you would wish to speak to him of these matters alone or in company.

Thank you, Socrates, for your consideration of me. For certainly a stranger finding his way into great cities, and persuading the flower of the youth in them to leave the company of their other kinsmen or acquaintance, and live with him, under the idea that they will be improved by his conversation, ought to be very cautious; great jealousies are occasioned by his proceedings, and he is the subject of many enmities and conspiracies. I maintain the art of the Sophist to be of ancient date; but that in ancient times the professors of the art, fearing this odium, veiled and disguised themselves under various names, some under that of poets, as Homer, Hesiod, and Simonides, some as hierophants and prophets, as Orpheus and Musaeus, and some, as I observe, even under the name of gymnastic-masters, like Iccus of Tarentum, or the more recently celebrated Herodicus, now of Selymbria and formerly of Megara, who is a first-rate Sophist. Your own Agathocles pretended to be a musician, but was really an eminent Sophist; also Pythocleides the Cean; and there were many others; and all of them, as I was saying, adopted these arts as veils or disguises because they were afraid of the envy of the multitude. But that is not my way, for I do not believe that they effected their purpose, which was to deceive the government, who were not blinded by them; and as to the people, they have no understanding, and only repeat what their rulers are pleased to tell them. Now to run away, and to be caught in running away, is the very height of folly, and also greatly increases the exasperation of mankind; for they regard him who runs away as a rogue, in addition to any other objections which they have to him; and therefore I take an entirely opposite course, and acknowledge myself to be a Sophist and instructor of mankind; such an open acknowledgment appears to me to be a better sort of caution than concealment. Nor do I neglect other precautions, and therefore I hope, as I may say, by the favor of heaven that no harm will come of the acknowledgment that I am a Sophist. And I have been now many years in the profession — for all my years when added up are many — and there is no one here present of whom I might not be the father. Wherefore I should much prefer conversing with you, if you do not object, in the presence of the company.

As I suspected that he would like to have a little display and glory in the presence of Prodicus and Hippias, and would gladly show us to them in the light of his admirers, I said: But why should we not summon Prodicus and Hippias and their friends to hear us?

Very good, he said.

Suppose, said Callias, that we hold a council in which you may sit and discuss. This was determined, and great delight was felt at the prospect of hearing wise men talk; we ourselves all took the chairs and benches, and arranged them by Hippias, where the other benches had been already placed. Meanwhile Callias and Alcibiades got up Prodicus and brought in him and his companions.

When we were all seated, Protagoras said: Now that the company are assembled, Socrates, tell me about the young man of whom you were just now speaking.

I replied: I will begin again at the same point, Protagoras, and tell you once more the purport of my visit: this is my friend Hippocrates, who is desirous of making your acquaintance; he wants to know what will happen to him if he associates with you. That is all I have to say.

Protagoras answered: Young man, if you associate with me, on the very first day you will return home a better man than you came, and better on the second day than on the first, and better every day than you were on the day before.

When I heard this, I said: Protagoras, I do not at all wonder at hearing you say this: even at your age, and with all your wisdom, if any one were to teach you what you did not know before, you would become better no doubt: but please to answer in a different way; I will explain how by an example. Let me suppose that Hippocrates, instead of desiring your acquaintance, wished to become acquainted with the young man Zeuxippus of Heraclea, who has newly come to Athens, and he were to go to him as he has gone to you, and were to hear him say, as he has heard you say, that every day he would grow and become better if he associated with him: and then suppose that he were to ask him, " In what would he be better, and in what would he grow? " Zeuxippus would answer, " In painting." And suppose that he went to Orthagoras the Theban, and heard him say the same, and asked him " In what would he become better day by day? " he would reply, " In flute-playing." Now I want you to make the same sort of answer to this young man and to me, who am asking questions on his account. When you say that on the first day on which he associates with you he will return home a better man, and on every day will grow in like manner — in what, Protagoras, will he be better? and about what?

When Protagoras heard me say this, he replied: You ask questions fairly, and I like to answer a question which is fairly put. If Hippocrates comes to me he will not experience the sort of drudgery with which other Sophists are in the habit of insulting their pupils; who, when they have just escaped from the arts, are taken and driven back into them by these teachers, and made to learn calculation, and astronomy, and geometry, and music (he gave a look at Hippias as he said this); but if he comes to me, he will learn that which he comes to learn. And this is prudence in affairs private as well as public; he will learn to order his own house in the best manner, and he will be best able to speak and act in the affairs of the state.

Do I understand you, I said; and is your meaning that you teach the art of politics, and that you promise to make men good citizens?

That, Socrates, is exactly the profession which I make.

Then, I said, you do indeed possess a noble art, if there is no mistake about this; for I will freely confess to you, Protagoras, that I have a doubt whether this art is capable of being taught, and yet I know not how to disbelieve your assertion. And I ought to tell you why I am of opinion that this art can not be taught or communicated by man to man. I say that the Athenians are an understanding people, as indeed they are esteemed by the other Hellenes. Now I observe that when we are met together in the assembly, and the matter in hand relates to building, the builders are summoned as advisers; when the question is one of ship-building, then the ship-builders; and the like of other arts which they think capable of being taught and learned. And if some person offers to give them advice who is not supposed by them to have any skill in the art, even though he be good-looking, and rich, and noble, they don't listen to him, but laugh at him, and hoot him, until either he is clamored down and retires of himself; or if he persist, he is dragged away or put out by the constables at the command of the prytanes. This is their way of behaving about the arts which have professors. When, however, the question is an affair of state, then everybody is free to have a say — carpenter, tinker, cobbler, sailor, passenger; rich and poor, high and low — any one who likes gets up, and no one reproaches him, as in the former case, with not having learned, and having no teacher, and yet giving advice; evidently because they are under the impression that this sort of knowledge can not be taught. And not only is this true of the state, but of individuals; the best and wisest of our citizens are unable to impart their political wisdom to others: as for example, Pericles, the father of these young men, who gave them excellent instruction in all that could be learned from masters, in his own department of politics taught them nothing; nor did he give them teachers, but they were allowed to wander at their own free will in a sort of hope that they would light upon virtue of their own accord. Or take another example: there was Cleinias the younger brother of our friend Alcibiades, of whom this very same Pericles was the guardian; and he being in fact under the apprehension that Cleinias would be corrupted by Alcibiades, took him away, and placed him in the house of Ariphron to be educated; but before six months had elapsed, Ariphron sent him back, not knowing what to do with him. And I could mention numberless other instances of persons who were good themselves, and never yet made any one else good, whether friend or stranger. Now I, Protagoras, when I reflect on all this, am inclined to think that virtue can not be taught. But then again, when I listen to your words, I am disposed to waver; and I believe that there must be something in what you say, because I know that you have great experience, and learning, and invention. And I wish that you would, if possible, show me a little more clearly that virtue can be taught. Will you be so good?

That I will, Socrates, and gladly. But what would you like? Shall I, as an elder, speak to you as younger men in an apologue or myth, or shall I argue the question?

To this several of the company answered that he should choose for himself.

Well, then, he said, I think that the myth will be more interesting.

Once upon a time there were gods only, and no mortal creatures. But when the time came that these also should be created, the gods fashioned them out of earth and fire and various mixtures of both elements in the inward parts of the earth; and when they were about to bring them into the light of day, they ordered Prometheus and Epimetheus to equip them, and to distribute to them severally their proper qualities. Epimetheus said to Prometheus: " Let me distribute, and do you inspect." This was agreed, and Epimetheus made the distribution. There were some to whom he gave strength without swiftness, or again swiftness without strength; some he armed, and others he left unarmed; and devised for the latter some other means of preservation, making some large, and having their size as a protection, and others small, whose nature was to fly in the air or burrow in the ground; this was to be their way of escape. Thus did he compensate them with the view of preventing any race from becoming extinct. And when he had provided against their destruction by one another, he contrived also a means of protecting them against the seasons of heaven; clothing them with close hair and thick skins sufficient to defend them against the winter cold and summer heat, and for a natural bed of their own when they wanted to rest; also he furnished them with hoofs and hair and hard and callous skins under their feet. Then he gave them varieties of food, — to some herb of the soil, to others fruits of trees, and to others roots, and to some again he gave other animals as food. And some he made to have few young ones, while those who were their prey were very prolific; and in this way the race was preserved. Thus did Epimetheus, who, not being very wise, forgot that he had distributed among the brute animals all the qualities that he had to give, — and when he came to man, who was still unprovided, he was terribly perplexed. Now while he was in this perplexity, Prometheus came to inspect the distribution, and he found that the other animals were suitably furnished, but that man alone was naked and shoeless, and had neither bed nor arms of defence. The appointed hour was approaching in which man was to go forth into the light of day; and Prometheus, not knowing how he could devise his salvation, stole the mechanical arts of Hephaestus and Athene, and fire with them (they could neither have been acquired nor used without fire), and gave them to man. Thus man had the wisdom necessary to the support of life, but political wisdom he had not; for that was in the keeping of Zeus, and the power of Prometheus did not extend to entering into the castle of heaven, in which Zeus dwelt, who moreover had terrible sentinels; but he did enter by stealth into the common workshop of Athene and Hephaestus, in which they used to pursue their favorite arts, and took away Hephaestus' art of working by fire, and also the art of Athene, and gave them to man. And in this way man was supplied with the means of life. But Prometheus is said to have been afterwards prosecuted for theft, owing to the blunder of Epimetheus.

Now man, having a share of the divine attributes, was at first the only one of the animals who had any gods, because he alone was of their kindred; and he would raise altars and images of them. He was not long in inventing language and names; and he also constructed houses and clothes and shoes and beds, and drew sustenance from the earth. Thus provided, mankind at first lived dispersed, and there were no cities. But the consequence was that they were destroyed by the wild beasts, for they were utterly weak in comparison of them, and their art was only sufficient to provide them with the means of life, and would not enable them to carry on war against the animals: food they had, but not as yet any art of government, of which the art of war is a part. After a while the desire of self-preservation gathered them into cities; but when they were gathered together, having no art of government, they evil intreated one another, and were again in process of dispersion and destruction. Zeus feared that the race would be exterminated, and so he sent Hermes to them, bearing reverence and justice to be the ordering principles of cities and the bonds of friendship and conciliation. Hermes asked Zeus how he should impart justice and reverence among men: — should he distribute them as the arts are distributed; that is to say, to a favored few only, — for one skilled individual has enough of medicine, or of any other art, for many unskilled ones? Shall this be the manner in which I distribute justice and reverence among men, or shall I give them to all? To all, said Zeus; I should like them all to have a share; for cities can not exist, if a few only share in the virtues, as in the arts. And further, make a law by my order, that he who has no part in reverence and justice shall be put to death as a plague of the state.

And this is the reason, Socrates, why the Athenians and mankind in general, when the question relates to carpentering or any other mechanical art, allow but a few to share in their deliberations; and when any one else interferes, then, as you say, they object, if he be not of the favored few, and that, as I say, is very natural. But when they come to deliberate about political virtue, which proceeds only by way of justice and wisdom, they are patient enough of any man who speaks of them, as is also natural, because they think that every man ought to share in this sort of virtue, and that states could not exist if this were otherwise. I have explained to you, Socrates, the reason of this phenomenon.

And that you may not suppose yourself to be deceived in thinking that all men regard every man as having a share of justice and every other political virtue, let me give you a further proof, which is this. In other cases, as you are aware, if a man says that he is a good flute-player, or skilful in any other art in which he has no skill, people either laugh at him or are angry with him, and his relations think that he is mad and go and admonish him; but when honesty is in question, or some other political virtue, even if they know that he is dishonest, yet, if the man comes publicly forward and tells the truth about his dishonesty, in this case they deem that to be madness which in the other case was held by them to be good sense. They say that men ought to profess honesty whether they are honest or not, and that a man is mad who does not make such a profession. Their notion is, that a man must have some degree of honesty; and that if he has none at all he ought not to be in the world.

I have been showing that they are right in admitting every man as a counsellor about this sort of virtue, as they are of opinion that every man is a partaker of it. And I will now endeavor further to show that they regard this virtue, not as given by nature, or growing spontaneously, but as capable of being learned and acquired by study. For injustice is punished, whereas no one would instruct, or rebuke, or be angry at those whose calamities they suppose to come to them either by nature or chance; they do not try to alter them, they do but pity them. Who would be so foolish as to chastise or instruct the ugly, or the diminutive, or the feeble? And for this reason; they know, I imagine, that this sort of good and evil comes to them by nature and chance; whereas if a man is wanting in those good qualities which come to men from study and exercise and teaching, and has only the contrary evil qualities, men are angry with him, and punish him and reprove him. And one of those evil qualities is impiety and injustice, and they may be described generally as the opposite of political virtue. When this is the case, any man will be angry with another, and reprimand him, — clearly under the impression that by study and learning the virtue in which he is deficient may be acquired. For if you will think, Socrates, of the effect which punishment has on evil-doers, you will see at once that in the opinion of mankind virtue may be acquired; for no one punishes the evil-doer under the notion, or for the reason, that he has done wrong, — only the unreasonable fury of a beast acts in that way. But he who desires to inflict rational punishment does not retaliate for a past wrong, for that which is done can not be undone, but he has regard to the future, and is desirous that the man who is punished, and he who sees him punished, may be deterred from doing wrong again. And he implies that virtue is capable of being taught; as he undoubtedly punishes for the sake of prevention. This is the notion of all who retaliate upon others either privately or publicly. And the Athenians, too, like other men, retaliate on those whom they regard as evil-doers; and this argues them to be of the number of those who think that virtue may be acquired and taught. Thus far, Socrates, I have shown you clearly enough, if I am not mistaken, that your countrymen are right in admitting the tinker and the cobbler to advise about politics, and also that they deem virtue to be capable of being taught and acquired.

There yet remains one difficulty which has been raised by you about the sons of good men. What is the reason why good men teach their sons the knowledge which is gained from teachers, and make them wise in that, but do nothing towards improving them in the virtues which distinguish themselves? And here, Socrates, I will leave the apologue and take up the argument. Please to consider: Is there or is there not some one quality in which all the citizens must be partakers, if there is to be a city at all? In the answer to this question is contained the only solution of your difficulty; there is no other. For if there be any such quality, and this quality or unity is not the art of the carpenter, or the smith, or the potter, but justice and temperance and holiness and, in a word, manly virtue — if this is the quality of which all men must be partakers, and which is the very condition of their learning or doing anything else, and if he who is wanting in this, whether he be a child only or a grown-up man or woman, must be taught and punished, until by punishment he becomes better, and he who rebels against instruction and punishment is either exiled or condemned to death under the idea that he is incurable — if, I say, this be true, and nevertheless good men have their sons taught other things and not this, do consider how extraordinary would be their conduct. For we have shown that they think virtue capable of being taught and inculcated both in private and public; and yet, notwithstanding this, they teach their sons lesser matters, ignorance of which does not involve the punishment of death: but those things, the ignorance of which may cause death and exile to those who have no knowledge or training —

aye, and confiscation as well as death, and, in a word, may be the ruin of families — those things, I say, they are supposed not to teach them, — not to take the utmost care that they should learn. That is not likely, Socrates.

Education and admonition commence in the first years of childhood, and last to the very end of life. Mother and nurse and father and tutor are quarrelling about the improvement of the child as soon as ever he is able to understand them: he can not say or do anything without their setting forth to him that this is just and that is unjust; this is honorable, that is dishonorable; this is holy, that is unholy; do this and abstain from that. And if he obeys, well and good; if not, he is straightened by threats and blows, like a piece of warped wood. At a later stage they send him to teachers, and enjoin them to see to his manners even more than to his reading and music; and the teachers do as they are desired. And when the boy has learned his letters and is beginning to understand what is written, as before he understood only what was spoken, they put into his hands the works of great poets, which he reads at school; in these are contained many admonitions, and many tales, and praises, and encomia of ancient famous men, which he is required to learn by heart, in order that he may imitate or emulate them and desire to become like them. Then, again, the teachers of the lyre take similar care that their young disciple is temperate and gets into no mischief; and when they have taught him the use of the lyre, they introduce him to the poems of other excellent poets, who are the lyric poets; and these they set to music, and make their harmonies and rhythms quite familiar to the children, in order that they may learn to be more gentle, and harmonious, and rhythmical, and so more fitted for speech and action; for the life of man in every part has need of harmony and rhythm. Then they send them to the master of gymnastic, in order that their bodies may better minister to the virtuous mind, and that the weakness of their bodies may not force them to play the coward in war or on any other occasion. This is what is done by those who have the means, and those who have the means are the rich; their children begin education soonest and leave off latest. When they have done with masters, the state again compels them to learn the laws, and live after the pattern which they furnish, and not after their own fancies; and just as in learning to write, the writing-master first draws lines with a style for the use of the young beginner, and gives him the tablet and makes him follow the lines, so the city draws the laws, which were the invention of good lawgivers who were of old time; these are given to the young man, in order to guide him in his conduct whether as ruler or ruled; and he who transgresses them is to be corrected, or, in other words, called to account, which is a term used not only in your country, but also in many others. Now when there is all this care about virtue private and public, why, Socrates, do you still wonder and doubt whether virtue can be taught? Cease to wonder, for the opposite would be far more surprising.

But why then do the sons of good fathers often turn out ill? Let me explain that, — which is far from being wonderful, if, as I have been saying, the very existence of the state implies that virtue is not any man's private possession. If this be true — and nothing can be truer — then I will ask you to imagine, as an illustration, some other pursuit or branch of knowledge which may be assumed equally to be the condition of the existence of a state. Suppose that there could be no state unless we were all flute-players, as far as each had the capacity, and everybody was freely teaching everybody the art, both in private and public, and reproving the bad player as freely and openly as every man now teaches justice and the laws, not concealing them as he would conceal the other arts, but imparting them — for all of us have a mutual interest in the justice and virtue of one another, and this is the reason why every one is ready to teach justice and the laws; — suppose, I say, that there were the same readiness and liberality among us in teaching one another flute-playing, do you imagine, Socrates, that the sons of good flute-players would be more likely to be good than the sons of bad ones? I think not. Would not their sons grow up to be distinguished or undistinguished according to their own natural capacities as flute-players, and the son of a good player would often turn out to be a bad one, and the son of a bad player to be a good one, and all flute-players would be good enough in comparison of those who were ignorant and unacquainted with the art of flute-playing? In like manner I would have you consider that he who appears to you to be the worst of those who have been brought up in laws and humanities, would appear to be a just man and a master of justice if he were to be compared with men who had no education, or courts of justice, or laws, or any restraints upon them which compelled them to practise virtue — with the savages, for example, whom the poet Pherecrates exhibited on the stage at the last year's Lenaean festival. If you were living among men such as the man-haters in his Chorus, you would be only too glad to meet with Eurybates and Phrynondas, and you would sorrowfully desire the rascality of this part of the world. And you, Socrates, are discontented, and why? Because all men are teachers of virtue, each one according to his ability, and you say that there is no teacher. You might as well ask, Who teaches Greek? For of that too there will not be any teachers found. Or you might ask, Who is to teach the sons of our artisans this same art which they have learned of their fathers? He and his fellow-workmen have taught them to the best of their ability, — but who will carry them further in their arts? And you would certainly have a difficulty, Socrates, in finding a teacher of them; but there would be no difficulty in finding a teacher of those who are wholly ignorant. And this is true of virtue or of anything; and if a man is better able than we are to promote virtue ever so little, that is as much as we can expect. A teacher of this sort I believe myself to be, and above all other men to have the knowledge which makes a man noble and good; and I give my pupils their money's-worth, and even more, as they themselves confess. And therefore I have introduced the following mode of payment: — When a man has been my pupil, if he likes he pays my price, but there is no compulsion; and if he does not like, he has only to go into a temple and take an oath of the value of the instructions, and he pays no more than he declares to be their value.

Such is my Apologue, Socrates, and such is the argument by which I endeavor to show that virtue may be taught, and that this is the opinion of the Athenians. And I have also attempted to show that you are not to wonder at good fathers having bad sons, or at good sons having bad fathers, as may be seen in the sons of Polycleitus, who are of the same age as our friends Paralus and Xanthippus, and who are very inferior to their father; and this is true of many other artists. But I ought not to say the same as yet of Paralus and Xanthippus themselves, for they are young and there is still hope of them.

Protagoras ended, and in my ear

" So charming left his voice, that I the while
  Thought him still speaking; still stood fixed to hear."

At length, when I saw that he had really finished, I gradually recovered consciousness, and looking at Hippocrates, I said to him: O son of Apollodorus, how deeply grateful I am to you for having brought me hither; I would not have missed the speech of Protagoras for a great deal. For I used to imagine that no human care could make men good; but I know better now. Yet I have still one very small difficulty which I am sure that Protagoras will easily explain, as he has already explained so much. For if a man were to go and consult Pericles or any of our great speakers about these matters, he might perhaps hear as fine a discourse; but then if any one has a question to ask of any of them, like books, they can neither answer nor ask; and if any one challenges the least particular of their speech, they go ringing on in a long harangue, like brazen pots, which when they are struck continue to sound unless some one puts his hand upon them; whereas our friend Protagoras can not only make a good speech, as he has already shown, but when he is asked a question he can answer briefly; and when he asks he will wait and hear the answer; and this is a very rare gift. Now I, Protagoras, have a little question that I want to ask of you, and if you will only answer me that, I shall be quite satisfied. You were saying that virtue can be taught; — that I will take upon your authority, and there is no one to whom I am more ready to trust. But I marvel at one thing about which I should like to have my mind set at rest. You were speaking of Zeus sending justice and reverence to men; and several times while you were speaking justice, and temperance, and holiness, and all these qualities, were described by you as if together they made up virtue. Now I want you to tell me truly whether virtue is one whole, of which justice and temperance and holiness are parts; or whether all these are only the names of one and the same thing: that is the doubt which still lingers in my mind.

There is no difficulty, Socrates, in answering that the qualities of which you are speaking are the parts of virtue which is one.

And are they parts, I said, in the same sense in which mouth, nose, and eyes, and ears, are the parts of a face; or are they like the parts of gold, which differ from the whole and from one another only in being larger or smaller?

I should say that they differed, Socrates, in the first way; as the parts of a face are related to the whole face.

And do men have some one part and some another part of virtue? Or if a man has one part, must he also have all the others?

By no means, he said; for many a man is brave and not just, or just and not wise.

Why then, I said, courage and wisdom are also parts of virtue?

Most undoubtedly, he said; and wisdom is the noblest of the parts.

And they are all different from one another? I said.
Yes.

And each of them has a distinct function like the parts of the face; — the eye, for example, is not like the ear, and has not the same functions; and the other parts are none of them like one another, either in their functions, or in any other way? Now I want to know whether the parts of virtue do not also differ in themselves and in their functions; as that is clearly what the simile would imply.

Yes, Socrates, you are right in that.

Then, I said, no other part of virtue is like knowledge, or like justice, or like courage, or like temperance, or like holiness?

No, he answered.

Well then, I said, suppose that you and I inquire into their natures. And first, you would agree with me that justice is of the nature of a thing, would you not? That is my opinion, would not that be yours also?

Yes, he said; that is mine also.

And suppose that some one were to ask us, saying, O Protagoras, and you Socrates, what about this thing which you just now called justice, is it just or unjust? And I were to answer, just: and you — would you vote for me or against me?

With you, he said.

Thereupon I should answer to him who asked me, that justice is of the nature of the just: would not you?

Yes, he said.

And suppose that he went on to say: Well now, is there such a thing as holiness? — we should answer, Yes, if I am not mistaken?

Yes, he said.

And that you acknowledge to be a thing — should we admit that?

He assented.

And is this a sort of thing which is of the nature of the holy, or of the nature of the unholy? I should be angry at his putting such a question, and should say, Peace, man; nothing can be holy if holiness is not holy. What do you say to that? Would you not answer in the same way?

Certainly, he said.

And then after this suppose that he came and asked

us, What were you saying just now? Perhaps I may not have heard you rightly, but you seemed to me to be saying that the parts of virtue were not the same as one another. I should reply, You certainly heard that said, but you did not, as you think, hear me say that; for Protagoras gave the answer, and I did but ask the question. And suppose that he turned to you and said, Is this true, Protagoras? and do you maintain that one part of virtue is unlike another, and is this your position? how would you answer him?

I could not help acknowledging the truth of what he said, Socrates.

Well then, Protagoras, assuming this, and supposing that he proceeded to say further, Then holiness is not of the nature of justice, nor justice of the nature of holiness, but of the nature of unholiness; and holiness is of the nature of the not just, and therefore of the unjust, and the unjust is unholy; how shall we answer him? I should certainly answer him on my own behalf that justice is holy, and that holiness is just; and I would say in like manner on your behalf also, if you would allow me, that justice is either the same with holiness, or very nearly the same; and I would most assuredly say that justice is like holiness and holiness is like justice; and I wish that you would tell me whether I may be permitted to give this answer on your behalf, and whether you would agree with me.

He replied, I can not simply agree, Socrates, to the proposition that justice is holy and that holiness is just, for there appears to me to be a difference between them. But what matter? if you please I please; and let us assume, if you will, that justice is holy, and that holiness is just.

Pardon me, I said; I do not want this " if you wish " or " if you will " sort of argument to be proven, but I want you and me to be proven; and I mean by this that the argument will be best proven if there be no " if."

Well, he said, I admit that justice bears a resemblance to holiness, for there is always some point of view in which everything is like every other thing; white is in a certain way like black, and hard is like soft, and the most extreme opposites have some qualities in common; even the parts of the face which, as we were saying before, are distinct and have different functions, are still in a certain point of view similar, and one of them is like another of them. And you may prove that they are like one another on the same principle that all things are like one another; and yet things which are alike in some particular ought not to be called alike, nor things which are unlike in some particular, however slight, unlike.

And do you think, I said, in a tone of surprise, that justice and holiness have but a small degree of likeness?

Certainly not, he said; but I do not agree with what I understand to be your view.

Well, I said, as you appear to have a difficulty about this, let us take another of the examples which you mentioned instead. Do you admit the existence of folly?

I do.

And is not wisdom the very opposite of folly?

That is true, he said.

And when men act rightly and advantageously they seem to you to be temperate or moderate?

Yes, he said.

And moderation makes them moderate?

Certainly.

And they who do not act rightly act foolishly, and in thus acting are not moderate?

I agree to that, he said.

Then to act foolishly is the opposite of acting moderately?

He assented.

And foolish actions are done by folly, and moderate or temperate actions by moderation?

He agreed.

And that is done strongly which is done by strength, and weakly which is done by weakness?

He assented.

And that which is done with swiftness is done swiftly, and that which is done with slowness, slowly?

He acknowledged that.

And if anything is done in the same way, that is done by the same; and if anything is done in an opposite way, by the opposite?

He agreed.

Once more, I said, is there anything beautiful?

Yes.

To which the only opposite is the ugly?

There is no other.

And is there anything good?

There is.

To which the only opposite is the evil?

There is no other.

And there is the acute in sound?

True.

To which the only opposite is the grave?

There is no other, he said, but that.

Then every opposite has one opposite only and no more?

He assented.

Then now, I said, let us recapitulate our admissions. First of all we admitted that everything has one opposite and not more than one?

To that we assented.

And we admitted also that what was done in opposite ways was done by opposites?

Yes.

And that which was done foolishly, as we also admitted, was done in the opposite way to that which was done moderately?

Yes.

And that which was done moderately was done by moderation or temperance, and that which was done foolishly by folly?

He agreed.

And that which is done in opposite ways is done by opposites?

Yes.

And one thing is done by moderation or temperance, and quite another thing by folly?

Yes.

And those are opposite ways?

Certainly.

And therefore done by opposites. Then folly is the opposite of moderation or temperance?

That is evident.

And do you remember that folly has already been acknowledged by us to be the opposite of wisdom?

He assented.

And we said that everything has only one opposite?

Yes.

Then, Protagoras, which of the two assertions shall we renounce? One says that everything has but one opposite; the other that wisdom is distinct from temperance or moderation, and that both of them are parts of virtue; and that they are not only distinct, but unlike, both in themselves and in their functions, like the parts of a face. Which of these two assertions shall we renounce? For both of them together are certainly not in harmony; they do not accord or agree:

for how can they be said to agree if everything is assumed to have only one opposite and not more than one, and yet folly, which is one, has clearly the two opposites — wisdom and temperance? Is not that true, Protagoras? I said. What else would you say?

He assented, but with great reluctance.

Then temperance and wisdom are the same, as before justice and holiness appeared to us to be nearly the same. And now, Protagoras, I said, do not let us be faint-hearted, but let us complete what remains. Do you think that an unjust man can be temperate in his injustice?

I should be ashamed, Socrates, he said, to acknowledge this, which nevertheless many may be found to assert.

And shall I argue with them or with you? I replied.

I would rather, he said, that you should argue with the many first, if you will.

Whichever you please, if you will only answer me and say whether you are of their opinion or not. My object is to test the validity of the argument; and yet the result may be that I and you who ask and answer may also be put on our trial.

Protagoras at first made a show of refusing, as he said that the argument was not encouraging; at length, however, he consented to answer.

Now then, I said, begin at the beginning and answer me. You think that some men are moderate or temperate, and yet unjust?

Yes, he said; let that be admitted.

And moderation is good sense?

Yes.

And good sense is good counsel in doing justice?

Granted.

If they succeed, I said, or if they don't succeed?

If they succeed.

And you would admit the existence of goods?

Yes.

And is the good that which is expedient for man?

Yes, indeed, he said; and there are some things which may be inexpedient, and yet I call them good.

I thought that Protagoras was getting ruffled and excited; he seemed to be setting himself in an attitude of war. Seeing this, I minded my business and gently said: —

When you say, Protagoras, that things inexpedient are good, do you mean inexpedient for man only, or inexpedient altogether? and do you call the latter good?

Certainly not the last, he replied; for I know of many things, meats, drinks, medicines, and ten thousand other things, which are partly expedient for man, and partly inexpedient; and some which are expedient for horses, and not for men; and some for oxen only, and some for dogs; and some for no animals, but only for trees; and some for the roots of trees and not for their branches, as for example, manure, which is a good thing when laid about the roots, but utterly destructive if thrown upon the shoots and young branches; or I may instance olive oil, which is mischievous to all plants, and generally most injurious to the hair of every animal with the exception of man, but beneficial to human hair and to the human body generally; and even in this application (so various and changeable is the nature of the benefit) that which is the greatest good to the outward parts of a man, is a very great evil to his inward parts: and for this reason physicians always forbid their patients the use of oil in their food, except in very small quantities, just sufficient to take away the disagreeable sensation of smell in meats and sauces.

When he had given this answer, the company cheered him. And I said: Protagoras, I have a wretched memory, and when any one makes a long speech to me I never remember what he is talking about. As then, if I had been deaf, and you were going to converse with me, you would have had to raise your voice; so now, having such a bad memory, I will ask you to cut your answers short, if you would take me with you.

What do you mean? he said: how am I to shorten my answers? shall I make them too short?

Certainly not, I said.

But short enough? he said.

Yes, I said.

Shall I answer what appears to me to be short enough, or what appears to you to be short enough?

I have heard, I said, that you can speak and teach others to speak about the same things at such length that words never seemed to fail, or with such brevity that no one could use fewer of them. Please therefore, if you talk with me, to adopt the latter or more compendious method.

Socrates, he replied, many a battle of words have I fought, and if I had followed the method of disputation which my adversaries desired, as you want me to do, I should have been no better than another, and the name of Protagoras would have been nowhere.

I saw that he was not satisfied with his previous answers, and that he would not play the part of answerer any more if he could help; and I considered that there was no call upon me to continue the conversation; so I said: Protagoras, I don't wish to force the conversation upon you if you had rather not, but when you are willing to argue with me in such a way that I can follow you, then I will argue with you. Now you, as is said of you by others and as you say of yourself, are able to have discussions in shorter forms of speech as well as in longer, for you are a master of wisdom; but I can not manage these long speeches: I only wish that I could. You, on the other hand, who are capable of either, ought to speak shorter as I beg you, and then we might converse. But I see that you are disinclined, and as I have an engagement which will prevent my staying to hear you at length (for I have to be in another place), I will depart; although I should have liked to have heard you.

Thus I spoke, and was rising from my seat, when Callias seized me by the hand, and in his left hand caught hold of this old cloak of mine. He said: We can not let you go, Socrates, for if you leave us there will be an end of our discussions: I must therefore beg you to remain, as there is nothing in the world that I should like better than to hear you and Protagoras discourse. Do not deny the company this pleasure.

Now I had got up, and was in the act of departure. Son of Hipponicus, I replied, I have always admired, and do now heartily applaud and love your philosophical spirit, and I would gladly comply with your requests, if I could. But the truth is that I can not. And what you ask is as great an impossibility to me, as if you bade me run a race with Crison of Himera, when in his prime, or with some one of the long or day course runners. To that I should reply, that I humbly make the same request to my own legs; and they can't comply. And therefore if you want to see Crison and me in the same stadium, you must bid him slacken his speed to mine, for I can not run quickly, and he can run slowly. And in like manner if you want to hear me and Protagoras discoursing, you must ask him to shorten his answers, and keep to the point, as he did at first; if not, how can there be any discussion? For discussion is one thing, and making an oration is quite another, according to my way of thinking.

But you see, Socrates, said Callias, that Protagoras may fairly claim to speak in his own way, just as you claim to speak in yours.

Here Alcibiades interposed, and said: That, Callias, is not a fair statement of the case. For our friend Socrates admits that he can not make a speech — in this he yields the palm to Protagoras; but I should be greatly surprised if he yielded to any living man in the power of holding and apprehending an argument. Now if Protagoras will make a similar admission, and confess that he is inferior to Socrates in argumentative skill, that is enough for Socrates; but if he claims a superiority in argument as well, let him ask and answer — not, when a question is asked, having recourse to shifts and evasions, and instead of answering, making a speech at such length that most of his hearers forget the question at issue (not that Socrates is likely to forget — I will be bound for that, although he may pretend in fun that he has a bad memory). And Socrates appears to me to be more in the right than Protagoras; that is my opinion, and every man ought to say what he thinks.

When Alcibiades had done speaking, some one — Critias, I believe — went on to say: O Prodicus and Hippias, Callias appears to me to be a partisan of Protagoras. And this led Alcibiades, who loves opposition, to take the other side. But we should not be partisans either of Socrates or Protagoras; let us rather unite in entreating both of them not to break up the discussion.

Prodicus added: That, Critias, seems to me to be

well said, for those who are present at such discussions ought to be impartial hearers of both the
speakers; remembering, however, that impartiality is
not the same as equality, for both sides should be im-
partially heard, and yet an equal meed should not be
assigned to both of them; but to the wiser a higher
meed should be given, and a lower to the less wise.
And I as well as Critias would beg you, Protagoras
and Socrates, to grant our request, which is, that you
will argue with one another and not wrangle; for
friends argue with friends out of good will, but only
adversaries and enemies wrangle. And then our meeting will be delightful; for in this way you, who are
the speakers, will be most likely to win esteem, and
not praise only, among us who are your audience;
for esteem is a sincere conviction of the hearers' souls,
but praise is often an insincere expression of men
uttering words contrary to their conviction. And
thus we who are the hearers will be gratified and not
pleased; for gratification is of the mind when receiving wisdom and knowledge, but pleasure is of the
body when eating or experiencing some other bodily
delight. Thus spoke Prodicus, and many of the company applauded his words.

Hippias the sage spoke next. He said: All of you
who are here present I reckon to be kinsmen and
friends and fellow-citizens, by nature and not by law;
for by nature like is akin to like, whereas law is the
tyrant of mankind, and often compels us to do many
things which are against nature. How great would
be the disgrace then, if we, who know the nature of
things, and are the wisest of the Hellenes, and as such
are met together in this city, which is the metropolis of
wisdom, and in the greatest and most glorious house
of this city, should have nothing to show worthy of
this height of dignity, but should only quarrel with

one another like the meanest of mankind. I do pray and advise you, Protagoras, and you, Socrates, to agree upon a compromise. Let us be your peacemakers. And do not you, Socrates, aim at this precise and extreme brevity in discourse, if Protagoras objects, but loosen and let go the reins of speech, that your words may be grander and become you better. Neither do you, Protagoras, go forth on the gale with every sail set out of sight of land into an ocean of words, but let there be a mean observed by both of you. Do as I say. And let me also suggest and suppose further, that you choose an arbiter or overseer or president; he will keep watch over your words and reduce them to their proper length.

This proposal was received by the company with universal approval; and Callias said that he would not let me off, and that I was to choose an arbiter. But I said that to choose an umpire of discourse would be unseemly; for if the person chosen was inferior, then the inferior or worse ought not to preside over the better; or if he was equal, neither would that be well; for he who is our equal will do as we do, and what will be the use of choosing him? And if you say " Let us have a better then," to that I answer that you can not have any one who is wiser than Protagoras. And if you choose another who is not really better, and whom you only say is better, to put another over him as though he were an inferior person would be an unworthy reflection on him; not that, as far as I am concerned, any reflection is of much consequence to me. Let me tell you then what I will do in order that the conversation and discussion may go on as you desire. If Protagoras is not disposed to answer, let him ask and I will answer; and I will endeavor to show at the same time how, as I maintain, he ought to answer: and when I have answered as many questions as he likes to ask, let him in like manner answer; and if he seems to be not very ready at answering the exact questions, you and I will unite in entreating him, as you entreated me, not to spoil the discussion. And this will require no special arbiter: you shall all of you be arbiters.

This was generally approved, and Protagoras, though very much against his will, was obliged to agree that he would ask questions; and when he had put a sufficient number of them, that he would answer in his turn those which he was asked in short replies. He began to put his questions as follows: —

I am of opinion, Socrates, he said, that skill in poetry is the principal part of education; and this I conceive to be the power of knowing what compositions of the poet are correct, and what are not, and how they are to be distinguished, and of explaining them when asked. And I propose to transfer the question which you and I have been discussing to the domain of poetry, speaking as before of virtue, but in reference to a passage of a poet. Now Simonides says to Scopas the Son of Creon the Thessalian: —

" Hardly on the one hand can a man become truly good; built four-square in hands and feet and mind, a work without a flaw."

Do you know the poem? or shall I repeat the whole?

There is no need, I said; for I am perfectly well acquainted with the ode, of which I have made a careful study.

Very good, he said. And do you think that the ode is a good composition, and true?

Yes, I said, both good and true.

But if there is a contradiction, can the composition be good or true?

No, not in that case, I replied.

And is there not a contradiction? he asked. Reflect.

Well, my friend, I have reflected.

And does not the poet proceed to say, " I do not agree with the word of Pittacus, albeit the utterance of a wise man; hardly," says he, " can a man be good." Now you will observe that this is said by the same poet.

I know that, I said.

And do you think, he said, that the two sayings are consistent?

Yes, I said, I think they are (at the same time I could not help fearing that there might be something in what he said). And do you think otherwise? I said.

Why, he said, how can he be consistent in saying both? First of all, premising as his own thought, " Hardly can a man become truly good; " and then a little further on in the poem, forgetting, and blaming Pittacus and refusing to agree with him, when he says, " Hardly can a man be good," which is the very same thing. And yet when he blames him who says the same with himself, he blames himself; so that he must be wrong either in his first or his second assertion.

Many of the audience cheered and applauded this. And I felt at first giddy and faint, as if I had received a blow from the expert hand of a boxer, when I heard his words and the sound of the cheering; and to confess the truth, I wanted to get time to think what the meaning of the poet really was. So I turned to Prodicus and called him. Prodicus, I said, Simonides is a countryman of yours, and you ought to come to his rescue. I think that I must summon you to my aid, like the river Scamander in Homer, who, when beleaguered by Achilles, asks Simois to aid him, saying:

" Brother dear, let us both together stay the force of the hero."

And I summon you, for I am afraid that Protagoras will make an end of Simonides. Now is the time to rehabilitate Simonides, by the application of your charming philosophy of synonyms, which distinguishes " will " and " wish " and many similar words which you mentioned in your admirable speech. And I should like to know whether you would agree with me; for I am of opinion that there is no contradiction in the words of Simonides. And first of all I wish that you would say whether, in your opinion, Prodicus, " being " is the same as " becoming."

Not the same, certainly, replied Prodicus.

Did not Simonides first set forth, as his own view, that " Hardly can a man become truly good? "

Quite right, said Prodicus.

And then he blames Pittacus, I said, not for saying the same as himself, as Protagoras imagines, but for saying something different; for Pittacus does not say as Simonides says, that hardly can a man become good, but hardly can a man be good: and our friend Prodicus says that being, Protagoras, is not the same as becoming; and if they are not the same, then Simonides is not inconsistent with himself. I dare say that Prodicus and many others would say, as Hesiod says, " Hardly can a man become good, for the gods have placed toil in front of virtue; but when you have reached the goal, then the acquisition of virtue, however difficult, is easy."

Prodicus heard and approved; but Protagoras said: Your correction, Socrates, involves a greater error than is contained in the sentence which you are correcting.

Alas! I said, Protagoras; then I am a sorry physician, and do but aggravate a disorder which I am seeking to cure.

The fact, he said, is as I have stated.

How is that? I asked.

The poet, he replied, could never have made such a mistake as to say that virtue, which in the opinion of all men is the hardest of all things, can be easily acquired.

Well, I said, and how fortunate this is that Prodicus should be of the company, for he has a wisdom, Protagoras, which, as I imagine, is more than human and of very ancient date, and may be as old as Simonides or even older. Learned as you are in many things, you appear to know nothing of this; but I know, for I am a disciple of his. And now, if I am not mistaken, you do not understand the word " hard " in the sense which Simonides intended; and I must correct you, as Prodicius corrects me when I used the word " dreadful " as a term of praise. If I say that Protagoras is a dreadfully wise man, he asks me if I am not ashamed of calling that which is good dreadful; and then he explains to me that the term " dreadful " is always taken in a bad sense, and that no one speaks of being dreadfully healthy or wealthy or wise, but of dreadful war, dreadful poverty, dreadful disease, meaning by the term " dreadful," evil. And I think that Simonides and his countrymen the Ceans, when they spoke of " hard " meant " evil," or something which you do not understand. Let us ask Prodicus, for he ought to be able to answer questions about the dialect of Simonides. What did he mean, Prodicus, by the term " hard? "

Evil, said Prodicus.

And therefore, I said, Prodicus, he blames Pittacus for saying, " Hard is the good," just as if that were equivalent to saying, Evil is the good.

Yes, he said, that was certainly his meaning; and he is twitting Pittacus with ignorance of the use of terms, which in a Lesbian, who has been accustomed to speak a barbarous language, is natural.

Do you hear, Protagoras, I asked, what our friend Prodicus is saying? And have you an answer for him?

You are all wrong, Prodicus, said Protagoras; and I know very well that Simonides in using the word "hard" meant what all of us mean, not evil, but that which is not easy — that which takes a great deal of trouble. Of this I am positive.

I said: I also incline to think, Protagoras, that this was the meaning of Simonides, and that our friend Prodicus was quite aware of this, but he thought that he would make fun, and try if you could maintain your thesis; for that Simonides could never have meant the other is clearly proved by the context, in which he says that God only has this gift. Now he can not surely mean to say that to be good is evil, when he afterwards proceeds to say that God only has this gift, and that this is the attribute of him and of no other. For if this be his meaning, Prodicus would impute to Simonides a character of recklessness which is very unlike his countrymen. And I should like to tell you, I said, what I imagine to be the real meaning of Simonides in this poem, if you will test what, in your way of speaking, would be called my skill in poetry; or if you would rather, I will be the listener.

Protagoras hearing me offer this, replied: As you please; and Hippias, Prodicus, and the others, told me by all means to do as I proposed.

Then now, I said, I will endeavor to explain to you my opinion about this poem. There is a very ancient philosophy which is more cultivated in Crete and Lacedaemon than in any other part of Hellas, and there are more philosophers in those countries than anywhere else in the world. This, however, is a secret which the Lacedaemonians deny; and they pretend to be ignorant, just because they do not wish to have it thought that they rule the world by wisdom, like the Sophists of whom Protagoras was speaking, and not by valor of arms; considering that if the reason of their superiority were disclosed, all men would be practising their wisdom. And this secret of theirs has never been discovered by the imitators of Lacedaemonian fashions in other cities, who go about with their ears bruised in imitation of them, and have the caestus bound on their arms, and are always in training, and wear short cloaks; for they imagine that these are the practices which have enabled the Lacedaemonians to conquer the other Hellenes. Now when the Lacedaemonians want to unbend and hold free conversation with their wise men, and are no longer satisfied with mere secret intercourse, they drive out all these laconizers, and any other foreigners who may happen to be in their country, and they hold a philosophical *séance* unknown to the strangers: and they themselves forbid their young men to go out into other cities (in this they are like the Cretans), in order that they may not unlearn the lessons which they have taught them. And in these cities not only men but also women have a pride in their high cultivation. And you may know that I am only speaking the truth in attributing this excellence in philosophy to the Lacedaemonians, by this token: If a man converses with the most ordinary Lacedaemonian, he will find him seldom good for much in general conversation, but at any point in the discourse he will be darting out some notable saying, terse and full of meaning, with unerring aim; and the person with whom he is talking seems to be like a child in his hands. And many of our own age and of former ages have noted that the true Lacedaemonian type of character has the love of philosophy even stronger than the love of gymnastics; they are conscious that only a perfectly educated man is capable of uttering such expressions. Such were Thales of Miletus, and Pittacus of Mytilene, and Bias of Priene, and our own Solon, and Cleobulus the Lindian, and Myson the Chenian; and seventh in the catalogue of wise men was the Lacedaemonian Chilo. All these were lovers and emulators and disciples of the culture of the Lacedaemonians, and any one may perceive that their wisdom was of this character, consisting of short memorable sentences, which individuals uttered. And they met together and dedicated in the temple of Apollo at Delphi, as the first-fruits of their wisdom, the far-famed inscriptions, which are in all men's mouths, " Know thyself," and " Nothing too much."

Why do I say all this? I am explaining that this Lacedaemonian brevity was the style of primitive philosophy. Now there was a saying of Pittacus which was privately circulated and received the approbation of the good, " Hard to be good." And Simonides, who was ambitious of the fame of wisdom, was aware that if he could overthrow this saying, then, as if he had won a victory over some famous athlete, he would carry off the palm among his contemporaries. And if I am not mistaken, he composed the entire poem with the secret intention of damaging that saying.

Let us all unite in examining his words, and see whether I am speaking the truth. Simonides must have been a lunatic, if, in the very first words of the poem, wanting to say only that to be good is hard, he inserted μέν, " on the one hand " (on the one hand to become good is hard); there would be no possible reason for the introduction of   unless you suppose him to speak with a hostile reference to the words of Pittacus. Pittacus is saying "Hard to be good," and he says, controverting this, "No, the truly hard thing, Pittacus, is to become good," not joining "truly" with "good," but with "hard." Not the hard thing is to be truly good, as though there were some truly good men, and there were others who were good but not truly good (that would be a very simple observation, and quite unworthy of Simonides); but you must suppose him to make a trajection of the word (ἀλαθέως), construing the saying of Pittacus thus (and let us imagine Pittacus to be speaking and Simonides answering him): "O my friends," says Pittacus, "hard to be good," and Simonides answers, "In that, Pittacus, you are mistaken, the difficulty is not to be good, but on the one hand, to become good, four-square in hands and feet and mind, without a flaw — that is hard truly." This way of reading the passage accounts for the insertion of (μέν) "on the one hand," and for the use of the word "truly," which is rightly placed at the end; and all that follows tends to prove that this is the meaning. A great deal might be said in praise of the details of the poem, which is a charming piece of workmanship, and very finished, but that would be tedious. I should like, however, to point out the general intention of the poem, which is certainly designed in every part to be a refutation of the saying of Pittacus. For he speaks in what follows a little further on as if he meant to argue that although there is a difficulty in becoming good, yet this is possible for a time, and only for a time. But having become good, to remain in a good state and be good, as you, Pittacus, affirm, that is not possible, and is not granted to man; God only has this blessing; "but man can not help being bad when the force of circumstances overpowers him." Now whom does the force of circumstances overpower in the command of a vessel? — not the private individual, for he is always overpowered; and as one who is already prostrate can not be overthrown, but only he who is standing upright and not he who is prostrate can be laid prostrate, so the force of circumstances can only be said to overpower him who has resources, and not him who is at all times helpless. The descent of a great storm may make the pilot helpless, or the severity of the season the husbandman or the physician; for the good may become bad, as another poet witnesses: —

" The good are sometimes good and sometimes bad."

But the bad does not become bad; he is always bad. So that when the force of circumstances overpowers the man of resources and skill and virtue, then he can not help being bad. And you, Pittacus, are saying, " Hard to be good." Now there is a difficulty in becoming good; and yet this is possible: but to be good is an impossibility; " for he who does well is the good man, and he who does ill is the bad." But what sort of doing is good in letters? and what sort of doing makes a man good in letters? Clearly the knowing of them. And what sort of well-doing makes a man a good physician? Clearly the knowing of the art of healing the sick. " But he who does ill is the bad." Now who becomes a bad physician? Clearly he who is in the first place a physician, and in the second place a good physician; for he may become a bad one also: but none of us unskilled individuals can by any amount of doing ill become physicians, any more than we can become carpenters or anything of that sort; and he who by doing ill can not become a physician at all, clearly can not become a bad physician. In like manner the good may become deteriorated by time, or toil, or disease, or other accident (the only real ill-doing is the deprivation of knowledge), but the bad man will never become bad, for he is always bad; and if he were to become bad, he must previously have been good. Thus the words of the poem tend to show that on the one hand a man can not be continuously good, but that he may become good and may also become bad; and again that " they are the best for the longest time whom the gods love."

All this relates to Pittacus, as is further proved by the sequel. For he adds: " Therefore I will not throw away my life in searching after the impossible, hoping in vain to find a perfectly faultless man among those who partake of the fruit of the broad-bosomed earth; and when I have found him to tell you of him " (this is the vehement way in which he pursues his attack upon Pittacus throughout the whole poem): " but him who does no evil voluntarily I praise and love; — not even the gods war against necessity." All this has a similar drift, for Simonides was not so ignorant as to say that he praised those who did no evil voluntarily, as though there were some who did evil voluntarily. For no wise man, as I believe, will allow that any human being errs voluntarily, or voluntarily does evil and dishonorable actions; but they are very well aware that all who do evil and dishonorable things do them against their will. And Simonides never says that he praises him who does no evil voluntarily; the word " voluntarily " applies to himself. For he was under the impression that a good man might often compel himself to love and praise an· other, and that there might be an involuntary love, such as a man might feel to an ungainly father or mother, or to his country, or something of that sort. Now bad men, when their parents or country have any defects, rejoice at the sight of them, and expose them to others, and find fault with them and denounce them under the idea that the rest of mankind will be less likely to take them to task and reproach them when they neglect them; and this makes them exaggerate their defects, in order that the odium which is necessarily incurred by them may be increased: but the good man dissembles his feelings, and constrains himself to praise them; and if they have wronged him and he is angry, he pacifies his anger and is reconciled, and compels himself to love and praise his own flesh and blood. And Simonides, as is probable, considered that he himself had often had to praise and magnify a tyrant or the like, much against his will, and he also wishes to imply to Pittacus that he is not censorious and does not censure him. "For I am satisfied," he says, "when a man is neither bad nor very stupid, and when he knows justice (which is the health of states), and is of sound mind, I will find no fault with him, for I am not given to finding fault, for there are innumerable fools" (implying that if he delighted in censure he might have abundant opportunity of finding fault). "All things are good with which evil is unmingled." In these latter words he does not mean to say that all things are good which have no evil in them, as you might say "All things are white which have no black in them," for that would be ridiculous; but he means to say that he accepts and finds no fault with the moderate or intermediate state. "I do not hope," he says, "to find a perfectly blameless man among those who partake of the fruits of the broad-bosomed earth, and when I have found him to tell you of him; in this sense I praise no man. But he who is moderately good, and does no evil, is good enough for me, who love and approve every one" (and here observe that he uses a Lesbian word, ἐπαίνημι, because he is addressing Pittacus, —

" who love and approve every one voluntarily," says, " who does no evil: " and that the stop should be put after " voluntarily ") ; but there are some whom I involuntarily praise and love. And you, Pittacus, I would never have blamed, if you had spoken what was moderately good and true; but I do blame you because, wearing the appearance of truth, you are speaking falsely about the greatest matters." And this, I said, Prodicus and Protagoras, I take to be the true meaning of Simonides in this poem.

Hippias said: I think, Socrates, that you have given a very good explanation of this poem; but I have also an excellent interpretation of my own which I will expound to you, if you will allow me.

Nay, Hippias, said Alcibiades; not now, but another time. At present we must abide by the compact which was made between Socrates and Protagoras, to the effect that as long as Protagoras is willing to ask, Socrates should answer; or that if he would rather answer, then that Socrates should ask.

I said: I wish Protagoras either to ask or answer as he is inclined; but I would rather have done with poems and odes, if you do not object, and come back to the question about which I was asking you at first, Protagoras, and by your help make an end of that. The talk about the poets seems to me like a commonplace entertainment to which a vulgar company have recourse; who, because they are not able to converse or amuse one another, while they are drinking, with the sound of their own voices and conversation by reason of their stupidity, raise the price of flute-girls in the market, hiring for a great sum the voice of a flute instead of their own breath, to be the medium of intercourse among them: but where the company are real gentlemen and men of education, you will see no flute-girls, nor dancing-girls, nor harp-girls; and they have no nonsense or games but are contented with one another's conversation, of which their own voices are the medium, and which they carry on by turns and in an orderly manner, even though they are very liberal in their potations. And a company like this of ours, and men such as we profess to be, do not require the help of another's voice, or of the poets whom you can not interrogate about the meaning of what they are saying; people who cite them declaring, some that the poet has one meaning, and others that he has another; and there arises a dispute which can never be put to the proof. This sort of entertainment they decline, and prefer to talk with one another, and try one another's mettle in conversation. And these are the sort of models which I desire that you and I should imitate. Leaving the poets, and keeping to ourselves, let us try the mettle of one another and of the truth in conversation. And if you have a mind to ask I am ready to answer; or if you would rather, do you answer, and give me the opportunity of taking up and completing our unfinished argument.

I made these and some similar observations; but Protagoras would not distinctly say which he would do. Thereupon Alcibiades turned to Callias, and said: — Do you think, Callias, that Protagoras is fair in refusing to say whether he will or will not answer? for I certainly think that he is unfair; he ought either to proceed with the argument, or distinctly to refuse to proceed, that we may know his intention; and then Socrates will be able to discourse with some one else, and the rest of the company will be free to talk with one another.

I think that Protagoras was really made ashamed by these words of Alcibiades, and when the prayers of Callias and the company were superadded, he was

at last induced to argue, and said that I might ask
and he would answer.

So I said: Do not imagine, Protagoras, that I have
any other interest in asking questions of you but that
of clearing up my own difficulties. For I think that
Homer was very right in saying that " When two go
together, one sees before the other," for all men who
have a companion are readier in deed, word, or
thought; but if a man " sees a thing when he is alone,"
he goes about straightway seeking until he finds some
one to whom he may show his discoveries, and who
may confirm him in them. And I would rather hold
discourse with you than with any one, because I think
that no man has a better understanding of most things
which a good man may be expected to understand and
in particular of virtue. For who is there, but you? —
who not only claim to be a good man and a gentleman,
for many are this, and yet have not the power of
making others good. Whereas you are not only good
yourself, but also the cause of goodness in others.
Moreover such confidence have you in yourself, that
although other Sophists conceal their profession, you
proclaim in the face of Hellas that you are a Sophist
or teacher of virtue and education, and are the first
who demanded pay in return. How then can I do
otherwise than invite you to the examination of these
subjects, and ask questions and take advice of you?
Indeed, I must. And I should like once more to have
my memory refreshed by you about the questions
which I was asking you at first, and also to have your
help in considering them. If I am not mistaken the
question was this: Are wisdom and temperance and
courage and justice and holiness five names of the
same thing? or has each of the names a separate un-
derlying essence and corresponding thing having a
proper function, no one of them being like any other

of them? And you said that the five names were not the names of the same thing, but that each of them had a separate object, and that all of them were parts of virtue, not in the same way that the parts of gold are like each other and the whole of which they are parts, but as the parts of the face are unlike the whole of which they are parts and one another, and have each of them a distinct function. I should like to know whether this is still your opinion; or if not, I will ask you to define your meaning, as I shall not take you to task if you now make a different statement. For I dare say that you may have said what you did only in order to make trial of me.

I answer, Socrates, he said, that all these qualities are parts of virtue, and that four out of the five are to some extent similar, and that the fifth of them, which is courage, is very different from the other four, as I prove in this way: You may observe that many men are utterly unrighteous, unholy, intemperate, ignorant, who are nevertheless remarkable for their courage.

Stop, I said; that requires consideration. When you speak of brave men, do you mean the confident, or another sort of nature?

Yes, he said; I mean the impetuous, ready to go at that which others are afraid to approach.

In the next place you would affirm virtue to be a good thing, of which good thing you assert yourself to be a teacher.

Yes, he said; I should say the best of all things, as I am a sane man.

And is it partly good and partly bad, I said, or wholly good?

Wholly good, and that in the highest degree.

Tell me then; who are they who have confidence in diving into a well?

I should say, the divers.

And the reason of this is that they have knowledge?

Yes, that is the reason.

And who have confidence in fighting on horseback — the skilled horsemen or the unskilled?

The skilled.

And who in fighting with light shields — the peltasts or the nonpeltasts?

The peltasts. And that is true of all other things, he said, if that is your point: those who have knowledge are more confident than those who have no knowledge, and they are more confident after they have learned than before.

And have you not seen persons utterly ignorant, I said, of these things, and yet confident about them?

Yes, he said, I have seen persons very confident.

And are not these confident persons also courageous?

In that case, he replied, courage would be a base thing, for the men of whom we are speaking are surely madmen.

Then who are the courageous? Are they not the confident?

Yes, he said; and I still maintain that.

And those, I said, who are thus confident without knowledge are really not courageous, but mad; and in that case the wisest are also the most confident, and being the most confident are also the bravest, and upon that view again wisdom will be courage.

Nay, Socrates, he replied, you are mistaken in your remembrance of what was said by me. When you asked me, I certainly did say that the courageous are the confident; but I was not asked whether the confident are the courageous; for if you had asked me that, I should have answered "not all of them:" and what I did answer you have not disproved, although you proceed to show that those who have knowledge are more courageous than they were before they had knowledge, and more courageous than others who have no knowledge; and this makes you think that courage is the same as wisdom. But in this way of arguing you might come to imagine that strength is wisdom. You might begin by asking whether the strong are able, and I should say " Yes; " and then whether those who know how to wrestle are not more able to wrestle than those who do not know how to wrestle, and more able after than before they had learned, and I should assent. And when I had admitted this, you might use my admissions in such a way as to prove that upon my view wisdom is strength; whereas in that case I should not have admitted, any more than in the other, that the able are strong, although I have admitted that the strong are able. For there is a difference between ability and strength; the former is given by knowledge as well as by madness or rage, but strength comes from nature and a healthy state of the body. And in like manner I say of confidence and courage, that they are not the same; and I argue that the courageous are confident, but not all the confident courageous. For confidence may be given to men by art, and also, like ability, by anger and madness; but courage comes to them from nature and the healthy state of the soul?

I said: You would admit, Protagoras, that some men live well and others ill?

He agreed to this.

And do you think that a man lives well who lives in pain and grief?

He does not.

But if he lives pleasantly to the end of his life, don't you think that in that case he will have lived well?

I do.

Then to live pleasantly is a good, and to live unpleasantly an evil?

Yes, he said, if the pleasure be good and honorable.

And do you, Protagoras, like the rest of the world, call some pleasant things evil and some painful things good? — for I am rather disposed to say that things are good in as far as they are pleasant, if they have no consequences of another sort, and in as far as they are painful they are bad.

I do not know, Socrates, he said, whether I can venture to assert in that unqualified manner that the pleasant is the good and the painful the evil. Having regard not only to my present answer, but also to the rest of my life, I shall be safer, if I am not mistaken, in saying that there are some pleasant things which are not good, and that there are some painful things which are good, and some which are not good, and that there are some which are neither good nor evil.

And you would call pleasant, I said, the things which participate in pleasure or create pleasure?

Certainly, he said.

Then my meaning is, that in as far as they are pleasant they are good; and my question would imply that pleasure is a good in itself.

According to your favorite mode of speech, Socrates, let us inquire about this, he said; and if the result of the inquiry is to show that pleasure and good are really the same, then we will agree; but if not, then we will argue.

And would you wish to begin the inquiry? I said; or shall I begin?

You ought to take the lead, he said; for you are the author of the discussion.

May I use this as an illustration? I said. Suppose some one who is inquiring into the health or some other bodily quality of another: — he looks at his face and at the tips of his fingers, and then he says, Uncover your chest and back to me that I may have a better view: — that is the sort of thing which I desire in this speculation. Having seen what you opinion is about good and pleasure, I am minded to say to you: Uncover your mind to me, Protagoras, and reveal your opinion about knowledge, that I may know whether you agree with the rest of the world. Now the rest of the world are of opinion that knowledge is a principle not of strength, or of rule, or of command: their notion is that a man may have knowledge, and yet that the knowledge which is in him may be overmastered by anger, or pleasure, or pain, or love, or perhaps fear, — just as if knowledge were a slave, and might be dragged about anyhow. Now is that your view? or do you think that knowledge is a noble and commanding thing, which can not be overcome, and will not allow a man, if he only knows the difference of good and evil, to do anything which is contrary to knowledge, but that wisdom will have strength to help him?

I agree with you, Socrates, said Protagoras; and not only that, but I, above all other men, am bound to say that wisdom and knowledge are the highest of human things.

Good, I said, and true. But are you aware that the majority of the world are of another mind; and that men are commonly supposed to know the things which are best, and not to do them when they might? And most persons of whom I have asked the reason of this have said that those who did thus were overcome by pain, or pleasure, or some of those affections which I was just now mentioning.

Yes, Socrates, he replied; and that is not the only point about which mankind are in error.

Suppose, then, that you and I endeavor to instruct and inform them what is the nature of this affection, which is called by them being overcome by pleasure, and which, as they declare, is the reason why they know the better and choose the worse. When we say to them: Friends, you are mistaken, and are saying what is not true, they would reply: Socrates and Protagoras, if this affection of the soul is not to be described as being overcome by pleasure, what is it, and how do you call it? Tell us that.

But why, Socrates, should we trouble ourselves about the opinion of the many, who just say anything that happens to occur to them?

I think, I replied, that their opinion may help us to discover the nature and relation of courage to the other parts of virtue. If you are disposed to abide by our recent agreement, that I should lead in the way in which I think that we shall find the truth best, do you follow; but if you are disinclined, never mind.

You are quite right, he said; and I would have you proceed as you have begun.

Well then, I said, let me suppose that they repeat their question, What account do you give of that which, in our language, is termed being overcome by pleasure? I should answer them thus: Listen, and Protagoras and I will endeavor to show you. When men are overcome by eating and drinking and other sensual desires which are pleasant, and they, knowing them to be evil, nevertheless indulge in them, is not that what you would call being overcome by pleasure? That they will admit. And suppose that you and I were to go on and ask them again: In what way do you say that they are evil, — in that they are pleasant and give pleasure at the moment or because they cause

disease and poverty and other like evils in the future?
Would they still be evil, if they had no attendant evil
consequences, simply because they give the consciousness of pleasure of whatever nature? Would they
not answer that they are not evil on account of the
pleasure which is immediately given by them, but on
account of the after consequences — diseases and the
like?

I believe, said Protagoras, that the world in general
would give that answer.

And in causing diseases do they not cause pain?
and in causing poverty do they not cause pain; —
they would agree to that also, if I am not mistaken?

Protagoras assented.

Then I should say to them, in my name and yours:
Do you think them evil for any other reason, except
that they end in pain and rob us of other pleasures: —
that again they would admit?

We both of us thought that they would.

And then I should take the question from the opposite point of view, and say: Friends, when you
speak of goods being painful, do you not mean
remedial goods, such as gymnastic exercises and
military services, and the physician's use of burning,
cutting, drugging, and starving? Are these the
things which are good but painful? — they would
assent to that?

He agreed.

And do you call them good because they occasion
the greatest immediate suffering and pain; or because, afterwards, they bring health and improvement of the bodily condition and the salvation of
states and empires and wealth? — they would agree
to that, if I am not mistaken?

He assented.

Are these things good for any other reason except

that they end in pleasure, and get rid of and avert pain? Are you looking to any other standard but pleasure and pain when you call them good? — they would acknowledge that they were not?

I think that they would, said Protagoras.

And do you not pursue after pleasure as a good, and and avoid pain as an evil?

He assented.

Then you think that pain is an evil and pleasure is a good: and even pleasure you deem an evil, when it robs you of greater pleasures than it gives, or causes greater pain than the pleasures which it has. If, however, you call pleasure an evil in relation to some other end or standard, you will be able to show us that standard. But you have none to show.

I do not think that they have, said Protagoras.

And have you not a similar way of speaking about pain? You call pain a good when it takes away greater pains than those which it has, or gives pleasure greater than the pains: for I say that if you have some standard other than pleasure and pain to which you refer when you call actual pain a good, you can show what that is. But you can not.

That is true, said Protagoras.

Suppose, again, I said, that the world says to me: Why do you spend many words and speak in many ways on this subject? Excuse me, friends, I should reply; but in the first place there is a difficulty in explaining the meaning of the expression " overcome by pleasure; " and the whole argument turns upon this. And even now, if you see any possible way in which evil can be explained as other than pain, or good as other than pleasure, you may still retract. But I suppose that you are satisfied at having a life of pleasure which is without pain. And if you are satisfied, and if you are unable to show any good or evil which

does not end in pleasure and pain, hear the consequences: — If this is true, then I say that the argument is absurd which affirms that a man often does
evil knowingly, when he might abstain, because he is
seduced and amazed by pleasure; or again, when you
say that a man knowingly refuses to do what is good
because he is overcome at the moment by pleasure.
Now that this is ridiculous will be evident if only we
give up the use of various names, such as pleasant and
painful, and good and evil. As there are two things,
let us call them by two names — first, good and evil,
and then pleasant and painful. Assuming this, let us
go on to say that a man does evil knowing that he
does evil. But some one will ask, Why? Because he
is overcome, is the first answer. And by what is he
overcome? the inquirer will proceed to ask. And we
shall not be able to reply " By pleasure," for the name
of pleasure has been exchanged for that of good. In
our answer, then, we shall only say that he is overcome.
" By what? " he will reiterate. By the good, we shall
have to reply; indeed we shall. Nay, but our questioner will rejoin with a laugh, if he be one of the
swaggering sort, That is too ridiculous, that a man
should do what he knows to be evil when he ought not,
because he is overcome by good. Is that, he will ask,
because the good was worthy or not worthy of conquering the evil? And in answer to that we shall
clearly reply, Because it was not worthy; for if it
had been worthy, then he who, as we say, was overcome by pleasure, would not have been wrong. But
how, he will reply, can the good be unworthy of the
evil, or the evil of the good? Is not the real explanation that they are out of proportion to one another,
either as greater and smaller, or more and fewer?
This we can not deny. And when you speak of being
overcome — what do you mean, he will say, but that

you choose the greater evil in exchange for the lesser good? This being the case, let us now substitute the names of pleasure and pain, and say, not as before, that a man does what is evil knowingly, but that he does what is painful knowingly, and because he is overcome by pleasure, which is unworthy to overcome. And what measure is there of the relations of pleasure to pain other than excess and defect, which means that they become greater and smaller, and more and fewer, and differ in degree? For if any one says: " Yes, Socrates, but immediate pleasure differs widely from future pleasure and pain " — To that I should reply: And do they differ in any other way except by reason of pleasure and pain? There can be no other measure of them. And do you, like a skilful weigher, put into the balance the pleasures and the pains, near and distant, and weigh them, and then say which outweighs the other. If you weigh pleasures against pleasures, you of course take the more and greater; or if you weigh pains against pains, you take the fewer and the less; or if pleasures against pains, then you choose that course of action in which the painful is exceeded by the pleasant, whether the distant by the near or the near by the distant; and you avoid that course of action in which the pleasant is exceeded by the painful Would you not admit, my friends, that this is true? I am confident that they can not deny this.

He agreed with me.

Well then, I shall say, if you admit that, be so good as to answer me a question: Do not the same magnitudes appear larger to your sight when near, and smaller when at a distance? They will acknowledge that. And the same folds of thickness and number; also sounds, which are in themselves equal, are greater when near, and lesser when at a distance. They will grant that also. Now supposing that happiness consisted in making and taking large things, what would be the saving principle of human life? Would the art of measuring be the saving principle, or would the power of appearance? Is not the latter that deceiving art which makes us wander up and down and take the things at one time of which we repent at another, both in our actions and in our choice of things great and small? But the art of measurement is that which would do away with the effect of appearances, and, showing the truth, would fain teach the soul at last to find rest in the truth, and would thus save our life. Would not mankind generally acknowledge that the art which accomplishes this is the art of measurement?

Yes, he said, the art of measurement.

Suppose, again, the salvation of human life to depend on the choice of odd and even, and on the knowledge of when men ought to choose the greater or less, either in reference to themselves or to each other whether near or at a distance; what would be the saving principle of our lives? Would not knowledge? — a knowledge of measuring, when the question is one of excess and defect, and a knowledge of number, when the question is of odd and even? The world will acknowledge that, will they not?

Protagoras admitted that they would.

Well then, I say to them, my friends; seeing that the salvation of human life has been found to consist in the right choice of pleasures and pains, — in the choice of the more and the fewer, and the greater and the less, and the nearer and remoter, must not this measuring be a consideration of excess and defect and equality in relation to each other?

That is undeniably true.

And this, as possessing measure, must undeniably also be an art and science?

They will agree to that.

The nature of that art or science will be a matter
of future consideration; the demonstration of the existence of such a science is a sufficient answer to the
question which you asked of me and Protagoras. At
the time when you asked the question, if you remember, both of us were agreeing that there was nothing
mightier than knowledge, and that knowledge, in
whatever existing, must have the advantage over
pleasure and all other things; and then you said that
pleasure often got the advantage even over a man
who has knowledge; and we refused to allow this, and
you said: O Protagoras and Socrates, if this state is
not to be called being overcome by pleasure, tell us
what it is; what would you call it? If we had immediately and at the time answered " Ignorance,"
you would have laughed at us. But now, in laughing
at us, you will be laughing at yourselves: for you also
admitted that men err in their choice of pleasures and
pains; that is, in their choice of good and evil, from
defect of knowledge; and you admitted further that
they err, not only from defect of knowledge in general, but of that particular knowledge which is called
measuring. And you are also aware that the erring
act which is done without knowledge is done in ignorance. This, therefore, is the meaning of being overcome by pleasure; — ignorance, and that the greatest.
And our friends Protagoras and Prodicus and Hippias declare that they are the physicians of ignorance;
but you, who are under the mistaken impression that
ignorance is not the cause, neither go yourselves, nor
send your children, to the Sophists, who are the teachers of these things — you take care of your money
and give them none; and the result is, that you are
the worse off both in public and private life: — Let
us suppose this to be our answer to the world in general. But I would like now to ask you, Hippias, and

you, Prodicus, as well as Protagoras (for the argument is to be yours as well as ours), whether you think that I am speaking the truth or not?

They all thought that what I said was entirely true.

Then you agree, I said, that the pleasant is the good, and the painful evil. And here I would beg my friend Prodicus not to introduce his distinction of names, whether he is disposed to say pleasurable, delightful, joyful. However and in whatever way he rejoices to name them, I will ask you, most excellent Prodicus, to answer this in my sense.

Prodicus laughed and assented, as did the others.

Then, my friends, I said, what do you say to this? Are not all actions, the tendency of which is to make life painless and pleasant, honorable and useful? The honorable work is also useful and good?

This was admitted.

Then, I said, if the pleasant is the good, nobody does anything under the idea or conviction that some other thing would be better and is also attainable, when he might do the better. And this inferiority of a man to himself is merely ignorance, as the superiority of a man to himself is wisdom.

They all assented.

And is not ignorance the having a false opinion and being deceived about important matters?

To that they also unanimously assented.

Then, I said, no man voluntarily pursues evil, or that which he thinks to be evil. To prefer evil to good is not in human nature; and when a man is compelled to choose one of two evils, no one will choose the greater when he might have the less.

All of us agreed to every word of this.

Well, I said, there is a certain thing called fear or terror; and here, Prodicus, I should particularly like to know whether you would agree with me in defining this fear or terror as expectation of evil.

Protagoras and Hippias agreed, but Prodicus said that this was fear and not terror.

Never mind about that, Prodicus, I said; but let me ask whether, if our former assertions are true, a man will pursue that which he fears when he need not? Would not this be in contradiction to the admission which has been already made, that he thinks the things which he fears to be evil; and no one will pursue or voluntarily accept that which he thinks to be evil.

That also was universally admitted.

Then, I said, these, Hippias and Prodicus, are our premisses; and I would beg Protagoras to explain to us how he can be right in what he said at first. I do not mean in what he said quite at first, for his first statement, as you may remember, was that whereas there were five parts of virtue none of them was like any other of them; each of them had a separate func· tion. To this, however, I am not referring, but to the assertion which he afterwards made that of the five virtues four were nearly akin to each other, but that the fifth, which was courage, differed greatly from the others. And of this he gave me the following proof. He said: You will find, Socrates, that some of the most impious, and unrighteous, and intemperate, and ignorant of men are among the most courageous; and that is a proof that courage is very different from the other parts of virtue. I was surprised at his saying this at the time, and I am still more surprised now that I have discussed the matter with you. So I asked him whether by the brave he meant the confident. Yes, he replied, and the impetuous or goers. (You may remember, Protagoras, that this was your answer.)

He acknowledged the truth of this.

Well then, I said, tell us against what are the courageous ready to go — against the same as the cowards?

No, he answered.

Then against something different?

Yes, he said.

Then do cowards go where there is safety, and the courageous where there is danger?

Yes, Socrates, that is what men say.

That is true, I said. But I want to know against what the courageous are ready to go — against dangers, believing them to be dangers, or not against dangers?

No, said he; that has been proved by you in the previous argument to be impossible.

That, again, I replied, is quite true. And if this has been rightly proven, then no one goes to meet what he thinks to be dangers, since the want of self-control, which makes men rush into dangers, has been shown to be ignorance.

He assented.

And yet the courageous man and the coward alike go to meet that about which they are confident; so that, in this point of view, the cowardly and the courageous go to meet the same things.

And yet, Socrates, said Protagoras, that to which the coward goes is the opposite of that to which the courageous goes; the one, for example, are ready to go to battle, and the others are not ready.

And is going to battle honorable or disgraceful? I said.

Honorable, he replied.

And if honorable, then already admitted by us to be good; for all honorable actions we have admitted to be good.

That is true; and to that opinion I shall always adhere.

True, I said. But which of the two are they who, as you say, are unwilling to go to war, which is a good and honorable thing?

The cowards, he replied.

And yet, I said, that which is good and honorable is also pleasant?

That, he said, was certainly admitted.

And do the cowards knowingly refuse to go to the nobler, and pleasanter, and better?

The admission of that, he replied, would belie our former admissions.

But does not the courageous man also go to meet the better, and pleasanter, and nobler?

That must be admitted.

And the courageous man has no base fear or base confidence?

True, he replied.

And if not base, then honorable?

He admitted this.

And if honorable, then good?

Yes.

But the fear and confidence of the coward or foolhardy or madman, on the contrary, are base?

He assented.

And these base fears and confidences originate in ignorance and uninstructedness?

True, he said.

Then as to the motive from which the cowards act, do you call that cowardice or courage?

I should say cowardice, he replied.

And have they not been shown to be cowards through their ignorance of dangers?

Assuredly, he said.

And because of that ignorance they are cowards?

He assented.

And the reason why they are cowards is admitted by you to be cowardice?

He assented.

Then the ignorance of what is and is not dangerous is cowardice?

He nodded assent.

But surely courage, I said, is opposed to cowardice?

Yes.

And the wisdom which knows what are and are not dangers is opposed to the ignorance of them?

To that again he nodded assent.

And the ignorance of them is cowardice?

To that he very reluctantly nodded assent.

And the knowledge of that which is and is not dangerous is courage, and is opposed to the ignorance of these things?

At this point he would no longer nod assent, but was silent.

And why, I said, do you neither assent nor dissent, Protagoras?

Finish the argument by yourself, he said.

I only want to ask one more question, I said. I want to know whether you still think that there are men who are most ignorant and yet most courageous?

You seem to have a great ambition to make me answer, Socrates, and therefore I will gratify you, and say, that this appears to me to be impossible consistently with the argument.

My only object, I said, in continuing the discussion, has been the desire to ascertain the relations of virtue and the essential nature of virtue; for if this were clear, I am very sure that the other controversy which has been carried on at great length by both of us — you affirming and I denying that virtue can be taught — would also have become clear. The result of our discussion appears to me to be singular. For if the argument had a human voice, that voice would be heard laughing at us and saying: Protagoras and Socrates, you are strange beings; there are you who were saying that virtue can not be taught, contradicting yourself now in the attempt to show that all things are knowledge, including justice, and temperance, and courage, — which tends to show that virtue can certainly be taught; for if virtue were other than knowledge, as Protagoras attempted to show, then clearly virtue can not be taught; but if virtue is entirely knowledge, as you, Socrates, are seeking to show, then I can not but suppose that virtue is capable of being taught. Protagoras, on the other hand, who started by saying that it might be taught, is now eager to show that it is anything rather than knowledge; and if this is true, it must be quite incapable of being taught. Now I, Protagoras, perceiving this terrible confusion of ideas, have a great desire that they should be cleared up. And I should like to carry on the discussion until we ascertain what virtue is, and whether capable of being taught or not, lest haply Epimetheus should trip us up and deceive us in the argument, as he forgot to provide for us in the story; and I prefer your Prometheus to your Epimetheus: of him I make use whenever I am busy about these questions in Promethean care of my own life. And if you have no objection, as I said at first, I should like to have your help in the inquiry.

Protagoras replied: Socrates, I am not of a base nature, and I am the last man in the world to be envious. I can not but applaud your enthusiasm in the conduct of an argument. As I have often said, I admire you above all men whom I know, certainly above all men of your age; and I believe that you will become very eminent in philosophy. Let us come back to the subject at some future time; at present we had better turn to something else.

By all means, I said, if that is your wish; for I too ought long since to have kept the engagement of which I spoke before, and only tarried because I could not refuse the request of the noble Callias. This finished the conversation, and we went our way.

EUTHYDEMUS

INTRODUCTION

The Euthydemus is, of all the Dialogues of Plato, that in which he approaches most nearly to the comic poet. The mirth is broader, the irony more sustained, the contrast between Socrates and the two Sophists, although veiled, penetrates deeper than in any other of his writings. Even Thrasymachus, in the Republic, is at last pacified, and becomes a friendly and interested auditor of the great discourse. But in the Euthydemus the mask is never dropped; the accustomed irony of Socrates continues to the end.

Socrates narrates to Crito a remarkable scene in which he has himself taken part, and in which the two brothers, Dionysodorus and Euthydemus are the chief performers. They are natives of Chios, who have been exiled from Thurii, and in former days had appeared at Athens as teachers of rhetoric and of the art of fighting in armor. To this they have now added a new fighting accomplishment — the art of Eristic, or fighting with words, which they are likewise willing to teach " for a consideration." But they can also teach virtue in a very short time and in the very best manner. Socrates, who is always on the look out for teachers of virtue, is interested in the youth Cleinias, the grandson of the great Alcibiades, and is desirous that he should have the benefit of their instructions. He is quite ready to fall down and worship them; although the greatness of their professions does arouse in his mind a temporary incredulity.

A circle gathers round them, in the midst of which are Socrates, the two brothers, the youth Cleinias, who is watched by the eager eyes of his lover Ctesippus, and others.

The performance begins; and such a performance as might well seem to require an invocation of Memory and the Muses. It is agreed that the brothers shall question Cleinias. " Cleinias," says Euthydemus, " who learn, the wise or the unwise? " " The wise," is the reply; given with blushing and hesitation. " And yet when you learned you did not know and were not wise." Then Dionysodorus takes up the ball: " Who are they who learn

1055

dictation of the grammar-master; the wise boys or the foolish boys?" "The wise." "Then after all the wise learn." "And do they learn," said Euthydemus, "what they know or what they do not know?" "The latter." "And dictation is a dictation of letters?" "Yes." "And you know letters?" "Yes." "Then you learn what you know." "But," retorts Dionysodorus, "is not learning acquiring knowledge?" "Yes." "And you acquire that which you have not got already." "Then you learn that which you do not know."

Socrates is afraid that the youth Cleinias may be discouraged at these repeated overthrows. He therefore explains to him the nature of the process to which he is being subjected. The two strangers are not serious; there are jests at the mysteries which precede the enthronement, and he is being initiated into the mysteries of the sophistical ritual. This is all a sort of horse-play, which is now ended. The exhortation to virtue will follow, and Socrates himself (if the wise men will not laugh at him) is desirous of carrying on such an exhortation, by way of example to them, according to his own poor notion. He proceeds to question Cleinias. The result of the investigation may be summed up as follows: —

All men desire good; and good means the possession of goods, such as wealth, health, beauty, birth, power, honor; not forgetting the virtues and wisdom. And yet in this enumeration the greatest good of all is omitted. What is that? Good fortune. But what need is there of good fortune when we have wisdom already: — in every art and business are not the wise also the fortunate? This is admitted. And again, the possession of goods is not enough; there must be a right use of them as well, and this can only be given by knowledge: in themselves they are neither good nor evil, but knowledge and wisdom are the only good, and ignorance and folly the only evil. The conclusion is that we must get "wisdom." But can wisdom be taught? "Yes," says Cleinias. Socrates is delighted at the ingenuousness of the youth relieving him from the necessity of discussing one of his great puzzles. "As wisdom is the only good, he must become a philosopher, or lover of wisdom." "That I will," says Cleinias.

After Socrates has given this specimen of his own mode of instruction, the two brothers recommence their exhortation to virtue, which is of quite another sort.

"You want Cleinias to be wise?" "Yes." "And he is not wise yet?" "No." "Then you want him to be what he is not, and not to be what he is? — not to be — that is, to perish. Pretty lovers and friends you must all be!"

Here Ctesippus, the lover of Cleinias interposes in great excitement, thinking that he will teach the two Sophists a lesson of good manners. But he is quickly entangled in the meshes of their sophistry; and as a storm seems to be gathering Socrates pacifies him with a joke, and Ctesippus then says that he is not reviling the two Sophists, he is only contradicting them. "But," says Dionysodorus, "there is no such thing as contradiction. When you and I describe the same thing, or you describe one thing and I describe another, how is there any contradiction in that?" Ctesippus is unable to reply.

Socrates has already heard of the denial of contradiction, and would like to be informed by the great master of the art, "What is the meaning of this?" Do they mean that there is no such thing as error, ignorance, falsehood? Then what are they professing to teach? The two Sophists complain that Socrates is ready to answer what they said a year ago, but is "non-plussed" at which they are saying now. "What does the word 'non-plussed' mean?" Socrates is informed in reply that words are lifeless things, and lifeless things have no sense or meaning. Ctesippus again breaks out, and again has to be pacified by Socrates, who renews the conversation with Cleinias. The two Sophists are like Proteus in the variety of their transformations, and he, like Menelaus, hopes to restore them to their natural form.

He had arrived at the conclusion that philosophy must be studied. And philosophy is the possession of knowledge; and knowledge must be of a kind which is profitable, and in which knowledge and use coincide. What knowledge is there which is of such a nature? Not the knowledge which is required in any particular art; nor again the art of the composer of speeches, who knows how to write them, but can not speak them, although he too must be admitted to be a kind of enchanter of wild animals. Neither is the knowledge for which we are searching the knowledge of the general. For the general makes over his prey to the statesman, as the huntsman does to the cook, or the taker of quails to the keeper of quails; he has not the use of that which he acquires. The two inquirers, Cleinias and Socrates, are described as wandering about in a wilderness, vainly searching after the art of life and happiness. At last they fix upon the kingly art, as having the desired sort of knowledge. But the kingly art only gives men those goods which are neither good nor evil: and if we say further that it makes us wise, in what does it make us wise? Not in special arts, such as cobbling or carpentering, but only in itself: or say again that it makes us good, there is no answer to the question, "good in what?" At length in despair Cleinias and Socrates turn to the "Dioscuri" and request their aid.

Euthydemus argues that Socrates know something; and as he can not know and not know, he can not know some things and not know others, and therefore he knows all things: he and Dionysodorus and all other men know all things. "Do they know shoemaking, etc.?" "Yes." The sceptical Ctesippus would like to have some evidence of this extraordinary statement: he will believe if Euthydemus will tell him how many stumps of teeth Dionysodorus has, and if Dionysodorus will give him a like piece of information about Euthydemus. Even Socrates is incredulous, and indulges in a little raillery at the expense of the brothers. But he restrains himself, remembering that if the men who are to be his teachers think him stupid they will take no pains with him. Another fallacy is produced which turns on the absoluteness of the verb "to know." And here Euthydemus is caught "napping," and is induced by Socrates to confess that "he does not know the good to be unjust." Socrates recommends him to call his brother Dionysodorus to his assistance, as Heracles called his nephew Iolaus. Dionysodorus rejoins that Iolaus was no more the nephew of Heracles than of Socrates. For a nephew is a nephew, and a brother is a brother, and a father is a father, not of one man only, but of all; nor of men only, but of dogs and sea-monsters. Ctesippus makes merry with the consequences which follow: "Much good has your father got out of the wisdom of his puppies."

But, says Euthydemus, unabashed, "Nobody wants much good." Medicine is a good, arms are a good, money is a good, and yet there may be too much of them in wrong places. "No," says Ctesippus, "there can not be too much gold." "And would you be happy if you had three talents of gold in your belly, a talent in your plate, and a stater in either eye?" Ctesippus, imitating the new wisdom, replies, "And do not the Scythians reckon those to be the happiest of men who have their skulls gilded and see the inside of them?" "Do you see," retorts Euthydemus, "what has the quality of vision or what has not the quality of vision." What has the quality of vision?" "And you see our garments?" "Yes." "Then our garments have the quality of vision." A similar play of words follows. which

is successfully retorted by Ctesippus, to the great delight of
Cleinias, who is rebuked by Socrates for laughing at such solemn
and beautiful things.

"But are there any beautiful things? And if there are such,
are they the same or not the same as absolute beauty?" Socrates
replies that they are not the same, but each of them has some
beauty present with it. "And are you an ox because you have an
ox present with you?" After a few more similar amphiboliae, in
which Socrates, like Ctesippus, in self-defence borrows the
weapons of the brothers, they both confess that the two heroes
are invincible; and the scene concludes with a grand chorus
of shouting and laughing, and a panegyrical oration from
Socrates:

First, he praises the indifference of Dionysodorus and Euthydemus to public opinion; for most persons would rather be refuted by such arguments than use them in the refutation of
others. Secondly, he remarks upon their impartiality; for they
stop their own mouths, as well as those of other people. Thirdly,
he notes their liberality, which makes them give away their secret
to all the world: they should be more reserved, and let no one
be present at this exhibition who does not pay them money; or
better still they might practise on one another only. He concludes with a respectful request that they will take him and
Cleinias as their disciples.

Crito tells Socrates that he has heard one of the audience
criticize severely this wisdom, — not sparing Socrates himself
for countenancing such an exhibition. Socrates asks what manner of man was this censorious critic. "Not an orator, but a
great composer of speeches." Socrates understands that he is an
amphibious sort of animal, half philosopher, half politician; one
of a class who have the highest opinion of themselves, and a spite
against philosophers, whom they imagine to be their rivals. They
are a class who are very likely to get mauled by Euthydemus and
his friends, and have a great notion of their own wisdom; for
they imagine themselves to have all the advantages and none of
the drawbacks both of politics and of philosophy. They do not
understand the principles of combination, and hence are ignorant
that the union of two good things which have different ends
produces a compound inferior to either of them taken separately.

Crito is anxious about the education of his children, one of
whom is growing up. The description of Dionysodorus and
Euthydemus suggests to him the reflection that the professors

of education are strange beings. Socrates consoles him with the remark that the good in all professions are few, and recommends that "he and his house," should continue to serve philosophy, and not mind about its professors.

———

There is a stage in the history of philosophy in which the old is dying out, and the new has not yet come into full life. Great philosophies like the Eleatic or Heraclitean, which have enlarged the boundaries of the human mind, begin to pass away in words. They subsist only as forms which have rooted themselves in language — as troublesome elements of thought which can not be either used or explained away. The same absoluteness which was once attributed to abstractions is now attached to the words which are the signs of them. The philosophy which in the first and second generation was a great and inspiring effort of reflection, in the third becomes sophistical, verbal, eristic.

It is this stage of philosophy which Plato satirizes in the Euthydemus. The fallacies which are noted by him appear trifling to us now, but they were not trifling in the age before logic, in the decline of the earlier Greek philosophies, at a time when language was first beginning to perplex human thought. Besides he is caricaturing them; they probably received more subtle forms at the hands of those who seriously maintained them. They are patent to us in Plato, and we are inclined to wonder how any one could ever have been deceived by them; but we must remember also that there was a time when the human mind was only with great difficulty disentangled from such fallacies.

To appreciate fully the drift of the Euthydemus, we should imagine a mental state in which not individuals only, but whole schools during more than one generation, were animated by the desire to exclude the conception of rest, and therefore the very word "thus" from language; in which the ideas of space, time, matter, motion, were proved to be contradictory and imaginary; in which the nature of qualitative change was a puzzle, and even differences of degree, when applied to abstract notions, were not understood; in which contradiction itself was denied; in which, on the one hand, it was affirmed that every predicate was true of every subject, and on the other hand, that no predicate was true of any subject; and that nothing was, or was known, or could be spoken. Let us imagine disputes carried on with religious earnestness and more than scholastic subtlety, in which the catchwords of philosophy are completely detached from their context. To such disputes the humor, whether of Plato in the ancient, or of Pope and Swift in the modern world, is the natural enemy. Nor must we forget that in modern times there is no fallacy so gross, no trick of language so transparent, no abstraction so barren and unmeaning, no form of thought so contradictory to experience, which has not been found to satisfy the minds of philosophical inquirers at a certain stage, or when regarded from a certain point of view only. The peculiarity of the fallacies of our own age is that we live within them, and are therefore generally unconscious of them.

Aristotle has analyzed several of the same fallacies in his book " De Sophisticis Elenchis," which Plato, with equal command of their true nature, has preferred to bring to the test of ridicule. At first we are only struck with the broad humor of this " reductio ad absurdum: " gradually we perceive that some important questions begin to emerge. Here, as everywhere else, Plato is making war against the philosophers who put words in the place of things, who tear arguments to tatters, who deny predication, and thus make knowledge impossible. Two great truths seem to be indirectly taught through these fallacies: (1) The uncertainty of language, which allows the same words to be used in different meanings, or with different degrees of meaning: (2) The necessary limitation or relative nature of all phenomena. Plato is aware that his own doctrine of ideas, as well as the Eleatic Being and Not-being, alike admit of being regarded as verbal fallacies.

Contrasted with the exhibition of the Sophists are the two discourses of Socrates in several respects: (1) In their perfect relevancy to the subject of discussion, whereas the Sophistical discourses are wholly irrelevant: (2) In their inquiring sympathetic tone, which encourages the youth, instead of " knocking him down," after the manner of the two Sophists: (3) In the absence of any definite conclusion — for while Socrates and the youth are agreed that philosophy is to be studied, they are not able to arrive at any certain result about the art which is to teach it. This is a question which will hereafter be answered in the Republic and the Politicus.

The characters of the Dialogue are easily intelligible. There is Socrates once more in the character of an old man; and his equal in years, Crito, the father of Critobulus, like Lysimachus in the Laches, his fellow demesman, to whom the scene is narrated, and who once or twice interrupts with a remark after the manner of the interlocutor in the Phaedo, and adds his commentary at the end; Socrates makes a playful allusion to his money-getting habits. There is the youth Cleinias, the grandson of Alcibiades, who may be compared with Lysis, Charmides, Menexenus, and other ingenuous youths out of whose mouths Socrates draws his own lessons, and to whom he always seems to stand in a kindly and sympathetic relation. Crito will not believe that Socrates has not improved or perhaps invented the answers of Cleinias. The name of the grandson of Alcibiades, who is described as long dead, and who died at the age of forty-four, in the year 404 B. C., suggests not only that the intended scene of the Dialogue could not have been earlier than 404, but that as a fact this Dialogue, which is probably one of the earliest of the Platonic writings, could not have been composed before 390 at the soonest, and probably even later. Ctesippus, who is the lover of Cleinias, has been already introduced to us in the Lysis, and seems there too to deserve the character which is here given him, of a somewhat uproarious young man. But the chief study of all is the picture of the two brothers, who are unapproached in their effrontery, equally careless of what they say to others and of what is said to them, and never at a loss. They are " Arcades ambo et cantare pares et respondere parati." Some superior degree of wit or subtlety is attributed, however, to Euthydemus, who continues the conversation when Dionysodorus has been put to silence.

The epilogue or conclusion of the Dialogue has been criticized as inconsistent with the general scheme. Such a criticism is like similar criticisms on Shakespeare, and proceeds upon a narrow notion of the variety which the Dialogue, like the drama, seems to admit. Plato in the abundance of his dramatic power has chosen to write a play upon a play, just as he often gives us an argument within an argument. At the same time he takes the opportunity of assailing another class of persons who are as alien from the spirit of philosophy as Euthydemus and Dionysodorus. The Eclectic, the Syncretist, the Doctrinaire, have been apt to have a bad name both in ancient and modern times. The persons whom Plato ridicules in the epilogue to the Euthydemus are of this class. They occupy a border-ground between philosophy and politics; they are free from the dangers of politics, and at the same time use philosophy as a means of serving their own interests. Plato quaintly describes them as making two good things, philosophy and politics, a little worse by perverting the objects of both.

Education is the common subject of all Plato's earlier Dialogues. The concluding remark of Crito, that he has a difficulty in educating his two sons, and the advice of Socrates to him that he should not give up philosophy because he has no faith in philosophers, seems to be a preparation for the more peremptory declaration of the Meno that " Virtue can not be taught because there are no teachers."

EUTHYDEMUS

PERSONS OF THE DIALOGUE.

SOCRATES, *who is the narrator*
   of the Dialogue.
CRITO.
CLEINIAS.

EUTHYDEMUS.
DIONYSODORUS.
CTESIPPUS.

SCENE:— The Lyceum.

Crito. WHO was the person, Socrates, with whom you were talking yesterday at the Lyceum? There was such a crowd around you that I could not get within hearing, but I caught a sight of him over their heads, and I made out, as I thought, that he was a stranger with whom you were talking: who was he?

Socrates. There were two, Crito; which of them do you mean?

Cri. The one who was seated second from you on the right-hand side. In the middle was Cleinias the young son of Axiochus, who has wonderfully grown; he is only about the age of my own Critobulus, but he is much forwarder and very good-looking: the other is thin and looks younger than he is.

Soc. He whom you mean, Crito, is Euthydemus; and on my left hand there was his brother Dionysodorus, who also took part in the conversation.

Cri. Neither of them are known to me, Socrates; they are a new importation of Sophists, as I should imagine. Of what country are they, and what is their line of wisdom?

Soc. As to their origin, I believe that they are natives of this part of the world, and have migrated

1065

from Chios and Thurii; they were driven out of
Thurii, and have been living for many years past in
this region. As to their wisdom, about which you ask,
Crito, they are wonderful — consummate! I never
knew what the true pancratiast was before; they are
simply made up of fighting, not like the two Acarna-
nian brothers who fight with their bodies only, but
this pair are perfect in the use of their bodies and have
a universal mode of fighting (for they are capital at
fighting in armor, and will teach the art to any one
who pays them): and also they are masters of legal
fence, and are ready to do battle in the courts; they
will give lessons in speaking and pleading, and in
writing speeches. And this was only the beginning
of their wisdom, but they have at last carried out the
pancratiastic art to the very end, and have mastered
the only mode of fighting which had been hitherto
neglected by them; and now no one dares look at
them: such is their skill in the war of words, that they
can refute any proposition whether true or false.
Now I am thinking, Crito, of putting myself in their
hands; for they say that in a short time they can
impart their skill to any one.

Cri. But, Socrates, are you not too old? there may
be reason to fear that.

Soc. Certainly not, Crito; as I will prove to you,
for I have the consolation of knowing that they began
this art of disputation which I covet, quite, as I may
say, in old age; last year, or the year before, they had
none of their new wisdom. I am only apprehensive
that I may bring the two strangers into disrepute, as
I have done Connus the son of Metrobius, the harp-
player, who is still my music-master; for when the
boys who also go to him see me going, they laugh at
me and call him grandpapa's master. Now I should
not like the strangers to experience this sort of treat-

ment, and perhaps they may be afraid and not like
to receive me because of this; and therefore, Crito,
I shall try and persuade some old men to go along
with me to them, as I persuaded them to go to Connus, and I hope that you will make one: and perhaps
we had better take your sons as a bait; they will want
to have them, and will be willing to receive us as pupils
for the sake of them.

Cri. I see no objection, Socrates, if you like; but
first I wish that you would give me a description of
their wisdom, that I may know beforehand what we
are going to learn.

Soc. I will tell you at once; for I can not say that
I did not attend: the fact was that I paid great attention to them, and I remember and will endeavor to
tell you the whole story. I was providentially sitting
alone in the dressing-room of the Lyceum in which
you saw me, and was about to depart, when as I was
getting up I recognized the familiar divine sign: so
I sat down again, and in a little while the two brothers Euthydemus and Dionysodorus came in, and several others with them, whom I believe to be their disciples, and they walked about in the covered space;
they had not taken more than two or three turns when
Cleinias entered, who, as you truly say, is very much
improved: he was followed by a host of lovers, one of
whom was Ctesippus the Paeanian, a well-bred youth,
but also having the wildness of youth. Cleinias saw
me from the entrance as I was sitting alone, and at
once came and sat down on the right hand of me, as
you describe; and Dionysodorus and Euthydemus,
when they saw him, at first stopped and talked with
one another, now and then glancing at us, for I particularly watched them; and then Euthydemus came
and sat down by the youth, and the other by me on
the left hand; the rest anywhere. I saluted the broth-

ers, whom I had not seen for a long time; and then I said to Cleinias: These two men, Euthydemus and Dionysodorus, Cleinias, are not in a small but in a large way of wisdom, for they know all about war, — all that a good general ought to know about the array and command of an army, and the whole art of fighting in armor: and they know about law too, and can teach a man how to use the weapons of the courts when he is injured.

They heard me say this, and I was despised by them; they looked at one another, and both of them laughed; and then Euthydemus said: Those, Socrates, are matters which we no longer pursue seriously; they are secondary occupations to us.

Indeed, I said, if such occupations are regarded by you as secondary, what must the principal one be; tell me, I beseech you, what that noble study is?

The teaching of virtue, Socrates, he replied, is our principal occupation; and we believe that we can impart it better and quicker than any man.

My God! I said, and where did you learn that? I always thought, as I was saying just now, that your chief accomplishment was the art of fighting in armor; and this was what I used to say of you, for I remember that this was professed by you when you were here before. But now if you really have the other knowledge, O forgive me: I address you as I would superior beings, and ask you to pardon the impiety of my former expression. But are you quite sure about this, Dionysodorus and Euthydemus: the promise is so vast, that a feeling of incredulity will creep in.

You may take our word, Socrates, for the fact.

Then I think you happier in having such a treasure than the great king is in the possession of his kingdom. And please to tell me whether you intend to exhibit this wisdom, or what you will do.

That is why we are come hither, Socrates; and our purpose is not only to exhibit, but also to teach any one who likes to learn.

But I can promise you, I said, that every unvirtuous person will want to learn. I shall be the first; and there is the youth Cleinias, and Ctesippus: and here are several others, I said, pointing to the lovers of Cleinias, who were beginning to gather round us. Now Ctesippus was sitting at some distance from Cleinias; and when Euthydemus leaned forward in talking with me, he was prevented from seeing Cleinias, who was between us; and so, partly because he wanted to look at his love, and also because he was interested, he jumped up and stood opposite to us: and all the other admirers of Cleinias, as well as the disciples of Euthydemus and Dionysodorus, followed his example. And these were the persons whom I showed to Euthydemus, telling him that they were all eager to learn: to which Ctesippus and all of them with one voice vehemently assented, and bid him exhibit the power of his wisdom. Then I said: O Euthydemus and Dionysodorus, I earnestly request you to do myself and the company the favor to exhibit. There may be some trouble in giving the whole exhibition; but tell me one thing, — can you make a good man only of him who is convinced that he ought to learn of you, or of him also who is not convinced? either because he imagines that virtue is not a thing which can be taught at all, or that you two are not the teachers of it. Say whether your art is able to persuade such an one nevertheless that virtue can be taught; and that you are the men from whom he will be most likely to learn.

This is the art, Socrates, said Dionysodorus, and no other.

And you, Dionysodorus, I said, are the men who

among those who are now living are the most likely
to stimulate him to philosophy and the study of virtue?

Yes, Socrates, I rather think that we are.

Then I wish that you would be so good as to defer
the other part of the exhibition, and only try to persuade the youth whom you see here that he ought to
be a philosopher and study virtue. Exhibit that, and
you will confer a great favor on me and on every one
present; for the fact is that I and all of us are extremely anxious that he should be truly good. His
name is Cleinias, and he is the son of Axiochus, and
grandson of the old Alcibiades, cousin of the Alcibiades that now is. He is quite young, and we are
naturally afraid that some one may get the start of
us, and turn his mind in a wrong direction, and he may
be ruined. Your visit, therefore, is most happily
timed; and I hope that you will make a trial of the
young man, and converse with him in our presence, if
you have no objection.

These were pretty nearly the expressions which I
used; and Euthydemus, in a lofty and at the same
time cheerful tone, replied: There can be no objection, Socrates, if the young man is only willing to
answer questions.

He is quite accustomed to that, I replied; for his
friends often come and ask him questions and argue
with him; so that he is at home in answering.

What followed, Crito, how can I rightly narrate?
for not slight is the task of rehearsing infinite wisdom,
and therefore, like the poets, I ought to commence
my relation with an invocation to Memory and the
Muses. Now Euthydemus, if I remember rightly,
began nearly as follows: O Cleinias, are those who
learn the wise or the ignorant?

The youth, overpowered by the question, blushed,

and in his perplexity looked at me for help; and I, knowing that he was disconcerted, said: Don't be afraid, Cleinias, but answer like a man whichever you think; for my belief is that you will derive the greatest good from their questions.

Whichever he answers, said Dionysodorus, leaning forward in my ear and laughing, I prophesy that he will be refuted, Socrates.

While he was speaking to me, Cleinias gave his answer: the consequence was that I had no time to warn him of the predicament in which he was placed, and he answered that those who learned were the wise.

Euthydemus proceeded: There are those whom you call teachers, are there not?

The boy assented.

And they are the teachers of those who learn — the grammar-master and the lyre-master used to teach you and other boys; and you were the learners?

Yes.

And when you were learners you did not as yet know the things which you were learning?

No, he said.

And were you wise then?

No, indeed, he said.

But if you were not wise you were unlearned?

Certainly.

You then, learning what you did not know, were unlearned when you were learning?

The youth nodded assent.

Then the unlearned learn, and not the wise, Cleinias, as you imagine.

At these words the followers of Euthydemus, of whom I spoke, like a chorus at the bidding of their director, laughed and cheered. Then, before the youth had well time to recover, Dionysodorus took him in hand, and said: Yes, Cleinias; and when the grammar-master dictated to you, were they the wise boys or the unlearned who learned the dictation?

The wise, replied Cleinias.

Then after all the wise are the learners and not the unlearned; and your last answer to Euthydemus was wrong.

Then followed another peal of laughter and shouting, which came from the admirers of the two heroes, who were ravished with their wisdom, while the rest of us were silent and amazed. This Euthydemus perceiving, determined to persevere with the youth; and in order to heighten the effect went on asking another similar question, which might be compared to the double turn of an expert dancer. Do those, said he, who learn, learn what they know, or what they do not know?

Dionysodorus said to me in a whisper: That, Socrates, is just another of the same sort.

Good heavens, I said; and your last question was so good!

Like all our other questions, Socrates, he replied, — inevitable.

I see the reason, I said, why you are in such reputation among your disciples.

Meanwhile Cleinias had answered Euthydemus that those who learned learn what they do not know; and he put him through a series of questions as before.

Don't you know letters?

He assented.

All letters?

Yes.

But when the teacher dictates to you, does he not dictate letters?

He admitted that.

Then if you know all letters, he dictates that which you know?

He admitted that also.

Then, said the other, you do not learn that which he dictates; but he only who does not know letters learns?

Nay, said Cleinias; but I do learn.

Then, said he, you learn what you know, if you know all the letters?

He admitted that.

Then, he said, you were wrong in your answer.

The word was hardly out of his mouth when Dionysodorus took up the argument, like a ball which he caught, and had another throw at the youth. Cleinias, he said, Euthydemus is deceiving you. For tell me now, is not learning acquiring knowledge of that which one learns?

Cleinias assented.

And knowing is having knowledge at the time?

He agreed.

And not knowing is not having knowledge at the time?

He admitted that.

And are those who acquire those who have or have not a thing?

Those who have not.

And have you not admitted that those who do not know are of the number of those who have not?

He nodded assent.

Then those who learn are of the class of those who acquire, and not of those who have?

He agreed.

Then, Cleinias, he said, those who do not know learn, and not those who know.

Euthydemus was proceeding to give the youth a third fall; but I knew that he was in deep water, and therefore, as I wanted to give him a rest, and also in order that he might not get out of heart, I said to him consolingly: You must not be surprised, Cleinias, at the singularity of their mode of speech: this I say because you may not understand what they are doing with you; they are only initiating you after the manner of the Corybantes in the mysteries; and this answers to the enthronement, which, if you have ever been initiated, is, as you will know, accompanied by dancing and sport; and now they are just prancing and dancing about you, and will next proceed to initiate you; and at this stage you must imagine yourself to have gone through the first part of the sophistical ritual, which, as Prodicus says, begins with initiation into the correct use of terms. The two strange gentlemen wanted to explain to you, as you do not know, that the word " to learn " has two meanings, and is used, first, in the sense of acquiring knowledge of some matter of which you previously have no knowledge, and also, when you have the knowledge, in the sense of reviewing this same matter done or spoken by the light of this knowledge; this last is generally called " knowing " rather than " learning; " but the word " learning " is also used, and you did not see that the word is used of two opposite sorts of men, of those who know, and of those who do not know, as they explained. There was a similar trick in the second question, when they asked you whether men learn what they know or what they do not know. These parts of learning are not serious, and therefore I say that these gentlemen are not serious, but only in fun with you. And if a man had all that sort of knowledge that ever was, he would not be at all the wiser; he would only be able to play with men, tripping them up and oversetting them with distinctions of words. He would be like a person who pulls away a stool from some one when he is about to sit down, and then laughs and claps his hands at the sight of his friend sprawling on the ground. And you must regard all that has passed hitherto as merely play. But now I am certain that they will proceed to business, and keep their promise (I will show them how); for they promised to give me a sample of the hortatory philosophy, but I suppose that they wanted to have a game of play with you first. And now, Euthydemus and Dionysodorus, I said, I think that we have had enough of this. Will you let me see you exhibiting to the young man, and showing him how he is to apply himself to the study of virtue and wisdom? And I will first show you what I conceive to be the nature of the task, and what I desire to hear; and if I do this in a very inartistic and ridiculous manner, do not laugh at me, for I only venture to improvise before you because I am eager to hear your wisdom: and I must therefore ask you to keep your countenances, and your disciples also. And now, O son of Axiochus, let me put a question to you: Do not all men desire happiness? And yet, perhaps, this is one of those ridiculous questions which I am afraid to ask, and which ought not to be asked by a sensible man: for what human being is there who does not desire happiness?

There is no one, said Cleinias, who does not.

Well, then, I said, since we all of us desire happiness, how can we be happy? — that is the next question. Shall we not be happy if we have many good things? And this, perhaps, is even a more simple question than the first, for there can be no doubt of the answer.

He assented.

And what things do we esteem good? No solemn sage is required to tell us this, which may be easily answered; for every one will say that wealth is a good.

Certainly, he said.

And are not health and beauty goods, and other personal gifts?

He agreed.

Now, can there be any doubt that good birth, and power, and honors in one's own land, are goods?

He assented.

And what other goods are there? I said. What do you say of justice, temperance, courage: do you not verily and indeed think, Cleinias, that we shall be more right in ranking them as goods than in not ranking them as goods? For a dispute might possibly arise about this. What then do you say?

They are goods, said Cleinias.

Very well, I said; and in what company shall we find a place for wisdom — among the goods or not?

Among the goods.

And now, I said, think whether we have left out any considerable goods.

I do not think that we have, said Cleinias.

Upon recollection, I said, indeed I am afraid that we have left out the greatest of them all.

What is that? he asked.

Fortune, Cleinias, I replied; which all, even the most foolish, admit to be the greatest of goods.

True, he said.

On second thoughts, I added, how narrowly, O son of Axiochus, have you and I escaped making a laughing-stock of ourselves to the strangers.

Why do you say that?

Why, because we have already spoken of fortune, and are but repeating ourselves.

What do you mean?

I mean that there is something ridiculous in putting fortune again forward, and saying the same thing twice over.

He asked what was the meaning of this, and I replied: Surely wisdom is good fortune; even a child may know that.

The simple-minded youth was amazed; and, observing this, I said to him: Do you not know, Cleinias, that flute-players are most fortunate and successful in performing on the flute?

He assented.

And are not the scribes most fortunate in writing and reading letters?

Certainly.

Amid the dangers of the sea, again, are any more fortunate on the whole than wise pilots?

None, certainly.

And if you were engaged in war, in whose company would you rather take the risk — in company with a wise general, or with a foolish one?

With a wise one.

And if you were ill, whom would you rather have as a companion in a dangerous illness — a wise physician, or an ignorant one?

A wise one.

You think, I said, that to act with a wise man is more fortunate than to act with an ignorant one?

He assented.

Then wisdom always makes men fortunate: for by wisdom no man could ever err, and therefore he must act rightly and succeed, or his wisdom would be wisdom no longer. At last we somehow contrived to agree in a general conclusion, that he who had wisdom had no longer need of fortune. I then recalled to his mind the previous state of the question. You remember, I said, our making the admission that we should be happy and fortunate if many good things were present with us?

He assented.

And should we be happy by reason of the presence of good things, if they profited us not, or if they profited us?

If they profited us, he said.

And would they profit us, if we only had them and did not use them? For example, if we had a great deal of food and did not eat, or a great deal of drink and did not drink, should we be profited?

Certainly not, he said.

Or would an artisan, who had all the implements necessary for his work, and did not use them, be any the better for the possession of all that he ought to possess? For example, would a carpenter be any the better for having all his tools and plenty of wood, if he never worked?

Certainly not, he said.

And if a person had wealth and all the goods of which we were just now speaking, and did not use them, would he be happy because he possessed them?

No indeed, Socrates.

Then, I said, a man who would be happy must not only have the good things, but he must also use them; there is no advantage in merely having them?

True.

Well, Cleinias, but if you have the use as well as the possession of good things, is that sufficient to confer happiness?

Yes, in my opinion.

And may a person use them either rightly or wrongly?

He must use them rightly.

That is quite true, I said. And the wrong use of a thing is far worse than the non-use; for the one is an evil, and the other is neither a good nor an evil. You admit that.

He assented.

Now in the working and use of wood, is not that which gives the right use simply the knowledge of the carpenter?

Nothing else, he said.

And surely, in the manufacture of vessels, knowledge is that which gives the right way of making them?

He agreed.

And in the use of the goods of which we spoke at first — wealth and health and beauty, is not knowledge that which directs us to the right use of them, and guides our practice about them?

Knowledge, he replied.

Then in every possession and every use of a thing, knowledge is that which gives a man not only good fortune but success?

He assented.

And tell me, I said, O tell me, what do possessions profit a man, if he have neither sense nor wisdom? Would a man be better off, having and doing many things without wisdom, or a few things with wisdom? Look at the matter thus: If he did fewer things would he not make fewer mistakes? if he made fewer mistakes would he not have fewer misfortunes? and if he had fewer misfortunes would he not be less miserable?

Certainly, he said.

And who would do least — a poor man or a rich man?

A poor man.

A weak man or a strong man?

A weak man.

A noble man or a mean man?

A mean man.

And a coward would do less than a courageous and temperate man?

Yes.

And an indolent man less than an active man?

He assented.

And a slow man less than a quick; and one who had dull perceptions of seeing and hearing less than one who had keen eyes?

All this was mutually allowed by us.

Then, I said, Cleinias, the sum of the matter appears to be that the goods of which we spoke before are not to be regarded as goods in themselves, but the degree of good and evil in them depends on whether they are or are not under the guidance of knowledge: under the guidance of ignorance, they are greater evils than their opposites, inasmuch as they are more able to minister to the evil principle which rules them; and when under the guidance of wisdom and virtue, they are greater goods: but in themselves they are nothing?

That, he said, appears to be certain.

What then, I said, is the result of all this? Is not this the result — that other things are indifferent, and that wisdom is the only good, and ignorance the only evil?

He assented.

Let us consider this further point, I said: Seeing that all men desire happiness, and happiness, as has been shown, is gained by a use, and a right use, of the things of life, and the right use of them, and good fortune in the use of them, is given by knowledge, — the inference is that every man ought by all means to try and make himself as wise as he can?

Yes, he said.

And the desire to obtain this treasure, which is far more precious than money, from a father or a guardian or a friend or a suitor, whether citizen or stranger — the eager desire and prayer to them that they would impart wisdom to you, is not at all dis-

honorable, Cleinias; nor is any one to be blamed for
doing any honorable service or ministration to any
man, whether a lover or not, if his aim is wisdom. Do
you agree to that, I said?

Yes, he said, I quite agree, and think that you are
right.

Yes, I said, Cleinias, if only wisdom can be taught,
and does not come to man spontaneously; for that is
a point which has still to be considered, and is not yet
agreed upon by you and me.

But I think, Socrates, that wisdom can be taught,
he said.

Best of men, I said, I am delighted to hear you say
that; and I am also grateful to you for having saved
me from a long and tiresome speculation as to
whether wisdom can be taught or not. But now, as
you think that wisdom can be taught, and that wisdom
only can make a man happy and fortunate, will you
not acknowledge that all of us ought to love wisdom,
and that you in particular should be of this mind and
try to love her?

Certainly, Socrates, he said; and I will do my best.

I was pleased at hearing this; and I turned to
Dionysodorus and Euthydemus and said: That is an
example, clumsy and tedious I admit, of the sort of
exhortations which I desire you to offer; and I hope
that one of you will set forth what I have been saying
in a more artistic style: at any rate take up the inquiry where I left off, and next show the youth
whether he should have all knowledge; or whether
there is one sort of knowledge only which will make
him good and happy, and what that is. For, as I
was saying at first, the improvement of this young
man in virtue and wisdom is a matter which we have
very much at heart.

Thus I spoke, Crito, and was all attention to what

was coming. I wanted to see how they would approach the question, and where they would start in their exhortation to the young man that he should practise wisdom and virtue. Dionysodorus the elder spoke first. Everybody's eyes were directed towards him, perceiving that something wonderful might shortly be expected. And certainly they were not far wrong; for the man, Crito, began a remarkable discourse well worth hearing, and wonderfully persuasive as an exhortation to virtue.

Tell me, he said, Socrates and the rest of you who say that you want this young man to become wise, are you in jest or in real earnest?

(I was led by this to imagine that they fancied us to have been jesting when we asked them to converse with the youth, and that this made them jest and play, and being under this impression, I was the more decided in saying that we were in profound earnest.) Dionysodorus said:

Reflect, Socrates; you may have to deny your words.

I have reflected, I said; and I shall never deny my words.

Well, said he, and so you say that you wish Cleinias to become wise?

Undoubtedly.

And he is not wise as yet?

At least his modesty will not allow him to say that he is.

You wish him, he said, to become wise and not to be ignorant?

That we do.

You wish him to be what he is not, and no longer to be what he is.

I was thrown into consternation at this.

Taking advantage of my consternation he added:

You wish him no longer to be what he is, which can only mean that you wish him to perish. Pretty lovers and friends they must be who want their favorite not to be, or to perish!

When Ctesippus heard this he got very angry (as a lover might) and said: Strangers of Thurii — if politeness would allow me I should say, You be ——. What can make you tell such a lie about me and the others, which I hardly like to repeat, as that I wish Cleinias to perish?

Euthydemus replied: And do you think, Ctesippus, that it is possible to tell a lie?

Yes, said Ctesippus; I should be mad to deny that.

And in telling a lie, do you tell the thing of which you speak or not?

You tell the thing of which you speak.

And he who tells, tells that thing which he tells, and no other?

Yes, said Ctesippus.

And that is a distinct thing apart from other things?

Certainly.

And he who says that thing says that which is?

Yes.

And he who says that which is, says the truth. And therefore Dionysodorus, if he says that which is, says the truth of you and no lie.

Yes, Euthydemus, said Ctesippus; but in saying this, he says what is not.

Euthydemus answered: And that which is not is not.

True.

And that which is not is nowhere?

Nowhere.

And can any one do anything about that which has

no existence, or do to Cleinias that which is not and is nowhere?

I think not, said Ctesippus.

Well, but do rhetoricians, when they speak in the assembly, do nothing?

Nay, he said, they do something.

And doing is making?

Yes.

And speaking is doing and making?

He agreed.

Then no one says that which is not, for in saying that, he would be doing nothing; and you have already acknowledged that no one can do what is not. And therefore, upon your own showing, no one says what is false; but if Dionysodorus, says anything, he says what is true and what is.

Yes, Euthydemus, said Ctesippus; but he speaks of things in a certain way and manner, and not as they really are.

Why, Ctesippus, said Dionysodorus, do you mean to say that any one speaks of things as they are?

Yes, he said, — all gentlemen and truth-speaking persons.

And are not good things good, and evil things evil?

He assented.

And you say that gentlemen speak of things as they are?

Yes.

Then the good speak evil of evil things, if they speak of them as they are?

Yes, indeed, he said; and they speak evil of evil men. And if I may give you a piece of advice, you had better take care that they don't speak evil of you, since I can tell you that the good speak evil of the evil.

And do they speak great things of the great,

rejoined Euthydemus, and warm things of the warm?

Yes, indeed, said Ctesippus; and they speak coldly of the insipid and cold dialectician.

You are abusive, Ctesippus, you are abusive!

Indeed, I am not, Dionysodorus, he replied; for I love you and am giving you friendly advice, and, if I could, would persuade you not to make so uncivil a speech to me as that I desire my beloved, whom I value above all men, to perish.

I saw that they were getting exasperated with one another, so I made a joke with him and said: O Ctesippus, I think that we must allow the strangers to use language in their own way, and not quarrel with them about words, but be thankful for what they give us. If they know how to destroy men in such a way as to make good and sensible men out of bad and foolish ones — whether this is a discovery of their own, or whether they have learned from some one else, this new sort of death and destruction, which enables them to get rid of a bad man and put a good one in his place — if they know this (and they do know this — at any rate they said just now that this was the secret of their newly-discovered art) — let them, in their phraseology, destroy the youth and make him wise, and all of us with him. But if you young men do not like to trust yourselves with them, then *fiat experimentum in corpore senis;* I will be the Carian on whom they shall operate. And here I offer my old person to Dionysodorus; he may put me into the pot, like Medea the Colchian, kill me, pickle me, eat me, if he will only make me good.

Ctesippus said: And I, Socrates, am ready to commit myself to the strangers; they may skin me alive, if they please (and I am pretty well skinned by them already), if only my skin is made at last, not like that of Marsyas, into a leathern bottle, but into a piece of virtue. And here is Dionysodorus fancying that I am angry with him, when I am really not angry at all; I do but contradict him when he seems to me to be in the wrong: and you must not confound abuse and contradiction, O illustrious Dionysodorus; for they are quite different things.

Contradiction! said Dionysodorus; why, there never was such a thing.

Certainly there is, he replied; there can be no question of that. Do you, Dionysodorus, maintain that there is not?

You will never prove to me, he said, that you have heard any one contradicting any one else.

Indeed, he said; then now you may hear Ctesippus contradicting Dionysodorus. Are you prepared to make that good?

Certainly, he said.

Well, then, are not words expressive of things?

Yes.

Of their existence or of their non-existence?

Of their existence. For, as you may remember, Ctesippus, we just now proved that no man could affirm a negative; for no one could affirm that which is not.

And what does that signify, said Ctesippus; you and I may contradict all the same for that.

But can we contradict one another, said Dionysodorus, when both of us are describing the same thing? Then we must surely be speaking the same thing?

He admitted that.

Or when neither of us is speaking of the same thing? For then neither of us says a word about the thing at all?

He granted that also.

But when I describe something and you describe

another thing, or I say something and you say nothing — is there any contradiction? How can he who speaks contradict him who speaks not?

Here Ctesippus was silent; and I in my astonishment said: What do you mean, Dionysodorus? I have often heard, and have been amazed, to hear this thesis of yours, which is maintained and employed by the disciples of Protagoras, and others before them, and which to me appears to be quite wonderful and suicidal, as well as destructive, and I think that I am most likely to hear the truth of this from you. The dictum is that there is no such thing as falsehood; a man must either say what is true or say nothing. Is not that your position?

He assented.

But if he can not speak falsely, may he not think falsely?

No, he can not, he said.

Then there is no such thing as false opinion?

No, he said.

Then there is no such thing as ignorance, or men who are ignorant; for is not ignorance, if there be such a thing, a mistake of facts?

Certainly, he said.

And that is impossible?

Impossible, he replied.

Are you saying this as a paradox, Dionysodorus; or do you seriously maintain that no man is ignorant?

Do you refute me? he said.

But how can I refute you, if as you say, falsehood is impossible?

Very true, said Euthydemus.

Neither did I tell you just now to refute me, said Dionysodorus; for how can I tell you to do that which is not?

O Euthydemus, I said, I have but a dull conception

of these subtleties and excellent devices of wisdom; I am afraid that I hardly understand them, and you must forgive me therefore if I ask a very stupid question: if there be no falsehood or false opinion or ignorance, there can be no such thing as erroneous action, for a man can not fail of acting as he is acting — that is what you mean?

Yes, he replied.

And now, I said, I will ask my stupid question: If there is no such thing as error in deed, word, or thought, then what, in the name of goodness, do you come hither to teach? And were you not just now saying that you could teach virtue best of all men, to any one who could learn?

And are you such an old fool, Socrates, rejoined Dionysodorus, that you bring up now what I said at first — and if I had said anything last year, I suppose that you would bring that up — but are non-plussed at the words I have just uttered?

Why, I said, they are not easy to answer; for they are the words of wise men: and indeed I have a great difficulty in knowing what you mean in that last expression of yours, "that I am non-plussed at them." What do you mean by that, Dionysodorus? You must mean that I have no refutation of them. Tell me if the words have any other sense.

No, he said; the sense or meaning of them is that there is a difficulty in answering them; and I wish that you would answer.

What, before you, Dionysodorus? I said.

Answer, said he.

And is that fair?

Yes, quite fair, he said.

Upon what principle? I said. I can only suppose that you are a very wise man, who comes to us in the character of a great logician, and who knows when to answer and when not to answer — and now you won't open your mouth at all, because you know that you ought not.

You prate, he said, instead of answering. But if, my good sir, you admit that I am wise, answer as I tell you.

I suppose that I must obey, for you are master. Put the question.

Are the things which have sense alive or lifeless?

They are alive.

And do you know of any word which is alive?

I can not say that I do.

Then why did you ask me what sense my words had?

Why, because I was stupid and made a mistake. And yet, perhaps, I was right after all in saying that words have a sense; — what do you say, wise man? If I was not in error, and you do not refute me, all your wisdom will be non-plussed; but if I did fall into error, then again you are wrong in saying that there is no error, — and this remark was made by you not quite a year ago. I am inclined to think, however, Dionysodorus and Euthydemus, that this argument is not very likely to advance: even your skill in the subtleties of logic, which is really amazing, has not found out the way of throwing another and not falling yourself.

Ctesippus said: Men of Chios, Thurii, or however and whatever you call yourselves, I wonder at you, for you seem to have no objection to talking nonsense.

Fearing that there would be high words, I endeavored to soothe Ctesippus, and said to him: To you, Ctesippus, I must repeat what I said before to Cleinias — that you don't understand the peculiarity of these philosophers. They are not serious, but, like the Egyptian wizard, Proteus, they take different forms and deceive us by their enchantments: and let us, like Menelaus, refuse to let them go until they show us their real form and character. When they are in earnest their full beauty will appear: let us then beg and entreat and beseech them to shine forth. And I think that I had better show them once more the form in which I pray to behold them. I will go on where I left off before, as well as I can, in the hope that I may touch their hearts and move them to pity, and that when they see me deeply serious, they may also be serious. You, Cleinias, I said, shall remind me at what point we left off. Did we not agree that philosophy should be studied? and was not that our conclusion?

Yes, he replied.

And philosophy is the acquisition of knowledge?

Yes, he said.

And what knowledge ought we to acquire? Is not the simple answer to that, A knowledge that will do us good?

Certainly, he said.

And should we be any the better if we went about having a knowledge of the places where most gold was hidden in the earth?

Perhaps we should, he said.

But have we not already proved, I said, that we should be none the better off, even if without trouble and digging all the gold that there is in the earth were ours? And if we knew how to convert stones into gold, the knowledge would be of no value to us, unless we also knew how to use the gold? Do you not remember? I said.

I quite remember, he said.

Nor would any other knowledge, whether of money-making, or of medicine, or of any other art which knows only how to make a thing, and not to use that

which is made, be of any use to us. Is not that
true?

He agreed.

And if there were a knowledge which was able to
make men immortal, without giving them the knowledge of the way to use the immortality, neither would
there be any use in that, if we may argue from the
analogy of the previous instances?

To all this he agreed.

Then, my dear boy, I said, the knowledge which we
want is one that uses as well as makes?

True, he said.

And our desire is not to be skilful lyre-makers, or
artists of that sort; far otherwise: for with them the
art which makes is one, and the art which uses is another. Having to do with the same, they are divided;
for the art which makes and the art which plays on the
lyre differ widely from one another. Am I not right?

He agreed.

And clearly we do not want the art of the flute-
maker; for that is another of the same sort?

He assented.

But suppose, I said, that we were to learn the art
of making speeches — would that be the art which
would make us happy?

I think not, rejoined Cleinias.

And what proof have you of that? I asked.

I see, he replied, that there are some composers of
speeches who do not know how to use the speeches
which they make, just as the makers of lyres do not
know how to use the lyres; and also some who are of
themselves unable to compose speeches, but are able
to use the speeches which the others make for them;
and this proves that the art of making speeches is not
the same as the art of using them.

Yes, I said; and that I think is a sufficient proof

that the art of making speeches is not one which will make a man happy. And yet I did think that the art which we are seeking might be discovered in that direction; for the composers of speeches, whenever I meet them, always appear to me to be very extraordinary men, Cleinias, and their art is lofty and divine, and no wonder. For their art is a part of the great art of enchantment, and hardly, if at all, inferior to it: and whereas the art of the enchanter is a mode of charming snakes and spiders and scorpions, and other monsters and pests, this art acts upon dicasts and ecclesiasts and bodies of men, for the charming and consoling of them. Do you agree with me?

Yes, he said, I think that you are quite right.

Whither then shall we go, I said, and to what art shall we have recourse?

I do not see my way, he said.

But I think that I do, I replied.

And what is your notion? asked Cleinias.

I think that the art of the general is the one the possession of which is most likely to make a man happy.

I do not think that, he said.

Why not? I said.

The art of the general is surely an art of hunting mankind.

What of that? I said.

Why, he said, no art of hunting extends beyond hunting and capturing; and when the prey is taken they can not use it; but the huntsman or fisherman hands it over to the cook, and the geometricians and astronomers and calculators (who all belong to the hunting class, for they do not make their diagrams, but only find out that which was previously contained in them) — they, I say, not being able to use but only to catch their prey, hand over their inventions to the dialecticians to be applied by them, if they have any sense in them.

Good, I said, fairest and wisest Cleinias. And is this true?

Certainly, he said; just as a general when he takes a city or a camp hands over his new acquisition to the statesman, for he does not know how to use them himself; or as the quail-taker transfers the quails to the keeper of them. If we are looking for that art which is to make us blessed, and which is able to use that which it makes or takes, the art of the general is not the one, and some other must be found.

Cri. And do you mean to say, Socrates, that the youngster said that?

Soc. Are you incredulous, Crito?

Cri. Indeed, I am; for if he said that, I am of opinion that he needs neither Euthydemus nor any one else to be his instructor.

Soc. Perhaps I may have forgotten, and Ctesippus was the real answerer.

Cri. Ctesippus! nonsense.

Soc. All I know is that I heard these words, and that they were not spoken either by Euthydemus or Dionysodorus. I dare say, my good Crito, that they may have been spoken by some superior person. That I heard them I am certain.

Cri. Yes, indeed, Socrates, by some one a good deal superior, as I should be disposed to think. But did you carry the search any further, and did you find the art which you were seeking?

Soc. Find! my dear sir, no indeed. And we cut a poor figure; we were like children after larks, always on the point of catching the art, which was always getting away from us. But why should I repeat the whole story? At last we came to the kingly art, and inquired whether that gave and caused happiness, and then we got into a labyrinth, and when we thought we were at the end, came out again at the beginning, having still to seek as much as ever.

Cri. How did that happen, Socrates?

Soc. I will tell you; the kingly art was identified by us with the political.

Cri. Well, and what came of that?

Soc. To this royal or political art all the arts, including that of the general, seemed to render up the supremacy, as to the only one which knew how to use that which they created. This seemed to be the very art which we were seeking — the art which is the source of good government, and which may be described, in the language of Aeschylus, as alone sitting at the helm of the vessel of state, piloting and governing all things, and utilizing them.

Cri. And were you not right, Socrates?

Soc. You shall judge, Crito, if you are willing to hear what followed; for we resumed the inquiry, and a question of this sort was asked: Does this kingly art, having this supreme authority, do anything for us? To be sure, was the answer. And would not you, Crito, say the same?

Cri. Yes, I should.

Soc. And what would you say that the kingly art does? If medicine were supposed to have supreme authority over the subordinate arts, and I were to ask you a similar question about that, you would say that it produces health?

Cri. I should.

Soc. And what of your own art of husbandry, supposing that to have supreme authority over the subject arts — what does that do? Does it not supply us with the fruits of the earth?

Cri. Yes.

Soc. And what does the kingly art do when invested with supreme power? Perhaps you may not be ready with an answer?

Cri. Indeed I am not, Socrates.

Soc. No more were we, Crito. But at any rate you know that if this is the art which we were seeking, it ought to be useful?

Cri. Certainly.

Soc. And surely it ought to do us some good?

Cri. Certainly, Socrates.

Soc. And Cleinias and I had arrived at the conclusion that knowledge is the only good?

Cri. Yes, that was what you were saying.

Soc. All the other results of politics, and they are many, as for example, wealth, freedom, tranquillity, were neither good nor evil in themselves; but the political science ought to make us wise, and impart wisdom to us, if that is the science which is likely to do us good, and make us happy.

Cri. Yes; that was the conclusion at which you had arrived, according to your report of the conversation.

Soc. And does the kingly art make men wise and good?

Cri. Why not, Socrates?

Soc. What, all men, and in every respect? and teach them all the arts, — carpentering, and cobbling, and the rest of them?

Cri. I do not think that, Socrates.

Soc. But then what is this knowledge, and what are we to do with it? For it is not the source of any works which are neither good nor evil, nor of any knowledge, but the knowledge of itself; what then can it be, and what are we to do with it? Shall we say, Crito, that it is the knowledge by which we are to make other men good?

Cri. By all means.

Soc. And in what way will they be good and useful? Shall we repeat that they will make others good, and that these others will make others again, without ever determining in what they are to be good; for we put aside the results of politics, as they are called. Why, here is iteration; as I said, we are just as far, if not farther, than ever from the knowledge of the art or science of happiness.

Cri. Indeed, Socrates, you do appear to have got into a great perplexity.

Soc. Thereupon, Crito, seeing that I was on the point of shipwreck, I lifted up my voice, and earnestly entreated and called upon the strangers to save me and the youth from the whirlpool of the argument; they were our Castor and Pollux, I said, and they should be serious, and show us in sober earnest what that knowledge was which would enable us to pass the rest of our lives in happiness.

Cri. And did Euthydemus show you this knowledge?

Soc. Yes, indeed; he proceeded in a lofty strain to the following effect: Would you rather, Socrates, said he, that I should show you this knowledge about which you are doubting, or shall I prove that you already have it?

What, I said, are you blessed with such a power as this?

Indeed I am.

Then I would much rather that you should prove me to have such a knowledge; at my time of life that will be more agreeable than having to learn.

Then tell me, he said, do you know anything?

Yes, I said, I know many things, but not anything of much importance.

That will do, he said. And would you admit that anything is what it is, and at the same time is not what it is?

Certainly not.

And did you not say that you knew something?

I did.

If you know, you are knowing.

Certainly, of the knowledge which I have.

That makes no difference; — and must you not, if you are knowing, know all things?

Certainly not, I said, for there are many other things which I do not know.

And if you do not know, you are not knowing.

Yes, my friend, I said, I am not knowing of that which I do not know.

Still you are not knowing, and you said just now that you were knowing; and therefore you are and are not at the same time, and in reference to the same things.

That sounds well, Euthydemus; and yet I must ask you to explain how I have that knowledge which we were seeking; — since a thing can not be and not be, and if I know one thing I know all, for I can not be knowing and not knowing at the same time, and if I know all things, I must have that knowledge as well. May I not assume that to be your ingenious notion?

Out of your own mouth, Socrates, you are convicted, he said.

Well, but, Euthydemus, I said, has that never happened to you; for if I am only in the same case as you and our beloved Dionysodorus, I can not greatly mind that. Tell me then, you two, do you not know some things, and not know others?

Certainly not, Socrates, said Dionysodorus.

What do you mean, I said; do you know nothing?

Nay, he replied, we do know something.

Then, I said, you know all things, if you know anything?

Yes, all things, he said; and that is as true of you as of us.

O, indeed, I said, what a wonderful thing, and what a great blessing! And do all other men know all things or nothing?

Certainly, he replied; they can not know some things, and not know others, and be at the same time knowing and not knowing.

Then what is the inference? I said.

They all know all things, he replied, if they know one thing.

O heavens, Dionysodorus, I said, I see now that you are in earnest; hardly have I got you to that point. And do you really know all things, including carpentering and leather-cutting?

Certainly, he said.

And do you know stitching?

Yes, indeed we do, and cobbling, too.

Yes.

And do you know things such as the numbers of the stars and of the sand?

Certainly; did you think that we should say No to that?

By Zeus, said Ctesippus, interrupting, I only wish that you would give me some proof which would enable me to know whether you say truly.

What proof shall I give you? he said.

Will you tell me how many teeth Euthydemus has? and Euthydemus shall tell how many teeth you have.

Will you not take our word that we know all things?

Certainly not, said Ctesippus; you must further tell us this one thing, and then we shall know that you are speaking the truth; if you tell us the number, and we count them, and you are found to be right, we will believe the rest. They fancied that Ctesippus was making game of them, and they refused, and contented themselves with saying, in answer to each of his questions, that they knew all things. Ctesippus at last began to throw off all restraint; no question was too bad for him; he would ask them if they knew the foulest things, and they, like wild boars, came rushing on his blows, and fearlessly replied that they did. At last, Crito, I too was carried away by my incredulity, and asked Euthydemus whether Dionysodorus could dance.

Certainly, he replied.

And can he vault upon swords, and turn upon a wheel, at his age? has he got to such a height of skill as that?

He can do anything, he said.

And did you always know this?

Always, he said.

When you were children, and at your birth?

They both said that they did.

This we could not believe. And Euthydemus said: You are incredulous, Socrates.

Yes, I said, and I might well be incredulous, if I did not know that you are wise men.

But if you will answer, he said, I will make you confess to similar marvels.

Well, I said, there is nothing that I should like better than to be self-convicted of this, for if I am really a wise man, which I never knew before, and you will prove to me that I know and have always known all things, there is nothing in life that would be a greater gain to me than that.

Answer then, he said.

Ask, I said, and I will answer.

Do you know something, Socrates, or nothing?

Something, I said.

And do you know with what you know, or with something else?

With what I know; and I suppose that you mean with my soul?

Are you not ashamed, Socrates, of asking a question when you are asked?

Well, I said; but then what am I to do? for I will do what you bid; when I do not know what you are asking, you tell me to answer nevertheless, and not to ask again.

Why, you surely have some notion of my meaning, he said.

Yes, I replied.

Well then answer according to your notion of my meaning.

Yes, I said; but if the question which you ask in one sense is understood and answered by me in another, will that please you — if I answer what is not to the point?

That will please me very well; but will not please you equally well, as I imagine.

I certainly will not answer unless I understand you, I said.

You won't answer, he said, according to your view of the meaning, because you are an old fool and pedant.

Now I saw that he was getting angry with me for drawing distinctions, when he wanted to catch me in his springes of words. And I remembered that Connus was always angry with me when I opposed him, and then he neglected me, because he thought that I was stupid; and as I was intending to go to Euthydemus as a pupil, I thought that I had better let him have his way, as he might think me a blockhead, and refuse to take me. So I said: You are a far better dialectician than myself, Euthydemus, for I have never made a profession of the art, and therefore do as you say; ask your questions once more, and I will answer.

Answer then, he said, once more, whether you know what you know with something, or with nothing.

Yes, I said; I know with my soul.

The man will go on adding to the question; for, said he, I did not ask you with what you know, but whether you know with something.

My ignorance, I said, led me to answer more than you asked, and I hope that you will forgive that. And now I will answer simply that I always know what I know with something.

And is that something, he rejoined, always the same, or sometimes one thing, and sometimes another thing?

Always, I replied, when I know, I know with this.

Will you not cease adding to your answers?

My fear is that this word " always " may get us into trouble.

You, perhaps, but certainly not us. And now answer: Do you always know with this?

Always; since I am required to withdraw the words " when I know."

You always know with this, or, always knowing, do you know some things with this, and some things with something else, or do you know all things with this?

All that I know, I replied, I know with this.

There again, Socrates, he said, the addition is superfluous.

Well, then, I said, I will take away the words, " that I know."

Nay, take nothing away; I desire no favors of you; but let me ask: Would you be able to know all things, if you did not know all things?

Quite impossible.

And now, he said, you may add on whatever you like, for you confess that you know all things.

I suppose that is true, I said, if my qualification implied in the words, "that I know," is not allowed to stand; and so I do know all things.

And have you not admitted that you always know all things with that which you know, whether you make the addition of when you know them or not? for you have acknowledged that you have always and at once known all things, that is to say, when you were a child, and at your birth, and when you were growing up, and before you were born, and before the heaven and earth existed, you knew all things if you always know them; and I swear that you shall always continue to know them if I am of the mind to make you.

But I hope that you will be of that mind, reverend Euthydemus, I said, if you are really speaking the truth, and yet I a little doubt your power to accomplish this unless you have the help of your brother Dionysodorus; then you may do it. Tell me now, for although in the main I can not doubt that I really do know all things, when I am told so by men of your prodigious wisdom — how can I say that I know such things as this, Euthydemus, that the good are unjust; come, do I know that or not?

Certainly, you know that.

What do I know?

That the good are not unjust.

Quite true, I said; and I have always known that; but the question is, where did I learn that the good are unjust?

Nowhere, said Dionysodorus.

Then, said I, I do not know this.

You are ruining the argument, said Euthydemus to

Dionysodorus; he will be proved not to know, and then after all he will be knowing and not knowing at the same time.

Dionysodorus blushed.

I turned to the other, and said, What do you think, Euthydemus? Does not your omniscient brother appear to you to have made a mistake?

What, replied Dionysodorus in an instant; am I the brother of Euthydemus?

Thereupon I said, Please not to interrupt, my good friend, or prevent Euthydemus from proving to me that I know the unjust to be the good; such a lesson you might at least allow me to learn.

You are running away, Socrates, said Dionysodorus, and refusing to answer.

No wonder, I said, for I am not a match for one of you, and *a fortiori* I must run away from two. I am no Heracles; and even Heracles could not fight against the Hydra, who was a she-sophist, and had the wit to shoot up many new heads when one of them was cut off; especially when he saw a second monster of a sea-crab, who was also a Sophist, and appeared to have newly arrived from a sea voyage, bearing down upon him from the left, opening his mouth and biting. Then he called Iolaus, his nephew, to his help, and he ably succored him; but if my Iolaus, who is Patrocles the statuary, were to come, he would make a bad business worse.

And now that you have delivered yourself of this strain, said Dionysodorus, will you inform me whether Iolaus was the nephew of Heracles any more than he is yours?

I suppose that I had best answer you, Dionysodorus, I said, for you will insist on asking — that I pretty well know — out of envy, in order to prevent me from learning the wisdom of Euthydemus.

Then answer me, he said.

Well then, I said, I have only to say in answer, that Iolaus was not my nephew at all, but the nephew of Heracles; and his father was not my brother Patrocles, but Iphicles, who has a name rather like his, and was the brother of Heracles.

And is Patrocles, he said, your brother?

Yes, I said, he is my half brother, the son of my mother, but not of my father.

Then he is and is not your brother.

Not by the same father, my good man, I said, for Chaeredemus was his father, and mine was Sophroniscus.

And was Sophroniscus and Chaeredemus a father?

Yes, I said; the former was mine, and the latter his father.

Then, he said, Chaeredemus is not a father.

He is not my father, I said.

But can a father be other than a father? or are you the same as a stone?

I certainly do not think that I am a stone, I said, though I am afraid that you may prove me one.

Are you not other than a stone?

I am.

And being other than a stone, you are not a stone; and being other than gold, you are not gold.

Very true.

And so Chaeredemus, he said, being other than a father, is not a father.

I suppose that he is not a father, I replied.

For if, said Euthydemus, taking up the argument, Chaeredemus is a father, then Sophroniscus, being other than a father, is not a father; and you, Socrates, are without a father.

Ctesippus retorted: And is not your father in the same case, for he is other than my father?

Assuredly not, said Euthydemus.

Then he is the same?

He is the same.

I can not say that I like the connection; but is he only my father, Euthydemus, or is he the father of all other men?

Of all other men, he replied. Do you suppose that he is a father and not a father?

Certainly, I did imagine that, said Ctesippus.

And do you suppose that gold is not gold, or that a man is not a man?

They are not "*in pari materia,*" Euthydemus, said Ctesippus, and you had better take care, for it is monstrous to suppose that your father is the father of all.

But he is, he said.

What, of men only, said Ctesippus, or of horses and all other animals?

Of all, he said.

And your mother, too, is the mother of all?

Yes, our mother too.

Yes; and your mother has a progeny of sea-urchins then?

Yes; and yours, he said.

And gudgeons and puppies and pigs are your brothers.

And yours too.

And your papa is a dog.

And so is yours, he said.

If you will answer my questions, said Dionysodorus, I will soon extract the same admissions from you, Ctesippus. You say that you have a dog.

Yes, a villain of a one, said Ctesippus.

And he has puppies?

Yes, and they are very like himself.

And the dog is the father of them?

Yes, he said, I certainly saw him and the mother of the puppies come together.

And is he not yours?

To be sure he is.

Then he is a father, and he is yours; ergo, he is your father, and the puppies are your brothers.

Let me ask you one little question more, said Dionysodorus, quickly interposing, in order that Ctesippus might not get in his word: You beat this dog?

Ctesippus said, laughing, Indeed I do; and I only wish that I could beat you instead of him.

Then you beat your father, he said.

I should have had far more reason to beat yours, said Ctesippus; what could he have been thinking of when he begat such wise sons? much good has this father of you and other curs got out of your wisdom.

But neither he nor you, Ctesippus, have any need of much good.

And have you no need, Euthydemus? he said.

Neither I nor any other man; for tell me now, Ctesippus, if you think it good or evil for a man who is sick to drink medicine when he wants it; or to go to war armed rather than unarmed.

Good, I say. And yet I know that I am going to be caught in one of your charming puzzles.

That, he replied, you will discover, if you answer; for seeing that you admitted medicine to be good for a man to drink, when wanted, must it not be good for him to drink as much as possible — a cartload of hellebore will not be too much for him?

Ctesippus said: Certainly not, Euthydemus, if he who drinks be as big as the statue of Delphi.

And if, he said, in war it be good to have arms, he ought to have as many spears and shields as possible?

Very true, said Ctesippus; and do you think that

he ought to have one shield only, Euthydemus, and one spear?

I do.

And would you arm Geryon and Briareus in that way?

Considering the skill which you and your companion have in fighting in armor, I thought that you would have known better. Here Euthydemus held his peace, and Dionysodorus returned to the previous answer.

Don't you think the possession of gold is good?

Yes, said Ctesippus, and the more the better.

And to have money everywhere and always is a good.

Certainly, a great good, he said.

And you admit that gold is a good?

I have admitted that, he replied.

And ought not a man then to have gold everywhere and always, and as much as possible in himself, and may he not be deemed the happiest of men who has three talents of gold in his belly, and a talent in his head, and a stater of gold in either eye?

Yes, Euthydemus, said Ctesippus; and the Scythians count them the happiest and bravest of men who have gold in their own skulls (that is only another instance of your manner of speaking about the dog and father), and what is still more extraordinary, they drink out of their own skulls gilt, and see the inside of them, and hold their own heads in their hands.

And do the Scythians and others see that which has the quality of vision, or that which has not? said Euthydemus.

That which has the quality of vision clearly.

And you also see that which has the quality of vision? he said.

Yes, I do.

Then do you see our garments?

Yes.

Then our garments have the quality of vision.

They can see to any extent, said Ctesippus.

What can they see?

Nothing; but you, my sweet man, may perhaps imagine that they do not see; and certainly, Euthydemus, you do seem to me to have been caught napping when you were not asleep, and that if it be possible to say and say nothing — that is what you are doing.

And may not a person speak and be silent? said Dionysodorus.

Impossible, said Ctesippus.

Or be silent and speak.

That is still more impossible, he said.

But when you speak of stones, wood, iron bars, do you not speak (of them) silent?

Not when I pass a smithy; for then the iron bars make a tremendous noise and outcry if they are touched: so that here your wisdom is strangely mistaken; please, however, to tell me how you can be silent when speaking (I thought that Ctesippus was put upon his mettle because Cleinias was present).

When you are silent, said Euthydemus, are you not silent about all things?

Yes, he said.

Then the speaking are silent, if speaking things are included in all things.

What, said Ctesippus, are not all things silent?

Certainly not, said Euthydemus.

Then, my good friend, do they all speak?

Yes; those which speak.

Nay, said Ctesippus, but the question which I ask is whether all things are silent or speak?

Neither and both, said Dionysodorus, quickly interposing; I am sure that you will be " non-plussed " at that answer.

Here Ctesippus, as his manner was, burst into a roar of laughter; he said, That brother of yours, Euthydemus, has got into a dilemma; all is over with him. This delighted Cleinias, whose laughter made Ctesippus ten times as uproarious; but I can not help thinking that the rogue must have picked up this answer from them; for there has been no wisdom like theirs in our time. Why do you laugh, Cleinias, I said, at such solemn and beautiful things?

Why, Socrates, said Dionysodorus, did you ever see a beautiful thing?

Yes, Dionysodorus, I replied, I have seen many.

Were they other than the beautiful, or the same as the beautiful?

Now I was in a great quandary at having to answer this question, and I thought that I was rightly served for having opened my mouth at all: I said however, They are not the same as absolute beauty, but they have beauty present with each of them.

And are you an ox because an ox is present with you, or are you Dionysodorus, because Dionysodorus is present with you?

I don't like to hear you say that, I replied.

But how, he said, by reason of one thing being present with another, will one thing be another?

Is that your difficulty? I said. For I was beginning to imitate their skill, on which my heart was set.

Yes, he answered, and I and all the world are in a difficulty about the non-existent.

What do you mean, Dionysodorus, I said. Is not the honorable honorable and the base base?

That, he said, is as I please.

And do you please?

Yes, he said.

Also you will admit that the same is the same, and the other other; for surely the other is not the same; I should imagine that even a child will hardly have any difficulty about this. But, I think, Dionysodorus, that you must have intentionally missed the last question; for in general you seem to me to be a good workman, and to do the dialectician's business excellently well.

What, said he, is the business of a good workman? tell me, in the first place, whose business is hammering?

The smith's.

And whose the making of pots?

The potter's.

And who has to kill and skin and mince and boil and cook?

The cook, I said.

And if a man does his business he does rightly?

Certainly.

And the business of the cook is to cut up and skin; you have admitted that?

Yes, I have admitted that, but you must not be too severe upon me.

Then if some one were to kill, mince, boil, roast the cook, he would do his business, and if he were to hammer the smith, and pot the potter, he would do their business.

Poseidon, I said, this is the crown of wisdom; can I ever hope to have such wisdom of my own?

And would you be able, Socrates, to recognize this wisdom when it has become your own?

Certainly, I said, if you will allow me.

What, he said, do you think that you know what is your own?

Yes, I do, subject to your correction; for you are

the bottom, and Euthydemus is the top, of all my wisdom.

Is not that which you would deem your own, he said, that which you have in your own power, and which you are able to use as you would desire, for example, an ox or a sheep — would you not think that your own which you could sell and give and sacrifice to any god whom you pleased, and that which you could not give or sell or sacrifice you would think not to be in your own power?

Yes, I said (for I was certain that something good would come of the questions, which I was impatient to hear); yes, such things only are mine.

Yes, he said, and you would mean by animals living beings?

Yes, I said.

You admit then, that those animals only are yours with which you have the power to do all these things which I was just naming.

I admit that.

Then, after an ironical pause, in which he seemed to be thinking of something great, he said: Tell me, Socrates, have you an ancestral Zeus? Here anticipating the final move which was to enclose me in the net, in the attempt to get away, I gave a desperate twist and said: No, Dionysodorus, I have not.

What a miserable man you must be then, he said; you are not an Athenian if you have no ancestral gods or temples, or any other good.

Nay, Dionysodorus, I said, do not be rough; good words, if you please; in the way of religion I have altars and temples, domestic and ancestral, and all that other Athenians have.

And have not other Athenians, he said, an ancestral Zeus?

That name, I said, is not to be found among the

Ionians, whether colonists or citizens of Athens; an ancestral Apollo there is, who is the father of Ion, and a family Zeus, and a Zeus guardian of the phratry, and an Athene guardian of the phratry. But the name of ancestral Zeus is unknown to us.

No matter, said Dionysodorus, for you admit that you have Apollo, Zeus, and Athene.

Certainly, I said.

And they are your gods, he said.

Yes, I said, my lords and ancestors.

At any rate they are yours, he said, did you not admit that?

I did, I said; what is going to happen to me?

And are not these gods animals? For you admit that all things which have life are animals; and have not these gods life?

They have life, I said.

And are they not animals?

They are animals, I said.

And you admitted that of animals those are yours which you could give away or sell or offer in sacrifice, as you pleased?

I did admit that, Euthydemus, and I have no way of escape.

Well then, said he, if you admit that Zeus and the other gods are yours, can you sell them or give them away, or do what you will with them, as you would with other animals?

At this I was quite struck dumb, Crito, and lay prostrate. Ctesippus came to the rescue.

Bravo, Heracles, brave words, said he.

Bravo Heracles, or is Heracles a bravo? said Dionysodorus.

Poseidon, said Ctesippus, what awful distinctions. I will have no more of them; the pair are invincible.

Then, my dear Crito, there was universal applause
of the speakers and their words, and what with laughing and clapping of hands and rejoicings the two men
were quite overpowered; for hitherto only their partisans had cheered at each successive hit, but now the
whole company shouted with delight until the columns
of the Lyceum returned the sound, seeming almost
to sympathize in their joy. To such a pitch was I
affected myself, that I made a speech, in which I
acknowledged that I had never seen the like of their
wisdom; I was their devoted servant, and fell to
praising and admiring of them. What marvellous
dexterity of wit, I said, enabled you to acquire this
great perfection in such a short time? There is much,
indeed, to admire in your words, Euthydemus and
Dionysodorus, but there is nothing that I admire more
than your magnanimous disregard of any opinion —
whether of the many, or of the grave and reverend
seigniors — which is not the opinion of those who are
like minded with you. And I do verily believe that
there are few who are like you, and would approve
of your arguments; the majority of mankind are so
ignorant of their value, that they would be more
ashamed of employing them in the refutation of others
than of being refuted by them. I must further express my approval of your kind and public-spirited
denial of all differences, whether of good and evil,
white or black, or any other; the result of which is
that, as you say, every mouth is stopped, not excepting your own, which graciously follows the example
of others; and thus all ground of offence is taken
away. But what appears to me to be more than all
is, that this art and invention of yours is so admirably
contrived, that in a very short time it can be imparted
to any one. I observe that Ctesippus learned to imitate you in no time. Now this quickness of attain-

ment is an excellent thing; but at the same time I would advise you not to have any more public entertainments; there is a danger that men may undervalue an art which they have so easy an opportunity of learning; the exhibition would be best of all, if the discussion were confined to your two selves; but if there must be an audience, let him only be present who is willing to pay a handsome fee; — you should be careful of this; — and if you are wise, you will also bid your disciples discourse with no man but you and themselves. For only what is rare is valuable; and water, which, as Pindar says, is the best of all things, is also the cheapest. And now I have only to request that you will receive Cleinias and me among your pupils.

Such was the discussion, Crito; and after a few more words had passed between us we went away. I hope that you will come to them with me, since they say that they are able to teach any one who will give them money, however old or stupid. And one thing which they said I must repeat for your especial benefit, — that not even the business of making money need hinder any man from taking in their wisdom with ease.

Cri. Truly, Socrates, though I am curious and ready to learn, yet I fear that I am not like minded with Euthydemus, but one of the other sort, who, as you were saying, would rather be refuted by such arguments than use them in refutation of others. And though I may appear ridiculous in venturing to advise you, I think that you may as well hear what was said to me by a man of very considerable pretensions — he was a professor of legal oratory — who came away from you while I was walking up and down. "Crito," said he to me, "are you attending to these wise men?" "No, indeed," I said to him;

" I could not get within hearing of them, there was such a crowd." " You would have heard something worth hearing if you had." " What was that?" I said. " You would have heard the greatest masters of the art of rhetoric discoursing." " And what did you think of them?" I said. " What did I think of them," he said; " what any one would think of them who heard them talking nonsense, and making much ado about nothing." That was the expression which he used. " Surely," I said, " philosophy is a charming thing." " Charming!" he said; " what simplicity! philosophy is nought; and I think that if you had been present you would have been ashamed of your friend — his conduct was so very strange in placing himself at the mercy of men who care not what they say, and fasten upon every word. And these, as I was telling you, are supposed to be the most eminent professors of their time. But the truth is, Crito, that the study and the men themselves are both equally mean and ridiculous." Now his censure of the pursuit, Socrates, whether coming from him or from others, appears to me to be undeserved; but as to the impropriety of holding a public discussion with such men, I confess that I thought he was in the right about that.

Soc. O Crito, they are marvellous men; but what was I going to say? What manner of man was he who came up to you and censured philosophy; was he an orator who himself practises in the courts, or an instructor of orators, who makes the speeches with which they do battle?

Cri. He was certainly not an orator, and I doubt whether he had ever been into court; but they say that he knows the business, and is a clever man, and composes wonderful speeches.

Soc. Now I understand, Crito; he is one of an

amphibious class, whom I was on the point of mentioning — one of those whom Prodicus describes
as on the border-ground between philosophers and
statesmen — they think that they are the wisest of
all men, and that they are generally esteemed the
wisest; nothing but the rivalry of the philosophers
stands in their way; and they are of the opinion that
if they can prove the philosophers to be good for nothing, no one will dispute their title to the palm of wisdom, for that they are really the wisest, although they
are apt to be mauled by Euthydemus and his friend,
when they get hold of them in conversation. This
opinion which they entertain of their own wisdom is
very natural; for they have a certain amount of philosophy, and a certain amount of political wisdom;
there is reason in what they say, for they argue that
they have just enough of both, while they keep out
of the way of all risks and conflicts and reap the fruits
of their wisdom.

Cri. What do you say of them, Socrates? There
is certainly something specious in that notion of theirs.

Soc. Yes, Crito, there is more speciousness than
truth; they can not be made to understand the nature
of intermediates. For all persons or things, which are
intermediate between two other things, and participant of them — if one of these two things is good
and the other evil, are better than the one and worse
than the other; but if they are in a mean between two
good things which do not tend to the same end, they
fall short of either of their component elements in the
attainment of their ends. Only in the case when the
two component elements which do not tend to the
same end are evil is the participant better than either.
Now, if philosophy and political action are both good,
but tend to different ends, and they participate in
both, and are in a mean between them, then they are

talking nonsense, for they are worse than either; or, if the one be good and the other evil, they are better than the one and worse than the other; only on the supposition that they are both evil could there be any truth in what they say. I do not think that they will admit that their two pursuits are either wholly or partly evil; but the truth is, that these philosopher-politicians who aim at both fall short of both in the attainment of their respective ends, and are really third, although they would like to stand first. There is no need, however, to be angry at this ambition of theirs — they may be forgiven that; for every man ought to be loved who says and manfully pursues and works out anything which is at all like wisdom: at the same time we shall do well to see them as they really are.

Cri. I have often told you, Socrates, that I am in a constant difficulty about my two sons. What am I to do with them? There is no hurry about the younger one, who is only a child; but the other, Critobulus, is getting on, and needs some one who will improve him. I can not help thinking, when I hear you talk, that there is a sort of madness in many of our anxieties about our children: — in the first place, about marrying a wife of good family to be the mother of them, and then about heaping up money for them — and yet taking no care about their education. But then again, when I contemplate any of those who pretend to educate others, I am amazed. They all seem to me to be such outrageous beings, if I am to confess the truth: so that I do not know how I can advise the youth to study philosophy.

Soc. Dear Crito, do you not know that in every profession the inferior sort are numerous and good for nothing, and the good are few and beyond all price: for example, are not gymnastic and rhetoric and money-making and the art of the general, noble arts?

Cri. Certainly they are, in my judgment.

Soc. Well, and do you not see that in each of these arts the many are ridiculous performers?

Cri. Yes, indeed, that is very true.

Soc. And will you on this account shun all these pursuits yourself and refuse to allow them to your son?

Cri. That would not be reasonable, Socrates.

Soc. Do you then be reasonable, Crito, and do not mind whether the teachers of philosophy are good or bad, but think only of philosophy herself. Try and examine her well and truly, and if she be evil seek to turn away all men from her, and not your sons only; but if she be what I believe that she is, then follow her and serve her, you and your house, as the saying is, and be of good cheer.

ION

INTRODUCTION

THE Ion is the shortest, or nearly the shortest, of all the writings which bear the name of Plato, and is not authenticated by any early external testimony. The grace and beauty of this little work supply the only, and perhaps a sufficient, proof of its genuineness. The plan is simple, and the dramatic interest consists entirely in the contrast between the irony of Socrates and the transparent vanity and childlike enthusiasm of the rhapsode Ion. The theme of the Dialogue may possibly have been suggested by the passage of Xenophon's Memorabilia (iv. 2, 10) in which the rhapsodists are described by Euthydemus as "very precise about the exact words of Homer, but very foolish themselves."

Ion the rhapsode has just come to Athens; he has been exhibiting in Epidaurus at the festival of Asclepius, and is intending to exhibit at the festival of the Panathenaea. Socrates admires and envies the rhapsode's art — for he is always well dressed and in good company — in the company of good poets and of Homer, who is the prince of them. In the course of conversation the admission is elicited from Ion that his skill is restricted to Homer, and that he knows nothing of inferior poets, such as Hesiod and Archilochus; — he brightens up and is wide awake when Homer is being recited, but is apt to go to sleep at the recitations of any other poet. "And yet, surely, he who knows the superior ought to know the inferior also; — he who can judge of the good speaker is able to judge of the bad. And poetry is a whole; and he who judges of poetry by rules of art ought to be able to judge all poetry." This is confirmed by the analogy of sculpture, painting, flute-playing, and the other arts. The argument is at last brought home to the mind of Ion, who asks how this contradiction is to be solved. The solution given by Socrates is as follows: —

The rhapsode is not guided by rules of art, but is an inspired person who derives a mysterious power from the poet; and the poet, in like manner, is inspired by the God. The poets and their interpreters may be compared to a chain of magnetic rings suspended from one another, and from a magnet. The magnet is the Muse, and the large ring which comes next in order is the poet himself; then follow the rhapsodes and actors, who are rings of inferior power; and the last ring of all is the spectator. The poet is the inspired interpreter of the God, and the rhapsode is the inspired interpreter of the poet, and this is the reason why some poets, like Tynnichus, are the authors of single poems, and some rhapsodes the interpreters of single poets.

Ion is delighted at the notion of being inspired, and acknowledges that he is beside himself when he is performing; — his eyes rain tears and his hair stands on end. Socrates is of opinion that a man must be mad who behaves in this way at a festival when there is nothing to trouble him. Ion is confident that Socrates would never think him mad if he could only hear his embellishments of Homer. Socrates asks whether he can speak well about everything in Homer. " Yes, indeed he can." " What about things of which he has no knowledge?" Ion answers that he can interpret anything in Homer. But, rejoins Socrates, when Homer speaks of the arts, as for example, of chariot-driving, or of medicine, or of prophecy, or of navigation — will he, or will the charioteer or physician or prophet or pilot be the better judge? Ion is compelled to admit that every man will judge of his own particular art better than the rhapsode. He still maintains, however, that he understands the art of the general as well as any one. " Then why in this city of Athens, in which men of merit are always being sought after, is he not at once appointed a general?" Ion replies that he is a foreigner, and the Athenians and Spartans will not appoint a foreigner to be their general. " No, that is not the real reason. But Ion has long been playing tricks with the argument; like Proteus, he transforms himself into a variety of shapes, and is at last about to escape in the disguise of a general. Would he rather be regarded as inspired or dishonest?" Ion eagerly embraces the alternative of inspiration.

The Ion, like the other earlier Platonic Dialogues, is a mixture of jest and earnest, in which no definite result is obtained, but some Socratic or Platonic truths are allowed dimly to appear.

The elements of a true theory of poetry are contained in the notion that the poet is inspired. Genius is often said to be unconscious, or spontaneous, or a gift of nature: that genius is akin to madness is a popular aphorism of modern times. The greatest strength is often observed to have an element of limitation. It is said, too, that the force of nature must have its way, and is incapable of correction or improvement. Reflections of this kind may have been passing before Plato's mind when he describes the poet as inspired, or when, as in the Apology, he speaks of poets as the worst critics of their own writings — anybody taken at random from the crowd is a better interpreter of them than they are of themselves. They are sacred persons, "winged and holy things," who have a touch of madness in their composition, and should be treated with every sort of respect, but not allowed to live in a well-ordered state.

In the Protagoras the ancient poets are recognized by Protagoras himself as the original sophists; and this family resemblance may be traced in the Ion. The rhapsode belongs to the realm of imitation and of opinion: he professes to have all knowledge, which is derived by him from Homer, just as the sophist professes to have all wisdom, which is contained in his art of rhetoric. Even more than the sophist he is incapable of appreciating the commonest logical distinctions; his great memory remarkably contrasts with his inability to follow the steps of the argument. And in his highest dramatic flights he has an eye to his own gains.

The old quarrel between philosophy and poetry, which in the Republic leads to their final separation, is already working in the mind of Plato, and is embodied by him in the contrast between Socrates and Ion. Yet, as in the Republic, Socrates shows a sort of sympathy with the poetic nature. Also, the manner in which Ion is affected by his own recitations affords a lively illustration of the power which, in the Republic, Socrates attributes to dramatic performances over the mind of the performer. His allusion to his embellishments of Homer, in which he declares himself to have surpassed Metrodorus of Lampsacus and Stesimbrotus of Thasos, seems to show that, like them, he belonged to the allegorical school of interpreters. The circumstance that nothing more is known of him may be adduced in confirmation of the argument that this truly Platonic little work is not a forgery of later times.

ION

PERSONS OF THE DIALOGUE

SOCRATES. ION.

Socrates. WELCOME, Ion. Are you from your native city of Ephesus?

Ion. No, Socrates; but from Epidaurus, where I attended the festival of Asclepius.

Soc. And do the Epidaurians have contests of rhapsodes at the festival?

Ion. O yes, and of all sorts of musical performers.

Soc. And were you one of the competitors — and did you succeed?

Ion. I obtained the first prize of all, Socrates.

Soc. Well done; and I hope that you will do the same for us at the Panathenaea.

Ion. And I will, please heaven.

Soc. I often envy the profession of a rhapsode, Ion; for you have always to wear fine clothes and to look as beautiful as you can is a part of your art. Then, again, you are obliged to be continually in the company of many good poets; and especially of Homer, who is the best and most divine of them; and to understand him, and not merely learn his words by rote, is a thing greatly to be envied. And no man can be a rhapsode who does not understand the meaning of the poet. For the rhapsode ought to interpret the mind of the poet to his hearers, and he can not do this well unless he knows what he means. All this is greatly to be envied.

Ion. That is true, Socrates; and that has certainly been the most troublesome part of my art; and I believe that I can speak about Homer better than any man; and that neither Metrodorus of Lampsacus, nor Stesimbrotus of Thasos, nor Glaucon, nor any one else that ever was, had as good ideas about Homer as I have, or as many of them.

Soc. I am glad to hear that, Ion; for I see that you will not refuse to acquaint me with them.

Ion. Certainly, Socrates; you ought to hear my embellishments of Homer. I think that the Homeridae should give me a golden crown as a reward for them.

Soc. I shall take an opportunity of hearing them at some future time. But just now I should like to ask you a question: Does your art extend to Hesiod and Archilochus, or to Homer only?

Ion. To Homer only; and that appears to me to be quite enough.

Soc. Are there any things about which Homer and Hesiod agree?

Ion. Yes; I am of opinion that there are a good many.

Soc. And can you interpret better what Homer says, or what Hesiod says, about these matters in which they agree?

Ion. I can interpret them equally well, Socrates, where they agree.

Soc. But what about matters in which they do not agree? — for example, about divination, of which both Homer and Hesiod have something to say.

Ion. Very true.

Soc. Well now, would you or a good prophet be a better interpreter of what these two poets say, whether they agree or disagree, about divination?

Ion. A prophet.

Soc. But if you were a prophet, would you not be able to interpret them when they disagree as well as when they agree?

Ion. Clearly.

Soc. Well then, how come you to have this skill about Homer, but not about Hesiod or the other poets? Does not Homer speak of the same themes which all other poets handle? Is not war his great argument? and does he not speak of human society and of intercourse of men, good and bad, skilled and unskilled, and of the gods conversing with one another and with mankind, and about what happens in heaven and in the world below, and the generations of gods and heroes? Are not these the themes of which Homer sings?

Ion. Very true, Socrates.

Soc. And do not the other poets sing of the same?

Ion. Yes, Socrates; but not in the same way as Homer.

Soc. What! in a worse way?

Ion. Yes, in a far worse.

Soc. And Homer is better?

Ion. He is incomparably better.

Soc. And yet surely, my dear friend Ion, in a discussion about arithmetic, where many people are speaking, and some one person speaks better than the rest, any one can judge who is the good speaker?

Ion. Yes.

Soc. And he who judges of the good will be the same as he who judges of the bad speakers?

Ion. The same.

Soc. And he will be the arithmetician?

Ion. Yes.

Soc. Well, and in discussions about the wholesomeness of food, when many persons are speaking, and one speaks better than the rest, will he who recognizes the better speaker be a different person from him who recognizes the worse, or the same?

Ion. Clearly the same.

Soc. And who is he, and what is his name?

Ion. A physician.

Soc. And speaking generally, in all discussions in which the subject is the same and many men are speaking, will not he who knows the good know the bad speaker also? Or if he does not know the bad, neither will he know the good.

Ion. True.

Soc. Is not the same person skilful in both?

Ion. Yes.

Soc. And you say that Homer and the other poets, such as Hesiod and Archilochus, speak of the same things, although not in the same way; but the one speaks well and the other not so well?

Ion. Yes; and I am right in saying that.

Soc. And if you know the good speaker, you would also know that the inferior speakers are inferior?

Ion. That is true.

Soc. Then, my dear friend, can I be mistaken in saying that Ion is equally skilled in Homer and in other poets, since he himself acknowledges that the same person will be a good judge of all those who speak of the same things; and that almost all poets do speak of the same things?

Ion. What then, Socrates, is the reason why I lose attention and go to sleep and have absolutely no ideas, when any one speaks of any other poet; but when Homer is mentioned, I wake up at once and am all attention and have plenty to say?

Soc. That, my friend, is easily explained. No one can fail to see that you speak of Homer not by any art or knowledge. If you were able to speak of him by rules of art, you would have been able to speak of all other poets, for poetry is a whole.

Ion. Yes.

Soc. And when any one acquires any other art as a whole, the same may be said of them. Would you like me to explain my meaning, Ion?

Ion. Yes, indeed, Socrates; I wish that you would: for I love to hear you wise men talk.

Soc. I wish, Ion, that we could be truly called wise: but the truth is that you rhapsodes and actors, and the poets whose verses you sing, are wise; and I am a common man, who only speaks the truth. For do but consider what a very common and trivial thing this is, which I have said — a thing which any man might say; that when a man has acquired a knowledge of a whole art, the inquiry into good and bad is one and the same. Let us think about this; is not the art of painting a whole?

Ion. Yes.

Soc. And there are and have been many painters good and bad?

Ion. Yes.

Soc. And did you ever know any one who was skilful in pointing out the excellences and defects of Polygnotus the son of Aglaophon, but incapable of criticizing other painters; and when the work of any other painter was produced, went to sleep and was at a loss and had no ideas; but when he had to give his opinion about Polygnotus, or whoever the painter might be, woke up and was attentive and had plenty to say?

Ion. No indeed, I never did.

Soc. Or did you ever know of any one in sculpture, who was skilful in expounding the merits of Daedalus the son of Metion, or of Epeius the son of Panopeus, or of Theodorus the Samian, or of some other individual sculptor; but when the works of other sculptors were produced, was at a loss and went to sleep and had nothing to say?

Ion. No indeed, I never did.

Soc. And if I am not mistaken, you never met with any one among flute-players or harp-players or singers to the harp or rhapsodes who was able to discourse of Olympus or Thamyras or Orpheus, or Phemius, the rhapsode of Ithaca, but was at a loss when he came to speak of Ion of Ephesus, and had no notion of his merits or defects?

Ion. I can not deny that, Socrates. Nevertheless I am conscious in my own self that I do speak better and have more to say about Homer than any other man, and this is the general opinion. But I do not speak equally well about others — tell me the reason of this?

Soc. I perceive, Ion; and I will proceed to explain to you what I imagine to be the reason of this. This gift which you have of speaking excellently about Homer is not an art, but, as I was just saying, an inspiration; there is a divinity moving you, like that in the stone which Euripides calls a magnet, but which is commonly known as the stone of Heraclea. For that stone not only attracts iron rings, but also imparts to them a similar power of attracting other rings; and sometimes you may see a number of pieces of iron and rings suspended from one another so as to form quite a long chain: and all of them derive their power of suspension from the original stone. Now this is like the Muse, who first gives to men inspiration herself; and from these inspired persons a chain of other persons is suspended, who take the inspiration from them. For all good poets, epic as well as lyric, compose their beautiful poems not as works of art, but because they are inspired and possessed. And as the Corybantian revellers when they dance are not in their right mind, so the lyric poets are not in their right mind when they are composing their beautiful strains: but when falling under the power of music and metre they are inspired and possessed; like Bacchic maidens who draw milk and honey from the rivers, when they are under the influence of Dionysus, but not when they are in their right mind. And the soul of the lyric poet does the same, as they themselves tell us; for they tell us that they gather their strains from honied fountains out of the gardens and dells of the Muses; thither, like the bees, they wing their way. And this is true. For the poet is a light and winged and holy thing, and there is no invention in him until he has been inspired and is out of his senses, and the mind is no longer in him: when he has not attained to this state, he is powerless and is unable to utter his oracles. Many are the noble words in which poets speak of actions like your own words about Homer; but they do not speak of them by any rules of art: only when they make that to which the Muse impels them are their inventions inspired; and then one of them will make dithyrambs, another hymns of praise, another choral strains, another epic or iambic verses — and he who is good at one is not good at any other kind of verse: for not by art does the poet sing, but by power divine. Had he learned by rules of art, he would have known how to speak not of one theme only, but of all; and therefore God takes away the minds of poets, and uses them as his ministers, as he also uses diviners and holy prophets, in order that we who hear them may know that they speak not of themselves who utter these priceless words in a state of unconsciousness, but that God is the speaker, and that through them he is conversing with us. And Tynnichus the Chalcidian affords a striking instance of what I am saying: he wrote nothing that any one would care to remember but the famous paean which is in every one's mouth, and is one of the finest poems ever written, and is certainly an invention of the Muses, as he himself says. For in this way the God would seem to indicate to us and not allow us to doubt that these beautiful poems are not human, or the work of man, but divine and the word of God; and that the poets are only the interpreters of the Gods by whom they are severally possessed. Was not this the lesson which the God intended to teach when by the mouth of the worst of poets he sang the best of songs? Am I not right, Ion?

Ion. Yes, indeed, Socrates, I feel that you are; for your words touch my soul, and I am persuaded somehow that good poets are the inspired interpreters of the Gods.

Soc. And you rhapsodists are the interpreters of the poets?

Ion. That again is true.

Soc. Then you are the interpreters of interpreters?

Ion. Precisely.

Soc. I wish you would frankly tell me, Ion, what I am going to ask of you: When you produce the greatest effect upon the spectators in the recitation of some striking passage, such as the apparition of Odysseus leaping forth on the floor, recognized by the suitors and casting his arrows at his feet, or the description of Achilles rushing at Hector, or the sorrows of Andromache, Hecuba, or Priam, — are you in your right mind? Are you not carried out of yourself, and does not your soul in an ecstasy seem to be among the persons or places of which she is speaking, whether they are in Ithaca or in Troy or whatever may be the scene of the poem?

Ion. That proof strikes home to me, Socrates. For

I must confess that at the tale of pity my eyes are filled with tears, and when I speak of horrors, my hair stands on end and my heart throbs.

Soc. Well, Ion, and what are we to say of a man who at a sacrifice or festival, when he is dressed in holiday attire, and has gold crowns upon his head, of which nobody has robbed him, appears weeping or panic-stricken in the presence of more than twenty thousand friendly faces, when there is no one spoiling or wronging him; — is he in his right mind or is he not?

Ion. No indeed, Socrates, I must say that strictly speaking he is not in his right mind.

Soc. And are you aware that you produce similar effects on most of the spectators?

Ion. Yes indeed, I am; for I look down upon them from the stage, and behold the various emotions of pity, wonder, sternness, stamped upon their countenances when I am speaking: and I am obliged to attend to them; for unless I make them cry I myself shall not laugh, and if I make them laugh, I shall do anything but laugh myself when the hour of payment arrives.

Soc. Do you know that the spectator is the last of the rings which, as I am saying, derive their power from the original magnet; and the rhapsode like yourself and the actors are intermediate links, and the poet himself is the first link of all? And through all these the God sways the souls of men in any direction which he pleases, and makes one man hang down from another. There is also a chain of dancers and masters and undermasters of bands, who are suspended at the side, and are the rings which hang from the Muse. And every poet has a Muse from whom he is suspended, and by whom he is said to be possessed, which is nearly the same thing; for he is taken possession of. And from these first rings, which are the poets, depend others, some deriving their inspiration from Orpheus, others from Musaeus; but the greater number are possessed and held by Homer. Of which latter you are one, Ion — possessed by Homer; and when any one repeats the verses of another poet you go to sleep, and know not what to say; but when any one recites a strain of Homer you wake up in a moment, and your soul leaps within you, and you have plenty to say, for not by art or knowledge about Homer do you say what you say, but by divine inspiration and by possession; just as the revellers too have a quick perception of that strain only which is appropriated to the God by whom they are possessed, and have plenty of dances and words for that, but take no heed of any other. And you too, Ion, when the name of Homer is mentioned have plenty to say, and nothing to say of others. And the reason of this is, that you praise Homer not by art but by divine inspiration: and this is the answer to your question.

Ion. That is good, Socrates; and yet I doubt whether you will ever have eloquence enough to persuade me that I praise Homer only when I am mad and possessed; and if you could hear me speak of him I am sure that you would never think that.

Soc. I should like very much to hear you, but not until you have answered a question which I have to ask. On what part of Homer do you speak well? — not surely about every part?

Ion. There is no part, Socrates, about which I do not speak well: of that I can assure you.

Soc. Surely not about things in Homer of which you have no knowledge?

Ion. And what is there of which Homer speaks of which I have no knowledge?

Soc. Why! does not Homer speak in many passages about arts? For example, about driving; if I can only remember the lines I will repeat them.

Ion. I remember, and will repeat them.

Soc. Tell me then, what Nestor says to Antilochus, his son, where he tells him to be careful of the bend at the horse race in honor of Patroclus.

Ion. " Bend gently," he says, " in the polished chariot to the left of them, and give the horse on the right hand a touch of the whip, and shout — and at the same time slacken his rein. And when you are at the goal, let the left horse draw near, yet so that the nave of the well-wrought wheel may not even seem to touch the extremity; and keep from catching the stone." [1]

Soc. Enough. Now, Ion, will the charioteer or the physician be the better judge of the propriety of these lines?

Ion. The charioteer, clearly.

Soc. And will the reason be that this is his art, or will there be any other reason?

Ion. No, that will be the reason.

Soc. And every art is appointed by God to have knowledge of a certain work; for that which we know by the art of the pilot we do not know by the art of medicine?

Ion. Certainly not.

Soc. Nor do we know by the art of the carpenter that which we know by the art of medicine?

Ion. Certainly not.

Soc. And this is true of all the arts; — that which we know with one art we do not know with the other? But let me preface this question by another: You admit that there are differences of arts?

Ion. Yes.

Soc. You would argue, as I should, that when the subject of knowledge is different, the art is also different?

[1] Il. xxiii. 335.

Ion. Yes.

Soc. Yes; for surely, if the subject of knowledge were the same, there would be no meaning in saying that the arts were different, — if they both gave the same knowledge. For example, I know that here are five fingers, and you know the same. And if I were to ask whether I and you became acquainted with this fact by the help of the same science of arithmetic, you would acknowledge that we did?

Ion. Yes.

Soc. Tell me, then, what I was going to ask you just now, — whether this holds universally? Must the same art have the same subject of knowledge, and any others have other subjects of knowledge?

Ion. That is my opinion, Socrates.

Soc. Then he who has no knowledge of a particular art will have no right judgment of the sayings and doings of that art?

Ion. That is true.

Soc. Then which will be a better judge of the lines of Homer which you were reciting, you or the charioteer?

Ion. The charioteer.

Soc. Why, yes, because you are a rhapsode and not a charioteer.

Ion. Yes.

Soc. And the art of the rhapsode is different from that of the charioteer?

Ion. Yes.

Soc. And if a different knowledge, then a knowledge of different matters?

Ion. Yes.

Soc. You know the passage in which Hecamede the concubine of Nestor is described as giving to the wounded Machaon a posset, as he says,

" Made with Pramnian wine; and she grated cheese of goat's milk with a brazen knife, and at his side there was an onion which gives a relish to drink." [1]

Would you say now that the art of the rhapsode or the art of medicine was better able to judge of these lines?

Ion. The art of medicine.

Soc. And when Homer says,

" And she descended into the deep like a leaden plummet, which, set in the horn of ox that ranges in the fields, rushes along carrying death among the ravenous fishes," — [2]

will the art of the fisherman or of the rhapsode be better able to judge of the propriety of these lines?

Ion. Clearly, Socrates, the art of the fisherman.

Soc. Come now, suppose that you were to say to me: Since you, Socrates, are able to assign different passages in Homer to their corresponding arts, I wish that you would tell me what are the passages the excellence of which ought to be judged of by the prophet and prophetic art, and you shall see how readily and truly I will answer you. For there are many such passages, particularly in the Odyssee; as, for example, the passage in which Theoclymenus of the house of Melampus says to the suitors: —

" Wretched men! what is happening to you? Your heads and your faces and your limbs underneath are shrouded in night; and the voice of lamentation bursts forth, and your cheeks are wet with tears. And the vestibule is full, and the court is full, of ghosts descending into the darkness of Erebus, and the sun has perished out of heaven, and an evil mist is spread abroad." [3]

And there are many such passages in the Iliad also; as for example in the description of the battle near the rampart, where he says: —

[1] Il. x. 638, 630.   [2] Il. xxiv. 80.   [3] Od. xx. 351.

" As they were eager to pass the ditch, there came to them an omen: a soaring eagle, holding back the people on the left, bore a huge bloody dragon in his talons, still living and panting; nor had he yet resigned the strife, for he bent back and smote the bird which carried him on the breast by the neck, and he in pain let him fall from him to the ground into the midst of the multitude. And the eagle, with a cry, was borne afar on the wings of the wind." [1]

These are the sort of things which I should say that the prophet ought to consider and determine.

Ion. And you are quite right, Socrates, in saying that.

Soc. Yes, Ion, and you are right also. And as I have selected from the Iliad and Odyssee for you passages which describe the office of the prophet and the physician and the fisherman, do you, who know Homer so much better than I do, Ion, select for me passages which relate to the rhapsode and the rhapsode's art, and which the rhapsode ought to examine and judge of better than other men.

Ion. All passages, I should say, Socrates.

Soc. Not all, Ion, surely. Have you already forgotten what you were saying? A rhapsode ought to have a better memory.

Ion. Why, what am I forgetting?

Soc. Do you not remember that you declared the art of the rhapsode to be different from the art of the charioteer?

Ion. Yes, I remember.

Soc. And you admitted that being different they would have different subjects of knowledge?

Ion. Yes.

Soc. Then upon your own showing the rhapsode, and the art of the rhapsode, will not know everything.

Ion. I dare say, Socrates, that there may be exceptions.

[1] Il. xii. 200.

Soc. You mean to say that he will not know the subjects of the other arts. As he does not know all of them, which of them will he know?

Ion. He will know what a man ought to say and what a woman ought to say, and what a freeman and what a slave ought to say, and what a ruler and what a subject.

Soc. Do you mean that a rhapsode will know better than the pilot what the ruler of a sea-tossed vessel ought to say?

Ion. No; the pilot will know that best.

Soc. Or will the rhapsode know better than the physician what the ruler of a sick man ought to say?

Ion. He will not.

Soc. But he will know what a slave ought to say?

Ion. Yes.

Soc. Suppose the slave to be a cowherd; the rhapsode will know better than the cowherd what he ought to say in order to soothe the rage of infuriated cows?

Ion. No, he won't.

Soc. But he will know what a spinning-woman ought to say about the working of wool?

Ion. No.

Soc. But he will know what a general ought to say when exhorting his soldiers?

Ion. Yes, that is the sort of thing which the rhapsode will know.

Soc. Well, but is the art of the rhapsode the art of the general?

Ion. I am sure that I should know what a general ought to say.

Soc. Why, yes, Ion, because you may possibly have a knowledge of the general's art; and you may also have a knowledge of horsemanship as well as of the lyre: in that case you would know when horses were well or ill managed. But suppose I were to ask you: By the help of which art, Ion, do you know whether horses are well managed, by your skill as a horseman or as a performer on the lyre —what would you answer?

Ion. I should reply, as a horseman.

Soc. And if you judged of performers on the lyre, you would admit that you judged of them as performers on the lyre, and not as horsemen?

Ion. Yes.

Soc. And in judging of the general's art, do you judge of that as a general or a rhapsode?

Ion. That appears to me to be all one.

Soc. What do you mean? Do you mean to say that the art of the rhapsode and of the general is the same?

Ion. Yes, one and the same.

Soc. Then he who is a good rhapsode is also a good general?

Ion. Certainly, Socrates.

Soc. And he who is a good general is also a good rhapsode?

Ion. No; I don't say that.

Soc. But you do say that he who is a good rhapsode is also a good general?

Ion. Certainly.

Soc. And you are the best of Hellenic rhapsodes?

Ion. Far the best, Socrates.

Soc. And are you the best general, Ion?

Ion. To be sure, Socrates; and Homer was my master.

Soc. But then, Ion, what in the name of goodness can be the reason why you, who are the best of generals as well as the best of rhapsodes in all Hellas, go about as a rhapsode instead of being a general? Do you think that the Hellenes want a rhapsode with his golden crown, and do not want a general?

Ion. Why, Socrates, the reason is, that my countrymen, the Ephesians, are the servants and soldiers of Athens, and don't need a general; and you and Sparta are not likely to have me, for you think that you have enough generals of your own.

Soc. My good Ion, did you never hear of Apollodorus of Cyzicus?

Ion. Who may he be?

Soc. One who, though a foreigner, has often been chosen their general by the Athenians: and there is Phanosthenes of Andros, and Heraclides of Clazo-menae, whom they have also appointed to the command of their armies and to other offices, although aliens, after they had shown their merit. And will they not choose Ion the Ephesian as their general, and honor him, if he prove himself worthy? Were not the Ephesians originally Athenians; and Ephesus is no mean city? But, indeed, Ion, if you are correct in saying that by art and knowledge you are able to praise Homer, you don't deal fairly with me, and after all your professions of knowing many glorious things about Homer, and promises that you would exhibit them to me, do only deceive me, and will not even explain at my earnest entreaties what is the art of which you are a master. You have literally as many forms as Proteus; and now you go all manner of ways, twisting and turning, and, like Proteus, become all manner of people at once, and at last slip away from me in the disguise of a general, in order that you may escape exhibiting your Homeric lore. And if, as I was saying, you have art, then I should say that in falsifying your promise that you would exhibit Homer, you are not dealing fairly with me. But if, as I believe, you have no art, but speak all these beautiful words about Homer unconsciously under his inspiring influence, then I acquit you of dishonesty, and shall only say that you are inspired. Which do you prefer to be thought, dishonest or inspired?

Ion. There is a great difference, Socrates, between them; and inspiration is the far nobler alternative.

Soc. Then, Ion, I shall assume the nobler alternative; and attribute to you in your praises of Homer inspiration, and not art.

GORGIAS

1. THE GOOD MAN DESIRES, NOT A LONG, BUT A VIRTUOUS LIFE

THE Gorgias, like several other writings of Plato, is not easily summarized under a single head, although numerous commentators and editors have attempted the task. We shall, perhaps, not be far wrong if we say that the dialogue is intended to set forth the final victory of truth and righteousness over falsehood and injustice; but we have to travel by many winding roads in order to reach our goal. There is a true rhetoric which convinces us of sin, and a false rhetoric which places evil in a specious light, and "makes the worse appear the better cause." Again, there is a true art of politics which considers only the welfare of the state, and a bastard kind which flatters the multitude and brings ruin on the city. Lastly, there is the contrast between the just man who is happy "even though he suffer undeservedly," and the wicked, who, if they escape punishment in this life, receive fitting chastisement in another world. The lesson or "moral" is pointed by a myth which shows how futile are the falsehoods and conventions of human life, when the soul comes to appear before the judgment-seat of the sons of Zeus in Hades.

The dialogue probably belongs to a middle period of the Platonic writings. It seems to be later than the Phaedrus, which also treats of Rhetoric true and false, but is written in a lighter and more playful vein; it can scarcely come after the Republic, in which the triumph of justice again furnishes a guiding principle of the whole discourse. Thus it may be described as a resumption of the one, and a preparation for the other. A further reason for assigning the dialogue to a later rather than to an earlier date is to be found in the appearance of that austerity or bitterness of tone which marks several of Plato's most important works, e. g. the Statesman and the Laws, and which we may indulge our fancy by attributing in a measure to the circumstances of his life.

1141

The characters of the dialogue, besides the familiar figure of Socrates, are Gorgias, the famous Sophist; Polus, his young disciple, the same whose " Licymnian diction " is ridiculed in the Phaedrus, and Callicles, a wealthy Athenian and friend of Gorgias, not otherwise known to us. Chaerophon, the " excitable " admirer of Socrates, also appears in the prologue, although he does not share in the subsequent discussion. Gorgias himself plays a somewhat subordinate part; and neither he nor his confident and forward pupil, Polus, can offer any substantial resistance to the dialectical prowess of Socrates, that " hero of argument." Callicles, coming to the rescue of Polus, maintains against Socrates " the law of nature," or the principle that " might is right; " he, however, is in turn vanquished, and grudgingly admits " that he is almost convinced " of the truth of his opponent's words. This is the most serious portion of the dialogue; but the earnestness is slightly veiled as usual by the irony of Socrates, which really helps to heighten the effect.

. . . The connection of the passage which is here quoted with what immediately precedes is as follows: — Callicles has been asserting that virtue is a mere sham or convention, and that the unjust man is happy so long as he prospers in his career of crime. Socrates protests against such an impious doctrine, and declares that the unjust is only happy when he is punished for his wickedness. Callicles says that this is absurd; for will not the tyrant be able to put the just man to death or treat him in any cruel manner which he pleases? The answer according to Socrates is that life in itself is of little value; the just man simply desires a good life, whether short or long, happy or miserable. He then proceeds in his half-jesting manner to support his thesis by humorous instances of life-saving arts which are held in little esteem among mankind.

Cal. You always contrive somehow or other, Socrates, to invert everything: do you not know that he who imitates the tyrant will, if he has a mind, kill him who does not imitate him and take away his goods?

Soc. Excellent Callicles, I am not deaf, and I have heard that a great many times from you and from Polus and from nearly every man in the city, but I wish that you would hear me too. I dare say that he will kill him if he has a mind — the bad man will kill the good and true.

Cal. And is not that just the provoking thing?

Soc. Nay, not to a man of sense, as the argument shows: do you think that all our cares are to be directed to prolonging life to the uttermost, and to the study of those arts which secure us from danger always; like that art of rhetoric which saved men in courts of law, and which you recommend me to cultivate?

Cal. Yes, truly, and very good advice too.

Soc. Well, my friend, but what do you think of the art of swimming; does that appear to have any great pretensions?

Cal. No, indeed.

Soc. And yet surely swimming saves a man from death, and there are occasions on which he must know how to swim. And if you despise the swimmers, I will tell you of another and greater art, the art of the pilot, which not only saves the souls of men, but also their bodies and properties from the extremity of danger, just like rhetoric. But this art is modest and unpresuming, and has no airs or pretences of doing anything extraordinary, and, in return for the same salvation which is given by the pleader, demands only two obols, if the voyage is from Aegina to Athens, or for the longer voyage from Pontus or Egypt at the utmost two drachmae, for the great benefit of saving the passenger and his wife and children and goods, and disembarking them safely at the Piraeus; and he who is the master of the art, and has done all this, gets out and walks about on the sea-shore by his ship in an unassuming way. For he is a philosopher, you must know, and is aware that there is no certainty as to which of his fellow-passengers he has benefited, and which of them he has injured in not allowing them to be drowned. He knows that they are just the same when he disembarked them as when they embarked, and not a whit better either in their bodies or in their souls; and he considers that if a man who is afflicted by great and incurable bodily diseases is only to be pitied for having escaped, and is in no way benefited by him in having been kept alive; much more must this be true of one who has great and incurable diseases, not in his body, but in his soul, which is the more honorable part of him; neither is life worth having nor of any profit to him, whether he be saved from the sea, or the law-courts, or any other devourer; — he knows that the bad man had better not live, for he can not live well.

And this is the reason why the pilot, although he is our savior, is not usually conceited, any more than the engineer, who is not a whit behind either the general, or the pilot, or any one else, in his saving power, for he sometimes saves whole cities. Is there any comparison between him and the pleader? And yet, Callicles, if he were to talk in your grandiose style, he would bury you under a mountain of words, declaring and insisting that we ought all of us to be engine-makers, and that they are the only realties; he would have plenty to say. Nevertheless you despise him and his art, and sneeringly call him an engine-maker, and you will not allow your daughters to marry his son, or marry your son to his daughters. And yet, on your principle, what justice or reason is there in this? What right have you to despise the engine-maker, and the other whom I was just now mentioning? I know that you will say, " I am better, and better born." But if the better is not what I say, and virtue consists only in a man saving himself and his, whatever may be his character, then your censure of the engine-maker, and of the physician, and of the other arts of salvation, is ridiculous.

O my friend! I want you to see that the noble and the good may possibly be something different from saving and being saved, and that he who is truly a man ought not to care about living a certain time: — he knows, as women say, that none can escape the day of destiny, and therefore he is not fond of life; he leaves all that with God, and considers in what way he can best spend his appointed term; — whether by assimilating himself to that constitution under which he lives, as you at this moment have to consider, how you may become as like as possible to the Athenian people, if you intended to be dear to them, and to have power in the state; whereas I want you to think and see whether this is for the interest of either of us; — I would not have us risk that which is dearest on the acquisition of this power, like the Thessalian enchantresses, who, as they say, bring down the moon from heaven at the risk of their own perdition.

ALCIBIADES I

SOCRATES HUMILIATES ALCIBIADES BY SHOWING HIM HIS INFERIOR-
ITY TO THE KINGS OF LACEDAEMON AND OF PERSIA

There is little substantial reason to doubt the genuineness of the vast majority of the writings which have come down to us under the name of Plato. A few works, however, have been preserved, which are of a less certain character. Of these a small proportion may actually be dialogues written by Plato at an early period of his life, or in hours when the Muses were unpropitious, or they may be the work of members of his school to which, by a natural confusion, his own name has come to be affixed. The remainder and larger number appear to belong to a later date, and are so unmistakably inferior to the undoubted compositions of Plato, that it is hardly possible seriously to maintain their authenticity.

The First Alcibiades is a good specimen of the former class. It is by no means without merit, and is clearly and simply written. The principal ground for suspicion is that it seems to be merely a rewriting of the theme which occupies a considerable space in the Symposium, — the relations of Socrates to Alcibiades. But the color and glow of the master are wanting: everything betrays the feeble hand of the copyist who is striving to imitate some work of original genius.

The characters of the Dialogue are only two, Socrates and Alcibiades, and no attempt is made to describe the scene or the surroundings. Alcibiades, who is on the point of entering public life, is cross-examined by Socrates as to his fitness for the career of a statesman. Alcibiades at first is confident that he is thoroughly prepared; but Socrates by a series of questions entangles him in self-contradictions, and finally reduces him to a humiliating confession of ignorance. He does not even, as the Delphian inscription recommends, "know himself," and much less is he capable of managing the affairs of others.

The passage which follows is a humorous contrast between the greatness and wealth of the Kings of Sparta and Persia and the insignificance of Alcibiades, both in respect of birth and means. The satire which it conveys on the statesmen of Athens is quite in the spirit of Plato; and we must suppose the writer, if not really Plato himself, to have had in mind the depreciatory references to Pericles and other public men in the Gorgias and the Statesman. And it may have been one at least of the objects with which the Dialogue was composed to exhibit the unfitness and incapacity of the politicians of the time, as well as to show that Socrates was not justly to be blamed for the wickedness and folly of some of those who called themselves his disciples. (Cp. Socrates' defence of himself against this charge in the Apology.)

Soc. You surely know that our city goes to war now and then with the Lacedaemonians and with the great king?

Al. True enough.

Soc. And if you meant to be the ruler of this city, would you not be right in considering that the Lacedaemonian and Persian kings are your true rivals?

Al. I believe that you are right.

Soc. Oh no, my friend, I am quite wrong, and I think that you ought rather to turn your attention to Midias the quail-breeder and others like him, who manage our politics; in whom, as the women would remark, you may still see the slaves' cut of hair, cropping out in their minds as well as on their pates; and they come with their barbarous lingo to flatter us and not to rule us. To these, I say, you should look, and then you will have no need to take any heed of yourself in this noble contest; you will not have to trouble yourself either with learning what has to be learned, or practising what has to be practised, or with any other sort of preparation for a political career.

Al. I think, Socrates, that you are right in that; I do not suppose, however, that the Spartan generals or the great king are really different from anybody else.

Soc. But, my dear friend, do consider what this is which you are saying.

Al. What shall I consider?

Soc. In the first place, will you be more likely to take care of yourself, if you are in a wholesome fear and dread of them, or if you are not?

Al. Clearly, if I have such a fear of them.

Soc. And do you think that you will sustain any injury if you take any care of yourself?

Al. No, I shall be greatly benefited.

Soc. And this is one very important respect in which that notion of yours is bad.

Al. True.

Soc. In the next place, consider that what you say is probably false.

Al. How is that?

Soc. Let me ask you whether better natures

are likely to be found in noble races or not in noble races?

Al. Clearly in noble races,

Soc. Are not those who are well born and well bred most likely to be perfect in nature?

Al. Certainly.

Soc. Then let us compare our antecedents with those of the Lacedaemonian and Persian kings; are they inferior to us in descent? Have we not heard that the former are sprung from Heracles, and the latter from Achaemenes, and that the race of Heracles and the race of Achaemenes go back to Perseus, son of Zeus?

Al. Why, so does mine go back to Eurysaces, and he to Zeus!

Soc. And mine, noble Alcibiades, to Daedalus, who, by the way of Hephaestus, also goes back to Zeus. But, for all this, we are far inferior to them. For they are descended " from Zeus," through a line of kings — either kings of Argos and Lacedaemon, or kings of Persia which they have always possessed, and at various time have been sovereigns of Asia, as they now are; whereas, we and our fathers were but private persons. How ridiculous would you be thought for making a parade of your ancestors and of Salamis the island of Eurysaces, or of Aegina, the habitation of the still more ancient Aeacus to Artaxerxes, son of Xerxes. You should consider how inferior we are to them both in the derivation of our birth and in other particulars. Did you never observe how great is the property of the Spartan kings? And their wives are under the guardianship of the Ephori, who are public officers, and watch over them, in order to preserve the purity of the Heracleid blood.

And the Persian king far surpasses them; for no one ever entertains a suspicion that a prince of Persia can have any other father. Such is the awe which invests the person of the queen, that she needs no other guard. And when the heir of the kingdom is born, all the subjects of the king feast; and the day of his birth is forever afterwards kept as a holiday and time of sacrifice by all Asia; whereas, when you and I were born, Alcibiades, as the comic poet says, the neighbors hardly knew of the important event. After the birth of the royal child, he is tended, not by a good-for-nothing woman-nurse, but by the best of the royal eunuchs, who are charged with the care of the child, and especially with the fashioning and formation of his limbs, in order that he may be as fair as possible; and this being their calling, they are held in great honor. And when the young prince is seven years old he is put upon a horse and taken to the riding-masters and begins to go out hunting. And at fourteen years of age he is handed over to the royal schoolmasters, as they are termed: these are four chosen men, reputed to be the best among the Persians of a certain age; and one of them is the wisest, another the justest, a third the most temperate, and a fourth the most valiant. The first instructs him in the magianism of Zoroaster, the son of Oromasus, which is the worship of the Gods, and teaches him also the duties of his royal office; the second, who is the justest, teaches him always to speak the truth; the third, or most temperate, forbids him to allow any pleasure to be lord over him, that he may be accustomed to be a freeman and king indeed, — lord of himself first, and not a slave; the most valiant makes him bold and fearless, telling him that if he fears he is to deem himself a slave; whereas Pericles gave you, Alcibiades, for a tutor Zophyrus the Thracian, a slave of his with whom he could do nothing else.

I might enlarge on the nurture and education of

your rivals, but that would be tedious; and what I
have said is a sufficient sample of what remains to
be said. I have only to remark, by way of contrast,
that no one cares about your birth or nurture or education, or, I may say, about that of any other Athenian, unless he has a lover who takes care of him.
And if you cast an eye on the wealth, the luxury,
the garments with their flowing trains, the anointings
with myrrh, the multitudes of attendants, and all the
other bravery of the Persians, you will be ashamed
when you discern your own inferiority; or if you
would look at the temperance and orderliness and
ease and grace and magnanimity and courage and
endurance and love of toil and desire of glory and
ambition of the Lacedaemonians — in all these respects you will regard yourself as a child in comparison of them. Nay, even in wealth, if you are inclined
to think much of that, I must reveal to you the true
state of the case; for if you form an estimate of the
wealth of the Lacedaemonians, you will see that our
possessions fall far short of theirs. For no one here
can compete with them either in the extent and fertility of their own and the Messenian territory, or
in the number of their slaves, and especially of the
Helots, or of their horses, or of the animals which
feed on the Messenian pastures.

But I have said enough of this: and as to gold and
silver, there is more of them in Lacedaemon than in
all the rest of Hellas, for during many generations
gold has been always flowing in to them from the
whole Hellenic world, and often from the barbarian
also, and never flowing out, as in the fable of Aesop,
the fox said to the lion, "The prints of the feet of
those going in are distinct enough;" but who ever
saw the trace of money going out of Lacedaemon?
and therefore you may safely infer that the inhab-

itants are the richest of the Hellenes in gold and silver, and their kings are the richest of them, for the greater part of this harvest goes to their kings, and they have also a tribute paid to them, which is very considerable. Yet the Spartan wealth, though great in comparison of the wealth of the other Hellenes, is as nothing in comparison of that of the Persians and their kings. Why, I have been informed by a credible person who went up to the king [at Susa], that he passed through a large tract of excellent land, extending for nearly a day's journey, which the people of the country called the queen's girdle, and another, which they called her veil; and several other fair and fertile districts, which were reserved for the adornment of the queen, and are named after her several habiliments. Now, I can not help thinking to myself, What, if some one were to go to Amestris, the wife of Xerxes and mother of Artaxerxes, and say to her, There is a certain Dinomachè, whose whole wardrobe is not worth fifty minae — and that will be more than the value — and she has a son who is possessed of a three-hundred acre patch at Erchiae, and he has a mind to go to war with your son — would she not wonder to what this Alcibiades trusts for success in the conflict? " He must rely," she would say to herself, " upon his training and wisdom — these are the things which Hellenes value." And if she heard that this Alcibiades who is making the attempt is not as yet twenty years old, and is wholly uneducated, and that when his lover tells him that he ought to get education and training first, and then go and fight the king, he refuses, and says that he is well enough as he is, would she not be amazed, and ask, " On what, then, does the youth rely? " And if we reply that he relies on his beauty, and stature, and birth, and mental endowments, she would

think that we were mad, Alcibiades, when she compared the advantages which you possess with those
of her own people.   And I believe that Lampido,
the daughter of Leotychides, the wife of Archidamus
and mother of Agis, all of whom were kings, would
have the same feeling; if, in your present uneducated
state, you were to turn your thoughts against her
son, she, too, would be equally astonished.   But how
disgraceful, that we should not have as high a notion
of what is required in us as our enemies' wives have
of the qualities which are required in their assailants!
O my friend, be persuaded by me and hear the Delphian inscription, " Know thyself; " deem these
kings to be our antagonists, who are not such as you
think, but quite of another sort, and we can only
overcome them by pains and skill.   And if you fail
in the required qualities, you will fail also in becoming renowned among Hellenes and Barbarians, which
you seem to desire, as no other man ever desired anything.

PARMENIDES

THE MEETING OF SOCRATES AND PARMENIDES AT ATHENS.   CRITICISM OF THE IDEAS

THE Parmenides is perhaps the most difficult of all the dialogues of Plato, and one of a group which are not very attractive to the reader who has not been initiated into the " mysteries
of dialectic." The subject is the Doctrine of Ideas, those metaphysical abstractions which occupied the mind of Plato more or
less during the greater part of his life. They have often been
supposed to be the keystone of his system, on which all his other
thoughts and conceptions depend for stability.

This view, however, goes beyond the truth.   It is a mistake to
imagine that Plato had in view a complete scheme of philosophy,
which he endeavored to draw out in a series of treatises.   His
genius was unsystematic and irregular; he was almost as much

a poet as a philosopher; and the testimony of his own writings is sufficient to show that he fell at various periods under the influence of different teachers. The Ideas ought rather to be treated by us as an attempt to convey Plato's conviction that there was a truth unrealized beyond sense, which could only be grasped by the mind when freed from the thraldom of the body. But he was greatly perplexed by the difficulty of finding an adequate expression of his thoughts, and he was perfectly conscious of the many and serious objections which could be urged against his own doctrines.

In the Parmenides, which we may reasonably consider a work of Plato's later years, he has reached a stage at which he is able by an extraordinary effort of intellectual power to produce a criticism of the Ideas which he himself can not refute. Yet he hints by the mouth of Parmenides that he is still convinced of their reality and existence; for, without abstract ideas, thought and reasoning would be impossible. And in the Sophist he resumes the topic with more success, and clears away some of the obstacles to his theory which in the Parmenides had appeared to him to be insuperable.

WE went from our home at Clazomenae to Athens, and met Adeimantus and Glaucon in the Agora. Welcome, said Adeimantus, taking me by the hand; is there anything which we can do for you in Athens?

Why, yes, I said, I am come to ask a favor of you.

What is that? he said.

I want you to tell me the name of your half-brother, which I have forgotten; he was a mere child when I last came hither from Clazomenae, but that was a long time ago; your father's name, if I remember rightly, is Pyrilampes?

Yes, he said, and the name of our brother, Antiphon; but why do you ask?

Let me introduce some countrymen of mine, I said; they are lovers of philosophy, and have heard that Antiphon was in the habit of meeting Pythodorus, the friend of Zeno, and remembers certain arguments

which Socrates and Zeno and Parmenides had together, and which Pythodorus had often repeated to
him.

That is true.

And could we hear them? I asked.

Nothing easier, he replied; when he was a youth
he made a careful study of the pieces; at present his
thoughts run in another direction; like his grandfather, Antiphon, he is devoted to horses. But, if
that is what you want, let us go and look for him;
he dwells at Melita, which is quite near, and he has
only just left us to go home.

Accordingly we went to look for him; he was at
home, and in the act of giving a bridle to a blacksmith
to be fitted. When he had done with the blacksmith,
his brothers told him the purpose of our visit; and
he saluted me as an acquaintance whom he remembered from my former visit, and we asked him to
repeat the dialogue. At first he was not very willing,
and complained of the trouble, but at length he consented. He told us that Pythodorus had described
to him the appearance of Parmenides and Zeno; they
came to Athens, he said, at the great Panathenaea;
the former was, at the time of his visit, about 65 years
old, very white with age, but well favored. Zeno
was nearly 40 years of age, of a noble figure and fair
aspect; and in the days of his youth he was reported
to have been beloved of Parmenides. He said that
they lodged with Pythodorus in the Ceramicus, outside the wall, whither Socrates and others came to
see them; they wanted to hear some writings of
Zeno, which had been brought to Athens by them for
the first time. He said that Socrates was then very
young, and that Zeno read them to him in the absence
of Parmenides, and had nearly finished when Pythodorus entered, and with him Parmenides and Aris-

toteles who was afterwards one of the Thirty; there was not much more to hear, and Pythodorus had heard Zeno repeat them before.

When the recitation was completed, Socrates requested that the first hypothesis of the first discourse might be read over again, and this having been done, he said: What do you mean, Zeno? Is your argument that the existence of many necessarily involves like and unlike, and that this is impossible, for neither can the like be unlike, nor the unlike like; is that your position? Just that, said Zeno. And if the unlike can not be like, or the like unlike, then neither can the many exist, for that would involve an impossibility. Is the design of your argument throughout to disprove the existence of the many? and is each of your treatises intended to furnish a separate proof of this, there being as many proofs in all as you have composed arguments, of the non-existence of the many? Is that your meaning, or have I misunderstood you?

No, said Zeno; you have quite understood the general drift of the treatise.

I see, Parmenides, said Socrates, that Zeno is your second self in his writings too; he puts what you say in another way, and half deceives us into believing that he is saying what is new. For you, in your compositions, say that the all is one, and of this you adduce excellent proofs; and he, on the other hand, says that the many is naught, and gives many great and convincing evidences of this. To deceive the world, as you have done, by saying the same thing in different ways, one of you affirming and the other denying the many, is a strain of art beyond the reach of most of us.

Yes, Socrates, said Zeno. But although you are as keen as a Spartan hound in pursuing the track, you do not quite apprehend the true motive of the performance, which is not really such an artificial piece of work as you imagine; there was no intention of concealment effecting any grand result — that was a mere accident. For the truth is, that these writings of mine were meant to protect the arguments of Parmenides against those who ridicule him, and urge the many ridiculous and contradictory results which were supposed to follow from the assertion of the one. My answer is addressed to the partisans of the many, and intended to show that greater or more ridiculous consequences follow from their hypothesis of the existence of the many if carried out, than from the hypothesis of the existence of the one. A love of controversy led me to write the book in the days of my youth, and some one stole the writings, and I had therefore no choice about the publication of them; the motive, however, of writing, was not the ambition of an old man, but the pugnacity of a young one. This you do not seem to see, Socrates; though in other respects, as I was saying, your notion is a very just one.

That I understand, said Socrates, and quite accept your account. But tell me, Zeno, do you not further think that there is an idea of likeness in the abstract, and another idea of unlikeness, which is the opposite of likeness, and that in these two, you and I and all other things to which we apply the term many, participate; and that the things which participate in likeness are in that degree and manner like; and that those which participate in unlikeness are in that degree unlike, or both like and unlike in the degree in which they participate in both? And all things may partake of both opposites, and be like and unlike to themselves, by reason of this participation. Even in that there is nothing wonderful. But if a person could prove the absolute like to become unlike, or the absolute unlike to become like, that, in my opinion, would be a real wonder; not, however, if the things which partake of the ideas experience likeness and unlikeness — there is nothing extraordinary in this. Nor, again, if a person were to show that all is one by partaking of one, and that the same is many by partaking of many, would that be very wonderful? But if he were to show me that the absolute many was one, or the absolute one many, I should be truly amazed. And I should say the same of other things. I should be surprised to hear that the genera and species had opposite qualities in themselves; but if a person wanted to prove of me that I was many and also one, there would be no marvel in that. When he wanted to show that I was many he would say that I have a right and a left side, and a front and a back, and an upper and a lower half, for I can not deny that I partake of multitude; when, on the other hand, he wants to prove that I am one, he will say, that we who are here assembled are seven, and that I am one and partake of the one, and in saying both he speaks truly. Or if a person shows that the same wood and stones and the like, being many are also one, we admit that he shows the existence of the one and many, but he does not show that the many are one or the one many; he is uttering not a wonder but a truism. If, however, as I was suggesting just now, we were to make an abstraction, I mean of like, unlike, one, many, rest, motion, and similar ideas, and then to show that these in their abstract form admit of admixture and separation, I should greatly wonder at that. This part of the argument appears to be treated by you, Zeno, in a very spirited manner; nevertheless, as I was saying, I should be far more amazed if any one found in the ideas themselves

which are conceptions, the same puzzle and entangle-
ment which you have shown to exist in visible objects.

While Socrates was saying this, Pythodorus
thought that Parmenides and Zeno were not altogether pleased at the successive steps of the argument; but still they gave the closest attention, and
often looked at one another, and smiled as if in admiration of him. When he had finished, Parmenides
expressed these feelings in the following words: —

Socrates, he said, I admire the bent of your mind
towards philosophy; tell me now, was this your own
distinction between abstract ideas and the things
which partake of them? and do you think that there
is an idea of likeness apart from the likeness which
we possess, or of the one and many, or of the other
notions of which Zeno has been speaking?

I think that there are such abstract ideas, said
Socrates.

Parmenides proceeded. And would you also make
abstract ideas of the just and the beautiful and the
good, and of all that class of notions?

Yes, he said, I should.

And would you make an abstract idea of man distinct from us and from all other human creatures,
or of fire and water?

I am often undecided, Parmenides, as to whether
I ought to include them or not.

And would you feel equally undecided, Socrates,
about things the mention of which may provoke a
smile? — I mean such things as hair, mud, dirt, or
anything else that is foul and base; would you suppose that each of these has an idea distinct from the
phenomena with which we come into contact, or not?

Certainly not, said Socrates; visible things like
these are such as they appear to us, and I am afraid
that there would be an absurdity in assuming any

idea of them, although I sometimes get disturbed, and begin to think that there is nothing without an idea; but then again, when I have taken up this position, I run away, because I am afraid that I may fall into a bottomless pit of nonsense, and perish; and I return to the ideas of which I was just now speaking, and busy myself with them.

Yes, Socrates, said Parmenides; that is because you are still young; the time will come when philosophy will have a firmer grasp of you, if I am not mistaken, and then you will not despise even the meanest things; at your age, you are too much disposed to look to the opinions of men. But I should like to know whether you mean that there are certain forms or ideas of which all other things partake, and from which they are named; that similars, for example, become similar, because they partake of similarity; and great things become great, because they partake of greatness; and that just and beautiful things become just and beautiful, because they partake of justice and beauty?

Yes, certainly, said Socrates, that is my meaning.

And does not each individual partake either of the whole of the idea or of a part of the idea? Is any third way possible?

Impossible, he said.

Then do you think that the whole idea is one, and yet being one, exists in each one of many?

Why not, Parmenides? said Socrates.

Because one and the same existing as a whole in many separate individuals, will thus be in a state of separation from itself.

Nay, replied the other; the idea may be like the day which is one and the same in many places, and yet continuous with itself; in this way each idea may be one and the same in all.

I like your way, Socrates, of dividing one into many; and if I were to spread out a sail and cover a number of men, that, as I suppose, in your way of speaking, would be one and a whole in or on many — that will be the sort of thing which you mean?

I am not sure.

And would you say that the whole sail is over each man, or a part only?

A part only.

Then, Socrates, the ideas themselves will be divisible, and the individuals will have a part only and not the whole existing in them?

That seems to be true.

Then would you like to say, Socrates, that the one idea is really divisible and yet remains one?

Certainly not, he said.

Suppose that you divide greatness, and that of many great things each one is great by having a portion of greatness less than absolute greatness — is that conceivable?

No.

Or will each equal part, by taking some portion of equality less than absolute equality, be equal to some other?

Impossible.

Or suppose one of us to have a portion of smallness; this is but a part of the small, and therefore the small is greater; and while the absolute small is greater, that to which the part of the small is added, will be smaller and not greater than before.

That is impossible, he said.

Then in what way, Socrates, will all things participate in the ideas, if they are unable to participate in them either as parts or wholes?

Indeed, he said, that is a question which is not easily determined.

Well, said Parmenides, and what do you say of another question?

What is that?

I imagine that the way in which you are led to assume the existence of ideas is as follows: — You see a number of great objects, and there seems to you to be one and the same idea of greatness pervading them all; and hence you conceive of a single greatness.

That is true, said Socrates.

And if you go on and allow your mind in like manner to contemplate the idea of greatness and these other greatnesses, and to compare them, will not another idea of greatness arise, which will appear to be the source of them all?

That is true.

Then another abstraction of greatness will appear over and above absolute greatness, and the individuals which partake of it; and then another, which will be the source of that, and then others, and so on; and there will be no longer a single idea of each kind, but an infinite number of them.

But may not the ideas, asked Socrates, be cognitions only, and have no proper existence except in our minds, Parmenides? For in that case there may be single ideas, which do not involve the consequences which were just now mentioned.

And can there be individual cognitions which are cognitions of nothing?

That is impossible, he said.

The cognition must be of something?

Yes.

Of something that is or is not?

Of something that is.

Must it not be of the unity, or single nature, which the cognition recognizes as attaching to all?

Yes.

And will not this unity, which is always the same in all, be the idea?

From that, again, there is no escape.

Then, said Parmenides, if you say that other things participate in the ideas, must you not say that everything is made up of thoughts or cognitions, and that all things think; or will you say that being thoughts they are without thought?

But that, said Socrates, is irrational. The more probable view, Parmenides, of these ideas is, that they are patterns fixed in nature, and that other things are like them, and resemblances of them; and that what is meant by the participation of other things in the ideas, is really assimilation to them.

But if, said he, the individual is like the idea, must not the idea also be like the individual, in as far as the individual is a resemblance of the idea? That which is like, can not be conceived of as other than the like of like.

Impossible.

And when two things are alike, must they not partake of the same idea?

They must.

And will not that of which the two partake, and which makes them alike, be the absolute idea [of likeness]?

Certainly.

Then the idea can not be like the individual, or the individual like the idea; for if they are alike, some further idea of likeness will always arise, and if that be like anything else, another and another; and new ideas will never cease being created, if the idea resembles that which partakes of it?

Quite true.

The theory, then, that other things participate in

the ideas by resemblance, has to be given up, and some other mode of participation devised?

That is true.

Do you see then, Socrates, how great is the difficulty of affirming self-existent ideas?

Yes, indeed.

And, further, let me say that as yet you only understand a small part of the difficulty which is involved in your assumption, that there are ideas of all things, which are distinct from them.

What difficulty? he said.

There are many, but the greatest of all is this: — If an opponent argues that these self-existent ideas, as we term them, can not be known, no one can prove to him that he is wrong, unless he who is disputing their existence be a man of great genius and cultivation, and is willing to follow a long and laborious demonstration — he will remain unconvinced, and still insist that they can not be known.

How is that, Parmenides? said Socrates.

In the first place, I think, Socrates, that you, or any one who maintains the existence of absolute ideas, will admit that they can not exist in us.

Why, then they would be no longer absolute, said Socrates.

That is true, he said; and any relation in the absolute ideas, is a relation which is among themselves only, and has nothing to do with the resemblances, or whatever they are to be termed, which are in our sphere, and the participation in which gives us this or that name. And the subjective notions in our mind, which have the same name with them, are likewise only relative to one another, and not to the ideas which have the same name with them, and belong to themselves, and not to the ideas.

How do you mean? said Socrates.

I may illustrate my meaning in this way, said Parmenides: — A master has a slave; now there is nothing absolute in the relation between them; they are both relations of some man to another man; but there is also an idea of mastership in the abstract, which is relative to the idea of slavery in the abstract; and this abstract nature has nothing to do with us, nor we with the abstract nature; abstract natures have to do with themselves alone, and we with ourselves. Do you see my meaning?

Yes, said Socrates, I quite see your meaning.

And does not knowledge, I mean absolute knowledge, he said, answer to very and absolute truth?

Certainly.

And each kind of absolute knowledge answers to each kind of absolute being?

Yes.

And the knowledge which we have, will answer to the truth which we have; and again, each kind of knowledge which we have, will be a knowledge of each kind of being which we have?

Certainly.

But the ideas themselves, as you admit, we have not, and can not have?

No, we can not.

And the absolute ideas or species, are known by the absolute idea of knowledge?

Yes.

And that is an idea which we have not got?

No.

Then none of the ideas are known to us, because we have no share in absolute knowledge?

They are not.

Then the ideas of the beautiful, and of the good, and the like, which we imagine to be absolute ideas, are unknown to us?

That appears to be the case.

I think that there is a worse consequence still.

What is that?

Would you, or would you not, say, that if there is such a thing as absolute knowledge, that must be a far more accurate knowledge than our knowledge, and the same of beauty and other things?

Yes.

And if there be anything that has absolute knowledge, there is nothing more likely than God to have this most exact knowledge?

Certainly.

But then, will God, having this absolute knowledge, have a knowledge of human things?

And why not?

Because, Socrates, said Parmenides, we have admitted that the ideas have no relation to human notions, nor human notions to them; the relations of either are in their respective spheres.

Yes, that has been admitted.

And if God has this truest authority, and this most exact knowledge, that authority can not rule us, nor that knowledge know us, or any human thing; and in like manner, as our authority does not extend to the gods, nor our knowledge know anything which is divine, so by parity of reason they, being gods, are not our masters; neither do they know the things of men.

Yet, surely, said Socrates, to deprive God of knowledge is monstrous.

These, Socrates, said Parmenides, are a few, and only a few, of the difficulties which are necessarily involved in the hypothesis of the existence of ideas, and the attempt to prove the absoluteness of each of them; he who hears of them will doubt or deny their existence, and will maintain that even if they do exist, they must necessarily be unknown to man, and he will think that there is reason in what he says, and as we were remarking just now, will be wonderfully hard of being convinced; a man must be a man of real ability before he can understand that everything has a class and an absolute essence; and still more remarkable will he be who makes out all these things for himself, and can teach another to analyze them satisfactorily.

I agree with you, Parmenides, said Socrates; and what you say is very much to my mind.

And yet, Socrates, said Parmenides, if a man, fixing his mind on these and the like difficulties, refuses to acknowledge ideas or species of existences, and will not define particular species, he will be at his wit's end; in this way he will utterly destroy the power of reasoning; and that is what you seem to me to have particularly noted.

Very true, he said.

But, then, what is to become of philosophy? What resource is there, if the ideas are unknown?

I certainly do not see my way at present.

Yes, said Parmenides; and I think that this arises, Socrates, out of your attempting to define the beautiful, the just, the good, and the ideas generally, without sufficient previous training. I noticed your deficiency, when I heard you talking here with your friend Aristoteles, the day before yesterday. The impulse that carries you towards philosophy is noble and divine — never doubt that — but there is an art which often seems to be useless, and is called by the vulgar idle talking; in that you must train and exercise yourself, now that you are young, or truth will elude your grasp.

And what is the nature of this exercise, Parmenides, which you would recommend?

That which you heard Zeno practising; at the same time, I give you credit for saying to him that you did not care to solve the perplexity in reference to visible objects, or to consider the question in that way; but only in reference to the conceptions of the mind, and to what may be called ideas.

Why, yes, he said, there appears to me to be no difficulty in showing that visible things experience likeness or unlikeness or anything else.

Quite true, he said; but I think that you should go a step further, and consider not only the consequences which flow from a given hypothesis, but the consequences which flow from denying the hypothesis; and the exercise will be still better.

What do you mean? he said.

I mean, for example, that in the case of this very hypothesis of Zeno's about the many, you should inquire not only what will follow either to the many in relation to themselves and to the one, or to the one in relation to itself and the many, on the hypothesis of the existence of the many, but also what will follow to the one and many in their relation to themselves or to one another, on the opposite hypothesis. Or if likeness does or does not exist — what will follow on either of these hypotheses to that which is supposed, and to other things in relation to themselves and to one another, and the same of unlikeness; and you may argue in a similar way about motion and rest, about generation and destruction, and even about existence and non-existence; and in a word, whatever you like to suppose as existing or non-existing, or experiencing any sort of affection. You must look at what follows in relation to the thing supposed, and to any other things which you choose, — to the greater number, and to all in like manner; and you must also look at other things in relation to themselves and to anything else which you choose, whether you suppose that they do or do not exist, if you would train yourself perfectly and see the real truth.

THEAETETUS

THE Theaetetus is a dialogue for which it is peculiarly difficult to assign a place in the series of the Platonic writings. In style it belongs rather to the earlier class, having many affinities to such works as the Protagoras or the Meno. But in the order of thought it is nearest akin to the Sophist and the Statesman, with which also it appears to be expressly connected by Plato.

The only indication of date which is furnished by the Dialogue itself is the mention in the prologue of the fighting near Corinth. This, however, contains an element of uncertainty. If the Corinthian War (B. C. 394-387) is intended (which is most probably the case), Plato must at least have passed his fortieth year when he wrote the Theaetetus. Or, if the reference is to the later operations in B. C. 369, when Iphicrates was in command at the Isthmus, we must refer the composition of the work to a correspondingly later time in Plato's life.

The principal subject of the dialogue is a discussion of the nature of knowledge and the manner in which it is received by us through perception and sensation. It takes the form chiefly of a criticism of the doctrine of Protagoras that "man is the measure of all things," which is identified with the Heracleitean theory that "all is in a flux," and is explained by Socrates to mean that all knowledge is relative, both in the intellectual and the moral sphere.

Neither of the two passages which follow relate to the main theme. They have the character of digressions, which pleasantly help to beguile the long and sometimes tedious course of the discussion. And we are inclined perhaps to sympathize with Theodorus, when he is dragged back by the indefatigable Socrates into the direct path, and to say that we "prefer the digressions to the argument itself."

1. SOCRATES, A MIDWIFE AND THE SON OF A MIDWIFE

Socrates is here humorously described by one of those figures of speech in which Plato takes such delight, as the midwife who delivers men of their thoughts and ideas, "the fair and immortal children of the mind," of whom he discourses in the Symposium. For Socrates is unlike any other of the great teachers of mankind; he does not convey ideas to his hearers, but elicits their intellectual conceptions from them, more sometimes, as Theaetetus says, "than was ever in them."

This is part of his mission, or rather, perhaps, another way of describing it; and when the thought comes to the light, he tries and tests it in every way to see whether it is the genuine offspring of wisdom, or the spurious progeny of self-conceit and vanity. Nor can we wonder that the "parents of the child," when it was condemned and pronounced wanting by the merciless judge, were apt to "fall into a rage," and fancied that they had been "deprived of some cherished possession."

Soc. SUCH are the midwives, whose work is a very important one, but not so important as mine; for women do not bring into the world at one time real children, and at another time idols which are with difficulty distinguished from them; if they did, then the discernment of the true and false birth would be the crowning achievement of the art of midwifery — you would think that?

Theaet. Yes, I certainly should.

Soc. Well, my art of midwifery is in most respects like theirs; but the difference lies in this — that I attend men and not women, and I practise on their souls when they are in labor, and not on their bodies; and the triumph of my art is in examining whether the thought which the mind of the young man is bringing to the birth is a false idol or a noble and true creation. And like the midwives, I am barren, and the reproach which is often made against me, that I ask questions of others and have not the wit to answer them myself, is very just; the reason is, that the god compels me to be a midwife, but forbids me to bring forth. And therefore I am not myself wise, nor have I anything which is the invention or

offspring of my own soul, but the way is this: —
Some of those who converse with me, at first appear
to be absolutely dull, yet afterwards, as our acquaintance ripens, if the god is gracious to them, they all
of them make astonishing progress; and this not
only in their own opinion but in that of others. There
is clear proof that they have never learned anything
of me, but they have acquired and discovered many
noble things of themselves, although the god and I
help to deliver them.

And the proof is, that many of them in their ignorance, attributing all to themselves and despising me,
either of their own accord or at the instigation of
others, have gone away sooner than they ought; and
the result has been that they have produced abortions
by reason of their evil communications, or have lost
the children of which I delivered them by an ill bringing up, deeming lies and shadows of more value than
the truth; and they have at last ended by seeing
themselves, as others see them, to be great fools.
Aristides, the son of Lysimachus, is one of this sort,
and there are many others. The truants often return
to me and beg that I would converse with them again
— they are ready to go down on their knees — and
then, if my familiar allows, which is not always the
case, I receive them, and they begin to grow again.
Dire are the pangs which my art is able to arouse
and to allay in those who have intercourse with me,
just like the pangs of women in childbirth; night
and day they are full of perplexity and travail which
is even worse than that of the women. So much for
them. And there are others, Theaetetus, who come
to me apparently having nothing in them; and as I
know that they have no need of my art, I coax them
into another union, and by the grace of God I can
generally tell who is likely to do them good. Many

of them I have given away to Prodicus, and some to other inspired sages.

I tell you this long story, friend Theaetetus, because I suspect, as indeed you seem to think yourself, that you are in labor — great with some conception. Come then to me, who am a midwife and the son of a midwife, and try to answer the question which I will ask you. And if I abstract and expose your first-born, because I discover upon inspection that the conception which you have formed is a vain shadow, do not quarrel with me on that account, as the manner of women is when their first children are taken from them. For I have actually known some who were ready to bite me when I deprived them of a darling folly; they did not perceive that I acted from good will, not knowing that no god is the enemy of man (that was not within the range of their ideas); neither am I their enemy in all this, but religion will never allow me to admit falsehood, or to stifle the truth. Once more, then, Theaetetus, I repeat my old question, " What is knowledge?" and do not say that you can not tell; but quit yourself like a man, and by the help of God you will be able to tell.

2. THE LAWYER AND THE PHILOSOPHER

The description of the lawyer and the philosopher in the Theaetetus is one of the most striking delineations of character in all the writings of Plato. The two types of men are opposed to one another with perfect skill and completeness. The contrast intended by Plato is the same as that which has always existed among mankind under various names and disguises. Aristotle has it in view when he speaks of the " life of action " and the " life of speculation," and a similar difference also appears in another age as the " secular " and the " religious life."

The philosopher is the man of thought and reflection, who dwells apart from others in a world of his own imagination. His mind is absorbed in the contemplation of the eternal and divine;

he can not condescend to the things " which lie at his feet." He sees the faults and follies of human nature so clearly that he is incapacitated for action.   But if he has almost too little of the mundane spirit, his rival and opponent is wholly taken up with the matters of daily life.   He is the man of affairs, who is unable to snatch an hour from business for solitude and meditation, and whose horizon is bounded by the narrow limits of self-interest. The higher impulses of his nature have withered and died in this arid atmosphere.   He is a match for the philosopher in the law courts and the senate; but when he is drawn into a philosophical argument, what a laughing-stock does he become to the wise man!

This is a picture which Plato is never weary of painting: — the philosopher and the politician in the Euthydemus; the philosopher and the man of the world in the Gorgias; the true and the false rhetorician in the Phaedrus, are all variations of the same theme.   The union of the two characters in one person is the favorite dream of Plato; the philosopher is to be the king in the state, or, at least, the princes of this world must be trained and educated in the school of philosophy.

Soc. Here is a new question offering, Theodorus, which is likely to be still longer than the last.

Theod. Well, Socrates, we have plenty of leisure.

Soc. That is true, and your remark recalls to my mind an observation which I have often made, that those who have passed their days in the pursuit of philosophy are ridiculously at fault when they have to appear and plead in court.   How natural is this!

Theod. What do you mean?

Soc. I mean to say, that those who from their youth upwards have been knocking about in the courts and such like places, compared with those who have received a philosophical education, are slaves, and the others are freemen.

Theod. In what is the difference seen?

Soc. In the leisure of which you were speaking, and which a freeman can always command; he has his talk out in peace, and, like ourselves, wanders at will from one subject to another, and from a second to a third, if his fancy prefers a new one, caring not whether his words are many or few; his only aim is to attain the truth. But the lawyer is always in a hurry; there is the water of the clepsydra driving him on, and not allowing him to expatiate at will; and there is his adversary standing over him, enforcing his rights; the affidavit, which in their phraseology is termed the brief, is recited; and from this he must not deviate. He is a servant, and is disputing about a fellow-servant before his master, who is seated, and has the cause in his hands; the trial is never about some indifferent matter, but always concerns himself; and often he has to run for his life. The consequence has been, that he has become keen and shrewd; he has learned how to flatter his master in word and indulge him in deed; but his soul is small and unrighteous. His slavish condition has deprived him of growth and uprightness and independence; dangers and fears, which were too much for his truth and honesty, came upon him in early years, when the tenderness of youth was unequal to them, and he has been driven into crooked ways; from the first he has practised deception and retaliation, and has become stunted and warped. And so he has passed out of youth into manhood, having no soundness in him; and is now, as he thinks, a master in wisdom. Such is the lawyer, Theodorus. Will you have the companion picture of the philosopher, who is of our brotherhood; or shall we return to the argument? Do not let us abuse the freedom of digression which we claim.

Theod. Nay, Socrates, let us finish what we were about; for you truly said that we belong to a brotherhood which is free, and are not the servants of the argument; but the argument is our servant, and must wait our leisure. Where is the judge or spec-

tator who has a right to censure or control us, as he
might the poets?

Soc. Then, as this is your wish, I will describe the
leaders; for there is no use in talking about the
inferior sort. In the first place, the lords of philosophy have never, from their youth upwards, known
their way to the Agora, or the dicastery, or the council, or any other political assembly; they neither see
nor hear the laws or votes of the state written or
spoken; the eagerness of political societies in the
attainment of offices — clubs, and banquets, and
revels, and singing-maidens, do not enter even into
their dreams. Whether any event has turned out well
or ill in the city, what disgrace may have descended
to any one from his ancestors, male or female, are
matters of which the philosopher no more knows
than he can tell, as they say, how many pints are
contained in the ocean. Neither is he conscious of
his ignorance. For he does not hold aloof in order
that he may gain a reputation; but the truth is, that
the outer form of him only is in the city; his mind,
disdaining the littlenesses and nothingnesses of human things, is " flying all abroad," as Pindar says,
measuring with line and rule the things which are
under and on the earth and above the heaven, interrogating the whole nature of each and all, but not
condescending to anything which is within reach.

Theod. What do you mean, Socrates?

Soc. I will illustrate my meaning, Theodorus, by
the jest which the clever, witty Thracian handmaid
made about Thales, when he fell into a well as he
was looking up at the stars. She said, that he was
so eager to know what was going on in heaven, that
he could not see what was before his feet. This is a
jest which is equally applicable to all philosophers.
For the philosopher is wholly unacquainted with his

next door neighbor; he is ignorant, not only of what he is doing, but whether he is or is not a human creature; he is searching into the essence of man, and is unwearied in discovering what belongs to such a nature to do or suffer different from any other; — I think that you understand me, Theodorus?

Theod. I do, and what you say is true.

Soc. And thus, my friend, on every occasion, private as well as public, as I said at first, when he appears in a law-court, or in any place in which he has to speak of things which are at his feet and before his eyes, he is the jest, not only of Thracian handmaids but of the general herd, tumbling into wells and every sort of disaster through his inexperience. He looks such an awkward creature, and conveys the impression that he is stupid. When he is reviled, he has nothing personal to say in answer to the civilities of his adversaries, for he knows no scandals of any one, and they do not interest him; and therefore he is laughed at for his sheepishness; and when others are being praised and glorified, he can not help laughing very sincerely in the simplicity of his heart; and this again makes him look like a fool. When he hears a tyrant or king eulogized, he fancies that he is listening to the praises of some keeper of cattle — a swineherd, or shepherd, or cowherd, who is being praised for the quantity of milk which he squeezes from them; and he remarks that the creature whom they tend, and out of whom they squeeze the wealth, is of a less tractable and more insidious nature. Then, again, he observes that the great man is of necessity as ill-mannered and uneducated as any shepherd — for he has no leisure, and he is surrounded by a wall, which is his mountain-pen. Hearing of enormous landed proprietors of ten thousand acres and more, our philosopher deems this to be a

trifle, because he has been accustomed to think of
the whole earth; and when they sing the praises of
family, and say that some one is a gentleman because he has had seven generations of wealthy ancestors, he thinks that their sentiments only betray the
dulness and narrowness of vision of those who utter
them, and who are not educated enough to look at
the whole, nor to consider that every man has had
thousands and thousands of progenitors, and among
them have been rich and poor, kings and slaves, Hellenes and barbarians, many times over. And when
some one boasts of a catalogue of twenty-five ancestors, and goes back to Heracles, the son of Amphitryon, he can not understand his poverty of ideas.
Why is he unable to calculate that Amphitryon had
a twenty-fifth ancestor, who might have been anybody, and was such as fortune made him, and he had
a fiftieth, and so on? He is amused at the notion
that he can not do a sum, and thinks that a little
arithmetic would have got rid of his senseless vanity.
Now, in all these cases our philosopher is derided by
the vulgar, partly because he is above them, and also
because he is ignorant of what is before him, and
always at a loss.

Theod. That is very true, Socrates.

Soc. But, O my friend, when he draws the other
into upper air, and gets him out of his pleas and
rejoinders into the contemplation of justice and injustice in their own nature and in their difference
from one another and from all other things; or from
the commonplaces about the happiness of kings to
the consideration of government, and of human happiness and misery in general — what they are, and
how a man should seek after the one and avoid the
other — when that narrow, keen, little legal mind is
called to account about all this, he gives the philos-

opher his revenge; for dizzied by the height at which he is hanging, and from which he looks into space, which is a strange experience to him, he being dismayed, and lost, and stammering out broken words, is laughed at, not by Thracian handmaidens or any other uneducated persons, for they have no eye for the situation, but by every man who has not been brought up as a slave. Such are the two characters, Theodorus: the one of the philosopher or gentleman, who may be excused for appearing simple and useless when he has to perform some menial office, such as packing up a bag, or flavoring a sauce or fawning speech; the other, of the man who is able to do every kind of service smartly and neatly, but knows not how to wear his cloak like a gentleman; still less does he acquire the music of speech, or hymn the true life which is lived by immortals or men blessed of heaven.

Theod. If you could only persuade everybody, Socrates, as you do me, of the truth of your words, there would be more peace and fewer evils among men.

Soc. Evils, Theodorus, can never perish; for there must always remain something which is antagonist to good. Of necessity, they hover around this mortal sphere and the earthly nature, having no place among the gods in heaven. Wherefore, also, we ought to fly away thither, and to fly thither is to become like God, as far as this is possible; and to become like him, is to become holy and just and wise. But, O my friend, you can not easily convince mankind that they should pursue virtue or avoid vice, not for the reasons which the many give, in order, forsooth, that a man may seem to be good; — this is what they are always repeating, and this, in my judgment, is an old wives' fable. Let them hear the truth: In God is no unrighteousness at all — he is altogether righteous; and there is nothing more like him than he of us, who is the most righteous. And the true wisdom of men, and their nothingness and cowardice, are nearly concerned with this. For to know this is true wisdom and manhood, and the ignorance of this is too plainly folly and vice. All other kinds of wisdom or cunning, which seem only, such as the wisdom of politicians, or the wisdom of the arts, are coarse and vulgar. The unrighteous man, or the sayer and doer of unholy things, had far better not yield to the illusion that his roguery is cleverness; for men glory in their shame — they fancy that they hear others saying of them, " these are not mere good-for-nothing persons, burdens of the earth, but such as men should be who mean to dwell safely in a state." Let us tell them that they are all the more truly what they do not know that they are; for they do not know the penalty of injustice, which above all things they ought to know — not stripes and death, as they suppose, which evil-doers often escape, but a penalty which can not be escaped.

Theod. What is that?

Soc. There are two patterns set before them in nature: the one, blessed and divine, the other godless and wretched; and they do not see, in their utter folly and infatuation, that they are growing like the one and unlike the other, by reason of their evil deeds; and the penalty is, that they lead a life answering to the pattern which they resemble. And if we tell them, that unless they depart from their cunning, the place of innocence will not receive them after death; and that here on earth, they will live ever in the likeness of their own evil selves, and with evil friends — when they hear this they in their superior cunning will seem to be listening to fools.

Theod. Very true, Socrates.

Soc. Too true, my friend, as I well know; there is, however, one peculiarity in their case: when they begin to reason in private about their dislike of philosophy, if they have the courage to hear the argument out, and do not run away, they grow at last strangely discontented with themselves; their rhetoric fades away, and they seem to be no better than children. These, however, are digressions from which we must now desist, or they will overflow, and drown our original argument; to which, if you please, we will now return.

Theod. For my part, Socrates, I would rather have the digressions, for at my age I find them easier to follow; but if you wish, let us go back to the argument.

SOPHIST

THE PRE-SOCRATIC PHILOSOPHERS AND THEIR PUZZLES

The Sophist, like the Parmenides, deals with metaphysical problems and puzzles, and with the Doctrine of the Ideas. The form which it takes is an inquiry into the nature and character of the Sophist or pretender to wisdom, who is exhibited in an odious light as the opposite to the true philosopher, ambitious, shallow, mercenary, disputatious, a sorcerer who makes that which is not appear to be.

But, the question is asked, how can " not-being " exist? This, which seems to us an almost meaningless fallacy, was to Plato and his contemporaries a real philosophical difficulty. And accordingly he proceeds to show that the separation of the spheres of the absolute and the relative, of being and not-being, which had been taught by Parmenides and his followers, could not be maintained. All ideas are not incompatible, although some are. Being, for instance, partakes both of rest and motion; whereas rest and motion are inconsistent. Not-being is only the negation of being, just as not-motion or rest is the negation of motion.

In the course of the discussion Plato gives a sketch of the history of Greek philosophy, which is interesting in itself, and is also the first attempt of the kind which is known to us. It is, as we might expect, only an outline of which we are left to fill up the details to the best of our power. Plato divides the philosophers who preceded him into several schools or sects: —

(1) The early Ionian philosophers, like Pherecydes (B. C. 560), who maintained the existence of two or three principles, such as heat and cold, moist and dry, and declared that these were sometimes united and sometimes at strife:

(2) The Eleatics, who derived their origin from Xenophanes (B. C. 540), and Parmenides (B. C. 504), and taught that "the many was also one," and "asserted the unity of the Universe:"

(3) "The Ionian and Sicilian Muses" (Heracleitus, B. C. 504), and Empedocles (B. C. 443), who combined the tenets of Pherecydes and the Eleatics; Heracleitus affirming that plurality and unity were in perpetual process of union and division by love and hate, while Empedocles supposed that they were in regular alternation to each other.

These somewhat crude and primitive philosophers were succeeded by more subtle teachers, whom Plato regards as his principal opponents. He has not clearly stated to whom he is referring; but he appears to have in view chiefly the Megarian School, or, possibly, the early Cynics, who delighted in verbal questions and disputes about being and not-being, and "found no end, in wandering mazes lost."

Lastly, there were the Idealists, by whom is probably intended a School who held in some form a Doctrine of Ideas; and the fierce and uncouth sect of the Materialists, who dragged heaven to earth, and believed in nothing except the evidence of their senses.

Into the midst of this warfare of words Plato has to descend. His object is not so much to put forward opinions of his own, as to gain from the different combatants the truest part of that for which they were fighting. He was by temperament an Eclectic, in the best sense of the term, and during the whole of his life, we find him indefatigable in the search after truth, and ready to welcome her from whatever side she appeared.

The principal character in this dialogue is taken by a Stranger from Elea, " a disciple of Parmenides and Zeno, and a true philosopher."

Str. WILL you, then, forgive me, and, as your words imply, be contented if I slightly flinch from the grasp of such a sturdy argument?

Theaet. Certainly, I will.

Str. There is also another request which I have to make.

Theaet. What is that?

Str. That you will promise not to regard me as a parricide.

Theaet. Why do you say that?

Str. I mean to say that, in self-defence, I must test the philosophy of my father Parmenides, and try to prove by main force that in a certain sense not-being is, and that being is not.

Theaet. Some attempt of the kind is clearly needed.

Str. Yes, a blind man, as they say, might see that, and, unless a decision on this point is obtained, no one when he speaks of false words, or false opinion, or idols, or images, or imitations, or apparitions, or about the arts which are concerned with them, can avoid falling into ridiculous contradictions.

Theaet. Most true.

Str. And therefore I must venture to lay hands on my father's argument; for, if I am to be scrupulous, I must entirely give the matter up.

Theaet. Nothing in the world should ever induce us to do that.

Str. I have a third little excuse which I wish to offer.

Theact. What is that?

Soc. You heard me say what I have always felt and still feel — that I have no heart for this argument?

Theaet. I did.

Str. I tremble at the thought of what I have said,

and expect that you will deem me mad, when you hear of my sudden changes and shiftings; let me therefore observe to you, that I am proceeding with the argument entirely out of regard for you.

Theaet. You certainly need not fear my bad opinion, or that I shall impute any impropriety to you, if you attempt to establish your refutation; take heart, therefore, and proceed.

Str. And where shall I begin the perilous enterprise? I think that the road which I had better take is ———

Theaet. Which? — Let me hear.

Str. I think that we had better, first of all, consider the points which at present are regarded as self-evident, lest we should have fallen into some confusion about them, and be too ready to assent to one another, fancying that we have the means of judging.

Theaet. Say more clearly what you mean.

Str. I think that Parmenides, and all who undertook to determine the number and nature of existence, talked to us in rather a light and easy strain.

Theaet. How did they talk to us?

Str. As if we had been children, to whom they repeated each their own particular mythus or story; — one said that there were three principles at one time warring in a manner with one another, and then at peace again; and they were married and begat children, and brought them up; and another spoke of two principles, — a moist and dry, or hot and cold, which he brought together and gave in marriage to one another. The Eleatics in our part of the world say that all things are many in name, but in nature one; this is their mythus, which begins with Xenophanes, and is even older. Then there are Ionian, and in more recent times Sicilian muses, who have conceived the thought that to unite the two principles is safer; and they say that being is one and many, which are held together by enmity and friendship, ever parting, ever meeting, as the more potent masters of harmony assert, while the general ones do not insist on the perpetual strife and peace, but admit a relaxation and alternation of them; peace and friendship sometimes prevailing under the sway of Aphrodite, and then again diversity and war, by reason of a principle of strife. Whether any of them spoke the truth in all this is hard to determine; antiquity and famous men should have reverence, and not be liable to such insinuations. Yet one thing may be said of them without offence:

Theaet. What is that?

Str. That they went on their several ways with a good deal of disdain of people like ourselves; they did not care whether they took us with them, or left us behind them.

Theaet. How do you mean?

Str. I mean to say, that when they talk of one, two, or more elements, which are or have become or are becoming, or again of heat mingling with cold, and in some other part of their works assume separations and combinations of them, — tell me, Theaeteetus, do you understand what they mean by these expressions? When I was a younger man, I used to fancy that I understood quite well what was meant by the term " not-being," which is our present subject of dispute; and now you see in what a perplexity we are landed.

Theaet. I see.

Str. And very likely we have been getting into the same difficulty about " being," and yet may fancy that when anybody utters the word, we understand him and are in no difficulty, although we still admit that we are ignorant of not-being, when the truth is, that we are equally ignorant of both.

Theaet. I dare say.

Str. And the same may be said of all the subjects of the previous discussion.

Theaet. True.

Str. Most of them may be deferred for the present; but we had better now consider the chief captain and leader of them.

Theaet. I suppose that you are speaking of being, and you want to take this first, and discover what they mean who use the word?

Str. You follow close at my heels, Theaetetus. For the right method, I conceive, will be to call into our presence and interrogate the dialectic philosophers. To them we will say, " O ye, who speak of hot and cold, or of any other two principles of which the universe consists, what term is this which you apply to both of them, and what do you mean when you say that both and each of them are? How are we to understand the word " are?" Are we to suppose that there is a third principle over and above the other two, and that there are three in all, and not two, according to your notions? For clearly you can not say that one of the two principles is being, and yet attribute being equally to both of them; for, whichever of the two is identified with being, they would be one and not two."

Theaet. Very true.

Str. You mean, then, to call the sum of both of them " being?"

Theaet. I suppose so.

Str. Then, friends, we shall reply to them, the answer to that is plainly that the two will thus be resolved into one.

Theaet. Most true.

Str. Since, then, we are in a difficulty, please to tell us what you mean, when you speak of being; for there can be no doubt that you always from the first understood your own meaning, whereas we once thought that we understood you, but now we are in a great strait. Please to begin by explaining this matter to us, and let us no longer fancy that we understand you, when we entirely misunderstand you. There will be no impropriety in our thus inquiring either of the dualists or of the pluralists?

Theaet. Certainly not.

Str. And what about the assertors of the all and one — must we not endeavor to ascertain from them what they mean by " being? "

Theaet. By all means.

Str. Then let us ask a question of them: — One, you say, alone is? Yes, they will reply.

Theaet. True.

Str. And, again, being is?

Theaet. Yes.

Str. And is being the same as one, and do you apply two names to the same thing?

Theaet. What will be their answer to that, Stranger?

Str. It is clear, Theaetetus, that he who asserts the unity of being will find a difficulty in answering this or any other question.

Theaet. How is that?

Str. To admit of two names, and to affirm that there is nothing but unity, is surely ridiculous?

Theaet. Certainly.

Str. And equally irrational to admit that a name has any real existence?

Theaet. How is that?

Str. If the name is distinguished from the thing, that supposes two things.

Theaet. Yes.

Str. And yet he who identifies the name with the thing will be compelled to say that the name is of nothing, or if he says that the name is of something, then the name will be the name of a name, and of nothing else.

Theaet. True.

Str. The one in the same way will be only one of one, and although absolute unity, will be of a mere name.

Theaet. Certainly.

Str. And would they say that the whole is other than the one being, or the same with it?

Theaet. To be sure they will and do say that.

Str. If the one is a whole, as Parmenides sings, —

> " Every way like the fulness of a well-formed sphere,
> Equally balanced from the centre on every side,
> And must needs be neither greater nor less,
> Neither on this side nor on that — "

then being has a centre and extremes, and, having these, must also have parts.

Theaet. True.

Str. And that which has parts may have the attribute of unity in all the parts, and in this way being all and a whole, may be one?

Theaet. Certainly.

Str. But that of which this is the condition can not be absolute unity?

Theaet. How is that?

Str. Because, according to right reason, that which is absolutely one ought to be affirmed to be indivisible.

Theaet. Certainly.

Str. But this indivisible, if made up of parts, will contradict reason.

Theaet. I understand.

Str. Shall we say that being is one and a whole only as having the attribute of unity? Or shall we say that being is not a whole at all?

Theaet. That is a hard alternative to offer.

Str. Most true; for being having in a certain sense the attribute of unity, is yet proved not to be the same as unity, and the all is therefore more than one.

Theaet. Yes.

Str. And yet if being be not a whole in having the attribute of one, and there being such a thing as an absolute whole, then being lacks something of the nature of being?

Theaet. Certainly.

Str. Upon this view, again, being having a defect of being, will become not-being?

Theaet. True.

Str. And, again, the all becomes more than one, for being and the whole will each have their separate nature.

Theaet. Yes.

Str. But if the whole does not exist at all, all the previous difficulties remain the same, and there will be the further difficulty, that besides having no exist. ence, being can never have come into existence.

Theaet. Why is that?

Str. Because that which comes into existence always comes into existence as a whole, so that he who does not give whole a place among existences, can not speak either of essence or generation as being.

Theaet. Yes, that certainly appears to be true.

Str. Again; how can that which is not a whole have any quantity? For that which is of a certain quantity must necessarily be of that quantity taken as a whole.

Theaet. Exactly.

Str. And there will be innumerable other points,

each of them involving infinite perplexity to him who
says that being is either one or two.

Theaet. The difficulties which are already appearing prove this; for one objection connects with another, and they are always increasing in difficulty
and eliciting fresh doubts about what has preceded.

Str. We are far from having exhausted the more
exact thinkers who treat of being and not-being. But
let us be content to leave them, and proceed to view
those who speak less precisely; and we shall find as
the result of all, that the nature of being is quite as
difficult to comprehend as that of not-being.

Theaet. Then now we are to go to the others.

Str. There appears to be a sort of war of Giants
and Gods going on among them; they are fighting
about the nature of essence.

Theaet. How is that?

Str. Some of them are dragging down all things
from heaven and from the unseen to earth, and seem
determined to grasp in their hands rocks and oaks;
of these they lay hold, and are obstinate in maintaining, that the things only which can be touched or
handled have being or essence, because they define
being and body as one, and if any one says that what
is not a body exists they altogether despise them, and
will hear of nothing but body.

Theaet. I have often met with such men, and terrible fellows they are.

Str. And that is the reason why their opponents
cautiously defend themselves from above, out of an
unseen world, mightily contending that true essence
consists of certain intelligible and incorporeal ideas;
the bodies of the materialists, which are maintained
by them to be the very truth, they break up into little
bits by their arguments, and affirm them to be generation and not essence. O, Theaetetus, there is an end-

less war which is always raging between these two armies on this ground.

Theaet. True.

Str. Let us ask each of them, in turn, to give an account of that which they call essence.

Theaet. How shall we get that out of them?

Str. With those who make being to consist in ideas, there will be less difficulty, for they are civil people enough; but there will be very great difficulty, or rather an absolute impossibility, in arguing with those who drag everything down to matter. I will tell you what I think that we must do.

Theaet. What is that?

Str. Let us, if we can, really improve them; but if this is not possible, let us imagine them to be better than they are, and more willing to answer in accordance wih the rules of argument, and then their opinion will be more worth having; for that which better men acknowledge has more weight than that which is acknowledged by inferior men. And we are no respecters of persons, but seekers of the truth.

STATESMAN

THE REIGN OF CRONOS

THE Statesman is a companion piece to the Sophist, which it much resembles in style and manner of treatment. It contains a picture of the ideal statesman or ruler who is "set over against" his rival, the mere politician. The true king or statesman is the superior of his fellow citizens, and governs them by knowledge and not by power. His rule is better than that of the law: for the law is fixed and unbending, whereas the individual can allow himself to be guided by circumstances. But since this "king by nature" is scarcely or never to be found among men, they prefer to submit to one of the various "imperfect forms of government."

There was an age, however, when mankind was ruled in the true sense of the word. This was in the time of Cronos, those happy days during which the human race lived in Paradisiacal innocence under the government of Divine Shepherds, who were appointed by Cronos himself. Our present and far inferior state is due to the revolutions of the Universe.

In the beginning, the course of the world was guided by the hand of God; but when the appointed number of generations had been born from the earth and had returned again to her, the Creator ceased His directing care; the Universe fell to chaos, and all living creatures perished. A new race succeeded; the evil which is inherent in matter reasserted itself, and the world went from bad to worse, until the Creator at last again interposed, and restored order to creation. At the same time He introduced a new principle of life; the earth no longer brought forth men and animals, but they reproduced their species, each after their kind. Men were at first poor and helpless; gradually, however, by the aid of the Gods, they learned the arts of life and formed themselves into communities.

In this remarkable myth Plato, while adding confirmation by the example of the rule of Cronos to the argument respecting the true nature of government, is also enabled to set forth in a poetical form his solution of two different problems which seem to have been a frequent subject of his thoughts — (1) the existence of evil, and (2) the growth of human society.

(1) He is sorely perplexed, as men have been in all ages, by the existence of evil in the Universe. He saw everywhere the marks of design; yet the efforts of the Designer appeared liable to be thwarted by some malignant influence. And this power or principle of evil he supposed to be, not a " Prince of Darkness," who was opposed on almost equal terms to the Deity, but an inherent quality of matter, against which even the Creator was not wholly able to contend. Hence also he was led to place between the Creator and the Creation an intermediate order of divine beings who execute " their Father's will in the best and wisest manner which they can."

(2) The growth of civilization was a subject of much curiosity to the Greeks. Their lively and reflective minds were deeply stirred by what they were able to learn of the ancient history of the East and of Egypt. They felt how truly they might be called a " race of children; " for their national history was brief and hardly more than a mass of inconsistent legends and traditions, while the Egyptian priests could recite to Herodotus the

names of " 330 kings who reigned in Egypt between the days of Menes and his own time." Moreover, short and imperfect as was their knowledge of the events of the past, they were well aware that great revolutions had happened, and that kingdoms which had once been powerful had fallen into decay, while others had succeeded in their place.

They were easily led, therefore, to the conclusion that " there had been many destructions of mankind," and that civilization had grown up by slow and painful efforts among the survivors of some deluge or other catastrophe, such as had become familiar to their minds from the legends of the deluges of Ogyges and Deucalion or the destruction of the earth by Phaëthon. Plato recurs once more to this subject in the Third Book of the Laws, where we shall find him treating of the manner in which the several forms of government may be supposed to have developed among men.

The conversation is between the Eleatic Stranger of the " Sophist " and the younger Socrates, who is not a relation of his namesake.

Str. LET us make a beginning, and travel by a different road.

Υ. *Soc.* What road?

Str. I think that we may have a little amusement; there is a famous tale, of which a good portion may with advantage be interwoven, and then we may resume our series of divisions, and proceed along that path until we arrive at the summit or desired end. Shall we do as I say?

Υ. *Soc.* By all means.

Str. Listen, then, to a tale which a child would love to hear, and you are not too old to be amused as a child.

Υ. *Soc.* Let me hear.

Str. There did really happen, and will again happen, like many other events of which ancient tradition has preserved the record, the portent which is traditionally said to have occurred in the quarrel of Atreus and Thyestes. You remember what that was?

ϒ. *Soc.* I suppose that you mean the token of the golden lamb?

Str. No, not that; but another part of the story, which tells how the sun and the stars rose in the west, and set in the east, and that the god reversed their motion, and gave them that which they have at present as a testimony to the right of Atreus.

ϒ. *Soc.* Yes; that is certainly related.

Str. Again, we have been often told of the kingdom of Cronos.

ϒ. *Soc.* Yes, very often.

Str. Did you ever hear that the men of former times were earth-born, and not begotten of one another?

ϒ. *Soc.* Yes, that is also an old tradition.

Str. All these stories, and ten thousand others which are still more wonderful, have a common origin; many of them have been lost in the lapse of ages, or exist only as fragments; but the origin of them is what no one has told, and may as well be told now; for the tale is suited to throw light on the nature of the king.

ϒ. *Soc.* Very good; and I hope that you will give the whole story, and leave out nothing.

Str. Listen, then. There is a time when God goes round with the world, which he himself guides and helps to roll; and there is a time, on the completion of a certain cycle, when he lets go, and the world being a living creature, and having originally received intelligence from its author and creator, turns about and revolves in the opposite direction.

ϒ. *Soc.* Why is that?

Str. Why, because only the most divine things of all are unchangeable, and body is not included in this class. Heaven and the universe, as we have termed them, although they have been endowed by the

Creator with many glories, partake of a bodily nature, and therefore can not be entirely free from perturbations. But the heavenly motion is, as far as possible, single and in the same place, and in relation to the same; and is therefore only subject to a reversal, which is the least alteration possible. For the lord of all moving things is alone able to move of himself; and to think that he can go at one time in one direction and at another time in another, is unlawful. Hence we must not say that the world is either self-moved always, or that the universe is made to go round by God in two opposite courses; or that two Gods, having intelligence, oppose one another in the movement of the world. But as I have already said (and this is the only remaining alternative) the world is guided by an accompanying divine power and receives life and immortality by the appointment of the Creator, and then, when let go again, moves spontaneously, being let go at such a time as to have, during infinite cycles of years, a reverse movement: this is due to exquisite perfection of balance, and the size of the universe; which is the greatest of bodies, and turns on the smallest pivot.

Υ. *Soc.* All that description seems to be very reasonable indeed.

Str. Let us now reflect upon what has been said, and try to comprehend the nature of this great mythological wonder, which has been called by us, and assuredly is, the cause of the other wonders.

Υ. *Soc.* To what are you referring?

Str. To the reversal of the motion of the universe.

Υ. *Soc.* How was that the cause of the others?

Str. Of all changes in the heavens, this is to be deemed the greatest and mightiest.

Υ. *Soc.* I should imagine that.

Str. And may be supposed to have resulted in the

greatest changes to the human beings who were the inhabitants of the world at the time.

Υ. *Soc.* That, again, is not unlikely.

Str. And animals, as we know, are seriously affected by great changes of many different kinds happening together.

Υ. *Soc.* Very true.

Str. Hence there necessarily occurred a great destruction of them, which extended also to the life of man; few survivors of the race were left, and those who remained became the subjects of several novel and remarkable phenomena, and of one in particular, which is simultaneous with the revulsion, and took place at the time when the transition was made to the cycle opposite to that in which we live.

Υ. *Soc.* What was that?

Str. The life of all animals first came to a stand, and the mortal nature ceased to be or look older, and was then reversed and grew young and delicate; the white locks of the aged darkened again, and the cheeks of the bearded man became smooth, and he was restored to his original youth; the bodies of the young grew finer and smaller, continually by day and night returning and becoming assimilated to the nature of a newly-born child in mind as well as body; in the succeeding stage they wasted away and wholly disappeared. And the bodies of those who had died by violence quickly passed through the like changes, and in a few days were no more seen.

Υ. *Soc.* Then how, Stranger, were the animals created in those days; and in what way were they begotten of one another?

Str. It is evident, Socrates, that there was no such thing in the then order of nature as the procreation of animals from one another; the primeval race, who were given back from the earth, was the one then in existence; and of this tradition, which is now-a-days often unduly discredited, our ancestors, who came into existence immediately after the end of the first period and at the beginning of this, are the heralds to us. For mark how consistent the sequel of the tale is; after the return of age to youth, follows the return of the dead, who are lying in the earth, to life; the wheel of their existence has been turned back, and they come together and rise and live in the opposite order, unless God has carried any of them away to some other lot. And these are the so-called earth-born men who, according to the tradition, of necessity came into existence, and this is the explanation of the term.

Υ. *Soc.* Certainly that is quite consistent with what has preceded; but let me interrupt you to ask whether the life which you said existed in the reign of Cronos was in that cycle of the world, or in this? For the change in the course of the stars and the sun might certainly have occurred in either.

Str. I see that you enter into my meaning; — no, that blessed and spontaneous life does not belong to the present cycle of the world, but to the previous one, in which God superintended the whole revolution of the universe; and the parts of the universe were distributed under the rule of certain inferior deities, which is the way in some places still. There were demigods, who were the shepherds of the various species and herds of animals, and each one was in all respects sufficient for those of whom he was the shepherd; neither was there any violence, or devouring of one another, or war or quarrel among them; and I might tell of ten thousand other blessings, which belonged to that dispensation. Now, the reason why the old fable speaks of the spontaneous life of man is as follows. In those days God himself was their shepherd, and ruled over them, just as man, who is by comparison a divine being, still rules over the animals. Under him there were no governments or separate possessions of women and children. For all men rose again from the earth, having no memory of any past events; and they had no property or families, but the earth gave them abundance of fruits, which grew on trees and shrubs unbidden, and were not planted by the hand of man. And they dwelt naked, and mostly in the open air, for the temperature of their seasons was mild; and they had no beds, but lay on soft couches of grass, which grew plentifully out of the earth. Such was the life of man in the days of Cronos, Socrates; the character of our present life, which is said to be under Zeus, you know from your own experience. Can you, and will you, determine which of them you deem the happier?

Y. *Soc.* I can not.

Str. Then shall I determine for you as well as I can?

Y. *Soc.* By all means.

Str. Suppose that the children of Cronos, having this boundless leisure, and the power of holding intercourse, not only with men but with the animal creation, had used all these advantages with a view to philosophy, conversing with the animals as well as with one another, and learning of every nature which was gifted with any special power, and was able to contribute some special experience to the store of wisdom, there would be no difficulty in determining which was the happier. Or, again, if they had merely eaten and drunk until they were full, and told stories to one another, and to the animals — such stories as are now told of them — in this case also, as I should imagine, the answer would be easy. But as there is no satisfactory reporter of the desires and thoughts of those times, I think that we must leave the question unanswered, and go at once to the point of the tale, and then we will proceed on our journey.

In the fulness of time, when the change was to take place, and the earth-born race had all perished, and every soul had fallen into the earth and been sown her appointed number of times, the governor of the universe let the helm go, and retired to his place of view; and then Fate and innate desire reversed the motion of the world. Then, also, all the other deities who share the rule of the supreme power, being informed of what was happening, let go the parts of the world of which they were severally the guardians. And the world turning round with a sudden shock, having received an opposite impulse at both ends, was shaken by a mighty earthquake, producing a new destruction of all manner of animals. After a while the tumult and confusion and earthquake ceased, and the universal creature, once more at peace, attained to a calm, and settled down into his own orderly and accustomed course, having the charge and rule of himself and of all other creatures, and remembering and executing the instructions of the Father and Creator of the world, more particularly at first, but afterwards with less exactness.

The reason of the falling off was the admixture of matter in the world; this was inherent in the primal nature, which was full of disorder, until attaining to the present cosmos or order. From God, the constructor, the world indeed received every good, but from a previous state came elements of violence and injustice, which, thence derived, were implanted in the animals. While the world was producing animals in unison with God, the evil was small, and great the good which worked within, but in the process of separation from him, when the world was let go, at first all proceeded well enough; then, as time went on, there was more and more forgetting, and the old discord again entered in and got the better, and burst forth; and at last small was the good, and great was the admixture of the elements of evil, and there was a danger of universal ruin of the world and the things in the world. Wherefore God, the orderer of all, seeing that the world was in great straits, fearing that all might be dissolved in the storm, and go to the place of chaos and infinity, again seated himself at the helm; and reversing the elements which had fallen into dissolution and disorder when left to themselves in the previous cycle, he set them in order and restored them, and made the world imperishable and immortal.

And this is the whole tale, of which the first part will suffice to illustrate the nature of the king. For when the world returned to the present cycle of generation, the age of man again stood still, and another change was the result. The small creatures which had almost disappeared grew in stature, and the newly-born children of the earth became grey and died and sank into the earth again. All things changed, imitating and following the condition of the universe, and agreeing with that in their mode of conception and generation and nurture; for no animal was any longer allowed to come into being in the earth through the agency of other creative beings, but as the world was ordained to be the lord of his own progress, in like manner the parts were ordained to grow and generate and give nourishment, as far as they could, of themselves, impelled by a similar movement.

And so we have arrived at the real end of this discourse; for although there might be much to tell of the lower animals, and of the reasons and causes of their changes, about men there is not much, and that little is more to the purpose. Deprived of the care of God, who had possessed and tended them when, in process of time, most of the animals who were by nature intractable had grown wild, they were left helpless and defenceless, and were torn in pieces by them; moreover, in the first ages they carried on the struggle for existence without arts or resources; the food which once grew spontaneously had failed, and they knew not how to procure any more, because no necessity had hitherto compelled them. For all these reasons they were in a great strait; wherefore, also the gifts spoken of in the old tradition were imparted to them by the gods, together with the indispensable knowledge and information of their uses; fire was given to us by Prometheus, the arts by Hephaestus and his fellow-worker (Athene), seeds and plants by others. Out of these human life was framed; since the care of the Gods, as I was saying, had now failed men, and they had to order their course of life for themselves, and were their own masters, just like the universal creature, whom they imitate and follow, ever living and being born into the world, at one time after this manner, at another time after another manner.

PHILEBUS

THE FIRST TASTE OF LOGIC. THE ART OF DIALECTIC

The Philebus is one of the more purely metaphysical dialogues of Plato, and was probably composed in his later years. The subject of the work may be briefly said to be, — " Pleasure in relation to Knowledge and to the Good," or, " The place of Pleasure in the life of man." Pleasures are divided into two classes, the pure and the impure kind; the latter have no part in the virtuous life; the former are allowed, but are placed last in the scale of goods. First comes measure; second, symmetry; third, reason; fourth, knowledge; fifth, the pure pleasures.

The passage which follows does not relate to the principal thesis of the dialogue, but is rather an account of the method in which Plato thinks that such an inquiry should be pursued. This is the " Dialectic " of which we so often hear in the Platonic writings. Yet there is a difference in his language in the Philebus when compared with that which he employs in other works, and especially in the Republic and Symposium. In these dialogues Dialectic is spoken of as the " steps " by which we mount from sensible objects to the contemplation of true being or the eternal beauty. This vague conception is not further explained by Plato in the Republic, and in the Sophist, the Statesman, and the Philebus, he returns to the more prosaic notion of Dialectic which he has already stated in the Phaedrus, where it is said to be the art by which the philosopher is enabled to divide things into their species, " according to the natural formation, where the joint is, not breaking any part as a bad carver might."

It is, therefore, a logical process of division and subdivision, closely analogous to what Aristotle calls his " customary method by which the compound is resolved into the elements or least parts of the whole." This seems to have been merely a passing phase of Plato's philosophy, when in his " warfare on behalf of mind " he felt the necessity, as he himself expresses it, " of hav-ing weapons of another make from those which he used before." In the Laws Dialectic occupies a far less important place, and is only the name given to the mode of carrying on the argument by question and answer, which affords a " suitable pastime " for the days of old age.

Soc. GOOD; and where shall we begin this great and comprehensive battle, in which such various points are at issue? Shall we begin thus?

Pro. How shall we begin?

Soc. We say that the one and many are identified by the reasoning power, and that they run about everywhere together, in and out of every word which is uttered, as they have done in all time present as well as past, and this will never cease, and is not now beginning, but is, as I believe, an everlasting quality of reason, as such, which never grows old in us. Any young man, when he first tastes these subtleties, is delighted, and fancies that he has found a treasure of wisdom; in the first enthusiasm of his joy he sets (not every stone, but) every thought rolling, now converting the many into the one, and kneading them together, now unfolding and dividing them; he puzzles himself first and above all, and then he proceeds to puzzle his neighbors, whether they are older or younger, or of his own age — that makes no difference; neither father nor mother does he spare; no human being who has ears is safe from him, hardly even his dog, and a barbarian would have no chance with him, if an interpreter could only be found.

Pro. Considering, Socrates, how many we are, and that all of us are young men, is there not a danger that we and Philebus may conspire and attack you, if you speak evil of us? Yet we understand; and if there is any better way or manner of quietly escaping out of all this trumoil and perplexity, and arriving at the truth, we hope that you will guide us into that way, and we will do our best to follow, for the inquiry in which we are engaged, Socrates, is not a small one.

Soc. Not a small one, my boys, as Philebus calls you, and there neither is nor ever will be a better than my own favorite way, which has nevertheless already often deserted me in the hour of need.

Pro. Tell us what that is?

Soc. One which may be easily explained, but is by no means easy of application, and is the parent of all the discoveries of the art.

Pro. Say only what.

Soc. A gift of heaven, which, as I conceive, the gods tossed into the world by the hands of some Prometheus. together with a blaze of fire; and the ancients, who were our betters and nearer the gods than we are, handed down the tradition, that all things which are supposed to exist draw their existence from the one and many, and have the finite and infinite in them as a part of their nature: seeing, then, that such is the order of the world, we too ought in all our investigations to assume that there is one idea of everything; this unity we shall be sure to find, and having found, we may next proceed to look for two, if there be two, or, if not, then for three or some other number, subdividing each of these units, until at last the original one is seen, not only as one and many and infinite, but also in some definite number; the infinite must not be suffered to approach the many until the entire number of the species intermediate between unity and infinity has been found out, — then, and not till then, we may rest from division, and all the remaining individuals may be allowed to pass into infinity.

This, as I was saying, is the way of considering and learning and teaching one another, which the gods have handed down to us. But the wise men of our time are either too quick or too slow in conceiving plurality in unity. Having no method, they make their one and many anyhow, and from unity pass at once to infinity, without thinking of the intermediate steps. And this, I repeat, is what makes the difference between the mere art of disputation and true dialectic.

TIMAEUS

1. THE TALE OF SOLON

THE Timaeus is connected by Plato himself with the Republic and the Critias. Socrates is supposed to have recounted on the following day the conversation recorded in the Republic to a circle of friends who have promised to deliver in turn a discourse upon some philosophical topic. The persons named are Timaeus, a citizen of Locri in Italy, Hermocrates, probably the famous Syracusan general, and Critias, the Athenian, who has previously appeared in the Charmides and Protagoras. A fifth member of the group, whose name is not mentioned, is said to have been absent through illness.

We hear nothing of any other auditors, and we miss the dramatic or artistic setting which enhances the effect of the earlier Platonic writings. In these respects the Timaeus seems akin to the Sophist and the Statesman, which it also resembles in the circumstance that Socrates is no longer the chief speaker, but a stranger who has come on a visit to Athens. Here Timaeus is the protagonist, no doubt because, as a native of Southern Italy, he could fitly expound a theory of the Cosmos which was to a considerable extent based upon Pythagorean ideas. His task is to explain how the world came into being, and how man and the animals were created. Before, however, Timaeus commences his speech, Critias relates in outline a story which he proposes to take for his theme on the morrow.

This is the famous legend of Atlantis, the great island which once existed in the Atlantic and afterwards sank beneath the waves. The tale has exercised a curious power of attraction over the imagination, which has lasted almost to our own time: the site of Atlantis has been gravely debated by learned writers, and has formed the subject of many treatises. Yet the story is probably only the birth of Plato's prolific fancy, or rests at most upon a vague tradition of a land beyond the Atlantic which had reached Athens from the Western Mediterranean. For it is not unreasonable to suppose that the nations who lived upon the verge of the great ocean may have dreamed of a " New World " on the other side, which their fancy would paint in bright and alluring colors as the seat of an ancient and primitive civilization. And it is even possible that the adventurous Phoenicians may have gained a knowledge of one or more of the Atlantic islands which would gradually come to the ears of the Greek sailors and merchants.

However this may be, the object of Plato in narrating the legend is clearly enough indicated by him. He wishes to picture, as he himself says, " the ideal state engaged in a conflict with her neighbors, and showing by her actions and the magnanimity of her words a result worthy of her training." He invents, therefore, an imaginary Athenian commonwealth which is supposed to have existed many centuries ago, and to have waged a victorious war with the people of Atlantis. This is at the same time an allegory or another version of the unceasing struggle between the Hellenes and the Barbarian, which so greatly occupied the Greek mind; and Plato's use of the legend may be compared to the manner in which Herodotus turns the ancient myth into a prelude of the Persian War.

Atlantis is the typical Barbarian power, like Babylon or Egypt, full of luxury and vain pomp and glory; while Athens is the Hellenic state, " endowed with slender means," but strong in the virtue and patriotism of its citizens. The conflict is unequal; yet the issue is not doubtful. Hellenic valor and discipline prevail, as they did when the Athenians and their allies triumphed over the unwieldy hosts of Persia on the plains of Marathon, or when Xenophon led the Ten Thousand through the heart of the Persian empire to the shores of the Pontus.

Crit. THEN listen, Socrates, to a strange tale which is, however, certainly true, as Solon, who was the wisest of the seven sages, declared. He was a relative and a great friend of my great-grandfather, Dropidas, as he himself says in several of his poems; and Dropidas told Critias, my grandfather, who remembered and told us: — That there were of old great and marvellous actions of the Athenians, which have passed into oblivion through time and the destruction of the human race, and one in particular, which was the greatest of them all, the recital of which will be a suitable testimony of our gratitude to you, and also a hymn of praise true and worthy of the goddess, which may be sung by us at the festival in her honor.

Soc. Very good. And what is this ancient famous action of which Critias spoke not as a mere legend, but as a veritable action of the Athenian state, which Solon recounted?

Crit. I will tell an old-world story which I heard from an aged man; for Critias was, as he said, at that time nearly ninety years of age, and I was about ten years of age. Now the day was that day of the Apaturia which is called the registration of youth, at which, according to custom, our parents gave prizes for recitations, and the poems of several poets were recited by us boys, and many of us sang the poems of Solon, which were new at the time. One of our tribe, either because this was his real opinion, or because he thought that he would please Critias, said that in his judgment Solon was not only the wisest of men, but also the noblest of poets. The old man, as I very well remember, brightened up at this and said, smiling: Yes, Amynander, if Solon had only, like other poets, made poetry the business of his life, and had completed the tale which he brought with him from Egypt, and had not been compelled, by reason of the factions and troubles which he found stirring in this country when he came home, to attend to other matters, in my opinion he would have been as famous as Homer or Hesiod, or any poet.

And what was the poem about, Critias? said the person who addressed him.

About the greatest action which the Athenians ever did, and which ought to have been the most famous, but which, through the lapse of time and the destruction of the actors, has not come down to us.

Tell us, said the other, the whole story, and how and from whom Solon heard this veritable tradition.

He replied: — At the head of the Egyptian Delta, where the river Nile divides, there is a certain district which is called the district of Sais, and the great city of the district is also called Sais, and is the city from which Amasis the king was sprung. And the citizens have a deity who is their foundress; she is called in the Egyptian tongue Neith, and is asserted by them to be the same whom the Hellenes called Athene. Now the citizens of this city are great lovers of the Athenians, and say that they are in some way related to them.

Thither came Solon, who was received by them with great honor; and he asked the priests, who were most skilful in such matters, about antiquity, and made the discovery that neither he nor any other Hellene knew anything worth mentioning about the times of old. On one occasion, when he was drawing them on to speak of antiquity, he began to tell about the most ancient things in our part of the world — about Phroneus, who is called "the first," and about Niobe; and after the Deluge, to tell of the lives of Deucalion and Pyrrha; and he traced the genealogy of their descendants, and attempted to reckon how many years old were the events of which he was speaking, and to give the dates. Thereupon, one of the priests, who was of a very great age, said: O Solon, Solon, you Hellenes are but children, and there is never an old man who is an Hellene. Solon hearing this, said, What do you mean?

I mean to say, he replied, that in mind you are all young; there is no old opinion handed down among you by ancient tradition; nor any science which is hoary with age. And I will tell you the reason of this. There have been, and will be again, many destructions of mankind arising out of many causes; the greatest have been brought about by the agencies of fire and water, and other lesser ones by innumerable other causes. There is a story which even you have preserved, that once upon a time Phaëthon, the son of Helios, having yoked the steeds in his father's chariot, because he was not able to drive them in the path of his father, burned up all that was upon the earth, and was himself destroyed by a thunderbolt. Now, this has the form of a myth, but really signifies a declination of the bodies moving around the earth and in the heavens, and a great conflagration of things upon the earth recurring at long intervals of time; when this happens, those who live upon the mountains and in dry and lofty places are more liable to destructions than those who dwell by rivers or on the seashore. And from this calamity the Nile, who is our never-failing savior, saves and delivers us.

When, on the other hand, the gods purge the earth with a deluge of water, among you, herdsmen and shepherds on the mountains are the survivors, whereas those of you who live in cities are carried by the rivers into the sea. But in this country, neither at that time nor at any other, does the water come from above on the fields, having always a tendency to come up from below, for which reason the things preserved here are said to be the oldest. The fact is, that wherever the extremity of winter frost or of summer sun does not prevent, the human race is always increasing at times, and at other times diminishing in numbers. And whatever happened either in your country or in ours, or in any other region of which we are informed — if any action which is noble or great or in any other way remarkable has taken place, all that has been written down of old, and is preserved in our temples; whereas you and other nations are just being provided with letters and the other things which States require; and then, at the usual period, the stream from heaven descends like a pestilence, and leaves only those of you who are destitute of letters and education; and thus you have to begin all over again as children, and know nothing of what happened in ancient times, either among us or among yourselves.

As for those genealogies of yours which you have recounted to us, Solon, they are no better than the tales of children; for in the first place you remember one deluge only, whereas there were many of them; and in the next place, you do not know that there dwelt in your land the fairest and noblest race of men which ever lived, of whom you and your whole city are but a seed or remnant. And this was unknown to you, because for many generations the survivors of that destruction died and made no sign. For there was a time, Solon, before the great deluge of all, when the city which now is Athens, was first in war and was preëminent for the excellence of her laws, and is said to have performed the noblest deeds and to have had the fairest constitution of any of which tradition tells, under the face of heaven. Solon marvelled at this, and earnestly requested the priest to inform him exactly and in order about these former citizens.

You are welcome to hear about them, Solon, said the priest, both for your own sake and for that of the city, and above all, for the sake of the goddess who is the common patron and protector and educator of both our cities. She founded your city a thousand years before ours, receiving from the Earth and Hephaestus the seed of your race, and then she founded ours, the constitution of which is set down in our sacred registers as 8000 years old. As touching the citizens of 9000 years ago, I will briefly inform you of their laws and of the noblest of their actions; and the exact particulars of the whole we will hereafter go through at our leisure in the sacred registers themselves. If you compare these very laws with your own you will find that many of ours are the counterpart of yours as they were in the olden time. In the first place, there is the caste of priests, which is separated from all the others; next there are the artificers, who exercise their several crafts by themselves and without admixture of any other; and also there is the class of shepherds and that of hunters, as well as that of husbandmen; and you will observe, too, that the warriors in Egypt are separated from all the other classes, and are commanded by the law only to engage in war; moreover, the weapons with which they are equipped are shields and spears, and this the goddess taught first among you, and then in Asiatic countries, and we among the Asiatics first adopted. Then as to wisdom, do you observe what care the law took from the very first, searching out and comprehending the whole order of things down to prophecy and medicine (the latter with a view to health) ; and out of these divine elements drawing what was needful for human life, and adding every sort of knowledge which was connected with them.

All this order and arrangement the goddess first imparted to you when establishing your city; and she chose the spot of earth in which you were born, because she saw that the happy temperament of the seasons in that land would produce the wisest of men. Wherefore the goddess who was a lover both of war and of wisdom, selected and first of all settled that spot which was the most likely to produce men likest herself. And there you dwelt, having such laws as these and still better ones, and excelled all mankind in all virtue as became the children and disciples of the gods.

Many great and wonderful deeds are recorded of your State in our histories. But one of them exceeds all the rest in greatness and valor. For these his-

tories tell of a mighty power which was aggressing
wantonly against the whole of Europe and Asia, and
to which your city put an end. This power came forth
out of the Atlantic Ocean, for in those days the Atlantic was navigable; and there was an island situated
in front of the straits which you call the columns of
Heracles; the island was larger than Libya and Asia
put together, and was the way to other islands, and
from the islands you might pass to the whole of the
opposite continent which surrounded the true ocean;
for this sea which is within the Straits of Heracles
is only a harbor, having a narrow entrance, but that
other is a real sea, and the surrounding land may be
most truly called a continent.

Now in this island of Atlantis there was a great
and wonderful empire which had rule over the whole
island and several others, as well as over parts of the
continent, and, besides these, they subjected the parts
of Libya within the columns of Heracles as far as
Egypt, and of Europe as far as Tyrrhenia. The vast
power thus gathered into one, endeavored to subdue
at one blow our country and yours and the whole of
the land which was within the straits; and then, Solon,
your country shone forth, in the excellence of her virtue and strength, among all mankind; for she was
first in courage and military skill, and was the leader
of the Hellenes. And when the rest fell off from her,
being compelled to stand alone, after having under-
gone the very extremity of danger, she defeated and
triumphed over the invaders, and preserved from slavery those who were not yet subjected, and freely
liberated all the others who dwell within the limits
of Heracles. But afterwards there occurred violent
earthquakes and floods; and in a single day and night
of rain all your warlike men in a body sank into the
earth, and the island of Atlantis in like manner dis-

appeared, and was sunk beneath the sea. And that is the reason why the sea in those parts is impassable and impenetrable, because there is such a quantity of shallow mud in the way; and this was caused by the subsidence of the island.

I have told you shortly, Socrates, the tradition which the aged Critias heard from Solon. And when you were speaking yesterday about your city and citizens, this very tale which I am telling you came into my mind, and I could not help remarking how, by some coincidence not to be explained, you agreed in almost every particular with the account of Solon; but I did not like to speak at the moment. For as a long time had elapsed, I had forgotten too much, and I thought that I had better first of all run over the narrative in my own mind and then I would speak. And for this reason I readily assented to your request yesterday, considering that I was pretty well furnished with a theme such as the audience would approve, and to find this is in all such cases the chief difficulty.

And therefore, as Hermocrates has told you, on my way home yesterday I imparted my recollections to my friends in order to refresh my memory, and during the night I thought about the words and have nearly recovered them all. Truly, as is often said, the lessons which we have learned as children make a wonderful impression on our memories, for I am not sure that I could remember all that I heard yesterday, but I should be much surprised if I forgot any of these things which I have heard very long ago. I listened to the old man telling them, when a child, with great interest at the time; he was very ready to teach me, and I asked him about them a great many times, so that they were branded into my mind in ineffaceable letters. As soon as the day broke I began to repeat them to my companions, that they as well as myself might have a material of discourse.

And now, Socrates, I am ready to tell you the whole tale of which this is the introduction. I will give you not only the general heads, but the details exactly as I heard them. And as to the city and citizens, which you yesterday described to us in fiction, let us transfer them to the world of reality; this shall be our city, and we will suppose that the citizens whom you imagined, were our veritable ancestors — the same of whom the priest was telling; they will perfectly agree, and there will be no inconsistency in saying that the citizens of your republic are these ancient Athenians.

2. THE BALANCE OF MIND AND BODY

The Timaeus, after the close of the Introduction, is a monologue unbroken by any of the auditors. Timaeus gives a description of the Cosmos, in which he enlarges upon the Creation of the World and of Man, the Starry System, the Four Elements, the Senses, the Nature of Disease, the Parts of the Soul, the Fate of the Soul after Death, and other kindred topics. Towards the end of his discourse he takes occasion to speak of a subject, which, although not immediately connected with the main scheme of the work, is of the highest interest and importance — the relation of the Soul to the Body, and the influence which each of them exercises upon the other.

Plato is here enforcing from a rather different side the lesson which he has already taught us in the Republic, that the cultivation of the mind and the training of the body ought to be pursued in common. He perhaps exaggerates the necessity of harmony between the soul and the bodily frame; for many instances might be quoted in which the very weaknesses and infirmities of the body seem not to have hindered, but even to have quickened and stimulated, the intellectual powers. Yet it is also hardly possible to doubt that a certain sobriety and sanity of judgment is enjoyed by the happy possessor of a healthy and robust constitution. He is freer from morbid and unwholesome thoughts, and his outlook on life is brighter and more cheerful.

In this respect Plato may have been to some extent influenced by the antipathy to deformity and suffering which forms a marked characteristic of the Hellenic temper: and the same spirit is apparently betrayed by the manner in which he speaks of the inutility of attempting to contend against disease, just as in the Republic he derides Herodicus, the " inventor of valetudinarianism," who taught men to protract a useless existence to extreme old age, and to spend on the care of their bodies the time which would have been better employed on the improvement of their minds.

There is a corresponding inquiry concerning the modes in which the mind and the body are to be treated, and by what means they are preserved, on which I may and ought to enter; for it is more our duty to speak of the good than of the evil. Everything that is good is fair, and the fair is not without measure, and the animal who is fair may be supposed to have measure. Now we perceive lesser symmetries and comprehend them, but about the highest and greatest we have no understanding; for with a view to health and disease, and virtue and vice, there is no symmetry or want of symmetry greater than that of the soul to the body; and this we do not perceive, or ever reflect that when a weaker or lesser frame is the vehicle of a great and mighty soul, or conversely, when they are united in the opposite way, then the whole animal is not fair, for it is defective in the most important of all symmetries; but the fair mind in the fair body will be the fairest and loveliest of all sights to him who has the seeing eye. Just as a body which has a leg too long, or some other disproportion, is an unpleasant sight, and also, when undergoing toil, has many sufferings, and makes violent efforts, and often stumbles through awkwardness, and is the cause of infinite evil to its own self — in like manner we should conceive of the double nature which we

call the living being; and when in this compound
there is an impassioned soul more powerful than the
body, that soul, I say, convulses and disorders the
whole inner nature of man; and when too eager in
the pursuit of knowledge, causes wasting; or again,
when teaching or disputing in private or in public,
and strifes and controversies arise, inflames and dissolves the composite frame of man and introduces
rheums; and the nature of this is not understood by
most professors of medicine, who ascribe the phenomenon to the opposite of the real cause. And once
more, when a body large and too much for the soul
is united to a small and weak intelligence, seeing that
there are two desires natural to man, — one of food
for the sake of the body, and one of wisdom for the
sake of the diviner part of us — then, I say, the motions of the stronger principle, getting the better and
increasing their own power, but making the soul dull,
and stupid, and forgetful, engender ignorance, which
is the greatest of diseases.

There is one protection against both: — that we
should not move the body without the soul or the soul
without the body, and thus they will aid one another,
and be healthy and well balanced. And therefore the
mathematician or any one else who devotes himself to
some intellectual pursuit, must allow his body to have
motion also, and practise gymnastic; and he who
would train the limbs of the body, should impart to
them the motions of the soul, and should practise
music and all philosophy, if he would be called truly
fair and truly good.

And in like manner should the parts be treated,
and the principle of the whole similarly applied to
them; for as the body is heated and also cooled within
by the elements which enter in, and is again dried up
and moistened by external things, and experiences

these and the like affections from both kinds of motions, the result is that the body if given up to motion when in a state of quiescence is overmastered and destroyed; but if any one, in imitation of that which we call the foster-mother and nurse of the universe, will not allow the body to be at rest, but is always producing motions and shakings, which constantly react upon the natural motions both within and without, and by shaking moderately the affections and parts which wander about the body, brings them into order and affinity with one another according to the theory of the universe which we were maintaining, he will not allow enemy placed by the side of enemy to create wars and disorders in the body, but he will place friend by the side of friend, producing health.

Now of all motions that is the best which is produced in a thing by itself, for it is most akin to the motion of the intelligent and the motion of the universe; but that motion which is caused by others is not so good, and worst of all is that which moves the parts of the body, when prostrate and at rest, in parts only and by external means; wherefore also that is the best of the purifications and adjustments of the body which is effected by gymnastic; next is that which is effected by carrying the body, as in sailing or any other mode of conveyance which is not fatiguing; the third sort of motion may be of use in a case of extreme necessity, but in any other will be adopted by no man of sense: I mean the purgative treatment of physicians; for diseases which are not attended by great dangers should not be irritated by purgatives, for every form of disease is in a manner akin to the living being — for the combination out of which they were formed has an appointed term of life and of existence. And the whole race and every animal has his appointed natural time, apart from violent casualties; for the triangles are originally framed with power to live for a certain time, beyond which no man can prolong his life. And this holds also of the nature of diseases, for if any one regardless of their appointed time would destroy nature by purgatives, he only increases and multiplies them. Wherefore we ought always to manage them by regimen, as far as a man can spare the time, and not provoke a disagreeable enemy by medical treatment.

Let this much be said of the general nature of man, and of the body which is a part of him, and of the manner in which a man may govern himself and be governed best, and live most according to reason: and we must begin by providing that the governing principle shall be the fairest and best possible for the purpose of government. But to discuss such a subject accurately would be a sufficiently long business of itself. As a mere supplement or sequel of what has preceded, it may be summed up as follows. As I have often said, that there are three kinds of soul located within us, each of them having their own proper motions —so I must now say in the fewest words possible, that the one part, if remaining inactive and ceasing from the natural motion, must necessarily become very weak, but when trained and exercised then very strong. Wherefore we should take care that the three parts of the soul are exercised in proportion to one another.

Concerning the highest part of the human soul, we should consider that God gave this as a genius to each one, which was to dwell at the extremity of the body, and to raise us like plants, not of an earthly but of a heavenly growth, from earth to our kindred which is in heaven. And this is most true; for the divine power suspended the head and root of us from that place where the generation of the soul first began, and thus made erect the whole body. He, therefore, who is always occupied with the cravings of desire and ambition, and is eagerly striving after them, must have all his opinions mortal, and, as far as man can be, must be all of him mortal, because he has cherished his mortal part. But he who has been earnest in the love of knowledge and true wisdom, and has been trained to think that these are the immortal and divine things of a man, if he attain truth, must of necessity, as far as human nature is capable of attaining immortality, be all immortal, as he is ever serving the divine power; and having the genius residing in him in the most perfect order, he must be preëminently happy.

Now there is only one way in which one being can serve another, and this is by giving him his proper nourishment and motion. And the motions which are akin to the divine principle within us are the thoughts and revolutions of the universe. These each man should follow, and correct those corrupted courses of the head which are concerned with generation, and by learning the harmonies and revolutions of the whole, should assimilate the perceiver to the thing perceived, according to his original nature, and by thus assimilating them, attain that final perfection of life, which the gods set before mankind as best, both for the present and the future.

CRITIAS

OR THE ISLAND OF ATLANTIS

THE legend of Atlantis is resumed in the Critias, but the story is abruptly broken off a short way from the commencement. Why the work was not completed by Plato, we can not say. He may have found the task too difficult even for his artistic powers. The theme would scarcely bear elaboration, nor could the result, we may think, have been entirely satisfactory. Allegory and satire have generally been most successful in proportion to their shortness; longer writings of this class are apt to retain only a romantic or a poetical interest for the reader, while their deeper meaning is forgotten or ignored.

It is, however, possible that Plato may have been compelled by circumstances of which we are ignorant to " leave half-told " the myth of Atlantis. We may please ourselves, if we choose, by imagining that the second or third journey which Plato is alleged to have made to Sicily was the cause of the interruption. Yet such a conjecture does not give us any real assistance, and we must be content to let the question, like so many other literary problems, remain without an answer.

Timaeus. How thankful I am, Socrates, that I have arrived at last, and, like a weary traveller after a long journey, may now be at rest! And I pray the being who always was of old, and has now been by me declared, to receive and preserve my words, in so far as they have been spoken truly and acceptably to him; and if unintentionally I have said anything wrong, I pray that he will impose upon me a fitting retribution, and the proper retribution of him who errs is to set him in the right way. Wishing, then, that for the future I may speak truly concerning the generation of the gods, I pray them to give me knowledge, which of all medicines is the most perfect and best. — That is my prayer. And now I deliver the argument into the hands of Critias, according to our agreement.

Critias. And I, Timaeus, accept the trust, and as you at first said that you were going to speak of high matters, and begged that some allowance might be extended to you, I must request the same or a greater allowance for what I am about to say. And although I very well know that I am making an ambitious and a somewhat rude request, I must not be deterred by that. For will any man of sense deny that you have spoken well? I can only attempt to show that my theme is more difficult, and claims more indulgence than yours; and I shall argue that to seem to speak well of the gods to men is far easier than to speak well of mortals to one another: for the inexperience and utter ignorance of his hearers about such matters is a great assistance to him who has to speak of them, and we know how ignorant we are concerning the gods. But I should like to make my meaning clearer, if you will follow me.

All that we are any of us saying can only be imitation and assimilation. For if we consider how the works of the painter represent bodies divine and heavenly, and the different degrees of gratification with which the eye of the spectator receives them, we shall see that we are satisfied with the artist who is able in any degree to imitate the earth and its mountains, and the rivers, and the woods, and the universe, and the things that are and move therein, and further, that knowing nothing precise about such matters, we do not examine or analyze the painting; all that is required is a sort of indistinct and deceptive mode of shadowing them forth. But when a person endeavors to paint the human form we are quick at finding out defects, and our familiar knowledge makes us severe judges of any one who does not render every point of similarity; and this is also true of discourse; we are satisfied with a picture of divine and heavenly things which has very little likeness to them; but we are more precise in our criticism of mortal and human things. Wherefore if at the moment of speaking we can not suitably express what we mean, you must excuse us, considering that to form approved likenesses of human things is the reverse of easy. This is what I want to suggest to you, and at the same time to beg, Socrates, that I may have not less, but more indulgence conceded to me in what I am about to say. Which favor, if I am right in asking, I hope that you will be ready to grant.

Socrates. Certainly, Critias, we will grant that, and we will grant the same by anticipation to Hermocrates, who has to speak third; for I have no doubt that when his turn comes a little while hence, he will make the same request which you have made. In order, then, that he may provide himself with a fresh beginning, and not be compelled to say the same things over again, let him understand that the indulgence is already extended by anticipation to him. And now, friend Critias, I will announce to you the judgment of the theatre. They are of opinion that the last performer was wonderfully successful, and that you will need a great deal of indulgence if you are to rival him.

Hermocrates. The warning, Socrates, which you have addressed to him, I must also regard as applying to myself. But remember, Critias, that faint heart never yet raised a trophy; you must go and attack the argument like a man. First invoke Apollo and the Muses, and then let us hear you sing the praises of your ancient citizens.

Crit. Friend Hermocrates, you who are stationed last and have another in front of you, have not lost heart as yet; whether you are right or not, you will soon know; meanwhile I accept your exhortations and encouragements. But in addition to the gods whom you have mentioned, I would specially invoke Mnemosyne; for all the important part of what I have to tell is dependent on her favor, and if I can recollect and recite enough of what was said by the priests and brought hither by Solon, I doubt not that I shall satisfy the requirements of this theatre. To that task then I will at once address myself.

Let me begin by observing first of all, that nine thousand was the sum of years which had elapsed since the war which was said to have taken place between all those who dwelt outside the pillars of Heracles and those who dwelt within them; this war I am now to describe. Of the combatants on the one side, the city of Athens was reported to have been the ruler and to have directed the contest; the combatants on the other side were led by the kings of the islands of Atlantis, which, as I was saying, once had an extent greater than that of Libya and Asia; and when afterwards sunk by an earthquake, became an impassable barrier of mud to voyagers sailing from hence to the ocean. The progress of the history will unfold the various tribes of barbarians and Hellenes which then existed, as they successively appear on the scene; but I must begin by describing first of all the Athenians, as they were in that day, and their enemies who fought with them; and I shall have to tell of the power and form of government of both of them. Let us give the precedence to Athens:

In former ages, the gods had the whole earth distributed among them by allotment; there was no quarrelling; and you can not suppose that the gods did not know what was proper for each of them to have; or, knowing this, that they would seek to procure for themselves by contention that which more properly belonged to others. Each of them obtained righteously by lot what they wanted, and peopled their own districts ; and when they had peopled them they tended us human beings who belonged to them as shepherds tend their flocks, excepting only that they did not use blows or bodily force, as the manner of shepherds is, but governed us like pilots from the stern of a vessel, which is an easy way of guiding animals, by the rudder of persuasion, taking hold of our souls according to their own pleasure; — thus did they guide all mortal creatures.

Now different gods had their inheritance in different places which they set in order. Hephaestus and Athene, who were brother and sister, and sprang from the same father, having a common nature, and being united also in the love of philosophy and of art, both obtained as their allotted region this land, which was naturally adapted for wisdom and virtue; and there they implanted brave children of the soil, and put into their minds the order of government; their names are preserved, but their actions have disappeared by reason of the destruction of those who had the tradition, and the lapse of ages. For the survivors of each destruction, as I have already said, dwelt in the mountains; they were ignorant of the art of writing, and had heard only the names of the chiefs of the land, and a very little about their actions. The names they gave to their children out of affection, but of the virtues and laws of those who preceded them, they knew only by obscure traditions; and as they themselves and their children were for many generations in want of the necessaries of life, they directed their attention to the supply of their wants, and of that they discoursed, to the neglect of events that had happened in times long passed; for mythology and the inquiry into antiquity are introduced into cities when they have leisure, and when they see the necessaries of life already beginning to be provided, but not before. And this is the reason why the names of the ancients have been preserved to us without their deeds. This I infer because Solon said that the priests in their narrative of that war mentioned most of the names which are recorded prior to the time of Theseus, such as Cecrops, and Erechtheus, and Erichthonius, and Erysichthon, and the names of the women in like manner. Moreover, the figure and image of the goddess show that at that time military pursuits were common to men and women, and that in accordance with that custom they dedicated the armed image of the goddess as a testimony that all animals, male and female, which consort together, have a virtue proper to each class, which they are all able to pursue in common.

Now the country was inhabited in those days by various classes of citizens; — there were artisans, and there were husbandmen, and there was a warrior class originally set apart by divine men; these dwelt by themselves, and had all things suitable for nurture and education; neither had any of them anything of their own, but they regarded all things as common property; nor did they require to receive of the other citizens anything more than their necessary food. And they practised all the pursuits which we yesterday described as those of our imaginary guardians. Also about the country the Egyptian priests said what is not only probable but also true, that the boundaries were fixed by the Isthmus, and that in the other direction they extended as far as the heights of Cithaeron and Parnes; the boundary line came down towards the plain, having the district of Oropus on the right, and the river Asopus on the left, as the limit towards the sea. The land was the best in the world, and for this reason was able in those days to support a vast army, raised from the surrounding people. And a great proof of this fertility is, that the part which still remains may compare with any in the world for the variety and excellence of its fruits and the suitableness of its pastures to every sort of animal; and besides beauty the land had also plenty.

How am I to prove this? and of what remnant

of the land then in existence may this be truly said?
I would have you observe the present aspect of the
country, which is only a promontory extending far
into the sea away from the rest of the continent, and
the surrounding basin of the sea is everywhere deep
in the neighborhood of the shore. Many great deluges have taken place during the nine thousand years,
for that is the number of years which have elapsed
since the time of which I am speaking; and in all the
ages and changes of things, there has never been any
settlement of the earth flowing down from the mountains as in other places, which is worth speaking of;
it has always been carried round in a circle and disappeared in the depths below.

The consequence is, that in comparison of what
then was, there are remaining in small islets only the
bones of the wasted body, as they may be called; all
the richer and softer parts of the soil having fallen
away, and the mere skeleton of the country being left.
But in former days, and in the primitive state of the
country, what are now mountains were only regarded
as hills; and the plains, as they are now termed, of
Phelleus were full of rich earth, and there was abundance of wood in the mountains. Of this last the
traces still remain, for there are some of the mountains which now only afford sustenance to bees,
whereas not long ago there were still remaining roofs
cut from the trees growing there, which were of a
size sufficient to cover the largest houses; and there
were many other high trees, bearing fruit and abundance of food for cattle. Moreover, the land enjoyed
rain from heaven year by year, not, as now, losing
the water which flows off the earth into the sea, but
having an abundance in all places, and receiving and
treasuring up in the close clay soil the water which
drained from the heights, and letting this off into the

hollows, providing everywhere abundant streams of fountains and rivers; and there may still be observed indications of them in ancient sacred places, where there are fountains; and this proves the truth of what I am saying.

Such was the natural state of the country, which was cultivated, as we may well believe, by true husbandmen, who were lovers of honor, and of a noble nature, and did the work of husbandmen, and had a soil the best in the world, and abundance of water, and in the heaven above an excellently tempered climate. Now the city in those days was arranged on this wise; in the first place the Acropolis was not as now. For the fact is that a single night of excessive rain washed away the earth and laid bare the rock; at the same time there were earthquakes, and then occurred the third extraordinary inundation, which immediately preceded the great destruction of Deucalion. But in primitive times the hill of the Acropolis extended to the Eridanus and Ilissus, and included the Pnyx and the Lycabettus as a boundary on the opposite side to the Pnyx, and was all well covered with soil, and level at the top, except in one or two places. Outside the Acropolis and on the sides of the hill there dwelt artisans, and such of the husbandmen as were tilling the ground near; at the summit the warrior class dwelt by themselves around the temples of Athene and Hephaestus, living as in the garden of one house, and surrounded by one enclosure.

On the north side they had common houses, and had prepared for themselves winter places for common meals, and had all the buildings which they needed for the public use, and also temples, but unadorned with gold and silver, for these were not in use among them; they took a middle course between meanness and extravagance, and built moderate

houses in which they and their children's children
grew old, and handed them down to others who were
like themselves, always the same. And in summer-
time they gave up their gardens and gymnasia and
common tables and used the southern quarter of the
Acropolis for such purposes. Where the Acropolis
now is there was a single fountain, which was extinguished by the earthquake, and has left only a few
small streams which still exist, but in those days the
fountain gave an abundant supply of water, which
was of equal temperature in summer and winter.
This was the fashion in which they lived, being the
guardians of their own citizens and the leaders of the
Hellenes, who were their willing followers. And
they took care to preserve the same number of men
and women for military service, which was to continue through all time, and still is, — that is to say,
about twenty thousand.

Such were the ancient Athenians, and after this
manner they righteously administered their own land
and the rest of Hellas; they were renowned all over
Europe and Asia for the beauty of their persons and
for the many virtues of their souls, and were more
famous than any of their contemporaries. And next,
if I have not forgotten what I heard when I was a
child, I will impart to you the character and origin
of their adversaries. For friends should not keep
their stories to themselves, but have them in common.

Yet, before proceeding further in the narrative, I
ought to warn you, that you must not be surprised if
you should hear Hellenic names given to foreigners.
I will tell you the reason of this: Solon, who was
intending to use the tale for his poem, made an investigation into the meaning of the names, and found
that the early Egyptians in writing them down had
translated them into their own language, and he re-

covered the meaning of the several names and re-translated them, and copied them out again in our language. My great-grandfather, Dropidas, had the original writing, which is still in my possession, and was carefully studied by me when I was a child. Therefore if you hear names such as are used in this country, you must not be surprised, for I have told you the reason of them. The tale, which was of great length, began as follows: —

I have before remarked in speaking of the allot-ments of the gods, that they distributed the whole earth into portions differing in extent, and made themselves temples and sacrifices. And Poseidon, re-ceiving for his lot the island of Atlantis, begat chil-dren by a mortal woman, and settled them in a part of the island, which I will proceed to describe. On the side towards the sea and in the centre of the whole island, there was a plain which is said to have been the fairest of all plains and very fertile. Near the plain again, and also in the centre of the island at a distance of about fifty stadia, there was a mountain not very high on any side. In this mountain there dwelt one of the earth-born primeval men of that country, whose name was Evenor, and he had a wife named Leucippe, and they had an only daughter who was called Cleito. The maiden was growing up to womanhood, when her father and mother died; Poseidon fell in love with her and had intercourse with her, and breaking the ground, inclosed the hill in which she dwelt all round, making alternate zones of sea and land larger and smaller, encircling one an-other; there were two of land and three of water, which he turned as with a lathe, out of the centre of the island, equidistant every way, so that no man could get to the island, for ships and voyages were not as yet heard of. He himself, as he was a god,

found no difficulty in making special arrangements
for the centre island, bringing two streams of water
under the earth, which he caused to ascend as springs,
one of warm water and the other of cold, and making
every variety of food to spring up abundantly in the
earth.

He also begat and brought up five pairs of male
children, dividing the island of Atlantis into ten
portions; he gave to the first-born of the eldest pair
his mother's dwelling and the surrounding allotment,
which was the largest and best, and made him king
over the rest; the others he made princes, and gave
them rule over many men, and a large territory.
And he named them all; the eldest, who was the king,
he named Atlas, and from him the whole island and
the ocean received the name of Atlantic. To his twin
brother, who was born after him, and obtained as his
lot the extremity of the island towards the pillars of
Heracles, as far as the country which is still called
the region of Gades in that part of the world, he gave
the name which in the Hellenic language is Eumelus,
in the language of the country which is named after
him, Gadeirus. Of the second pair of twins he called
one Ampheres, and the other Evaemon. To the third
pair of twins he gave the name Mneseus to the elder,
and Autochthon to the one who followed him. Of
the fourth pair of twins he called the elder Elasippus,
and the younger Mestor. And of the fifth pair he
gave to the elder the name of Azaes, and to the
younger that of Diaprepes. All these and their descendants were the inhabitants and rulers of divers
islands in the open sea; and also, as has been already
said, they held sway in the other direction over the
country within the pillars as far as Egypt and Tyrrhenia.

Now Atlas had a numerous and honorable family,

and his eldest branch always retained the kingdom,
which the eldest son handed on to his eldest for many
generations; and they had such an amount of wealth
as was never before possessed by kings and potentates,
and is not likely ever to be again, and they were furnished with everything which they could have, both in
the city and country. For because of the greatness
of their empire many things were brought to them
from foreign countries, and the island itself provided
much of what was required by them for the uses of
life. In the first place, they dug out of the earth
whatever was to be found there, mineral as well as
metal, and that which is now only a name and was
then something more than a name, orichalcum, was
dug out of the earth in many parts of the island, and
with the exception of gold was esteemed the most
precious of metals among the men of those days.
There was an abundance of wood for carpenter's
work, and sufficient maintenance for tame and wild
animals.

Moreover, there were a great number of elephants
in the island, and there was provision for animals of
every kind, both for those which live in lakes and
marshes and rivers, and also for those which live in
mountains and on plains, and therefore for the animal
which is the largest and most voracious of them. Also
whatever fragrant things there are in the earth,
whether roots, or herbage, or woods, or distilling drops
of flowers or fruits, grew and thrived in that land;
and again, the cultivated fruit of the earth, both the
dry edible fruit and other species of food, which we
call by the general name of legumes, and the fruits
having a hard rind, affording drinks and meats and
ointments, and good store of chestnuts and the like,
which may be used to play with, and are fruits which
spoil with keeping, and the pleasant kinds of dessert

which console us after dinner, when we are full and
tired of eating — all these that sacred island lying
beneath the sun, brought forth fair and wondrous in
infinite abundance. All these things they received
from the earth, and they employed themselves in constructing their temples and palaces and harbors and
docks; and they arranged the whole country in the
following manner: —

First of all they bridged over the zones of sea which
surrounded the ancient metropolis, and made a passage into and out of the royal palace; and then they
began to build the palace in the habitation of the god
and of their ancestors. This they continued to ornament in successive generations, every king surpassing
the one who came before him to the utmost of his
power, until they made the building a marvel to behold for size and for beauty. And beginning from
the sea they dug a canal of three hundred feet in width
and one hundred feet in depth, and fifty stadia in
length, which they carried through to the uttermost
zone, making a passage from the sea up to this, which
became a harbor, and leaving an opening sufficient to
enable the largest vessel to find ingress. Moreover,
they divided the zones of land which parted the zones
of sea, constructing bridges of such a width as would
leave a passage for a single trireme to pass out of one
into another, and roofed them over; and there was a
way underneath for the ships; for the banks of the
zones were raised considerably above the water. Now
the largest of the zones into which a passage was cut
from the sea was three stadia in breadth, and the zone
of land which came next of equal breadth; but the
next two, as well the zone of water as of land, were
two stadia, and the one which surrounded the central
island was a stadium only in width.

The island in which the palace was situated had **a**

diameter of five stadia. This and the zones and the bridge, which was the sixth part of a stadium in width, they surrounded by a stone wall, on either side placing towers, and gates on the bridges where the sea passed in. The stone which was used in the work they quarried from underneath the centre island, and from underneath the zones, on the outer as well as the inner side. One kind of stone was white, another black, and a third red, and as they quarried, they at the same time hollowed out rocks double within, having roofs formed out of the native rock. Some of their buildings were simple, but in others they put together different stones which they intermingled for the sake of ornament, to be a natural source of delight. The entire circuit of the wall, which went round the outermost one, they covered with a coating of brass, and the circuit of the next wall they coated with tin, and the third, which encompassed the citadel, flashed with the red light of orichalcum.

The palaces in the interior of the citadel were constructed on this wise: — In the centre was a holy temple dedicated to Cleito and Poseidon, which remained inaccessible, and was surrounded by an enclosure of gold; this was the spot in which they originally begat the race of the ten princes, and thither they annually brought the fruits of the earth in their season from all the ten portions, and performed sacrifices to each of them. Here, too, was Poseidon's own temple of a stadium in length, and half a stadium in width, and of a proportionate height, having a sort of barbaric splendor. All the outside of the temple, with the exception of the pinnacles, they covered with silver, and the pinnacles with gold. In the interior of the temple the roof was of ivory, adorned everywhere with gold and silver and orichalcum; all the other parts of the walls and pillars and floor they lined with orichalcum. In the temple they placed statues of gold — there was the god himself standing in a chariot — the charioteer of six winged horses — and of such a size that he touched the roof of the buildings with his head; around him there were a hundred Nereids riding on dolphins, for such was thought to be the number of them in that day. There were also in the interior of the temple other images which had been dedicated by private individuals. And around the temple on the outside were placed statues of gold of all the ten kings and of their wives, and there were many other great offerings both of kings and of private individuals, coming both from the city itself and the foreign cities over which they held sway. There was an altar too, which in size and workmanship corresponded to the rest of the work, and there were palaces, in like manner, which answered to the greatness of the kingdom, and the glory of the temple.

In the next place, they used fountains both of cold and hot springs; these were very abundant, and both kinds wonderfully adapted to use by reason of the sweetness and excellence of their waters. They constructed buildings about them and planted suitable trees; also cisterns, some open to the heaven, others which they roofed over, to be used in winter as warm baths; there were the king's baths, and the baths of private persons, which were kept apart; also separate baths for women, and others again for horses and cattle, and to each of them they gave as much adornment as was suitable for them. The water which ran off they carried, some to the grove of Poseidon, where were growing all manner of trees of wonderful height and beauty, owing to the excellence of the soil; the remainder was conveyed by aqueducts which passed over the bridges to the outer circles; and there were many temples built and dedicated to many gods; also gardens and places of exercise, some for men, and some set apart for horses, in both of the two islands formed by the zones; and in the centre of the larger of the two there was a race-course of a stadium in width, and in length allowed to extend all round the island, for horses to race in. Also there were guard-houses at intervals for the body-guard, the more trusted of whom had their duties appointed to them in the lesser zone, which was nearer the Acropolis; while the most trusted of all had houses given them within the citadel, and about the persons of the kings. The docks were full of triremes and naval stores, and all things were quite ready for use. Enough of the plan of the royal palace. Crossing the outer harbors, which were three in number, you would come to a wall which began at the sea and went all round: this was everywhere distant fifty stadia from the largest zone and harbor, and enclosed the whole, meeting at the mouth of the channel towards the sea. The entire area was densely crowded with habitations; the canal and the largest of the harbors were full of vessels and merchants coming from all parts, who, from their numbers, kept up a multitudinous sound of human voices and din of all sorts night and day.

I have repeated his descriptions of the city and the parts about the ancient palace nearly as he gave them, and now I must endeavor to describe the nature and arrangement of the rest of the country. The whole country was described as being very lofty and precipitous on the side of the sea, but the country immediately about and surrounding the city was a level plain, itself surrounded by mountains which descended towards the sea; it was smooth and even, but of an oblong shape, extending in one direction three thousand stadia, and going up the country from the sea, through the centre of the island, two thousand stadia; the whole region of the island lies towards the south, and is sheltered from the north. The surrounding mountains he celebrated for their number and size and beauty, in which they exceeded all that are now to be seen anywhere; having in them also many wealthy inhabited villages, and rivers, and lakes, and meadows supplying food enough for every animal, wild or tame, and wood of various sorts, abundant for every kind of work.

I will now describe the plain, which had been cultivated during many ages by many generations of kings. It was rectangular, and for the most part straight and oblong; and what it wanted of the straight line followed the line of the circular ditch. The depth, and width, and length of this ditch were incredible, and gave the impression that such a work, in addition to so many other works, could hardly have been wrought by the hand of man. But I must say what I have heard. It was excavated to the depth of a hundred feet, and its breadth was a stadium everywhere; it was carried round the whole of the plain, and was ten thousand stadia in length. It received the streams which came down from the mountains, and winding round the plain and touching the city at various points, was there let off into the sea. From above, likewise, straight canals of a hundred feet in width were cut in the plain, and again let off into the ditch towards the sea: these canals were at intervals of an hundred stadia, and by them they brought down the wood from the mountains to the city, and conveyed the fruits of the earth in ships, cutting transverse passages from one canal into another, and to the city. Twice in the year they gathered the fruits of the earth — in winter having the benefit of the rains, and in summer introducing the water of the canals.

As to the population, each of the lots in the plain had an appointed chief of men who were fit for military service, and the size of the lot was to be a square of ten stadia each way, and the total number of all the lots was sixty thousand. And of the inhabitants of the mountains and of the rest of the country there was also a vast multitude having leaders, to whom they were assigned according to their dwellings and villages. The leader was required to furnish for the war the sixth portion of a war-chariot, so as to make up a total of ten thousand chariots; also two horses and riders upon them, and a light chariot without a seat, accompanied by a fighting man on foot carrying a small shield, and having a charioteer mounted to guide the horses; also, he was bound to furnish two heavy armed, two archers, two slingers, three stone-shooters, and three javelin-men, who were skirmishers, and four sailors to make up the complement of twelve hundred ships. Such was the order of war in the royal city — that of the other nine governments was different in each of them, and would be wearisome to narrate.

As to offices and honors, the following was the arrangement from the first. Each of the ten kings in his own division and in his own city had the absolute control of the citizens, and in many cases, of the laws, punishing and slaying whomsoever he would. Now the relations of their governments to one another were regulated by the injunctions of Poseidon as the law had handed them down. These were inscribed by the first men on a column of orichalcum, which was situated in the middle of the island, at the temple of Poseidon, whither the people were gathered together every fifth and sixth years alternately, thus giving equal honor to the odd and to the even number. And when they were gathered together they con-

sulted about public affairs, and inquired if any one
had transgressed in anything, and passed judgment
on him accordingly, and before they passed judgment
they gave their pledges to one another on this wise: —
There were bulls who had the range of the temple of
Poseidon; and the ten who were left alone in the
temple, after they had offered prayers to the gods
that they might take the sacrifices which were acceptable to them, hunted the bulls, without weapons, but
with staves and nooses; and the bull which they
caught they led up to the column; the victim was
then struck on the head by them and slain over the
sacred inscription. Now on the column, besides the
law, there was inscribed an oath invoking mighty
curses on the disobedient.

When therefore, after offering sacrifice according
to their customs, they had burned the limbs of the bull,
they mingled a cup and cast in a clot of blood for each
of them; the rest of the victim they took to the fire,
after having made a purification of the column all
round. Then they drew from the cup in golden vessels, and pouring a libation on the fire, they swore
that they would judge according to the laws on the
column, and would punish any one who had previously transgressed, and that for the future they
would not, if they could help, transgress any of the
inscriptions, and would not command or obey any
ruler who commanded them, to act otherwise than according to the laws of their father Poseidon. This
was the prayer which each of them offered up for
himself and for his family, at the same time drinking and dedicating the vessel in the temple of the
god, and after spending some necessary time at
supper, when darkness came on, and the fire about
the sacrifice was cool, all of them put on most beautiful azure robes, and, sitting on the ground, at

night, near the embers of the sacrifices on which they had sworn, and extinguishing all the fire about the temple, they received and gave judgment, if any of them had any accusation to bring against any one; and when they had given judgment, at daybreak they wrote down their sentences on a golden tablet, and deposited them as memorials with their robes.

There were many special laws which the several kings had inscribed about the temples, but the most important was the following: — That they were not to take up arms against one another, and they were all to come to the rescue if any one in any city attempted to overthrow the royal house; like their ancestors, they were to deliberate in common about war and other matters, giving the supremacy to the family of Atlas. And the king was not to have the power of life and death over any of his kinsmen unless he had the assent of the majority of the ten kings.

Such was the vast power which the god settled in the lost island of Atlantis; and this he afterwards directed against our land on the following pretext, as traditions tell: For many generations, as long as the divine nature lasted in them, they were obedient to the laws, and well-affectioned towards the gods, who were their kinsmen; for they possessed true and in every way great spirits, practising gentleness and wisdom in the various chances of life, and in their intercourse with one another. They despised everything but virtue, not caring for their present state of life, and thinking lightly of the possession of gold and other property, which seemed only a burden to them; neither were they intoxicated by luxury; nor did wealth deprive them of their self-control; but they were sober, and saw clearly that all these goods are increased by virtuous friendship with one another, and that by excessive zeal for them, and honor of

them, the good of them is lost and friendship perishes with them.　By such reflections and by the continuance in them of a divine nature, all that which
we have described waxed and increased in them; but
when this divine portion began to fade away in them,
and became diluted too often and with too much of
the mortal admixture, and the human nature got the
upper hand, then they, being unable to bear their
fortune, became unseemly, and to him who had an
eye to see, they began to appear base, and had lost
the fairest of their precious gifts; but to those who
had no eye to see the true happiness, they still appeared glorious and blessed at the very time when
they were filled with unrighteous avarice and power.
Zeus, the god of gods, who rules with law, and is able
to see into such things, perceiving that an honorable
race was in a most wretched state, and wanting to
inflict punishment on them, that they might be chas-
tened and improve, collected all the gods into his
most holy habitation, which being placed in the centre of the world, sees all things that partake of generation.　And when he had called them together, he
spake as follows: —

THE LAWS

We have now reached the work which seems to have occupied
the last years of Plato's long life, the " swan song " with which
he takes his leave of the world (*Phaedo*).　The Laws may be
called either a remodelling of the Republic, or a companion
treatise on a slightly altered theme.　The question, in Aristotle's
language, is no longer, " What State is best in the abstract? "
but " What State is the best relatively to circumstances? "　In
every respect the two Dialogues form a striking contrast.
　　The Republic is written with the greatest literary skill, and
with the utmost grace and refinement: the Laws are ill composed,

and put together without order or purpose; the dialogue is halting and badly sustained; the language is harsh and obscure. Yet the later work had also some merits such as are hardly possessed in an equal degree by any other composition of Plato, and which render it one of the most remarkable remains of Classical Antiquity.

There is a singular power of insight in many passages, and an exalted moral tone pervades the whole. It is marked, too, by an earnestness and intensity of feeling which rather remind us of a Jewish prophet than of an Hellenic philosopher. The veil of irony and humor behind which Plato has hitherto concealed his deepest reflections is cast aside, and he preaches, as it were, to us so eagerly and sincerely that the utterance of his thoughts is impeded, and he can no longer clothe them with an artistic dress.

These peculiarities of the Laws have been made a reason for throwing a doubt upon the genuineness of the Dialogue, though without any real ground. The deficiency of arrangement, the faults of language, the contradictions and obscurities, which are unquestionably to be discovered in the Laws, become intelligible when we consider that it was written by Plato in the decline of his life, and most probably never received its final shape from him. And on the other hand, the extraordinary genius which is everywhere manifested in the work, forbids us to suppose that the author could have been any other than Plato. The reader, if he will not allow himself to be deterred by the uncouth exterior, but will persist in his perusal until the dialogue has grown thoroughly familiar to him, will find a rich reward; the irregularities and difficulties will gradually disappear from view, and he will recognize " as familiar friends " the spirit of inquiry and the love of truth, which are no less characteristic of the Laws than of all the other writings of Plato.

The persons of the dialogue are three old men, an Athenian, to whom no name is given, Megillus a Spartan, Cleinias a Cretan. They are walking together from Cnosus to the cave and Temple of Zeus, and spend the time, as becomes the citizens of such famous states, in discoursing on laws and government. After the conversation has proceeded to a considerable length, Cleinias announces that he is one of the commissioners appointed by the Cnosians to establish a new colony in Crete, and begs his companions to assist him in drawing up a constitution. This they consent to do, and the Athenian, (for he is the only speaker of importance), accordingly details the institutions which he thinks suitable for the proposed State.

BOOK I

The First Book opens with a criticism of the Lacedaemonian and Cretan institutions.

Both have a single object in view, — to inspire courage in war. But the lawgiver should have regard to all the virtues, and not to one only. Better is he who has temperance and courage than he who has courage alone; and better also is he who is faithful in civil strife than he who is merely a good soldier. Peace, again, is better than war; reconciliation than conquest. Moreover, there are two kinds of courage: a courage which arms a man against fear, and teaches him to endure hardships; and a courage which inspires him to resist the insidious assaults of pleasure and desire. Neither quality ought to be wanting in him who aims at being perfect in virtue.

How can this nobler spirit be implanted in the citizens of a state? Clearly they must be educated from the first to fight against the temptations of pleasure, just as children are taught in their earliest years to play at the occupations which they will one day follow in earnest. There must be festive gatherings, presided over by sober "rulers of the feast," at which there will be a free use of wine under proper regulations. For wine is a test of character, — " *in vino veritas*," says the proverb, and the older citizens especially will only show their real natures under its stimulating influence.

1. THE TRUE NATURE OF EDUCATION

We have already seen how deep an interest Plato, like many other of the great Greek philosophers, took in the subject of education. It may indeed be doubted whether the most advanced of modern nations have established systems of education which would wholly satisfy the aspirations of Plato and Aristotle.

In this passage Plato gives expression to the important principle that children should be trained from the first with an eye to the callings which they will pursue in after-life. And we have ourselves begun to realize that education does not begin and end merely with a knowledge of books; but that the eye and the hand require training no less than the ear and the mind. Nor is the advantage of such studies by any means confined to those who will find them of practical service hereafter; for there is no child who will not receive benefit from a knowledge of drawing or an acquaintance with the simpler mechanical arts, even though he may never need to use them in order to gain a livelihood.

Ath. You seem to be quite ready to listen; and I am also ready to perform as much as I can of an almost impossible task, which I will nevertheless attempt. At the outset of the discussion, let me define the nature and power of education; for this is the way by which our argument must travel onwards to the God Dionysus.

Cle. Let us proceed, if you please.

Ath. Well, then, if I tell you what are my notions of education, will you tell me whether you agree with them?

Cle. Let us hear.

Ath. According to my view, he who would be good at anything must practise that thing from his youth upwards, both in sport and earnest, in the particular way which the work requires; for example, he who is to be a good builder, should play at building children's houses; and he who is to be a good husbandman, at tilling the ground; those who have the care of their education should provide them when young with mimic tools. And they should learn beforehand the knowledge which they will afterwards require for their art. For example, the future carpenter should learn to measure or apply the line in play; and the future warrior should learn riding, or some other exercise for amusement, and the teacher should endeavor to direct the children's inclinations and pleasures by the help of amusements, to their final aim in life. The sum of education is right training in the nursery. The soul of the child in his play should be trained to that sort of excellence in which when he grows up to manhood he will have to be perfected. Do you agree with me thus far?

Cle. Certainly.

Ath. Then let us not leave the meaning of education ambiguous or ill-defined. At present, when we speak in terms of praise or blame about the bring-ing-up of each person, we call one man educated and another uneducated, although the uneducated man may be sometimes very well educated for the calling of a retail trader, or of a captain of a ship, and the like. For we are not speaking of education in this sense of the word, but of that other education in virtue from youth upwards, which makes a man eagerly pursue the ideal perfection of citizenship, and teaches him how rightly to rule and how to obey. This is the only training which, upon our view, would be characterized as education; that other sort of training, which aims at the acquisition of wealth or bodily strength, or mere cleverness apart from intel-ligence and justice, is mean and illiberal, and is not worthy to be called education at all. But let us not quarrel with one another about the name, provided that the proposition which has just been granted hold good; to wit, that those who are rightly educated generally become good men. Neither must we cast a slight upon education, which is the first and fairest thing that the best of men can ever have, and which, though liable to take a wrong direction, is capable of reformation. And this work of reformation is the great business of every man while he lives.

Cle. Very true; and we quite agree with you.

2. MAN THE PUPPET OF THE GODS

The Laws, as we have previously had occasion to observe, are pervaded by a tone of pessimism and bitterness, which appears to have grown upon Plato during his later years. The world is a stage on which men and women play their several parts in the tragi-comedy of life: human affairs are hardly worthy of serious consideration: the incurable wickedness of man makes the work of the legislator a sad necessity; for even in the best-governed states evil natures which are proof against instruction and admonition will spring up like weeds in a fair garden.

Plato himself was not unconscious that this feeling sometimes carried him too far: "You have a low opinion of mankind, stranger," says Megillus to the Athenian on one occasion. It may have been due partly to the chilling effect of age, which, while it sharpened the mental vision, diminished enthusiasm and hope in a proportionate degree. In the earlier dialogues, at least, there is a brighter and serener atmosphere; but in the Republic and the Theaetetus Plato begins to moralize upon the pettiness and insignificance of mortal things; and in the Statesman he speaks of men and governments in the same depreciatory manner which is so marked in the Laws.

Ath. Let us look at the matter in this way: May we not regard every living being as a puppet of the Gods, which may be their plaything only, or may be created with a purpose; for that is a matter which we can not certainly know? but this we know, that these affections in us are like cords and strings, which pull us different and opposite ways, and to opposite actions; and herein lies the difference between virtue and vice. The argument tells me, that every man ought to follow one of these cords and not let go, but pull with that against all the rest; and this is the sacred and golden cord of reason, called by us the common law of the State; there are others also which are hard and of iron, but this is soft because golden; and there are various other kinds. Now we ought always to coöperate with the lead of the best, which is law. For inasmuch as reason is beautiful and gentle, and not violent, her rule must needs have ministers in order to help the golden principle in vanquishing the other principles. And thus the moral tale about our being puppets will not be lost, and the meaning of the expression " superior or inferior to a man's self " will become clearer; as also that in this matter of pulling the strings of the puppet, cities as well as individuals should live according to reason; the individual attaining reason in himself, and the city receiving reason from some god, or from the legislator who knows, making that her law in her intercourse with herself and with other states. In this way virtue and vice will be more clearly distinguished by us.

BOOK II

In the Second Book Plato continues the subject of education. During the early years of life children are educated by perceptions of pleasure and pain, and the pleasure is chiefly conferred by means of dance and song. These, which are the gifts of our " kind playfellows the gods," should not be left unregulated, as is now the case; they should be fixed and established by law after the manner of the Egyptians. The criterion of excellence in music should be pleasure, yet not the pleasure of the base or the foolish; the pleasant, the just, and the noble will be declared by the law to be identical. There will be three choruses at our festivals, one of children, another of youth, a third of elder men from thirty to sixty; and all will utter the same strain, — " that virtue and happiness are inseparable." The aged, too, who can not sing, will tell stories to the like effect, as with the voice of an oracle. The elder men may be permitted some indulgence in wine, which will warm their hearts and overcome their diffidence; to children and the young in general it will be forbidden. Our fifty-year-old choristers must be true judges of music, well grounded in the principles of harmony and rhythm.

But how can they receive the necessary training? If they are allowed to drink without regulation at their festivals, they will be disorderly and mutinous; and therefore, as we have before said, they must have sober rulers of the feast, men of ripe age and experience, who will enforce discipline among them, and teach them to choose good and fitting melodies and reject those which are unsuitable.

A final word may be added about the use of wine: — Drinking must be kept under strict control, and only tolerated at all in a few cases which will be determined by the legislator.

THE HABIT OF DRINKING NOT TO BE ENCOURAGED IN THE STATE

With the concluding words of the Second Book Plato completes the discussion of the question: — Whether his future citizens may be permitted to drink wine? The inquiry has a modern sound; and we perhaps wonder that Plato should raise it. For intoxication was not a national vice among the Greeks, but rather a mark of barbarism. The "paradise of drunkenness," which Musaeus sang, was, we may suppose, an idea derived with the Orphic mysteries from Thrace. We know, indeed, that drinking was fashionable among certain circles at Athens, yet this may have been a custom borrowed from the Persians or Macedonians, or the Sicilian tyrants. And when Plato tells us that he had seen "all Tarentum drunk at the Dionysia," we must remember that he is speaking of a religious festival; and that the intoxication was hardly more than the gaiety and infectious lightheartedness of a Southern race enjoying a holiday. The Hellenic temperament was in general averse to excess: even in matters of food and drink the Greek was abstemious, and conscious of a limit which should not be passed.

It is probable that Plato's prohibition of wine is due to Spartan influence. The sentiment grew partly out of the ascetic dislike of pleasure which the institutions of Lycurgus had impressed on the Spartans, and partly out of the feeling that a habit which might "deprive a man of his wits" at some critical moment was a dangerous vice for the citizens of a Greek state who personally took part in war and in government (cp. Shakespeare, Othello A. ii, sc. 3: — "O that men should put an enemy in their mouths to steal away their brains!").

Plato, therefore, will only allow a limited use of wine in his new colony. He has already strictly forbidden it to the young, while permitting, perhaps as much in jest as earnest, some indulgence to the aged. And now he seriously declares his conviction that men and women engaged in the various pursuits of life, whether in war or peace, ought entirely to refrain from the perilous habit. We have had a wider experience than Plato, and our motives of action are not entirely the same; but we, too, seem inclined more and more to return to the old Hellenic ideals, and to insist that our youth shall be educated in an atmosphere of sobriety and temperance.

The reader may compare a passage from the Politics of Aristotle, (vii. 17, §1), where, speaking of the rearing of children, he says: — "It would appear from the example of animals, and of those nations who desire to create the military habit, that the food which has most milk in it is best suited to human beings; but the less wine the better, if they would escape diseases."

Ath. One part of this subject has been already discussed by us, and there remains another part to be discussed?

Cle. Exactly.

Ath. I have first to add a crown to my discourse about drink, if you do not object.

Cle. What is that?

Ath. I would say that if a city seriously means to adopt this practice of drinking, under due regulation and with a view to the enforcement of temperance; and in like manner, and on the same principle, will allow of other pleasures, designing to gain the victory over them — in this way all of them may be used. But if the State makes only an amusement of it, and whoever likes may drink whenever he likes, and with whom he likes, and add to this any other indulgences, I shall never agree or allow that this city or this man should adopt such a usage of drinking. I would go farther than the Cretans and Lacedaemonians, and am disposed rather to the law of the Carthaginians, that no one while he is on a campaign should be allowed to taste wine at all; but I would say that he should drink water during all that time, and that in the city no slave, male or female, should ever drink wine; and that no rulers should drink during their year of office, nor pilots of vessels, nor judges while on duty should taste wine at all; nor any one who is going to hold a consultation about any matter of importance, nor in the day-time at all, unless in consequence of exercise or as medicine; nor again at night, when any one, either man or woman, is minded to get children. There are numberless other cases also in which those who have good sense and good laws ought not to drink wine, so that if what I say is true, no city will meet many vineyards. Their husbandry and their way of life in general will follow an appointed order, and their cultivation of the vine will be the most limited and moderate of their employments. And this, Stranger, shall be the crown of my discourse about wine, if you agree.

Cle. Excellent: we agree.

BOOK III

Plato now diverges abruptly to another part of his theme: — the origin of the various forms of government.

There have been many destructions of mankind by deluges and other catastrophes in past ages. And after each calamity society has grown up again in the same way: — First, the isolated families live under the rule of the eldest; next, several families live under one chief; thirdly, cities are built, small, originally, and on high ground; fourthly, the cities become larger and are built in the plains; and lastly, confederations or nations are formed by the union of a number of cities.

Such a confederation was the mighty Dorian league of Sparta, Argos, and Messenè, and its history will furnish us with an important lesson. Why did this union fail? Because the balance of power was not observed in two out of the three states, Argos and Messenè. Sparta, by a happier fate, obtained a better regulated constitution; and she only has retained her original greatness. . . . A similar lesson is taught by the history of Persia and Athens; unbridled tyranny has ruined the one, and excessive freedom the other.

At this point Cleinias mentions the new Cretan colony, and requests the aid of his companions.

THE ORIGIN OF GOVERNMENT

The growth and development of human society was a subject of keen interest to the Greek philosophers. They knew very little of the history of the past; but their scanty information merely served to stimulate and intensify their curiosity. The long-recorded antiquity of the East offered a striking contrast to the brief and imperfect annals of Hellas. And it seemed natural to resort for an explanation to the ancient traditions which told how parts of the earth had often been destroyed, sometimes by fire and sometimes by water. There had been many civilizations in the progress of time: man had not proceeded so far along the road to perfection as he would have done, because the fruit of his labors was perpetually liable to be swept away by some overwhelming catastrophe. And then society had to be reconstructed from the very base: the knowledge of antiquity had perished; the arts were lost; and the human race was only represented by a few scattered shepherds and herdsmen. The stages by which mankind advanced from barbarism are related in much the same manner by Aristotle in the First Book of the Politics as by Plato in the Laws, and their account is no doubt true, in the main, at least, to the history of Hellas.

The earliest form of society in which there is no common head, and each family is an independent unit, is, though rare, still to be met with among primitive races, and was once widely prevalent. The family gives place to the tribe or clan, which is little more than a union of families under a single head. But civilization progresses, and the necessities of defence and protection impel men to collect together in settlements. City life begins at this point, and the Hellene, accustomed to the small polities of his own country, could hardly rise beyond the city to the formation of a great nation.

The ancients, we may also remark, fell into the error of supposing that such changes were more uniform than they really were. They did not understand the degree to which men are affected by circumstances; how, for instance, level and fertile plains, such as those of Egypt and Assyria, afford a natural field for the growth of large and highly organized communities, while impenetrable forests and rugged mountains are the appropriate refuge of weak and barbarous races, like the Arcadians or the Epeirots, who are thus enabled to retain their independence at the cost of progress in the arts of civilization.

Athenian Stranger. Enough of this. And what, then, is to be regarded as the origin of government? Will not a man be able to judge best from a point of view in which he may behold the progress of states and their transitions to good or evil?

Cleinias. What do you mean?

Ath. I mean that he might watch them from the point of view of time, and observe the changes that take place in them during infinite ages.

Cle. How is that?

Ath. Why, do you think that you can reckon the time which has elapsed since cities first existed and men were citizens of them?

Cle. Hardly.

Ath. But you are sure that it must be vast and incalculable?

Cle. Quite true.

Ath. And have there not been thousands and thousands of cities which have come into being and perished during this period? And has not every place had endless forms of government, and been sometimes rising and at other times falling, and again improving or waning?

Cle. Certainly.

Ath. Let us endeavor to ascertain the cause of these changes; for that will probably explain the first origin and succession of states.

Cle. Very good. You shall endeavor to impart your thoughts to us, and we will make an effort to understand you.

Ath. Do you believe that there is any truth in ancient traditions?

Cle. What traditions?

Ath. The traditions about the many destructions of mankind which have been occasioned by deluges and diseases, and in many other ways, and of the preservation of a remnant.

Cle. Every one is disposed to believe them.

Ath. Let us imagine one of them: I will take the famous one which was caused by a deluge.

Cle. What are we to think about that?

Ath. I mean to say that those who then escaped

would only be hill shepherds, — small sparks of the human race preserved on the tops of mountains.

Cle. Clearly.

Ath. Such survivors would necessarily be unacquainted with the arts of those who live in cities, and with the various devices which are suggested to them by interest or ambition, and all the wrongs which they contrive against one another.

Cle. Very true.

Ath. Let us suppose, then, that the cities in the plain and on the sea-coast were utterly destroyed at that time.

Cle. Let us suppose that.

Ath. Would not all implements perish and every other excellent invention of political or any other sort of wisdom utterly fail at that time?

Cle. Why, yes, my friend; and if things had always continued as they are at present ordered, how could any discovery have ever been made even in the least particular? For it is evident that the arts were unknown during thousands and thousands of years. And no more than a thousand or two thousand years have elapsed since the discoveries of Daedalus, Orpheus and Palamedes, — since Marsyas and Olympus invented music, and Amphion the lyre, — not to speak of numberless other inventions which are but of yesterday.

Ath. Have you forgotten, Cleinias, the name of a friend who is really of yesterday?

Cle. I suppose that you mean Epimenides.

Ath. The same, my friend; for his ingenuity does indeed far overleap the heads of all your great men; what Hesiod had theorized about long before, he converted into a fact, as you declare.

Cle. Yes, that is our tradition.

Ath. After the great destruction, may we not suppose that the state of man was something of this sort: — There was a fearful, illimitable desert and a vast expanse of land; a herd or two of oxen would be the only survivors of the animal world; and there might be a few goats, hardly enough to support the life of those who tended them in the beginning of things.

Cle. True.

Ath. And of cities or governments or legisation, about which we are now talking, do you suppose that they could have any recollection at all?

Cle. They could not.

Ath. And out of this state of things has there not sprung all that we now are and have: cities and governments, and arts and laws, and a great deal of vice and a great deal of virtue?

Cle. What do you mean?

Ath. Why, my good friend, how can we possibly suppose that those who knew nothing of all the good and evil of cities could have attained their full development, whether of virtue or of vice?

Cle. I understand your meaning, and you are quite right.

Ath. But, as time advanced and the race multiplied, the world came to be what the world is.

Cle. Very true.

Ath. Doubtless the change was not made all in a moment, but little by little, during a very long period of time.

Cle. That is to be supposed.

Ath. At first, they would have a natural fear ringing in their ears which would prevent their descending from the heights into the plain.

Cle. Of course.

Ath. The fewness of the survivors would make them desirous of intercourse with one another; but then the means of travelling either by land or sea would have been almost entirely lost, as I may say, with the loss of the arts, and there would be great difficulty in getting at one another; for iron and brass and all metals would have become confused, and would have disappeared; nor would there be any possibility of extracting them; and they would have no means of felling timber. Even if you suppose that some implements might have been preserved in the mountains, they would quickly have worn out and disappeared, and there would be no more of them until the art of metallurgy had again revived.

Cle. There could not have been.

Ath. In how many generations would this be attained?

Cle. Clearly, not for many generations.

Ath. During this period, and for some time afterwards, all the arts which require iron and brass and the like would disappear.

Cle. Certainly.

Ath. Faction and war would also have died out in those days, and for many reasons.

Cle. How would that be?

Ath. In the first place, the desolation of these primitive men would create in them a feeling of affection and friendship towards one another; and, in the second place, they would have no occasion to fight for their subsistence, for they would have pasture in abundance, except just at first, and in some particular cases; on this pasture-land they would mostly support life in that primitive age, having plenty of milk and flesh, and procuring other food by the chase, not to be despised either in quantity or quality. They would also have abundance of clothing and bedding, and dwellings, and utensils either capable of standing on the fire or not; for the plastic and weaving arts do not require any use of iron: God has given these two arts to man in order to provide him with necessaries, that, when reduced to their last extremity, the human race may still grow and increase.

Hence in those days there was no great poverty; nor was poverty a cause of difference among men; and rich they could not be, if they had no gold and silver, and such at that time was their condition. And the community which has neither poverty nor riches will always have the noblest principles; there is no insolence or injustice, nor, again, are there any contentions or envyings among them. And therefore they were good, and also because of what would be termed the simplicity of their natures; for what they heard of the nature of good and evil in their simplicity they believed to be true, and practised. No one had the wit to suspect another of a falsehood, as men do now ; but what they heard about Gods and men they believed to be true, and lived accordingly; and therefore they were in all respects such as we have described them.

Cle. That quite accords with my views, and with those of my friend here.

Ath. Would not many generations living on in this way, although ruder, perhaps, and more ignorant of the arts generally, and in particular of those of land or naval warfare, and likewise of other arts, termed in cities legal practices and party conflicts, and including all conceivable ways of hurting one another in word and deed; — although inferior to those who lived before the deluge, or to the men of our day in these respects, would they not, I say, be simpler and more manly, and also more temperate and in general more just? The reason of this has been already explained.

Cle. Very true.

BOOK IV

In the Fourth Book the new colony is further discussed, and some first principles of government are laid down.

The site proposed for the city is at a considerable distance from the sea, and this is an advantage: for maritime states are unstable and given to the pursuit of gain. The colonists are to be Hellenes, and Peloponnesians will have the preference.

The legislator, like other artists, requires favorable conditions for the exercise of his art; and the greatest good fortune which can befall him is that he should be aided in his work by a young tyrant, who possesses both virtue and absolute power. But such a conjunction occurs very rarely in the course of ages.

What is to be the constitution? Modern states are governed in the selfish interests of the ruling class; in our commonwealth the law will be supreme, and the rulers will be only the ministers of the law.

The citizens will be exhorted by the legislator to follow virtue, and to pay due honor to Gods and to parents. His words will be a general prelude to legislation; and the laws, which should be clearly and precisely stated, should each likewise have a preamble, intended to explain the law and make men more inclined to obey it.

1. THE VIRTUOUS TYRANT

The idea of the " virtuous tyrant " who supplies the force necessary to set the new machinery of government in motion, is a somewhat paradoxical expression of a thought which has arisen in the minds of many philosophers and political writers. It is not, perhaps, an impossible task to frame an imaginary polity which would be an improvement upon any constitution known to exist in the world. But how can the legislator induce or compel mankind to obey his commands? The answer seems obvious: — Let him for a short time enjoy absolute power, or let his efforts be seconded by some " benevolent despot " or " savior of society," and the rest will be easy; — to use the language of Plato in the familiar passage of the Republic, " the evils of the world will only cease when philosophers are kings or kings are philosophers."

To the Greek especially such a conception was natural. He was inclined to exaggerate the power of the legislator to alter the entire character of a nation, as Lycurgus was supposed to have done at Sparta; and the rapid rise of Hellenic civilization prevented him from clearly seeing that states grow rather than are made, and are, like men, "conditioned by their circumstances." The uncertain equilibrium of the small Greek commonwealths and the violent changes which they underwent, — from aristocracy or oligarchy to tyranny, from tyranny to democracy, from democracy to oligarchy again, — also contributed to strengthen this feeling. In the larger and more solidly based communities of modern Europe, on the other hand, the continuity of history is generally better maintained, and the reform of existing institutions, which, in the words of Aristotle, "is no less difficult a task than the establishment of new ones," is the principal object of the statesman's efforts.

Ath. And might not this be also said of legislation as well as of other things; even supposing all other circumstances favorable, the true legislator is still required, from time to time, to provide for the happiness of the state?

Cle. That I admit.

Ath. In each case the artist would be right in praying for certain favorable conditions, under which he would only require to exercise his art?

Cle. That is very true.

Ath. And all other artists, if they had to offer up their prayers, would ask a similar boon?

Cle. Certainly.

Ath. And the legislator would do the same thing which they did?

Cle. I believe that he would.

Ath. "Come, legislator," we will say to him; "and what are the conditions which you require of us previously to organizing your state?" What ought to be his answer to this? Shall I give the answer of the legislator?

Cle. Very good.

Ath. He will say — "Give me a state which is governed by a tyrant, and let the tyrant be young and have a good memory; let him be quick at learning, and of a courageous and noble nature; let him have that which, as I said before, is the inseparable companion of all the other parts of virtue, if there is to be any good in them."

Cle. I suppose, Megillus, that this companion virtue of which the Stranger speaks, must be temperance?

Ath. Yes, Cleinias, temperance in the vulgar sense, not that which in the exaggerated language of some philosophers is demonstrated to be prudence, but that which is the natural gift of children and animals, and makes some of them live continently and others incontinently, but when isolated was, as we said, hardly worth reckoning in the catalogue of goods. I think that you must understand mý meaning?

Cle. Certainly.

Ath. Then our tyrant must have this as well as the other qualities, if the state is to acquire the form of government which is most conducive to happiness in the best manner and in the shortest time; for there neither is nor ever will be a better or speedier way of establishing a polity than this.

Cle. By what possible arguments, Stranger, can any one ever persuade another that he is right in saying that?

Ath. There is surely no difficulty in seeing, Cleinias, that this is according to the order of nature?

Cle. You would assume, as you say, a tyrant who was young, temperate, quick at learning, having a good memory, courageous, of a noble nature?

Ath. Yes; and you must add fortunate; and his good fortune must be that he is the contemporary of a great legislator, and that some happy chance brings them together. When this has been accomplished, God has done all that He can ever do for a state which

He desires to be eminently prosperous; He has done this in an inferior degree for a state in which there are two such rulers, and in the third degree when there are three. The difficulty increases with the increase of the number, and diminishes with the diminution of the number.

Cle. You mean to say, I suppose, that the best government is produced from a tyranny, and originates in a good lawgiver and an orderly tyrant, and most easily and rapidly passes out of such a tyranny into a perfect form of government; and, in the second degree, out of an oligarchy; and, in the third degree, out of a democracy: is not that your meaning?

Ath. Not so; I mean rather to say that the change is best made out of a tyranny; and secondly, out of a monarchy; and thirdly, out of some sort of democracy; fourthly, in the capacity for improvement, comes oligarchy, which has the greatest difficulty in admitting of such a change, because the government is in the hands of a number of potentates. I am supposing that the legislator is by nature of the true sort, and that his strength is united with that of the chief men of the state; and when he is strongest, and, at the same time, there are the fewest persons concerned, as in a tyranny, there the change is likely to be easiest and most rapid.

Cle. How is that? I do not understand.

Ath. And yet I have repeated what I am saying a good many times; but I suppose that you have never seen a city which is under a tyranny?

Cle. No; I can not say that I have any great desire to see one.

Ath. And yet, where there is a tyranny, you might certainly see that of which I am now speaking.

Cle. What do you mean?

Ath. I mean that you might see how, without trouble and in no very long period of time, the tyrant, if he wishes, can change the manners of a state; he has only to go in the direction of virtue or of vice, whichever he prefers, he himself setting an example in his own person, praising and countenancing some actions, and reproving and setting a note of dishonor upon others.

Cle. But how can we imagine that the citizens in general will at once follow the example set to them; or how can he have this power both of persuading and of compelling them?

Ath. Let no one, my friends, persuade us that there is any quicker and easier way in which laws act upon states than when the rulers lead: such changes never have, nor ever will, come to pass is any other way. The real impossibility or difficulty is of another sort, and is rarely surmounted in the course of ages; but when this is once effected in a state, ten thousand or rather all blessings follow.

Cle. Of what are you speaking?

Ath. The difficulty is to find the divine love of temperate and just institutions existing in any powerful forms of government, whether in a monarchy or oligarchy of wealth or of birth. You might as well hope to reproduce the character of Nestor, who is said to have excelled all men in the power of speech, and yet more in his temperance. This, however, according to the tradition, was in the times of Troy; in our own days there is nothing of the sort; but if such an one either has or ever shall come into being, or is now among us, blessed is he and blessed are they who hear the wise words that flow from his lips. And this may be said of power in general: When the supreme power in man coincides with the greatest wisdom and temperance, then the best laws are by nature framed and the best constitution; but in no other way will they ever come into being. And I would have what I am saying regarded as a sort of divination and declaration that, in one point of view, there may be a difficulty for a city to have good laws, but that there is another point of view in which nothing can be easier or sooner effected, granting our supposition.

2. THE LIFE OF VIRTUE

The Laws, among other singular features, are remarkable for the number of addresses and exhortations which they contain, and which take the place of the dialectical arguments of the earlier dialogues. The following passage is one of these discourses, supposed to be addressed to the newly-arrived colonists, and intended to inform them of the moral and religious principles by which their life would have to be guided. There appears to us something strange in a legislator giving such admonitions to a band of settlers; the Greek philosopher saw no boundary fixed between ethics and politics, between the legal and the moral code.

The ideal State which Plato has outlined in the Laws exemplifies this tendency in the highest degree. The community may be compared in Platonic phraseology to the soul which pervades and animates the whole body. The citizens are to have a certain mould impressed upon them from their first entrance into the world to the time when they take leave of it. The children are to be educated in a uniform manner, and no allowance is made for individual fancies and peculiarities. A round of duties is prescribed for the citizens, and the women are, as far as possible, to share the training and occupations of the men.

Plato is not unaware that many of his minute regulations can not be enforced by law; but he thinks that the approbation of the legislator and the force of public opinion will ensure their acceptance. He does not sufficiently realize the feeble and unprogressive character which such a community would assume. There would be no spring of life or energy among the young: no career for promising talent: no expansion of mind or thought. If Plato could have seen his dreams carried into effect, he would have found that he had purchased uniformity by the loss of much that is most valuable in the existence of nations and individuals.

Ath. And now, what is to be the next step? May we not suppose the colonists to have arrived, and proceed to make our speech to them?

Cle. Certainly.

Ath. " Friends," we say to them, — " God, as the old tradition declares, holding in His hand the beginning, middle, and end of all that is, moves according to His nature in a straight line towards the accomplishment of His end. Justice always follows Him, and is the punisher of those who fall short of the divine law. To that law, he who would be happy holds fast, and follows it in all humility and order; but he who is lifted up with pride, or money, or honor, or beauty, who has a soul hot with folly, and youth, and insolence, and thinks that he has no need of a guide or ruler, but is able himself to be the guide of others, he, I say, is left deserted of God; and being thus deserted, he takes to him others who are like himself, and dances about in wild confusion, and many think that he is a great man, but in a short time he pays a penalty which justice can not but approve, and is utterly destroyed, and his family and city with him. Wherefore, seeing that human things are thus ordered, what should a wise man do or think, or not do or think? "

Cle. Every man ought to make up his mind that he will be one of the followers of the God; there can be no doubt of that.

Ath. Then what sort of action is agreeable to the God, and becoming in his followers? There is an old saying, that " like agrees with like, with measure measure," but things which have no measure agree neither with themselves nor with the things which have measure. Now, God is the measure of all things, in a sense far higher than any man could be, as the common saying affirms. And he who would be dear to God must, as far as is possible, be like Him and such as He is. Wherefore the temperate man is the friend of God, for he is like Him; and the intemperate man is unlike Him, and different from Him, and unjust. And the same holds of other things, and this is the conclusion, which is also the noblest and truest of all sayings: — that for the good man to offer sacrifice to the Gods, and hold converse with them by means of prayers and offerings and every kind of service, is the noblest and best of all things, and also the most conducive to a happy life, and very fit and meet. But with the bad man, the opposite of this holds: for the bad man has an impious soul, whereas the good is pure; and from one who is polluted, neither a good man nor God is right in receiving gifts. And therefore the unholy waste their much service upon the Gods, which, when offered by any holy man, is always accepted of them.

Such is the mark at which we ought to aim. But what weapons shall we use, and how shall we direct them? In the first place, we affirm that next after the Olympian Gods, and the Gods of the State, honor should be given to the Gods below; they should receive everything in even numbers, and of the second choice, and of evil omen, while the odd numbers and the first choice, and the things of lucky omen, are given to the Gods above, by him who would rightly hit the mark of piety. Next to these Gods, a wise man will do service to the demons or spirits, and then to the heroes, and after them will follow the sacred places of private and ancestral Gods, having their ritual according to law.

Next comes the honor of living parents, to whom, as is meet, we have to pay the first and greatest and oldest of all debts, considering that all which a man has belongs to those who gave him birth and brought

him up, and that he must do all that he can to minister
to them: first, in his property; secondly, in his person; and thirdly, in his soul; paying the debts due
to them for the care and travail which they bestowed
upon him of old, in the days of his infancy, and which
he is now to pay back to them when they are old and
in the extremity of their need. And all his life long
he ought never to utter, or to have uttered, an unbecoming word to them; for of all light and winged
words he will have to give an account; Nemesis, the
messenger of justice, is appointed to watch over them.
And we ought to yield to our parents when they are
angry, and let them satisfy their feelings in word or
deed, considering that, when a father thinks that he
has been wronged by his son, he may be expected to
be very angry. At their death, the most moderate
funeral is best, neither exceeding the customary expense, nor yet falling short of the honor which has
been usually shown by the former generation to their
parents; and let a man not forget to pay the yearly
tribute of respect to the dead, honoring them chiefly
by omitting nothing that conduces to a perpetual remembrance of them, and giving a reasonable portion
of their fortune to the dead. Doing this, and living
after this manner, we shall receive our reward from
the Gods and those who are above us; and we shall
spend our life for the most part in good hope.

BOOK V

The Fifth Book of the Laws falls naturally into two divisions: —

(1) The first part is a long monologue of the Athenian, in
which the citizens are further instructed in ethical and moral
principles. . . . The soul is to be duly honored as the divinest
element of man's nature. A mean state of the bodily habits is
to be desired, and excess must also be shunned in the acquisition

of property. . . . Reverence should be paid to the elder; and
our duties towards kindred, strangers, and suppliants, are to be
scrupulously fulfilled. . . . In the relations of life a man should
be just, faithful, sincere, unenvious. Injustice is involuntary;
the unjust are to be pitied, and only the incurable punished. . . .
Selfishness should be avoided. . . . Men should have a true taste
for pleasure, and the highest pleasures are those of a temperate
life.

(2) The preamble thus finished, we turn to the construction
of the state. . . . The citizens are to be 5040 in number, and
each of them will receive an equal allotment of land. The constitution will be, not the best, but the second best; communism
must be abandoned, being unsuited for citizens reared as ours
will have been. Population must be regulated by various devices,
and no addition or diminution permitted. . . . The accumulation
of wealth will be discouraged. A little money may be coined,
of a kind, however, which will not pass current elsewhere. Dowries may not be given, and usury will be disallowed. The state
is to be virtuous, not wealthy; both at once it can not be. A
good education is far above riches. . . . The citizens will be
divided into four classes according to a property qualification;
and there will be twelve tribes, with a presiding deity assigned
to each. . . . The legislator must pay great attention to numerical proportions and ratios in the arrangement of his state; and
he must also encourage the citizens to study Arithmetic, which is
an invaluable mental training.

1. THE HONOR OF THE SOUL. PRECEPTS FOR A VIRTUOUS LIFE

The opening of the Fifth Book of the Laws is one of the most
noble and striking passages in all the writings of Plato. In
solemn and earnest language he lays down the principles which
are to guide the soul on her " voyage through life." He wishes
his citizens to have true notions respecting the objects of human
existence; they are not to regard the accumulation of wealth as
the end to which they are to " devote their most serious endeavors," or to degrade themselves by self-indulgence and luxury.
They will be the citizens of a State which will have few rivals
on earth, and they must strive to be worthy of her.

Plato perceives clearly that, without this ethical foundation,
the best laws and institutions will be of little avail; and, although
he is aware that even " in a State which is perfectly adapted for
virtue " the evil passions of men will bear their inevitable fruit,

he is not disposed to relax his efforts for the improvement of the human race. He remains to the end an idealist, though his estimate of mankind has sunk lower and lower with advancing years. He is filled with disappointment and despair; his spirit is more bitter and pessimistic than in earlier and brighter days; yet he can not bring himself to think that the repeated admonitions and exhortations of the legislator will fall unheeded on the ears of the citizens.

Like Socrates in the Phaedo, he feels that he is soon about to go to " other Gods who are wise and good; " and he would fain stay one brief moment before he takes the final journey, and address a few last words of encouragement and advice to all who will listen to him. The pathos and impressiveness of this parting discourse are greatly heightened by a dignified and lofty tone which was justified by age and the consciousness of a life spent in the service of virtue.

Athenian Stranger. Listen, all ye who have just now heard the laws about Gods, and about our dear forefathers: — Of all the things which a man has, next to the Gods, his soul is the most divine and most truly his own. Now in every man there are two parts: the better and superior part, which rules, and the worse and inferior part, which serves; and the ruler is always to be preferred to the servant. Wherefore I am right in bidding every one next to the Gods, who are our masters, and those who in order follow them, to honor his own soul, which every one seems to honor, but no one honors as he ought; for honor is a divine good, and no evil thing is honorable; and he who thinks that he can honor the soul by word or gift, or any sort of compliance, not making her in any way better, seems to honor her, but honors her not at all. For example, every man, in his very boyhood, fancies that he is able to know everything, and thinks that he honors his soul by praising her, and he is very ready to let her do whatever she may like. But I mean to say that in acting thus he only injures his soul, and does not honor her; whereas, in our opinion, he ought to honor her as second only to the Gods.

Again, when a man thinks that others are to be blamed, and not himself, for the errors which he has committed, and the many and great evils which befell him in consequence, and is always fancying himself to be exempt and innocent, he is under the idea that he is honoring his soul; whereas the very reverse is the fact, for he is really injuring her. And when, disregarding the word and approval of the legislator, he indulges in pleasure, then again he is far from honoring her; he only dishonors her, and fills her full of evil and remorse; or when he does not endure to the end the labors and fears and sorrows and pains which the legislator approves, but gives way before them, then, by yielding, he does not honor the soul, but by all such conduct he makes her to be dishonorable; nor when he thinks that life at any price is a good, does he honor her, but yet once more he dishonors her; for the soul having a notion that the world below is all evil, he yields to her, and does not resist and teach or convince her that, for aught she knows, the world of the Gods below, instead of being evil, may be the greatest of all goods. Again, when any one prefers beauty to virtue, what is this but the real and utter dishonor of the soul? For such a preference implies that the body is more honorable than the soul; and this is false, for there is nothing of earthly birth which is more honorable than the heavenly, and he who thinks otherwise of the soul has no idea how greatly he undervalues this wonderful possession; nor, again, when a person is willing, or not unwilling, to acquire dishonest gains, does he then honor his soul with gifts? — far otherwise; he sells her glory and honor for a small piece of gold; but all the gold which is under or upon the earth is not to be given in exchange for virtue.

In a word, I may say that he who does not estimate the base and evil, the good and noble, according to the standard of the legislator, and abstain in every possible way from the one and practise the other with all his might, does not know that he is most foully and disgracefully abusing his soul, which is the divinest part of man; for no one, as I may say, ever considers that which is declared to be the greatest penalty of evil-doing — namely, to grow into the likeness of bad men, and growing like them to fly from the conversation of the good, and be cut off from them, and cleave to and follow after the company of the bad. And he who is joined to them must do and suffer what such men by nature do and say to one another, which suffering is not justice but retribution; for justice and the just are noble, whereas retribution is the suffering which waits upon injustice; and whether a man escape or endure this, he is miserable, — in the former case, because he is not cured; in the latter, because he perishes in order that the rest of the world may be saved.

Speaking generally, our glory is to follow the better and improve the inferior, which is susceptible of improvement, in the best manner possible. And of all the possessions which a man has, the soul is by nature most inclined to avoid the evil, and search out and find the chief good; and having found, to dwell with the good, during the remainder of life. Wherefore the soul also is second in honor; and third, as every one will perceive, comes the honor of the body in natural order. Having determined this, we have next to consider which of the honors given to the body are genuine, and which are not genuine. This appears to me to be the business of the legislator, and

he intimates that they are to be ranked in the following order: — Honor is not to be given to the fair,
or the strong, or the swift, or the tall, or the healthy
body (although this would be the opinion of many),
any more than to their opposites; but the mean states
of all these habits are by far the safest and most moderate; for the one extreme makes the soul braggart
and insolent, and the other illiberal and mean; and
the possession of money, and property, and distinction, beats to the same tune. The excess of any of
these is apt to be a source of hatreds and divisions
among states and individuals; and the defect of them
is commonly a cause of slavery.

And, therefore, I would not have any one fond of
heaping up riches for the sake of his children, in order
that he may leave them as rich as possible. For the
possession of great wealth is of no use, either to them
or to the state. The condition of youth which is free
from flattery, and at the same time not in need of the
necessaries of life, is the best and most harmonious
of all, being in accord and agreement with our nature, and making life to be most entirely free from
sorrow. Let parents, then, bequeath to their children
not riches, but the spirit of reverence. We, indeed,
fancy that they will inherit reverence from us, if we
rebuke them when they show a want of reverence.
But this quality is not really imported to them by
the present style of admonition, which only tells them
that the young ought always to be reverential. A
sensible legislator will rather exhort the elders to
reverence the younger, and above all to take heed that
no young man sees or hears him doing or saying anything base; for where old men have no shame, there
young men will most certainly be devoid of reverence.
The best way of training the young, is to train yourself at the same time; not to admonish them, but

to be seen always doing that of which you would admonish them.

He who honors his kindred, and reveres those who share in the same Gods, and are of the same blood and family, may fairly expect that the Gods who preside over generation will be propitious to him, and will quicken his seed. And he who deems the services which his friends and acquaintances do to him, greater and more important than they themselves deem them, and his own favors to them less than theirs to him, will have their good will in the intercourse of life. And surely in his relations to the state and his fellow-citizens, he is by far the best, who rather than the Olympic or any other victory of peace or war, desires to win the palm of obedience to the laws of his country; and who, of all mankind, is the person reputed to have obeyed them best during his whole life.

In his relations to strangers, a man should consider that a contract is a most holy thing, and that all concerns and wrongs of strangers are more directly dependent on the protection of God, than the wrongs done to citizens; for the stranger having no kindred and friends, is more to be pitied by Gods and men. Wherefore, also, he who is able to assist him is more zealous in his cause; and he who is most able is the divinity and god of the stranger, who follows in the train of Zeus, the god of strangers. And for this reason, he who has a spark of caution in him, will do his best to pass through life without sinning against the stranger. And of offences committed, whether against strangers or fellow-countrymen, that against suppliants is the greatest. For the God who witnessed to the agreement made with the suppliant, becomes in a special manner the guardian of the sufferer; and he will certainly not suffer unavenged.

Thus we have nearly described the manner in which

a man is to act about his parents, and himself, and his own affairs; and in relation to the state, and his friends, and kindred, both in what concerns his own countrymen, and in what concerns the stranger. I will now describe what manner of man he must be who would best pass through life in respect of those other things which are not matters of law, but of praise and blame only; in which praise and blame educate a man, and make him more tractable and amenable to the laws which are about to be imposed.

Truth is the beginning of every good to the Gods, and of every good to man; and he who would be blessed and happy, should be from the first a partaker of the truth, that he may live a true man as long as possible, for then he can be trusted; but he is not to be trusted who loves voluntary falsehood, and he who loves involuntary falsehood is a fool. Neither condition is to be desired, for the untrustworthy and ignorant has no friend, and as time advances he becomes known, and lays up in store for himself isolation in crabbed age when life is on the wane: so that, whether his children or friends are alive or not, he is equally solitary.

Worthy of honor, too, is he who does no injustice, and of more than twofold honor if he not only does no injustice himself, but hinders others from doing any; the first may count as one man, the second is worth many men, because he informs the rulers of the injustice of others. And yet more highly to be esteemed is he who coöperates with the rulers in correcting the citizens as far as he can — he shall be proclaimed the great and perfect citizen, and bear away the palm of virtue. The same praise may be given about temperance and wisdom, and all other goods which may be imparted to others, as well as acquired by a man for himself; he who imparts them shall be honored as the man of men, and he who is willing yet is not able, may be allowed the second place; but he who is jealous and will not, if he can help, allow others to partake in a friendly way of any good, is deserving of blame: the good, however, which he has, is not to be undervalued because possessed by him, but to be acquired by us to the utmost of our power. Let every man, then, freely strive for the prize of virtue, and let there be no envy. For the unenvious nature increases the greatness of states — he himself contends in the race and defames no man; but the envious, who thinks that he ought to get the better by defaming others, is less energetic himself in the pursuit of true virtue, and reduces his rivals to despair by his unjust slanders of them. And thus he deprives the whole city of the proper training for the contest of virtue, and diminishes her glory as far as in him lies.

Now every man should be spirited, but he should also be gentle. From the cruel, or hardly curable, or altogether incurable acts of injustice done by others, a man can only escape by fighting and defending himself, and conquering, and by never ceasing to punish them; and no man who is not of a noble spirit is able to accomplish this. As to the actions of those who do evil, but evil which is curable, in the first place, let us remember that the unjust man is not unjust of his own free will. For no man of his own free will would choose to possess the greatest of evils, and least of all in the most honorable part of himself. And the soul, as we said, of a truth is deemed by all men the most honorable. In the soul, then, which is the most honorable part of him, no one, if he could help, would admit, or allow to continue the greatest of evils. The unjust and the unfortunate are always to be pitied in any case; and one can afford to forgive as well as pity, him who is curable, and refrain and calm one's anger, not giving way to passion, and continuing wrathful with feminine bitterness. But upon him who is incapable of reformation and wholly evil, the vials of our wrath should be poured out; wherefore, I say, that good men ought, when occasion arises, to be both gentle and passionate.

The greatest evil to men, generally, is one which is innate in their souls, and which a man is always excusing in himself and never correcting; I mean, what is expressed in the saying, " that every man by nature is and ought to be his own friend." Whereas the excessive love of self is in reality the source to each man of all offences; for the lover is blinded about the beloved, so that he judges wrongly of the just, the good, and the honorable, and thinks that he ought always to prefer his own interest to the truth. But he who would be a great man, ought to regard what is just, and not himself or his interests, whether in his own actions, or those of others. Through a similar error, men are induced to fancy that their own ignorance is wisdom, and thus we who may be truly said to know nothing, think that we know all things; and because we will not let others act for us in what we do not know, we are compelled to act amiss ourselves. Wherefore, let every man avoid excess of self-love, and condescend to follow a better man than himself, not allowing any false shame to stand in the way.

There are also lesser matters than these which are often repeated, and with good reason; a man should recollect them and remind himself of them. For when a stream is flowing out, there should be water flowing in too; and recollection is the flowing in of failing knowledge. Therefore I say that a man should refrain from excess either of laughter or tears, and should exhort his neighbor to do the same; he should veil his immoderate sorrow or joy, and seek to behave with propriety, whether his genius be set at good fortune, or whether at the crisis of his fate, when he seems to be mounting high and steep places, the Gods oppose him in some of his enterprises. Still he may hope, that when calamities supervene upon the blessings which the God gives him, he will lighten them and change existing evils for the better; and as to the goods which are the opposite of these evils, he will not doubt that they will be ever present with him, and that he will be fortunate. Such should be men's hopes, and such should be the exhortations with which they admonish one another, never losing an opportunity, but on every occasion distinctly reminding themselves and others, of all these things both in jest and earnest.

2. THE BEST AND THE SECOND-BEST STATE

In the passage which follows, Plato explains the relation between the perfect state of the Republic and the commonwealth described in the Laws. He holds to the opinion that the government of philosophers and the community of women, children, and property are necessary to the highest and best form of the state, although he now concedes that men as they exist in the world are unfitted to live under such institutions. In the Laws, therefore, communism is abandoned, and the rulers are only magistrates whose training has been chiefly of a practical kind. The place of communism is, however, supplied to some extent by the limits imposed upon the accumulation of wealth, by the common education which is given to men and women, and also by the extension of the common meals to women.

The constitution of the new or " second-best " state can hardly be said with propriety to be " next to the perfect form." It has no ideal character, but is an aristocratic government of an ordinary Greek type. The citizens are divided into four clsases according to a property qualification; the more important magistracies, though nominally open to all, are practically confined to men of wealth and position by means of complicated methods of election; the Assembly is reduced to a mere shadow, having no functions of importance, and subject to the control of the Senate.

The distrust of the popular element which Plato shows throughout these arrangements is somewhat remarkable when we consider that he is proposing to construct a state in which there would be no proletariate; for the citizens are to be in a middle condition, equally removed from the extremes of wealth and poverty, and are forbidden to trade or to engage in husbandry. Evidently he is still influenced by his dislike to the city populace of Athens; he forgets that he is legislating for a community of an entirely different nature. This is one of several inconsistencies which are found in the Laws, and may be compared with the manner in which Plato praises the life of peace and yet gives his whole commonwealth a military cast resembling that of Sparta, or in which, while denouncing the evils caused by riches, he makes the distinction of classes and the right to office rest upon the possession of property.

And now comes the movement of the pieces from the sacred line as in the game of draughts. The form of constitution being unusual, may excite wonder when mentioned for the first time; but, upon reflection and trial, will appear to us, if not the best, to be the second best. And yet a person may not approve this form, because he thinks that sort of legislation is ill adapted to a legislator who has not despotic power. The truth is, that there are three forms of government, the best, the second and third best, which we may just mention, and then leave the selection to the ruler of the settlement. Following this method in the present instance, let us speak of that state which is first and second and third in excellence, and then leave to Cleinias, or to any one who has any choice, the selection of that form of polity which he approves in his own country.

The first and highest form of the state and of the government and of the law is that in which there pre-

vails most widely the ancient saying, that " Friends
have all things in common." Whether there is now,
or ever will be, this communion of women and children and of property in which the private and individual is altogether banished from life, and things
which are by nature private, such as eyes and ears
and hands, have become common, and in some way
see and hear and act in common, and all men express
praise and blame, and feel joy and sorrow, on the
same occasions, and the laws unite the city to the
utmost, — whether all this is possible or not, I say
that no man, acting upon any other principle, will
ever constitute a state more exalted in virtue, or truer
or better than this. Such a state, whether inhabited
by Gods or sons of Gods, will make them blessed
who dwell therein; and therefore to this we are to
look for the pattern of the state, and to cling to this,
and, as far as possible, to seek for one which is like
this. The state which we have now in hand, when
created, will be nearest immortality in the next degree; and, after that, by the grace of God, we will
complete the third one. And, we will begin by speaking of the nature and origin of the second.

Let them at once distribute their land and houses,
and not till the land in common, since this sort of
constitution goes beyond their proposed origin, and
nurture, and education. But in making the distribution, let the several possessors feel that their particular lots also belong to the whole city; and as the
land is the parent, let them tend this more carefully
than children do their mother. For she is a goddess
and their queen, and they are her mortal subjects.
Such also are the feelings which they ought to entertain to the Gods and demi-gods of the country. And
in order that the distribution may always remain,
they ought to consider further that the present num-

ber of families should be always retained, and neither increased nor diminished.

This may be secured for the whole city in the following manner: — Let the possessor of a lot leave the one of his children who is his best beloved, and one only, to be the heir of his dwelling, and his successor in the duty of ministering to the Gods, the family and the state, as well the living as those who are departed; but of his other children, if he have more than one, he shall give the females in marriage according to the law to be hereafter enacted, and the males he shall distribute as sons to such of the citizens as have no children, and are willing, if possible; or if there is no one willing, and particular individuals have too many children, male or female, or too few, as in the case of barrenness — in all these cases let the highest and most honorable magistracy created by us, judge and determine what is to be done with the redundant or deficient, and devise a means that the number of 5040 houses shall always remain the same. There are many ways of accomplishing this; for they in whom generation is affluent may be made to refrain, and, on the other hand, special care may be taken to increase the number of births by rewards and stigmas, and by the instruction and admonition of the younger by their elders — in this way the object may be attained.

And if after all there be very great difficulty about the preservation of the 5040 houses, and there be an excess of citizens, owing to the too great love of those who live together, and we are at our wit's end, there is still the old device often mentioned by us of sending out a colony, which will part friends with us, and be composed of suitable persons. If, on the other hand, there come a wave bearing a deluge of disease, or a plague of war, and the inhabitants become much fewer than the appointed number by reason of mortality, you ought not to introduce citizens of spurious birth and education, if this can be avoided; but even God is said not to be able to fight against necessity.

3. RICHES AND GODLINESS

There is hardly any subject in the Laws on which Plato speaks with greater emphasis and frequency than on his determination to banish from his state the ills which arise out of excessive wealth and the pursuit of gain: " no gold or silver Plutus," as he says in one passage, " shall dwell in our city." To effect this object he proposes: — (1) to make the lot inalienable; (2) to abolish dowries; (3) to debar the citizens from money-making, and from receiving usury; (4) to forbid the acquisition of property beyond a certain limit; (5) to restrict the power of bequest in various ways. He is aware that the worst evils owe their origin to the accumulation of wealth in a few hands, and he may have had in mind the decadent condition of Sparta, which, accord-ing to Aristotle, was largely due to a similar cause.

The only impracticable part of his plan is, probably, the enact-ment which fixes a limit to the acquisition of wealth. In modern times we should be more inclined to suggest the imposition of a graduated property tax on the owners of large incomes, the re-sumption of the " unearned increment " by the state, or the ex-action of heavy " death duties." The other proposals of Plato seem to be derived from the actual practice of Hellenic states, or at least to have been put forward by previous writers and thinkers. For the inequalities of property had been from the earliest times the " very spring and fountain of revolutions " in the cities of Hellas, which were, as Plato and Aristotle agree in telling us, rent asunder by the endless quarrel of rich and poor.

But although Plato hopes by wise legislation to diminish, if not entirely to destroy, this great social danger, he is not igno-rant of the truth on which Aristotle afterwards enlarges, that " it is more important to equalize the desires than the possessions of men." Here is the province of education, which is the basis and foundation of the whole state. By its aid he expects to render his citizens " receptive of virtue," while the Spartan sever-ity and simplicity of their training will raise them above the lower instincts of their nature, and make them docile and obedi-ent to the guiding hand of the legislator.

The intention, as we affirm, of a reasonable statesman, is not what the many declare to be the object of
a good legislator; namely, that the state for which
he is advising should be as great and as rich as possible, and should possess gold and silver, and have
the greatest empire by sea and land; — this they
imagine to be the true object of legislation, at the
same time adding, inconsistently, that the true legislator desires to have the city the best and happiest
possible.   But they do not see that some of these
things are possible, and some of them are impossible;
and he who orders the state will desire what is possible, and will not indulge in vain wishes or attempts
to accomplish that which is impossible.

The citizen must indeed be happy and good, and
the legislator will seek to accomplish this; but very
rich and very good at the same time he can not be,
not, at least, in the sense in which the many speak
of riches.   For they describe by the term " rich," the
few who have the most valuable possessions, although
the owner of them be a rogue.   And if this be true,
I can never assent to the doctrine that the rich man
will be happy; he must be good as well as rich.   And
good in a high degree, and rich in a high degree at
the same time, he can not be.

Some one will ask, why is this?   And we shall
answer, — because acquisitions which come from unjust, as well as just sources, are more than double
those which come from just sources only; and the
sums which are expended neither honorably nor disgracefully, are only half as great as those which are
expended honorably, and on honorable purposes.
Thus, if one acquires double and spends half, the
other who is in the opposite case can not possibly be
wealthier than he.   One of them is a good man, and
the other — I am speaking of the saver and not of

the spender — is not always bad; he may indeed be
utterly bad, but, as I was saying, a good man he
never is. For he who receives money unjustly as
well as justly, and spends neither justly nor unjustly,
will be a rich man if he be also thrifty. On the other
hand, the utterly bad is in general profligate, and
therefore poor; while he who spends on noble objects, and acquires wealth by just means only, can
hardly be remarkable for riches, any more than he
can be very poor. The argument then is right, in
declaring that the very rich are not good, and, if they
are not good, they are not happy.

But the intention of our laws was, that the citizens
should be as happy as possible, and as friendly as
possible to one another. And men who are always
at law with one another, and amongst whom there
are many wrongs done, can never be friends to one
another, but only those among whom crimes and law-
suits are few and slight. Therefore, we say that gold
and silver ought not to be allowed in the city, nor
much of the vulgar sort of trade which is carried on
by lending money, or rearing the meaner kinds of live
stock; but only the produce of agriculture, and only
so much of this as will not compel us in pursuing it
to neglect that for the sake of which riches exist, —
I mean, soul and body, which without gymnastics,
and without education, will never be worth anything;
and therefore, as we have said not once but many
times, the care of riches should have the last place
in our thoughts.

For there are in all three things about which every
man has an interest; and the interest about money,
when rightly regarded, is the third and lowest of
them: midway comes the interest of the body; and,
first of all, that of the soul; and the state which we
are describing will have been rightly constituted if

it ordains honors according to this scale. But if, in any of the laws which have been ordained, health be preferred to temperance, or wealth to health and temperate habits, that law must clearly be wrong. Wherefore, also, the legislator ought often to impress upon himself the question — "What do I want?" and "Do I attain my aim, or do I miss the mark?" In this way, and in this way only, he may acquit himself and free others from the work of legislation.

BOOK VI

The Sixth Book, like the Fifth, may be divided into two parts. (1) The mode of appointing the chief magistrates and officials of the new state is described. These include Guardians of the Law, Military Officers, a Council or Senate, Priests, Interpreters of Sacred Matters, Temple Treasurers, Wardens of the City, of the Agora, and of the Country, Rural Police, Directors of Music and Gymnastic, a Minister of Education, Judges of Public and Private Causes. (2) A commencement is made with legislation; and laws concerning Marriage, Slaves, Common Meals, Registration of Births, Age for Military and Political Service, are enacted.

BOOK VII

In the Seventh Book the subject of education is resumed and completed.

During the first three years of life children will chiefly require attention to their bodily growth and development. They must not be allowed to walk, lest their tender limbs should become distorted by too early exercise; but, since motion is highly beneficial to them, they must be constantly carried about by their nurses. And motion is no less good for the soul: it quiets fear and promotes courage and cheerfulness. The children should be kept free from pain, yet not be spoiled by too much pleasure.

From three to six they may pass their time in sports and games. . . . At the age of six, boys, and girls, too, if they like, should commence to learn military exercises and the use of weapons: they must be taught to employ both hands with equal skill.

Education has two branches: — gymnastic, or the training of the body, and music, or the cultivation of the soul. All gymnastic must be practised with a view to war. Music should be simple, and conform to fixed types; for even in amusement innovation is dangerous. The law will prescribe certain principles, from which the composers are not to depart. But with what object are our citizens to learn music? We reply: — In order that they may be better fitted to live the life of peace, propitiating the Gods by dance and song, which is a nobler occupation than the pursuits of war.

Education is to be common to all. Both gymnastic and music must be taught to boys and girls alike. Women should be a help to the state in the hour of peril, and not a useless burden, as they are in most cities. . . . The citizens must lead an active life, rising early and taking little rest.

At daybreak boys must go to school, where they will spend three years in learning to read and write, and three more in the study of music. The compositions which the children commit to memory must be carefully selected. The music must be such as can be readily acquired by every one. Dancing is of two kinds; there is the dance of peace and the dance of war; both must be of a serious and dignified character. Comedy may be performed only by slaves and hirelings. The tragic poets must submit their plays to the censor, before they can be allowed to exhibit.

Three subjects of education remain: — Arithmetic, Geometry, Astronomy. (1) Arithmetic is an invaluable aid to knowledge, and every freeman should strive to gain skill in it. (2) Geometry is too much neglected by the Hellenes: it will be an easy and innocent study for our scholars. (3) Astronomy is useful in many ways, and teaches us correct notions about the Sun and Moon and the other Gods in Heaven.

A word may be added about hunting. Lazy sports, such as angling and fowling, are objectionable. Let our youth confine themselves to the chase of land animals by day with dogs and horses, which will be a test of their endurance and courage.

1. THE GOOD CITIZEN MUST NOT LEAD AN INACTIVE LIFE

The life of strenuous activity which Plato imposes on his citizens, both in the Republic and in the Laws, is probably a reflection of the restless energy of the Athenians in the days of their greatness, when, in the familiar words of Thucydides, "they knew no holiday except to do their duty, and deemed the quiet of inaction to be as tedious as the most tiresome business." We may also, perhaps, see in it a trace of Plato's own character and habits; for he shows in several passages of his writings a certain impatience or dislike of sickness and weakness which suggests that he himself had never felt the restraint of "Theages' bridle."

He was well aware, too, that idleness was a fertile source of evil both to the individual and to the state, and he would have agreed with the modern moralist that "it is only in some corner of the brain which we leave empty that Vice can obtain a lodging." His citizens, therefore, are subjected to a discipline which is almost monastic in its severity, although the austere spirit of the cloister is far removed from the cheerfulness and gaiety of Hellenic life. And if, like Adeimantus in the Republic, we were to object that such an existence would be no better than that of a soldier who is compelled to be ever on duty, Plato's reply would still be the same: — That his aim in founding the state was not the disproportionate happiness of a privileged class, but the greatest happiness of the whole.

Ath. What will be the manner of life among men who may be supposed to have their food and clothing provided for them in moderation, and who have entrusted the practice of the arts to others, and whose husbandry committed to slaves paying a part of the produce, brings them a return sufficient for men living temperately; who, moreover, have common tables in which the men are placed apart, and near them are the common tables of their families, of their daughters and mothers, which, day by day, the rulers, male and female, are to dismiss, when they have inspected them and seen to their mode of life; after which the magistrate and his attendants shall honor with libations those Gods to whom that day and night are dedicated, and then go home? To men whose lives are thus ordered, is there no work to be done which is necessary and fitting, but shall each one of them live fattening like a beast? That, we say, is neither just nor honorable, nor can he who lives in that way fail of meeting his due, and the due reward of the idle fatted beast is that he should be torn in pieces by some other valiant beast whose fatness is worn down by labors and toils. These regulations, if we duly consider them, will never perfectly take effect under present circumstances, nor as long as women and children and houses and all other things are the private property of individuals; but if we can attain the second-best form of polity, with that we may be satisfied. And to men living under this second polity, there remains a work to be accomplished which is far from being small or mean, and is, in truth, the greatest of all works, ordained by the appointment of righteous law. For the life which is wholly concerned with the virtue of body and soul may truly be said to be twice, or more than twice, as full of toil and trouble as the pursuit after Pythian and Olympic victories, which debars a man from every employment of life. For there ought to be no bye-work which interferes with the due exercise and nourishment of the body, or the attainments and habits of the soul. Night and day are not long enough for the accomplishment of their perfection and consummation; and to this end all freemen ought to arrange the time of their employments during the whole course of the twenty-four hours, from morning to evening and from evening to the morning of the next sunrise.

There may seem to be some impropriety in the legislator determining minutely the little details of the management of the house, including such particulars as the duty of wakefulness in those who are to be perpetual watchmen of the whole city; for that any citizen should continue during the whole night in sleep, and not be seen by all his servants, always the first to awake and the first to rise — this, we say, should be deemed base and unworthy of a freeman, whether the regulation is to be called a law or only a practice; also that the mistress of the house should be awakened by some of her handmaidens instead of herself first awakening them, is what her slaves, male and female, and her children, and, if that were possible, everything in the house should regard as base. If they rise early, they may all of them do much of their public and of their household business, as magistrates in the city, and masters and mistresses in their private houses, before the dawn. Much sleep is not required by nature, either for our souls or bodies, or for the actions in which they are concerned. For no one who is asleep is good for anything, any more than if he were dead; but he of us who has the most regard for life and reason keeps awake as long as he can, reserving only so much time for sleep as is expedient for health; and much sleep is not required, if the habit of not sleeping be once formed. Magistrates in states who keep awake at night are terrible to the bad, whether enemies or citizens, and are honored and reverenced by the just and temperate, and are useful to themselves and to the whole state.

2. THE EDUCATION OF THE YOUNG

The scheme of education which is laid down in the Laws is thoroughly Hellenic in character, and seems to agree in the main with the course of instruction which was actually followed in Greek schools.

Plato expects the children to acquire their "rudiments" in the comparatively short space of three years; for when he speaks of "learning to read and write" it is natural to suppose that he includes under the term elementary arithmetic, and, probably, drawing. We must remember, however, that the curriculum of a Greek school in his time was necessarily simple; there were no lessons in history or geography or grammar, and no religious teaching: all that the child learned of these subjects was derived from the innumerable verses of Homer and other poets which he committed to memory.

Music is deferred to a rather late age, thirteen, and is also only to be studied for three years. Plato regards music as a means towards the attainment of virtue, and as an "innocent pleasure" for the citizens. They are not to pursue the art beyond a certain point, or to aim at complete proficiency. Here Plato follows the common Greek sentiment, which considered the skill of the professional artist a "vulgar thing," beneath the dignity of the freeman.

It is not easy to gather from Plato's language, either in the Republic or in the Laws, in what way he intended that women should be educated. In both dialogues he tells us that the two sexes are to learn music and gymnastic on an equal footing. But in the present passage he appears to have the boys only in view; nothing whatever is said about the girls. If he meant that they should be left to receive instruction at home, according to the general custom, when and as much as the parents pleased, this is hardly in agreement with the high position which he assigns to women in the state. It may perhaps be a concession to popular prejudice, like the abandonment of communism. (It should be remarked, however, that in a previous passage, he speaks of "school buildings for boys and girls.")

His ideal of education is in many ways rather Spartan than Athenian, although in an earlier part of the work he is disposed to criticize the Lacedaemonian institutions. He admires, and desires to imitate, the manner in which the Spartans made "education the business of the State, and took the greatest pains about their children." He has failed to remember how feeble and stunted the intellectual life of Sparta became under the discipline of Lycurgus; nor does he reflect that the "city of the Magnetes" would have offered little or no scope for the growth and development of mental powers such as his own.

Athenian Stranger. When the day breaks, the time has arrived for youth to go to their schoolmasters. Now neither sheep nor any other animals can live without a shepherd, nor can children be left without tutors, or slaves without masters. And of all animals the boy is the most unmanageable, inasmuch as he has the fountain of reason in him not yet regulated; he is the most insidious, sharp-witted, and insubordinate of animals. Wherefore he must be bound with many bridles; in the first place, when he gets away from mothers and nurses, he must be under the management of tutors on account of his childishness and foolishness; then, again, being a freeman, he must have teachers, and be educated by them in anything they teach and must learn what he has to learn; but he is also a slave, and in that regard any freeman who comes in his way may punish him and his tutor and his instructor, if any of them does anything wrong; and he who comes across him and does not inflict upon him the punishment which he deserves, shall incur the greatest disgrace; and let the guardian of the law, who is the guardian of education, see to him who coming in the way of the offences which we have mentioned, does not chastise them when he ought, or chastises them in a way which he ought not; let him keep a sharp look-out, and take especial care of the training of our children, directing their natures, and always turning them to good according to the law. . . .

A fair time for a boy of ten years old to spend in letters is three years; at thirteen years he should begin to handle the lyre, and he may continue at this for another three years, neither more nor less, and whether his father or himself like or dislike the study, he is not to be allowed to spend more or less time in learning music than the law allows. And let him who disobeys the law be deprived of those youthful honors of which we shall hereafter speak. Hear, however, first of all, what the young ought to learn in the early years of life, and what their instructors ought to teach them. They ought to be occupied with their letters until they are able to read and

write; but the acquisition of perfect beauty or quickness in writing, if nature has not stimulated them to
acquire these accomplishments in the given number
of years, they should let alone. And as to the learning of compositions committed to writing which are
unaccompanied by song, whether metrical or without
rhythmical divisions, compositions in prose, as they
are termed, having no rhythm or harmony — seeing
how dangerous are the writings handed down to us
by many writers of this class — what will you do with
them, O most excellent guardians of the law? or,
how can the lawgiver rightly direct you about them?
I believe that he will be in great difficulty.

Cle. What is the nature of this perplexity,
Stranger, under which you seem to be laboring?

Ath. That is a fair question, Cleinias, and to you,
who are my partners in the work of education, I must
state the difficulties of the case.

Cle. To what do you refer in this instance?

Ath. I will tell you. There is a difficulty in opposing many myriads of mouths.

Cle. Well, and have we not already opposed the
popular voice in many important enactments?

Ath. That is quite true; and you mean to imply
that the road which we are taking may be disagreeable to some but is agreeable to as many others, or if
not to as many, at any rate to persons not inferior
to the others, and in company with them you bid me,
at whatever risk, proceed along the path of legislation
which has opened out of our present discourse, and
to be of good cheer, and not to faint.

Cle. Certainly.

Ath. And I do not faint; I say, indeed, that we
have a great many poets writing in hexameter,
trimeter, and all sorts of measures; some who are
serious, others who aim only at raising a laugh, in

which the aforesaid myriads declare that the youth who are rightly educated should be brought up and saturated; they should be constantly hearing them read at recitations, and learning them, getting off whole poets by heart; while others select choice passages and long speeches, and make compendiums of them, saying that these shall be committed to memory, and that in this way a man is to be made good and wise by varied experience and learning. And you want me to say plainly in what they are right and in what they are wrong.

Cle. Yes, I do.

Ath. But how can I in one word rightly comprehend all of them? I am of opinion, and, if I am not mistaken, there is a general agreement, that every one of these poets has said many things well and many things the reverse of well; and if this be true, then I do affirm that much learning brings danger to youth.

Cle. Then how would you advise the guardian of the law to act?

Ath. In what respect?

Cle. I mean to what pattern should he look as his guide in permitting the young to learn some things and forbidding them to learn others. Do not shrink from answering.

Ath. My good Cleinias, I rather think that I am fortunate.

Cle. In what?

Ath. I think that I am not wholly in want of a pattern, for when I consider the words which we have spoken from early dawn until now, and which, as I believe, have been inspired by Heaven, they appear to me to be quite like a poem. When I reflected upon all these words of ours, I naturally felt pleasure, for of all the discourses which I have ever learned or heard, either in poetry or prose, this seems to me to be the justest, and most suitable for young men to hear; I can not imagine any better pattern than this which the guardian of the law and the educator can have. They can not do better than advise the teachers to teach the young these and the like words, and if they should happen to find writings, either in poetry or prose, or even unwritten discourses like these of ours, and of the same family, they should certainly retain them, and commit them to writing. And, first of all, the teachers themselves should be constrained to learn and approve them, and, any of them who will not, shall not be employed by them as colleagues, but those whom they find agreeing in their approval, they shall make use of and shall commit to them the instruction and education of youth. And here and on this wise let my fanciful tale about letters and teachers of letters come to an end.

BOOK VIII

The Eighth Book treats of a variety of subjects which are more or less loosely connected.

(1) There are to be daily sacrifices, monthly feasts dedicated to the Twelve Gods, and festivals for men and for women.

(2) Military pastimes and tournaments shall be regularly held, in order that the citizens may be better prepared for war. This is an excellent practice, which is commonly neglected, first, because men are absorbed by the pursuit of gain, and, secondly, because existing states are ruled by selfish partisans who have no regard to the common weal. Also there must be races for armed runners, conflicts in armor, and horse races, three kinds of each, one of boys, another of youths, and a third of men: and similar competitions must be arranged for girls and women, in which they will take part according to their age.

(3) The mention of these various contests and festivals in which men and women meet together serves to introduce a difficult and vexed topic, — the relation of the sexes. Licentiousness is utterly abominable. Men should live in moderation, as nature

enjoins, and not fall below the level of the beasts. If the law cannot ensure this, at least we must insist upon some observance of decency.

(4) There must be laws relating to (a) husbandmen and the cultivation of the soil, (b) artisans, (c) imports and exports, (d) division of produce, (e) the arrangement of hamlets and country dwellings, (f) market regulations, (g) resident aliens.

BOOK IX

With the Ninth Book the criminal code of the new State commences.

Laws are enacted against Temple robbing, Treason, Theft. . . . Capital causes are to go before the Guardians of the Law and a Court of Select Judges.

A distinction is drawn between voluntary and involuntary crimes; or, as it would be better to say, between " injustice " and " hurt." There are many causes of crime and motives of action, but all may be brought under these two heads.

Homicide is divided into various classes: — (1) the killing of another by accident or misadventure: (2) homicide committed in anger, whether with or without premeditation: (3) killing in self-defence: (4) deliberate murder, a crime which is due to three causes, — avarice, ambition, fear: (5) suicide: (6) slaying a thief or burglar or other persons engaged in unlawful acts. An animal which kills a man is to be slain and cast beyond the border.

In cases of wounding, with or without intent to kill, much may be left to the law courts, if they are well constituted. The degree of premeditation has to be borne in mind when fixing the punishment.

Lastly, there is the kindred crime of assault, and in this also the different cases must be distinguished, and appropriate penalties laid down for each.

BOOK X

In the Tenth Book Plato deals with the offences of those who disbelieve in the Gods or have erroneous notions concerning them. They are divided into three classes: — (1) Atheists: (2) men who, although they acknowledge the existence of the Gods, think that they take no care of us; or, (3), imagine that they may be propitiated by gifts. Each class is solemnly reasoned with before the law is declared, in the hope that the offenders may be brought to a better frame of mind.

(1) The existence of the Gods is proved by the order of the Universe and by the general belief of mankind. Nowadays there are many who assert that chance rules the world, and that law and religion are mere conventions designed to protect the weak against the strong. They falsely suppose that the four elements came into being before the soul, whereas the soul is really prior to all that is material. She alone is self-moved and the origin of motion in other things. But there are two souls, a good and an evil, and it is the good soul which moves the sun, the moon, and the other heavenly bodies and carries them round in their orbits. And as this soul of good is certainly a Divine Principle, we may truly say that " the Universe is full of Gods."

(2) The opinion that the Gods exist, yet take no heed of human affairs, grows up when men see the unrighteous prospering in the land. They forget that the Gods, who are all-wise and all-good, can not fitly be compared to unworthy artists, attending only to the great and neglecting the small. Man is made for the Universe, the part for the whole, not the whole for the part. Providence designs that good shall triumph over evil, but there is an element of free will and choice in the soul, and we must each in some degree work out our own destiny. The good soul at every change of existence goes to a better place; the soul which has done evil sinks lower and lower into the abyss. This is the justice of Heaven which none may escape.

(3) The third and wickedest class of unbelievers can not be addressed with patience: — they who say that the Gods can be propitiated by gifts and sacrifices, must conceive them to resemble the vilest of men who will betray their trust to gain a paltry bribe.

After the prelude comes the law. The more innocent unbelievers shall be punished with five years' imprisonment, and, in case of a second offence, with death. The worst sort, mendicant priests and the like, who offer " for a consideration " to win the favor of Heaven and to bring up the dead from Hades, shall be imprisoned during life, and never again hold intercourse with their fellows, and when they die, their bodies shall be cast beyond the borders. . . . There shall be no religious rites in private houses: all public worship must take place in the Temples of the State, under the direction of duly appointed priests and priestesses.

The Tenth Book of the Laws is a peculiarly interesting instance of the manner in which that work is related to the Republic. The main ideas are the same; the difference is chiefly one of tone and emphasis. We have already made acquaintance in the Republic with the threefold errors of men respecting the Gods; and now Plato returns to the attack with renewed vigor and zeal.

He first undertakes to prove the existence of the Gods, a subject upon which in his previous writings he had only lightly touched. His arguments, like those which he employs in the Phaedo to demonstrate the immortality of the soul, are not satisfactory or convincing to us; but we, too, feel the force of the appeal which he makes to the better mind of the world in all ages, and acknowledge, as we contemplate the order of the Universe, that God is everywhere. These thoughts move us, as no metaphysical arguments can, and, — slightly to change Plato's own metaphor, — we cling fast to the instinctive belief in the existence of God, as our support in passing through the flood of doubt and discussion.

When, however, Plato proceeds to speak with passionate sincerity of the Goodness of God and His care for His creatures, he is on firmer ground, and we are still more at one with him. He is perplexed to understand how evil can find a place in the scheme of Providence, and discovers the solution in the idea that all things work together to a common end, — the victory of good. His language is vague, but he appears to speak of evil as a principle which is inherent in matter, and can not be eliminated even by the Creator ("There must always remain something which is antagonistic to good"). On the other hand, he supposes that there is in man a real, though limited, freedom of the will, which is assisted in the struggle against evil by the general tendency of the Universe. Life is thus at once the school of character, and the preparation for the world to come.

On the third class of offenders, — those who believe that the Gods favor the wicked in return for their gifts, — Plato does not waste much argument. In his eyes they are moral outlaws, and their opinions must be stamped out of the State like a pestilence. Yet in the law which he proceeds to enact, he distinguishes, as in other cases of unbelief, between a greater and a lesser degree of guilt. The more serious offenders, in his opinion, are they who make a gain out of the fears and terrors of man-

kird, and lead the weak and foolish into the extravagancies of
superstition. We can scarcely say that we know of grave social
evils which had arisen from such a cause in his day; but he is
speaking almost in "a prophetic strain," and his words are in a
measure justified by the corruptions of religion in the Roman
Empire and in Mediæval and Modern Europe.

The somewhat intolerant temper which Plato exhibits is remarkable in a Greek philosopher of the Fourth Century B. C.
We may observe, however, that his zeal is directed against what
he considers an injury to the moral well-being of the State. His
feeling is different to the ordinary Greek sentiment, which only
objected to "new Gods" as an innovation on the established
order of things, and had little or nothing to do with ethical principles; and it is equally removed from the fanaticism with which
we are more familiar, and which endeavors to force upon all by
any or every means the adoption of a series of dogmatic propositions.

We have already said in general terms what shall
be the punishment of sacrilege, whether fraudulent
or violent, and now we have to determine what is to
be the punishment of those who speak or act insolently
toward the Gods. But first we must give them an
admonition which may be in the following terms: —
No one ever intentionally did any unholy act, or
uttered any unlawful word, retaining a belief in the
existence of the Gods, but he must have supposed one
of three things, — either that they did not exist, —
that is the first possibility, or secondly, that if they
did they took no care of man. or thirdly, that they
were easily appeased by sacrifices, or turned from
their course by prayers.

Cle. What shall we say or do to these persons?

Ath. My good friends, let us first hear the jests
which I suspect that they in their superiority will
utter against us.

Cle. What jests?

Ath. They will make some provoking speech of

this sort: O inhabitants of Athens, and Sparta, and Cnosus, they will reply, in that, you speak truly; for some of us deny the very existence of the Gods, while others, as you say, are of opinion that they do not care about us; and others that they are turned from their course by gifts. Now we have a right to claim, as you yourself allowed, in the matter of the laws, that before you are hard upon us and threaten us, you should argue with us and convince us — you should first attempt to teach and convince us that there are Gods; — let that be shown to us by reasonable evidences — and also that they are too good to be unrighteous, or to be propitiated, or turned from their course by gifts. For when we hear these and the like things said of them by those who are esteemed to be the best of poets, and orators, and prophets, and priests, and innumerable others, the thoughts of most of us are not set upon abstaining from unrighteous acts, but upon doing them and making atonement for them. When lawgivers profess that they are gentle and not stern, we think that they should first of all use persuasion to us, and show us the existence of Gods, if not in a better manner than other men, at any rate in a truer; and who knows but that we shall hearken to them? If then our request is a fair one, please to accept our challenge.

Cle. But is there any difficulty in proving the existence of the Gods?

Ath. How would you prove their existence?

Cle. How? In the first place, the earth and the sun, and the stars and the universe, and the fair order of the seasons, and the division of them into years and months, furnish proofs of their existence; and also there is the fact that all Hellenes and barbarians believe in them.

Ath. I am afraid, my sweet friend, though I will

not say I am ashamed, of the contempt with which
the profane will be likely to assail us. For you do
not understand the nature of their complaint, and
fancy that their minds rush into impiety only from
a love of sensual pleasure.

Cle. Why, Stranger, what other reason is there?

Ath. One which you who live in another part of
the world would never guess.

Cle. What is that?

Ath. A very grievous sort of ignorance which is
imagined to be the greatest wisdom.

Cle. What do you mean?

Ath. At Athens there are tales preserved in writing which the virtue of your state, as I am informed,
refuses to admit. They speak of the Gods in prose
as well as verse, and the oldest of them tell of the
origin of the heavens and the world, and as they proceed not far from the beginning they narrate the birth
of the Gods, and how after they were born they be-
haved to one another. Whether these stories have a
good or a bad influence I should not like to be severe
upon them, because they are ancient; but I must say,
that looking at them with reference to the duties of
children to their parents I can not praise them, or
think that they are useful, or at all true. Of the
words of the ancients I have nothing more to say;
and I should wish to say of them only what is pleasing to the God. But as to our younger generation
and their wisdom, I can not let them off when they
do mischief. For do but mark the effect of their
words: when you and I argue that there are Gods,
and produce the sun, moon, and stars as Gods or
divine beings, if we would listen to the aforesaid philosophers we should say that they are earth and stones
only, which can have no care at all of human affairs.

and that all this is a cooking up of words and a make-believe.

Cle. One such teacher, O Stranger, would be bad enough, and you imply that there are many of them, which is worse.

Ath. Well, then; what shall we say or do? — shall we assume that some one is accusing us among unholy men, and that they, and not we, are the real defendants in the matter of legislation; they will say of us — How dreadful that we should legislate on the supposition that there are Gods! and shall we make a defence? or shall we leave them and return to our laws, lest the preamble should become longer than the law? For the discourse will certainly extend to great length, if we are to treat the impiously disposed as they desire; partly arguing with them, as they demand, partly frightening them, or inspiring aversion in them, and then proceed to the requisite enactments.

Cle. Yes, Stranger; but then how often have we repeated already that there is no reason why brevity should be preferred to length; for there is nobody to hurry us, and it would be paltry and ridiculous to prefer the shorter to the better. It is a matter of no small consequence, that our reasons in proof of the assertion, that there are Gods, and that they are good, and regard justice more than men, should carry some sort of conviction with them. This would be the best and noblest preamble of all our laws. And therefore, without impatience, and without hurry, let us summon as far as possible all the power of persuasion which we possess, and unreservedly consider the whole matter.

Ath. When I see you thus earnest, I feel impelled to offer up a prayer, and can no longer refrain. Tell me, I say, who can preserve calmness, having to speak of the existence of the Gods? For he must hate and abhor the men who are and have been the cause of these words of ours; I speak of those who will not believe the words which they have heard as babes and sucklings from their mothers and nurses, who used them as charms, both in jest and earnest, whom also they have heard and seen offering up sacrifices and prayers — sights and sounds delightful to children — of their parents sacrificing in the most earnest manner on behalf of them and of themselves, and with eager interest talking to the Gods, and beseeching them, as though they were firmly convinced of their existence; moreover, they see and hear the genuflexions and prostrations which are made by Hellenes and barbarians to the rising and setting sun and moon, in all the various turns of good and evil fortune, not as if they thought that there were no Gods, but as if there could be no doubt of their existence, and no suspicion of their non-existence; when men, knowing all these things, despise them on no real grounds, as would be admitted by all who have any particle of intelligence, and when they force us to say what we are now saying, how can any one in gentle terms remonstrate with the like of them, when he has to begin by proving to them the very existence of the Gods? Yet the attempt must be made; for it would be unseemly that one-half of mankind should go mad with lust, and the other half in righteous indignation at them. Our address to these lost and perverted natures should not be spoken in passion; let us suppose ourselves to select some one of them, and gently reason with him, smothering our anger: — O my son, we say to him, you are young, and the advance of time will make you reverse many of the opinions which you now hold. Wait, therefore, until the time comes, and do not attempt to judge of high matters at present; and that is the highest of which you think nothing — to know the Gods rightly and to live accordingly. And in the first place let me indicate to you one point which is of great importance and of the truth of which I am quite certain: — You and your friends are not the first who have held this opinion about the Gods. There have always been persons more or less numerous who have had the same disorder. I have known many of them, and can tell you this, that no one who had taken up in youth this opinion, that the Gods do not exist, ever continued in the same until he was old; the two other notions certainly do continue in some cases, but not in many; the notion, I mean, that the Gods exist, but take no heed of human things, and also the notion that they do take heed of them, but are easily propitiated with sacrifices and prayers. What may be the true doctrine, if you are patient, and take my advice, you will hereafter discover, by the help of the legislator and of others. In the meantime take heed lest you offend about the Gods. For the duty of the legislator is and always will be to teach you the truth of these matters.

Cle. Your address, Stranger, thus far, is excellent.

Ath. And now we are to address him who, believing that there are Gods, believes also that they take no heed of human affairs: O thou best of men (this is what we will say to him), in believing that there are Gods you are led by some affinity to them, which attracts you towards your kindred and makes you honor and believe in them. But the fortunes of evil and unrighteous men in private as well as public life, which, though not really happy, are wrongly counted happy in the judgment of men, and are sung or spoken of by poets and prose writers, draw you aside from your natural piety. Perhaps you have seen impious men growing old and leaving their children's children in high offices, and that shakes your faith; you have known or heard or been yourself an eye-witness of many monstrous impieties, and have beheld men by these criminal means from small beginnings reaching the pinnacle of greatness, and considering all these things you do not like to accuse the Gods of them, because they are your relatives; and so from some want of reasoning power, and also from an unwillingness to find fault with them, you are led to believe that they exist indeed, but have no thought or care of human things.

Now, that your present evil opinion may not grow to still greater impiety, and that we may if possible use arguments which may drive away the pollution of error, we will add another argument to that which we addressed to him who utterly denied the existence of the Gods. And do you, Megillus and Cleinias, answer for the young man as you did before; and if any difficulty arises in the course of the argument, I will take the word out of your mouths, and carry you over the river as I did before.

Cle. Very good; do as you say, and we will help you as well as we can.

Ath. There will surely be no difficulty in proving to him that the Gods care about the small as well as about the great. For he was present and heard what was said, that they are perfectly good, and that the care of all things is most entirely natural to them.

Cle. He certainly heard that.

Ath. Let us consider together in the next place what we mean by this virtue which we ascribe to them. Surely we should say that to possess mind belongs to virtue, and the contrary to vice?

Cle. Certainly.

Ath. Yes; and courage is a part of virtue, and cowardice of vice?

Cle. True.

Ath. And the one is dishonorable, and the other honorable?

Cle. To be sure.

Ath. And the one, like other meaner things, is a human quality, but the Gods have no part in anything of the sort?

Cle. No one will deny that.

Ath. But do we imagine carelessness and idleness and luxury to be virtues? What do you think?

Cle. Certainly not.

Ath. They rank under the opposite class?

Cle. Yes.

Ath. And their opposites would fall under the opposite class?

Cle. Yes.

Ath. But can we suppose that one who takes care of great and small will be luxurious and heedless and idle, like those whom the poet compares to stingless drones?

Cle. And the comparison is a most just one.

Ath. Surely God must not be supposed to have a nature which he himself hates? — and if any one dares to say anything of that sort, he must not be allowed for a moment.

Cle. He must not — of course not.

Ath. Should we not on any principle be entirely mistaken in praising any one who has some special business entrusted to him, he having a mind which takes care of great matters and no care of small ones? Reflect; he who acts in this way, whether he be God or man, must act from one of two principles.

Cle. What are they?

Ath. Either he must think that the neglect of the

small matters is of no consequence to the whole, or if they are of consequence, and he neglects them, his conduct must be attributed to carelessness and indolence. Is there any other way in which his neglect can be explained? For, surely, he will not neglect anything, whether small or great, from any impossibility of taking care of all — or be careless about those things of which an inferior being, who has not the power, whether God or man, might be unable to take care.

Cle. Impossible.

Ath. Now, then, let us examine the offenders, who both alike confess that there are Gods, but with a difference, — the one saying that they may be appeased, and the other that they have no care of small matters — there are three of us and two of them, and we will say to them: In the first place, you both acknowledge that the Gods hear and see and know all things, and that nothing can escape them which is matter of sense and knowledge: — do you admit this?

Cle. Yes.

Ath. And do you admit also that they have all power which mortals and immortals can have?

Cle. They will, of course, admit this also.

Ath. And surely we three and they two — five in all — have acknowledged that they are good and perfect.

Cle. Assuredly.

Ath. But, if they are such as we conceive them to be, can we possibly suppose that they ever act in the spirit of carelessness and indolence? For in us inactivity is the child of cowardice, and carelessness of inactivity and indolence.

Cle. Most true.

Ath. Then not from inactivity and carelessness is

any God ever negligent; for he has no cowardice in him.

Cle. That is very true.

Ath. Then the alternative which remains is, that if the Gods neglect the lighter and lesser concerns of the universe, they neglect them because they know that they ought not to care about such matters; what other alternative is there but that they have no knowledge?

Cle. There is none.

Ath. And, O most excellent and best of men, do I understand you to mean that they are ignorant, and do not know that they ought to take care, or that they know and yet like the meanest sort of men, knowing the better choose the worse because they are overcome by pleasures and pains?

Cle. Impossible.

Ath. Do not all human things partake of the nature of soul? And is not man the most religious of all animals?

Cle. That is certainly true.

Ath. Surely we say that all mortal creatures are the property of the Gods, to whom also the whole of heaven belongs?

Cle. Certainly.

Ath. And, now, whether a person says that these things to the Gods are great or small — in either case the Gods who own us and who are the most careful and the best of owners, are not likely to neglect us. There is also a further consideration.

Cle. What is that?

Ath. Sensation and power are in an inverse ratio to each other in respect to their ease and difficulty.

Cle. What do you mean?

Ath. I mean that there is greater difficulty in seeing and hearing the small than the great, but more facility in moving them and controlling them and taking care of them than of their opposites.

Cle. Far more.

Ath. Suppose the case of a physician who is willing and able to cure some living thing as a whole, — how will the whole fare at his hands, if he takes care only of the greater and neglects the lesser?

Cle. Certainly not well.

Ath. No better would be the result with pilots or generals, or householders or statesmen, or any other class, if they neglected the small and regarded only the great; — as the builders say, the larger stones do not lie well without the lesser.

Cle. Of course not.

Ath. Let us not, then, deem God inferior to human workmen, who, in proportion to their skill, finish and perfect their works, small as well as great, by one and the same art; or that God, the wisest of beings, who is willing and able to extend His care to all things, like a lazy good-for-nothing, wants a holiday, and takes no thought of smaller and easier matters, but of the greater only.

Cle. Never, Stranger, let us admit such a supposition about the Gods; which is both impious and false.

Ath. I think that we have now said enough to him who charges the Gods with neglect.

Cle. Yes.

Ath. He has been forced to acknowledge that he is in error, but he still seems to me to need some consolation.

Cle. What consolation will you offer him?

Ath. Let us say to the youth: " The ruler of the universe has ordered all things with a view to the preservation and perfection of the whole, and each part has an appointed state of action and passion; and the smallest action or passion of any part affecting the minutest fraction has a presiding minister. And one of these portions of the universe is thine own, stubborn man, which, however little, has the whole in view; and you do not seem to be aware that this and every other creation is for the sake of the whole, and in order that the life of the whole may be blessed; and that you are created for the sake of the whole, and not the whole for the sake of you. For every physician and every skilled artist does all things for the sake of the whole, directing his effort towards the common good, executing the part for the sake of the whole, and not the whole for the sake of the part. And you are annoyed because you do not see how that which is best for you is, as far as the laws of the creation admit of this, best also for the universe." Now, as the soul combining first with one body and then with another undergoes all sorts of changes, either of herself, or through the influence of another soul, all that remains to the master of the game is that he should transpose the pieces; sending the better nature to the better place, and the worse into the worse, and so assigning to them their proper portion.

Cle. How do you mean?

Ath. I am proposing a plan which may be supposed to make the care of all things easy to the Gods. For if any one did not form or fashion all things with a view to the whole, — if, for example, he formed a living element of water out of fire, instead of forming many things out of one, or one out of many, not at random, but in regular order of the first or second or third degree, the transmutation would have been infinite; but now the ruler of the world has a wonderfully easy task.

Cle. How is that?

Ath. In this way: — When the king saw that our actions had life, and that there was much virtue in them and much vice, and that the soul and body, although not eternal, were indestructible, like the Gods of popular opinion (for if either of them had been destroyed, there would have been no generation of animals) ; and when he observed that the good of the soul was by nature designed to profit men, and the evil to harm them — he, seeing all this, contrived so to place them in each of the parts that their position might in the easiest and best manner procure the victory of good and the defeat of evil in the whole. And he contrived a general plan by which a thing of a certain nature found a certain seat and room. But the formation [1] of qualities he left to the wills of individuals. For every one of us is made pretty much what he is by the bent of his desires and the nature of his soul.

Cle. Yes, that is probably true.

Ath. Then all things which have a soul change, and possess in themselves a principle of change, and in changing move according to law and the order of destiny: lesser changes of nature move on level ground, but greater crimes sink into the abyss, that is to say, into Hades and other places in the world below, of which the very names terrify men, and about which they dream that they live in them absent from the body. And when the soul changes greatly, either for the better or worse, by her own impulse or the strong influence of others, when she has communion with divine virtue and becomes divine, she is carried into another and better place, which is also divine and perfect in holiness; and when she has communion with evil, then she also changes the place of her life.

" For that is justice of the Gods who inhabit heaven." [2]

---

[1] Reading τοῦ τοίου.   [2] Hom. Odyss. 19. 43.

O youth or young man, who fancy that you are neglected by the Gods, know that if you become worse you shall go to the worse souls, or if better to the better, and in every succession of life and death you will do and suffer what like may fitly suffer at the hands of like. This is a divine justice, which neither you nor any other unfortunate will ever glory in escaping, and which the ordaining powers have specially ordained; take good heed of them, for a day will come when they will take heed of you.

If thou sayest: — I am small and will creep into the depths of the earth, or I am high and will fly up to heaven, you are not so small or so high but that you shall pay the fitting penalty, either in the world below or in some yet more savage place still to which thou shalt be conveyed. This is also the explanation of the fate of those whom you saw, who had done unholy and evil deeds, and from small beginnings had become great, and you fancied that from being miserable they had become happy; and in their actions, as in a mirror, you seemed to see the universal neglect of the Gods, not knowing how they make all things work together and contribute to the great whole. And thinkest thou, bold man, that thou shouldst not know this; he who knows not this can never see any true form or say any true word touching the happiness or unhappiness of life? If Cleinias and this reverend company succeed in proving to you that you know not what you say of the Gods, then will God help you; but should you desire to hear more, listen to what we say to the third opponent, if you have any understanding left in you. For I think that we have sufficiently proved the existence of the Gods, and that they have a care of man, — that they are appeased by wicked men, and take gifts is what

I will not allow, and what every man should disprove to the utmost of his power.

Cle. Very good; let us do as you say.

Ath. Well, then, by the Gods themselves I conjure you to tell me, — if they are to be propitiated, how are they to be propitiated? Who are they, and what is their nature? Must not the eternal administrators of heaven be at least rulers?

Cle. True.

Ath. And to what earthly rulers can they be compared, or who to them? How in the less can we find an image of the greater? Are they charioteers of contending pairs of steeds, or pilots of vessels? Perhaps they might be compared to the generals of armies, or they might be likened to physicians providing against the strife of bodily disease, or to husbandmen observing anxiously the effects of the seasons or the growth of plants; or perhaps to shepherds of flocks. For as we acknowledge the heaven to be full of many goods and also of evils, and of more evils than goods, there is, as we affirm, an immortal conflict going on among us, which requires marvellous watchfulness; and in that conflict the Gods and demigods are our allies, and we are their property. Injustice and insolence and folly are the destruction of us, and justice and temperance and wisdom are the salvation of us; and the place of these latter is in the life of the Gods, and of their virtues some vestige may occasionally be discerned among mankind. But upon this earth there dwell souls who have an unjust spirit, and they, like brute animals, fawn upon their keepers, who may be dogs or shepherds, or may be the best and most perfect masters; and upon these, as the wicked declare, they prevail by flattery and prayers and incantations, and are allowed to make their gains with impunity. And this sin, which is termed dishonesty, is the same evil as that which is called disease in living bodies or blight in the seasons, and in cities and governments has another name, which is injustice.

Cle. Quite true.

Ath. That is what he must say who declares that the Gods are always lenient to the doers of unjust acts, who divide the spoil with them. That is as if wolves might be supposed to toss a portion of their prey to the dogs, and they, mollified by the gift, suffered them to tear the flocks. What but this will he say who maintains that the Gods are to be propitiated?

Cle. That is what he will say.

Ath. And to whom of the abovementioned classes of guardians would any man gravely compare the Gods? Will he say that they are like pilots, who are themselves turned away from their duty by draughts of wine and the savor of fat, and at last overturn both ship and sailors?

Cle. Certainly not.

Ath. And surely they are not like charioteers who are bribed to give up the victory to other chariots?

Cle. That would be a fearful image of the Gods.

Ath. Nor are they like generals, or physicians, or husbandmen, or shepherds; and no one would compare them to dogs who have been silenced by wolves.

Cle. Do not be profane.

Ath. And are not all the Gods the chiefest of all guardians, and do they not guard our highest interests?

Cle. Yes; the chiefest.

Ath. And shall we say that those who guard our noblest interests, and are the best of guardians, are inferior in virtue to dogs, and to men even of moderate excellence, who would never betray justice, for the sake of gifts which unjust men impiously offer them?

Cle. Certainly not; nor is such a notion to be endured, and he who holds this opinion may be fairly singled out and characterized as of all impious men the wickedest and most impious.

Ath. Then are the three assertions — that the Gods exist, and that they take care of men, and that they will not be entreated to injustice, now sufficiently demonstrated? May we say that they are?

Cle. You have our entire assent to your words.

Ath. I have spoken with vehemence because I was jealous of evil men; and I will tell you, dear Cleinias, what is the reason of my jealousy. I would not have them suppose that the wicked having the superiority in argument, may do as they like in accordance with their various imaginations about the Gods; and this zeal has led me to speak more vehemently; but if we have at all succeeded in persuading the men to hate themselves and love their opposites, the preamble of our laws about impiety will not have been spoken in vain.

Cle. So let us hope; and even if we have failed, the style of our argument will not discredit the lawgiver.

BOOK XI

In the Eleventh Book Plato takes up another part of legislation, — that which regulates dealings between man and man.

Laws are enacted concerning Treasure Trove, Deposited Property, Runaway Slaves, Freedmen, Sale of Goods, Fraudulent Sale of Slaves, Adulteration, Retail Trade, Contracts, Wills and Testamentary Bequests, Intestacy, Orphans, Family Disputes and Quarrels, Divorce, Neglect of Parents, Poisoning and Witchcraft, Lunatics, Abuse and Ridicule, Beggars, Witnesses and False Witness, Dishonesty of Advocates.

1. THE EVILS OF RETAIL TRADE, AND THE CURE OF THEM

There was probably no feeling more deeply implanted in the Greek mind than that which taught the essentially "vulgar" character of retail trade. And this is worthy of peculiar remark because the Greeks were themselves the keenest of traders and merchants. They expelled the Phoenicians from their trading stations in the Mediterranean; they went to Tartessus for silver and other metals, — to the shores of the Baltic for amber, — to the steppes of Scythia for grain; they travelled, like Pytheas, to Britain and "farthest Thule" in search of new openings for commerce. No doubt, in Greece, not less than in England, the scale of the operations made a difference to the manner in which they were regarded. The wealthy aristocrat might employ his slaves in a workshop, or let them out for hire as artisans and mechanics: he could not without social degradation, to use Plato's humorous language, "open a shop or keep a tavern." Moreover, and this sentiment also is by no means unknown among ourselves, there appears to have been a distinction drawn between the trader retired with a fortune and the man who was actually engaged in trade. At least, Aristotle asserts that it was not uncommon in oligarchies to allow only those to hold office who had left business for a period of ten years or more.

In most of his previous writings Plato has shown that he shared in the general prejudice; and in the Republic, even while he acknowledges that retail trade is one of the primary necessities of life in the social community, he adds that "in well-ordered states the retailers are commonly those who are the weakest in bodily strength, and therefore of little use for any other purpose." In the Laws, however, he takes a step further. He has told us in the Fourth Book that a city of merchants and shop-keepers will be "unfriendly and unfaithful, both to her own citizens and to other nations;" but now he begins to reflect that it would be much to the good of the state, if the better class of men and women would follow the pursuits of trade, and turn away the reproach which at present clings to them.

The wish, he admits, is futile; the insatiable desire for riches will always throw an insurmountable obstacle in the way. Here he exhibits the characteristic tone which runs through the Laws: — He has still, in this latest hour of his life, a consuming zeal for the improvement of mankind. Yet the "creeping touch" of age has saddened his temper, and lowered his estimate of the world, and he can not persuade himself that the human race will ever "make it their first and last and constant and all-absorbing aim to exceed in virtue."

After the practices of adulteration naturally follow practices of retail trade. Concerning these, we will first of all give a word of counsel and reason, and the law shall come afterwards. Retail trade in a city is not by nature intended to do any harm, but quite the contrary; for is not he a benefactor who reduces the inequalities and immeasurabilities of goods to equality and measure? And this is what the power of money accomplishes, and the merchant may be said to be appointed for this purpose. The hireling and the tavern-keeper, and many other occupations, some of them more and others less seemly — all alike have this object; — they seek to satisfy our needs and equalize our possessions. Let us then endeavor to see what is this dishonor and appearance of unseemliness, and what is the accusation brought against retail trade, in order that if not entirely we may yet partially remove the objection by law. To effect this is no easy matter, and implies a great deal of virtue.

Cle. What do you mean?

Ath. Dear Cleinias, the class of men is small — they must have been rarely gifted by nature, and trained by education, who, when compelled by wants and desires of every sort, are able to hold out and observe moderation, and when they might make a great deal of money are sober in their wishes, and prefer a moderate to a large gain. But the mass of mankind are the very opposite: their desires are unbounded, and when they might gain in moderation they prefer gains without limit; wherefore all that relates to retail trade and merchandise, and keeping of taverns, is denounced and numbered among dishonorable things. For if what I trust may never be and will not be, we were to compel, if I may venture to say a ridiculous thing, the best men everywhere to keep taverns for a time, or carry on retail trade, or do anything of that sort; or if, in consequence of some dire necessity, the best women were compelled to take to a similar calling, then we should know how agreeable and pleasant all these things are? And if they were carried on according to pure reason, all such occupations would be held in honor, and those who practised them would be deemed parents or nurses; but now that a man goes to desert places and builds houses which can only be reached by long journeys, for the sake of retail trade, and receives strangers who are in need at the desired resting-places, or gives them sweet calm when they are tossed by the storm, or cool shade in the heat; and then instead of behaving to them as friends, and showing the duties of hospitality to those whom he has received under his roof, treats them as enemies and captives who are at his mercy, and will not release them until they have paid the highest, most exorbitant, and base price, — these are the sort of practices, and foul evils they are, which cast a reproach upon the succor of adversity. And the legislator ought always to be devising a remedy for evils of this sort.

There is an ancient saying, which is also a true one — " To fight against two opponents is a difficult thing," as is seen in diseases and in many other cases. And in this case also the war is against two enemies — wealth and poverty; one of whom corrupts the soul of man with luxury, while the other drives him by pain into utter shamelessness. What remedy can a city of sense find against this disease? In the first place, they must have as few as possible of the retail class; and in the second place, they must assign the occupation to that class of men whose corruption will be the least injury to the state; and in the third place, they must devise some way whereby the followers of these occupations themselves will not readily fall into habits of unbridled shamelessness and meanness.

2. THE HONOR OF PARENTS

The respect for age which is everywhere apparent in the Laws may be partly explained by the natural feeling of Plato, writing in the decline of life; but it is also, we can not doubt, due to the influence which Spartan customs and institutions exercised over his mind. The sentiment had a strong hold in a community which preserved so many traces of the patriarchial age of society wherein the eldest bore rule, " because with them government originated in the authority of a father and mother." In the busy city life of Athens, the elder was apt to be pushed aside by his younger and stronger rival; and we observe a similar tendency in the democratic nations of modern times.

At Athens, however, the worship of ancestors still underlay the whole fabric of social and domestic existence, and, probably, as in some Eastern countries, may have retained vitality when other parts of the national religion were in more or less complete decay; and this primitive belief must have helped to maintain a degree of consideration in the young towards their parents and elders. Such a disposition was most welcome to Plato, both for its own sake, and because it would encourage the mildness of temper and subordination to authority which he desired to see incorporated in the citizens of his new State.

And therefore he indicts a brief prelude to the law concerning the right treatment of parents, in which his ancient power of language once again seems to return to him, and in words of singular beauty and pathos he urges upon the young the duty of paying reverence and veneration to the aged, who are far more potent for good and ill than the lifeless statues of the Gods.

Neither God, nor a man who has understanding, will ever advise any one to neglect his parents. To a discourse concerning the honor and dishonor of parents, a prelude such as the following, about the service of the Gods, will be a suitable introduction: — There are ancient customs about the Gods which are universal, and they are of two kinds: some of the Gods we see with our eyes and honor them, of others we honor the images; raising statues of them which we adore; and though they be lifeless, yet we imagine that the living Gods have a good will and gratitude to us on this account. Now, if a man has a father or mother, or their father or mother treasured up in his house stricken in years, let him consider that no statue can be more potent to grant his requests than they are, who are sitting at his hearth, if only he knows how to show true service to them.

Cle. And what do you call the true mode of service?

Ath. I will tell you, O my friend, for such things are worth listening to.

Cle. Proceed.

Ath. Oedipus, as tradition says, when dishonored by his sons, invoked on them the fulfilment of those curses from the God which every one declares to have been heard and ratified by the Gods, and Amyntor in his wrath invoked curses on his son Phoenix, and Theseus upon Hippolytus, and innumerable others have also called down wrath upon their children, which is a plain proof that the Gods listen to the imprecations of parents against their children; for the curses of a parent are, as they ought to be, mighty against his children as no others are. And shall we suppose that the prayers of a father or mother who is specially dishonored by his or her children, are heard by the Gods in accordance with nature; and that if a man is honored by them, and in the gladness of his heart earnestly entreats the Gods in his prayers to do them good, he is not equally heard, and that they do not minister to his request? If not, they would be very unjust ministers of good, and that we affirm to be contrary to their nature.

Cle. Certainly.

Ath. May we not think, as I was saying just now, that we can possess no image which is more honored by the Gods, than that of a father or grandfather, or of a mother stricken in years? whom when a man honors, the heart of the God rejoices, and he is ready to answer their prayers. And, truly, the figure of an ancestor is a wonderful thing, far higher than that of a lifeless image. For when they are honored by us, they join in our prayers, and when they are dishonored, they utter imprecations against us; but lifeless objects do neither. And, therefore, if a man makes a right use of his father and grandfather and other aged relations, he will have the best of all images which can procure him the favor of the Gods.

Cle. That is excellent.

Ath. Every man of understanding fears and respects the prayers of his parents, knowing well that many times and to many persons they have been accomplished. Now, these things being thus ordered by nature, good men think that they are the gainers by having aged parents living, to the end of their life, or if they depart early, they are deeply lamented by them; and to the bad they are very terrible. Wherefore let every man honor with every sort of lawful honor his own parents agreeably to what has now been said.

BOOK XII

The Twelfth Book continues the subject of legislation. — It contains laws respecting Heralds, Theft, Failure of Service, Desertion, Throwing away of Arms and Cowardice in War, Examiners and Censors of Magistrates and the Burial Rites of those who die holding this office, Oaths in Courts of Justice, Neglect of Public Duties, Foreign Travel and the Reception of Strangers, Surety, Right of Search, Limitation of Time in Disputes about Property, Intimidation of Witnesses or Competitors, Receiving Exiles, Making private War or Peace, Taking Bribes, Registration and Assessment of Property, Offerings to the Gods, Suits at Law and their Execution.

Thus the regulations for the round of civil life are concluded; and Plato proceeds to add a few words upon the disposal of the dead. Interment must take place in ground which is unfit for cultivation; the mounds must be low and the stones small. Funerals are to be simple; the amount spent upon them will be fixed by law. Public lamentations and processions through the streets will not be permitted.

Finally, Plato deals with the question, — How can the permanence of his institutions be assured? He proposes to establish an assembly called the " Nocturnal Council," composed of the ten oldest guardians, of all those who have gained the prize of virtue, of the Director and the ex-Director of Education, and of those who have travelled to see the institutions of other countries, besides an equal number of younger colleagues between thirty and forty, appointed one by each of the seniors. The Council will be " the mind of the State," and its members will know the true object of laws, which is not power or wealth or freedom, but virtue. Now virtue is one, although we distinguish four virtues, — courage, temperance, wisdom, justice; and the guardians of the State ought to understand the nature of virtue, and be far better teachers of it than any chance poet or wandering sophist. They will require a special training for this purpose; and they must also have a right knowledge of the Gods, and be firmly grounded in the belief that the soul is prior to the body, and that soul and mind rule the Universe.

The Nocturnal Council, of which the members are men who have been educated in such ideas, will be the salvation of the whole State. If it can be duly established and set up, then will our City become a waking reality and not the mere imagination of a dream.

1. THE GOOD STATE IN ITS INTERCOURSE WITH THE WORLD

The following passage treats of a subject in respect to which the customs of ancient states were singularly unlike those of modern communities. The Hellenic cities were divided by barriers of race, of dialect, of manners, of civil and social institutions, and within their walls the rich were at constant feud with the poor, the oligarch with the democrat: — "all men," says Cleinias at the very beginning of the long discourse, "are always at war with one another." The traditions of past ages lingered, especially in the more backward states, and "stranger" and "enemy" continued to be almost synonymous terms.

In this regard, as in every other, Sparta and Athens represented the opposite poles of Hellenic sentiment. Sparta remained the rude warrior state with the virtues and vices and prejudices of primæval days. The stranger was an object of suspicion and dread; and the "harsh and morose" practice of expelling foreigners from the land, — the so-called "Xenelasia," — was often enforced, while the young men were forbidden to go out into other countries. But at Athens the prevailing conditions were of another kind: the democratic government was less haughty and exclusive: the habits of daily life were free and unconstrained: commercial interests were strong: and in culture and intelligence the city was the "school of Hellas," and the resort of strangers from the whole Hellenic world.

We are not surprised, therefore, to observe that Plato when he comes to speak of travel and the reception of foreigners, endeavors, in his usual fashion, to combine Athenian and Spartan ideas. He is true to his native origin, and is unwilling to exchange Attic grace and freedom for the blunt and unsociable manners of the Lacedaemonians, "whose existence was modelled after that of a camp." Moreover he is aware that the criticism of the world is by no means to be despised. Yet he is afraid that the distasteful spirit of innovation will find new entrance into the commonwealth, if the love of wandering is too much encouraged. And so he draws up an ingenious scheme, which will, he hopes, secure a due amount of intercourse with other lands, and at the same time keep the desire of change in subordination. The modern reader, however, will hardly be able to sympathize with him, or to refrain from the remark that a wider experience of the course of history would most probably have led him to a different conclusion.

Athenian. Now, a state which makes money from the cultivation of the soil only, and has no foreign trade, must consider what it will do about the emigration of its own people to other countries, and the reception of strangers from elsewhere. About these matters the legislator has to consider, and he will begin by using his influence as far as he can.

The intercourse of cities with one another is apt to create a confusion of manners; strangers are always suggesting novelties to strangers. When states are well governed by good laws the mixture causes the greatest possible injury; but seeing that most cities are the reverse of well ordered, the confusion which arises in them from the reception of strangers, and from the citizens themselves expatiating in other cities, whenever any one young or old desires to travel abroad at any time or to go anywhere, is of no consequence. And, on the other hand, the refusal to receive others and to allow their own citizens to go to other places is utterly impossible, and to the rest of the world is likely to appear ruthless and uncivilized; we call the practice by the name xenelasia or banishment of strangers, which is a hard word, and is descriptive of hard and morose ways, as men think. And to be thought or not to be thought well of by the rest of the world is no light matter; for the many are not so far wrong in their judgment of who are bad and who are good, as they are removed from the nature of virtue in themselves. Even bad men have a divine instinct which guesses rightly, and very many who are utterly depraved form correct notions and judgments about the differences of good and bad.

Wherefore also the generality of cities are right in exhorting men to value a good reputation in the world, for there is no truth greater and more important than this — that he who is really good (I am speaking of him who would be perfect), seeks for reputation, with, but not without, the reality of goodness. And our Cretan colony ought also to acquire the fairest and noblest reputation for virtue from other men; and there is every reason to expect that, if the reality answers to the idea, there will be few like her among well-ordered cities, beholding the face of the sun and of the other Gods. Wherefore, in the matter of emigration to other countries and the reception of strangers, we enact as follows: — In the first place, let no one be allowed to go anywhere at all into a foreign country who is less than forty years of age; and no one shall go in a private capacity, but only in some public one, as a herald, or on an embassy, or on a sacred mission. Foreign travel when on an expedition or in war is not to be included among travels authorized by the state. To Apollo at Delphi and to Zeus at Olympia and to Nemea and to the Isthmus citizens should be sent to take part in the sacrifices and games dedicated to these Gods; and they should send as many as possible, and the best and fairest that can be found, and they will make the city renowned at holy meetings in time of peace, procuring a glory which shall be the converse of that which is gained in war; and when they come home they shall teach the young that the institutions of other states are inferior to their own. And they shall send spectators of another sort, if they have the consent of the guardians, being such citizens as desire to look a little more at leisure at the doings of other men; and these no law shall hinder.

For a city which has no experience of good and bad men or intercourse with them, can never be thoroughly and perfectly civilized, nor, again, can the citizens of a city properly observe the laws by habit only, and without an intelligent understanding of them. And there always are in the world a few inspired men whose acquaintance is beyond price, and who spring up quite as much in ill-ordered as in well-ordered cities. And he who lives in a well-ordered city should be ever tracking them out, going forth by sea and land to seek after him who is incorruptible — seeking to establish more firmly the good institutions which they have, and amending what is deficient; for without this examination and inquiry a city will never continue perfect any more than if the examination is ill-conducted.

2. THE BURIAL OF THE DEAD

Few subjects, as Plato has discovered, occasion more trouble to the legislator, than the disposal of the dead. The deepest feelings and the most unreasonable prejudices of mankind unite to increase the difficulty; and religion is so intimately bound up everywhere with the sentiment of veneration and respect for the departed, that it becomes almost impossible to alter the prevailing practices except by a slow and gradual process of enlightenment.

The regulations which Plato desires to introduce are admirable, and contain much which is worthy of our serious consideration. He expressly enjoins that the dead are to be interred in remote and barren spots; and this was easy to effect in a rugged and mountainous country, like Greece, where there are extensive districts which can never be brought under cultivation. He would certainly have censured the customs of European nations, which long permitted the dead to be placed in sacred buildings and in churchyards amid the crowded populations of cities, and which still allow large tracts of soil to be diverted from their natural purpose " of affording sustenance to the living."

Cremation, we observe with some surprise, is not mentioned by him, either here or in a previous passage relating to the burial of the Censors. The rite was probably more common in the heroic ages of Greece than in the historic period; but it is alluded to by Herodotus in the story of King Darius and the Callatians, and also by Thucydides in his description of the Plague at Athens. Plato may have thought that it would not be required in a state such as the Cnosian colony, chiefly composed of husbandmen spread over a wide area of territory. In our own day it appears to be the best solution of a very difficult question.

The preference of Plato for short epitaphs and simple monuments will meet with general approval in modern times. He shared in full measure the moderation and restraint which marked the Hellenic character; the bad taste and adulation by which our memorials of the dead are too often disfigured would have been revolting to him. And we, when we look with regret upon the " heavy load " which by-gone generations have left to us, may well wish that Plato's rules could have been put in force four or five centuries ago.

The same good sense appears in his law against extravagant expenditure upon funerals. This has been in every age a source of mischief, and has contributed much to the impoverishment of the people. It is one of the evils which are universally deplored, but which no efforts seem able to exterminate. And even Plato, the boldest and most undaunted of reformers, acknowledges that great concessions must be made in these matters to the weakness of human nature. The legislator must have resort to " persuasion rather than to force; " and we may be allowed to borrow Plato's own language, and to say that " men will listen with more gentleness and good-will to the precepts of the lawgiver, if their souls are prepared to receive his words; even a little done in the way of conciliation gains their ear, and is always worth having."

Thus is a man born and brought up and begets and brings up his own children, and has his share of dealings with other men, and suffers if he has done wrong to any one, and receives satisfaction if he has been wronged, and so at the appointed time, under the dominion of the laws, he grows old, and meets his end in the order of nature. Concerning the dead of either sex, the religious ceremonies which may fittingly be performed, whether appertaining to the Gods of the under world or of this, shall be decided by the interpreters with absolute authority. Their

sepulchres are to be in places which are not cultivated, and there shall be no monuments to them,
either large or small, but they shall occupy that part
of the country which is naturally adapted for receiving and concealing the bodies of the dead with as
little hurt as possible to the living. No man, living
or dead, shall deprive the living of the sustenance
which the earth, our mother, is naturally inclined to
bear to them. And let not the mound be piled higher
than would be the work of five men completed in five
days; nor shall the stone which is placed over the
spot be larger than would be sufficient to receive the
praises of the dead included in four heroic lines. Nor
shall the laying-out of the dead continue for a longer
time than is sufficient to distinguish between him who
is in a trance only and him who is really dead, and
speaking generally, the third day after death will be
a fair time for carrying out the body to the sepulchre.

Now we must believe the legislator when he tells
us that the soul is in all respects superior to the body,
and that even in life what makes each one of us to
be what we are is only the soul; and that the body
follows us about in the likeness of each of us, and
therefore, when we are dead, the bodies of the dead
are rightly said to be our shades or images; for that
the true and immortal being of each one of us which
is called the soul goes on her way to other Gods —
that before them she may give an account — an
inspiring hope to the good, but very terrible to the
bad, as the laws of our fathers tell us, which also say
that not much can be done in the way of helping a
man after he is dead. But the living — he should be
helped by all his kindred, that while in life he may
be the holiest and justest of men, and after death
may have no great sins to be punished in the world

below. If this be true, a man ought not to waste his substance under the idea that all this lifeless mass of flesh which is in process of burial is connected with him; he should consider that the son, or brother, or the beloved one, whoever he may be, whom he thinks he is laying in the earth, has gone away to complete and fulfil his own destiny, and that his duty is rightly to order the present, and to spend moderately on the lifeless altar of the Gods below.

But the legislator does not intend moderation to be taken in the sense of meanness. Let the law, then, be as follows: — The expenditure on the entire funeral, of him who is of the highest class, shall not exceed five minae, and for him who is of the second class, three minae, and for him who is of the third class two minae, and for him who is of the fourth class one mina, will be a fair limit of expense. The guardians of the law ought to take especial care of the different ages of life, whether childhood or manhood, or any other age. And at the end of all, let there be some one guardian of the law presiding, who shall be chosen by the friends of the deceased to superintend, and let it be glory to him to fulfil well and with moderation the offices of the dead, and a discredit to him if they are not well fulfilled. Let the laying out and other ceremonies be in accordance with the law, and the lawgiver who is also a citizen may concede something to custom. It would be monstrous to command any man to weep or abstain from weeping over the dead, but he may forbid cries of lamentation, and not allow the voice of the mourner to be heard outside the house; also, he may forbid the bringing of the dead body into the open streets, or the processions of mourners in the streets, and may require that before daybreak they should be outside the city. Let these, then, be our laws relating to such matters, and let him who obeys be free from penalty; but he who disobeys even a single guardian of the law shall be punished by them all in a fitting penalty.

Episode #41 – *The Red Menace - Pa*

Isaiah 33:22

Welcome to Wisconsin, the Land of Cheese
    and… Jellyfish?.....*45*
So How do Jellyfish Fossilize.....*47*
A Trip to the Quarry *48*

Why this is Good Evidence for
    Creationists *49*
Animal Scrabble *53*

Episode #42 – *The Ancient City of the Jaguar - Part I ....*   *54*

Romans 5:12

Chichen Itza.....*54*
The Story in Genesis Explains Many Things
    About Our World.....*57*
If Genesis is not True the Way it is Written,
    Other things do not Make Sense *59*

Problem of Time *60*
Communication Breakdown *62*
The Problem of the Symbolic *63*

Episode #43 – *The Ancient City of the Jaguar - Part II ....*   *64*

Acts 17

Acts 17.....*64*
Mystery Animal – the Armadillo *65*
Spider Money.....*67*

Yucca, Yucca.....*67*
Mayan Ruins Maze.....*69*
People are Valuable.....*74*

Episode #44 – *Darwin's Fiery Mountain - Part I ....*   *75*

Psalm 104

Evolution's Two-stroke Engine *75*
Mutations: The First Stroke of the
    Evolutionary Engine....*76*
The Galapagos Islands.....*78*
Building Blocks Activity.....*79*
The Tortoise.....*80*
Evolution's Engine Needs a Mechanic! *82*

After Their Kind.....*83*
The Master Mechanic Makes No
    Mistakes *84*
Natural Selection and the Evolutionary
    Engine.....*85*
What is a Species Anyway?.....*87*
Summary.....*90*

Episode #45 – *Darwin's Fiery Mountain - Part II* *91*

Genesis 8:17

The Flightless Cormorant....*91*
The Iguana.....*92*

Volcano Disaster Recovery.....*94*
Animal Classification Game.....*96*

Episode #46 – *Darrow's Bluff* *97*

Matthew 10:33 & 34

The Scopes Trial.....*97*
Two Worldviews *98*
The Characters of the Trial.....*100*

The Science of the Trial.....*101*
End of the Scopes Trial.....*107*
Scopes Crossword Puzzle.....*108*

Episode #47 – *The Descent from Sandia Peak - Part I* *110*

Colossians 3:20

Mountain Climber Joe.....*110*
Biomes....*110*

Activity –- Help Mountain Joe.....*114*
Forest Fires have a Purpose.....*116*

Episode #48 – *The Descent from Sandia Peak - Part II* *118*

Psalm 139

Monarch Butterflies.....*119*
Hummingbird.....*120*
Roadrunner.....*121*

Skunk.....*122*
Children you are a Blessing.....*123*
Eco-Trivia....*124*

Getting the Most From This Study Guide

The Jonathan Park Audio Adventures were produced to help children and families have a strong foundation on which to build their faith! Unfortunately, many live as if their belief in the Bible is just another brand of religion. However, God has given us a gift that we often take for granted – He has asked us to believe in truth! Sadly, many Christians are intimidated by evolutionary ideas and told that the Word of God has been disproven by science. The truth is that if God really created the universe, animals, and mankind like He said in Genesis, we should be able to investigate this world and find evidence that what He says is true... and we do!

Think about the difference between the Christian and evolutionary worldviews. If evolution is true, then there is no God and we are the product of random evolutionary processes. As nothing more than a bunch of molecules, we have no purpose in life. On the other hand, if we were created, it means that we were made especially by a loving Creator who has a unique purpose for each of our lives! This difference can completely change a person's life! Truly knowing that God's Word is true is a foundation that will change every aspect of a child's life. That's what we hope to accomplish with the Jonathan Park project – to teach families about scientific evidence that is in harmony with God's Word.

We've designed the audio adventures so families can enjoy them in their cars – while on trips or just running errands. They can listen at home or during family devotional time. Our goal is to provide exciting adventures that run deep with creation apologetics and Biblical lessons. We hope that you enjoy them regardless of where you listen to them!

This Jonathan Park Study Guide has been designed to maximize teaching from each episode in the Jonathan Park Series. Our hope is that after listening to each Jonathan Park Audio Adventure, parents will sit down with their children and work through the information provided in this booklet. Here's how we recommend you use this guide with your child:

1. Listen to an episode from the Jonathan Park: The Hunt for Beowulf – Album #5.
2. Begin your study by praying with your child. Pray that God will teach you truth and continue to build your faith.
3. In the Table of Contents, we've listed Scripture references for each episode. Spend time reading through this section of God's Word.
4. Next, open this Study Guide to the corresponding section. The information is arranged in bite-

sized nuggets – each builds upon the previous one. Read through the information with your child and relate it back to the Word of God.

5. Let the child ask questions, and help them find answers. This Study Guide may be the key to unlocking doubts that a child has. Always follow up a child's question. Refer to other creation science resources, or make a commitment to search for the answer together. These questions are excellent ways to take them deeper into God's Word.

6. End in prayer. Thank the Lord for the specific things He has taught during this time.

While this Study Guide is designed to address *scientific* issues, we have also created devotionals that focus on the *Biblical* aspect of the topics presented on each episode of Jonathan Park. In addition, we have also prepared Real Adventures – activities that can be used to reinforce the information within this booklet. For these devotionals and activities, go to www.JonathanPark.com and click on "Real Adventures".

"But sanctify the Lord God in your hearts: and be ready always to give an answer to every man that asketh you a reason of the hope that is in you with meekness and fear."

- I Peter 3:15

Creation Week

Do you remember what God created on which day? Here are some pictures to remind you of the order of creation.

Find the days on the chart where God created the air, sea, and land animals.

On which day did He create humans?

All life on earth was created within this one week.

Did you know that this means that humans and dinosaurs lived at the same time ?!!.

Evidence for Man's co-existence with Dinosaurs in History

Have you ever heard stories about dragons? Do you think that dragons could have actually been dinosaurs?

Dinosaur

The word dinosaur which means 'terrible reptile' in Latin, wasn't invented until 1842 by an Englishman named Sir Richard Owen, but the word "dragon" or its equivalent has been used in many cultures for hundreds of years.

1842

The Chinese have a word "kong long" which means terrible dragon. They do not have the word dinosaur. The Chinese were using this word years before people dug up a dinosaur bone. So when we read really old stories about dragons it is possible that 'dragon' may have been the old original word for what we now call dinosaurs.

恐龍

Ancient legends about dragons, and man's encounters with them, are found all around the world, and dragon images have been found on the Ishtar Gate of Babylon, in Egyptian hieroglyphs and Ethiopian sketches, on the fronts of Viking ships, on Aztec temples, on cliffs above the Mississippi River, and on bones carved by Inuits, a tribe of Native peoples in Alaska.

This may be evidence that humans and dinosaurs did live together at one time.

Oseberg Viking Ship
A bras-wood plate excavated in 1904 in Oseberg, Norway.
Ship believed to be from around 800 AD.

This is the Welsh flag with a dragon on it.

China is very well known for its use of dragons in its culture.

This dragon is very artistic and stylized but is similar to the Welsh flag that we saw before.

Dragons and the Bible

The word 'dragon' in Hebrew is "tannim" and is used over 20 times in the Old Testament.

In Job, we are given two very detailed descriptions of dinosaur-like creatures: Behemoth and Leviathan.

Behemoth

"Behold now behemoth, which I made with thee; he eateth grass as an ox. Lo now, his strength is in his loins, and his force is in the navel of his belly. He moveth his tail like a cedar: the sinews of his stones are wrapped together. His bones are as strong pieces of brass; his bones are like bars of iron. He is the chief of the ways of God: he that made him can make his sword to approach unto him. Surely the mountains bring him forth food, where all the beasts of the field play. He lieth under the shady trees, in the covert of the reed, and fens. The shady trees cover him with their shadow; the willows of the brook compass him about. Behold, he drinketh up a river, and hasteth not: he trusteth that he can draw up Jordan into his mouth. He taketh it with his eyes: his nose pierceth through snares." Job 40:15-24

Now go back and circle all the words in this paragraph that describe Behemoth, like "strength" and "tail." What type of animal does this sound like to you?

Leviathan

"Canst thou draw out leviathan with an hook? or his tongue with a cord which thou lettest down? Canst thou put an hook into his nose? or bore his jaw through with a thorn? Who can open the doors of his face? his teeth are terrible round about. His scales are his pride, shut up together as with a close seal. One is so near to another, that no air can come between them. They are joined one to another, they stick together, that they cannot be sundered. By his neesings a light doth shine, and his eyes are like the eyelids of the morning. Out of his mouth go burning lamps, and sparks of fire leap out. Out of his nostrils goeth smoke, as out of a seething pot or caldron. His breath kindleth coals, and a flame goeth out of his mouth. In his neck remaineth strength, and sorrow is turned into joy before him. The flakes of his flesh are joined together: they are firm in themselves; they cannot be moved. His heart is as firm as a stone; yea, as hard as a piece of the nether millstone. When he raiseth up himself, the mighty are afraid: by reason of breakings they purify themselves. The sword of him that layeth at him cannot hold: the spear, the dart, nor the habergeon. He esteemeth iron as straw, and brass as rotten wood. The arrow cannot make him flee: slingstones are turned with him into stubble. Darts are counted as stubble: he laugheth at the shaking of a spear. Sharp stones are under him: he spreadeth sharp pointed things upon the mire. He maketh the deep to boil like a pot: he maketh the sea like a pot of ointment." Job 41:1-2. 14-31

*"So is this great and wide sea, wherein are things creeping innumerable, both small and great beasts. There go the ships: there is that **leviathan**, whom thou hast made to play therein."* Psalm 104:25-26

What images do these descriptions bring to mind? Below, draw a picture of what you think Leviathan looked like.

11

Evidence of Humans and Dinosaurs Living at the Same Time

Petroglyphs
Petroglyphs are drawings or carvings made on rocks made by people living a long time ago.

Natural Bridges Monument in Utah.
Under one of the rock bridges in this state park there is a drawing that appears to be a dinosaur, that is thought to be made by the Anasazi Indians. They lived between 400 A.D. to 1,300 A.D.

Hava supai Canyon in Arizona.
There is a picture of an animal standing on its hind legs that resembles a dinosaur.

San Rafael Reef in Utah.
In Black Dragon Canyon there is a large carving of what resembles a Pterosaur-a flying reptile. About 200 miles away from the canyon, fossil tracks have been found that may have been made by a Pterosaur.

Figurines from Acambaro, Mexico. In 1944, over 33,000 ceramic figures were found and many look like dinosaurs.

So Where Did They Go?

As you have read, there is quite a lot of evidence in history that dragons may actually be dinosaurs and that they lived at the same time as humans. Because dinosaurs were created on day 6 as we talked about earlier, we know that they most likely were also on Noah's ark during the flood. However, many dinosaurs were killed in the flood or went extinct during climate changes after that. This may be why we now find only their bones. However, those bones can tell us a lot!

Geological Evidence for Dinosaurs

Dinosaur Graveyards

Dinosaur fossils have been found all over the world, many of them in what are known as dinosaur graveyards.

Dinosaur graveyards got their name because there are many fossilized animals buried in the same place. Unlike human graveyards, that are orderly and neat, dinosaur graveyards are a jumbled mess. There are no headstones telling you who or what they were and when the animal died. If there were then we would have no problem determining how old a fossil was! But we are not so fortunate.

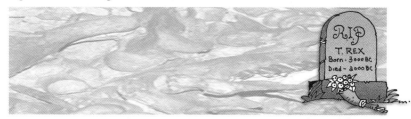

How do you think that a bunch of animals could become buried in the same place without being put there by a person?

A. They were all in a train accident.

B. They ate too much bubble gum.

C. A large flood drowned them and carried their bodies there.

In England on the Isle of Wight, scientists have discovered a dinosaur graveyard with fossils of a Baryonyx, Iguanadon, Brachiosaur, Eotyrannus, Polacanthus, and more.

Dinosaur Forensics

Finding fossils and putting them back together correctly is like examining the evidence of a crime scene. A dinosaur expert must prepare the fossil very carefully if he wants as complete a picture of what happened as possible. Below is an example of the process scientists often use to extract and preserve fossils.

Fossil Preparation Process

The first thing that has to be done is to stabilize the specimen. When the fossil dries tiny cracks develop, so really thin glue is carefully put in the cracks so that the fossil does not break apart. Sometimes it is brought back to the lab in a plaster wrap similar to the one you will make at the end of this chapter.

Secondly, the fossil is uncovered with pneumatic hammers. These are tiny jackhammers that chip away the rock from the fossil. They have to be very careful not to touch the fossil with the hammer or they could break it so this is done under a microscope.

Next, there is still a thin layer that covers the fossil so a microsandblaster is used to complete the cleaning. A microsandblaster is another tiny tool that blows abrasive powder on the fossil to clean it off.

Finally, the rock that the fossil is imbedded in is cleaned up. The chisel marks are smoothed out to make the specimen look good.

Now that the fossil parts are prepared, they can be put together and studied.

English Dinosaur

In 1990 in England on the Isle of Wight, Steve Hutt discovered a Brachiosaur-like dinosaur. However, after the fossils were prepared and put back together, it was determined that parts of it were missing, including the dinosaur's head, neck, tail, and back legs. It was also evident from the original sediment that surrounded it that it had once been submerged in water.

Interpreting the Results

Based on the evidence, two very different conclusions were reached by two different groups: the evolutionists and the creationists.

The evolutionists decided that:	The creationists determined that:
1. It was missing its head, neck, tail, and legs because it had been attacked and killed by another animal.	1. The dinosaur was killed by a torrential flood.
2. What was left of it then sunk to the bottom of a swamp.	2. During that violent upheaval, various pieces of its body became separated from each other.
3. It was then gradually covered by sediment for millions of years as it fossilized.	3. Those pieces were then buried in a jumbled mess in the sediment left behind by the water.

Problems with the evolutionist's explanation:

1. There is no evidence that the animal was attacked by another dinosaur.
2. The sediment that surrounded the dinosaur indicates that it was left by large amounts of water, not by a stagnate swamp.
3. If it had died in a swamp, it should have decayed and rotted away, not fossilized.

What's the point?

So who cares about dragons, petroglyphs, figurines, fire breathing Leviathan, and fossil graveyards?

Evolutionary scientists would say that dragons are mythical creatures that did not really exist so they couldn't have been dinosaurs. They would also say that dinosaurs and humans lived millions of years apart so they could not have lived at the same time.

Creation scientists would say that the evidence we have talked about indicates that the dragon legends around the world may actually be talking about dinosaurs, indicating that dinosaurs and humans lived at the same time. We find dinosaur "artwork" around the world that seems to confirm this idea. Also fossil graveyards are evidence for a world wide flood–the flood of the Bible!

Making Your Own Fossil Cast

Materials:

Plaster of Paris
Bucket
Mixing stick
Water

Mud
Toothbrush
Tiny pick
Small paint
brush

Procedure:

Find, or make a thick muddy pool in your garden. The mud should be thick like clay. Make an imprint of your footprint, handprint, a fern press, or a pet print in the mud. Leave it to dry. Follow the directions on the plaster package for mixing in the bucket. Poor the plaster into the imprint that you made and leave it to set or harden. Return to carefully lift up the plaster cast. You may need to use a stick or dull knife to cut around the outside of the plaster to lift it out. Turn it over and inspect your cast. Use a toothbrush, old dentist tool, and small brush to clean off your cast. Be very careful not to damage the imprint with your cleaning techniques!

Eeeewwww what is that smell?
It smells like rotten eggs!

If you've ever gotten a whiff of sulfur, it's a smell you're not likely to soon forget! It has a very strong odor that resembles the smell of a spoiled egg.

The words "Iwo" and "Jima" are Japanese for "sulfur" and "island" or "Sulfur Island." Because Iwo Jima is a volcanic island and is still an active volcano, sulfur gas is constantly leaking out of hot vents on the island's surface, giving the air a sulfer smell... hence it's name!

The island of Iwo Jima, located in the Pacific Ocean, is part of the Ogasawara Islands south of Japan and was a Japanese base during WWII where a famous battle was fought and many people lost their lives. The island is of great historic interest as well as scientific interest.

There are several types of volcanoes around the world:

Cinder cones-simplest volcano formed from particles and blobs of lava ejected from the crater from a central vent.

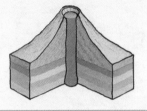

Composite volcanoes- are built of alternating layers of lava flows, volcanic ash, cinders, blocks, and bombs. Mount St. Helen's and Mount Fuji in Japan are two examples.

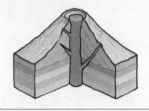

Shield volcanoes- are built of fluid lava flows such as those in Hawaii.

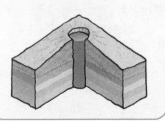

Lava domes-built by thick bulbous masses of lava such as the center of Mount St. Helen's.

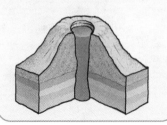

A **caldera** is a volcanic feature, a depression, formed by the collapse of the volcano into itself. A very well known caldera is Crater Lake in Oregon which used be called Mount Mazama.

Iwo Jima is inside a caldera that is about 9 km wide. In the last 100 years it has had several small eruptions.

There are two main domes on the island.

Because of magma flowing into an underground pool about a mile and a half below the caldera floor, the island is actually being lifted up, and has been growing an average of about 7 inches per year for more than 400 years. Since the Marines raised the flag on Mt. Suribachi, the dome has raised about 33 feet.

Volcanoes and the Flood

Iwo Jima is a present-day example of volcanic activity. Creation scientists study volcanoes to answer questions like, "Where did such colossal amounts of water come from?" and "What were the 'Fountains of the great deep' that we read about in Genesis 7:11?" The more they explore, the more interesting evidence they find, particularly on the ocean's floor. Let's look at some of the unique features found on the bottom of the ocean!

Explorers have found extraordinary features on the ocean floor, including black smokers, volcanic vents, and underwater calderas.

A **black smoker** is a chimney-like structure on the bottom of the ocean where very hot water, chemicals and gasses spew out. The chimney structure is made from sulfur coming from under the earth's crust that has hardened onto the volcanic rocks. They are called black smokers because the hot mineral water mixes with the cold ocean water and tiny particles form that make the vent water look black.

On the Southern Ural mountains of Russia, scientists have found actual fossils of ancient black smoker chimneys. They have also found fossils of the animals that lived around the vents which are the same as those in present day vent communities.

Around these black smokers have accumulated wonderful creatures that you do not find anywhere else, such as huge tube worms, crabs, and giant clams. The creatures have adapted to the hot temperatures of the water and use the chemicals that come out of the smoker to live. Black smokers may be left over "fountains of the great deep" that helped to flood the earth in Noah's flood.

Volcanic vents, found on the ocean floor, spew very hot water, near 350 degrees Celsius, into the ocean. The hot water comes up from openings in the crust of the earth.

An **underwater caldera** is similar to the Iwo Jima caldera but it is on the ocean floor. They are also called submarine calderas and were formed by a huge volcanic eruption on the ocean floor. Underwater calderas were recently discovered with in the last 20 years, and many of those are off the coast of Japan in the Pacific Ocean. There is one named Myojin Knoll Caldera, 4000ft. below the surface and it is 4 miles across, the same size as Crater Lake! In 1996 they discovered a huge ore deposit of gold, silver, and other minerals inside this caldera that may be worth over a billion dollars. The eruptions that created these giant calderas may have been a source of large amounts of water.

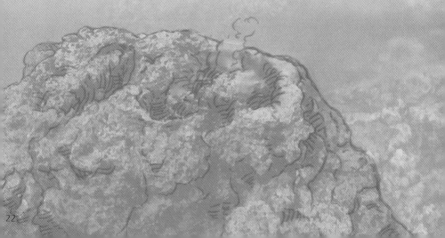

Have you always thought that all the water from Noah's flood fell as rain from the sky?

As you carefully read Genesis 7:11, you will notice that this may not have been the only source of water.

Volcanoes exploding on the ocean floor may have provided water to help flood the earth during Noah's flood. Volcanoes not only release hot magma but also water.

When Mount St. Helen's erupted, 90% of that eruption was water.

When hot magma came in contact with the cold ocean water, it would have made super-heated steam clouds that would release mass amounts of water into the atmosphere. This steam would make more water available to flood the earth.

Large composite volcanoes (near water level) when they erupt, often fall inward on themselves and suck water into itself causing huge tsunamis. In 1883, a volcano, Krakatoa, erupted in Indonesia. It's collapse created a tidal wave that killed 36,000 people.

Spewing Forth Experiment

Materials:

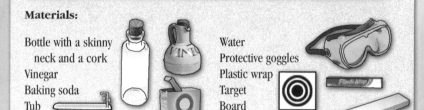

Bottle with a skinny
   neck and a cork
Vinegar
Baking soda
Tub

Water
Protective goggles
Plastic wrap
Target
Board

Procedure:
Place 1/2 cup of vinegar in the bottle and set aside for later. Put about a table spoon of baking soda onto the center of a small piece of plastic wrap. The plastic wrap should be about 3 square inches. Grab the four corners of the wrap and loosely twist together. Quickly push the wrap and its contents into the bottle and replace the cork. Place the bottle into a position slanted up with a board so that you think it will hit the target. Stand back and wait for the cork to be spewed forth into the air. Adjust the distance between the bottle and the target so that you can make the mark. Try this as many times as you would like.

Fill a bucket with water. Make sure that the water level is able to cover the bottle and cork when it is placed in the bucket, about one inch or more. Follow the same procedure as above for placing the baking soda into the bottle. You may need to first put in some fresh vinegar in the bottle. Quickly place the soda into the bottle, cork, and place the bottle into the bucket of water. Stand back and wait to see what happens. As with most experiments you may need to tinker with the materials to get the desired results, such as gently shaking the bottle to mix the soda and vinegar. The baking soda in the vinegar when corked should build up pressure and then eventually explode out of the bottle shooting the cork into the air. Adjust the amount of soda and vinegar to change the results.

Rock Layers

The Precambrian Cardenas Basalt rock layer that is found in the Grand Canyon appears to be volcanic rock that may have been laid down during a huge water event.

Fossil Conditions

The flood and volcanoes provide the conditions for fossils to be made.
Silica mixed with hot water is the perfect solution for making great fossils. These two things would be present during volcanic eruptions.

> The Chinle formation found at Ghost Ranch is a volcanic layer where thousands of dinosaur fossils are found. There are many of these layers through out the earth.

Layers of volcanic rocks, water and silica, and lots of fossils are evidence that volcanoes may have been erupting during the flood.

What is all this in a nut shell?

In this episode, we learned that

(1) Iwo Jima is an example of a caldera that is formed when a composite volcano explodes under or near the surface of water.

(2) Hot water comes from the earth's crust under the ocean through black smokers, volcanic vents, and past volcanoes exploding, forming submarine calderas.

(3) The conditions for layers of rocks and fossil formation are perfect during volcanic activity and the presence of lots of water.

God is Powerful

Psalm 104:32 - *He looketh on the earth, and it trembleth: he toucheth the hills, and they smoke.*

Psalm 97:5 - *The hills melted like wax at the presence of the LORD, at the presence of the Lord of the whole earth.*

Creation is often used in the Bible to describe God's might and power, showing us that He is in control of our natural world, sustaining all things, and upholding all things. It draws us to have reverence and awe for His power, wisdom, and character.

Iwo Jima is part of the Ogasawara Islands, south of Japan. A unique beauty and variety of animal life is found here, both on land and in the surrounding Pacific Ocean.

One of these is the Humpback Whale. The humpback whale is one of the most well known whales in the Pacific Ocean and is frequently seen in the waters near Iwo Jima.

Humpback whales are active whales that like to jump out of the water (this is called breaching), splash with their tail fluke, and sing.

Their favorite foods are a type of shrimp called krill and small schooling fish, and they have a very unique way of "fishing" called "bubble netting." Several whales dive underneath a school of fish and then swim up while blowing out bubbles around the fish. This bubble net causes the fish to gather together into one large group. Then the whales swim into the school and gulp down fish.

Migration

Migration means to travel from one location to another. People sometimes migrate from cold areas in the winter to warm areas. Whales do the same. They migrate from the cold waters that have lots of food in the summer to the warm waters in the wintertime. This trip happens every year and is about 6,000 miles-worth of swimming!

Every year they migrate to one of three wintering grounds.

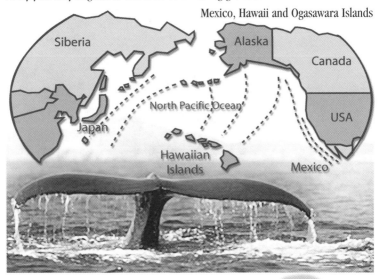

The whales that stay for the winter in the Ogasawara Islands migrate back to the Aleutian Islands of Alaska.

Why do you think that a whale would want to migrate to one of the three places mentioned for the winter months? (For the same reason that many people like to go to Florida and Arizona for the winter). It's warmer!

Scientists do not know for sure how the whales know where and when to migrate, but they have a few ideas:

Guesses for when they migrate:

| Length of days change from summer to winter | Cooler water temperature in the winter | Less food available in the winter | Inner clock that signals the time to migrate |

Guesses for direction they migrate:

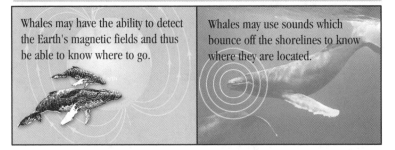

| Whales may have the ability to detect the Earth's magnetic fields and thus be able to know where to go. | Whales may use sounds which bounce off the shorelines to know where they are located. |

Scientists think that the whale's inner ears may be involved.
In 2000, whales whose inner ears believed to be damaged became beached possibly because they lost their direction.

Even though scientists do not know how whales know when and where to migrate, it is a part of the design of this amazing animal. They have been created with abilities that humans cannot figure out, but that are needed for them to be able to survive.

Sand Tiger Sharks

Sand Tiger Sharks, also found in the waters off the island of Iwo Jima, are another example of design found in animals. They have special abilities that make them very well suited for life in the ocean.

Design Features:

Olfactory Organ (smell)

A sharks nostril can detect the smell of blood one part per million from 1mile away, or roughly the equivalent of 10 drops in an average-size pool full of water!

Eyesight

Special reflective pigment in the back of the eye that acts like a mirror to reflect light so that they can see in very dim light. It is the same reflection that you see in a cat's eye when light shines on them at night.

Crazy Fact
The sand tiger shark is one of the only sharks that changes its buoyancy (its ability to float) by "burping." It gulps air and saves it in its stomach and lets out air when it comes to the surface.

Hearing

They can hear from a couple of miles away. They are attracted to low frequencies such as the low frequencies that an injured or dieing fish would make.

Lateral Line

Lateral line is a series of fluid filled grooves on the sides of the fish. These canals help the fish to feel vibrations, movement, sound, and pressure changes in the water.

Ampullae of Lorenzini

This fancy name is for special cells that are located at the base of the sharks snout, lower jaw, and around the eyes. They detect the electric fields that other fish give off.

As we have just read, God has given both the Humpback Whale and the Sand Tiger Shark incredibly unique mechanisms that help them to survive, and instincts that even scientists cannot explain! It's almost as if they're following an internal code that is telling them what to do—or are they?

DNA

What could these letters represent? They stand for deoxyribonucleic acid. It carries your genetic code. Your genes determine many things about you such as hair color, height, and whether or not you will have freckles.

A T C G are the abbreviations for the chemicals that make up the proteins which make your hair brown or eyes green. The order and number of the chemicals in the code are de-coded or translated by your cells with another molecule called RNA.

RNA and the Navajo Code Talkers

In 1942 a missionary's son named Philip Johnston persuaded the military that the Navajo language would form a great basis for an unbreakable code. The Japanese were known to be amazing code breakers and had broken all the codes that the military had used. The US Marines ended up with 400 Navajo code talkers that transmitted important battle information over the telephone and radio.

The Code

This is how it worked. For each letter of our alphabet the 'code talker' would say a Navajo word that would translate into an English word that began with the letter they wanted to pass on. So a 'b' could be represented by several Navajo words like those for 'bug', 'bow', or 'buffalo'.

This code was so good because the Navajo language was spoken by very few people outside the Navajo themselves and was an unwritten language. With the help of the code talkers the battle of Iwo Jima was won.

RNA is like the Navajo code talkers; without RNA your body would not know the meaning of the code.

The code is like a foreign language, such as Navajo, and is not understood unless it is learned or interpreted. Information like that in a code always comes form a source.

Think about a sewing pattern like one for a mitten.

This pattern gives you the information for making mittens. And the thread holds it all together. DNA is like the thread in the mitten. It holds the code for all life and holds everything together. The thread of DNA is found in all living organisms. It is also unique in every organism. No two DNA codes are the same. That's why even twins aren't exactly the same. They may look alike, but they each have a different set of DNA that makes them different in other ways. Each code or pattern is different because each organism is unique.

Secret Code Game

Here is a code. Can you decipher its meaning?

7 15 4   9 19   3 18 5 1 20 15 18

HINTS

Each group of underlined represent one word. This code is a three-word sentence.

Make your own secret code message and give it to someone to see if they can de-code it.

Conclusion: The Case for Design

What we have been talking about here are cases for design.

Inside our case we can find what we know:

Information must come from somewhere. Information has been only found to come from intelligence.

DNA is complex information in a code and makes unique organisms.

If all information must come from somewhere, and that somewhere must be an intelligent source, a source intelligent enough to create incredibly complex DNA codes that are unique to each and every living thing that exists, has ever existed, or will exist, that fits better with the Creation account of Genesis than with random evolution, don't you think?

Answer: **God is Creator.** Each letter of the alphabet is given a number beginning with A being 1 and so on.

34

Animal Scramble

Instructions:

Make a copy and cut out each square of the animal scramble and put the pieces back together in a way that makes a picture of an animal. You will be able to figure out what the picture of the animal is when it is correctly assembled.

Start off with a scrambled picture and put it together.

Please Don't Squish that Jellyfish!

Have you ever been walking down an ocean beach and come across what looks like a big blob of clear gel lying on the sand? If so, you probably found what remained of a jellyfish that accidentally washed up on shore. And if you're like many visitors to the beach, you may have even accidentally stepped on one! Yuk!

So what is a Jellyfish? Is it really a fish?

Starfish and jellyfish have sort of been misnamed. Neither of them are actually fish, but fall into a category that also includes coral because of the way they develop. This is a diagram of the way a jellyfish grows from an egg to an adult.

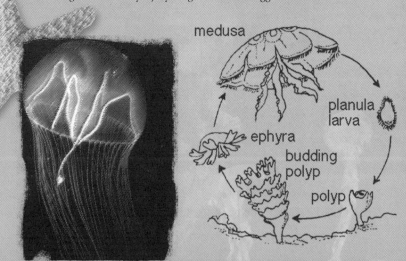

medusa

planula larva

ephyra

budding polyp

polyp

There are many different types of jellyfish, ranging in size from the smallest, called the Irukandji, which is 1 1/2 inches across, to the Lion's Mane jellyfish, that can be up to 8 feet wide and have tentacles almost 200 feet long!

Lion's Mane Jellyfish

Irukandji Jellyfish

What are jellyfish made of anyway?

Jellyfish are made mostly of water, between 95-98%! Their body has two layers and between the layers is a jelly-like substance. If a jellyfish washed ashore, the water would disappear and the body of the jellyfish would flatten.

Make some Jell-O Jellyfish

To experience the texture of a jellyfish first-hand, follow the directions on a box of Jell-O. The consistency of this type of Jell-O is like the consistency of the gelatin-like substance found in the bell of most jellyfish.

Jellyfish Design

Even what appears to be a blob of jelly is a complicated, designed organism!!

What a swimmer!

The bell or sac is the body part that the jellyfish uses to swim.
Muscles around the rim of the sac squeeze it closed very quickly causing water to shoot out like jet propulsion.

Sea Nettle

Jellyfish Propulsion Activity

Materials:

Water in a bathtub

Balloon

Procedure:
- Fill a bathtub or large sink up with water.
- Fill a balloon with water. (This is like the jelly filling its bell with water)
- Squeeze the opening of the balloon shut by holding it with your fingers.
- With that same hand push the balloon under the water, then let go of the balloon and watch the water push the balloon across the tub as it is released. This is similar to how a jellyfish gets pushed through the water.

What a hunter!

Jellyfish get their food by using their harpoon stinging cells called nematocysts that are found on their tentacles.

The harpoon is triggered by touch or movement.

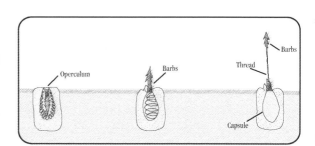

The man-made harpoon is very similar to the harpoon that God made for the jellyfish!

Don't Touch That Jelly!

Although they may appear to be harmless blobs of goo, many types of jellyfish are actually extremely poisonous, even to humans, and can sting you even after they've washed up on shore. So if you just can't resist examining one you find on the sand, poke it with a stick or something other than your fingers, especially if its tentacles are still attached!

This is a picture of a Sea Wasp or box jelly. The sting from this type of jelly can kill a human very quickly.

39

Some jellyfish find nourishment through their amazing symbiotic relationship with algae. The word "symbiotic" means two animals living in harmony with each other without hurting each other.

This is how the relationship works: The jellyfish lets the algae come in and live inside its tissues, providing it with both a sheltered "apartment" and also with access to the one thing it needs to produce its food ... sunlight! The jellyfish does this by inverting itself on the shallow bottom of the ocean with its tentacles floating upward, enabling the algae to get as much sunlight as possible.

Upside-down jellyfish

Then, after a "batch" has been made, the jellyfish releases a special chemical that signals the algae to share some of its food with the jellyfish! What an amazing design! Does that sound like an "evolutionary accident" to you?

Man O' War fish: another symbiotic relationship.

These are very special fish that are called Man O' War fish. They spend most of their time among the tentacles of the Man O' War jellyfish! How do they survive? They are immune to the sting of the jelly. They live among the tentacles and clean up after the jelly. So the fish gets food and housing while serving the jellyfish!

What a sailor!

Jellies move about the ocean not only through
jet propulsion but also by using the natural
ocean currents. There is lots of food for the
jellies to eat in the currents.

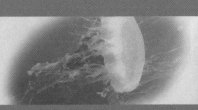

What a light!

Many organisms in the ocean and on land do something very amazing. They can
make light! This ability is called Bioluminescence or florescence.

Bioluminescence

> Bio = life
> Lumen = light
>
> This fancy word means the making of
> light by a living organism.

Organisms that give off light

On land
Fire flies
Glow worms

In water
Shrimp
Squid
Fish
Jellyfish

Purpose:

1. A way to scare away enemies with a flash of light
2. A lure to draw prey closer to be eaten
3. Attract a mate

This deep sea Angler Fish uses its
bioluminescent lure to catch food.

Think about that. An animal that can make its own light inside its body tissue. Can you do that? As people, we have only invented a way to flip a switch to il**lumin**ate a room. These animals have their own light switch inside their body.

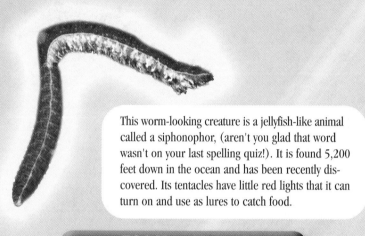

This worm-looking creature is a jellyfish-like animal called a siphonophor, (aren't you glad that word wasn't on your last spelling quiz!). It is found 5,200 feet down in the ocean and has been recently discovered. Its tentacles have little red lights that it can turn on and use as lures to catch food.

Did You Know?

A defense of shrimp is to vomit out a shining cloud of light. This type of bioluminescence is to scare away the shrimp's enemies.

The shrimp in your refrigerator may glow in the dark. The USDA gets calls every year from upset people who say that their imitation crabmeat is glowing. This is from the bioluminescence present in the seafood.

What's the point?

After all this talk about jellyfish and bioluminescence what should we remember?

1. Let your light shine!

Mathew 5:14-16 says *"¹⁴Ye are the light of the world. A city that is set on an hill cannot be hid. ¹⁵Neither do men light a candle, and put it under a bushel, but on a candlestick; and it giveth light unto all that are in the house. ¹⁶Let your light so shine before men, that they may see your good works, and glorify your Father which is in heaven."*

We have a light inside us as well! Oh, it may not light up an actual room like physical light, but it is even more important! Our light comes from God, the source of all light in the world.

We need to show our spiritual "light" to those around us, so that they can see God's love and truth.

2. Jellyfish are not just blobs of jelly, but are ...

- Swimmers
- Hunters
- Sailors
- And Some Make Light

What an incredible example of design! Even though it is a relatively "simple" creature, its incredible design and important relationship with other creatures around it speaks of a carefully planned blueprint by a master designer, rather than of a convenient accident!

Making a Jellyfish Model

Materials:

Coffee filter (cone or flat shape)
Colored string (become tentacles)
Floral wire
Wire cutters
Hole punch

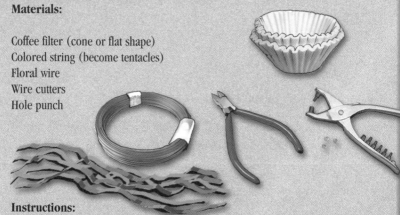

Instructions:

Punch at least 10 holes around the open bottom edge of the filter or as many as you want. Cut different lengths of string. Thread a piece of string through each hole. Tie the knot closest to the filter and let the long end dangle down. Cut the same number and length of floral wire. Twist the wire around the string and bend into any desired tentacle-like shape. Punch two holes at the top of the filter and thread a string through in order to hang the jellyfish.

Welcome to Wisconsin, the land of cheese and ... jellyfish?

Have you ever been to Wisconsin?

Even if you haven't, you've probably heard about things they are famous for, like their cheese. What you probably didn't know however, is that Wisconsin is also home to a very important discovery ... jellyfish fossils!

Greetings from Mosinee

In central Wisconsin, near the town of Mosinee is a place called the Krukowski Rock Quarry. A quarry is a place where large amounts of rock are dug out of the ground or a hillside and used to build roads, highways, houses, and many other things. The Krukowski Quarry though, is no ordinary rock pit! Large amounts of fossilized jellyfish have been found there.

Evolutionists say that these fossils date back to the Cambrian period of evolutionary history, but Creationists believe these jellyfish provided evidence for a worldwide flood. But more on that later ....

What are jellyfish doing in Wisconsin?

So how did fossils end up so far from the ocean? Evolutionists think that millions of years ago, this part of the United States was near the equator, (the equator is the invisible line around the center of the earth), and that it was surrounded by islands, lagoons, and bays, resembling present-day Florida. And it was heavily populated with jellyfish.

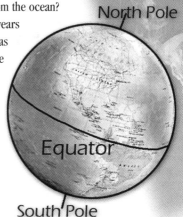

Why is a jellyfish fossil so important?

It is amazing that jellyfish have been fossilized. Can you think of why?

_____

_____

_____

_____

_____

Most of the fossils we find today come from what are called "hard-bodied" creatures, or animals that had bones and teeth or a hard exterior. Because of these hard parts of their structure, they fossilize easily due to their hearty nature. But jellyfish are very different. These fossils are made from animals that have no hard bones and are so fragile that they are nearly impossible to fossilize. In fact, Charles Darwin once said "No organism wholly soft can be preserved." These fossils prove that he was wrong.

The evolutionary theory for the fossilization of the Jellyfish

Evolutionists believe that the fossils found in the quarry are part of the Cambrian layer, a time period that they claim occurred about "500 million years ago". They suggest that jellyfish swam into the sandy shores of ancient Wisconsin as they migrated, hunted for prey, and reproduced. They then claim that strong tides, possibly from storms, could have washed the jellyfish up on the shore, and because no natural predators had yet evolved to eat them, the waves gradually buried them with course sand and they fossilized. Creationists believe, however, that all the evidence points to something quite different! Let's go to the quarry and examine the evidence!

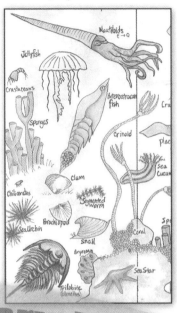

Evolutionary Time

100 Million

200 Million

300 Million

400 Million

500 Million

A Trip to the Quarry

Below is a key we'll be using as we examine what we find. The eyes will note what we actually observe at the quarry, the mouth will point to what the evolutionists say, and the star will give the creationist explanation. After we look at the initial evidence, we'll go to a modern-day beach and find out what happens today. Ok, ready?

Key:

👀	**What we See**
👄	**What Evolution Says**
☆	**What Creationists Say**

Evidence #1

👀	Perfectly preserved jellyfish fossils
👄	No predators had evolved yet to eat them
☆	Even if no predators, why didn't they decay?

An example from the beach: Birds

If you have been to the beach you have probably noticed birds such as seagulls eating things that are washed up on the shore, maybe even one picking at a dead or dehydrated jellyfish.

When animals wash up on the shore there is usually another animal that will eat it before it would have a chance to become a fossil. Evolutionists believe that no predators had evolved yet to eat the jellyfish, and so they simply laid on the beach until they fossilized!

Why this is good evidence for creationists:

Even assuming that there were no other predators present, there are three problems with this evolutionary theory:

First, why didn't the jellyfish rapidly decay after lying out on the beach instead of fossilizing - especially in direct sunlight?

Second, when a jellyfish washes up on a beach, it pumps its bell in an attempt to get back to the water, leaving behind little rings in the sand. There are no rings around these fossils

Third, since a jellyfish is 96% water, it would dry out and shrink if it lay out on the sand in the air. There is no evidence that these jellyfish ever changed size.

What does all this point to? It shows very rapid fossilization of the jellyfish. This is excellent evidence for creation and the worldwide Flood!

Evidence #2

👀	Fossils of jellyfish in rippled sand
👃	Waves created the ripples as they washed the jellyfish up on the beach
☆	Waves washing up on a beach won't create ripples

An example from the Beach: Sand Castles

Have you ever built a sand castle on the beach and watched the waves wash it away? Or stood in one place on the sand as the waves wash back and forth over your feet? As the waves come in there are ripples in the sand and as the waves go back out the sand is smoothed out again. Waves on a beach don't leave behind ripples.

Evolutionists say that the jellyfish were washed up on shore and then many more waves covered them with sand and they fossilized. HOWEVER, the jellyfish are preserved in rippled sand. If they were gradually covered by many waves of sand, there should be no ripples.

Why ripples are great evidence for the Flood model:

The only place where we see ripples that aren't washed away is underwater. This implies that the jellyfish didn't wash up on shore, but were deposited and fossilized underwater. Also, the only way the impression of a ripple can be fossilized is by another layer of fine silt coming to rest on top of it. This also can only happen rapidly underwater.

Evidence #3

👀	Fossilized jellyfish buried in 7 layers over 12 feet high
🧢	Created by one or more tropical storms -- possibly over thousands of years
☆	For jellyfish to have fossilized once was almost impossible, but several times over thousands of years? Great evidence for the flood

An example from the beach: Sand Cave

Have you ever dug a big hole or cave in the sand? As you were digging did you notice that the sand grains are not all the same as you dig down. There are layers of colors and sizes of grains as you go down.

These jellyfish were fossilized in coarse sand like the coarse sand you may have found when digging a sand cave. When an animal is buried in coarse sand compared to tiny silt, more oxygen comes in contact with the jellyfish, causing faster decay. Evolutionists believe that these seven layers were possibly laid down over thousands of years by many different storms, each time fossilizing a new layer of jellyfish in the sand.

Why these layers are excellent evidence for creation:

As we've already seen, it is almost impossible for a jellyfish to fossilize, especially the way we find at the quarry. Any extended exposure to air, sun, or predators would have made it impossible. It must be under exactly the right conditions: rapidly and underwater. Because of this, to say these jellyfish might have fossilized several times is unreasonable. It is much better evidence for a catastrophic, worldwide flood that quickly laid down the layers of sediment, and fossilized the jellyfish underwater.

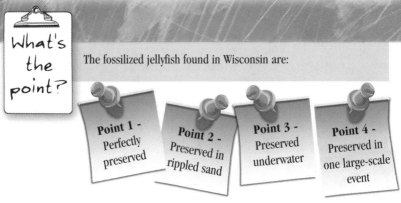

What's the point?

The fossilized jellyfish found in Wisconsin are:

Point 1 - Perfectly preserved

Point 2 - Preserved in rippled sand

Point 3 - Preserved underwater

Point 4 - Preserved in one large-scale event

Meaning- The discovery of fossilized jellyfish has been a victory for creation scientists! While evolutionists have had to readjust their theories to adapt to this new evidence, creationists see how this once again substantiates the Bible's account of a worldwide flood. While this jellyfish discovery fits perfectly with what the creation model would expect, it doesn't fit with what the evolutionary theory would predict.

Animal Scramble

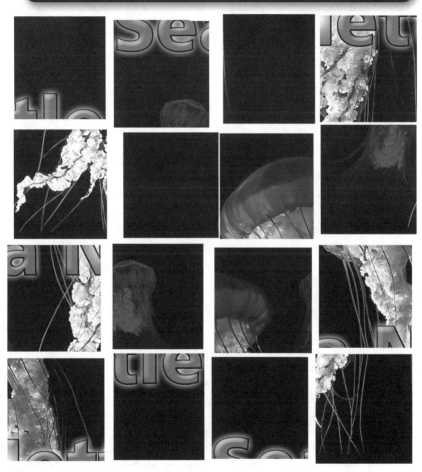

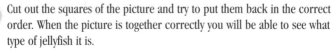

Cut out the squares of the picture and try to put them back in the correct order. When the picture is together correctly you will be able to see what type of jellyfish it is.

The following two chapters based on Jonathan Park and the Ancient City of the Jaguar take place in a very old city in Mexico, on the Yucatan Peninsula. As you listen to the events in the episodes, follow some of their movements with this map.

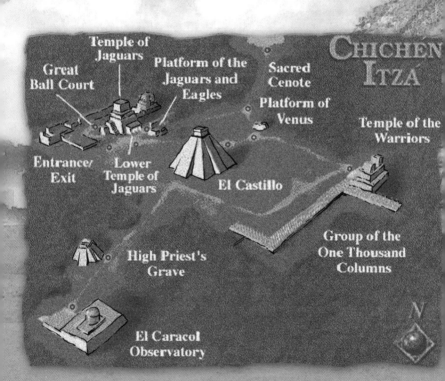

CHICHEN ITZÁ

Temple of Jaguars

Great Ball Court

Platform of the Jaguars and Eagles

Sacred Cenote

Platform of Venus

Temple of the Warriors

Entrance/ Exit

Lower Temple of Jaguars

El Castillo

Group of the One Thousand Columns

High Priest's Grave

El Caracol Observatory

The Mayans used sunlight in many ways in their buildings and worship. For example, the pyramid, "El Castillo" (castle in Spanish) is a solar calendar. There are 91 steps on each side and 1 for the top. This makes 365, representing the days in a year. At the spring and fall equinox, the corner of the pyramid casts a shadow on the side of the stairway. This shadow looks like the body of the snake connected to the giant carved heads at the bottom of the stairs. As the sun moves -- so does the shadow -- making it look like the snake is descending down the side of the stairs! They understood the movement of the sun very well but they did not know the true source of light: God the Creator.

Studying ancient cultures is very interesting. By studying the ruins of the Mayan culture you can see that they did not know the God of the Bible.

Many cultures do not have an understanding of the Bible.
They have a creation story **BUT** it has parts of a Biblical story and other parts all mixed up together.

One of the ancient Mayan creation stories is an example. You will see what is meant by this as you read the following:

"In the beginning there were only the Creators, Tepeu and the Feathered Serpent, Gucumatz, in the void and the waters. These two sat together and thought. They glittered with sun power. Whatever they thought and whatever they said came into being."

Underline the parts of this story that are similar to the Biblical creation story.

Missionaries can use these similarities to connect the culture's stories to the true creation story of the Bible.

There is little knowledge in these cultures about the true God being the Creator, sin, or that Jesus died on the cross for that sin. So it is a perfect strategy for missionaries, or you, to begin telling these cultures about God from the beginning of the Bible.

You can see from the Mayan story that you can not assume that the word 'God' is talking about the God of the Bible. They may think you are talking about one of their many gods like Tepeu or Gucumatz.

In our American culture today, there are also people who have grown up not going to church and so the word 'God' can mean different things to them too.

This strategy of witnessing starting at the beginning of the Bible is called Creation Evangelism.

The story in Genesis explains many things about our world.
Genesis means "beginnings". In Genesis, we learn why we must work, why we wear clothes, and about the first marriage between one man and one woman.

Why do we work?

Read Genesis 2: 17-19
We work because after sin, God said that man's work would be very hard, toiling with the thorns and thistles from the ground.

Why do we wear clothes?

After sin, God made the first sacrifice of a lamb for two reasons:
1. Because blood is needed to pay for sin.
2. He used the skin of the lamb for Adam and Eve's clothes

Why do we get married?

Adam and Eve were the first man and woman to be married. It is here that God gave us the example of what this relationship is supposed to be like.

Why is there evil in the world?

Bad things happen in this world because sin entered the world through Adam and Eve. Satan now has power on the earth, and people continue to chose to do bad things. That is why Christians have the Holy Spirit to help us make good choices.

Genesis and Revelation are like Book ends.

Genesis is the first book of the Bible and Revelation is the last book.
Genesis tells us how things began and Revelation tells us how things will end.

Perfection

Genesis tells about the perfect Garden of Eden.
Revelation tells us about the return to a perfect eternity.

Sin

Genesis tells us about the fall into sin.
Revelation tells about the restoration from sin.

Light

In Genesis, God made light that came from a source other than the sun.
In Revelation, it says that in eternity there will no longer be a need for the sun, because the light will come from the Lord himself.

The books of Genesis and Revelation bring balance and hope to the whole Bible.

If Genesis is not true the way it is written, other things do not make sense.

Put on your critical thinking hats and try to think about these questions.
Which diagram shows gradual change?

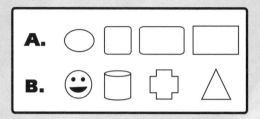

A.

B.

Looking at this evolutionary picture, can you see how it shows gradual change?

If humans evolved from an ape-like ancestor gradually over a long time, when did they become made in God's image – and separate from the animals? (Remember the picture is only an artists drawing)

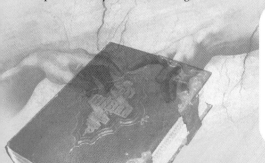

Genesis says that humans were made from the beginning "in God's image". So gradual change as the picture shows from apes into humans could NOT have happened and does not make sense.

Problem of Time

6 days of creation vs Millions of years of evolution.

If there was not an actual time
when the real Adam and Eve
committed the first sin, where
did it come from?

With out the Bible, there is no point in time when this happened.

Do you know what a timeline is?
It is a way of drawing out events that have taken place through time.
Draw a time line of your life.

Look at the following time lines.

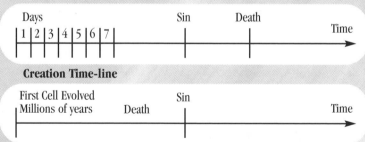

According to the creation timeline, there was no death before sin.
According to the Evolution timeline there was death before sin.

Genesis says that death came as a result of Adam & Eve's sin. But if you try to make the days of creation into long periods of time, there would have to be millions of years where animals died before sin came into the world.

However, Romans 5:12 says, *"Wherefore, as by one man sin entered into the world, and death by sin; and so death passed upon all men, for that all have sinned."*.

Death came as a result of sin. If death was just a natural part of the world, and not the penalty for sin, then Jesus died for no reason.

It is important for you to understand this point. Can you explain it in your own words?

_____
_____
_____
_____
_____
_____

Communication Breakdown

Have you ever had a miscommunication with your parents, brother or sister? It is usually not too hard to explain what the problem is when everyone is willing to listen.

Some people say Genesis is just a simple story that God wrote so humans could understand, but really when God created it was so complicated, that He couldn't explain it to humans. So they say the Biblical creation story is not how it really happened..

This argument does not make sense. God is the creator of the universe. He would certainly be able to communicate clearly what he meant! If God could not figure out how to tell us what really happened then God is a pretty bad communicator and not the God we know in the Bible.

The Problem of Order

Days of Creation

Millions of years ago

This is the order of evolution. Do the orders match? NO

The order of evolution and Genesis are completely different. If God was just telling us a little story about evolution or long periods of times –He did so in the wrong order.

Do you know what a symbol is?
It is a sign that is given a meaning just like a red light in the street means stop and a green light means go.

The Cross is a Christian symbol representing Jesus' sacrifice for our sins.

A blue sign with a large white H on it means Hospital.

There are fancier symbols that are more complicated.

Some people say Genesis is a symbolic story. They believe that science has proven evolution. So they are changing God's account of Creation and changing it to fit with man's theories and ideas.

However, when you accept what God said, you can see that true science is in agreement with the literal reading of Genesis.

When you understand the meaning of Genesis it becomes easier to share your faith with others.

Have you ever shared about God to a friend? It is sometimes hard to know how to start. Here is a model that you can use found in Acts 17:16-34 says...

¹⁶ Now while Paul waited for them at Athens, his spirit was stirred in him, when he saw the city wholly given to idolatry. ¹⁷Therefore disputed he in the synagogue with the Jews, and with the devout persons, and in the market daily with them that met with him. ¹⁸Then certain philosophers of the Epicureans, and of the Stoicks, encountered him. And some said, What will this babbler say? other some, He seemeth to be a setter forth of strange gods: because he preached unto them Jesus, and the resurrection. ¹⁹And they took him, and brought him unto Areopagus, saying, May we know what this new doctrine, whereof thou speakest, ²⁰For thou bringest certain strange things to our ears: we would know therefore what these things mean. ²¹(For all the Athenians and strangers which were there spent their time in nothing else, but either to tell, or to hear some new thing.) ²²Then Paul stood in the midst of Mars' hill, and said, Ye men of Athens, I perceive that in all things ye are too superstitious. ²³For as I passed by, and beheld your devotions, I found an altar with this inscription, TO THE UNKNOWN GOD. Whom therefore ye ignorantly worship, him declare I unto you. ²⁴God that made the world and all things therein, seeing that he is Lord of heaven and earth, dwelleth not in temples made with hands; ²⁵Neither is worshipped with men's hands, as though he needed any thing, seeing he giveth to all life, and breath, and all things; ²⁶And hath made of one blood all nations of men for to dwell on all the face of the earth, and hath determined the times before appointed, and the bounds of their habitation; ²⁷That they should seek the Lord, if haply they might feel after him, and find him, though he be not far from every one of us: ²⁸For in him we live, and move, and have our being; as certain also of your own poets have said, For we are also his offspring. ²⁹Forasmuch then as we are the offspring of God, we ought not to think that the Godhead is like unto gold, or silver, or stone, graven by art and man's device. ³⁰And the times of this ignorance God winked at; but now commandeth all men every where to repent: ³¹Because he hath appointed a day, in the which he will judge the world in righteousness by that man whom he hath ordained; whereof he hath given assurance unto all men, in that he hath raised him from the dead. ³²And when they heard of the resurrection of the dead, some mocked: and others said, We will hear thee again of this matter. ³³So Paul departed from among them. ³⁴Howbeit certain men clave unto him, and believed: among the which was Dionysius the Areopagite, and a woman named Damaris, and others with them.

Paul's Model

First, identify the true Creator God

Second, share with them how we are his creation

Third, show them how we rebelled in sin

Last, explain that Jesus paid our penalty for sin

If Paul had been visiting the Mayans he may have used this model with them. In their culture they worshiped many gods and did not recognize the true creator God. One thing that the Mayans worshiped was the Jaguar. This animal is found on the Yucatan Peninsula. Other interesting animals that are found there are the armadillo, spider monkey, and the yucca moth and yucca plant.

Mystery Animal

Can you guess what animal this is?

Ears like a mule

Eyes like a pig

Claws like a bear

Head like a lizard

Snout like a hog

Tail like a rat

The Nine-banded Armadillo are the kind that live in the Yucatan. However, the Three Banded Armadillo can roll themselves into a ball when they are scared. They roll-up by bringing their tail up to their head both fit into slots in the armor. This leaves no soft parts exposed.

What do you think the armadillo's armor is made from?

Armadillo Armor

The armor consists from boney plates, covered by tough, horny skin. Each of the armadillo's plates is separated by a section of skin which makes his armor suit flexible!

The Armadillo's Inner Winter Coat

You know when you wear your warm winter coat to keep your body warm many times the top half of your body is warm but your legs may still be cold. The armadillo does not have this problem!

They have a special net of arteries and blood vessels known as the *reta mirabila*. That is Latin for "miraculous net". Arteries that supply blood to the legs give their warmth back to the body before the blood goes into the legs. So the heat is kept inside the body, and not lost through the legs.

Spider Monkey

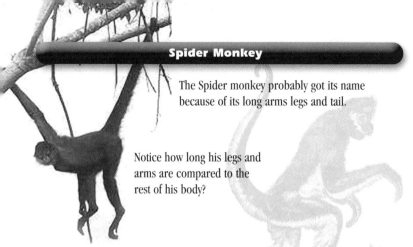

The Spider monkey probably got its name because of its long arms legs and tail.

Notice how long his legs and arms are compared to the rest of his body?

Does your Mom or Dad have a little machine they use to spread fertilizer around the lawn?

The Spider Monkeys are responsible for spreading seeds around the jungle. These monkeys eat many fruits whole including the seeds. Then they move on to somewhere else. When these seeds work their way through the monkey's digestive system, they are left behind somewhere else in the jungle.

Yucca, Yucca

Yucca—does something not taste very good?

That's not what I mean. Yucca is this plant!

What is so grand about a Yucca plant and moth?

The amazing way that the plant and moth depend on each other.

The female flies to a Yucca flower and gathers pollen into a sticky ball, using her special mouth.

The Yucca moth has the ability to find another Yucca plant that has not yet been pollinated by another moth.

When inside the flower, the moth injects her eggs into the flower. Then she stuffs the sticky pollen ball right inside.

Then the flowers begin producing seeds that will make new plants. When the moth eggs hatch they begin to eat the left-over seeds.

Without the plant the moth would die, and without the moth, the plant would die. God has designed a way in which these two depend completely upon each other. Just as we are supposed to depend completely on God our creator!

Find your way through the Mayan Ruins Maze.

START

Begin where it says START. Follow the
pathways to each number in the correct
order. When you reach a number, read
the fact or question for that number on the following page.

7. God's Design

6.

8. Lost!!

9.

El Ca

5.

Temple of Jaguar

4.

3.

Great Ball Court

2.

1.

St

70

71

1. As you travel through the ruins you run into an armadillo! Armadillos are designed with armor. Two sheilds to protect their front and back. Bendable armor around their middle and boney rings around their tail.

2. Play a game in the Great Ball Court.
The courts were similar to soccer fields. There were raised stone hoops placed at each end. The game was a cross between soccer and basketball. A hard rubber ball was used. The game is played like soccer with out using hands, and a score is made by putting the ball through the hoop. The court is about the size of a football field.

3. Did you know?
Armadillos can gulp in air into their stomach and intestines so that they float like a balloon in the water!

4. The Temple of Jaguars.
The Jaguar is a large cat that lives on the Yucatan Peninsula. It was revered by the Mayans. This temple has several stone carved Jaguars in it.

5. You have to walk through part of the jungle to get to the next ruin.
You see an amazing monkey hanging by its tail in a tree. What kind of monkey could it be?

6. The monkey you saw is called a Spider Monkey.
They have a 'prehensile' tail. Which means 'to grasp'. The underside of the tip of his tail has ridged skin which helps him hold onto things. He can use it to grab onto tree limbs, to use as a fifth leg, or to stabilize himself when reaching out.

7. Explain how the armadillo shows God's design of the animal.

8. OH NO!
You have lost your way in the ruins and it is getting dark. What are you going to do?

9. **This pyramid is called El Castillo.** It is an amazing show of the Mayans architectural and astronomical knowledge. It is thought that many human sacrifices were made here.

10. **The Yucca plant** has a special partner that is designed to help the plant and in turn the plant helps the partner. Do you know what kind of relationship this is called?

11. **The Yucca plant** produces pollen that's much stickier than other flowers. The pollen can not be carried off by the wind. It is also too sticky for bees. The only thing that can pollinate these flowers so they don't die out is a special insect.

12. **The Yucca plant and the Yucca moth have a symbiotic relationship.** The moth pollinates the yucca while the yucca provides a place for the moth to lay its eggs and food for its young.

13. **The Temple of the Warriors and 1000 columns.** Every 52 years the Mayans would tie up a sheaf of years representing the end of one of their cycles.

14. **You have met a friend And have had a good conversation with him/her.** You have the opportunity to share about God with them. How would you go about sharing?

15. **High Priests Grave.** Don't be fearful around graves because you have the Holy Spirit with in you. God has power over all things.

16. **El Caracole is an astronomical observatory.** They made a stone dome with windows at precise points so that stars can be seen through a certain window on certain dates.

Circle the drawing that shows what is the most valuable.

A giant SUV

All the money that you can imagine

A ray of sunshine in the rain

Human being

Happiness on a sad day

SAD DAY

Cultures are made up of people.

When a culture does not value its people, the people are treated as throw away things, it will eventually lead to the fall of that culture. It appears that the Mayan culture did not value its people. We know this because they would offer human sacrifices to their gods.

Have you ever been treated badly?
It does not make you feel valued. God values you and that is why He had his son die for you on the cross.

Psalm 33:11-13 says
"The counsel of the LORD standeth for ever, the thoughts of his heart to all generations. Blessed is the nation whose God is the LORD; and the people whom he hath chosen for his own inheritance. The LORD looketh from heaven; he beholdeth all the sons of men."

This is talking about how God sees, blesses, and values everyone on the earth!

IN GOD WE TRUS

Evolution's Two-stroke Engine

Have you ever built or owned a model airplane that actually flies in the air? If you have, it probably had a two-stroke engine that enabled it to fly.

What is a two-stroke engine and how does it work?

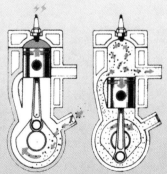

A two-stroke engine is basically a smaller version of the four-stroke engine you find in cars and trucks. In a two-stroke engine, the piston moves up for the first stroke. Then a sparkplug fires, creating a small explosion, driving the piston down again for the second stroke, completing the revolution.

Evolutionists are always talking about animals changing into other animals, but what do they say actually makes the changes?

Evolution

What are the two components that actually make the evolution engine go?

Two things called mutation and natural selection.

How do they work?

It is like a two-stroke engine.

The upward stroke is mutations and the downward stroke is natural selection. These two working together is what supposedly makes evolution go.

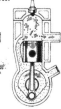

Natural Selection   **Mutation**

Mutations: The first stroke in the evolutionary engine

Mutations are mistakes in an animal's genetic code.
The genetic code is the blueprint for how an animal will grow.
There are four letters that are used to represent the genetic code (also called DNA): they are A, C, T, and G.

This is part of a genetic code: **AAGGCT**

Sometimes, a mistake occurs when a cell makes a copy of its genetic code when it reproduces. In the following copy from the code above there is a mistake: **AAGGT**

Can you find the mistake?

This is part of another genetic code: **GGAACTC**

These are two copies of the code above. Which one has the mistake?

GGACTC   **GGAACTC**

What is the mistake?_____

As you probably found, part of the code was left out; the second letter A. This mistake, called a deletion, deviates from the original code and results in a mutation.

Evolutionists believe that the right types of mistakes could actually change an animal for the better.

On the Galapagos Island you will find many interesting animals that evolutionists use to support their theory.

The Galapagos Islands

The Galapagos Islands are about 600 miles off the coast of Ecuador in South America. They are well known because of Darwin's visit in the 1830's.

Darwin was on a ship named the H.M.S. Beagle, owned by the Queen of England at that time. The purpose of the voyage was to explore the lower coast of South America. Darwin was aboard the ship to learn about the animals and natural resources along the journey.

When Charles Darwin returned home he began to create his theory of evolution. He was influenced by the finches (a type of bird) that he brought back from the Galapagos and the other varieties of animals on the islands.

The Islands have a great variety and uniqueness that Darwin had never seen before. There are scientists doing research on the islands still today.

Once a Block always a Block

What qualities make the two blocks different?   What qualities make the two blocks the same?

One of these blocks is very different than the others. Circle the different one.

Activity
"Building Blocks"

Materials:

Paper   Scissors   Glue

Copy of these 'blocks'

Instructions:

Copy and cut out each block and place them into groups of like qualities. You decide on the groups such as number of holes, shape, pattern etc. Write your groups on a piece of paper and place each block under the group name. There can be different ways to group your blocks. After you are happy with the way that you have grouped them you can glue them to your page.

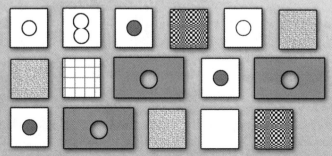

Now that you have categorized your blocks, think of them as one type of animal, such as a wild rabbit. Rabbits can have many different colors, sizes, lengths of hair, and whisker type. Like the blocks, animals like the rabbit have been placed into categories.

What's the point?

The point is that there are many varieties of animals in a kind but they are still the same animal. Once a block always a block. Once a rabbit always a rabbit!

On the Galapagos Islands, there is a tortoise who belongs to the species group called geochelone elephantopus. Evolutionists have named 15 different types of tortoises that belong to this group.

Can you observe some differences between these two tortoises?

hoodensis   vandenburghi

The 15 types of tortoises can be divided into two general types:

domed and saddle-backed.

In the **domed tortoises**, the front edge of the shell forms a low line over the neck.

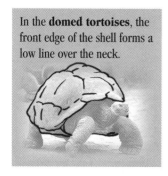

In the **saddle-backed tortoises**, the front edge arches high over the neck.

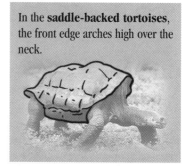

Can you see this in the pictures?

Each type looks a little different so evolutionists think that they are changing in different ways. It is said that they are on the road to becoming a new evolved animal.

Now apply what you just learned about the blocks to the tortoises. Some have hood shaped shells and some have saddle shaped shells. Does this mean they are evolving into a different animal other than a tortoise? Explain your answer.

Remember, "once a block always a block."

Evolutionists think that mutations are responsible for these changes.

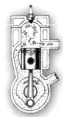

Mutations

- mistakes made in the genetic information of the animal over time.

This is the first stroke of the evolutionary engine.

There is something wrong with the evolutionary engine!
The problem is that it is well documented that mutations are usually bad for the animal, causing it harm.

However, evolutionists say that tons of good mutations made enough new information to turn a single cell into a tortoise.

Evolution's Engine Needs a Mechanic!

When mistakes in the genetic information are seen, they actually work in the opposite direction that the theory requires, which is to make good mutations. Instead we almost always observe a loss of information, resulting in harmful mutations.

The Evolutionary Engine does not work!

What can actually be seen is that lions are lions and bears are bears.

Oh My! We never see an animal like this!

We see animals with different colors and habits but we do not see an animal becoming a different animal.

After their kind

In Genesis chapter 1, verse 24 it says, *"And God said, Let the earth bring forth the living creature after his kind, cattle, and creeping thing, and beast of the earth after his kind: and it was so."*

DADDY!

God uses the phrase "after their kind" many times throughout the creation story in Genesis. To us this means that bears only make baby bears and lions only make baby lions. A lion can not make a baby bear!

Creationists say that the variety we see was already programmed into the DNA of these tortoises. They are just showing different variations of the original kind made by the Creator. It is very different than mutations.

Even though these tortoises can vary and adapt, they are still tortoises. They do not have the ability to slowly become a different animal.

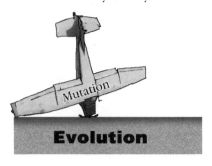

Evolution

Creation

Remember those finches Darwin brought back from the Galapagos?
This is what he observed:

Leaves

Insects

Seeds

Tools

Buds / Fruit

Grubs

Observe the beaks of the finches. What do you notice about the sizes and shapes?

_____
_____
_____

The pictures show the varieties of finches, just like the varieties of blocks.

Evolutionists say that each beak type was made by mutation(s) and is possibly a new species of finch. They believe this shows that the birds are evolving.

This is where natural selection comes in.

Some of the finches have adapted so that they have long beaks. They are better able to poke into holes to retrieve grubs. This gives them an advantage over the other finches. According to evolutionary thought, if grubs ever became the only food, these finches would continue to live while the others would eventually die out. In this scenario nature selected or chose the food source and so chose the best suited beak type to eat those grubs.

This is natural selection.

We *do* observe that Natural Selection does play a role in adaptation. It influences variety that was pre-programmed into an animal. We also see how animals showing bad mutation, such as a severely deformed beak, would not survive if it could not eat its food. So natural selection allows this mutation to die out. So Natural Selection works against evolutionary theory. It often keeps bad mutants from surviving to pass on the mutation.

What's the point?

The problem is when evolutionists claim that Natural Selection helps direct mutations to slowly create new animals. We do not observe this to be true!

What is a species anyway?

Recall the blocks.

If you grouped the blocks in this manner:

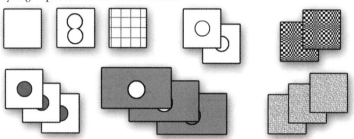

A block classifier could give each little group of blocks a different species name. However, when it comes to animals, different species are not supposed to breed with each other.

If this block   and   this block bred together to make a new block,

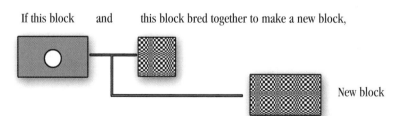

New block

a scientist may give this a new species name but the problem is that it is still a block because the two original blocks bred together.

Evolutionists would give each of the finches with different beak types a different species name. 'Species' does not mean that it is a new animal.

Just like the blocks above, Darwin's finches can breed together. This was observed in a strong weather change in the 1970's and 1980's which caused the varieties of finches to breed together. This shows that they are NOT new species!

So a 'species' *should* be defined as a group of animals that can not breed together to make babies. However, often a new species is named because a new variety is found. This is not a true species. It is also not evolution, but pre-designed variety in a kind of animal.

Notice the sizes of beaks of these two birds. If these two finches bred together, they may have a baby with a medium sized beak. This is designed variety.

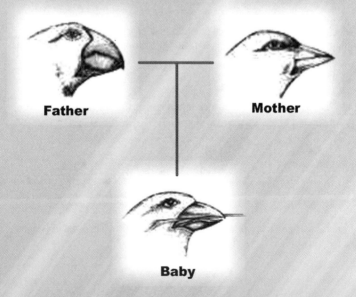

Father

Mother

Baby

Finch beaks are sort of like flavors of ice cream!

There are many flavors of ice cream but no matter what the flavor it is still ice cream. Do you have a favorite flavor of ice cream?

I like this one... this one... that one... and that one also.

Well, the finches have a favorite food and beak shape. If their beak is large and pointed their favorite food is seeds because their beak is the best for cracking open seeds. If it is slender and pointed it is best for getting insects to eat.

What's the point?

No matter what the size and shape of the beak they are still a finch adapted to eat and live where it is best suited.

Summary

The two stroke engine of evolution does not work. Mutations cause the engine to move backwards and natural selection just helps an animal adapt to its surroundings and gets rid of the bad mutations. The animals often show new varieties-not species-- of animals that may be able to survive better.

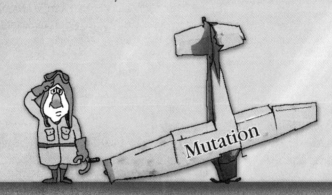

Evolution

The Bottom Line

Since we do observe natural selection happening, the REAL PROBLEM is when evolutionists use the small adaptations and new varieties to say that this is how one animal actually becomes another animal. This is called macro-evolution and it does not happen! It can not be observed.

The jump from small adaptations to one animal becoming a totally different animal is unbridgeable.

There are some other interesting animals found on the Galapagos Islands of which are also said to support evolution. Let's take a look.

The Flightless Cormorant

Cormorants are found all around the world. God has designed them with webbed feet, the end of their bill is hooked so that they can catch fish, and they are also excellent swimmers.

There is a type of cormorant that lives on the Galapagos Islands that cannot fly. These birds still have wings, and they use them to swim. God *might* have made the flightless cormorant separately from the others with flight.

However, it may also be that they may have simply lost their ability to fly. This bird has adapted to become an excellent swimmer and does not need to fly in order to survive.

Does this support evolution?

Remember that evolutionists say that a mutation must cause an animal to be better. BUT if the cormorant simply lost its ability to fly, this is *a loss of information, not a gain*. Again, this is backwards from evolution.

Mutation

Once again the evolutionary plane has crashed.

Evolution

91

The Iguana

Land-dwelling Iguana

Marine Iguana

The land iguana feed on prickly pear cactus. They get most of their water from the cactus - and can go long periods of time without water. They also burrow into the ground to escape the heat.

The marine iguana feeds on algae and seaweed found in the water. They have become efficient swimmers and move onto land to warm themselves.

Land and marine dwelling iguanas are probably from the same created kind because they can breed. That is good evidence that at one time these two iguanas came from the same group.

Why would the thought that 'marine and land iguanas came from a single type of iguana' not be considered evolution?

_____

_____

_____

_____

_____

_____

It is variations that were already in their genes. God made the Iguana with the ability to adapt to the water and to the land.

This shows God's wisdom to place design inside of design. Not only did He make the iguana, but he designed the adaptations that they express.

Psalm 104 talks about all the wonderful varieties of animals that the Lord has made. In verse 24 it says, *"O LORD, how manifold are thy works! in wisdom hast thou made them all: the earth is full of thy riches."*

Volcano disaster recovery

When Mount Saint Helen's erupted in 1980, it killed much of the forests, habitats and animals living in the area. Many people thought that it would take a very long time to recover. But in 20 years many of the original types of animals returned.

Before Mount Saint Helens erupted, there were many herds of elk that would move in and out of the area. After the eruptions, many of the elk returned to eat the new plant growth and then began to have twins. The rate that they were having babies was one of the highest ever seen. God designed it this way so they could quickly repopulate the devastated area.

Cumbre volcano on the island of Fernandina is an active volcano in the Galapagos. It has erupted over 20 times since 1813. Many land iguanas, vegetation and other animals' lives were lost in these eruptions. This volcano continues to be active even over the last few decades.

These natural disasters that happen today give us clues about the huge world-wide flood described in the Bible.

The Bible says that the Lord sent a world-destroying flood. All of the land-dwelling, air breathing animals not in the ark were killed. The entire earth was like the area around Fernandina and Mt. Saint Helen's, life mostly destroyed.

After the flood waters dried, God told Noah and the animals to leave the ark in Genesis 8:17, *"Bring forth with thee every living thing that is with thee, of all flesh, both of fowl, and of cattle, and of every creeping thing that creepeth upon the earth; that they may breed abundantly in the earth, and be fruitful, and multiply upon the earth."*

It was God's will for the animals that were preserved on the ark to fill the earth again. He created all the kinds with the ability to leave the ark, and spread out around the world and adapt to their special environments.

We can observe from natural disasters that it is possible for an area to recover from devastation in a rather short amount of time.

GAME

What group do I fit in?

Draw a line from the picture of the animal to the group that it belongs to.

Reptile   **Mammal**   **Bird**

Charles Darwin's book, *The Origin of Species*, published in 1859, pushed the theory of evolution to the front of the scientific and public world. At that time it was accepted by some but rejected by most.

By the 1920's however, the theory of evolution was becoming more accepted in society. Many parents, nevertheless, wanted to protect their children from being taught the theory in school, and so took legal action.

As a result, laws were created that actually made it illegal to teach evolution in the school systems. The Bulter Act was one of these laws, and was passed in the state of Tennessee in 1925.

However, this law was quickly challenged by a group called the ACLU, which stands for the American Civil Liberties Union, and was taken to court.

The case was called the Scopes Trial. A teacher named John Scopes was on trial for teaching evolution, but instead of the case focusing on teaching an illegal theory, it became about the two worldviews of evolution and creation.

Two Worldviews

A worldview is the way that a person sees or views the world. Not how they literally see it with their eyes, such as one person thinking the earth looks round and another believing it looks flat...

...but a worldview is what we believe and how we answer basic questions like:

- What is the universe's origin?

- Where did the earth come from?

- How did we get here?

Two of the foundations of a worldview:

-Belief about the origin of the world

-View of morality

Belief about the origin of the world

Creation worldview

The earth was created by God through His power as He spoke it into existence.

Evolution worldview

The earth happened by chance processes.

View of morality

Are there rules to live by?

Creation worldview

A Biblical Christian world-view says "yes," God gave us morality"-rules to live by that are made to provide for and protect us. Deuteronomy 7:11 says *"Thou shalt there-fore keep the commandments, and the statutes, and the judg-ments, which I command thee this day, to do them."*

Evolution worldview

Evolution's worldview says that there are not really any rules to live by, and that we must make up our own. We can change the rules when needed to best fit the situation or circumstance.

A closer look at the Scopes Trial

The Scopes Trial, also known as the "Scopes Monkey Trial" was a defining moment in our society for many reasons. Let's take a better look at the people and the issues that were involved:

The Characters of the Trial

Dayton, TN-the town where it all took place.

Dayton, TN

John Scopes- the teacher on trial for teaching evolution

Clarence Darrow-the lawyer for the American Civil Liberties Union (ACLU) in favor of evolution.

William Bryan-the lawyer in favor of creation.

The trial was designed by the ACLU to become a spectacle, like a Circus, hence the nickname "monkey trial." The evolutionists were portrayed as smart and highly educated, while the Christians were made to look like ignorant country people. Unfortunately, this plot was in many ways successful through the spin and publicity of radio and newspapers.

The Science of the Trial

Scientists weren't allowed to *testify* at the trial. So the judge excused the jurors, and allowed the scientific evidence to be read into the court's record.

The evidence brought out at the trial in favor of evolution:

Vestigial Organs   **Apemen Fossils**

Vestigial Organs Evidence

The first piece of evidence used by evolutionists in the trial was Vestigial Organs. Vestigial Organs are structures in man or animals that are thought to have "no use." Evolutionists said these structures once had a purpose, but as an organism evolved, the organ lost its purpose, creating "useless junk."

Examples:

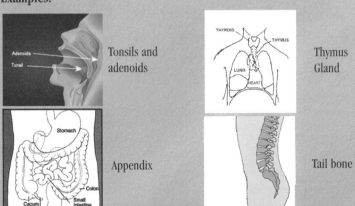

Tonsils and adenoids

Thymus Gland

Appendix

Tail bone

But for some, one persons junk is another's treasure!

Scientists have now found that these "left-over" organs actually do have a purpose!

 Appendix: Originally called "junk," it is now known to be part of the immune system.

 Tailbone: Was said to be a "leftover" from our ancestors (monkeys) that had tails, but we now know that it is very import because it is where important muscles are hooked.

 Tonsils and adenoids: Tonsils which are at the back of your throat, and adenoids which are behind your nose, were both thought to not have any purpose, but are now known to help your body fight infections.

 Thymus gland: A gland that is behind your sternum bone in your chest, it was also thought to be useless, but it has been found that it also helps your immune system, especially when you are young.

Conclusion of the Vestigial Organ evidence:
Again, it's all about worldview. In Psalm 139:16, it says, *"Thine eyes did see my substance, yet being unperfect; and in thy book all my members were written, which in continuance were fashioned, when as yet there was none of them."* If a person believes that man was created by God in His image, then they will also believe that He didn't make man with any "extra or junk" parts, but that every part of our body has a specific purpose, even if we don't necessarily understand what it is. If a person believes in evolution, however, then the human race itself is simply a collection of "lucky mistakes" and there is no purpose or order for anything.

Apemen Fossils Evidence

Another piece of evidence used by evolutionists in the Scopes trial was that of "Apemen Fossils." This refers to fossils that are thought to be Ape-like humans that lived a very long time ago. Scientists have made a "family tree" that tries to show how humans evolved from apes.

Evolutionary Tree

A family tree is a chart that shows the many different people in your family's history, both who they were and where they were fit in time in your family.

How far back can you make your family tree go? Ask your parents and your grandparents to help you make a family tree. Here is an example.

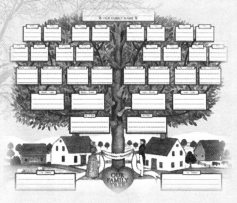

103

There are four ape-man fossils supposedly in the human family tree that were presented at the Scopes trial:

Piltdown Man

The "Piltdown Man" fossil is comprised of the crushed skull of a woman and a jaw bone that supposedly resembles that of a chimp.

However, it is now known that this "fossil" was actually a practical joke. It was no ape-man but was a human skull and a chimp jawbone that were intentionally put together and made to look really old.

Heidelberg Man

The "Heidelberg Man" is the fossil of a skull that is supposedly mostly human with some ape-like features. Its jawbone, nose, and teeth are unusually broad, and massive in size and shape. It is now known as Neanderthal Man. Creation scientists believe the evidence shows that it was fully human.

Australopithecus
(pronounced oss-trah-loh-PITH-ek-us)

This is a specific group of fossils, the most famous of which has been nicknamed "Lucy" by scientists. Lucy is supposedly mostly ape with some human-like features, but there is lots of disagreement about this group of fossils. Many scientists have become convinced that it was simply an ape.

Java Man

The "Java Man" consists only of a fossil of the top of a skull, two teeth, and a leg bone (the femur). The skull showed a large, far back forehead and big heavy ridges where the eyebrows would be like an ape, but the leg and teeth looked like a humans. There is still much debate over the validity of this fossil. It appears that the fossils used for Java Man may not have even come from the same individual (they were found a ways apart). Even some evolutionists don't accept Java Man as an ancestor to humans.

Have you ever seen a poster like this? It may make human evolution look very real, but BE CAREFUL! Remember that when you look at things like this, they are just artists drawings of what evolutionists THINK that the fossils MIGHT have looked like and are based on the assumption that man evolved in the first place. This "evidence" has been created to support the evolutionary worldview. It is not built on the actual evidence. REMEMBER also that an entire skeleton has never been found, but only pieces. They have never discovered a half-man, half ape!

Conclusion of the "Apemen" evidence:

Evolutionists want you to think that human evolution is a sure thing, but the truth is that it is very confusing and not "scientifically sound" like TV and books make it out to be. There is tons of guessing that happens when giving fossils the right names, putting the right pieces together, and their ages.

Creationists have a strong case for the unique creation of human beings.

The trial ended with the evolutionist lawyer Darrow making the argument that evolution was true and that the Christians had no evidence to support creation.

Bryan who was the Christian lawyer was not even allowed to make the case for creation or make his closing statements.

After the trial, many Christians were embarrassed to admit any longer that they were believers because of the way they were portrayed. However, in Mathew 10:32-33 it says: *"Whosoever therefore shall confess me before men, him will I confess also before my Father which is in heaven. But whosoever shall deny me before men, him will I also deny before my Father which is in heaven."*

What does this verse mean to you?

_____

_____

It is important to remain faithful to God even when it is hard or seems embarrassing to do so. Faith is not based on things that you can see. If it was, then faith would be easy and wouldn't really be faith at all! There is however, much science that supports the Bible, and this helps to build up our faith. It is essential that you know what this evidence is so you can defend your faith when someone challenges you.

What's the point?

- Vestigial organs like the appendix and tail bone do have a purpose.
- There is no such thing as an ape-man.
- Faith should not be based solely on the latest "scientific evidence."
- It is important to learn how to defend your faith.

Crossword Puzzle

Across

1. In 1925, this law made it illegal to teach evolution.

4. The last name of the evolutionist Lawyer.

8. Ape-(wo)man fake.

9. The fossil group of Lucy are actually _____.

10. This organ helps the immune system.

11. God's _____ provide for us and protect us.

Down

2. The last name of the teacher on trial for teaching evolution.

3. How we see the world is called a _____.

5. One person's trash is another person's _____.

6. Vestigial organs are also called _____.

7. Important muscles are hooked onto this bone.

12. The state where the first law against evolution was passed.

601

Answer:

Mountain Climber Joe

Have you ever climbed a mountain or just gone on a hike? Mountain Climber Joe is climbing the Sandia Mountains in New Mexico. He has discovered some very exciting things as he climbs. As he goes up the mountain he notices that the trees and animals change, the air temperature gets cooler and the ground is wetter. These three things are part of different 'biomes' – or "life-zones" we find in nature.

Biomes

A biome is a large geographical area which has particular plant and animal groups that are adapted to live in that environment. Biomes can consist of many ecosystems with their own set of plants and animals. Sometimes these ecosystems are also called biomes, life zones, or eco-regions. These terms can all mean the same thing.

BIOMES

This is a diagram of the world's general biomes.

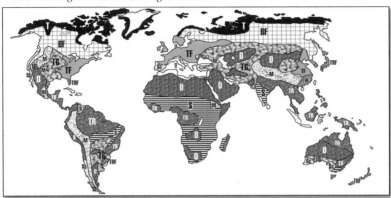

Different biomes include areas like:
Deserts (D)
Savanna (S)
Grasslands (G)
Scrub brushlands (Sc)
Mountains (M)

Tropical rain forests (TR)
Boreal forests (BF)
Temperate forest (TF)
Temperate rain
   forest (TRF)

Four different
types of
forests

Notice the biomes of the United States. List them here:

Sandia Mountains are a range near Albuquerque,
New Mexico. The highest point is 10,678.

Biomes change as you go across the United States and as you go up in elevation. Mountain ranges have very complex zones.

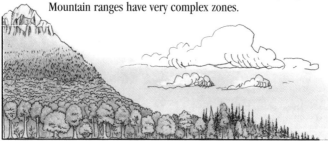

The things that cause the zones:

Elevation (the number of feet the land rises above the level of the sea)
Rainfall (amount of rain per year)
Temperature (how warm or cold the air feels)

In the Sandias, we see four of these different biomes as we climb in elevation.

The highest zone gets 30 - 35 inches of rain and is dominated by Spruce and Fir trees.

Then we find Douglas Fir Trees that get between 25 – 30 inches of rain.

The next area is covered by Ponderosa Pines, and usually gets 18 - 26 inches of rain.

The lower parts of the Mountains are populated with Juniper trees. It rains about 8 -20 inches a year.

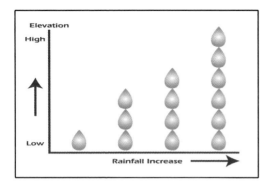

This graph illustrates that the amount of rain increases as you go up in elevation.

Look at the graph by reading the labels and how the water drops get taller from left to right. In your own words write out what the graph is telling you.

_____

_____

_____

Three Big Ideas about Biomes

By interpreting the meaning of the graph you discovered one of the big ideas about biomes. Here are all of them:

- The amount of rain increases as you go up in elevation (from the graph).
- Air temperature decreases as you go up in elevation.
- Plant and animal types vary with the change in elevation.

The amazing thing is that the Creator has made animals that fit perfectly into each one of these ecosystems. The plants, animals, and trees all work together to make each zone unique.

Activity -- Help Mountain Climber Joe:

Make a copy of this activity. You will make a diagram of the mountain that shows the characteristics of each zone found on the Sandia Mountains. The characteristics are:

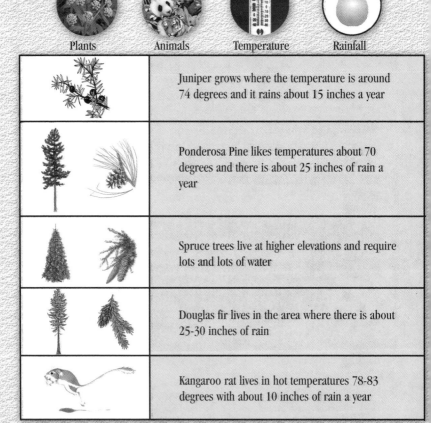

| Plants | Animals | Temperature | Rainfall |

	Juniper grows where the temperature is around 74 degrees and it rains about 15 inches a year
	Ponderosa Pine likes temperatures about 70 degrees and there is about 25 inches of rain a year
	Spruce trees live at higher elevations and require lots and lots of water
	Douglas fir lives in the area where there is about 25-30 inches of rain
	Kangaroo rat lives in hot temperatures 78-83 degrees with about 10 inches of rain a year

114

Instructions:

Read through the facts that are next to each picture.
Copy and cut out the pictures of each plant and animal. Help Climber Joe
describe each biome by gluing the pictures to the diagram of the mountain in
the zone where they live(on page 116). Use the facts about rainfall and
temperature to make sure that you place them in the right biome on the
mountain.

	Mule Deer lives in the forest from 5000 ft to 11000 feet
	Squirrel lives in and eats ponderosa pine tree
	Monarch passes through and rests in trees
	Striped skunk likes to live in the desert, woodlands, or grassy plains
	Road runner is designed to live in the hot desert
	Humming bird can be seen through out the zones

Diagram of Sandia Mountain Biomes

Sandia Crest about 11,000 feet high

Cold air temperatures

30-35 inches
of rain

25-30 inches
of rain

Hot air
temperatures

18-26 inches
of rain

8-20 inches
of rain

Elevation at Sandia base 5,000 feet

Forest fires have a purpose!

Lightning strikes start natural forest fires in forests all around the world, and the Sandia Mountains are no exception. These types of fires are healthy for the forest because it burns fallen leaves, wood, underbrush, and diseases, but does not kill the trees. Park managers now set controlled fires to help keep the forest healthy.

Forests become overgrown when natural fires are prevented from burning the dry underbrush. When a fire finally starts, it burns out of control killing everything in its path.

Thick barked trees, such as ponderosa pines, are protected from moderate fires. The bark protects the softer parts of the tree.

In some forests thin barked trees, like the Black Spruce, have special cones called 'serotinous' that remain closed while on the tree. While a fire may damage the bark of the tree, the heat opens the cones and the seeds are dispersed to the forest floor ensuring that if the tree dies, new ones will grow. What an incredible design by the Creator to restore a forest!

The Sandia forest has a natural cycle after a fire. When a fire burns, it opens up the thick Spruce forests so that light shines on the forest floor. Aspen trees can sprout because of the new sunlight. The aspen trees make new shade for the little new spruce trees to grow back.

Find the animals in the forest on the mountain. Circle and color them.

Monarch Butterfly

Monarch Butterflies are beautiful insects. Do you know the difference between a moth and a butterfly? You can tell the difference because a butterfly has club shaped antennae and moths have comb-like feathery antennae. Monarch butterflies actually can fly long distances and moths do not.

Butterfly   Moth

Every year all Monarchs migrate to special places. One is west of the Rocky Mountains, and the other is to the East. The Eastern path starts in Canada and goes all the way down to Mexico City. This is the route that goes through the Sandia Mountains of New Mexico.

The map shows the different routes that the Monarchs take to get to their breeding grounds.

Yes, insects as simple as a butterfly know how to navigate a long distance. New scientific research shows that they may have an internal clock and use the timing of the rising, setting, and direction of the sun to find their way.

It's been shown that a butterfly blown a hundred miles off course by a huge wind is able to find their way back!

Hummingbird

Hummingbirds don't actually hum with their voice, but when they fly their wings move so fast that they make a humming sound.

They can move their wings 80 times a second and fly up to 60mph in any direction—forward, backwards, right, left, up, down, and even upside-down.

Hummingbirds also have the ability to hover in the air by tilting their body to 45 degrees. Did you know that ideas for a helicopter came from these incredible birds? They flap their wings in the shape of a figure eight, and turn the bottom of their wings upward.

Their tongue is also pretty special, because they would not be able to get enough food to sustain their energy level if it wasn't shaped into channels to hold the nectar as they curl it back into their mouth. They can stick their tongue inside the flower 13 times per second!

Roadrunner

Roadrunners can run up to 17 mph and would rather do that than fly because they are not the greatest flyer. Their tail helps them to steer and slow down like the rudder of a boat. Because God gave them such speed, they can actually grab a humming bird right out of the air! It can also kill a rattlesnake by grabbing its tail and pounding its head on the ground. They also have a special eyelid called a nictitating membrane. It closes for protection when they catch prey like a snake or lizard.

One place that roadrunners like to live is in the lower elevations of the Sandia Mountains. It is designed to conserve water, and have a gland in their nose that gets rid of excess salt, which they need because of the heat in which they live. Roadrunners have a dark patch under their feathers on their skin. It is so that the sun will warm their body in the mornings.

The roadrunner is perfect for living in their habitat!

Skunk

If you threaten a skunk, it will bend its body into a "U" shape and point both its head and back end at you. Then it will squeeze some special muscles which squirt an oily mixture out two glands from underneath the tail, creating a spray.

The spray has chemicals that contain sulfur—that are what makes it smell so much. The chemicals are very sticky so the smell is hard to get off.

The skunk lives in the Sandia Mountains where it is suitable for nesting and there is lots of food. Skunk mothers always give birth in the spring because the baby is suspended from developing until the timing is right when there is lots of food.

Children, you are a blessing!

Speaking of babies, children are a wonderful blessing from the Lord! Psalm 139 is a wonderful Psalm about God knowing everything about you, because He formed you and knew you even before you were knitted together in your mother's womb. Verse 14 says *"I will praise thee; for I am fearfully and wonderfully made: marvelous are thy works; and that my soul knoweth right well."*

Psalm 127 4-6 says *"As arrows are in the hand of a mighty man; so are children of the youth. Happy is the man that hath his quiver full of them: they shall not be ashamed, but they shall speak with the enemies in the gate."*

When you become a parent yourself you will more fully understand what a great treasure children and families are! God knew what He was doing when he designed humans to be born as babies and grow up in the care of a family. ***You are special!***

What's the point?

All of creation points to God the creator!

Biomes are places where climate, geography, and animals are interdependent on one another. There is a special place for each plant and animal in the environment. We can see by studying these places that God had every detail in mind when designing the earth. The Sandia Mountains, Monarch butterflies, humming birds, road runners, and skunks show us God's design.

To put the icing on the cake, He created each child unique, special, and as blessings to us. He has a special place for you in the world just as He does for plants and animals. You are even more special because he created you in His image!

123

Eco-Trivia

Instructions

Photocopy the pages with the trivia cards. Cut them out and make two piles, one that is for the cards that say BONUS and the other for the Trivia card. (If you use up all the cards, make some of your own to add to the pile.) Place them face down on the table. Choose small natural items like a piece of bark from a tree, leaves, seeds, or small rocks to be your game pieces. Two or more people may play at a time.

How to play:

Roll the number cube to determine who goes first. The person with the highest number begins play. This person then draws a trivia card. The card is read by another player and then the person who drew the card must answer the question. If the correct answer is given, they then roll the number cube and move ahead that number of spaces on the game board. If the player answered the question correctly, he or she may also try to answer a BONUS card question. If this is answered correctly, they may now move ahead one additional space. Place each used card at the bottom of the pile of cards. The next person continues play in a clock-wise direction until 'Finish' is reached. The first person to reach the end is the Eco-Trivia Champion!

Trivia Card

A large geographical area which has particular plant and animal groups that are adapted to that environment.

Biome

Trivia Card

Does it get warmer or colder as you go up in elevation on a mountain?

Colder

Trivia Card

Does it rain more or less as you go up in elevation on a mountain?

More

Trivia Card

Name one reason that the types of plants change as you go up a mountain.

More rain, higher elevation, or cooler temperatures

Trivia Card

Are natural forest fires healthy for a forest?

Yes

Trivia Card

Does a butterfly or a moth have a club shaped antennae?

Butterfly

Trivia Card

How do Monarch butterflies find their way when they are migrating?

Inner clock, or sun rising and setting

Trivia Card

Do humming birds actually hum with their voices?

No

Trivia Card

What part on the hummingbird makes a humming sound?

Their wings

125

Trivia Card

How many times a second can humming bird's wings move?

☞ 80 times

Trivia Card

Can a roadrunner kill a rattle snake?

☞ Yes

Trivia Card

Can a road runner catch a humming bird right out of the air?

☞ Yes

Trivia Card

Road runners are designed to conserve what?

☞ Water

Trivia Card

Why does a skunk's spray smell so bad?

☞ Sulfur

Trivia Card

What time of the year do skunks usually give birth?

☞ Spring

Trivia Card

Where is the road runner's special gland?

☞ On his nose

Trivia Card

How does a striped skunk stand as it is going to spray you with its smell?

☞ In the shape of a "U"

Trivia Card

What do hummingbirds eat?

☞ Nectar

126

Bonus

What elevations of the Sandia Mountains get the most rain?

Higher elevations

Bonus

How much rain do Ponderosas trees need to live?

18-26 inches a year

Bonus

What type of plant lives where it only rains 8-20 inches a year?

Juniper

Bonus

In a Sandia Spruce forest after a fire, what type of tree will grow?

Aspen

Bonus

Why are natural forest fires good for a forest?

Kills disease, burns underbrush

Bonus

What is the name of the membrane that protects a road runners eyes?

Nictitating membrane

Bonus

How many general Biomes are there in the Sandia Mountains?

4

Bonus

Do you know what biome that you live in?

Bonus

How high is the Sandia Crest?

10,678 feet high

Start

128

Finish
You are the
o-Trivia Champion!